D1265879

The Complete Costume Dictionary

Elizabeth J. Lewandowski

The Scarecrow Press, Inc.
Lanham • Toronto • Plymouth, UK
2011

Published by Scarecrow Press, Inc.
A wholly owned subsidiary of The Rowman & Littlefield Publishing Group, Inc.
4501 Forbes Boulevard, Suite 200, Lanham, Maryland 20706
http://www.scarecrowpress.com

Estover Road, Plymouth PL6 7PY, United Kingdom

British Library Cataloguing in Publication Information Available

Library of Congress Cataloging-in-Publication Data

Lewandowski, Elizabeth J., 1960–
  The complete costume dictionary / Elizabeth J. Lewandowski ; illustrations by Dan Lewandowski.
     p. cm.
  Includes bibliographical references.
  ISBN 978-0-8108-4004-1 (cloth : alk. paper) — ISBN 978-0-8108-7785-6 (ebook)
  1. Clothing and dress—Dictionaries. I. Title.
  GT507.L49 2011
  391.003—dc22   2010051944

∞™ The paper used in this publication meets the minimum requirements of American National Standard for Information Sciences—Permanence of Paper for Printed Library Materials, ANSI/NISO Z39.48-1992. Printed in the United States of America

For Dan.
Without him, I would be a lesser person.

It is the fate of those who toil at the lower employments of life, to be rather driven by the fear of evil, than attracted by the prospect of good; to be exposed to censure, without hope of praise; to be disgraced by miscarriage or punished for neglect, where success would have been without applause and diligence without reward.

Among these unhappy mortals is the writer of dictionaries; whom mankind have considered, not as the pupil, but the slave of science, the pioneer of literature, doomed only to remove rubbish and clear obstructions for the paths through which naming and Genius press forward to inquest and glory, without bestowing a smile on the humble drudge that facilitates their progress. Every other author may aspire to praise; the lexicographer can only hope to escape reproach; and even this negative recompense has been yet granted very few.

—Dr. Samuel Johnson, preface to *The English Dictionary*

Contents

Acknowledgments

Many people made this book possible. I want to offer my special thanks to the following people for their inspiration and assistance: to my husband, Dan, for his computer wizardry; to Dan and to Aaron Solomon for their assistance in making many of the 19th-century illustrations possible; to Jessica McCleary and Stephen Ryan at Scarecrow Press for believing in this project and prodding me regularly to keep at it; to the interlibrary loan librarians at Midwestern State University who never turned me away when I came asking them for yet another obscure book; to the reference section librarians at libraries across Texas who helped me with access to their rare book collections; to LaLonnie Lehman, fellow costume designer, who encouraged me to turn this project from a private list of fun words into a book; to my fellow faculty members at Midwestern State University who encouraged me to finish this daunting task; to the members and officers of the U.S. Institute for Theatre Technology (USITT) who constantly challenge themselves and others to improve themselves and expand the world of theater; and to my dear friends who understood when I went into hibernation to finish this project.

The illustration of the shako is dedicated to the memory of Karen Tursi (1959–2010). She used to wear a shako like this, and she made it look good.

Finally, my thanks to my parents, Dr. Donald R. and Caroline Schertz, both educators, who instilled in me from a very young age the desire to read, learn, ask questions, and challenge myself to continually grow intellectually.

Introduction

When I began this project 15 years ago, it started in my search for understanding the terminology used in an 18th-century diary written by one of my ancestors. As the years passed, I began to run across more costume terms that were new to me. I jotted them down and began collecting them on notecards. When the notecards threatened to take over my office, the project moved to computer files. When the computer files grew, the project became a book. You never know where the search for knowledge will take you!

In the appendices, I have categorized the terms in three ways (when possible): by country of origin, by type of word, and by time period of origin. The time periods were chosen using Lucy Barton's *Historic Costume for the Stage* (Boston: Walter H. Baker, 1935), a standard referred to in many texts of the 20th century.

In my research I have accessed as many books as were available to me. I have attempted to categorize these terms as carefully as possible, but inevitably there will be mistakes. These errors are mine alone—the errors of a researcher lost in their passion for the project. Errata, additional terms, definitions, and other comments can be sent to the author by visiting mostlyharmlessweb.com. Along the way, I learned that each new age creates its own fashions and its own language for the fashions of the past. The pace at which these fashions change is rapidly accelerating. In five or 10 years, the world will have added hundreds of new clothing terms. I challenge the next generation of lovers of fashion and costume to record those words for posterity.

A

à gomito: Renaissance (1450–1550 C.E.). Italy. A sleeve that was cut full at the top and narrow at the wrist.

à gozzo: *See* à gomito.

'a 'iku: United States of America. Hawaii. High collar; stiff collar.

à jour: France. Lace of drawn work or another openwork.

à la Byron: Romantic (1815–1840 C.E.). France. Man's unstarched, floppy cravat.

à la chale: Bustle (1865–1890 C.E.). In 1868, a heart-shaped neckline.

à la du Barry corsage: Crinoline (1840–1865 C.E.). France. Popular from 1850 to 1867, a bodice with stomacher-shaped front.

à la Farare: Late Georgian (1750–1790 C.E.). France. In 1787, a woman's wide-brimmed, very high crowned bonnet that was trimmed with three feathers and eschelles.

à la Figaro: Late Georgian (1750–1790 C.E.). France. Garments in the fashion of the country costumes worn in the 1784 production of *The Marriage of Figaro*.

à la George V: (1910–1919 C.E.). United Kingdom. Named for King George V who popularized the fashion, a man's soft woolen cap with a short visor-style brim.

à la Grecque corsage: Crinoline (1840–1865 C.E.). France. Popular from 1850 to 1867, a bodice with a low, square, off-the-shoulder décolletage. The bodice had vertical pleats extending from the shoulders to the center front waist.

à la jardiniere: Romantic (1815–1840 C.E.). Austro-Hungarian Empire. An 1830s sleeve style featuring short, tight sleeves that were ruched just below the shoulder.

à la Louis XV corsage: Crinoline (1840–1865 C.E.). France. A bodice with the center section in the shape of a stomacher.

à la George V

à la Maintenon: Early Georgian (1700–1750 C.E.). France. Coiffure made fashionable by Mme de Maintenon.

à la Marie Stuart: Crinoline (1840–1865 C.E.). United States of America. Woman's evening wreath with a point in the center front.

à la Marlborough: Late Georgian (1750–1790 C.E.). France. Ladies' fashion named for John Churchill, first duke of Marlborough (1650–1722 C.E.).

à la Napoleon: Romantic (1815–1840 C.E.). France. Man's untied cravat worn crossed in front.

à la plaquette: Late Georgian (1750–1790 C.E.). France. In 1787, a woman's hairstyle where the hair was worn in spherical shapes by the ears.

à la Raphael: Bustle (1865–1890 C.E.). In 1868, a square neckline.

à la Titus: Directoire and First Empire (1790–1815 C.E.). France. A woman's hairstyle resembling the hair of a person condemned to the guillotine. It was often worn with a red ribbon tied snugly around the neck.

à la Victime: *See* à la Titus.

à la vielle: Crinoline (1840–1865 C.E.). Form of quilling.

à l'espignole: Crinoline (1840–1865 C.E.). Fan that folded at the joint.

A line: (20th century). Triangular or A-shaped dress worn belted or unbelted. *See also* trapeze.

à l'innocence reconnue: Late Georgian (1750–1790 C.E.). France. In 1770s, a skirt fashion popularized from trial of a cook-maid.

a tsi'kin: United States of America. Blackfoot Indians' moccasins.

a 'ula: United States of America. Hawaii. Reddish; brownish.

a-a: Borneo. Open slit.

'a'a lole: United States of America. Hawaii. European cloth.

'a'a moni: United States of America. Hawaii. A purse.

'a'a niu: United States of America. Hawaii. Coconut cloth.

1

'a'a puhaka: United States of America. Hawaii. Girdle; belt.

'a'a'a: United States of America. Hawaii. Coconut cloth.

aaca: India. Sari border.

'a'ahu: United States of America. Hawaii. Generic term for clothing.

'a'ahu a po'o: United States of America. Hawaii. A helmet.

'a'ahu ali'i: United States of America. Hawaii. A type of colored tapa worn by people of rank.

'a'ahu makaloa: United States of America. Hawaii. A long malo.

'a'ahu 'oihana piha: United States of America. Hawaii. A dress uniform.

'a'ahu pawehe: United States of America. Hawaii. A garment made from a patterned mat.

aal: India. Red dye used in fabric painting. It was made from the roots of *Morinda tinctoria* and *Morinda cintrifolia*.

'a'amo'o: United States of America. Hawaii. Gauze; snakeskin.

aar: India. An awl used in embroidery.

'abā: *See* cogā.

aba: 1. Palestine. A robe in the shape of a folded rectangle that is left unseamed at the sides and is held in position by cords or ties under the arms. Worn by both sexes, it is four feet long and five feet wide. It is commonly made of woven camel or goat hair or coarse woolen in dark solids or stripes. *See also* abayah. 2. *See* zibun. 3. Portugal. Skirt. 4. *See* chuga.

abaaya: Palestine and United Arab Emirates. A woman's black wool cloak which envelopes the body. It may be elaborately embroidered down the front, on the side gores, and at the hem.

abaca: Philippine Islands. Manila hemp from trunk of abaca plant, *Musa textilis*, used to make straw hats.

abaissé: France. Lowered, as a hem or waistline.

abalone: United States of America. Mollusk shell lined with mother-of-pearl and used to make buttons, beads, and ornaments.

aba-posztó: Hungary. Coarse woolen fabric.

abarenoshi: Japan. Wild abalone strips.

abayah: 1. Palestine. Man's cloak. 2. Egypt. Cloak.

abb: Term used by weavers to indicate the warp yarn or the inferior part of the fleece at the edge.

abba: *See* aba.

ábbasi: India. Cloth dyed magenta.

abbé cape: Tiered shoulder cape.

abbot's cloth: Rough, canvaslike cotton fabric woven in basket weave; similar to monk's cloth.

abe: Nigeria. Ikat.

abenet: Long sash worn by Jewish high priest.

abgar: Bulgaria. Cotton cloth pouch worn on a cord over the shoulder.

ab-i-hawa: India. Literally "woven air," a kind of muslin.

ab-i-rawan: India. Literally "running water," a kind of muslin.

abillement: *See* biliment.

abiti: *See* vestiti.

abito da pantalone: Italy. Pantaloon.

abiyad: Palestine. White.

abla: Pakistan. Tiny mirrors attached with embroidery to the fabric.

abnet: Jewish. Long, linen or wool embroidered scarf or sash worn by a high priest or officer.

Abocchnai: India. A wedding shawl embroidered in silk or cotton with motifs of flowering bushes.

abolla: Roman (753 B.C.E.–323 C.E.). Red, rectangular military cloak made of linen or silk and worn fastened at neck; similar to the Greek chlamys.

abougedid: Abyssinia. Cotton sheeting.

abrasam: India. A generic term for silk fabrics.

abrigo: Spain. Coat.

abrigo cruzado: Spain. Double-breasted coat.

abrigo en forma de capa: Spain. Dolman coat.

abrigo polo: Spain. Polo coat.

abrigo raglan: Spain. Raglan coat.

abrigo trinchera: Spain. Trench coat.

absinthe: Bustle (1865–1890 C.E.). In 1871, a greenish gray color.

abu hizz ahmar: Palestine. Fabric with linen weft and silk warp.

abu miten: Palestine. Fabric with narrow purple stripe between wider red pink stripes.

abu sab'in: Palestine. Fabric with narrow red pink stripe between wider white stripes.

ac: Romania. Needle.

ac cu gămălie: Romania. Pin.

Academician: (1950–1960 C.E.). Man's hairstyle with high side part.

acajou: France. Mahogany color.

acala cotton: United States of America. Cotton variety grown extensively in Texas, Oklahoma, and Arkansas. Staple length is 1-1/16 inches.

acanalado: Spain. Crepoline.

acanthus: A foliage design based on the Mediterranean plant, *Acanthus spinosus*.

acca: Early Gothic (1200–1350 C.E.). Silk fabric with gold threads woven in. Believed to have been made in Acre, a Syrian seaport.

accollé: France. To be entwined around the neck; collared. *See also* acollé.

accordion pleats: Narrow pleats resembling an accordion.

accroche-coeur: France. Little flat curl of hair worn at the temple.

ačē attāmitō: Ethiopia. King's gold ring worn on the right hand.

ačē gumbō: Ethiopia. King's silver staff with gold wire wound around it.

ače kéčō: Ethiopia. King's gold armlet worn on the right forearm.

ače saččō: Ethiopia. King's gold necklace.

Acele: Trade name by DuPont for rayon made using the acetate process.

acessório: Portugal. Accessory.

aceta: Cellulose acetate rayon.

acetaat: Holland. Acetate.

acetate: (1920–1930 C.E.). United States of America. One of the first man-made fibers. Patented in 1925 by Celanese Corporation.

acetato: Portugal and Spain. Acetate.

acetato de celulosa: Spain. Cellulose acetate.

acetinado: Portugal. Satiny; silky.

ach: *See* al.

achates: Roman (753 B.C.E.–323 C.E.). Agate.

achchhadanaka: India. Short shoulder wrap.

achkan: India. Man's high-collared coat. *See also* sherwani.

acid dye: Type of dye used on animal fibers that requires acid and heat as assist. It works particularly well on protein fibers.

acier: Bustle (1865–1890 C.E.). In 1883, a steel gray color.

ackhan: India. A long, flowing coat.

ačō: Ethiopia. Gold.

acock: To be turned up at an angle.

acollé: France. To be entwined or encircling the neck. *See also* accollé.

acordonado Bedford: Spain. Bedford cord.

acorn: 1. Small military motif representing rank and corps. 2. Ornamental knob on men's hat cords.

acrilan: Liquid derivative of natural gas and air used in creating challis and other fibers.

Acrilon: Trade name for fabric made from acrylic fiber.

acrobatic shoe: Lightweight leather shoe with a buckskin sole.

acroc: Hook or clasp.

acrylic: Light, but bulky, man-made fiber.

acter: Bustle (1865–1890 C.E.). In 1875, a steel gray color.

acton: Early Gothic (1200–1350 C.E.). Jacket worn under the armor. *See also* gambeson.

acus: Roman (753 B.C.E.–323 C.E.). Hairpin or bodkin of copper, bone, or silver.

ada: Lithuania. Leather.

Ada canvas: Square mesh canvas used for needle work.

adaabo: Ghana. Royal breastplate of gold.

adaftō: Ethiopia. Silver earrings.

adagan: Ireland. Gaelic word for a little hat or a cap.

adai: India. A jacquard-like device used in Kanchipuram.

adamas: 1. Very hard precious stone; a diamond. 2. Roman (753 B.C.E.–323 C.E.). Diamond.

adana: India. An imported stuff from Aden.

adanudo cloth: High grade cotton, silk, or rayon fabric.

adarque: Renaissance (1450–1550 C.E.). Heart-shaped buckler.

adata: Lithuania. Needle.

adati: India. Fine, light cotton fabric from Bengal, India.

addhacina: India. A gauzelike silk cloth.

ade: Yoruba beaded crown with a veil of rope beads.

adelaide: Romantic (1815–1840 C.E.). United Kingdom. A steel blue color.

Adelaide blue: Romantic (1815–1840 C.E.). A steel blue color.

Adelaide boot: Romantic (1815–1840 C.E.). United Kingdom. Popular from 1830 to 1865, an ankle-high, side-laced boot with patent leather toe and heel. It was sometimes fringed or fur trimmed at the top. Named for Adelaide of Saxe-Coburg.

Adelaide boot

Adelaide wool: Fine merino wool from Adelaide, Australia.

Adèle: Crinoline (1840–1865 C.E.). 1. In April 1856, a woman's moiré scarf en tablier trimmed with a puff of ribbon and a deep fringe. 2. In May 1856, a woman's light mantle with three flounces. It was intended for wear at watering place.

adhivasa: India. Outer garment.

adhivikartana: India. A divided skirt.

adhotari: India. A fine cotton dupatta.

adhranga: India. Deep blue.

adinkra cloth: Ghana. Fabric stumped with abstract designs.

adire cloth: Nigeria. Fabric created using batik.

adire eleko: Nigeria. Process of using starch paste as a resist on fabric.

adjagba beads: Ghana. Beads made of pulverized European glass bottles and beads.

Admiralty cloth: United Kingdom. Melton cloth.

Adonis wig: Late Georgian (1750–1790 C.E.). Very fashionable, very expensive wig of fine gray or white hair.

adonize: To dress up; to dandify.

adoucir: France. To soften.

adrianople: Bustle (1865–1890 C.E.). Introduced in 1876, an unglazed cotton lining fabric. In 1880, the term applied to a red calico fabric printed with arabesques.

adriatic green: Bustle (1865–1890 C.E.). Introduced in 1873, a bluish green color.

adrienne: *See* sack gown.

adzalotí: Greece. Counted or measured stitch.

aegis: Greek (3000–100 B.C.E.). Animal skin that was worn with the head of the animal resting on the chest of the wearer.

aegyptium: Egyptian (4000–30 B.C.E.). Perfume made from almond oil, cinnamon, honey, orange blossoms, and henna.

aeolian: Lightweight fabric with cotton warp and silk weft. *See also* eolienne.

aerdhaite: Ireland. Gaelic word for being sky colored.

aerophane: Directoire and First Empire (1790–1815 C.E.). Introduced in 1820, a fine crimped crepe.

aeroplane umbrella: (1910–1920 C.E.). Umbrella with French-carved ivory handle cut to resemble aviators. Two of the six ribs were shorter, creating an airplane-wing shape.

aetherial: Romantic (1815–1840 C.E.). United Kingdom. A sky blue color.

afe: Samoa. A hem.

afef: Egyptian (4000–30 B.C.E.). Stylized fly amulet.

Affe: Germany. Monkey fur.

Affenpeltz: Germany. Monkey fur.

affiquet: Renaissance (1450–1550 C.E.). France. Brooch pinned to the upturned hat brim.

afia: Nigeria. A Tiv man's ceremonial hat.

afrikin: Biblical (unknown–30 C.E.). Hebrew man's breeches.

afshan: India. A spangle.

afterwelt: In women's stockings, the intermediate part of the stocking top between the leg and the welt.

agaat: Holland. Agate.

agabanee: Syria. Cotton fabric embroidered in silk.

agait: Ireland. Gaelic word for agate.

agal: Palestine. Fillet of thick wool or goat's hair cords which wraps around the head, holding in place the kaffiyeh. It is often wrapped in gold and silver threads. *See also* 'aqal.

agala: India. A deep brown stuff.

agamid: Philippine Islands. Strong inner bark of plant used to make cloth and rope.

agate: Chalcedony used to make jewelry. It is most commonly gray or white.

Agatha robe: Directoire and First Empire (1790–1815 C.E.). Introduced in 1800, a soft muslin dress held closed with clasps on the shoulders and worn open on the left over the skirt. It had snug-fitting short sleeves.

agave: Mexico. Fleshy leaved plant used to create cordage.

agbada: 1. Yoruba man's heavyweight gown worn over the buba. It is also called *gbariye*. 2. Nigeria. Man's cape of brilliantly colored cotton with printed motifs. It is worn with loose trousers.

agemaki: Meizi (1867–1912 C.E.). Japan. Literally "rolled-up locks," a woman's formal hairstyle.

aghetto: *See* punta.

agihila: *See* agala.

Agilon: Trademarked stretch nylon yarn.

aglet: Early Gothic (1200–1350 C.E.) and Elizabethan (1550–1625 C.E.). Point or metal piece that capped a string used to attach two pieces of the garment together, i.e., sleeve and bodice.

agneau: France. Lamb fur.

agneau du Tibet: France. Tibet lamb fur.

agneau karakul: France. Breitschwantz fur.

agnelin: France. Lambskin with wool left on.

agnellino de Persia: Italy. Persian lamb.

agnello: Italy. Lamb.

Agnes Sorel bodice: Crinoline (1840–1865 C.E.). United Kingdom. Introduced in 1861, a square-necked day bodice with bishop sleeves.

Agnes Sorel corsage: Crinoline (1840–1865 C.E.). United Kingdom. Popular from 1851 to 1867, the bodice of a pelisse-robe with a square neckline and bishop sleeves.

Agnes Sorel style: Crinoline (1840–1865 C.E.). France. Introduced in 1861, the princess line.

ago: Italy. Needle.

ago duku: Ashanti. Velvet cloth.

Agra gauze: Very fine, plain weave silk gauze with a stiff finish.

agrafe: Early Gothic (1200–1350 C.E.). France. A hook, clasp, or buckle used as a fastening for clothing.

agrafes de centure: Bustle (1865–1890 C.E.). In imitation of ancient jewelry, a three-chain trim; the middle chain for a watch, and the others for a key and seal.

agraffe: Early Gothic (1200–1350 C.E.). France. Fastening consisting of lever and eyelet and used to close armor.

agrafka: Poland. Safety pin.

agrandir: France. To enlarge.

agrements: France. Trimmings or ornaments.

águamarinha: Portugal. Aquamarine, the gemstone.

agugello: *See* punta.

aguja: Spain. Needle.

agulha de tricô: Portugal. Knitting needle.

agulhade: *See* pennbazh.

agun-pat sari: India. Flame colored sari.

ahaddha: India. A strapped shoe.

'ahapi'i: United States of America. Hawaii. Worn by chiefs, a tapa dyed with kukui bark.

ahata tantrika: *See* anahata.

'ahiehie: United States of America. Hawaii. A silvery gray color.

'ahina: United States of America. Hawaii. 1. Blue denim. 2. Blue dye.

ahinvala: India. A silk fabric from Anahilwada.

aho: Maori. The woof of fabric.

ah'ta qua o weh: United States of America. Iroquois moccasins.

'ahu: United States of America. Hawaii. Generic term for an upper body garment.

'ahu hinano: United States of America. Hawaii. A soft mat garment plaited from pandanus flowers.

ahuasca: Bolivia. Warp faced cloth.

ahuaska: *See* avaska.

ahuayo: Bolivia. Woman's mantle.

'ahuna: United States of America. Hawaii. Coat; garment.

'ahunali'i: United States of America. Hawaii. A red striped tapa worn by chiefs.

'ahuua: United States of America. Hawaii. A raincoat made of dried ti leaves tied to a net.

'ahu'ula: United States of America. Hawaii. A feather cape, formerly worn by high chiefs and kings.

ái: China. The color snow white.

ai: Samoa. Sew; seam.

'a'i: United States of America. Hawaii. Neck of a garment.

'a'i kala: United States of America. Hawaii. Collar.

ai ling: (1900–1910 C.E.). United States of America. Chinese Hawaiian term for a woman's three-quarter-inch-high collar.

Aida canvas: Square mesh canvas used for needlework.

aigeallan: Ireland. Gaelic word for a breast pin, jewel, or earring.

aigilean: Ireland. Gaelic word for a tassel or earring.

aiglet: *See* aglet.

aigrette: France. Feather or plume from an egret or heron.

aiguille: France. Needle.

aiguille a reprises: France. Darning needle.

aiguille a tricoter: France. Knitting needle.

aiguillette: Early Georgian (1700–1750 C.E.). France. Bow of ribbon that was worn on the right shoulder of a man's coat. It was the decorative remnant of the ties that once held up the sword belt.

ailanthus silk: Wild silk from the Attacus atlas moth.

ailbheag: Ireland. Gaelic word for a ring.

ailbheag cluais: Ireland. Gaelic word for an earring.

ailbheagan airgid: Ireland. Gaelic word for silver rings.

aile: France. Wing.

aile de pigeon: Late Georgian (1750–1790 C.E.). France. Popular in 1750s and 1760s, a man's pigeon-winged wig with two stiff horizontal rolls of hair above the ears (pigeon wings) and smooth on the top and sides.

'a'ilepe: United States of America. Hawaii. Ruffles or folds around the neck.

ailerons: Renaissance (1450–1550 C.E.). Spain. Short, floating sleeves.

ailette: Early Georgian (1700–1750 C.E.). France. Protective forged iron or steel shoulder plate in armor; the forerunner of the epaulet.

àilleag: Ireland. Jewel.

'ainakini: United States of America. Hawaii. Navy blue cotton cloth.

aincis: Ireland. Gaelic word for a skin or hide.

āinne: Ireland. Old Gaelic word for finger ring.

ainyi: Burma. Double-breasted blouse or jacket.

airmchrios: Ireland. Gaelic word for a military shoulder belt.

airplane cloth: Plain weave, water-repellent fabric used on airplanes. Presently used in shirts.

aision: Ireland. Gaelic word for a diadem.

aizome momen: Japan. Indigo-dyed cotton.

'ajami: Palestine. Woman's brightly colored girdle.

ajarakh: India. A predominantly indigo colored cloth with block printing. It is worn by Muslin men as turbans and/or lungis.

ajári: Greece. Inferior silver.

ajina: India. Generic term for an animal skin.

ajina yajnopavita: India. A deerskin worn over the left shoulder by Hindu ascetics.

Ajorstick: Germany. Hem stitch.

ajour: *See* à jour.

ajrak: Pakistan. Hand-blocked wrapping shawl.

ajsu: Bolivia. Often worn over a wool dress (almilla), an overskirt worn fastened at the waist with a belt.

ajuar: Spain. Trousseau.

akaaka: United States of America. Hawaii. White, very thin tapa.

akaka: *See* akaaka.

'akala: United States of America. Hawaii. Pink; pink tapa.

akalpa: India. A generic term for clothes.

akambo: Ghana. Face marking (disfiguring).

akane: Japan. The red dye made from madder.

akanjo: Madagascar. Shirt or smock.

akanjobe: *See* akanjo.

akathorasbhagarvakomala: India. Very soft fabric.

aka-ume-zome: Japan. A red plum color.

akcha watana: Ecuador. Tape used for winding women's hair.

akcha watarina: Ecuador. Quichua term for a band worn woven around a woman's hair.

akertjes: Holland. Tassels.

aketon: *See* acton.

akhi laj: India. Literally "complete shame," the veil worn over the face, down to the waist and covering the arms, allowing no part of the body to be visible.

'aki: United States of America. Hawaii. Hair switch.

ákna: Greece. Red dye for the hair.

akoko: Nigeria. Yoruba woman's one-yard-wide cloth made in Igbomina Province.

akome: Japan. The inner robe of the sokutai costume.

akongo: Tiv. Worn by women, broad strip of openwork joined to a narrow strip of cloth.

akpwem: Tiv. All white cloth worn only by men.

aksamit: Poland. Velvet.

aksamitka: Slovakia. Velvet hat band worn by married men.

aksu: Bolivia. Incan woman's dress.

aksun: India. A fine, painted Chinese silk.

akwaba doll: Ghana. Doll worn tied at waist by young girls as a sign that the wearer is unmarried.

al: India. Morindin, a dye, from the roots of Indian mulberry.

al hilel: United Arab Emirates. Needle.

ala: Spain. Brim.

alaballee: *See* alliballi.

alabaster: White.

alabere: Nigeria. Adire where the pattern is stitched with needle and thread.

alacha: Lightweight Oriental silk or cotton fabric.

aladire: Nigeria. Skilled dyer of adire.

aladzás: Greece. Cotton material.

alajah: *See* aleejah.

alaka: India. Curled locks of hair.

alaménes: Greece. Women with their festival costume.

ālamgīrī: India. Decorated fabric.

ālamjarī: India. Decorated fabric.

alamode: Restoration (1660–1700 C.E.) to Early Georgian (1700–1750 C.E.). A lightweight silk.

Alampasand: India. Literally "world pleasing," a hat style created by Wajid 'Ali Shah (r. 1837–1857 C.E.), the last king of Oudh. It was a cardboard base covered in satin that rose straight up from the forehead with a muslin or net bag which hung over the back of the neck.

alan dangi: Turkmenistan. Woman's circular diadem worn tilted back on the head. It is worn with the yaluk.

ala-niho: United States of America. Hawaii. Long tattoo stripe.

alankara: India. A generic term for jewelry.

'alapaka: United States of America. Hawaii. Alpaca.

alapine: *See* alepine.

al-aqrāq al-zarrariyya: Arabia. Sandals with gilded laces native to Bijāya.

alari: Nigeria and Yorube. Silk fiber dyed deep red woven into strips that are then sewn into wrappers.

alas: Renaissance (1450–1550 C.E.). Spain. Wings.

alaska: 1. Overshoe. 2. Yarn of cotton and wool.

Alaska sable: Misnomer for skunk fur.

alaulau: United States of America. Hawaii. Generic term for clothes.

alb: Elizabethan (1550–1625 C.E.). White linen tunic with fitted sleeves worn by priests as the second vestment in Mass.

alba velvet: *See* jacquard velvet.

albagcā: India. Waistcoat worn over the coat.

albangala: Elizabethan (1550–1625 C.E.) Piece goods from India for export to United Kingdom.

Albanian hat: Elizabethan (1550–1625 C.E.). France. Popularized by Henri IV, a high-crowned hat decorated with a feather.

Albanian robe: Crinoline (1840–1865 C.E.). Popular from 1840 to 1870, a flounced garment that had colored stripes woven into edging.

albatross: Lightweight, soft, wool, plain weave fabric. Named for the albatross bird because of its downy breast.

albe: Holland. Alb.

alberoce: Morocco. Jewish man's burnouse of black wool.

Albert boots: Crinoline (1815–1840 C.E.). United Kingdom. Worn from 1840 to 1870, side-laced boots with a fabric top and patent leather toes. They frequently had mother-of-pearl buttons down the front.

Albert cape: Crinoline (1840–1865 C.E.). Man's driving cape with a seamless back.

Albert cloth: Double-sided wool fabric with a different pattern on each side; used for overcoats.

Albert collar: Crinoline (1840–1865 C.E.). United Kingdom. Man's separate standing, starched white linen collar introduced around 1850. It fastened at the back to button on the shirt.

Albert crepe: Crinoline (1840–1865 C.E.). Introduced in 1862, a fine, black silk crepe worn for mourning.

Albert driving-cape: Crinoline (1840–1865 C.E.). United Kingdom. Introduced in 1860, very loose Chesterfield made without a seam down the center back.

Albert jacket: Crinoline (1840–1865 C.E.). United Kingdom. Popular around 1848, a man's very short, single-breasted, skirted coat without a breast pocket.

Albert overcoat: Crinoline (1840–1865 C.E.). United Kingdom. Man's loose, mid-calf length, fly front overcoat with small shoulder cape, a long back vent, and vertical breast pockets.

Albert pot: Crinoline (1840–1865 C.E.) to Bustle (1865–1890 C.E.). United Kingdom. Introduced in 1844, a military shako named for Prince Albert.

Albert riding coat: Crinoline (1840–1865 C.E.). United Kingdom. Introduced in 1841, man's single-breasted, full-skirted coat with wide collar, narrow lapels, and hip pockets.

Albert shoe: Crinoline (1840–1865 C.E.). United Kingdom. Named for Prince Albert, a man's slipper with a vamp that formed a tongue on the instep.

Albert shoe
Dover Publications

Albert top frock: Crinoline (1840–1865 C.E.) to 1900. United Kingdom. Popular from 1860s to 1890, man's overcoat cut like frock coat with three-inch-wide velvet collar, short waist, long skirts, and flap hip pockets. In 1893, it became a double-breasted, very long, close-fitting coat.

Albert watch-chain: Bustle (1865–1890 C.E.). United Kingdom. Introduced around 1870, a heavy chain worn by men that reached across the front of the vest from one welted pocket to the other.

albói: *See* touca.

Alboni: Crinoline (1840–1865 C.E.). 1. In 1853, a rich, one-piece mantilla that was slightly gathered at the shoulders and had a small hood with an ornate tassel at the point. 2. In 1855, a scarf-like mantilla cut in a narrow crescent shape. It had a gathered tulle border and was trimmed with ornamental gimp or braid on tulle. 3. In 1856, a woman's velvet cloak with a border of moire antique trimmed with looped and tasseled fringe. The hood was lined with velvet and trimmed with a bow.

albornoz: 1. Renaissance (1450–1550 C.E.). Spain. Hooded cape that is worn with a marlota. 2. Spain. Bathrobe.

Albuera: Crinoline (1840–1865 C.E.). In 1854, a square-fronted silk mantilla with a wide neckline, scalloped hem, and bow at the front of the neck. It was embroidered and trimmed with fringe.

albusado: Spain. Blousing.

alcah: India. To be striped.

Alcamina: Crinoline (1840–1865 C.E.). In 1857, a woman's muslin summer scarf with a scalloped edge embroidered with polka dots and two volants edged in the same way.

alceste: Crinoline (1840–1865 C.E.). Introduced in 1862, a woman's white silk bonnet covered in white crepe and trimmed with black lace and white feathers. The inside of the bonnet was trimmed with lobelia blue velvet and black lace.

alchah: India. Corded silk fabric.

alcorque: Elizabethan (1550–1625 C.E.). Spain. Cork-soled shoe.

aleejah: Early Georgian (1700–1750 C.E.). Corded silk fabric from Turkestan.

Alençon lace: France. Floral design on fine net ground; referred to as queen of French handmade needlepoint laces. The original handmade Alencon was a fine needlepoint lace made of linen thread. It was made in Alencon, France.

Alençon point: Two thread lace, forming octagons and squares.

alepin: 1. United States of America. Turkish-Syrian fabric imported into the Southwest via Mexico. 2. Spain. Bombazine.

alepine: Early Georgian (1700–1750 C.E.). Silk and wool or mohair and cotton blend fabric often worn for mourning.

alesan: Cafe au lait color.

Alesjo: Africa. Tuareg man's headcloth.

alessandrino: Renaissance (1450–1550 C.E.). Violet blue fabric or color.

alexander: Early Gothic (1200–1350 C.E.). Striped silk fabric.

alexander twill: Twill weave alpaca lining fabric.

Alexandra collar: Crinoline (1840–1865 C.E.). In 1863, a lady's collar with a Prince of Wales feather stitched on in colored cotton.

Alexandra jacket: Crinoline (1840–1865 C.E.). United Kingdom. Introduced in 1863, a woman's postillioned day jacket made with small revers and collar. The sleeves had epaulettes and small cuffs.

Alexandra petticoat: Crinoline (1840–1865 C.E.). United Kingdom. Introduced in 1863, a woman's poplin day petticoat with a wide plaid border at the hem.

Alexandrine: Crinoline (1840–1865 C.E.). In 1856, a woman's scarf en tablier trimmed with a full puff of ribbon and deep fringe.

alezan: Bustle (1865–1890 C.E.). France. In 1888, a dark reddish brown color.

alfaiate: Portugal. Tailor.

alfi: India. A grass green color.

alfiler: Spain. Pin.

alfinete: Portugal. Pin; tie pin.

alforja: Bolivia and Peru. Woven saddle bag.

alforje: Portugal. Pannier.

Algerian purse: (20th century). Purse made from Algerian leather; often tooled and embossed with gold.

Algerian stripe: Rough, knotted cotton and silk blend fabric in alternating stripes on a cream ground.

algerienne: Bustle (1865–1890 C.E.). In 1867, a kind of poil de chevre.

algerine: Crinoline (1840–1865 C.E.). Introduced in 1840, a twilled shot silk in green and poppy or blue and gold.

algibeira: Portugal. Pocket.

algodão: Portugal. Cotton.

algodón: Ecuador, Guatemala, and Spain. Cotton.

alhaya: *See* joya.

aliança: Portugal. Wedding ring.

alicante: Bustle (1865–1890 C.E.). In 1882, a golden brown color.

Alice blue: (1930–1949 C.E.). United States of America. Medium light blue color favored by Alice Roosevelt when she lived in the White House.

Alice mantle: Crinoline (1840–1865 C.E.). In 1854, a woman's cloak that was fitted in front like a vest and was loose in the back like a mantle. It was heavily embroidered and had heavy twisted fringe.

Alice Maud: Crinoline (1840–1865 C.E.). In 1855, a woman's heavy carriage mantle pleated onto a square yoke. The mantle was trimmed with galloon and fringe.

alicula: Roman (753 B.C.E.–323 C.E.). Traveler's cloak with sleeves and cowl, often red in color. It was worn over the tunica.

álises: Greece. Rows of chains used for ornamentation.

alizarin: Romantic (1815–1840 C.E.). First introduced in 1831, a purplish red dye made from madder root. In 1869, a synthetic method for producing dye was developed; the first synthetic dye.

alizarina: Spain. Alizarine; madder.

aljófar: Renaissance (1450–1550 C.E.). Spain. Seed pearls.

aljuba: Renaissance (1450–1550 C.E.). Spain. Marlota.

alkhalak: India. A knee-length frock coat worn by the army.

alkhaliq: India. A close-fitting coat.

alkilla: Hausa. Black and white checked fabric.

all: Ireland. Gaelic word for white or foreign.

allapeen: *See* alepine.

alleja: *See* aleejah.

alli churana: Ecuador. Literally "good clothing," a generic term for synthetic clothing.

alliance: France. Wedding ring.

alliballi: Directoire and First Empire (1790–1815 C.E.). India. Muslin.

allieballie: *See* alliballi.

alligator: Tanned hide of alligator used for shoes, handbags, luggage, and other accessories.

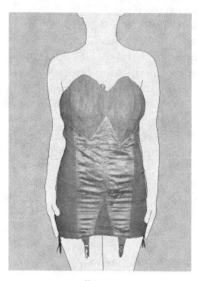

all-in-one
See also photospread (Undergarments).

all-in-one: 1. (1920–1930 C.E.). Combination brassiere and corselet for larger women. 2. (1930–1939 C.E.). Combination brassiere and corselet made from lastex, a two-way stretch fabric. It was made without stays.

allongé: France. To be lengthened, elongated, or stretched.

alloutienne: France. Sturdy silk with slight slub used for evening gloves.

allover: Pattern or design that is repeated over the entire surface of the fabric.

all-rounder: Crinoline (1840–1865 C.E.). Introduced in 1854, a man's stiff shirt collar that completely encircled the neck.

allucciolati: Renaissance (1450–1550 C.E.). Silk velvet with shiny loops of silver or gold that rise above the pile.

allura mai-kai: Nigeria. Pin for woman's headcloth.

alma: Silk twill weave fabric.

Alma: Crinoline (1840–1865 C.E.). 1. In March 1855, a woman's velvet cloak with elbow-length yoke and skirt box-pleated in back and flat in the front. It was trimmed with ostrich feathers. 2. In May 1855, a mantilla with a box-pleated flounce and trimmed with satin ribbon. 3. In November 1855, a cloak with a quilted taffeta lining. The cloak was trimmed with velvet fringe on the false yoke and sleeves.

alma brown: Crinoline (1840–1865 C.E.). Copper brown.

Alma Escharpe: Crinoline (1840–1865 C.E.). In 1856, a shawl with a vandyked flounce. The shawl was trimmed with checkered galloon.

almain coat: Renaissance (1450–1550 C.E.). Germany. Man's short, snug, jacket with flared skirts and long hanging sleeves.

almain hose: Elizabethan (1550–1625 C.E.). Men's very loose, paned hose with large pullings-out.

almain rivet: Elizabethan (1550–1625 C.E.). Suit of light half armor made with breast and back split.

almayne rivet: Renaissance (1450–1550 C.E.). Suit of light half armor.

almenadas: Renaissance (1450–1550 C.E.). Spain. Battlemented edges.

almerian: Crinoline (1840–1865 C.E.). Introduced in 1862, a woman's heavy black silk shawl edged in six rows of ruffles around the outer edge and trimmed with ruching down the center front.

almete: Spain. A tilting helm.

almilla: Bolivia. Woman's wool dress.

almizclera: Renaissance (1450–1550 C.E.). Spain. Muskrat.

almoner: *See* aumoniere.

almuce: Late Gothic (1350–1450 C.E.) to Renaissance (1450–1550 C.E.). Fur or fur-lined hood worn in severe weather.

almuzi: Late Gothic (1350–1450 C.E.). Italy. Men's hoods that were worn around the head with a wide collar on the shoulders.

alnage: United Kingdom. Former measurement of cloth, roughly equal to 45 inches. *See also* aune; ell.

alner: *See* aumoniere.

aloe hemp: The agave, a plant which produces fiber similar to hemp.

aloe lace: Delicate lace made from aloe fibers.

aloha shirt: (1930–1940 C.E. and after). Brightly printed silk shirt in imitation of a Hawaiian man's garment. It is generally worn outside the trousers.

alpaca: Romantic (1815–1840 C.E.). 1. Long hair of Peruvian alpaca, a type of llama. 2. Fine soft wool fabric, often with cotton warp.

alpaga: France. Alpaca.

alpagas: Italy. Alpaca.

alpago: Crinoline (1840–1865 C.E.). Introduced in 1843, a strong satin delaine.

Alpaka: Germany. Alpaca.

alpargata: Ecuador, France, Guatemala, Italy, Portugal, and Spain. Sandal of woven hemp or rope with shaped sole and straps. *See also* espadrille.

alpine: Crinoline (1840–1865 C.E.). Introduced in 1862, a young lady's traveling suit comprised of shirt, jacket, and skirt. The skirt was trimmed with two rows of velvet from the front waist center to the hem and on each side of the center seam. The center strip was one inch wide and the outer strips were one-half inch wide. A row of black velvet buttons ran inside the outer rows of velvet. On the skirt waist were two tabs trimmed in velvet. The jacket was closed in front, short and cutaway to the hips on the sides; trimmed in velvet and buttons. The sleeves were wide and pleated at the shoulders with two pleats. The fullness at the bottom of the jacket sleeves was contained with velvet edged lozenge shaped tabs.

alpine hat: Man's soft felt hat with low crown.

alpine jacket: Bustle (1865–1890 C.E.). Introduced in 1876, a man's double-breasted jacket with a center back pleat and vertical side pockets.

Alsatian: Crinoline (1840–1865 C.E.). United States of America. Plain black beaver mantle for mourning, trimmed with bands of rep.

Alsatian bow: Large, flat bow with a loose knot, used in millinery.

alta costura: Spain. Haute couture.

alta moda: Italy. Haute couture.

altibajo: Renaissance (1450–1550 C.E.). Spain. Figured velvet.

altita: Romania. Embroidered part of upper portion of woman's sleeve.

alto e basso: Velvet with two pile heights.

aluta luxor: Roman (753 B.C.E.–323 C.E.). Heavy leather boots that were softened with alum.

amabejhu: Rhodesia. Ndebele man's everyday garment consisting of two skins tied around the waist and hanging down in front and in back.

amadis: 1. Late Georgian (1750–1790 C.E.). Snug sleeve that fastened at the wrist. 2. Directoire and First Empire (1790–1815 C.E.). Woman's long, full sleeve with puffs at intervals down the arm.

amadis sleeve: Restoration (1660–1700 C.E.). Introduced in 1684 by Mlle le Rochois, actress, a snug sleeve that continued onto the back of the hand. It was fashionable again in 1830s and 1850s.

amageta: Japan. Rainy weather sandals with high wooden cleats and protective toe covers.

amalia: Greece. Woman's national costume of an embroidered chemise that shows at the neck of a low-cut silk dress. It is worn with a fitted, embroidered, waist-length, velvet jacket.

amanqonqo: Rhodesia. Ndebele. Large beads used on a woman's waistband.

amant: Greenland. Hood on woman's jacket. The hood is large enough to be used to carry a baby.

amanyatelo: Rhodesia. Ndebele term for sandals.

amaranth: Purple color tinged with red.

amaranthus color: Directoire and First Empire (1790–1815 C.E.). United States of America. Very fashionable in 1802, a soft pinkish purple color.

amarelo: Portugal. Yellow color.

amarillo: Spain. Yellow color.

amaua: Tiv. Entirely black fabric worn by both men and women.

amazon collar

amautik: Quilted parka worn by the Inuit.

amazon: Wool fabric in satin or twill weave with a raised nap.

amazon collar: Crinoline (1840–1865 C.E.). Woman's standing collar with a gap in the center front. It was particularly popular on blouses when finished off with a black ribbon necktie.

amazon corsage: Crinoline (1840–1865 C.E.). Popular for informal attire in 1840s, a plain buttoned bodice with a small white cambric collar and cuffs.

amazon corset: Crinoline (1840–1865 C.E.). Horsewoman's corset with elastic lacings.

amazon plume: Long, soft ostrich feather with the end curled inward to cover the stem.

amazone: France. Riding habit.

amazones: *See* pleureuses.

âmbar: Portugal. Amber.

ambara: *See* amsuka.

ambaram: *See* amsuyam.

ambari: *See* qatifah-i-purbi.

amber: Fossil resin that may be cloudy, opaque, or transparent and may be reddish brown, yellow, honey colored, or even black.

ambergris: Waxy substance used in the manufacture of perfume.

ambo: Spain. Two-piece suit.

ambohai: India. A mango green color.

'ameki: United States of America. Hawaii. Amethyst.

amelie: Romantic (1815–1840 C.E.). Azure color.

amelle: Romantic (1815–1840 C.E.). United Kingdom. A blue color.

amen: Romantic (1840–1865 C.E.). Fine figured lasting.

American: Romantic (1815–1840 C.E.). United Kingdom. Color of mistletoe.

American badger: Rough, long-haired, white fur with a black band just below the tip.

American blade: (20th century). United States of America. Coat with broad shoulders and with extra fullness at upper arm and center back to prevent seam strain.

American broadtail: Pelts of South American lamb, aged one day to nine months, that are sheared very close and processed to resemble broadtail.

American cloth: British name for American oilcloth.

American green: Romantic (1815–1840 C.E.). United States of America. A green color. *See also* forester's green.

American shoulders: (20th century). Characteristic broad, straight, padded shoulders of American men's coats before World War II. *See also* epaules Americaines.

American trousers: Crinoline (1840–1865 C.E.). United Kingdom. From 1857, men's trousers with the fabric gathered onto a narrow waistband that buckled in the rear.

American vest: Crinoline (1840–1865 C.E.). United Kingdom. Popular from the 1860s on, a man's single-breasted collarless vest that buttoned high. *See also* French vest.

americana: Spain. Jacket.

amess: *See* almuce.

amethist: Holland. Amethyst.

amethyst: Quartz ranging in color from violet to purple. It is commonly used in jewelry. The darker the hue, the more valuable it is.

amethystus: Roman (753 B.C.E.–323 C.E.). Amethyst, a gemstone.

ameti: *See* 'ameki.

ametist: Ireland. Gaelic word for amethyst.

ametista: Portugal. Amethyst.

amhcha: Ireland. Gaelic word for a cravat.

amice: Linen strip that is laid hood-like over the head and then dropped to the shoulders and tied into position around the body. It is the first liturgical vestment to be put on by priests for Mass. It developed from Roman neckcloth.

amictorium: Roman (753 B.C.E.–323 C.E.). Wrapped garment.

amictus: Roman (753 B.C.E.–323 C.E.). Generic term referring to all draped outer garments.

amido: Portugal. Starch.

amigaut: Early Gothic (1200–1350 C.E.). France. Slit at the neck of a woman's surcoat.

amincir: France. To make thin; to look slender.

Amish dress: Characteristic plain dark dress of Christian Mennonites or "Plain People" consisting of garments that fasten with hooks and eyes, having no buttons or other form of decoration. Because of their use of hooks and eyes, the Mennonites were once referred to as hookers.

amlag: Ireland. Gaelic word for a curl or ringlet.

ammana: India. A large wound turban worn by Muslims.

amônières sarrasinoises: Late Gothic (1350–1450 C.E.). France. Literally "Saracen almsbags," the term referred to bags that hung from the girdle to carry coins for the poor.

amortir: France. To fade, as a color.

amphibole: Bustle (1865–1890 C.E.). In 1872, a green gray color.

amphimalla: Roman (753 B.C.E.–323 C.E.). Cloth unshorn on both sides.

amphitapa: *See* amphimalla.

amplificateur

amplificateur: (1900–1910 C.E.). Camisole with several heavy frills sewn around the bust.

ampyz: Greek (3000–100 B.C.E.). Woman's diadem.

amsuka: India. 1. A smooth, shining veil. 2. A generic term for clothing. *See also* vastra.

amsu-patta: India. Fine silk.

amsuyam: India. A generic term for cloth.

amulet: Object worn as protection against bad luck or evil.

amuleto: Portugal. Amulet.

amusse: Byzantine and Romanesque (400–1200 C.E.). Small cape with hood worn by nobility and monks.

amuva: India. Bright green.

Amy Robsart satin: Romantic (1815–1840 C.E.). Introduced in 1836, a satin fabric with a white ground with white flowers traced in gold thread or plain colored flowers traced in silver thread.

amyan ikondo: Tiv. Man's dark blue cloth with red checks.

amys: *See* almuce.

an nouveau desire: Late Georgian (1750–1790 C.E.). Trim with interlacings of ermine or striped gauze. The name derived from the son hoped for in the pregnancy of Marie Antoinette in 1778.

anabas: Early Georgian (1700–1750 C.E.). Cheap cotton fabric.

anacholus: Greek (3000–100 B.C.E.). Undertunic.

anacu: 1. Peru. Woman's wrap skirt. 2. Peru. Long, full, cotton tunic.

anadem: Renaissance (1450–1550 C.E.). Chaplet or wreath of flowers for head.

anaglyph: Low relief ornament, as a cameo.

anágua: Portugal. Petticoat.

anahata: India. Any uncalendered fabric.

anaku: Ecuador and Guatemala. Inca term for a woman's pleated, wrapped skirt.

analabos: Cloak decorated by crosses and worn by monks in Eastern Church.

analav: Kerchief with symbols worn by nuns in Russian Church.

anamite: 1. Color of string or the color of unbleached muslin. 2. Natural, unbleached, neutral color.

ananas: Bustle (1865–1890 C.E.). In 1882, a pineapple color.

anantu hwinie: Ashanti. Garters worn below the knee.

anaranjado: Spain. Orange color.

anart garbh: Ireland. Gaelic word for coarse linen.

Anasazi stripe twill: United States of America. Self-patterned twill cloth distinguished by black or brown, red, and white weft bands.

Anatolian silk: Turkey. Fair quality silk.

Anatolian wool: Turkey. Long, medium fine wool used in making carpets.

anbijāniyya: Arabia. Simple woolen cloak.

Andaluse cape: Crinoline (1840–1865 C.E.). United Kingdom. Introduced in 1846, a woman's outdoor silk cape trimmed in volants of crepe lisse.

Andalusia: Crinoline (1840–1865 C.E.). In 1855, a woman's embroidered velvet cloak that was trimmed at the yoke with three strand tassels. The sleeves were cut in reverse scallops. The skirt was box pleated to the yoke.

andalusian: Romantic (1815–1840 C.E.). Introduced in 1825, a fine open washing silk with broché pattern.

Andalusian: Crinoline (1840–1865 C.E.). 1. In 1856, a poult de soie mantilla with the back cut in gores. The flounce was pleated in reverse folds. The mantilla was trimmed with gimp, rosettes, and looped fringe. 2. In 1857, a woman's talma with a deep lace bertha and rich passementerie. 3. In 1858, a lace mantilla with a deep flounce that ended in scallops.

andalusian casaque: Directoire and First Empire (1790–1815 C.E.). United Kingdom. Introduced in 1809, a woman's evening wear tunic that fastened down the center front and sloped away to below the knees in back.

andrienne: *See* sack gown.

androsame: Switzerland. Swiss military hat that resembles a bicorne with a spout-like crease in the center front. In France, the androsmane; in United Kingdom and the United States, the kevenhuller.

androsman: *See* androsame.

androsame

androsmane: *See* androsame.

anelace: *See* anlace.

Aneline shawl: Crinoline (1840–1865 C.E.). In 1861, a square shawl of silk, crepe, or grenadine, plain or embroidered. It was trimmed with a flounce of lace.

anello: Italy. Finger ring.

anga: India. Ankle-length dress with tight-fitting long sleeves.

angada: India. Armlet.

angadh: Ireland. Gaelic word for a shirt gusset.

angarkha: India. A tunic with a side fastening.

angarkhi: India. Garment that closes with a tie on the right shoulder.

angavastra: *See* pachedī.

angel overskirt: (1890–1899 C.E.). United Kingdom. Woman's day short upper skirt made with two long points, one on each side.

angel sleeve
Dover Publications

angel skin: Waxy, smooth, dull finish applied to satin.

angel sleeve: Bustle (1865–1890 C.E.). United Kingdom. Introduced in 1889, the name applied to long square panels on some mantles that reached from the shoulder to the ground.

angelus cap: Type of peasant handkerchief cap.

anger: Tiv. Man's cloth of alternating strips of blue and white.

angi: India. A blouse.

angia: India. Light, waist-length jacket with elbow-length sleeves.

anglaise: Crinoline (1840–1865 C.E.). Used from 1840 on, the term applied to the collar and its fold on a waistcoat.

angle-fronted coat: Bustle (1865–1890 C.E.). United Kingdom. Popular from 1870 to 1880, a variation of the man's single-breasted morning coat in which the front was cut away to expose the waistcoat beneath. The bottom corners of the coat were cut at obtuse angles rather than curves.

Anglesea: Trade name for curve in men's hat brims.

angleterre: Small needlepoint loops worked on an edge.

Anglo-Greek bodice: Romantic (1815–1840 C.E.). United Kingdom. Popular in the 1820s, a woman's bodice with wide lapels that were often edged in lace.

anglo-merino: Directoire and First Empire (1790–1815 C.E.). United Kingdom. Introduced around 1810, a very fine fabric made from George III's merino flock.

Anglo-Saxon embroidery: Old-style embroidery with the design outlined in long stitches and couched in metal thread.

angora: Turkey. Twill weave, soft, woolly fabric made of angora cat, angora rabbit, or angora goat fur.

Angora goat: Wiry, lustrous, strong fur of angora goat; usually white. The fibers are four to seven inches in length.

Angora rabbit: 1. Very fine, silky hair from specific breed of rabbit. It is very lightweight and warm. 2. Soft, wooly fur of angora rabbit. The fur is clipped or plucked from the animal.

Angoulême bonnet: Romantic (1815–1840 C.E.). France. Ladies' bonnet with a high crown, commonly worn tied at the side.

Angoulême hat: Directoire and First Empire (1790–1815 C.E.) to Bustle (1865–1890 C.E.). United States of America. Popular from 1800 to 1870, a narrow brimmed hat with a high fluted crown. It was named for the daughter of Marie Antoinette.

Angouleme spencer: Romantic (1815–1840 C.E.). United States of America. New spencer style introduced in 1815.

Angoulême tippet: Directoire and First Empire (1790–1815 C.E.) to Bustle (1865–1890 C.E.). United States. Popular from 1800 to 1870, a satin tippet trimmed in swansdown.

angrakhâs: India. Jewish man's turban.

angulia: India. Finger ring.

anguliya: India. Finger ring.

anguliyaka: India. Finger ring.

anguri: India. Light canary yellow.

angusti clavi: *See* clavi.

angūthī: India. Small finger ring with precious stones.

anhaho: India. A variegated or patterned headscarf.

añil: Spain. Indigo.

aniline: Dye derived from aniline or any organic dye.

anima: Elizabethan (1550–1625 C.E.). Armor made with back and breast of horizontal lames.

anime: Renaissance (1450–1550 C.E.). Italy. A coat of plates that were joined together with sliding rivets.

anjonp'in: Korea. Safety pin.

ankanjo: Madagascar. A Western-style dress.

ankh: Egyptian (4000–30 B.C.E.). Decorative symbol of life in the shape of a cross.

ankle-breeches: Elizabethan (1550–1625 C.E.). Colloquialism for Spanish breeches or Spanish hose.

ankle-jacks: Crinoline (1840–1865 C.E.). United Kingdom. Worn in 1840s, men's short boots that were fitted to the ankles and closed with five eyelets on the outside of the foot.

anlace: Early Gothic (1200–1350 C.E.). Short sword or dagger.

anlet: Elizabethan (1550–1625 C.E.). Ring in mailed armor.

Anne Boleyn mob: Directoire and First Empire (1790–1815 C.E.). United States of America. Name for fashionable dress cap in 1807.

annelet: *See* anlet.

Annette Kellerman: (1920–1930 C.E.). United States of America. Mass produced by Jantzen in 1920, a woman's one-piece sleeveless swimsuit that ended about two inches above the knee. It was named for the famous swimmer who wore this style as early as 1909.

annulet: *See* anlet.

anorak: Hip-length, hooded jacket for Arctic wear.

anserine: Early Georgian (1700–1750 C.E.). Silk and wool blend fabric first introduced for the funeral of Prince George I of Denmark in 1708.

antaravasaka: India. Robe.

antariya: India. Woman's lower garment.

antelope: Soft, velvety leather from the flesh side of the skin of the antelope gazelle of Africa. It is usually brownish or silver tan in color.

anteojos: Renaissance (1450–1550 C.E.). Spain. Eyeglasses.

anteri: 1. Balkans. Short white undervest worn by both genders. 2. Turkey. Long robe.

anterí: *See* kaváði.

anterne: Early Georgian (1700–1750 C.E.). Wool and silk or mohair and cotton blend fabric.

antery: Turkey. Man's vest that often reaches to below the knee.

anthrax: Roman (753 B.C.E.–323 C.E.). Garnet, a gemstone.

antigropolis: Crinoline (1840–1865 C.E.). United Kingdom. Popular in the 1850s, a man's high leather gaiter that fastened at the side.

antique bodice: Romantic (1815–1840 C.E.). United Kingdom. Popular from 1836 to 1849, a woman's long-waisted bodice that ended in a long, sharp point in the center front.

antique finish: Weathered or satin finish on leather created through the application of wax and oil.

antique lace: Darned bobbin lace.

antique satin: Heavy, dull-faced satin.

antique taffeta: Taffeta made with slubbed yarn.

Antoinette: Crinoline (1840–1865 C.E.). In 1855, a mantle with a fitted body. The mantle was trimmed with wide tartan ribbon and had a double pelerine.

Antwerp lace: Restoration (1660–1700 C.E.) to Early Georgian (1700–1750 C.E.). Rare bobbin lace with basket motif.

Antwerp pot lace: Rare bobbin lace with a pot of flowers in the design.

anuenue: United States of America. Hawaii. Scallop-like design on tapa.

ānulus: Roman (753 B.C.E.–323 C.E.). Finger ring.

anyam: Borneo. To weave.

ao: China. Qing dynasty (1644–1911 C.E.). Han woman's semi-formal, elaborately decorated, upper garment of silk damask with a curved front with a toggle closure. The informal ao had narrower, plainer borders and was made of cotton.

áo: Vietnam. Generic term for clothes.

áo bà-ba: Vietnam. Loose blouse.

áo baðò-suy: Vietnam. Pardessus.

áo bành-tô: Vietnam. Suit coat; jacket.

áo bò: Vietnam. Denim jacket.

áo bông: Vietnam. Quilted dress.

áo cam-bào: Vietnam. Imperial robe made from brocade.

áo cánh: Vietnam. Blouse.

áo cà-sa: Vietnam. Monk's robe.

áo choàng: Vietnam. Cloak; mantle.

áo côc: Vietnam. Blouse; shirt.

áo cut: Vietnam. Blouse; shirt.

áo da: Vietnam. Woolen dress.

áo dài: Vietnam. Vietnamese dress.

áo ðai-trào: Vietnam. Formal dress.

áo da-le: Vietnam. Mess jacket.

áo ðan: Vietnam. Sweater.

áo dãu: Vietnam. Soldier's uniform.

áo ði mura: Vietnam. Raincoat.

áo ðuôi-tôm: Vietnam. Tailcoat.

áo giáp: Vietnam. Armor.

áo gi-lê: Vietnam. Waistcoat.

áo kép: Vietnam. Lined dress.

áo lan: Vietnam. Diving suit.

áo lanh lót vài bông: Vietnam. Parka.

áo len: Vietnam. Sweater.

áo lông: Vietnam. Fur coat.

áo lót: Vietnam. Undergarment.

áo lót mình: Vietnam. Undershirt.

áo mão: Vietnam. Mandarin's bonnet and gown.

áo muta: Vietnam. Raincoat.

áo ngù: Vietnam. Bathrobe.

áo nit: Vietnam. Undershirt.

áo njt: Vietnam. Undershirt.

áo tam: Vietnam. Swimsuit.

áo thày-tu: Vietnam. Priest's robe.

áo thung: Vietnam. Academic gown.

áo toi: Vietnam. Raincoat; poncho.

áo vét-tông: Vietnam. Suit coat; jacket.

áo xiêm: Vietnam. Clothes.

áo xõng: Vietnam. Clothes.

aodach solus: Ireland. Gaelic word for white or light colored clothing.

aodach tiusail: Ireland. Gaelic word for comfortable clothing.

aoerfóni: Greece. The overlapping opening of a skirt.

aoidai: Vietnam. A woman's long fitted sheath with side slits to the waist. It is worn over long trousers.

ao-iro: Japan. Yellowish green color.

aozuri: Japan. A fabric rubbed with a blue dye.

áp long-bào: Vietnam. Imperial robe with a dragon design.

'apa memea: Samoa. Brass or copper.

'apamemea: Samoa. Copper.

aparan: Ireland. Gaelic word for an apron.

aparsaig: Ireland. Gaelic word for a knapsack.

apavartaka: India. Pearl necklace with alternating gold globules.

apch'ima: Korea. Apron.

apg'erbt: Lithuania. To clothe or dress.

apikaklé: Lithuania. Collar.

apkakle: Lithuania. Collar.

aplatir: France. To flatten.

apo Ifa: Yoruba diviner's beaded bag.

apo kula: United States of America. Hawaii. Gold bracelet.

apo lima: United States of America. Hawaii. Bracelet.

apo papale: United States of America. Hawaii. Hatband.

apodesme: Greek (3000–100 B.C.E.). Wool, linen, or chamois leather band worn as a brassiere.

Apollo: Romantic (1815–1840 C.E.). Bright gold color.

Apollo corset: Directoire and First Empire (1790–1815 C.E.). United Kingdom. Worn by either gender, a whalebone corset.

Apollo knot: Romantic (1815–1840 C.E.). United Kingdom. Popular from 1824 to 1838, plait of false hair looped and wired on top of a woman's coiffure.

apotygma: Greek (3000–100 B.C.E.). Overfold on chiton.

apparel: Elizabethan (1550–1625 C.E.). Strips or square of embroidery.

appas postiches: Directoire and First Empire (1790–1815 C.E.). France. False breasts.

Appenzell embroidery: Switzerland. Very fine drawn work on white linen or lawn. This embroidery originated in the Swiss canton of Appenzell.

appicciolato: Renaissance (1450–1550 C.E.). Italy. Damask silk.

appilion: Biblical (unknown–30 C.E.). Hebrew word for pallium.

apple green: Vivid yellow green color.

applebloom: Early Gothic (1200–1350 C.E.). Fabric similar in shade to apple blossoms.

appleblue: *See* applebloom.

applicazione: Italy. Tuck embroidery.

applique: a piecing process using small cutouts of fabric sewn onto a background fabric.

aprapadina: India. 1. Woman's lower garment. 2. A long robe that reaches to the toes.

apredyti: *See* apvilkti.

aprenti: *See* apvilkti.

apricot: Pale tint of orange.

apron: Length of fabric hemmed at the bottom edge, gathered or pleated to a waistband, and tied in the center back. It may or may not have a bib. It is worn for both utilitarian and decorative purposes.

apron front: Boot or a shoe with oval-shaped apron, similar to that on a moccasin.

apron tunic: (20th century). Tunic with an overskirt that is cut away in back, giving the illusion of an apron.

aprūn: Ireland. Apron.

apruoce: Lithuania. Bracelet.

apsiustas: Lithuania. Cloak.

ápvilkti: Lithuania. To clothe or to dress. Also called apredyti and aprenti.

'aqal: Palestine. Man's headrope, most commonly black, sometimes white. It is made of wool, camel hair, or cotton. *See also* agal.

'aqal mqassab: Palestine. Man's ornamental headropes.

'aqd anbar: *See* qladet 'anbar.

'aqd wazari: Palestine. Necklace of flat figure-eight pieces of silver.

aqrāq: Arabia. Cork-soled sandals.

aquamarine: Semi-precious stone of light blue to blue green color.

aquatic shirt: Romantic (1815–1840 C.E.). United Kingdom. Popular from 1830 on, a man's cotton striped or checked shirt decorated with sporting designs.

aquerne: Early Gothic (1200–1350 C.E.). Fur of squirrel.

ara: *See* tirchha.

arabesque: Ornamental geometrically balanced pattern.

Arabian embroidery: Elaborate Oriental embroidery.

Aragonese bonnet: Romantic (1815–1840 C.E.). United Kingdom. Introduced in 1834, a silk bonnet with an arched front brim and pyramid-shaped crown.

araignée méditant un crime: Restoration (1660–1700 C.E.). France. Shade of gray.

arak-chin: India. Worn by the Brahmins of Sind, a white or colored cotton cap much like a smoking cap.

aralac: Casein base fiber similar to wool.

araluck: India. Waistcoat with elbow-length sleeves.

Aramis mantelet: Crinoline (1840–1865 C.E.). In 1850s, a mantelet with loose hanging sleeves. The mantelet was cut round in back and came to a point in front.

Aran Isle sweater: V or round necked sweater knit in traditional Irish design.

araneous: Early Gothic (1200–1350 C.E.). Embroidery.

aranzel: *See* fustao.

arápis: Greece. Apron ornament.

'araqiyeh: Palestine. Married woman's skull-cap.

aratae: Japan. A rough cloth.

aratóbocskor: Hungary. Moccasins made from worn out boots.

'arayjeh: *See* menajel.

arba kanphoth: Hebrew. Rectangle of fabric, usually wool, about three feet long and one foot wide. It has an opening for the head and tassels at all four corners.

arcari: Romantic (1815–1840 C.E.). In late 1830s, a woman's half cap worn back on the head. It was often tied under the chin with a ribbon. The half cap was made of lace, ribbon, and rosebuds.

arched collar: Directoire and First Empire (1790–1815 C.E.). Introduced in 1814, a high collar that was curved to fit the throat and turned slightly under beneath the chin.

arc'henad: *See* botez.

arc'henad-kambr: France. Breton for slipper.

Arctic: Crinoline (1840–1865 C.E.). In 1855, a velvet talma covered with netting that ended in tassels. The talma was fringed on the lower edge.

arctic hare: Russia. Long-haired rabbit with blue fur with white, tan, or bluish gray guard hairs.

arctics: (20th century). Rubberized overshoes.

ardhaguchchha: India. Necklace of 24 strings of pearls.

ardhamanavaka: India. Necklace of 10 strings of pearls.

ardhi laj: India. Literally "half shame," a veil worn over the face and down to the waist. It is worn in the presence of the senior relative in the home.

ardhoruka: India. Upper body garment; long coat.

Ardil: Trade name for protein fiber made from peanuts.

ardilla: Spain. Squirrel.

ardilla gris: Spain. Petit-gris.

ardilla parda: Spain. Imitation sable.

ardoise: France. Slate color.

arfanítica: Greece. Chemise.

argaman: Hebrew. Red purple.

argent: France. Silver.

Argentan lace: France. Edging, insertion, or band of lace. It was originally a French needlepoint lace made of fine linen thread.

argentine: Silvery substance made from fish scales and used to make fake pearls.

Argentine cloth: Glazed tarlatan or open weave cheesecloth.

argênteo: Portugal. Silvery.

argentería: Renaissance (1450–1550 C.E.). Spain. Silver gilt.

arghwani: India. A deep red color.

argile: Bustle (1865–1890 C.E.). In 1872, the color of potter's clay.

argolas: Portugal. Earrings.

argūbō: Ethiopia. Kafa large white cloak.

argyle: Multicolored diamond pattern. Argyll is the name of a Scottish clan after which this pattern is named.

arhi: *See* aar.

ari: India. A small awl with a notch used to embroider a chain stitch.

Ariadne sleeve: Crinoline (1840–1865 C.E.). In 1861, a small bishop sleeve with a pointed cap.

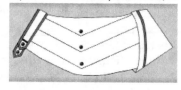
Ariadne sleeve

Aridex: DuPont's name for the water repellent wax emulsion used on cotton, rayon, and wool fabrics.

Arimatsu shibori: Japan. A coarse tie-dye done on cotton in Arimatsu.

ario: Samoa. Silver.

arisard: Scotland. Woman's mantle or plaid that reached from head to feet and was worn draped at the waist.

arkhalukh: Caucasus. Woman's outer garment worn belted at the waist. The sleeves were trimmed with silver buttons or chain links.

armadura: Portugal. Armor.

armadura del busto: *See* corazza.

armatura: Italy. Armor.

armazine: Early Georgian (1700–1750 C.E.). Strong corded silk fabric used for women's gowns and men's waistcoats.

armbaand: Denmark. Bracelet.

armband: Holland and Sweden. Bracelet.

Armband: Germany. Bracelet.

Ärmel: Germany. Sleeve.

Ärmelaufschlag: Germany. Cuffs.

Armenian cloak: Crinoline (1840–1865 C.E.). United Kingdom. Fashionable in 1850s and 1860s, a man's overcoat cut in one piece except for the velvet collar.

Armenian lace: A fine, needle-made, knotted handmade edging lace.

Armenian mantle: Crinoline (1840–1865 C.E.). Popular 1847–1850, a woman's cloak with lace or gimp trim.

Armenian rat: Greek (3000–100 B.C.E.). Ermine.

Armenian toque: Romantic (1815–1840 C.E.). Introduced in 1817, a small tulle and satin turban trimmed with feathers and spangled with silver.

armes à l'épreuve: Renaissance (1450–1550 C.E.). France. Pistol-proof armor.

armet: 1. Late Gothic (1350–1450 C.E.). Small iron or steel helmet with movable visor in front and a brim in back. 2.

armet

Elizabethan (1550–1625 C.E.). Round helmet worn by horsemen in the tiltyard.

armil: *See* armilla.

armilausa: Late Gothic (1350–1450 C.E.). Short cloak or cape worn over armor.

armilla: Greek (3000–100 B.C.E.). Bracelets.

armillae: *See* brachiāle.

arming bolster: Elizabethan (1550–1625 C.E.). Padding worn at the waist under armor.

arming doublet: Elizabethan (1550–1625 C.E.). Padded leather garment worn under armor.

arming points: Elizabethan (1550–1625 C.E.). Point-tipped strong pieces of twine that held mail gussets in place beneath the armpits, in the elbows, and in the knees.

arming-bonett

arming-bonett: Renaissance (1450–1550 C.E.). Padded cap worn under the helmet.

arming-hose: Renaissance (1450–1550 C.E.). Long hose worn under leg armor.

arminho: Portugal. Ermine.

armiño: Spain. Ermine.

armoire: Bustle (1865–1890 C.E.). Introduced in 1880, a very thick corded silk.

armoisin: France. Silk taffeta fabric used for linings.

armozeau: Romantic (1815–1840 C.E.). Introduced in 1820s, a silk similar to lute string but not as thick.

armozeen: *See* armazine.

armozine: *See* armazine.

Armspange: *See* Armband.

armure: 1. Early Gothic (1200–1350 C.E.). Fabric with a woven pattern resembling chain link armor. 2. Crinoline (1840–1865 C.E.). Introduced in 1850, a rich silk and wool fabric with an almost invisible pattern resembling chain or triangles. 3. Stiff, rich fabric of silk, cotton, rayon, wool, or blends. It is patterned in small designs to suggest chain armor.

armure cannelée: Renaissance (1450–1550 C.E.). France. Fluted armor.

armure satinee: Silk fabric with fine twill armure face and satin back.

armure-laine: Heavy corded or ribbed fabric with silk warp and wool weft.

armurette: Bustle (1865–1890 C.E.). Introduced in 1874, a very soft, silky mohair.

army green: (1950–1960 C.E.). United States of America. Introduced in 1954, a new color for uniforms.

Arnel: Trademark name for synthetic fabric made from cellulose triacetate.

arokah: India. Brilliants.

aronui: New Zealand. Maori. A fine cloak of the best quality flax worn only by the leading chiefs. The body of the cloak is made of unbleached flax and the borders were of black, white, and red flax.

arpillera: Spain. Burlap.

arqalix: Iran. Woman's short, tight jacket.

arracadas: Mexico. Crescent-shaped earrings.

Arragon: Crinoline (1840–1865 C.E.). In 1857, a woman's checked, two-thirds circle pardessus with a flounce and a bias cut hood. The hood was trimmed with three large tassels.

Arragonese: Crinoline (1840–1865 C.E.). 1. In 1854, a yoked velvet cloak. The skirt was box-pleated in front. The cloak was embroidered and had a narrow collar. 2. In February 1860, a black silk pardessus with unusual bagged sleeves, bertha trim, and crocheted fringe.

arras: France. Tapestry, originally designed in Arras, France.

Arras lace: France. Bobbin lace originating in Arras.

Arrasene embroidery: Embroidery done with chenille cord creating a velvet appearance.

arrêter: France. To fasten.

arricciatura: Italy. 1. Trim of lace and ribbons fastened in small folds around a handkerchief hem. 2. Curliness.

arrondir: France. To round; to shape into a circle.

arrowhead: Embroidered triangle at the ends of seams on tailored garments.

arroxeado: Portugal. Purplish.

arruivado: Portugal. Reddish, especially pertaining to hair.

arsi: India. A thumb ring set with a mirror.

artificial silk: (1910–1920 C.E.). United States of America. In 1910, American Viscose Company began commercial development of a fabric similar to pure silk; produced from wood pulp, corn protein, and chemical compounds. It was named rayon. Rayon first appeared in garments in a 1915 line by Gabrielle Chanel.

artificial wool: (1920–1929 C.E.). Introduced in United States of America in 1926, short lengths of rayon filaments, crimped, spun and woven or knitted.

artois: Late Georgian (1750–1790 C.E.). Popular with both genders, a long coat topped with three or four short capes. It was named for Count of Artois, brother of Louis XVI (later Charles X of France). It became fashionable again from 1824 to 1830.

artois buckle: Late Georgian (1750–1790 C.E.). United Kingdom. Fashionable from 1775 to 1788, a man's very large shoe buckle.

as: Egyptian (4000–30 B.C.E.). Prince's lock; the plait worn by a prince down one side of the head.

asagi: Japan. Light blue color.

asanoha: Japan. An allover hemp leaf design.

asargado: Spain. Twill.

asaweri: Palestine. Cotton and silk fabric.

asawir 'iradh: Palestine. Wide silver bracelets.

asayib: United Arab Emirates. Circlet used to hold a burqa in place.

asbeh ruwaysiyeh: Palestine. Headband.

Asbestall: Trade name for fabric made of asbestos and nylon yarns.

asbestos: Known to cause cancer, a fireproof fabric of long, straight fibers.

ascanta: Ecuador and Guatemala. Man's felt sombrero with a broad brim.

ascot tie: Bustle (1865–1890 C.E.). Man's scarf with horizontal ends worn tied in a knot and then crossed diagonally, usually held in place with stick pin.

ashantee: Bustle (1865–1890 C.E.). In 1875, a new gray color.

ashasana: India. Decorative border or fabric.

ashida: Japan. High clogs to wear in the rain.

ashifuki: Japan. Foot towel.

ashigappa: United States of America. Hawaii. Literally "leg covering," pants.

ashi-maki: Japan. The cords that tie some trousers at the ankles.

ashinaka-zori: Japan. Straw sandals.

ashira: Tiv. Man's cloth of a white strip edged in blue.

ashish: Tiv. Red openwork cloth worn only by women.

ashrafi: Arabia. Cotton textile.

asi-ebi: Nigeria. Literally "family cloth," aso-oke worn by all members of a family.

asimojórdano: Greece. Neck ornament.

ásimozúnaro: Greece. Belt of chains from which hangs the knife.

asinan: *See* okana.

asisa: Ibo. Blue and white cloth with openwork.

asli: India. A honey color.

asmani: India. Sky blue.

asmar: Palestine. Dark blue color.

asmodée: (1890–1899 C.E.). Black etamine striped with one-inch old rose silk bands.

aso-alake: Nigeria. Wrapper of ikat.

aso-oke: Nigeria. Yoruba handwoven cloth.

asooch: Elizabethan (1550–1625 C.E.). Term meaning that garment was worn diagonally across the body instead of in the normal position.

asparsanumeya: India. Thin, transparent fabric.

áspri: Greece. Festival and bridal costumes.

asprocéndi: Greece. Embroidery made with white thread.

assam cotton: East India. Rough, short staple cotton.

assili cotton: Egypt. Cotton with a golden yellow, strong 1-1/4-inch staple.

assisi embroidery: Form of cross-stitch.

astar: India. A generic term for any kind of silk lining.

astracán: Spain. Persian lamb fur.

Astracan de laine: Crinoline (1840–1865 C.E.). In 1861, a new rough textured trim.

astrakan: 1. Hide of the karakul lamb from Central Asia. *See also* Persian lamb. 2. France and Italy. Astrakhan fur.

Astrakan: Germany. Astrakan fur.

astrakhan: Made in Astrakan, Russia, a woven fabric with loops or curls on face. The pile is mohair or wool and the ground is wool or cotton.

Asturian: Crinoline (1840–1865 C.E.). In 1857, a woman's cloth or velvet cloak trimmed with a network of passementerie and mini-tassels. The cloak also had a beaded fringe.

aswashka: Ecuador and Guatemala. Woven textile.

'at'a': Navajo. Feather.

ata: 1. Biblical (unknown–30 C.E.). Band with gold or silver thread sewn on neck edge of tallith. 2. India. The tucking of the sari.

atataakoro: Ghana. White cloth with indigo blue stripes.

atef: Egyptian (4000–30 B.C.E.). Double crown of Egypt consisting of both the red wicker crown of Lower Egypt and the white felt crown of Upper Egypt.

ati: *See* ata.

atigi: Caribou fur parka worn by Inuit with the fur toward the inside. The fur around the hood is wolverine.

atka: India. Man's long, close-fitting cloak made in a bright color and embroidered with gold thread.

Atlas: Germany. Satin.

atlas: 1. Elizabethan (1550–1625 C.E.) to Late Georgian (1750–1790 C.E.). India. Smooth silk fabric. 2. Turkey. Lightweight silk satin.

atlas khasu: India. A generic term for satin.

atlas silk: India. Silk from Attacus atlas moth. *See also* ailanthus silk.

atole: Guatemala. Sizing.

atrocelado: Renaissance (1450–1550 C.E.). Spain. Trimmed.

atshi: India. Deep red.

atsuita: Japan. Stiff brocaded silk.

attaby: Early Gothic (1200–1350 C.E.). Silk fabric. *See also* tabby.

attāmitō: Ethiopia. Men's earrings; women's finger rings.

attiffet: Renaissance (1450–1550 C.E.). Woman's headdress that created an arc across the top of the head that was surmounted by a veil that fell to a point on the brow.

attigra: Nigeria. A man's elaborate, heavy velvet gown embroidered with metallic threads. It is worn for ceremonial and special occasions.

attila: Crinoline (1840–1865 C.E.). Hungary. Tunic.

attush: Japan. Worn by the Ainu, long tunics made from the inner bark of the elm tree.

au dekls: Lithuania. Linen cloth.

au globe fixé: Late Georgian (1750–1790 C.E.). France. In 1778, a woman's hairstyle.

aubergine: (1890–1899 C.E.). Rich reddish brown color.

auburn: Reddish brown color.

aubusson stitch: Vertical canvas stitch.

audeklas: Lithuania. Linen.

Audobon plumage law: (1900–1910 C.E.). Law passed to prevent the extinction of various native birds and to prevent the importation or sales of various feathers.

Aufschlag: Germany. Lapel.

Augsburg checks: Germany. Small check gingham fabric made for export.

Augusta: Charles I and the Commonwealth (1625–1660 C.E.). Fustian.

Augusta cloth: Crinoline (1840–1865 C.E.). United States of America. Fabric made in Augusta, Georgia.

'auli: Samoa. Clothes iron.

aulmoniere: *See* aumoniere.

aumoniere: Early Gothic (1200–1350 C.E.). France. Embroidered silk pouch that hung from the girdle or belt.

aumuce: *See* almuce.

aune: France. Old fabric measure of 45 inches.

aupakaksiki: India. A 27-inch square of cloth worn tied over the chest and anchored on the left shoulder.

aupakasaki: India. Woman's bodice worn tied on the left shoulder.

Âu-phuc: Vietnam. Western clothes.

aurifère: Crinoline (1840–1865 C.E.). France. Fawn color with a tint of gold.

aurifrisium: *See* opus phrygium.

aurna: India. Woolen cloth.

'auro: Samoa. Gold.

aurora: Romantic (1815–1840 C.E.). Shell pink.

aurum filatum cyprense: Byzantine and Romanesque (400–1200 C.E.). Gold thread.

aurum tractitium: Byzantine and Romanesque (400–1200 C.E.). Gold thread made from gold wire.

Ausstattung: Germany. Trousseau.

Australian wool: Australia. Fine quality wool from Spanish merino sheep.

Austrian belt: Leather-clad metal belt worn around the waist. The belt features screws that, when tightened, render the waist a perfect circle.

Austrian knot: Heavy, black silk braid ornament appliqued on military uniforms in loops.

Austrian shade cloth: Austria. Cotton shade fabric with wide stripes of crinkled surface.

Austurian: Crinoline (1840–1865 C.E.). In 1858, a woman's circular cloth wrap with a bertha. The wrap was gathered on a string at the waist and trimmed with black velvet on a taffeta ground.

Author: (1950–1960 C.E.). Man's hairstyle.

automobile veil: Large protective veil worn by women in early days of cars.

âu-trang: Vietnam. Western clothes.

autruche: France. Ostrich.

autui: Maori. Four-inch cloak pins of whalebone or boars' tusks.

autumn tea brown: China. Yuan dynasty. Shade of brown.

'ava: Samoa. Beard.

ava cotton: India. Cotton.

'avaaluga: Samoa. Moustache.

avaghataka: India. Pearl necklace.

avagraha: India. Woman's lower garment worn to cover genitalia.

avagunthana: India. Worn by women, a long fabric piece worn over the head and sometimes over a part of the face.

avampiés: Renaissance (1450–1550 C.E.). Spain. Gaiters.

avasakthika: *See* paryastika.

avaska: Peru. Naturally colored llama wool or cotton fabric.

Ave Maria lace: Elizabethan (1550–1625 C.E.). France. Variation on Val lace made in Dieppe, France.

avental: Portugal. Apron.

aventurine: Romantic (1815–1840 C.E.). Murrey color.

avignon: Romantic (1815–1840 C.E.). Silk taffeta for coat linings.

avika: India. Sheep's wool or fabric from sheep's wool.

aviver: France. To brighten; to polish.

avocado: Greenish yellow color.

avondcape: *See* sortie.

avonet: Persia. Rug wool from three-year-old sheep.

avqueton: *See* hoqueton.

avve: Norway. Waistband.

awakipa: *See* ribete.

awana: Ecuador and Guatemala. Backstrap loom.

awarua: Australia. Maori dogskin cloak with alternating strips of black and white.

awase-bodokko: Japan. A simple lined garment.

awasqa: Inca. A rough cloth for domestic use.

awayu: Bolivia and Peru. Woman's shawl.

awning: Heavy, brightly colored, sometimes striped canvas.

awondwa: Ghana. The color yellow.

aya: Japan. A patterned silk with a simple geometric motif on a twilled ground.

Aylesham: Early Gothic (1200–1350 C.E.). United Kingdom. Fine linen made in Aylesham, Norfolk.

aymilla: Bolivia. Dress with a very full skirt that reaches to below the knees. The lower edge is trimmed with machine embroidery.

Ayrshire: Directoire and First Empire (1790–1815 C.E.) to Crinoline (1840–1865 C.E.). Scotland. Introduced in Scotland c1814, a dainty white embroidery on linen and cotton. It became a major home industry until the middle of the 19th century.

Ayrshire work: *See* Ayrshire.

azafran: Spain. Saffron color.

Azetat: Germany. Acetate.

azr: *See* izar.

azufar: Renaissance (1450–1550 C.E.). Spain. Bleaching (of the hair).

azul: Ecuador, Guatemala, and Portugal. Blue.

azulado: Portugal. Azure.

azulmarinho: Portugal. Navy blue.

azur: 1. Hungary. Black or white felt greatcoat with full-length broad lapels and enormous sleeves. It was generally worn like a cloak, without the arms in the sleeves. It was elaborately decorated with applique. 2. France. Azure.

azure: Romantic (1815–1840 C.E.). United Kingdom. Sky blue color.

azuren: *See* hemelsblauw.

azurline: Crinoline (1840–1865 C.E.). In 1861, a new bright blue color.

azuur: *See* hemelsblauw.

azzurro: Italy. Azure.

B

baalto: *See* zibun.

babador: Portugal. Bib.

babadu: Ashanti. Weft designed silk cloth.

babag: Ireland. Gaelic word for tassel or fringe.

baban: Ireland. Gaelic word for bobbin.

babero: Spain. Bib; pinafore.

babet bonnet: Romantic (1815–1840 C.E.). United Kingdom. Introduced in 1839, woman's small tulle evening bonnet that sat at the back of the head and covered the ears. It was trimmed with lace and small roses.

babet cap: Romantic (1815–1840 C.E.). Popular from 1836 to the 1840s, woman's muslin morning cap with small caul, trimmed with ribbon.

babhaid: Ireland. Gaelic word for tassel.

babiche: Algonquin. Cord or thong of rawhide or sinew.

babouche: Muslim. Old style heel-less slipper, often of embroidered leather.

baboutcha: *See* kheaya el kebira.

babushka: (1930–1940 C.E.). United States of America. Brightly printed scarf worn around the head and tied under the chin. Named for the Russian word for grandmother.

baby blue: Pastel blue.

baby bodice: Bustle (1865–1890 C.E.). United Kingdom. Woman's square-necked day bodice with vertical pleats down the center front and a large basque. In 1897, the neck had a threaded ribbon to draw it and was worn with a wide side sash.

baby cap: Elizabethan (1550–1625 C.E.). United Kingdom. Popular woman's coif.

baby delaine: *See* delaine wool.

baby doll pajama: (1950–1960 C.E. to present). United States of America. Woman's popular sleepwear set consisting of a loose sleeveless or short-sleeved, flared top and very short bloomers.

baby doll shoe: Shoe with short, wide, round toe.

baby flannel: Plain weave, lightweight cotton fabric used to make children's underwear and clothes.

baby French heel: Crinoline (1840–1865 C.E.). United Kingdom. Popular from 1850 to 1867, small, low heel with an inward curve.

baby lace: *See* Valenciennes lace.

baby Louis heel: (1900–1910 C.E.). Low heel with an inward curve.

baby pink: Pastel pink.

baby pins: Tiny gold bar pins, commonly worn in pairs.

baby ribbon: Extremely narrow white or pastel ribbon.

baby Stuart cap: 1. Charles I and the Commonwealth (1625–1660 C.E.) to present. Woman's small cap similar to baby's bonnet. 2. Child's decoratively edged lace cap.

Babylonian work: Babylonia. Embroidery worn on linen or wool with a rosette design.

babylonica stromata: Roman (753 B.C.E.–323 C.E.). Tapestries depicting animals from Oriental lore and mythology.

babysokje: Holland. Baby bootee.

baccello di piselli: Italy. Peascod.

bacchante: Bustle (1865–1890 C.E.). In 1884, red purple.

bacchetta: Italy. Walking stick.

bachelik: *See* bachlik.

bachelor shoes: *See* brogans.

bachlik: Bustle (1865–1890 C.E.). Short hooded cape ending in a large tassel.

bach-ngoc: Vietnam. White jade.

bacinet: *See* bascinet.

backlik: *See* bachlik.

backsters: United Kingdom. Dyke makers' leather boots on wood platforms.

backstitch: Horizontal stitches moving right to left.

back-strap shoe: Sling pump.

baço: Portugal. Dark brown.

back-strap shoe
See also photospread
(Foot and Legwear).

badami: India. An almond color.

badan: India. Short, double-breasted, narrow-sleeved jacket.

badana: Renaissance (1450–1550 C.E.). Spain. Sheepskin.

badara: India. A variety of silk.

Baden hemp: Excellent quality hemp.

badger: Fur of the badger; a coarse, durable, black hair mixed with white, gray, or tan.

badger whiskers: Crinoline (1840–1865 C.E.). United States of America. Fashion prescribed for the U.S. Navy in 1841 by honorable George E. Badger, Secretary of the Navy. Consisted of whiskers no lower than one inch below the ear and even with the mouth.

badhani: India. From 300 B.C.E. to 700 C.E., a tie-dyed cloth.

badine: Late Georgian (1750–1790 C.E.). France. Woman's fashionable version of shepherdess's crook.

badiyān: *See* badan.

bādlā: *See* kāmdānī.

badshah pasand: India. Lavender color.

badstof: Holland. Terry cloth.

baende: Byzantine and Romanesque (400–1200 C.E.). United Kingdom. Band of metal or gold-embroidered fabric. Possibly for the head.

baeta: Portugal. Baize.

bafota: Madagascar. Plain white cotton cloth.

bafota malandy: Madagascar. New white cotton cloth.

baft: Renaissance (1450–1550 C.E.). Coarse cotton fabric in natural or red and blue.

bafta: 1. India. A kind of calico, made especially at Baroch. 2. India. Silk fabric. 3. Kenya. Glazed bleached calico.

bag bodice: Bustle (1865–1890 C.E.). In 1883, woman's day blouse with pouch front.

bag bonnet: Directoire (1790–1815 C.E.). From 1800 to 1810, woman's day bonnet with a loosely gathered crown.

bag cap: Late Gothic (1350–1450 C.E.). Man's turban-like cap with a fur band and an ornament.

bag Holland: Elizabethan (1550–1625 C.E.). Fine quality linen.

bag plastron: Bustle (1865–1890 C.E.). United Kingdom. Introduced in 1884, plastron for a day bodice that sagged in the front, forming a bag.

bag sheeting: Closely woven even weave cotton fabric used for salt and sugar bags.

bag wig: Early Georgian (1700–1750 C.E.). Worn early in the period for informal wear and fashionable on formal occasions with the younger set after 1730 C.E., man's wig with a ponytail at the back and the front hair brushed into a foretop which often included the man's natural hair. A bag, usually black, covered

bag wig

the ponytail. The bag was usually tied with strings to a black bow at the nape of the neck.

bagalbandi: India. A short fitted coat with a double flap in front. It has tapering full sleeves. *See also* mirjai.

bagazia: *See* muszuj.

bagdad: Bustle (1865–1890 C.E.). 1. Introduced in 1872, striped Eastern silk. 2. Introduced in 1886, pinkish brick dust color.

bagdad wool: Iran. Black or brownish carpet wool.

bagging: Coarse fabric of jute, cotton used for making bags.

bagging shoe: Renaissance (1450–1550 C.E.). Man's loose shoe for country wear.

bagh: 1. India. A Punjabi woman's shawl worn to weddings. It is embroidered in silk floss. 2. Pakistan. Woman's heavily embroidered head shawl worn for ceremonial occasions.

bagheera: Fine, uncut pile velvet that is rough and resistant to crushing.

bagnolette: Early Georgian (1700–1750 C.E.). Woman's small hooded cap that fastened at the neck and gathered around the feet.

bagpipe sleeve: *See* bellows sleeve.

bags: *See* unmentionables.

bague: France. Finger ring.

baguette: Early Gothic (1200–1350 C.E.). Lappet of mail.

bag-waistcoat: *See* bag plastron.

bahia sheeting: Brazil. Cotton fabric.

bahirivasani: India. Woman's ankle-length sari-like garment worn belted.

bahu: India. An armlet.

bahut: Early Georgian (1700–1750 C.E.). Masquerade dress or domino.

bai na yi: China. Ming dynasty. Richly patched shui tian yi.

bài ngá: Vietnam. Ivory badge of office.

bai shou yi: China. Type of burial dress.

bai tong: China. White copper alloy popular with the Han in the Qing dynasty (1644–1700 C.E.).

baiberek: Restoration (1660–1700 C.E.). Russia. Silk fabric.

báibù: China. Plain white fabric.

baigneuse: Late Georgian (1750–1790 C.E.). Popular 1775–1790, large, tucked negligee cap worn while bathing.

baigneuse

bainbergs: Early Gothic (1200–1350 C.E.). Shin guard in a suit of armor.

bàin-dearg: Ireland. Flesh colored.

bainin: Ireland. Handwoven woolen fabric.

bairam: *See* beiramee.

bairami: India. A high-quality muslin.

bairēad: Ireland. 1. Phrygian cap. 2. *See* caipín.

báisè: China. 1. White color. 2. *See* baize.

baiseuse: France. Patch worn at the corner of the mouth; the "kiss" patch.

baishan: China. Man's sleeveless coat worn as everyday dress.

baisser: France. To lower.

baiya: Timbuktu. Gold spiral nose ring.

baize: 1. China. Under the Zhengde emperor (r. 1505–1521 C.E.), sixth and seventh rank of embroidery on a gown; animal with a two-horned dragon's head and a scaly lion's body. Also called baise. 2. Renaissance (1450–1550 C.E.). Thick woolen fabric. 3. Thin serge.

baizi: India. Light indigo color.

bajera: *See* enagua.

baju: 1. Malaysia. Short, loose, short-sleeved white cotton jacket. 2. Indonesia. Shirt and sarong combination making the traditional dress. 3. India. An armlet for the upper arm. 4. Indonesia. Woman's short jacket made from single piece of fabric. 5. Borneo. Coat.

baju bodo: Celebes. A blouse.

baju kurung: Indonesia. Full upper garment.

baju panjang: Indonesia. A long sleeved garment worn over the kain or the sarong.

baka: India. A fop.

bakar: Bosnia. Copper.

Bakelite: (1900–1910 C.E.). Plastic patented by Leo Baekeland in 1907. Used to create dress accessories like buttons, buckles, etc.

bakhrama: India. Crested turban.

bakkebaarden: Holland. Side whiskers.

bakku: Sikkim. Long-sleeved coat that fastens at neck and on one side.

bakou: *See* baku.

baku: Ceylon. Fine, lightweight straw.

bakwala: Nigeria. Round cap.

bal: Woman's low-heeled ankle boot worn for bicycling.

bála: Greece. Forehead.

balaba: India. Persian cape.

bālābandī: India. Short-waisted jacket.

balaclava: (1910s to present). Heavy wool helmet-like crocheted or knitted hat. First worn in World War I by soldiers and derives its name from the Balaclava coast of Russia.

balagnie cloak: Charles I and the Commonwealth (1625–1660 C.E.). France. Elegant cape with a deep collar that was held in place with cords around the collar. It could be worn over one or both shoulders.

Balaklava: Crinoline (1840–1865 C.E.). In 1855, gros d'Afrique mantilla with box-pleated flounce. Trimmed with pearl-edged braid on an insertion lace.

balandran: *See* caban.

balandrana: Early Gothic (1200–1350 C.E.) to Renaissance (1450–1550 C.E.). Traveler's cloak with hood and large sleeves.

balantine: Directoire and First Empire (1790–1815 C.E.). Woman's handbag that hung free from the belt. *See also* reticule; ridicule.

balaq: Turkmenistan. Woman's trousers that taper to the ankle. Upper part is made of plain fabric and legs of an embroidered fabric.

balayeuse: Bustle (1865–1890 C.E.). Ruffle on the inside hem of woman's skirt to protect it from the ground.

balbriggan: Ireland. Unbleached cotton fabric with a fleecy back. Popular for men's winter undergarments, called balbriggans.

baldachin: Rich, embroidered or brocaded silk fabric woven with silk or gold threads.

baldekin: Late Gothic (1350–1450 C.E.). Silk fabric like brocade woven with gold thread.

baldrés: *See* badana.

baldric: *See* baldrick.

baldrick: Elizabethan (1550–1625 C.E.). Band of fabric, ribbon, or leather used to hold the sword; later worn for decorative purposes.

baleen: Early Gothic (1200–1350 C.E.). Tough substance in upper jaw of a whale. Used for armor and later for stays under the name whalebone.

balein: Holland. Baleen.

baleinage: France. Boning.

baleine: 1. *See* baleen. 2. France. To bone.

balerino: *See* balayeuse.

balernos: Bustle (1865–1890 C.E.). In 1874, soft, silky mohair fabric.

balesses: Renaissance (1450–1550 C.E.). United Kingdom. Rose pink spinel.

balg: Ireland. Gaelic word for a leather bag.

balga: Timbuktu. Slipper.

balgan: Ireland. Gaelic word for wallet or satchel.

balg-bannaig: Ireland. Gaelic word for bannock bag.

balg-thional: Ireland. Gaelic word for wallet.

bali: India. A ring-type earring with a pearl strung on it.

balibuntal: *See* ballibuntl.

balílà: China. Paris green.

baline: 1. Rough wool or cotton fabric. 2. Jute or hemp.

Balkan blouse: Bustle (1865–1890 C.E.). Woman's long-waisted bodice cut full at the bottom edge with a belt at the hips. Long full sleeves that gathered onto wristbands. Made from linen, lawn, or voile. Often colorfully cross-stitched.

ball: Ireland. Gaelic word for any part of the male or female dress.

ballantine: *See* reticule.

ballerina dress: Mid-calf-length dress for dinner or evening.

ballet-skirt: Bustle (1865–1890 C.E.). United Kingdom. Introduced in 1883, tulle evening skirt on a silk or satin base. Top layer of tulle commonly spotted with stars, pearls, or beetle wings to sparkle. Often worn with a velvet or satin bodice.

ballibuntal: *See* ballibuntl.

ballibuntl: Philippine Islands. Fine, shiny, smooth straw similar to baku straw.

balloon cloth: Closely woven, fine cotton fabric originally used for balloons and dirigibles.

balloon hat: Late Georgian (1750–1790 C.E.). Popular from 1783 to 1785, woman's gauze hat with a huge balloon-shaped crown and a wide brim. Celebration of Lunardi and the balloon.

balloon skirt: Voluminous skirt.

balloon sleeve: Gay Nineties (1890–1900 C.E.). Woman's sleeve cut full to elbow, fitted in the forearm.

ballpark blue: Pastel blue color.

ballroom neckcloth: Romantic (1815–1840 C.E.). United Kingdom. Popular in 1830s, man's white starched neckcloth worn with the end held crossing in the front with a pin.

ball-serice: Ireland. Gaelic word for beauty spot.

balmacaan: (20th century). Loose-fitting overcoat, fuller at the bottom than the top, usually with raglan sleeves. Originated in Scotland.

balmoral
See also photospread
(Foot and Legwear).

balmoral: 1. Crinoline (1840–1865 C.E.). United Kingdom. Introduced by Prince Albert around 1853, laced shoe or half-boot. Later in 1890s, a tennis shoe. 2. United Kingdom. Strong, heavy twill weave fabric with stripes of red, blue, and black. 3. Kind of woman's cheap petticoat.

balmoral bodice: Bustle (1865–1890 C.E.). United Kingdom. Introduced in 1867, postillion corsage with short basques.

balmoral cap: Flat tam-o'-shanter.

balmoral cloak: Crinoline (1840–1865 C.E.). In 1852, woman's sleeveless, hooded, short cloak.

balmoral cloth: United Kingdom. Twill weave fabric striped in red, gray, blue, or black.

balmoral crape: (1890–1900 C.E.). United Kingdom. Introduced in 1895.

balmoral jacket: Bustle (1865–1890 C.E.). In 1867, woman's jacket cut like a waistcoat and buttoning to the throat. In 1870, more tailored version with belt and cuffs.

balmoral mantle: Bustle (1865–1890 C.E.). In 1866, woman's cashmere, cloth, or velvet cape.

balmoral petticoat: Crinoline (1840–1865 C.E.) to Bustle (1865–1890 C.E.). United Kingdom. Red and black wool petticoat. Popularly worn under a long dress looped up for walking from 1860 to 1870s.

balneari: Roman (753 B.C.E.–323 C.E.). Bath clothes.

balneri: Biblical (unknown–30 C.E.). Hebrew's bath clothes.

balones: Ecuador and Guatemala. Very full knee breeches.

balt: 1. Ireland. Gaelic word for the welt of a shoe; a belt or the selvedge of fabric. 2. Romania. Narrow belt with brass ornaments.

baltaich: Ireland. Gaelic word for a welt, belt, or border.

bälte: Sweden. Belt.

balteum: Roman (753 B.C.E.–323 C.E.). Pair of belts.

balteum militare: Roman (753 B.C.E.–323 C.E.). Military belt.

balteus: Roman (753 B.C.E.–323 C.E.). Baldric or leather girdle. *See also* cīnctus.

baltion: Greek (3000 B.C.E.–100 B.C.E.). Pair of belts.

baluchar: Directoire (1790–1815 C.E.) to Gay Nineties (1890–1900 C.E.). India. A silk brocade sari made with supplementary weft motifs of diagonal rows of small flowers.

balusu: Indonesia. Sa'dan-Toraja armband of white shelkl.

Balz: Germany. Old High German term for belt.

balza: 1. *See* balzana. 2. Italy. Flounce.

balzana: Renaissance (1450–1550 C.E.). Italy. Trim around the hem of a gown.

balzarine: Romantic (1815–1840 C.E.). Introduced in the 1830s, cotton and worsted fabric.

balzerine: Bustle (1865–1890 C.E.). Introduced in 1889, narrow striped grenadine overlaid with wide silk crepe stripes.

balzo: Renaissance (1450–1550 C.E.). Italy. Large, round headdress that hid the wearer's head.

bamagia: Renaissance (1450–1550 C.E.). Italy. Linen or cotton fabric used for interfacing.

bambak: Armenia. Cotton.

bambergs: Early Gothic (1200–1350 C.E.). Armor for the shin. *See also* bainbergs.

bambino hat: (1930–1940 C.E.). Wide-brimmed hat that framed the face like a halo. Named for the paintings of the Christ Child by Luca della Robbia.

bambulo: Bustle (1865–1890 C.E.). Introduced in 1885, coarse, translucent canvas.

bamkyinie: Ashanti. Umbrella used for state occasions.

bams: Sailors' leather gaiters.

bàn: Ireland. White.

bàn chài quan áo: Vietnam. Clothes brush.

ban hi: China. Tang dynasty. Woman's upper garment.

bana: India. Robes.

banador: Spain. Bathing suit.

banafsai: India. Purple.

banat: India. Silken lace embroidered with gold or silver wire.

banco: Ecuador and Guatemala. Base of a spinning wheel.

band: 1. Elizabethan (1550–1625 C.E.). Turned-down collar. 2. *See* lint.

band strings: Elizabethan (1550–1625 C.E.). Laces or strings used to tie the band or ruff together.

banda arricciata: Italy. Flounce; ruffle.

bandanna: Red or blue cotton handkerchief distinguished by its white or colored paisley-shaped ornaments.

Banddurchzug: Germany. Trimming insertion.

bandeau: 1. Narrow brassiere. 2. Narrow filet for the head.

bandeau beehive crown hat: (1910–1920 C.E.). Woman's velvet turban-shaped hat with ostrich plumes. Worn very low on the head.

bandekin: *See* baldekin.

bandelet: Filet.

bandelette: *See* bandelet.

bandera: Bolivia. Bright, multicolored poncho with even-width stripes.

band-gale-kā-coat: India. Short coat with fitted neck.

bandhana-krtsna: India. Worn from 300 to 700 C.E., shoes with more than three fasteners.

bandeau beehive crown hat

bandhani: India. The resist technique used in tie-dye.

bandhej: *See* bandhani.

bandi: India. A sleeveless bagalbundi.

bāndiā angarkhā: India. Short, fitted, long-sleeved coat that fastens with tapes on the chest or at the side.

bandileer: Elizabethan (1550–1625 C.E.). Leather baldrick popularized by musketeers who wore them over the left shoulder.

banditti: Directoire and First Empire (1790–1815 C.E.). Small, decorative bunch of feathers worn on women's bonnets.

bandle: 1. Ireland. Homespun, coarse linen that is woven two feet wide. 2. Scotland, United Kingdom. Old fabric measurement two feet wide.

bandle linen: Ireland. Homemade linen.

bandleg brief: Woman's panty style with strip of ribbing around leg opening.

bandolier: *See* bandileer.

bandolier cloth: United States. Bed sheeting dyed olive drab and used in army and navy as belts for carrying cartridges.

bandore: Early Georgian (1700–1750 C.E.). Woman's mourning headdress with black veil.

bandore peak: Early Georgian (1700–1750 C.E.). Woman's mourning black bonnet that curved to a point over the center of the forehead.

bandvai gujarati: India. Saris from Gujarat.

bane: Borneo. A necklace.

Bangalore cap: India. A black felt fez-shaped cap.

bangbangan: Java. Red on white color combination used in fabric.

bàn-gheal: Ireland. Milk white color.

bangkok: Fine, light straw.

bangle: India. Bracelet of colored glass.

bangle bracelet: Round, rigid bracelet.

bành-tô: Vietnam. Topcoat.

banker's blue: (1950–1960 C.E.). Dark blue color.

bankuo: Ashanti. Weft-designed cotton cloth.

Banlon: Patented crimped knit yarn.

bann-amh'cha: Ireland. Gaelic word for neckband of a shirt.

bann-bhràghad: Ireland. 1. Cravat. 2. Front band of a woolen or cotton shirt.

bann-bhràighe: Ireland. Cape.

bann-dùirn léine: Ireland. Shirt wristband.

bann-muineal: Ireland. Gaelic word for collar.

bannockburn: Scotland. Tweed fabric made in Bannock. Used in suits and topcoats.

baño reservado: Ecuador and Guatemala. Indigo.

bante: Nigeria. Triangular loincloth.

banyan: 1. Restoration (1660–1700 C.E.) to Late Georgian (1750–1790 C.E.). Man's dressing gown cut like coat of the period. Often made of Indian linen, silk, or velvet. In 1780s, worn outdoors in the country. 2. India. Undershirt, originally of muslin, now made from blends.

banzhi: China. Thumb ring.

ba'o barit: Borneo. Printed beads.

ba'o bata': *See* let.

bao bó: Vietnam. Sackcloth.

ba'o burur: Borneo. Heavy cornelian beads.

ba'o rawir: Borneo. Small elongated orange beads.

bao táo: Vietnam. Sackcloth.

bao tou: China. Rectangular scarf of black cotton or gummed silk held on the head with a woven band.

baori: Japan. A style of hat.

báosha zhiwù: China. Muslin.

Bär: Germany. Bear fur.

bar pin: Three-inch-long, narrow breast pin of platinum or gold, often set with row of gems.

bar shoe: Shoe with bar or buckle across the instep.

barani: India. A type of upper coat.

baranice: Slovakia. Plain lambskin cap with earflaps.

barasi: India. Vedic period. Cloth from the fibers of the red-flowered rhododendron.

bar shoe
See also photospread (Foot and Legwear).

baratea: Spain. Barathea.

barathea: Silk and cotton blend fabric with pebbly weave resembling chain armor.

barba: Portugal. Beard or whiskers.

barbante: Portugal. Thread.

barbe: 1. Byzantine and Romanesque (400–1200 C.E.). Piece of fabric, often linen, worn under the chin. Commonly worn by widows or persons in mourning. 2. Renaissance (1450–1550 C.E.). Hood supported by wire that dipped low over the forehead into a point.

barbe

barbel: Romantic (1815–1840 C.E.). In 1827, pompadour blue.

barber's apron: Plastic circular cape worn to protect clothes during haircut. Fastens at nape of neck.

barbette: *See* barbe.

barbichet: Woman's headdress made like poke bonnet but with lappets.

barboteuse: France. Rompers.

Barbour jacket: United Kingdom. Country all-weather coat made of waterproof waxed cotton.

barbui: Romania. Fan-shaped pleats.

barbúli: Greece. Fine red kerchief worn like a turban.

barbute

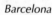

Barcelona

barbute: Late Gothic (1350–1450 C.E.). Helmet of Italian origin that covered most of the face. Allegedly worn by Joan of Arc.

barcelona: Spain. Kerchief or twilled silk worn around the neck or head.

Barcelona: Crinoline (1840–1865 C.E.). Name given to various forms of women's outerwear.

Barcelona scarf: Denmark. Woman's scarf of patterned silk.

Barchent: Germany. Fustian.

barclod: *See* ffedog.

bard: India. A large wrapper.

barège: Romantic (1815–1840 C.E.). Introduced in 1819, translucent silk and wool blend fabric.

barège Anglais: Crinoline (1840–1865 C.E.). Summer weight dress fabric.

barège de laine: Crinoline (1840–1865 C.E.). Woolen and cotton fabric.

barège de Pyrenees: Crinoline (1840–1865 C.E.). Introduced in 1850, barege printed with flowers.

barège-grenadine: Bustle (1865–1890 C.E.). Introduced in 1877, cotton and jute blend barege.

baret: Holland. Biretta.

Barett: *See* barrette.

baréza: Greece. Woolen winter veil.

Bargello stitch: Upright canvas stitch.

bari: India. Bengal cotton.

barito: Romania. Cloth foot wraps.

barjura: *See* svechchhitika.

bark cloth: 1. Fabric made of soaked inner bark of tree and then dyed or ornamented. 2. Modern fabric imitating appearance of tree bark.

bark crepe: Rough crepe fabric imitating tree bark.

barkit: Early Georgian (1700–1750 C.E.). Slang term for dirt hardened onto the hair.

barleycorn: 1. Early Georgian (1700–1750 C.E.) Figured fabric with small regular design. 2. Basket weave with floats.

barleycorns: *See* wheat ears.

barlingham: Early Gothic (1200–1350 C.E.). United Kingdom. Taffeta woven in Barlingham.

barmcloth: Early Gothic (1200–1350 C.E.). Leather apron worn by workmen.

barmecloth: *See* barmcloth.

barmfell: Early Gothic (1200–1350 C.E.) to Late Gothic (1350–1450 C.E.). Workman's leather apron.

barmillion: United Kingdom. Fustian made in Manchester.

barmskin: *See* barmfell.

barn-door britches: United States of America. Front-fall trousers.

baro: Philippine Islands. Woman's wide sleeved blouse.

baronduki: Russia. Misspelling of burunduki, a chipmunk.

Baronette: Trade name for rayon.

barong tagalong: Philippine Islands. Shirt or blouse worn instead of dinner jacket.

barouche: Directoire and First Empire (1790–1815 C.E.). Snug, three-quarter-length coat with full sleeves. Closed down the front with gold buttons and belted at the waist.

barpour: Crinoline (1840–1865 C.E.). Introduced in 1847, twilled silk and wool blend fabric.

barraca: Portugal. Big umbrella.

barracan: 1. Palestine. Length of cloth worn wrapped around body and drawn over head and shoulders. Worn as cloak, mantle, or coat. Originally made of coarse camlet. 2. Fabric of goat or camel hair.

barracano: Coarse Bedouin cloth blanket.

barragan: *See* barracan.

barraighin: Ireland. Gaelic word for miter.

barras: Holland. Canvas or linen for neckcloths.

barratee: *See* barathea.

barratine: Restoration (1660–1700 C.E.) to Directoire (1790–1815 C.E.). United States of America. Popular from 1697 to 1800, silk fabric used for petticoats and stomachers.

barre: Silk fabric striped selvage to selvage.

barrel hose: Elizabethan (1550–1625 C.E.). Men's full breeches.

barrel purse: Cylindrical bag with two handles that connect on the flat sides of the barrel. Commonly opens on one side with a flap.

barrel sash: Worn by hussars, a sash with a large number of cords that passed through tubes.

barret: Renaissance (1450–1550 C.E.). Spain. Flat cap commonly slashed, puffed, and embroidered.

barrete: Portugal. Barret.

barrette

barrette: 1. Renaissance (1450–1550 C.E.). Italy. A flat, four-cornered velvet cap worn by men. 2. Elizabethan (1550–1625 C.E.). France. Hat similar to biretta but with stiff, turned up brim. Lining of brim was generally different color than rest of hat and was often embroidered, trimmed, slashed, or puffed. Varied greatly in size. In Germany, called the Barett.

barrettino: Italy. Long, knitted red or black stocking cap favored by fishermen and farmers.

barrie: *See* barry.

barros miudas: India. A Portuguese term for colored opaque beads.

barrow coat: Baby bunting or flannel wrap used to wrap up baby. Usually bag shaped with attached cap.

barry: Slang for underskirt or petticoat.

baršun: *See* samt.

barthaube: Renaissance (1450–1550 C.E.). Germany. Chin guard of plate.

barvell: United States of America. Coarse leather apron.

bas: France. Literally "stocking."

bas à cotes: France. Ribbed or openwork stockings.

bas à jour: *See* bas à cotes.

bas de laine: France. Wool stockings.

bas de soie: France. Silk stockings.

bas de soy: *See* bas de soie.

basane: Directoire and First Empire (1790–1815 C.E.). Strip of woven bronze lace.

basc: 1. Ireland. Gaelic word for the color red. 2. *See* muince.

baschina: Italy. Basque.

bascinet: Late Gothic (1350–1450 C.E.). Round, pointed helmet without a visor or throat piece.

basco: Italy. Beret.

base coat: Renaissance (1450–1550 C.E.). Man's jerkin with pleated, knee-length skirt, short sleeves, and square neckline.

baselard: Early Gothic (1200–1350 C.E.). Ornamental dagger.

basen: *See* bazan.

bases: Renaissance (1450–1550 C.E.). Cartridge-pleated, knee-length skirts of rich material worn by men.

bashlik: Russia. Hood.

bashlyk: 1. (1950–1959 C.E.). Fitted cloth hood worn covering the ears. 2. India. A Scythian pointed felt cap.

bashōfu: Japan. A fabric made from the banana plantain fiber.

basil: Tanned sheepskin used for shoe linings.

basin de laine: Crinoline (1840–1865 C.E.). Introduced in 1855, thick, wool dimity ribbed on one side.

basinet: *See* bascinet.

basing: Byzantine and Romanesque (400–1200 C.E.). Rectangular cloak of fur worn by men.

basket weave: Plain weave using paired threads.

basma: 1. *See* batistă. 2. Turkey. Printed cloth.

basmak: 1. *See* sapog. 2. Turkey. Shoe; sandal.

basque: Crinoline (1840–1865 C.E.). France. Short, skirt-like ending of woman's bodice.

basque belt: Romantic (1815–1840 C.E.). Corset-like garment worn by many men in 1830s and 1840s to create the slim-waisted look.

basque beret: France. Round, flat, soft wool cap worn by Basque peasants.

basque shirt: Knitted woolen jersey shirt woven in contrasting horizontal stripes.

basque waistband: Bustle (1865–1890 C.E.). In 1867, woman's bodice with five vandyked tabs as basque.

basque-habit: Bustle (1865–1890 C.E.). Woman's bodice with square basques.

basquin body: Crinoline (1840–1865 C.E.). Woman's bodice cut with basque in one with bodice.

basquina: Spain. Overskirt.

basquine: 1. Renaissance (1450–1550 C.E.). Restraining underbodice of heavy material. 2. Elizabethan (1550–1625 C.E.). Boned, hip-length bodice similar to corset.

Basquine: Crinoline (1840–1865 C.E.). In 1856, woman's unlined cloak with wide, loose sleeves.

basquine a l'espagnole: Crinoline (1840–1865 C.E.). In 1857, woman's silk or satin jacket with basque cut in deep scallops edged with silk braid and lace. Sleeves trimmed like basque. Lappets around neck imitating collar.

basta cloth: Indonesia. Fabric with yellow ground and red motif.

bastão: Portugal. Walking stick; cane.

baston con anima: Italy. Gadget cane.

bata: Portugal. Dressing gown.

bata corta: Spain. Smock.

bata de casa: Spain. Housedress.

bata de mañana: Spain. Dressing gown.

batakari: Ghana. Smock.

batas: Lithuania. Boot.

batavia: Twill.

batavia cloth: Philippine Islands. Straw and cotton or silk fabric used for drapery.

bateau neckline: 1. Boat-shaped neckline. 2. Crinoline (1840–1865 C.E.). Wide, low neckline on women's garments.

bath-throid: Ireland. Gaelic word for helmet.

bâti: France. The outlining thread couched on a lace pattern.

baticol: Renaissance (1450–1550 C.E.). Spain. Burnished steel breeches.

batik: Indonesia. Method of resist dyeing developed in Java. Wax is used as resist, leaving slight streaking in pattern where dye permeates cracks in resist.

batilla: Ecuador. A shoulder wrap.

batín: Spain. Smoking jacket.

batina: Portugal. Cassock.

Batist: Germany. Batiste.

batist: Germany and Holland. Batiste; cambric.

batistă: Romania. Handkerchief.

batista: Italy and Spain. Batiste.

batiste: France. Sheer, finely woven, plain weave, cotton fabric named for inventor Baptiste Chambrai, French weaver in the 13th century.

batiste de laine: Crinoline (1840–1865 C.E.). In 1855, new fabric.

batiste de soie: Silk batiste.

batom: Portugal. Lipstick.

batswing: Soft wool or cotton fabric, usually taupe in color.

Battenburg jacket: Bustle (1865–1890 C.E.). Woman's short outdoor jacket.

Battenburg lace: Rough form of Renaissance lace used for dresses and draperies. *See also* Renaissance lace.

Battist: Germany. Cambric.

battle jacket: (1910–1920 and 1940–1950 C.E.). Single-breasted, waist-length man's jacket worn during World War I.

batts: Charles I and the Commonwealth (1625–1660 C.E.). Woman's popular black leather shoe with medium heel that fastened with latchet or buckle.

batuz work: Embroidery with attached metal plates.

batwat: Late Gothic (1350–1450 C.E.). Small padded cap worn under helmet.

batwing: (20th century). Sleeve with deep armseye.

batyst: Poland. Batiste.

batz: Guatemala. Cotton thread.

baudekin: Elizabethan (1550–1625 C.E.). Brocade of silk and gold.

baudekyn: *See* baudekin.

baudricke: *See* baldrick.

baugr: Norway. Old Norse word for bracelet.

baum marten: Soft, durable fur of the European brown marten.

Baumwolle: Germany. Cotton.

Baumwollsamt: Germany. Velveteen.

bauson skin: Renaissance (1450–1550 C.E.). Skin of badger.

bautta: Italy. Black cloak with hood deep enough to cover face of wearer.

bavaglio: Italy. Bib.

bavalla: Italy. Fabric woven from silk waste and combings.

bavarel: France. Woman's corset cut straight in front and reaching high point in back where it fastened. Worn outside dress.

bavarette: Elizabethan (1550–1625 C.E.). Child's bib.

Bavarian dress-style: Romantic (1815–1840 C.E.). Introduced in 1826, carriage dress trimmed with rows of bands down front of the garment.

Bavarian lace: Simple bobbin lace of linen or cotton thread.

Bavarian pelisse robe: Romantic (1815–1840 C.E.). Popular from 1815 to 1835, dress trimmed with two rows reaching from shoulder to hem.

bavette: Late Georgian (1750–1790 C.E.). Bib of an apron.

bavlna: Czechoslovakia. Cotton.

bavlnka: Slovakia. Girl's skirt, white with wide red stripes, that is worn to indicate that she is of marriageable age.

bavolet: 1. Renaissance (1450–1550 C.E.). Woman's headdress made of strip of linen that descended from top of the head to the shoulders. 2. Crinoline (1840–1865 C.E.). Flounce. 3. Ruffle at back edge of woman's bonnet.

bawdrech: Baldric or necklace.

bawdric: *See* baldrick.

bawełna: Poland. Cotton.

bayadère: Bustle (1865–1890 C.E.). Introduced in 1869, striped silk and wool fabric made in plain or twill weave.

bayadère poplin: Crinoline (1840–1865 C.E.). In 1862, poplin with narrow silver stripe.

bayeta: 1. Ecuador and Guatemala. Plain-weave woolen fabric. 2. Bolivia. Coarse woolen fabric. 3. Spain. An English red cloth.

bayeta de lishtas: Ecuador. A woman's shoulder wrap.

bayō: Ethiopia. Pointed leather cap.

bayonnaise: Bustle (1865–1890 C.E.). In 1879, similar to tamise cloth.

bays: *See* baize.

bayt al-sham: Palestine. Plain white cotton used for underdresses.

bazan: Early Gothic (1200–1350 C.E.). Sheepskin tanned in oak or birch bark.

bazayl: Palestine. Flannelette for men's nightwear and women's dresses.

Bazna: Algeria. Woman's silk sash.

bāzūband: India. Armlet with folding bands.

bēabhar: Ireland. Gaelic word for beaver.

beach coat: (20th century). Short, loose coat of terry cloth or toweling used for beachwear.

bead lace: Strip of black tulle with beads sewn on in motifs.

beading stitch: A line of small overcast holes.

bēag: United Kingdom. Old English word for bracelet.

beah: Byzantine and Romanesque (400–1200 C.E.). United Kingdom. Ring for the finger, arm, neck, or head.

beanie: (1940–1950 C.E.). Calotte.

beannag: Ireland. Gaelic word for kerchief, the corner of a plaid, skirt, linen coif, or shawl.

bearams: *See* beiramee.

bearding: In a quilt, the batting fibers that migrate to the surface of the quilt top.

bearing cloth: Elizabethan (1550–1625 C.E.). Robe or large square of heavy silk cloth used to carry a child to his/her baptism.

bearm-clap: Byzantine and Romanesque (400–1200 C.E.). United Kingdom. Apron.

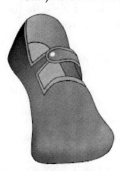

bear's paw
See also photospread
(Foot and Legwear).

bear's paw: Renaissance (1450–1550 C.E.). Padded shoes.

bearskin: A grenadier cap covered in fur.

bearskin pants: Greenland. Men's white bearskin pants.

beatelle: *See* betteela.

beatilla: Renaissance (1450–1550 C.E.). Spain. Hood of sheer material that reached to the back and the chest.

Beatrice: Crinoline (1840–1865 C.E.). United States of America. Introduced 1860, nine-flounced spring dress.

Beatrice parasol: Crinoline (1840–1865 C.E.). United Kingdom. Popular parasol of the 1860s named for the youngest daughter of Queen Victoria.

Beatrice twill: United Kingdom. Twill weave fabric, usually cotton, but sometimes a worsted or alpaca blend.

beattillia: *See* betteela.

beau-catcher: 1. Curl worn in middle of woman's forehead. Also called spit curl. 2. Bustle (1865–1890 C.E.). In 1866, long ribbon tied at back of bonnet.

beaudoy: Early Georgian (1700–1750 C.E.). Worsted fabric used for stockings.

beaupers: Renaissance (1450–1550 C.E.). Linen.

beauty patches: Roman to modern times. Small, black velvet shapes worn on the face, throat, and breast.

beauty spot veil: Gay Nineties (1890–1900 C.E.). Veiling with sparsely powdered velvet spots.

beauvais embroidery: France. Tapestry-like form of embroidery.

beaver: 1. Elizabethan (1550–1625 C.E.). Moveable face guard on helmet. 2. Hat made of beaver fur or imitation fur. 3. Short-haired, durable fur with dense pile from the *Castor canadensis*.

beaver cloth: Heavyweight, woolen fabric with soft finish and thick nap used to make overcoats.

beaver fustian: *See* beaverteen.

beaverteen: Romantic (1815–1840 C.E.). Cotton twilled fabric with warp drawn up into loops.

bebed: Java. A rectangular textile worn wrapped around men's hips.

bebedi: *See* pheta.

beche-cashmere: Crinoline (1840–1865 C.E.). Introduced in 1848, soft wool fabric thicker than flannel.

beck: Renaissance (1450–1550 C.E.). Beak shaped portion of hood worn in 1500–1525.

bed jacket: (20th century). Short jacket worn when resting in bed.

bedelarmband: Holland. Charm bracelet.

bedford cloth: Sturdy fabric with lengthwise ribs made from wool, silk, cotton, synthetics, or blends. *See also* Bedford cord.

Bedford cord: United States of America. Worsted, ribbed fabric used for riding habits, livery, suits, and children's clothes.

Bedfordshire Maltese lace: Black silk or cream cotton bobbin lace.

Bedfordshire plaited lace: A bobbin lace in which the ground is formed of wheat ears in a square formation.

bedla: Egypt. Woman's floor length A-line gown with full sleeves.

bedong: Borneo. Woman's waistband.

bedrukt katoen: Holland. Calico.

bedrukte katoenen stof: Holland. Cotton print.

bee chaha'ohí: Navajo. Umbrella.

beech marten: *See* baum marten.

beefeater: Brimmed black hat with flat, high crown.

bee-gum hat: Popular term for high silk hat.

beehive bonnet: Directoire and First Empire (1790–1815 C.E.). Hive-shaped bonnet of straw that tied under chin with ribbon.

beehive coiffure: (1950–1960 C.E.). Woman's hairstyle built on back combed base.

beehive hat: Directoire and First Empire (1790–1815 C.E.) and 1910–1914. Large, beehive-shaped hat that came down far over the head. Popular from 1910 to 1914.

beenwindsel: Holland. Puttee.

beer jacket: (1920–1930 and 1930–1940 C.E.). Simple cotton or linen flannel jacket popular with male college students.

beetling: Lustrous treatment for cotton and linen fabrics.

beffschen: Switzerland. Plain neck band.

beg: Byzantine and Romanesque (400–1200 C.E.) to Renaissance (1450–1550 C.E.). United Kingdom. Middle English word for bracelet.

begadim levanim: Biblical (unknown–30 C.E.). Hebrew's white clothes.

beggar's lace: *See* Bavarian lace.

beguin: 1. Byzantine (400–1200 C.E.). Introduced in 12th century, three-piece fine linen cap. 2. Renaissance (1450–1550 C.E.). Felt or velvet cap. 3. Early Georgian (1700–1750 C.E.). Linen cap worn under the wig.

bei xin: China. Sleeveless waistcoat worn by boys.

bei yen: China. In the Qing dynasty (1644–1911 C.E.), long drop ornament hung from back of chao zhu.

bei ze: China. In the Ming dynasty (1368–1644 C.E.), a narrow robe which met in the center front and tied at the chest. It was worn for informal wear or as an underrobe.

bei zi: China. Ming dynasty. Narrow sleeved or sleeveless dress with front opening.

beidài: China. Suspenders.

bèifú: China. Army clothing.

beige: 1. Natural or undyed fabric. 2. Cotton, worsted, or rayon twill weave fabric. 3. Light tan or ecru color. 4. *See* grege. 5. Bustle (1865–1890 C.E.). Introduced in 1874, coffee colored wool vicuna fabric.

beige damasse: Bustle (1865–1890 C.E.). In 1876, loose, light woolen tissue.

beiramee: Elizabethan (1550–1625 C.E.) India. Cotton fabric for export. *See also* bairami.

bekatapu: Borneo. Wearing a war cap.

bekecs: *See* kodmon.

bekengkang: Borneo. To be striped.

beksis: Lithuania. Trousers.

béla: Greece. Nickname for a blonde woman.

belcher: Blue kerchief with white spots with blue centers. Popularized by Jim Belcher, English pugilist.

béledzík: Greece. Bracelet.

belette: Early Gothic (1200–1350 C.E.) to Elizabethan (1550–1625 C.E.). Jewel or ornament.

Belgian lace: Pillow lace from Belgium.

Belgian linen: Bustle (1865–1890 C.E.). Introduced in 1879, thick, damask-like, cream colored linen with colored pattern.

Belgian split straw: Narrow straw plaiting.

Belgium Venise: A needle lace made to imitate 17th-century Venetian raised lace.

Belgrave shoe: Romantic (1815–1840 C.E.). A woman's calfskin, low-heeled evening shoe. The back of the shoe extended up behind the ankle, gladiator-style. The tongue-less shoe laced from the ball of the foot to the top of the ankle.

Belgrave shoe

beli potouri: Bulgaria. White wool trousers worn over futsami gashti.

bell bottoms: (1960–1970 C.E.). Trousers with wide, flaring bottoms.

bell hoop: *See* cupola coat.

bell suit: (1950–1959 C.E.). Woman's skirted suit where the jacket is nipped in at the waist and has a padded bell-shaped hipline.

bellboy hat: (1910–1920 C.E.). United States of America. Late in decade, woman's high-crowned, small visored hat with plume or bow in the front.

Belle: Crinoline (1840–1865 C.E.). In 1853, silk mantilla with deep collar trimmed with a border of silk folds and deep fringe.

belling: Norway. Hide from the legs of a reindeer.

Belliz: Germany. Fur.

bellotas: Peru. Woolen pompons often used as trim on hats.

bell suit
See also photospread (Women's Wear).
Dover Publications

bellows pocket: Pocket on man's sporting coat cut with large inward pleat, allowing great expansion.

bellows sleeve: Late Gothic (1350–1450 C.E.). Gathered sleeve with cuff and long vertical slit through which arm passed.

belodreshnik: Bulgaria. Men's "white dress": narrow trousers and Slavic top.

belongkon: Java. Intricately folded turban sewn from an ikat.

belti: *See* lindi.

Belvidera: Crinoline (1840–1865 C.E.). In 1857, shawl-shaped lace net scarf with Greek applique.

Bemberg: United States of America. Trademark name for a rayon made by American Bemberg Corporation.

ben'àn: China. Aniline.

benares: India. Silk and metal tissue fabric.

benayeq: Israel. Side panels in woman's gown.

benayiq: Palestine. Side panels of woman's gown.

bend: Byzantine and Romanesque (400–1200 C.E.). United Kingdom. Headband.

benda: Renaissance (1450–1550 C.E.). Italy. Length of veiling used to wrap around and through the hair.

bendera: Kenya. Red cotton fabric.

bendigo: Poor man's skin cap.

bend-leather: Charles I and the Commonwealth (1625–1660 C.E.) to Late Georgian (1750–1790 C.E.). Leather from back and flanks of an animal used to make jack boots.

benerica: Renaissance (1450–1550 C.E.). Spain. Scallop shell pattern.

benevretsi: Bulgaria. Trousers with tight-fitting legs that are worn low on pelvis and fastened with belt of string.

bengal: India. Striped cotton gingham made in Bengal, India.

bengal stripes: India. Cheap cotton fabric with stripes on white ground.

bengalina: Spain. Bengaline.

bengaline: Bustle (1865–1890 C.E.) to present. Introduced in 1869, very light mohair in solid color or brocaded with small flowers and corded.

bengaline constellation: Gay Nineties (1890–1900 C.E.). In 1892, a bengaline with two sized spots resembling moons and stars.

bengaline de soie: Silk, plain weave, corded fabric.

bengaline poplin: Bustle (1865–1890 C.E.). Introduced in 1865, poplin with thick cord.

bengaline russe: Gay Nineties (1890–1900 C.E.). Introduced in 1892, shot wool and silk blend.

beni: Japan. Red; deep red.

benjamin: Directoire and First Empire (1790–1815 C.E.). Man's close-fitting overcoat.

benjy: Slang term for waistcoat.

benn: Scotland. Colored silk sash.

benoiton chains: Bustle (1865–1890 C.E.). France. Popular in 1866, chains of metal or jet that hung from the chignon to the bosom.

bents: 1. Renaissance (1450–1550 C.E.). Support for stays made from bunches of hollow stemmed reeds. 2. Elizabethan (1550–1625 C.E.). Strips of whalebone or rushes used to create the shape of bum rolls and farthingales.

bequin: France. Plain white linen cap named for Beguines, order of nuns.

beram: *See* beiramee.

beramen: Palestine. Woman's extra-long gown. The excess fabric is pulled up and draped over a belt (shuwayhiyyeh).

berber: Light satin fabric.

berdash: Wide cravat.

beret: Round wool or felt cap made from circle with edge drawn up with string to fit head. Believed to date to Ancient Greece. Today cap is made in sized felt and tiny tail (tontarra) is sewn on to cover eye of cap.

beret basque: France. Beret.

beret de marin: France. Cap ribbon.

beret sleeve: Romantic (1815–1840 C.E.). United Kingdom. Short sleeve made from wide circle of fabric and stiffened with muslin; similar to beret.

beretta: Medium-large draped beret.

berettino: Renaissance (1450–1550 C.E.). Italy. Shade of gray, bordering on black. Favored by Isabella d'Este.

berger: Restoration (1660–1700 C.E.). Curl of hair at nape of neck that hung to shoulder.

bergere hat: Early Georgian (1700–1750 C.E.) to Directoire and First Empire (1790–1815 C.E.). Large straw hat with flexible brim and low crown.

Beringt: Renaissance (1450–1550 C.E.). Germany. Ringed mail.

Berlin canvas: Coarse, square mesh embroidery fabric.

Berlin gloves: Romantic (1815–1840 C.E.) to present. Knitted cotton gloves.

Berlin wool: Embroidery yarn of merino wool.

Berlin work: Embroidery done on Berlin canvas, usually form of cross-stitch.

Berlins: Germany. Gloves similar to Woodstock gloves.

bermejo: Spain. Vermillion.

bermellon: Spain. Vermillion.

Bermuda fagoting: Fagoting on wrong side of fabric.

bermuda shorts: Pair of shorts that end just above the knee. Made of drill or cotton.

bernec: Romania. Woolen braid used to fasten skirt at waist.

Bernhardt mantle: Bustle (1865–1890 C.E.). France. Short outdoor cape named for actress Sarah Bernhardt.

bernia: Renaissance (1450–1550 C.E.). Spain. Cloak of shaggy woolen cloth.

beronis: *See* beiramee.

berretino: Italy. Skull-cap worn by cardinals.

berretto: Italy. Cap.

berretto alla marinara: Italy. Hat ribbon.

bersagliere: Italy. Black glazed felt hat with plume worn by Italian army rifle corps.

bersáña: Greece. Small chains with coins worn as part of the bridal headdress.

berta: Italy. Bertha.

bertha: Romantic (1815–1840 C.E.). Wide collar popular on women's gowns. Accented dropped shoulder line. Often made of lace.

bertha

Berthe: Germany. Bertha.

bertita: Romania. Narrow embroidered band on wrist of shirt.

berundjuk: Turkey. Woman's at-home white silk chemise.

beryl: Semiprecious stone colored blue green, yellow, pink, and white.

beryllus: Roman (753 B.C.E.–323 C.E.). Aquamarine, a gemstone.

besague: 1. Early Gothic (1200–1350 C.E.) to Late Gothic (1350–1450 C.E.). Knight's horn-like staff. 2. Renaissance (1450–1550 C.E.). Small plates to protect the armpits.

beshmet: Russia. Military quilted jacket.

Bessarabian lamb: Coarse type of Persian lamb.

besshe: Early Gothic (1200–1350 C.E.). An animal fur, probably squirrel.

bestickt: Germany. To be quilted.

bete: Romania. Three to four meter long braid of dyed wool worn by women as sash.

beteele: East India. Muslin once used for petticoats.

beten: Early Gothic (1200–1350 C.E.). Embroidery on garments.

Bethlehem headdress: 1. Muslim. Woman's tarboosh in red or green on which were sewn coins to represent her dowry. When woman was married, white veil was worn over hat. 2. (1920–1930 C.E.). Hat shaped like a truncated cone and trimmed with veil or coins.

Betsie: Directoire and First Empire (1790–1815 C.E.). Multitiered lace collar named for Queen Elizabeth I. By 1807, collar could have as many as seven falls of lace.

Betsie

betteela: India. Kind of muslin.

betúnici: Greece. Festival costume of a newly married woman.

betweens: Small, thin needles used to quilt.

beuk: Holland. Woman's upper body garment.

beul-a-theach: Ireland. Gaelic word for band on a pair of trousers.

beur: India. Bodice.

beurs: Holland. Purse.

bevor: *See* beaver.

bewar: *See* beur.

bewdley cap: *See* Monmouth cap.

bez: *See* platno.

béza: Greece. Head kerchiefs.

bezelikia: *See* bezelitsa.

bezelitsa: Greece. Wide bracelets.

bezulánky: Slovakia. Green woolen skirts that are worn in winter.

bhaga: India. A cloth woven from the fiber of the bhag tree.

bhagawān: India. Loincloth.

bhagela: India. A modern term for bhaga.

bhairnavasani: India. The earliest form of skirt; a tubular cloth held up in gathers around the waist by a girdle.

Bhayyā-cap: India. White cap.

bhrameraka: India. Lock of hair on forehead.

bhurra: United Kingdom. English plain weave cotton fabric with basket weave border used for African native clothes.

bi xi: China. Long narrow panel on front of a robe, through which belt is drawn.

biàn: China. 1. Man's cap. 2. Braid of hair.

biancherie dammaschinate: Italy. Damask linen.

bianchetto: Renaissance (1450–1550 C.E.). Italy. White cloth, maybe wool.

bianco: Italy. White.

biànxié: China. Slippers.

bias: The diagonal of the fabric weave.

bib blouse: High-necked, back-buttoned blouse with plastron front.

bib-cravat: Restoration (1660–1700 C.E.). Man's bib-like cravat.

bibe: Portugal. Pinafore; child's apron.

Biber: Germany. Beaver.

bibi capote

bicorne

Biberhaar: Germany. Beaver hair.

bibi bonnet: Romantic (1815–1840 C.E.). United Kingdom. Woman's bonnet with sides tilted upward.

bibi capote: Romantic (1815–1840 C.E.). Popular in 1830s, any capote with projecting brim. Shaped like baby's bonnet.

bibila: Turkey. A form of open, knotted needle lace.

bibíla: Greece. Fine lace.

bibizári: Greece. Fine silk fabric used for the wedding chemise.

bice: *See* besshe.

bích-không: Vietnam. Azure blue.

bich-ngoc: Vietnam. Emerald.

bicoquet: Late Gothic (1350–1450 C.E.). France. Steel hood with pointed top that left face uncovered.

bicorne: Late Georgian (1750–1790 C.E.). Developed from Swiss military hat, had flaps in front and back with highest point being in center front, or side to side with highest point in center. Worn by men.

bicycle bal: Bustle (1865–1890 C.E.). Low-heeled, lace-up leather or canvas shoe worn for bicycling.

bicycle clip: (1950–1960 C.E.). Simple velvet or satin band worn in hair for evening.

bidang: 1. Borneo. Woman's short tubular skirt decorated with ikat. 2. Borneo. Woman's knee-length petticoat. 3. Malaysia. Woman's short wrapped skirt of handwoven cotton.

bidémña: Greece. Fine, twisted wool or silk thread for embroidery.

biec: Vietnam. Green colored.

biedermeier: Germany. Style of dress similar to French crinoline.

bielizna: Poland. Underwear.

bietle: Native American. Deerskin jacket worn by Apache women.

bietta: Bright red cloth.

biézhen: China. Safety pin or brooch.

bifid beard: Saxon's beard, parted in the center.

Big Look: (1970–1980 C.E.). Fashion for oversized tops, frequently paired with tight pants or leggings.

bigarré: France. Checkered.

bigdai tsivonim: Biblical (unknown–30 C.E.). Hebrew's colored clothes.

bigean: Ireland. Gaelic word for cap.

biggen: *See* beguin.

biggin: 1. *See* beguin. 2. Renaissance (1450–1550 C.E.). Baby's bonnet.

biggon: *See* beguin.

biggonet: Woman's cap, often with earpieces.

bigio: Renaissance (1450–1550 C.E.). Italy. Gray.

bignere: Married Hamar woman's torque with penis-shaped decoration.

bigotera: Spain. Metal contrivance worn overnight in the moustaches to give them a cockleshell twist.

bigouden: France. Jackets worn by both sexes and trimmed in red bold silk designs copied from Celts.

bihari: India. A high quality muslin from Bihar Sharif.

bijel: Bosnia. White colored.

bìji: China. Serge.

bijou: France. Jewel.

Bijou: Crinoline (1840–1865 C.E.). In 1856, woman's mantua silk mantle shaped at waist with four box-pleats. Trimmed with bretelles, fancy galloon, and heavy fringe.

*Big Look
See also photospread
(Women's Wear).
Dover Publications*

bijouterie: France. Gold or fancy jewelry.

bijoutier: *See* joaillier.

bikini: (1940–1950 C.E.). Originally created by the House of Heim, Paris, woman's two-piece bathing dress.

bikini chain belt: (1960–1969 C.E.). Narrow gold chain worn with bikini or hip-huggers.

bikla: Hungary. Characteristic white skirt of tulle, fine linen, or cambric. Five or six could be worn at one time.

bil: Dress worn by the Navajo women that is made from two rectangular handwoven pieces of fabric tied at one shoulder and belted at the waist.

bìlán: China. Dark blue.

bilbo: Elizabethan (1550–1625 C.E.). Spain. Sword made in Bilbao, famed for its fine steel blades.

bilboquets: Early Georgian (1700–1750 C.E.) to Bustle (1865–1890 C.E.). Small rolls of pipe cleaners used to set wigs.

bili javali: India. A white cloth.

biliment: Elizabethan (1550–1625 C.E.). Woman's elaborate, delicate headdress made of lace with gold threads, beads, jewels, gauze, and a feather.

bill: Elizabethan (1550–1625 C.E.). Military pole made from staff about six feet long and spiked axe blade.

billicock: United Kingdom. Hard felt hat with round crown. Examples include the derby, the bowler, or the melon.

billiment: 1. *See* biliment. 2. Elizabethan (1550–1625 C.E.). Decorative border, often of gold and jewels, used on the upper edge of a French hood.

billment: *See* biliment.

billycock: *See* billicock.

bilqusak: Turkmenistan. Striped silk scarf worn by unmarried women tied around hip.

bìlù: China. Dark green.

bím: Vietnam. Lock or tress of hair.

bina: India. A star-shaped forehead ornament.

binary chiton: Greek (3000–100 B.C.E.). Robe formed from two rectangles that joined at shoulders with pins or ties.

binche lace: Flemish. Bobbin lace with floral scrolls on net ground. Originally a handmade bobbin lace of linen thread made in a town in Belgium.

binde: 1. Byzantine and Romanesque (400–1200 C.E.). United Kingdom. Headband, typically worn by secular married women. 2. *See* kupkeh.

binder: Early Georgian (1700–1750 C.E.). Band of flannel worn by babies to support back.

bindi: India. A forehead ornament; a spangle.

binette: *See* full bottomed wig.

bingata: 1. Japan. Okinawan paste-resistant dyeing technique. 2. Japan. Stenciled and dyed Okinawan textiles.

bingle: Hair cut short enough to be above nape of neck.

binh-phuc: Vietnam. Military uniform.

binnogue: Ireland. Woman's peasant headdress.

biodag: Scotland. Dirk.

biorān: Ireland. Pin.

biorraid: Ireland. Gaelic word for helmet or cap with a scoop on it.

birawō: Ethiopia. Silver

birbíla: Greece. Fine, golden lace kerchief worn at the waist.

bird of paradise: Romantic (1815–1840 C.E.). Straw color.

birda: Egypt. A 1-1/2-by-4-meter rectangle worn as wrap.

birdseye: Small geometric diaper pattern woven into fabric with dot in middle to resemble bird's eye.

birdseye pique: Pique fabric with birdseye pattern.

biretta: Elizabethan (1550–1625 C.E.). Non-liturgical cap worn by Catholic officials consisting of stiff square cap with three or four projections rising above crown.

biretz: Reversible wool or wool blend fabric with twill weave on one side and cord on other.

birinji: India. Brass colored.

birisi: Ghana. 1. Native woven black fabric worn by chief when in mourning. 2. The color indigo blue.

birisii: *See* birisi.

birnetsi: Bulgaria. Men's full-bottomed trousers with fitted legs trimmed with black braid on seams.

birodo: Japan. Velvet.

biron: Java. Blue on white color combination used in fabric.

birritta: Sardinia. Long stocking hat of orbace wool or felt.

birrus: Greek (3000–100 B.C.E.). Thick hooded red cloak.

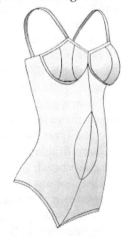

biretta
See also photospread (Headwear).

birthday suit: A woman's one-piece undergarment that is bra, girdle, and panties in one piece. So called because it prevents the wearer from having panty lines, suggesting that the wearer is in her "birthday suit," i.e., naked under her clothing.

Bisamratte: Germany. Muskrat.

Biscayan: Crinoline (1840–1865 C.E.). In 1858, woman's pardessus trimmed with black lace and cord. It had mousquetaire sleeves.

bise: *See* besshe.

biser: Bosnia. Pearl.

bisette: Restoration (1660–1700 C.E.). Coarse bobbin lace.

birthday suit

bìsha: China. Black armband.

bishop: Bustle (1865–1890 C.E.). Horsehair bustle.

bishop cotton: *See* bishop's lawn.

bishop sleeve

bishop sleeve: (1900 to present). Woman's long, full sleeve gathered onto the wristband.

bishop's blue: Directoire and First Empire (1790–1815 C.E.). Introduced in 1809, purplish blue.

bishop's knot: Romantic (1815–1840 C.E.). Popular from 1836 to 1849, two ends of ribbon which fell from bonnet to shoulder.

bishop's lawn: Fine lawn.

bishop's mantle: Elizabethan (1550–1625 C.E.). Germany. Worn by the Landsknechts, a deep mail cape, often with a standing collar. It was worn over the armor.

bisht: 1. United Arab Emirates. A man's large cloak worn draped from the shoulders. 2. Palestine. A woman's sleeveless coat.

bisshe: *See* besshe.

bister: *See* bistre.

bistre: Dark brown.

bi-swing: A man's sportswear jacket with a pleat in the center back to allow extra movement.

bít-tãt: Vietnam. Socks; stockings.

bít-tãt tay: Vietnam. Gloves.

bitug: Philippine Islands. Amulet.

bitusca: Romania. Shepherd's sheepskin coat.

bivertina: Spain. Beaverteen.

bivouac mantle: Directoire and First Empire (1790–1815 C.E.). United Kingdom. Introduced in 1814, woman's loose, ankle-length mantle with high collar. Frequently scarlet in color and lined with ermine.

bizou: France. Breton for finger ring.

bizuteria: Poland. Jewelry.

bla lome: Sierra Leone. A gown presented to the father of the bride as part of the bride price.

black bear: Durable, fine, dark brown fur from black bear of North America.

black lace: Elizabethan (1550–1625 C.E.) to Restoration (1660–1700 C.E.). Black lace made in Bayeaux, France, and popularized by Spanish Infanta.

black turquoise: Jet.

black-a-lyre: Early Gothic (1200–1350 C.E.). Black cloth from Brabant.

blackerybond: Renaissance (1450–1550 C.E.). Long narrow ribbons of black-a-lyre.

blackwork: Renaissance (1450–1550 C.E.). Of Spanish origin, black counted embroidery on white linen.

blaireau: France. Badger fur.

blană: Romania. Fur.

blanc: 1. Bustle (1865–1890 C.E.). In 1886, blue white. 2. France. White.

blanc haubert: Renaissance (1450–1550 C.E.). France. Coat of mail.

blancard: Early Georgian (1700–1750 C.E.). France. Strong linen fabric.

blanchet: Early Gothic (1200–1350 C.E.). Doublet, generally white, sometimes fur lined.

blanco: Ecuador, Guatemala, and Spain. White.

blanco cremoso: Spain. Off white.

blangkon: Indonesia. Man's turban-like headdress.

blanket cloth: Heavy reversible fabric made in two-color jacquard weave.

blanket coat: *See* Hudson Bay coat.

blatta: Purple.

blau: Germany. Blue.

blaukappe: *See* spitzkappe.

blaunchmer: Early Gothic (1200–1350 C.E.). A fur, animal unknown, presumably white in color.

blaundemer: *See* blaunchmer.

blaundever: *See* blaunchmer.

blauner: *See* blaunchmer.

blauw: Holland. Blue.

blauwe duffel: Holland. Pilot cloth.

blazer: Bustle (1860–1890 C.E.). Man's lightweight jacket.

blazer cloth: A striped flannel.

blé de Turquie: Crinoline (1840–1865 C.E.). In 1863, rich shade of yellow.

blé mur: Bustle (1865–1890 C.E.). In 1876, color of ripe wheat.

blé vert: Bustle (1865–1890 C.E.). In 1876, color of half-ripe wheat.

bleu: France. Blue.

bleu Anglais: Bustle (1865–1890 C.E.). In 1884, Gordon blue.

bleuté: France. Bluish.

blezer: Poland. Blazer.

bliand: Byzantine and Romanesque (400–1200 C.E.). Early version of chemise, cut full or slit on sides.

bliant: *See* bliand.

bliaunt: *See* bliand.

bliaus: *See* bliand.

blistering: Slashing.

block: Mold used to shape a hat.

bloeja: Norway. Veil.

blonda: Spain. Lace trim.

blonde: Lightweight, shiny, unbleached silk lace made with varying sizes of yarn.

blonde lace: Fine silk bobbin lace, originally white.

blonde net: Washable cotton net.

blonder: Norway. Metallic woven ribbon.

blondes de Caen: France. A bobbin lace made in Caen.

blondine: Gay Nineties (1890–1900 C.E.). Pale nut shade.

bloomers: 1. Crinoline (1840–1865 C.E.). Loose trousers for women, influenced by Oriental styles. Popularized by Amelia Bloomer in 1851. 2. (1900–1910 C.E.). Women's loose underdrawers, frequently gathered below knee.

blousant: France. Blousing.

blouse polonaise: Bustle (1865–1890 C.E.). In 1873, double-breasted polonaise.

blouse suit: *See* Russian suit.

blousette: Sleeveless blouse.

blucher: Late Georgian (1750–1790 C.E.). Laced shoe invented by Field Marshall von Blucher, commander of the Prussian forces at Waterloo. Quarters of shoe reached up and met over instep where laced together.

blue fox: Fox fur with mixture of gray, brown, and misty blue hairs.

blue john: Crinoline (1840–1865 C.E.). United Kingdom. A corruption of the French word *bleu-jaune*; a semiprecious stone used in jewelry.

bluebonnet: Scotland. Traditional cap of shepherd, soldier, and gentleman, a one-piece, woven cap of dark blue wool with blue or red tuft on top. May be decorated with ribbon cockade, sprig of evergreen, and/or feather to signify rank within clan.

bluet: Plain blue fabric, usually cotton or wool.

bluey: Australia. Bushman's shirt, usually blue.

bluff edge: Hand-felled edge of cloth coat bound with braid.

Blumenkränzchen: Germany. Garland.

blusa: 1. Italy, Portugal, and Spain. Blouse. 2. Guatemala. Blouse of foreign inspiration.

blusa de operário: *See* camisa de muiher.

blusante: Italy. Blousing.

blusão: Portugal. Windbreaker.

Blusig: Germany. Blousing.

bluska: Poland. Blouse.

bluza: Bosnia. Blouse.

bó: China. Silks.

bô cánn: Vietnam. Suit; dress.

boa: Long neck scarf of fur, feathers, tulle, or lace. It was six to eight feet long in the late 19th century. It was revived in the 1930s and 1960s.

boat neck: *See* bateau neckline.

boater: Bustle (1865–1890 C.E.) to 1930s. Man's sennit straw sailor hat, usually shellacked, with a very flat brim and crown.

boater

boban: Ireland. Gaelic word for bobbin.

bobbin lace: Lace that is worked on pillow around pins marking out design.

bobbinet: Fine, machine-made net with a hexagonal mesh.

bobina: Portugal. Bobbin.

bobo: *See* calcao.

bob-wig: Early Georgian (1700–1750 C.E.). Man's wig with ends turned up or "bobbed." Gradually accepted for all classes for undress.

bob-wig
See also photospread (Headwear).

bocací: Spain. Buckram.

bocaran: Renaissance (1450–1550 C.E.). Spain. Buckram. *See also* bocací.

boccaccino: Renaissance (1450–1550 C.E.). Italy. Cotton or linen fabric used to line sleeves.

bocskor: Hungary. Heelless leather shoes.

bôd-da: Andaman islands. Belts made from the pandanus leaf.

bodice: Upper part of woman's dress.

bodies, pair of: Elizabethan (1550–1625 C.E.). Under-bodice supported with whalebone, wood, or steel.

bodkin: Elizabethan (1550–1625 C.E.). 1. Dagger. 2. Hair ornament. 3. Something used to curl women's hair. 4. Tool used to punch holes in fabric.

bodkin cloth: Elizabethan (1550–1625 C.E.). Rich silk and gold fabric.

bodkin-beard: Renaissance (1450–1550 C.E.) to Elizabethan (1550–1625 C.E.). Man's long, pointed beard.

bodom beads: *See* adjagba beads.

body coat: Romantic (1815–1840 C.E.). Tailoring term referring to outer garment of a suit.

body shirt: (1960–1970 C.E.). Man's shirt that tapered to waist, fitting body contours.

body stichet: Renaissance (1450–1550 C.E.). Woman's rigid corset.

body stocking: (1960–1970 C.E.). United States of America. Stretch suit consisting of leotard and stockings in one piece that reached from neck to toe.

body-stychet: Renaissance (1450–1550 C.E.). United Kingdom. Corset.

bœlte: Denmark. Belt.

boemio: Elizabethan (1550–1625 C.E.). Spain. Half-length, formal cloak of taffeta or velvet, sometimes lined with fur.

boershabijt: Elizabethan (1550–1625 C.E.). Holland. Peasant dress.

bofeta: Ethiopia. Cotton cloth.

bögatya: Hungary. Men's very wide trousers made from four to eight widths of 55–60 cm wide fabric and held on with drawstring (gatyamadzag).

bogazie: *See* musui.

Bohemian lace: Coarse net resembling braid.

bohemio: Renaissance (1450–1550 C.E.). Spain. Short cape. *See also* ferreruelo.

Boi: Germany. Baize.

boicionn: Ireland. Gaelic word for goat skin.

boideachan: Ireland. Gaelic word for bodkin.

boiled shirt: United States of America. Man's white shirt with starched bosom.

boiled-off silk: Silk with natural gum removed.

boina: 1. Portugal. Cap. 2. Spain. Round wool cap.

boina vasca: Spain. Beret.

boineid: 1. Ireland. Gaelic word for bonnet. 2. Scotland. Balmoral or Glengarry bonnet.

boineid bhall-ach: Ireland. Gaelic word for tartan bonnet.

boineid biorach: Ireland. Gaelic term for Glengarry bonnet.

boineid chath-dath: *See* boineid bhall-ach.

bois: Wood brown color.

bois de rose: 1. Bustle (1865–1890 C.E.). France. Introduced in 1866, light red brown. 2. (1940–1949 C.E.). Grayed red orange color.

boiseid: Ireland. Gaelic term for belt or girdle.

boisson: Late Georgian (1750–1790 C.E.). France. Popular in 1780s, woman's short, hooded cloak.

boje: Nigeria. Wealthy man's white cotton damask trousers with a very wide drawstring waist and short, narrow legs. The trousers are embroidered.

bokani: India. A sequined or embroidered turban band.

bokashi: Japan. Color gradation or shading.

bokasyn: Renaissance (1450–1550 C.E.). Type of fustian.

bokshandschoen: Holland. Boxing glove.

bolero: Crinoline (1840–1865 C.E.). Short jacket, often having rounded corners in front.

bolero toque: Bustle (1865–1890 C.E.). Introduced in 1887, woman's small velvet, astrakhan, or fur toque with black trim.

bolgar: *See* bulgar.

bolia: Greece. A bride's long white or cream colored lightweight scarf.

bolivar: Lightweight, fine, wool flannel, often dyed gray.

Bolivar hat: Romantic (1815–1840 C.E.). Hat trimmed with tartar ribbons and violets.

bolivia: Soft, plush wool fabric used for women's coats.

Bolivia cloth: Soft, all wool, pile fabric. Tufts of pile usually in diagonal or vertical rows.

boliviano: *See* bandera.

bollinger: Crinoline (1840–1865 C.E.). United Kingdom. Popular from 1858 to 1860s, man's hat with bowler crown and narrow brim and knob in middle of crown. Originally worn by cab drivers. *See also* hemispherical hat.

Bologna crape: Elizabethan (1550–1625 C.E.). A lightweight silk mourning crape.

boloya: India. Ivory bangles worn by married women.

bolsicón: Ecuador. Spanish style skirt with horizontal pleats at the hem and gathered on a waistband.

bolsillo: Spain. Pocket.

bolso: Spain. Handbag.

boltrachan: Ireland. Gaelic word for perfume.

bò-lu: Vietnam. Smock blouse.

bò-lu-dông: Vietnam. Jacket; lumber jacket; windbreaker.

bolzegin: Loose, baggy boots.

bombachas: Uruguay. Popularized by gauchos, these long, full pantaloons are gathered at ankles and worn with silver-studded leather belt.

bombanas: Straw fiber from bombanassa plant.

bombards: Loose, baggy, padded breeches.

bombasette: *See* bombazet.

bombasino: Renaissance (1450–1550 C.E.). Italy. Cotton or cotton and linen fabric used to line doublets.

bombast: Renaissance (1450–1550 C.E.). Padding of wool, flax, or hair used to fill out padded garments of period.

bombazet: Thin, worsted plain or twill weave fabric.

bombazina: Spain. Bombazine.

bombazine: Lightweight, lustrous, twill weave, silk, and worsted fabric used for mourning.

bombe: France. Rounded.

bombei: Kenya. Cheap lightweight cotton.

bomber cloth: Strong durable fabric in broken twill weave used for home furnishings.

bombetta: Italy. Bowler.

bombycina: Byzantine and Romanesque (400–1200 C.E.). Transparent silk textiles.

bombycine: Made of silk.

bomuld: Denmark. Cotton.

bomull: Sweden. Cotton.

bōna: *See* coilēar.

Bonaparte helmet: Directoire and First Empire (1790–1815 C.E.). Woman's white silk bonnet that gathered onto black velvet forehead band. Trimmed with laurel leaves and ostrich feather.

bondita: Romania. Sleeveless sheepskin vest.

boné: *See* boina.

bone lace: *See* bobbin lace.

boneette: Bustle (1865–1890 C.E.). Introduced in 1877, wool and silk blend fabric with damask print.

bông: Vietnam. Cotton.

bongos: Zambia. Grass cloth.

bongrace: Renaissance (1450–1550 C.E.). Woman's headdress which came to point over forehead. Made of silk, velvet, or chiffon. Sometimes had pearl or jewel in center.

bonnaz: Embroidery on Bonnaz sewing machine.

bonnes grâces: France. Border for furnishings, wider than passementeries and usually made of lace.

bonnet à barbes: Romantic (1815–1840 C.E.). Evening headdress of lace, ribbon, and roses.

bonnet à flamme: 1. France. Military hat. 2. Elizabethan (1550–1625 C.E.). Decorative border, often of gold and jewels, used on the upper edge of a French hood.

bonnet à la crête de coq: Late Georgian (1750–1790 C.E.). France. Woman's cap in shape of cock's comb.

bonnet à la laitière: Late Georgian (1750–1790 C.E.). France. Cap in milkmaid style.

bonnet à la moresque: Late Georgian (1750–1790 C.E.). France. Cap in the Moorish fashion.

bonnet à la Richard: Late Georgian (1750–1790 C.E.). France. Woman's hat in medieval style.

bonnet à la victoire: Late Georgian (1750–1790 C.E.). France. Woman's hat decorated with laurel leaves.

bonnet assassin: Crinoline (1840–1865 C.E.). United Kingdom. Introduced in 1844, a lace cap.

bonnet aux trois ordres réunis: Late Georgian (1750–1790 C.E.). France. In 1789, woman's gauze miter-shaped bonnet. Embroidered with olive leaves and trimmed with bands of white taffeta. Included cockade.

bonnet beehive: Romantic (1815–1840 C.E.). Woman's straw hat with crown shaped like beehive. Trimmed with ribbon to tie under chin.

bonnet cabriolet: Early Georgian (1700–1750 C.E.) to Bustle (1865–1890 C.E.). Cabriolet-shaped bonnet with bows under chin.

bonnet de police: France. Policeman's forage cap.

bonnet demi-negligee: Late Georgian (1750–1790 C.E.). France. Woman's informal hat.

bonnet négligée: Late Georgian (1750–1790 C.E.). France. Woman's at-home hat.

bonnet pamela: Romantic (1815–1840 C.E.). Tall crowned straw bonnet trimmed with daffodils and ribbons.

bonnet rond: Reign of Louis XV. Lower class woman's bonnet with two flaps that covered sides of face.

bonnet sylphide: *See* bonnet à barbes.

bonneterie: France. Hosiery.

bonneto: Jewish. Turban.

Bonnie and Clyde: (20th century). Dark gray or dark blue pin-striped suit worn with full-cut trousers. Popular with both genders.

bont: Holland. Checked cotton from the Indies.

booie sum: Bustle (1865–1890 C.E.). United States of America. Chinese Hawaiian term for a vest.

book linen: Firm linen used to stiffen men's shirt collars.

boomwol: *See* katoen.

boonie hat: *See* bush hat.

boorka: Afghanistan. Ground-length cloak.

boot cuff

boot cuff: Early Georgian (1700–1750 C.E.). Popular from 1727 to 1740s, very deep, turned back cuff on man's coat.

boot hose: Restoration (1660–1700 C.E.). Decorative topped short leggings worn under boots. Decorative top edge of sheer white linen trimmed with wide lace was folded over top of the boot. Worn by men.

bootee: Boot with short leg.

bootikin: Late Georgian (1750–1790 C.E.). Soft boot of wool and oiled silk. Commonly worn as cure for gout.

bootee

boquilha: Portugal. Cigar- or cigarette-holder.

borada crape cloth: Bustle (1865–1890 C.E.). A cheap mourning fabric.

borak: *See* burak.

boratto: Elizabethan (1550–1625 C.E.). Light fabric made from silk and fine wool.

borceguí: Elizabethan (1550–1625 C.E.). Spain. Buskin.

bord: France. Brim.

borda: *See* aba.

bordado: 1. Spain. Embroidery. 2. Portugal. Embroidery.

bordado a mano: Spain. Hand embroidery.

bordado con calados: Spain. Drawn work.

bordado con perlas: Spain. Beaded work.

bordado cortado: Spain. Cutout embroidery.

bordado en blanco: Spain. Household linen embroidery.

bordado plano: Spain. Satin stitch.

bordado suizo: Spain. Guipure.

bordāra pyjamā: India. Full straight-legged trousers.

borde: Spain. Hem.

bordeaux: The color claret.

borduurwol: Holland. Crewel.

boreal: Bustle (1865–1890 C.E.). In 1886, shade of brown.

borgal: *See* bulgar.

Borgana: Trademark name for deep-piled fake fur used in woman's coat.

borgeon: Bustle (1865–1890 C.E.). In 1889, light green tinged with yellow.

Borghesé: Crinoline (1840–1865 C.E.). United States of America. Woman's hairstyle with back hair in heavy Grecian knot ending in braid forming bandeau. Quite short in front.

börk: Turkmenistan. Unmarried woman's embroidered skull cap with jeweled finial (qubpa).

borla: 1. Portugal. Academic cap; tassel. 2. Spain. Tassel.

borrillonnées: Crinoline (1840–1865 C.E.). France. In 1852, alternating rows of Swiss insertion and puffings.

borsa: 1. Ireland. Gaelic word for purse. 2. Italy. Purse.

borsalino: Italy. Hand constructed hat of fur that was aged for three years built on felted base which is aged for four years.

borst: Holland. Stomacher.

borstplaat: Holland. Breastplate.

borstrok: Holland. Vest.

Borte: *See* Tresse.

bortspeld: *See* broche.

boscele: *See* pestelci.

bosom bottles: Late Georgian (1750–1790 C.E.). Small containers of tin or glass that held small amount of water and single flower. Some bodices were constructed with pouches to hold the bottles.

bosom flowers: *See* bosom bottles.

bosom friends: Directoire and First Empire (1790–1815 C.E.) to Crinoline (1840–1865 C.E.). Flannel, wool, or fur chest protectors.

bosom shirt: Shirt with starched, plaited, or tucked bosom.

bosphore green: Crinoline (1840–1865 C.E.). Sea green.

bosses: Early Gothic (1200–1350 C.E.). Decorative cauls worn by women on each side of the head to contain large braids of hair. Often worn with veil.

Boston net: Leno weave curtain fabric.

bota: Czechoslovakia, Portugal, and Spain. Boot.

Botany: Trademark name for fabric manufactured by Botany Mills, Inc.

Botany wool: Australia. Fine merino wool from Botany Bay.

botão: Portugal. Button.

botas: Wales. Boot.

botchi: Japan. A woman's hood common in the snowy regions of Niigata.

bote: Byzantine and Romanesque (400–1200 C.E.) to Renaissance (1450–1550 C.E.). United Kingdom. Middle English word for boot.

bote cuello: Spain. Boat neckline.

boteh: India. The paisley motif.

botez: France. Breton for boot.

botforti: Russia. Cuirassier boots.

boti: Norway. Old word for boot.

botina: Portugal. Half-boot.

botinicos: Renaissance (1450–1550 C.E.). Spain. Little boots.

botoeira: *See* casa de botão.

botón: Spain. Button.

boton suelto con espiga: Spain. Shirt stud.

botoun: Byzantine and Romanesque (400–1200 C.E.) to Renaissance (1450–1550 C.E.). United Kingdom. Middle English word for button.

botte: France. Man's boot.

botte à genouillere: France. Jackboot.

bottekin: Small boot.

bottine: 1. Romantic (1815–1840 C.E.). Introduced in 1836, woman's beige gored boot with leather tip and elastic inserts. Invented for Queen Victoria. *See also* Jemima. 2. France. General term referring to woman's boot.

bottle-green: Directoire (1790–1815 C.E.) to Crinoline (1840–1865 C.E.). Dark blue green, popular from 1800 to 1860.

bottoni: Renaissance (1450–1550 C.E.). Italy. Buttons. Used as important decorative detail. Sometimes of silk or silver or gilt.

bòtuinn: Ireland. Boot.

botwm: Wales. Button.

boubou: Wodaabe man's long, loose, sleeveless robe.

Bouc: Germany. Bracelet.

bouche: Plain weave, undyed, wool or wool and cotton blend fabric used for shirts by clergy in southern Europe.

bouchette: Early Gothic (1200–1350 C.E.). Buckle that fastened lower part of breastplate to upper part.

bouchons de carafe: Bustle (1865–1890 C.E.). France. Earrings made of diamonds the size of decorative bottle stoppers.

bouclé: France. Rough textured, soft knitted fabric used in making sportswear and sweaters.

boucle d'oreille: France. Earring.

boucle d'oreille à la guillotine: Directoire (1790–1815 C.E.). France. Earring style representing small guillotine topped with red cap and with pendant decapitated crowned head.

boudoir cap: Late Georgian (1750–1790 C.E.) to Bustle (1865–1890 C.E.). Woman's lace-edged cap worn over undressed hair.

bouffant mecanique: Romantic (1815–1840 C.E.). France. Introduced in 1828, spring reaching from top of corset to outer edge of sleeve to support its extreme size.

bouffante sleeve: Romantic (1815–1840 C.E.) to Crinoline (1840–1865 C.E.). Puffed sleeve.

bouffette: France. Ribbon bow or tassel.

bouffon: Gay Nineties (1890–1900 C.E.). Introduced in 1893, a shade darker than eau de nil.

bouffron: Gay Nineties (1890–1900 C.E.). In 1893, a light tan.

Boug: Germany. Old High German word for bracelet.

bouillion: Romantic (1815–1840 C.E.). France. Puffed trim popular on women's garments.

bouillioné: France. To be shirred or gathered.

boukrania: Egyptian (4000–30 B.C.E.). Cow-shaped amulet with curved lyre-shaped horns.

boulanger: Bustle (1865–1890 C.E.). France. In 1888, bright red.

boulanger umbrella: Bustle (1865–1890 C.E.). Popular in 1880s, umbrella with sabre hilt shaped handle, named for French general.

bouleau: Bustle (1865–1890 C.E.). In 1872, birch color.

boulevart: Renaissance (1450–1550 C.E.). Worn from 1450 to 1500, unfashionable short hose that covered only groin and upper thighs. Tied to belt.

boumwolle: *See* Kattūn.

bouquet de corsage: Crinoline (1840–1865 C.E.). Corsage worn at waist.

bouracan: Bustle (1865–1890 C.E.). Introduced in 1867, ribbed poplin.

bourbon cotton: Cotton with extra-long, silky fiber.

bourbon hat: Romantic (1815–1840 C.E.). France. Woman's blue satin hat trimmed with fleur-de-lis of pearls. Fashionably worn to celebrate return of royal family to Paris.

bourbon lace: Lace made with cording on net ground.

bourdalou: Charles I and the Commonwealth (1625–1660 C.E.) to present. Fine grosgrain ribbon used around crown of hat.

bourdon: Early Gothic (1200–1350 C.E.). Five-foot-long pilgrim's staff with iron spike at bottom to assist in climbing. Had pierced knob on top that held palm branch, the symbol of pilgrims, and unscrewed to hold relics.

bourdon lace: Net lace with corded edge.

bourette: Bustle (1865–1890 C.E.). Introduced in 1877, twill weave wool fabric with colored blubs.

bourette mousse: Bustle (1865–1890 C.E.). In 1877, woven fabric with looped face.

bourguignotte

bourguignotte: Late Gothic (1350–1450 C.E.). France. Iron helmet with cheek pieces and sometimes nosepiece.

bournouse: Crinoline (1840–1865 C.E.). Hooded knee-length mantle, often fringed. Worn by women. Also spelled burnous.

bourré: To be stuffed or wadded.

bourrelet: 1. Late Gothic (1350–1450 C.E.). Padded roll, part of woman's headdress. 2. Late Georgian (1750–1790 C.E.). Padded head cap worn by very young to protect head from injury.

bourse: France. Purse.

bourserie en lisse: France. Type of bag or purse woven on a loom.

boutis: France. A type of embroidery from Marseilles and maritime Provence.

bouton: France. Button.

bouton d'or: Bustle (1865–1890 C.E.). France. In 1888, golden yellow.

boutonnage: France. Closing.

boutonnière: 1. (20th century). Real or artificial flower worn in buttonhole of left lapel of man's coat. 2. France. Buttonhole.

bouton-pression: France. Snap fastener.

boutons d'oreille: Small drop earrings.

bouwen: Elizabethan (1550–1625 C.E.) to Charles I (1625–1660 C.E.). Holland. Overskirts.

bovelna: *See* medvilnė.

bow blouse: Blouse with jabot-bow formed from collar.

bow shoes: China. Ming dynasty. Worn by women with bound feet, shoes with high soles of camphor wood.

bowler: *See* derby.

box cloth: Tightly woven, woolen overcoating pulled and shrunk to resemble felt. Mostly waterproof.

box coat: Romantic (1815–1840 C.E.). Introduced around 1830, straight, loose, beige coat worn by coachmen. Sometimes had cape.

box pleat: Pair of pleats where outer edges face opposite directions.

boxers: Men's undergarments made like shorts.

bō-y: Vietnam. Cotton underpants.

boyang: Band worn by laborers around trouser leg below knee to restrain it.

bozal: Ecuador. A closed double chain stitch.

brabant: France. Sturdy linen fabric.

bracach: Ireland. Gaelic word for being grayish.

bracaille: Ireland. Gaelic word for bracelet.

bracan: Ireland. Gaelic word for glove.

braccae: Byzantine and Romanesque (400–1200 C.E.). United Kingdom. Trousers.

braccas: Byzantine and Romanesque (400–1200 C.E.). United Kingdom. Trousers. *See also* braccae.

braccialetto: Italy. Bracelet.

bracco: Byzantine and Romanesque (400–1200 C.E.). Semi-close-fitting leg covering worn over hose; may be worn with or without cross gartering.

bracconiere: Late Gothic (1350–1450 C.E.) to Elizabethan (1550–1625 C.E.). Armored hip-length skirt made of overlapping steel plates.

bracecloth: *See* paño berbi.

bracelet cuff: Cuff of metal, lace, ribbon, or other material, wider than average bracelet.

bracelet sleeve: Sleeve reaching below elbow.

bracelet tie: Ankle strap shoe.

bracelete: Portugal. Bracelet.

bracer: Late Gothic (1350–1450 C.E.). United Kingdom. A set of complete armor for the arms.

braces: Crinoline (1840–1865 C.E.). United Kingdom. Suspenders, usually elastic, crossing shoulders and used to support trousers. Worn by men.

brachiāle: Roman (753 B.C.E.–323 C.E.). Bracelet.

bracken: Scotland. Type of tartan plaid.

braconniere: Late Gothic (1350–1450 C.E.). Hip-length skirt of steel that hinged on one side and fastened with buckles on the other. Disappeared from use in armor by 17th century.

bractiates: Byzantine and Romanesque (400–1200 C.E.). Pins used to fasten garments closed.

braecce: Byzantine and Romanesque (400–1200 C.E.). United Kingdom. Trousers.

Braganza: Crinoline (1840–1865 C.E.). In 1856, woman's velvet carriage mantle with point in front and round in back. Trimmed with figured velvet plush and broad lace flounce.

bragas: Spain. Wide, loose trousers.

bragetto: Renaissance (1450–1550 C.E.). Italy. Codpiece.

bragoenen: Elizabethan (1550–1625 C.E.). Holland. Padded wheels worn around armseye.

bragon braz: Spain. Full trousers.

bragou: France. Breton for trousers.

bragou-braz: France. Popularized by Breton peasant men, dark blue linen, full cut trousers gathered onto self-belt and ending in knee cuffs.

bragueta: Elizabethan (1550–1625 C.E.). Spain. Codpiece.

braguette: Early Gothic (1200–1350 C.E.). 1. France. Armor equivalent to codpiece. 2. *See* brayette.

braguilha: Portugal. The fly on a pair of trousers.

brahón: Renaissance (1450–1550 C.E.). Spain. Armseye trim.

braiel: *See* breech-girdle.

braies: *See* bracco.

brāislēad: Ireland. Bracelet.

bràist: Ireland. 1. Brooch. 2. Bracelet.

bràisteachan: Ireland. Little brooch.

braistich: Ireland. Gaelic word for brooch.

brakan: *See* breakan.

branc: Renaissance (1450–1550 C.E.). Woman's smock.

branched velvet: Early Gothic (1200–1350 C.E.). Figured velvet.

brandenbourgs: Romantic (1815–1840 C.E.) to Crinoline (1840–1865 C.E.). Popular from 1836 to 1849, a number of cords and tassels used to trim women's clothing in military style.

Brandenburg: Restoration (1660–1700 C.E.) to Romantic (1815–1840 C.E.). Man's loose-fitting overcoat.

Brandenburg fringe: Directoire and First Empire (1790–1815 C.E.). Introduced in 1812, twisted silk fringe.

brandestoc: United Kingdom. Walking stick with a hidden sword.

brandistocchi: Italy. Walking stick with a hidden sword.

brangenybé: Lithuania. Jewel.

brangus akmuo: *See* brangenybé.

brannamh: Ireland. Gaelic word for coat of mail.

branquidão: Portugal. White color.

Branscombe point: A form of tape lace.

bransoletka: Poland. Bracelet. *See also* naramiennik.

braoig: France. Breton for jewel.

bras-fhalt: Ireland. Gaelic word for head hair.

bras-ghruag: Ireland. Gaelic word for curled hair.

braslet': Russia. Bracelet.

brassard: 1. Early Gothic (1200–1350 C.E.). Armor for arm. 2. Black or white armband worn for mourning. 3. White ribbon worn on arm of first communicants in Roman Catholic Church.

brasserole: 1. Early Gothic (1200–1350 C.E.) to Restoration (1660–1700 C.E.). Young girl's camisole. 2. Elizabethan (1550–1625 C.E.). Man's quilted jacket.

brassière: Renaissance (1450–1550 C.E.). France. Small bolero-like garment of black silk or velvet that was worn by women under robe.

brat: Ireland. Worn by both sexes, a large, semi-circular, woolen mantle.

brățară: Romania. Bracelet.

brat-dhearg: Ireland. Gaelic word for being red veiled or covered in red.

bratt: Byzantine and Romanesque (400–1200 C.E.). United Kingdom. Cloak.

braun: Germany. Brown.

brayer: *See* breech-girdle.

brayes: Ireland. Early Gothic (1200–1350 C.E.). Drawers.

brayette: 1. Early Gothic (1200–1350 C.E.). Armored skirt of overlapping bands. 2. Steel petticoat, similar to a baguette.

brazalete: Spain. Bracelet.

Brazilian corded sarcenet: Romantic (1815–1840 C.E.). Introduced in 1820, colored sarcenet with thick, white cotton cord running through it.

brazowy: Poland. Brown.

breaban-deiridh: Ireland. Gaelic word for heel-piece for a shoe.

breaban-toisich: Ireland. Gaelic word for the fore-sole of a shoe.

breacán: *See* breakan.

breacan-feile: Scotland. Traditional Highland dress, piece of tartan, usually two yards wide and four to six feet long, doubled, wrapped around waist, belted, and drawn up over head.

breacan-guaille: Scotland. The plaid.

breac-liath: Ireland. Gaelic word for being grayish.

breadeen: Restoration (1660–1700 C.E.). Ireland. Homespun fabric.

breakan: Ireland. Woolen fabric.

breast hook: *See* stay hook.

breast knot: Early Georgian (1700–1750 C.E.) to Romantic (1815–1840 C.E.). Small bow of colored ribbon worn on bosom of woman's dress.

breathnas: Ireland. Gaelic for the tongue of a buckle.

brec: *See* broc.

brēc: United Kingdom. Old English word for trousers.

brech: Byzantine and Romanesque (400–1200 C.E.) to Renaissance (1450–1550 C.E.). United Kingdom. Middle English word for trousers.

brec-hraegl: Byzantine and Romanesque (400–1200 C.E.). United Kingdom. Trousers.

brede: Obsolete term for braid or embroidery.

bredon: Renaissance (1450–1550 C.E.). Italy. Fabric pieces which hung from backs of armseye, perhaps the waist.

bredzon: Switzerland. Man's thick twill smock with short, puffed sleeves.

breeches: Renaissance (1450–1550 C.E.). Leg coverings made in one piece, either cut from fabric or knitted.

breech-girdle: Early Gothic (1200–1350 C.E.). Running string that drew in pair of breeches at waist.

breichled: Wales. Bracelet.

brēid: *See* ēadach.

bréid: Ireland. Married woman's square linen head kerchief that is fastened with silk cords or metal pins.

bréid geal: Ireland. White headdress.

bréid-bronn: Ireland. Apron.

bréidín: *See* breadeen.

bréid-uchd: Ireland. 1. Stomacher. 2. Bib.

brēit: Ireland. Old Gaelic word for cloth.

breitschwantz: France and Spain. Broadtail fur.

Breitschwantz: 1. Hides from the naturally aborted fetuses of the karakul lamb (*Ovis aries platyura*). 2. Germany. Broadtail fur.

breloque: Ornament which hangs from man's watch chain.

breost-lin: Byzantine and Romanesque (400–1200 C.E.). United Kingdom. Linen band to bind breast or wrap for corpse.

breost-rocc: Byzantine and Romanesque (400–1200 C.E.). United Kingdom. Garment covering the chest.

bretelle: Decorative suspender, common in European national peasant dress styles.

bretenne lace: *See* Bretonne lace.

brethyn: Wales. Cloth.

breton: Woman's hat style based on Brittany peasant hat with flat crown and rolled back brim.

Bretonne lace: Thick colored-thread embroidery on net ground. It is used to trim lingerie, dress accessories and fancy linens.

breug-chiabh: Ireland. Gaelic word for a wig or peruke.

brewer's cap: Knitted stocking cap.

brezarau: Romania. Twisted hemp cord used as drawstring on women's smocks.

brezekouki: Greece. A woman's deep red silk belt.

brezikúci: Greece. Red silk bridal belt.

brial: Renaissance (1450–1550 C.E.). Spain. Dress.

brichette: Renaissance (1450–1550 C.E.). Armor for loins and hips.

bridal lace: Type of reticella lace.

bride: 1. Loop, bar, or tie in needlework. 2. Slender thread connecting parts of design in lace. 3. Bonnet string.

bride lace: Elizabethan (1550–1625 C.E.). Blue ribbon tied around rosemary and given as wedding favor. Commonly worn on hats of wedding guests.

brides: Romantic (1815–1840 C.E.). United Kingdom. Wide ribbon ties on women's bonnets.

bridgwater: Renaissance (1450–1550 C.E.). Broadcloth.

bridle-gauntlet: An elbow-length gauntlet worn on the left hand.

brigandine: 1. Late Gothic (1350–1450 C.E.). Armored corset of overlapping metal plates sewn between layers of canvas. 2. Elizabethan (1550–1625 C.E.). Velvet jacket lined with canvas and small overlapping plates of steel.

Brighton nap: Directoire and First Empire (1790–1815 C.E.). Wool fabric with knots on face.

bril: Holland. Spectacles.

brilhante: Portugal. Diamond.

brillantes: Bolivia. Chemical aniline dyes.

brillianette: Early Georgian (1700–1750 C.E.). Glazed wool fabric in stripes and flowers. *See also* calamanco.

brilliante: 1. Crinoline (1840–1865 C.E.). In 1851, fabric like jaconet with tiny raised figures. 2. Ecuador. Clear plastic bead.

brilliantine: Lustrous, plain or twill weave cotton and mohair blend fabric used for jacket linings.

brilliants: Crinoline (1840–1865 C.E.). Introduced in 1863, silk fabric with white ground patterned in damask.

brim: Palestine. Cotton or cotton and linen blend fabric, undyed or dyed blue.

brim caqui: Portugal. Khaki.

brin: 1. Stout linen fabric. 2. One of sticks in a fan.

brinco: Portugal. Earring; pendant.

briolette: Pear- or oval-shaped stone.

briosaid: Ireland. Gaelic word for a belt or girdle.

brissimi: Greece. Dark red or purple silk.

brīste: Ireland. Trousers.

Bristol red: Renaissance (1450–1550 C.E.). Red fabric.

British warm: (1940–1950 C.E.). United Kingdom. Short coat of thick blue wool that closed with wooden toggles and cloth loops. Originally naval surplus. Officially called "duffer" and later called "duffle coat."

Brittany: France. Cotton or cotton and linen blend fabric.

Brittany cloth: *See* Brittany.

Brittany work: France. Embroidery of Breton peasant.

brîu: Romania. A 10 to 35 cm wide, 3 to 4 m long woolen sash worn by men and women.

briuki-dudochki: (1960–1970 C.E.). Russia. Straight-legged pants.

brium: Ireland. Gaelic word for helmet.

brk: Bosnia. Moustache.

broadcloth: Tightly woven, plain weave cotton fabric.

broadtail lamb: Fragile fur with a moiré-like surface. Usually black in color.

broc: 1. Byzantine and Romanesque (400–1200 C.E.). United Kingdom. Men's short trousers. By 13th century, also applied to woman's garment. The plural is *brec*. 2. Ireland. Gaelic word for gray.

brōc: Ireland. Old Gaelic word for trousers.

brocade: Rich, elegant fabric decorated with embroidery or fabric in a jacquard weave.

brocado: Spain. Brocade.

brocado raso de pelo: Renaissance (1450–1550 C.E.). Spain. Brocaded satin velvet.

brocantine: Gay Nineties (1890–1900 C.E.). Introduced in 1898, fine wool fabric brocaded with silk.

brocart: France. Brocade.

brocatel: Spain. Brocatelle.

brocatelle: 1. Small patterned brocade. 2. Directoire and First Empire (1790–1815 C.E.). Italy. Gold or silk brocade fabric.

brocatine: Fabric with raised patterns woven to imitate embroidery.

brocato: Spain. Brocade.

broccato: Italy. Brocade.

broche: 1. Holland. Brooch. 2. France. Spindle. 3. Silk or cotton fabric with a satin pattern.

broché: To be woven with a raised figure or to be embossed.

broché shawl: Paisley shawl woven in different colored strips.

broché silk serge: Bustle (1865–1890 C.E.). In 1872, soft, thick, twilled silk with black background and colored figures.

brochetta: *See* fermaglio.

brochette: France. Small brooch.

brodé: France. Embroidered.

brodekin: Renaissance (1450–1550 C.E.). United Kingdom. Man's calf-high boot.

brodequin: 1. Romantic (1815–1840 C.E.). Popular in 1830s, women's boots of velvet or satin that were trimmed with fringe around upper edge. 2. France. Child's boot.

broderie: France. Embroidery.

broderie anglaise: 1. Crinoline (1840–1865 C.E.) to Gay Nineties (1890–1900 C.E.). Bold embroidery of different shaped eyelets arranged to form a pattern. Used on women's and children's clothing and accessories. 2. (1910–1920 C.E.). Openwork embroidery on cambric or linen. 3. (1920–1930 C.E.). Cheruit design gown with lampshade sleeves, crepe underskirt trimmed with chiffon overpanels.

broderie en blanc: France. Household linen embroidery.

broderie en jais: France. Embroidery in which glass cylindrical beads are inserted on the embroidery yarn.

broderie perse: Literally "Persian embroidery," an applique cut from a printed fabric picture.

broek: Holland. Trousers.

brœkr: Norway. Old word for trousers.

broekrok: Holland. Culottes.

broella: Early Gothic (1200–1350 C.E.). Rough fabric worn by peasants and monks.

brōg: Ireland. Shoe.

brogan tionndaidh: Scotland. Ghillie-style shoe.

brogans: Crinoline (1840–1865 C.E.). Shoes with wooden or thick leather soles that were pegged to a sturdy leather upper. They were often studded at the toe with brass tacks.

bròg-bhréid: Ireland. Sandal.

bròg-chalpach: Ireland. Boot.

brogetie: Elizabethan (1550–1625 C.E.). Coarse brocade.

bròg-fhiodha: Ireland. Sabot.

broglio-broglio: Early Georgian (1700–1750 C.E.). Camlet.

brogs: Elizabethan (1550–1625 C.E.). Ireland. Men's long breeches.

brogues: Renaissance (1450–1550 C.E.). Scotland. Rough shoes of undressed leather.

broigne: Byzantine and Romanesque (400–1200 C.E.). France. Long tunic of skin or canvas with metal rings sewn on it. Worn by cavalrymen as form of defensive armor.

broith: Ireland. Gaelic word for carnation color.

broithdheanta: Ireland. Gaelic word for flesh colored.

broiudneireachd: Ireland. Gaelic word for embroidery.

brok: 1. Byzantine and Romanesque (400–1200 C.E.). Ireland. Hose or trews. 2. Macedonia. Madder used as a dye.

brokaat: Holland. Brocade.

Brokat: Germany. Brocade.

brolly: United Kingdom. Slang for umbrella.

bròn: Ireland. Mourning dress.

bronnach: Ireland. Gaelic word for belt or girdle.

bronze: Dark brown color with tint of green.

broom skirt: Full skirt given wavy plait by drying around handle of broom.

broszka: Poland. Brooch.

brown Holland: Unbleached or partially bleached linen fabric.

brown linen: Unbleached linen.

brown sheeting: Unbleached sheeting.

broz: France. Breton for skirt.

brucag: Ireland. Gaelic word for eyelet.

Bruch: Germany. Old High German word for trousers.

brud: Norway. Woman's bridal coronet.

Bruges lace: Belgium. Bobbin lace similar to guipure tape.

bruin: Holland. Brown.

bruinneadach: Ireland. Gaelic word for apron.

bruki: Russia. Breeches.

brumánika: Greece. Pleated dickey.

brummaggem: United Kingdom. Costume jewelry made in Birmingham.

Brummel: (1920–1930 C.E.). United Kingdom. A dandy.

Brummel bodice: Directoire and First Empire (1790–1815 C.E.) to Romantic (1815–1840 C.E.). Man's corset worn in imitation of Beau Brummel.

brun: France. Brown.

brunatny: *See* brazowy.

brune: France. Brunette.

brunete: Early Gothic (1200–1350 C.E.). Wool fabric dyed and used for tunics and stockings.

bruno: Italy. Brown.

Brunswick: Early Georgian (1700–1750 C.E.). Germany. Woman's fitted riding coat.

Brunswick cloth: Renaissance (1450–1550 C.E.). Germany. Linen fabric.

Bruoch: Germany. Trousers.

bruschino: Renaissance (1450–1550 C.E.). Italy. Dark red.

brushed rayon: Napped rayon fabric.

brushed wool: Knit fabric with a nap. Usually contains mohair.

Brussels bobbin lace: A fine part lace grounded with drochel net.

Brussels camlet: Late Georgian (1750–1790 C.E.). Poplin used for riding habits.

Brussels edging: Lace formed by series of buttonhole stitches, leaving small loop on surface.

Brussels ground: Six sided mesh for lace.

Brussels lace: Belgium. Any lace made in Brussels.

Brussels needle lace: A flat tape lace made with very fine thread.

Brussels net: A machine-made net.

Brussels point: Crinoline (1840–1865 C.E.). Lace with pattern of sprigs.

Brussels wire-ground: Silk mesh for lace.

brustfleck: Austria. Man's vest without front opening. Strings cross in back and tie in front.

Brustharnisch: Germany. Cuirasse.

bruststück: Renaissance (1450–1550 C.E.). Germany. Breastplate.

brusttuch: Poland. Jewish woman's ornamented plastron.

Brutus cut: Directoire and First Empire (1790–1815 C.E.). Man's hairstyle with hair combed forward over forehead, long sideburns, and hair reaching over top of collar.

Brutus head wig: Directoire and First Empire (1790–1815 C.E.). Man's cropped wig with disheveled appearance.

bryczesy: Poland. Breeches.

bù: China. Fabric.

buac: Ireland. Gaelic word for unbleached linen.

buaicean: Ireland. Gaelic word for veil.

buatais: Ireland. Boot.

buba: West Africa. 1. Overblouse with set-in sleeves, straight sides, and straight, elbow-length sleeves. 2. Yoruba man's narrow, tunic-like skirt.

bùbó: China. Cotton and silk fabric.

bubou: Romania. Fleece coat.

bubu: Africa. An oversized shirt.

bubúces: Greece. Embroidery on the hem of the chemise.

bucaran: Spain. Buckram.

buchai: Borneo. Fringe.

Buchanan: (1920–1930 C.E.). United States of America. In 1924, a dandy. Named for the English stage star, Jack Buchanan.

bucket-top boot: Charles I and the Commonwealth (1625–1660 C.E.). Boots that are very wide at top. Often boot top is folded over to form a large cuff. Worn by men.

bucket-top boot

Buckingham lace: Common lace, similar to Alencon.

Buckinghamshire lace: Renaissance (1450–1550 C.E.) to present. Fine bobbin lace with simple design.

buckled wig: Early Georgian (1700–1750 C.E.). Man's wig with tight curls (buckles) worn above ears.

buckler: Elizabethan (1550–1625 C.E.) to Restoration (1660–1700 C.E.). Small shield of metal or wood with metal spike in center and strap across back.

buckram: Renaissance (1450–1550 C.E.) to present. Coarse open weave linen or cotton fabric sized with glue. Used for bombasting, shaping garments and hats.

bucksain: Crinoline (1840–1865 C.E.). Man's padded greatcoat with wide sleeves.

buckskin: Directoire and First Empire (1790–1815 C.E.). 1. Popular name for tan leather riding gaiter. 2. Fine, stretchy leather.

Buddun khas: India. A muslin.

budge: Elizabethan (1550–1625 C.E.). Lambskin worn with wool on outside.

bufanda: 1. Spain. Muffler; scarf. 2. Ecuador. A warp-resistant patterned scarf.

buff: 1. Light, brownish yellow. 2. Buffalo skin. 3. Coat of buff leather.

buff jerkin: Elizabethan (1550–1625 C.E.) to Restoration (1660–1700 C.E.). Military jacket of leather or hide.

buffalo cloth: Heavy, twilled fabric with long nap. Used to make wool lap robes.

buffin: Renaissance (1450–1550 C.E.) to Restoration (1660–1700 C.E.). Form of camlet.

buffon: Late Georgian (1750–1790 C.E.). Popular in the 1780s, a large, often starched handkerchief, worn bunched in the center front of a gown.

buffonts: Late Georgian (1750–1790 C.E.) to Directoire and First Empire (1790–1815 C.E.). Gauze scarf worn to fill in neckline of décolleté gown. Worn puffed out in "pouter pigeon" line.

bufle: Renaissance (1450–1550 C.E.). Coat of buff leather.

bughma: Turkey. Choker necklace.

bughmeh: Palestine. Choker necklace.

bugis: United Kingdom. Colored fabrics woven with border on only one side and made for export.

bugle: Tube-shaped ornament.

buhl: Form of elaborate decoration using tortoiseshell, ivory, and colored metals.

búi tó: Vietnam. Bun; chignon.

búi tóc: *See* búi tó.

bui-bui: 1. Madagascar. Moroni woman's wide black robe. 2. Swahili. Woman's hooded black cloak.

buidhe: Ireland. Gaelic word for yellow colored or golden colored.

buidhe-bhan: Ireland. Gaelic word for buff colored.

buidhe-dhonn: Ireland. Gaelic colored auburn colored.

buidhe-ruadh: Ireland. Gaelic word for bay colored.

buidhe-shoilleir: Ireland. Gaelic word for amber colored.

buidh-liath: Ireland. Gaelic word for pale yellow colored.

builg: *See* balg.

buill: *See* ball.

buis: Holland. Jacket. *See also* rok. During the Elizabethan era in English-speaking countries, it was called the jerkin.

bujka: Hungary. Blue cloth jacket.

bukhani: India. A scarf or sash worn by bridegrooms in Kutch and Saurashtra.

bukser: Denmark. Trousers.

bukskin: Holland. Buckskin cloth.

bul: Byzantine and Romanesque (400–1200 C.E.). United Kingdom. Early in 11th century, woman's ornament or brooch.

bulavka: Russia. Pin.

bulbulchasm: India. Heavy silk with nightingale eye-shaped embroidery.

búles: Greece. Embroidery for the everyday chemise.

bulgar: India. Russian leather.

bulgara cira: India. A silk or velvet from Bulgaria.

bulgare pleat: Bustle (1865–1890 C.E.). United Kingdom. Introduced in 1875, double box pleat on women's skirts that was narrower at waist than at hem. Held in place with elastic strips on inside.

Bulgarian cloth: Bustle (1865–1890 C.E.). United Kingdom. Introduced in 1883, cream colored satin with silver and colored threads worked into it.

Bulgarian embroidery: Brightly colored embroidery on coarse linen.

bulger: *See* bulgar.

bulgha: Egypt and United Arab Emirates. Soft, yellow leather slippers favored by peasants.

bulghar: *See* bulgar.

bulla: Greek. Locket with charm inside. Given to child at nine days of age and worn by girls until marriage and by boys until manhood (age 16).

bulldog toe: (20th century). Shoe toe that is rounded and blunt.

bullet-hole lace: A patterned machine lace with rows of large, round holes.

bullgarry: *See* bulgar.

bullion embroidery: Embroidery done with gold wires.

bullion hose: *See* French hose.

bullion lace: Heavy lace made with gold or silver threads.

bull's head fringe: Charles I and the Commonwealth (1625–1660 C.E.). Woman's hairstyle with large forehead curls.

bullycock: Bustle (1865–1890 C.E.). Type of bowler.

búloma: Greece. Red, turban-like kerchief worn on the face by a bride.

bumbac: Romania. Cotton.

bum-barrel: Elizabethan (1550–1625 C.E.). United Kingdom. Padded roll used to extend hipline.

bum-freezer: (1920–1930 C.E.). United Kingdom. Term referring to the shorter lengths of men's coats.

bumper: Netherlands. Silk cap with thick roll of black yarn covering top and sides of head. Provides protection for delicate bones of small child.

bunda: Hungary. Long, sleeveless, embroidered sheepskin coat or cloak lined with fur. Made from 3-1/2 to 15 skins.

bundi: India. Man's sleeveless shirt.

bunga bau: Indonesia. Sa'dan-Toraja light yellow bead.

buningr: *See* klœði.

bunny suit: Fitted, footed, one-piece pajamas.

buntal: Fine, white straw fiber.

bunte Sportjacke: Germany. Blazer.

buntes Kopftuch: Germany. Bandanna.

bunting: 1. Bustle (1865–1890 C.E.). Introduced in 1881, coarse form of nun's cloth. 2. Colored cotton fabric similar to cheesecloth.

bur'a': Egypt. Face veil of crocheted silk yarn.

burak: 1. Borneo. White. 2. Palestine. Plain white cotton used for underdresses.

burano lace: Italy. Needlepoint lace on a square mesh.

buratto: Elizabethan (1550–1625 C.E.). Handwoven canvas with needlepoint pattern worked on top.

buratto lace: Renaissance (1450–1550 C.E.) to present. Italy. Filet lace.

burausu: Japan. A blouse.

burberry cloth: Waterproof cloth.

burchanka: *See* koshoulya.

burchena riza: Bulgaria. Smock gathered to neck and with triangular shoulder gores.

burdash: *See* berdash.

burdeos: Spain. Claret.

bure: 1. Bustle (1865–1890 C.E.). Introduced in 1874, coarse wool fabric with wide diagonal rib. 2. France. Drugget.

bureau: Coarse heavy fabric.

burel: Early Gothic (1200–1350 C.E.). Coarse dark red wool fabric.

burga: United Arab Emirates. Woman's full face veil.

burganet: *See* bourguignotte.

burgonet: *See* bourguignotte.

burgoyne: Bustle (1865–1890 C.E.). In 1879, shade of plum brown.

burgundy: Bluish red color.

burial blanket: United States of America. Southwestern blanket with figures woven in black or another somber color on a white ground.

burian: *See* bureau.

buridan: Romantic (1815–1840 C.E.). In 1836, horizontally striped silk.

buriel: Peru. Undyed, demi-colored wool.

buriti: Leaf of Brazilian palm used to make straw hats.

burka: 1. Enveloping garment worn by Mohammedan women covering them from head to toe with eyeholes or strips of lace for eyes. 2. Caucasus. Thick, trapezoidal cloak or sheepskin or astrakhan that doubles as tent.

burlap: Coarse, heavy, plain weave jute, hemp, or cotton fabric. *See also* hessian.

burlet: Coif or hood.

burnet: Early Gothic (1200–1350 C.E.). 1. Light brown fabric. 2. Dark brown.

burnley: United Kingdom. Gray cotton fabric.

burnous: 1. *See* bournouse. 2. United Arab Emirates. Hooded mantle.

burnouse: Crinoline (1840–1865 C.E.). France. Cloak in imitation of Moorish mantle.

burnsides: Side whiskers so named for General A. E. Burnside. *See also* sideburns.

buros: Biblical (unknown–30 C.E.). Hebrew's cloak with attached cape.

burqa: Egypt. Face veil.

burqah: Afghanistan. Woman's dark cloak.

burqo: Palestine. Woman's harness-like face veil.

burqu: Turkey. Woman's face veil.

burqu': United Arab Emirates. Woman's face veil.

burrah: Striped, plain weave, cotton fabric worn by African natives.

burrail collar: Romantic (1815–1840 C.E.). Popular in 1832, man's greatcoat collar that could be worn standing or flat.

bursa: Roman (753 B.C.E.–323 C.E.). Purse.

buruncek: Turkey. Blouse.

burunduki: Fur of Siberian chipmunk.

burung hook: Java. The phoenix symbol.

burzighino: Sardinia. White linen trousers worn gathered into black gaiters or leggings.

busby: Early Georgian (1700–1750 C.E.). Tall fur shako.

busc: *See* busk.

bush hat: (1960–1970 C.E.). United States of America. A soft Army hat with a round crown and a wide brim.

bush jacket: *See* safari jacket.

busht: Palestine. A black and white or red and white striped woolen fabric used for men's cloaks.

busk: Renaissance (1450–1550 C.E.). Stiff piece of wood, metal, or whalebone set in stomacher to help give flat fronted look of period in women's garments.

busk point: Elizabethan (1550–1625 C.E.). Lacing to hold busk in place.

buske: *See* busk.

buskins: 1. *See* brodekin. 2. Elizabethan (1550–1625 C.E.). Short, loose stocking of expensive fabric worn by pope. 3. Directoire and First Empire (1790–1815 C.E.). Calf-high, laced boot based on the style of the cothurnes.

busq: *See* busk.

busque: *See* busk.

busserull: Norway. Man's workshirt.

bust bodice: Gay Nineties (1890–1900 C.E.). White coutil breast support worn above corset. Laced in front and back.

bust forms: (1930–1940 C.E.). Molded foam rubber pads worn in brassiere to firm up small bosom.

bust improver
Dover Publications

bust improver: *See* bust forms.

bustehouder: Holland. Brassiere.

Buster Brown collar: (1900–1910 C.E.). United States of America. Wide, round, starched collar usually worn with Windsor tie. Named for character Buster Brown.

Buster Brown suit: (1910–1920 C.E.). United States of America. Boy's suit consisting of double breasted tunic-shirt with stiff, detachable, white Peter Pan collar, large bow tie, and short bloomer trousers.

bustian: Elizabethan (1550–1625 C.E.). Coarse fabric.

bustier: Strapless, waist-length, long-line bra. Frequently closes in front.

bústos: Greece. A kind of vest.

but: Poland. Boot.

buta: India. A textile pattern of a large floral cone.

butcher boy blouse: Loose smock-like blouse.

butcher's linen: Rough linen used for butcher's aprons and jackets.

buti: India. A textile pattern of a small floral cone.

butter cloth: *See* cheesecloth.

butterfly bow sleeve: Gay Nineties (1890–1900 C.E.). United Kingdom. In 1895, a woman's evening sleeve with deep pleats that were suggestive of wings.

butterfly bun: China. Woman's hairstyle.

butterfly cap: Late Georgian (1750–1790 C.E.). Popular in 1750s and 1760s, woman's small lace cap that was wired in shape of butterfly. Worn on top of head.

butterfly headdress: Late Gothic (1350–1450 C.E.). Worn over tall hennin; made of semitransparent linen and draped and wired to resemble butterfly.

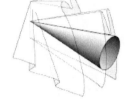

butterfly headdress

butternut: Homespun, twill weave, cotton fabric and dyed brown with dye from butternut tree.

buttery cotton: Cotton fabric creamy or light brown in color.

butti: India. The flower design used in textiles.

button: Small solid object with eye at base or two eyes through object used as decoration or fastening.

butung: Philippine Islands. Man's pouch-like cloth bag worn hung from the belt.

buty turystyczne: Poland. Walking boots.

buzáña: Greece. Embroidery on the siguni.

buzu: Iran. Handwoven wool fabric.

buzunar: Romania. A purse.

bwoom: Zaire. Helmet-style mask.

byal ruchenik: Bulgaria. White kerchief worn over cherven ruchenik by bride for first 40 days of marriage.

byala houta: Bulgaria. Second apron worn over primary apron.

byatilha: *See* betteela.

bycocket: Early Gothic (1200–1350 C.E.) to Elizabethan (1550–1625 C.E.). High crowned, wide brimmed hat with point in center front or back.

bycoket: *See* bycocket.

byramee: *See* beiramee.

byrampaut: *See* beiramee.

byrams: *See* beiramee.

byramy: *See* beiramee.

Byrd cloth: (20th century). Lightweight, strong, water repellant, wind resistant cotton fabric designed to replace fur parka on polar expeditions of Richard E. Byrd.

byrnie: Early Gothic (1200–1350 C.E.). Coat of chain or linked mail.

Byron collar: Romantic (1815–1840 C.E.). Unstarched collar left open at throat. Often combined with loosely tied scarf.

byrrus: *See* birrus.

byssine: Early Gothic (1200–1350 C.E.). Fine fabric.

byssus: Egyptian (4000–30 B.C.E.). Yellowish flax used to create linen for mummy wrappings.

byxor: Sweden. Trousers.

byzantine: Bustle (1865–1890 C.E.). Introduced in 1881, dull, semitransparent silk and wool blend fabric.

byzantine embroidery: Romantic (1815–1840 C.E.) to Bustle (1865–1890 C.E.). Appliqué work combined with heavy stitches.

byzantine granité: Bustle (1865–1890 C.E.). Introduced in 1869, dark brown wool fabric with a few gold threads woven into it.

bzima: Berber pin or fibula.

C

cabaan: United Arab Emirates. White fabric scarf.

cabachon: Decorative trim of ribbon that has been pleated or twisted and then mounted on button or piece of cardboard.

caballeras postizas: Spain. False hair.

caballeros: Fine Spanish wool popular in United Kingdom.

caban: 1. Late Gothic (1350–1450 C.E.) to present. Wide sleeved coat that is not sewn on sides. Worn belted. 2. France. Gabardine.

cabaset: *See* cabasset.

cabasset: Elizabethan (1550–1625 C.E.). Round, high crowned, narrow brimmed steel helmet.

çabat: Persia. Bast shoe.

cabbage: United Kingdom. Tailor's clippings.

cabbage shoestring: Elizabethan (1550–1625 C.E.) to Restoration (1660–1700 C.E.). Man's large shoe rose.

cabbage-ruff: Elizabethan (1550–1625 C.E.). Large ruff in soft folds.

cabeca: East Indies. Fine silk.

cabeleira: Portugal. Wig.

cabeleira postiça: *See* peruca.

cabeleirerio: Portugal. Hairdresser; wigmaker.

cabesa: Spain. Raw wool from Estramadura.

cabestrillo: Elizabethan (1550–1625 C.E.). Spain. Thick gold chain worn draped over one shoulder and under opposite shoulder.

cabin boy breeches: (20th century). Short, snug knee pants that laced at knee.

cable cord: Soft, twisted cotton cord used for pipings, shirrings, etc. *See also* constitution cord.

cable knit: Knit with heavy cord in raised loped stripe.

cable net: Heavy cotton yarn net with large mesh. Used for curtains and draperies.

cabos: *See* clavos.

cabot: Gray, plain weave, cotton webbing.

cabra de China: Spain. Chinese goat.

cabretta leather: Skin of cabretta, hairy sheep; used in gloves and shoes.

cabriole: Late Georgian (1750–1790 C.E.). Popular from 1755 to 1757, carriage-shaped ornament worn in hair.

cabriolet: Directoire and First Empire (1790–1815 C.E.). Carriage-shaped hat with silk trimmings.

cabrito: Spain. Dankal goat.

cabron: France. Kid leather.

çabut: Turkmenistan. Woman's short-sleeved coat.

cacci: Roman (753 B.C.E.–323 C.E.). Shoe made with separate top and sole. Laced over instep and tied around ankle. When worn by patricians, they were leather and encrusted with gold or silver ornaments and pearls.

caceres: Spain. Medium quality wool.

cache corset: Camisole.

cachecol: Portugal. Neckerchief; stole.

cache-folies: Directoire and First Empire (1790–1815 C.E.). France. Small wigs worn by women to hide cropped hair popularized during Revolution.

cachelaid: Charles I and the Commonwealth (1625–1660 C.E.). France. Literally "hide-ugly," small black velvet masks.

cachemira: *See* cahemir.

cachemire: 1. France. Cashmere. 2. Bustle (1865–1890 C.E.). Introduced in 1876, fine wool and silk fabric with Eastern patterns.

cachemire de soie: Fine twilled silk fabric with cashmere-like finish.

cachemire marguerite: Bustle (1865–1890 C.E.). Italy. In 1883, medium-weight durable silk made in Genoa.

cachemire royal: Bustle (1865–1890 C.E.). Introduced in 1889, fabric resembling cashmere with silk back.

cache-peigne: Crinoline (1840–1865 C.E.) to Bustle (1865–1890 C.E.). France. Popular from 1850 to 1967, headdress of net and ribbon that held hair in back of head.

cachimira: Ecuador. Fine wool.

cachou: Bustle (1865–1890 C.E.). Dead leaf brown.

caciula: Romania. Red felt fez.

cack: Infant's shoe with soft leather sole and no heel.

cactli: Mexico. Aztec sandals.

cadach: Wales. Handkerchief.

cadadh: Ireland. Gaelic word for a tartan or a fabric used to make hose.

cadanette: Charles I and the Commonwealth (1625–1660 C.E.). Lovelock worn over one shoulder and tied with ribbon or string. Worn by both genders.

cādar: India. Veil.

cadās: *See* canach.

caddice: *See* caddis leather.

caddice garter: Renaissance (1450–1550 C.E.) to Elizabethan (1550–1625 C.E.). Servant's garter of rough silk.

caddie: Slouch hat.

caddis leather: Renaissance (1450–1550 C.E.) to Restoration (1660–1700 C.E.). Leather from Cadis.

caddow: Ireland. Woolen mantle.

caddy: *See* caddie.

cadena: *See* puntada limeña.

cadenat: Directoire and First Empire (1790–1815 C.E.). Piece of jewelry intended to hold hair.

cadeneta: Guatemala and Mexico. Machine-made chain stitch.

cadenette: *See* cadanette.

cadenilla: Renaissance (1450–1550 C.E.). Spain. A stitch like the chain stitch.

caderas postizas: Renaissance (1450–1550 C.E.). Spain. Padded false hips.

cadet blue: Dark grayish blue color.

cadet cloth: Sturdy bluish gray, blue, gray, or indigo and white fabric used for uniforms in boys' military schools, like West Point. Heavyweight and durable.

cadet gray: Grayed blue color.

cadet jacket: *See* Nehru jacket.

cadge: To bind edge of garment.

cadogan: Late Georgian (1750–1790 C.E.). Man's wig with wide, flat braid that was folded up on itself and then tied. Named for first Earl of Cadogan (1674–1726).

cadows: *See* caddow.

čadu: Ethiopia. Dime girl's pubic covering made of ivory cylinders engraved with black dots and held by a leather belt to the waist.

caefing: Byzantine and Romanesque (400–1200 C.E.). United Kingdom. Hairpin or head ornament for women.

caeles: Byzantine and Romanesque (400–1200 C.E.). United Kingdom. Sock.

caen: France. Woolen serge.

caeppe: Byzantine and Romanesque (400–1200 C.E.). United Kingdom. Cap, hood, or hooded cloak. Possibly only for ecclesiastical use.

cafe: Spain. Brown.

cafe au lait: Light, creamy brown color.

cafe claro amarillento: Spain. Tan.

cafe rojizo: Spain. Sorrel color.

caffa: Renaissance (1450–1550 C.E.) to Restoration (1660–1700 C.E.). A rich silk fabric.

caffoy: Early Georgian (1700–1750 C.E.) to Late Georgian (1750–1790 C.E.). Fabric similar to damask.

caftan: Loose coat-like robe with very long sleeves worn tied around waist. Usually of silk and cotton blend.

cage: Crinoline (1840–1865 C.E.) to Bustle (1865–1890 C.E.). United Kingdom. Nickname for artificial crinoline; petticoat with whalebone hoops, wire, or watchstring.

cage Americaine: Crinoline (1840–1865 C.E.). France. Petticoat in which only bottom half was covered with fabric, upper half only boning.

cage empire: Crinoline (1840–1865 C.E.) to Bustle (1865–1890 C.E.). Popular from 1861 to 1869, slightly trained petticoat made of 30 steel hoops that increased in size as they approached the ground.

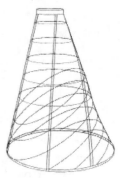

cage
See also photospread (Undergarments).

cagoule: 1. Byzantine and Romanesque (400–1200 C.E.). Hooded, semicircular cape of cloth or fur. Worn by peasants. 2. France. Balaclava.

cahemir: Spain. Cashmere.

cahouk: Egypt. A red, yellow, or green, low, cylindrical, shako-like hat.

cái: Vietnam. Parasol.

cai-ao: Annam. Long chemise with long, fitted sleeves.

caichóu: China. Colored silk fabric.

caicmhe: Ireland. Gaelic word for a neck ornament.

caille: Ireland. Gaelic word for a hood, veil, or a cowl.

caillouté: France. Pebbled.

cailmhion: Ireland. Gaelic word for light helmet.

cailmleid: Ireland. Gaelic word for camlet.

caimmse: *See* lēne.

càin: Ireland. White.

cainb: Ireland. Gaelic word for sackcloth.

cainb-aodach: Ireland. Gaelic word for canvas.

cainsil: Byzantine and Romanesque (400–1200 C.E.). Very fine fabric of simple weave.

caipīn: Ireland. Cap.

càiqing: China. Dark grayish green color.

caiquan: Annam. Long trousers; white for men, black for women.

cairel: Renaissance (1450–1550 C.E.). Spain. Passementerie.

cairtidh: Ireland. Gaelic word for bark colored.

caisbheart: Ireland. Gaelic word for footwear.

cais-chiabh: Ireland. Gaelic word for curl or ringlet.

caisean-feusaig: Ireland. Gaelic word for moustache.

caisreag: Ireland. Gaelic word for curl or ringlet.

caissia: Greek (3000–100 B.C.E.). Headdress; style unknown.

caita: Romania. Thin cloth cap.

caite: Guatemala. Sandal with leather back and wood or hide sole. The sandal is held in place with leather thongs.

caite
See also photospread (Foot and Legwear).

cake hat: Gay Nineties (1890–1900 C.E.). Man's soft felt, low-crowned hat similar to alpine hat.

cakresvari: India. Silk from Chakrabari.

caksire: *See* hlace.

calaber: Early Gothic (1200–1350 C.E.) to Late Gothic (1350–1450 C.E.). Fur of gray squirrel.

calais val: Heavy version of Valenciennes lace.

calamanco: Satin weave wool fabric that is plain, striped, or checked. *See also* brillianette.

calamatta: Italy. Ungummed silk.

calamistrum: Roman (753 B.C.E.–323 C.E.). Curling iron.

calanaka: *See* candataka.

calani: *See* candataka.

calanika: India. An antariya worn in between the legs and then wrapped around the hips.

calash: Late Georgian (1750–1790 C.E.). Woman's hat made to cover wigs with top that folded back like the top of carriage. Hoops were made of reed or whalebone.

calasiris: Egyptian (4000–30 B.C.E.). Semitransparent tunic worn with knotted belt.

calata: Late Gothic (1350–1450 C.E.). Italy. Closed helmet that hid the face.

calash

calavia: India. An extremely light stuff.

calbhthas: Ireland. Gaelic word for half boot or bulskin.

calc: Byzantine and Romanesque (400–1200 C.E.). United Kingdom. Man's simple sandal.

calçado: *See* sapata.

calção: Portugal. Pantaloons.

calção de banho: Portugal. Bathing trunks.

calção de montaria: Portugal. Riding breeches.

calcarapedes: Crinoline (1840–1865 C.E.). In 1860s, men's rubber galoshes.

calças: Portugal. Trousers.

calças de couro: Portugal. Buckskins.

calce: Early Gothic (1200–1350 C.E.). Long tight stockings with gusset in back to add movement.

calceolus: Roman (753 B.C.E.–323 C.E.). Light form of calceus for women.

calcetería: Spain. Hosiery.

calcetin: Spain. Hose.

calcetines: Spain. Long socks.

calceus: Roman (753 B.C.E.–323 C.E.). Shoe or half-boot reaching up to calf.

calceus patricius: Roman (753 B.C.E.–323 C.E.). Low shoe with straps that laced up leg. Worn only by senators.

calcheña llijlla: Bolivia. Llijlla with black bands.

caldron: Reddish copper or brown color.

cale: Renaissance (1450–1550 C.E.). Bag, often of black velvet, worn in combination with gabled headdress or French hood to conceal hair.

calêche: France. Hood.

caleçons: 1. Byzantine and Romanesque (400–1200 C.E.). Spain, France. Drawers. 2. Elizabethan (1550–1625 C.E.) to Restoration (1660–1700 C.E.). Men's linen drawers. 3. Elizabethan (1550–1625 C.E.) to Restoration (1660–1700 C.E.). Women's riding garment.

Caledonian cap: Romantic (1815–1840 C.E.). Popular in 1817, woman's small close-fitting cap trimmed with black feathers.

Caledonian brown: Dull reddish yellow.

Caledonian silk: Directoire and First Empire (1790–1815 C.E.). Introduced in 1810, fabric similar to poplin but with silkier surface.

calendering: A mechanical finishing process for fabrics that produces a surface effect, such as glazing.

calfskin: Strong, supple leather.

calibri: Bustle (1865–1890 C.E.). In 1868, shot velvet.

calico: Elizabethan (1550–1625 C.E.) to present. Plain weave, lightweight, printed cotton fabric originally imported from India.

calicó: Portugal. Calico.

calico china button: Crinoline (1840–1865 C.E.). United States of America. Early mass produced buttons designed to coordinate with China calico fabrics.

California: Crinoline (1840–1865 C.E.). France. Intense yellow color. Originally called bouton d'or.

Californian embroidery: Pre-Spanish embroidery done with animal cords and fishbone needles.

caliga: 1. Roman (753 B.C.E.–323 C.E.). Enclosed shoe with thick nailed sole worn by soldiers and centurions. 2. Stocking worn by bishops.

caligula: *See* caliga.

calimanco: Elizabethan (1550–1625 C.E.). Glazed fabric.

call: Ireland. Gaelic word for veil.

callaid: Ireland. Gaelic word for a cap or a wig.

caliga
See also photospread (Foot and Legwear).

calmuc: Loose, twill weave woolen fabric with nap.

calotte: Plain skull-cap often having tab on center top. In China, worn by men. Married men have red tab and wear white tab when in mourning.

calpac: Renaissance (1450–1550 C.E.) to present. Russian Cossack officer's high astrakhan cap.

calque: France. Pricked paper pattern used for tracing.

calton: Elizabethan (1550–1625 C.E.) to Restoration (1660–1700 C.E.). Coarse fabric similar to frieze.

calum labrada: Ecuador and Guatemala. Decorated or embroidered fabric, possibly calico.

calva: Renaissance (1450–1550 C.E.). Spain. Skull or bowl of helmet.

calypso chemise: Directoire and First Empire (1790–1815 C.E.). Popular in 1790s, a woman's colored muslin, round gown worn with loose over robe.

calyptra: Byzantine (400–1200 C.E.). Headdress of emperor in shape of polygon.

calza: Italy. Short breeches.

calzado: Spain. Footwear. *See also* zapato.

calzamaglia: Italy. Leotards.

calzas conpies: Renaissance (1450–1550 C.E.). Spain. Footed hose.

calzas enteras: Renaissance (1450–1550 C.E.). Spain. Long hose.

calzas largas: Renaissance (1450–1550 C.E.). Spain. Long hose.

calzatura: Italy. Shoe.

calzaz de aguja: Elizabethan (1550–1625 C.E.). Spain. Knit hose.

calzettoni: Italy. Long socks.

calzón: Ecuador, Guatemala, and Mexico. Men's full-length, full-cut trousers.

calzón bombacho: Spain. Panties.

calzoncillo: Mexico. 1. Pair of trousers traditionally made of homespun. Cut varies widely in different regions. 2. Women's long drawers.

calzoneras: Mexico. Trousers that button on each side.

calzoni: Italy. Breeches.

camaca: Early Gothic (1200–1350 C.E.) to Late Gothic (1350–1450 C.E.). Rich, heavy, silk or silk and cotton blend fabric. Often figured.

camacaa: *See* kamkhab.

camada: *See* casaco.

camafeu: Portugal. Cameo.

camag: Ireland. Gaelic word for curl or ringlet.

camaieu: France. Brooch; cameo.

camail: 1. Early Gothic (1200–1350 C.E.). Chain-mail hood. 2. Crinoline (1840–1865 C.E.). Introduced in 1842, woman's waist-length or calf-length cloak with armseyes and small falling collar. Lined with silk in summer or cashmere, satin, or velvet in winter.

camalag: Ireland. Gaelic word for curl or ringlet.

camall: *See* kambala.

camara: Czechoslovakia. Man's tailed jacket with low standing collar, decorative braid clasps, and black silk buttons.

cámara: Renaissance (1450–1550 C.E.). Spain. Wardrobe.

camarera mayor: Renaissance (1450–1550 C.E.). Spain. Empress's wardrobe mistress.

camargo: Bustle (1865–1890 C.E.). Panniered jacket worn over waistcoat. Named for Marie Camargo, French dancer of 18th century.

camargo hat: Romantic (1815–1840 C.E.). Introduced in 1836, woman's small evening hat with brim that reached up in front.

camargo puff: Bustle (1865–1890 C.E.). Introduced in 1868, woman's puff skirt formed by looping up back of overskirt on pannier dress.

cămaşă: Romania. Shirt.

camauro: Former cap of pope; ermine-trimmed, red velvet cap.

camayeux silk: Crinoline (1840–1865 C.E.). Introduced in 1850, colored chiné silk.

cambaia: *See* comboy.

cambali: *See* kambala.

câm-bào: Vietnam. Brocade robe.

cambay: *See* comboy.

cambaye: India. Lightweight cotton fabric.

cambelloto: Renaissance. Wool fabric originally made of camel or goat hair.

cambja: *See* comboy.

cambolim: India and Portugal. Cloak.

camboy: *See* comboy.

cambraia: Italy and Portugal. Cambric.

cambray: Spain. Chambray.

cambray liso: Spain. Cambric.

cambresine: 1. France. Good quality linen and cotton fabrics that are finished to resemble linen. 2. Early Georgian (1700–1750 C.E.). France. Made in Cambrai, France; fine linen.

cambric: 1. Elizabethan (1550–1625 C.E.). France. Manufactured in Cambrai, France, thin fine linen used for ruffs, collars, shirts, and handkerchiefs. 2. Lightweight glazed cotton fabric.

cambridge coat: Bustle (1865–1890 C.E.) to 20th century. Introduced in 1870, man's single- or double-breasted lounge coat with center back vent with four patch pockets. By 1880, single-breasted reefer.

cambridge paletot: Crinoline (1840–1865 C.E.). Introduced in 1855, man's large, full-length overcoat with wide sleeves and wide turned back cuffs. Wide lapels reached to hem.

câm-châu: Vietnam. Pongee.

camee: Holland. Cameo.

camel: Medium light brown color.

caméléon: 1. Crinoline (1840–1865 C.E.). Popular around 1859, woman's boot with upper having small ornamental holes to reveal stockings. 2. Crinoline (1840–1865 C.E.). Introduced in 1840s, silk shot in three colors. By 1850, it was called shot poplin.

cameleon antique: Gay Nineties (1890–1900 C.E.). Introduced in 1892, a silk with changeable effect.

cameleurion: Roman (753 B.C.E.–323 C.E.). Hemispherical crown worn by Caesars.

camelin: Early Gothic (1200–1350 C.E.). Fabric of camel or goat hair.

cameline: *See* camelin.

camelite: Bustle (1865–1890 C.E.). In 1872, reddish plum.

cameloleopard: Romantic (1815–1840 C.E.). French beige.

camelot: France. A tabby.

camel's hair cloth: Thick, warm, lightweight, twill weave fabric with glossy face made from camel's hair, mohair, or cow hair. Usually light tan in color.

cameo: Stone carved in relief to show woman's head, usually in white against pastel background.

camericke: *See* cambric.

camibockers: (1910–1919 C.E.). United Kingdom. Woman's combination undergarment of batiste, crepe de Chine, or silk. *See also* teddies; teddy-bears.

camicia: Italy. Shirt.

camicia da donna: Italy. Chemise

camicia rossa: Italy. Red shirt popularized by Garibaldi, Italian patriot.

camiciuola: Italy. Waistcoat.

cami-knickers

cami-knickers: (1920–1930 C.E.). Woman's undergarments combining bodice and panties.

Camilla mantelet: Crinoline (1840–1865 C.E.). In 1854, silk mantelet trimmed with four rows of Honiton lace at neck and same at waist.

camisa: 1. *See* chemise. 2. Ecuador and Guatemala. Tailored shirt. 3. Spain. Shirt.

camisa chaki picada: Ecuador. A woman's blouse with a scalloped hem.

camisa de baixo: Portugal. Straightjacket.

camisa de força: Portugal. Straightjacket.

camisa de homem: Portugal. Shirt.

camisa de lã: Portugal. Jersey shirt.

camisa de la tela amarilla: Ecuador. The traditional cotton shirt that is made to look like a tunic without any shaping or sleeves. The sides of the garment are sewn to simulate armseyes.

camisa de muiher: Portugal. Smock.

camisa de rigor: Portugal. Dress shirt.

camisa de senhoras: Portugal. Chemise.

camisa polo: Spain. Polo shirt.

camise: Byzantine and Romanesque (400–1200 C.E.). Loose, lightweight shirt, smock, or tunic.

camiseiro: Portugal. Shirtmaker.

camiseta: 1. Ecuador and Guatemala. Shirt. 2. Portugal and Spain. Undershirt.

camiseta con mangas cortas: Spain. T-shirt.

camiseta de mujer: Spain. Tank top.

camisola: Portugal. Nightshirt; camisole.

camisole: 1. Lace trimmed underbodice with narrow straps. 2. Woman's short negligee jacket. 3. Man's jacket or jersey. 4. Restoration (1660–1700 C.E.). France. Waistcoat.

camisole neckline: Straight horizontal neckline with shoulder straps.

camisón: Peru. Thin cotton blouse.

camlee: *See* kambala.

camlet: Mixed material fabric.

cammaka: 1. Early Gothic (1200–1350 C.E.). Expensive fabric, probably of silk and camel hair. Used for royal and ecclesiastical garments. 2. *See* kamkhab.

cammakara: India. A cobbler.

cammello: Italy. Camel.

cammocca: *See* kamkhab.

câm-nhung: Vietnam. Silk velvet.

camoca: *See* camaca; kamkhab.

camocas: Early Gothic (1200–1350 C.E.) to Renaissance (1450–1550 C.E.). Rich silk fabric, often striped in gold and silver. Made in Palestine.

camocato: *See* kamkhab.

camocho: Renaissance (1450–1550 C.E.) to Restoration (1660–1700 C.E.). Italy. Silk fabric.

campagus: Byzantine (400–1200 C.E.). Ankle-high shoe that laced over instep.

campaign coat: Restoration (1660–1700 C.E.). United Kingdom. Long military coat worn by common soldier from 1667.

campaign hat: (1910–1920 C.E.). United States of America. Broad brimmed felt hat with quartered indentations in crown, encircled by cord. Worn by World War I doughboys.

campaign wig: Restoration (1660–1700 C.E.) to Early Georgian (1700–1750 C.E.). Popular until 1750 C.E., powdered wig with large curls on top and long curls hanging down back. The back curls were sometimes bound or braided into two or three bunches.

campaign wig

campaigne: 1. A fringed or indented braid. 2. Restoration (1660–1700 C.E.). A simple, net grounded, straight lace.

Campan: Crinoline (1840–1865 C.E.). In 1855, a fitted, moire antique pelisse trimmed with tufted velvet galloon and lace flounce.

campane: *See* campaigne.

campanoni d'ori: Italy. Large buttons worn down front of doge's mantle.

campera: Spain. Windbreaker.

campos: Spain. Wool fabric.

câm-y: Vietnam. Brocade garment.

can: Vietnam. Cane; walking stick.

canabhas: Ireland. Gaelic word for canvas.

canach: Ireland. Cotton.

canache: Plume of feather tips, usually ostrich.

Canadian embroidery: Primitive embroidery of Canadian Indians that was done with porcupine quills and animal skin strips.

canaichean: Ireland. Gaelic word for cotton.

cañamazo doblado: Elizabethan (1550–1625 C.E.). Spain. Hempen canvas.

cañari: Bolivia. Woman's wide, heavy underbelt.

canarie jaune: France. Canary yellow.

canary yellow: Bright, slightly reddish yellow.

canavaccio: Italy. Canvas.

cancan dress: Gay Nineties (1890–1900 C.E.). France. Style popularized by cancan dancers in Paris, France, in 1890s. Includes basque bodice with large sleeves, long full skirt, and great number of ruffled petticoats.

cân-ðai: Vietnam. Ceremonial dress.

candakanta: India. Long, loose coat with a front opening.

candanhār: India. A layered gold necklace.

candataka: India. 1. A petticoat. 2. A sewn skirt.

candlewick: 1. Late Gothic (1350–1450 C.E.). Manservants' rough material. 2. Present. Tufted cotton material.

candongas: Ecuador. Large, round earrings.

candramā: India. Moon-shaped ornament.

candys: Persia. Seventh to fourth century B.C.E. Linen or wool garment. First recorded garment with set-in sleeves.

cane color: Elizabethan (1550–1625 C.E.). Yellowish white color.

canepin: France. Kidskin.

canevas: France. Canvas.

canezou
Dover Publications

canezou: 1. Directoire and First Empire (1790–1815 C.E.) to Crinoline (1840–1865 C.E.). France. Introduced in 1820s as white sleeveless spencer. By the 1830s, it was short, pointed cape that did not cover arms. By 1850s, it was fancy muslin fichu with lace and ribbons that covered front and back of torso. 2. *See* corsage.

canezou spencer: Romantic (1815–1840 C.E.). Woman's transparent, collared, sleeved, short overbodice tucked into a sash at the waist.

cang: China. Dark green color.

cangan: China. Rough cotton fabric.

canganes: China. Cloth from Kaga.

cangcang: China. Gray.

cangee: Yoke-like collar.

canghuáng: China. Greenish yellow color.

cánh dán: Vietnam. Brown.

cánh-kien: Vietnam. Purple.

cành-phuc: Vietnam. Police uniform.

caniche: Curly tufted fabric used for jackets.

canille: Weave with stripes broken at intervals with knot, giving effect of bamboo cane.

canions: Elizabethan (1550–1625 C.E.). Very tight upper stocks. Worn by men.

canipo: Peru. Worn on the head, Incan large circular patens of gold or silver.

canne: France. Walking stick.

canne à système: France. Gadget cane.

cannelé: To be woven in flutes or creased or sewn into fluted surface.

cannellato: Italy. Crepoline.

cannequin: Renaissance (1450–1550 C.E.) to Late Georgian (1750–1790 C.E.). White cotton fabric from East Indies.

cannes demi-solde: France. Flat cane containing a sword.

cannes-dard: France. Cane containing a stiletto.

cannetille: Directoire and First Empire (1790–1815 C.E.). 1. Weave forming interlocking checks. 2. Lacy braid of gold or silver thread.

cannon sleeves: Elizabethan (1550–1625 C.E.). Padded, stiffened, full-cut gown sleeves that were fitted at wrist.

canoque: Bustle (1865–1890 C.E.). In 1879, golden brown.

canotier: France. Straight brimmed, flat crowned hat popularized by boatmen.

cân-quac: Vietnam. Woman's handkerchief.

cantab hat: Directoire and First Empire (1790–1815 C.E.). Introduced in 1806, woman's straw day hat with narrow rectangular brim and flat crown.

cantaloon: Elizabethan (1550–1625 C.E.). Another name for camlet.

canton crepe: Soft crepe fabric with bias ribs, originally made of silk in Canton, China.

canton flannel: Strong cotton, twill weave flannel with long nap on one side. Used for interlinings, infant wear, and sleepwear.

canton linen: *See* swatow grass cloth.

cantoon: Directoire and First Empire (1790–1815 C.E.) to Bustle (1865–1890 C.E.). Fabric similar to fustian, but with fine cord on one side and satin face on other side.

canura: Romania. Woolen thread.

cañutillos: Renaissance (1450–1550 C.E.). Spain. Bugle beads.

canvas: 1. Heavy, strong cotton, linen, or synthetic fabric. 2. Cross-stitch fabric.

caoxié: China. Straw sandals.

cap à la Charlotte Corday: Directoire and First Empire (1790–1815 C.E.). France. Woman's soft cap with frill around face and worn tied with ribbon at neck. Named for Charlotte Corday.

cap of maintenance: United Kingdom. Symbol of rank that is carried on cushion before ruler of United Kingdom at coronation. Made of scarlet velvet and trimmed with ermine.

cap sleeve: Small sleeve, just covering shoulder.

cap tóc: Vietnam. Hairpin.

capa: 1. Elizabethan (1550–1625 C.E.). Spain. Wide, circular, hooded cloak worn by men. 2. Romantic (1815–1840 C.E.). Flowing evening cloak. 3. Portugal. Rain cape. 4. *See* manto.

capa corta: Spain. Cape.

capa larga: Spain. Cloak.

capa magna: Hooded cloak worn by cardinals in Roman Catholic Church.

capa morisca: Spain. Burnoose.

capacete: Portugal. Helmet.

capacete de Indias: Spain. Sun helmet.

capacho: Bolivia. Man's shoulder bag.

capadüsli: Switzerland. Woman's small gold-trimmed cap.

cap-a-pie armour: Elizabethan (1550–1625 C.E.). Complete suit of armor, reaching head to toe.

capash: Greece. Flowing scarf.

cape a l'espanole: *See* capa.

cape net: Stiff cotton net.

capela: *See* touca.

capelina: Renaissance (1450–1550 C.E.). Italy. Skull-cap of steel.

capeline (modeled)

capeline

capeline: 1. Soft brimmed hat. 2. Early Gothic (1200–1350 C.E.). Metal skullcap worn by soldiers. From French word for hood. 3. Early Gothic (1200–1350 C.E.). A woman's hood, popularly worn by nuns and widows. 4. France. A woman's hood, commonly attached to a short capelet.

capellar: Renaissance (1450–1550 C.E.). Spain. Hooded cloak.

caperuza: Renaissance (1450–1550 C.E.). Spain. Hood.

capeskin: Durable glove leather from skin of South African haired sheep.

capichola: Spain. Faille.

capilla: Renaissance (1450–1550 C.E.). Spain. Hood.

capillamentum: Roman (753 B.C.E.–323 C.E.). Wig.

capirote: Renaissance (1450–1550 C.E.). Spain. Cap.

capisayo: Ecuador and Guatemala. Vest; poncho.

capitonné: France. To be stuffed or padded.

capitonné embroidery: Decorative tufting on furniture.

capixaij: Guatemala. Man's long, rectangular cloak with an opening for the head. May be worn belted.

capixay: Guatemala. Man's woolen long coat.

capka: *See* cepice.

capot: Romantic (1815–1840 C.E.). Introduced in 1816, woman's evening hood of cardinal red silk handkerchief.

capota: Portugal. Cap; headdress.

capote: 1. Early Georgian (1700–1750 C.E.) to Bustle (1865–1890 C.E.). Woman's cap that fitted around chignon, with wide brim that framed face. 2. *See* poke bonnet. 3. Ecuador, Guatemala, and Portugal. Cloak; mantle.

capot-ribot: Directoire and First Empire (1790–1815 C.E.). Black velvet pillbox hat with black triangular curtain on back and sides. Lined in red, green, or violet.

capouch: Elizabethan (1550–1625 C.E.). Monk's cowl or hood. Also hood of cloak.

cappa: Byzantine and Romanesque (400–1200 C.E.). United Kingdom. Cap. Possibly only for ecclesiastical use.

cappa clausa: Early Gothic (1200–1350 C.E.). Closed cope.

cappa magna: Ceremonial robe worn by cardinals and bishops.

cappa nigra: Early Gothic (1200–1350 C.E.). Black choir cope.

cappadine: Waste from silk cocoon remaining after silk has been removed.

cappe: Byzantine and Romanesque (400–1200 C.E.) to Renaissance (1450–1550 C.E.). United Kingdom. Middle English term for a cap.

cappelina: Late Gothic (1350–1450 C.E.). Light steel helmet that fitted snugly to the head.

cappeline: Hat blank with brim formed but body unblocked.

cappello: Italy. Hat.

cappello a cencio: Italy. Cloth hat.

cappello a cilindro: Italy. Top hat.

cappello a lobbia: Italy. Homburg.

cappello a tagliere: Italy. Broad-brimmed hat.

cappello a tesa larga: Italy. Squash hat.

cappello da uomo: Man's trilby.

cappello di paglia: Italy. Straw hat.

cappello floscio: Italy. Slouch hat.

cappucio: Italy. Hood; cowl.

capra china: Italy. Chinese goat fur.

capri: Bluish green.

capri blue: Deep sea blue.

capri pants: Women's tapered leg pants that end just above ankle, sometimes with slit over ankle bone.

caprice: Crinoline (1840–1865 C.E.). Introduced in 1846, woman's loose, sleeveless evening jacket that reached down to rounded point in back.

capriole: *See* cabriolet.

capuce: *See* capuchon.

capuch: Elizabethan (1550–1625 C.E.). Cloak's hood.

capucha: Portugal. Hood; bonnet.

capuche: Crinoline (1840–1865 C.E.). In 1850s, woman's silk-lined muslin bonnet.

capuchin: 1. Late Georgian (1750–1790 C.E.). Hooded cloak similar to those worn by Capuchin friars.

2. Crinoline (1840–1865 C.E.). Introduced in 1862, red brown like cinnamon. 3. Bustle (1865–1890 C.E.). Gray cashmere or alpaca dust cloak that was lined in red or striped surah. The cloak had a peaked hood.

capuchinho: Portugal. Small hood or cowl.

capuchon: Byzantine and Romanesque (400–1200 C.E.). Hood, often with tail (known later as the liripipe), and usually attached to cape.

capucine: Canary yellow.

capulet: France. Hood worn by peasant women.

caputium: Elizabethan (1550–1625 C.E.). Hood worn by scholars and ecclesiastics.

caputrock: Late Georgian (1750–1790 C.E.). Austria. Overcoat.

capuz: *See* touca.

capuz de frade: Portugal. Cowl.

caqui: Spain. Khaki.

cáqui: Portugal. Khaki.

cà-rá: Vietnam. Diamond.

carabitina: Greek. Sandal worn by peasants.

caracal: Lynx fur.

caracalla: Byzantine and Romanesque (400–1200 C.E.). Long sleeved, narrow, fitted garment, sometimes hooded.

caraco: Late Georgian (1750–1790 C.E.). Gown à la francaise that ended at hip, making peasant-style jacket.

caraco á la française: Late Georgian (1750–1790 C.E.). France. Caraco with watteau pleats.

caraco á la polonaise: Late Georgian (1750–1790 C.E.). France. Caraco with lower front edge curving around to back.

caraco ácoqueluchon: Late Georgian (1750–1790 C.E.). France. Caraco with hood or cowl.

caraco gown: Late Georgian (1750–1790 C.E.). Long basqued gown with peplum. Often trained.

caracul: Russia. Astrakhan fur.

caracul cloth: Heavy woolen fabric resembling Persian lamb.

caracul lamb: Sleek, soft fur with high luster.

caracule: Gay Nineties (1890–1900 C.E.). Astrachan with wide curl in hair.

caracule material: Gay Nineties (1890–1900 C.E.). In 1894, a flannel lining fabric with crocodile mohair surface.

caradori: Crinoline (1840–1865 C.E.). In 1858, woman's silk summer mantle with fitted body and deep lace flounce.

caramel: Reddish yellow.

carana: India. Kilts.

carapa: Croatia and Serbia. Stocking.

čarapa: Bosnia. Stocking.

carapuça: Portugal. Funnel-shaped blue felt cap with pipe pointing up and holding sprig of rosemary. Worn by both genders before WWI and is now worn rarely, and then only by women.

caravan: Late Georgian (1750–1790 C.E.). In 1765, early version of calash.

carbunculus: *See* anthrax.

carcaille: Late Gothic (1350–1450 C.E.). Flaring collar reaching to ears. Common on houppelandes and pourpoint, it was often trimmed with fur for winter wear.

carcaille

carcanet: Elizabethan (1550–1625 C.E.). Gold or jeweled necklace, bracelet, or hair ornament.

carda: Early Gothic (1200–1350 C.E.) to Late Gothic (1350–1450 C.E.). France. Cloth of unknown origin used in making surcoats.

cardado: Spain. Any shaggy uncombed wool fabric.

cardador: Ecuador and Guatemala. Person who cards fleece.

cardato: Italy. Any shaggy uncombed wool fabric.

cardigan: Crinoline (1840–1865 C.E.) to present. Knitted sweater that opened down front.

cardinal: 1. Gay Nineties (1890–1900 C.E.). Woman's waist-length, hoodless cloak. 2. *See* Talma cloak. 3. Crinoline (1840–1865 C.E.). In 1864, lady's collar ending in pleated muslin tabs. 4. First Empire (1790–1815 C.E.). United States of America. Scarlet hooded wool cloak.

cardinal cloth: Red wool fabric used in some vestments.

cardinal pelerine: Crinoline (1840–1865 C.E.). Popular in 1840s, woman's deep lace evening bertha split in center.

cardinal red: Bright red, darker than scarlet.

cardinal white: Elizabethan (1550–1625 C.E.). White undyed wool homespun.

cardows: Elizabethan (1550–1625 C.E.). Tasseled cords on man's ceremonial robe.

carechale: *See* marechal.

careless: Romantic (1815–1840 C.E.). United Kingdom. Man's loose overcoat with full cape and wide collar. Made without waist seam.

çargat: Iran. Woman's transparent veil.

Cariola: Crinoline (1840–1865 C.E.). In 1858, woman's striped burnous with pointed hood.

carkanett: Ireland. Weight of jewelry.

carkanette: *See* carcanet.

carkenet: *See* carkanett.

çârma: Algeria. Jewish woman's long, cone-shaped headdress on metal framework.

carmagnole: Directoire and First Empire (1790–1815 C.E.). Italy. Man's short-skirted coat with wide, turned down collar and rows of metal buttons. Worn by Italian workmen and later adopted by French Revolutionaries. Commonly worn with redingote, clogs, and Phrygian cap.

carmakt: *See* padukakrt.

carmeillette: 1. *See* capuchon. 2. Romantic (1815–1840 C.E.). In 1837, woman's short evening cloak with hood and long sleeves.

carmeline: 1. Bustle (1865–1890 C.E.). Introduced in 1870, fine wool fabric. 2. Persian wool.

carmelite: 1. Bustle (1865–1890 C.E.). Introduced in 1872, reddish-plum color. 2. Gay Nineties (1890–1900 C.E.). Fabric similar to thin beige but more open in weave.

carmeñola: Spain. Man's small, fitted cap.

carmezim: Portugal. Crimson.

carmim: Portugal. Carmine.

carmin: 1. Italy. Carmine. 2. Spain. Carmine.

carmine: 1. Directoire and First Empire (1790–1815 C.E.). Bright red color popular in 1817. 2. (1940–1949 C.E.). Red color with blue tint.

carminio: Italy. Carmine.

carnagan: Romantic (1815–1840 C.E.). Popular in the 1820s, cloth commonly used for trousers.

carnation: Elizabethan (1550–1625 C.E.). Flesh color.

carnaza: Elizabethan (1550–1625 C.E.). Flesh side of a hide.

carnelian: 1. Variety of chalcedony used in jewelry. 2. Flesh red.

carnival: Type of reticella lace.

carolina beaver: Beaver fur imported from Carolina. Inferior to Canadian fur.

caroline: 1. France. Twill weave, woolen dress fabric. 2. Stovepipe hat.

caroline corsage: Romantic (1815–1840 C.E.). United Kingdom. Popular in the 1830s, woman's evening corsage with narrow lace fall in deep V shape.

caroline hat: Restoration (1660–1700 C.E.) to Early Georgian (1700–1750 C.E.). Man's hat of Carolina beaver, commonly worn by servants.

caroline sleeve: Romantic (1815–1840 C.E.). Popular in 1830s, woman's day dress sleeve that was very full to elbow and then fitted to wrist.

caroline spencer: Directoire and First Empire (1790–1815 C.E.). Spencer with pelerine cape that was made of white kerseymere and trimmed with light blue satin cut on bias.

caroubier: Bustle (1865–1890 C.E.). In 1876, new color.

carpenter's apron: Fabric or leather half apron with pouch-like pockets to carry small tools, screws, etc. Worn on a belt.

caroline sleeve

carpet slippers: Crinoline (1840–1865 C.E.) to 20th century. United Kingdom. Worn from around 1840, men's bedroom slippers with uppers made of German wool woven like carpet.

carpmeal: Renaissance (1450–1550 C.E.) to Late Georgian (1750–1790 C.E.). United Kingdom. Coarse cloth used for linings.

carpmeal white: Renaissance (1450–1550 C.E.) to Elizabethan (1550–1625 C.E.). Fabric used for hose linings.

carpote: Crinoline (1840–1865 C.E.). Woman's small hat worn with ties beneath chin.

carranes: 1. Ireland. Leather footwear. 2. Isle of Man. Rough calfskin shoes made with hair still on. Laced with leather thongs.

carreau: France. Check or square design.

carreau amazone: Gay Nineties (1890–1900 C.E.). In 1891, a dark blue and light sky blue check fabric.

carrel: Renaissance (1450–1550 C.E.) to Elizabethan (1550–1625 C.E.). Silk and homespun fabric.

carrez de gaze: France. A type of needlework lace.

carriage boot: Woman's protective outer boot.

carriages: Elizabethan (1550–1625 C.E.). Straps that hung from belt and were used to support sword.

carrick: Bustle (1865–1890 C.E.) to 20th century. Long woman's dust cloak with three capes.

carrickmacross: Crinoline (1840–1865 C.E.) to 1890s. Cut muslin work.

carrickmacross lace: Ireland. Lace with appliqued motifs connected by knotted hexagonal lace.

carrodary: Early Georgian (1700–1750 C.E.) to Directoire and First Empire (1790–1815 C.E.). Original name of cherryderry.

carrot color: Red yellow.

çarsof: Turkey. Woman's outer garment consisting of large rectangle with drawstring at waist. Worn draped over head and falls to feet.

carthage cymar: Directoire and First Empire (1790–1815 C.E.). Introduced in 1809, fancy net scarf with gold embossed border that was worn attached to one shoulder and hanging down back to knees.

carthagena: Long staple West Indian cotton.

cartisane: Parchment strip wrapped in silk or metal thread and used in lace to give raised effect.

cartola: Portugal. Top hat.

cartoose collar: Elizabethan (1550–1625 C.E.). Standing collar with pickadils on upper edge.

cartridge pleat: Round pleat shaped as if to hold a cartridge.

cartwheel: Flat, wide, low-crowned, stiff-brimmed, straw or felt hat.

casa de botão: Portugal. Buttonhole.

casaca: Portugal. Dress coat; frock coat; tail coat.

cartwheel

casaco: Portugal. Coat.

casaco de peles: Portugal. Fur coat.

casaco esportiva: Portugal. Blazer.

casaco para uso caseiro: Portugal. Housecoat.

casag: Ireland. Gaelic word for long coat.

casag-mharcachd: Ireland. Gaelic word for riding coat.

casair: Ireland. Gaelic word for buckle.

casaque: 1. Charles I and the Commonwealth (1625–1660 C.E.). Greatcoat with large sleeves with revered cuffs. Usually three-quarter length. 2. Restoration (1660–1700 C.E.). France. Surcoat. 3. Crinoline (1840–1865 C.E.). Woman's fitted jacket that had a deep basque and buttoned to neck.

casaque bodice: Bustle (1865–1890 C.E.). Introduced in 1873, woman's fitted bodice with deep front basque.

casaquin: Early Georgian (1700–1750 C.E.) to Late Georgian (1750–1790 C.E.). Woman's at-home dressing gown.

casaquin bodice: Bustle (1865–1890 C.E.). Woman's tailed fitted day bodice that buttoned down front. Worn with untrained skirt that was two inches off ground.

casaquin en juste: Late Georgian (1750–1790 C.E.). France. Woman's short, fitted, hip-length jacket.

casaweck: Romantic (1815–1840 C.E.) to Crinoline (1840–1865 C.E.). Popular from 1836 to around 1850, woman's short, quilted, sleeved mantle with velvet, silk, or satin collar. Trimmed in fur, velvet, or lace.

casbans: Directoire and First Empire (1790–1815 C.E.) to 1890s. Heavy cotton fabric used for linings.

cascade: Jabot.

cascade waistband: Crinoline (1840–1865 C.E.) to Bustle (1865–1890 C.E.). United Kingdom. Woman's waistband that was fringed in jet pendants.

casco: 1. Italy. Crash helmet. 2. Spain. Helmet; crash helmet.

casco coloniale: Italy. Sun helmet.

caseac: Romania. Woman's triangular kerchief with tassels.

cased body: 1. Elizabethan (1550–1625 C.E.). United Kingdom. Man's sleeveless jerkin worn over doublet. 2. Romantic (1815–1840 C.E.). Woman's bodice with rows of horizontal pleats across chest.

cased sleeve: Directoire and First Empire (1790–1815 C.E.) to Romantic (1815–1840 C.E.). United Kingdom. Woman's long sleeve with horizontal bands of insertion.

casement cloth: Sheer drapery fabric of silk, rayon, cotton, or blend in light colors.

casemira: Portugal. Cashmere.

casentino: Italy. Red coachman's coat lined in green.

casha: Soft wool fabric, similar to flannel, used for dresses, blouses, and coats.

cashmere: Very fine, soft wool from undercoat of cashmere goats. Naturally white, gray, tan, or blend. Used to make high quality fabric.

cashmere de baize: Crinoline (1840–1865 C.E.). Silk and worsted fabric used for travelling dresses.

cashmere shawl: Romantic (1815–1840 C.E.) to 20th century. Square or oblong shawl either woven or embroidered. Woven version was woven in sections and more costly. Best quality shawls were 3.5 yards by 1.5 yards. Characteristic pattern was cone design.

cashmere syrien: Crinoline (1840–1865 C.E.). Very fine, soft twill weave cashmere.

cashmere twill: Gay Nineties (1890–1900 C.E.). Cotton fabric imitating French cashmere.

cashmere work: India. Embroidery done on cashmere, often including inlaid applique.

cashmerette: Lightweight, twill weave cotton fabric with slight nap.

cashmerienne: Bustle (1865–1890 C.E.). Introduced in 1880, fine wool fabric with twill on both sides.

cashmire de bège: Crinoline (1840–1865 C.E.). In 1855, new fabric.

casimir: France, Spain. Cassimere. *See also* kerseymere.

casimir de soie: Crinoline (1840–1865 C.E.). Introduced in 1853, silk and wool blend fabric that looked like shot silk.

casimira: Portugal. Kerseymere.

casimiro: Italy. Cassimere.

casket cloth: Cotton warp and wool, silk, or rayon weft fabric.

casōg: Ireland. Coat.

caspian: Gay Nineties (1890–1900 C.E.). In 1897, a dull green.

casque: 1. *See* helm. 2. France. Crash helmet.

casque à la Tarleton: Directoire and First Empire (1790–1815 C.E.). France. Peaked leather helmet with bearskin crest.

casque colonial: France. Sun helmet.

casquetel: Small, lightweight, open helmet without visor.

casquette: 1. Crinoline (1840–1865 C.E.). Popular in 1863–1864, woman's straw hat with low brim. Trimmed in black velvet and ostrich feathers. 2. France. Hat.

cassenet: Romantic (1815–1840 C.E.). Summer dress fabric.

cassimere: Medium weight, woolen fabric made in twill, plain, and fancy weaves.

cassimerette: Cheap grade of cassimere used for boys' suit.

cassinette: Fabric with cotton warp and wool or wool blend weft.

cassis: 1. Late Gothic (1350–1450 C.E.). Italy. Small, fitted metal helmet. 2. Bustle (1865–1890 C.E.). In 1875, black currant color with slight hint of blue.

cassock: Restoration (1660–1700 C.E.). Man's doublet which from 1650 to 1670 was lengthened sometimes to knee. Worn belted or beltless. Later became daily wear of Roman Catholic and Church of United Kingdom clergy.

cassock mantle: Bustle (1865–1890 C.E.). United Kingdom. Worn in 1880s, woman's short sleeved, knee-length cloak that gathered on shoulders and down center back.

cassock vest: Crinoline (1840–1865 C.E.). United Kingdom. Worn in 1850s by Tractorian High Church officials, clerical waistcoat that buttoned on shoulder.

castagnino: Italy. Nut brown.

castanho: Portugal. Brown. *See also* cor.

castaño: Spain. Hazel.

castellan delaine: Bustle (1865–1890 C.E.). In 1872, new fabric.

Castiglione: Crinoline (1840–1865 C.E.). In 1858, woman's cloth cloak with deep collar. Trimmed with strips of arabesque plush and buttons.

Castilian

Castilian: Crinoline (1840–1865 C.E.). 1. In 1853, cloak made from 5-1/2 widths of velvet 36 inches long and lined with silk. Removable hood. 2. In 1857, woman's woolen talma with bertha and lower edge trimmed with fringe. Talma was trimmed with 10 rows of passementerie. 3. In 1859, summer burnous trimmed with quilled ribbon and chenille tassels.

castillian red: Bright, intense, slightly yellowish red.

castle: Renaissance (1450–1550 C.E.). United Kingdom. Variety of helmet.

castle hat: (1910–1920 C.E.). In 1913, a woman's hat with crushed crown with assymetric brim and trimmed with feather bunch on one side.

castor: 1. Elizabethan (1550–1625 C.E.) to Bustle (1865–1890 C.E.). Beaver hat. 2. Bustle (1865–1890 C.E.). Introduced in 1872, brownish gray. 3. *See* beaver cloth. 4. France and Spain. Beaver fur.

castor gray: Yellow green.

castorina: Spain. Beaver cloth.

castorino: Italy. Nutria.

castoro: Italy. Beaver fur.

casul: Byzantine and Romanesque (400–1200 C.E.). United Kingdom. Cloak or chasuble. Possibly only an ecclesiastical term.

casulo: Portugal. Chasuble.

cas-urladh: Ireland. Gaelic word for curled lock.

catagan: Bustle (1865–1890 C.E.). Popular from 1870 to 1875, chignon of ringlet or braids worn at base of back of head and tied with ribbon.

catagan head-dress: Bustle (1865–1890 C.E.). Introduced in 1889, woman's hairstyle with hair braided in back and tied up with ribbon. Popular with older schoolgirls.

catagan net: Bustle (1865–1890 C.E.). Popular in 1870s, woman's hairnet worn over catagan.

cataloon: *See* catalowne.

catalowne: Elizabethan (1550–1625 C.E.) to Restoration (1660–1700 C.E.). Inferior camlet.

catalpha: Elizabethan (1550–1625 C.E.) to Restoration (1660–1700 C.E.). Silk fabric.

cater-cap: Renaissance (1450–1550 C.E.) to Restoration (1660–1700 C.E.). Man's four-cornered cap worn by academicians.

catgut: Plain weave fabric made from hardspun linen yarn.

Catgut lace: Elizabethan (1550–1625 C.E.) to Late Georgian (1750–1790 C.E.). Trade name for type of lace, not really from catgut.

cathedral beard: Elizabethan (1550–1625 C.E.) to Directoire and First Empire (1790–1815 C.E.). American. Wide, square cut beard worn by dignitaries of Church.

Catherine wheel farthingale: Elizabethan (1550–1625 C.E.). United Kingdom. Popular from 1580 to around 1620, woman's farthingale in tub shape. *See also* wheel farthingale.

cati: France. Gloss; luster.

catiole: France. Marriage coif.

cát-két: Vietnam. Visored cap.

çatma: Turkey. Fine, tightly woven, lustrous velvet made in Bursa from late 15th century on.

catogan: Late Georgian (1750–1790 C.E.) to Directoire and First Empire (1790–1815 C.E.). Popular from 1760 to late 1790s, man's wig with wide, flat queue that folded up and tied with black ribbon.

catogan

catrinta: Romania. Woman's apron. Vertical stripes and designs.

catrintoi: Romania. Woman's apron worn behind. Horizontal stripes and designs.

catskin: Silk hat of inferior quality.

catto: India. A veil.

catula: India. A pendant.

caubagalā: *See* badan.

caubeen: Ireland. Slang term for any hat, particularly old ones.

caucho pargate: Ecuador. Sandals made from rubber tires.

caudebec hat: Restoration (1660–1700 C.E.) to Late Georgian (1750–1790 C.E.). Man's beaver felt hat, originally from Caudebec, Normandy.

caul: 1. Byzantine and Romanesque (400–1200 C.E.). Close-fitting hairnet worn by women of upper class. 2. Early Gothic (1200–1350 C.E.) to Charles I (1625–1660 C.E.). Trellis-work cap of silk thread or gold. Sometimes lined with silk or worn with veil. 3. Restoration (1660–1700 C.E.) to Late Georgian (1750–1790 C.E.). Net on which a wig was constructed. 4. Early Georgian (1700–1750 C.E.) to Bustle (1865–1890 C.E.). Soft crown of woman's cap.

cauliflower wig: Late Georgian (1750–1790 C.E.). United Kingdom. Man's curled bob-wig worn by coachmen.

caungeantries: Renaissance (1450–1550 C.E.) to Elizabethan (1550–1625 C.E.). Fabric with worsted warp and silk weft.

caurimauri: Late Gothic (1350–1450 C.E.) to Renaissance (1450–1550 C.E.). Coarse fabric.

caushets: Obsolete term for corsets.

causia: Greek. Thessalonian traveling hat. Worn by actors to suggest having been traveling.

cavalier boot: 1. High boot with flaring cuff. 2. Man's house slipper.

cavalier cuff: Deep gauntlet cuff.

cavalier sleeve: Romantic (1815–1840 C.E.). United Kingdom. Common in 1830s, woman's day sleeve that was full to elbow and then tight to wrist. Tied along outside edge with ribbons.

cavallino: Italy. Pony.

Cavalry: Germany. Cavalry twill.

cavalry: France, Italy, and Spain. Cavalry twill.

cavalry twill: Double twill weave worsted, cotton, or rayon fabric.

cavanhaque: Portugal. Goatee.

ca-vát: Vietnam. Necktie.

cawdebink: *See* caudebec hat.

caxon: Early Georgian (1700–1750 C.E.) to Late Georgian (1750–1790 C.E.). Man's tie-wig worn for undress. Generally white or light colored.

cayenne: France. Unbleached linen.

cazapo: Italy. Spanish rabbit fur much used for men's hats.

cazavacka: France. Sacque.

cazenou: Crinoline (1840–1865 C.E.). Woman's short, sleeveless jacket.

ccahua: *See* unku.

ccahuas: Bolivia. Tunics.

cchipas: India. Person who prints fabric with handblocks.

cchok: Korea. Married woman's fist-sized bun held in place with twitkkoji.

ceabet: Norway. Standing collar.

ceadach: Ireland. Gaelic word for coarse fabric; veil or mantle.

cealt: Ireland. Gaelic word for apparel.

cealtar: Ireland. Gaelic word for thick, gray broadcloth.

ceanna-bhrat: Ireland. Gaelic word for headdress.

ceann-aodach: Ireland. Gaelic word for headdress; miter or turban.

ceann-bhàrr: Ireland. Any male headdress.

ceann-bhàrr eas-buig: Ireland. Bishop's miter.

ceann-bheart: Ireland. Gaelic word for helmet.

ceann-éideadh: Ireland. 1. Headdress. 2. Turban. 3. Miter.

ceapsâ: Romania. Woman's bonnet.

ceara: Ireland. Gaelic word for red colored.

čebatas: *See* batas.

cebolão: Portugal. Silver watch.

cebot: Russia. Boot.

cebtí: Spain. Renaissance. In 1493, a popular silk fabric.

Cebu hemp: *See* abaca.

ceimhleag: Ireland. Gaelic word for fillet.

ceimh-mhileach: Ireland. Gaelic word for hair bodkin.

ceimh-phion: *See* ceimh-mhileach.

ceint: Late Gothic (1350–1450 C.E.) to Renaissance (1450–1550 C.E.). Sash, girdle, or belt.

ceinture: France. Girdle.

ceinture dragonne: Crinoline (1840–1865 C.E.). Introduced in 1862, waistband resembling corselet in front. Closed in back with tabs and buttons. Made in two contrasting colors such as black and violet or white and mauve.

céire: Ireland. 1. Dark gray. 2. Drab brown.

cela: *See* amsuka.

celada de engole: Renaissance (1450–1550 C.E.). Spain. Ridged helmet with a serrated comb and a pointed visor.

celadon: Bustle (1865–1890 C.E.). In 1889, new color.

Celadon green: Light, soft gray green.

celam: *See* amsuyam.

Celanese: Trade name for synthetic fiber made using acetate process.

Celastic: Fabric impregnated with plastic.

celeste: 1. France. To be celestial. 2. Bustle (1865–1890 C.E.). In 1867, blue color.

celestial: Romantic (1815–1840 C.E.). United Kingdom. Sky blue.

cellular cloth: Leno weave, porous fabric used for underwear.

celluloid: Bustle (1865–1890 C.E.). Plastic invented in 1883.

celtic weave: Basket weave.

cemes: Byzantine and Romanesque (400–1200 C.E.). United Kingdom. Male child's shirt.

cendal: Early Gothic (1200–1350 C.E.) to Elizabethan (1550–1625 C.E.). Silk fabric similar to taffeta.

cendré: France. Ash color.

cendre de rose: Bustle (1865–1890 C.E.). Introduced in 1872, gray color with pink cast.

cendryn: Early Gothic (1200–1350 C.E.) to Late Gothic (1350–1450 C.E.). Gray fabric.

cenojil: *See* liga.

cento: Garment made of patches.

centre de Cedra: Bustle (1865–1890 C.E.). In 1874, ashy gray.

centro: Ecuador. A Spanish style skirt that is gathered or pleated onto a waistband.

centro de lana: Peru. Plain woolen skirt that is gathered at the waist.

ceòis: *See* cias.

cepec: 1. Russia. Hood. 2. Slovakia. Cap worn by married women.

cepice: Czechoslovakia. Cap.

cepken: Turkey. Man's bolero-like, sleeveless, elaborately embroidered jacket.

cepök: Hungary. Low boot that laces on side.

cepure: Lithuania. Hat; hood.

cerata: Portugal. Oilcloth.

cereja: Portugal. Cherry red.

Cerevis: Germany. Small, brimless, round cap similar to pillbox.

cereza: Spain. Cerise.

cerise: Cherry-like color.

cermuk: Indonesia. Small mirror pieces embroidered onto fabric.

ceroulas: Portugal. Drawers; long johns.

cerrada: Elizabethan (1550–1625 C.E.). Spain. Center back.

cerulea: Portugal. Cerulean.

cerulean blue: *See* cyan blue.

ceruse: Renaissance (1450–1550 C.E.) to Late Georgian (1750–1790 C.E.). Cosmetic used to whiten face, once made of white lead.

cervelière: Early Gothic (1200–1350 C.E.). Fitted steel cap.

cervelliera: Late Gothic (1350–1450 C.E.). Italy. Fitted steel cap.

ceryphalos: Greek (3000–100 B.C.E.). Bandage-like fillet.

cerzideira: Portugal. Seamstress.

cestus: Greek (3000–100 B.C.E.). Woman's girdle, either simple cord or wide, fancy belt.

cetim: Portugal. Satin.

cetrino: Spain. Chartreuse.

cettelle: Renaissance (1450–1550 C.E.). Spain. Kirtle.

ceylon: United Kingdom. Plain weave, cotton shirting fabric.

ceylonette: United Kingdom. All cotton fabric.

chachal: Guatemala. Woman's necklace of beads and silver coins.

chach'im': *See* panul.

chaconada: Spain. Jaconet.

chaconne: Restoration (1660–1700 C.E.). Ribbon that wrapped around neck and fell to chest, forming narrow cravat.

chaddar: Iran. Shawl or mantle.

chadder: India. Hand spun, handwoven fabric.

chadidāra sādi: *See* dadiyā.

chadoe: Charles I and the Commonwealth (1625–1660 C.E.). East Indian printed cotton or cotton blend fabric.

chadri: *See* burqa.

chaetpit: Korea. Gray.

chaffers: Renaissance (1450–1550 C.E.). United Kingdom. Embroidered lapels of gabled hood.

chagae: Korea. Mother of pearl.

chagrin: Silk fabric with pebbled face resembling leather.

chai: China. Woman's hairpin.

chai-chieh-p'ai: *See* zhaijiepai.

chaila: India. Printed saris worn by unmarried girls.

chain buckle: Early Georgian (1700–1750 C.E.). Curled wig.

chain lace: An openwork braid.

chain stitch: A stitch made of interlocking flat links.

chaine de forçat: Romantic (1815–1840 C.E.). Heavy gold chain attached to watch or monocle.

chain-hole: Bustle (1865–1890 C.E.) to 20th century. Hole for watch-chain sewn between two buttonholes on waistcoat.

chainse: Byzantine and Romanesque (400–1200 C.E.). France. Full, ankle-length garment with long straight sleeves. Worn belted under the bliaud.

chainsil: *See* cainsil.

chaisel: Early Gothic (1200–1350 C.E.) to Late Gothic (1350–1450 C.E.). Fine linen used for smocks.

chajutbit: Korea. Purple.

chakchiri: Russia. Hussar breeches worn with boots.

chak'et: Korea. Jacket.

chakva chir: India. Fine shawls trimmed with golden lace.

chakvidar: India. Muslim turban.

chal: Spain. Shawl; collar.

chalana: India. Loose or close-fitting trouser.

chalanika: India. Women's mid-thigh-length under-shorts.

chalcedony: Wax-like quartz used in jewelry.

chalchihuitl: Mexico. Jade.

chaldera: Spain. Copper color.

châle: France. Shawl. *See also* manta.

châle de brodie: Crinoline (1840–1865 C.E.). In 1853, large shawl trimmed with deep fringe.

chaleco: Ecuador and Spain. Vest.

chalet: Turkestan. Kandys-type garment, often quilted or padded.

chalina: 1. Ecuador. Shawl. 2. Peru. Single man's rectangular shawl with fringes on the ends. 3. Spain. Scarf.

chalinet: *See* challis.

chalk stripe: Light stripe in suiting fabrics.

challapata: Bolivia. Special poncho worn by the local chieftain.

challie: *See* challis.

challis: Soft, lightweight, plain weave fabric.

chalmyeon: Greek (3000–100 B.C.E.). Long narrow chlamys for women.

chalong phra ong long raja: Thailand. Sua yarn worn by a member of the court.

chalwar: Turkey. Women's ankle-length, red silk trousers worn at home.

chàm: Vietnam. Indigo.

châm: Vietnam. Pin; needle.

chaman: Chile and Peru. Woman's jacket that is embroidered at cuffs and borders.

chamarre: Renaissance (1450–1550 C.E.) to Elizabethan (1550–1625 C.E.). France. Large square of fabric with T-shaped opening for neck. Collar was attached to crosspiece of T and neck opening revered back. Sleeves cut full at top that were often lined with fur.

chambangi: Korea. Farmer's knee breeches.

chambard mantle: Crinoline (1840–1865 C.E.). United Kingdom. Woman's three-quarter-length, sleeved, hooded mantle with deep pleats in back.

chambergo: Spain. Squash hat.

chambertine: Bustle (1865–1890 C.E.). Introduced in 1872, wool and linen blend fabric for light dress.

chambery gauze: Bustle (1865–1890 C.E.). In 1869, very thin fabric.

chamblette: Elizabethan (1550–1625 C.E.). Plain weave, silk fabric.

chambord: Ribbed woolen fabric.

chambray: 1. Bustle (1865–1890 C.E.). Introduced in 1880s, thick, strong zephyr. 2. Bustle (1865–1890 C.E.). Cotton gingham used for bonnets. 3. Plain weave cotton fabric made with colored warp and white weft.

chameau: France. Camel.

chameleon: Changeable fabric created by having warp and weft threads of different colors.

chamelia: India. Golden yellow.

chamford mantle: Crinoline (1840–1865 C.E.). United Kingdom. First appearing in 1850, velvet or satin hooded cloak, similar to shawl, with deep fold in back.

chamlet: Camlet.

chamma: 1. Abyssinia. Worn by both men and women, a three yard long, two to four yard wide piece of fabric worn draped around the shoulders. 2. Ethiopia. Traditional outer garment made from one piece of cotton. Woman's version may be embroidered.

chammarros: Mexico. Cloak in Chiapas.

chammer: Renaissance (1450–1550 C.E.) to Elizabethan (1550–1625 C.E.). United Kingdom. Man's rich, sleeved gown worn open.

chamois: Suede-finished undersplit of lamb or sheep skins.

chamois cloth: Knitted or woven cotton fabric napped to resemble chamois.

chamoisette: Fine knitted cotton fabric used for gloves.

chamoisuede: Fine knitted cotton fabric for gloves.

chamot: Korea. Nightgown.

champ: France. Refers to the ground of a lace.

champagne: Light, pale gold.

champai: India. Saffron yellow.

champaigne cloth: *See* champeyn.

champeyn: Late Gothic (1350–1450 C.E.) to Renaissance (1450–1550 C.E.). Fine linen fabric.

chana-chani: India. A hempen cloth.

chanbagala: India. A man's vest with four fastenings.

chancellor: Early Georgian (1700–1750 C.E.) to Late Georgian (1750–1790 C.E.). Man's wig, style unknown.

chanchanko: Japan. A sleeveless kimono jacket for toddlers.

chanclas: Guatemala and Mexico. Plastic or rubber thong sandals.

chandail: 1. Spencer sweater. 2. France. Sweater.

chandal: Spain. Sweatshirt.

chandarvo: India. Canopy cloth.

chandataka: India. Woman's undergarment; petticoat.

chandlo: India. Vermillion caste mark on a woman's forehead.

chandtara: India. Muslin with floral embroidery.

Chanel suit: (1920–1930 C.E.). United States of America. Woman's day suit consisting of severely straight skirt and jacket. Almost a uniform.

cháng: China. 1. Cloak. 2. Skirt worn in ancient times.

chang fu: China. Charles I and the Commonwealth (1625–1660 C.E.) to 1910s. Man's basic long robe with standing collar.

chang guan: China. Green bamboo bark headdress worn by civil officials while making sacrifices.

chang shan: China. Qing dynasty (1644–1911 C.E.). Han man's side-fastening ordinary gown. Curved front opening with loop and toggle closures. Long tapering sleeves.

changalli: Ecuador. A kind of apron.

changeable taffeta: Taffeta woven with warp of one color and weft of another. Appears to change color as light hits it from various angles.

changgap: Korea. Pairs of gloves or mittens.

changhwa: Korea. Top boots.

chángkù: China. Trousers.

chang-ot: Korea. Woman's full-sleeved cloak worn with draped skirt.

chángpáo: China. Long gown or robe.

chángshan: China. Long, unlined gown.

chàngtongwà: China. Stockings.

chaniyo: India. Long, gathered silk skirt.

channavira: India. Crossbelt on the chest.

channon cloth: Late Gothic (1350–1450 C.E.). Worsted fabric.

chantilly: A dainty, machine-made bobbin lace of silk made with a fine hexagonal mesh ground and pattern. Originally it was a bobbin lace of raw silk. Later the term referred to a black version of the lace.

chao dai: China. Qing dynasty (1644–1911 C.E.). Man's woven silk girdle.

ch'ao fu: China. Manchu imperial robe for formal court functions.

chao gua: China. Qing dynasty (1644–1911 C.E.). Woman's court vest with deep armseyes and sloping shoulder seams.

chao guan: China. Qing dynasty (1644–1911 C.E.). Winter hat worn by emperor, male members of imperial family and high officials. Red floss silk padded crown and brim of sable or fox fur.

chao pao: China. Qing dynasty (1644–1911 C.E.). Man's court robe. Short, side-fastening jacket connected to skirt with pleated aprons.

chao zhu: China. Qing dynasty (1644–1911 C.E.). Necklace of 108 small beads separated with four larger beads. Both ornamental and served as abacus. Female version had two extra necklaces, worn crossed from shoulder to opposite underarm.

ch'aokua: China. Ch'ing dynasty. Full-length vest worn by Manchu women.

chapan: Afghanistan. Folded over coat or robe.

chaparajos: Worn by cowboys to protect their legs from brush and thorns, strong leather breeches that covered only front of legs.

chape: 1. Byzantine and Romanesque (400–1200 C.E.). Cape, sometimes slit at sides, with cap sleeves or long, loose sleeves. 2. Piece that holds buckle to strap.

chape à aige: Early Gothic (1200–1350 C.E.). France. Rain cape.

chapeau: France. Hat.

chapeau à borne: Switzerland. Grape pickers' large straw hat.

chapeau à la Basile: Late Georgian (1750–1790 C.E.). France. Woman's headdress named for character in *The Marriage of Figaro*.

chapeau à la Cérès: Late Georgian (1750–1790 C.E.). France. Woman's hat trimmed with wheat, symbol of Ceres, Roman goddess of harvest.

chapeau à la Charlotte: Late Georgian (1750–1790 C.E.). France. Woman's headdress in style of one worn by Queen Charlotte of United Kingdom.

chapeau à la Chérubin: Late Georgian (1750–1790 C.E.). France. Woman's hat named for character Cherubino in *The Marriage of Figaro*.

chapeau à la Colonne: Late Georgian (1750–1790 C.E.). France. Woman's hat named for French Minister of Finance, Charles-Alexandre de Calonne.

chapeau à la Devonshire: Late Georgian (1750–1790 C.E.). France. French version of English style hat.

chapeau à la Grenade: Late Georgian (1750–1790 C.E.). France. Hat with pomegranate button to hold feathers in place. Named for French conquest of island in Caribbean.

chapeau à la turque: Late Georgian (1750–1790 C.E.). France. Hat of unclear description.

chapeau à l'égyptienne: Late Georgian (1750–1790 C.E.). France. Puffed handkerchief with lace edge that was worn as cap and was held on with aigrette of two heron feathers.

chapeau à l'italienne: Late Georgian (1750–1790 C.E.). France. Woman's cap in style of those worn during Italian Renaissance.

chapeau à plumes: France. Hat with plumes.

chapeau au bateau renversé: Late Georgian (1750–1790 C.E.). France. Woman's large bonnet with white gauze veil that reached to waist.

chapeau claque: France. Gibus.

chapeau de Cardinal: Late Georgian (1750–1790 C.E.). France. In 1776, woman's straw hat bound with red ribbon. Popular during trial of Cardinal de Rohan.

chapeau de paille: France. Straw hat.

chapeau d'homme: France. Man's trilby.

chapeau jockei: Late Georgian (1750–1790 C.E.). France. Hat in style of those worn by jockeys.

chapeau melon: *See* bowler hat.

chapeau mou: France. Squash hat.

chapeau souple: France. Slouch hat.

chapeau-bras: 1. Early Georgian (1700–1750 C.E.) to Late Georgian (1750–1790 C.E.). France. Small false hat shaped like tricorne, but flat. Carried by dandies under arm, rather than wearing hat which might disarrange hair. 2. Directoire and First Empire (1790–1815 C.E.). Woman's crush bonnet introduced in 1814 by Mrs. Bell, London dressmaker.

chapel d'acier: Renaissance (1450–1550 C.E.). France. Steel war-hat.

chapel de Montauban: Renaissance (1450–1550 C.E.). France. Steel war-hat made at Montauban.

chapel-de-fer: Early Gothic (1200–1350 C.E.). France. Iron skull-cap, sometimes with brim.

chapeleiro: Portugal. Hatmaker.

chapelle-de-fer: *See* chapel-de-fer.

chapeo: Spain. Parasol.

chaperone: 1. Late Gothic (1350–1450 C.E.). Caped hood with long liripipe which was sometimes worn draped around shoulders. Later worn with face opening over top of head and cape drooping decoratively over side. 2. Charles I (1625–1660 C.E.). Woman's soft, informal hood worn tied under chin.

chapéu cardinalício: Portugal. Cardinal's scarlet hat.

chapiron: Renaissance (1450–1550 C.E.). Spain. French hood.

chapkan: *See* balaba.

chaplet: Wreath or garland worn like fillet, often worn as symbol of honor.

chappals: India. Sandals.

chaps: Shortened form of chaparajos.

chapska: Early Georgian (1700–1750 C.E.). Poland. Fur-trimmed cap with square crown.

chaqué: Spain. Morning coat.

chaqueta: Spain. Heavy fabric or leather jacket worn by cowboys.

chaqueta corta de marino: Spain. Reefer.

chaqueta corta y gruesa: Spain. Lumberjack's jacket.

chaqueta deportiva: Spain. Blazer.

chaqueta para casa: Spain. Smoking jacket.

chaquira: Ecuador and Guatemala. Decorative beads.

charahuilla: Chile. Men's very wide trousers worn tied at ankles.

charak: Korea. Skirt.

charan dharan: India. Shoes.

charanalankara: India. Ordinary anklet or toe ring.

chargat: Turkmenistan. Woman's triangular shawl worn over alan dangi and yaluk.

charicari: Directoire and First Empire (1790–1815 C.E.). Leather, chamois, buckskin, or suede cavalry overalls that were sewn in the instep and had buttoned up sides on scalloped outer seam.

chariwari: *See* esquavar.

charka: India. A hand-powered floor spinning wheel.

charkha: *See* charka.

charlotte: Late Georgian (1750–1790 C.E.). Woman's wide, tightly gathered hat on brim with wide flounce. Named for Queen Charlotte of United Kingdom.

Charlotte Corday bonnet: Bustle (1865–1890 C.E.). United Kingdom. Woman's outdoor hat with tall, soft crown gathered to narrow brim with frill. Wide ribbon covered place where crown and brim met. Pendant strings.

Charlotte Corday cap: Crinoline (1840–1865 C.E.). United Kingdom. Named for Charlotte Corday, a heroine of the French Revolution known for being the murderer of Jean-Paul Marat. A lingerie cap designed as a variation of the mob cap worn during the French Revolution and trimmed with ribbons, flounces, lace, and flowers.

Charlotte Corday cap (early Crinoline) Dover Publications

Charlotte Corday cap (late Crinoline)

charm: *See* chatelaine.

charm bracelet: Bracelet with pendant charms.

charm ring: Talisman ring.

charm string: Bustle (1865–1890 C.E.). Popular in 1880s, woman's necklace of small buttons of various styles.

charmè: Mexico. Silk velvet.

charmeen: Fine worsted fabric with twill.

charmelaine: Fabric with twill back.

charmés: Spain. Charmeuse.

charmeuse: (20th century). Satin formal dress fabric with dull back and shiny face.

charmeuse felt: Soft, lightweight felt with lustrous face.

charol: Spain. Patent leather.

charoul: Egypt. A man's very full, ankle-length trousers.

charretera: Spain. Epaulet.

chartreuse: Yellow green.

charuot: Korea. Sack dress.

charvet: France. Elegant silk fabric in irregular twill weave.

charvet et fils de Paris: *See* charvet.

charwa: China. Worn by Yi women, woolen felt cape with square shoulders. Usually of black fabric and piped in a color.

chásè: China. Dark brown.

ch'aska: *See* t'ikita.

chasseur: Bustle (1865–1890 C.E.). In 1872, hunter's green.

chasu: Korea. Embroidery.

chasuble: 1. Early Gothic (1200–1350 C.E.). Circular outer garment with head opening. 2. Silk or metallic fabric T-shaped cape worn in the Catholic Church. 3. France. Jumper.

chasujong: Korea. Amethyst, a gem.

châtain: France. Nut brown.

chatelaine: 1. Renaissance (1450–1550 C.E.) to 20th century. Long metal chain that fastened around woman's waist, pinned to skirt. Had a variety of attachments, including keys, mirror, scent box, pincushion. 2. Crinoline (1840–1865 C.E.). Small ring attached to watch chain. From it hung small fobs.

chatelaine bag: (20th century). Small bag attached to belt. Worn by women.

chatiagne: Bustle (1865–1890 C.E.). In 1889, dark oak color.

chaton: France. Setting of gem.

chatoyante: Crinoline (1840–1865 C.E.). Introduced in 1847, thin wool fabric with gray ground having wide check.

chatta: India. Umbrella.

chattra: India. An umbrella, the symbol of royalty.

chau: Crinoline (1840–1865 C.E.). United States of America. Chinese Hawaiian term for a crude fabric that is one-third cotton and two-thirds silk.

chatelaine bag Dover Publications

châu báu: Vietnam. Generic term for precious pearls.

chau fu: China. Qing dynasty (1644–1911 C.E.). Man's court dress consisting of chao pao, pi ling, hat, girdle, necklace, and boots.

chāubwalī jootī: India. Close-fitting embroidered slippers with pointed toes.

chaudron: Bustle (1865–1890 C.E.). In 1882, copper red.

chaugoshia: India. A cap made of four panels which meet in a point at the top of the crown. In the 19th century, it was worn informally at court.

chaulari: India. A four-stringed necklace.

chaume: Bustle (1865–1890 C.E.). In 1876, new color.

chauri: India. A fly whisk made from an ox tail.

chausettes: France. Socks.

chausse: *See* epitoga.

chaussembles: Late Gothic (1350–1450 C.E.). Nobility's hose with leather soles. Were sometimes worn without other shoes.

chausses: Byzantine and Romanesque (400–1200 C.E.). Leg coverings of fabric, stitched to fit.

chausses en bourses: Elizabethan (1550–1625 C.E.). France. Breeches that were full at bottom.

chausses larges à l'antique: France. Galligaskins.

chausses semellées: Late Gothic (1350–1450 C.E.). France. Footed tights.

chaussette: *See* chaussettes.

chaussette montant: France. Long socks.

chaussons: Renaissance (1450–1550 C.E.). Trews or breeches of chain mail.

chaussure: France. Shoe.

chaussures à cric: Elizabethan (1550–1625 C.E.). France. Heeled shoes.

chaussures à pont-levis: *See* chaussures à cric.

chayazome: Japan. Summer kimono.

cheater's cloth: A fabric printed with an allover quilt design, intended to look like a pieced quilt top.

cheats: 1. Restoration (1660–1700 C.E.). Men's waistcoats with front made from elaborate fabric and back from cheap fabric. 2. Romantic (1815–1840 C.E.). Man's shirt with collar attached already.

chechia: 1. Arabia. Cylindrical skullcap with tuft on top. 2. Tall hat similar to fez.

chechias: Tunisia. Tight-fitting round felt hat.

cheesecloth: Loosely woven, plain weave, lightweight cotton fabric. Thin and very flimsy. Originally used to wrap around pressed cheese.

chef's apron: One-piece apron of canvas, terry, or other heavy fabric.

cheklaton: Early Gothic (1200–1350 C.E.) to Late Gothic (1350–1450 C.E.). Scarlet or gold fabric.

chekmak: Turkey. Silk and cotton blend fabric with gold threads woven into it.

chela: India. Woman's upper garment.

chele: Early Gothic (1200–1350 C.E.). Fur from marten's throat.

chelsea: Flat collar with pointed ends that meet in front in deep V.

Chelsea boot
See also photospread
(Foot and Legwear).

Chelsea boot: (1960–1970 C.E.). Man's ankle-high boot with elastic gores on sides.

Chelsea collar: (1960–1970 C.E.). Long-pointed man's collar.

chelum: Borneo. Black.

chemical lace: A form of machine embroidery with the pattern worked in a vegetable fiber on a silk ground.

chemiloon: Woman's one-piece combination of chemise and drawers.

chemise: 1. Byzantine (400–1200 C.E.). Long-sleeved undergarment that showed beneath sleeves of women's garments. 2. Early Gothic (1200–1350 C.E.) By this time, sometimes colored. 3. Crinoline (1840–1865 C.E.). Linen, homespun, or cotton knee-length gar-

ment with square neck. 4. Bustle (1865–1890 C.E.). In 1876, pleated gussets were introduced to assist in shaping bust. In 1880s, elaborately trimmed. By 1890, replaced with combinations. 5. France. Shirt.

chemise à la greque: Directoire and First Empire (1790–1815 C.E.). France. High-waisted gown with small puffed sleeves and slightly gathered skirt.

chemise à la Reine: Late Georgian (1750–1790 C.E.). France. Popularized by Marie Antoinette, a loose, unfitted gown with deep décolletage worn sashed at waist.

chemise à l'anglaise: Directoire and First Empire (1790–1815 C.E.). United Kingdom. Lingerie gown with crushed satin sash. Worn in winter and summer.

chemise de nuit: France. Nightgown.

chemise d'homme: France. Shirt.

chemise dress: Dress that hangs straight from shoulders.

chemise gown: Directoire and First Empire (1790–1815 C.E.). United Kingdom. Muslin gown with sleeves cut full at shoulder and fitted at wrist. Fitted at waist where it tied with sash.

chemisette: 1. Early Georgian (1700–1750 C.E.) to Late Georgian (1750–1790 C.E.). Prussia. Cuirassier's waistcoat. 2. Romantic (1815–1840 C.E.). White muslin or cambric wrap to fill décolletage of gown.

chemisette

chemisier: France. Shirtwaist.

chènbù: China. Lining fabric.

cheney: Elizabethan (1550–1625 C.E.) to Late Georgian (1750–1790 C.E.). Wool or worsted fabric. Possibly nickname for Philip and Cheney.

chéng: China. Orange.

chenille: Directoire and First Empire (1790–1815 C.E.) to 20th century. 1. Fringed ribbon used as trim. 2. Caterpillar-shaped ornament on carabineer helmet. 3. Fabric with tufted, velvety pile.

chenille blonde: A silk or other light thread lace with chenille used to outline the geometric pattern.

chenille embroidery: Velvety embroidery of fine chenille.

chenille lace: France. Bobbin lace with silk honeycomb ground filled in with thick stitches and outlined in white chenille.

chènkù: China. Underpants.

chènqún: China. Underskirt or petticoat.

chènshan: China. Shirt.

chènyí: China. Underclothes.

cheo: Afghanistan. Woman's long black cotton robe worn pulled up into pouch at waist.

cheongsam
See also photospread
(Women's Wear).

cheongsam: American. Oriental style gown ending four to five inches above knee with side slit of eight to ten inches.

chepeneag: Hungary and Romania. Overcoat.

Cherbourg: Crinoline (1840–1865 C.E.). In 1858, silk walking dress en tablier with checked trim of velvet ribbon. It had velvet buttons.

cherkeska: 1. Russia. Circassian long-waisted outer garment. 2. Caucasus. Fitted, front-opening jacket with full skirt and standing collar. Reaches to mid-thigh.

chermisi: *See* chermisino.

chermisino: Italy. Crimson.

chernodreshnik: Bulgaria. Men's black dress; trousers that are full at hips and fitted at knee with waist-length jacket.

cherry: Bright red color, yellowish red in hue.

cherryderry: Early Georgian (1700–1750 C.E.) to Late Georgian (1750–1790 C.E.). India. Cotton fabric similar to gingham.

cherusque: Directoire and First Empire (1790–1815 C.E.). Lace border on neck of women's décolleté gowns or starched lace collarettes of court costume.

cherusse: *See* cherusque.

cherven ruchenik: Bulgaria. Red kerchief worn by newly married woman for first 40 days of marriage.

Chesterfield overcoat: Bustle (1865–1890 C.E.). Man's fitted overcoat with hidden buttons and velvet collar.

chestnut: Brown with yellowish tint.

cheval de frise: France. Crisscross dress trim.

Chevalier bonnet: Bustle (1865–1890 C.E.). In 1870s, bonnet made completely of jet beads.

chevaux de frise: *See* cheval de frise.

cheveril: Elizabethan (1550–1625 C.E.). Very flexible kid leather.

chevesaille: Early Gothic (1200–1350 C.E.). France. Decorative border on neck of garment.

Cheviot: Germany. Cheviot.

cheviot: 1. Bustle (1865–1890 C.E.). France. Introduced in 1880, soft, shaggy faced, twill weave, wool fabric in tiny stripes and checks. Originally made from Cheviot sheep. 2. Striped or checked cotton shirting.

cheviot tweed: Tweed fabric with diagonally twilled or chevron pattern.

chevre: France. Goatskin.

chèvre de Chine: France. Chinese goat fur.

chèvre de Mongolie: France. Mongolia fur.

chevreau: France. Goatskin.

chevrette: France. Thin goatskin.

chevron: Originally a heraldic device, but in the early 19th century this inverted V motif began to be used as part of military ranking notation.

chevron de laine: Bustle (1865–1890 C.E.). Germany. Introduced in 1878, fine twill weave fabric with every other line being reverse twill.

cheyne lace: *See* chain lace.

cheyney: Romantic (1815–1840 C.E.). Worsted or woolen fabric with pattern printed on prior to weaving, creating shadow design.

chhint: India. Chintz.

chi: China. A foot (35 cm).

chi fu: China. Manchu imperial robe with a diaper pattern.

chí hong: Vietnam. Pink thread, the symbol of marriage.

chianetta: Renaissance (1450–1550 C.E.). Helmet.

chiang chau: Bustle (1865–1890 C.E.). United States of America. Chinese Hawaiian term for a raw silk and cotton fabric with a shiny black surface. It was thinner than sang chau.

chicken: India. Embroidery.

chicken skin glove: Elizabethan (1550–1625 C.E.) to Bustle (1865–1890 C.E.). Glove made of chicken skin and worn by women to soften and whiten their hands while they slept.

chickenwalla: India. Itinerant dealer in embroidered handkerchiefs, petticoats, etc.

chicon: India. Fine white embroidered sari fabric.

chicoree: Romantic (1815–1840 C.E.). France. Material cut with edge left raw.

chiffon: Gay Nineties (1890–1900 C.E.) to present. Delicate silk barege or grenadine. Now, a very light, sheer, open mesh, plain weave fabric.

chiffon batiste: Very lightweight, sheer batiste.

chiffon crepe: Sheer, light crepe.

chiffon lace: Chiffon embroidered in silk yarn.

chiffon net: High quality, black silk net.

chiffon taffeta: Quality, lightweight, sheer taffeta that is soft and lustrous.

chiffon velvet: Very soft, lightweight silk pile velvet.

chifón: Spain. Chiffon.

chifón terciopelo: Spain. Chiffon velvet.

chigap: Korea. Purse.

chignon: Knot or mass of hair on back of head.

chignon flottant: Late Georgian (1750–1790 C.E.). Woman's hairstyle incorporating ringlets or curls hanging over back of neck.

chignon strap: Band that loops beneath hair in back to hold woman's hat in place.

chihèsè: China. Russet color.

chìhóng: China. Crimson.

chiiwaun: Thailand. Buddhist monk's upper garment.

chijimi: Japan. Crepe.

chikan: India. Whitework.

chikara-age: Japan. Shoulder pleat giving uplifting effect.

ch'ilbo norigae: Korea. Cloisonné pendants.

child's pudding: Child's small round hat that hides padding to protect their skulls.

Chilkat blankets: Canada. Goat hair blankets made by Chilkat Tlingit women.

chillo: India. Brightly colored cotton fabric.

chillu: *See* utcu.

chilum: *See* chelum.

ch'ima: Korea. Skirt part of national costume.

chimere: Elizabethan (1550–1625 C.E.). Long, sleeveless ecclesiastical gown in black satin or silk that opened down center front.

chimi: Bolivia. Two colors blended together.

chimir: Romania. A 15–25 cm wide leather belt.

chimney pot hat: Crinoline (1840–1865 C.E.). Tall top hat with almost no brim. Worn by men.

chimpato: Peru. Colored woolen cords worn woven in a woman's hair.

chimphullani: India. A woman's short skirt.

chimney pot hat

chimpita: Peru. Narrow chumpi.

chin stays: Romantic (1815–1840 C.E.). Popular in late 1820s to late 1830s, frills of tulle or lace on some bonnet strings that made frill around chin when tied.

China calico: Crinoline (1840–1865 C.E.). United States of America. Fashionable and affordable fabric imported from Calcutta, India.

china cola: India. Sleeveless, metal armor, probably of Chinese origin.

China cotton: China. Cotton used for comforters and quilts.

China damask: Bustle (1865–1890 C.E.). Introduced in 1879, two-color cotton damask with palm pattern.

China gauze: Bustle (1865–1890 C.E.). Introduced in 1878, light colored gauze sprinkled with tufts of silk floss.

China grass: Bustle (1865–1890 C.E.). Introduced in 1870, plain weave fabric of China grass used for summer waistcoats.

china patta: India. Chinese silk of a golden color.

China ribbon: Narrow, inexpensive ribbon.

China silk: Thin, transparent, plain weave, silk or silk blend fabric. Sometimes colored and figured.

chinacholaka: India. Royal person's outer garment.

Chinaseide: Germany. China silk.

Chinaziege: Germany. Chinese goat fur.

chinbunhongui: Korea. Cherry colored.

chinchilla: France and Spain. Blue gray fur of South American rodent, the *Chinchilla brevicaudata*.

chinchillà: Italy. Chinchilla fur.

Chinchilla: Germany. Chinchilla fur.

chinchilla cloth: 1. Crinoline (1840–1865 C.E.). Thick woolen velvet overcoating fabric. 2. Heavy, tufted fabric, usually of wool.

chin-clout: Elizabeth (1550–1625 C.E.). Large square of fabric worn over the chin by country women.

chiné: Fabric in which warp is dyed before weaving, creating mottled appearance.

chinela: Renaissance (1450–1550 C.E.) to Elizabethan (1550–1625 C.E.). Spain. Mule.

Chinese badger: China. Long-haired fur of badger.

chinese green: Romantic (1815–1840 C.E.). United Kingdom. Malachite green.

Chinese mink: China. Light yellowish fur of animal similar to mink.

chinese spenser: Directoire and First Empire (1790–1815 C.E.). United Kingdom. Introduced in 1808, woman's very short jacket or spencer that had two long points in front.

Chinese Venise: Venetian lace made in China.

chingmul: Korea. Generic term for cloth.

chinhongsaek: Korea. Scarlet.

chinius: Romania. Man's sleeveless, drugget coat.

chinju: Korea. Pearl.

chino: Twill weave cotton fabric, mercerized and Sanforized.

chinó: Portugal. Chignon; wig.

chint: United States of America. Native American term for chintz.

chintes: Chintz.

chintz: Plain weave, brightly colored printed and waxglazed linen.

chip hat: Late Georgian (1750–1790 C.E.). Woman's hat woven from thin wooden strips.

chipana: Peru. Incan wristlets and armlets of gold or silver.

chip'angi: Korea. Walking stick; cane.

chiquetades: *See* slashings.

chirimen: Japan. Dull luster silk crepe used for blouses, dresses, and kimonos.

chirinka: Russia. Square of silk or muslin embroidered in metallic thread or edged in gold fringe or tassels.

chiripá: Argentina. Worn into 20th century. Skirt formed by wrapping square woolen blanket around hips. It was held up by sturdy elaborate silver belt.

chisamus: Early Gothic (1200–1350 C.E.). Fur of unknown origin.

chita: Portugal. Calico.

chitão: Portugal. Printed cotton; chintz.

chite: 1. Restoration (1660–1700 C.E.). India. Painted linen. 2. Romania. Long fringes of colored wool.

chitika: *See* ruchika.

chiton: Greek (3000–100 B.C.E.). Tunic, usually undergarment, held in position by fibula.

chitra: Sanskrit word for variegated.

chitragupita: India. A veil.

chitta: 1. Iran. Speckled or multicolored cloth. 2. Sanskrit word for spotted cloth.

chitterlings: Restoration (1660–1700 C.E.) to Directoire and First Empire (1790–1815 C.E.). United Kingdom. Linen or lace frills on front of men's shirts.

chivaret: Charles I and the Commonwealth (1625–1660 C.E.) to Late Georgian (1750–1790 C.E.). Wool fabric.

chivarras: Mexico. Leggings.

chivarros: *See* chivarras.

chiveret: Elizabethan (1550–1625 C.E.) to Late Georgian (1750–1790 C.E.). Popular woolen fabric.

chlaine: Greek (3000–100 B.C.E.). Wool cloak worn by shepherds and warriors.

chlamus: Greek (3000 B.C.E.–100 B.C.E.). Cloak.

chlamydon: Greek (3000–100 B.C.E.). Short wrap worn from right shoulder under left arm. Worn mostly by women.

chlamys: Greek (3000–100 B.C.E.). Short, light, trapeze-shaped garment worn draped in various ways.

chloene: Greek (3000–100 B.C.E.). Coarse wool garment worn hooked on one shoulder and wrapped under opposite arm.

chlopok: Russia. Cotton.

chobawi: Korea. Woman's silk hat worn in winter.

choclos: Peru. Silver earrings.

chocolat au lait: Crinoline (1840–1865 C.E.). In 1864, brown color.

chocolate: Dark reddish brown.

choga: India. Man's long sleeved, long skirted cloak that opened down front and fastened above waist.

choggā: India. Fan-shaped gold jewelry worn on turbans.

choggi: Korea. Waistcoat.

chogon: Korea. Jacket part of national costume.

chogori: Korea. Jacket.

choi-ngon: Vietnam. Crown.

choker: 1. High necklace. 2. High stiff neckcloth.

chokki: Korea. Man's vest.

choksaek: Korea. Red.

chokturi: Korea. Bride's delicate crown that is beaded and decorated with flowers and small pendants.

chol: Korea. Hair bow.

chola derby: Bolivia. Woman's brown, black, or beige bowler hat.

cholaka: India. Woman's transparent, ankle-length, white silk garment. *See also* choli.

cholana: India. Dhoti worn as shorts.

cholee: *See* choli.

choli: India. Short-sleeved, low cut bodice, usually of cotton.

ch'olmo: Korea. Helmet.

Cholo coat: Trade name for short sports coat.

cholst: Russia. Coarse linen cloth.

chompas: Ecuador. Sweaters.

ch'on: Korea. Cloth.

chonbok: Korea. Sleeveless out coat worn by scholars.

chong er: China. Pearl or piece of jade hung by an ear of mian guan.

chong kra ben: Laos and Thailand. Manner of draping fabric around the loins like an Indian dhoti.

chongbok: Korea. Formal dress.

chongjagwan: Korea. Scholar's three tiered hat. Named for Northern Sung Neo-Confucian scholar, Cheng I (1033–1103).

ch'ongsaek: Korea. Blue.

chope: India. A phulkari shawl made by the maternal grandmother of a bride for presentation at the wedding. It is embroidered with a double darning stitch so the pattern is identical on both sides of the shawl.

chopines: Elizabethan (1550–1625 C.E.). Spain. Usually made of cork or wood and covered with velvet or leather, high clogs worn to keep one's shoes out of muck and mire. Originally worn in the Middle East by women.

chopines
See also photospread
(Foot and Legwear).

Chorhemd: Germany. Surplice.

chorni: India. Pantaloons that are tight from the knee down.

ch'oroksaekui: Korea. Green.

chorrock: *See* Messrock.

chou: France. Soft rosette or knot of velvet, satin, ribbon, or lace and used as trim on women's dresses.

chóu: China. Silk fabric.

chou hat: France. Hat with soft, crushed crown.

chóuduàn: China. Silks and satins.

chouquette: France. Crocheted straw hat.

choux: Restoration (1660–1700 C.E.). Woman's chignon.

chóuzi: China. Silk fabric.

chrisom: Child's baptismal gown.

chrome leather: Leather tanned in mineral process.

chromo embroidery: Embroidery done over colored paper pattern.

chrysogaitana: Greek. Type of surface embroidery, usually in gold.

chrysolithus: *See* topazon.

chrysoprase: Bustle (1865–1890 C.E.). In 1869, popular pale green gemstone.

chu: China. Red.

chuàn: China. Bracelet.

chuandài: China. General term for apparel or dress.

chuanzhuó: China. General term for apparel or dress.

chubut wool: Argentina. Fine quality merino wool.

chuca: Peru. Very ordinary fabric.

chu-chu: China. Long chain of 108 stones.

chucu: Bolivia. Conical cap.

chuda: India. Man's hair-lock worn on top of head. *See also* kesapasa.

chudamani: India. Crown ornament with pearls.

chudan: Korea. Silks and satins.

chuddah: *See* chuddar.

chuddar: India. Mantle or shawl made from strip of cotton cloth three yards long. Worn by men only.

chudder: *See* chuddar.

chuởi hat trai: Vietnam. Pearl necklace.

chuga: India. A knee-length kurta.

chugata: Japan. Allover stenciled pattern.

chugha: India. Coat worn over a tunic by the Kushans.

chukka boot: (1930–1940 C.E.). United States of America. Popular for sportswear, almost ankle-high, heavy soled boot that tied high on instep.

chukker shirt: Short sleeved, open necked polo shirt.

chuku: *See* ñañaca.

chulja: Korea. Tape measure.

chulla cara: Ecuador. Monochrome poncho.

chullo: 1. Long stocking cap, as long as 18 inches. 2. Bolivia. Pointed knit cap with earflaps.

ch'ullu: Bolivia and Peru. Knitted cap.

chullu: *See* shukina.

chumbi: Ecuador and Guatemala. Incan belt.

chumbi banderilla: Ecuador. Belt used to tie the anaku.

chumpi: 1. Peru. Sash. 2. Bolivia and Peru. Belt.

chun sam: Bustle (1865–1890 C.E.). United States of America. Chinese Hawaiian term for a long sleeved tunic of dark material that opened down the front and fastened with six coral buttons whose heads were made of hard black rubber. It had a tight collar worn flapped down.

chunadi: India. Kind of odhni.

chunari: India. Cotton and silk blend fabric that is tie-dyed.

chundadi: India. A veil-cloth.

chungch'imak: Korea. Long-sleeved robe worn by scholars.

chungjolmo: Korea. Soft hat; felt hat.

chungsanmo: Korea. Derby.

chunnat: India. The front pleats of the dhoti.

chunzhuang: China. Spring clothes.

chuo: *See* zhuo.

chuoi: Vietnam. Necklace.

chupa: 1. Spain. Waistcoat. 2. Tibet. Long, surplice-front robe.

chupetes: *See* choclos.

chupkun: India. Long robe worn by most men.

chuppaun: Uzbekistan. Coat or tunic worn by Tartars.

churajuna: Ecuador. Quichua traditional dress.

churna-kuntala: India. Curled ringlets of hair.

churridah: India. Woman's silk or cotton leggings.

chusi: Peru. Very thick and coarse fabric.

chuspa: Peru. Shoulder bag. *See also* alforja.

ch'uspa: Bolivia. Incan coca bag.

ch'úspa: Ecuador and Guatemala. Incan small bag for carrying coca leaves.

chusta: Poland. Linen cloth.

chusteczka: Poland. Handkerchief.

chustka: Poland. Kerchief.

chutki: India. Twisted lace overlaid with tiny glass beads.

chya mun bo: Crinoline (1840–1865 C.E.). United States of America. Chinese Hawaiian term for a crude cotton fabric with a twill weave.

chymer: *See* chammer.

chyrpy: Turkey. Women's cloaks.

ciabhag: Ireland. Gaelic word for small ringlet or whisker.

ciabh-chasta: Ireland. Gaelic word for curled lock of hair.

cialdini apron: Crinoline (1840–1865 C.E.). Introduced in 1862, decorative apron made from gores of gray chiné moire. It had a velvet plastron in the center with cutouts of horizontal diamonds revealing moire beneath. It was trimmed in black lace and buttons.

ciarpa de' Scozzesi: Italy. Plaid.

ciarsūr: Ireland. Handkerchief.

cias: Ireland. Gaelic word for skirt.

ciasan: *See* cias.

cicilian cloth: Bustle (1865–1890 C.E.). Basket weave mohair, very soft and drapable.

cicimus: *See* chisamus.

cicisbeo: Bow or knot of ribbon used to trim accessories.

ciclaton: *See* cheklaton.

ciclatoun: Early Gothic (1200–1350 C.E.). Very rich woven fabric of unknown origin.

cicuilli: Aztec. Sleeveless jacket.

cidaris: 1. Jewish priest's tiara. 2. Crown of ancient Persian kings.

ciel blue: Bustle (1865–1890 C.E.). In 1869, palest sky tint with silver shimmer.

ciemne okulary: Poland. Tinted glasses.

cifatten: Romantic (1815–1840 C.E.). Ghana. Robes made from Turkish or Indian cut silk.

ciferšlus: *See* rajferšlus.

cifraszür: Hungary. Decorated szür.

cihrai: India. Flesh colored.

cilice: Early Gothic (1200–1350 C.E.). Commonly brown or black, hair shirt worn by monks.

cillāwālī: India. Turban made from two different pieces of fabrics.

cimarosa: Crinoline (1840–1865 C.E.). Introduced in 1862, woman's bonnet with brim of rose silk, crown of figured illusion, and neck cape of white blonde. It was trimmed in rose ribbons and black lace.

cimds: Lithuania. Glove.

cimeira: Portugal. Crest of a helmet.

cimier: Early Gothic (1200–1350 C.E.). Ornament on top of helmet. Also referred to the helmet itself.

cina: India. A silk from China.

cinamsuka: India. Silk from China.

cinch belt: (1940–1949 to 1950–1959 C.E.). Wide belt of elastic or cloth, worn very tight.

cīnctus: Roman (753 B.C.E.–323 C.E.). Man's belt. *See also* balteus.

cinctus gabinus: Roman (753 B.C.E.–323 C.E.). Garment for solemn occasions.

cinde kenanga: Java. A batik pattern.

cinde parang: Java. A batik pattern.

cinde wilis: Java. A batik pattern.

cînduse: Romania. Woman's low-necked, black woolen frock.

cineflone: Roman (753 B.C.E.–323 C.E.). Slave who used a curling iron on women's heads.

cineraire: Bustle (1865–1890 C.E.). Red purple.

cingătoare: Romania. Belt.

cingillum: Roman (53 B.C.E.–323 C.E.). Woman's belt.

cingle: Girdle; sash; belt.

cingulum: 1. *See* cīnctus. 2. Early Gothic (1200–1350 C.E.). Band or belt worn by women under their breasts or by men to tuck up skirt for exercise.

cingulum militare: Late Gothic (1350–1450 C.E.). Man's broad hip belt of metal plaquettes that were jointed or mounted on leather. Sword worn suspended from this belt.

cingulum militiae: Roman (753 B.C.E.–323 C.E.). Military waist-belt. Term rarely used before third century C.E.

cini: India. Chinese blue.

cinnamon: Grayish brown.

cinnteagan: Ireland. Gaelic word for coarse cloth.

cinta: 1. Spain. Ribbon. 2. Spain. Hat band. 3. Ecuador. Band worn woven around a woman's hair. 4. Portugal. Girdle; sash.

cintaliga: Portugal. Garter belt.

cinto: 1. Spain. Waistband. 2. Portugal. Girdle.

cintura: Italy. Girdle.

cinturão: Portugal. Wide sash or belt.

cinturón: Spain. Belt.

cinzento: Portugal. Gray.

cioda: Croatia and Serbia. Pin.

ciolar: Ireland. Gaelic word for linsey-woolsey.

ciondolino: *See* orecchino.

cioppa: Renaissance (1450–1550 C.E.). Italy. Full overgown with hanging sleeves which were often lined with fur or silk. It often had rich fur around facings.

ciorap: Romania. Stocking.

ciotag: Ireland. Gaelic word for little scarf.

cipcic: Romania. Woman's small cap.

cipela: 1. *See* obuca. 2. Poland. Shoe.

cipka: Croatia and Serbia. Lace.

cipky: *See* krajky.

çipsip: Turkey. Woman's indoor slippers.

cīra: India. Kind of odhni.

cirb: Ireland. Gaelic word for skirt.

circas: Germany. Cassimere.

circassian: Wool and cotton fabric with diagonal weave.

circassian bodice: Romantic (1815–1840 C.E.). United Kingdom. Woman's bodice in folds from shoulders and crossing waist.

circassian hat: Directoire and First Empire (1790–1815 C.E.). Introduced in 1806, woman's hat similar to gipsy hat but with fanciful crown.

circassian sleeve: Directoire and First Empire (1790–1815 C.E.). Worn by children in 1807, short sleeve that looped up in front.

circassian wrapper: Directoire and First Empire (1790–1815 C.E.). Similar to night chemise. Very low bodice and sleeves of stripes of alternating fabrics.

circassians: Twilled lining fabric originally made of mohair, later of rayon or cotton and wool.

circassienne gown: Late Georgian (1750–1790 C.E.). Variation of polonaise gown with double sleeves.

circingle: Girdle worn over cassock.

circular: Gay Nineties (1890–1900 C.E.). Ankle-length cape lined with squirrel fur, fancy flannel, or surah silk.

circumfolding hat: Romantic (1815–1840 C.E.). United Kingdom. Worn in 1830s, man's round, low-crowned dress hat that folded flat to carry under arm.

ciré: A heavy, lustrous lace usually sold as a wide flouncing.

ciruela: Spain. Plum.

ciselé velvet: Bustle (1865–1890 C.E.). Introduced in 1876, fabric with satin ground and raised pattern in velvet.

čist: *See* bijel.

citra-kapardaka: India. Either a printed calico or a figured fabric.

citravastra: India. A patterned cloth.

citrine: Yellow or yellowish green color, like a lemon.

citron: Greenish yellow.

cittalam: India. A type of variegated fabric.

ciupag: Bulgaria. Woman's short jacket.

civet cat: Hide of the *Spilogale putorius*, a member of the skunk family but with a white patterned coat.

civette: France. Fur of the civet cat.

cizma: Croatia and Serbia. Boot.

cizmă: Romania. Boot.

clabaran: Ireland. Gaelic word for patten.

clac: Spain. Gibus.

clach-mhara: Ireland. Gaelic word for an aquamarine.

claidheamh-mor: Scotland. Great sword.

clair de lune: Color ranging from pale greenish blue to lavender gray.

clann: Ireland. Gaelic word for lock of hair.

clap: Byzantine and Romanesque (400–1200 C.E.). United Kingdom. Garment for both genders.

clāp: United Kingdom. Old English word for cloth.

clapes: Byzantine and Romanesque (400–1200 C.E.). United Kingdom. Term for clothes.

clāpes: United Kingdom. Old English word for clothing. *See also* rēaf.

claque: Collapsible hat.

clarence: Romantic (1815–1840 C.E.). United Kingdom. Man's boot with triangular gusset of soft leather and eyelets for lacing.

clarence blue: Directoire and First Empire (1790–1815 C.E.). Introduced in 1811, color similar to Cambridge blue.

claret: Claret wine color.

Clarissa Harlowe bonnet: Bustle (1865–1890 C.E.). United Kingdom. Woman's large bonnet of leghorn straw and lined with velvet.

Clarissa Harlowe corsage: Crinoline (1840–1865 C.E.). United Kingdom. Woman's evening dress with off-the-shoulder neckline and short sleeves with two or three lace falls.

clavi: Roman (753 B.C.E.–323 C.E.). Purple bands that vertically decorated tunics of Roman dignitaries.

clavos: Renaissance (1450–1550 C.E.). Spain. Aglets.

clawhammer tails: Directoire and First Empire (1790–1815 C.E.). Man's coat with straight cutaway front and very long tails in back.

Clay worsted: United Kingdom. Heavy fabric with diagonal weave.

cleachd: Ireland. Gaelic word for ringlet of hair.

cleachdag: *See* cleachd.

clearc: Ireland. Gaelic word for lock of hair or bright yellow colored.

cleòc: Ireland. Mantle or cloak.

cleòca Gaidhealach: Scotland. Inverness cape.

cleòcan: Ireland. Scarf.

cleopatra: Gay Nineties (1890–1900 C.E.). In 1893, a magenta color.

cliabh: Ireland. Gaelic word for straightjacket.

cliabhan-ceangail: Ireland. Gaelic word for bodice.

clinquant: France. To glitter, as with gold or silver.

cloak: Loose outer wrap.

cloak-bag breeches: Elizabethan (1550–1625 C.E.). United Kingdom. Men's trousers cut very full and gathered above knee. Decorated with points or ribbon rosette or bow.

clōca: Ireland. Cloak. *See also* brat.

cloche

clog

cloche: (1920–1930 C.E.). Close-fitting, bell-shaped hat.

cloche de feutre: France. Felt cloche.

cloche de fieltro: Spain. Felt cloche.

cloche di feltro: Italy. Felt cloche.

clock: 1. Triangular insertion in garment to widen it at that point. 2. Originally, embroidery to cover seams of clock insertion; later it meant embroidery on ankles, gored or not.

clock-mutch: Holland. Cap worn by women.

clœp: *See* clāp.

clog: 1. Elizabethan (1550–1625 C.E.) to 20th century. Wooden soled shoe or sandal with leather upper. Originally developed to protect inner shoe from elements. 2. *See* mantell.

clòimh: Ireland. Wool.

cloissoné: Form of enameling.

cloister cloth: Rough, canvaslike, basket weave drapery fabric.

cloke: Byzantine and Romanesque (400–1200 C.E.) to Renaissance (1450–1550 C.E.). United Kingdom. Cloak.

clokey: United States. Cloque.

cloky: *See* clokey.

cloqué: France. Having appearance of being blistered.

close cap: Elizabethan (1550–1625 C.E.). Small cap, similar to baby cap, worn by women and children. Elderly men often wore version of linen, lace, silk, brocade, or velvet.

close-gauntlet: Renaissance (1450–1550 C.E.). A mitten gauntlet with a latch to attach the finger-ends to the cuff so as to make the hand's grasp unbreakable.

clot: Renaissance (1450–1550 C.E.) to Elizabethan (1550–1625 C.E.). Heavy shoe soled in iron commonly worn by laborers.

cloth of gold: Late Gothic (1350–1450 C.E.) to present. Material woven with a warp of real gold theatre and a weft of silk. Occasionally, both warp and weft are of gold.

cloth rash: *See* rash.

clothe: Byzantine and Romanesque (400–1200 C.E.) to Renaissance (1450–1550 C.E.). United Kingdom. To clothe or dress.

clotidienne: Romantic (1815–1840 C.E.). Introduced in 1833, ribbon striped satin.

cloud: Bustle (1865–1890 C.E.). In 1870s, woman's long scarf worn as outdoor headdress for evening.

clouded cane: *See* Malacca cane.

clouded lustrings: Late Georgian (1750–1790 C.E.). Lustring with pale patterns on it.

clove: United Kingdom. Measure of fabric, 7.7 pounds.

cluas-sheud: Ireland. Gaelic word for ear jewel.

clubwig: *See* cadogan.

cluny lace: Bobbin lace of heavy ivory linen or cotton thread in paddle or wheel pattern.

cluthachadh: Ireland. Gaelic word for clothing.

cly: Renaissance (1450–1550 C.E.). Common term for pocket.

clytie knot: Woman's hairstyle involving hair being arranged in loose knot at nape of neck, in style of bust of Clytie, Greek nymph.

cnaep: Byzantine and Romanesque (400–1200 C.E.). Fastener, brooch, or button.

cnàimh-deud: Ireland. Ivory.

cnaipe: Byzantine and Romanesque (400–1200 C.E.). Ireland. Button.

cnap: Ireland. Gaelic word for button.

cnapan-trusgaidh: Ireland. Gaelic word for button.

cneaball: Ireland. Gaelic word for garter of thrums worn tied around the hose.

cneap: *See* cnap.

cneap-tholl: Ireland. Gaelic word for buttonhole.

cnemides: Armor of shaped hide or bronze.

cnemis: Roman (753 B.C.E.–323 C.E.). Leather, brass, or bronze protective leggings worn by soldiers.

cô' con: Vietnam. Detachable collar.

cô' tay: Vietnam. Cuff.

coachman's coat: Heavy double-breasted coat with large metal buttons.

coācta: Roman (753 B.C.E.–323 C.E.). Felt.

coalman's hat: Felt hat with deep fantail in back.

coalscuttle bonnet: Directoire and First Empire (1790–1815 C.E.). Woman's bonnet with huge shovel-like brim in front.

coamery: Isle of Man. Long, circular, homespun mantle.

coat shirt: Gay Nineties (1890–1900 C.E.). United Kingdom. Man's shirt that opened and buttoned down front. *See also* tunic shirt.

coat-dress
See also photospread (Women's Wear). Dover Publications

coat-bodice: Bustle (1865–1890 C.E.). In 1880s, woman's day bodice with long basques, high neck, outside pockets, and buttons down front. Pleats in back like man's frock coat.

coat-dress: (1960–1970 C.E.). Tailored dress with pockets and closures similar to those found on outerwear. It was often made of fabrics similar to those used in men's suits.

coatee: Directoire and First Empire (1790–1815 C.E.). In 1802, short coat or spencer.

coating velvet: Silk or rayon velvet with closely woven pile, so tight that when folded no break in pile is observable.

coatlet: Gay Nineties (1890–1900 C.E.). United Kingdom. In 1899, a woman's velvet or fur short coat with fan-shaped collar with large revers. Sometimes frogged and braided.

coat-sleeve: Bustle (1865–1890 C.E.). United Kingdom. Woman's sleeve cut like the sleeve of a man's coat, i.e., straight, tubular with slight curve at elbow and narrowing at wrist. In 1870s, often worn with mousequetaire cuff.

coazzone: Renaissance (1450–1550 C.E.). Italy. Wide braid or roll of hair, sometimes with ribbon woven into it, that hung down back.

cobalt blue: Medium greenish blue color.

cobceab: Clog-like shoe.

cobhrach: Ireland. Gaelic word for foam white.

coburg: Wool and cotton twill weave fabric.

Coburg bonnet: Romantic (1815–1840 C.E.). In 1816, soft crowned bonnet that tied under chin.

Coburg cap: Woman's cap with high crown of silver tissue. Popular at opera.

cobweb lawn: Elizabethan (1550–1625 C.E.). Around 1600, very fine transparent lawn.

cocar: Portugal. Rosette.

cocarde: France. Rosette or ornament of ribbon worn on hat. In French Revolution, became national party symbol called cockade.

coccarda: Italy. Cockade.

coccum: Greek (3000–100 B.C.E.). 1. The color scarlet. 2. Scarlet fabric.

cochall: Byzantine and Romanesque (400–1200 C.E.). Ireland. Elbow-length, closely cowled or hooded mantle made from many pieces of fabric.

cochineal: 1. Red dye made from bodies of insects. 2. Bright yellowish red.

cochinilla: Ecuador. Quichua word for cochineal.

cochl: *See* mantell.

cochlach: Ireland. Gaelic word for hairlace.

cochull: Ireland. Gaelic word for cowl.

cockade: *See* cocarde.

cockers: Early Georgian (1700–1750 C.E.) to Bustle (1865–1890 C.E.). 1. Rough knee-high boot worn by laborers, shepherds, and countrymen. 2. Leggings that buckle or button and strap under foot.

cockle: 1. Shell worn by pilgrims on travels. 2. Ringlet or curl.

cockle hat: Elizabethan (1550–1625 C.E.). United Kingdom. Hat with scallop shell on it to symbolize pilgrimage to shrine of St. James of Compostella in Spain.

cocktail apron: Decorative half apron of purely decorative nature.

cocktail dress: (20th century). Party dress for late afternoon.

cocoa: Dark brown, slightly lighter than chocolate.

cocrez: *See* cockers.

cocuzzolo o cupola: Italy. Hat crown.

coda: India. A cadar.

codiarte: Guatemala. Man's long wool tunic.

codini: Italy. Large carved bead of coral used in jewelry.

Codovec: Trade name for beaver hat.

codpiece: Elizabethan (1550–1625 C.E.) to Charles I (1625–1660 C.E.). Stuffed fabric appendage at front opening of men's hose.

cod-placket: Renaissance (1450–1550 C.E.) to Late Georgian (1750–1790 C.E.). Term meaning front opening in men's breeches.

codrington: Crinoline (1840–1865 C.E.). United Kingdom. Man's single- or double-breasted wrapper or loose overcoat resembling Chesterfield.

coeffes: France. Coifs.

cœppe: *See* hœtt.

coeur de melon: Crinoline (1840–1865 C.E.). In 1863, color of the inside of a melon.

coffer headdress: Renaissance (1450–1550 C.E.). Woman's box-shaped headdress worn with hair braided on each side of head.

cofia: Spain. Coif.

cofia de tranzado: Renaissance (1450–1550 C.E.). Spain. Woman's headdress consisting of a tube worn over the braid and attached to the cap.

cofta: Romania. Skirt.

cogā: India. Angaraklh that reaches to below the knees.

coggers: Early Georgian (1700–1750 C.E.) to Romantic (1815–1840 C.E.). Men's stiff leather gaiters that buttoned up side and had strap under instep.

cogware: Early Gothic (1200–1350 C.E.). Coarse fabric similar to frieze.

čoha: Croatia. Richly embroidered, long coat of light, pulled woolen white wool. It had tapered sleeves and a hemline widened with gores. It was worn over the shoulders. It fastened on the chest with leather straps.

coif: Small fitted cap worn by both genders.

coif cooil corran: Isle of Man. Sickle-shaped coif worn by older women.

coif-de-mailles: Early Gothic (1200–1350 C.E.). Coif of mail.

coiffe: France. Headdress.

coiffette: Early Gothic (1200–1350 C.E.). Skull-cap of iron worn by soldiers.

coiffure à la Ceres: Crinoline (1840–1865 C.E.). In 1854, diadem of small flowers.

coiffure à la Chinoise: Directoire and First Empire (1790–1815 C.E.). Woman's hairstyle with hair drawn to topknot. Loose curls hung on each side of the face.

coiffure à la conseillere: Late Georgian (1750–1790 C.E.). France. Hairstyle in which top is curled and rest falls straight in back and in large curls on sides. Unpowdered and left its natural color.

coiffure à la Dauphine: Late Georgian (1750–1790 C.E.). France. Hairstyle with four large curls at sides to frame back hair. Named for wig style worn by Dauphin.

coiffure à la Eurydice: Late Georgian (1750–1790 C.E.). France. Woman's hairstyle.

coiffure à la Flore: 1. Late Georgian (1750–1790 C.E.). France. Woman's hairstyle. 2. Crinoline (1840–1865 C.E.). In 1854, crown of brightly colored flowers.

coiffure à la herisson: *See* hedgehog haindo.

coiffure à la Junon: Late Georgian (1750–1790 C.E.). France. Woman's hairstyle.

coiffure à la moutonne: France. Restoration (1660–1700 C.E.). Woman's hairstyle with bangs and bobbed and crimped hair on the sides.

coiffure à la Ninon: France. Elizabethan (1500–1625 C.E.). France. Woman's hairstyle with short ringlet bangs, shoulder curls, and back knot. Named for Ninon l'Eclos, Parisian leader of fashion.

coiffure à la Pomone: Crinoline (1840–1865 C.E.). In 1854, diadem headdress of fruits and leaves.

coiffure à la qu' es aco: Late Georgian (1750–1790 C.E.). France. In 1774, woman's hair fashion that included three plumes at back of the head.

coiffure à la Reine: Late Georgian (1750–1790 C.E.). France. Woman's hairstyle.

coiffure à la zazzera: France. Man's hairstyle with ends curled under.

coiffure à l'Agnes Sorel: Romantic (1815–1840 C.E.) to Crinoline (1840–1865 C.E.). France. Popular from 1836 to 1849, woman's hairstyle with bangs in front and a knot on back.

coiffure à l'anglomane: Late Georgian (1750–1790 C.E.). France. Woman's hairstyle arranged in exaggerated English style.

coiffure à l'enfant: Late Georgian (1750–1790 C.E.). France. Woman's hairstyle.

coiffure à l'indisposition: Directoire and First Empire (1790–1815 C.E.). France. Woman's fancy cap made of lace and muslin worn around 1812.

coiffure au chien couchant: Late Georgian (1750–1790 C.E.). France. Literally, "like a recumbent dog," a hairstyle with two large curls on sides that reached down to the shoulders.

coiffure Egyptienne: Crinoline (1840–1865 C.E.). In 1857, woman's headdress made from two bandeaux of groseille colored velvet embroidered with gold. Had lotus flower on one side and bow on other, decorated with hieroglyphics.

coiffure en bouffons: Directoire and First Empire (1790–1815 C.E.). France. Woman's hairstyle with tufts of crimped hair over temples and fringe (garcette) over forehead.

coiffure en cadenettes: 1. Elizabethan (1550–1625 C.E.). France. Hairstyle worn by both genders with lock of hair wound in ribbons that fell on either side of face. 2. Early Georgian (1700–1750 C.E.). Man's hairstyle in which two long locks were held in back with ribbon.

coiffure en chien couchant: Late Georgian (1750–1790 C.E.). France. Woman's hairstyle.

coiffure en moulin à vent: Late Georgian (1750–1790 C.E.). France. Woman's hairstyle.

coiffure en parterre galant: Late Georgian (1750–1790 C.E.). France. Woman's hairstyle.

coiffure en raquette: Elizabethan (1550–1625 C.E.). France. Supported by a hoop, a woman's hairstyle with hair swept up around the face and puffed over temples.

coiffure Eugenie: Crinoline (1840–1865 C.E.). France. In 1860, green velvet foliage diadem trimmed with daisies and ornaments of gold.

coiffure Louis Trieze: Crinoline (1840–1865 C.E.).

France. In 1860, mauve velvet toque trimmed with amethyst and white ostrich feather.

coiffure Maintenon: Crinoline (1840–1865 C.E.). In 1863, toufet of short curls atop the head, ringlets behind ears, back hair in bow or puffs.

coiffure Zouave: Crinoline (1840–1865 C.E.). In 1860, green velvet and gold trim on bandeau of white ostrich feathers.

coilēar: Ireland. Collar.

coileir: Ireland. Gaelic word for collar or necklace.

coilichin: Ireland. Gaelic word for large cravat or muffler.

coin de feu: Crinoline (1840–1865 C.E.). France. Introduced in 1848, woman's wide sleeved short coat that closed at neck. Made of velvet, cashmere, or silk and worn indoors.

cointise: Early Gothic (1200–1350 C.E.) to Late Gothic (1350–1450 C.E.). France. To be extreme or unusual in fashion.

coire: Ireland. Gaelic word for ring or girdle.

cōirighim: Ireland. To clothe or to dress.

cojin para hacer puntilla: Spain. Lace-pillow.

cokar: India. Close-fitting gold necklace with pearls on it.

coke: Crinoline (1840–1865 C.E.). United Kingdom. Nickname for the bowler, so called for William Coke who first commissioned the hat.

cokers: *See* cockers.

col: France. Collar.

cola: India. A young girl's tunic.

colaka: *See* cola.

colan: Romania. Woman's belt.

colar: Portugal. Necklace.

colar de pérolas: Portugal. String of pearls.

colbac: Spain. Busby.

colbacco: Italy. Busby.

colback: Directoire and First Empire (1790–1815 C.E.). Drum-shaped military hat covered in fur with laced crown. Often had plume in front.

Colbert embroidery: France. Embroidery with worked background outlining unworked designs.

colberteen: *See* colbertine.

colbertine: Charles I and the Commonwealth (1625–1660 C.E.) to Early Georgian (1700–1750 C.E.). Coarse French lace named for J.B. Colbert, Minister of Finance. Unpopular by mid-18th century.

colcha de renda: Portugal. Bertha.

colchete: Portugal. Hook and eye.

coler: 1. Wales. Collar. 2. Byzantine and Romanesque (400–1200 C.E.) to Renaissance (1450–1550 C.E.). United Kingdom. Middle English word for collar or necklace.

colera: Mexico. Man's open-front vest made from two widths of red and white striped fabric. Embroidered and fringed.

colête: Portugal. Waistcoat.

coli: India. Short jacket.

colier: Romania. Necklace. *See also* ghiordan.

collana: Italy. Necklace.

collar: Spain. Necklace.

collar à la Vandyke: Crinoline (1840–1865 C.E.). Guipere lace collar worn tied close at throat.

collar canvas: Fabric used in theatrical corset.

collar of esses: Decorative collar made of interlocking S designs.

collar velvet: Thick velvet with short pile used for velvet collars on overcoats.

collare: *See* collo.

Colleen Bawn cloak: Crinoline (1840–1865 C.E.) to Bustle (1865–1890 C.E.). Popular from 1850 to 1867, white grenadine cloak with large cape that was supported by rosettes in back.

collerette: Directoire and First Empire (1790–1815 C.E.). France. Ruff of lace or cotton, part of historical revival movement.

collet: *See* col; guleron.

collet monte: Charles I and the Commonwealth (1625–1660 C.E.). France. Linen collar with card or tin base. *See also* rotonde.

colletin: 1. Vestment cloth worn around neck by priests in Catholic Church. 2. Late Gothic (1350–1450 C.E.).Piece of plate armor worn over shoulders and around neck.

colletto: *See* collo.

colley-westonward: Renaissance (1450–1550 C.E.) to Elizabethan (1550–1625 C.E.). United Kingdom. Term meaning gone awry, referring to fashion of wearing mandilion sideways on the body.

collier: 1. France. Collar-like necklace. 2. *See* halsketting.

collier de chien: Dog collar–style necklace.

collo: Italy. Collar.

collodion silk: *See* artificial silk.

colmar: Early Georgian (1700–1750 C.E.). France. Fan fashionable during reign of Queen Anne (1702–1714 C.E.).

colobium: 1. Roman (753 B.C.E.–323 C.E.). Sleeveless tunic. 2. Byzantine (400–1200 C.E.). Similar to Greek kolobus, made of linen or wool and sewn on sides and at the shoulder. Occasionally it was sewn all in one piece.

colonial pump: (1900–1910 C.E.). New name for the Molière.

color aceitung: Spain. Olive.

colorado: 1. Renaissance (1450–1550 C.E.). Spain. Red. 2. Ecuador and Guatemala. Red.

colorante acido: Spain. Acid dye.

colori corozoso: Renaissance (1450–1550 C.E.). Italy. Mourning colors which were dull dark colors, shades of mulberry, blue, green, brown, and black.

Colson: Crinoline (1840–1865 C.E.). In 1859, poile de chevre dress with plain, round corsage and plain, very full skirt.

coltrui: Holland. Polo necked sweater.

Columbine: Crinoline (1840–1865 C.E.). In 1854, richly embroidered mantilla trimmed with seven inch netted fringe. It was trimmed down center front with double row of silk puffing and had a waist knot. Collar and cuffs were of embroidered cambric and edged in tatting.

comadreja: Spain. Weasel.

comadreja de Siberia: Spain. Kolinsky fur.

combed helmet: Crinoline (1840–1865 C.E.). United Kingdom. Cloth-covered cork helmet with a raised spine running from the top down the back. It had a lightly curved brim like a bowler.

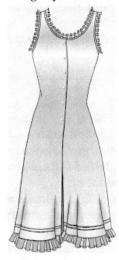

combinations

combinations: Gay Nineties (1890–1900 C.E.). United Kingdom. Several varieties of woman's underwear made in one piece were so called: chemise-drawers-pantaloons (1892), pantaloon-petticoat (1897), and bodice-pantaloon-petticoat (1898).

comboy: 1. Ceylon. Long, wrapped, colorful skirt worn by both men and women as part of national dress. 2. India. Skirt or kilt of white calico.

comforter: Crinoline (1840–1865 C.E.). United Kingdom. Worn from 1840s, man's wool scarf worn wrapped around neck in cold weather.

comforts: Directoire and First Empire (1790–1815 C.E.). United Kingdom. In 1800, double soled sandals.

còmhdach: Ireland. Generic term for clothing.

comh-dhualadh: Ireland. Gaelic word for embroidery.

com-le: Vietnam. Suit of clothes.

comley: *See* kambala.

commode: *See* fontanges.

common dress: *See* undress.

common gingham: Coarse gingham.

comperes: France. Small false front on the front of bodice suggesting a waistcoat.

cô'n bào: Vietnam. Imperial robe.

concertina cloth: Gay Nineties (1890–1900 C.E.). In 1892, a corded silk fabric with silk shot through it.

conch: 1. Renaissance (1450–1550 C.E.). France. Full-length wrap with wired standing collar. 2. Elizabethan (1550–1625 C.E.). France. Shell-shaped, gauze or crepe hat built on a tin frame worn primarily by widows.

conch hat: Hat of palmetto leaves.

concha: Belt worn by both Navajo men and women. Made of silver ornaments on leather strap.

conchiglie cipree: Italy. Cowries.

conciu: Romania. 1. Woman's finely embroidered headdress. 2. Knot of plaited hair worn on crown of head. 3. Band around which woman's hair is gathered.

condra: Hungary. Man's jacket of homespun fabric.

conejo: Spain. Rabbit fur.

coney: Nickname for rabbit fur.

confezione: Italy. Tailored clothing.

confidents: Restoration (1660–1700 C.E.). 1. Small curls of hair by the ears. 2. Silk hood that tied under the chin.

congbái: China. Very light blue.

conglù: China. Pale yellowish green.

congo: Bustle (1865–1890 C.E.). In 1883, a rich burnished coppery gold.

Congo cloth: Trade name for all rayon fabric.

congo red: First direct cotton colors, discovered in 1884 by Boettigen.

congress gaiter: Bustle (1865–1890 C.E.). Ankle-high boot with leather or cloth top and elastic gusset in the sides instead of laces.

congress shoe: *See* congress gaiter.

connaught: Cotton foundation fabric used for embroidery.

conque: *See* conch.

considerations: *See* panniers.

Constance: Crinoline (1840–1865 C.E.). United States of America. In May, 1860, seven flounced spring dress.

constitution cord: Very heavy corded cotton fabric. *See also* cable cord.

constitutionals: *See* constitution cord.

contado: Mexico. Zoque Indian counted embroidery.

Continental: (1950–1960 C.E.). Man's hairstyle.

continental hat: *See* androsame.

contoushe: *See* kontush.

convent cloth: Solid color, plain weave woolen fabric once used for nun's apparel.

conversation bonnet: Directoire and First Empire (1790–1815 C.E.). United Kingdom. Fashionable in 1807, chip bonnet with flaring brim. Usually lined with silk that matched the ribbon trim which went around crown and tied in bow on top of the bonnet.

conversation hat: Directoire and First Empire (1790–1815 C.E.). Fashionable in 1803, woman's hat similar to the conversation bonnet but with brim wrapping around entire hat.

convertible collar: Straight collar, made to be worn up or down.

convertible jumper: Sleeveless dress worn in different ways: with sweater for casual wear, with blouse for day wear, and alone for evening.

convolvulus: Gay Nineties (1890–1900 C.E.) In 1895, a shade of purple.

cony: Rabbit skin.

cool gown: China. Song dynasty. Gown used as everyday dress by officials; later a mourning gown.

cool pants: *See* hot pants.

coolie hat

coolie hat: Usually made of woven straw, a round, widely conical hat.

coomassie: Bustle (1865–1890 C.E.). In 1875, new gray color.

coothay: India. Striped satin fabric.

copa: 1. Sides of crown of hat. 2. Spain. Hat crown.

copatain: Elizabethan (1550–1625 C.E.). Hat with high conical crown.

cope: Liturgical vestment in Catholic Church; embroidered or brocaded semicircular cape that fastens across chest with wide ornamental band. Vestigial hood in back.

Copenhagen blue: Medium light grayish blue.

cophia: Renaissance (1450–1550 C.E.). Coif of mail.

copitank: *See* copitain.

copotain: Elizabethan (1550–1625 C.E.). Woman's hat with high crown and small brim. Revived 1640–1665 as sugarloaf.

copper: Brown with yellowish red tint.

coppo: Renaissance (1450–1550 C.E.). Italy. Skull of a helm or helmet.

copricappa: Sardinia. Cape.

coq: *See* coque.

coquard: Elizabethan (1550–1625 C.E.). Worn by Swiss and German knights, satin cap with plumes.

coque: France. 1. Loop or looped bow of ribbon used as trim. 2. Long, iridescent, black and green feathers of rooster used as trim on hats.

coquearde: Tuft of rooster feathers.

coquelicot: Bustle (1865–1890 C.E.). France. In 1888, blood red.

coqueluche: France. Hood or cowl.

coquette: Decorative patch worn on lips.

coquillage: France. Trim resembling shells.

coquille: France. Edging or ruching in shell shape.

coquillicot feathers: Directoire and First Empire (1790–1815 C.E.). United States. Stiff bunch of rooster feathers used as hat trim in 1802.

cor: Portugal. Brown. *See also* castanho.

cor de laranja: Portugal. Orange.

cor de rosa: Portugal. The color rose.

Cora mantle: Crinoline (1840–1865 C.E.). In October, 1859, silk or poplin mantle made in imitation of the toga.

coracinus color: Greek (3000–100 B.C.E.). Black wool.

coraco Eugenie: Crinoline (1840–1865 C.E.). In 1855, lightweight fabric jacket.

coral: Medium bright red orange.

coral currant button: Crinoline (1840–1865 C.E.). United Kingdom. Used after 1845, currant-shaped, coral button used on men's waistcoats.

Coralie: Crinoline (1840–1865 C.E.). In 1855, woman's crocheted basket-shaped purse.

Coraline: Crinoline (1840–1865 C.E.). In November, 1859, highly decorated mantle of black cloth with square sleeves.

coramo: India. Pajama.

coranā: India. Narrow trousers.

corano: India. Trousers cut loose to the knee and fitted below the knee.

corazza: 1. Crinoline (1840–1865 C.E.). Worn after 1845, man's cambric or cotton fitted shirt that buttoned down back. 2. Italy. Cuirass. 3. *See* pettabotta.

corbata: Spain. Necklace; necktie.

corbata ascot: Spain. Ascot.

corbeau: France. Very dark green, almost black in color.

corchete: Spain. Hook and eye; hook.

corcuir: Ireland. Gaelic word for red color or purple colored.

corcur: Ireland. Gaelic word for scarlet.

corcurachd: Ireland. Gaelic word for purple.

corde du Roi: France. Corduroy.

cordeliere: 1. Renaissance (1450–1550 C.E.). France. Long chain which hung from girdle and held small items. Worn by women. Also, knotted girdle worn by Franciscan friars. 2. Crinoline (1840–1865 C.E.). Introduced in 1846, silk and wool blend fabric.

cordellate: 1. Renaissance (1450–1550 C.E.). Spain. Grogram. 2. Peru. Coarse wool fabric used for trousers and blankets.

cordero: Spain. Lamb.

cordero del Rusia: Karakul.

cordero del Tibet: Spain. Tibet lamb.

cordero mongoliano: Spain. Mongolia fur.

cordey cap: Directoire and First Empire (1790–1815 C.E.). United Kingdom. Popular from 1795 to 1799, woman's large crowned hat with wide lace brim that was trimmed with cockades or ribbon bows.

cordobán: Elizabethan (1550–1625 C.E.). Spain. Goatskin.

cordoban leather: Goatskin, tanned simply.

cordões de sapatos: Portugal. Shoelace.

cordon: Decorative cord, lace, or braid used as a fastening or to indicate rank.

cordon de soulier: France. Shoelace.

cordon de zapatos: Spain. Shoelace.

cordoncillo con alma: Spain. Gimp.

cordonero: Renaissance (1450–1550 C.E.). Spain. Passementerie maker.

cordoni: Greece. A woman's chest ornament of multiple chains from which hang medallions, coins, and ornaments.

cordonnet: Raised edge of military braid.

cordouan: Elizabethan (1550–1625 C.E.). France. Black or colored soft leather.

cordovan: Dark reddish brown.

Cordovan: Crinoline (1840–1865 C.E.). In 1856, woman's cloth cloak with velvet passementerie and buttons of same.

corduroy: Plain or twill weave, cut pile fabric with wide or narrow wales.

cordwain: Early Gothic (1200–1350 C.E.). Cordovan or Spanish leather.

cordy: Felt hat.

cordyback hat: *See* caudebec hat.

corinna: Romantic (1815–1840 C.E.). Introduced in 1837, richly flowered silk fabric.

corinth blue: Romantic (1815–1840 C.E.). Color of calamine.

corinthe green: Crinoline (1840–1865 C.E.). Light green.

corium: Roman (753 B.C.E.–323 C.E.). 1. Leather. 2. Upper body leather made of overlapping scales or flaps of leather.

cork rump: Late Georgian (1750–1790 C.E.). United Kingdom. Woman's bustle made from pad stuffed with cork.

corked shoes: Renaissance (1450–1550 C.E.) to Elizabethan (1550–1625 C.E.). Women's shoes with wedge-shaped cork heels.

corking pins: Large pins used to hold hair in place.

cornalia: Early Gothic (1200–1350 C.E.). Jewish woman's pointed veil. *See also* cornu.

corned shoe: Renaissance (1450–1550 C.E.). United Kingdom. Wide-toed shoe.

corner cap: Renaissance (1450–1550 C.E.) to Restoration (1660–1700 C.E.). Cap with three or four corners worn with academic or ecclesiastical dress.

cornet: 1. Long point of a hood. 2. Renaissance (1450–1550 C.E.). Woman's cap with point on top. 3. Elizabethan (1550–1625 C.E.) to Late Georgian (1750–1790 C.E.). Woman's linen headdress.

cornet hat: Directoire and First Empire (1790–1815 C.E.). United Kingdom. Woman's hat with gathered crown and narrow brim.

cornet skirt: Gay Nineties (1890–1900 C.E.). United Kingdom. In 1892, a woman's day skirt with slightly gored front section measuring 40 inches at hem and darted at waist. Back was cut on bias and trained in semicircle.

cornette: 1. Renaissance (1450–1550 C.E.). France. Long pendant strips of fabric like English liripipe and tippet. 2. Directoire and First Empire (1790–1815 C.E.). France. Woman's bonnet with gathered crown and brim worn turned down. Worn tied under chin with small ribbon bow.

cornette à la Diane: Romantic (1815–1840 C.E.). France. Worn in 1815, small bonnet with crescent-shaped front.

cornflower: Medium purplish blue.

corno: Italy. Tall conical felt hat worn by Venetian doges.

cornu: Italy. Venetian doge's brocade, satin, or velvet cap. *See also* cornalia.

coroa: Portugal. Crown; wreath.

corolla: Dainty folds in front of nun's hat.

coron: Ireland. Gaelic word for crown or coronet.

coron Muire: Ireland. Gaelic word for rosary of beads.

coron òir: Ireland. Crown of gold.

corona: 1. Circlet or fillet, often of gold, worn as part of ecclesiastical vestments. 2. Roman (753 B.C.E.–323 C.E.). Crown or garland awarded for distinguished service.

corona etrusca: Roman (753 B.C.E.–323 C.E.). Wreath of gold leaves, set with jewels and tied with ribbons that was held over the head of a general when making his triumphal entry into Rome.

corona muralis: Roman (753 B.C.E.–323 C.E.). Band of gold with turreted upper edge awarded for bravery in siege.

corona navalis: Roman (753 B.C.E.–323 C.E.). Gold band decorated with ship prows awarded for naval service to the Empire.

corona radiata: Roman (753 B.C.E.–323 C.E.). Headdress of divinity suggesting rays of the sun.

coronal: Coronet; crown.

coronation braid: Filled cotton cord.

coronet: Byzantine and Romansque (400–1200 C.E.). Ornamental circlet worn on head.

corozoso: Late Gothic (1350–1450 C.E.). Dark mourning colors of mulberry, blue, brown, green, and black.

corp a baleine: *See* corps piqué.

corpetto: Italy. Bodice.

corpiño: 1. Peru. Sleeveless vest. 2. Spain. Bodice.

corps piqué: Renaissance (1450–1550 C.E.) to Late Georgian (1750–1790 C.E.). France. Fitted quilted camisole with busk of varnished wood to stiffen it. In 17th and 18th centuries, whaleboned underbodice that laced and was held in position with shoulder straps. Replaced in late 18th century by a corset.

corredo: Italy. Trousseau.

correia articulada: Portugal. Chain belt.

corr-léine: Ireland. Shirt of armor.

corsage: 1. Byzantine and Romanesque (400–1200 C.E.). Snug, sleeveless jacket worn over bliaut. Resembles a corset. Worn by women. 2. Small bouquet of flowers worn pinned on woman's bosom. 3. France. Woman's jacket.

corsage à la Maintenon: Romantic (1815–1840 C.E.) to Crinoline (1840–1865 C.E.). France. Worn from 1836 to 1849, shaped bodice with ribbon knots down center front.

corsage à la vierge: Romantic (1815–1840 C.E.). Austro-Hungarian Empire. Term for bertha.

corsage en corset: Romantic (1815–1840 C.E.) to Crinoline (1840–1865 C.E.). France. Worn from 1836 to 1849, fitted evening bodice with seams similar to those in corset.

corsage en Fourreau: Romantic (1815–1840 C.E.) to present. Style of cutting the bodice in one with the skirt by a central panel at the back.

corse: 1. Byzantine and Romanesque (400–1200 C.E.). Snug, sleeveless jacket made of leather or metal disks. Worn over man's tunic or bliaut. 2. Spain. Corset. 3. Italy. Corset.

corselet: Early Gothic (1200–1350 C.E.). Piece of armor covering torso.

corset: 1. Early Gothic (1200–1350 C.E.). Long or short sleeveless surcoat worn by men. 2. Late Gothic (1350–1450 C.E.) to Renaissance (1450–1550 C.E.). Woman's gown that laced in front and was fur lined for winter. 3. Elizabethan (1550–1625 C.E.) to Late Georgian (1750–1790 C.E.). Bodice, with or without sleeves, supported by two busks. 4. Directoire and First Empire (1790–1815 C.E.) to 20th century. Boned bodice whose shape varied depending on vagaries of fashion.

corset batiste: Stout, plain weave fabric, sometimes containing an elastic weft.

corset cover
Dover Publications

corset cover: Garment worn to cover corset.

corset dress: Fetish dress laced like a corset. It hobbles the wearer.

corset frock: Directoire and First Empire (1790–1815 C.E.). Woman's dress with corset-shaped bodice with three gores on each side of the breast, short sleeves, and short skirt. Laced up the back with white silk cord.

corset lace: Narrow tape used for lacing corsets.

corset waist: United States of America. Long-line bra.

corsetka: Ukraine. Woman's three-quarter-length, fitted, sleeveless jacket that fastens to one side.

Corsican tie: *See* Napoleon necktie.

corso: India. Type of odhni.

corte: Guatemala. Wraparound skirt; skirt length.

cós: Portugal. Waistband of a garment.

cosar: Ireland. Gaelic word for coat or mantle.

cosetto: *See* corse.

cosh-boy: (1950–1960 C.E.). Teddy boy.

cossack cap: Russia. Tall, brimless, cur or lamb's wool cap worn by Cossacks.

cossack hat: Directoire and First Empire (1790–1815 C.E.). United States of America. Introduced in 1812, woman's hat with helmet-shaped crown, turned back brim edged in pearls, and small bunch of feathers on one side.

cossack trousers: Very full trousers worn by various mounted troops.

cossacks: Directoire and First Empire (1790–1815 C.E.) to Crinoline (1840–1865 C.E.). United Kingdom. Worn from 1814 to around 1850, men's trousers that pleated onto a waistband and tied around ankles with ribbon drawstring. Initially baggy, but by 1820 no longer needed drawstrings. In 1830, double instep straps were added, and in 1840, single instep strap remained.

cossas: India. Plain cotton fabric.

costeleta: Portugal. Sideburns.

costume á la Constitution: Directoire and First Empire (1790–1815 C.E.). France. Dress of red, white, and blue striped or flowered fine lawn or muslin. Worn with red sash and helmet-shaped cap.

costume au grand Figaro: Late Georgian (1750–1790 C.E.). France. Woman's short jacket cut in man's style and waistcoat-like bodice worn with sash.

costureira: Portugal. Dressmaker.

costureiro: Portugal. Ladies' tailor.

cot: 1. Guatemala. Huipil; blouse or tunic. 2. Wales. Coat.

cota: *See* casaco.

còta: Ireland. Petticoat.

còta biorach dubh: Ireland. Black, tailed coat; morning coat.

cóta coirí: Ireland. Bride's red petticoat. Worn on special occasions throughout her life.

còta de chadadh nam ball: Ireland. Coat of spotted tartan.

còta-ban: Ireland. Flannel petticoat.

còta-bhioran: Ireland. Knitted petticoat.

còta-cathdath: Ireland. Tartan coat.

còta-craicinn: Ireland. Skin coat.

còta-fada: Ireland. Frock coat.

còta-gearr: Ireland. Short, tartan or scarlet coat with short cutaway tail.

còta-glas: Ireland. Gray coat.

còta-goirid: Ireland. Jacket.

còta-uisge: Ireland. Waterproof coat.

cotan: Ireland. Cotton.

còtan: Ireland. 1. Little petticoat. 2. Little coat.

cote: Byzantine and Romanesque (400–1200 C.E.). Long tunic with sleeve cut in one with garment. Length varied from calf to foot.

cote à armer: France. Surcoat.

cote de Cheval: France. Corded fabric with characteristic warp rib used to make riding costumes.

cote de Genève: Bustle (1865–1890 C.E.). In 1874, light rep.

cotehardie: Early Gothic (1200–1350 C.E.) to Renaissance (1450–1550 C.E.). Long gown that opened in front with full-cut sleeves, sometimes hanging sleeves. Also referred to as dressing gown.

côtelé: 1. Bustle (1865–1890 C.E.). Introduced in 1865, thick ribbed silk. 2. Spain. Corduroy.

cotelé fino: Spain. Pin corduroy.

cotelette: Bustle (1865–1890 C.E.). Introduced in 1881, stocking-woven wool without stretch.

cotelettes: *See* cotellae.

coteline: 1. Thin white fabric, often corded. 2. Bustle (1865–1890 C.E.). Introduced in 1886, faille and wool blend in black.

cotellae: Early Gothic (1200–1350 C.E.). Sideless gown.

coteron: Little coat.

cothurnes: Greek (3000–100 B.C.E.). Calf-high boot favored by huntsmen; a shoe with very thick cork sole worn by actors to make them appear taller.

cotillion: Black and white striped fabric.

còt'-iochdair: Ireland. 1. Undercoat. 2. Under petticoat.

cotla-gearr: Scotland. Highlander's single-breasted, cutaway jacket worn with or without vest. Day version of tweed or worsted.

cotón: 1. Mexico. Sleeved shirt or tunic. 2. France. Cotton. 3. Peru. Woman's large, long back smock with long sleeves. 4. *See* cotoun.

cotone: Italy. Cotton.

cô-tông: Vietnam. Cotton.

cotonia: *See* kuttan.

cotorina: Mexico. Man's front-opening, sleeveless, wool vest.

cotoun: Byzantine and Romanesque (400–1200 C.E.) to Renaissance (1450–1550 C.E.). United Kingdom. Cotton.

cotswold: Renaissance (1450–1550 C.E.). High quality wool from Cotswold sheep.

cotta: *See* cote.

cotta de maglia: Renaissance (1450–1550 C.E.). Italy. Coat of mail.

cotta d'ecclesiastico: Italy. Surplice.

cottage bonnet: Directoire and First Empire (1790–1815 C.E.). In 1808, woman's straw bonnet with wide brim.

cottage cloak: Romantic (1815–1840 C.E.) to Bustle (1865–1890 C.E.). Cloak with hood or cap that tied beneath chin.

cottage front: Directoire and First Empire (1790–1815 C.E.) to Romantic (1815–1840 C.E.). United Kingdom. Popular from 1800 to 1820, woman's day bodice with space in front showing blouse over which front laced together.

cotte: *See* cote.

cotte d'armes: France. Tabard.

cottereau: Early Gothic (1200–1350 C.E.). France. Overskirt for riding.

cotton: Fiber from cotton plant. Fibers range in length from 1/2 inch to 2-1/2 inches.

cotton back satin: Satin made with silk or rayon warp and cotton weft.

cotton cambric: *See* cambric.

cotton crepe: Lightweight cotton fabric with crepe face used for dresses, gowns, spreads, etc.

cotton flannel: Plain or twill weave cotton fabric with soft nap on one or both sides.

cotton foulard: Cotton fabric made to imitate silk foulard.

cotton pongee: Soft, lustrous, silky, plain weave cotton fabric.

cotton taffeta: Plain weave fabric of cotton and mercerized yarns, usually in woven stripe.

cotton velvet: *See* velvet.

cottonade: Stout, twill weave, cotton fabric used for trousers and cheap suiting.

cottonette: Cotton and wool blend fabric.

còt'-uachdair: Ireland. Overcoat.

cotun: Ireland. Gaelic word for coat of mail.

coturno: Portugal. Buskin.

cotwm: Wales. Cotton.

couching stitch: Straight or slanted tight stitch used to achieve raised effect.

couchouc: Romantic (1815–1840 C.E.). In 1820s, India rubber used for garters and stays.

coudières: Late Gothic (1350–1450 C.E.). France. Long hanging tab on cotehardie sleeves.

couleur-de-roi: Renaissance (1450–1550 C.E.). France. Tawny color.

countenances: Elizabethan (1550–1625 C.E.). France. In 1550, very first muffs to be carried by women.

coups de vent: Directoire and First Empire (1790–1815 C.E.). France. Man's hairstyle with loose bangs.

couraça: Portugal. Cuirasse.

coureur: Directoire and First Empire (1790–1815 C.E.). France. Very fitted caraco with short basques.

couroncon: Bustle (1865–1890 C.E.). In 1889, melon green.

couronne: France. Ornamental loop on cordonnet edging point lace.

couronne Ristori: Crinoline (1840–1865 C.E.). In 1857, wreath headdress of silk oak-leaves and acorns.

courreges: (1950–1960 C.E.). France. Lined and fur-topped goulashes. Usually white real or imitation leather.

court habit: *See* habit.

court plaster: Late Georgian (1750–1790 C.E.). Beauty patches.

court sleeve cuff: *See* manchette de cour.

court tie: Oxford tie.

Courtauld crape: Gay Nineties (1890–1900 C.E.). United Kingdom. A crimped, dull, black mourning crape.

Courtauld's new silk crepe: Gay Nineties (1890–1900 C.E.) In 1894, a silk crepe almost as thin and soft as chiffon.

courtepy: Late Gothic (1350–1450 C.E.). France. Very short overgarment usually with high collar. Often particolored or embroidered.

courtepye: *See* courtepy.

couter: Elbow piece of armor.

couters: Early Gothic (1200–1350 C.E.). The disc-shaped plates attached to the elbows of a hauberk.

coutil: 1. Crinoline (1840–1865 C.E.) to 20th century. France. Introduced in the 1840s, lightweight jean. 2. Strong, tightly woven, herringbone twill weave cotton fabric made from medium weight yarns.

couvre-chef: France. White muslin headscarf.

couvrechef: France. Woman's headdress, veil, or head-scarf.

couvre-oreille: France. Earmuff.

cover: Spain. Cover coat.

cover coat: Coarse wool Batavia twill with pronounced diagonal wales.

Covercoat: Germany. Cover coat.

coverslut: Garment, like apron, worn to cover other clothes.

covert: Diagonal twill weave, durable, medium-weight fabric in variety of blends.

cowbandi: India. Waist-length, sleeveless, fitted jacket.

cowboy boots
See also photospread
(Foot and Legwear).

cowboy hat

cowboy boots: High-heeled riding boots with fancy stitching on top.

cowboy hat: Brimmed felt hat with creased crown.

cowes: Gay Nineties (1890–1900 C.E.). United Kingdom. Man's evening jacket without tails. Popularized by the Prince of Wales for semi-formal evening dress. Later called dinner jacket.

cowichan sweater: (20th century). Canada. Sweater with American Indian pattern in black and white or black and gray.

cowl: 1. Monk's hood. 2. Scotland. Nightcap. 3. Soft fold or drape of material in neckline.

cowl collar: 1. (1930–1940 C.E.). Large, shoulder-length, circular collar. 2. (1980–1989 C.E.). Draped turtleneck collar.

coxa: Iran. Mantle.

coxcomb: Cap with strip of notched red cloth, once worn by licensed court jesters.

coxcombs: *See* wheat ears.

coyoichcatl: Mexico. Aztec term for coyote-colored cotton.

crackle net: Net with mesh of crackle designs.

crackow shoes: *See* pigaches.

cracow: *See* pigaches.

crà-gheal: Ireland. Light red.

crakow: Shoe with long pointed toe.

crambaid: Ireland. Gaelic word for buckle.

cramignole: Renaissance (1450–1550 C.E.) to Elizabethan (1550–1625 C.E.). Man's cap with turned-up brim. In late 15th century, made of velvet; by early 17th century, of lighter stuff.

cramoisi: France. Crimson.

cran: Romantic (1815–1840 C.E.). In 1830s, V-shaped gap in man's suit coat collar.

crane color: Elizabethan (1550–1625 C.E.). Grayish white.

cranky checks: United Kingdom. Check fabric with colors woven in, most commonly blue and white check.

crants: Early Gothic (1200–1350 C.E.) to Late Georgian (1750–1790 C.E.). Chaplet of flowers or gold and gems.

crapand: Early Georgian (1700–1750 C.E.). In 1745, ribbon used to tie man's hair in ponytail at back of head.

crapaud: *See* bag wig.

crapaud mort d'amour: Restoration (1660–1700 C.E.). France. Light green.

crapaud saisi: Restoration (1660–1700 C.E.). France. Medium green.

crape: Late Georgian (1750–1790 C.E.). 1. To make one's hair curly or frizzy. 2. Mourning gauze of black silk.

craponne: Cheap, stout guipere.

craquelé net: Firm net woven in zigzag pattern giving appearance of cracked glass.

crash: Coarse, cotton, linen, rayon, or blend, plain weave fabric with rough irregular face.

Cravanette: Trade name for waterproof finish.

cravat: Charles I (1625–1660 C.E.) to 20th century. Loose, ornamental neckwear favored by men. Generally included band around the neck secured in variety of styles.

cravat cocodes: Crinoline (1840–1865 C.E.). In 1863, lady's large riding cravat worn tied in knot.

cravat strings: Restoration (1660–1700 C.E.). United Kingdom. Worn from 1665 to 1680s, colored ribbon worn around cravat ends and tied in bow under the chin. More formal version appeared later.

cravate: 1. France. Necktie; cravat. 2. France. Provencal little white cap of ribbon or lace.

cravate à-la Bergami: Romantic (1815–1840 C.E.). France. Similar to cravate a la Byron.

cravate cocodes: Crinoline (1840–1865 C.E.). France. Fashionable in 1863, woman's large bow cravat worn with habit shirt and standing collar.

cravate de bureaucrate: Crinoline (1840–1865 C.E.). France. High, tight, black cravat that was stiffened with whalebone and stuffed with horsehair.

cravate mathématique: Romantic (1815–1840 C.E.). France. Cravat with folds all horizontal forming two acute angles.

cravatta: Italy. Necktie; cravat.

cravenette: Gay Nineties (1890–1900 C.E.) In 1899, the process which made fibers water resistant.

crea: Spain. Linen or cotton fabric.

crèach: Ireland. Gray.

cream: Very light yellow.

creedmore: Cheap, heavy, blucher-cut shoe favored by workmen.

crema: Spain. Cream color.

cremallera: Spain. Zipper.

cremallera separable: Spain. Separating zipper.

creme de cachemire lace: Bustle (1865–1890 C.E.). In 1876, ecru or cream colored lace of fine cashmere wool.

cremesino: Renaissance (1450–1550 C.E.). Italy. Deep crimson dye made from tiny insects brought in from India.

cremisi: Late Gothic (1350–1450 C.E.). Premium quality red.

Cremona cravat: Early Georgian (1700–1750 C.E.). Worn in 1702, plain ribbon decorated with gathers on each edge.

cremorne: Bustle (1865–1890 C.E.). Introduced in 1872, faint reddish brown.

cremyll: Early Gothic (1200–1350 C.E.) to Late Gothic (1350–1450 C.E.). Cotton openwork or lace.

creoles: Late Georgian (1750–1790 C.E.). Worn by both genders, loop earrings.

crêpe: Any of number of fabrics with characteristic crinkled or puckered surface.

crepe aerophane: Crinoline (1840–1865 C.E.). In 1861, new fabric.

crepe anglaise: (20th century). United Kingdom. French term for English black and white mourning crape.

crepe back satin: Heavy, drapable fabric with satin face and crepe back, commonly made from rayon.

crepe charmeuse: Soft, dull luster silk used for dresses, evening wear, and some linings.

crepe de Chine: Very lightweight, fine, plain weave silk fabric.

crepe de laine: Fine, lightweight, plain weave woolen fabric.

crépe de Suisse: Crinoline (1840–1865 C.E.). In 1860, dress fabric.

crepe georgette: Silk, silk and rayon, or silk and cotton highly creped fabric.

crepe imperial: Bustle (1865–1890 C.E.). United Kingdom. A wool crape.

crepe lisse: Thin, smooth, glossy silk fabric that feels like crepe.

crepe maretz: Crinoline (1840–1865 C.E.). In 1862, new fabric.

crepe marocain: Heavy, plain weave silk, cotton , rayon, or blend fabric.

crepe meteor: Fine, lightweight silk crepe with satin face on one side.

crepe myosotis: (1930–1940 C.E.). Crimped silk mourning crepe with soft finish.

crepe plissé: Thin, lightweight cotton crepe with puckered stripes in direction of warp.

crepe poplin: Bustle (1865–1890 C.E.). Introduced in 1871, silk and wool blend fabric, crinkly like crepe.

crepe royal: Bustle (1865–1890 C.E.). Introduced in 1889, transparent crepe de Chine.

crepe rubber: Rubber with creped surface used in soles of shoes.

crepe-de-china: Portugal. Crepe de Chine.

crepeline: Bustle (1865–1890 C.E.). Popular in 1870s, cheap substitute for crepe de Chine.

crepelle: (1900–1910 C.E.). France. A cheap silk and wool mourning fabric.

crepida: Roman (753 B.C.E.–323 C.E.). Half shoe or sandal with leather or fabric sole that enclosed heel and sides of foot and fastened across instep with laces through eyelets.

crepida
See also photospread (Foot and Legwear).

crepine: 1. Directoire and First Empire (1790–1815 C.E.). Trim of very long knotted fringes. 2. French silk dress fabric.

crepoline: Wool dress fabric.

crepon: Bustle (1865–1890 C.E.) to present. 1. Introduced in 1866, China crepe with soft, silky surface. 2. Introduced in 1882, wool, silk, or blend fabric like very heavy crepe. 3. Gay Nineties (1890–1900 C.E.). Popular in 1890s, woolen fabric creped to appear puffed between stripes of squares.

crepon milleraye: Gay Nineties (1890–1900 C.E.). France. In 1896, a finely striped crepon.

crepon Persian: Gay Nineties (1890–1900 C.E.). France. In 1896, a crepon with oriental patterns.

crep-satén: Spain. Satin crepe.

crespe: Elizabethan (1550–1625 C.E.). France and Italy. A lightweight crimped type of gauze used for mourning dress.

crespine: Early Gothic (1200–1350 C.E.) to Late Gothic (1350–1450 C.E.). Open-weave net worn over women's hair with barbette and filet.

crespo: Italy. Crepe.

crespón: Spain. Crepe.

crespón arena: Spain. Sand crepe.

crespón de Cantón: Spain. Canton crepe.

Crespón de China: Spain. Crepe de Chine.

crespón de lana: Spain. Wool crepe.

crespón georgette: Spain. Georgette.

crespón marroqui: Spain. Marocain.

crespón musgo: Spain. Crepe mousse.

crespón romano: Spain. Crepe romaine.

cress cloth: *See* crest cloth.

crest cloth: Late Gothic (1350–1450 C.E.) to Elizabethan (1550–1625 C.E.). Type of linen used for linings.

cresta: *See* touca.

Crete lace: Greece. Colored flax lace made on Crete.

cretinta: *See* pastura.

cretona: Spain. Cretonne.

cretonne: Bustle (1865–1890 C.E.) to present. Introduced in 1867, a twill weave, unglazed cotton fabric printed in colors.

creve-coeur: Restoration (1660–1700 C.E.). France. Curled hair worn by women at nape of neck.

creves: *See* slashings.

crevette: France. Pinkish color of shrimp.

crew neckline: (20th century). Close-fitting, round neckline without collar.

crewel work: Any embroidery made with lightly twisted, two-ply worsted yarn.

criardes: Early Georgian (1700–1750 C.E.). Early pannier made of underskirts of gummed linen.

cricket: *See* tellex.

cricket sweater: Tennis sweater.

cridhachan: Ireland. Gaelic word for small brooch or buckle worn at the breast.

Crimea: Crinoline (1840–1865 C.E.). 1. In 1854, woman's satin cloak, lined with taffeta. It had an 18-inch cape with 14-inch skirt box-pleated on. It was trimmed with noeuds of black velvet ribbon. 2. In 1856, woman's moire antique carriage cloak trimmed with satin galloon and lined with silk.

crimson: Deep red with hint of blue.

crinc: Byzantine and Romanesque (400–1200 C.E.). United Kingdom. Shoe, possibly not fitted, but laced.

crinkle cloth: *See* seersucker.

crinoletta: Bustle (1865–1890 C.E.). Whalebone or steel bustle covered in flounces.

crinolette: Bustle (1865–1890 C.E.). Worn from 1868 to around 1873, small cage crinoline hoop in back only.

crinolette petticoat: Bustle (1865–1890 C.E.). Worn in 1870 and revived in 1883, petticoat cut flat in front and with half circle steel hoops in back and flounces on bottom back.

crinolina: Italy and Spain. Crinoline.

crinoline: Crinoline (1840–1865 C.E.). France. Originally horsehair cloth used for officers' collars. Later used for women's underskirts to support skirts. Around 1850, replaced by many petticoats, starched and boned. Around 1856, light metal cage was developed.

crios: Ireland. Gaelic word for belt or girdle.

criosan: Ireland. Gaelic word for a small belt or apron.

criosan biodag: Scotland. Dirk belt. Wide belt (2-1/2 to 3 inches) of black morocco or patent leather with ornamented silver buckle. Dirk worn suspended from belt.

crios-ceangail: Ireland. Gaelic word for belt.

crios-claidheimh: Ireland. Gaelic word for sword belt.

crioslachan: Ireland. Gaelic word for a bag worn hung from the girdle.

crios-muineil: Ireland. Gaelic word for a necklace or a neckband.

crios-pheilear: Ireland. Gaelic word for bandolier.

crios-tarsainn: Ireland. Gaelic word for shoulder belt.

crisp: Early Gothic (1200–1350 C.E.) to Elizabethan (1550–1625 C.E.). 1. Lawn. 2. Woman's head veil. 3. Curl of hair.

crispin: Romantic (1815–1840 C.E.) to Crinoline (1840–1865 C.E.). 1. Introduced in 1826, collarless coat used by actresses to keep them warm when waiting in wings. 2. Introduced in 1839, man's evening cloak with very large sleeves. Silk lined, wadded, and quilted. 3. Introduced in 1842, woman's short mantle of cashmere, satin, or velvet with short cape that fitted snugly around neck. Cut on bias and often wadded.

crispin cloche: Crinoline (1840–1865 C.E.). Introduced in 1842, woman's bell-shaped, knee-length crispin.

crispine: Byzantine and Romanesque (400–1200 C.E.). Headdress made of gold net and pearls.

crispinette: *See* crispine.

criss: 1. Late Gothic (1350–1450 C.E.). Man's girdle. 2. Isle of Man. Man's girdle made of two- to three-inch-wide knitted band of brightly colored wool. Worn wrapped twice around waist and then tied. 3. Ireland. Gaelic word for girdle.

cristygrey: Late Gothic (1350–1450 C.E.). Fur taken from animal's head or crest.

crn: Poland. Black colored.

crnac: Poland. The color black.

crò snàthaid: Ireland. Eye of a needle.

cròchach: Ireland. Saffron colored.

crochag: Ireland. Gaelic word for ear pendant.

croché: Portugal. Crochet work.

crocking: To rub off unfixed dye or paint from fabric.

crocodile: Alligator leather.

crocus: Late Georgian (1750–1790 C.E.). United States of America. Coarse linen fabric worn by slaves and common folk.

crò-dhearg: Ireland. 1. The color saffron. 2. Red.

croiméal: Ireland. Moustache worn without beard.

croise cloth: Bustle (1865–1890 C.E.). In 1874, lightly twilled wool fabric in unbleached shades.

croisgileid: Ireland. Gaelic word for a triangle of fabric worn tied around an infant's head.

croîtor: Romania. Tailor.

croizette blue: Bustle (1865–1890 C.E.). In 1876, new color.

Cromwell collar: Bustle (1865–1890 C.E.). United Kingdom. Popular in 1880s, woman's deep turned over collar worn with morning dress.

Cromwell shoe: 1. Bustle (1865–1890 C.E.). United Kingdom. Worn from 1869 to 1889, tongued shoe with buckle similar to those worn during mid-1600s. 2. (20th century). Beginning in the 1920s, a shorter toed version of the mid-1600s shoe popularly worn by women.

Cromwell shoe (Bustle period) Dover Publications

Cromwell shoe (20th century)

cronnt: Ireland. Gaelic word for green or gray.

crook and flail: Egyptian (4000–30 B.C.E.). Royal insignia carried by a pharaoh consisting of a crook, similar to a shepherd's hook, possibly symbolic of the pharaoh as the shepherd of his people, and a flail, possibly symbolic of a shepherd's whip or a fly-whisk. Together they denote the authority and power of the leader.

crop: Late Georgian (1750–1790 C.E.). Short hairstyle worn as prevention against tax on hair-powder.

croppes: Renaissance (1450–1550 C.E.). Fur made from pieces cut from rump of animal.

croquet boots: Bustle (1865–1890 C.E.). Introduced in 1865, woman's boot of morocco leather often with fancy toe-caps. Top edge had tassels in front and back and it laced up.

croquis: France. Fashion sketch.

cross aigrette: Short feathers from under wings of egret.

cross fox: Fox fur that is mix of black or silver and red fox. Black cross over shoulders and down back.

cross gartering
See also photospread
(Foot and Legwear).

cross gartering: Elizabethan (1550–1625 C.E.). Bands, ribbons, or strips of fabric or leather worn crisscrossed below knees. Worn by men.

cross pocket: Early Georgian (1700–1750 C.E.) to Late Georgian (1750–1790 C.E.). Pocket with horizontal opening.

cross-cloth: Elizabethan (1550–1625 C.E.). United Kingdom. Band of fabric worn across forehead in connection with coif. Also worn at night as wrinkle preventative.

cross-stitch: Cross formed by two slanted stitches.

crotalia: Roman (753 B.C.E.–323 C.E.). Women's earrings made of pear-shaped beads that rattled like castanets with any movement.

crottin: Bustle (1865–1890 C.E.). In 1888, blonde color.

Crown pearl: (1930–1940 C.E.). A new color.

crubhas: Ireland. Gaelic word for crimson.

crubhasg: Ireland. Gaelic word for crimson.

cruches: Restoration (1660–1700 C.E.). Women's small forehead curls.

cruinneacan: Ireland. Gaelic word for coronet.

crumenal: Obsolete term for purse.

crùn: Ireland. 1. Crown. 2. Garland of flowers.

crùn-easbuig: Ireland. Bishop's miter.

crusene: Byzantine and Romanesque (400–1200 C.E.). United Kingdom. Man's fur or skin garment.

crushed strawberry: Gay Nineties (1890–1900 C.E.). In 1891, a new color; shade of red.

crushed velvet: Velvet with irregular surface.

cruth-lachd: Ireland. Gaelic word for sword girdle.

cruz churuku: Ecuador. A rough diamond-shaped weave.

crven: Poland. Red colored.

crvena boja: Poland. Red.

crys: Wales. Shirt.

crystallus: Roman (753 B.C.E.–323 C.E.). Rock crystal.

csakora cut: Romantic (1815–1840 C.E.). Austro-Hungarian Empire. Popular style of tailoring involving diagonally cut piece of fabric overlapping front area of the dolman below the waist.

csepesz: Hungary. Married woman's black frilled bonnet.

csispkèsköttö: Hungary. Green apron with lace trim.

csizma: Romantic (1815–1840 C.E.). Austro-Hungarian Empire. Boot.

cuach-chiabh: Ireland. Gaelic word for ringlet.

cuach-fhalt: Ireland. Gaelic word for curled hair.

cuaran: 1. Ireland. Gaelic word for sock; brogue of untanned skin; sandal; buskin or slipper. 2. Renaissance (1450–1550 C.E.) to Restoration (1660–1700 C.E.). Scotland. Highlander's knee-high boot.

Cuban heel: Heel with straight sides.

cubhrag: Ireland. Gaelic word for infant's flannel shawl.

cubica: 1. Fine, worsted shalloon used for linings. 2. Spain. A fabric.

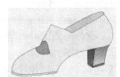

Cuban heel

cubital: Sleeve covering arm from wrist to elbow.

cubitière: Early Gothic (1200–1350 C.E.). France. Piece of plate armor for elbow.

cubù: China. Coarse fabric.

cuculla: Roman (753 B.C.E.–323 C.E.). Oblong piece of fabric with opening for head used by all classes as protection from weather. Later became part of dress for Benedictine monks as form of scapular.

cucullus: Roman (753 B.C.E.–323 C.E.). Hood on working clothes.

cudamani: India. A lotus-shaped hair ornament.

cudari: *See* badhani.

cūdīdār: India. Trousers cut loose at the waist and fitted at the ankle.

cūdō: Roman (753 B.C.E.–323 C.E.). Skin helmet.

cudon: Italy. Leather skull cap held on with a chin strap.

cue de Paris: Bustle (1865–1890 C.E.). United States of America. Bustle padded with horsehair.

cuecas: Portugal. Shorts.

cueitl: Mexico. Aztec woman's ankle-length, wraparound skirt.

cuello: Spain. Collar.

cuello bebés: Spain. Baby collar.

cuello bote: Spain. Boat collar.

cuello burberry: Spain. Burberry collar.

cuello capuchon: Spain. Cowl neckline.

cuello chal: Spain. Shawl collar.

cuello chino: Spain. Mao collar.

cuello de pajarita: Spain. Wing collar.

cuello eton: Spain. Eton collar.

cuello mandarín: Spain. Mandarin collar.

cuenta: Ecuador and Guatemala. Bead.

cuerbully: *See* cuir-bouilli.

cuero: Spain. Leather.

cuero de ante: Spain. Chamois.

cuero de cerdo: Spain. Pigskin.

cuero de cocodrilo: Spain. Alligator leather.

cuero de marroqui: Spain. Morocco leather.

cuero napa: Spain. Nappa leather.

cuerpo: Ecuador. Body of a blouse.

cuerpo baxo: Renaissance (1450–1550 C.E.) to Elizabethan (1550–1625 C.E.). Spain. Quilted, boned, sleeveless bodice worn with basquine.

cufaica: Romania. Blouse.

cuff link: Fastening device that connects the two sides of a cuff.

cuff strings: Elizabethan (1550–1625 C.E.). Thin ties used to hold cuff in place.

cuffia: 1. Byzantine and Romanesque (400–1200 C.E.). United Kingdom. Late 10th-century women's headdress. 2. Italy. Bonnet.

cuffie: *See* cuffia.

çuga: Iran. Short jacket.

cuha: Hungary and Turkey. Woven woolen fabric.

cui: China. 1. Pure white. 2. Emerald green.

cuille: Ireland. Gaelic word for black fabric.

cuìlù: China. Emerald green.

cuir: 1. France. Leather. 2. Crinoline (1840–1865 C.E.). In 1862, new shade of brown; literally, "leather."

cuirass tunic: Bustle (1865–1890 C.E.). United Kingdom. Introduced in 1874, woman's plain, fitted tunic worn with cuirasse bodice.

cuirasse bodice
Dover Publications

cuirasse bodice: Bustle (1865–1890 C.E.). United Kingdom. Introduced in 1874, woman's long, fitted and boned day bodice that reached below hips. Often made of different fabric than the dress. Sleeves matched trim.

cuirasse tunic: Bustle (1865–1890 C.E.). From 1874 to 1878, woman's masculine cut tunic.

cuir-bouilli: Early Gothic (1200–1350 C.E.). France. Hard, boiled leather used of armor.

cuircinn: Ireland. Gaelic word for woman's headdress.

cuirie: Early Gothic (1200–1350 C.E.). France. Armored mittens.

cùirnean: Ireland. Brooch.

cuish: *See* cuisse.

cuissard: *See* cuisse.

cuissart: *See* cuisse.

cuisse: Early Gothic (1200–1350 C.E.). Plate armor piece for front of the thighs.

cuivre: France. Copper color.

cukar: Late Gothic (1350–1450 C.E.). Side pieces of woman's horned headdress.

cul de crin: Late Georgian (1750–1790 C.E.). In 1788, woman's bustle.

cul de Paris: Restoration (1660–1700 C.E.). In 1680s, woman's bustle.

cul postiche: Late Georgian (1750–1790 C.E.). False bums or rumps.

culaidh-aodaich: Ireland. Gaelic word for suit of clothes.

culaidh-bainnse: Ireland. Gaelic word for wedding suit.

culan: Early Gothic (1200–1350 C.E.). Ireland. Man's hairstyle where front was shaved and hair remained in back. Forbidden in 1297.

culeco: Peru. Large shirt of white cotton embroidered with colored threads.

culet: Early Gothic (1200–1350 C.E.). Defensive armor that covered buttocks.

culgah: *See* culgee.

culgee: 1. India. Jeweled plume worn on turban. 2. India. Figured silk fabric.

culok: Russia. Sock.

culot: Elizabethan (1550–1625 C.E.). France. Men's very short and tight breeches.

culote: Portugal. Riding breeches.

culotte: 1. Restoration (1660–1700 C.E.). Men's breeches that tied below knee. 2. France. Breeches.

culotte courte: France. Knee breeches.

culpait: Byzantine and Romanesque (400–1200 C.E.). Ireland. Large collar.

cumábù: China. Burlap.

cumáoyàng: China. Coarse wool.

cumbe: Ecuador and Guatemala. Fine fabric, usually a double faced tapestry.

cumbe camentera: Ecuador and Guatemala. Incan fine cloth decorated with brightly colored feathers.

Cumberland corset: Romantic (1815–1840 C.E.). United Kingdom. Worn from 1815 to 1820s, man's corset worn by dandies.

Cumberland hat: Romantic (1815–1840 C.E.). United Kingdom. Worn in 1830s, man's tall hat with eight inch crown that tapered toward top and narrow brim turned up on sides.

cumbi: 1. Bolivia. Tapestry cloth. 2. *See* cumpi.

cumbly: *See* kambala.

cumhais: Ireland. Gaelic word for selvedge.

cumly: *See* kambala.

cummerbund: Wide, pleated sash belt, usually in satin. Worn by men with formal wear and by women more casually.

cummul: *See* kambala.

cumpi: Peru. Fine fabric of vicuna or cotton.

cūndad: India. Tie-dyed red scarf.

cunnī: India. Scarf.

cunua: Romania. Bride's wreath of cardboard, paper, flowers, beads, and small mirrors.

cuoio: Italy. Leather.

cuoroncou: Bustle (1865–1890 C.E.). France. In 1888, medium yellow green.

cupola coat: Early Georgian (1700–1750 C.E.) to Late Georgian (1750–1790 C.E.). Worn from around 1710 to 1780, popular term for domed petticoat of whalebone or cane hoops.

cuppalium: India. A freshly dyed fabric.

cuprius: Roman (753 B.C.E.–323 C.E.). Copper.

curace: Cuirass.

cùrainn: Ireland. Coarse woolen fabric or flannel.

cùrainn-chneas: Ireland. Flannel.

curch: Late Georgian (1750–1790 C.E.). United States of America. Plain, close-fitting cap worn by women.

curchef: *See* curch.

curea: *See* cingătoare.

curi: Peru. Tribal woman's disc that is worn hanging from a pierced lower lip.

curled silk: Directoire and First Empire (1790–1815 C.E.). United States of America. Introduced in 1814, new fabric for bonnets.

curling: Trim of lace and ribbons stitched in tight fold on handkerchief hem.

curling-cloud crown: China. Song dynasty. Emperor's blue crown made with 24 one-inch-long beams.

curls à la Greque: Directoire and First Empire (1790–1815 C.E.). Worn after 1801, waving curls close to face.

curóugé: China. Rough-tanned leather.

currac: Ireland. Gaelic word for woman's cap.

curracag: Ireland. Gaelic word for hood.

curricle cloak: Directoire and First Empire (1790–1815 C.E.). United Kingdom. Worn from 1801 to 1806, woman's half or three-quarter length cloak that was fitted at waist. Front borders curved away from waist. Edged in lace or fur.

curricle coat: Romantic (1815–1840 C.E.). In 1820s, woman's long coat with lapels.

curricle dress: Directoire and First Empire (1790–1815 C.E.). United Kingdom. Popular from 1794 to 1803, woman's gown with over-tunic or half robe of net. Short sleeved and opened down front. Sometimes worn with habit shirt.

curricle pelisse: Romantic (1815–1840 C.E.). United Kingdom. Worn in 1820s, woman's pelisse with three capes.

cursey cloth: *See* kersey.

curtain drapery: Bustle (1865–1890 C.E.). North America. Term for pannier folds. *See also* hip bags.

cushion headdress: Romantic (1815–1840 C.E.). Term for padded roll worn in Late Gothic (1350–1450 C.E.) era.

curtain drapery
Dover Publications

cushion work: *See* opus pulvinarium.

cushionet: Elizabethan (1550–1625 C.E.) to Charles I (1625–1660 C.E.). Woman's bustle worn with farthingale to lift it in back.

cushma: 1. *See* kushma. 2. Peru. Tribal man's long, wide tunic.

cusma: Romania. Old-fashioned fur cap.

cut linen work: Elizabethan (1550–1625 C.E.). Form of embroidery where groups of threads are removed by cutting.

cut velvet: Fine, knife-cut silk velvet.

cutar: India. A plain white calico.

cutaveica: Romania. Blouse.

cutaway: Man's one-button formal coat with skirt cut away in front, forming tails in back.

cut-fingered gloves: Early Georgian (1700–1750 C.E.). Women's gloves with tips of fingers removed.

cut-fingered pumps: Renaissance (1450–1550 C.E.). United Kingdom. Men's shoes that were slashed over toes.

cuth-bhàrr: Ireland. Helmet.

cuth-bharran: Ireland. Gaelic word for hood.

cutlets: *See* dundrearys.

cutout embroidery: Buttonhole stitch with interior cut out.

cut-fingered pumps
See also photospread
(Foot and Legwear).

cuttanee: Elizabethan (1550–1625 C.E.) to Late Georgian (1750–1790 C.E.). East Indian linen used for shirts, cravats.

cutwork: Embroidery from which parts of the ground are cut away.

cutworks: *See* wheat ears.

cuyuscate: Guatemala. Brown cotton.

cuzhi xianwéi: China. Acetate fiber.

cyan blue: Strong blue color with green tint.

cyanus: Roman (753 B.C.E.–323 C.E.). Lapis lazuli.

cyclamen: Dull blue red.

cyclas: Early Gothic (1200–1350 C.E.). Cut in one piece, this overgarment had hole in center for head. Sometimes lined with fur or silk.

cymar: Woman's loose garment or scarf.

cynara: Heavy, sheer rayon crepe similar to romaine.

cypress: Bustle (1865–1890 C.E.). Dark green.

Cyprian gold: Early Gothic (1200–1350 C.E.). Italy. White linen thread sheathed in gold.

cyprus: Renaissance (1450–1550 C.E.) to Restoration (1660–1700 C.E.). Fine, black silk crepe worn as mourning veil or for hatbands. Made in Cyprus.

cyrtel: Byzantine and Romanesque (400–1200 C.E.). United Kingdom. Man's tunic or woman's gown. Originally short. Of wool or fur.

czapka: Poland. Cap or caul. *See also* kall.

czapska: Directoire and First Empire (1790–1815 C.E.). Poland. Military cap with square top and visor in front. Worn first by Polish troops in French service under Napoleon.

czarina: Crinoline (1840–1865 C.E.). In 1854, woman's wrap with caped yoke and box-pleated skirt. Had arm slits and scalloped lower edge and was embroidered.

czarny: Poland. Black colored.

czarny jak smola: Poland. Jet black.

czechoslovakian embroidery: Brightly colored geometric shapes on linen.

czepek: Poland. Bonnet.

czepesz: Romania. Woman's starched lace bonnet.

czerwony: Poland. Red.

czólka: Poland. Stiff tiara with ribbons and bunch of flowers and feathers on one side.

D

da: Vietnam. Wool; felt.

da boc-can: Vietnam. Box calf leather.

da dai: China. Zhuong dynasty. Women's silk girdle.

da láng: Vietnam. Patent leather.

da linh: Vietnam. Chamois.

da lon: Vietnam. Pigskin.

dáábalii: Navajo. Shawl.

dabao: China. Long, broad girdle.

dacca muslin: One of very earliest textiles, made in Dacca, India, from locally grown cotton.

dacca silk: Embroidery silk.

dàchang: China. Outer garment.

Dachs: Germany. Badger fur.

Dacron: DuPont's trade name for its polyester fiber.

dadhikali: India. A very white wrapper with an indented decoration on the borders.

dadiyā: India. Sari with a zigzag pattern.

dadong: Borneo. Shawl.

dagba gulai: Sierra Leone. Literally "nursing dress," cloth presented to the mother of the bride as part of the bride price.

dagged: Renaissance (1450–1550 C.E.). 1. Appliqué of petal-shaped pieces of material. 2. Snipped edges on garment.

daglā: See cogā.

Dagmor blue: Bustle (1865–1890 C.E.). In 1867, very rich deep blue.

dagswain: Late Gothic (1350–1450 C.E.) to Elizabethan (1550–1625 C.E.). Very coarse fabric.

dàguà: China. Unlined long gown.

dàhóng: China. Bright red.

dai fong chau: Crinoline (1840–1865 C.E.). United States of America. Chinese Hawaiian term for a soft, processed silk with a thick texture.

dai kou: China. Literally "pocket mouths," patch pockets inside jacket.

dai seong siu kwun: Bustle (1865–1890 C.E.). United States of America. Chinese Hawaiian term for pantaloons.

daikou: China. Ming belt buckle.

dàilù: China. Dark green.

daimana: See kaimana.

daimon: Japan. Literally "big crest," a square cut coat emblazoned with large family crests.

daishi: China. Ming belt plaque.

daisy belle: Solid color cotton fabric.

Daisy cloth: Trade name for twill weave outing flannel.

daku: Hungary. Embroidered sheepskin waistcoat. Worn by women and some men.

dalahany: Madagascar. Finest silk cloth.

dalc: See dalk.

dalephuc: Vietnam. Evening dress.

dali dali: Indonesia. Sa'dan-Toraja pendant.

dalian: China. Layered jacket worn by wrestlers.

dalk: Byzantine and Romanesque (400–1200 C.E.) to Renaissance (1450–1550 C.E.). Term usually refers to a pin, but it may also mean brooch, clasp, or buckle. See also prēon.

dalkr: Norway. Old word for pin.

dalmatic: See dalmatica.

dalmatica: 1. Roman (753 B.C.E.–323 C.E.). Long, T-shaped garment made of white Dalmatian wool and trimmed with vertical purple bands. Considered effeminate garment. 2. Byzantine (400–1200 C.E.). T-shaped garment worn by both genders, decorated with two vertical stripes reaching from shoulder to hem. One of most important garments of period. 3. Elizabethan (1550–1625 C.E.). Mass vestment of rich fabric. Bishop's version was fringed on both sleeves and sides and worn under chasuble. Deacon's was fringed only on left side and sleeves. Never worn under cope.

dalmatikon: Biblical (unknown–30 C.E.). Hebrew word for dalmatica.

dalmonas: See kišené.

dam boo lau: Bustle (1865–1890 C.E.). United States of America. Chinese Hawaiian term for a cloth vendor.

damas: France. Damask. Also damassé.

damas lisere: Silk damask in which jacquard is outlined in gold.

Damascene lace: Imitation Honiton lace of sprigs and braids joined with corded bars.

damascening: *See* damasking.

damaschino: Renaissance (1450–1550 C.E.). Italy. Monochrome damask with satin ground and sateen pattern.

damasco: 1. Italy. Damask. 2. Portugal. Damask. 3. Spain. Damask.

damascus: *See* damask.

damasellours: *See* damasin.

damasin: Elizabethan (1550–1625 C.E.) to Late Georgian (1750–1790 C.E.). Silk brocaded with metal threads.

damask: Silk, linen, cotton, rayon, or blend fabric in jacquard weave, originally from Damascus, patterned with self-colored foliage and animals. May be all white, piece dyed, or woven in colors.

damaskin: Brocatelle or damask with gold or silver flower patterns.

damasking: Sword blade inlaid with gold or silver.

damassé: To be woven like damask.

damassin: 1. *See* damaskin. 2. Damask or brocade fabric with floral patterns woven in gold or silver threads.

Damast: Germany. Damask.

damast: Holland. Damask.

damer: Palestine. Man's broadcloth jacket.

dameslarrje: Holland. Woman's bootee.

damesmantel: Holland. Pelisse.

Damhirschfell: Germany. Doeskin.

damier: France. Check pattern.

dam-thanh: Vietnam. Light green.

ðan: Vietnam. Red.

dan garagai: Nigeria. Wealthy man's rainy season sandals with raised wooden soles.

dan kura: Nigeria. Wealthy man's handspun indigo cotton turban. The cotton has a glossy surface.

Danakillisches Böcklein: Germany. Dankal goat fur.

dancing clog: Shoe with thin wooden sole for tap dancing.

dancing phoenix bun: China. Woman's hairstyle.

danda: India. A mace, the emblem of power or the eternal order.

dandaprakara: India. A striped silk fabric.

dandine: (1920–1930 C.E.). France. Man's black Shetland wool morning coat worn with striped trousers. Not a popular fashion.

dandizette: Romantic (1815–1840 C.E.). Female dandy of 1816–1820 who stood in Grecian bend.

dandy collar: Deep pointed shirt collar.

dang: China. Crotch of trousers.

dangdong: 1. Borneo. Men's cotton ceremonial shawl. 2. Sarawak. Shawl.

d'Angri: Crinoline (1840–1865 C.E.). In 1858, woman's moire basquine with square bertha.

ðang-ten: Vietnam. Lace.

Danish embroidery: Embroidery from Denmark.

Danish trousers: Bustle (1865–1890 C.E.). United Kingdom. In 1870s, open-legged trouser popular with boys that reached just below the knee. Worn with jacket.

daniyu: India. Studded gold collar.

Danjuro cha: Japan. A bright brown tea color named for actor Ichikawa Danjuro.

dankalia capretto della: Italy. Dankal goat fur.

dankalie: France. Ermine fur.

da-n-katanga: Hausa. Cotton cloth with small amounts of red and black.

dannocks: Late Georgian (1750–1790 C.E.). Heavy gloves.

danpiàn yanjìng: China. Monocle.

dànqing: China. Light greenish blue.

danshichi-goshi: Japan. White and rust checkered pattern.

dansiki: Nigeria. Yoruba man's sleeveless tunic with large armholes and a round neckline.

dantelă: Romania. Lace.

dantelez: France. Breton for lace.

danyi: China. Unlined garment.

dàoguàjinzhong: China. Fuchsia.

darázsolás: Hungary. Smocking.

dārgums: Lithuania. Jewel.

darned lace: Lace with pattern filled in with needlework.

daróc: *See* condra.

darpana: India. The mirror, the emblem of wisdom and illusion.

darpe: Iran. Women's voluminous trousers.

Darro: Crinoline (1840–1865 C.E.). 1. In 1855, mantilla with box-pleated ruffle. Trimmed with ruches of pink taffeta. 2. In 1857, woman's taffeta mantilla with double tabs in front and point in back. The hood had large tassel. It was trimmed with needlework embroidery.

dart: Tapering; stitched tuck in garment.

darzi: India. A tailor.

das: Holland. Cravat; necktie.

dasa: India. A border.

dashiki: Long, loose robe with slit neckline and full sleeves. Derived from Saharan styles.

dasko: Norway. Man's small purse.

dastar: India. Turban of fine muslin worn by Delhi nobles.

dastar boongga: India. Indigo blue turban worn by the warrior class Sikhs.

dastar khana: India. Floorspread.

dastmal: Iran. Unmarried woman's large triangular veil worn over klaw-i jnan. Ends are tied loosely and thrown over shoulders.

date-eri: Japan. Under-collar worn instead of under-kimono.

date-gera: Japan. A straw coat.

datemaki: Japan. An undersash used for a kimono and its undergarment.

datil: Coconut palm whose leaves are used to make rope hats.

datilado: Elizabethan (1550–1625 C.E.). Spain. Date colored.

dauni: India. Chaplet of gold or silver.

dauphiness: Late Georgian (1750–1790 C.E.). United States. Style of women's mantle.

Davao hemp: *See* abaca.

Davy Crockett cap: (1950–1960 C.E.). Coonskin cap with tail in back.

dây bang: Vietnam. Ribbon.

dây giãy: Vietnam. Shoelace.

de Berri: Romantic (1815–1840 C.E.). United Kingdom. Light blue.

de caracolillo: Mexico. Spanish word for purple skirts.

de France: Romantic (1815–1840 C.E.). United Kingdom. Blue.

de frivolité: Late Georgian (1750–1790 C.E.). France. To be touched with frivolity or whimsy.

de lazo: Renaissance (1450–1550 C.E.). Spain. With lacing.

de Roi: Romantic (1815–1840 C.E.). United Kingdom. Light blue.

de todo lazo: Elizabethan (1550–1625 C.E.). Spain. Completely laced.

deacaid: Ireland. Gaelic word for jacket; waistcoat or bodice.

dead Spaniard: Elizabethan (1550–1625 C.E.). Pale grayish tan.

dead white: Gay Nineties (1890–1900 C.E.). In 1894, a white with hint of blue.

dealg: *See* biorān.

dealg-fhuilt: Ireland. Gaelic word for hairpin.

dealg-gualainn: Ireland. Gaelic word for the pin that holds the plaid on the left shoulder.

dearg: Ireland. Gaelic word for crimson.

deargan: Ireland. Gaelic word for red dye.

death lace: Czechoslovakia. Black lace with white outline with three white points in each scallop.

death's head button: Late Georgian (1750–1790 C.E.). Domed button with thread or metal twist.

debajero: Ecuador. Pleated skirt.

deboan: *See* lasoa.

debrum: Portugal. Hem; edging; border.

debutante slouch: (1910–1920 C.E.). Fashionable stance for young women involving hands being placed on hips with pelvis thrown forward, de-emphasizing bustline.

décolletage: Low-cut or décolleté neckline or yoke.

dedo: Nigeria. Tanned sheepskin worn by Wodaabe men as a loincloth.

deerskin: Skin of deer.

deerstalker hat: Tweed hat with peak in front and in back.

defrise: France. To be uncurled.

degenkoppel: Holland. Sword belt.

degenstok: Holland. Sword cane.

deguisement: France. Fancy dress.

degummed silk: Silk from which gum has been removed in hot soap solution.

dehri: India. A disc-shaped earring.

deiji'éé': Navajo. Shirt.

deirge: Ireland. Gaelic word for the color red.

deerstalker hat
See also photospread
(Headwear).

deise: Ireland. Gaelic word for a suit of clothes.

deise-mharcachd: Ireland. Gaelic word for a riding habit.

dekmantel: *See* schoudermantel.

del: Mongolia. Calf-length, surplice-front, belted robe.

delaine: Lightweight, plain weave dress fabric.

delaine wool: From the French, literally "of wool." Originally a high-quality woolen for women's clothing, the term now applies to any plain weave, compactly woven woolen fabric.

delantal: Spain. Apron.

delantal de cintura: Spain. Half apron.

delft blue: Soft medium blue.

delg: Ireland. Old Gaelic word for pin.

Delhi work: India. Embroidery in chain and satin stitches with metal and silk threads.

delinere: Medium quality linen popular in Europe.

delmonas: *See* kišené.

demerara: Raw cotton from Guiana.

demi-castor: Elizabethan (1550–1625 C.E.) to Early Georgian (1700–1750 C.E.). France. Beaver hat made partly of coney.

demicaul: *See* bonnet à barbes.

demiceint: Renaissance (1450–1550 C.E.). France. Worn by women, second belt of hinged metal plaques worn down on hips.

demi-converti: Directoire and First Empire (1790–1815 C.E.). France. Man's outercoat with tall, folded-down collar, sleeves cut full at shoulder, narrow knee-length tails, and cutaway to waist in front. It could be worn with the fronts buttoned back or buttoned up double breasted.

demi-gown: Renaissance (1450–1550 C.E.). Man's short gown worn when riding.

demijambe: Early Gothic (1200–1350 C.E.). France. Armor piece for front of leg.

demi-manche: Half sleeve.

demi-mousseline: France. Very lightweight cotton or linen fabric.

demipauldron: Renaissance (1450–1550 C.E.). Piece of armor for shoulder, used to join body and arm pieces.

demiplume: Medium- or half-length ostrich plume.

demi-surtout: Romantic (1815–1840 C.E.). United Kingdom. In 1818, man's lightweight fitted overcoat.

demi-tablier: Late Georgian (1750–1790 C.E.). France. Short apron.

demi-tunique: Directoire and First Empire (1790–1815 C.E.). France. Woman's three-quarter length, short-sleeved summer jacket.

demi-turban: Directoire and First Empire (1790–1815 C.E.). Soft muslin or gauze scarf worn tied around head in soft bow. Fashionable from 1800 to 1812.

demivambrace: Early Gothic (1200–1350 C.E.). Piece of protective armor worn on forearm on top of mail.

demob: (1940–1949 C.E.). United Kingdom. Man's simple single-breasted, three-pocket jacket.

de-mob suit: (1940–1950 C.E.). United Kingdom. Ready-made suit issued to soldiers who had been demobilized.

demysent: Late Gothic (1350–1450 C.E.). Half girdle worn by women with only front half decorated.

demy-teste: Renaissance (1450–1550 C.E.). United Kingdom. Steel skull-cap.

ðen lánh: Vietnam. Shining black.

dendeki: Palestine. Rusty-red cotton used for women's headdresses.

dengue: Spain. Cape.

dengxinróng: China. Corduroy.

denim: Early Georgian (1700–1750 C.E.) to 20th century. Stout, twill weave, cotton fabric with white fill and navy warp. Name shortened from serge de Nimes.

denkuro-zome: Japan. A fabric with a pattern of balls inside diamonds.

Denmark cock: Late Georgian (1750–1790 C.E.). United Kingdom. Man's tricorne hat with brim cocked up in back and down in front.

Denmark satin: Satin twill weave fabric.

dentalium: A mollusk with a thinly pointed shell. It is used to make beads.

dentelle: *See* passemente.

dentelle Angleterre: France. A cheap tape lace made mainly in Austria.

dentelle Arabe: Tunisia. Edging lace.

dentelle aux fuseaux: France. Bobbin lace.

dentelle cachmire: Bustle (1865–1890 C.E.). In 1867, Cluny-style lace woven of brightly colored wool.

dentelle d'application: France. Lace where decoration is sewn to foundation.

dentelle de Cambrai: Crinoline (1840–1865 C.E.). France. Silk lace made in Cambrai.

dentelle de fil: France. Thread lace.

dentelle de la vierge: France. Wide Dieppe point lace.

dentelle de laine: Crinoline (1840–1865 C.E.). Worsted lace.

dentelle renaissance: France. A form of tape lace.

dentelle torchon: Bustle (1865–1890 C.E.). In 1876, linen lace forming geometric designs.

dentes de loup: Romantic (1815–1840 C.E.). Pointed, serrated trim.

deogir: India. A famous muslin from Deogir.

deraa: Morocco. Man's long, loose shirt of blue cotton with a big pocket.

derby: Crinoline (1840–1865 C.E.) to today. United States of America. Traditionally made from felt, a rigid, dome-shaped hat with a short curled brim. In the United Kingdom, it is referred to as a bowler or bowler hat.

derby

Derby shoe: Boot or shoe with eyelet tabs stitched on top of vamp.

ðerdan: Croatia and Serbia. Necklace.

derekas ing: Hungary. Man's short shirt.

deriband: India. Thin fabric.

derrara: Africa. Man's long, loose blue shirt with large front pocket.

Derby shoe
See also photospread (Foot and Legwear).

derries: India. Cotton dress good made from colored yarns, mostly blue and brown.

dervish tulle: Coarse, shiny, stiff tulle.

desborrador: Ecuador and Guatemala. Person who takes the cloth off the loom.

Desdemona: Crinoline (1840–1865 C.E.). In 1857, woman's cloth cloak trimmed with fringe of jet beads.

desero: India. Thread.

deshilado: Renaissance (1450–1550 C.E.). Spain. Drawn work.

deshret: Egyptian (4000–30 B.C.E.). Red Crown of Egypt; a low cylinder with a point in the center back and a spiral in the center front. It was made of red linen or leather on a frame.

desoy: Early Georgian (1700–1750 C.E.) to Directoire and First Empire (1790–1815 C.E.). United States. Rough silk fabric used for men's clothing.

desplegada: Peru. Thickly pleated skirt.

dessous: France. On a hat, area below brim.

desvadusya: India. A diba silk from Persia.

detachi: Japan. Tight trousers.

detente: Peru. Small piece of embroidered fabric of religious importance.

Dettingen cock: Early Georgian (1700–1750 C.E.) to Directoire and First Empire (1790–1815 C.E.). Man's tricorne with brim equally cocked in front and back.

deuil: France. Mourning.

devadusa: India. A smooth fabric.

devagiru: India. A fine muslin from Devagiri.

devanga: India. A silk cloth.

devanga-cira: India. A brocaded diba silk.

devantiere: Charles I (1625–1660 C.E.) to Restoration (1660–1700 C.E.). France. Woman's riding costume that was split up back.

device: Early Gothic (1200–1350 C.E.) to Late Gothic (1350–1450 C.E.). Distinguishing emblem used to represent person or family.

devil skin: United Kingdom. Corduroy.

Devonshire: Named for the Duchess of Devonshire, to have the lower two ribs removed in order to have a smaller waist.

Devonshire brown: Directoire and First Empire (1790–1815 C.E.). Introduced in 1813, rich reddish brown.

Devonshire hat: Late Georgian (1750–1790 C.E.). In 1783, woman's very large hat with large brim and deep crown.

Devonshire lace: Honiton lace.

dhablo: India. Tie-dyed black woolen veil.

dhammilia: India. An elaborate hairstyle consisting of flowers, pearls, and jewels.

dhanak: India. Narrow silver lace.

dhanush: India. Bow.

dhardi: *See* kināri.

dharmasastra: India. Sanskrit religious laws that include socio-religious clothing prescriptions.

dhautakanseya: India. A bleached silk or raw silk fabric.

dhautapatta: India. A washed silk fabric.

dhautavata: *See* dhota-patta.

dhile paenche: India. Trousers with loose ankle openings.

dhota-patta: India. A bleached silk.

dhotar: *See* dhoti.

dhotara: *See* dhoti.

dhotee: *See* dhoti.

dhoti: 1. Iran. Long loincloth worn wrapped around loins, pulled between the legs, and tucked at the waist. 2. India. Lightweight cotton fabric used for loincloth.

dhumani: India. The color brown.

dhumarai: India. An emerald green fabric.

dhurrie: Thick cotton or wool rug or carpet.

diadem: Crown.

diadem bonnet: Bustle (1865–1890 C.E.). United Kingdom. Introduced in 1869, woman's lace and velvet headdress that formed diadem above forehead and tied with ribbon below chignon.

diadem comb: Romantic (1815–1840 C.E.). United Kingdom. Popular in 1830s, wide curved comb with high ornament shaped like diadem. Worn with evening dress.

diadem fanchon bonnet: Bustle (1865–1890 C.E.). United Kingdom. Popular in 1869, one-inch-wide headdress trimmed with tulle or ruching and aigrette of feathers or flowers. It fastened beneath chin with lappets and satin bow.

diamanté: France. To be set with diamonds.

Diamond dyes: Bustle (1865–1890 C.E.). United States of America. Dyes that required no mordant.

dian: China. Indigo blue.

Diana Vernon bonnet: Bustle (1865–1890 C.E.). United Kingdom. Woman's large, low-crowned, wide-brimmed bonnet.

Diana Vernon hat: Bustle (1865–1890 C.E.). United Kingdom. Woman's country shallow crowned straw hat with wide brim that curved up on one side. It tied under chin with wide ribbons.

diaopí: China. Fur of the marten.

diaper: 1. Byzantine and Romanesque (400–1200 C.E.). Cloth of one color woven in ornamental pattern. 2. Allover repetitive pattern.

diaper cloth: Soft, absorbent, bleached cotton fabric used to make infants' diapers. May be dobby, plain, or twill weave.

diaphane: Thin silk or cotton fabric with transparent design.

diaraogenn: *See* tavancher.

diasper: Early Gothic (1200–1350 C.E.). A silk textile woven from a glossy woof thread.

diaspurum: *See* diasper.

dibahae cin: India. Chinese brocade.

dickey: False shirt front.

didjee: *See* darzi.

Dieppe ground: Simple square mesh ground of twisted threads.

Dieppe point lace: Elizabethan (1550–1625 C.E.) to Late Georgian (1750–1790 C.E.). France. Valenciennes type bobbin lace made in Dieppe, France.

digitalia: Roman (753 B.C.E.–323 C.E.). Gloves.

dikkeh: Palestine. 1. Drawstring used to gather sirwal. 2. Fringed band.

dikky: *See* tikkeh.

dilak bedong: Borneo. Sash.

dilbahar: *See* badshah pasand.

dildo: Restoration (1660–1700 C.E.) to Late Georgian (1750–1790 C.E.). Sausage-shaped curl on man's wig.

dilge: Renaissance (1450–1550 C.E.). Germany. Leg-guard for jousts.

dilhil: Navajo. Jet black.

dillad: 1. Wales. Clothing. 2. France. Breton for clothing.

dilladu: *See* gwisgo.

dīllat: Ireland. Gaelic word for clothing.

dilun: China. Polyester fiber.

dima: 1. Ethiopia. Red. 2. Palestine. Striped cotton fabric used for men's coats.

dimayeh: *See* qumbaz.

dimie: Romania. Homespun thick, woolen drugget used for overcoats and winter clothes.

dimii: Bulgaria. Men's trousers with wide legs, ending below knees. Ornamented on bottom edge.

dimity: India. Semi-sheer, lightweight cotton fabric first made in Damietta. Popularly used for summer dresses, aprons, and pinafores.

din: Bustle (1865–1890 C.E.). United States of America. Chinese Hawaiian term for satin.

dindilliam: India. A type of embroidered fabric.

dinh cúc: Vietnam. Large-head needle.

dinner cap: Directoire and First Empire (1790–1815 C.E.). Woman's white satin and lace cap popular in 1812.

dinner jacket: *See* cowes.

diphera: Crinoline (1840–1865 C.E.). Introduced in 1852, fine soft kid leather used for women's bonnets.

diphtera: Greek (3000–100 B.C.E.). Cloak made from animal skin or thick wool.

diplax: Greek (3000–100 B.C.E.). Woman's version of chloene.

diploidion: Greek (3000–100 B.C.E.). Woman's chiton worn with portion above waist doubled.

Directoire bonnet: Bustle (1865–1890 C.E.). United Kingdom. Popular from 1878 to 1880, woman's bonnet with square, high crown, brim that fitted over the ears and spread out over the forehead.

Directoire coat: 1. Bustle (1865–1890 C.E.). United Kingdom. Popular from 1869 to 1889, woman's ankle-length coat cutaway in front and skirted only in back. 2. Bustle (1865–1890 C.E.). In 1888, day bodice, made single- or double-breasted and cutaway in front and skirted to ankles in back. Had tight, cuffed sleeves. Worn with habit shirt and wide folded sash.

Directoire hat: Bustle (1865–1890 C.E.). United Kingdom. Introduced in 1888, larger version of Directoire bonnet.

Directoire jacket: Bustle (1865–1890 C.E.). United Kingdom. Introduced in 1888, day bodice similar to Directoire coat but made without the skirt.

Directoire knickers: (1910–1920 C.E.). Woman's fitted knickers with elastic waist and knees.

Directoire skirt: Gay Nineties (1890–1900 C.E.) United Kingdom. In 1895, a seven gore day skirt in which the four back gores were fluted. Lined and stiffened with horsehair and measuring 13–18 feet around the hem.

Directoire swallow-tail coat: Bustle (1865–1890 C.E.). United Kingdom. Introduced in 1888, term referring to back of Directoire coat in which the tails were cut with deep center vent.

Director: (1950–1960 C.E.). Man's hairstyle with slight wave on crown.

directory suit: (20th century). Suit with high waist and short cutaway jacket, in the lines of men's suits from Directoire period.

dirge: *See* darzi.

dirndl: Very full skirt like those worn in Tyrolese festival dress.

dirzee: *See* darzi.

disa: Nigeria. A blue striped scarf.

diseño: Spain. Design.

diseño a cuadro: Spain. Checks.

diseño a cuadros escocés: Spain. Plaid.

diseño a rayas: Spain. Striped.

diseño con lunares: Spain. Polka dots.

diseño raya de alfiler: Spain. Pin striped.

diseño tradicional de piñones: Spain. Paisleyed.

disfraz: Spain. Fancy dress.

dish dasha: Iraq. Man's ankle-length white shirt that buttons from neck to waist.

disissik: Indonesia. Sa'dan-Toraja ceremonial head-cloth that is placed on a corpse.

diszmagyar: Romantic (1815–1840 C.E.). Austro-Hungarian Empire. Jewel studded gala costume.

dittos: Late Georgian (1750–1790 C.E.) to 20th century. Term referring to man's suit being cut of one fabric.

dival: Turkey. Goldwork.

dival isi: Turkey. Embroidery formed by couching flat gold strip backwards and forwards over stiff card, giving satin-like effect.

divided skirt: Bustle (1865–1890 C.E.). United Kingdom. Introduced in 1882 by Lady Harbeton for bicycling, short kilted skirt cut to conceal division between legs.

divolgatore: Italy. Blazer.

divorce corset: Romantic (1815–1840 C.E.). United Kingdom. Introduced in 1816, padded metal triangle in woman's corset which pushed between the breasts to separate them.

divyasudha: India. A good quality starch.

diyugi: United States of America. Navajo term for serape-shaped blankets made for everyday use. Loosely woven of thick, soft yarns.

diz: *See* kalets.

dizge: Turkey. Flat textile woven as a long, narrow belt.

djebba: Tunisia. Summer version of the kadroun.

djedda: Bustle (1865–1890 C.E.). Introduced in 1866, poil de chevre with silk spots.

djéli: Greece. White embroidery along the chemise hem.

djellaba: Morocco. Three-quarter length cloak.

djersa: Woolen fabric used for jerseys.

djnne-djnne: Timbuktu. A woman's hairstyle with a queue in front and another in back. It is trimmed with beads and silver triangles.

djore: Tibet. A pendant shaped like a thunderbolt.

djorro-marabu: Timbuktu. A line of hair left on a man's shaven head.

djubba: Algeria. Jewish woman's ankle-length gown.

dlùth: Ireland. The warp of fabric.

do: Vietnam. Dark blue colored.

dò choé: *See* dò chói.

dò chói: Vietnam. Bright red.

dò chót: *See* dò chói.

ðò orí: Vietnam. Dark red.

ðõ sô gai: Vietnam. Mourning clothes.

do twarzy: Poland. Face powder.

dobby cloth: Any fabric woven on a dobby loom.

doblados todos: Renaissance (1450–1550 C.E.). Spain. Lined throughout.

dobladura: Spain. Fold.

dobuku: Japan. Outer garment worn over armor.

dochu-gi: Japan. Traveling cape.

docrease: India. Striped muslin.

dodo: 1. Sudan. Woman's sarong. 2. Indonesia. Sa'dan-Toraja woman's skirt.

dodot: Indonesia (Java). Skirt cloth four times the size of a kain. Worn draped and folded as an overskirt by officials and members of the court.

dodowa: Ashanti. Bobbin.

doeskin: 1. Very smooth, tightly woven, fine quality woolen fabric made from merino wool. 2. Heavyweight, twill weave cotton fabric finished with short nap on one side. 3. Suede-finished leather from sheep and lamb skins. 4. Leather made from skin of the doe.

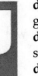

dofuku

dofuku: Japan. Samurai's outer garment.

dog collar: Wide necklace worn snug around neck.

dogaline: Early Gothic (1200–1350 C.E.) to Elizabethan (1550–1625 C.E.). Italy. Venetian fashion featuring a straight, loose gown with wide sleeves. The lower edge of sleeve was pinned up to the shoulder, revealing undergown sleeve.

dogi: Japan. A sleeveless coat.

dogskin: Elizabethan (1550–1625 C.E.) to Late Georgian (1750–1790 C.E.). Heavyweight sheepskin leather used for hunting or hawking gloves.

đôi bít-tất: Vietnam. Pair of socks.

đôi bông: Vietnam. Pair of earrings.

Doitsu ahina: United States of America. Hawaiian term for blue denim imported from Germany.

dolaktanka: Bulgaria. Short-sleeved coat.

dolama: Bulgaria. Long-sleeved coat that opens in front.

doll hat: (1930–1940 C.E.). United States of America. Introduced in 1938 by Schiaparelli, tiny explosion of flowers and feathers held on the head by ribbon that tied under chin.

Dolly Varden bonnet: Bustle (1865–1890 C.E.). United Kingdom. Popular from 1868 to 1889, woman's beaver bonnet that tied with ribbon and was trimmed with crystal and silver bird.

Dolly Varden cap: Bustle (1865–1890 C.E.). United Kingdom. Popular in 1888, small cap of gathered lace and ribbon worn with teagown.

Dolly Varden dress: Bustle (1865–1890 C.E.). United Kingdom. Popular from 1868 to 1889, revival version of panniered polonaise gown of Georgian periods.

Dolly Varden hat: Bustle (1865–1890 C.E.). United Kingdom. Worn from 1871 to 1875, woman's low crowned, wide brimmed, straw hat with minimal trim that was worn at forward angle and tied under chignon with ribbon.

Dolly Varden polonaise: Bustle (1865–1890 C.E.). United Kingdom. Introduced in 1871, chintz or cretonne polonaise gown worn with bright silk petticoat

that was flowered or quilted. Winter version of flannel or cashmere printed in chintz pattern. Favored by middle and lower classes.

dolman: Romantic (1815–1840 C.E.). Austro-Hungarian Empire. Coat or jacket that was worn under mente. Cut straight from shoulder seams or fitted to waist from which it flared out. Fastened with loops and buttons.

dolman sleeve: Sleeve very wide at armseye, fitted at wrist.

dolmanette: Gay Nineties (1890–1900 C.E.). Crocheted dolman that tied at neck with large ribbon bow.

doloman: Russia. Hussar jacket.

Dom pedro: Brazil. Heavy work shoe.

domette: Crinoline (1840–1865 C.E.). Loosely woven flannel with cotton warp and woolen weft.

domino: Early Georgian (1700–1750 C.E.). Cloak, often black, that was worn to masquerades.

donariere: Bustle (1865–1890 C.E.). France. Introduced in 1869, woman's round hood of quilted satin with sleeved pelerine.

dolman sleeve

Doncaster riding coat: Crinoline (1840–1865 C.E.). United Kingdom. Worn in 1850s, man's loose Newmarket coat.

donegal: Originally thick homespun woolen fabric from Donegal, Scotland. Now any tweed with colorful thick slubs woven in irregularly.

đông-hồ đeo tay: Vietnam. Wristwatch.

đông-ho quá quít: Vietnam. Pocket watch.

Dongola kid: Sheep, goat, or kangaroo skin.

doni: Nigeria. A gown worn by the chief. It has four studs for closure.

donje rublje: Bosnia. Underwear.

donkerblauw: Holland. Mazarine blue.

donn: Ireland. Gaelic word for brown.

donn laugh-na-h-éilde: Ireland. Fawn brown.

Donna Maria: Romantic (1815–1840 C.E.). Long sleeve that was full to elbow and fitted to wrist.

donn-ghlas: Ireland. Gaelic word for ash colored.

donn-uaine: Ireland. Gaelic word for an olive brown color.

donsu: Japan. Silk satin damask.

don't mentions: *See* unmentionables.

dooputty: India. Dupatta.

dootl'izh: Navajo. Blue.

dop: *See* knoop.

dopairi: India. Indoor cap or two half-moon shapes sewn together.

dopatta: India. Silk or muslin scarf that is often decorated with gold or silver threads.

dorado: Yellowish orange.

doramché: Bulgaria. Sleeveless clat.

doré: France. Golden.

dorea: *See* doriya.

dorelet: Early Gothic (1200–1350 C.E.). Hairnet embroidered with jewels.

dori: India. Thread or chain stitch.

doria: 1. India. Cotton fabric with stripes of various widths. 2. Swahili. Colored muslin.

doric chiton

doric chiton: Greek (3000–100 B.C.E.). Worn by all Greek women after sixth century B.C.E., wool chiton with upper edge folded down over breast. Folded around one side of the body, pinned at shoulders, and held in place with girdle. Often dyed indigo, madder, or saffron. In Corinth and Attica, sewn together down side below waist.

dorina: Bosnia. Checkered cloak that covers wearer from head to toe.

doriya: India. Striped or checked fine muslin.

dormeuse

dormeuse: Late Georgian (1750–1790 C.E.). Soft ladies' cap with ruched border that fitted the head snugly, covering the cheeks. Held on with ribbon that tied on top of the head. For day, it had pinners and brim that turned up at the nape.

dormilonas: Peru. Fourteen carat gold filigree earrings.

dormouse: *See* dormeuse.

dornag: Ireland. Gaelic word for a glove or gauntlet.

dorneck: Renaissance (1450–1550 C.E.). United Kingdom. Linen fabric made in Norfolk used for servant's clothes.

dornick: 1. France. Any fabric made in Tournai. 2. Scotland. Damask-like fabric made in Dornoch.

dorn-nasq: Ireland. Gaelic word for a bracelet.

dorretteen: Directoire and First Empire (1790–1815 C.E.). Made in Norwich, silk and wool twist with thin invisible stripes introduced in 1792.

d'Orsay coat: Romantic (1815–1840 C.E.). United Kingdom. Introduced in 1838, man's overcoat shaped like a pilot coat but fitted at waist with a long dart. Slashed or flapped pockets in knee-length skirts and no pleats, folds, or hip buttons. The plain sleeves trimmed with three or four horn or gambroon buttons.

d'Orsay pump
See also photospread
(Foot and Legwear).

d'Orsay pump: Romantic (1815–1840 C.E.). In 1830s, shoe with cutaway sides and low, wide heel.

d'Orsay roll: Romantic (1815–1840 C.E.). United Kingdom. In late 1830s, high beaver hat had full rolling brim named for Count Gabriel d'Orsay (1801–1852).

Dorset thread button: Early Georgian (1700–1750 C.E.) to Romantic (1815–1840 C.E.). Underwear button made on brass wire ring covered in white cotton threads that radiated out from center.

dorsetteen: Early Georgian (1700–1750 C.E.) to Late Georgian (1750–1790 C.E.). Fabric with worsted warp and silk weft.

dorso: Renaissance (1450–1550 C.E.). Italy. Back of the gauntlet.

dos: Renaissance (1450–1550 C.E.). Spain. Back-plate of a cuirass.

dosan-banntraich: Ireland. Gaelic word for a braid.

doschella: Hindu. Long shawl.

doshala: India. Pair of shawls.

doshāllā: India. Round skirted court robe that tied on the right side.

doso: Ashanti. Fiber kilt.

dosooty: *See* do-suti.

dossière: Renaissance (1450–1550 C.E.). France. The back-piece of the cuirass.

do-suta: *See* do-suti.

do-suti: India. Cheap cotton woven with doubled threads.

doti: India. Coarse cotton cloth woven by Dhers.

dotted swiss: *See* swiss muslin.

dotted Venetian bars: Venetian bars with French knots.

dou: China. Pocket.

dou bo: China. Qing dynasty. Cape, originally made of palm fiber and hemp.

dou dou: China. Qing dynasty (1644–1911 C.E.). Han woman's cotton or silk, small triangular upper body garment. Covered the breasts and stomach. Held on with silver chain or tape. Often embroidered.

dou niu: China. Under Zhengde emperor (r. 1505–1521), first rank of embroidery on gowns; three or four clawed dragons with downward curving horns.

dou wu: China. Zhuong dynasty. Helmet.

douanier: Bustle (1865–1890 C.E.). In 1879, shade of blue.

double: Renaissance (1450–1550 C.E.). United Kingdom. To be lined.

double bouffant sleeves: Romantic (1815–1840 C.E.). United Kingdom. Popular from 1832 to 1836, woman's short puffed evening sleeve with horizontal band dividing it into two puffs. Revived in 1855 as day sleeve with band placed just above the elbow.

double cuff: Shirt cuff turned back to make two cuff thicknesses.

double damask: Fine linen, cotton, or rayon and cotton damask.

double ikat: Indonesia. Ikat process requiring the binding and dyeing of both warp and weft threads.

double knit: Firm, often reversible, fabric made on special loom with double set of needles.

double-face satin: Satin fabric with two warps and one weft which create satin effect on both sides of fabric.

doublet: Renaissance (1450–1550 C.E.) to Restoration (1660–1700 C.E.). Variety of gambesson made in rich cloth. Began in military and later worn by civilians. Sixteenth and seventeenth centuries, standard man's garment. *See also* pourpoint.

doublure: France. Lining.

doublure du chapeau: France. Hat lining.

doudoukur: China. Child's sun suit.

doudu: China. Baby bib. Also called tou-tu.

douillette: 1. Directoire and First Empire (1790–1815 C.E.). France. Woman's winter quilted pelisse. 2. Romantic (1815–1840 C.E.). By 1830s, redingote with caped pelerine of merino, cashmere, or satin, made with wide sleeves.

douillette à la Russienne: Directoire and First Empire (1790–1815 C.E.). France. Woman's cloak with warm, usually wadded, lining fashionable after 1802.

doulì: China. Bamboo hat.

doupeng: China. Cape.

doupion: Silk thread made from two cocoons. Thread is irregular and thick. Used in slubbed fabrics.

douzi: China. Pocket.

dowlas: Elizabethan (1550–1625 C.E.). Coarse linen from Brittany used by lower classes for shirts and smocks.

downy calves: Late Georgian (1750–1790 C.E.). United Kingdom. False pads worn by men in appropriate places in tights to produce more attractive legs.

DPM: (1970–1980 C.E.). Scotland. Literally "disruptive pattern material," a camouflage fabric used to make military uniforms.

draad: Holland. Thread.

drab: Early Georgian (1700–1750 C.E.). Thick, strong, wool fabric in dull brown or gray color.

drab style: Directoire and First Empire (1790–1815 C.E.). From 1800 to 1810, the muted colors of pale browns, olives, and yellows that predominated women's fashion.

drabbet: United Kingdom. Coarse linen fabric in drab color.

drabužis: Lithuania. Clothing.

draft: *See* amen.

dragocennost': Russia. Jewel.

dragon's blood cane: Early Georgian (1700–1750 C.E.). Man's cane made from frond stems of the Dragon Palm from Malay.

dragoonka: Russia. Dragoon cap introduced under Alexander III. The name was shortened from dragoonskia shapka.

dragoonskia shapka: *See* dragoonka.

dragulj: Croatia and Serbia. Jewel.

drahokam: *See* klenot.

drana: *See* vadmala.

drap: 1. Soft, silky wool twill. 2. France. Cloth.

drap d'Alma: France. Twilled fabric.

drap d'Argent: France. Cloth of silver.

drap de Berry: France. Woolen fabric made in berry.

drap de billard: France. Baize.

drap de France: Bustle (1865–1890 C.E.). France. Introduced in 1871, double twilled cashmere.

drap de Paris: Crinoline (1840–1865 C.E.). France. Introduced in 1860, very fine soft fabric.

drap de soldat: Bustle (1865–1890 C.E.). In 1878, very heavy cloth.

drap de velours: Crinoline (1840–1865 C.E.). France. Introduced in 1861, thick soft velvet-like fabric.

drap de Venice: Bustle (1865–1890 C.E.). France. Introduced in 1866, ribbed poplin.

drap d'eté: France. Literally "cloth of summer," light twill weave woolen fabric.

drap d'or: France. Cloth of gold.

drap feutre: France. Felt cloth.

drap fourreau: Bustle (1865–1890 C.E.). France. Introduced in 1867, thick smooth fabric with plush face on one side.

drap laitiere: Bustle (1865–1890 C.E.). In 1874, striped woolen fabric.

drap o drapé: Italy. Drap.

drap ou drapé: France. Drap.

drap roulier: Bustle (1865–1890 C.E.). In 1874, woolen fabric.

drapanos rubai: *See* drabuzis.

Drapé: Germany. Drap.

drape cut: (1930–1940 C.E.). United Kingdom. The broad shouldered, high belted men's suits popularized by Frederick Scholte, tailor to the Prince of Wales. This fashion was later renamed the American cut.

drapi: India. 1. Woman's embroidered coat. 2. A close-fitting embroidered vest worn by both sexes. 3. Cloak.

drapo: Italy. Silk cloth.

drappus: *See* textum.

drawboys: Early Georgian (1700–1750 C.E.) to Late Georgian (1750–1790 C.E.). Figured materials made on looms where treadles were run by boys.

drawers: Renaissance (1450–1550 C.E.) to 20th century. Undergarments worn by both genders made from linen or hide.

drawings out: *See* pullings out.

drawn bonnet: Woman's bonnet made by gathering fabric over hoops of cane, reed, or wire.

drawn seams: Seams that have been lapped and stitched down.

drawn thread work: A technique in which threads are removed from the ground to form an open weave fabric.

drawers
Dover Publications

drawn work: Elizabethan (1550–1625 C.E.) to 20th century. Form of linen decoration where threads are removed. *See also* lacis.

dreach-bhuidhe: Ireland. Gaelic word for "beautifully yellow."

dreadnought: Heavy, unattractive, woolen fabric used for outer garments.

dreas: Ireland. Gaelic word for dress.

drebe: *See* vadmala.

drebes: Lithuania. Clothing.

drebnieks: Lithuania. Tailor.

dreieckige Faltung: Germany. Handkerchief folded so that only one corner appears out of the pocket.

Dreispitz: Germany. Tricorn.

Dresden point lace: Germany. Drawn work made in Dresden on ground of fine linen.

Dresden silk: Silk fabric decorated with small floral effects.

Dresden work: Late Georgian (1750–1790 C.E.). Muslin with drawn thread embroidery. It was stronger than lace so was used for garments in daily use.

dress clip: Crinoline (1840–1865 C.E.). United Kingdom. In 1840s, metal hook was attached to waist of many women's garments. From the hook hung a chain with clip at end to hitch up skirt when walking. Often in shape of Negro's head.

dress elevator: *See* porte-jupe pompadour.

dress flannel: Napped woolen fabric.

dress holder: Bustle (1865–1890 C.E.). United Kingdom. In 1870s, fancy dress clip with two chains and clips.

dress improver: Bustle (1865–1890 C.E.). Small bustle in 1880s.

dress linen: Firm, plain weave linen fabric.

dress lounge: Bustle (1865–1890 C.E.). United Kingdom. Worn after 1888, man's informal evening jacket worn only when ladies were not present.

dress protector: Crinoline (1840–1865 C.E.) to 20th century. United Kingdom. From 1840s, crescent shaped piece of fabric sewn into bottom of armseyes to prevent sweat stains.

dreumelthoelje

dress Wellington: Romantic (1815–1840 C.E.) to Crinoline (1840–1865 C.E.). United Kingdom. Worn from 1830 to around 1850, man's evening dress boot that resembled slipper and stocking made in one piece. It reached to just below knee.

dresse: *See* clothe.

dreumelthoelje: Elizabethan (1550–1625 C.E.). Holland. A brimless hat similar to a fez.

drilbu: Tibet. A pendant shaped like a tiny bell.

dríli: Greece. Cotton material used to make everyday clothing.

drill: Stout twill weave linen made from coarse yarns.

drillette: United Kingdom. Satin weave cotton fabric.

driubhlach: Ireland. Gaelic word for cowl.

driving-cape: *See* Albert driving-cape.

drobé: Lithuania. Fine linen cloth.

drògaid: Ireland. 1. Drugget. 2. Linsey-woolsey. 3. Russet.

droghette: Italy. Droguet.

droguet: Directoire and First Empire (1790–1815 C.E.). Coarse wool fabric with cotton, silk, or linen warp. Used formerly for coarse clothing, petticoats, and coats.

droguete: Portugal. Droguet.

droineach: Ireland. Gaelic word for a ragged garment.

Droop Snoot: *See* Flying Saucer.

drugget: *See* droguet.

druid's cloth: Rough, basket weave fabric similar to monk's cloth.

druin: Ireland. Gaelic word for needlework or embroidery.

drum farthingale: *See* farthingale.

Drummond: United Kingdom. Twill weave worsted.

du Barry corsage: Crinoline (1840–1865 C.E.). United Kingdom. Introduced in 1850, woman's evening dress fashion with ruching reaching from shoulders to form under-stomacher.

du Barry sleeve: Crinoline (1840–1865 C.E.). United Kingdom. Introduced in 1850, woman's large day sleeve with bouffant above elbow and one above wrist.

dual: Ireland. Gaelic word for a lock of hair.

dualadh: Ireland. Gaelic word for embroidery.

duàn: China. Satin.

duandàyi: China. Short overcoat.

duantongxue: China. Ankle boots.

duànwén: China. Satin weave.

duànzi: China. Satin.

dubbahah: Palestine. Tassel.

dubhach: Ireland. Gaelic word for black dye.

dubh-bhuidhe: Ireland. Gaelic word for a dark yellow.

dubh-ghlas: Ireland. Gaelic word for dark gray.

dubh-ghorm: Ireland. Gaelic word for dark blue.

dubh-ruadh: Ireland. Gaelic word for dark red.

ducape: Corded silk fabric.

duchess: Restoration (1660–1700 C.E.). Ribbon bow worn on fontange.

Duchess: Crinoline (1840–1865 C.E.). In 1854, woman's plain cloak trimmed with velvet strips.

duchesse: Heavy, soft fabric.

Duchesse: Crinoline (1840–1865 C.E.). In 1853, gilet-scarf with fitted bodice. Ended in deep knotted fringe.

duchesse lace: A lace similar in look to Honiton, it is a pillow lace made of linen thread.

duchesse pleat: Bustle (1865–1890 C.E.). United Kingdom. Introduced in 1875, series of four box pleats on each side of center back of woman's skirt.

duchesse satin: Lustrous satin weave fabric with plain back.

duchowny: Poland. Jewish scholar's fur cap.

duck: Strong, tightly woven linen or cotton, plain or rib weave fabric. Lighter and finer than canvas.

duck-billed shoes: Renaissance (1450–1550 C.E.). Slipper-like shoes with very wide, square toes.

duck-hunter: Crinoline (1840–1865 C.E.) to present. Man's short, striped linen jacket worn by waiters.

dudda: Ethiopia. Skin skirt for a Sidamo woman.

dudhai kanjai: India. Pearl gray.

dudhia khaki: India. Light slate gray.

duffel: Coarse woolen fabric.

duffer: *See* British warm.

duffle coat: *See* British warm.

dugme: *See* puce.

ðui: Vietnam. Silk; shantung.

duibleid: Ireland. Gaelic word for doublet.

duikerpak: Holland. Diving suit.

duire: Ireland. Gaelic word for dirk.

dukr: *See* klœði.

dukula: India. A woven silk or white fabric.

dukulottariya: India. Upper body garment; wrapper or shawl.

dulamás: Greece. Sleeved festival vest.

dulándle: Hungary. Large white tulle veil with corner embroidered in colored crewel. Worn by brides for first few years of their marriage.

dulápi: Greece. Material that has been beaten with wooden paddles.

dulband: Iran. Local name for Muslim turban.

dulbén: Greece. White cotton kerchief worn on the head.

dulboka pazva: Bulgaria. Deep fold in smock above waist.

dullemoese: Denmark. Nightcap.

duluma: Romania. Man's folk jacket edged with braid.

dun: Dull grayish brown.

dundreary whiskers: *See* dundrearys.

dundrearys: Crinoline (1840–1865 C.E.). Very long men's side whiskers.

ðung: Vietnam. Trouser crotch.

dungaree: 1. India. Coarse calico fabric. 2. Overalls.

dunkelblau: Germany. Blue black.

dunne ochtendjas: Holland. Negligee.

dunniattham: India. A woman's loincloth.

dunstable: Plated straw hat.

dunster: Early Gothic (100–1350 C.E.). United Kingdom. In early 14th century, a broadcloth made in Somersetshire, United Kingdom.

dupattā: India. Mantle or veil.

dura'ah: Palestine. Woman's plain, short-sleeved, front-opening coat. Usually made from cotton, mostly in indigo blue.

durance: Renaissance (1450–1550 C.E.) to Late Georgian (1750–1790 C.E.). United Kingdom. Durable wool fabric made in Norwich.

durazno: Spain. Peach color.

Durene: Trade name for woven or knitted fabrics of mercerized yarns.

Duretta: Trade name for middy twill or jean.

duretty: *See* durance.

durol bedyeli: A hairstyle worn by a widow during the last week of her mourning period.

durol bedyeli puDaaDo: Africa. A hairstyle worn by a bride during the last week of the period of seclusion before entering into marriage.

durol cakaol: Africa. A hairstyle worn by young girls and married women.

durol chuddito: Africa. A hairstyle worn by a widow during her five month period of seclusion.

durol pila dorungol: Africa. A hairstyle worn by a young mother during the week following her return to her husband with their newborn.

durol tyeli: Africa. A hairstyle worn by a mother during the three weeks following the naming ceremony of her newborn child.

durol yesool: Africa. A hairstyle worn by little girls.

duroy: Early Georgian (1700–1750 C.E.). Coarse wool fabric similar to tammy.

durra'a: *See* dura'ah.

durzi: Palestine. Indigo dyed cotton fabric used for women's dresses.

dusa: India. Woolen chaddar.

dushagreia: Russia. Woman's embroidered, padded jacket of brocade or velvet.

dushegreya: Russia. Man's short, padded, and lined jacket with long sleeves. Made from scarlet damask or red velvet.

dust gown: Elizabethan (1550–1625 C.E.). Outer gown worn when riding.

dust of Paris: Crinoline (1840–1865 C.E.). Ecru.

dust of ruins: Romantic (1815–1840 C.E.). Color of a squirrel.

dust ruffle: *See* balayeuse.

duster: Long, lightweight coat.

dusya: India. A costly woolen cloth.

Dutch blue: Shade of blue lighter and brighter than navy.

Dutch bonnet: Directoire and First Empire (1790–1815 C.E.). United States of America. Straw bonnet fashionably worn turned up in front and back after 1802.

Dutch cap: Holland. Lace or embroidered muslin cap with point at top and wings that flare away at sides.

duster

Dutch cap

Dutch cloak: Elizabethan (1550–1625 C.E.). United Kingdom. Man's short cloak with wide sleeves. Often heavily trimmed with braids.

Dutch collar: Narrow, close fitting collar.

Dutch lace: A misnomer for a dense Flemish bobbin lace.

Dutch neckline: Neckline cut two inches below throat.

Dutch skeleton dress: Romantic (1815–1840 C.E.). United Kingdom. Popular fashion for young boys consisting of a high-waisted coat, ankle-length trousers, and frilled collar. There were three vertical rows of buttons on the coat.

Dutch waist: Elizabethan (1550–1625 C.E.). United Kingdom. Worn from around 1580 to 1620, woman's bodice with square cut waist that was worn with wheel farthingale.

dutis: Spain. Dhoti.

dutty: Elizabethan (1550–1625 C.E.). Fine cloth.

duvetina: Spain. Duvetyne.

duvetine: *See* duvetyn.

duvetyn: Soft, twill weave fabric with suede on one side.

Duvillier wig: Early Georgian (1700–1750 C.E.). Man's long, high dress wig.

dux collar: Crinoline (1840–1865 C.E.) to 20th century. United Kingdom. Worn from 1860s, man's shallow standing collar with corners turned down in front.

dux collar

dvipadi: India. Trousers.

dwete 'ka: Ashanti. Silver bangles.

Dynel: Trade name for acrylic.

dzaan: Tiv. Woman's cloth of narrow stripes alternating colors, like black and white.

dzákos: Greece. Small vest or bodice worn over the chemise.

dzep: Croatia and Serbia. Pocket.

dZi bead: Tibet. A bland and white or dark brown bead of etched or treated agate.

E

e sa: Bustle (1865–1890 C.E.). United States of America. Chinese Hawaiian term for a thin woolen material popular with both sexes. It was rather expensive and was used for chun sams.

'ea malani: United States of America. Hawaii. Light brown.

'ea 'ula: United States of America. Hawaii. Wine colored.

eabonach: Ireland. Gaelic word for ebony colored.

ēadach: Ireland. Clothing.

ēaduighim: See cōirighim.

eaglewood brown: China. Yuan dynasty. Shade of brown.

ear string: Elizabethan (1550–1625 C.E.). Eccentricity of period, black string worn through hole in left ear and hung on shoulder.

earcap: Cap with tabs that cover the ears.

eared shoe: Renaissance (1450–1550 C.E.). Square-toed shoe.

earlet: Obsolete name for earring.

earlock: Lock of hair worn by ear.

earradh: Ireland. Gaelic word for clothing.

earthquake dress: Late Georgian (1750–1790 C.E.). United Kingdom. Following two earthquakes in London in March 1750, fashion developed for warm gowns to wear outside overnight in case of a third earthquake.

Easter bonnet: New hat worn on Easter Sunday.

eau de veau: Directoire and First Empire (1790–1815 C.E.). United States of America. Cosmetic used in 1808.

ebbelo: Morocco. Thin white face-veil.

ebo: Japan. A man's small black cap.

ebolo: Nigeria. Cloth used in funerals.

ebomvu: Rhodesia. Ndebele term for the color red.

ebon: Black.

eboni: See 'eponi.

eboshi: Japan. A nobleman's stiff black hat.

ebosi: See ebo.

ebu: Nigeria. A gown worn only by the king.

eburneo: Spain. Ivory color.

ecaille work: France. Decorative needlework that used quill pieces sewn on fabric to resemble scales.

écarlate: France. Scarlet.

ecarlate blanches: Early Gothic (1200–1350 C.E.). Pale crimson.

eccelide: Romantic (1815–1840 C.E.). Introduced in 1837, cashmere and silk blend fabric, chiné and striped.

echancre: France. To be slashed.

echarpe: France. Scarf worn wrapped around a hat.

echelle: France. Ladder-like motif, like lacing on a woman's bodice.

echelon: Restoration (1660–1700 C.E.). France. Worn on ladies' stomacher, these bows graduated in size from top to bottom gradually getting smaller.

echizen: Japan. High quality silk dress fabric.

ecorce: Bustle (1865–1890 C.E.). Bark color.

ecossais: France. Two-color fabric woven in lengthwise, alternating satin stripes and plain weave stripes.

écossaise hat: Crinoline (1840–1865 C.E.). Scotland. Woman's hat cut higher in front than in back. Ribbon hangs down back.

ecrouellique: Directoire and First Empire (1790–1815 C.E.). France. Woman's cravat.

ecru: Color of unbleached cotton.

ecru silk: Unbleached silk.

ecureuil: France. Imitation sable.

edau: Wales. Thread.

eddimō: Ethiopia. King's green cloak ornamented with gold and silver.

Edelmarder: Germany. Marten.

edged Venetian bars: Variation of Venetian bars.

Editor: (1950–1960 C.E.). Man's hairstyle with high side part, both sides swept up.

Edo kanoko: Japan. A purple painted kanoko.

eel skirt: Gay Nineties (1890–1900 C.E.). United Kingdom. In 1899, a woman's day skirt that was cut on bias into five gores. All the gores except the center front had circular hems. It fastened in front or on side and was fitted over the hips and flared to ground.

eelskin sleeve: Elizabethan (1550–1625 C.E.). Woman's close fitting sleeve. Fashionable again in 1880 and 1881.

eelskin trousers: Bustle (1865–1890 C.E.). In 1880s, very tight trousers worn by dandies.

een broek: Holland. Pair of trousers.

'éétsoh 'álts'íígíí: Navajo. Jacket.

effronter: France. Decorative patch worn on nose.

'efu 'efu: Samoa. Gray color.

egasuri: Japan. A pictorial kasuri.

egeni bitte: Ibo. Cloth made of broad strips in various shades of blue.

eggplant: Bronze purple.

eggshell: Yellowish white.

eglantine: Crinoline (1840–1865 C.E.). In 1853, a cloak that was semi-fitted in the body. Lined with silk.

egret: Plume of egret or heron.

Egyptian brown: Directoire and First Empire (1790–1815 C.E.). United Kingdom. Brown.

Egyptian cloth: Bustle (1865–1890 C.E.). Introduced in 1866, soft silk and wool blend fabric.

Egyptian cotton: Egypt. Long-staple, fine, strong, brownish cotton.

Egyptian indigo: Indigo dye from the shrub *Cracca apolinea* in southern Europe.

Egyptian lace: Knotted lace, often beaded.

eha: Namibia. Man's back ornament of leather, metal, and beaten wire.

éhuáng: China. Light yellow.

ehuatl: Mexico. Aztec military garment covered with feathers.

ei: Japan. The streamer on a nobleman's hat.

Eichhörnchen: Germany. Squirrel fur.

éideadh: Ireland. Generic term for clothing.

eiderdown: 1. Soft down from breast and body of eider duck. 2. Lightweight fabric, knitted or woven with nap on one or both sides.

eillets panaches: Bustle (1865–1890 C.E.). In 1880, a dress where the skirt was covered with alternating narrow pleated flounces of two colors.

eip'uron: Korea. Apron.

eis wool: Fine, glossy, wiry woolen yarn used for scarves.

Eisenhower jacket: (1940–1949 C.E.). United States of America. Man's khaki waist-length military jacket with convertible collar, shoulder yoke, front-opening banded waist, and long, cuffed sleeves. Popularized by General Eisenhower during World War II and worn by civilians after the war.

Eisenkappe: Renaissance (1450–1550 C.E.). Germany. Skull-cap of steel.

ekavali: India. Single string of pearls necklace.

ekaveni: India. Woman's single long braid.

ekawa: Japan. Painted leather.

'ekemau'u: United States of America. Hawaii. Burlap.

eko: *See* lafun.

ekpe cloth: *See* ukara.

el costal: Mexico. Zoque Indian woman's wraparound skirt worn with a large fold (la bolsa) in front.

elastic: Cording, thread, or fabric woven from India rubber.

elastic hat: *See* opera hat.

elastic net: *See* flexible net.

elastic-sided boots: Romantic (1815–1840 C.E.). In 1836, shoes with gussets of elastic on each side.

elatch: Restoration (1660–1700 C.E.). India. Striped silk.

elatcha: *See* elatch.

elbas: Palestine. Women's early pants of thick handwoven cotton. Lower legs were richly embroidered.

Elbert Hubbard tie: Dark tie about nine inches wide and cut on bias that was worn tied like a Windsor tie.

elbow cloak: Renaissance (1450–1550 C.E.) to Elizabethan (1550–1625 C.E.). Man's short cloak.

elbow cuff: Early Georgian (1700–1750 C.E.). Woman's turned-back cuff on elbow-length sleeves.

elbow gauntlet: Renaissance (1450–1550 C.E.). Metal or leather glove with cuff that reached to the shoulder.

elbow sleeve: Sleeve reaching to or just below sleeve.

elbow-cops: Renaissance (1450–1550 C.E.). Elbow-pieces of plate armor.

elderberry: Bustle (1865–1890 C.E.). In 1868, gray purple.

eldergreen: Bustle (1865–1890 C.E.). In 1882, dark green.

'ele hiwa: United States of America. Hawaii. Jet black.

electoral cloth: *See* biretz.

electra cloth: Cotton or silk and synthetic blend umbrella fabric.

electrum: Roman (753 B.C.E.–323 C.E.). Amber, the stone.

'ele'ele: United States of America. Hawaii. Black.

'ele'ele kanikau: United States of America. Hawaii. Black crepe worn for mourning.

elegant: France. Fashionable man.

eleganté: France. Fashionable woman.

'ele'i: United States of America. Hawaii. Shiny black.

elek: Bulgaria. Sleeveless jacket.

elephant cloth: Bustle (1865–1890 C.E.). Introduced in 1869, fabric made of twisted flax cord, appearing to have been woven like a basket.

elephant pants: Trousers with very wide legs.

elephant sleeve: 1. Romantic (1815–1840 C.E.). United Kingdom. Appearing around 1830, woman's very large day sleeve made in a light fabric. Majority of fullness hung toward cuff resembling elephant's ear. 2. Crinoline (1840–1865 C.E.). In 1854, large cape on Moldavian mantle.

'eleuli: United States of America. Hawaii. Grayish black.

elevator shoes: Shoes with raised inner sole.

eleven gore ripple skirt: Gay Nineties (1890–1900 C.E.). United Kingdom. In 1895, a woman's 11-gore day skirt that was fitted at hips and full at bottom (up to 20 feet in circumference). Hem was lined and stiffened with horsehair.

Eliottine silk: Knitting silk.

ell: Measurement of length often applied to fabric. Varied from country to country, hence in United Kingdom it was 45 inches; in Scotland 37.2 inches; and in the Netherlands 27 inches.

ellementes: Elizabethan (1550–1625 C.E.) to Restoration (1660–1700 C.E.). Worsted fabric.

elliotine silk: Knitting silk.

elliptic collar: Crinoline (1840–1865 C.E.). United Kingdom. Introduced in 1853, patent detachable collar with fronts reaching higher than back.

elminetta: Early Georgian (1700–1750 C.E.) to Late Georgian (1750–1790 C.E.). Thin cotton fabric.

elmo di giostra: Renaissance (1450–1550 C.E.). Italy. Tilting-helm.

elysian: Romantic (1815–1840 C.E.). Woolen fabric with diagonal nap used for overcoats.

embozalada: *See* puntada limeña.

embroidered batiste: Allover embroidered eyelet.

'emelala: United States of America. Hawaii. Emerald.

emerala: *See* 'emelala.

emerald: Bright green.

emeraude: Bustle (1865–1890 C.E.). France. In 1888, deep emerald green.

Emily: Crinoline (1840–1865 C.E.). In 1855, silk mantilla trimmed with shamrock embroidered and sewing-silk fringe.

eminence: 1. Romantic (1815–1840 C.E.). United Kingdom. Color of crushed strawberry. 2. Gay Nineties (1890–1900 C.E.). In 1893, a violet color with splash of red.

eminii: Bulgaria. Flat, stitched leather shoes.

empeines: Renaissance (1450–1550 C.E.). Spain. Bands over the instep of a shoe.

emperor shirt: Crinoline (1840–1865 C.E.). United Kingdom. Worn from 1850 to 1860s, man's red flannel shirt worn by gentlemen in the country.

empire bodice: Bustle (1865–1890 C.E.). United Kingdom. Introduced in 1889, woman's evening bodice that gave appearance of being high waisted by a number of silk scarves being draped across front and tied on side or back.

empire cap: Crinoline (1840–1865 C.E.). In 1860, woman's small bonnet that tied under the chin. It was trimmed with ribbon.

empire jupon: Crinoline (1840–1865 C.E.). United Kingdom. Gored petticoat with two or three steel hoops at bottom; worn from 1850 to 1867.

empire skirt: Bustle (1865–1890 C.E.). United Kingdom. Worn from 1888 to the 1890s, day skirt that gathered at waist and ended with gathered ruffle at hem. For evening, it was ruched at the hem and embroidered with flowers. In 1892, day version had two straight panels in front and two triangular gores on each side. Slightly trained.

Empress: Crinoline (1840–1865 C.E.). 1. In June 1854, silk mantelet cut low in neck. Trimmed with falls of lace and ribbon. 2. In November 1854, velvet pelerine with back box-pleated to yoke. It was elaborately embroidered.

empress cloth: 1. Double faced, twill weave, wool or wool and cotton blend fabric. 2. Calico with red and yellow pattern.

Empress Eugenie hat: Crinoline (1840–1865 C.E.). Popularized by Empress Eugenie for riding and traveling, this hat had a flat crown and a rolled brim with ribbons trailing down the back.

empress gauze: Fine flowered, satin weave fabric with silk gauze ground and linen figures.

Empress pardessus: Crinoline (1840–1865 C.E.). In 1855, cloth or velvet pardessus trimmed with fur. Particularly popular in France.

empress petticoat: Bustle (1865–1890 C.E.). United Kingdom. Introduced in 1866, woman's evening dress petticoat gored at waist, reaching eight yards in circumference at hem with yard long train. It was trimmed with deep flounce above knee and was substituted for the cage crinoline.

en beret: Crinoline (1840–1865 C.E.). France. After 1840, arrangement of woman's hair and cap.

en Cavalier: Crinoline (1840–1865 C.E.). In 1858, woman's riding habit with cavalier style collar and embroidered cambric cuffs. Jacket was trimmed with buttons.

en coeur: France. Heart-shaped neckline.

en colimaçon: Directoire and First Empire (1790–1815 C.E.). France. Woman's hairstyle arranged like a snail.

en coulisse: Crinoline (1840–1865 C.E.). France. After 1840, arrangement of puffs as trim.

en dos d'ane: Late Georgian (1750–1790 C.E.). In 1780, man's hairstyle with ponytail and side pieces.

en échelle de Jacob: Late Georgian (1750–1790 C.E.). France. To be trimmed in shape of Jacob's ladder.

en fourreau lace: Late Georgian (1750–1790 C.E.). France. To be tightly laced to body like sheath.

en manche: Crinoline (1840–1865 C.E.). France. After 1840, to be made with cuffs.

en Marquise: Crinoline (1840–1865 C.E.). Square neckline.

en platitude: Late Georgian (1750–1790 C.E.). France. Term meaning ruchings.

en pouf: Late Georgian (1750–1790 C.E.). France. To be tufted.

en pouf à la Luxembourg: Late Georgian (1750–1790 C.E.). France. To be worn in tufted style. Introduced in Luxembourg Gardens in Paris.

en ravanche: Crinoline (1840–1865 C.E.). France. Arrangement of flowers and ribbon worn on head and tilted toward left eye.

en tablier: Crinoline (1840–1865 C.E.). France. To give apron effect.

en tout cas: United Kingdom. Combination umbrella and parasol. It was often brightly colored and without external trim. It had an elaborate handle and plain cover. It was an English invention with a French name that waned in popularity after 1908.

'ena: Samoa. Light brown.

'ena'ena: Samoa. Brown.

'ena'ena mumu: Samoa. Auburn.

enagua: 1. Mexico. Woman's skirt gathered to waistband. Trimmed with flounces or lace. 2. Spain. Slip; petticoat. 3. Ecuador. White cotton petticoat. 4. Mexico. Made by the Zoque Indians, a handwoven huipil.

enagua de lana: Spain. Balmoral petticoat.

enarme: Early Gothic (1200–1350 C.E.). Attachments on back of shield by which it was held to the arm.

enbraude: Early Gothic (1200–1350 C.E.). To be embroidered.

encaje: Spain. Lace.

encaje chantilli: Spain. Chantilly lace.

encaje de aguja: Spain. Needlepoint lace.

encaje de àngel: Spain. Angel lace.

encaje de bolillos: Spain. Bobbin lace.

encaje de Lila: Spain. Lille lace.

encaje de Malinas: Spain. Malines lace.

encaje de malla cuadrada: Spain. Filet lace.

encaje de Milano: Spain. Milano lace.

encaje estrecho de algodón: Spain. Torchon lace.

encaje frivolité: Spain. Tatting lace.

encaje hecho a maquina: Spain. Nottingham lace.

encaje suizo: Spain. Guipure.

encarnado: Renaissance (1450–1550 C.E.). Spain. Reddish.

encerado: Portugal. Oilcloth.

end of the day: Glass canes so named because they were created by glass blowers at the end of the work day.

endima: Morocco. Jewish woman's buckled belt, embroidered with gold thread. Matches color of the dress.

engageantes: Early Georgian (1700–1750 C.E.). France. Lace cuffs with two or three graduated ruffles which were worn commonly on women's gowns.

engkudu: Borneo. Red.

English bars: Long Venetian bars.

English chain: Romantic (1840–1865 C.E.). Chatelaine.

English cottage bonnet: *See* bibi bonnet.

English edging: *See* angleterre.

English embroidery: Fine eyelet embroidery.

English farthingale: Elizabethan (1550–1625 C.E.). Worn from 1580s to 1620s, woman's roll farthingale without any flattening of line in front.

English foot: High fashioned hose with seam on each side of foot.

English gown: Late Georgian (1750–1790 C.E.). Long, simple gown of rich, simple fabric.

English hood: Renaissance (1450–1550 C.E.). Worn from 1500 to 1540s, woman's hood and under cap combination. The hood was wired in front to form pointed arch above the forehead. The under cap completely covered hair after around 1525. The back of hood hung loosely until 1525, when it evolved into two lappets that were sometimes worn pinned up.

English mohair: Bustle (1865–1890 C.E.). In 1871, wiry cotton and wool blend suiting.

English nightgown: Early Georgian (1700–1750 C.E.). Unboned informal dress.

English ringlet: Early Georgian (1700–1750 C.E.). Ringlets worn on either side of the face.

English rosette: Embroidery stitch.

English scarlet: (1930–1940 C.E.). A new color.

English velveteen: Bustle (1865–1890 C.E.). New velveteen.

English work: 1. Byzantine and Romanesque (400–1200 C.E.). Very fine Anglo-Saxon embroidery made from seventh to tenth century. 2. Renaissance (1450–1550 C.E.). United Kingdom. Gold thread embroidery with silk figures.

English wrap: Crinoline (1840–1865 C.E.). In 1840s, man's double-breasted paletot-sac similar to loose Chesterfield.

engreynen: Early Gothic (1200–1350 C.E.). To dye the thread before weaving.

enjoueé: France. Decorative patch worn on fold of mouth when laughing.

enredo: Mexico. Aztec woman's wraparound skirt.

enredos: Mexico. Woman's wrap skirt.

enseigne: France. Pilgrim's badge.

ensign blue: Dark navy blue.

ensign cloth: Plain weave cotton or linen fabric used for bunting and flags.

entre-deux: France. Very narrow insertion lace used in fine lingerie.

entretela: 1. Portugal. Gusset. 2. Spain. Interfacing.

entretela fusible: Spain. Fusible interfacing.

envelope bag: Envelope shaped handbag.

envelope combination: (1910–1920 C.E.). In 1915, a woman's one piece undergarment made with ribbon shoulder straps, drawstring neckline, and button front closure.

envuelto: Guatemala. Wraparound skirt.

eobhrat: Ireland. Gaelic word for headdress.

eolica: Spain. Eolienne.

eolienne: Plain weave, silk and worsted or silk and cotton fabric with cross cord. Similar to poplin but lighter in weight. *See also* aeolian.

eolienne diagonal: Gay Nineties (1890–1900 C.E.). In 1892, an eolienne with diagonal stripes.

'epane: United States of America. Hawaii. Apron.

epanechka: Russia. Short, circular cape worn by women for visits and holidays.

epangeline: Bustle (1865–1890 C.E.). Introduced in 1868, wool rep-like material.

epani: *See* 'epane.

epaules Americaines: Gay Nineties (1890–1900 C.E.). French term for American shoulders.

epaulet: Shoulder ornament intended to widen shoulder line.

epaulet sleeve: Sleeve extended over shoulder.

epauleti: Russia. Epaulets.

epaulette: Shoulder strap of a corset.

épaulière: Early Gothic (1200–1350 C.E.). France. Shoulder piece reaching from backpiece to breastplate in armor.

ephod: Hebrew. Two rectangular pieces of linen roughly 30 inches by 10 inches joined over shoulder with 10-inch-long straps. Worn on top of the robe with girdle similar to those worn by Levites that wrapped around the body and tied in front. Worn by the high priest.

epingeaua: *See* chepeneag.

épingle: France. Pin brooch.

epingle: France. Fine, lustrous, silk fabric that is ribbed or corded.

épingle à chevaux: France. Hairpin.

epingles de nourrice: Gay Nineties (1890–1900 C.E.). In 1891, very large gold-headed pins.

epingline: Silk or rayon and worsted fabric with crepe surface.

epingline chevron soie: Gay Nineties (1890–1900 C.E.). In 1891, plum corded ground with watered design in black and gold.

epingline flotté soie: Gay Nineties (1890–1900 C.E.). In 1891, a brown and red striped fabric with diagonal rows of black and gold.

epingline raye: Crinoline (1840–1865 C.E.). In 1862, tissue with appearance of uncut velvet.

epinglorie brochée: Crinoline (1840–1865 C.E.). In 1862, cotton and wool blend.

epitoga: Roman (753 B.C.E.–323 C.E.). Cloak worn over the toga. Later, it was a wide, unbelted robe with bell sleeves. In 13th century, it reappeared as an academic robe.

epomine: *See* epitoga.

eponge: Soft fabric made with nubby, twisted yarn.

'eponi: United States of America. Hawaii. Ebony.

equipage: Early Georgian (1700–1750 C.E.). Ornamental case that hung from chatelaine and held knife, scissors, thimble, etc.

er: China. Jade or pearl earring.

er dang: China. Pearl or jade ear ornament.

erdif: Berber woman's square anklets.

erhuán: China. Earrings.

eri: 1. Japan. A long collar. 2. India. A type of wild silk produced mainly in Assam.

erinoid: Gay Nineties (1890–1900 C.E.). Introduced around 1897, plastic made from powdered milk.

ermellini: Renaissance (1450–1550 C.E.). Italy. Highly valued fur, ermine. Used primarily on edges of garments like necklines and sleeves.

ermellino: Italy. Ermine.

ermine: 1. Early Gothic (1200–1350 C.E.). Most valued of all furs, reserved by law for royalty. Took its name from Herminia (Armenia). 2. Hide of the *Mustela erminea*, a member of the weasel family with a white coat in winter and a beige coat in summer. The tail of the animal is black.

ešarpa: *See* marama.

esawra: *See* swar.

escaffignons: 1. Byzantine and Romanesque (400–1200 C.E.). In 12th century, light shoe in rich fabric. 2. Renaissance (1450–1550 C.E.). Very tight flat shoes that were slashed on top.

escarelle: *See* aumoniere.

escarlata: Spain. Crimson; scarlet.

escarlata subido: Spain. Hunter's pink.

escarlate: Portugal. Scarlet.

escarpins: Directoire and First Empire (1790–1815 C.E.). Heeled, pointed toed shoes of soft leather.

eschapins: *See* escaffignons.

esclaud: Holland. A wooden shoe, often referred to as a clog, worn in factories, mines, and farms.

esclaud
See also photospread (Foot and Legwear).

esclavage: Late Georgian (1750–1790 C.E.). France. Woman's necklace made of several gold chains that were draped across bosom. Named for resemblance to slave fetters.

esclavina: Spain. Bertha.

esclavine: *See* sclavyn.

esclote: *See* esclaud.

escocés: Spain. Tartan.

escoffion: Late Gothic (1350–1450 C.E.). Tall headdress, sometimes in shape of two horns. Commonly had veil around yard square.

escote: Spain. Neckline.

escote en U: Spain. Scoop neckline.

escuaypiles: Aztec. Manta and cotton fabric.

escudete: Spain. Gusset.

Escurial: Crinoline (1840–1865 C.E.). In 1856, Lyons silk scarf-shawl trimmed with black velvet edged with lace.

esgid: Wales. Shoe.

Eskimo cloth: Heavy napped overcoating fabric in plain colors or broad stripes.

Esmerelda: Crinoline (1840–1865 C.E.). In 1850, fitted silk pardessus trimmed with two rows of lace.

esmoquin: Spain. Tuxedo.

esmouchoir: Fly whisk or fan.

esono: Ashanti. Red dye.

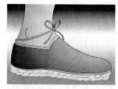

espadrille
See also photospread (Foot and Legwear).

espadrille: Rope-soled shoe with canvas or leather upper. *See also* alpargata.

espartilho de senhora: Portugal. Corset.

esparto: Rough fabric of esparto grass.

espèce d'ouvrage à jour: France. Rickrack.

espécie de jaqueta: Portugal. Spenser.

esprits: Directoire and First Empire (1790–1815 C.E.). France. Aigrettes worn upright in hair or hat; worn after 1802.

espuelas: Ecuador and Guatemala. Barberry.

espulgeata: Renaissance (1450–1550 C.E.). Spain. Defleaed.

espuma: Ecuador and Guatemala. Thread of synthetic material.

esquavar: Late Georgian (1750–1790 C.E.). Prussia. Military closely fitted trousers. They were worn with leather breeches.

esqui: Portugal. Snowshoe.

esquilo: Portugal. Squirrel.

esquirole: Renaissance (1450–1550 C.E.). Spain. Squirrel.

estaches: Late Gothic (1350–1450 C.E.). France. Strings that tied hose to doublet.

estameña: Renaissance (1450–1550 C.E.). Spain. Serge.

estamene: Coarse worsted, loosely woven fabric.

estameya: *See* sobrepantalón rajado.

estamine: Bustle (1865–1890 C.E.). Introduced in 1876, thick serge.

estampado: Portugal. Printed cloth.

esterhazy: Romantic (1815–1840 C.E.). Silver gray.

estofado: Renaissance (1450–1550 C.E.). Spain. Stuffed with cotton.

estofée: Renaissance (1450–1550 C.E.). Spain. Quilted.

estopa: Portugal. Lockram.

estopilla: Spain. Cheesecloth.

estrain: Early Gothic (1200–1350 C.E.). Straw used for hat making.

Estramadura: Crinoline (1840–1865 C.E.). In 1855, full circle cloak trimmed with plush and velvet bands.

estrella: Plain weave, silk crepe.

estrich: *See* estrith.

estridge: *See* estrith.

estrith: Renaissance (1450–1550 C.E.) to Elizabethan (1550–1625 C.E.). Felted material made from ostrich feather down.

északi: *See* haraszt.

ētach: *See* dīllat.

etam: Ashanti. Girl's loincloth.

etamine: Lightweight, open plain weave fabric made from variety of yarns. Made in variety of weights.

etamine broché: Gay Nineties (1890–1900 C.E.). France. In 1896, a semitransparent fabric.

etapi: Namibia. Man's pleated cotton skirt. At one time, it was made of hide.

etibo: Nigeria. A man's long shirt worn with a wrapper or trousers.

ētim: Ireland. Gaelic word meaning to clothe or to dress.

ētiuth: *See* dīllat.

étoffe: France. Cloth. *See also* drap.

étoffe écossaise: France. Plaid.

etoile: Lustrous satin fabric used for dresses.

étole: France. Stole.

Eton cap: United Kingdom. Fitted cap with visor similar to those worn by boys at Eton College.

Eton collar: Large, stiff, turnover collar originally worn by students at Eton College, United Kingdom.

Eton jacket: Bustle (1865–1890 C.E.). United Kingdom. Fashionable for women, a short jacket with lapels, similar to those worn by boys at Eton College.

Etruscan cloth: Bustle (1865–1890 C.E.). Introduced in 1873, rough fabric similar to terry.

Eton collar

etu: 1. Nigeria. Narrow band of finely woven fabric that is dyed deep blue black and used for funerals. 2. Yorube. Natural fiber black cloth speckled with white.

etui: Elizabethan (1550–1625 C.E.). France. Term for equipage that first appeared in 1610.

Eugenie blue: Crinoline (1840–1865 C.E.). Color of a pale cornflower.

Eugenie hat: Crinoline (1840–1865 C.E.). Named for Empress Eugenie, a woman's small hat with brim turned up on left side or on both sides. It was worn trimmed with ostrich plumes and tilted to the right.

Eugenie purse: Crinoline (1840–1865 C.E.). In 1855, woman's small crocheted bag.

Eulalie: Crinoline (1840–1865 C.E.). In 1855, crocheted, tulip-shaped purse.

Eureka: Crinoline (1840–1865 C.E.). In 1857, woman's basque with deep, scalloped flounce that was removable to serve as a shawl.

eventail: France. Fan.

eveque: Gay Nineties (1890–1900 C.E.). In 1897, purple.

everlastings: *See* durance.

ewu: Yorubu beaded garments.

exametum: *See* samite.

exhibition checks: Crinoline (1840–1865 C.E.). United Kingdom. Large checked fabric used for trousers in 1851, the year of the Great Exhibition.

exomia: Greek (3000–100 B.C.E.). Sleeveless chiton worn pinned on one shoulder by athletes and workmen. Often made of sheepskin or leather.

exomide: Greek (3000–100 B.C.E.). Very short sleeveless tunic worn open down right side by lower classes.

express stripes: Strong, warp faced, cotton fabric with equal width stripes of white and dark blue.

external high shoes: China. Ming dynasty. Shoes with exterior wooden soles.

eyelash: Fabric with fringed surface resembling eyelashes.

eyelet doublet: Elizabethan (1550–1625 C.E.). United Kingdom. Doublet of twine or thread knitted all over in eyelets or buttonholes. It resembled macramé or tatting.

eyelet embroidery: Dress fabric characterized by eyelets of other machine-embroidered figures.

ezo nisbiki: Japan. A brocade on a satin ground with the design threads floated across the back of the fabric.

ezor: Biblical (unknown–30 C.E.). Loincloth worn by Jewish men.

F

fa guan: China. Han dynasty (206 B.C.E.–7 C.E.). Judge's headdress.

fa'amalu: Samoa. Umbrella.

fa'amau: Samoa. Button.

fa'ataelama: Samoa. Dark brown.

face: Side of fabric with better appearance.

faces: Directoire and First Empire (1790–1815 C.E.). United Kingdom. Flat lock of hair that outlined the face of dandies.

fachalina: Ecuador and Guatemala. Woman's head-cloth and shoulder wrap.

fachalina de cabeza: Ecuador. A headcloth.

fachallina: Ecuador. A shawl.

facing silk: Lightweight, tightly woven fabric, often imitation silk.

facings: 1. Byzantine and Romanesque (400–1200 C.E.). In 12th century, edging of fur on elegant garments especially when garments were lined with less expensive fur. 2. Early Georgian (1700–1750 C.E.). Long band, often decorated, that trimmed gown à la francaise. It was narrow on the bodice and wider on the skirt. 3. (20th century). Portion of garment that reverses to the inside to bind garment openings, such as armseyes, necklines.

facitergium: Roman (753 B.C.E.–323 C.E.). Handkerchief for wiping the face.

facóli: 1. Greece. Every day. 2. Greece. White cotton band worn tied around the head by newly married women.

faconné: France. To be figured.

Fadam: Germany. Thread.

Faden: Germany. Thread.

faglia: Italy. Faille.

fail: Ireland. Gaelic word for ring or earring. *See also* foil.

faileach-an: Ireland. Gaelic word for earring.

faille: 1. France. Glossy, silk, rib weave fabric with light cross grain. 2. Nun's hood, veil, or scarf that covers head and shoulders.

faille crepe: Crepe with pebbled surface.

faille taffeta: Taffeta with obvious crosswise ribs.

faillette: Gay Nineties (1890–1900 C.E.). In 1898, a soft, rib weave, wool fabric with gloss.

failtean: Ireland. Headband.

faina: Italy. Stone marten.

fāinne: Ireland. Finger ring.

fàinne-pòsaidh: Ireland. Wedding ring.

Fair Isle sweater: United Kingdom. Bright, colorful sweater.

faitheam: Ireland. Gaelic word for hem or the border of a garment.

faixa: Portugal. Belt; ribbon.

faja: 1. Argentina. Worn by gauchos, woolen sash worn wrapped several times around the waist. 2. Ecuador and Guatemala. Cloth belt.

faja rizada: Spain. Shirring.

faja-calzón: Spain. Panty-girdle.

fàjia: China. Hairpin.

fajin: Spain. Sash.

fakhtai: India. Dove gray.

falánróng: China. Flannel.

falbala: 1. Restoration (1660–1700 C.E.). On woman's three-quarter or elbow-length sleeve, the ruffle of lace. 2. *See* Duvillier wig.

Falbel: Germany. Furbelow.

falda: 1. Renaissance (1450–1550 C.E.). Spain. Train of a skirt. 2. Spain. Skirt.

falda combinación: Spain. Half-slip.

falda con peto: Spain. Sun suit.

falda con tabla añadida: Spain. Gored skirt.

falda envuelta: Spain. Wraparound skirt.

falda escocesa: Spain. Kilt.

falda o tesa: Italy. Brim of a hat.

falda-pantalón: Spain. Culottes.

falbala

faldellin: Bustle (1865–1890 C.E.). Peru. In the 1880s, a calf-length skirt.

faldetta: 1. Crinoline (1840–1865 C.E.). Woman's colored taffeta, waist-length mantle with deep lace flounce on hem. It had wide sleeves. 2. Malta. Woman's black silk hood and cap combination. The hood is supported with whalebone, cardboard, or wire to form peak. It is black except in Zabbar and Zeitun where it is blue.

faldia: Renaissance (1450–1550 C.E.). Italy. Linen underskirt that was supported by horizontal bands that were padded with cotton wool or linen.

falding: Early Gothic (1200–1350 C.E.). Coarse wool fabric similar to frieze.

faldita: Spain. Basque.

faldrilla: Renaissance (1450–1550 C.E.). Spain. Underskirt.

Faliero: Crinoline (1840–1865 C.E.). In 1850, woman's cloak trimmed with galloon and twisted fringe.

Falkland Island wool: Rough cheviot wool produced in Falkland Islands.

fall: 1. Ornamental cascade of lace or other fabric. 2. Wiglet. 3. Renaissance (1450–1550 C.E.). Worn with gable headdress, a black silk or velvet bag to conceal the hair. Similar to the cale. 4. Early Georgian (1700–1750 C.E.). Buttoned flap on front of man's breeches or trousers. 5. Directoire and First Empire (1790–1815 C.E.). Loose back piece of woman's hood.

falla contrama crespón: Spain. Tissue faille.

fallaing: Byzantine and Romanesque (400–1200 C.E.). Ireland. Coarse mantle.

fal-lal: *See* falbala.

fallal: Gaudy ornament.

falling band: 1. Elizabethan (1550–1625 C.E.). Wide, flat collar usually of sheer white fabric, with or without lace edging. 2. Charles I (1625–1660 C.E.) to present. Collar with two tabs that hang on breast. Still worn by some Protestant ministers.

falling ruff: Charles I and the Commonwealth (1625–1660 C.E.). Full, unsupported neck ruff.

falluing: Ireland. Gaelic term for a mantle or robe.

falnis: Biblical (unknown–30 C.E.). Hebrew cloak or mantle.

falpalà: Italy. Furbelow.

false front: 1. False bangs. 2. Dickey.

false gown: Early Georgian (1700–1750 C.E.). United Kingdom. Fitted bodice with gathered skirt. It had a ribbon sash that tied in back. Referred to as false gown since it was not open over fancy petticoat, but was all in one piece.

false hips: Early Georgian (1700–1750 C.E.) to Late Georgian (1750–1790 C.E.). United Kingdom. From 1740s to 1760s, women wore side hoops that precursed panniers.

false sleeves: Late Gothic (1350–1450 C.E.). Late 14th-century fashion, wearers began by allowing unbut-

toned part of sleeve to hang freely. Later these narrowed to decorative panels that hung from elbow. These panels were often of contrasting fabric.

falsies: *See* bust forms.

falt-dhealg: Ireland. Gaelic word for hairpin.

fält-teken: Charles I and the Commonwealth (1625–1660 C.E.). Sweden. Military scarves.

faluchos: Spain. Cocked hat.

falwe: Early Gothic (1200–1350 C.E.). Yellow.

famalniya: Biblical (unknown–30 C.E.). Hebrew's leggings.

familla: Oman. Sash.

fan hoop: Early Georgian (1700–1750 C.E.). Pyramid-shaped petticoat that was flat in front and back, forming fan-shaped base for the gown.

fan parasol: Directoire and First Empire (1790–1815 C.E.) to Crinoline (1840–1865 C.E.). United Kingdom. Woman's small parasol with hinge in stick that allowed the fabric end to be tilted up and used as a fan.

fan pleats: Pleats radiating from central point.

fana: Early Gothic (1200–1350 C.E.) to Late Gothic (1350–1450 C.E.). United Kingdom. Generic term for cloth.

fanbù: China. Canvas.

fanchon: Romantic (1815–1840 C.E.). From the 1830s, small head kerchief worn by women. Term later referred to lace trim around the ears on day caps. *See also* half handkerchief.

fanchon cap: Crinoline (1840–1865 C.E.). Woman's lace or tulle cap with ear lappets.

fancies: 1. Charles I and the Commonwealth (1625–1660 C.E.) to Restoration (1660–1700 C.E.). United Kingdom. Popular from 1650s to 1670s, ribbon trim worn on men's breeches. Amount of trim per pair was usually 72 yards, but could be in excess of 250 yards. 2. Any fabric with patterned weave.

fandaráca: Greece. Embroidery design worn by older women.

fandewai: Sierra Leone. White cotton cloth.

Fane: Germany. Cloth.

fanfreluche bodice: Bustle (1865–1890 C.E.). United Kingdom. Introduced in 1888, woman's day bodice that gathered at neck and shoulders and sloped to a point at top of the corset.

fangchóu: China. Soft, plain weave, silk fabric.

fanling: China. Turndown collar.

fantail hat: Late Georgian (1750–1790 C.E.). Tricorne hat with fan-shaped back brim that was cocked to look like fan. Fashionable for riding with both genders.

fantail wig: Early Georgian (1700–1750 C.E.). Wig with ponytail shaped into several curls.

fantasia: Guatemala. Costume jewelry.

fàqia: China. Hairpin.

faraguja: Egypt. Over-robe worn by men in learned professions.

farajiyyat: India. Robe similar to durra.

farala: Spain. Flounce.

farandine: Elizabethan (1550–1625 C.E.) to Restoration (1660–1700 C.E.). Silk and hair or wool blend fabric.

farba: 1. Poland. Dye. 2. Bosnia. Dye.

farda: Portugal. Uniform.

fardegalijn: Elizabethan (1550–1625 C.E.). Holland. Farthingale.

fargal: India. Raincoat.

fargī: India. Short coat worn over the jama.

farmer's satin: Durable cotton or cotton and rayon blend fabric in satin weave used primarily for lining.

farmer's silk: *See* Venetian cloth.

farous: Iraq. Loincloth.

farrajiyah: Morocco. Full coat with very wide, long sleeves.

farrukhshāhi: India. Type of turban.

farthingale: Renaissance (1450–1550 C.E.) to Elizabethan (1550–1625 C.E.). Linen underskirt with wire supports which, when shaped, produced a variety of dome, bell, and oblong shapes. *See also* verdugado.

farthingale breeches: Elizabethan (1550–1625 C.E.) to Late Georgian (1750–1790 C.E.). From 17th to 18th centuries, men's breeches were padded out like farthingale under the theory that they would protect wearer from poniard thrusts.

farthingale sleeves: Elizabethan (1550–1625 C.E.). Large sleeves, head of which were held out with wire, reeds, or whalebone.

fartuch: Poland. Apron.

fartuk: Russia. Apron. *See also* perednik.

fartuszek: Poland. Pinafore.

farwah: United Arab Emirates. Thick sheep wool overcoat.

Fasanerfeder: Germany. Pheasant's feather.

fascia: Roman (753 B.C.E.–323 C.E.). Bands of varying widths worn tied around head, waist, arm, etc.

fasciatrella: Italy. Colored cloth worn over tovaglia.

fascinator: (20th century). Square or triangular head covering for women. Made of silk, lace, net, or other delicate fabrics.

fasgadan: Ireland. Gaelic word for umbrella.

fashion waist: (19th century). Tailoring term for length on man's coat from base of the collar to the waist seam.

fat quarter: One quarter of a square yard of fabric, cut 18 x 22 inches.

fatas: Russia. Beautiful veil of diaphanous silk or cotton. Often embroidered in gold or silver and edged with gold fringe.

Fatima robe: Directoire and First Empire (1790–1815 C.E.). United States of America. Short overgown with elbow-length sleeves that were slit up front and held together with decorative buttons. Fashionably worn over muslin gown in 1800.

fatiota: Portugal. Clothes.

fato: Portugal. Suit of clothes.

fatumar saki: Nigeria. Handspun cotton cap with earflaps.

faufautu: Samoa. Headcloth worn as protection from the weather.

fausse montre: Late Georgian (1750–1790 C.E.). France. Fashion for wearing second watch, a fake.

Faust slipper: Man's house shoe similar to the Romeo. It is high cut and has a V-shaped cut on each side.

Fausthandschuh: Germany. Mitten.

Faustling: *See* Fausthandschuh.

fautre: Renaissance (1450–1550 C.E.). France. Thigh armor.

favoris: *See* dundrearys.

favorite: Late Georgian (1750–1790 C.E.). United States of America. Lock of hair worn on temples by women.

favors: *See* galants.

favourite: *See* favorite.

fawn: Yellowish dark tan.

faxiolion: Greek (3000–100 B.C.E.). Handkerchief.

fayi: China. Clothes worn by Buddhist or Taoist priests at religious ceremonies.

fazolo: Late Georgian (1750–1790 C.E.). Italy. Handkerchief.

fazzelkappe: *See* spitzkappe.

fazzoletto: Renaissance (1450–1550 C.E.). Italy. Silk or linen kerchief commonly worn tucked into neckline of dress.

fearnothing: *See* dreadnought.

fearnothing jacket: Early Georgian (1700–1750 C.E.) to Romantic (1815–1840 C.E.). Man's jacket made of dreadnought worn by seafaring men, sportsmen, laborers, and apprentices.

fearnought: *See* dreadnought.

feather cloth: Fabric with fluff on surface for softness.

featherbrush skirt: Gay Nineties (1890–1900 C.E.). United Kingdom. In 1898, a woman's day skirt of light material made with overlapping flounces below knee.

featherstitch: Decorative stitch made of blanket stitches in zigzag line.

feather-top wig: Late Georgian (1750–1790 C.E.). United Kingdom. Worn by parsons and sportsmen, a man's wig with feather toupee, commonly made from drake or mallard feathers.

feax-clap: Byzantine and Romanesque (400–1200 C.E.). United Kingdom. Cloth or band for hair.

feax-net: Byzantine and Romanesque (400–1200 C.E.). United Kingdom. Hairnet.

feax-preon: Byzantine and Romanesque (400–1200 C.E.). United Kingdom. Hairpin.

Feder: Germany. Feather.

fedora: Bustle (1865–1890 C.E.). Felt or velour man's hat with medium height crown, usually creased in middle.

Feh: Germany. Squirrel belly fur.

fei: China. Red.

fei yu: China. Under the Zhengde emperor (r. 1505–1521 C.E.), the second rank of embroidery on gowns; winged dragon with forked fishtail.

feihóng: China. Bright red.

feileadh-beag: Scotland. Little kilt worn as early as 1639. Short kilt with knife pleats.

feilt: Ireland. Felt.

feisè: China. Light pink.

fel: Byzantine and Romanesque (400–1200 C.E.). United Kingdom. Full-length skin or leather garment worn by monks.

feldr: Norway. Old word for cloak.

Felix: Crinoline (1840–1865 C.E.). In 1855, collared, sleeved sacque. It had moss appliqué and guipure on lower edge.

félkabát: *See* rokk.

felon: Russia. Robe worn in religious ceremonies.

félpa: Greece. Cotton cloth with a velvety texture.

felt: Non-woven fabric of pressed fibers.

felted knitting: Renaissance (1450–1550 C.E.). Process in which knitted garment, usually made too large, is soaked, rubbed, and pounded to create felt.

feltr: France. Breton for felt.

feltro: Italy. Felt.

feluca: Italy. Cocked hat.

femina: Feathers from female ostrich.

feminalia: Roman (753 B.C.E.–323 C.E.). Men's knee-length drawers worn by Roman troops in Northern climes.

femoralia: *See* feminalia.

fenetres d'enfer: Late Gothic (1350–1450 C.E.). Arms-eyes of women's surcoat.

feng huang: China. Phoenix symbol.

fengjìng: China. Goggles.

féngmào: China. Cowl-like winter hat.

fenhóng: China. Pink.

fents: Renaissance (1450–1550 C.E.). Spain. Openings in a garment.

feòil-dhaith te: Ireland. Flesh colored.

feòil-dhath: Ireland. The color carnation.

ferace: Turkey. Long, dark coat with close-fitting, round neck and wide, elbow-length sleeves.

ferenn: Ireland. Gaelic word for sword belt.

feridge': Turkey. Woman's loose, ankle-length cloak made of silk or wool.

ferka: Egypt. Woman's large, rectangular wrap with yellow, white, and black braid.

fermaglio: Renaissance (1450–1550 C.E.). Italy. Brooch or hat pin often worn on shoulder, headdress, sleeve, or bodice. Many had a figure in relief.

fermail: Late Gothic (1350–1450 C.E.). Buckle or brooch.

ferozai: India. Turquoise blue.

ferradura: *See* sapata.

ferraiuolo: Italy. Mantle.

ferreruelo: Elizabethan (1550–1625 C.E.). Spain. Long or short capa with high collar. *See also* bohemio.

ferret: Elizabethan (1550–1625 C.E.) to Restoration (1660–1700 C.E.). Narrow silk or cotton ribbon.

ferret-silke: Early Gothic (1200–1350 C.E.). Coarse silk.

ferris waist: (20th century). Brand name for fitted waist worn mainly by young girls. It had button tabs to hold the supporters.

ferroniere: Romantic (1815–1840 C.E.). France. Fine chain, ribbon, or thin leather thong worn around forehead with small jewel in center of forehead.

ferroniere

ferrule: End cap on umbrella, cane, etc.

fers: Elizabethan (1550–1625 C.E.). Metal buttons worn as decoration on dress of woman of rank.

fersing: *See* rokolya.

fertuch: Slovakia. Apron.

fessagida: Hausa. Cotton cloth with a broad band of silk.

feston: France. Buttonhole stitch.

festones: Ecuador. Horizontal pleats.

festoons: Early Georgian (1700–1750 C.E.). Curved garlands of fabric or flowers worn on women's garments.

festoul: Morocco. Long, fine silk sash used to tie up Jewish woman's hair.

festracht: Austria. General term referring to festival dress.

fetel: Byzantine and Romanesque (400–1200 C.E.). United Kingdom. Belt or girdle; particularly the sword belt.

fetels: Byzantine and Romanesque (400–1200 C.E.). United Kingdom. Belt or bag; possibly a purse that was suspended from girdle.

Fettschwanzschaf: Germany. Karakul.

fettuccia: *See* nastro.

Feuerwiesel: Germany. Kolinsky fur.

feur: France. Breton for fur.

feusag-bheòil: Ireland. Moustache.

feutre: 1. Bustle (1865–1890 C.E.). In 1872, felt gray. 2. France. Felt.

fez: Turkey. Brimless, felt cap worn with tassel.

ffedog: Wales. Apron.

ffwr: Wales. Fur.

fîal: *See* caille.

fiapo: Portugal. Fine thread.

fiber lace: Lace made from aloe, banana, or pineapple fibers.

fiber silk: Artificial silk.

Fiberglas: Trade name for products made of glass fibers.

fibre chamoise: (1900–1910 C.E.). Stiff, paper-like fabric used to line and reinforce the fashionable balloon sleeves.

fibula: Roman (753 B.C.E.–323 C.E.). Pin or brooch.

ficelle: Bustle (1865–1890 C.E.). In 1882, very thick lace.

ficheall: Ireland. Gaelic word for buckle.

fichu: Late Georgian (1750–1790 C.E.). Shoulder scarf of lightweight, sometimes transparent fabric, worn with different styles of gowns by women.

fichu Antoinette: Crinoline (1840–1865 C.E.). United Kingdom. Introduced in 1857, woman's summer morning fine muslin fichu that was trimmed in black lace and narrow velvet ribbon. It fastened in back with small bow and covered the shoulders like a shawl and crossed at center front waist.

fichu Antoinette

fichu Corday: Romantic (1815–1840 C.E.). United Kingdom. Introduced in 1837, grenadine gauze fichu that crossed bosom, tying in back. It had a wide hem that a ribbon ran through.

fichu la Valiere: Bustle (1865–1890 C.E.). France. Introduced in 1868, fichu worn with front edges pinned together, not crossing as usual.

fichu menteur: Late Georgian (1750–1790 C.E.). France. Woman's fichu that was worn draped to exaggerate figure, particularly the bust.

fichu raphael: Bustle (1865–1890 C.E.). France. Introduced in 1867, white tulle or lace fichu that was square over shoulder. It was worn with a high-necked bodice.

fichu Ristori: Crinoline (1840–1865 C.E.). In 1856, pelerine-shaped fichu worn with ends crossed in front and tied with bows. Named for French actress Mme Ristori.

fichu-canezou: Romantic (1815–1840 C.E.). France. Woman's deep collar that fell from neck of a bodice but did not cover the arms. It was sometimes made with small ruff.

fichu-pelerine: Romantic (1815–1840 C.E.). France. Worn after 1825, large white fichu, often having double cape and turndown collar. The front had knee-length fichu ends that were worn under belt.

fichu-robings: Romantic (1815–1840 C.E.). United Kingdom. In 1820s, flat trim sewn to bodice to imitate fichu.

ficka: Sweden. Pocket.

field cap: Lightweight soft cloth cap of any of a number of shapes, mainly worn for military undress use.

field service cap: *See* field cap.

fieltro: 1. Elizabethan (1550–1625 C.E.). Spain. Three-quarter length double riding cape with button-up collar and hood. 2. Spain. Felt.

fifele: Byzantine and Romanesque (400–1200 C.E.). United Kingdom. Buckle or brooch.

fig leaf: Crinoline (1840–1865 C.E.) to Bustle (1865–1890 C.E.). United Kingdom. Woman's small ornamental, bibless apron of black silk.

Figaro jacket: Crinoline (1840–1865 C.E.) to 1890s. Worn with waistcoat, a variation of zouave jacket, it was a snug bolero-type jacket with epaulets.

figgery: Ornaments.

figgragulþ: Early Gothic (1200–1350 C.E.) to Late Gothic (1350–1450 C.E.). United Kingdom. Finger ring.

figurero: Charles I and the Commonwealth (1625–1660 C.E.). Woolen fabric.

figuretto: Charles I and the Commonwealth (1625–1660 C.E.). Expensive flowered fabric, perhaps woven with metallic threads.

figury: Late Gothic (1350–1450 C.E.) to Renaissance (1450–1550 C.E.). Figured satin and velvet fabric.

fijne: Holland. Broadcloth.

fijne punt: Holland. Needlepoint.

fil: France. Thread.

fil de Chevre: Crinoline (1840–1865 C.E.). In 1862, new fabric.

fil de retour: A line of thread in a needle lace.

fil de vierge: Gay Nineties (1890–1900 C.E.). In 1891, tulle veil studded with pearls or blue stones.

fil tiré: France. Drawn work that is filled in with needlework.

fila ab'eti: Nigeria. Earflaps on a Yoruba man's labarikada.

filati: Greece. Thread.

filbert: Pale brown with grayish tint.

filé: Directoire and First Empire (1790–1815 C.E.). France. Smooth metallic thread that was wound on silk or linen core.

filead: Ireland. Gaelic word for fillet.

filemot: *See* phillamot.

filet: 1. Net lace with square mesh. 2. Strip or ribbon.

filet brodé: Embroidered net.

filet lace: Lace with square knotted mesh ground.

filete: Ecuador. Scallop work.

filetto: Renaissance (1450–1550 C.E.). Italy. Edge of hem, occasionally trimmed in fur.

fili tirati: Italy. Drawn-thread work.

filibeg: Scotland. Modern knee-length kilt.

filigree: Delicate ornamental openwork.

filleadh beag: Early Georgian (1700–1750 C.E.) to present. Small kilt.

fillet: Narrow band or ribbon worn around head.

filo: Italy. Thread.

filozella: Charles I and the Commonwealth (1625–1660 C.E.). Double camlet.

filozetta: *See* filozella.

filt: Denmark and Sweden. Felt.

filum: Roman (753 B.C.E.–323 C.E.). Thread.

Filz: Germany. Felt.

Filzglocke: Germany. Felt cloche.

Filztuch: Germany. Felt cloth.

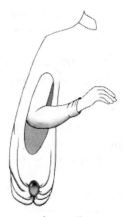

finestrella

finger gauntlet
Dover Publications

fimbria: Italy. Skirt.

finestrella: Renaissance (1450–1550 C.E.). Italy. The opening in hanging sleeve through which the arm passes.

finger gauntlet: Late Gothic (1350–1450 C.E.). A gauntlet with the fingers protected by separate lames, not in the more commonly glove shape.

fingerstall: Glove finger.

fingroms: Early Georgian (1700–1750 C.E.) to Late Georgian (1750–1790 C.E.). Coarse serge made at Stirling.

finic: Ireland. Gaelic word for jet.

finica: Greece. Silver, egg-sized ornaments worn by a bride on her hair.

finnesko: Lapland. Treated reindeer skin boots with fur on outside.

fiocco: Italy. Bow.

fionnadh: Ireland. Fur.

fir: Romania. Thread.

firmale: Renaissance (1450–1550 C.E.). Spain. Brooch.

firmament: Charles I and the Commonwealth (1625–1660 C.E.) to Restoration (1660–1700 C.E.). Filet set with gems.

firmla: Morocco. Vest that reaches below hips.

firozi: India. Turquoise color.

fish net: Net with very large mesh.

fisher: Species of American marten with rich, dark brown underhair and long, black overhairs.

fishtail: Bustle (1865–1890 C.E.). The nickname given to the narrow bustle and train popular in the later years of the period.

fishwife skirt: Full peasant skirt of striped fabric.

fîstîc: *See* catrinta.

fita: Portugal. Ribbon.

fitchet: Early Gothic (1200–1350 C.E.) to Renaissance (1450–1550 C.E.). France. Vertical placket in gown skirt or cape.

fitelho: Portugal. Narrow ribbon.

fitili: Greece. A thick yellow cotton yarn.

Fitzherbert hat: Late Georgian (1750–1790 C.E.). Introduced in 1786, modified balloon hat for women with oval brim and raised crown.

five hole lace: One of the earliest and most widespread bobbin lace grounds, it is worked with four pairs of

fishtail
Dover Publications

thread which form five small holes where they meet at intersections.

fivela: Portugal. Buckle.

flabells: Gay Nineties (1890–1900 C.E.). Italy. Great circular fan used on state occasions.

Flachs: Germany. Flax.

Flahs: Germany. Flax.

flame: Brilliant scarlet.

flame embroidery: *See* Florentine embroidery.

flamme de punch: Crinoline (1840–1865 C.E.). In 1864, new color resembling the light from a punch bowl.

flammeum: Roman (753 B.C.E.–323 C.E.). Dark flame-colored marriage veil worn by brides. It covered wearer completely. Bridegroom removed veil after they had arrived at their home. Some matrons continued to wear it after their wedding.

flandan: Restoration (1660–1700 C.E.). Woman's cap with lace-edged lappets.

Flanders serge: Elizabethan (1550–1625 C.E.) to Restoration (1660–1700 C.E.). United Kingdom. Worsted fabric.

flange heel: Shoe heel that flares out at bottom.

flange shoulder: Shoulder with pleat that reaches over sleeve.

flann: Ireland. Gaelic word for blood red.

flannach: Ireland. Gaelic word for purple.

flann-dhearg: Ireland. Gaelic word for purple.

flannel: Soft, lightweight, twill or plain weave, cotton fabric with slight nap on one or both sides.

flannelette: Bustle (1865–1890 C.E.) to 20th century. United States of America. Introduced in 1876, lightweight, plain weave, cotton fabric with one side twilled and other plush. *See also* kimono flannel.

flanyela: Romania. Flannel.

flashdance top: Based on designs for movie *Flashdance*. Knit shirt with short sleeves and large neckline.

flat crepe: Fine, tightly woven, lustrous crepe.

flax: Plant from which linen is made.

flaxen: Straw color.

Flaxon: Trade name for crisp finish on cotton.

flea: Late Georgian (1750–1790 C.E.). Puce color.

flea-fur: Renaissance (1450–1550 C.E.) to Elizabethan (1550–1625 C.E.). Vernacular name for marten or sable stole.

fleax: United Kingdom. Old English word for flax.

Fleckenskunk: Germany. Fur of the civet cat.

fleco: Spain. Fringe.

fleco bullion: Spain. Bullion fringe.

fleco morisco: Spain. Macramé.

fleece: Any heavy, napped, or pile fabric with fleece-like surface.

Flehtan: Germany. Braid.

Flemysshe cloth: Early Gothic (1200–1350 C.E.). Linen.

flesh: Tint of red orange.

fleshings: Directoire and First Empire (1790–1815 C.E.). Flesh-colored tights.

fleur de lis: Conventionalized iris flower motif that is royal emblem of France.

fleur de lys: *See* fleur de lis.

fleur de peche: Crinoline (1840–1865 C.E.). In 1860, new trim color.

fleur de soufre: Bustle (1865–1890 C.E.). In 1879, pale shade of sulfur yellow.

fleur de thé: Bustle (1865–1890 C.E.). In 1880, cotton fabric as fine as lawn.

fleur volant: France. Ornamental loop in point lace pattern.

fleuron: Ornament in shape of a flower.

flex: Byzantine and Romanesque (400–1200 C.E.) to Renaissance (1450–1550 C.E.). United Kingdom. Middle English word for flax.

flexible net: Closely woven, leno weave, millinery fabric of cotton. Made in white or cream.

flexine: Gay Nineties (1890–1900 C.E.). In 1892, a reddish slate color.

flieder: Early Gothic (1200–1350 C.E.) to Restoration (1660–1700 C.E.). Germany. Jewish woman's pointed veil.

fliegende Nachtrok: *See* volanten.

flight boot: (1940–1949 C.E.). United States of America. Chukka boot popularized by aircraft carrier attendants in World War II. Natural, flesh-side out leather upper with non-skid sole. It became official equipment on all carriers.

flimsies: Slang for women's undergarments.

flip: *See* krave.

flipe: Renaissance (1450–1550 C.E.) to Elizabethan (1550–1625 C.E.). Fold or flap on cap brim.

Flitter: Germany. Sequins.

flitter braid: Very light braid covered in sequins.

float: Portion of yarn in fabric that floats above two or more other threads.

flocket: Renaissance (1450–1550 C.E.) to Elizabethan (1550–1625 C.E.). Woman's long, loose garment.

floconné: France. Small, white flakes on colored ground.

floddermuts: Holland. Woman's loose cotton cap.

flokati: Greece. Slipper sock.

floki: *See* pofi.

flor: Sweden. 1. Veil. 2. Fine cloth.

flóra: Greece. White embroidery threads.

Flora: Crinoline (1840–1865 C.E.). In 1855, shawl with box-pleated skirt. It trimmed with bands of glacé silk and gimp. Large ornamental bow between shoulder blades.

floramedas: Elizabethan (1550–1625 C.E.) to Restoration (1660–1700 C.E.). Flowered or figured fabric.

florence: 1. Directoire and First Empire (1790–1815 C.E.). Lightweight silk taffeta. 2. Crinoline (1840–1865 C.E.). In 1840s, corded barege or grenadine used for linings. 3. France. Sarsenet.

Florence satin: Directoire and First Empire (1790–1815 C.E.). Used in 1802 and after, thin, soft satin.

florentine: Bustle (1865–1890 C.E.). 1. Introduced in 1867, yellow color with bronze tint. 2. Heavy silk fabric.

Florentine: Crinoline (1840–1865 C.E.). In 1857, woman's taffeta shawl. Bertha trimmed with box-pleated ruffle, as was lower edge of shawl. Shawl was trimmed with passementerie and Tom Thumb fringe.

Florentine embroidery: Canvas embroidery where stitches are worked in zigzag pattern.

Florentine hat: Italy. Large straw hat.

Florentine leather: Italy. Fine leather tooled in gold and colors from Florence.

Florentine neckline: Very wide boat neckline.

Florentinerhut: Germany. Boater.

florinelle: Late Georgian (1750–1790 C.E.) to Directoire and First Empire (1790–1815 C.E.). United Kingdom. Made in Norwich, glazed brocade that was striped and flowered.

Florodora Girl costume: Based on chorus costumes from *Florodora*, the ensemble included full, fluffy skirt, lace-trimmed, bishop sleeved bodice that gathered at waist and picture hat.

floss silk: A very shiny untwisted raw silk.

flossing: Crinoline (1840–1865 C.E.). Stitching used to encase corset bones in place.

flotation jacket: Self-inflating life preserver.

flots: Overlapping rows of ribbon or lace arranged as loops.

flounce: Late Georgian (1750–1790 C.E.) to 20th century. Band of fabric or lace that is fluted and attached to garment by its upper edge only.

flounce à disposition: Crinoline (1840–1865 C.E.). France. Worn after 1851, flounce woven with same border pattern as the dress.

flourish: Renaissance (1450–1550 C.E.) to Elizabethan (1550–1625 C.E.). To ornament profusely.

flower bottle: Bustle (1865–1890 C.E.). Worn in 1865, small glass bottle for flowers that was worn by some men in buttonhole in left lapel of morning coat. Piece of wide ribbon was sewn under lapel to hold bottle in position.

flower hole: Crinoline (1840–1865 C.E.) to 20th century. United Kingdom. From 1840s on, small buttonhole appeared in left lapel of coat for flower stem or flower bottle.

flower pot hat: 1. Elizabethan (1550–1625 C.E.). United Kingdom. Worn by both men and women, a felt hat shaped like an inverted flower pot and surrounded with a short curled brim. 2. (1960–1969 C.E.). Similar to the earlier version, a woman's hat of straw or felt, usually without a brim.

flower pot hat

flow-flow: Bustle (1865–1890 C.E.). United Kingdom. Graduated fall of colored ribbon loops that trimmed bodice front of women's gowns.

floxine: Gay Nineties (1890–1900 C.E.). In 1892, a red with tint of lilac.

flues: Feather fibers on each side of feather stem.

flügelmütze: Prussia. Mirliton.

flurt-silke: Early Gothic (1200–1350 C.E.). Figured silk.

flushing hat: Directoire and First Empire (1790–1815 C.E.). In 1809, woman's hat similar to gipsy hat with under crown to fit wearer snugly.

flushings: Romantic (1815–1840 C.E.). Heavy wool fabric similar to duffels.

fluting: Narrow pleats.

fluweel: Holland. Velvet.

fly plaid: Scotland. A tartan scarf attached to the left shoulder and falling to the bottom of the kilt.

flycap: Elizabethan (1550–1625 C.E.) to Late Georgian (1750–1790 C.E.). United Kingdom. Woman's cap with lappets on sides.

fly-fringe: Early Georgian (1700–1750 C.E.) to Bustle (1865–1890 C.E.). Fringe of cord and silk tufts.

flying Josie: *See* joseph.

Flying Saucer: (1950–1960 C.E.). United States of America. Man's hairstyle with horizontal part across the head from ear to ear.

fly's wing: Romantic (1815–1840 C.E.). United Kingdom. Gray.

fly-suit: Early Georgian (1700–1750 C.E.) to Late Georgian (1750–1790 C.E.). Loose negligee gown.

fob pocket: Charles I and the Commonwealth (1625–1660 C.E.) to present. Small pocket in breeches.

fob ribbon: Early Georgian (1700–1750 C.E.) to Crinoline (1840–1865 C.E.). Short ribbon worn by men reaching from watch to fob pocket. It often held seals and watch key.

fo-bhuidhe: Ireland. Gaelic word for tawny or yellowish color.

foca: Italy and Spain. Seal fur.

focale: Roman (644 B.C.E.–323 C.E.). Knotted scarves worn by warriors on campaign.

fóci: Greece. Leather belt.

fodera: Italy. Lining.

fodra: Romania. Fan-shaped cuff on woman's smock.

fogle: Directoire and First Empire (1790–1815 C.E.) to Bustle (1865–1890 C.E.). Vernacular term for silk handkerchief.

foil: Ireland. Gaelic word for bracelet. *See also* fail.

foileid: Ireland. Gaelic word for wimple.

fol: Trinidad. Heart-shaped panel in a garment.

fola: Ireland. Gaelic word for garment.

follette: Early Georgian (1700–1750 C.E.). France. Another name for a fichu.

folly bells: Late Gothic (1450–1550 C.E.). United Kingdom. Series of small bells hung from girdle, shoulder belt, or neckband.

foloara: Madagascar. Woman's cotton head covering.

fond: France. Flat crown.

fond à la marriage: A variety of point de Paris.

fond clair: France. Simple twist net ground of the bucks point type.

fond de casserole: Gay Nineties (1890–1900 C.E.). In 1891, a coppery red.

fond double: Point de Paris made with four pairs of thread.

fond simple: *See* fond clair.

fong chau: (1920–1930 C.E.). United States of America. Chinese Hawaiian term for a medium-quality silk.

fontanges: Restoration (1660–1700 C.E.). France. Woman's upswept hairstyle that was held in place by ribbon and surmounted by various caps and accessories.

fools hood: Fisherman's stocking cap.

foot-mantle: Early Gothic (1200–1350 C.E.). Petticoat worn by women on horseback to keep their gowns clean.

footing: Fine cotton net one-half inch to six inches wide used for ruffling.

forage cap: Directoire and First Empire (1790–1815 C.E.) to Crinoline (1840–1865 C.E.). United Kingdom. Man's cap with round flat crown with its edge stiffened with cane, front visor, tassel in the center of crown, and sometimes leather chin strap. In 1829, adapted by the military.

for-bhrat: Ireland. Gaelic word for cloak or outer garment.

forcella: Italy. Hairpin.

fore-and-aft cap: Bustle (1865–1890 C.E.). Cap with visor-type brim in front and back. Popularized by literary character, Sherlock Holmes.

forel: United Kingdom. Border or selvage.

forepart: Elizabethan (1550–1625 C.E.). Decorative fabric insert in front of woman's bodice.

foresleeve: Part of sleeve covering forearm.

forest cloth: Renaissance (1450–1550 C.E.) to Late Georgian (1750–1790 C.E.). Good quality woolen fabric from Forest of Dean.

forest green: Dark green.

forest white: Renaissance (1450–1550 C.E.) to Restoration (1660–1700 C.E.). White homespun fabric made in Peniston. Red or blue colored version was called Peniston.

forester's green: Romantic (1815–1840 C.E.). United States of America. Bright green color popular in 1817. *See also* American green.

forestry cloth: United States of America. Kind of olive drab flannel originally made for U.S. Forestry Service.

forfar: Scotland. Coarse, heavy linen fabric once made in Forfarshire.

forked beard: Late Gothic (1350–1450 C.E.). Beard with two points.

förkläde: Sweden. Apron.

forklœde: Denmark. Apron.

fôrma: Portugal. Hat block; shoe last.

Fornarina: Crinoline (1840–1865 C.E.). In 1850, fitted pardessus trimmed with gimp and thin fringe.

forro: Spain. Lining.

forro de sombrero: Spain. Hat lining.

fortop: *See* toupee.

Fortuny print: Italy. Art fabric made for Fortuny in Venice using secret printing process giving cotton cloth the look of antique brocade.

Fortuny tea gown: (1910–1920 C.E.). France. Fortuny design for clinging gown in Grecian line made of durable silk with neckline that gathered on a silk cord. Fabric was usually plaited, and sometimes trimmed with stencils, beads, or gold and silver tracery.

fo-ruadh: Ireland. Gaelic word for reddish brown.

fot: *See* klœði.

fota: 1. Ethiopia. Woman's shawl. 2. Romania. Oblong, black woolen skirt.

fotaforkle: Norway. Apron with a wide border above the hem.

fotgewaed: Byzantine and Romanesque (400–1200 C.E.). United Kingdom. Footwear of monks.

fouine: France. Stone marten.

foulard: 1. Soft, washable satiny silk with small figures on dark or light ground. 2. Soft, fine, twill weave cotton fabric. 3. Handkerchief of silk foulard. 4. Holland. Bandana.

foulard de laine: Crinoline (1840–1865 C.E.). In 1861, fabric resembling alpaca.

foulard poile de chevre: Bustle (1865–1890 C.E.). France. Introduced in 1870, fabric of goat's hair similar to foulard.

foulé: Bustle (1865–1890 C.E.). France. Introduced in 1882, soft and velvety fabric similar to casimir.

foulinenn: *See* feur.

foundation net: Coarse, sized net used in hat understructure.

foundi: Greece. A chemise embroidered in silk thread.

foundling bonnet: Bustle (1865–1890 C.E.). United Kingdom. Woman's hat with small stiff brim, soft plush crown, and ties for bow under chin.

fouraschka: Russia. Field cap.

fourchette: Small piece of leather set between fingers in glove.

fouriaux: Byzantine and Romanesque (400–1200 C.E.). France. In first half of 12th century, these long silk sheaths enclosed two long braids of hair commonly worn by ladies of rank.

four-in-hand: Bustle (1865–1890 C.E.). Necktie tied in slipknot.

fourisseur d'arme: France. Armorer.

fourreau dress: Crinoline (1840–1865 C.E.). Introduced in 1864, princess style dress that buttoned down front.

fourreau skirt: Crinoline (1840–1865 C.E.). Introduced in 1864, gored morning skirt that was fitted at waist and full over crinoline.

fourreau tunic: Crinoline (1840–1865 C.E.). Introduced in 1864, upper skirt (tunic) that was cut in one with bodice. It measured six yards at hem. The double skirt was worn for evening.

fourrure: France. Fur.

fox: Fur of the *Vulpes vulpes*, a fur with long, soft fur in various shades.

foynes: Early Gothic (1200–1350 C.E.). Skin of a polecat.

frac: Late Georgian (1750–1790 C.E.) to Crinoline (1840–1865 C.E.). France. From 1767, man's informal garment with turndown collar that was wider than coat. It evolved into formal, basqued jacket that was cutaway in front.

fragrance on the surface of the soles: China. Ming dynasty. Flat-soled shoes worn by older women.

fragrant leaves: *See* external high shoes.

fraise: 1. Renaissance (1450–1550 C.E.) to Elizabethan (1550–1625 C.E.). France. Small ruffle on edge of standing collar. 2. Romantic (1815–1840 C.E.). Piece of embroidered muslin trimmed in ruching that was worn folded across woman's bosom and pinned in place. Appeared with carriage dress as replacement for cravat.

fraise à la confusion: *See* falling ruff.

fraise à la Gabrielle: Crinoline (1840–1865 C.E.). In 1857, woman's ruff of quilled muslin edged with narrow Valenciennes.

fraka: Poland. Dress coattails.

frakke: Denmark. Coat.

fralda: *See* aba.

framboise: Bustle (1865–1890 C.E.). In 1882, raspberry color.

Francis the First sleeve: Crinoline (1840–1865 C.E.). In 1861, short puffed sleeve for evening.

Franco-Cuban heel: Narrow Cuban heel.

franela: Spain. Flannel.

franela de Canton: Spain. Canton flannel.

franela ligera: Spain. Baby flannel.

frangipani gloves: Perfumed gloves.

frangipani perfume: Restoration (1660–1700 C.E.). France. Perfume named for the marquis who discovered that perfume could be held in liquid form by using alcohol.

franja: Portugal. Fringe.

franjas: Renaissance (1450–1550 C.E.). Spain. Fringes.

fraternity pin: Pin containing Greek letters representing fraternity. It often had tiny pearls around the rim. A guard chain with symbols for chapter name is often attached. Woman's version is sorority pin.

frazada: Ecuador. Blanket.

fregio: Italy. Frieze.

freiseau: Byzantine and Romanesque (400–1200 C.E.). France. Twelfth-century term for decorative hair comb.

French back serge: Fine worsted serge made with extra warp on back.

French back twill: Worsted suiting fabric.

French bearer: Romantic (1815–1840 C.E.). Bearer band on men's breeches that were made with falls.

French boa: Romantic (1815–1840 C.E.). Worn after 1829, woman's long round tippet of swansdown, fur, or feathers. Reappeared in 1890s.

French bottoms: Romantic (1815–1840 C.E.). Men's trouser legs that were cut wider at hem than above.

French cambric: Finest grade of cambric.

French chalk: Soft, absorbent chalk used as cleaning agent to absorb grease and perspiration.

French chip: Soft, durable but expensive chip straw.

French cloak: Renaissance (1450–1550 C.E.) to Restoration (1660–1700 C.E.). Worn draped informally over the left shoulder, a man's long, circular or semi-circular cape with square flat collar or shoulder cape.

French bottoms

French crepe: Very lightweight, plain weave, silk or rayon crepe.

French cuff: 1. Man's coat cuff with side slit that buttoned. 2. Crinoline (1840–1865 C.E.). Beginning in 1850s, wide shirt cuff that linked at wrist and buttoned higher up.

French dart: Dart formed by joining vertical darts from shoulder and waistline.

French fall: Charles I and the Commonwealth (1625–1660 C.E.). Style of shoe.

French foot: Hose with one seam in middle of sole.

French frock: Late Georgian (1750–1790 C.E.) to Directoire and First Empire (1790–1815 C.E.). Worn from 1770s to around 1800, man's full dress coat trimmed with gold embroidered buttons.

French gigot sleeves: Gay Nineties (1890–1900 C.E.). United Kingdom. Woman's sleeve with cuff that extended onto back of hand. Style was introduced by Sarah Bernhardt.

French gingham: Fine, soft gingham.

French gores: Directoire and First Empire (1790–1815 C.E.). United Kingdom. Gores in day skirt that

French gigot sleeves

first eliminated gathers at the waist.

French heel: Curved, high heel.

French hood: Renaissance (1450–1550 C.E.) to Elizabethan (1550–1625 C.E.). Popular from 1521 to 1590, woman's headdress with small stiff bonnet that was worn far back on head. Front curved forward to cover the ears and was trimmed in ruching. Falling back from the cap was curtain of pleated fabric. Held in place with chin strap.

French heel

French hose: Elizabethan (1550–1625 C.E.). United Kingdom. Worn from 1550 to 1610, men's paned trunk hose worn with canions.

French jet: Gay Nineties (1890–1900 C.E.). Jet pieces applied to fabric.

French kid: Fine quality kid leather.

French knot: Ornamental embroidery knot.

French merino: Fine grade merino wool.

French net: Directoire and First Empire (1790–1815 C.E.). Net introduced in 1807 for evening gowns.

French opening vest: Crinoline (1840–1865 C.E.). Man's vest cut low in front to show the shirt.

French percale: High quality percale.

French pocket: Charles I and the Commonwealth (1625–1660 C.E.) to Restoration (1660–1700 C.E.). Horizontal slit pocket with flap cover.

French polonaise: *See* Irish polonaise.

French ruff: Elizabethan (1550–1625 C.E.). Worn from 1580 to around 1610, man's very large cartwheel ruff.

French serge: Finely twilled serge.

French sleeves: Elizabethan (1550–1625 C.E.). Worn from 1550 to 1600, men's detachable pinked or paned sleeves.

French vest: Crinoline (1840–1865 C.E.) to Bustle (1865–1890 C.E.). Worn in 1860s, man's high-buttoned waistcoat with short lapels. *See also* American vest.

French work: Romantic (1815–1840 C.E.). Embroidery insertions in front of a woman's bodice.

frenello: Renaissance (1450–1550 C.E.). Italy. String of pearls or a ribbon twisted around hair and silk veiling strips and worn in hair as an ornament. Frequently had jewel in center front.

fret: Late Gothic (1350–1450 C.E.). Gold wire trellised cap to hold hair.

frette: *See* fret.

friar's cloth: Coarse textured, basket weave, drapery fabric.

friendship bracelet: (20th century). Bracelet consisting of links of metal, each piece given by a friend, and later assembled.

Fries: Germany. Frieze.

fries: Holland. Frieze.

frieze: 1. Renaissance (1450–1550 C.E.). Thick wool fabric worn by lower classes. 2. To raise the nap on a fabric. 3. To embroider. 4. Present. Thick, heavy fabric with a raised surface of uncut loops.

frilal: Border or ornamental ribbon.

frileuse: Crinoline (1840–1865 C.E.). France. Introduced in 1847, woman's quilted satin or velvet pelerine that was fitted at the back at the waist and had long, loose sleeves.

frill: Renaissance (1450–1550 C.E.) to 20th century. Gathered piece of trim that suggests a ripple.

frilling: Crinoline (1840–1865 C.E.) to Bustle (1865–1890 C.E.). United Kingdom. Gathered piece of stiff white muslin worn at neck and wrists of a woman's bodice. Often worn by widows in 1870s and 1880s.

friponne: *See* jupe.

frippery: Tawdry finery.

frisa: Portugal. Frieze.

frise: France. Frieze.

frilling

frisé: France. Pile fabric of uncut loops.

frisé brocade: Bustle (1865–1890 C.E.). Introduced in 1885, brocade with pile pattern.

frisette: 1. Fringe or bangs of hair worn on forehead. 2. Padding in underskirts.

frislet: Elizabethan (1550–1625 C.E.). Small ruffle.

friso: Portugal. Band or fillet.

frisure d'or: Renaissance (1450–1550 C.E.). Gold or silver embroidery.

frivolité: France. Tatting.

frizado: Renaissance (1450–1550 C.E.) to Restoration (1660–1700 C.E.). Heavy worsted fabric similar to baize.

frizé: *See* frisé.

frizette: *See* frisette.

frizz wig: Late Georgian (1750–1790 C.E.). Man's wig that was crimped all over.

frock coat: Romantic (1815–1840 C.E.). Man's coat with long skirts of same length all around the body.

frog: Romantic (1815–1840 C.E.). Ornamental cord fastening of Oriental influence consisting of loop and toggle.

frog pocket: Crinoline (1840–1865 C.E.). Pocket in the side seam of men's breeches cut with rectangular flap and secured with a button.

frock coat

frog-mouthed helm: Late Gothic (1350–1450 C.E.). A jousting helmet.

froissé: France. To be crumpled or crushed.

froncés: France. Close bouillonnee; curliness.

frontiere: *See* Mary Stuart cap.

frontje: Holland. Shirt front.

frontlet: 1. Late Gothic (1350–1450 C.E.). Small chain or loop of fabric worn across brow from large headdress. 2. Renaissance (1450–1550 C.E.) to Elizabethan (1550–1625 C.E.). Band worn around forehead with a coif.

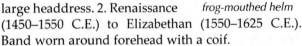

frog-mouthed helm

frontone de berretto: Italy. Flat crown of a hat.

frose paste: Renaissance (1450–1550 C.E.) to Elizabethan (1550–1625 C.E.). Paste paper often associated with French hoods.

frou-frou: Bustle (1865–1890 C.E.). Introduced in 1870, satin similar to washing cloth.

frou-frou dress: Bustle (1865–1890 C.E.). Introduced in 1870, day dress worn with short muslin tunic, skirts of which were rounded in front. Worn with light silk underskirt that was trimmed in many pinked flounces.

frou-frou gauze: Bustle (1865–1890 C.E.). In 1870, thin solid color grenadine with surface coloring imitating crepe.

frounce: Late Gothic (1350–1450 C.E.) to Elizabethan (1550–1625 C.E.). Pleated or gathered flounce.

frouting: Elizabethan (1550–1625 C.E.) to Restoration (1660–1700 C.E.). To rub sweet perfumed oil into a garment.

frouze: Restoration (1660–1700 C.E.) to Early Georgian (1700–1750 C.E.). Wig worn to cover a bald head.

fruncidas: Renaissance (1450–1550 C.E.). Spain. Gathered.

fruncido: Spain. Curliness.

frúta: Greece. Beads.

frutilla: Ecuador. A belt woven with small diamond figures.

fterotó: Greece. Embroidery design on the old wedding chemise.

fú: China. Clothes.

fu ku: China. Men's pleated ankle-length breeches with fullness looped up at knees.

fu tou: China. 1. Ming dynasty (1368–1644 C.E.). Lacquered black, a man's official hat. Round, gauze cap with two stiff wings at back. 2. Tang dynasty. Silk turban made of handkerchief with four corners cut into ribbons.

fuafuati: Samoa. Lock of hair.

fuaigheal: Ireland. Gaelic word for seam.

fūan: Ireland. 1. Old Gaelic word for coat. *See also* inar. 2. Outer garment worn by both sexes.

fuchina: Mexico. Purple aniline dye.
fuchou: China. Poplin.
Fuchs: Germany. Fox fur.
fuchsia: Purplish red.
Fuchsie: Germany. Fuchsia.
fucus: Roman (753 B.C.E.–323 C.E.). Rouge.
fudag: Ireland. Gaelic word for shoe strap.
füdzö: Hungary. Closing flap on bodice.
fue: Samoa. Fly whisk.
fufuo: Ghana. The color white.
fugi: Japan. Wisteria fiber coats.
fugitive coat: Directoire and First Empire (1790–1815 C.E.). Introduced in 1807, pelisse that opened down front. Descendent of flying Josie.
fugu: Ghana. Man's loose smock worn with short trousers.
fuigheag: Ireland. Gaelic word for thrum.
fuiliche: Ireland. Gaelic word for blood red.
fuilidh: Ireland. Gaelic word for blood red.
fuine: Italy. Wolf fur.
fuji: Japan. Plain spun silk fabric made in Fuji.
fukás: Greece. Wool belt.
fukube-dana: Japan. A facial mask.
fu-la: Vietnam. Scarf.
full bottomed wig: Restoration (1660–1700 C.E.). Light wig invented for Louis XIV by Sieur Binet, wigmaker.
full slops: *See* slops.
fuller's chalk: *See* fuller's earth.
fuller's earth: Clay used to remove grease and perspiration from hats. Usually a gray powder.
fulu: Samoa. Feather.
fumee: Bustle (1865–1890 C.E.). In 1872, smoke brown.
fumee de Londres: Bustle (1865–1890 C.E.). In 1884, tint of London smoke.
funda: Biblical (unknown–30 C.E.). Hebrew's money belt.
fúndes: Greece. Tassels worn attached to braids of hair.
fúndi: Greece. Chemise.
fundilho: Portugal. Seat of trousers.
fúndítses: Greece. Fringes on the seguni.
fundo de agulha: Portugal. Eye of a needle.
fungomi: Japan. Woman's trousers.

furisode

funnel collar: Collar fitted at neckline, flaring outward at top.
funnel sleeve: *See* pagoda sleeve.
fuo: China. Zhuong dynasty. Axe-shaped embroidered ornament hung from waist. Precursor of bixi.
furashka: Russia. Forage cap.
furbelow: *See* flounce.
furisode: Japan. A kimono with long, bag-like sleeves.

furoshiki: Japan. Kerchief made of plain or patterned cotton, muslin, or flannel.
furoshiki-botchi: *See* furoshiki.
furre: Byzantine and Romanesque (400–1200 C.E.) to Renaissance (1450–1550 C.E.). United Kingdom. Middle English word for fur.
fürtuchsklemmer: Austria. Large brooch.
fusa: Japan. Tassel.
fuseau: France. Bobbin.
fuselli: Italy. Bobbins.
Fusex shirt: (1930–1940 C.E.). United Kingdom. A man's shirt with a self-stiffening collar.
fusi: Samoa. Belt.
fustă: Romania. Skirt.
fústa: Greece. Petticoat or skirt.
fustaine: France. Fustian.
fustan: 1. Late Georgian (1750–1790 C.E.). Peru. In the 1780s, a petticoat ruffle. 2. Spain. Fustian; dimity.
fustanéles: *See* fustanella.
fustanella: Greece. Short, pleated, white skirt worn by men as part of national dress.
fustão: Portugal. Fustian.
fustar: Romania. Man's puckered shirt.
fuste: Guatemala and Peru. Cotton underskirt.
fustein: Holland. Fustian.
fustian: Byzantine and Romanesque (400–1200 C.E.) to Bustle (1865–1890 C.E.). United Kingdom. Cotton or cotton and flax fabric popular with the Normans. Cistercians were forbidden to wear anything but linen or fustian. First such was made in United Kingdom in Norwich. Wool fustian was made as early as 1336.
fustian anapes: Charles I and the Commonwealth (1625–1660 C.E.). Italy. Fustian from Naples.
fusube: Japan. Tie-dyed and smoked leather.
fusuma: Japan. Indian silk with designs in nonmetallic thread.
futa: Egypt. Piece of fabric.
fúta: Greece. Apron; festival apron.
futro: Poland. Fur coat.
Futter: Germany. Lining.
Fütterung: Germany. Lining.
fututam: Ghana. White cloth.
fuubu: *See* batakari.
fuya: 1. Celebes. Manila hemp. 2. Indonesia. Bark cloth.
fúzhuang: China. Dress; clothing.
fycheux: Byzantine and Romanesque (400–1200 C.E.). Fur of polecat.

G

gaas: Holland. Gauze.

gåat adahke: Norway. Antler or brass plate that hangs from a woman's belt from which hang a small purse, needle-case, etc.

gabā: India. Vest.

ga-ba-ðin: Vietnam. Gabardine.

gaban: Spain. Overcoat.

gabán: Guatemala. Woolen overcoat.

gabano: Renaissance (1450–1550 C.E.). Italy. Sleeved, open mantle.

gabardina: Spain. Gabardine.

gabardine: 1. Renaissance (1450–1550 C.E.) to Elizabethan (1550–1625 C.E.). Wide sleeved, long, loose overcoat worn with or without girdle. It ceased to be fashionable after 1560s, but it remained popular in lower classes. 2. Bustle (1865–1890 C.E.). Introduced in 1879, waterproof Egyptian cotton fabric. 3. Tightly woven, twilled fabric with high sheen.

gabardyna: Poland. Gabardine.

gabbano: 1. *See* gabano. 2. *See* palandrano.

gaberdine: 1. Smock frock. 2. Late Gothic (1350–1450 C.E.). Jewish mantle. 3. Any cloak or mantle. 4. Laborer's loose garment.

gable headdress: Renaissance (1450–1550 C.E.). United Kingdom. Stiffened, elaborate headdress shaped like gable that often reached as low as the shoulders. It was especially popular with matrons.

gábmaga: Norway. Woman's reindeer hide boots.

gabnel: Bustle (1865–1890 C.E.). Princess style dress.

gable headdress

Gabrielle dress: Bustle (1865–1890 C.E.). United Kingdom. Introduced in 1865, day dress with bodice and center skirt section cut in one. Three large box-pleats in back of gored skirt or one on each side and one in center back.

Gabrielle sleeve: Romantic (1815–1840 C.E.). United Kingdom. Popular from 1815 to 1835, woman's sleeve cut full at armseye and tapering slightly to forearm where it ended in deep cuff with lace band.

gacchakā-kī-turrī: India. Crested plume made of gold or silver ribbon worn on top of a turban.

gach: India. Bobbinet cloth.

gadar: India. Long, wide coat.

gadget cane: Cane or walking stick which conceals an object, like a sword or a flask.

gadget stick: *See* gadget cane.

gadlings: Late Gothic (1350–1450 C.E.). United Kingdom. Low spikes over the fingertips.

gadlyngs: Early Gothic (1200–1350 C.E.). Steel plates or bosses on gauntlets.

gadroon: Gay Nineties (1890–1900 C.E.). Inverted pleat or flute used as trim on caps and cuffs. Also used popularly on dress skirts.

gaforinha: Portugal. Curled hair of a Negro.

gage de Inde: Crinoline (1840–1865 C.E.). Muslin de soie; very thin silk tissue.

gaghra: India. A full skirt worn by women in western India.

gahper: Norway. Woman's headdress.

gahra gulabi: India. Dark pink.

gai pee jau sa: Crinoline (1840–1865 C.E.). United States of America. Chinese Hawaiian term for a maroon-colored silk crepe used for underclothes.

gaib: United Arab Emirates. Pocket.

gaine: 1. Sheath. 2. Girdle.

Gainsborough bonnet: Bustle (1865–1890 C.E.). United Kingdom. Introduced in 1877, woman's velvet fitted hat with high front brim and a wide crown. Often trimmed with roses.

Gainsborough hat: Late Georgian (1750–1790 C.E.). Wide-brimmed ladies' hat decorated with ribbons and feathers. Commonly found in paintings by Gainsborough.

gairda: Early Gothic (1200–1350 C.E.) to Late Gothic (1350–1450 C.E.). United Kingdom. Girdle.

gairgre: Ireland. Gaelic word for pilgrim's dress.

gaitan: Russia. Peasant woman's chest ornament.

gaiter: 1. Fabric or leather covering for ankle and lower calf that buckled or buttoned on side. It sometimes had a strap under the instep. 2. Ankle-high shoe with elastic sides. Meant to imitate shoe worn with gaiter.

gaiter bottoms: Crinoline (1840–1865 C.E.). United Kingdom. Popular cut of bottom of men's trousers.

gajajin: India. A bark-strip garment of the ascetic.

gajavadi: India. 1. A fabric decorated with an elephant pattern. 2. A closely woven cotton stuff.

gajipali: India. The silk from Ghazipur.

galabijeh: Egypt. Gown worn by fellahin.

galabiyeh bi wist: Egypt. Woman's waisted dress.

galante: Late Georgian (1750–1790 C.E.). France. Decorative patch worn in middle of the cheek.

galants: Charles I and the Commonwealth (1625–1660 C.E.). France. Ties or loops of ribbon used as decoration on women's garments.

galão: Portugal. Gold lace; silver lace.

galashiels: Scotland. Tweeds made in district of same name.

galatea: 1. Sturdy, satin or twill weave, cotton fabric used for children's play clothes. 2. Child's sailor crowned straw hat.

Galatea comb: Gay Nineties (1890–1900 C.E.). United Kingdom. Decorative hair comb with long teeth and fancy handle.

Galatea hat: Gay Nineties (1890–1900 C.E.). United Kingdom. Child's hat of Chinese or Japanese plait straw made with sailor crown and turned up brim.

galea: Early Gothic (1200–1350 C.E.). Leather helmet.

galerilla: Elizabethan (1550–1625 C.E.). Spain. One piece gown.

galero: Late Gothic (1350–1450 C.E.). Italy. Wide-brimmed red hat with 30 hanging bows. Worn by cardinals.

galerum: Byzantine and Romanesque (400–1200 C.E.). Fitted helmet of undressed skin.

galerus: *See* galerum.

galilla: Small inside collar.

gallang: Indonesia. Brass ankle-rings worn by Sa'dan-Toraja women of high status.

gallants: Charles I and the Commonwealth (1625–1660 C.E.). Small ribbon bows worn in the hair and on the clothing as trim.

gallér-szür: Hungary. Large, gored, circular cape.

gallicae: Byzantine and Romanesque (400–1200 C.E.). Low shoe with thick sole worn laced closed.

galligaskins: Elizabethan (1550–1625 C.E.). Loose knee-length trousers. *See also* gaskin.

galliochios: Pattens.

Gallo-Greek bodice: Romantic (1815–1840 C.E.). United Kingdom. Popular in 1820s, bodice with narrow flat trim reaching from shoulders to just above waist.

gallone: Italy. Galloon.

galloon: Narrow tape or metal lace on a ribbon.

galloshoes: Renaissance (1450–1550 C.E.) to Elizabethan (1550–1625 C.E.). Wooden soled overshoes.

gallowses: Early Georgian (1700–1750 C.E.) to Bustle (1865–1890 C.E.). Cloth suspenders with hooks and eyes.

galluses: *See* gallowses.

galocha: 1. Portugal. Galosh. 2. Elizabethan (1550–1625 C.E.). Spain. Wooden-soled shoe.

galoche: 1. Late Gothic (1350–1450 C.E.) to Elizabethan (1550–1625 C.E.). Wooden platform with strap attached to it to fit over shoe. It was worn to keep feet raised from ground. *See also* arctics. 2. France. Galosh.

galon: 1. *See* galloon. 2. Holland. Galloon.

galon d'argent: France. Silver lace.

galon d'or: France. Gold lace.

galoscia: Holland. Galosh.

galosh: Overshoe.

galosses: *See* galloshoes.

galuchat: 1. Ornamented shagreen. 2. Kind of sharkskin.

galyac: *See* galyak.

galyak: Very flat, glossy fur from lamb, kid, or goat.

gãm: Vietnam. Brocade.

gãm vóc: Vietnam. Brocade and satin.

gamanjunni: Norway. Turned-up toe on shoes or boots.

gamashes: Elizabethan (1550–1625 C.E.) to Restoration (1660–1700 C.E.). Worn from 1590s to 1700, men's long, loose, cloth leggings that buttoned. Worn on horseback or on foot as protection from mud spatters.

gambade: Long gaiter that was attached like a stirrup to the saddle. Worn to protect wearer from mud spatters.

gambado: *See* gambade.

gambeson: Early Gothic (1200–1350 C.E.) to Late Gothic (1350–1450 C.E.). Defensive coat of leather, or quilted and padded fabric. Worn as protection under armor and later became civilian garment known as juppe, gippon, pourpoint, or doublet.

gambeto: Spain. Short wool topcoat.

gamboised cuisses: India. Early Gothic (1100–1250 C.E.). Quilted thigh defenses.

gambroon: Twill weave fabric of linen, wool, or a blend used for linings.

gamcha: India. A cloth that may serve as both the turban and the loincloth.

gammadion: Ecclesiastical emblem used in church embroideries created from positioning of four gammas in shape of cross.

gamoshes: Restoration (1660–1700 C.E.). United States. Men's high boots.

gamp: Crinoline (1840–1865 C.E.) to Bustle (1865–1890 C.E.). Popular name for the umbrella, named for Mrs. Gamp in Dickens's *Martin Chuzzlewit*.

gamsbart: Austria. Thick chamois plume worn on Tyrolese hats.

gamurra: Renaissance (1450–1550 C.E.). Italy. Woman's garment, perhaps similar to houppelande.

gamuza: Spain. Suede; chamois.

gàn: China. Dark purple.

ganache: Early Gothic (1200–1350 C.E.). Robe with short caped sleeves.

gandhaki: India. Light yellow.

gandoora: *See* gandoura.

gandoura

gandoura: Algeria. African sleeveless robe.

gandurah: *See* gandoura.

gangasagara: India. A fine silk from Bengal.

gangetic: Roman (753 B.C.E.–323 C.E.). The best quality muslin from India.

gangkai: China. Steel helmet.

gànqing: China. Dark purple.

gansbauch: Elizabethan (1550–1625 C.E.). Germany. Literally "goose belly," German term for peascod belly.

ganse: Cord.

gansey: Knitted jacket or jersey.

gansy: *See* gansey.

gant: France. Glove.

gants de chevreau: France. Kid gloves.

gants de Swède: Crinoline (1840–1865 C.E.). In 1862, undressed kid gloves with embroidered backs.

gants Régence: Bustle (1865–1890 C.E.). In 1878, long, dull kid gloves that laced.

gao: China. In ancient China, thin white silk.

gaogenxié: China. High-heeled shoes.

gaopí: China. Lambskin.

gaosù: China. White mourning clothes.

gáppte: Norway. Woman's long, wide tunic with a V-neck.

garacolū: India. Bride's red sari with wide, many colored borders.

garannō: Ethiopia. Cloak.

garanza: Renaissance (1450–1550 C.E.). Italy. Dye creating variety of colors from red to purple to black. *See also* madder.

garcettes
See also photospread
(Headwear).

garbbhasutra: India. A fine variety of muslin.

garbh-chulaidh: Ireland. Gaelic word for frieze coat.

garcettes: Charles I and the Commonwealth (1625–1660 C.E.). France. A woman's short curls worn on the forehead; bangs.

garchola: India. Literally "house garment," a grid-patterned sari.

garçon d'honneur: France. Page.

garde Français: Crinoline (1840–1865 C.E.). In 1864, lady's muslin collar trimmed with lace.

gardebras: Early Gothic (1200–1350 C.E.). Piece of armor that protected arm.

garde-collet: Early Gothic (1200–1350 C.E.). Ridge on pauldron that protected the neck.

garde-corps: Early Gothic (1200–1350 C.E.) to Late Gothic (1350–1450 C.E.). Loose, flowing garment with short sleeves or sleeveless that was worn by both genders.

gardecors: *See* garde-corps.

garde-de-rein: Early Gothic (1200–1350 C.E.). Kidney guard in suit of armor.

garduña: Spain. Stone marten.

gare: Nigeria. Middle-class man's very wide, white cotton gown with one large chest pocket.

garha: *See* gurrah.

gari: Borneo. Garment; clothes.

Garibaldi blouse: Crinoline (1840–1865 C.E.). Woman's loose blouse worn in 1859 in honor of Italian hero.

Garibaldi blouse
See also photospread
(Women's Wear).

Garibaldi bodice: Crinoline (1840–1865 C.E.). United Kingdom. Worn in 1860s, woman's day bodice that fell loosely over the waistband or had a number of tiny tucks from neck to waist. Worn with or without a jacket.

Garibaldi hat: Crinoline (1840–1865 C.E.). Woman's braided pillbox hat.

Garibaldi jacket: Crinoline (1840–1865 C.E.). United Kingdom. Woman's shirt of red cashmere, decorated with black cord, braid, and buttons.

Garibaldi sleeve: Crinoline (1840–1865 C.E.). United Kingdom. In 1860s, woman's full sleeve that gathered onto wristband.

Garibaldi bodice

Worn with thin morning or afternoon dresses.

garlicks: Elizabethan (1550–1625 C.E.) to Restoration (1660–1700 C.E.). Linen made in Prussian Silesia.

garnache: *See* ganache.

garnement: Early Gothic (1200–1350 C.E.). Term meaning garment.

garnet: Late Georgian (1750–1790 C.E.). Dark pink, almost magenta.

garrankee: Sierra Leone. Shoemaker.

garri cloth: Sierra Leone. Hand printed cotton fabric made using wax resist technique.

garrick greatcoat: Directoire and First Empire (1790–1815 C.E.). Caped overcoat.

garrison cap: (1940–1950 C.E.). United States of America. Army enlisted man's soft, folding overseas cap.

gartain: Scotland. Garter. Traditionally one yard long and worn tied in snaoin gartain (garter knot). Usually green or red.

gartan: Ireland. Gaelic word for bonnet or garter.

garter: 1. Ribbon that tied around leg to hold up stocking. 2. Band at bottom of pair of knee-breeches.

garter belt: Band with supporters worn around waist and used to support stockings.

garvín: Renaissance (1450–1550 C.E.). Spain. Hairnet.

garza: Italy. Gauze.

gash: Scotland. To be well dressed.

gasieng: *See* gasing.

gasing: Borneo. Spinning-wheel.

gaskin: Short for galligaskin.

gassa: Italy. Bow.

gassed lace: Lace made with thread that has been passed through gas flame to burn off any extra fibers.

gatĕ: Slovakia. Men's wide, coarse linen trousers.

Gates of Hell: Renaissance (1450–1550 C.E.). So called by church leaders, laced openings in women's bodices.

gates of Paris cloth: *See* brocatelle.

gatos de lomos: Renaissance (1450–1550 C.E.). Spain. Catskins.

gātrikāgranthi: India. Swastika-shaped knot of fabric.

gatto civetta: Italy. Fur of the civet cat.

gatugatu: Samoa. Bark-cloth.

gatya: Hungary. Men's linen pantaloons cut from rectangles.

gatyamadzag: Hungary. Drawstring.

gau: Vietnam. The cuffs on a pair of trousers.

gau chau: Bustle (1865–1890 C.E.). United States of America. Chinese Hawaiian term for the finest chau fabric. It came in three forms: 1) jee ma sa (rough textured), 2) din mui sa (medium textured), and 3) lai kee wat chau (very smooth textured). It was a glazed black gossamer material with a brown undersurface.

gau dai hai: (1900–1910 C.E.). United States of America. Literally "boat shoes," Chinese Hawaiian term for women's embroidered cloth shoes with a high, thick sole that tapered up toward the ends.

gau liang: (1900–1910 C.E.). United States of America. Chinese Hawaiian term for a high collar.

gaucho belt: (1960–1969 C.E.). Leather and metal medallion and chain belt.

gaucho blouse: Full, loose blouse.

gaucho hat: Wide brimmed, high crowned hat.

gaucho pants: Calf-length pants with tapered legs. In imitation of pants worn by gauchos in Argentina.

gauffré: France. Term for various embossed patterns pressed into fabric.

gaufrure: France. The couching of parallel lines of yarns to produce a waffle-like pattern.

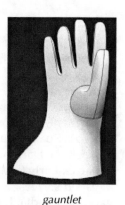

gauntlet

gauging: Romantic (1815–1840 C.E.). Type of fine cartridge pleating.

gaunaka: India. A very rough cloth.

gauntlet: Elizabethan (1550–1625 C.E.). Elbow-length glove with decorative backs.

gauntlet cuff: Deep flared cuff as on gauntlets.

gausapa: Roman (753 B.C.E.–323 C.E.). Type of psila.

gauze: Sheer, lightweight, leno weave fabric.

gavacha: Guatemala. Apron.

gay: Vietnam. Very red.

gayado: Renaissance (1450–1550 C.E.). Spain. Striped.

gayas: Renaissance (1450–1550 C.E.). Spain. Stripes.

gaza: Poland. Gauze.

gazar: France. Loosely woven silk fabric; gauze.

gaze: Portugal. Gauze; tissue.

Gaze: Germany. Gauze.

gaze à bouquets: Late Georgian (1750–1790 C.E.). France. Gauze fabric printed in floral pattern.

gaze de Chambery: Bustle (1865–1890 C.E.). In 1867, fine silk gauze striped with brightly colored stripes.

gaze de fantaisie: Late Georgian (1750–1790 C.E.). France. Gauze fabric with fancy trim.

gaze d'Orient: Crinoline (1840–1865 C.E.). In 1855, new fabric.

gaze gauffree: Gay Nineties (1890–1900 C.E.). In 1893, a diaphanous crepe.

gaze neige: Bustle (1865–1890 C.E.). In 1876, new lace.

gazeline barege: Bustle (1865–1890 C.E.). Introduced in 1877, semi-transparent fabric made from llama wool.

gazzatum: Gauze silk or linen made in Gaza, Palestine.

gbariye: *See* agbada.

ge dai: China. Zhou dynasty. Leather girdle.

geal: Ireland. Gaelic word for white.

geamantan: *See* ilic.

gebauw: Holland. Fabric.

gebreid of geweven ondergoed: Holland. Hosiery.

gebreid vest: Holland. Cardigan.

gebreide muts: Holland. Stocking cap.

gedilim: Biblical. Twisted cord tassel.

geel: Holland. Yellow.

geer: Holland. Gusset.

gefrens: Renaissance (1450–1550 C.E.). Fringe worn at back of woman's head.

gegendas: Gay Nineties (1890–1900 C.E.). Corset with steel stays.

geideal: Ireland. Gaelic word for fan.

Gekko shirt: (1980–1990 C.E.). A man's striped shirt with a white color and cuffs. It was named for the character Gordon Gekko in *Wall Street* (1988), played by Michael Douglas.

geklede jas: Holland. Frock coat.

geknauften kogeln: Late Gothic (1350–1450 C.E.). Germany. Gugel that buttoned in center front.

gelb: Germany. Yellow.

geldem: Ethiopia. Knee-length loincloth.

gelumbė: Lithuania. Manufactured cloth.

gemelos: Spain. Cufflinks; studs.

geminal ring: Betrothal ring.

gemma: Roman (753 B.C.E.–323 C.E.). Jewel.

gemme: *See* iuele.

gemmews: Renaissance (1450–1550 C.E.). Jaws of hanging bag.

gen: China. Heel of a shoe.

genappe cloth: Crinoline (1840–1865 C.E.). Introduced in 1863, wool and cotton blend fabric striped in two shades of same color.

genet: Fur of wildcat.

Geneva bands: White lawn or linen flaps worn on front of clerical dress.

Geneva embroidery: Embroidery similar to ticking.

Geneva gown: Ecclesiastical vestment made as long, loose gown with large sleeves.

Geneva hat: Charles I (1625–1660 C.E.). Man's broad brimmed, high crowned hat worn by Puritan ministers and others. Sometimes untrimmed.

Geneva printruff: Charles I and the Commonwealth (1625–1660 C.E.). United Kingdom. Puritan's small ruff based on those worn by Calvinists in Geneva.

Genoa cloak: *See* Italian cloak.

Genoa lace: Italy. Variety of laces made in Genoa in 17th century.

Genoa plush: Bustle (1865–1890 C.E.). Plush fabric with short, thick pile, similar to velvet.

Genoa velvet: 1. Late Georgian (1750–1790 C.E.). Italy. Brocaded silk velvet from Genoa. 2. Bustle (1865–1890 C.E.). Fabric with satin ground and velvet arabesques.

Genoese embroidery: Italy. Buttonhole embroidery done on cord on linen or muslin.

Genoese lace: Solid, scalloped bobbin laces decorated with wheat ear motifs.

genouillieres: 1. Early Gothic (1200–1350 C.E.). Protective knee piece in armor. 2. Renaissance (1450–1550 C.E.) to Elizabethan (1550–1625 C.E.). France. Fabric knee pieces that fit space between stockings and trunk hose.

genthulla: India. A bodice or a tunic.

gentish: Early Georgian (1700–1750 C.E.). Fabric from Ghent.

genuillieres: *See* genouillieres.

geolan: Ireland. Gaelic word for fan.

George: Nigeria. Ibo nickname for Indian madras.

georgette: Thin, lightweight, plain weave silk or rayon fabric that has creped face.

georgette crepe: Sheer, semi-transparent crepe.

Georgian cloth: Directoire and First Empire (1790–1815 C.E.). Introduced in 1806, lightweight broadcloth.

g'erbt: *See* apg'erbt.

gerele: Byzantine and Romanesque (400–1200 C.E.). United Kingdom. Term meaning garment or clothes, especially meaning finery.

gergueta: Ecuador. Black anaku that stops just below the knee.

gerife: Byzantine and Romanesque (400–1200 C.E.). United Kingdom. Term meaning a garment.

geringsing: Indonesia (Bali). Double ikat fabric.

German gown: Late Georgian (1750–1790 C.E.). Fitted gown with sack back, long sleeves, and front buttons.

German serge: Early Georgian (1700–1750 C.E.). Serge made with worsted warp and woolen weft. *See also* thunder and lightning.

German wool: *See* Berlin wool.

Gertrude: Flannel T-shaped robe worn by infants.

geru: India. Red ochre.

Geschützlafette: Germany. Barbette.

ge-scripla: Byzantine and Romanesque (400–1200 C.E.). United Kingdom. Term meaning men's clothes.

gestaltrock: Elizabethan (1550–1625 C.E.). Germany. Literally "form-coat," new name for the schaube.

gesteven overhemb: Holland. Boiled shirt.

gestreepte of geruite katoenen stof: Holland. Gingham.

geta: Japan. Similar to chopines, wooden clogs with horizontal boards that raise the feet from the ground. The clogs are held to the feet with velvet or cord thongs.

geta
See also photospread
(Foot and Legwear).

gewœde: *See* clāpes.

gewœdian: *See* scrydan.

ghabani: Palestine. Silk fabric.

ghabaniyyeh: Palestine. White kafiyyeh with golden yellow silk embroidery.

ghabi: Transvaal. A Ndebele girl's 9-1/2-inch-wide beaded panel worn over a fringed apron.

ghaggharo: India. A woman's short skirt.

ghaghara: India. Woman's short loincloth.

ghagra: India. Woman's pleated or gathered skirt.

ghagri: India. A simple, stitched skirt.

gharacholoo: India. Red bridal sari.

gharara: India. Woman's, full, flaring pants.

ghararas: India. Wedding outfits including a wrap 30–40 yards long.

gharcholu: India. Special wedding veil.

ghatra: Egypt. Worn under the futa, a headcloth that frames the forehead.

ghava-ye zananeh: Iran. Woman's long, narrow, tight-sleeved coat.

gheată: Romania. Shoe.

gherone: Italy. Gusset.

gheta: Japan. High wooden clogs.

ghillie: Scotland. Shoe that laces through loops instead of eyelets.

ghim bang: Vietnam. Safety pin.

ghiordan: Romania. Woman's fine bead necklace. *See also* colier.

ghiottone: Italy. Wolverine fur.

ghirlanda: Italy. Garland.

ghlîla: Algeria. Jewish woman's knee-length, décolleté vest with short sleeves.

ghost coat: (1930–1940 C.E.). United Kingdom. In 1939, a man's overcoat with a white proof finish that reflected in headlights for safety, but was dark enough for blackout conditions.

ghoutra: United Arab Emirates. Square of cotton fabric large enough to wrap around head.

ghudfeh: 1. Palestine. Woman's festive veil with wide embroidered panel on one or both short sides. 2. Palestine. Married woman's shawl. Usually cross-stitched with red the dominant color.

ghughi: *See* natiyo.

ghunghut: India. Veiling.

ghungru: India. An anklet with small bells.

ghutanna: India. Very tight trousers worn neatly gathered at the ankles.

ghutra: Arabia. Man's headscarf of cotton, rayon, linen, voile, silk, or shantung made in variety of colors and patterns. About four feet square (smaller for boys) and worn folded into triangle with two points over shoulders, and the third down the center back. Often worn over skullcap. It is held in position with an agal.

ghwayshat: Palestine. Glass bracelets.

giacca: Italy. Coat.

giacchetto: Italy. Coat of mail.

giall' antique: Italy. Color ancient yellow, named for a rich yellow marble.

giall-bhrat: Ireland. Gaelic word for neck-cloth or cravat.

giallo: Italy. Yellow.

giallo antico: *See* giall' antique.

giáp: Vietnam. Armor.

giáp-bào: Vietnam. Armor.

giáp-y: Vietnam. Armored coat.

giardinetti rings: Renaissance (1450–1550 C.E.) to Late Georgian (1750–1790 C.E.). Finger rings set to resemble flower bouquets, nosegays, and jardinieres.

giá-trang: Vietnam. Bride's trousseau.

giay ta: Vietnam. Slipper-like shoes.

giay tây: Vietnam. Western shoes.

giay tuyet: Vietnam. Snow shoes.

gibao: *See* saiote.

gibeciere: *See* aumoniere.

giboun: Crinoline (1840–1865 C.E.). Introduced in 1844, man's wide sleeved, loose cape that did not fasten, but hung open.

gibus: *See* opera hat.

gig coat: *See* curricle coat.

gige: *See* guige.

gigolo: (1920–1930 C.E.). High-crowned hat with center crease, narrow brim that turned up in the back and down in front.

gigot sleeve: (20th century). Full sleeve with greatest fullness at elbow.

gig-top: *See* Normandy bonnet.

gilaharā: India. Sari with a wide border.

gilbah: Egypt. Islamic woman's ankle-length robe with long sleeves and a high neck. Made in subdued colors of cotton or wool.

gi-lê: Vietnam. Vest; waistcoat.

gilet: France. Worn most commonly with suits, woman's sleeveless bodice made to resemble blouse.

gilet-veste: Late Georgian (1750–1790 C.E.). France. Man's short fronted waistcoat.

gillie: *See* ghillie.

gim: *See* gimstān.

Gimma: Germany. Old High German word for jewel.

gimme: Germany. Old word for jewel.

gimmoru: Japan. Indian silk with silver thread designs.

gimnasterka: Russia. Gymnastic shirt.

gimnel-ring: Late Gothic. A popular betrothal gift, two rings locked together that could be separated into two separate rings.

gimp: Silk, worsted, or cotton twist trim.

gimstān: Renaissance (1450–1550 C.E.). United Kingdom. Old English word for jewel.

gimsteinn: Norway. Old word for jewel.

giná: Egypt. Plain, black, coarse, heavy shawl.

gindhuam: India. A breastcloth.

Gingang: Germany. Gingham.

gingerline: Elizabethan (1550–1625 C.E.) to Restoration (1660–1700 C.E.). Fabric, sometimes reddish violet color.

gingham: Medium-weight, cotton or linen fabric woven with colored yarns in stripes, checks, or other patterns.

ginglers: Elizabethan (1550–1625 C.E.). Pair of man's spurs with metal drops that rattled against the rowel when the wearer walked, creating noise.

ginran: Japan. Use of metallic paper strips in woven cloth.

giogan: Ireland. Gaelic word for a brooch worn in the side of a Glengarry bonnet.

gioielle: *See* spillo da petto.

gioiello: Italy. Jewel.

giosān: *See* stoca.

gipciere: Early Gothic (1200–1350 C.E.). France. Pouch or purse.

gipon: Early Gothic (1200–1350 C.E.). Early form of doublet made from quilted fabric. Worn as undergarment. By mid-14th century, had become the doublet. *See also* jupe; jupon.

gippo: Short tunic.

gippon: *See* gipon.

gipsy bonnet
See also photospread
(Headwear).

gipser: *See* gipciere.

gipsy bonnet: Bustle (1865–1890 C.E.). Introduced in 1871, woman's small, flat bonnet worn on the crown of the head. It was trimmed with lace and feathers.

gipsy cloak: Romantic (1815–1840 C.E.). Woman's plain circular wrap with hood.

gipsy hat: Directoire and First Empire (1790–1815 C.E.) to Romantic (1815–1840 C.E.). United Kingdom. Popular from 1800 to 1830s, woman's straw or chip, wide brimmed hat with ribbon that ran over crown and brim and tied under chin.

giraffe comb: Bustle (1865–1890 C.E.). United Kingdom. Introduced in 1874, woman's high ornamental hair comb made of tortoiseshell.

girandole: Pendant piece of jewelry.

girdel: Byzantine and Romanesque (400–1200 C.E.) to Renaissance (1450–1550 C.E.). United Kingdom. Middle English word for belt.

girdelstede: Byzantine and Romanesque (400–1200 C.E.). Saxon word for waist.

girdle: 1. Flexible lightweight corset worn to confine figure, particularly the hipline. 2. Something that girds, as a belt.

girdle à la victime: Directoire and First Empire (1790–1815 C.E.). France. Worn in 1796, brightly colored sash worn by women over shoulders, crossing in back and tied around the waist.

girdle glass: Charles I and the Commonwealth (1625–1660 C.E.). United Kingdom. Hand mirror worn hanging from waist by women.

girike: Nigeria. Yoruba man's large, heavy agbada.

girki: Nigeria. Wealthy man's cotton damask gown.

girri: Ethiopia. Koma earrings.

Gitana: Crinoline (1840–1865 C.E.). 1. In 1850, velvet cloak that buttoned down the front. It had a small upright collar and was trimmed in black Brussels lace. 2. In 1855, Spanish broadcloth wrapper. It was trimmed with moss applique and heavy fringe.

gite: Early Gothic (1200–1350 C.E.) to Renaissance (1450–1550 C.E.). Gown.

gitzwart: Holland. Jet black.

giubea: Romania. Long, white drugget coat.

giumedanii: Romania. Man's long coat that fastens on one side.

giuvaer: Romania. Jewel.

giveh: Iran. Hand sewn shoes.

giwāti: *See* wāt.

gjorð: Norway. Old word for girdle.

gla Halstuch: USA. Married Amish woman's sleeveless capelet worn across the shoulders and forming a point in the center front and center back.

glacé kid: Polished glove leather.

glacé Marguerite: Crinoline (1840–1865 C.E.). In 1861, shot silk dress fabric.

Gladstone bag: Traveling bag with flexible sides that divides into two equal compartments that hinge open to lay flat. Named for W. E. Gladstone.

Gladstone collar: Bustle (1865–1890 C.E.). United Kingdom. Man's standing collar with the points flaring.

Gladstone overcoat: Bustle (1865–1890 C.E.). United Kingdom. Worn in 1870s, man's short, double-breasted overcoat with its shoulder cape and edges trimmed in astrakhan.

gland: France. Tassel.

glandkin: Renaissance (1450–1550 C.E.). Luxurious gown in royal wardrobe.

glas: Ireland. Gaelic word for gray.

glasag-muineil: Ireland. Gaelic word for locket.

glass cloth: Fabric made of glass yarns or covered in powdered glass used for polishing.

glass toweling: Plain or twill weave, smooth, checked fabric used for glassware towels.

glauco: Spain. Light green.

Glauvina pin: Romantic (1815–1840 C.E.). United Kingdom. Pin with detachable head, used as hair ornament.

glazed chintz: Chintz with glaze from being treated with paraffin and then calendered.

glazed kid: Kid leather polished with frosted glass cylinder.

glazendoek: Holland. Glass cloth.

gleindorch: *See* gwddfdorch.

glen checks: Any of the small, evenly checked designs that originated in Scotland.

Glengarry: Directoire and First Empire (1790–1815 C.E.) to 20th century. First appearing in 1805, wool cap with crease in top. Edges were bound with ribbon which hangs down back in streamers. Sides are stiffened. Often had red or blue tuft on top.

glenglen: Trinidad. Small round bell hung on the points of the Carnival Pierrot Grenade costume.

glib: Renaissance (1450–1550 C.E.). Ireland. Man's hairstyle where hair on front of head grew to cover eyes, but the rest was shaved above the ears. Forbidden in United Kingdom in 1537.

glinne: Ireland. Gaelic word for coat.

glissade: United Kingdom. Cotton lining fabric.

gloan: France. Breton for wool

glocken: Early Gothic (1200–1350 C.E.) to Late Gothic (1350–1450 C.E.). Germany. Circular cape.

glōf: Romanesque (400–1200 C.E.). United Kingdom. Glove.

glofi: Norway. Old word for glove.

gloria: Tightly woven silk and worsted, silk and cotton, or other blend fabric woven in diagonal twill. Primarily used to cover umbrellas.

glotón: Spain. Wolverine fur.

glouhché: Bulgaria. Woman's sleeveless, slightly flared, knee-length coat that opens in front.

glouton: France. Wolverine fur.

glove: Covering for hand with separate sheaths for each finger.

glove silk: Warp knit fabric used for gloves.

glove string: Early Georgian (1700–1750 C.E.). Ribbon or horsehair tie worn tied or buckled at elbow of woman's long glove.

glove-band: Charles I and the Commonwealth (1625–1660 C.E.) to Restoration (1660–1700 C.E.). Worn from c1640 to c1700, band of ribbon ties worn at the elbow of woman's glove to hold it in place.

gluga: Romania. Worn in bad weather, a tasseled or fringed woolen hood.

glùinean: Ireland. Garter.

glutton: Hide of the *Gulo luscus*, a cross between a wolf and a bear. The fur is brown with a characteristic beige forked pattern on the back of the animal.

goaly: Bustle (1865–1890 C.E.). Introduced in 1874, ecru silk, texture of fine canvas.

goatee: Chin beard trimmed to single point.

goat's hair fringe: Crinoline (1840–1865 C.E.). In 1864, new trim.

gob cap: U. S. Navy white cotton twill cap with round crown and turned-up stitched brim.

gobaishi: Japan. Black dye.

gobanji: United States of America. Hawaii. A plaid or check pattern.

gobelin blue: Bustle (1865–1890 C.E.). Introduced in 1887, gray blue.

goburan-ori: Japan. Tapestry weave in the Gobelin style.

god: France. Breton for a fold in a garment.

godalming: Early Gothic (1200–1350 C.E.). Calfskin leather made in Godalming.

goddess sleeve: Sleeve cut full from elbow to wrist with two gathered lines along fullness.

godell: France. Breton for pocket.

godet: Triangular piece of cloth set into garment for fullness or decoration.

godet pleat: Bustle (1865–1890 C.E.). Worn in 1870s, hollow, tubular pleat that widened downward on women's skirts.

godet skirt: Gay Nineties (1890–1900 C.E.). United Kingdom. In 1895, a woman's day skirt made with godet pleats on back and sides. Hem was often reinforced with a thin steel.

godo: Hausa. Fabric woven from thick black and white threads.

godrons: Type of Jewish ruff.

godweb: Byzantine and Romanesque (400–1200 C.E.). United Kingdom. Tenth-century term for richest fabric available, thick silken cloth in various colors.

godweb-cynn: Byzantine and Romanesque (400–1200 C.E.). United Kingdom. Cloak of fancy material.

goffer: To pleat, crimp, or flute.

goffered veil: *See* nebula headdress.

goffering: Process of fluting, waving, or pleating fabric.

go-go boot: (1960–1970 C.E.). Woman's calf-high white boot.

goirridh: Ireland. Gaelic word for fox colored.

gola: Portugal. Collar.

Golconda chintz: *See* Masulipatam chintz.

gold and silver kid: Kid leather gilded or silvered.

gold embroidery: Elaborate embroidery done with gold thread.

gold ingot bun: China. Woman's shoe-shaped bun.

gold kid: Kidskin with gold leaf applied.

gold lace: Lace of gold color or lace thread with gold.

golden tea brown: China. Yuan dynasty. Shade of brown.

gole: Early Gothic (1200–1350 C.E.) to Renaissance (1450–1550 C.E.). Cape on hood or chaperon.

golf cap: Man's visored flat cap.

golf cloth: Fine woolen fabric used for sportswear.

golf hose: Heavy woolen hose.

golf shoe: Sports shoe with cleats on the bottom.

golf skirt: Heavy ankle length wool skirt with flared bottom.

golf vest: Gay Nineties (1890–1900 C.E.). United Kingdom. In 1894, a man's single-breasted, collarless vest with side pockets and watch-pocket. Often made of knitted scarlet wool and bound with braid.

gólfi: Greece. Amulet.

golilla: Elizabethan (1550–1625 C.E.). Spain. Starched, round neckband.

goller: 1. Renaissance (1450–1550 C.E.). Germany. Flat, plain piece of fabric to which back and front of scholar's gown was sewn. 2. Austria. Woman's collar that covers throat and shoulders.

Gollier: *See* Krage.

golosh: United States of America. Shoe with wood or leather soles that was held on with instep straps.

gomeda lugadu: India. A short yellow waistcloth.

gömlek: Renaissance (1450–1550 C.E.) to present. Turkey. Woman's round-necked, white chemise.

gomushin: *See* komusin.

gonbaiz: Morocco. Jewish woman's red or green bodice trimmed with gold stripes and silver buttons.

gondolier net: Bustle (1865–1890 C.E.). In 1870s, wide mesh hairnet held in place with black bows.

gonella: Italy. Skirt.

gonelle: Roman (753 B.C.E.–323 C.E.) to Byzantine and Romanesque (400–1200 C.E.). Long tunic that was adopted as monastic dress. Originally worn by both genders, male version being only calf length, female version being ankle length.

gonellone: *See* gonelle.

gongzhuangkù: China. Overalls.

gonna: Italy. Skirt.

gonna pantalone: Italy. Pantskirt.

gonne: *See* gonelle.

goon lhiabbee: Isle of Man. Loose, dyed linen jacket with broad collar.

goose-turd: Elizabethan (1550–1625 C.E.). Yellowish green.

gooseturd greene: Renaissance (1450–1550 C.E.). Yellowish green.

gorchudd: Wales. Veil.

gordel: Holland. Girdle.

gördel: Sweden. Girdle.

Gordon blue: Bustle (1865–1890 C.E.). In 1884, gray blue.

gored bell skirt: Gay Nineties (1890–1900 C.E.). United Kingdom. In 1893, a woman's skirt cut with one center front panel, three to five side panels, and a back panel cut on the cross. Ten to 16 feet around at hem and had inner muslin or crinoline nine-inch ruffle.

Gore-Tex: (1970–1980 C.E.). Introduced in 1976, a fabric membrane that stops water from entering but allows perspiration to evaporate through it.

gorge à la Gabrielle d'Estrées: Late Georgian (1750–1790 C.E.). France. Neckline fashion named for Gabrielle d'Estrees (1563–1599), mistress of Henri IV.

gorge de pigeon: Late Georgian (1750–1790 C.E.). France. Changeable color, as in shot silk.

gorget: Early Gothic (1200–1350 C.E.). Piece of linen or silk that was worn by women draped over chin, neck, and shoulders and then pinned to hair on sides of face. Replaced the barbette.

gorgias: Renaissance (1450–1550 C.E.). Piece of gauze fabric used to fill décolleté of women's gowns.

gorgoran: Directoire and First Empire (1790–1815 C.E.). Heavy form of gros de Tours.

gorguera: Renaissance (1450–1550 C.E.). Spain. Paletot.

gorm: Ireland. Gaelic word for azure blue.

gorm-aotrom: Ireland. Gaelic word for light blue.

gorocana: India. The yellow pigment dye used for making the tilak (forehead mark) or for textiles.

gorra: Spain. Cap.

gorra deportiva: Spain. Tuque.

gorra escocesa: Spain. Tam-'o-shanter.

gorro: 1. Portugal. Red woolen or linen stocking cap; bonnet. 2. Spain. Tasseled, knitted stocking cap.

gorro de dormir: Spain. Nightcap.

gorro de marinero: Spain. Cap ribbon.

gorro de pieles: Spain. Busby.

gorrym: Isle of Man. Color blue.

gòrsaid: Ireland. Gorget.

gørsemi: *See* gimsteinn.

gorset: Poland. Corset.

goshodoki: Japan. Kosode style popular in the upper class.

goshpech: India. 1. The decorative band of a hat. 2. A shawl worn twisted around the head and ears as a turban.

gošŏ: Ethiopia. Copper.

gossamer: Very sheer, soft, gauzelike fabric made from fine silk yarns.

gossamer feathers: Downy feathers from under wings of goose.

gossamer satin: Directoire and First Empire (1790–1815 C.E.). Worn from 1813, thin, soft finish satin.

gót: Vietnam. The heel of a shoe.

gota: India. A variety of gold or silver lace.

gothic cap: Romantic (1815–1840 C.E.). United Kingdom. Woman's indoor morning cap with small crown and ruching around face.

goud: Holland. Gold.

goudbruin: Holland. Auburn.

gouden: Holland. Golden.

gougandine: Restoration (1660–1700 C.E.). France. Worn partially open in front, a laced corset popular during the reign of Louis XIV.

goura feather: Dainty, short feather from crown pigeon.

gourah feather: *See* goura feather.

gourgandine: Charles I and the Commonwealth (1625–1660 C.E.) to Restoration (1660–1700 C.E.). France. Woman's silk or velvet, front lacing corselette.

gourgourans: Romantic (1815–1840 C.E.). Introduced in 1835, dress fabric with light ground and white satin stripes.

gouriz: France. Breton for belt.

gousset: France. Gusset.

gouzougenn: France. Breton for collar.

govillam: India. A cloak.

gowce: Early Gothic (1200–1350 C.E.) to Renaissance (1450–1550 C.E.). Gusset.

gown: *See* gonelle.

gown à la française: Early Georgian (1700–1750 C.E.) to Late Georgian (1750–1790 C.E.). Fitted bodice with stomacher in front and two large pleats in the back reaching from neck to hem. Worn universally at first and became court gown until French Revolution.

gown à la levantine: Late Georgian (1750–1790 C.E.). Introduced ca. 1778, overgown that pinned in front and was worn open over underskirt. It had half sleeves.

gown à la polonaise: Late Georgian (1750–1790 C.E.). Woman's gown that fastened at top of bodice below which it was cut away to show waistcoat. It had sabot sleeves trimmed with petits bonhommes. Skirt was draped up in three panels over the underskirt.

gown à la sultane: Late Georgian (1750–1790 C.E.). Introduced in 1781, dress that was open over underskirt of contrasting color.

gown à la turque: Directoire and First Empire (1790–1815 C.E.). France. Introduced in 1799, elegant gown with fitted, pleated bodice, turndown collar, flaring sleeves, and draped belt worn tied over one hip.

gown à l'anglaise: Late Georgian (1750–1790 C.E.). Worn ca. 1778 to 1785, gown with long boned point in back that was worn over waistcoat. It had a skirt that was open in front to show an underskirt of same fabric.

gown à l'insurgente: Late Georgian (1750–1790 C.E.). France. Gown à l'anglaise with pagoda sleeves.

gown and coat: Late Georgian (1750–1790 C.E.). Woman's robe worn open over a petticoat.

grabanni: Lebanon. Machine embroidery.

Graham turban: Directoire and First Empire (1790–1815 C.E.). Introduced in 1811, woman's plaid silk bonnet worn with plume of black feathers.

Grain: Germany. Grain de poudre.

grain: The direction of the fabric, along the warp and weft threads.

grain de poudre: 1. Bustle (1865–1890 C.E.). In 1877, extremely soft silk tissue. 2. Very light, grainy wool fabric.

grain leather: Leather made from hair side of skin.

grains: *See* wheat ears.

graiveyaka: India. Man's neck ornament made of several rings.

gramalla: Late Gothic (1350–1450 C.E.). Jewish man's long outer gown.

gran gola: Elizabethan (1550–1625 C.E.). Spain. Large ruff.

grana: 1. Renaissance (1450–1550 C.E.). Italy. Red dye used as base for many colors. 2. *See* cochinilla.

grana encarnada: Renaissance (1450–1550 C.E.). Spain. Reddish woolen.

granaat: Holland. The gem, garnet.

granatza: Assyria. Long-sleeved gown.

grand broché: France. Any particularly spectacular brocaded silk weaving.

grand domino: Late Georgian (1750–1790 C.E.). Large cloak worn as disguise at carnivals. Later worn to cover masked ball costumes when traveling to the event.

grand habit: *See* habit.

grand habit de cour: Late Georgian (1750–1790 C.E.). France. In 1780s, formal costume for court occasions which included heavily boned bodice, elaborate lace sleeves, heavily trimmed pannier skirt with long train, all made from luxurious fabrics.

grand vair: *See* vair.

grande pelisse d'hiver: Late Georgian (1750–1790 C.E.). France. Large quilted cloak, often trimmed in fur.

grande redingote à l'allemande: Late Georgian (1750–1790 C.E.). Full-length redingote in German style.

grande robe à corps ouvert: Late Georgian (1750–1790 C.E.). France. Fancy gown that opened in front to show matching petticoat. Worn with wide panniers.

grande robe à la française: Late Georgian (1750–1790 C.E.). Richly trimmed gown worn with large panniers. It had loose pleats in back like all robes à la francaise.

grande-assiette sleeves: Late Gothic (1350–1450 C.E.). Man's sleeve cut to form round armseye.

granilla: Spain. Grain de poudre.

granit de laine: Crinoline (1840–1865 C.E.). In 1864, soft gray wool fabric speckled with dots of second color.

granite: Bustle (1865–1890 C.E.). Introduced in 1865, chiné woolen fabric in two shades of one color.

granite cloth: Durable, lightweight fabric in figured weave. Often made of wool yarns.

grannie skirt: Gay Nineties (1890–1900 C.E.) In 1893, a circular skirt made with flounces and tucks at knee. It had a velvet band around its sixteen to eighteen foot hem.

granny bonnet: Gay Nineties (1890–1900 C.E.). In 1893, an oversized bonnet with flaring brim and pot-shaped crown that was trimmed in feathers.

grano d'orzo: Renaissance (1450–1550 C.E.). Italy. Chain mail closed with a rivet.

grant: Ireland. Gaelic word for gray or green.

grape brown: China. Yuan dynasty. Shade of brown.

grass embroidery: United States. American Indian satin stitch embroidery done using colored grass for thread.

grassets: Early Georgian (1700–1750 C.E.) to Late Georgian (1750–1790 C.E.). United States. Popular from 1712 to 1768, dress fabric.

grasshopper green: Gay Nineties (1890–1900 C.E.). In 1892, a new color.

grau: Germany. Gray.

graundice: Renaissance (1450–1550 C.E.) to Elizabethan (1550–1625 C.E.). Head ornament.

grauw: *See* grijs.

gravata: Portugal. Necktie; cravat.

gray lilac: Romantic (1815–1840 C.E.). United Kingdom. Violet gray.

grazzets: *See* grassets.

gré: Ireland. Gaelic spelling of gray.

greatcoat: Large overcoat, commonly made of wool.

greatcoat dress: Directoire and First Empire (1790–1815 C.E.). United Kingdom. Dress cut like a greatcoat.

greaves: Roman (753 B.C.E.–323 C.E.) to 20th century. Accessory that covered leg from ankle to knee.

grebe: Ivory colored, smooth, down feather of grebe duck.

grebe cloth: Cotton fabric with downy surface on one side.

Grecian bend: Bustle (1865–1890 C.E.). Popular stance for women involving body being tilted forward from hips.

Grecian robe: Directoire and First Empire (1790–1815 C.E.). Popular from 1800 to 1805, pseudo-classic evening gown.

Grecian sandal: Directoire and First Empire (1790–1815 C.E.). Introduced in 1812, novel footwear for evening and street.

Grecian sleeve: Crinoline (1840–1865 C.E.). United

Kingdom. Introduced in 1852, woman's undersleeve that was slit on sides and then buttoned shut.

Grecque corsage: Crinoline (1840–1865 C.E.). United Kingdom. Popular in 1850, evening bodice that was pleated vertically to point in front and worn low on shoulders.

gredzens: Lithuania. Finger ring.

Greek embroidery: Applique in which stitch pattern to hold applied piece is repeated on ground.

Greek lace: Needlepoint lace like reticella.

Greek stripes: United Kingdom. Rough, plain weave cotton fabric made in dull stripes on dark blue ground.

Greek Venise: Fine reticello.

grege: France. Natural color of raw silk.

gregesque: Elizabethan (1550–1625 C.E.). Puffed venetians.

grego: Short coat with hood made of thick, rough fabric.

gregs: Sportsman's leggings.

gregues: Renaissance (1450–1550 C.E.) to Elizabethan (1550–1625 C.E.). France. Worn from 1515 to 1590, breeches.

greige: France. Unbleached, undyed fabric.

greige goods: Unfinished fabric in its natural state.

gréis: Ireland. Embroidery.

gréiseadaireachd: Ireland. Embroidery.

gréiseadh: Ireland. Embroidery.

gréis-obair: Ireland. Embroidery.

grelot: Crinoline (1840–1865 C.E.). United Kingdom. Ball fringe, popular on evening dresses.

grembiule: Italy. Apron.

gremial: Ecclesiastical dress. Silk or linen apron worn by a bishop when officiating.

grenadier cap: United Kingdom. Special cap worn by grenadiers. Originally a simple cloth cap, by the mid-18th century, this was a miter-shaped cap. The shape has continued to evolve through the years.

grenadierka: Russia. Grenadier cap.

grenadine: Fine, loose leno weave fabric of silk or wool.

grenadine rayée: Bustle (1865–1890 C.E.). In 1873, grenadine with white satin stripes.

Grenfell cloth: Firmly woven cotton fabric similar to Byrd cloth.

grian-sgàil: Ireland. Parasol; sunshade.

grian-sgàilean: Ireland. Little parasol.

gridelin: Early Georgian (1700–1750 C.E.). Soft blue gray.

grigio: Renaissance (1450–1550 C.E.). Italy. Gray.

grijs: Holland. Gray.

grijs blauw: Holland. Wedgwood blue.

grillage: Barred or grated ground in open spaces of lace.

grillé: France. Half-stitch work.

grin: Ireland. Gaelic word for green.

grinsing: Indonesia. Double-ikat textile. Considered national treasure and may not be exported.

gris: 1. *See* grise. 2. Italy. Gray. 3. Spain. Gray.

gris Anglaise: Bustle (1865–1890 C.E.). In 1867, lighter shade than steel with metallic cast.

gris de fer: Bustle (1865–1890 C.E.). In 1883, iron gray.

gris humo: Spain. Smoke gray.

gris parduzco: Spain. Taupe.

gris ratón: Spain. Taupe.

grisaglia: Italy. Grisaille.

grisaille: France. Cotton and wool fabric with figured design.

grisalho: Portugal. Gray colored.

grisalla: Spain. Grisaille.

grise: Early Gothic (1200–1350 C.E.). Expensive gray fur, probably squirrel or marten.

grisette: Sturdy, gray wool fabric.

Grisi: Crinoline (1840–1865 C.E.). In 1854, woman's satin cloak gathered on plain round yoke. Trimmed with scalloped guipure lace.

griza: Greece. A woman's long sleeveless vest of fine white wool. It is bordered in red wool.

grober Wollstoff: Germany. Droguet.

grobes Wollzeug: Germany. Kersey.

groen: Holland. Green.

grof weefsel: Holland. Linsey-woolsey.

grogram: Early Georgian (1700–1750 C.E.). Rough silk, mohair, and wool fabric that was often stiffened with gum.

groilleach: Ireland. Gaelic word for coarse cloth.

grommet: Metallic eyelet.

groppo: Italy. Knot.

gros: Strong fabric.

gros bleu: Bustle (1865–1890 C.E.). In 1873, blue black.

gros de Londres: Bustle (1865–1890 C.E.). 1. In 1870, very soft silk fabric with heavy reps like velours. 2. In 1883, lightweight silk fabric made in horizontal ribs.

gros de Naples: Directoire and First Empire (1790–1815 C.E.). Heavy silk fabric with ribbed ground.

gros de Rome: Bustle (1865–1890 C.E.). Crinkled silk.

gros de Suez: Bustle (1865–1890 C.E.). Introduced in 1867, silk with horizontal rib.

gros de Tours: Directoire and First Empire (1790–1815 C.E.). Tabby weave fabric with heavier weft than warp.

gros d'Eccose silk: Crinoline (1840–1865 C.E.). In 1863, new fabric.

gros drap: France. Kersey.

gros gren: Spain. Grosgrain.

gros point: Italy. Venetian point lace with large raised designs. *See also* gros point de Venise.

gros point de Venise: Italy. Heavy, raised Venetian point lace.

gros vair: *See* vair.

gros vilain vert: Early Georgian (1700–1750 C.E.). France. Literally "very dark green," green derived from yellow made with an iron mordant.

groseille: Crinoline (1840–1865 C.E.). In 1858, gooseberry color.

grosgrain: 1. France. To have heavy cross-grain ribs. 2. Heavy fabric or ribbon corded selvedge to selvedge.

grotetore: *See* gros de Tours.

ground: The bars or net which support a pattern in a piece of lace.

grun: 1. Morocco. Jewish woman's horned headdress. 2. Germany. Green.

grunong: Borneo. Small bells used as a fringe.

gu gu guan: China. Yuan dynasty. Tall birch-bark hat covered with black or red fabric. Trimmed with four to five foot long willow branches, flowers, and feathers. Worn by empress, emperor's concubines, and wives of high ministers.

guà: China. Unlined upper garment.

gua pi mao: China. Ming dynasty. Small, round skullcap made of gauze. Worn by commoners.

gualcas: Ecuador. Bead necklace.

gualescio: Renaissance (1450–1550 C.E.). Italy. Plain fabric, probably silk, used for linings.

guanaco: Thick, soft fur of wild South American animal related to the llama, the *Lama glama huanacas*. The fur ranges in color from red brown to white.

Guanako: Germany. Guanaco.

guanaquito: Fur of young guanaco. Camel colored with white belly.

guanmiãn: China. Royal hat.

guante: Spain. Glove.

guanto: Italy. Glove.

guanto senza dita: Italy. Mitten.

guard chain: Romantic (1815–1840 C.E.). United Kingdom. From c1825 on, small linked, long chain worn around neck and holding watch. Replaced the fob chain.

guard ring: Fitted finger ring worn above loose ring, to hold it in position.

guardamalleta: Spain. Lambrequin.

Guard-infanta: Elizabethan (1550–1625 C.E.). Spain. Literally "princess saver," oversized farthingale.

guards: Renaissance (1450–1550 C.E.) to Elizabethan (1550–1625 C.E.). Decorative fabric bands used to conceal seams in garments.

guarnache: Early Gothic (1200–1350 C.E.). Man's poncho-like garment.

guashmi: Ecuador and Guatemala. Tunic.

guayabera shirt: Cuba. Sports shirt developed from smock.

guayanilla: Strong, white, lustrous cotton from West Indies.

guazzerone: Renaissance (1450–1550 C.E.). Italy. Hemline border, sometimes trimmed in contrasting fabric.

guba: Hungary. Man's knee-length coat, sometimes hooded. Worn like a cloak.

guchccha: India. Necklace of 32 strings of pearls.

gudia: India. A cotton stuff from Bengal or Gauda.

guepiere: (1940–1950 C.E.). France. Small, lightweight corset.

gueridons: Late Georgian (1750–1790 C.E.). Panniers made of very large hoops fastened together with tape.

guernsey: Fitted, knitted, wool shirt worn by sailors.

guêtre: France. Gaiter.

gueules: Early Gothic (1200–1350 C.E.). Small, fur-lined shoulder cape worn with lower corners turned back.

gueuse: A light, net-grounded bobbin lace.

gugel: Late Gothic (1350–1450 C.E.). Germany. Man's hood worn in rough weather. It varied in size and shape.

gui yi: China. Han dynasty (206 B.C.E.–7 C.E.). Woman's robe with left front wrapped over right.

guige: Early Gothic (1200–1350 C.E.). Strap used to suspend shield from neck or shoulder.

guilloche: Decorative pattern using two or more intertwining lines. Often done in braid.

guimp: Early Gothic (1200–1350 C.E.) to Renaissance (1450–1550 C.E.). Light material used to surround woman's face.

guimpe: 1. Short blouse worn with a pinafore. 2. (1910–1919 C.E.). Chemisette with high collar worn to fill in neckline.

guinda: Spain. Cherry color.

guinea cloth: United Kingdom. Gray cotton fabric made for export to West Africa.

guinga: Spain. Gingham.

guingan: France. Gingham.

guipere de Bruges: *See* duchesse lace.

guipure: Heavy lace in large pattern with no ground or heavy net ground.

guipure arabe: Crinoline (1840–1865 C.E.). France. Heavy Duchesse-like lace made with a thick silk cordonnet.

guipure de Bruges: Old bobbin lace appearing to have been made with tape.

guirlande: France. Garland.

guirmean: Ireland. Gaelic word for indigo.

guirnalda: Spain. Garland.

guiseid: Ireland. Gaelic word for a gusset of a shirt and clocking on hose.

guiterre: Renaissance (1450–1550 C.E.). France. Small buckler of leather.

guj: India. An embroidered wedding blouse or coat.

gul yaqa: Turkmenistan. Unmarried woman's circular collar stud.

gulbadan: India. A silk warp-faced cloth in a multicolored, vertically striped design.

gulbi: India. The color pink.

güldenstick: Lithuania. Gold embroidery.

gul-e-anar: India. Scarlet.

gule-baqli: India. A flowered jamdani silk.

gulenar: India. Crimson.

guler: Romania. Collar.

guleras: *See* guler.

guleron: Early Gothic (1200–1350 C.E.). Cape on chaperon.

gulik holland: Early Georgian (1700–1750 C.E.). Very fine white linen used for shirts.

gul-i-sarrai: India. Silver gray.

gulix: *See* gulik holland.

gulpumbah: India. A light yellow color.

gun: China. Woman's skirt.

gun fu: China. Qing dynasty (1644–1911 C.E.). After 1759, imperial surcoat with four, eight, ten, or twelve embroidered medallions.

gun mian: China. Special ceremonial attire worn by men for sacrificial rites during Ming dynasty (1368–1644 C.E.).

gùn na h-eaglaise: *See* léine-bhàn.

gùn odhar: *See* léine-bhàn.

guna: *See* kabanica.

gunachan: Ireland. Gaelic word for little gown.

gunia: Hungary. Kandys.

gunji: India. A man's vest.

gunna: Byzantine (400–1200 C.E.). Long tunic.

gunoberonicia: *See* gunia.

gunpowder silk: Peru. Very fine silk used for mantas.

guo luo dai: China. Zhou dynasty. Waistband that fastened on ends with hooks (called dai gou). Often trimmed with gold, silver, or pearls.

guõc: Vietnam. Wooden shoe.

guosaga: Norway. Mostly red vuoddaga with yellow, green, blue, and white. It ends in a tassel.

gurača: Ethiopia. Black.

gurda: Ethiopia. Woman's sash of jet and hair with the loose ends hanging to the knees.

gurgurlya: Greece. Polychrome thread.

gurnakuntala: India. A man's hairstyle where the hair is curled and hangs loose to the shoulder.

gurrah: India. Coarse, thick muslin fabric.

Gürtel: Germany. Girdle.

Gurtil: Germany. Old High German word for girdle.

gusanillo: Spain. Chenille.

gusset: Small triangular or tapering piece of fabric or leather inserted into garment to strengthen or enlarge it.

gus-to-weh: United States of America. Iroquois feathered cap. It was a round skullcap covered in leather, layered in small turkey feathers, and topped with one large eagle feather.

gu'ut: Ethiopia. Koma necklace of one or more strands of beads, hoops, and amulets.

guzik: Poland and Portugal. Button.

guzjók: Greece. Vest worn open at the front.

guzzy: India. Very poor quality cotton cloth.

gwddfdorch: Wales. Necklace.

gwel: France. Breton for veil.

gwisg: *See* dillad.

gwisgo: Wales. To clothe or to dress.

gwiska: France. Breton for to clothe or dress.

gwiskamant: *See* dillad.

gwlan: Wales. Wool.

gwlanen: Wales. Woolen cloth.

gwregys: Wales. Belt.

gymschoentjes: Holland. Gym shoes.

gyolcs: Hungary. Cambric.

gyolocsfersling: Hungary. White gathered skirt.

gyöngyös bokréta: Hungary. Man's hat trimmed with beads.

gypciere: *See* gipciere.

gypsy blouse: (1960–1970 C.E.). Short-sleeved, drawstring blouse, cut full in the body.

gypsy cloak: *See* Gitana.

gyrdel: United Kingdom. Old English word for girdle.

gyrdel-hring: Byzantine and Romanesque (400–1200 C.E.). United Kingdom. Girdle buckle.

gyrdels: Byzantine and Romanesque (400–1200 C.E.). United Kingdom. Girdle or loincloth. Also a belt worn by monks. First occurred in eighth century.

gyrdels-hringe: *See* gyrdel-hring.

gyrðill: *See* gjorð.

H

haakwerk: Holland. Crochet.

Haarnadel: Germany. Hairpin.

haarspeld: Holland. Hairpin; bobby pin.

habaki: Japan. Leggings.

habassie: *See* ábbasi.

habergeon: Early Gothic (1200–1350 C.E.). Chain or ring mail jacket worn as part of armor.

habillement: *See* biliment.

habiller: France. To clothe or to dress.

habit: 1. Early Gothic (1200–1350 C.E.). A garment. 2. Elizabethan (1550–1625 C.E.) to Restoration (1660–1700 C.E.). Complete set of clothing; a suit. 3. Late Georgian (1750–1790 C.E.). Light justaucorps; the habit à la francaise.

habit à la française: *See* habit.

habit backed skirt: Bustle (1865–1890 C.E.). Full-length skirt flared to hem. Center back featured inverted pleat stitched partially down.

habit bodice: Bustle (1865–1890 C.E.). United Kingdom. Introduced in 1877, long cuirasse bodice with long basques in back worn open in front over a waistcoat.

habit de demi-gala: Late Georgian (1750–1790 C.E.). France. Dress style less formal than grand gala using less rich fabric and trim.

habit degage: Directoire and First Empire (1790–1815 C.E.). France. Double-breasted redingote cut away in front to show the waistcoat.

habit d'escalier: Late Georgian (1750–1790 C.E.). to Romantic (1815–1840 C.E.). France. Full evening dress with half robe and short sleeves. Sleeves were slit at bottom and laced up.

habit shirt

habit glove: Early Georgian (1700–1750 C.E.). United Kingdom. Woman's short riding glove.

habit noir: France. Man's black evening tailed suit.

habit shirt: Early Georgian (1700–1750 C.E.) to Crinoline (1840–1865 C.E.). Originally worn as part of riding costume, this dickey type shirt was 15 inches long in front and 11 inches long in back and tied on sides with tape. It had a stand collar and ruffled front that buttoned with two buttons. The sleeves were ruffled at wrist. In the 19th century, worn to fill in neckline of gown. In 1815, muslin or cambric ruff was added to neckline.

habit-redingote: Bustle (1865–1890 C.E.). United Kingdom. Introduced in 1879, princess polonaise with overskirt full-length in back and closed to knees in front.

habits: *See* vétements.

habkeh: Palestine. Literally "binding," a decorative stitch used on necklines and wrist openings.

habok: Korea. Summer clothes.

habutai: Japan. Literally "soft as down," thin, soft, plain weave, washable silk fabric. Heavier than China silk. *See also* Japanese silk.

habutaye: *See* habutai.

hacele: Byzantine and Romanesque (400–1200 C.E.). United Kingdom. Full-length cloak worn by both genders. In 10th and 11th centuries, sometimes hooded.

hachijo: Japan. Soft, plain weave silk.

hachimaki: United States of America. Hawaii. A head sweatband.

Hachul: Germany. Old High German term for cloak.

hacketon: *See* acton.

hackle: Plume used to decorate a headdress.

hadajuban: Japan. Woman's short-sleeved, thin camisole.

haer-naedl: Byzantine and Romanesque (400–1200 C.E.). United Kingdom. Hairpin.

haet: Byzantine and Romanesque (400–1200 C.E.). United Kingdom. Cap or hat.

haetera: Byzantine and Romanesque (400–1200 C.E.). United Kingdom. Men's clothes, particularly those belonging to the poor, often in rough condition.

haftel: Austria. Man's collarless, long jacket with contrasting neck and cuffs.

Häftler: United States of America. Word referring to the Amish people.

hagorah: Biblical (unknown–30 C.E.). Hebrew man's girdle.

Hahnenfeder: Germany. Cock feather.

haidate: Japan. Armored skirt.

haiduk: Early Georgian (1700–1750 C.E.). Austria and Hungary. Tall cylindrical felt cap.

haiena: United States of America. Hawaii. Yellowish; greenish.

haihúnshan: China. Sailor's striped shirt.

haik: Algeria. Long piece of cotton or wool handmade cloth which envelops the woman in public. Usually 6 to 6-1/2 yards long and 2 yards wide. It conceals entire body except the eyes which are hidden by a white veil.

haik royal: Egyptian (4000–30 B.C.E.). Transparent, lightly pleated, draped garment worn by royalty.

hailìsi cuni: China. Harris tweed.

ha'imanawa: United States of America. Hawaii. Thin, delicate, white tapa.

hainǎ: Romania. Coat; garment.

hainaka: United States of America. Hawaii. Handkerchief.

hainaka 'a'i: United States of America. Hawaii. Neckerchief.

hainaka lei: *See* hainaka 'a'i.

hainaka pa'eke: United States of America. Hawaii. Pocket handkerchief.

hainaka pakeke: *See* hainaka pa'eke.

haincelin: Late Gothic (1350–1450 C.E.). France. Riding garment with embroidered sleeves worn for effect rather than warmth. Became fashionable in 1386.

haïne: *See* îmbracaminte.

hair: Elizabethan (1550–1625 C.E.). Bright tan color.

hair à la Recamier: Directoire and First Empire (1790–1815 C.E.). United States of America. Introduced in 1802, hairstyle in which the woman's hair is drawn back from the left eyebrow.

hair à la Romaine: Directoire and First Empire (1790–1815 C.E.). Woman's hairstyle in which the hair is arranged in coils or braids that ring the head like a coronet.

hair line stripe: Black or dark blue suiting with single white yarn stripe.

hair shirt: Shirt or loincloth made of horsehair and worn next to the skin for penance.

hair strings: Crinoline (1840–1865 C.E.). United States of America. Small pieces of string tied to the hair.

hairbines: Late Georgian (1750–1790 C.E.). United Kingdom. Worsted, plain weave fabric with rough surface made in Norwich.

haircloth: Stiff, wiry fabric made with cotton warp and horsehair weft. Used to upholster chairs and sofas.

haircord: Plain weave cotton fabric with cords one-quarter inch apart.

hair-lace: Early Georgian (1700–1750 C.E.). Filet for hair.

hairnet: Net worn over hair to hold it in place.

hair-pin crochet: A delicate form of openwork created using a large hair pin and a hook.

hairpin lace: Insertion lace with looped edges and firm center.

haji: Japan. An Okinawan term for bashofu.

hakama: Japan. Pair of loose trousers that are on formal occasions worn over the kimono. Made of stiff silk in dark color and are open halfway up the sides. The fullness is pleated at top with six pleats in front and two in back. It is worn attached to a belt.

hakata: Japan. A thick rep.

hakimono: Japan. Footwear.

hakoseko: Japan. A brocaded ornamental purse worn tucked into the neckline of the kimono.

haku-e: Japan. Gold painting on cloth.

hakuls: *See* wasti.

halakea: United States of America. Hawaii. White tapa.

halba: *See* libá.

halchii': *See* lichii'.

haldi: India. Turmeric (used as a dye).

halecret: Renaissance (1450–1550 C.E.) to Elizabethan (1550–1625 C.E.). Corset favored by the Swiss.

halena: Czechoslovakia. Man's long, wide overcoat.

haleny: Slovakia. Greatcoats.

half bishop sleeve: Crinoline (1840–1865 C.E.). In 1862, sleeve cut plain at top, gathered at wrist to cuff.

half boot: Directoire and First Empire (1790–1815 C.E.) to Romantic (1815–1840 C.E.). Woman's low shoe worn after 1812.

half handkerchief: Early Georgian (1700–1750 C.E.) to Romantic (1815–1840 C.E.). Diagonal half of handkerchief worn on head or neck. From 1800

half bishop sleeve

to 1830, a woman's triangular cape worn pinned to crown of head with one point in back. After 1830s, it was called a fanchon.

half shirt: Renaissance (1450–1550 C.E.) to Late Georgian (1750–1790 C.E.). Man's short shirt with fancy front that was worn over plain shirt.

half silk: Late Georgian (1750–1790 C.E.). Fabric with a linen warp and a silk weft.

half-beaver: Charles I and the Commonwealth (1625–1660 C.E.) to Late Georgian (1750–1790 C.E.). Hat made of blend of beaver hair and another fur.

half-dress: Late Georgian (1750–1790 C.E.) to Crinoline (1840–1865 C.E.). Term referring to day dress and that dress worn to informal evening functions.

haling hands: Heavy gloves or mittens, usually wool, with leather palms worn by sailors and working men.

halja: Croatia and Serbia. Dress; coat.

haljine: *See* odjeca.

halka: Poland. Slip.

Hallingdal breeches: Norway. Men's yellow breeches that are finely embroidered.

halo: Round, flat bandeau open in the center to fit the head. It is placed inside a hat that is too large in order to make it fit.

halo hat: *See* bambino hat.

halsbaand: Denmark. Necklace.

halsband: Sweden. Necklace.

Halsband: Germany. Necklace.

Halsbinde: Germany. Necktie; cravat.

halsboord: Holland. Neckband.

Halsbouc: Germany. Necklace.

Halsboug: *See* Menni.

halsdoek: *See* hoofddoek.

halsgjørð: *See* men.

Halsgolt: *See* Halsbouc; Menni.

halshemd: Renaissance (1450–1550 C.E.). Germany. Material used to fill in neckline.

halsketting: Holland. Necklace.

halslijn: Holland. Neckline.

halsneusdoek: Elizabethan (1550–1625 C.E.). Holland. Neckerchief.

halssieraad: Holland. Carcanet.

halssnoer: Holland. Necklet.

halstuch: United States of America. Amish woman's shoulder cape.

Halstuch: Germany. Scarf.

halter top: (20th century). Bare-backed blouse with tie or loop of fabric around back of the neck.

haluk: Biblical (unknown–30 C.E.). Poor Jewish man's shirt.

ham: Byzantine and Romanesque (400–1200 C.E.). United Kingdom. Shirt.

hamaku'u: United States of America. Hawaii. To tie one's hair in a topknot.

hamarti: Abyssinia. Heavy brass bracelets.

Hamburg homespun: Denmark. Fabric with pale stripes.

Hamilton lace: Early Georgian (1700–1750 C.E.). Coarse lace with a diamond pattern.

hammercut beard: Elizabethan (1550–1625 C.E.) to Charles I and the Commonwealth (1625–1660 C.E.). Combination beard and moustache that formed a hammer shape, the beard forming the handle and the waxed moustache the head.

hammock cloth: Plain weave cotton fabric woven in brightly colored stripes.

hamo 'ula: United States of America. Hawaii. To dye something red.

hamsa: India. Embroidery pattern of the sacred goose.

hamsa mithuna: India. A decorative motif of a pair of swans.

hamsa-chihna-dukula-vana: India. Bridegroom's silk wedding dress embroidered with swans.

hamsakah: India. Anklets.

hana: Australia. Maori's all white cape.

hanao: Japan. Thongs on geta.

hànbèixin: China. Sleeveless undershirt.

hanbok: Korea. Term for the national costume.

hances: *See* cadach.

hancha: Japan. A sleeveless jacket with dyed patterns.

hand: 1. The tactile qualities of a fabric. 2. Crinoline (1840–1865 C.E.). United States of America. Unit of measure equal to four inches.

hand fall: Charles I and the Commonwealth (1625–1660 C.E.) to Restoration (1660–1700 C.E.). United Kingdom. Turned back, starched cuff trimmed in lace. It was often worn with a standing or falling band.

handboei: Holland. Bracelet.

handewarpes: Renaissance (1450–1550 C.E.). United Kingdom. White or colored fabric made in East Anglia.

handkerchief dress: Bustle (1865–1890 C.E.). United Kingdom. Introduced in 1880, dress made of fabric resembling large bandanas. Tunic was made from two bandanas with points almost reaching hem. Upper points show beneath the basque-like jacket-bodice.

handkerchief lawn: Soft cotton lawn.

handkerchief linen: Lightweight, very fine grade, plain weave linen.

handkerchief tunic: Overskirt where outer edges are corners that hang in pleats.

hand-ruffs: Elizabethan (1550–1625 C.E.) to Late Georgian (1750–1790 C.E.). United Kingdom. Wrist ruffles.

händschen: Switzerland. Gloves.

handschoen: Holland. Glove.

Handschuh: Germany. Glove.

hand-scio: Byzantine and Romanesque (400–1200 C.E.). United Kingdom. Mitten.

handske: Denmark and Sweden. Glove.

handu djere: Timbuktu. A half-moon pendant.

handubaek: *See* songabang.

haneeka: United States of America. Hawaiian word for handkerchief.

han-eri: Japan. An ornamental neckband for the undergarment of a kimono.

hanga-korbo: Timbuktu. Silver crescent earring with a large ball of amber and a small ball of coral on it.

hangers: Elizabethan (1550–1625 C.E.). Straps that hung from girdle and held the sword.

hanging sleeve: Late Gothic (1350–1450 C.E.) to Charles I and the Commonwealth (1625–1660 C.E.). Long sleeves slit from shoulder to wrist. Arm extended through upper part of sleeve.

hangra: 1. India. Striped silk sa. 2. Korea. Almost transparent sa silk with weft skipped at intervals to create parallel lines. Also made of ramie or cotton.

han-juban: Japan. Woman's undergarment.

hankotana: Japan. A face mask.

hanina: United States of America. Hawaii. A yellow sarong.

han'pa: United States of America. Dakota Indian's moccasins.

hāns: India. Close-fitting necklace with pearls and gems.

hansam: Korea. Long piece of white silk worn draped over a bride's hands held at chest level.

hanselin: *See* haincelin.

hànshan: China. Undershirt; t-shirt.

hansworst: Holland. Pantaloon.

hanten: Japan. A sailing jacket.

Hantschuoch: Germany. Glove.

Hantscuoh: Germany. Old High German term for glove.

hanzki: *See* glofi.

hao mao: China. Qing dynasty. Conical army hat.

haol

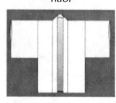

haori

haol: China. Long robe.

haori: Japan. Worn by both genders, a loose, knee-length, silk coat tied in front with silk cords.

happi: Japan. A workman's garment that indicates his trade.

hār: India. Gold necklace with pearls and gems.

Har: *See* Vlahs.

hara: India. Necklace.

harasekhara: India. White necklace.

haraszt: Hungary. Coarse woolen thread used for szür embroidered prior to 1880.

haravsti: India. Large pearl necklace.

harayasti: India. Necklace of one string of pearls.

harbeh: Palestine. Horseshoe-shaped padded roll worn atop the shatweh.

hardanger embroidery: Cutaway embroidery of triangles and diamonds used on the edges of women's garments.

harden: Renaissance (1450–1550 C.E.) to Restoration (1660–1700 C.E.). Common linen made with the coarsest hemp.

hardhanger cloth: Soft, mercerized, basket weave fabric in white or ecru.

hare pocket: Romantic (1815–1840 C.E.) United Kingdom. Large pocket inside skirt of a shooting jacket.

haren stof: Holland. Haircloth.

harem-hem skirt: (20th century). Soft hem, imitating the look of bloomers.

harir asli: Palestine. Pure plain silk for women's veils and men's headcloths.

harir nabati: 1. Palestine. Imported, imitation silk fabric. 2. Israel. Artificial silk.

hariry: *See* lasoa.

harisnya: Hungary. Men's gray or white homespun breeches worn over tight trousers with front drop-fly. Trimmed with red of black braid on sides. Held up with strap.

harlem stripes: Early Georgian (1700–1750 C.E.) to Late Georgian (1750–1790 C.E.). Holland. Linen.

harlequin plaid: Fabric with contrasting color diamond patterns.

harlot: Late Gothic (1350–1450 C.E.). Garment similar to modern tights.

harlots: Late Gothic (1350–1450 C.E.). In 1360s, man's parti-colored hose. Worn laced to paltocks.

harrateen: Early Georgian (1700–1750 C.E.). Coarse linen fabric used for curtains and bed furniture.

Harrie sack: Crinoline (1840–1865 C.E.). Introduced in 1862, boy's plain sack coat without lapels. It was trimmed around borders and down sleeve seam with braid in Grecian style.

harrington: Romantic (1815–1840 C.E.). Introduced in 1835, stout fabric used for winter overcoats.

harris: France, Italy, and Spain. Harry tweed.

harris tweed: Crinoline (1840–1865 C.E.) to Bustle (1865–1890 C.E.). Loosely woven, homespun tweed.

harry tweed: Wool tweed hand woven in the Outer Hebrides.

harsa: Nigeria. Wealthy man's turban of white cotton gauze.

Haru: *See* Flahs.

harvard sheeting: United Kingdom. Shirting fabric woven in a twill weave with colored stripes.

harvards: Gay Nineties (1890–1900 C.E.). Striped cotton shirting in two and two twill or plain weave.

haryani: India. A cloth of gold.

harzkappe: *See* gestaltrock.

Hasenhaar: Germany. Hare hair.

hashimi: Iraq. Woman's loose, long-sleeved tunic-dress.

hasp: Early Georgian (1700–1750 C.E.). Decorative hook and eye closure.

hastávali: India. Bracelets.

hasti: India. Ivory bangles.

hastrigánky: Slovakia. Fancy black lambskin caps.

hat à la reine: Crinoline (1840–1865 C.E.). France. Woman's Italian straw hat with shallow brim that turned down around small crown. Narrow hatband, ends of which hung down in back.

hat body: Hat blank.

hat screw: Late Georgian (1750–1790 C.E.) to Romantic (1815–1840 C.E.). Tool used to stretch a man's hat.

hata: 1. Ireland. Hat. 2. Japan. Loom.

hatakape: India. A sleeveless barabundi.

hatere: Early Gothic (1200–1350 C.E.). Term for attire.

hathisondaka: India. An antariya worn in elephant-trunk style.

hatt: Sweden. Hat.

hatta: 1. *See* kafiyyeh. 2. Sweden. Generic term for hat.

hattah: Palestine. Man's square head cloth of cotton, silk, and wool.

hattan: Japan. Twilled silk.

hatte: Sri Lanka. Woman's short sleeved, midriff length, fitted jacket or blouse.

hatter's plush: Silk or rabbit plush used to cover men's hats.

haube: 1. Late Gothic (1350–1450 C.E.). Germany. Coif. 2. Germany. Bonnet.

haubergeon
Dover Publications

haubergeon: Early Gothic (1200–1350 C.E.). France. Introduced c1340, mailed version of the hauberk that reached to mid-thigh. Worn over the hoqueton.

hauberjet: Woolen fabric.

hauberk: Early Gothic (1200–1350 C.E.). Shirt of mail.

haubert à maille double: *See* haubert doublier.

haubert clavey de double maille: *See* haubert doublier.

haubert doublier: Late Gothic (1350–1450 C.E.). France. Mail with two rings used for ordinary mail.

hau'ina: United States of America. Hawaii. Tapa sarong.

hauketon: *See* acton.

ha'ula: United States of America. Hawaii. Reddish.

ha'ula'ula: United States of America. Hawaii. Pink.

hault collet: Renaissance (1450–1550 C.E.). Spain. High collar.

hausse col: 1. Early Gothic (1200–1350 C.E.). Crescent shaped piece of metal worn to protect the throat. 2. Renaissance (1450–1550 C.E.) to Elizabethan (1550–1625 C.E.). Padded hip roll.

hausse cul: *See* hausse col.

haustuch: Switzerland. Homespun fabric.

haut de forme: France. Top hat.

haut-de-chausses: *See* trunk hose.

haute couture: France. High fashion.

havane: Crinoline (1840–1865 C.E.). France. In 1861, light coffee color.

havanese embroidery: Buttonhole embroidery worked on heavy fabric.

havannah: Crinoline (1840–1865 C.E.). In 1860, brownish olive green.

havelock: Lightweight fabric cover for military hat, long in back to protect the neck.

haze: Very light spray of a color.

hazel: Color of a brown hazelnut.

hè: China. Brown.

he'a: United States of America. Hawaii. Blood red.

headrail: Byzantine and Romanesque (400–1200 C.E.). Veil or headdress.

head-side: The lower, often scalloped, edge of a lace border.

heafod-clap: Early Gothic (1200–1350 C.E.). United Kingdom. Headcloth. Worn by religious women in 13th century.

heafod-gewaede: Byzantine and Romanesque (400–1200 C.E.). United Kingdom. Women's headdress, probably a veil.

healsbēag: *See* mene.

healsed: Byzantine and Romanesque (400–1200 C.E.). United Kingdom. Cloth for head or neck.

heart-breaker: Restoration (1660–1700 C.E.). Woman's long lock that corresponded to men's love lock.

heather: Purplish blue.

heaume: Early Gothic (1200–1350 C.E.). Large, heavy helmet.

heavy swell: Crinoline (1840–1865 C.E.). United Kingdom. In 1860s, ultra-fashionable gentleman.

hechtgrau: Crinoline (1840–1865 C.E.). In the 1860s, a pike gray fabric made from 50% natural wool and 50% blue wool.

hectorean: Greek (3000–100 B.C.E.). Man's hairstyle with short hair combed toward the back in curls.

hedbo embroidery: Denmark. Cutwork embroidery.

hed-clap: *See* heden.

heden: Byzantine and Romanesque (400–1200 C.E.). United Kingdom. Garment of fur, leather or sheepskin, worn by monks. In 10th and 11th centuries, it was sometimes hooded.

hedgehog hairdo: Late Georgian (1750–1790 C.E.). Woman's hairstyle cut short in front, frizzed, and worn high on head. First appeared in 1778. Particularly popular with the Macaronis.

hedvábí: Czechoslovakia. Silk.

heer: India. A term used for floss silk in western India.

heerpauke: Elizabethan (1550–1625 C.E.). Germany. Heavily padded, round breeches.

héfú: China. Kimono.

hei: China. Black.

hei jiao chou: China. Black gummed silk.

heiyanjìng: China. Sunglasses.

heko-obi: Japan. Wide sash worn wrapped around the waist two or three times and tied in back.

helaka: *See* sambelatra.

Helanca: Two-way stretch elastic fabric.

Helen cap: Crinoline (1840–1865 C.E.). Cap worked on honeycomb netting. Named for Grand Duchess Helen, sister-in-law of the emperor of Russia.

heliotrope: Purple blue tint.

hellviolet: Germany. Mauve.

helm: Military helmet made of leather or metal.

helmet: *See* helm.

helmet cap: Directoire and First Empire (1790–1815 C.E.). United Kingdom. Woman's day cap shaped like a helmet. It was usually made of strips of lace and embroidery and tied under the chin with ribbons.

helmet hat: Bustle (1865–1890 C.E.). United Kingdom. Often worn at the seaside, a fabric hat with helmet-shaped crown and narrow brim.

hema-netrapata: India. A golden yellow silk.

hemasutra: India. Necklace made of gold chain with one precious stone.

hemavaikaksha: India. Two long wreaths of flowers or pearls worn crossed on the chest. Mostly commonly worn by women.

hembras: Renaissance (1450–1550 C.E.). Spain. Eyes (to go with hooks).

hemd: Holland. Shirt.

Hemd: Germany. Shirt.

Hemde: Germany. Shirt.

hemelsblauw: Holland. Azure.

hemepe: Byzantine and Romanesque (400–1200 C.E.). United Kingdom. Worn by monks, sleeved shirt.

hemeÞe: *See* serc.

Hemidi: Germany. Old High German word for shirt.

hemispherical hat: Crinoline (1840–1865 C.E.). United Kingdom. Worn in 1850s and 1860s, man's hard felt bowl shaped hat with flat narrow brim. By 1858, it had a knob on the crown. *See also* bollinger.

hemming: Byzantine and Romanesque (400–1200 C.E.). United Kingdom. Rawhide sandal or boot.

hendira: *See* hiyyak.

hengjehuva: Norway. Literally "hanging cap," woman's old linen or cotton linen.

henke: *See* heuke.

Henley boater: Gay Nineties (1890–1900 C.E.). United Kingdom. In 1894, a blue or drab felt hat shaped like a boater.

henley shirt: Short-sleeved, collarless, knit shirt with a neckband and front button placket.

henna: Egypt. Dye from the shrub which creates a red orange dye.

hennin: Late Gothic (1350–1450 C.E.). Cone- or steeple-shaped women's headdress, commonly worn with a veil.

henri deux cape: Gay Nineties (1890–1900 C.E.). Woman's cape with square yoke.

Henrietta cloth: Gay Nineties (1890–1900 C.E.). Fine, twill weave fabric with silk warp and worsted weft, similar to a fine cashmere.

Henrietta glace: Bustle (1865–1890 C.E.). In 1889, silk warp varnished board fabric made by Bradford Mills.

Henrietta jacket: Gay Nineties (1890–1900 C.E.). Three-quarter length, loose jacket in deep color. It was lined in quilted satin or merv.

Henriette hat: Crinoline (1840–1865 C.E.). Introduced in 1862, woman's low crowned, small brimmed, straw hat trimmed with bands and folds of blue velvet.

Hentzen: Renaissance (1450–1550 C.E.). Germany. Mitten gauntlets.

heqat and nekhekh: *See* crook and flail.

Hercules braid: Crinoline (1840–1865 C.E.). Introduced ca. 1850, narrow black or white braid from one-half to four inches in width.

heremzi: Palestine. Silk taffeta in red, green, yellow, orange, or purple. It is 18–22 cm wide. Used for decorative patchwork on women's coats.

here-pād: United Kingdom. Old English word for a coat of mail.

herigaute: Early Gothic (1200–1350 C.E.). France. Housse worn open at sides with hanging sleeves.

herlot: Early Gothic (1200–1350 C.E.). String used to tie hose to paltock or sleeve to armseye.

hermelijn: Holland. Ermine.

Hermelin: Germany. Ermine.

hermine: France. Ermine.

Hermione: Crinoline (1840–1865 C.E.). In 1850, shawl-shaped taffeta mantelet trimmed with fringe.

hernani: Grenadine woven with silk warp and wool weft.

Heroldsrock: Germany. Tabard.

heron: Bustle (1865–1890 C.E.). France. In 1888, grayish drab color.

Herrenhut: Germany. Trilby.

herrenhutte: *See* ritterhute.

herreruelo: *See* ferreruelo.

herrete: *See* clavos.

herringbone: Irregular twill weave giving a zigzag effect.

herset: Egyptian (4000–30 B.C.E.). Cornelian (used for amulets).

Hershey bars: (1950–1960 C.E.). United States of America. Nickname for the Army's overseas service bars worn on the right cuff.

hertevel: Holland. Deerskin.

hessian: 1. Directoire and First Empire (1790–1815 C.E.) to Crinoline (1840–1865 C.E.). Man's black leather short riding boots that were calf high in back and curved up to point in front below the kneecap ending in a tassel. Top edge was sometimes bound in colored leather. 2. Rough hemp or jute and hemp blend fabric used for sacking. *See also* burlap.

hessian boot: *See* hessian.

het: Wales. Hat.

hetchi pansu: United States of America. Hawaii. Japanese term for boys' pants with buttonholes at the waist through which buttons attached to the shirt were buttoned.

heuke: Early Gothic (1200–1350 C.E.) to Renaissance (1450–1550 C.E.). Germany. Semi-

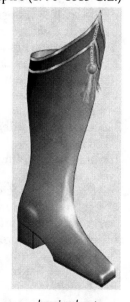

hessian boot
See also photospread
(Foot and Legwear).

circular cloak worn gathered at the shoulder where it was clasped or buttoned. It was worn lower on left than on right.

heume: France. Helmet.

heuz: France. Breton for boot.

heuze: Byzantine and Romanesque (400–1200 C.E.) to Early Gothic (1200–1350 C.E.). Tall leather thick soled boots in various heights.

hevilla: Renaissance (1450–1550 C.E.). Spain. Buckle.

hezaam: Arabia. Long woolen sash.

hezam: Morocco. Stiff, wide belt of gold embroidered velvet.

Hibernian embroidery: Satin and purl stitch embroidery done in colors on silk, velvet, or net.

Hibernian vest: Directoire and First Empire (1790–1815 C.E.). United States of America. Short jacket or spencer of velvet trimmed with fur.

hickory: Blue or brown and white striped, twill weave cotton shirting.

hickory shirting: *See* hickory.

hidarimae: Japan. The right, overlapping panel of the kimono.

hidim: *See* qumbaz.

hidim al-khal: Palestine. Coat of white silk presented by the groom to the bride's maternal uncle. Literally "the uncle's coat."

hieu-phuc: Vietnam. Mourning clothes.

highlows: Late Georgian (1750–1790 C.E.) to Bustle (1865–1890 C.E.). United Kingdom. Worn in the country, men's calf-high leather boots that laced up the front. In the 19th century, they were shorter, only ankle high, and more elegant.

hi-goza: *See* ki-gomo.

hijab: 1. Palestine. Amulet. 2. Literally "curtain" or "cover," a Muslim woman's traditional head covering. 3. Modest Muslim style of dress.

hijo marstiogutoguan: Indonesia. A circular cloth used in the birth rites.

hikeshi hanten: Japan. Thick fireman's jacket.

hikoni: United States of America. Hawaii. Tattoo on the forehead of an outcast.

hiladillo: Renaissance (1450–1550 C.E.). Spain. Ferret.

hilador: Ecuador and Guatemala. Spinner.

hilar: Ecuador and Guatemala. To spin.

hilda: Twill weave fabric with cotton warp and alpaca weft. Used for linings.

hili ha: United States of America. Hawaii. A four strand braid.

hili pa ha: *See* hili ha.

hili pa kolu: United States of America. Hawaii. A three strand braid.

hilo: Spain. Thread.

Himalaya carreau: Gay Nineties (1890–1900 C.E.). Very large check with shaggy half-inch line of long upstanding hairs.

himation: Greek. Rectangular shawl with weighted corners worn by philosophers over the left shoulder leaving the right arm free. Worn by married women as a shawl. Natural wool colored, white, brown, black, scarlet, crimson, or purple. Often embroidered.

himmelblau: Germany. Azure.

Himmutsatha: Biblical (unknown–30 C.E.). Hebrew man's red tunic.

himru: India. An intricately woven brocade with cotton for the warp.

hinaka: *See* hainaka.

hinaka 'a'i: *See* hainaka 'a'i.

hinaka paeke: *See* hainaka pa'eke.

hinarunaru: New Zealand. Maori term for poor quality weaving.

hingghi: Indonesia. Man's warp ikat garments woven in pairs. One is worn wrapped around the hips, the other as a shawl.

hinggi: Sumba. Large blankets worn in pairs. One is worn as a sarong, the other as a shoulder wrap.

hinggi kombu: Sumba. Man's ikat shawl.

hiogi: Japan. A folding fan made of thin slats of Japanese cypress wood.

hi'ohi'o: United States of America. Hawaii. Bright red color.

hip bags: Bustle (1865–1890 C.E.). Introduced in 1883, slang phrase for pannier folds. *See also* curtain drapery.

hip buttons: Restoration (1660–1700 C.E.) to Bustle (1865–1890 C.E.). United Kingdom. Pair of buttons found at top of a back vent in a man's jacket.

hip huggers: Pant with waistline dropped two to three inches below the natural waist.

hip spring: Ideal hip measurement minus waist measurement (9- to 13-inch difference).

Hippolita: Crinoline (1840–1865 C.E.). In 1857, woman's scarf-shaped moiré antique mantle. Had lace trimmed single flounce with hollow pleats. Trimmed with embossed velvet.

hipsters: (1960–1970 C.E.). Hip-hugging pants.

hiranya: India. Gold.

hiranyan atkan: India. A mantle adorned with gold.

hiranya-sraj: India. A gold garland.

hirauchi: Japan. Woman's ornamental hairpin.

hire: Japan. A lower-class person's ebosi.

hirivastra: *See* haryani.

hirosode: Japan. Wide sleeved kimono.

hiro-tana: *See* furoshiki.

hiscu: Bolivia. Sandals.

Hispania: Crinoline (1840–1865 C.E.). 1. In 1854, Spanish cloak where right front folded over left. It was trimmed with striped velvet galoon. 2. In 1856, woman's half-circle cloak with semicircular yoke. It had a box-pleated flounce and was trimmed with tufted plush and fringe.

historical shirt: Charles I and the Commonwealth (1625–1660 C.E.) to Restoration (1660–1700 C.E.). Man's shirt embroidered in religious subjects.

hitai-ebosi: Japan. A triangular piece of black silk cloth secured to the forehead by strings.

hitatare: Japan. A ceremonial costume of the samurai.

hitoe: Japan. Unlined garment.

hitta-zome: Japan. A type of dapple dyeing.

hive: Renaissance (1450–1550 C.E.) to Early Georgian (1700–1750 C.E.). High-crowned, hive-shaped, plaited straw hat with little or no brim.

hiyoku: Japan. An underkimono.

hiyyak: Morocco. Woolen material worn as a cloak.

hizam: Palestine. Man's sash.

hlace: Croatia and Serbia. Trousers.

hlače: *See* pantalone.

H-line: (1950–1960 C.E.). United States of America. Introduced by Dior in 1954, sheath dress with slight flare to hem.

ho: Japan. A nobleman's formal court robe.

hoa cà: Vietnam. Lilac colored.

hoa tai: Vietnam. Earring.

hoakakala: United States of America. Hawaii. Bracelet of the tusks of a hog or a dog.

hoàng-bò: Vietnam. Imperial robe.

hoàng-ngoc: Vietnam. Topaz.

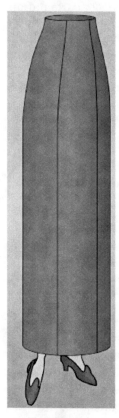

hobble skirt
See also photospread
(Women's Wear).

hobble skirt: (1910–1920 C.E.). Very narrow skirt that tapered at the hem, making walking difficult.

hock see hai: Crinoline (1840–1865 C.E.). United States of America. Chinese Hawaiian term for the front of men's white pigskin-soled shoes.

hod: Byzantine and Romanesque (400–1200 C.E.). United Kingdom. Hood, similar to monk's cowl.

hodden: Scotland. Woven fabric of undyed wool fleeces.

hodnhue: *See* hodnhuva.

hodnhuva: Norway. Literally "horned cap," starched cotton cap.

hodootl'izh: *See* dootl'izh.

hodtrene: Renaissance (1450–1550 C.E.). Curtain or lappets at back of a hood.

hoed: Holland. Hat.

hoedeband: Holland. Hatband.

hoepelrok: Holland. Crinoline.

hoesaek: Korea. Gray.

hœtt: United Kingdom. Old English word for hat.

hofkledij: Holland. Court dress.

hoge hoed: Holland. Top hat.

hoge laars: Holland. Jackboot.

hoge toneelschoen: Holland. Cothurnus.

hoge zijden: Holland. Opera hat.

hoggers: Plowman's boots.

hohos: Indonesia. Belt worn by a high-status person.

hoi nong hu: (1900–1910 C.E.). United States of America. Chinese Hawaiian term for a child's pair of trousers with the seam from the crotch point to the back waist left open.

hoju: Japan. A pearl design often shown with flames.

hok see hai: Bustle (1865–1890 C.E.). United States of America. Chinese Hawaiian term for Chinese-style shoes.

hokua: United States of America. Hawaii. Nape of the neck.

hol: Cambodia. Silk weft ikat fabric.

holán: Mexico. Ruffle of heavily starched lace or tulle that is worn at the hem of a woman's skirt.

holanda: Spain. Renaissance (1450–1550 C.E.). Fine linen.

Holbein work: Outline embroidery in double running stitch.

holbi: Norway. Border added to the bottom edge of a skirt.

holei: United States of America. Hawaii. Imported yellow dotted cloth.

holland: Fine, plain weave linen fabric.

Holland cloth: Early Gothic (1200–1350 C.E.) to Restoration (1660–1700 C.E.). Holland. Fine white linen lawn used for mourning caps and cuffs.

Holland shade cloth: Plain weave linen fabric with a finish that made it opaque.

hollie point lace: Early Gothic (1200–1350 C.E.) to Restoration (1660–1700 C.E.). Church lace in hollie stitch with religious designs.

hollie stitch: Type of buttonhole stitch.

hollmes: Charles I and the Commonwealth (1625–1660 C.E.). Fustian.

hollow lace: Renaissance (1450–1550 C.E.) to Elizabethan (1550–1625 C.E.). Braid lace used for edging.

hollow-cut velveteen: Velveteen with pile cut into designs.

holly point: Very close needlepoint.

Hollywood gauze: Rayon marquisette made in a leno weave.

holoku: United States of America. Hawaii. 1. Loose, sewn dress with a train and a yoke. It is based on the missionaries' Mother Hubbards. 2. Cloak; cape.

holomu: United States of America. Hawaii. Long, fitted dress.

holy point: *See* holly point.

Hombourg: France. Homburg.

hombrera: 1. Spain. Shoulder pad. 2. Ecuador. The yoke of a blouse.

homburg

homburg: Bustle (1865–1890 C.E.). Man's stiff felt hat with tapered and creased crown, rolled brim, and grosgrain ribbon. Made fashionable by the Prince of Wales.

homespun: 1. Loose, rough woolen fabric in a plain or twill weave. 2. Crude fabric of cotton, linen, jute, or blends.

homongi: Japan. A visiting kimono worn for special occasions.

honan: China. From Honan, a wild silk fabric that dyes uniformly.

hondorgo: Hungary. Bell-shaped skirt that covers the ankles.

honeycomb: Textured fabric woven to resemble a honeycomb.

honeycomb cloth: Weave used in toweling.

hóng: China. Red.

hòng-bào: Vietnam. Red mantle; ruby.

hong-ngoc: Vietnam. Ruby.

hongreline: Early Georgian (1700–1750 C.E.). France. Jacket favored by coachmen.

hongsaek: Korea. Red.

hóngyànyàn: China. Brilliant red.

Honiton lace: Elaborate bobbin lace.

Honiton point: Bustle (1865–1890 C.E.). In 1884, imitation lace with design outlined in silk.

honkar-ki-kalangi: India. Long crested cylindrical plume of gold or silver worn on top of the turban.

hoo: Bustle (1865–1890 C.E.). United States of America. Chinese Hawaiian term for pantaloons.

hoo geok kwun: *See* dai seong siu kwun.

hoo tau dai: Bustle (1865–1890 C.E.). United States of America. Chinese Hawaiian term for a belt.

hood: Mushroom-shaped, unblocked hat blank.

hoofdband: Holland. Headband.

hoofddoek: Holland. Handkerchief.

hoofdtooi: Holland. Headdress. *See also* kapsel.

hooftijsertgen

hooftijsertgen: Holland. A regional headdress, similar to a Juliet cap. Commonly made of lace, the cap has a round base and two rounded brim pieces, creating a heart shaped frame for the face.

hoop petticoat: Late Georgian (1750–1790 C.E.). United Kingdom. Term for panniers.

hoover apron: (1910–1920 C.E.). United States of America. Worn from 1914 to 1927, a wraparound, sleeved apron that originated during World War I in the Food Administration. Later, it was popularized for home wear.

hop-pada: Byzantine and Romanesque (400–1200 C.E.). United Kingdom. Literally "hoop-shaped," wide outer garment. Possibly for ecclesiastical use only.

hopsack: Gay Nineties (1890–1900 C.E.). Coarse woolen serge-canvas.

hopsacking: Coarse, plain weave fabric of cotton, linen, or rayon.

hoqueton: Renaissance (1450–1550 C.E.). Snug padded tunic worn as part of parade uniforms. Often decorated with gold and gems.

horitti: Korea. Belt.

horloger: France. Clock and watch maker.

hörr: *See* lin.

horrō: Ethiopia. Fringe of beads worn over the chest.

horsehair petticoat: 1. Renaissance (1450–1550 C.E.). Spain. Linen farthingale stiffened with horsehair. 2. Crinoline (1840–1865 C.E.). Another name for crinoline petticoat.

Hortense mantle: Crinoline (1840–1865 C.E.). United Kingdom. 1. Introduced in 1849, woman's three-quarter length mantle with falling collar and square, fringed waist-length cape. Named for Queen Hortense. 2. In 1854, round mantelet with rounded points. Beneath the points was a ruffle of vandyked Brussels net. Deep fall of lace was under the net.

horu: New Zealand. Maori term for the red ochre used in body painting.

Horus lock: Egyptian (4000–30 B.C.E.). Braid of false hair worn behind the right ear by fashionable women.

hosa: 1. Byzantine (400–1200 C.E.). Snug leg covering. 2. Byzantine and Romanesque (400–1200 C.E.). United Kingdom. Covering for lower leg and probably the foot also. Possibly leather boot. 3. Norway. Old Norse word for hosiery.

Hosa: Germany. Old High German term for hosiery.

hosan: Wales. Hose.

hose: *See* strømpe.

hoseaux: *See* heuze.

hose-bend: Byzantine and Romanesque (400–1200 C.E.). United Kingdom. Band worn around the leg, probably to secure the hosa.

hosen: *See* breeches.

Hosen: Germany. Trousers.

Hosenrock: Germany. Pantskirt.

hoso-zome: Japan. Fine-line dyeing in a spider-web design.

hot pants: (1960–1970 C.E.). United States of America. Extremely brief shorts.

hottr: Norway. Old word for hat.

hòugen: China. Heel of a shoe or sock.

hòujin: China. Back of a Chinese robe or jacket.

hounds ears: Restoration (1660–1700 C.E.). United Kingdom. In use from 1660s to 1680s, popular word for large coat cuffs fashionable at the time.

houndstooth check: Broken twill weave resembling a four pointed star.

hounscot say: Gay Nineties (1890–1900 C.E.). In 1891, a rough woolen serge-canvas.

houppe: Byzantine and Romanesque (400–1200 C.E.). France. Twelfth-century term for a tassel.

houppelande: Late Gothic (1350–1450 C.E.). Loose, large robe with wide, flaring sleeves and a tall collar, the carcaille, worn by both genders. Usually made of a rich fabric.

houppelande à mi-jambe: Late Gothic (1350–1450 C.E.). France. Early version of the haincelin.

houppelande courte: *See* haincelin.

houri-coat: Turkey. Kimono-like coat.

house dress: Bustle (1865–1890 C.E.). United Kingdom. Worn from 1877 on, woman's plain trained princess robe worn without corsets. By 1890, became the teagown.

household linen embroidery: White thread on white fabric embroidery.

housemaid skirt: Bustle (1865–1890 C.E.). United Kingdom. Introduced in 1884, plain skirt with five or six tucks near the hem. Worn at home by young women.

housse: Late Gothic (1350–1450 C.E.). France. Long, wide, sleeveless wrap or shawl, open at both sides and buttoned down the front or an outer garment with wide, short sleeves.

houta: Bulgaria. Apron.

houtje-touwtje-jas: *See* monty-coat.

houve: *See* huvet.

hovdatyet: Norway. Woman's headcloth.

how: Scotland. Hood or cap.

howling bags: Crinoline (1840–1865 C.E.). Slang term for trousers in a loud patterned fabric.

howve: *See* huvet.

hoxter: Crinoline (1840–1865 C.E.). Slang term for inside pocket of a coat.

hraegel: Byzantine and Romanesque (400–1200 C.E.). United Kingdom. Term meaning a garment or clothes. Used for both genders.

hraelung: *See* hraegel.

hring: Byzantine and Romanesque (400–1200 C.E.). United Kingdom. Ring, brooch, or neck-ring.

hringofinn serkr: Early Gothic (1200–1350 C.E.). Iceland. Shirt woven with ring mail.

hringr: Norway. Old Norse word for finger ring.

hrœgl: *See* clāpes.

hrycg-hraedel: Byzantine and Romanesque (400–1200 C.E.). United Kingdom. Garment, probably a cloak worn by both genders. Literally "back-cloth."

hsia-pei: China. Ch'ing dynasty. Calf-length vest worn by Han brides.

hua: Laos and Thailand. Waistband sewn to upper edge of woman's skirt.

hua yu: China. Peacock feathers.

huaaca: *See* huayaca.

huabù: China. Cotton print.

huádaní: China. Gabardine.

huaduan: China. Figured satin; brocade.

huáibiao: China. Pocket watch.

huaka: Bolivia. Belt.

huali: Peru. Full skirt that is gathered at the waist.

huallas: Bolivia. Mantle used for marriage ceremonies.

huallquepo: Bolivia. Coca bag.

huanaco: *See* guanaco.

huang ma qua: China. Yellow riding jacket awarded for bravery.

huángcàncn: China. Bright yellow.

huarache: Mexico. Sandal woven of strips of leather, usually in a light color, and sometimes with a heel strap.

huarizo: Soft fur of an animal that is a cross between a llama and an alpaca.

huayaca: Bolivia. Bag used to carry foodstuffs.

hūba: Germany. Old word for hood.

Hubbard cloth: Trade name for water repellent cotton fabric.

huccatoon: United Kingdom. Dyed cotton fabric made in Manchester for export to the United States.

huckaback: Absorbent cotton or linen fabric used for towels.

huckaback embroidery: Darned embroidery done on huckaback toweling.

Hudson Bay coat: Canada. Coat made from a Hudson Bay blanket, a woolen blanket woven with wide contrasting stripes.

hue: Denmark. Hat.

hueco de la manga: Spain. Armseye.

huepilli: Mexico. Sleeveless blouse or cotton cloth with an opening for the head worn by women. Style inherited from the Aztecs.

hù'er: China. Earflaps; earmuffs.

hufá: Iceland. Worn by women, a beret-style cap of black velvet surmounted by an etched gold cylinder through which is drawn a stout cord ending in a long black tassel.

hufa: Norway. Old word for cap.

hufe: Byzantine and Romanesque (400–1200 C.E.). United Kingdom. Hat.

hug-me-tight: Crinoline (1840–1865 C.E.) to Bustle (1865–1890 C.E.). United Kingdom. Worn from 1850 to 1867, hand-knitted or crocheted jacket with cape-like sleeves.

hugue: Byzantine and Romanesque (400–1200 C.E.). Woman's short sleeveless tunic.

Huguenot lace: Romantic (1815–1840 C.E.). Imitation lace on a muslin net ground on which cutouts are sewn.

hug-me-tight

hui yi: China. Song dynasty. Empress's dark blue gown ornamented with gold pheasants. It was trimmed with red bands decorated with clouds and dragons. Worn with the phoenix crown.

huicó: Mexico. Zoque Indian term for thread.

huif: Holland. Coif.

huik: Elizabethan (1550–1625 C.E.) to Restoration (1660–1700 C.E.). Flemish mantle that late in the century was combined with a felt hat with a tuft on top.

huila kaulike: United States of America. Hawaii. Disc wheel of a sewing machine.

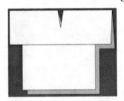

huipil

huipil grande

huipil: Guatemala and Mexico. Woman's long blouse made from four widths of fabric with a head-hole.

huipil grande: Mexico. Huipil with the neck and lower edges trimmed with lace flounces. Worn with sleeves hanging in front and behind.

huipil ranciado: Guatemala. Woman's blouse woven in jaspé.

huipile con labor: Mexico. Worn by the Zoque Indians, huipiles with an embroidered design.

huipilli: Mexico. Aztec term for a huipil.

huka pihi: United States of America. Hawaii. Buttonhook.

huke: 1. Late Gothic (1350–1450 C.E.). France. Tabard with front and back panels and occasionally with sleeves that was often worn belted. 2. Renaissance (1450–1550 C.E.) to Restoration (1660–1700 C.E.). Spain. Long veil that covered the female wearer to the knees or ankles. Evolved into the mantilla. 3. Malta. Long, black, cloth cloak of Moorish origin.

hukjinju: Korea. Black pearl.

hukkō: Ethiopia. Cap of skin.

hul: Netherlands. Woman's winged cap of white lace and embroidery. Worn only on special occasions.

hula saki: Nigeria. Tall domed cap of handwoven cotton. It is lined with shirting.

hula skirt: United States of America. Hawaiian grass skirt.

hule: Spain. Oilcloth.

hulle: *See* haube.

hulu: United States of America. Hawaii. Feather.

hulu hipa: United States of America. Hawaii. Woolen cloth.

huluhulu: United States of America. Hawaii. Flannel.

huma huatarina: Ecuador. Quichua word for head wrap.

Humboldt purple: Crinoline (1840–1865 C.E.). In 1863, new color.

humeral: Ecclesiastical dress. Veil or scarf worn around the shoulders by Roman Catholic clergy during the High Mass. It was descended from the chaperon.

hum-hum: Late Georgian (1750–1790 C.E.). United States of America. Coarse cotton fabric from India used to line garments from 1750 to 1770.

hummums: *See* hum-hum.

humu: United States of America. Hawaii. To sew.

humu kaulahao: United States of America. Hawaii. Chain stitch.

humu puka pihi: United States of America. Hawaii. Buttonhole stitch.

humuhumu ulana: United States of America. Hawaii. To darn.

hùmùjìng: China. Goggles.

humuka: United States of America. Hawaii. Cross-stitching.

humulau: United States of America. Hawaii. To embroider.

humupa'a: United States of America. Hawaii. Lock stitch.

humuwili: United States of America. Hawaii. Overcasting stitch.

hunakana'i: United States of America. Hawaii. Tapa with white and yellow dots.

Hungarian cord: Bustle (1865–1890 C.E.). Fashionably worn in 1867 and 1868, silk cord on the border of a trained skirt instead of the conventional braid.

Hungarian embroidery: Hungary. Flat- or stain-stitch embroidery done on peasant garments that is characterized by its bright colors.

Hungarian vest: Directoire and First Empire (1790–1815 C.E.). Woman's high collared, long sleeved jacket made with a scarf-like piece hanging from the left shoulder and crossing in the back to meet the belt.

Hungarian wrap: Directoire and First Empire (1790–1815 C.E.). United States of America. Introduced in 1809, a fashionable loose velvet cloak lined with silk and worn wrapped around the body.

hungback: Scotland. Lightweight tweed coat fabric.

Hungerland band: Charles I and the Commonwealth (1625–1660 C.E.). Woman's collar made of Hungerland lace.

Hungerland lace: Charles I and the Commonwealth (1625–1660 C.E.). Type of lace made at Halle in the Hungarian style.

hung-phuc: Vietnam. Mourning clothes.

hunhuáng: China. Pale yellow.

hunter green: Dark, slightly yellowish green.

hunter's pink: Brilliant scarlet velvet used for hunting coats.

hunting belt: Directoire and First Empire (1790–1815 C.E.). United Kingdom. In the 1820s, man's whalebone belt worn by dandies when hunting.

hunting necktie: Romantic (1815–1840 C.E.). United Kingdom. Worn from 1818 to 1830s, man's very wide necktie worn high on the neck with three creases on each side. Ends were crossed and pinned inside the coat.

hunting stock: (1890–1899 C.E.). United Kingdom. Man's large, cellular cloth necktie folded and tied twice around the neck, concealing the lack of a collar.

Huntley bonnet: Directoire and First Empire (1790–1815 C.E.). Introduced in 1814, woman's bonnet similar to a Scotch bonnet, made in twill weave plaid sarcenet and trimmed with a rosette and three feathers.

Huntley scarf: Romantic (1815–1840 C.E.). Scotch tartan scarf of silk or wool worn with ends pinned to left shoulder.

Huot: Germany. Hat.

hupé: *See* hufá.

hupodema: Hebrew. Sandals.

huque: Late Gothic (1350–1450 C.E.) to Renaissance (1450–1550 C.E.). France. Short flowing outer robe worn open at sides and often edged in fur and trimmed with embroidery or gems. Knights wore it open down the front.

hure: Early Gothic (1200–1350 C.E.) to Restoration (1660–1700 C.E.). 1. Shaggy hair on a man's head. 2. Cap made from animal skin with the hair left on it.

hurluburlu: Restoration (1660–1700 C.E.). Woman's hairstyle in which short curls were worn all over the head.

hurlupe: *See* hurluburlu.

hurricane cloth: Plied combed Egyptian cotton for luxury rainwear.

huru kurii: Australia. Maori's dogskin cloak made from whole skins.

huruhuru: *See* kaka hu kura.

húsè: China. Light green.

huso: Ecuador and Guatemala. Spindle.

hussar boots: Directoire and First Empire (1790–1815 C.E.) to Romantic (1815–1840 C.E.). United Kingdom. Worn from 1800 to 1820s, man's civilian boot style that reached the calf with slight point in front. Sometimes had turnover tops and was shod in iron.

Hussar buskins: Directoire and First Empire (1790–1815 C.E.). Knee-high boots with a heart-shaped peak at the center front, often decorated with a central tassel.

hussar jacket: Bustle (1865–1890 C.E.). United Kingdom. Braided and frogged jacket that was worn with

a waistcoat. Influenced by the military uniforms of the English in Egypt.

hussar point: Romantic (1815–1840 C.E.). United Kingdom. In 1820s, front edge of a man's waistcoat, had extreme points and even curved up over the hips on the sides.

Hut: Germany. Hat.

Hutband: Germany. Hat band.

Hutfutter: Germany. Hat lining.

Hutkopf: Germany. Hat crown.

huttu: Timbuktu. A silver plate worn in the middle of a woman's forehead.

huve: Late Gothic (1350–1450 C.E.). Woman's headdress resembling a tapered cornet with a veil.

huve

huvet: Late Gothic (1350–1450 C.E.). Hood.

huyèn-ðai: Vietnam. Black judo sash.

hvivklaede: Denmark. Woman's linen headscarf.

hwajang: Korea. Makeup.

hwajangbok: Korea. Bathrobe.

hwamunsa: Korea. Floral patterned sa silk.

hwangsaek: Korea. Yellow.

hwap'o: Korea. Canvas.

hwitel: Byzantine and Romanesque (400–1200 C.E.). United Kingdom. Piece of fabric, probably rectangular, used as a cloak. Originally of undyed fabric (literally "white"). Worn by both genders.

hyacinth: Medium lavender.

hyanggap norigae: Korea. Accessories with perfume cases.

hyangsu: Korea. Perfume.

Hyde Park bonnet: Directoire and First Empire (1790–1815 C.E.). Very fashionable in 1812, white satin bonnet trimmed with four white ostrich plumes.

hydrotobolic hat: Crinoline (1840–1865 C.E.). Man's hat with a ventilated crown made with a small hole in the center protected with wire gauze.

hyire: Ghana. White earth used as makeup.

hymo: Mohair and linen fabric used to reinforce body of coat.

I

iakepi: United States of America. Hawaii. Jasper.

iall: Ireland. Gaelic word for ribbon.

iallachrann: Ireland. Gaelic word for shoes.

iar: Ireland. Gaelic word for black.

iar-dhonn: Ireland. Gaelic word for brownish black.

iasepi: *See* iakepi.

ibante: Nigeria. Yoruba man's triangular loincloth.

ibobirin: Nigeria. Yoruba woman's six yard wrapper than hangs from breasts to calf.

iborun: Nigeria. Yoruba woman's veil.

ibrisimidzís: Greece. Silk worker.

iç tuman: Iran. Woman's printed cotton petticoat.

Iceland wool: Iceland. Lustrous wool produced in Iceland.

ichcahuipilli: Mexico. Aztec warrior's tunic of quilted cotton cloth. *See also* xicolli.

ichcatl: Mexico. Aztec term for white cotton.

ichella: Chile. Woman's long, fringed, woolen shawl.

ichi-dome: Japan. Woman's hairpin.

Ichimatsu: Japan. A checkered pattern named for the actor Sadokawa Ichimatsu.

Ida canvas: Open mesh fabric used for embroidery.

'ie: Samoa. Cloth.

'ie mafiafia: Samoa. Canvas.

'ie valavala: Samoa. Cheesecloth.

'ie-tonga: Polynesia. A six foot by five foot mat worn as a loincloth. Then ends are fringed and trimmed with a border of red feathers.

igaal: United Arab Emirates. Head circlet used to hold the ghoutra in place.

igbiri: Ekine word for an ankle circlet of locust beans.

igla: Croatia, Poland, Russia, and Serbia. Needle.

igne oyasi: Turkey. Finely worked needle lace made using crochet stitches and beadwork.

ihenga: India. Woman's short skirt.

ihram: 1. Combination of two white cotton wraps, one for the loin and one for the back, worn by the Mohammedan on pilgrimage to Mecca. 2. *See* ghoutra.

ihu kama'a: United States of America. Hawaii. The toe area of shoes.

ihupuni: Australia. Maori's dogskin cloak decorated with strips of black hair.

iie: Romania. Woman's smock.

ijara: India. A tapering pajama.

ijarbund: India. Pajama waist cord.

ijzergrauw: Holland. Iron gray.

ikan: Japan. A man's informal court costume.

ikar-hay: Tuareg. A woman's headcloth.

ikat: 1. Variety of chiné silk fabrics made in Java, Sumatra, etc. 2. *See* kasuri. 3. The resist-dyeing process in which designs are preserved in warp or weft by tying off small bundles of yarns to prevent dyeing.

iket: Java. Man's headcloth.

ikhdari: Palestine. Silk fabric with narrow red and green bands on a floral pattern.

ikori: Nigeria. Yoruba man's deep cylindrical hat.

ilaam: Zaire. General term for clothes.

ilbora: *See* irbora.

ilhó: Portugal. Eyelet.

'ili: United States of America. Hawaii. Leather.

'ili hinuhinu: United States of America. Hawaii. Patent leather.

'ili kuapo: United States of America. Hawaii. Belt.

'ili pale o kama'a: United States of America. Hawaii. The sole of shoes.

'ili pipi: United States of America. Hawaii. Leather; cowhide.

ilic: Bulgaria. Man's brown or red vest.

'ilio-hulu-papale: United States of America. Hawaii. Literally "hat-fur dog," the beaver.

illusion: Very fine, sheer tulle or net.

imbecile: Romantic (1815–1840 C.E.). 1. Worn from 1815 to 1835, woman's very full sleeve with horizontal folds from elbow to wrist. 2. Worn from 1829 to 1835, woman's very full day sleeve that gathered onto a cuff at the wrist.

îmbrăca: Romania. To clothe or to dress.

îmbrăcăminte: Romania. Clothing.

Imogen: Crinoline (1840–1865 C.E.). In 1857, silk mantle with two deeply pointed flounces edged with passementerie.

imperatrice: Crinoline (1840–1865 C.E.). 1. In 1862, woman's cravat bow. 2. In 1862, shade of blue.

imperial: 1. Crinoline (1840–1865 C.E.). Small beard, commonly worn with a waxed moustache. Begun by Napoleon III. 2. Crinoline (1840–1865 C.E.). Loose, fly-front paletot overcoat. 3. Early Gothic (1200–1350 C.E.). Gold-figured silk fabric introduced to Great Britain from Greece or the Orient.

Imperial: Crinoline (1840–1865 C.E.). In 1853, bias-cut mantle with heavy embroidery and a deep fringe.

Imperial gold: (1930–1940 C.E.). A new color.

imperial ottoman: Heavy, ribbed bengaline.

imperial sateen: Satin weave, heavy cotton fabric.

imperial serge: Soft, worsted, twill weave fabric.

imperial valley cotton: United States of America. Cotton grown in California.

imperial velvet: Bustle (1865–1890 C.E.). Introduced in 1870, fabric of equal width stripes of corded silk and velvet.

impilayoth: Biblical (unknown–30 C.E.). Hebrew socks or felt shoes.

impilia: Roman (753 B.C.E.–323 C.E.). Socks or felt shoes.

impiraperle: Italy. Bustle (1865–1890 C.E.). In the 1880s, a woman who strung beads for a living.

impiraressa: *See* impiraperle.

improver: *See* dress improver.

imurluc: Hungary. Wide mantle of natural color with a large collar which can be buttoned to the hood. It is richly embroidered with spirals and circles.

in: Romania. Flax.

in the gray: Natural fabric in the undyed state.

inaka yuzen: Japan. Country yuzen.

inar: 1. Byzantine and Romanesque (400–1200 C.E.). Fitted, sleeveless jacket. 2. *See* fūan.

încalţa minte: *See* gheată.

incarnat: Bustle (1865–1890 C.E.). In 1882, carnation red.

incarnate: Elizabethan (1550–1625 C.E.). Red.

Incroyable: Crinoline (1840–1865 C.E.). In 1856, woman's silk-lined cloth pardessus with a fitted body. The full skirt was pleated at the hip. The pagoda sleeves were slit to above the elbow. It was trimmed with galloon.

incroyable bows: Bustle (1865–1890 C.E.). Introduced in 1889, a number of large bows of lace and mousselaine de soie worn at the throat of Directoire costumes.

incroyable coat: Bustle (1865–1890 C.E.). Introduced in 1889, woman's long tailcoat with wide lapels. Worn with lace jabot and waistcoat in the afternoon, it was designed to imitate the swallow-tail look of the Directoire.

incwado: Rhodesia. Ndebele term for a penis sheath.

indaco: Italy. Indigo.

indanthrene dye: Kind of vat dye.

inde: Byzantine and Romanesque (400–1200 C.E.). To be azure colored.

inderlins: Early Georgian (1700–1750 C.E.) to Late Georgian (1750–1790 C.E.). Germany. Coarse hemp fabric from Hamburg.

indhoni: India. A padded ring worn on a woman's head to help her balance a load carried thereon.

India chintz: Chintz with large floral pattern.

India cloth: Short staple, low grade cotton.

India cotton: Heavy figured chintz used in upholstery.

India linen: Fine, cotton lawn woven in imitation of linen. It is slightly sized and usually bleached.

India muslin: India. Fine, soft, plain weave, cotton fabric.

India print: Plain weave cotton print with hand-blocked Oriental pattern.

India shawl: Expensive East Indian shawl, usually of figured or embroidered cashmere.

India silk: India. Soft, plain weave, silk fabric.

Indian: 1. Drawn muslin lace or muslin fabric. 2. Romantic (1815–1840 C.E.). United Kingdom. Green.

Indian dimity: Sheer, corded cotton fabric.

Indian embroidery: Any characteristic Oriental design worked by East Indian natives.

Indian gown: *See* Indian nightgown.

Indian green: Romantic (1815–1840 C.E.). Shade of green.

Indian head: Trade name for plain weave cotton fabric with soft finish.

Indian lamb: Fur of the caracul group.

Indian lawn: Light cotton muslin.

Indian necktie: Romantic (1815–1840 C.E.). United Kingdom. Man's muslin cravat, the ends of which were secured in front with a sliding ring.

Indian nightgown: Elizabethan (1550–1625 C.E.) to Late Georgian (1750–1790 C.E.). 1. Synonym for the banyan. 2. Woman's negligee.

Indian rubber: Romantic (1815–1840 C.E.). Patented in 1823.

Indian work: *See* Indian.

indienne: France. Bandanna.

indiennes: Elizabethan (1550–1625 C.E.) to Late Georgian (1750–1790 C.E.). Any painted or printed India muslin.

indigo: 1. Most precious dye, a deep purple red. 2. Reddish blue color.

Indigoblau: Germany. Indigo blue.

indispensible: Directoire and First Empire (1790–1815 C.E.) to Romantic (1815–1840 C.E.). United Kingdom. Used from 1800 to around 1820, small square or lozenge-shaped handbag of silk or velvet with a drawstring top and worn hanging from the arm on a ribbon.

indlugula: Rhodesia. Ndebele term for a warrior's ostrich feather headdress.

indrachchhanda: India. Necklace of 1,008 strings of pearls.

induere: *See* vestire.

indumentum: Roman (753 B.C.E.–323 C.E.). Any garment.

indusium: *See* tunica interior.

ineffibles: Romantic (1815–1840 C.E.). One of many euphemisms for breeches or trousers.

iner: Romania. Finger ring.

inexpressibles: Romantic (1815–1840 C.E.). One of many euphemisms for breeches or trousers.

infectore: Roman (753 B.C.E.–323 C.E.). Dyer of fleece wool.

infula: 1. Roman (753 B.C.E.–323 C.E.). Scarf-like band of red and white wool worn tied around the head as a sign of religious consecration. 2. Ecclesiastical dress. Tab at back of a bishop's miter. *See also* vexillum.

ingenue: Yellowish green.

injo chinju: Korea. Artificial pearl.

injogyonsa: Korea. Rayon.

ink gray: Bustle (1865–1890 C.E.). In 1874, nearly black gray.

inkin: 1. Japan. Imported Chinese fabric. 2. Japan. Kimono decoration of lacquer imprinted with gold leaf or gold dust.

inkle: Renaissance (1450–1550 C.E.) to Romantic (1815–1840 C.E.). Wool or linen tape, usually colored, used as a cheap binding or trim by the lower classes.

inner spring: Second busk underneath the busk, required in a very tight corset.

inro: Japan. Medicine box suspended from the obi.

insertion: Narrow lace with plain edge so it may be set into fabric.

insole: Inner or inside sole of shoe.

instita: Roman (753 B.C.E.–323 C.E.). Piece of fabric fastened under lower belt of stola to form train in back.

intaglio: Sunken or hollowed design in hard material, like a gem.

intarsia: Design knitted only into some sections on knitwear.

interala: *See* tunica interior.

interfacing: Woven or non-woven fabric used between layers to reinforce and stiffen collars, cuffs, etc.

interlining: Inner lining placed between lining and outer fabric.

internal high soles: China. Ming dynasty. Shoes with interior soles.

inti: Bolivia. In woven fabric, stylized diamonds symbolizing the sun.

intuiger: *See* ētim.

Inverness: Crinoline (1840–1865 C.E.) to 20th century. Worn after 1858, man's large, loose, knee-length overcoat with fitted collar and long cape. In 1870s, the cape only reached the sides where it joined the side seam. Often sleeveless in 1880s. Developed oversized armseyes in 1890s.

Inverness skirts: Scotland. The four pointed flaps which fall from the Highland doublet. Each flap is trimmed with lace and three buttons.

invisible zipper: Slide closing fastener designed so that no part of the fastener shows when closed.

io: New Zealand. Maori word for warp.

ionar: Ireland. Short jacket worn over the leine. The sleeves were slit on the underside to allow the leine sleeves to show.

ionaradh: Ireland. Gaelic word for clothing.

Ionian: Crinoline (1840–1865 C.E.). In 1856, woman's narrow scarf with two deep flounces. It was trimmed with satin puffing.

Ionic chiton: Greek (3000–100 B.C.E.). Evolved by 600 B.C.E., extra wide chiton of a thin woolen, linen, or gauze. Sewn together down the right side and pinned or buttoned at intervals down the arms. Very long, often worn trailing. It had an overfold at the waist, a kolpos.

Ionic chiton

ioring: *See* kwigoi.

ipingea: *See* imurluc.

ipingeaua: *See* chepeneag.

ipsiboe: Romantic (1815–1840 C.E.). Introduced in 1823, yellowish beige.

irbora: Ethiopia. Armlet worn by a man who has killed an elephant or an enemy.

irdan: Palestine. Wide pointed sleeves.

irege: *See* kamozi.

Irene Castle bob: (1910–1920 C.E.). Loosely waved, off-the-forehead women's hairstyle named for the dancer, Irene Castle.

irengan: Indonesia. Blue and brown fabric worn by widows.

iricinium: *See* ricinium.

iris: Medium lavender blue.

Irish crochet: Ireland. Needlepoint lace with medallions of a rose, a shamrock, or a leaf.

Irish lace: Ireland. Variety of lace styles made in Ireland.

Irish lawn: Ireland. Plain weave linen fabric.

Irish linen: Ireland. Plain weave, pure linen fabric.

Irish polonaise: Late Georgian (1750–1790 C.E.). United Kingdom. Worn from 1770 to 1775, day gown with fitted, décolleté bodice that closed down the front, pleated overskirt that was open in the front over a short underskirt.

Irish poplin: Ireland. Poplin with silk warp and worsted weft.

Irish work: Ireland. White embroidery on white ground.

iron-pot: Charles I and the Commonwealth (1625–1660 C.E.). United Kingdom. Iron helmet style favored by the soldiers of Oliver Cromwell.

'isāba: Palestine. Woman's headband used to fasten in place the 'agal.

Isabeau corsage: Crinoline (1840–1865 C.E.). United Kingdom. Introduced in 1846, woman's jacket-like bodice for morning wear open on the bottom and trimmed with galloon and silk buttons. Had high falling collar.

Isabeau sleeve: Crinoline (1840–1865 C.E.). Introduced in 1860s, woman's triangular sleeve with the point at the shoulder. Used on dresses, the pardessus, and the Maintenon cloak.

Isabeau style dress: Crinoline (1840–1865 C.E.). Worn in 1860s, day dress cut in one and fitted with goring. It had a row of buttons or rosettes down the front.

Isabella: Romantic (1815–1840 C.E.). The color cream.

Isabella color: Romantic (1815–1840 C.E.). United States. Dirty white color.

isallo: Bolivia. Mantle.

išānō: Ethiopia. Beads.

iscayo: 1. See isallo. 2. Bolivia. Ceremonial mantle worn by chieftain's wife.

ishdad: Palestine. Man's sash.

ishiwaba: Rhodesia. Ndebele term for a skin shirt worn by a woman.

ishi-zoko: Meiji (1876–1912 C.E.). Japan. Literally "stone soles," tabi with rubber soles.

ishkay fachalina: Ecuador. Quichua term for a woman's headwrap.

isi Diya: Natal. Worn by Zulu women, long untanned cowhide tunics.

isigula: Rhodesia. Ndebele term for a cloak.

Isir: Crinoline (1840–1865 C.E.). In 1854, cloak with deep front yoke and box-pleated back trimmed with eight rows of narrow velvet and a very rich fringe.

Isley green: Crinoline (1840–1865 C.E.). In 1863, new color.

ispahanis: Byzantine and Romanesque (400–1200 C.E.). Fabrics made in Almeria (Spain) from the eighth to the eleventh centuries.

istalla: Bolivia. Woman's coca bag.

istela: See itstela.

isticharion: Biblical (unknown–30 C.E.). Hebrew short-sleeved jacket.

itagbe: Ogboni. Woven by women, an intricately patterned shoulder cloth.

Italiaans stro: Holland. Leghorn straw.

Italian cloak: Renaissance (1450–1550 C.E.) to Restoration (1660–1700 C.E.). Man's short, hooded cloak.

Italian cloth: Strong, lightweight, lustrous fabric made with a satin or twill weave.

Italian collar: Notched shawl collar with the upper edge of the notch pointed and the lower edge curved.

Italian cut: Short irregular bob.

Italian farthingale: See wheel farthingale.

Italian ferret: Narrow silk braid.

Italian heel: Late Georgian (1750–1790 C.E.). United Kingdom. Small, peg-top heel that narrowed and then flared again at the sole. Made of wood covered in a colored kid leather, usually white or cream.

Italian heel

Italian nightgown: Late Georgian (1750–1790 C.E.). United Kingdom. Worn in 1770s, woman's semiformal day dress with boned, décolleté bodice, elbow-length sleeves, a long overskirt, and a contrasting underskirt. Overskirt could be worn hitched up like a polonaise.

Italian polonaise: See Irish polonaise.

Italian sleeve: Gay Nineties (1890–1900 C.E.) In 1891, a woman's sleeve cut full to elbow and fitted to wrist.

Italian slipper: Directoire and First Empire (1790–1815 C.E.). United States of America. Worn in 1812, heelless, flat slipper that was cut low on the foot.

Italien: Crinoline (1840–1865 C.E.). Introduced in 1862, woman's white chip bonnet with a long green feather around the brim. Tied under the chin with a green velvet crepe ribbon bow.

itar: Romania. Men's snug white trousers worn in winter.

itelli: Tuareg. The portion of veil covering the forehead.

itsembéri: Greece. Kerchief worn over the hair.

itstela: Biblical (unknown–30 C.E.). Hebrew shawl.

ityogaesi: Meizi (1867–1912 C.E.). Japan. A woman's hairstyle.

iuele: Byzantine and Romanesque (400–1200 C.E.) to Renaissance (1450–1550 C.E.). United Kingdom. Middle English word for jewel.

iupca: Romania. Skirt.

Ivanhoe cap: Romantic (1815–1840 C.E.). Introduced in 1820, popular cap named for Scott's novel of the same name.

ivory: White with a yellow orange tint.

ivory stitch: Restoration (1660–1700 C.E.) to Early Georgian (1700–1750 C.E.). A tightly knotted stitch used in working a dense needle lace.

iwede: Byzantine and Romanesque (400–1200 C.E.) to Renaissance (1450–1550 C.E.). United Kingdom. Middle English term for clothing.

ixcaco: See cuyuscate.

ixtle: Mexico. Fiber from the maguey plant that is used to make rope and decorated bags.

ixtli: Aztec. Maguey fiber.

iyegbe: Nigeria. Cut pile cloth woven in Owo. It is used by chiefs as a medicine cloth.

izār: 1. Syria. Large white or black cotton wrap worn by women when outside. 2. Berber word for haik. 3. India. Trousers.

izār baftā: India. Bifurcated trousers.

izaree: India. Izar.

izaribata: Japan. Looms.

iziketsho: Rhodesia. Ndebele term for bracelets.

iznaq: Palestine. Chain worn suspended from the sides of a shakkeh.

J

jaatl'óól: Navajo. Earring.

jabiru: Soft, almost furry plumage of stork-like bird.

jabot: Charles I and the Commonwealth (1625–1660 C.E.) to Romantic (1815–1840 C.E.). Elaborate tie at the top of a shirt.

jabot blouse: Blouse with jabot at collar.

jabul: Philippine Islands. Large mantle worn by women.

jacinth: Orange colored gemstone.

jack: Early Gothic (1200–1350 C.E.) to Renaissance (1450–1550 C.E.). United Kingdom. Padded military doublet made of up to 30 layers of fabric, quilted and fitted to the body.

jack boot: Elizabethan (1550–1625 C.E.) to Late Georgian (1750–1790 C.E.). Oversized boot that was generally large enough to wear a shoe or slipper inside it. It was lined with pockets to use to carry small items. It was made of jack leather, a leather coated with tar or pitch.

jack chain: Elizabethan (1550–1625 C.E.) to Restoration (1660–1700 C.E.). Decorative chain of figure eight links that joined at right angles.

jack leather: Elizabethan (1550–1625 C.E.) to Late Georgian (1750–1790 C.E.). Waxed leather painted with tar and used for boots.

Jack Tar suit: Bustle (1865–1890 C.E.) to Gay Nineties (1890–1900 C.E.). In 1880s and 1890s, boy's sailor suit with Jack Tar trousers.

Jack Tar trousers: Bustle (1865–1890 C.E.). In 1880s, men's yachting pants made without a side seam that were fitted to the knee and then flared to a 22-inch circumference. It was made with whole falls.

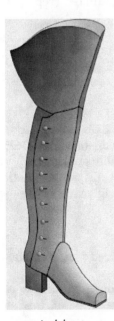

jack boot

jackanapes: Restoration (1660–1700 C.E.). Man's midriff-length, short sleeved jacket. Commonly worn with petticoat breeches.

jacket: Short, coat-like garment, with or without sleeves. Usually opens down front, reaching below hips.

jacket coat: Bustle (1865–1890 C.E.). Man's short jacket lined with wool.

Jackson shoes: *See* brogans.

Jacobean embroidery: Restoration (1660–1700 C.E.). United Kingdom. Embroidery characterized by a tree design ornamented in color with flowers, fruit, and birds.

jaconas: *See* jaconet.

jaconet: 1. Directoire and First Empire (1790–1815 C.E.). Fashionable in 1800 and after, thin cambric made in India for dresses and handkerchiefs. 2. Cotton fabric glazed on one side.

jaconette: *See* jaconet.

jacquard: Complex weave with intricate figured weave.

Jacquard velvet: Velvet woven with a cut-out or etched-out pile that creates a pattern.

jacqueminot: Gay Nineties (1890–1900 C.E.). In 1892, a rich shade of red.

jacquette: *See* courtepy.

jadara: India. A white silk worn by the bride during the marriage ceremony.

jade: Shade of green.

Jaeger underclothes: Bustle (1865–1890 C.E.). Introduced in 1880s by a German doctor, Dr. Jaeger, these wool underclothes were constructed to include both the trunk and limbs.

jaganath: United Kingdom. Coarse, plain weave, cotton fabric.

jahanaroho: India. A woman's short petticoat.

jais: France. Jet.

jaka: 1. Bulgaria. Collar. 2. *See* ogrlica.

jalaka: India. A metallic wire gauze used in making coats of mail.

jaleco: *See* colête.

jalika: India. Woman's hairnet.

jam: United Kingdom. Child's frock.

jāmā: India. Long cotton garment worn by Muslims in the northern areas of India.

jāmā chakmān: India. Knee-length coat with full sleeves.

jāmāah: *See* jāmā.

Jamaica shorts: Mid-thigh length shorts.

jamawar: India. A Kashmir shawl.

jamb: Early Gothic (1200–1350 C.E.). Piece of armor for the leg.

jambart: *See* jamb.

jambe: *See* jamb.

jambeau: *See* jamb.

jambee cane: Early Georgian (1700–1750 C.E.). Man's knotty bamboo walking stick from Jambi in Sumatra.

jambieres: Crinoline (1840–1865 C.E.). United States of America. Leather greaves.

jamdani: India. Hindu word for a figured or flowered muslin.

jamete: *See* xamete.

jamewar: India. Woolen jamdani.

jamiwar: India. An intricately woven brocade of a silk floral design on a wool background.

Jan de Bry coat: Directoire and First Empire (1790–1815 C.E.). France. Introduced in 1799, short-waisted coat with small revers and standing velvet collar that fastened shut with three buttons. It was cut away in front in curve to back where it ended in short, pointed tails. The sleeves were padded at the shoulders and were fitted down the arm where they ended in two buttons on the hand itself. Waistcoat showed beneath the jacket.

Jane: False bangs.

janghia: India. Short pants.

janna wa-nar: Samaria. Literally "heaven and hell," green and red striped fabric.

jansenistes: *See* panniers.

Janus cloth: Double-faced, worsted fabric with each side a different color.

Janus cord: Bustle (1865–1890 C.E.). Introduced in 1867, black rep of wool and cotton used for mourning clothing.

Jap marten: Durable, yellow fur of the Japanese marten often dyed the color of sable.

Jap mink: Light yellow fur of the mink from Japan with a dark stripe down the center back. It was often dyed to resemble American mink.

jap silk: *See* habutai.

japamala: Hindu prayer beads.

Japanese crepe: Japan. Imported plain weave cotton fabric with a twisted weft yarn that was made in Japan.

Japanese embroidery: Elaborate satin stitch embroidery made with colored silk or metal threads.

Japanese grass cloth: *See* Swatow grass cloth.

Japanese hat: Bustle (1865–1890 C.E.). United Kingdom. Worn in 1867 to 1869, woman's circular hat made without a crown and with a straw brim that sloped slightly downward. It was trimmed with ribbon and tied on with a bow below the chignon.

Japanese mink: Animal with short dark hair.

Japanese mocha: Glossy straw braid used to make cheaper grades of hats.

Japanese piqué: Bustle (1865–1890 C.E.). In 1872, soft twilled cotton.

Japanese pongee: Bustle (1865–1890 C.E.). Silk fabric with a smooth surface.

Japanese rose: Romantic (1815–1840 C.E.). Rose color.

Japanese silk: Bustle (1865–1890 C.E.). Introduced in 1867, silk fabric similar to alpaca. *See also* habutai.

Japanese velvet: Velvet with dyed designs.

japon: *See* rok.

japona: Portugal. Short jacket.

Japonais: Bustle (1865–1890 C.E.). In 1879, green blue.

jaque: Early Gothic (1200–1350 C.E.). France. Man's short, rough waistcoat worn by the poor.

jaquemar: (1898). Rich red.

jaqueta: Portugal. Jacket.

jaquette: 1. Early Gothic (1200–1350 C.E.) to Renaissance (1450–1550 C.E.). France. Style of coat, especially popular among the lower classes, cut like a tunic. 2. Bustle (1865–1890 C.E.). Woman's jacket inspired by the 17th-century hongreline. 3. France. Jacket.

jaquette coloriée: France. Blazer.

jarajari: India. An imported silk or brocade.

jarbā: India. Leather slippers.

jardiniere: 1. Design made of flowers, fruits, and leaves. 2. Pendant ornament on a woman's headdress. 3. France. Low ruffle. 4. Crinoline (1840–1865 C.E.). Introduced in 1841, striped and gauffered crepe patterned with small flowers.

jari: India. Gold thread.

jarrawiyah: Iraq. Man's turban or wrapped scarf.

jarreteira: Portugal. Garter.

jarretelle: France. 1. Stocking. 2. Sock supporter.

jarretiere: France. Garter.

jas: Holland. Coat.

jaseran: 1. Algeria. Chain mesh tunic. 2. Short linen jacket covered in thin metal plates. 3. Elizabethan (1550–1625 C.E.). Woman's high necklaces of thin gold chains.

jasey: Late Georgian (1750–1790 C.E.) to Romantic (1815–1840 C.E.). Man's cheap wig made of jersey wool yarn.

jasi: Kiamu. A round ear ornament.

jaspand: Holland. Coattail.

jaspe: Guatemala. Literally "marbelized," used of ikat-patterned threads in weaving.

jaspè: 1. Heavy drapery fabric woven in stripes of differing shades of the same hue. 2. Faint, broken striped effect.

jaspé: Guatemala. Tie-dyed linen.

jaspeado: Guatemala. Cloth woven with jaspé.

jasper: 1. Black and white fabric. 2. Green chalcedony. 3. Greenish yellow.

jastai: India. Gray.

jata-bhara: India. A heavy bundled topknot of matted hair worn by Hindu ascetics.

jata-mukuta: *See* jata-bhara.

jatun chumbi: Ecuador. A wide belt.

jaune: France. Yellow.

Java canvas: Basket weave canvas used as a base for embroidery.

Java cotton: Silky vegetable fiber.

Java stripes: Brightly striped cotton fabric.

Java supers: United Kingdom. Plain-weave cotton fabric.

jawara: India. Tassels tied on the turban behind the ear.

jazerant: Early Gothic (1200–1350 C.E.). Jacket made of small overlapping metal plates on a fabric base and worn as defensive garment.

jean: Twill weave cotton fabric.

Jean de Bry coat: *See* Jan de Bry coat.

jeanette: Romantic (1815–1840 C.E.). Introduced in 1836, woman's necklace made from a narrow band of hair or velvet and holding a small cross or heart.

jedwab: Poland. Silk.

jehla: Czechoslovakia. Needle.

jekkertje: *See* buis.

jelab: Morocco. Wide, wool blouse or hooded cloak.

jeléci: Greece. Woman's short, sleeveless vest.

jelek: Prussia. Woman's Turkish-inspired, short, sleeveless waistcoat.

jellab: *See* jelab.

jellaba: *See* jelab.

jellabia: *See* jelab.

jellib: *See* jelab.

jellick

jellick: Turkey. Woman's long coat with fitted waist that hangs open on the sides from the hips or a looser version of the same garment.

jelly bag: Man's soft washable nightcap.

jeltesta: Morocco. Jewish woman's flounced skirt.

jelteta: Morocco. Jewish woman's wide velvet skirt, usually the same color as the gonbaiz.

Jemima: Romantic (1815–1840 C.E.). United Kingdom. In 1836, fabric boot with elastic insertions and leather toe. Designed for Queen Victoria.

jemmy: Romantic (1815–1840 C.E.). Man's shooting coat with multiple pockets.

jemmy boots: Romantic (1815–1840 C.E.). Men's light riding boots, an upscale version of jockey boots.

jemmy cane: Early Georgian (1700–1750 C.E.) to Romantic (1815–1840 C.E.). Little switch carried by men under the arm. Particularly fashionable in 1750s and 1760s.

Jenny Bell: Crinoline (1840–1865 C.E.). In 1856, woman's unlined travelling mantle trimmed with galloon.

Jenny Lind costume: Crinoline (1840–1865 C.E.). United Kingdom. Popular from 1850 to 1867, dress with an off-the-shoulder neckline and hoop skirt with three lace ruffles. Popularized by Jenny Lind, the Swedish Nightingale.

Jenny Lind riding hat: Crinoline (1840–1865 C.E.). Low-crowned, moderate brimmed, black beaver hat. The brim turned up slightly on the sides. It was trimmed with broad band of velvet and satin ribbon with a rosette on the left.

Jenny Lind sortie de bal: Crinoline (1840–1865 C.E.). In 1862, wrap of white Venetian cord, trimmed with flounce of Spanish lace over border of colored silk.

jerga: 1. Ecuador. A coarse, twill weave cloth woven on the treadle loom. 2. Peru. Sackcloth.

jerkin: 1. Elizabethan (1550–1625 C.E.). Outer doublet with loose sleeves. 2. Charles I and the Commonwealth (1625–1660 C.E.) to Crinoline (1840–1865 C.E.). Military justaucorps adapted for civilian dress.

jerkin

jerkinet: Charles I and the Commonwealth (1625–1660 C.E.). Woman's jerkin.

jerry hat: United Kingdom. Round felt hat.

jérsei: Portugal. Jersey.

jersey: Bustle (1865–1890 C.E.) to 20th century. Introduced in 1879, elastic wool fabric that resembled fine knitting.

jersey sweater: Bustle (1865–1890 C.E.). Pullover sweater.

jessamine butter: Jasmine scented pomade.

jessamy gloves: Elizabethan (1550–1625 C.E.) to Restoration (1660–1700 C.E.). Popular jasmine scented gloves, often given to a bride and bridegroom.

jet: Rich black mineral coal which when polished is used in making ornaments and trim.

jet buttons: Romantic (1815–1840 C.E.). Worn in 1818 by women on boots that buttoned on the side.

jhaggā: India. Long, transparent, double-breasted bodice with a full skirt and full sleeves.

jhaggī: *See* beur.

jhalar: India. Fringe.

jhamaratali: India. A fine muslin of Bihar origin.

jhanbartali: India. A very fine quality muslin.

jhangias: India. Short drawers.

jhulwa: India. Jacket.

jhuna: India. A muslin.

jhuni: India. A fine quality muslin.

ji fu: China. Qing dynasty (1644–1911 C.E.). Man's sleeved, full-length gown and a curved, surplice right front. Worn belted for lesser court functions and official business.

ji guan: China. Qing dynasty (1644–1911 C.E.). Man's red silk fringe, dyed yak or horsehair version of the chao guan worn on semi-formal occasions. Woman's version was similar but with two wide embroidered streamers in the back and a red silk knot on the crown.

jiakè: China. Jacket.

jiaki-kanoko: Japan. Kanoko with a thin line of plain color between the dots.

jian: China. Fine silk.

jianchóu: China. Pongee.

jiàng: China. Deep red; crimson.

jiàngsè: China. Dark reddish brown.

jiàngzì: China. Dark reddish purple.

jianzhang: China. Epaulet.

jiao dai: China. Qing dynasty (1644–1911 C.E.). Han woman's rigid bamboo belt covered with red silk and ornamental plaques.

jiaxié: China. Rubber overshoes.

jiaxue: China. High rubber overshoes.

jibba: *See* jibbah.

jibbah: Smock.

jibbeh: Palestine. 1. Man's broadcloth coat, sometimes lined with sheepskin. 2. Coat-like outer garment worn by both sexes. *See also* dura'ah; jubbeh.

jièzhi: China. Finger ring.

jigari: India. The color blood red.

jigger button: Romantic (1815–1840 C.E.). Small hidden button that held back the wide lapel or rever on a double-breasted waistcoat.

jigger coat: Short informal coat.

jigha: India. A plume with an attached jewel worn on the turban.

jihaz: Palestine. Bride's trousseau; literally "equipment."

jika-tabi: Japan. A type of rubber-soled tabi used to walk directly on the ground.

jiljeleh: Palestine. Fabric with purple pink stripe.

jiljileh: Palestine. Silk fabric with plain red stripes at each border.

jillayeh: Palestine. Elaborately ornamented dura'ah.

Jim Crow hat: Crinoline (1840–1865 C.E.). Man's felt hat with wide, flapping brim.

jimbaori: Japan. A warrior's sleeveless camp coat worn over the armor.

jimi: India. A long, unstitched black or red woolen waist-cloth.

jimiki: India. A large drop earring with tassels.

jin be wun: Bustle (1865–1890 C.E.). United States of America. Chinese Hawaiian term for an applique pattern resembling a rising cloud.

jin huang: China. Literally "golden-yellow," an orange color restricted to the emperor's sons in 1759 C.E.

jin xian guan: China. Han dynasty (206 B.C.E.–7 C.E.). Scholar's headdress.

jin zi: China. Tang dynasty. Fixed turban worn atop the fu tou.

jinashi: *See* jinashi-nuihaku.

jinashi-nuihaku: Japan. A kimono completely covered with gold and embroidery.

jinnah cap: (1940–1950 C.E.). Pakistan. Karakul cap.

jinneh-u-nar: Palestine. Cotton fabric with a green silk stripe on one border and a red stripe on the other border.

jipijapa: 1. Spain. Panama hat. 2. Central and South American plant used to make Panama hats.

jiqa: Iran. Aigrette.

jiquilite: Guatemala. Indigo plant.

jirga poncho: Ecuador. A poncho of jerga.

jirkinet: Scotland. Woman's blouse or jacket.

jirnavastra: India. A generic term for old fabric. *See also* pataccara.

jirones: Renaissance (1450–1550 C.E.). Spain. Gussets or gores.

jíros: Greece. Women's hair arranged like a wreath on the head.

jiu: China. Bun; knot; chignon.

jjalbunyangbokbaji: Korea. Breeches.

joaillerie: France. Gem-set jewelry.

joaillier: France. 1. Jewelry. 2. Precious stone specialist.

joalharia: *See* pedraria.

Joan: Late Georgian (1750–1790 C.E.). Woman's small, fitted cap.

Joan-of-Arc bodice: Bustle (1865–1890 C.E.). United Kingdom. Introduced in 1875, woman's tight day bodice shaped like a corset that reached to the hips and was covered in jet or steel bead. Tight sleeves were frilled at the wrists.

Jocelyn mantle: Crinoline (1840–1865 C.E.). Introduced in 1852, woman's knee-length, double skirted mantle with three fringed capes and armseyes.

jockei: Directoire and First Empire (1790–1815 C.E.). Glorified epaulet or tippet.

jockey: Romantic (1815–1840 C.E.) to Bustle (1865–1890 C.E.). Worn from 1825 to 1870, flounce at the top of a sleeve that formed an epaulette.

jockey bonnet: Directoire and First Empire (1790–1815 C.E.). Introduced in 1806, woman's bonnet with full crown and visor that turned back from the face.

jockey boot: Restoration (1660–1700 C.E.) to Bustle (1865–1890 C.E.). Man's boot that ended just below the knee with turned top of lighter leather. They were pulled on by a leather loop on each side. *See also* top boot.

jockey boot

jockey cap: Restoration (1660–1700 C.E.) to 20th century. United Kingdom. Man's peaked cap of black velvet. In the 19th century, a light-colored silk cap was used for racing.

jockey sleeve: Restoration (1660–1700 C.E.) to 20th century. United Kingdom. Man's fitted sleeve with a small cuff.

jockey waistcoat

jockey waistcoat: Directoire and First Empire (1790–1815 C.E.) to 20th century. United Kingdom. Introduced in 1806, man's straight waistcoat that buttoned high with a low stand collar cut with a deep gap below the chin. Revived in 1884.

jocolo: Transvaal. Ndebele bride's beaded rectangular apron. It is 17-1/4 by 23-1/2 inches.

jodhpurs: (20th century). Riding breeches that are fitted in the seat, very full in the hips, tapering to the ankles where they fit snugly. Sometimes end in a strap under the foot.

joeb: Denmark. Skirt.

jofu: Japan. Fine handwoven linen fabric.

John Bull: Crinoline (1840–1865 C.E.). Man's 5-3/4-inch-high top hat.

joho: Swahili. Long robe-like dressing gown.

joinville: Crinoline (1840–1865 C.E.). United Kingdom. Worn from 1844 to 1855, man's wide bow necktie with square fringed ends.

jojky: Slovakia. Old woman's shapeless, flat-heeled boots.

jokey: *See* jockey.

jonc: France. Rigid bangle bracelet.

jonquille: Directoire and First Empire (1790–1815 C.E.). Introduced in 1811, fashionable shade of yellow.

jootī: India. Close-fitting embroidered leather slippers.

jordáni: Greece. Neck ornament; chest ornament.

jornea: Renaissance (1450–1550 C.E.). Spain. Sandwich-board style short outer garment.

jors: India. Bridegroom's pink or cream colored silk dhoti and chaddar with narrow gold borders.

jortiní fortescá: Greece. Feast day costume.

joseph: 1. Early Georgian (1700–1750 C.E.). Woman's green riding coat. 2. Directoire and First Empire (1790–1815 C.E.). Worn from 1800 to 1810, woman's outdoor garment similar to a long Jewish tunic with loose sleeves.

Josephine: Crinoline (1840–1865 C.E.). In 1856, bias cut, shawl-shaped mantilla. It was three-quarters of a yard from neck to peak. It was made of alternating rows of moiré antique and tulle. It was trimmed with velvet ribbon and heavy fringe.

josephine bodice: Bustle (1865–1890 C.E.). Introduced in 1879, woman's evening bodice with a very low and round décolletage and wide silk or satin belt draped in folds around the waist.

Josephine knot: Ornamental knot made of two loops with loose ends.

joshan: India. Armlet of gold or silver beads.

josie: Bustle (1865–1890 C.E.). Introduced in 1872, light yellowish olive color.

journade: Late Gothic (1350–1450 C.E.). Short, circular garment worn for riding. Initially it had large, full sleeves and later it had long, slit sleeves.

jouy: Cotton or linen fabric printed with reproductions of 18th-century French prints.

joya: Spain. Jewel.

joyau: *See* bijou.

ju: China. Zhou dynasty. Thin-soled, walking shoes made from material like hemp. Worn by officials at home.

juàn: China. Thin, tough silk.

juban: Japan. Silk or cotton undershirt.

jubba: *See* jubbah.

jubbah: Egypt and United Arab Emirates. Long outer garment with long loose sleeves worn over the kuftan.

jube: 1. *See* jupe. 2. Bulgaria. Sheepskin coat for winter trimmed with embroidery and colored applique. Usually long sleeved.

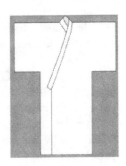

juban

jubeteros: Renaissance (1450–1550 C.E.). Spain. Doublet makers.

jubka: Russia. Skirt.

jubon: Renaissance (1450–1550 C.E.) to Restoration (1660–1700 C.E.). Spain. Worn by men under the doublet and by women under the galerilla, a long sleeved camisole that buttoned all down the front.

Juchten: Germany. Russian leather.

Judas color: Red.

Judenhut: Early Gothic (1200–1350 C.E.). Traditional pointed Jewish hat.

Judenkragen: Elizabethan (1550–1625 C.E.) to Crinoline (1840–1865 C.E.). Ruff worn by Jews.

jue: China. Zhou dynasty. Lightweight, convenient shoes made from sandal straw.

Jugendstil satin: Germany. Art Nouveau silk.

Jugoslavian embroidery: Geometrically designed embroidery done on coarse linen in bright colors.

júhóng: China. Tangerine color; reddish orange.

júhuáng: China. Orange color.

juive: Directoire and First Empire (1790–1815 C.E.). Calf-length douillette. *See also* tunic à la mameluck.

juk: Holland. Yoke.

jukh: Palestine. Broadcloth.

juk'ullu: Bolivia. Worn by young people to show their unmarried status, a knitted or crocheted cap with a front brim and long black flap.

Juliet: Woman's house slipper with high front and back and U-shaped gores on the sides.

Juliet

Juliet cap: Small, round, open mesh cap decorated with pearls or simulated jewels.

jullaha: India. A weaver.

jump suit: One-piece work or play suit.

jumper: 1. Man's hip-length shirt of sturdy fabric. 2. Woman's pull-on top.

jumps: 1. Restoration (1660–1700 C.E.). Woman's loose bodice. 2. Restoration (1660–1700 C.E.). Man's loose, thigh-length coat or jacket that buttoned down the front. It had full sleeves.

jungle cloth: Sturdy, tightly woven cotton fabric.

jungle fatigues: (1960–1970 C.E.). United States of America. Introduced in 1963, the Army tropical combat uniform.

jungle khassa: India. Muslin of great beauty.

junihitoe: Japan. Twelve unlined robes worn by court ladies.

juosta: Lithuania. Girdle.

juostos: Lithuania. Belts.

jupe: 1. Byzantine and Romanesque (400–1200 C.E.). Shirt or undergarment worn by both genders. Occasionally fur lined. *See also* gipon. 2. France. Skirt.

jupel: *See* gipon.

jupen: France. Breton for coat.

jupe-pantalon: France. Pantskirt.

jupon: Late Gothic (1350–1450 C.E.). France. Worn over the armor, this garment had the individual's symbol or coat of arms emblazoned on it. Sometimes referred to a petticoat.

juppe: *See* gambeson.

juppo: Austria. Dress with shoulder straps.

júrda: Greece. Short, dark blue (almost black) cloak worn with the shaggy wool on the inside.

jusi: Philippine Islands. Delicate dress fabric of pure silk.

justa: Latvia. Belt 12 to 15 cm wide, 2-1/2 to 4 m long.

justaucorps: Restoration (1660–1700 C.E.). Long coat, fitted in the body and full in the skirt, that buttoned down the front and had cuffed sleeves. Replaced the cassock around 1675.

justcoat: Early Georgian (1700–1750 C.E.). United Kingdom. Justaucorps.

juste au cou: France. Necklace fixed to a ribbon.

jute: Fiber used alone for sacking and mats. Blended with wool or silk for fabric.

juvel: Denmark and Sweden. Jewel.

juweel: Holland. Jewel.

Juwel: Germany. Jewel.

juwelen: Holland. Jewelry. *See also* kostbaarheden.

K

kaabe: Denmark. Cloak.

kaacha: India. The pleats of the dhoti tucked in the back.

kaachadi: *See* kaacha.

ka'ai: United States of America. Hawaii. Girdle of any kind.

k'aak'isaekui: Korea. Khaki colored.

ka'ako'o: United States of America. Hawaii. To belt.

kaap: Holland. Cape.

kaasdoek: Holland. Cheesecloth.

kabā: *See* cogā.

kabaa: *See* chuga.

kabal: Korea. Wig.

kabanica: 1. *See* plast. 2. Yugoslavia. Long hooded coat of brown or black woolen fabric. 3. Bosnia. Mackintosh.

kabari bandha: India. A woman's simple hairstyle in which the hair is twisted into a chignon or bun.

kabát: Czechoslovakia. Coat.

kabátek: Slovakia. Woman's bodice with a double pointed, angular neckline.

kabaya: Java. Lightweight, white cotton, outer jacket, often lace trimmed or embroidered that is worn with a sarong.

kabrí: Greece. American material.

kabuto: Japan. Armor helmet with decorative horns, center ornament and iron plates along the back lower edge.

kabuto-sita: Japan. An ebosi worn under the helmet by military leaders of the highest class.

kācali: India. Woman's open-backed, back-fastening bodice.

kācavo: *See* kācali.

káçes: Greece. Pleats.

kach: India. A Sikh man's knee-length breeches.

kachabia: Tunisia. Man's long woolen coat, often in black or dark brown.

kachali: *See* choli.

kachavo: *See* choli.

kachcha: India. A style of wearing the antariya in which the fabric is drawn up between the legs to form a trouser-like garment.

kachi: Japan. Victory; a black color favored by samurai.

kaci: India. A cotton stuff.

kaciyau pitha: India. Stiff from Kanchipuram.

kadā: India. Girdle.

kadali-garbha: India. A very soft silk.

kadémi: Greece. Large, dark belt with woven plant motifs.

kadifa: *See* samt.

kadife: Turkey. Velvet.

kadigi: India. Kohl.

kadillam: India. A waistcloth.

kadroun: Tunisia. Loose fitting coat worn open to the waist.

ka'ei papale: United States of America. Hawaii. Hatband.

ka'ei po'o: United States of America. Hawaii. Selvage of cloth.

k'aenbosu: *See* hwap'o.

kaeshi: Japan. A variety of komon with the dots of a lighter shade than the background.

kaffa: *See* caffa.

kaffiyeh: Arabia. Large, square, cotton handkerchief worn over the head and falling to the shoulders. It often has colored silk striped or figures and tassels. Worn with an agal.

kafiyyeh: Palestine. Man's headscarf; large square of fabric with warp fringes. Usually made of cotton, but can be wool, silk, or a silk and cotton blend. It is white, black, or patterned. It is worn folded diagonally into a triangle and held in place with an aqal.

kaftan: 1. *See* caftan. 2. Russia. All-purpose outer garment. It is a long, loose, heavy robe that overlaps, closing on the left side.

kaftani: Nigeria. Short-sleeved gown with slits at the sides and neck. It has four pockets.

kaftany: Poland. Long jacket.

kafuri: India. Straw color.

kaga-boshi: Japan. A type of hood made in a bag shape with openings for the eyes.

kageyapatte: India. Sackcloth.

kahan: Japan. A woman's leggings.

kahi: India. A deep blackish green color.

kahi 'omou: United States of America. Hawaii. A side or back comb used to hold the hair in place.

kahiko: United States of America. Hawaii. To wear finery.

kahiko kaua: United States of America. Hawaii. War finery.

kahu huruhuru: Australia. Maori general term for feather cloaks.

kahu kaakaapoo: Australia. Maori feather cloak trimmed with feathers of the kaakaapoo (*Strigops habroptilus*).

kahu kekeno: Australia. Maori cloak of sealskins.

kahu kiwi: Australia. Maori cloak covered with feathers of the kiwi.

kahu kura: Australia. Maori cloak covered with feathers of the native parrot.

kahu kuri: Australia. Maori dogskin cloaks.

kahu toi: Australia. Maori cloak made from cabbage tree leaves and fiber.

kahu waero: Australia. Maori cloak trimmed with tufts of white dog hair.

kaiapa: United States of America. Hawaii. Diaper.

kaidori: Japan. A long overkimono.

kaijia: China. Suit of armor.

kailiniai: Lithuania. Fur garment.

kailis: Lithuania. Fur.

kaimana: United States of America. Hawaii. Diamond.

kain: 1. Indonesia. Sarong made from tube of fabric 2-2/5 yards around, 1-2/3 yards long. 2. Java. Ankle-length skirt cloth.

kain bentenan: Celebes. Cotton woven textiles from Minahassa.

kain chelum: Borneo. Black fabric.

kain engkudu: Borneo. Red fabric.

kain kudu: India. A mantle with a faint horse design in warp ikat.

kain lemar: Thailand. Mat maii shoulder cloth.

kain lepas: Malaysia. Woman's skirt cloth worn wrapped around the hips. *See also* kain panjang.

kain mata: Borneo. Undyed fabric.

kain panjang: Indonesia. General word for fabric, but used specifically to refer to unseamed garment worn wrapped around the body. *See also* kain lepas.

kain prada: Bali. Fabric with gold applied to its surface.

kain sampin: Malaysia. Man's short sarong worn over a loose shirt and pants on festive occasions.

kain simbut: Indonesia. A sacred red textile.

kains: United Kingdom. Plain weave, cotton fabric made for export.

kaironan: Bustle (1865–1890 C.E.). In 1889, brown tinged with gold.

kaiser-rock: Bohemia. Common name for a man's coat.

kaishìmí: China. Cashmere.

kaisika: India. Man's head of curled hair.

kaitaka: New Zealand. Mat of fine flaxen material and made with an ornamental border. Worn as a mantle.

kaitsa: Bulgaria. Woman's halo-shaped hat trimmed with beads and coins. Worn from the wedding day until the birth of the first child.

kaj kulah: India. Literally "one who wears his hat awry," a fop or a dandy.

kājaliyā: India. Diagonally striped tie-dyed scarf in black.

kajuk hyokdae: Korea. Leather belt.

kaka hu kura: New Zealand. Maori feather cloak.

kakau uhi: United States of America. Hawaii. Solid tattoo pattern.

kakeda: Japan. Fine, raw silk fabric.

kake-eri: Japan. The piece of fabric covering the neckband of the kimono.

kaki: Holland. Khaki.

kakimea: United States of America. Hawaii. Cashmere.

kakinia: United States of America. Hawaii. Sateen.

kaki-sarasa: Japan. Hand-decorated sarasa.

kakla ruota: Lithuania. Necklace.

kaklaryšis: Lithuania. Necklace.

kakofnitch: Russia. Woman's headdress in tiara or diadem shape.

kakorízika: Greece. Second quality wool.

kaksha: India. Red seeds used for making ornaments.

kakshyabandha: India. A thick jeweled roll worn at an angle on the hips.

kaku obi: Japan. A man's narrow sash about five inches wide.

kaku-maki: *See* furoshiki.

kalabaku: India. A cummerbund of many strings.

kalabattu: India. A twisted thread made of silk and silver.

kalabattun: India. Gold, silver, or base metal thread wound around a silk thread, used for brocading and embroidery.

kalabi: Nigeria. Poor woman's rectangular headscarf.

kalabousenn: France. Breton for cap.

kalakamsuka: India. A black muslin or silk fabric.

kalakoa: United States of America. Hawaii. Calico.

kalam: India. A pen-like device used to draw out the pattern for embroidery.

kalambi: Borneo. Jackets, with or without sleeves, worn by both genders.

kalambi ara: Borneo. Coat of striped fabric.

kalamkari: East India. Cotton fabric with hand applied print.

kalandari: India. Silk cloth.

kalansuwa: Biblical (Unknown–30 C.E.). Hebrew word for the Persian hat. Hebrews were restricted to certain colors and trims in this style.

kala-pat sari: India. Black silk sari.

kalasakha: India. Jewelry worn on the back of the hand.

kalasiris: Egyptian (4000–30 B.C.E.). New Kingdom. Long fitted robe worn in several styles by both genders. It could be sleeveless, short and narrow, or long and wide. It could be woven or knitted in one piece or made in pieces and sewn together.

kalathaki: Greece. An antique ring.

kalauna: Samoa. Crown.

kalaunu: United States of America. Hawaii. Crown.

kalaunu bihopa: United States of America. Hawaii. Bishop's miter.

kalavadi: India. A cadar or duppatta of black silk.

kalavuka: India. A kamarband of many strings that are plaited together.

kaldoh: Abyssinia. A woman's apron made of skin.

kalekonuka: United States of America. Hawaii. Sardonyx.

kalets: Bulgaria. Gaiters.

kalewai: United States of America. Hawaii. Light brown tapa.

kalgan: Italy. Tibet lamb fur.

kalghi: Turkey. Culgee.

kalhoty: *See* spodky.

kalíca: Greece. Gold-embroidered, summer bridal shoes.

kalidar pyjama: India. A woman's legwear.

kaliki: United States of America. Hawaii. Corset; girdle.

kaliki waiu: United States of America. Hawaii. Brassiere; corset cover.

kalikia: Greece. A woman's shoe with a horseshoe shaped heel.

kalikone: United States of America. Hawaii. Cretonne.

kalima hamo: United States of America. Hawaii. Face cream.

kalimáfkia: Greece. High, flat-topped hats.

kall: 1. Late Gothic (1350–1450 C.E.) to Renaissance (1450–1550 C.E.). Unfinished back of headdress. 2. Netting foundation for wig. 3. Early Georgian (1700–1750 C.E.) to Bustle (1865–1890 C.E.). Woman's soft cap or bonnet. *See also* caul; fret.

kallača: Ethiopia. Konso man's phallic forehead ornament.

kálluwa: Ecuador and Guatemala. Backstrap loom.

kalmuck: Cotton or wool fabric with coarse, hairy nap.

kalmuks: Persia. Cotton or wool fabric with coarse, hairy nap. Coarsely dyed.

kalmus: Biblical (Unknown–30 C.E.). Hebrew cloak, like a chlamys.

kalómala: Greece. The best wool.

kalotje: Holland. Calotte.

kalpac: Uzbekistan. Pointed beige cap with three black felt lines.

kalpak: Turkey. A fur hat.

kalpáki: Greece. Man's large black melon-shaped hat.

kalpush: India. A Kashmiri red wool or brocade cap worn with its lower edge turned up.

kalsaek: Korea. Brown.

kaltsá: Greece. Stockings.

kaltsi: Bulgaria. Long gaiters.

kaltsoskúti: Greece. Wool fabric.

kaltsouni: Bulgaria. White woolen knee boot trimmed with black braid.

kaltsovelónes: Greece. Needles used of knitting stockings.

kalyptra: Greek (3000–100 B.C.E.). Woman's thin veil worn over the head and face.

kama'a: United States of America. Hawaii. Generic term for shoe.

kama'a hakahaka: United States of America. Hawaii. Literally "shoes with spaces," sandals.

kama'a hawele: United States of America. Hawaii. Sandals.

kama'a 'ie: United States of America. Hawaii. Braided sandals.

kama'a ili: United States of America. Hawaii. Leather shoes.

kama'a laholio: United States of America. Hawaii. Rubber shoes.

kama'a la'i: United States of America. Hawaii. Sandal made of ti leaf. It is worn for crossing lava.

kama'a lo'ihi: United States of America. Hawaii. Literally "tall shoes," boot.

kama'a pale wawae: United States of America. Hawaii. Slipper.

kama'a puki: United States of America. Hawaii. Boot.

kama'ehu: United states of America. Hawaii. Brownish; reddish brown.

kamakh: *See* heremzi.

kamakha: India. A brocade from China and Persia.

kamaki: United States of America. Hawaii. Generic term for garment.

kamalaharitacchaya: India. A yellowish green color.

kamalaveli: India. A stuff decorated with lotus flowers.

kamalena: United States of America. Hawaii. Yellow.

kamandha: India. Girdle.

kamarband: 1. India. A woman's sash. *See also* paryastika. 2. Iran. Woman's sash.

kamba iri: Timbuktu. A woman's bead bracelet.

kambal: India. Coarse wool shawl or blanket.

kambala: India. Coarse woolen cloth.

kambalaghana: India. A closely woven shawl.

kambánes: Greece. Large silver earrings.

kamben: Bali. A piece of batik worn wrapped around the hips and knotted at the waist. It reaches below the knee.

kamben cerik: Indonesia. A long, narrow strip of fabric worn over the shoulder or wrapped around the head. It was once used as a breast covering.

Kambrik: *See* Battist.

kāmdānī: India. Silver and gold wire embroidery on white fabric.

kamea: Poland. Cameo.

kameez: India. Tunic flared at the hip with a side slit.

kamelaukion: High brimless hat worn by Oriental priests.

Kamelhaar: Germany. Camel.

kame-nozoki: Japan. Light blue.

kamerjas: Holland. Dressing gown.

Kamfhandschuhe: Renaissance (1450–1550 C.E.). Germany. Gauntlet.

kamiks: Denmark. Sealskin boots worn with the hair on the inside.

kamis: 1. Embroidered, long undergarment worn sashed. 2. Ethiopia. Woman's chemise.

kamiselka: *See* kamizelka.

kamishimo: Japan. A wide shouldered formal samurai costume.

kamiz: India. A woman's tunic, usually worn with shalwar.

kamizelka: Poland. Waistcoat.

kamizóla: Greece. Vest with long, on-piece sleeves.

kamkha: India. A generic term for brocades. *See also* kamkhab.

kamkhab: India. Gold brocade. *See also* kamkha; kimkhab; kincob.

kamkho: India. Silk bodice.

kamkhwab: *See* kamkhab.

kammuri

kammuri: Japan. A skullcap worn by high noblemen, frequently featuring a curved taillike structure and tying under the chin with a narrow thong.

kamozi: Japan. False hair switches of human hair.

kampskatcha: Late Georgian (1750–1790 C.E.). Woman's fur-lined slipper with turned-up toe.

kampskatcha slipper: Late Georgian (1750–1790 C.E.). United Kingdom. Woman's slipper with pointed toe that turned up at tip. It had a high vamp and a low French heel.

kampū: Japan. An Okinawan hairstyle.

kampu anaku: Ecuador. An old-style pleated skirt.

kamr: Palestine. Tablet-woven belt, usually in red or brown wool, edged with yellow stripes.

kamrtušky: Slovakia. Cambrics.

kamrukhi: *See* chaugoshia.

kamsaek: Korea. Dark navy blue.

kamzar: India. Short coat.

kamzol: Russia. 17th century. Man's waistcoat cut shorter than the coat. Had long narrow sleeves and no pleats or collar.

kanakagi: United States of America. Hawaii. Literally "Hawaiian wear," a loose-fitting, simple dress.

kanakakamalaihkarna: India. Lotus-shaped ear ornament.

kanakakirita: India. Crown of gold.

kanakaneyura: India. Anklet.

kancala: India. An elaborate earring with pendants.

kanca-pat sari: India. Uncolored silk sari.

kanchali: India. Backless blouse with sleeves.

kanchanakumkumakambalanam: India. Saffron colored robe or woolen garment with gold threads woven into it.

kanchanakundala: India. Earring of pure gold.

kanchi: India. Gold belt.

kanchli: India. Corset.

kanchuka: India. Man's coat-like garment.

kanchulika: India. Woman's fabric bodice.

kancis: India. A hip girdle with bells.

kancuka: India. A bodice.

kancuyao: India. A coat of mail.

kandal: Trinidad. Tight-fitting satin or velvet breeches that end just above the knee.

kandaure: Indonesia. Woman's beaded collar or beaded pendant.

kanden-medare: Japan. An apron-skirt combination.

kandys: 1. Mede. Man's garment, wider at the foot than at the hip. It was so long that it was gathered in the front and at the sides and girdled. It had long sleeves that were wide at the wrist and tight at the armseye. 2. Assyria. Skirt of sheepskin.

kanekopa: United States of America. Hawaii. Kind of foreign cloth.

kangan: India. A bracelet.

kangaroo leather: Australia. Kangaroo-skin leather produced in Australia and tanned in the United States. One of best leathers for shoe uppers.

kangaroo stance: (1900–1910 C.E.). Woman's posture of forward thrown full bosom and hips thrust back. The posture was created by the corset. *See also* S curve.

kange: Kiunguja. Woman's tobe.

kanggan: Borneo. Chinese black calico.

kangha: India. A comb worn in a Sikh man's hair.

kaniki: 1. United Kingdom. Plain weave, cotton fabric dyed indigo or black. 2. Kenya. Indigo colored cloth.

Kanin: Germany. Rabbit fur.

kanjai: India. Smoke gray.

kanjian: China. Sleeveless jacket, usually padded or lined.

kanjiki: Japan. Snow shoes.

kankan: India. Gold bangle bracelet studded with precious stones.

kano cloth: United Kingdom. Coarse, heavy cotton fabric made for export.

kanoko: Japan. Fine-knotted tie-dyeing.

kanoko-zome: *See* kanoko.

kanonenstiefel: Germany. Jackboots.

kanseya: India. A woven silk.

kant: 1. Belgium and Holland. Lace.

kantha: India. 1. Torn fabric. 2. A short, broad, and flat necklace. 3. Cradle-cloth.

kanthamala: India. Dog-collar style necklace.

kanthī: India. Close-fitting gold necklace with pearls and gems.

kantje: Timbuktu. A small silver ornament worn in the middle of a woman's forehead.

kanto: Japan. Chinese striped fabrics.

kantopa: India. A flapped cap.

kanzashis: Japan. Ornamental hairpins.

kanzasi: Edo (1600–1867 C.E.). Japan. An ornamental hair comb.

kanzu: Swahili. Native shirt.

kaomi lole: United States of America. Hawaii. Sewing machine presser foot.

kap: *See* huif.

kapa: 1. Montenegro. Small pillbox hat with a crimson crown top to symbolize the blood shed by the ancestors for freedom and a black band to memorialize those who died in the 14th-century battle of Kosovo. Women decorate the top of theirs with small designs. 2. United States. Hawaiian fabric made of bark. 3. *See* siapo. 4. *See* feldr. 5. Bosnia, Croatia, and Serbia. Cap.

kápa: Greece. Small vest.

kapa ea: United States of America. Hawaii. Sapphire.

kapa 'ino'ino: United States of America. Hawaii. Sackcloth.

kapa kila: United States of America. Hawaii. Steel armor.

kapa komo: United States of America. Hawaii. Generic term for clothing.

kapa lau'i: United States of America. Hawaii. Plaited ti leaf textile.

kapaladharina: India. Necklace made of skull bones.

kaparda: India. Braid of hair.

kapasi: India. Light green.

kapdu: India. Hand embroidered blouse.

kapeila: United States of America. Hawaii. Sapphire.

kapeilo: *See* kapa ea.

kapelusz: Poland. Hat.

kapesník: Czechoslovakia. Handkerchief.

kapishay: Guatemala. Cloak.

kapitsáli: Greece. Kerchief or band of cloth which passes below the chin to connect to the fez.

kaplamás: *See* kaváði.

kapoto: Crete. Hooded coats.

Kapp: United States of America. Amish woman's head cap. The cap features a wide variety of fancy work and pleats. From age 12 until the woman is married, she wears a black Kapp for dress and a white one at home. After marriage, the Kapp is white at all times.

kappa: 1. Japan. Raincoat. 2. Sweden. Cloak.

kappa dachi: Japan. Literally "simple cut," a simple A-line dress.

kapparings: South Africa. Wooden sandals held on by a knob between the toes.

kappe: *See* kaabe.

kappel: *See* keppelche.

kapperoellike: Denmark. Woman's bonnet-shaped outdoor headdress of black velvet or colored calico. It is stiffened with cardboard.

kappie: Crinoline (1840–1865 C.E.). South Africa. Generic term for a lady's bonnet.

kappu: *See* kuzufu.

kapsa: 1. Czechoslovakia. Pocket. 2. Korea. Best quality of sa silk fabric.

kapsel: Holland. Coiffure. *See also* hoofdtooi.

kaptur: Poland. Hood.

kapuraveli: India. Plain silk fabric.

kapurnur: *See* qatifah-i-purbi.

kaput: Croatia and Serbia. Coat.

kaputula bombo: Swahili. 1. Shorts cut round in the hips, tapering to the legs. 2. Short shorts cut wide in the thighs.

kaputula forpoketa: Swahili. Shorts with two side pockets and two hip pockets.

kaputula ya Kenya: Swahili. Corduroy shorts.

Kapuze: *See* Mönchskappe.

kara: India. A steel bracelet worn on the right wrist by a Sikh man.

kara-aya: Japan. Plain-colored Chinese silk with a small woven design.

karabousenn: *See* kalabousenn.

karagumi: Japan. Highly complicated weaving technique used in producing decorative sashes.

karakchi: Korea. Ring.

karakul: *See* caracul.

karamil: Palestine. Hair ornaments.

karamini: Bustle (1865–1890 C.E.). Introduced in 1878, light wool fabric with lightly fleecy face.

kara-mushi: Japan. Ramie.

kara-nishiki: Japan. Chinese nishiki.

karanko geta: Japan. A dressy geta.

kara-nui: Japan. Embroidery with Chinese silk thread.

karaori: Japan. Silk brocaded with floss or gilded paper strips.

kara-ori: Japan. Literally "Chinese weaving," silk fabric imported from China.

karauna: *See* kalaunu.

karayari: India. Generic term for a thick cloth.

karazsia: Hungary. Tabby weave woolen made from the wool of merino sheep.

karbatkos: Lithuania. Lace.

karbelathehon: Biblical (Unknown–30 C.E.). Hebrew man's hat.

kardhani: India. Girdle.

Kardiert: Germany. Any shaggy uncombed wool fabric.

kareeta: Late Gothic (1350–1450 C.E.). Sweden. Cloth sack.

karfitsa: Greece. A large brooch decorated with stones.

karieliai: *See* kaklaryšis.

karigar: India. Literally "artist," a brocade weaver of Varansi.

kariginu: Japan. Originally a hunting costume, it is now the outfit worn by Shinto priests to minor services.

karinca: Romania. Striped, home-woven apron.

karitone: *See* kalikone.

kariyasu: Japan. Yellow dye.

karman: Russia. Pocket.

karmesin: Germany. Crimson.

karmijn: Holland. Carmine.

karminrot: Germany. Carmine.

karmozijnrood: Holland. Crimson.

karnabharana: India. Ear-drops.

karnabhusana: India. Earring.

karnapura: India. Earring.

karnavalaya: India. Round earring.

karnaysh: Palestine. White cotton fabric with crinkled stripes.

karnika: India. Flowerlike ear pendant.

karnotkilaka: India. Drum-shaped ear ornament.

karnphul: India. A flower-shaped earring.

karong: Borneo. Coverlet.

kaross: 1. South Africa. Square, rug-like garment made of skins. 2. Africa. Skin cloak worn by a bushman.

karpasa: India. A cotton fabric. *See also* badara.

karpata: India. A dirty or tattered cloth.

karppura-tilaka: India. A camphor white silk.

kartriz: Russia. Man's visored cap.

karure: New Zealand. Maori term for a heavy thread formed by twisting fibers by rolling them between the hands.

kasa: Japan. Man's basket-shaped straw hat.

kasaba: India. Woman's skullcap.

kasacken: Elizabethan (1550–1625 C.E.). Holland. Sleeveless over-jerkin.

kasaya: India. The color red ochre.

Kaschmir: Germany. Cashmere.

kaseyyaka: India. A high quality cotton or silk fabric.

kasha: France. Fine, softly napped, twill weave fabric made of cashmere goat wool.

kasha cloth: Plain weave, cotton flannel fabric.

kashabia: *See* kachabia.

kashmir: Palestine. Woman's ceremonial girdle. *See also* ishdad.

kasiam: India. A generic term for thin cloth.

kasida: India. Embroidery.

kasimea: *See* kakimea.

kasináci: Greece. Freehand stitch.

kasjmier: Holland. Cashmere.

kask: Crinoline (1840–1865 C.E.). Sweden. Spiked helmet.

kaska: Russia. Helmet.

kasket: Denmark. Cap.

kasni: India. Heliotrope color.

kassa: Senegal. Wool cloth.

kastanienbraun: Germany. Maroon.

kastanjebruin: Holland. Maroon.

kasturia: India. A musk-colored silk sari.

kasturiya: India. A musk-colored stuff.

kasumbi: India. Bright red.

kasumbo: *See* pomaco.

kasuri: Japan. 1. Cotton, silk, or linen fabric with a splash pattern, or the splash pattern itself. 2. Rare form of woman's kimono made of tsumugi silk.

kasuri no shatsu: Japan. Shirts of a sturdy fabric.

kasuti: India. Embroidery work of north Karnataka. The figurative designs are worked in cross-stitch and several different running stitches.

kasztanowaty: Poland. Chestnut colored.

kat: Korea. Top hat made of horsehair.

katab: India. Gujarati term for appliqué.

katabira: Japan. 1. Fine ramie fabric. 2. Unlined summer garment of ramie or bast.

kata-eri: Japan. Padded collar.

katagami: Japan. Paper dyeing stencils used on textiles.

kata-hazusi: Japan. The hairstyle of maids who serve a daimyo (feudal lord).

kataka: India. Bracelets.

katami-gawari: Japan. Literally "half-body garment," a garment with two sides of different colors or patterns.

katana jhuna: India. 1. A fine linen muslin. 2. A thin, coral colored linen striped or decorated with lotuses.

kata-ori: Japan. Tightly woven, fine textured fabric.

katapu: Borneo. Cap; war-cap.

katasárci: Greece. Undershirt.

katasuso: Japan. Literally "shoulders and hem," a garment in which the color and design are divided horizontally.

katatsuke: Japan. Use of fine rice paste resist in stencil resist dyeing.

kataza-kanoko: Japan. Kanoko in which the dots are more widely spaced than in honzo-kanoko.

kata-zome: Japan. Stencil dyeing. *See also* katazome.

katazome: Japan. Stencil dyeing. *See also* kata-zome.

kátça: Greece. Wool strands from a male goat used for decorating costumes.

Kate Greenaway costume: Bustle (1865–1890 C.E.) to 1890s. United Kingdom. Worn in 1880s and 1890s by small girls, Empire style dress with high waist, puffed short sleeves, and skirt trimmed with a narrow flounce. The whole was made from a light fabric patterned with flowers. Popularized by the illustrations of Kate Greenaway.

Katharine of Aragon lace: United Kingdom. A bobbin lace made with a scrolling tape pattern.

kathipa: India. A style of embroidery that utilizes geometric designs with one section in a horizontal pattern and the next in a vertical pattern.

katifés: Greece. Velvet.

katikinari: India. Cutwork used in borders.

katisutra: India. A string that suspends the hip-belt.

katitra: India. A waistcloth.

kat-no: Korea. Pleated cone of deep yellow colored, oiled paper that is worn as a rain hat.

kato manikia: Greece. Literally "lower sleeves," these ornamental lower sleeves are worn with the tzakos.

katoen: Holland. Cotton.

katoenfluweel: Holland. Velveteen.

katori: *See* kata-ori.

katra: Peru. Blanket of black sheep's wool decorated with a thick, wide, horizontal stripe woven in red wool. It is worn as a mantle.

katsura: Japan. Wig.

katsura-zutsumi: Japan. A white head shawl.

kattan: India. Waste selvedge in silk weaving. Used for stringing ornaments.

Kattūn: Germany. Old word for cotton.

kaula hoʻolewa: United States of America. Hawaii. Bracelets.

kaula li: United States of America. Hawaii. Lacing for shoes or corset.

kaula li kamaʻa: United States of America. Hawaii. Shoelace.

kaula uaki: United States of America. Hawaii. Watch chain.

kaun: *See* kin koot.

kaunace: Mesopotamian skirt of dressed leather.

kaunakes: Sumeria. Around 3,000 B.C.E., long-haired fur pelt worn as a skirt or a cape. Later, referred to a hairy cloth similar in appearance to the pelt.

kaupapa: New Zealand. Maori term for the body of a feather cloak made of dressed flax fiber.

kaupin: India. Upper body garment.

kauseya: India. A mulberry silk.

kauseyaka: India. Silk.

kaushambha: India. Silk garment dyes with kushumba (*Carthamus tinctorius*).

kausheya: India. A good quality tassar silk fabric.

kausumbha: India. A saffron colored cloth.

kaváði: Greece. Cotton or silk coat worn open down the center front. It has elbow-length or full-length sleeves.

kawa: 1. Iran. Short jacket. 2. Japan. Leather.

kawakī: India. Short dress.

kawiliwili humuhumu: United States of America. Hawaii. Sewing machine that is worked by hand, not by foot.

kawung: Java. Cotton.

kayabandh: India. A cummerbund or sash.

kazachock: Russia. Outer shirt.

kazaka: Madagascar. Man's suit jacket.

kazázis: Greece. Silk worker.

kazdodenný kroj: Slovakia. Everyday dress.

kazuifel: Holland. Chasuble.

kazuki: Japan. Special kimono worn as a head covering.

kažuoks: Lithuania. Fur.

ké deigo danineezi: Navajo. Boot.

kéʻachogii: Navajo. Galoshes.

kebat: Borneo. Ikat.

kebaya: Indonesia. Woman's blouse cut with curved seams on rectangles and no darts. Flares over hips and has gussets under the arms.

keččō: Ethiopia. Man's arm rings.

kecelja: *See* pregaca.

kedelys: Lithuania. Petticoat.

kediyun: India. White smock.

Keds: Trade name for rubber soled shoes.

kee ha hai: (1900–1910 C.E.). United States of America. Chinese Hawaiian term for Manchu style stilt shoes.

keear: Isle of Man. The color brown.

kefa: Iran. Loincloth.

keffieh: *See* kaffiyeh.

keffiyeh: *See* kaffiyeh.

keilhose: (1930–1940 C.E.). Skirt trousers with gusset.

kekryphalos: Greece. Handkerchief worn by women on head.

kela lole: United States of America. Hawaii. Tailor; dressmaker.

kelalin lambai: Borneo. Lacing stitch.

kelantan kain songket: Malaysia. Deep blue, green, maroon, or purple silk fabric shot with silver and gold thread.

kelinės: Lithuania. Trousers.

kelle: *See* kall.

kelt: Scotland. Heavy woolen suiting.

kemba: *See* foloara.

kemben: Java. Breast cloth worn by women instead of a blouse.

kemener: France. Breton for tailor.

keményszárú csizma: Hungary. Calf-high boots with hard uppers.

kemes: Early form of the chemise.

kemha: Turkey. Figured silk brocade.

kemp: Short, harsh wool.

kendal: Early Gothic (1200–1350 C.E.). United Kingdom. Coarse green fabric made in Westmorland.

kendal-green: *See* kendal.

kengkang: Borneo. Stripe.

kennel headdress: *See* gable headdress.

kente cloth: Ghana. Woven cloth. Literally "that which will not tear away under any conditions."

kenting: Late Georgian (1750–1790 C.E.). Fine linen made in Holland and imported to Ireland.

ke'oke'o maoli: United States of America. Hawaii. Good quality bleached muslin.

ke'oke'o pia: United States of America. Hawaii. Inferior bleached muslin.

ke'oke'o wai: United States of America. Hawaii. Bleached muslin.

keorai: India. Eggshell color.

kep quàn áo: Vietnam. Trouser clip.

kep tóc: Vietnam. Barrette; hairpin.

kepa: *See* siapo.

kepala: Indonesia. Literally "head," refers to a panel of contrasting color and design.

kepen': Belarus and Hungary. Overcoat.

kepen'ak: *See* kepen'.

kepenek: *See* coha.

kepi

kepi: Flat crowned military cap with a horizontal visor.

keppelche: Poland. Jewish man's skull-cap.

kepresh: Egyptian (4000–30 B.C.E.). War headdress of the Pharaoh, a tall tiara covered in projecting circles.

keptar: 1. Ukraine. Sleeveless sheepskin vest. 2. Romania. Bodice.

kepuré: Lithuania. Cap.

kera: Bhutan. Waistband or sash.

kera-mino: Japan. A woman's coat woven from the bark of the linden tree.

kere: Sumbawa. A brightly colored cotton plaid worn as a sarong.

keriya: India. A child's tight fitting, long sleeved jacket with a skirt-like border that flares out from the breastbone.

kermezot: Palestine. Silk and cotton blend fabric.

kerry cloak: Ireland. Long hooded cloak.

kersetka: Ukraine. Woman's sleeveless vest which fastens on the left. It was trimmed in black velvet and tape or zigzags. It may be as long as hip length.

kersey: Strong, twill or plain weave fabric with a wool or cotton warp. Usually ribbed.

kerseymere: Directoire and First Empire (1790–1815 C.E.). Strong, twill weave, wool fabric used for men's vests, coats, and breeches. *See also* casimir.

kerseynette: Cotton and worsted suiting.

kersrood: Holland. Cerise.

kes: India. A Sikh man's unshorn hair.

kesa: 1. Japan. Mantle. 2. Japan. Priest's robe.

k'eša: Lithuania. Pocket.

kesapasa: India. A woman's hairstyle in which the hair is looped close to the head in a long knot.

kesariya: India. Saffron colored.

kesdi: Turkey. An interlaced hand stitch.

kesg'han: India. Hair ribbon.

keshghan: India. Hair ribbon.

keshinui: Japan. Embroidered family crest.

kesho: Japan. Makeup.

ketesal: *See* kittysol.

kethoneth: Biblical (Unknown–30 C.E.). Mid-calf length tunic made of wool or linen.

ketl'óól: Navajo. Shoelace.

ketoh: Leather band worn around the wrist by Navajo men. Remnant of the bow guard.

kettle hat: Late Gothic (1350–1450 C.E.). Nickname for knight's iron helmet.

kettyl hat: Late Gothic (1350–1450 C.E.). Wide brimmed steel war hat.

kettyl hat

kettysol: *See* kittysol.

kevenhuller: *See* androsame.

keyhole neckline: Round neckline with wedge-shaped cut-out.

keyura: India. Armlets worn on the forearm. *See also* angada.

khaddar: India. Homespun cotton fabric.

khadi: India. A hand-spun, handwoven cloth.

khadi lehnga: India. A full-gathered skirt.

khaiki: Japan. All-silk fabric.

khajalia: India. A gold stuff.

khaki: 1. Sturdy cotton or wool fabric. 2. Light yellowish brown color, from East Indian word meaning earth color.

Khaki Kool: Trade name for sports silk with rough, crepe surface.

khalaga: *See* beramen.

khalat: Uzbekistan. Man's loose-fitting, knee-length, long sleeved cotton coat worn with colored handkerchief tied around the waist.

khalaty: (1960–1970 C.E.). Russia. Robes or housecoats.

khalkals: Berber woman's cylindrical anklets.

khalkhal: Persia. Women's heavy gold and silver anklets.

khallus: Bolivia. Small pocket inside ch'uspa.

khamar: *See* sualef ez zoher.

khamout: Burma. Conical straw hat.

khan ðôi ðàu: Vietnam. Turban.

khan mùi-soa: Vietnam. Handkerchief.

khan ngang: Vietnam. Mourning turban.

khan tang: *See* khan ngang.

khan tay: Vietnam. Handkerchief.

khan trùm: Vietnam. Veil.

khan tua: Vietnam. Fringed shawl.

khan vaông: Vietnam. Square scarf worn folded and tied under the chin.

khan voông: Vietnam. Scarf.

khanga: United Kingdom. Printed or color-woven cotton fabric.

khapusa: India. Boots that extend to above the knee.

kharaz azraq: Palestine. Blue bead bracelets.

kharita: *See* kareeta.

kharma: India. A floss silk.

kharwa: India. Deep red calico.

khasata: India. A fine variety of muslin.

khatim: Palestine. Signet ring.

khatwa: India. Appliqué work done in Bihar.

khawatim: Palestine. Finger rings.

khazz: India. Silk.

kheaya el kebira: Morocco. Gold embroidered slippers.

kheenkaub: *See* kamkhab.

khemkaub: *See* kamkhab.

khenmet: Egyptian (4000–30 B.C.E.). Red jasper.

khepesh: Egyptian (4000–30 B.C.E.). Curved sword.

kherqah: Palestine. Woman's Ramallah-embroidered veil.

khesbed: Egyptian (4000–30 B.C.E.). Lapis lazuli.

khiên-churong: Vietnam. Academic hood.

khila: India. Robes of honor.

khilat: India. Generic term for a set of clothes.

khimara: Egypt. Islamic woman's head covering of medium weight fabric in white or another subdued color.

khinkhwab: India. A brocade of silk with gold or silver wires woven in.

khirka: Robe or mantle worn by dervishes in Muslim countries.

khirkah: *See* khirka.

khirkidar: India. A flat style of turban made from a very long strip of muslin rolled into a rope.

khirki-dar-pagri: India. Literally "turban with window," dress turban with a band of brocade.

khirodaka: India. An ancient silk stuff.

khirqa: Palestine and United Arab Emirates. Married woman's veil worn over the smadeh. Usually made of natural or bleached handwoven linen.

kho: *See* bakku.

khombu: Indonesia. A rich red brown dye from the *Morinda citrifolia* root.

khopa: India. Woman's hairstyle with a coil of hair on the back of the head.

khsur: Palestine. Amber bracelets.

khuff: Turkey. Woman's pair of black boots for outdoor wear.

khuri: *See* qatifah-i-purbi.

khurkeh: Palestine. Woman's linen dress that is made very long and then bloused at the waist. Sleeves are fitted at the armseye and flared at the wrist. Front of the garment is elaborately embroidered as are the wrists and hem.

khusulka: India. The waistcloth of Buddhist monks.

kiber: *See* qumbaz.

kibr: United Arab Emirates. Man's hooded, striped cotton or silk robe.

kick pleat: Inverted pleat that adds fullness to straight skirts.

kickies: *See* unmentionables.

kid leather: Thin, soft leather made from very young milk-fed animals.

kidara: *See* ki-gomo.

kidaris: Mesopotamia. Ribbed tiara or embroidered hat worn by the king.

kidungas: United Kingdom. Printed or color-woven cotton scarves.

kiel: Holland. Blouse.

kierpce: Poland. Soft leather moccasin-type shoe.

kieszen': Poland. Pocket.

ki-gomo: Japan. A mat of rushes worn on the back to protect one from the sun.

ki-hachijo: Japan. Yellow hachijo silk.

kihachijo: Japan. A silk fabric made from silk yarns treated with a vegetable dye.

kihei: United States of America. Hawaii. Shawl.

kihei 'a'ahu no'eno'e: United States of America. Hawaii. Literally "colored garment cape," decorated cape.

kiing: Zaire. Raffia fiber used for sewing.

kiki skirt: (1910–1920 C.E.). Knee-length, form-fitting skirt, popularized by play of the name.

kiklikas: Lithuania. Woman's vest or corselet.

kikoi: Kenya. White cotton fabric with a colored border.

kikois: East African man's brightly colored cloth worn tied at the waist.

kila: India. Ear stud.

kilika: United States of America. Hawaii. Silk.

kilika lau: United States of America. Hawaii. Brocaded silk.

kilika nehe: United States of America. Hawaii. Taffeta.

killa: Bolivia. Half-moon shaped, brimmed cloth hat.

killu: Ecuador and Guatemala. Yellow.

kilmarnock: Early Georgian (1700–1750 C.E.). Scotland. Woolen serge made in Kilmarnock.

kilmarnock bonnet: Scotland. Broad topped, wool cap.

kilt: Scotland. Skirt of vertical pleats, usually of tartan plaid fabric.

kilted skirt: Bustle (1865–1890 C.E.). Popular for young boys in 1870, short skirt with deep pleats, based on the Highland costume.

kiltie tongue: Long shoe tongue that forms fringed flap over laces.

kim cài đầu: Vietnam. Pin; hairpin.

kim-bang: Vietnam. Safety pin.

kim-curong: Vietnam. Diamond.

kimkhab: India. Silk brocades with floral motifs.

kimkhwab: *See* kamkhab.

kim-khôi: Vietnam. Gold helmet.

kimmoru: Japan. Indian silk with gold thread designs.

kim-ngoc: Vietnam. Gold and jade.

kimono: Japan. Long gown with full sleeves.

ki-mô-nô: Vietnam. Kimono.

kimono dress: (20th century). Women's loose gown made in lines of a Japanese kimono. Popular around 1912.

kimono flannel: Soft, plain weave flannel.

kim-thoa: Vietnam. Gold hairpin.

kim-thuyen: Vietnam. Lamé.

kin koot: Korea. Gown.

kinamu: United States of America. Hawaii. Gingham.

kinãri: India. 1. A variety of gold or silver lace. 2. Sari's border.

kincob: Early Georgian (1700–1750 C.E.). Indian silk gauze embroidered in gold or silver flowers and other large figures.

kinderbroekje: Holland. Panties.

kinderschort: Holland. Pinafore.

king klipper: (1960–1970 C.E.). Man's five-inch-wide necktie.

kingcob: *See* kamkhab.

kính trang: Vietnam. Eyeglasses.

kinham: India. A thin black silk.

kinihama: *See* kinamu.

kiniki: Maori. A kilt.

kinkhab: *See* qatifah-i-purbi.

kinkhaib: *See* kincob.

kinkini: India. Anklet with small bells on it.

k'inkus: Bolivia. Woven zigzag pattern that creates a twill-like weave.

kinran: Japan. Gold brocaded fabric.

kinsha: Japan. Fine silk fabric; gold figured gauze.

kinu: Japan. Plain weave silk.

kinumo: Japan. Old-style of woman's dress with skirt and short coat.

kip: Raw or dressed pelt of young steer, cow, or horse.

kipini: Yao. Nose ornament.

kippe-sole: *See* kittysol.

kirdan: Palestine. Woman's silver choker necklace.

kirin: Korea. Animal with a horn and a flame from its mouth. Insignia for male members of the royal family.

kiri-osa: Japan. Embroidery using loose stitches couched with short cross threads.

kirita: India. 1. Man's gold diadem, sometimes ornamented with gems and pearls. 2. Man's turban.

kirita-mukuta: India. Man's conical hat with an ornament on top.

kirk: Turkey. Woman's ankle-length coat with short, tight sleeves. Often lined with fur and folded back from facings at the neck, front edge, and sleeve ends.

Kirmees: India. A muslin.

kirpas: India. A generic term for cotton fabric.

kirtle: Renaissance (1450–1550 C.E.) to Elizabethan (1550–1625 C.E.). Women's garment that was closefitting through the body and was full in the skirt. Evolved from the cotehardie.

kisaly: Madagascar. Woman's cotton shoulder wrap. *See also* lamba.

k'isas: Chile. Gradated stripes of color in a woven textile.

kišené: Lithuania. Pocket.

kisi: China. Brocade fabric.

kisibao: Swahili. A kind of waistcoat.

kiski: Macedonia. Red fringe.

kišni ogrtač: *See* kabanica.

kišobran: Bosnia. Umbrella.

kiss curl: *See* accroche-coeur.

kissing-strings: Early Georgian (1700–1750 C.E.). Strings used to tie a mob cap under the chin.

kiss-me-quick: Bustle (1865–1890 C.E.). United Kingdom. Worn from 1867 to 1869, popular name for a fashionable small bonnet.

kitamby: *See* lambahoany.

kite-high dandy: Crinoline (1840–1865 C.E.). United Kingdom. Man's 7-3/8-inch-high top hat.

kitel: Russia. Tunic.

kithaika: Charles I and the Commonwealth (1625–1550 C.E.). Russia. In 1654, a strong linen in plain white or a single color.

kitsol: *See* kittysol.

kittasol: *See* kittysol.

kittasole: *See* kittysol.

kittel: 1. Elizabethan (1550–1625 C.E.). Germany. Smock or coat worn by all classes with no skirt of tails. Cut in one piece, widening gradually from the shoulders. Usually worn with a girdle. Had long, not wide sleeves. Generally hung to the knee or below. Usually plain. 2. Hebrew. White cotton gown worn by orthodox Jews for solemn ceremonies and for burial. 3. Crinoline (1840–1865 C.E.). Austria. Lightweight, convenient linen tunic worn by the infantry when in Italy.

kittesaw: *See* kittysol.

kittisal: *See* kittysol.

kittsol: *See* kittysol.

kittysol: India. Slang for umbrella.

kittysoll: *See* kittysol.

kitysol: *See* kittysol.

kiver: Shako.

kkokkaot: Korea. Children's gala dress.

kkwemaeda: Korea. To darn.

kläda: Sweden. To clothe or to dress.

kläde: Sweden. Cloth.

kläder: Sweden. Clothing.

klaft: Egyptian (4000–30 B.C.E.). Pharaoh's striped fabric headdress on which a sparrow hawk was woven. Worn over the temples and tied or pinned behind the base of the head.

klapa: Poland and Portugal. Lapel.

klapbroek: Late Georgian (1750–1790 C.E.). South Africa. Breeches with a flap-fly front.

klapong sirat: Borneo. Man's waistcloth with decorated flap in back.

klapove hitl: *See* lappenmutze.

Klapphut: Germany. Gibus.

klashnik: Bulgaria. Thick wrap of wool and goat's hair.

klaw-i jnan: Iran. Unmarried woman's pillbox hat.

klaw-i pyawan: Iran. Crocheted skull cap.

kleeden: Holland. To clothe or to dress.

kleederen: Holland. Clothing.

kleedermaker: Holland. Literally "clothes maker," tailor.

kleeding: *See* kleederen.

kleiden: Germany. To clothe or to dress. *See also* woeten.

kleider: Germany. Clothing.

Kleiderrock: Germany. Jumper.

kleidunge: *See* kleit.

Kleinod: *See* Juwel.

kleinood: *See* juweel.

kleinōt: *See* gimme.

kleit: Germany. Old word for clothing.

klejnot: Poland. Jewel.

klenot: Czechoslovakia. Jewel.

kletje: Elizabethan (1550–1625 C.E.). Holland. Collarette.

klídja: Greece. Embroidery or black cloth bands on the siguni.

klier: Elizabethan (1550–1625 C.E.). Holland. Diminutive name for a collar.

klimatáca: Greece. Embroidery for everyday chemises.

klistó jiléci: Greece. Bride's vertically buttoned vest.

klobouk: Czechoslovakia. Hat.

klobuk: 1. Croatia and Serbia. Hat. 2. Poland. High cap.

klœða: Norway. Old word meaning to clothe or to dress.

klœde: Denmark and Germany. 1. To clothe or to dress. 2. Cloth.

klœder: Denmark and Germany. Clothing.

klœði: Norway. 1. Old word for clothing. 2. Old word for cloth.

klompen: Holland. Heavy wooden shoe; a sabot.

klonári: Greece. Embroidery design for chemises of newly married women.

klöppel: Germany. Bobbin.

klos: Holland. Bobbin.

klosant: Belgium. Bobbin lace.

kluteen: Romantic (1815–1840 C.E.). Introduced in 1815, French figured and striped silk used for women's spensers and pelisses.

kna: Greece. Henna staining of bride's hands.

knap: Denmark. Button.

knapp: Sweden. Button.

knee breeches: Elizabethan (1550–1625 C.E.) to 20th century. Worn from 1570s on, men's breeches that closed below the knee.

knee buckles: Restoration (1660–1700 C.E.) to Romantic (1815–1840 C.E.). United Kingdom. Buckles that secured the knee-bands on men's breeches.

knee-band: Restoration (1660–1700 C.E.) to Romantic (1815–1840 C.E.). Band that closed the knee breeches below the knee.

knee-fringe: Restoration (1660–1700 C.E.). United Kingdom. Worn from 1670 to 1675, fringe of ribbons worn around the base of open breeches.

knee-piece: Restoration (1660–1700 C.E.). Top portion of boot hose.

knee-string: Elizabethan (1550–1625 C.E.) to Late Georgian (1750–1790 C.E.). United Kingdom. Ties for gathering in the breeches below the knee.

knevel: *See* snor.

Knickebockers: Germany. Knickerbockers.

knickerbockers: 1. Bustle (1865–1890 C.E.). Knee-length men's trousers. Named for Father Knickerbocker. 2. Introduced in 1867, thick, coarse wool fabric, sometimes speckled.

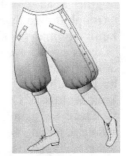

knickerbockers

kniebroek: *See* kuitbroek.

Kniehosen: Germany. Knee-breeches.

kniepe: Lithuania. Pin.

Kniestrümpfe: Germany. Long socks.

knife pleats: Series of small, hard pleats, all facing the same direction.

knight's blue: (1930–1940 C.E.). A new color.

knijpbril: Holland. Pince-nez.

knipling: 1. Denmark. Lace. 2. Norway. Metal lace.

kniplinger: Denmark. Lace.

knipmuts: Holland. Woman's broad lille lace bonnet with long tail at nape of neck.

knobkerry: South Africa. Walking stick.

knoflik: Czechoslovakia. Button.

knol: Holland. Jade.

knoop: Holland. Button.

knoopsgat: Holland. Buttonhole.

knop: 1. Early Gothic (1200–1350 C.E.). Button or tassel. 2. *See* knoop.

knopehaak: Holland. Buttonhook.

Knopf: Germany. Button.

Knöpflers: United States of America. Word referring to Mennonites.

Knopfloch: Germany. Buttonhole.

Knopflochblume: *See* Knopfloch.

knypkis: *See* saga.

k'o ssŭ: China. Silk tapestry.

kobaltblauw: Holland. Powder blue.

Kobe flannel: Japan. Similar to challis, only finer and more closely woven.

kobe gani: Timbuktu. A silver thumb ring.

kobene: Ghana. Vermillion red Ashanti cloth worn when the chief has just lost a close relative.

kobene cloth: *See* kobene.

kochi: India. The tucked in portion of the pleats of the sari.

kodmen: Hungary. Short coat.

ködmön: Hungary. Woman's sleeved, embroidered lambskin jacket that reaches to the waist. It has standing collar and is trimmed in fur.

kodongsaek: Korea. Brown; reddish brown.

kodot: Korea. Outer garment.

kodulch'i: Korea. Ceremonial white cuffs on a jacket.

koffo: Indonesia. Manila hemp.

kogai: Japan. A large, thick bar to which a woman's hair is fastened.

kogel: *See* gugel.

kogin: Japan. White cotton thread embroidered on rough indigo linen.

kohl: Egyptian (4000–30 B.C.E.). Black cosmetic used to make up the eyes and eyebrows.

kohlschwartz: *See* pechschwartz.

kojinė: Lithuania. Stocking.

kokade: Russia. Cockade.

Kokarde: Germany. Cockade.

kokechi: Japan. Tie-dyeing.

koketsu: Japan. Tie-dyeing.

ko-kinran: Japan. Ancient kinran.

kokoo: Ghana. The color red.

kokoshnik: Russia. Most valued part of a peasant woman's holiday costume. Shape of this elaborately trimmed headdress varies widely in different regions.

kokowai: *See* horu.

koksya: India. 1. A cloth that covers the genitals. 2. The border of a garment.

kola: 1. Pakistan. Man's little round embroidered hat. 2. Persia. Turban. 3. Samoa. Collar.

kolah: Persia. Brimless black lamb or cloth cap in a turban shape.

kólan: Greece. Silver belt.

kolaristó: Greece. Cotton petticoat.

kolbe: Elizabethan (1550–1625 C.E.). Man's hairstyle in a bowl shape.

kol'co: Russia. Finger ring.

kolczyk: Poland. Earring.

kolder: Elizabethan (1550–1625 C.E.). Holland. Soft leather jerkin.

kolinsky: Italy. Chinese or Siberian mink (*Mustela sibirica*) with straight, silky fur that is dyed brown to mimic sable.

Kolinsky: Germany. Kolinsky fur.

kolitsa: Bulgaria. Black woolen shawl worn wrapped around the fur cap, ends hanging down in back.

koller: Bustle (1865–1890 C.E.). Prussia. Front buttoning, long tunic worn by cuirassiers.

kolnierz: Poland. Collar.

koloa: United States of America. Hawaii. Long cane with a crook.

kolob: Biblical (Unknown–30 C.E.). Hebrew person's linen tunic.

kolobium: Greek (3000–100 B.C.E.). One-piece shirt-like garment worn by men. Opened on side for the arm and was often woven in one piece.

kolobus: Greek (3000–100 B.C.E.). Worn in fourth-century B.C.E., chiton made of two pieces of fabric that were sewn together at shoulders and sides, leaving openings for the head and arms. Often worn girded at the waist.

koloka: United States of America. Hawaii. Cloak; cape.

kolonáto: Greece. Mourning chemise.

kolor granatowy: Poland. Navy blue.

kolor khaki: Poland. Khaki, the color.

kolpak: Poland. High, sable hat trimmed with plush.

kolpos: Greek (3000–100 B.C.E.). Bloused part of the chiton at the waist.

komag: Norway. Man's reindeer hide boots.

komager: Norway. Worn by Lapps, soft heelless bootees.

komānam: India. Loincloth.

kombologion: Greek Orthodox knotted rosary.

kombu: Indonesia. Red dye made from the roots of the *Morinda citrifolia*.

kombukta: Korea. Dark red.

komo humuhumu: United States of America. Hawaii. Thimble.

komo lima: United States of America. Hawaii. Ring.

komon: Japan. A small allover design done by stencil resist dyeing.

Komparu: Japan. Ko-kinran design named for family of Noh actors.

komp'uruda: Korea. Dark blue.

komun: Korea. Black.

komusin: Korea. Rubber shoes with turned up toes.

kon: Japan. Dark blue.

konam: India. Loincloth.

kondó: Greece. Sleeveless chemise.

kondosa: Japan. A thick, dark blue paper that is pasted to the inside of a hairknot.

konfederatka: *See* czapka.

kon-gasuri: Japan. A cotton kasuri dyed with vegetable indigo dye.

kongdan: Korea. Silk satin fabric.

kontush: Poland. Generously cut caftan-shaped mantle.

koo: China. Dark blue everyday clothing.

kooi: Japan. Baby-carrying sash.

ko'oko'o 'amana: United States of America. Hawaii. Literally "tee-shaped cane," cane with a handle.

kooletah: Buttonless fur coat that pulls on over the head and is worn by Eskimos.

koong-soo: Korea. Professional embroidery.

koopuu: Australia. Maori plain inner garment.

koorhemd: *See* superplie.

kopa: Australia. Maori flax sandal that folds around the foot.

kopako: United States of America. Hawaii. Topaz.

kopča: Bosnia. A buckle.

kopeniak: Hungary and Poland. Overcoat.

Kopftuch: Germany. Head scarf.

kopin: India. Man's narrow coat-like dress.

köpönyeg: Hungary. Mantle.

kopplak: Holland. Large woolen headscarf woven in colorful pattern.

koprena: Croatia and Serbia. 1. Gauze; crepe. 2. Veil.

koprina: Bulgaria. Sort of silk.

kopseró: Greece. Woven embroidery design for the apron.

koreddō: *See* garannō.

korenka: Bulgaria. Apron called bark due to hardness of the fabric.

Korin-nami: Japan. A favored decorative pattern of waves.

kornaysh: Palestine. Silk crepe fabric.

kornek: France. Lace coif.

kornish: Egypt. Hem ruffle.

korona: Poland. Crown.

koronka: Portugal. Lace.

koronki: Poland. Lace.

korowai: New Zealand. Maori term for a large, fine cloak.

korozen: Japan. Yellowish brown.

korsaza: Madagascar. Brassiere.

korset: Holland. Corset.

Korsett: Germany. Corset.

kort wollen jasje: Holland. Spencer.

korte: Holland. Breeches.

korte pruik: Holland. Bob wig.

korum: Korea. Two sashes used to tie the chogori.

koruna: Russia. Maiden's filet.

kosa: India. A fabric dyed in safflower.

kosárky: Slovakia. Hat plumes.

koshi: Japan. Plaid design.

koshiate: Japan. Shin guards for armor.

koshihimo: Japan. Waist-ties.

koshimaki: Japan. 1. Summer garment of the samurai. 2. Woman's loincloth. 3. Underskirt.

koshipiri: Japan. A style of kimono.

koshoulya: Bulgaria. Smock of the bridal costume.

kosi: Samoa. Gauze.

kosile: Czechoslovakia. Shirt.

kosírek: Slovakia. Plume worn by an unmarried man on his hat.

kosnyo: Bulgaria. Hungary. Bodice closed with a flap called the fudzo.

kosode

kosode: Japan. Kimono with only a small sleeve opening. The forerunner of the modern kimono.

kosovorotka shirt: Russia. Man's traditional peasant shirt with band collar, long full sleeves, and asymmetrical front opening. Made of cotton, silk, or wool.

Kossuth: Crinoline (1840–1865 C.E.). Low-crowned, soft, flat hat introduced by the Hungarian patriot, Louis Kossuth, in 1851.

k'ossuyom: Korea. Moustache.

kostbaarheden: *See* juwelen.

kostim: Serbo-Croation. 1. Costume. 2. Swimsuit.

kostium damski: Poland. Lady's suit.

kostuum: Holland. Costume.

kosula: Poland. Shirt.

kósula: Greece. Chemise.

kosulja: Croatia and Serbia. Shirt.

kosuru: Japan. Small vine scroll pattern.

koszula damska: Poland. Chemise.

koszula meska: Poland. Shirt.

kotai: *See* lhani.

kote: Japan. Armored and chain mail sleeves.

koteny: Hungary. Very decorative apron.

koti oversaizi: Swahili. A long, Edwardian style coat.

kötö: *See* koteny.

kotoñs: France. Breton for cotton.

kotuly: Czechoslovakia. Large, round brooches.

kountouch: Early Georgian (1700–1750 C.E.). Poland. Long, sleeveless coat.

kous: Holland. Stocking.

kova sheberosho: Biblical (Unknown–30 C.E.). Hebrew's head covering.

ko-watari-tozan: Japan. An early striped cotton.

koyava: India. A wrapper stuffed with cotton.

koynek: 1. Turkmenistan. Woman's loose-fitting, ankle-length dress. 2. Iran. Woman's long-sleeved tabard.

koza: Croatia, Russia, and Serbia. Leather.

kozesina: Czechoslovakia. Fur.

kozhoushé: Bulgaria. Fur coat.

kozhukh: Ukraine. Enveloping sheepskin coat. Style depends on the shape of the skins.

kozsók: Hungary. Woman's hip-length sheepskin coat embroidered with silk.

kozuch: Poland. Sheepskin.

kraag: Holland. Collar.

krachoom: Thailand. Peaked red hat worn by naak (candidate for priesthood).

krage: Sweden. Collar.

Krage: Germany. Collar.

Kragen: Germany. Collar.

kragna: Serbian. Goller.

krajky: Czechoslovakia. Lace.

krambuno: Indonesia. Sa'dan-Toraja sunshade made from leaves of the fan-palm.

kras: Iran. Woman's dress with a full gathered skirt and straight sleeves.

kraspeda: Hebrew. Decorative borders.

Kräuseln: Germany. Curliness.

krauss: (1920–1930 C.E.). United Kingdom. Man's skirted coat; usually worn with checkered trousers.

kravata: Bosnia. Necktie.

Kravatte: Germany. Necktie.

krave: Denmark. Collar.

krawat: Poland. Necktie; cravat.

Krawatte: *See* Halsbinde.

krawiec: Poland. Tailor.

kredemnon: Greek (3000–100 B.C.E.). Woman's veil worn to conceal face.

kredka: Poland. Lipstick.

krejci: Czechoslovakia. Tailor.

krekls: Lithuania. Shirt.

kremezi: Greece. Red outlining thread.

Krempe: Germany. Brim.

krepis
See also photospread
(Foot and Legwear).

krepis: Roman (753 B.C.E.–323 C.E.). Light, thin soled sandal worn laced to ankle.

Krepp: Germany. Crape.

Kreuzstich: Germany. Cross-stitch.

krez: France. Breton for shirt.

krimija: *See* kanseya.

krimmer: Gray lamb fur.

Krinoline: Germany. Crinoline.

kripani: India. Scissors.

krochmal: Poland. Starch.

krojac: Croatia and Serbia. Tailor.

kroplap: *See* neerstick.

krósça: Greece. Gold lace knitted with real gold on spindles.

krosto: Greece. The rolled section of the tsemberi.

krótkie spodnie: Poland. Knickerbockers.

kroumir

kroumir: France. A soft leather slipper-like shoe.

krpce: Slovakia. Rough leather moccasins.

kruang tok: Laos. Special outfit worn by the oldest son at his parent's burial.

krul: *See* ringetje.

krulletje: *See* ringetje.

kruneforkle: Norway. Apron with embroidered stylized crowns.

krupáca: Greece. Embroidery design for the everyday chemise.

kruseler headdress: Late Gothic (1350–1450 C.E.). Germany. Woman's headdress of looped braids.

kruzeno: Russia. Lace.

kruzhevo: Russia. Lace.

krzno: Croatia and Serbia. Fur.

k'sa: Tuareg man's draped cloak, about six yards long. Worn over a kumya and pantaloons.

kselitsi: Greece. The jeweled ornament worn on the front edge of the tsemberi.

kshat: *See* sherihah.

Kshauna: India. Linen.

kshouma: India. Linen.

ksirodaka: India. A light silk stuff.

ksoulia: Greece. A bride's small fez covered with coins.

ktef: Morocco. Jewish woman's velvet chemise.

ku: China. Qing dynasty (1644–1911 C.E.). Trousers made from tubes of fabric that were joined with gussets in the crotch. Had a cotton waistband.

ku zhe: China. Northern man's pleated coat and breeches.

kuakalikea: United States of America. Hawaii. Cloth with white on its edges.

kubba: Afghanistan. Tunic.

kubba'ah: *See* libbadeh.

kubi najûn kudo: Korea. Low-heeled shoes.

kubi nop'ûn kudu: Korea. High-heeled shoes.

kudtā: India. Long coat; long sleeved tunic.

kuduggun: Korea. Shoestring.

kueka: United States of America. Hawaii. Sweater.

kuffieh: *See* kaffiyeh.

kufia: Tunisian Hebrew woman's pantaloons that are fitted to the ankle.

kufiyeh: *See* kaffiyeh.

kuftan: Egypt. Robe.

kugel: *See* gugel.

kugunni: Timbuktu. A silver ring with an ovoid projection.

kui humahuma: United States of America. Hawaii. Needle.

kui kaiapa: United States of America. Hawaii. Safety pin.

kui kele: United States of America. Hawaii. Large needle.

kui lihilihi: United States of America. Hawaii. Crochet hook.

kui ulana: United States of America. Hawaii. Knitting needle.

kuiki: United States of America. Hawaii. To quilt.

kuitbroek: Holland. Knee-breeches.

kuka: United States of America. Hawaii. Coat.

kuka ua: *See* kuka weke.

kuka weke: United States of America. Hawaii. Raincoat.

kuka'a: United States of America. Hawaii. Bolt of cloth.

kuka'aila: United States of America. Hawaii. Literally "oiled coat," raincoat. *See also* kukaua and kukaweke.

kukaenalo: United States of America. Hawaii. Unbleached muslin.

kukaua: *See* kuka'aila.

kukeweke: *See* kuka'aila.

kulah: 1. India. A stiffened and slightly domed cap worn under the turban. 2. Iran, Turkey. High, cylindrical felt hat.

kulahā: India. High cap.

kulah-e kordi: Iran. Married woman's turban made from fringed scarf trimmed with sequins and braid.

kulahī: India. Child's cap that covers the ears.

kulah-i pahlavi: Turkey. A peaked cap similar to the French kepi.

kule: Korea. Girl's richly embroidered, winter silk hat worn on outings. Has several wide ribbons with silk tassels in the back. Held on with sashes under the chin.

kulgie: *See* culgee.

kulia: United States of America. Hawaii. Twill.

kullah: Persia. Pointed skullcap.

kullu: Timbuktu. A C-shaped bracelet of silver or iron.

kum: Palestine. Tight sleeves.

kumach: Russia. Fustian.

kumbi: India. Silky fiber from a white silk-cotton tree.

kumbit: Korea. The color gold.

kumkuma: India. The color saffron.

kummul: *See* kambala.

kumpi: Inca. A fine cloth.

kumshigye: Korea. Gold watch.

kumya: 1. Morocco. Shirt that fastens down the front with closely set buttons and loops. 2. Tuareg man's sleeveless bodice.

kunba: India. A round crown.

kundala: India. A simple ring or circle earring.

kundalas: India. Ear-drops.

kundura: *See* cipela.

kuning: Borneo. Yellow.

kunka unku: Bolivia and Peru. Man's poncho.

k'unmori: Korea. Woman's large ceremonial hairstyle.

kunna: Timbuktu. A filigree hair ornament.

kunono: United States of America. Hawaii. Bright red.

kuntunkuni: 1. Ashanti. Widow's skirt. 2. Ghana. Dark brown cotton or linen cloth.

kuokvilna: Lithuania. Cotton.

kupasi: Afghanistan. Woman's headdress made of a heavy fabric rectangle that hangs down the back. Ornamented with cowrie shells, beads, pompons, and bells.

kupe'e: United States of America. Hawaii. Bracelet; anklet.

kupe'e niho 'ilio: United States of America. Hawaii. Dog-tooth anklets.

kupiah: Indonesia. Velvet cap.

kupkeh: Poland. Jewish woman's lace cap trimmed with flowers and birds.

kuppasam: India. A man's jacket.

kuras: Holland. Cuirass.

Kürass: *See* Brustharnisch.

kurira: India. Woman's horn-shaped coiffure.

kuri-ume: Japan. Purple with tints of yellow and red.

kurligatka: Bulgaria. Apron.

kurni: Ethiopia. Ten cubit garment given to the father of the bride by the groom.

kuro: Japan. Black.

kuro montsuki haori: Japan. Man's black silk haori worn for school ceremonies and mourning.

kurochō: Japan. A dark blue robe worn by women at weddings.

kuro-ume-zome: Japan. Dark purplish red color.

kurpasaka: India. Royal person's long, sleeveless coat; woman's bodice.

kurpasika: India. Woman's bodice-like garment.

kurpė: Lithuania. Shoe.

kursés: Greece. Gold lace.

kurta: 1. India. Of Parthian, Kushan, and Scythian origin, an undershirt with a four-pointed hem and ruched sleeves. 2. India. A long shirt. 3. Africa. Smock-like long white cotton shirt.

kurta pyjama: India. Tunic and trousers ensemble.

kurteh: Turkmenistan. Married woman's elaborately embroidered coat worn with the left armseye over the headdress.

kurtéles: Greece. Purchased ribbon.

kurti: 1. India. Long, sleeveless blouse worn over a backless blouse. 2. Turkestan. Woman's sleeved mantle worn over the head. 3. Hungary and Romania. Blue or black short jacket.

kurtka: 1. Late Georgian (1750–1790 C.E.). Poland. Short jacket with high collar and short tails edged with wide colored band. The tails were worn loose in winter and hooked back together in summer. 2. Russia. Short jacket.

kuru: New Zealand. Maori ear pendant.

Kurume-gasuri: Japan. Kasuri from Kurume.

Kurze hose: Germany. Shorts.

kusabhia: India. A safflower-dyed cloth.

kusak: 1. Bulgaria. Short, sleeveless jacket. 2. Turkey. Embroidered waist girdle whose ends are tied in a looped bow in front.

kushak: Russia. Soldier's girdle.

kushma: Ecuador and Guatemala. Man's tunic, similar to the Inca unku. It functions as a shirt.

kusi: Edo (1600–1867 C.E.). Japan. An ornamental hair comb.

kusljak: Hungary and Yugoslavia. Man's mantle of coarse homemade woolen fabric.

kusma: *See* 'unku.

kussabi: United Arab Emirates. Sleeveless, knee-length tunic.

kusti: India. Woolen cord worn as a girdle by the Parsis.

kusulaka: India. Woman's skirt.

kutapa: India. Tibetan shawls.

kutchi bharat: India. A form of embroidery made by using an awl (aar).

kutsani gashti: Bulgaria. Inner pair of trousers of cotton. Worn under beli potouri.

kuttan: India and Persia. Flax or linen cloth.

kutusoff hat: Directoire and First Empire (1790–1815 C.E.). Introduced in 1813, cloth cap that turned up in front, tied under the chin, and was finished with a feather. Named for the Russian general.

kutusoff mantle: Directoire and First Empire (1790–1815 C.E.). Made in fabric to match the kutusoff hat, had high puckered collar and shoulder width lapels. Fastened at neck with a brooch.

ku'uwelu: United States of America. Hawaii. Sarong.

kuvaa kisivilyan: Swahili. To wear civilian clothes. This term refers to policemen in off-duty clothing.

kuvala: India. A short sari that reaches to just below the genitals.

kuvinda: India. A weaver.

k'uyu: Bolivia. Made from handspun sheep's wool, a white cloth.

kuze: Czechoslovakia. Leather.

kuzufu: Japan. A cloth woven from kuzu vine.

kuzununo: *See* kuzufu.

kwasida adinkera: Ghana. White or yellow cloth with bands of yellow, black, red, and white.

kwef: Poland. Veil.

kwigoi: Korea. Earring.

kwitsa pargates: Ecuador. A young girl's sandals.

kwun: Bustle (1865–1890 C.E.). United States of America. Chinese Hawaiian term for a skirt.

kyahan: Japan. Leggings.

kyaphi: Egyptian (4000–30 B.C.E.). A perfume, supposedly the favorite of Cleopatra.

kyara-abura: Edo (1600–1867 C.E.). Japan. Literally "aloewood oil," a cosmetic paste of solid fat used to shape a man's knot of hair.

kyne: Greek (3000–100 B.C.E.). Soldier's leather helmet.

kyonjingmul: Korea. Silk fabrics.

kyorhon panji: Korea. Wedding ring.

kyorhon yak'on panji: Korea. Engagement ring.

Kyo-zome: Japan. Dyeing done in Kyoto.

kyrbasia: Mesopotamia. Hat similar to the Phrygian bonnet.

kyrtill: *See* kirtle.

L

la: Early Gothic (1200–1350 C.E.) to Late Gothic (1350–1450 C.E.). Sweden. Bride's chaplet, an embroidered band or fabric band decorated with silver ornaments.

lã: Portugal. Woolen fabric.

la bolsa: Mexico. Large fold in the front of a Zoque Indian woman's skirt (el costal).

la Bretelle: Crinoline (1840–1865 C.E.). In 1856, woman's cloak trimmed with broad moiré or velvet ribbon.

la Ciré: Cotton fabric combining seersucker, piqué, and leno characteristics.

la coiffure Diane: Crinoline (1840–1865 C.E.). In 1858, pearl ornament held in place on the chignon by a gold or silver arrow.

la comptesse Walewski: Crinoline (1840–1865 C.E.). In 1854, gossamer lace shawl embroidered with glossy straw. It had an embroidered flounce.

la Equestrienné: Crinoline (1840–1865 C.E.). In 1858, woman's cloth habit. Skirt was trimmed with velvet buttons. Short jacket was trimmed with the same and loops of braid. Habit included a habit-shirt and sleeves of cambric.

la Esmeralda: Crinoline (1840–1865 C.E.). In 1850, mantilla with a fitted body. Skirt had two deep falls of white lace. Elbow-length sleeves were finished with two white lace falls.

la Grange: Crinoline (1840–1865 C.E.). In 1858, woman's cloth basquine with a waist-length bertha. It was trimmed with velvet ribbon in a Greek pattern and fringe.

la Hermione: Crinoline (1840–1865 C.E.). In 1850, semi-fitted, glacé silk mantilla. It was trimmed with six rows of quilled ribbon.

la Manuela: Crinoline (1840–1865 C.E.). In 1855, black taffeta Spanish mantilla trimmed with a deep sewing-silk fringe and a row of Guipure lace.

la Marguerite: Crinoline (1840–1865 C.E.). Velvet mantle closely fitted in the bodice with a full sacque skirt. Edged in therry velvet.

la Mignene: Crinoline (1840–1865 C.E.). In 1856, woman's mantle with three volants.

la Ophelia: Crinoline (1840–1865 C.E.). In 1850, mantilla trimmed at the hem, elbow, front, and back seams with a double puff of silk. It had a single fall of lace from the bottom edge, a double fall on the sleeves.

la pliant: Gay Nineties (1890–1900 C.E.). Steel invention from 1896 which held out the hem of women's skirts in the back. Could be used in different skirts.

la Princesse: Crinoline (1840–1865 C.E.). Worn for evening, a wire-framed, velvet-covered cap trimmed with braided ribbon.

la Puritana: *See* Puritan.

lá sen: Vietnam. Semi-circular collar on a blouse.

la Stella: Crinoline (1840–1865 C.E.). In 1850s, mantilla that was lightly fitted in the body. The basquin had two flounces with deep scallops. Sleeves flared to the wrist.

la Princesse

la vierge: Crinoline (1840–1865 C.E.). Literally "infant's waist," bodice with the front gathered in a fan shape.

la'a: United States of America. Hawaii. Width of cloth.

laars: Holland. Boot.

la'au su'isu'i: Samoa. Sewing machine.

labaada: *See* chuga.

labādā: *See* cogā.

labang: Borneo. White.

labarikada: Nigeria. Yoruba man's close-fitting cap with earflaps.

label cloth: Sized cotton fabric used for tags and labels.

labong: Borneo. 1. Man's handkerchief, usually decorated. 2. Man's cap of woven cane.

labrada: Renaissance (1450–1550 C.E.). Spain. Embroidered.

labret: Mayan. Lip-plug worn through a perforation in the lower lip.

lacca: Renaissance (1450–1550 C.E.). Italy. Precious red dye.

lacerna: Greek (3000–100 B.C.E.). Coarse wool, short circular cape worn by the lower classes.

lacet: 1. Silk or cotton braid used in lace. 2. Braid used to cover seams in upholstery.

Lachen: *See* Tuoch.

lachet: *See* herlot.

lacing protector: Placket of fabric that spans the gap between the lacing on a corset. This allows the lacing to draw smoothly and protects the wearer's skin.

lacing studs: Gay Nineties (1890–1900 C.E.). In 1897, oval brass hooks used on men's shoes for lacing.

lacis: Square net foundation on which darned laces are made.

lad: Norway. From the old Norse word, hlað or hlaða (to lay something in a certain order, on top of each other or side by side). Headdress decorated with ornaments attached to an unseen base layer of fabric.

laddie, come follow me: *See* beau-catcher.

läder: Sweden. Leather.

ladva: India. Literally "sweet," a small round tattoo on a woman's chin.

Lady Alice sleeve: Crinoline (1840–1865 C.E.). In 1861, small bishop sleeve gathered to cuffed band.

Lady Diana hat

Lady Diana hat: Crinoline (1840–1865 C.E.). In 1862, leghorn straw hat with double turn.

lady's cloth: Variety of lightweight, woolen broadcloth.

la'ei: Samoa. Clothes.

laeloa: United States of America. Hawaii. Kind of wine red cotton cloth.

lafa'if: Palestine. Attached to the smadeh, two long bands of fabric used to bind the hair. Held on with silver chin chain.

laffayef-: Palestine. Woman's hairband.

laffeh: Palestine. Man's turban made from Syrian silk or cotton fabric, often striped or checked. Fringed on the ends.

lafun: Nigeria. Starch paste used as a resist.

laggosszárú csizma: *See* keményszárú csizma.

lagidigba: Nigeria. Yoruba woman's waist beads.

lagos: Africa. Coarse, irregular, brownish cotton fabric.

lah: *See* qatifah-i-purbi.

lahalile: United States of America. Hawaii. Dark navy blue calico with a small white print or dots.

laharia: *See* leheria.

lahariyo: India. Zigzag-patterned scarf. *See also* lahasyo.

lahasyo: *See* lahariyo.

lahra patora: India. Skirts.

lai kee wat chau: Crinoline (1840–1865 C.E.). United States of America. Chinese Hawaiian term for a smooth, shiny, black chau with a rust colored undersurface. It was used to make holiday clothing.

Laibli: Germany. Sleeveless bodice that fastens down the front. The armseyes, neck, and front are decorated with braid. May be plain or embroidered.

lainakini: United States of America. Hawaii. Navy blue cloth.

laine: France. Worsted or woolen fabric.

laine foulard: Crinoline (1840–1865 C.E.). Introduced in 1861, silk and wool blend washing silk.

laipeid: Ireland. Gaelic word for lappet.

laj kadvu: India. The wearing of a veil over the face.

laj karvu: *See* laj kadvu.

lájbi: 1. Hungary. Black brocade waistcoat trimmed with metal, bone and glass buttons, and braid. 2. Romania. Vest.

lájish: Navajo. Glove.

laka: India. The border of a garment.

lake: 1. Clear purplish red. 2. Byzantine and Romanesque (400–1200 C.E.) to Renaissance (1450–1550 C.E.). United Kingdom. Middle English word for fine linen.

lakeke: United States of America. Hawaii. Jacket; blouse.

laken: Holland. Cloth.

lal: India. The color scarlet.

lalaga: Samoa. To weave.

lalatantuja: India. A variety of silk.

lalatika: India. Pendant worn on a chain in the center of a woman's forehead.

laliàn: China. Zipper.

lamak: 1. Indonesia. Long, narrow textiles used as hangings before shrines. 2. *See* phaa chet naa.

lāmann: *See* lāmind.

lamb mena: Madagascar. Literally "red cloth," burial shroud.

lamba: 1. Madagascar. Brightly colored shawl or mantle; generic term for fabric. 2. Fabric of date leaves made and worn by some African natives.

lamba maitso: Madagascar. Literally "green cloth," mourning fabric.

lamba soratra: Madagascar. Patterned fabric.

lambahoany: Madagascar. Man's hip wrap.

lamballe: Late Georgian (1750–1790 C.E.). Silk scarf trimmed in lace. Named for the Princesse de Lamballe.

Lamballe bonnet: Bustle (1865–1890 C.E.). United Kingdom. Introduced in 1865, very small straw bonnet with a slightly curved brim that was worn flat on the head and tied under the chin. Sometimes had a veil in back or lace lappets on the sides.

lambana: India. A long necklace.

lamboys: Late Gothic (1350–1450 C.E.) to Elizabethan (1550–1625 C.E.). Knee-length steel skirt worn as part of armor.

lambrequin: Early Gothic (1200–1350 C.E.). Scarf worn over the helmet as protection from the elements.

lambsdown: Heavy, knitted, wool fabric with a thick nap on one side.

lambskin: 1. Leather made from the skin of a lamb less than two months old. 2. Lambskin that has been dressed with the wool on it. 3. Cotton or wool fabric with a napped, fleecy surface. 4. White leather apron worn by freemasons.

lamé: 1. Directoire and First Empire (1790–1815 C.E.). Fabric woven of strips of metal. 2. Fabric made of metallic thread.

lamhain: Ireland. Glove.

làmhainn: Ireland. Glove; especially a kid glove.

làmhan: Ireland. Glove; gauntlet.

lamhas: Ireland. Old Gaelic word for glove.

làmh-fhàil: Ireland. Bracelet.

lāmind: Ireland. Old Gaelic word for glove.

Lamm: Germany. Lamb fur.

lammie: *See* lammy.

lammy: Sailor's quilted sweater.

lamouxa: Greece. Velvets.

lampas: 1. Directoire and First Empire (1790–1815 C.E.). Fabric with an elaborate, ornamental design. 2. Fabric with two or more color jacquard.

lampasi: Russia. Stripe down the side of dress trousers.

lampshade dress: (1910–1920 C.E.). Double tiered dress with the top tier wired out in the shape of a lampshade.

lan: Croatia and Serbia. Flax.

lan yu: China. Dark blue feathers from a crow's tail.

lana: Ecuador, Guatemala, Italy, and Spain. Wool.

lāna: Roman (753 B.C.E.–323 C.E.). Wool.

lana de alpaca: Spain. Alpaca wool.

Lancer jacket: Crinoline (1840–1865 C.E.). In 1859, woman's jacket with points at the hips. Had mousquetaire sleeves.

landrines: Louis XIII. Men's boots with flared tops that were turned down for riding.

landy: Madagascar. Silk.

láng: Vietnam. Black taffeta.

langar: India. Close-fitting anklet of gold or silver, studded with precious stones.

lange: Swaddling cloth.

Lange hose: Germany. Trousers; slacks.

langet: Late Gothic (1350–1450 C.E.) to Renaissance (1450–1550 C.E.). 1. Lace or thong for closing a garment. 2. Plume on a knight's helmet.

langettes: Late Gothic (1350–1450 C.E.). String of beads.

langgu lungping: Borneo. Earring.

langkit: Philippine Islands. Separately woven bands on a malong.

langooty: India. Small loincloth.

langoti: India. A narrow loincloth.

Langtry bonnet: Bustle (1865–1890 C.E.). Small, close-fitting bonnet. Named for the famous actress Lilly Langtry.

Langtry hood: Bustle (1865–1890 C.E.). United Kingdom. Worn in 1880s, woman's detachable hood worn with any outer garment.

languette: Romantic (1815–1840 C.E.). United Kingdom. Used from c1818 to 1822, flat trim used on skirts and pelisses.

languti: India. Loincloth.

lãnh: Vietnam. Taffeta.

lanilla estampada: Spain. Delaine.

lansdowne: Fine, wiry, plain or twill weave fabric with silk warp and worsted weft used for women's dresses.

lantern sleeve: Bell shaped sleeve with circular wrist.

lanumoana: Samoa. Blue.

lanzadera: Ecuador and Guatemala. Shuttle or bobbin.

lap: 1. Tab. 2. To fold over. 3. Part of garment covering lower part of body. 4. Folded section of garment used as a pocket.

lapa: Germany. Woman's white or pastel large padded headdress.

lapel: Part of garment that folds over, especially the front neckline of a garment.

lapel pin: Small pin worn on lapel.

lapela: Portugal. Coat lapel.

lapin: France and Italy. Loosely sheared fur of rabbit dyed in fanciful shade.

Lapin: Germany. Lapin fur.

lapiz lazuli: Semi-precious dark blue gemstone.

Lapland beaver: Crinoline (1840–1865 C.E.). Introduced in 1859, twill weave fabric with plush face used for capes and other outdoor garments.

Lapland bonnet: Lapland. Traditional four pointed bonnet. Three of the points were stuffed with down, the fourth served as a purse.

lap-mantle: Elizabethan (1550–1625 C.E.). Rug for the knees.

lapot: Russia. Shoe made of strips of the inner bark from the birch or lime tree and laced together.

lappa: 1. Nigeria. Ibo man's long skirt. It is a cloth worn wound around the middle and then twisted and tucked over at the top in front. On the Niger Delta, it is worn fastened on the side. 2. Sierra Leone. A length of cotton or silk cloth that is worn around the waist as a skirt.

lappa cloth: West African fabric made from narrow strips that are sewn together.

lapped sleeve: Short sleeve with portion of fabric folded to front or back simulating a seam.

lappenmutze: Poland. Jewish man's cap with ear flaps.

lappet: Early Georgian (1700–1750 C.E.) to Bustle (1865–1890 C.E.). Pendant pieces of headdress that hang on the sides or behind the head. Plain or trimmed in lace.

laranja: Portugal. Orange colored.

lärft: Sweden. Linen.

larga: *See* puntada recta.

lark: Pale buff color.

larkspur: Light blue with pale greenish tinge.

larrigan: Knee-high boot with a moccasin foot worn by lumbermen and trappers.

lāsa: Ireland. Lace.

lasdadh: Ireland. Gaelic word for lace.

laseh: Palestine. Rectangle of white silk or cotton netting with metallic wire. Worn by women as a head covering.

lashdóón: Navajo. Ribbon.

laska: Poland. Walking stick.

lasoa: Madagascar. A silk cloth.

lasting boots: Bustle (1865–1890 C.E.). Boots with the uppers made of black cashmere.

lasuor: China. Zipper.

latão: Portugal. Brass.

latch buckle: Lapped belt buckle with metal swivel closing.

latchet: Elizabethan (1550–1625 C.E.). Lace, thong, or strap that fastens shoe or sandal.

laticlaves: *See* clavi.

látsíní: Navajo. Bracelet.

Lätzchen: *See* Schurze.

lau: Indonesia. Women's waist garments that use beads and shells in embroidery as a form of decoration.

lau pahudu: Sumba. Women's sarongs.

lauhitaka: India. A red fabric.

laundry duck: Variety of wide duck fabrics used to cover rolls in laundry machines.

lauoho: United States of America. Hawaii. Literally "head leaf," the hair on the head.

lauoho ku'i: United States of America. Hawaii. Literally "added hair," a hair switch.

láurea: Portugal. Crown of laurel.

lava-lava: Samoa. Loincloth of printed calico worn by the natives.

lavaliere: Restoration (1660–1700 C.E.). Necklace with a pendant, popularized by Louise de la Valiere, mistress of Louis XIV.

lavanda: Italy and Spain. Lavender.

lavende: France. Lavender.

lavender: Romantic (1815–1840 C.E.) to present. United Kingdom. Light violet color.

Laveuse costume: Bustle (1865–1890 C.E.). Introduced in 1876, day dress with an overskirt (tunic) that was folded up, draped on the sides, gathered in back, and buttoned in place.

Lavinia: Romantic (1815–1840 C.E.). Color of Wedgwood.

Lavinia hat: Directoire and First Empire (1790–1815 C.E.). Fashionable in 1807, variety of the gipsy hat.

lavreg: *See* bragou.

lawn: Elizabethan (1550–1625 C.E.) to 20th century. Originally made in Laon, France, fine linen or cambric used to make ruffs, cuffs, handkerchiefs, aprons, or shirts.

laylock: *See* lilac.

lazarines: *See* landrines.

lazo de entorchado: Spain. Frog.

lazouri: Greece. 1. A type of embroidery. 2. Cotton embroidery thread.

lazur: Poland. Azure.

lazúrja: Greece. Embroidery, embroidered the same on both sides.

lazurowy: Poland. Azure colored.

le Bijou: Crinoline (1840–1865 C.E.). In 1855, woman's wrap with a V-shaped yoke, a tulle skirt, and a pleated flounce. Trimmed with gauze ribbon and satin stripes.

le Caprice: Crinoline (1840–1865 C.E.). In 1855, sack cloak with cape sleeves. Trimmed with velvet, embroidery, and ostrich feathers.

le crapaud: Early Georgian (1700–1750 C.E.). Silk bag for the ponytail at the back of men's wigs.

le gilet: Late Georgian (1750–1790 C.E.). Sleeveless men's vest, with back of light fabric with lacing to make it fit the form.

le Gitana: Crinoline (1840–1865 C.E.). In 1856, hooded circular talma trimmed with plush.

la jupon Imperatrice: Crinoline (1840–1865 C.E.). In 1862, cambric petticoat heavily starched. Six yards in circumference. Supposedly invented by Empress Eugenie.

le printemps mantilla: Crinoline (1840–1865 C.E.). In 1854, one-piece silk mantilla that was trimmed with a deep fringe.

le Savage: Crinoline (1840–1865 C.E.). Fringe of feathers and jet.

leacadan: Ireland. Gaelic word for chin cloth or child's bib.

leading strings: Early Georgian (1700–1750 C.E.) to Crinoline (1840–1865 C.E.). Long narrow ribbons of fabric that were attached to the shoulders of small children's garments to hold them when they began to walk.

leadworks: *See* wheat ears.

leaf green: Medium green.

leather cloth: United Kingdom. Cheap variety of melton.

Leatherette: Trade name for paper or cloth imitation leather.

leatherine: Imitation leather made from calico with rubber coating.

leaves: *See* wheat ears.

lechugilla: Elizabethan (1550–1625 C.E.). Spain. Ruff.

lecric: Romania. Short, sleeved vest of thick feathers.

Leda cloth: Wool velvet. *See also* velours de laine.

leder: Holland. Leather.

Leder: Germany. Leather.

lederhosen: Austria. Form of leather shorts with ornately embroidered suspenders.

ledersen: Renaissance (1450–1550 C.E.). Germany. Combination legging and shoes.

leðr: Norway. Old word for leather.

leefekye: Renaissance (1450–1550 C.E.) to Elizabethan (1550–1625 C.E.). Bodice.

Leek button: Crinoline (1840–1865 C.E.). Patented in 1842, covered button with a flexible shank.

leetsoii: Navajo. Yellow.

lefhah: *See* shal.

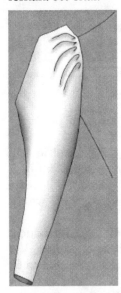

leg of mutton sleeves

leg of mutton sleeves: Romantic (1815–1840 C.E.). Worn from 1828 to 1837, popular sleeve with a huge puff at the top of the sleeve that narrows to a fitted wrist. Revived from 1893 to 1899.

leghorn: Finely plaited straw.

leheria: India. A resist dyeing technique.

lehnga: India. A style in which the antariya is worn like a skirt.

lei: 1. Samoa. Ivory. 2. United States of America. Hawaii. A garland or necklace of flowers, leaves, shells, ivy, feathers, or paper given as a sign of affection.

lei 'a'i: United States of America. Hawaii. Necktie.

lei ali'i: United States of America. Hawaii. Royal lei.

lei hala: United States of America. Hawaii. Lei of pandanus keys. It is considered bad luck.

lei hoaka: United States of America. Hawaii. Necklace of hog's tusks.

lei hulu: United States of America. Hawaii. Feather lei, formerly worn only by royalty.

lei kamoe: United States of America. Hawaii. Feather lei with the feathers tightly folded together.

lei kolona: United States of America. Hawaii. Literally "crown," a rosary.

lei korona: *See* lei kolona.

lei kukui: United States of America. Hawaii. Lei of candlenut seeds.

lei leho: United States of America. Hawaii. Lei of cowry shells.

lei niho 'ilio: United States of America. Hawaii. Dog-tooth necklace.

lei ole: United States of America. Hawaii. Dog-tooth lei.

lei 'opu'u: United States of America. Hawaii. Pointed whale tooth pendant.

lei palaoa: United States of America. Hawaii. Ivory pendant; necklace of beads of whale's teeth.

lei pani'o: United States of America. Hawaii. Lei with a spiral design of color.

lei papa: United States of America. Hawaii. Flat lei, as for a hat.

lei papahi: United States of America. Hawaii. Adornment of several leis.

lei pauku: United States of America. Hawaii. Lei with sections of varying colors.

lei pawehe: *See* lei pauku.

lei po'o: United States of America. Hawaii. Lei worn on the head.

lei wiliwili: United States of America. Hawaii. Lei of wiliwili seeds.

Leibchen: Germany. Bodice.

leiber: Bulgaria. Waist-length, sleeveless jacket.

leibi: Germany. Woman's fitted bodice or dress.

Leibli: *See* Laibli.

Leicester jacket: Crinoline (1840–1865 C.E.). United Kingdom. In 1857, man's British tailored lounge jacket.

lein: Early Gothic (1200–1350 C.E.) to Late Gothic (1350–1450 C.E.). United Kingdom. Linen.

Lein: *See* Flachs.

leine: Byzantine and Romanesque (400–1200 C.E.). Bulgaria. Sleeveless, ankle-length tunic in white or natural colors.

léine: Ireland. Large linen smock or shirt with wide sleeves worn by both genders. Usually dyed yellow. Also known as saffron shirt.

leine croich: Scotland. Saffron shirt of 24 ells worn belted at the waist. From 15th century, characteristic garment of Highlands.

léineag: Ireland. Little shirt.

léine-aifrionn: Ireland. Surplice.

léine-bhàn: Ireland. Smock worn by transgressors of ecclesiastical law.

léine-chaol: Ireland. White linen shirt.

léine-chròich: Ireland. Knee-length, saffron shirt or mantle worn by people of upper rank. It consisted of 24 ells of fabric and was worn belted around the waist.

Leinen: Germany. Linen.

léine-sheacair: Ireland. Narrow striped or pleated shirt.

léine-thuilinn: Ireland. Shirt of twilled linen.

léinteag: Ireland. Little shirt.

Leinwand: *See* Leinen.

leis-bheart: Ireland. Gaelic word for armor for the thigh or trousers.

leis-bhrat: Ireland. Gaelic word for a pair of trousers.

lejfa: Ecuador and Guatemala. Lye.

leki: United States of America. Hawaii. Tape used as dress trim.

lekmann detsmira: Morocco. Woman's separate white voile sleeves.

lelesepun: Celebes. Funeral shroud. *See also* poritutu roto.

lelieblank: Holland. Lily white.

lelingkok: Borneo. Zigzag.

lemba: Indonesia. Tiny pieces of mica sewn onto a garment.

lembe: Indonesia. The sacred shoulder wrap worn by royalty.

lemister: Renaissance (1450–1550 C.E.) to Elizabethan (1550–1625 C.E.). Fine wool used for knitted caps, commonly Herfordshire wool.

lemmetør klœde: Denmark. Handkerchief.

lemon yellow: Color of lemon fruit.

lemster: *See* lemister.

len: Czechoslovakia, Poland, and Russia. Flax.

lencería: Spain. Lingerie.

lenço: Portugal. Handkerchief.

lenço de sêda da india: Portugal. Bandanna.

lendener: Late Gothic (1350–1450 C.E.). Germany. Tight tunic of very tight but pliable leather, sometimes sleeveless, but usually with short sleeves. Elaborately trimmed.

lēne: Ireland. Old Gaelic word for shirt.

lenn: Ireland. Gaelic word for cloak. *See also* brat.

leno: Loose, open fabric in leno weave.

leno brocade: Leno fabric with a figure brocaded on it.

leno weave: Weave involving the yarns being twisted around each other in a figure eight.

lentejuela: Spain. Sequin; spangle.

Leonese: Crinoline (1840–1865 C.E.). In 1857, woman's cloth pardessus with a fitted basque, full skirt, and flowing sleeves. Deep bertha reached a point over the arms. Pardessus had border of plush.

leopard: 1. Short pale fawn or light orange fur with dark brown spots from the leopard (*Felix pardus*). 2. Italy and Spain. Leopard fur.

Leopard: Germany. Leopard fur.

léopard: France. Leopard fur.

leotard: Stretch material garment reaching from neck to groin. Originally developed by trapeze artist, Jules Leotard.

leotardo: Spain. Leotards.

lepela: Portugal. Lapel.

leÞer: United Kingdom. Old English word for leather.

leperhose: Byzantine and Romanesque (400–1200 C.E.). United Kingdom. Leather boot.

le-phuc: Vietnam. Formal dress.

leppi: Cameroon. Man's full-length robe.

ler: France. Breton for leather.

lerept: Norway. Old word for linen items.

lerion: Byzantine and Romanesque (400–1200 C.E.). Worn in 12th century, fur of the dormouse.

les shorts: *See* hot pants.

leso: Kiamu. Woman's tobe.

let: Borneo. Green and blue glassy beads.

lethar: Ireland. Gaelic word for leather.

leth-bhòt: Ireland. Buskin.

lether: Byzantine and Romanesque (400–1200 C.E.) to Renaissance (1450–1550 C.E.). United Kingdom.

Middle English word for leather.

leth-ruadh: Ireland. Gaelic word for reddish brown.

letnik: Russia. Outer garment that is part of holiday dress for women.

lettered silk: Originally, Oriental fabric decorated with letters, words, or sentences. Now, any such silk fabric.

lettice: Byzantine and Romanesque (400–1200 C.E.) to Late Gothic (1350–1450 C.E.). Pale gray fur similar to ermine.

lettice bonnet: Elizabethan (1550–1625 C.E.). Woman's warm bonnet of lettice cut to cover the ears.

lettice cap: *See* lettice bonnet.

lettice ruff: Elizabethan (1550–1625 C.E.). Ruff resembling lettuce.

lettuce green: Light yellowish green.

leug: Ireland. Gaelic word for precious stone or jewel.

leung mo: China. Traditional coolie hat.

levantine: 1. Romantic (1815–1840 C.E.). Used in 1820 and after, very soft velvet with a satin finish. 2. Crinoline (1840–1865 C.E.). Richly faced, twill weave silk, similar to surah. 3. Glossy faced, twill weave, cotton fabric.

levantine folicé: Romantic (1815–1840 C.E.). Introduced in 1837, soft rich silk with an arabesque pattern.

leviathan canvas: Coarse, open, double canvas used for Berlin work.

levite: Late Georgian (1750–1790 C.E.). Polonaise made of dimity or muslin and trimmed or bordered in chintz.

levite gown: Late Georgian (1750–1790 C.E.). Trained redingote.

Lexington cloak: Crinoline (1840–1865 C.E.). In 1856, woman's half-yoked, fitted front, velvet cloak trimmed with moiré buttons.

lézard: Bustle (1865–1890 C.E.). In 1872, lizard green.

lezim: Morocco. Silver clasp on the endema.

lhani: India. Parrot green.

lì: China. Large bamboo or straw hat with conical crown and broad brim.

li kakini: United States of America. Hawaii. Literally "tie stockings," garters.

li kaliki: United States of America. Hawaii. Corset lace.

li kama'a: United States of America. Hawaii. Shoelace.

liagh-dhealg: Ireland. Gaelic word for button.

liàn: China. White silk.

liang dang: China. Northern man's waistcoat.

liang dang kai: China. Wei, Jin, Southern and Northern dynasties. Hard metal or leather vest armor worn over heavy waistcoat.

liang mao: China. Flat circular hat of woven straw and bamboo with hole in center for crown of the head.

lià-njiaokù: China. Infant's footed pants.

liá-nyiqú-n: China. Woman's dress.

liars: Late Georgian (1750–1790 C.E.). Wires that supported the fichu.

liath: Ireland. Gaelic word for gray.

liath ghorm: Ireland. Gaelic word for cerulean blue.

liath-ghuirme: Ireland. Gaelic word for light blue.

liath-phurpur: Ireland. Gaelic word for mauve.

libá: Navajo. Gray.

libade: Romania. Short bodice of the cinduse.

libas: 1. Egypt. Very wide cotton pantaloons. 2. *See* sirwal.

libbadeh: Palestine. Man's white or gray felt cap worn over the taqiyeh and under the tarbush maghribi.

Liberty art silks: Bustle (1854–1890 C.E.). Made first in 1870s, artistically designed silk of an Indian weave.

Liberty bodice: Gay Nineties (1890–1900 C.E.) to 1960–1969 C.E. Boneless training corset for young girls.

liberty cap: Directoire and First Empire (1790–1815 C.E.). France. Soft, closely fitted cap worn as symbol of liberty.

liburnica: Biblical (Unknown–30 C.E.). Hebrew's cloak.

lichen: Bustle (1865–1890 C.E.). In 1872, mossy green.

lichíí: Navajo. Red.

lichtbruin: Holland. Nut brown.

licinium: Linen loincloth.

lid: Slang term for hat.

lie de Bordeaux: Bustle (1865–1890 C.E.). In 1874, deep claret color.

lièn: France. Breton for linen.

liencillo: Ecuador. Fine handwoven plain cotton cloth.

lienzo: 1. Ecuador. Handwoven plain-weave cotton cloth. 2. Spain. Linen.

lienzo de algodón: Spain. Broadcloth.

lienzo de la India: Renaissance (1450–1550 C.E.). Spain. East Indian cotton.

lierre lace: Gay Nineties (1890–1900 C.E.). In 1896, fine cream net sparsely figured.

lifú: China. Ceremonial dress.

liga: Elizabethan (1550–1625 C.E.). Spain. Garter.

lightfastness: The degree to which a dyed textile resists the color-destroying effects of light.

lightgroen: Holland. Pea green.

ligne empire: France. Empire line.

lihaf: Oman. Gauzy shawl worn by women over the head and shoulders and tucked under the chin.

lihilihi 'ula: United States of America. Hawaii. Narrow band of red, as on a shirt.

lijf: Elizabethan (1550–1625 C.E.). Holland. Décolleté bodice.

lijfje: Holland. Bodice.

lijnne: Norway. Shawl.

lijnwaad: *See* linnen.

lila: Holland. Lilac colored.

lilac: Late Georgian (1750–1790 C.E.) to present. Light tint of violet.

lilac gray: Pale lavender gray.

lilack: *See* lilac.

lila-röz: Poland. Mauve.

lilás: Portugal. Lilac colored.

lilina: United States of America. Hawaii. Linen; flax.

lilit: Borneo. Gold embroidered braid.

Lille à fond clair: Crinoline (1840–1865 C.E.). France. A bobbin lace with a simple unplaited ground and small motifs contoured with thicker thread.

Lille lace: Fine bobbin lace with the patterns outlined in a heavy, flat cordonnet.

Lily Benjamin: Romantic (1815–1840 C.E.). Common term for man's white overcoat.

lily feet: China. Term referring to the condition of feet when bound in the traditional manner. Style began in 1200 C.E. with the birth of the Princess Taki who was born with club feet. Her tiny feet were copied by binding the feet of infants. Foot binding became a penal offense in 1912.

Lily Langtry coiffure: Bustle (1865–1890 C.E.). Hairstyle popularized by English actress and friend of Edward VII, Lily Langtry. Low chignon with curls around forehead.

lima: United States of America. Hawaii. Sleeve.

lima puha'uha'u: United States of America. Hawaii. Puffed sleeve.

limào: China. Hat for formal dress.

limbrick: United Kingdom. Soft, lightweight, plain weave, cotton fabric.

lime green: Greenish yellow.

límec: Czechoslovakia. Collar

Limerick gloves: Late Georgian (1750–1790 C.E.) to Crinoline (1840–1865 C.E.). Woman's fine leather gloves, either short or long, said to be made from the skin of unborn lambs or calves.

Limerick lace: Machine-made net with a muslin applique and buttonhole edge.

limiste: Renaissance (1450–1550 C.E.). Spain. Woolen material.

limousine: Bustle (1865–1890 C.E.). Thick, rough woolen fabric.

Limpet trunks: (1930–1940 C.E.). United Kingdom. Men's swim trunks made from Lastex yarn and botany wool. They had no belt or side seams and fitted smoothly over the hips.

lin: 1. France and Ireland. Linen. 2. Norway. Old word for linen. 3. Norway. Bridal veil. 4. *See* lien.

lìn: Ireland. Old Gaelic word for linen.

lînă: Romania. Wool.

linaga: Transvaal. Ndebele bride's sheepskin cape.

linai: Lithuania. Flax.

lince: Italy and Spain. Lynx fur.

linchi: Ecuador. Knotted net tote bags.

Lincoln green: Elizabethan (1550–1625 C.E.). Best green dye, done in Lincoln, United Kingdom.

Lindbergh jacket: United States of America. Man's short overcoat with a fitted waistband and wrists. Popularized by the American flier, Charles Lindbergh, in his 1927 flight across the Atlantic.

lindi: Norway. Old Norse word for belt.

lindiana: Crepe weave, worsted, and silk fabric.

lindraki: Lithuania. Skirt.

linea imperio: Spain. Empire line.

linea impero: Italy. Empire line.

linen: Fabric made from stem of flax plant.

līnen: United Kingdom. Old English word for linen.

Līnen: Germany. Linen.

linen mesh: Open mesh knit fabric used for infants' shirts. Often of linen and cotton blend.

linene: Cotton fabric finished to imitate linen.

linenette: Cotton fabric made to imitate linen.

líng: China. Damask silk.

ling tao: China. Qing dynasty (1644–1911 C.E.). From 1850 to 1911, man's small, plain, stiffened collar that was worn over the pu fu. Made of silk, velvet, or fur and was sometimes worn with the pi ling.

ling yue: China. Qing dynasty (1644–1911 C.E.). Gold, jeweled collar inlaid with pearls and coral. Worn by imperial ladies on very formal occasions.

linge: France. White linen, or linen underwear.

lingerie hat: Lace or embroidery hat.

lingerie hem: Tiny rolled hem.

Lingette: Trade name for soft, satin weave, mercerized sateen woven in stripes of self-color.

lingjié: China. Bow tie.

lingjin: China. Neckerchief.

lingkòu: China. Collar button; collar stud.

lingüeta: Portugal. Tongue of a shoe.

lingzi: China. Collar.

linha: Portugal. Sewing thread.

linho: Portugal. Linen.

lini: Lithuania. Flax.

linne: *See* lärft.

linned: *See* lœrred.

linnen: Holland. Linen.

linnseach: Ireland. Gaelic word for linen fabric.

linnseach thrusaidh: Ireland. Gaelic word for linen packing cloth.

lino: 1. *See* tela de lino. 2. *See* lienzo.

lino irlandes: Spain. Irish linen.

linon: 1. Greek (3000–100 B.C.E.). Flax. 2. France. Cotton lawn.

linsey: United Kingdom. Strong, coarse, durable fabric.

linsey-woolsey: Elizabethan (1550–1625 C.E.) to present. United Kingdom. Coarse linen and wool or cotton and wool fabric made in Linsey, Suffolk.

linstock: Elizabethan (1550–1625 C.E.). Pike with branches shaped like a bird's head on each side to hold lighted match.

lint: Holland. Ribbon.

linteum: *See* līnum.

Lintrock: Germany. Skirt with linen strings.

līnum: Roman (753 B.C.E.–323 C.E.). Flax.

Līnwāt: *See* Līnen.

liocadan: Ireland. Gaelic word for chin cloth.

līon: Ireland. Linen.

lionceau: Bustle (1865–1890 C.E.). France. In 1888, dark fawn color.

lìon-cinn: Ireland. Hairnet.

lipa bannang: Celebes. Dark cotton plaid sarong.

lipa garrusu: Celebes. Reserved for nobility, a cotton sarong that is starched and rubbed with seashell to produce a glaze.

lipine: 1. Samoa. Ribbon. 2. United States of America. Hawaii. Ribbon.

lipine silika: Samoa. Silk ribbon.

liripipe: Early Gothic (1200–1350 C.E.). Long streamer attached to a headdress. Name comes from liripium.

liripium: Early Gothic (1200–1350 C.E.). Hood with pointed top.

lisè: China. Chestnut color; maroon.

liseré: 1. Directoire and First Empire (1790–1815 C.E.). Weft thread in a fabric. 2. Brightly finished, split straw braid. 3. Cord or braid used as binding.

lisle: Fabric made of lisle yarn, a fine, hard-twisted cotton thread. Named for the Flemish town where first made.

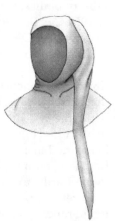

liripipe

Lisle lace: *See* Lille lace.

lisse: 1. Gay Nineties (1890–1900 C.E.). Introduced in 1894, uncrushable chiffon. 2. Filmy silk gauze.

lissto: Norway. Ribbon.

Lissue: United Kingdom. Trade name for fine mercerized cotton handkerchiefs.

lista: 1. Renaissance (1450–1550 C.E.). Italy. Strip of fabric applied to a garment to suggest a stripe. 2. Ecuador. Stripe.

listado: Bolivia. Striped.

listadoes: United Kingdom. Colored cotton fabric made for export.

listao ponch: Bolivia. Popular poncho with black or burgundy ground.

listónes: Mexico. Ribbons.

litewka: Directoire and First Empire (1790–1815 C.E.). Prussia. Winter overcoat.

litham: Bedouin. Distinguishing mark of dress, face-cloth worn by Tuareg women. Those of noble family wear black or blue and commoners wear white. Reveals the eyes, part of the forehead, and all of the cheeks.

little black dress: (1930–1940 C.E.). Integral part of every woman's wardrobe. Dress with simple lines, short or cap sleeves, full busted bodice, and slightly flared skirt suitable for day, cocktail, or theater wear. Introduced by Coco Chanel.

little girl collar: Narrow round collar, smaller than the Peter Pan collar.

little hennin: Renaissance (1450–1550 C.E.). Shortened cone headdress.

Little Lord Fauntleroy dress: Bustle (1865–1890 C.E.) to 20th century. Introduced in 1886, young boy's fashion made of a velvet tunic, velvet knickerbockers, and a wide lace collar, with a wide waist sash with the loose ends hanging to one hip.

little Venetian edging: Lace edging similar to Brussels edging.

Litze: *See* Tresse.

liùsb: Ireland. Woman's tattered skirt.

liver brown: Dull reddish brown.

livery lace: Early Georgian (1700–1750 C.E.) to Bustle (1865–1890 C.E.). Worsted braid woven with the household's design.

lizard: Leather from lizard skins.

lizhin: Navajo. Black.

ljubičast: Bosnia. Purple colored.

ljubičasta boja: Bosnia. Purple.

llacota: *See* llakolla.

llakolla: Bolivia and Peru. Large cloak.

llambu: Ecuador. Quichua term for a self-couching stitch.

llano: 1. Ecuador. Self-couching stitch. 2. Renaissance (1450–1550 C.E.). Spain. Plain.

llanque: Peru. A sandal.

llautu: 1. Ecuador and Guatemala. Incan headband worn wrapped around the head several times. 2. Peru. Fringed vicuna wool cord worn on the head as a sign of nobility in ancient times.

llawban: Wales. Felt.

llawto: Peru. Headband worn by the Inca emperor.

lledr: Wales. Leather.

lliain: Wales. Linen.

llica llica ahuaska: Peru. A thin fabric.

lliclla: 1. Bolivia. Cloak-like mantle. 2. Peru. Wrapping blanket.

lliglla: Ecuador. Quichua term for a woman's rectangular shawl worn pinned on the chest.

llijlla: Bolivia. Woman's mantle.

lliklla: 1. Ecuador. Aztec term for a shawl. 2. Bolivia and Peru. Worn as a shawl, two woven rectangles sewn together to form an almost square piece of fabric.

llin: Wales. Flax.

llodrau: Wales. Trousers.

llogell: Wales. Pocket.

lloq'e: Bolivia. Z-spun or S-spun yarn.

loafer: (1940–1950 C.E. to present). Slip-on leather shoe with a low heel. Based on the moccasin of American Indians.

loba: Renaissance (1450–1550 C.E.). Spain. Long, sleeveless garment.

lobas compridas: Renaissance (1450–1550 C.E.). Spain. Long gowns.

lobe: Spain. Wolf.

lobogó-s: Romania. Man's long, loose-sleeved shirt. Often has embroidered collar and cuffs.

lobster helmet: Charles I and the Commonwealth (1625–1660 C.E.). United Kingdom. Open helmet worn in English Civil War.

Lochstickerei: Germany. Broderie anglaise.

lockram: United Kingdom. Coarse, cheap linen fabric.

loden: 1. Thick, coarse, woolen, waterproof fabric. 2. Generally made in dark green or charcoal loden, a full-cut overcoat with a shoulder yoke.

loden green: Characteristic color of loden.

lodier: Charles I and the Commonwealth (1625–1660 C.E.) to Restoration (1660–1700 C.E.). Thick pad worn on the hips to increase their bulk.

lodix: Roman (753 B.C.E.–323 C.E.). Psila made in Verona.

lœder: Denmark and Germany. Leather.

loer: France. Breton for stocking.

lœrred: Denmark and Germany. Linen goods.

loft: The thickness and resilience of batting.

logia: Greece. Silk embroidery thread.

logwood brown: Reddish brown.

loincloth: Band of material worn around the hips like a short skirt.

lóipíní: *See* mairtíní.

lokalio: *See* lei kolona.

lokcan: Java. Silk slendang.

lole: United States of America. Hawaii. Generic term for clothes.

lole komo: *See* lole.

lole lauoho: United States of America. Hawaii. Sackcloth of hair.

lole moe po: United States of America. Hawaii. Literally "night-sleeping clothes," nightgown.

lole paikau: United States of America. Hawaii. Regalia.

lole wawae: United States of America. Hawaii. Trousers; pants.

lole wawae moe po: United States of America. Hawaii. Literally "trousers for night sleeping," pajamas.

lole wawae puha'uha'u: United States of America. Hawaii. Bloomers.

lomme: Denmark. Pocket.

lon: Vietnam. Stripe; chevron.

lona: Spain. Canvas; duck.

London cut: *See* drape cut.

London dust: Romantic (1815–1840 C.E.). French gray.

London Fog: Trademark name for classic poplin raincoat.

London mud: Romantic (1815–1840 C.E.). Dull dark brown.

London smoke: Romantic (1815–1840 C.E.). Gray.

long: China. Five-clawed dragon embroidery worn by the emperor, the empress's sons, princes, and some nobles.

long Duvallier: *See* Duvillier wig.

long johns: Slang term for thermal underwear.

long Melford: United Kingdom. Long stocking purse.

long pao: China. Qing dynasty (1644–1911 C.E.). Imperial ladies' semi-formal, official dress, a side-fastening robe embroidered with five-clawed dragons. Had long sleeves with horse hoof cuffs.

long-bào: Vietnam. Imperial robe.

longcloth: Fine, plain weave, cotton fabric with a soft finish.

long-con: Vietnam. Imperial robe.

long-drawers: India. Pajamas.

longline bra: Brassiere which reaches down to waist.

longotte: France. Coarse, stout, heavy, plain weave cotton fabric.

longyi: Burma. Sarong-like skirt.

Lonjumeau dress: Crinoline (1840–1865 C.E.). In 1858, walking dress with a Greek pattern of velvet or galloon. Had full sleeves. Corsage trimmed with bretelle.

lontra: Italy. Otter fur.

loo mask: Elizabethan (1550–1625 C.E.) to Late Georgian (1750–1790 C.E.). Half mask worn by women to cover only the upper part of the face.

looking glass silk: Gay Nineties (1890–1900 C.E.). Introduced in 1892, glacé fabric with trace of moiré.

loongee: Afghanistan. Blue silk and cotton blend handkerchief.

lopi: United States of America. Hawaii. Thread.

lopi ho'oholoholo: United States of America. Hawaii. Basting thread.

lopi huluhulu: United States of America. Hawaii. Worsted thread.

lopi kaholo: United States of America. Hawaii. Basting thread.

loraypu: Bolivia and Peru. Woven diamond pattern.

loretto: Elizabethan (1550–1625 C.E.) to Late Georgian (1750–1790 C.E.). Silk fabric used for waistcoats.

lorg-bheart: Ireland. Gaelic word for leg armor.

lorgnette: Small eyeglasses on ornamental handle.

lorica: Roman (753 B.C.E.–323 C.E.). Brass or bronze cuirass molded to fit the body following the line of the abdomen. Often decorated with metal reliefs and ornaments.

lorica hamata: Roman (753 B.C.E.–323 C.E.). Officer's lorica; mailed body armor.

lorica plumata: Roman (753 B.C.E.–323 C.E.). Mail made with very small scales on the surface. Uncommon.

lorica segmentata: Roman (753 B.C.E.–323 C.E.). Cuirass of iron strips articulated on leather straps. Had copper alloy fittings.

lorica squamata: Roman (753 B.C.E.–323 C.E.). Scale armor made from small metal sections wired to each other and sewn to fabric base.

loros: Byzantine and Romanesque (400–1200 C.E.). Scarf worn by the emperor.

lorum: Byzantine and Romanesque (400–1200 C.E.). Worn by Byzantine court from eighth to the 12th centuries, long narrow scarf, six to eight inches wide, and worn wrapped around the body. Evolved into long sash with head opening.

losse japon: Holland. Teagown.

lostenn: *See* broz.

lót: Vietnam. Garment lining.

loth: Ireland. Gaelic word for beard.

lotus flowers: *See* external high shoes.

lotus seeds: *See* external high shoes.

Lou Lura cloak: Crinoline (1840–1865 C.E.). In 1858, shawl with a double point in front. Bertha-style hood. Trimmed with velvet ribbon.

Louis XIII corsage: Crinoline (1840–1865 C.E.). United Kingdom. Introduced in 1850, woman's day corsage or a pelisse-robe that was open in the center to show a chemisette or cambric pleats or embroidery.

Louis XIV sleeve: Crinoline (1840–1865 C.E.). Introduced in 1850, sleeve that was widest at the bottom and trimmed with rows of fluted trim. Worn with undersleeve or engageante.

Louisa mantilla: Crinoline (1840–1865 C.E.). In 1853, mantilla with a circular back and scarf-shaped front. Flat collar. Edged with a very deep fringe.

Louise mantelet: Crinoline (1840–1865 C.E.). In 1854, loosely fitted silk mantelet trimmed with volants, embroidery, and fringe.

louisine: 1. Bustle (1865–1890 C.E.). Used in 1880s, very thin surah silk. 2. Lightweight silk fabric resembling taffeta.

lounge suit: Man's suit with broad shoulders, full chest, slim hips. Popular for business wear.

loup: 1. Half mask. 2. France. Wolf fur.

loutre: 1. Gay Nineties (1890–1900 C.E.). In 1892, a dark, rich brown. 2. France. Otter fur.

loutre de Sibérie: France. Kolinsky fur.

lovadi: India. Short woolen cadars.

lovat: Scotland. Heather color in tweeds.

love: Obsolete term for thin silk fabric.

love knot: Decorative knot of ribbon.

love lock: 1. Elizabethan (1550–1625 C.E.) to Charles I and the Commonwealth (1625–1660 C.E.). Curl of hair worn hanging over shoulder. 2. Late Georgian (1750–1790 C.E.). Long ringlet worn at right temple.

lovertje: Holland. Sequin.

lowell cloth: Crinoline (1840–1865 C.E.). United States of America. A cheap cloth made in Lowell, Massachusetts.

lower stocks: Elizabethan (1550–1625 C.E.). Silk or wool cloth stockings that showed beneath the upper stocks.

lowerings: Crinoline (1840–1865 C.E.). United States of America. Sacking cloth.

low-light: Darkest areas of color in a pattern.

lozi: Palestine. Almond-shaped pendant.

lu: China. Zhou dynasty. Shoes.

luan: China. Lesser phoenix.

lucco: Renaissance (1450–1550 C.E.). Italy. Originally from Florence, long gown that opened down the front and fastened at the neck. Slits on sides for arms. Worn by both genders.

Luchs: Germany. Lynx fur.

Lucia

Lucia: Crinoline (1840–1865 C.E.). A woman's decorative apron bordered with an accordion pleated ruffle and trimmed with knots of cording and tassels.

Lucie: Crinoline (1840–1865 C.E.). In 1856, woman's velvet mantle with guipure insertion and a flounce.

lucifer: Bustle (1865–1890 C.E.). 1. In 1869, deep wine color. 2. In 1880, color of brick dust.

luciole: Bustle (1865–1890 C.E.). France. In 1888, gendarme blue.

lucky bells: Gay Nineties (1890–1900 C.E.). In 1892, small bells worn on the chatelaine as part of Greek Revival.

luer: Norway. Caps.

lug: 1. Obsolete term for ear muff. 2. Dressy clothes.

lugadoo: India. Sari.

luhinga: East India. Petticoat.

lùireach: Ireland. Large cloak.

lùireach leathair: Ireland. Leather apron.

lùireach mhàilleach: Ireland. Coat of mail.

luirg-bheairt: Ireland. Gaelic word for leg armor.

lukini: United States of America. Hawaii. Perfume.

lukka: Lapland. Man's high-collared cape.

lulu ali'i: United States of America. Hawaii. Royal feather coat.

lumberjack: Short straight coat.

lumman: Byzantine and Romanesque (400–1200 C.E.). Ireland. Large mantle.

lunardi: *See* balloon hat.

lung p'ao: China. Manchu emperor's robe.

lungee: *See* lungi.

lunghi: Somalia. Length of cloth used as a man's robe.

lungi: India. Long cotton strip worn by Hindus as a loincloth, scarf, or turban.

lunula: Crescent shaped ornament in a necklace.

lupis: Finest grade of Manila hemp.

lupo: Italy. Wolf fur.

Lurex: Trade name for a glittery yarn made from aluminum foil coated with colored plastic film.

lurik: Indonesia. Checked-weave fabric.

luroi gà: Vietnam. Tongue of a shoe.

luroi-trai: Vietnam. Cap visor.

lurot: Vietnam. Turban silk.

lusekufte: Norway. Literally "flea-jerkin," black and white woven cardigan.

lustie-gallant: Elizabethan (1550–1625 C.E.). Light red.

lustre: Gay Nineties (1890–1900 C.E.). Mohair with shiny face.

lustrene: Thin, twill weave, cotton fabric.

lustrina: Guatemala. Mercerized embroidery cotton.

lustríña: Greece. Winter bridal shoes.

lustrine: *See* lustrene.

lustrini: Italy. Sequins.

lustring: *See* lutestring.

lutestring: Early Georgian (1700–1750 C.E.). Glossy silk fabric or a dress or ribbon made from this fabric.

lutherine: Early Georgian (1700–1750 C.E.) to Late Georgian (1750–1790 C.E.). Early form of lustre.

luto: 1. Spain. Mourning. 2. Bolivia. Mourning wear.

luto huipil: Guatemala. Mourning huipil.

luto poncho: Bolivia. Worn by widowers and funeral attendees, a poncho with very narrow woven bands and no ikat.

lutto: Italy. Mourning.

lu'u 'ili: United States of America. Hawaii. Tanner of skins and hides.

luva: Portugal. Glove.

Lycra: DuPont's version of a sturdy, nonrubber, elastic fiber. *See also* spandex.

lynx: Long-haired, gray to orange red, slightly mottled fur. Sometimes dyed black.

lyons loops: Bustle (1865–1890 C.E.). In 1865, velvet strips used to loop up woman's overskirt.

lyons velvet: Linen or cotton backed, stiff velvet with short pile.

M

M. B. waistcoat: *See* cassock vest.

ma canh gián: Vietnam. Dark brown.

mã da cam: Vietnam. Orange colored.

ma gua: 1. China. Qing dynasty (1644–1911 C.E.). Man's short, black satin jacket lined with blue silk. It had a small standing collar. Originally fastened to right, but later, closed in center front with five loops and buttons. 2. Crinoline (1840–1865 C.E.). United States of America. Chinese Hawaiian term for jacket of high quality black satin (din). It had sleeves that were 15 inches wide at the wrist and featured a narrow collar worn flapped down.

má hong: Vietnam. Rouge.

ma sa: Crinoline (1840–1865 C.E.). United States of America. Chinese Hawaiian term for a lightweight cotton fabric.

ma xue: China. Qing dynasty (1644–1911 C.E.). Mandarin man's black satin boots.

maa': Celebes. Sacred cloth.

ma'a taua: Samoa. Jewel.

maaporeth: Biblical (Unknown–30 C.E.). Hebrew napkin or apron.

mabiim: Zaire. Anklets.

mábù: China. 1. Gunny cloth; sackcloth; burlap. 2. Linen.

macabre: Romantic (1815–1840 C.E.). Introduced in 1832, light silk and wool combination textile figured in small patterns and edged with a Gothic border.

macacão: Portugal. Overalls.

macana: United Kingdom. Plain weave, soft, checked cotton fabric.

macaña: Ecuador. A warp-resist patterned shawl with fringed ends.

macaroni cravat: Late Georgian (1750–1790 C.E.). United Kingdom. Popular in 1770s, muslin cravat edged with lace and tied in bow under chin.

macaroni suit: Late Georgian (1750–1790 C.E.). Style of dress introduced by young men who had traveled in Italy. They founded the Macaroni Club in 1764 and popularized this style of dress in 1770s. The suit consisted of short, tight coat with very tight sleeves, tight striped trousers, dainty slippers, very small tricorne and frequently included nosegay of flowers worn on the left shoulder.

macassar oil: (1890–1900 C.E.). Man's hair oil.

macchavalaka: India. An antariya worn in a fish-tail style.

Macfarlane: Caped overcoat with slits in the sides to permit the hands to reach inside the garment for the pockets of the inner garment.

macica perlowa: Poland. Mother-of-pearl.

mackinaw: United States of America. Short, thick, double-breasted coat, frequently made of plaid wool. So named from its town of origin, Mackinac, Michigan.

mackinaw cloth: Heavy, durable fabric that is often double faced, with one side napped.

mackinaw hat: Coarse straw hat of varying shapes.

mackintosh: Romantic (1815–1840 C.E.) to present. United Kingdom. Introduced in 1836, short loose overcoat made of Mackintosh's patent India-rubber cloth. Came in drab or dark green.

maco: Long stranded cotton used in hosiery, underwear, etc.

ma-coual: Chinese. Wide sleeved jacket made of rich satin and worn by men of wealth.

macramé lace: Bulky knotted lace, usually fringed.

madagascar lace: Lace made in Madagascar with thread twisted into loops and scallops.

madapolam: Bustle (1865–1890 C.E.). In 1875, very heavy percale made with firm, hard twisted, round threads.

madas: *See* wata.

maddavina: India. A girdle with a pendant.

madder: Plant that yields bright red dye. *See also* garanza.

madeira embroidery: White embroidery on fine linen.

madow: Somalia. Black.

madras: India. Fine, hand-loomed cotton fabric with stripes or small woven designs.

madras gingham: United Kingdom. Brighter than usual madras.

madras muslin: Muslin with heavy figures, sometimes in color.

madras turban: Romantic (1815–1840 C.E.). United Kingdom. Introduced in 1819, women's turban made from a blue and orange Indian handkerchief.

madras work: Embroidery on bright silk handkerchiefs.

Madrid: Crinoline (1840–1865 C.E.). 1. In 1857, woman's cloth mantle with succession of capes trimmed with fringe. 2. In 1858, woman's hooded, circular silk mantle. Trimmed with mohair and chenille passementerie.

madvia: India. A stuff from Mandavi.

mae-dare: Japan. An apron.

mae-gami: Japan. A boy's forelock.

maekko moja: Korea. Straw hat.

mae-migoro: Japan. The front panel of a kimono.

mafors: Byzantine and Romanesque (400–1200 C.E.). Worn by women from sixth to 11th centuries, long narrow veil, generally covering the head and falling over the shoulders.

magatama: Japan. Comma-shaped beads.

mage: 1. Japan. Topknot. 2. Edo (1600–1867 C.E.). Japan. The main knot in a woman's hairstyle.

magenta: 1. Crinoline (1840–1865 C.E.). Introduced in 1860, first chemical dye to be used in dress material manufacture. Hailed as queen of colors. Named after battle of Magenta in 1859. 2. Vivid red purple color.

magiostrine: Italy. In Milan, the local name for a boater.

maglia piatta: Renaissance (1450–1550 C.E.). Italy. Ringed mail.

magliette: *See* punta.

magoja: Korea. Man's full-sleeved, dropped shoulder jacket.

mahadhana: India. A costly bleached silk.

maharatta: *See* Indian necktie.

maharmah: Turkey and Armenia. Muslin cloth worn over head and lower face by Turkish and Armenian women.

maheutres: Renaissance (1450–1550 C.E.). France. Cylindrical pads that were used to trim the shoulders of tight gippon sleeves to broaden the shoulders. Popular around 1450 C.E.

mahimudisahi: India. The finest muslin of Bengal origin.

mahmudi: India. Fine muslin.

mahogany: Dark red brown.

mahoîtres: Early Gothic (1200–1350 C.E.). France. Shoulder padding in gown or jacket.

mahrameh: Palestine. Christian man's red turban.

mahyu-salu: India. A red cloth from Mau.

mai: New Zealand. Maori. A rough, coarse flax cloak.

mai muka: Australia. Maori general term for all inner garments.

maiden hair: Elizabethan (1550–1625 C.E.). Bright tan.

maide's blush: Elizabethan (1550–1625 C.E.). Rose color.

mail: Flexible, mesh of interlocking metal rings.

mail coach: Romantic (1815–1840 C.E.). Very large neckcloth folded loosely around neck and tied in front. Usually white, often a cashmere shawl. Popular with dandies.

màilleach: Ireland. Armor.

màilleag: Ireland. Earring.

mailles carées: France. Square meshes as in Valenciennes lace.

maillot: Tightly fitted, one-piece swimsuit.

màineag: Ireland. Glove.

mainfaire: Renaissance (1450–1550 C.E.). Right-handed gauntlet.

Maintenon cloak: Crinoline (1840–1865 C.E.). United Kingdom. In 1860s, oversized black velvet cloak with wide sleeves enjoyed period of popularity. It was trimmed with deep pleated flounce covered in black guipure lace.

Maintenon corsage: Crinoline (1840–1865 C.E.). Close-fitting evening bodice trimmed with ribbon knots down center front and had lace fall at waist. Popular from 1839 through 1840s.

mairtíní: Renaissance. Ireland. Footless stockings.

mais: Bustle (1865–1890 C.E.). France. In 1888, straw color.

maístra: Greece. Woman who makes embroidery.

maiwai: Japan. Fisherman's ceremonial jacket.

maize: Soft yellow.

majestueuse: Patch in the center of the forehead.

majica: *See* podkošulja.

majithi: India. The color magenta.

major wig: Late Georgian (1750–1790 C.E.). United Kingdom. Military style of wig worn by male civilians. It had a toupee and two corkscrew curls tied at the nape of the neck where it forms a double queue.

majtki: Poland. Woman's panties.

makabala: India. Velvet.

makalena: United States of America. Hawaii. Fine muslin cloth.

makalena pu'u: United States of America. Hawaii. Dotted swiss cloth.

makarika: India. A hair ornament in the shape of a fish-crocodile.

makhi: India. Literally "fly," a small cross-shaped tattoo on a woman's cheek.

makhila: *See* pennbazh.

maki: *See* runa.

maki punta: Ecuador. A sleeve ruffle.

maki watana: Ecuador. A woman's wrist wrap.

makila: United States of America. Hawaii. Maui word for needle.

maku'a: United States of America. Hawaii. 1, Dark brown. 2. Topknot of hair.

maku'e: *See* maku'a.

mālā: 1. India. Garland of flowers. 2. Necklace of beads or jewels or gold.

mala: Portugal. Handbag.

mālāband: India. Chain of pearls with pendants.

malabar: Cotton handkerchief printed in bright colors and designs.

malabary: Madagascar. Man's long robe.

malacateras: Mexico. Women who spin yarn for a living.

Malacca cane: Early Georgian (1700–1750 C.E.) to Late Georgian (1750–1790 C.E.). Cane made from mottled or clouded stem of a malacca palm.

malafa: Nigeria. Split palm leaf sun hat with a wide brim and a conical crown.

malai: India. A gold coin necklace from southern India.

malak: Palestine. Most expensive silk fabric made in this country.

malak abu wardeh: Palestine. Expensive silk fabric with red floral pattern.

malamala sahi: India. The finest quality Bengal muslin.

malas: Palestine. Loose weave striped fabric.

malausiu: India. A silk stuff or damask from Malaya.

maldā: Ethiopia. Armlet worn only by those who have killed five men, five buffaloes, and five lions.

male: Norway. Eyelet; the plural is maler.

malines: 1. Bustle (1865–1890 C.E.). Introduced in 1885, closely woven canvas, appearing to be inter-woven. 2. Mechlin type lace made in Malines, Belgium.

malir: India. A cotton cloth woven on narrow looms and block printed in indigo blue.

maljor: Late Gothic (1350–1450 C.E.) to Renaissance (1450–1550 C.E.). Sweden. Lacing rings attached to a bodice. A ribbon or lace runs through the rings to hold the garment closed.

malle-molle: *See* malmal.

mallow-color: Crinoline (1840–1865 C.E.). In 1862, light shade of mauve.

malmal: India. Muslin.

malo: United States of America (Hawaii) and Samoa. Girdle or loincloth. Originally made of tapa cloth, now made of brightly dyed cotton.

malo kai: United States of America. Hawaii. Loincloth worn in the sea.

malo wai: United States of America. Hawaii. Loincloth wet in fresh water. It is taboo to wear this in the presence of a chief.

malong: Philippine Islands. Woman's sarong.

malong andon: Philippine Islands. Sarong ornamented with ikat patterns.

malong pandi: Philippine Islands. Man's sarong with horizontal stripes.

Maltese embroidery: Style of embroidery using small tassels worked on a surface of heavy material.

Maltese lace: 1. Bobbin lace similar to Mechlin and Val laces. 2. Guipure lace with simple geometric design featuring Maltese cross and dots.

malvenfarbig: *See* hellviolet.

malwa: Palestine. Silver wire bracelet.

malya: *See* mala.

mama chumbi: Ecuador and Guatemala. Literally "mother belt," a wide underbelt.

mama'o: United States of America. Hawaii. Greenish; light green.

mamelieres: Early Gothic (1200–1350 C.E.). Round steel armor plates covering the breasts.

mamelouk sleeve: Crinoline (1840-1864 C.E.). Sleeve made of several puffs from the shoulder to the wrist. Puffs were formed by tying ribbons along the arm.

mameluck: Directoire and First Empire (1790–1815 C.E.). Douillette with wide, pleated back.

mamelouk sleeve

mameluke: 1. Directoire and First Empire (1790–1815 C.E.). United States of America. Eastern style wrap fashionable in 1806. It hung from the shoulders in folds down the back. 2. Romantic (1815–1840 C.E.). Ladies' sleeve cut full to the wrist.

mameluke robe: Directoire and First Empire (1790–1815 C.E.). United States of America. First appearing in 1806, a trained full loose gown.

mameluke turban: Directoire and First Empire (1790–1815 C.E.). Introduced in 1804, a turban of white satin trimmed with large white feather.

mame-shibori: Japan. Early tie-dyeing which produced bean-shaped dots.

mamillare: *See* strophion.

mammelieres: Early Gothic (1200–1350 C.E.). Steel rondels that were fastened on either side of the breastplate. Chains hung from them to secure the helmet, sword, or misericorde.

mamoodie: *See* mahmudi.

manaeka: New Zealand. Maori. A showy timu.

manag: Ireland. Gaelic word for glove or mitten.

mañanita: Spain. Bedjacket.

mā-não: Vietnam. Agate.

manasasa: India. A fine quality muslin.

manavaka: India. Necklace of twenty strings of pearls.

mancebo: Portugal. Clothes hanger.

manche: France. Sleeve.

manche à gigot: France. Puffed sleeve.

mancheron: Renaissance (1450–1550 C.E.). Half sleeve of silk or velvet seen under the wide sleeves of gowns and houppelandes.

manchester: Holland. Corduroy.

Manchester velvet: Early Georgian (1700–1750 C.E.) to Late Georgian (1750–1790 C.E.). Cotton velvet.

manchetknoop: Holland. Cufflink.

manchette: France. Cuff or wristband.

manchette de cour: Directoire and First Empire (1790–1815 C.E.). French style sleeve made with English or alençon lace. Attached to dress with ribbon that matched color from the hairpiece. First introduced in 1793.

manchettes: Late Georgian (1750–1790 C.E.). Gauze or lace armbands set in between puffs and worn with gowns.

manchira: India. Pearl fringed fabric.

Manchu headdress: China. Woman's hairstyle where hair is set high on head and shaped into two wings at sides which are often glued into place and decorated with gems, coins, etc.

manchurian ermine: China. Fur of weasel.

mandā paradiyā: India. Sari with circular pattern on the border.

mandalia: India. A stuff from Mandalipathaka.

mandarin: Bustle (1865–1890 C.E.). 1. In 1873, Chinese blue. 2. In 1877, bright green.

mandarin coat: China. Long embroidered coat worn by mandarins.

mandarin collar: Narrow standing collar on fitted neckline.

mandarin collar

mandarin color: Orange or reddish yellow.

Mandarin hat: Crinoline (1840–1865 C.E.). United Kingdom. Ladies' black velvet porkpie hat trimmed with feathers on the back of the crown. Named for the French-British war with China.

mandarin sleeve: Kimono type sleeve.

mandel: India. 1. A round cap, often embroidered with gold and seed pearls. 2. A turban woven with silk and gold thread. 3. A woolen muffler worn rolled around the head like a turban.

Mandel: United States of America. Amish woman's long outer garment, like an overcoat.

mandeville: Charles I and the Commonwealth. Mandilion.

mandil: *See* sharb.

mandīl: Arabia. Common head veil.

mandiléño: Greece. Fine silk material.

mandili: Greece. Women's block printed scarves.

mandilion: Elizabethan (1550–1625 C.E.). Man's loose, hip-length jacket with fitted sleeves and open side seams. Often worn colley-westonward.

mandyas: Long outer garment similar to the cope. Worn by the clergy in the Eastern Church.

maneg: 1. Wales. Glove. 2. France. Breton for glove.

manege averte: France. Open ended sleeves.

manequim: Portugal. Tailor's dummy.

maneras: Renaissance (1450–1550 C.E.). Spain. Arm slits in a garment.

mang: China. Four-clawed dragon embroidery worn by lesser princes, nobles, and senior court officials in the Ming dynasty (1368–1644 C.E.).

mang ao: China. Qing dynasty (1644–1911 C.E.). Han woman's loose-fitting jacket. It had a plain round neck, bell sleeves, and a side opening. Usually red or blue.

mang chu: China. Qing dynasty (1644–1911 C.E.). Han woman's red or green silk skirt embroidered with dragons and phoenixes. First worn on the wedding day.

mang pao: China. Qing dynasty (1644–1911 C.E.). Four-clawed dragon long pao worn by noblewomen and officials' wives.

manga: 1. Mexico. Garment similar to the poncho; woven from wool with an opening for the head. Usually trimmed in velvet. 2. Portugal and Spain. Sleeve.

manga ahuecada: Spain. Puffed sleeve.

manga caída: Spain. Cap sleeve.

manga dolman: Spain. Dolman sleeve.

manga gitana: Spain. Magyar sleeve.

manga kimono: Spain. Kimono sleeve.

manga murciélago: Spain. Batwing sleeve.

manga raglán: Spain. Raglan sleeve.

mangaeka: *See* manaeka.

mangamelai: India. From southern India, a gold coin necklace set with gems.

mangas perdidas: Portugal. Hanging sleeve.

mangt'o: Korea. Mantle.

mang-tô: Vietnam. Topcoat.

manguito: Portugal. Mitten.

mangulsutra: India. A black and gold necklace.

mani: India. A pearl.

mani nupura: India. Anklets of jeweled beads.

maniakes: Byzantine and Romanesque (400–1200 C.E.). Collar worn by emperors.

manica: Roman (753 B.C.E.–323 C.E.). 1. Articulated armguard. 2. Italy. Long sleeve of a tunic. The sleeve covered the hand.

manica a buffo: Italy. Puffed sleeve.

maniche á comeo: Renaissance (1450–1550 C.E.). Italy. Women's elbow-length sleeves.

manicísco: Greece. Elbow-length sleeved garment worn under the anterí.

manifer: *See* mainfaire.

manik ata: Indonesia. Woman's necklace of gold and blood coral worn by the Sa'dan-Toraja.

manik barata: Indonesia. Sa'dan-Toraja black bead.

manik bura bura: Indonesia. Sa'dan-Toraja white bead.

manik kalaa': Indonesia. Sa'dan-Toraja pink bead.

manik sekke': Indonesia. Sa'dan-Toraja light blue bead.

manik tai anda': Indonesia. Sa'dan-Toraja shiny green bead.

manik tinggi: Indonesia. Sa'dan-Toraja dark red bead.

mani-karnika: India. Glass ear-ornaments.

manikéttia: Greece. Pair of cuffs.

mani-kundala: India. Earring inset with jewels.

Manila hemp: *See* abaca.

manilha: Portugal. Bracelet; armlet.

manilla: 1. Gay Nineties (1890–1900 C.E.). In 1897, yellowish beige. 2. Ecuador and Guatemala. Bracelet; arm wrap.

manilla brown: Directoire and First Empire (1790–1815 C.E.). Introduced in 1811, soft light shade, similar in color to hemp.

manillas: Ecuador. Bracelets.

maninupura: India. Anklet of precious stones.

maniple: Liturgical costume. 1. Ornamental handkerchief carried in the hand in the celebration of Mass. 2. Narrow band of fabric three feet long and decorated with three crosses. Worn over the left arm by priests at Mass.

manitergium: Roman (753 B.C.E.–323 C.E.). Handkerchief.

manivalaya: India. Bracelet made of conch shells.

manjira: India. 1. A stuff decorated with flowers. 2. Hollow anklets which make a tinkling sound as they move.

Manon robe: Crinoline (1840–1865 C.E.). United Kingdom. Worn from 1850 to 1867, this garment had a front that was cut in one piece and a pleat in the back, similar to the Watteau pleat, running from under the collar to the hem.

manopla: Renaissance (1450–1550 C.E.). Spain. Gauntlet.

manople: Renaissance (1450–1550 C.E.). Italy. Gauntlet.

manquitos: Peru. Oversleeves and stockings knitted with colored wool.

mant: Obsolete word for the mantilla.

manta: 1. Rough cotton cloth worn by lower classes in South America. Also refers to garments made from this fabric. 2. Guatemala. Plain white homespun cloth. 3. Ecuador and Portugal. Shawl. *See also* chale. 4. Romania. Cloak. 5. *See* phullu.

mantal: Ireland. Gaelic word for mantle.

Mantal: *See* Hachul.

mantaqa: Arabia. Sword belt.

mante: Restoration (1660–1700 C.E.). Short cape edged with lace ruffles and worn by women of high rank at court.

manteau: 1. Charles I and the Commonwealth (1625–1660 C.E.). Formal women's gown. 2. Restoration (1660–1700 C.E.). Loose, coat-like robe worn as negligee. Worn by women. 3. Restoration (1660–1700 C.E.). Woman's formal gown. Overskirt was looped back and held in place with ribbon bows. It had a train whose length determined the wearer's social position. Train was worn carried over the left arm, except in the presence of royalty, when it trained on the ground. 4. France. Cloak.

manteau à la cavaliere: Late Georgian (1750–1790 C.E.). Circular cape.

manteau à l'italienne: *See* manteau à la cavaliere.

manteau de cocher: Bustle (1865–1890 C.E.). In 1874, coachman's cape; Worth's polonaise with two pelerines.

mantee: Early Georgian (1700–1750 C.E.). Woman's sleeved coat worn open to show the stomacher and petticoat beneath it.

manteel: Early Georgian (1700–1750 C.E.). United Kingdom. Worn from 1730s to 1750s, scarf-like cape with long ends hanging in front and a hood in the back.

mantel: 1. Holland. Cloak. 2. *See* kappa. 3. *See* cloke.

Mantel: Germany. Cloak.

mantelet: Small mantle or short cloak.

mantelet à la grand mère: Crinoline (1840–1865 C.E.). Revived mantelet style trimmed with quillings of brocaded ribbon.

mantelet au lever de l'aurore: Late Georgian (1750–1790 C.E.). France. Short mantle for morning wear.

mantelet Isabelle: Crinoline (1840–1865 C.E.). Introduced in 1862, black silk mantelet with deep green and black fringe.

mantelette: Romantic (1815–1840 C.E.). Ladies' shaped shawl that fit the back of the body much like a jacket and reached to the knees in front.

manteline: Renaissance (1450–1550 C.E.). Short parade garment worn over the armor. Commonly decorated. Sometimes had a hood.

mantell: 1. Wales. Cloak. 2. France. Breton for cloak.

mantelletta: Short sleeveless robe of silk or wool worn by the clergy of the Roman Catholic Church.

mantellina: Renaissance (1450–1550 C.E.). Hood.

mantello: Italy. Cloak.

mantilla: Elizabethan (1550–1625 C.E.). Spain. Smaller version of the manto. Covered only head and shoulders.

mantille: Holland. Mantilla.

mantita: Bolivia. Extremely small mantle.

mantle: Early Georgian (1700–1750 C.E.). Long, winter version of the mante that buttoned down the front.

mantle and ring: Early Gothic (1200–1350 C.E.). Cloak and ring which were worn with the veil as a religious habit by widows.

mantle lace: Heavy, tasseled cord used in English ceremonial dress.

mantling: Early Georgian (1700–1750 C.E.). Rough blue check cotton cloth used in making aprons.

manto: 1. Renaissance (1450–1550 C.E.). Spain. Large shawl worn by women and young girls to cover the head, allowing only one eye to show. 2. Spain. Cloak.

manto de oraciones: Spain. Praying shawl.

manto de pescoço: Portugal. Plaid.

manto militar: Portugal. Tabard.

mantón de mantilla: Large embroidered shawl of silk crepe made in China and shipped to Spain where a deep fringe is added.

mantones de Manila: Ecuador. Shawls imported from the Far East via the Manila galleon trade.

mantua: 1. Early Georgian (1700–1750 C.E.). Formal gown with formal drapery in the back. Worn over boned bodice and with elaborate skirt. Popular in United Kingdom longer than elsewhere. 2. Early Georgian (1700–1750 C.E.) to Late Georgian (1750–1790 C.E.). A heavyweight silk, dyed black for mourning.

Mantua hose: Knitted silk stockings made in Mantua, Italy.

mantua maker: Charles I and the Commonwealth (1625–1660 C.E.) to Late Georgian (1750–1790 C.E.). Mantua tailor or dressmaker.

mantua marguerite: Crinoline (1840–1865 C.E.). France. Woman's velvet mantua in shawl shape. Trimmed with three rows of black lace headed with narrow silk braid.

mantua woman: Charles I and the Commonwealth (1625–1660 C.E.) to Late Georgian (1750–1790 C.E.). Mantua dressmaker.

mănuşă: Romania. Glove.

Manx plaid: Isle of Man. Small check pattern in scarlet and bright blue.

Mao jacket: *See* Nehru jacket.

máobù: China. Coarse cotton fabric.

máogé: China. Poplin.

màokuir: China. Skullcap.

maolag: Ireland. Gaelic word for footless stockings.

máolàio: China. Woolen fabric.

máolán: China. Darkish blue.

maolas: Ireland. Gaelic word for sandal.

maolua: United States of America. Hawaii. Kind of red tapa.

ma'oma'o: United States of America. Hawaii. 1. Green. 2. Green tapa.

máoyi: China. Woolen sweater.

máozhipin: China. Wool fabric.

màozi: China. Generic term for a hat.

mapache: Spain. Raccoon.

mapel: Zaire. Man's skirt.

mapoto: Transvaal. Ndebele wife's beaded rectangular apron (17-1/4 inches by 23-1/2 inches).

mappa: Roman (753 B.C.E.–323 C.E.). Combination handkerchief and washcloth. Also used to give signals at games.

mappelana: Italy. Woman's headdress.

mappula: *See* mappa.

maquillage: France. Makeup.

máquina de gasa: Mexico. Miniature sewing machine.

marabou: (20th century). 1. Feather trim made from feather of a stork. 2. Raw silk.

marabout: 1. Bustle (1865–1890 C.E.). Introduced in 1877, woolen, soft to the touch but looked rough. 2. Delicate, thin silk fabric.

marabout feathers: Directoire and First Empire (1790–1815 C.E.). Soft downy feathers from the tail and underside of the wings of the marabout stork. Very popular form of trim.

marabout silk: Thrown silk fabric.

marabù: Italy and Spain. Marabout.

Marabu: Germany. Marabout.

marafiya: Nigeria. Tall, domed cap made from a flour bag.

marakatajadara: India. An emerald green silk fabric.

marama: 1. Romania. Worn by matrons, long veil of thin white cotton or silk, embroidered and sequined, wound tightly around the head with an end hanging free at the back. 2. Bosnia. Scarf.

maramica: Croatia and Serbia. Handkerchief.

marate: Peru. Thick, hard sash.

marau: Borneo. Large cane.

marble silk: Silk fabric with mottled surface.

marbrinus: Late Gothic (1350–1450 C.E.). Worsted fabric woven with pale warp and colored weft that imitates marble.

marcasite: Glittering metal, looking like cut steel, used for jewelry.

marcel wave: (20th century). Type of artificial waving of the hair introduced by Marcel of France in 1907. Process was referred to as marcelling.

marcela: Spain. Marcella.

marceline: Directoire and First Empire (1790–1815 C.E.). Soft silk fabric similar to a light taffeta. Used for dresses.

marcella: Twilled cotton or linen, used for waistcoats.

marcelling: *See* marcel wave.

marchisite: Iron pyrites facet-cut and set in jewelry to resemble diamond cluster jewelry.

Marder: Germany. Marten fur.

marechal: Scent or perfume or scented hair powder.

marfil: Spain. Ivory color.

marfim: Portugal. Ivory.

Margaret of Valois: Crinoline (1840–1865 C.E.). Crinoline (1840–1865 C.E.). In 1856, woman's wide sleeve gathered at the top and bottom. Cap at top and deep cuff at the wrist.

margarita: Roman (753 B.C.E.–323 C.E.). A pearl.

margarite: Italy. A thin bead.

margaritte: Renaissance (1450–1550 C.E.). Spain. Large pearl.

margine: Lithuania. 1. Cloth of many colors. 2. Skirt.

Margot lace: Fancy fragile lace with a machine-embroidered design in a heavy cotton thread on a lightweight silk net.

marguerite: (19th century). Plastroned waistband or belt that laced in front and had tabs in the back.

Marguerite silk: Crinoline (1840–1865 C.E.). In 1861, new silk fabric.

mariage: France. Wedding.

Marian: Crinoline (1840–1865 C.E.). In 1856, woman's cloth travelling wrap that draped left over right. Trimmed with three rows of velvet ribbon and a mixed color fringe.

Marie Anglais bonnet: Bustle (1865–1890 C.E.). United Kingdom. Ladies' hat similar to a child's sailor hat although it was ornamented with flowers, feathers, and ribbon. Worn at back of the head and tied under the chin with a bow.

Marie Antoinette fichu: Crinoline (1840–1865 C.E.). 1. In 1856, woman's white fichu. 2. In 1859, white net fichu trimmed with puffings of tulle and narrow black or pink satin ribbon. Outer edges trimmed with three-inch-wide blonde.

Marie sleeve: Romantic (1815–1840 C.E.). Full sleeve that tied at intervals and at wrist to form puffs. Revived in 1872 as Marie-Antoinette sleeve.

Marie Stuart bodice: Romantic (1815–1840 C.E.). Introduced in 1828, tight evening bodice boned down front to a deep point.

Marie Stuart bonnet: Romantic (1815–1840 C.E.) to Bustle (1865–1890 C.E.). Worn from 1820s to around 1870, bonnet with brim that dipped in center over forehead. Particularly popular with widows. For dress occasions, made of white satin and trimmed with lace and colored ribbons.

Marie Stuart hat: Crinoline (1840–1865 C.E.). Introduced in 1849, evening dress hat of tulle with stiff brim that curled up with dip in the center of the forehead.

Marie-Antoinette sleeve: *See* Marie sleeve.

Marie-Louise blue: Crinoline (1840–1865 C.E.). Shade of light blue named for Empress.

marik: Borneo. Bead.

marinara: Italy. Sailor suit.

marine blue: Dark, grayed green blue color.

marineblauw: Holland. Navy blue.

marinera: Spain. Sailor suit.

mariner's cuff: Late Georgian (1750–1790 C.E.). United Kingdom. Small round cuff that had a vertical scalloped flap crossing it. Generally had three or four buttons.

marinière: France. Sailor suit.

marino faliero sleeve: Romantic (1815–1840 C.E.). Popular from 1830 to 1835, ladies' large hanging sleeve caught in at the elbow by a ribbon band. Named for the Byron drama of that name.

Marion: Crinoline (1840–1865 C.E.). In 1856, woman's velvet shawl trimmed with broad velvet ruffle with vandyked edge.

mariposa: Bustle (1865–1890 C.E.). 1. Introduced in 1872, washing sateen with stripes in plain and dotted fabric. 2. Woman's decorative triangular head scarf of mariposa trimmed with a deep fall of lace.

Mark of the Beast: *See* cassock vest.

Marlborough hat: Bustle (1865–1890 C.E.). United Kingdom. Large flat hat of lace and Tuscan straw. Trimmed with long shaded feathers and worn slightly to one side. Introduced in 1882.

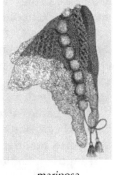

mariposa

marli: Fine net similar to tulle.

marlota: 1. Renaissance (1450–1550 C.E.). Spain. Loose garment worn in place of a jerkin. 2. Arabia. Sleeved outer garment.

marlotte: Renaissance (1450–1550 C.E.). Women's sleeved mantle worn open in the front. Fell in folds down the back. Had very short, puffed sleeves and standing collar. *See also* simarra.

marmot: Inexpensive, short thick fur. Used in imitation of mink.

marmota: Spain. Marmot.

marmotta: Italy. Raccoon fur.

marmotte: 1. Bustle (1865–1890 C.E.). In 1872, dark shade of ashes of roses. 2. France. Marmot.

marmotte bonnet: Romantic (1815–1840 C.E.). United Kingdom. Introduced in 1832, very small bonnet with narrow brim in the front.

marmotte cap: Romantic (1815–1840 C.E.). United Kingdom. Introduced in 1833, triangle of fabric worn far back on the head and tied under the chin. Worn during the day indoors.

maro: 1. New Zealand. Maori. An apron. 2. Polynesia. A loin girdle.

maro huka: New Zealand. Maori. Priest's flax fiber apron.

maro kaakaapoo: New Zealand. Maori. Apron of kaakaapoo (*Strigops habroptilus*).

maro kaukau: New Zealand. Maori. Apron made of rushes worn by women when they gather shellfish.

maro kopua: New Zealand. Maori. A triangular apron or girdle worn by girls of good families. It is made of finely dressed flax fiber.

maro kura: New Zealand. Maori. Apron covered with feathers of parrots and trimmed with pieces of shell.

maro kuta: New Zealand. Maori. A girl's apron made of grass.

maro waero: New Zealand. Maori. Apron trimmed with white dog hair.

maro waiapu: New Zealand. Maori. A woven apron ornamented with thrums.

marocain: Ribbed silk or wool crepe used for dress and dressmaker suits.

marocain crepe: Cross-ribbed crepe of wool, cotton, or silk.

maroon: Yellowish red.

marquis: Ladies' tricorne.

marquise: Crinoline (1840–1865 C.E.). Woman's morning slipper.

Marquise: Crinoline (1840–1865 C.E.). In 1854, silk pelisse with fitted body. Had lace flounce and three rows of goffered ribbon at the hem and around the yoke.

marquise bodice: Bustle (1865–1890 C.E.). United Kingdom. Ladies' evening bodice with frilled edge. Front was heart shaped.

marquise mantle: Romantic (1815–1845 C.E.). United Kingdom. Ladies' short mantlet of taffeta with short sleeves. Worn fitted to the waist in the back. Often trimmed with flounces and lace.

marquisette: Silk, cotton, rayon, or wool, lightweight, openwork fabric of the leno weave. Used for curtains and dresses.

marquisetto beard: Renaissance (1450–1550 C.E.). United Kingdom. Man's close-trimmed beard.

marramas: In 14th century, cloth of gold, made in the Orient. Principally used for ecclesiastical ornament.

marrom: Portugal. Brown.

marron: Spain. Maroon.

marseilles: France. Sturdy cotton fabric similar to piqué. Looks like quilted fabric. Used for bedspreads and drapery. Originally made in Marseilles, France.

Marseilles embroidery: Early Georgian (1700–1750 C.E.). France. All white needlework in which layers of fabric are stuffed and embroidered, the ground covered in little knots.

marseilles quilting: Romantic (1815–1840 C.E.). United States of America. Embossed, white woven cotton.

marsella: Heavy, bleached, twill weave, linen fabric.

marshmellow: Romantic (1815–1840 C.E.). United Kingdom. Soft rose color.

marsina: Late Georgian (1750–1790 C.E.). Italy. Man's tail coat.

marška: Lithuania. Linen cloth; fishing net.

maršliniai: Lithuania. Shirt.

marta: 1. Portugal. Sable. 2. Spain. Marten fur; squirrel belly fur.

marta cebellina: Spain. Sable.

marta comú: Spain. Marten.

marteaux: Bustle (1865–1890 C.E.). In 1873, heavy folds of hair held up by a comb.

marten: Soft, medium-weight fur from the weasel (*Martes martes*).

martingale belt: (1940–1950 C.E.). Half belt on back of a jacket or coat.

martingale breeches: Renaissance (1450–1550 C.E.) to Elizabethan (1550–1625 C.E.). United Kingdom. Breeches that had a moveable panel between the legs that was held to the belt with buttons and points.

martinpècheur: Bustle (1865–1890 C.E.). In 1872, kingfisher color.

martō: Ethiopia. Cotton loincloths.

martora: Italy. Marten fur.

martre: France. Marten.

martre zibeline: France. Sable.

marumage: Edo (1600–1867 C.E.). Japan. Literally "round chignon," a married woman's hairstyle.

maru-obi: Japan. A wide obi.

Mary Queen of Scots cap: Late Georgian (1750–1790 C.E.). United Kingdom. Indoor cap similar in line to that was popularized by Mary, Queen of Scots. Made of black cypress or gauze and was edged in French beads.

Mary Stuart: Crinoline (1840–1865 C.E.). In 1855, velvet and moiré antique cloak that was pleated in back to the yoke. Trimmed with watered braid.

Mary Stuart cap: Renaissance (1450–1550 C.E.). Heart-shaped cap popularized by Mary Stuart.

maryland: Bustle (1865–1890 C.E.). In 1873, nutria.

marynarka: Poland. Man's coat. *See also* kurtka.

mascaipacha: Peru. Red fringe on Inca man's headband.

mascaypacha: Peru. Royal Incan tassel of fine red wool woven into the llautu and worn in the middle of the forehead.

mascherata: Italy. Fancy dress.

masher: Bustle (1865–1890 C.E.). United Kingdom. Popular name for dandy of the period in 1880s and 1890s.

masher collar: Bustle (1865–1890 C.E.) to 1910s. United Kingdom. Very tall collar popularized by the masher in the 1880s and 1890s.

masher dust wrap: Bustle (1865–1890 C.E.). United Kingdom. Close-fitting Inverness with large arms-eyes and a cape. Worn by the mashers in 1880s.

mashi: India. Grass green.

mashru: Mixed fabric of silk and cotton. Originally worn only by Muslims. Named for the Arabic word for lawful because the Muslims are not allowed to wear pure silk while at prayer.

mashru sha'ri: India. A silk and goat hair blend fabric.

maskel lace: Late Gothic (1350–1450 C.E.) to Renaissance (1450–1550 C.E.). Spotted net lace.

maskotka: Poland. Amulet.

masla: *See* natiyo.

maspilli: *See* bottoni.

massereen blue: Late Georgian (1750–1790 C.E.). Dark purple.

Masulipatam chintz: Elizabethan (1550–1625 C.E.). A chintz made with a superior red dye.

mat kid: Fine kid leather finished to smooth, matte surface.

mat mii: Thailand. Weft ikat.

mata tioata: Samoa. Eyeglasses.

matab: Abyssinia. A silken cord carrying an amulet or charm. It is worn around the neck.

matara: Dark brown shade of dye used for seal fur.

mătase: Romania. Silk.

matelasé: Spain. Matelasse.

matelassé: 1. Bustle (1865–1890 C.E.). France. Introduced in 1874, firm silk woven to resemble quilting. 2. Fabric with woven designs in quilted effect. Made of wool, silk, rayon, or various blends. Quilting is stitched or embossed, but not woven in.

māteria: Roman (753 B.C.E.–323 C.E.). Material.

materija: *See* tkan'.

Mathilde: Directoire and First Empire (1790–1815 C.E.). Inspired by 1804–1805 exhibition of Queen Mathilde's Tapestry, the Bayeaux Tapestry; broad vertical band of embroidery popular on women's dress fronts. Later included band of embroidery around the hem of the dress and was referred to as inverted T or inverted Y.

Mathilde mantilla: Crinoline (1840–1865 C.E.). In 1859, brown or chocolate cloth mantilla trimmed with plaid velvet. Closed with mother-of-pearl buttons.

matinée: Crinoline (1840–1865 C.E.). United Kingdom. 1. Introduced in 1851, hooded pardessus worn outdoors over morning dress. Commonly made of jaconet or muslin. 2. Short breakfast robe. Opened in front and tied at the waist in a bow. It had a muslin flounce at the bottom hem and elbow. Hooded with a vandyked frill.

Matinee skirt: Crinoline (1840–1865 C.E.). In 1859, hooped underskirt with removable hoops.

Matrosenanzug: Germany. Sailor suit.

matschigote': Algonquin blanket worn as a cape.

matsuinui: Japan. Backstitched outline on embroidery.

matsu-nori: Japan. Paste used for studio dyed Yuzen.

matt stitch: Old term for surface embroidery done with satin stitches.

mattal: *See* lenn.

matte jersey: Dull tricot made of fine crepe yarns.

matting oxford: Oxford shirting with small basket weaves.

māu da giòi: Vietnam. Azure blue.

māu do: Vietnam. Gray.

Maud: Crinoline (1840–1865 C.E.). United Kingdom. Introduced in 1855, plaid fringed wrapper for ladies.

maud: Scotland. Gray plaid used as rug or shawl.

mauktika alankara: India. Ear ornament.

mauli: India. A turban.

mauli bandha: India. A elaborate style of turban.

mauli mani: India. A jeweled clasp for a turban.

Maulwurf: Germany. Mole.

mau'u-la 'ili: United States of America. Hawaii. Kind of calico with tiny figures.

mauve: Reddish violet.

Mauwiesel: Germany. Weasel fur.

mawa': *See* maa'.

mawaris: Palestine. Front and back seams of a gown.

maxi: (1960–1970 C.E.). Woman's ankle-length skirt.

maxtlatl: Mexico. Aztec loincloth.

maxtli: Guatemala. Breech cloth; loincloth.

may san: Vietnam. Ready-to-wear clothes.

mayad: Philippine Islands. Woman's sash.

mayāthir humr: Arabia. Tanned hides.

mayau: India. A silk stuff from Mayin.

may-ô: Vietnam. Undershirt.

mayūrakanthiā: India. Sari colored like the neck of a peacock.

Mazarin hood: Restoration (1660–1700 C.E.). France. Chaperon named for the niece of the cardinal, minister of Louis XIV.

Mazarine hood: Early Georgian (1700–1750 C.E.). Hood or headdress trimmed with lace. Introduced by Duchesse de Mazarin.

mazzette: Italy. Bobbin.

mbal: Zaire. Raffia cloth.

mbala: Zaire. Plain woven cloth used for most skirts.

mbala badinga: Zaire. A woven patterned raffia cloth used for some skirts.

m-cut collar: (19th century). Notch in shape of M between turned collar and lapel of a coat. First appeared in 1800, remaining in use until around 1870.

mdama kofe: Timbuktu. A ring with a miter-shaped projection.

meanaigean: Ireland. Gaelic word for gloves or mittens.

meanbh-ghàirdean: Ireland. Armlet.

mecca: Bustle (1865–1890 C.E.). Introduced in 1877, thinnest wool gauze with bits of silk in the wool.

mech: Russia. Fur.

Mechlin lace: Thin bobbin lace with a design of ornaments and flowers. Produced in Mechlin, Flanders, and very popular in the 18th century.

mechnesayim: Biblical (Unknown–30 C.E.). Jewish man's linen breeches that were worn low on the hips.

mechones: Renaissance (1450–1550 C.E.). Spain. Earlocks.

mechuelas: Renaissance (1450–1550 C.E.). Spain. Little locks of hair.

Mecklenburg cap: Late Georgian (1750–1790 C.E.). United Kingdom. Turban worn as indoor hat. Inspired by marriage of Charlotte of Mecklenburg to George III.

mecklenburgh: Late Georgian (1750–1790 C.E.). Wool damask with colored flowered stripes.

medaglio: *See* fermaglio.

medalionik: Poland. Locket.

medallion: Lace motif used to ornament lingerie, linens, etc.

me-ðay: Vietnam. Medal.

media: Spain. Stocking; hose.

medias: Ecuador and Guatemala. Stockings.

medias mangas: Renaissance (1450–1550 C.E.). Spain. Half sleeves.

medias y calcetines: Spain. Stockings.

Medici collar: Elizabethan (1550–1625 C.E.). Standing, lace-edged ruff worn high in the back and ending in a low décolletage. Popularized by portrait of Marie de Medici.

Medici dress: Bustle (1865–1890 C.E.). United Kingdom. Ladies' princess dress with a train, short sleeves, and a tablier front. Worn in 1870s.

Medici lace: French bobbin lace similar to insertion.

Medici sleeve: Romantic (1815–1840 C.E.). United Kingdom. Worn in 1830s, day sleeve puffed to elbow and then tight to the wrist.

Medina: Crinoline (1840–1865 C.E.). In 1856, woman's velvet cloak with deep yoke and deep frounce. Trimmed with a satin roll, ostrich plumes, and heavy fringe.

medley: Early Georgian (1700–1750 C.E.) to Late Georgian (1750–1790 C.E.). Wool cloth.

Medusa wig: Directoire and First Empire (1790–1815 C.E.). United Kingdom. Popular from 1800 to 1802, wig with many snakelike curls.

medvilnė: Lithuania. Cotton.

mefkat: Egyptian (4000–30 B.C.E.). Turquoise, a gemstone.

megamendung: Java. A cloud textile pattern.

megane: Japan. Eyeglasses.

meghadambara: India. Cloud-colored sari.

megha-udumbara: *See* meghavarna.

meghavarna: India. A black silk from Bengal.

mèi: China. Sleeve.

meia: Portugal. Stocking; hose; sock.

meia calça: Portugal. Panty hose.

meias de lã: Portugal. Worsted stockings.

méihóngsè: China. Plum color.

me'il: *See* kethoneth.

meisen: Japan. Plain weave silk fabric with a pattern of crosses created by hand-dyeing the yarn before weaving.

mejrevaló: Hungary. Woman's short, sleeveless, fur jerkin.

mekala: United States of America. Hawaii. Medal.

mekhala: India. Waist ornament.

mekkō: Ethiopia. Grass raincloth.

melange: France. Mixture of colors in weaving.

melas: Egypt. Woman's black overdress with a horizontal neckline.

melaya liff: Egypt. Rectangular wrap of nylon, silk, or other thin fabrics.

melbbang: Korea. Suspenders.

melemele: United States of America. Hawaii. Yellow.

melemele 'ili 'alani: United States of America. Hawaii. Orange yellow color.

mellay: Obsolete term for mixed color fabric.

mellény: *See* mellrevaló.

mellia: Tunisia. Six-yard length of cotton worn draped around the belt and then pinned at the shoulders.

melon

mellrevaló: Hungary. Waist jacket.

melon: Similar to the bowler or derby hat, a man's hard round crowned hat with a slightly curved brim.

melon bag: Handbag with gores resembling sides of melon.

melon hose: *See* trunk hose.

melon sleeve: Directoire and First Empire (1790–1815 C.E.). Worn from 1809 to 1815, ladies' evening sleeve was shaped like a melon, either short or elbow length. Often worn with a sheer sleeve reaching to the wrist.

melone: Germany. Bowler.

melote: Gothic. Sheepskin or coarse cloak worn by monks and friars while at work.

melppang: Korea. Suspenders.

melton: United Kingdom. Originally made in Melton, United Kingdom, short-napped, thick fabric of wool or cotton and wool blend. Similar to felt.

memele: *See* melemele.

men: Norway. Old word for necklace.

menagere: Switzerland. Short apron.

menajel: Palestine. Literally "sickles," a seam-joining stitch.

menat: Egyptian (4000–30 B.C.E.). Necklace, particularly one bearing symbol of goddess Hathor.

mendil: 1. Turkey. Embroidered handkerchief. 2. Palestine. Headscarf.

mendil hajj: Palestine. Mendil given to wives by husbands who have done the pilgrimage to Mecca. Made of orange silk with an allover pattern of flowers.

mene: United Kingdom. Renaissance (1450–1550 C.E.). United Kingdom. Old English word for necklace.

mengekudu: Java. Red vegetable dye.

Menni: Germany. Old High German word for a necklace.

mennuet: *See* mignonette.

mente: Romantic (1815–1840 C.E.). Austro-Hungarian Empire. Outer coat, often trimmed with fur, cut straight from the shoulder seams to the waist, then flaring out and ending at the knees or calves.

mentel: 1. Byzantine and Romanesque (400–1200 C.E.). United Kingdom. Cloak worn by both genders. Women fastened it with a brooch or pin. 2. *See* hacele.

mentel-preon: Byzantine and Romanesque (400–1200 C.E.). United Kingdom. Worn by women in 12th century, pin or brooch for fastening the mentel (cloak).

menteurs: *See* liars.

mentik: Russia. Hussar pelisse.

mentlíky: Slovakia. Dress coats.

mentonnières: Late Gothic (1350–1450 C.E.). Plate armor that guarded the throat and chin. Attached to the breastplate.

mentonnierres: Romantic (1815–1840 C.E.). Popular in 1820s and 1830s, pieces of tulle or lace sewn to edge of bonnet strings, which when tied, formed frill under the chin.

mentýk: Slovakia. White lamb's wool.

menu vair: *See* vair.

menyet: Egyptian (4000–30 B.C.E.). Ceremonial necklace made of green beads and a gold plaque. Carried or waved during religious ceremonies.

meo: Byzantine and Romanesque (400–1200 C.E.). United Kingdom. Sock worn by monks with the hosa.

mercury: Late Georgian (1750–1790 C.E.). United States of America. Style of cap popular in Boston around 1760.

merino: 1. Wool of the merino sheep. 2. Fine, soft dress fabric similar to cashmere. Originally made of merino sheep wool. 3. Fine wool yarn. 4. Guatemala. Cloth with any wool in it.

merinos: Holland. Merino.

merinos ecossais: Crinoline (1840–1865 C.E.). In 1862, wool fabric.

mériza: Greece. Wide gold lace similar to entre-deux.

merletto: Italy. Lace. *See also* trina.

merletto-trina chiaacchierino: Italy. Tatting lace.

mermaid's tail: Bustle (1865–1890 C.E.). United Kingdom. Nickname given to the train of a tied-back skirt; used from 1875 to 1882.

Merry Widow: (1950–1960 C.E.). United States of America. Introduced in 1952, long-line, strapless brassiere with feather-boning designed by Warner Foundations for Lana Turner in the film *Merry Widow*. It was usually non-lacing.

merry widow hat: (20th century). Extremely large picture hat popularized by the opera of the same name.

Mersea pattens: *See* backsters.

merveilleux: Lustrous silk or silk and cotton blend in twill weave. Used in coat linings.

mesal: Bulgaria. 1. Single-width kilt. 2. Three meter long kerchief with embroidered ornaments at ends.

mésange: Bustle (1865–1890 C.E.). In 1872, blue gray.

mescolato: Early Gothic (1200–1350 C.E.). Italy. Fabric made of threads, each dyed a different color.

mesh bag: (20th century). Bag made of metal links.

mesh bustle
Dover Publications

mesh bustle: Bustle (1865–1890 C.E.). A woman's pieced bustle made with several rounded pads of metal mesh.

mesofori: Greece. A petticoat with a hoop in the hem.

mess jacket: (1930–1940 C.E.) Introduced in 1930, jacket fashioned after the military dress jacket. Waist length, tail-less, and cut with a deep V in the back hem. It had large lapels and was commonly worn with a cummerbund.

messaline: Named for Messalina, wife of Roman emperor Claudius. Soft lightweight lustrous silk fabric in a satin weave. Usually in a solid color.

messaria: Greece. Triangular embroidery motifs.

messauria: Nigeria. A large sleeved shirt worn under the tilbi.

Messgewand: Germany. Chasuble.

Messrock: Germany. Cassock.

mest: Hebrew word for socks.

méstia: Greece. Soft slippers.

metal cloth: Decorative fabric of silk or cotton warp and metallic weft. Used in millinery and trim.

metal lace: Lace net on which designs are woven in metallic thread, by hand or machine.

metallic gauze: Romantic (1815–1840 C.E.). Introduced in 1820, gauze made in colors to imitate precious gems like emeralds, topaz, and amethysts.

mētelis: Lithuania. Cloak.

meteor crepe: Silk crepe.

metropolitan jacket: Crinoline (1840–1865 C.E.). Introduced in 1862, waist-length zouave cut away in front to reveal a shirt. Jacket had a small capelet with pagoda sleeves slit on outside to the elbow and trimmed with five rows of narrow velvet.

Metternich: Bustle (1865–1890 C.E.). In 1868, new shade of green.

meurtriers: Charles I and the Commonwealth (1625–1660 C.E.). Literally "murderer's knot," tie that when untied, releases all the hair.

mexican: Directoire and First Empire (1790–1815 C.E.). United Kingdom. Steel blue.

Mexican cloth: Bustle (1865–1890 C.E.). Introduced in 1865, strong, washable silk fabric.

Mexicans: United Kingdom. Various cotton fabrics made for export.

meyui: Japan. Konoko with small dark centered white dots.

mezail: Renaissance (1450–1550 C.E.). France. Visor.

mézeline: *See* brocatelle.

mezer: France. Breton for cloth.

mezz: Egypt. Woman's flat, embroidered slippers. Part of the indoor dress.

mezza mandolina: A form of lacis where the large square mesh is covered by a cobweb-like pattern of darned thread.

mezzaro: Crinoline (1840–1865 C.E.). Italy. Painted linen veil worn over the head and shoulders.

mezzo punto: Tape-based lace with needle-made fillings. Similar to gros point de Venise.

mian fu: China. Zhou dynasty. Sacrificial robes in varied colors and designs.

mian guan: China. Zhou dynasty. Dignified ceremonial headpiece worn to certain rites by emperors, kings, and officials.

miánbù: China. Cotton fabric.

miánkù: China. Cotton-padded trousers.

miánmáokù: China. Trousers of cotton interlock fabric.

miánmáoshan: China. Cotton jersey.

miánróng: China. Cotton velvet.

miányi: China. Cotton-padded clothes.

mica: Transparent mineral substance sometimes used in accessories.

middy blouse: (20th century). Young girl's blouse. Loose, unbelted, hip-length blouse with sailor collar. Based on the blouse worn by midshipmen in the U.S. Navy.

middy braid: Narrow, finely braided braid used on middy blouses and tailored dresses and coats.

middy twill: Cotton twill fabric similar to jean.

midi: (1960–1970 C.E.). Woman's mid-calf-length skirt.

midnight blue: Darkest navy blue.

midori: Japan. Very light green.

mighfar: Arabia. Cap or headcloth of mail worn under a helmet.

mignonette: 1. Crinoline (1840–1865 C.E.). Introduced in 1862, woman's black Thibet or Canton crepe mantelet embroidered with silk and bugle beads and trimmed with two rows of deep Guipere lace. 2. Inexpensive, thread lace with a fancy mesh ground.

mignonette green: Gay Nineties (1890–1900 C.E.). In 1897, a new color.

mignonette lace: Late Georgian (1750–1790 C.E.). Early form of bobbin lace. Very light and fine, similar to tulle. Fashionable for use on headdresses.

mikado: Bustle (1865–1890 C.E.). Introduced in 1875, silk alpaca that imitated Jap silk.

mikini humuhumu: United States of America. Hawaii. Sewing machine.

mikini lima: United States of America. Hawaii. Literally "hand mitten," glove.

miktorin: Biblical (Unknown–30 C.E.). Hebrew's wrapped garment, cloak, or scarf.

mila: Lithuania. Woolen homespun cloth.

milakatra: Peru. Katra with several wide red stripes.

Milan: Crinoline (1840–1865 C.E.). In 1864, color between salmon and corn.

Milan bonnet: Renaissance (1450–1550 C.E.). United Kingdom. Cap with crown like a beret and a rolled brim. Brim was often slit and the crown was sometimes slashed and trimmed.

Milan coat: Term referring to light armor.

Milan hat: Tailored fine straw hat.

Milan lace: Tape lace easily imitated by machine.

Milanese: 1. Silk or rayon warp-knit fabric with diagonal cross pattern used in gloves. 2. Bustle (1865–1890 C.E.). In 1874, glacé poplinette.

Milanese lace: Heavy Baroque bobbin lace.

Milanese taffeta: Bustle (1865–1890 C.E.). Introduced in 1880, semi-transparent silk fabric woven on the crossgrain.

Milanie: Crinoline (1840–1865 C.E.). In 1855, woman's crocheted purse with a tassel at the bottom.

milas: Lithuania. Woolen homespun cloth.

milfa: United Arab Emirates. Woman's face mask.

military frock coat: Romantic (1815–1840 C.E.) to Bustle (1865–1890 C.E.). United Kingdom. Frock coat with braided fronts, a roll collar, and no lapels. Worn by civilians from around 1820.

military stock: Late Georgian (1750–1790 C.E.) to Crinoline (1840–1865 C.E.). United Kingdom. Neckcloth stiffened with cardboard or leather and tied or buckled behind the nape of the neck. Frequently made of silk edged with kid.

milk and water: 1. Renaissance (1450–1550 C.E.). Cloth named for its color. 2. Elizabethan (1550–1625 C.E.). Bluish white.

milkmaid skirt: Bustle (1865–1890 C.E.). United Kingdom. Introduced in 1885, skirt in two-color striped material with overskirt that gathered at the waist. Worn for day dress only.

millefleurs: Kind of perfume.

millium: (1950–1960 C.E.). United States of America. Lining fabric of rayon and metal insulation.

millma sumbriru: Ecuador. A round, white hat of hand-fitted wool.

millma sumbru: Ecuador and Guatemala. Hat made from felted fleece.

milo lopi: United States of America. Hawaii. Distaff for spinning thread.

mimi-kakusi: Meizi (1867–1912 C.E.). Japan. Literally "hiding the ear," a woman's hairstyle.

min nap: Crinoline (1840–1865 C.E.). United States of America. Chinese Hawaiian term for a thin, cotton-padded jacket lined with dai fong chau. It opened down the front with six buttons or down the right breast with five buttons. It was more comfortable and less expensive than a ma gua.

minalim: Biblical (Unknown–30 C.E.). Hebrew shoes.

minart tunic: (1910–1920 C.E.). Belted, knee-length tunic with wire flared edge.

minda: Masai. A horseshoe-shaped brass ear ornament.

mindīl: *See* mandīl.

mînecare: Romania. Man's knitted woolen cuff worn over the wrist.

Minerva bonnet: Directoire and First Empire (1790–1815 C.E.). Fashionable in 1812, bonnet shaped like a helmet and featuring a long ostrich feather worn draped across the front.

ming guang kai: China. Wei, Jin, Southern and Northern dynasties. Iron or copper armor, highly shined.

mini: (1960–1969 C.E.). Woman's very short skirt.

miniceag: Ireland. Gaelic word for kidskin.

minicionn: Ireland. Gaelic word for calfskin.

minicionn-laoigh: Ireland. Gaelic word for kidskin.

minifalda: Spain. Miniskirt.

minigonna: Italy. Miniskirt.

minijupe: France. Miniskirt.

Minirock: Germany. Miniskirt.

minirok: Holland. Miniskirt.

miniver: Late Gothic (1350–1450 C.E.). Fur of unknown type used as trim. Today the term generally refers to ermine.

mink: Very durable fur of the weasel (*Mustela vison*). Best furs are bluish brown.

mino: Japan. An overcoat.

min-soo: Korea. Amateur embroidery.

mintaqa: Arabia. Military belt.

mintean: Romania. Man's long coat.

mintiyan: Palestine. Man's long-sleeved satin jacket.

Minuit: *See* mignonette.

minyiing: Zaire. Type of mask.

miotag: Ireland. Gaelic word for worsted glove.

miqna': *See* miqna'a.

miqna'a: Arabia. Face veil.

Mirandella: Crinoline (1840–1865 C.E.). In 1850, taffeta mantelet with black lace and figured ribbon.

mirchal: *See* morchal.

mirjāi: India. Bagalbandi that closes in the center front.

mirliton: 1. Late Georgian (1750–1790 C.E.). France. Elaborate version of haiduk. Tall black felt cap with long cloth tail. 2. Directoire (1790–1815 C.E.). Hussar hat with inverted funnel shape trimmed with cockade, plume, and cords.

miro: New Zealand. Maori. Thread created by twisting a fiber by rolling it between the hands.

miroir silk: Gay Nineties (1890–1900 C.E.). In 1892, a glace silk with hint of moiré.

mirror velvet: Gay Nineties (1890–1900 C.E.). Watered velvet that appeared to have reflections in it.

mirya: *See* nirya.

misaru: India. A cotton and silk blend fabric.

misè: China. Cream colored.

misericorde: Early Gothic (1200–1350 C.E.). Dagger of mercy, worn by knights on their right hip.

miser's purse: Late Georgian (1750–1790 C.E.) to Romantic (1815–1840 C.E.). Long, beaded, tube-shaped purse. *See also* stocking-purse.

mishlah: *See* bisht.

misofori: Greece. An everyday skirt.

misri: *See* qatifah-i-purbi.

misru: *See* mashru.

mission cloth: Rough, canvaslike fabric, similar to monk's cloth.

mission net: Leno weave fabric with a large mesh.

mistake: Directoire and First Empire (1790–1815 C.E.). Introduced in 1806, shaded silk used for ribbons.

mistake hat: Directoire and First Empire (1790–1815 C.E.). Introduced in 1804, ladies' hat made of straw or chip and had a tall flat-topped crown. Front brim turned up while the back brim turned down. Worn positioned on the back of the head.

mistral: Worsted fabric with a nub.

mitaine: France. Mitten.

miter: Liturgical costume. Headdress worn by bishops. High hat made of two pointed oval-like stiffened pieces of fabric. From the back hang two narrow fringed strips of fabric.

mitiafu: Samoa. Singlet.

mitile: Italy. Generic term for shell.

mitons: *See* moufles.

mitra: Scarf with ties on the ends so that it could be worn in a number of styles. In Persia, Arabia, and Asia Minor, worn like a turban. In Phrygia, worn as a cap with ties under the chin. The Greeks considered it an effeminate style.

mitt: Fingerless glove.

mitten gauntlet: Late Gothic (1350–1450 C.E.). A standard part of mail armor, a gauntlet glove with lames that covered the fingers in one piece like a mitten, rather than with individually jointed fingers.

mitten gauntlet
Dover Publications

mitten sleeve: Gay Nineties (1890–1900 C.E.). United Kingdom. Introduced in 1891, lace sleeve that fitted the arm snugly and reached to the knuckles.

mitu-ori: Japan. A man's tonsure made by creating a cylindrical shape in the back with the upper part bent forward.

mituwa: Meizi (1867–1912 C.E.). Japan. Literally "three loops," a woman's hairstyle.

mi'zar: 1. *See* izar. 2. Arabia. Knee-length pants.

mizz: Arabia. Snug fitting slippers made from a soft Cordovan leather.

mkufu: Swahili. Silver neck chain.

mlawlaw: Palestine. Couched embroidery design.

mo: Japan. 1. Skirt. 2. Fujiwara woman's pleated train.

mo gà: Vietnam. Light yellow.

moab: Bustle (1865–1890 C.E.). Popular from 1865 to 1870, turban with round crown.

Moabite turban: Romantic (1815–1840 C.E.). Popular in 1832, ladies' turban made of crepe with a feather on one side. Worn tilted to the back of the head.

moat collar: Narrow standing collar on a bateau neckline.

mob-cap: Late Georgian (1750–1790 C.E.). Large, round, soft lady's cap with a soft, full brim. Often made of muslin or linen and trimmed with lace and ribbons. Around 1780, had a pleated border and was edged in lace.

mobondam: Korea. Silk damask.

mocassin: Holland. Moccasin.

moccasin: Leather shoe or slipper.

mocha: Expensive, soft leather that is used for gloves. Sueded on both sides.

mochi: India. Male professional embroiderers.

moccasin

mock see hai: *See* hock see hai.

mockado: Renaissance (1450–1550 C.E.) to Late Georgian (1750–1790 C.E.). Imitation velvet, often made of wool.

mocota: India. Socks.

modacrylic: Synthetic textile fiber.

modano: Italy. Square mesh ground.

Modena: Crinoline (1840–1865 C.E.). In 1854, pelerine with gathered sleeves. Trimmed with two rows of taffeta galoon with a velvet edge.

Modena red: Romantic (1815–1840 C.E.). In 1827, a fushsia.

modeste: *See* jupe.

modestie: Early Georgian (1700–1750 C.E.). Decorative stomacher. In United Kingdom, called the modesty bit.

modesty bit: *See* modestie.

modesty piece: Early Georgian (1700–1750 C.E.) to Late Georgian (1750–1790 C.E.). Bit of lace or linen edged with lace pinned to the top of the corset to cover a low decolletage.

modrwy: Wales. Finger ring.

moegi: Japan. Bright green.

moelola: United States of America. Hawaii. Striped tapa.

moesje: Holland. Beauty spot.

mofeler: Renaissance (1450–1550 C.E.). United Kingdom. Scarf worn around the neck like a modern muffler.

mofeta: Spain. 1. Skunk. 2. Fur of the civet cat.

mofuku: Japan. Mourning wear.

mogadore: Ribbed silk fabric named for the Moroccan seaport. Used in making men's ties.

mogan: Ireland. Gaelic word for footless stocking; sock; blouse; or the leg of a pair of trousers or drawers.

mogan briogais: Ireland. Gaelic word for the leg of a pair of trousers.

moggan: Scotland. Long footless stocking or knitted sleeve.

mogul breeches: *See* pajama.

mohair: 1. Hair from the Angora goat. 2. Fabric like brilliantine. 3. Pile fabric with cotton or wool back and mohair pile.

moiré: 1. Watered or waved effect on fabric. 2. Bustle (1865–1890 C.E.). In 1886, cloudy white.

moiré française: Gay Nineties (1890–1900 C.E.). In 1893, a silken fabric with narrow water marks.

moiré velours: Gay Nineties (1890–1900 C.E.). Introduced in 1897, silk and wool mix watered velvet with large irregular pattern.

Moiréseide: Spain. Moleskin.

moirette: Gay Nineties (1890–1900 C.E.). Introduced in 1896, light worsted fabric with a watered surface. Slightly stiffened and used for petticoats.

moisson: France. Literally "harvest," refers to the use of golden wheat and tiny roses in trim.

moja: Korea. Brimless cap.

mojdī: India. Close-fitting leather slippers embroidered with gold or silver. They are similar to ballet shoes.

mòjing: China. Sunglasses.

mokasyny: Poland. Moccasins.

mokdori: Korea. Neckerchief.

mokgori: Korea. Necklace.

mok'kus sin: United States of America. Massachusetts's name for moccasins.

moktor: Korea. Muffler; scarf; boa.

mokume-shibori: Japan. Tie-dyeing in a wood grain pattern.

Moldavian mantle: Crinoline (1840–1865 C.E.). United Kingdom. Ladies' mantle with a long cape that fell over the arms in large folds that were referred to as elephant sleeves.

mole: Soft iridescent fur of the *Talpa Europaea*.

mole gray: Dark gray.

moleskin: Lightly napped fabric with a velvety finish.

moletón: Spain. Moleksin.

moletón reversible: Spain. Molleton.

molleton: Bustle (1865–1890 C.E.). Introduced in 1865, thick smooth surfaced flannel.

mollitan: *See* molleton.

molochine: Roman (753 B.C.E.–323 C.E.). A mallow-colored muslin from India.

molton: Holland. Swanskin.

mòlù: China. Blackish green.

momie cloth: Bustle (1865–1890 C.E.). Used in 1880s, cotton or silk and woolen blend that was similar to a fine crepe. Commonly black in color and used for mourning clothes.

momie crepe: Lightweight cotton crepe fabric.

momme: Japan. Unit of weight (3.75 grams) used to describe weight of silk fabric. The higher the momme, the heavier the fabric.

momohiki: Japan. Knee-length breeches or pantaloons.

momo-ware: Meizi (1867–1912 C.E.). Japan. Literally "parted peach," a woman's hairstyle.

mompe: Japan. Baggy trousers.

mon: Japan. Family crest.

monache: Roman (753 B.C.E.–323 C.E.). The best quality muslin from India.

monachino: Renaissance (1450–1550 C.E.). Italy. Reddish brown. Occasionally used as mourning color by widows and as a color for a utilitarian garment.

monastic silhouette: (1920–1930 and 1930–1940 C.E.). Dress resembling in cut that of a monk's robe. Hung loosely from the shoulders and was belted in at the waist.

mon-chirimen: Japan. Heavy crepe with a woven dot.

Mönchskappe: Germany. Cowl.

monétra: Greece. White cotton kerchief.

mong pao: (1900–1910 C.E.). United States of America. Chinese Hawaiian term for a traditional bridal mantle of red satin embroidered with colored silk and golden threads.

mongolia: Italy. Tibet lamb fur (*Ovis aries*) characterized by a light coat and long white ringlets.

Mongolia: Germany. Mongolia.

monial: Elizabethan. Enameled or jeweled ornament found on the ecclesiastical glove.

monīle: Roman (753 B.C.E.–323 C.E.). Necklace.

monjil: Elizabethan (1550–1625 C.E.). Spain. Widow's weeds.

monkey: Hide with long, black hair.

monkey skin: Crinoline (1840–1865 C.E.). Introduced in 1858, popular fabric for women's muffs.

monk's cloth: Rough, heavy, basket weave fabric of cotton and wool or linen and wool.

Monmouth cap: 1. Elizabethan (1550–1625 C.E.). United Kingdom. Tall crowned, brimless knitted cap. 2. United States of America. Originally made in Monmouth, known as Capper's Town, a popular flat, round cap with a disk-shaped crown.

monnikskap: Holland. Cowl.

mono: Spain. 1. Monkey fur. 2. Overalls.

monócula: Portugal. Monocle.

monograma: Spain. Monogram.

monogramma: Italy. Monogram.

monokini: Bottom half of bikini.

monpe: Japan. Baggy cotton trousers originally worn by farmers.

monsha: Japan. Woven silk gauze with pattern.

monster green: Romantic (1815–1840 C.E.). In 1827, a new color.

montagnac: Thick, soft, woolen overcoat fabric. Named for its inventor, Baron de Montagnac of France.

Montague curls: Bustle (1865–1890 C.E.). United Kingdom. Introduced in 1877, ladies' evening coiffure that included a crescent-shaped arrangement of curls glued to the forehead.

Montana: Crinoline (1840–1865 C.E.). In 1857, woman's lined talma of moiré antique with wide band of velvet. Closed with three frogs.

Montana peak: *See* campaign hat.

monté la haute: Charles I and the Commonwealth (1625–1660 C.E.). France. Wires used to raise and lower the hem of a dress.

montebello: Bustle (1865–1890 C.E.). Introduced in 1872, dark garnet.

Montebello: Crinoline (1840–1865 C.E.). In 1855, Chantilly lace mantilla with two deep flounces.

monteith: Named for its Scottish manufacturer. Cotton handkerchief featuring a colored background and a white design, created through the use of disperse dye.

montenegrin: 1. Ladies' fitted overgarment trimmed with braid and embroidery. 2. Close fitting hat.

montera: 1. Bolivia. Black molded-leather helmet shaped like a conquistador's helmet. It is often trimmed with sequins, rosettes, and small tassels. 2. Spain. Toreador hat.

montero: Elizabethan (1550–1625 C.E.). Rounded fur cap with a turned up brim.

monteroe: *See* montero.

Montespan: Romantic (1815–1840 C.E.). Ladies' sleeve with a full upper arm, a band at the elbow, and a forearm ruffle.

Montespan corsage: Crinoline (1840–1865 C.E.). United Kingdom. Snug-fitting ladies' evening bodice with a very low, square cut decolletage and deeply pointed waist in both front and back.

Montespan hat: Crinoline (1840–1865 C.E.). United Kingdom. Ladies' small round hat with a turned up brim. Included plume and was worn for evening.

Montespan pleats: Crinoline (1840–1865 C.E.). United Kingdom. Popular in 1859 and 1860s, series of large flat double or triple box pleats sewn to the waistband of a skirt.

Montespan sleeve: Romantic (1815–1840 C.E.). United Kingdom. Ladies' sleeve with a full upper arm, a band at the elbow, and a ruffle over the lower arm.

Montpensier cloth: Bustle (1865–1890 C.E.). Introduced in 1871, smooth soft cloth twilled on the reverse.

Montpensier mantle: Crinoline (1840–1865 C.E.). United Kingdom. Ladies' mantle that hung low in both the front and the back with slits up the sides to allow the arms to be free.

montsuki: Japan. A crested ceremonial kimono.

monty-coat: Holland. Duffel coat.

moonstone: Milky, translucent semi-precious stone.

mooree: *See* moorie.

moorie: India. Broad cloth exported to Straits of Malacca.

Moorish boot: Romantic (1815–1840 C.E.). Introduced in 1807, shoe of colored kid that laced in the front.

Moorish lace: Elizabethan (1550–1625 C.E.). Moroccan lace, similar to Maltese lace.

moquette: Heavy jacquard velvet.

morado: 1. Ecuador and Guatemala. Purple. 2. Spain. Magenta.

Moravian work: Directoire and First Empire (1790–1815 C.E.). Return to 16th-century cutwork with buttonholing at the edges. Early version of broderie anglaise.

morchal: India. Fan or fly whisk of peacock feathers.

moreen: 1. Early Georgian (1700–1750 C.E.) to Late Georgian (1750–1790 C.E.). Hardy cotton, wool, or blend fabric with a rib. Often had moiré surface. 2. Strong cotton and/or wool fabric used for upholstery and draperies.

morella: Charles I and the Commonwealth (1625–1660 C.E.). Fabric used for dresses and drapery.

morello: Renaissance (1450–1550 C.E.). Italy. Term referring to the color mulberry, one of the colori corozosi. Common for everyday dress.

Moresco: Crinoline (1840–1865 C.E.). 1. In 1856, woman's cloth cloak with deep Vs of velvet and buttons.

2. In 1857, woman's moiré shawl with a V front and back. Trimmed with fringe. 3. In 1858, woman's three-quarter-circle shawl trimmed with lace and passementerie.

moresque: To be decorated in the Moorish style.

morga: Guatemala. Heavy cloth; heavy weave, dark cotton skirt.

morganite: Rose colored beryl.

morikkoji: Korea. Woman's hairpin.

morion

morion: Renaissance (1450–1550 C.E.). Helmet with a curved brim.

morisco work: Renaissance (1450–1550 C.E.) to Elizabethan (1550–1625 C.E.). Form of couched embroidery using gold or silver thread working arabesque patterns.

moritkirum: Korea. Hair oil.

morning coat: Crinoline (1840–1865 C.E.). Gentleman's swallow-tail or curved skirted coat worn for formal morning wear.

morning glory skirt: (20th century). Ladies' skirt which was extremely fitted over the hips and then flared into a large bell at the hem.

morning gown: Late Georgian (1750–1790 C.E.). United Kingdom. Worn from late 18th century through 1830s, long loose indoor coat worn sashed.

moro: Zaire. Indigo.

morocco: Goatskin leather.

morone: Directoire and First Empire (1790–1815 C.E.). United Kingdom. Red.

morrales: Mexico. Handwoven shoulder bag carried by men.

Morresca: Crinoline (1840–1865 C.E.). In 1857, woman's cloak with bertha fitted to the shoulders.

morse: Pin or brooch used to secure the cope.

mortier: Worn by French lawyers, cap shaped like dentist's mortar bowl.

mortling: Obsolete term for wool from dead sheep.

moruori: Japan. Indian silk.

mös sa: Sweden. Cap.

mosaic gauze: Romantic (1815–1840 C.E.). Introduced in 1820, new variety of gauze.

mosalka: Poland. Hasidic Jew's silk skull-cap.

moschettos: Directoire and First Empire (1790–1815 C.E.). United Kingdom. Men's pantaloons made to fit over the boots like a gaiter.

moscovite: Bustle (1865–1890 C.E.). Wide, flat cords on satin surface of silk.

moscow: Heavy woolen overcoat fabric.

Moscow wrapper: 1. Crinoline (1840–1865 C.E.). Woman's 3/4 length, satin lined circular cape. 2. Bustle (1865–1890 C.E.). Introduced in 1874, man's full-cut overcoat with pagoda sleeves and a fly front.

Trimmed in astrakhan fur and had a turned collar of the same.

mosi: Korea. Ramie.

mosolin: *See* muslin.

moss cloth: Bustle (1865–1890 C.E.). Introduced in 1878, silk and wool blend fabric with a soft, rich, mossy surface.

moss green: Gray green.

mossy crepe: Crepe with a fine, mossy texture.

mosulrin: Korea. Muslin. *See also* okyangmok.

môt chiec: Vietnam. A sock.

môt ðôi: Vietnam. A pair of socks.

mothadā: India. Checkered tie-dye textiles.

mother hubbard: (20th century). Loose-fitting housedress.

Mother Hubbard cloak: Bustle (1865–1890 C.E.). United Kingdom. Ladies' three-quarter length coat with a high collar that tied shut. Made of plush, velvet, brocade, satin, or cashmere, lined and quilted. After 1882, vented in the back to allow draping over the bustle.

moti: 1. India. Glass beads, particularly Venetian Murano beads. 2. India. Beadwork. 3. Samoa. Scarification.

motia: India. Light red.

moticuri tamaru: India. A white stuff for export to Timar Island.

motiya: India. Pink.

motley: To be variegated in color.

moto-yui: Edo (1600–1867 C.E.). Japan. The strings used to tie up a woman's hairstyle.

mouche: France. Literally "fly," a small black patch on the face.

mouched: *See* mouchouer.

mouchoir: France. Handkerchief.

mouchoir Alma: Crinoline (1840–1865 C.E.). In 1855, embroidered pocket-handkerchief with rounded corners. Edged with narrow Valenciennes lace.

mouchoir de Venus: Charles I and the Commonwealth (1625–1660 C.E.). Handkerchief. It was often given as an amorous gift. A pink or blue one indicated warm feelings; mauve, tempestuous feelings or sadness.

mouchoir Victoria: Crinoline (1840–1865 C.E.). In 1855, pocket-handkerchief embroidered with a miniature flotilla and escutcheons in the corners.

mouchouer: France. Breton for handkerchief.

moufles: Early Gothic (1200–1350 C.E.). Fingerless gloves used for hunting or rough work. Later it meant the sleeve extension over the hand.

moulds: Elizabethan (1550–1625 C.E.). United Kingdom. Men's drawers that were bombasted. The balloon shaped breeches were supported by these.

moulinee: Plied multicolored yarns used in suiting.

moultan muslin: Crinoline (1840–1865 C.E.). Scotland. Muslin with a woven in pattern. Made in Glasgow, Scotland.

mountain moss: Crinoline (1840–1865 C.E.). Introduced in 1859, fabric similar to beaver fur. Came in solid colors and patterns and was used for loose capes.

mountero: *See* montero.

Mountmellick embroidery: White Irish embroidery.

mourning crepe: Dull semi-sheer crepe with moiré effect.

mousceline: *See* muslin.

mousquetaire: 1. Restoration (1660–1700 C.E.). France. Typical glove of the Cavalier; heavy gauntleted glove made in leather. Frequently embroidered and fringed in lace. 2. Crinoline (1840–1865 C.E.). Cloth coat trimmed with large buttons and ribbons. Popular around 1855.

mousquetaire cuff: Bustle (1865–1890 C.E.). Popular from 1868 to 1889, cuff with a crinkled effect.

mousquetaire mantle: Crinoline (1840–1865 C.E.). Introduced in 1847, ladies' black velvet mantle with short loose sleeves. Trimmed with braid, pockets, and had quilted satin lining.

mousquetaire sleeve: Crinoline (1840–1865 C.E.). Introduced in 1854 and revived in 1873, ladies' full sleeve with turned cuff, cut with deep points.

mousselin aboukir: Crinoline (1840–1865 C.E.). In 1855, new fabric.

mousseline: 1. Fine, soft French muslin. 2. Any lightweight, sheer, crisp fabric finer than muslin.

mousseline de laine: France. Lightweight wool muslin, often printed. Used for dresses. *See also* nun's cloth.

mousseline de soie: France. Transparent silk fabric, often figured. Called pineapple fabric when stiffened. Used in making foundations, dresses, blouses.

mousseline grenadine: Bustle (1865–1890 C.E.). In 1871, fine tarlatane.

mousseline soie: Bustle (1865–1890 C.E.). In 1872, silk muslin.

mouth veil: Veil draped across the face to cover only the mouth and chin area.

mouton: Processed lambskin.

mouw: Holland. Sleeve.

moyle: Mule.

Mozambique: Crinoline (1840–1865 C.E.). Introduced in 1865, silk broché wool grenadine.

mozetta: Worn by some church dignitaries, hooded cape.

mozzetta: *See* mozetta.

mpttull: *See* feldr.

mrezhera prestilka: Bulgaria. Apron joined with net in a horizontal seam.

msayyaha: Palestine. Silk kafiyyeh.

mshona wa Elizabethi: Swahili. A dress with a circular opening at the neck.

mshona wa mwavuli: Swahili. Literally "umbrella cut," a flared skirt.

mshona wa Rosi: Swahili. A dress with a V-neck in both front and back.

mu da: Vietnam. Felt hat.

mu mán: Vietnam. Mourning cap.

mu miên: Vietnam. Crown.

mua: Samoa. Stripe.

muaré: Spain. Moiré.

mubaf: India. Broad fillet.

mubarshi bakin fara: Nigeria. White muslin turban worn by middle-class men.

muckender: Early Georgian (1700–1750 C.E.). Handkerchief, napkin, or bib.

mudang morikkoji: Korea. Shaman's hairpins.

muddi: India. Two small connected finger rings studded with gems.

mudhahhab: Arabia. Fabric gilded on the surface.

mudrika: India. A signet ring.

muduveya javali: India. Wedding fabric.

muff: Separate, tube shaped covering for woman's hands. Worn for warmth.

muff bracelet: Restoration (1660–1700 C.E.). Ladies' small muff worn on the wrist.

muff string: Ribbon from which hung the muff.

muffetees: Early Georgian (1700–1750 C.E.) to Crinoline (1840–1865 C.E.). 1. Small wrist muffs worn to protect the wrist ruff during card play or for warmth. 2. Small muffs sewn shut at one end and worn over the hand for warmth.

muffin hat: Crinoline (1840–1865 C.E.). United Kingdom. Popular in 1860s, man's flat crowned, round, country hat with a narrow turned-up brim.

muffler: Heavy scarf worn around throat.

mufflers: Byzantine and Romanesque (400–1200 C.E.). United Kingdom. Armored mittens.

mufti: Term referring to clothing of an officer of the English army or navy when in civilian dress.

muga: India. One of best wild silks.

mugiwara bō: Japan. Hat woven out of barley straw.

mui dát: Vietnam. Cape.

muibaf: India. Hari ribbon.

muince: Ireland. Gaelic word for necklace.

muinead: Ireland. Gaelic word for collar or necklace.

muinge: Ireland. Gaelic word for collar.

muintorc: *See* muince.

mukhmal: Palestine. Velvet fabric.

mukhta: India. Embroidery pattern of comb ducks.

mukhu-wara: Peru. Thick white cotton apron with split legs worn by men to protect their trousers from thorns.

mukla: Egypt. Wide, formal turban worn by religious men.

mukluk: Moccasin-like sports shoe.

muktajala: India. Hairnet of pearls.

muktavali: India. Single string pearl necklace.

muktika-hara: India. Pearl necklace with three strings with 32, 64, and 108 pearls respectively.

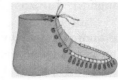

mukluk
See also photospread
(Foot and Legwear).

mukut: India. A crown.

mukuta: India. A cap, tiara, or crest.

mukyeeng: Zaire. Type of mask.

mulabbada: Arabia. Felted wrap.

mulberry: Reddish blue.

mule

mule: 1. (1910–1920 C.E.). Women's high-heeled slipper with no back. 2. Any slip-on shoe with no back.

muletón de lana: Spain. Duffel cloth.

muleus: Roman (753 B.C.E.–323 C.E.). Magistrate's red or violet colored boots.

mull: Soft, sheer, plain weave fabric of cotton or silk and cotton blend.

Muller-cut-down
See also photospread
(Headwear).

Muller-cut-down: Bustle (1865–1890 C.E.). United Kingdom. Popular name for a man's half-height top hat. Named after the 1864 murderer whose half-height hat led to his recognition and arrest.

mullu: Ecuador. Quichua word for a woman's many stranded necklace.

mullutuma: Bolivia. Network of colored braiding on huaka.

mulmul: India. Soft, thin muslin.

mulmul khas: India. A royal muslin that is very fine and lightweight.

mulmull: *See* malmal.

mulot: Bustle (1865–1890 C.E.). In 1885, field mouse color.

multipointed fold: Where all four corners of a handkerchief emerge from a pocket.

mumavadi: India. A waxed rainproof cloth.

mummy brown: Romantic (1815–1840 C.E.). In 1827, a new color.

mummy cloth: 1. Cotton, silk, or rayon crepe suede for dresses. 2. Sheer fabric, similar to fabric of ancient Egypt. 3. Loosely woven fabric in which mummies were wrapped.

mumu sesega: Samoa. Orange color.

mumusali: Samoa. Scarlet color.

muna-medare: Japan. A style of apron.

mundasa: India. A turban or a cloth worn wrapped around a turban.

mundash: India. General term for a headdress.

mundāsi: *See* talepā.

mundil: Turban elaborately decorated with metallic embroidery.

mundir: Russia. Uniform jacket.

mungo: Inferior fabric made from woolen rags.

muoddá: Norway. Fur tunic.

murabba: Egypt. Square neckline.

muraja: India. A girdle.

murasaki: Japan. Purple; a purple dye.

murassa-jadau: India. Ornament worn on the pagdi.

murchal: *See* morchal.

murkī: India. Small gold ring worn pierced through the earlobe.

murmel: Italy. Marmot fur.

Murmeltier: Germany. Marmot fur.

murray: Bustle (1865–1890 C.E.). In 1884, new color between violet and claret.

murrey: 1. Early Gothic (1200–1350 C.E.). Mulberry color. 2. Elizabethan (1550–1625 C.E.). Purplish red.

murry: Elizabethan (1550–1625 C.E.) to Restoration (1660–1700 C.E.). Mulberry color.

musa: Persia. Fur cloak with wide sleeves.

musaftaj: Arabia. Stiff linen.

musayyar: Arabia. Luxurious striped silk.

muscadin: Directoire and First Empire (1790–1815 C.E.). In 1790s, term referring to an overdressed and musk-perfumed patriot.

muscadine: Directoire and First Empire (1790–1815 C.E.). Musk-scented pastille. Name was extended to mean the effeminate men who, overdressed, commonly wore this scent, and carried a long walking stick.

Muscovite: 1. Crinoline (1840–1865 C.E.). In 1854, woman's velvet cloak with wide fur trim. 2. Bustle (1865–1890 C.E.). Introduced in 1884, thick corded silk.

Muscovite velvet: Bustle (1865–1890 C.E.). Introduced in 1883, velvet brocade on a ribbed silk ground.

muselina: Spain. Muslin.

muselina de la india: Spain. India muslin.

musequí: Renaissance (1450–1550 C.E.). Spain. Large puff (as in a sleeve).

musette bag: Canvas or leather wallet hung from a shoulder strap and carried by soldiers.

mush: United Kingdom. Slang for umbrella.

musha"ara: Arabia. Furry shoes from Yemen.

mushajjar: *See* qatafah-i-purbi.

mushal: *See* shash.

mushroom: Small, round-crowned hat with a turned-down brim.

mushroom hat: Bustle (1865–1890 C.E.). United Kingdom. Popular in 1870s and 1880s, ladies' straw mushroom-shaped hat elaborately trimmed with ribbon, flowers, or a bird.

mushroom sleeve: Gay Nineties (1890–1900 C.E.). United Kingdom. Introduced in 1894, ladies' short evening sleeve pleated into the armseye and trimmed with a lace frill.

mushru: Indian cotton backed satin.

musk melon bun: China. Woman's hairstyle.

muskrat: Short, silky, straight fur in silver to brown or dyed to simulate sealskin, mink, or sable.

muslin: Plain weave, natural colored, cotton fabric.

muslin de laine: Fine, lightweight, plain weave, worsted fabric.

muslin deaths: Directoire and First Empire (1790–1815 C.E.). United Kingdom. Nickname for very sheer muslin gowns. They were so called due to the number of deaths of wearers brought on by chills.

muslinet: Thick muslin or light cotton fabric.

musqin: India. Musk.

musquash: United Kingdom. Muskrat skin.

mussolen: *See* muslin.

mussolina: Italy. Muslin.

mussolo: *See* muslin.

must deviles: *See* mustardevelin.

mustard: Yellowish green.

mustard villars: *See* mustardevelin.

mustardevelin: Renaissance (1450–1550 C.E.). Mixed blend gray woolen fabric. Made in Montivilliers in Normandy.

mustardevillers: *See* mustardevelin.

musui: Hungary. Skirt.

muszuj: Hungary. Woman's wide skirt with smocked pleats. Not sewn in center front. Of black or dark blue satin or cotton. Has wide band at the bottom, often embroidered. The two front corners are tucked in the waist to expose the petticoat.

mùtan: Ireland. 1. Muff. 2. Thick glove. 3. Fingerless glove.

mutarraz bil-dhahab: Arabia. Fabric embroidered with gold thread.

mutch: Snug cap of linen or muslin worn by old women and babies.

mutton leg sleeve

mutria: Spain. Otter.

muts: Holland. Cap. *See also* baret.

mutsje: *See* huif.

mutsuki: Japan. Baby diaper.

mutton leg sleeve: Crinoline (1840–1865 C.E.). Worn by women, a full cut sleeve that was heavily pleated where it was set into the dropped shoulder and gathered onto a wristband. The style evolved from the leg-of-mutton sleeves of the earlier Romantic period.

muttonchops: Crinoline (1840–1865 C.E.). Men's large sideburns extending onto the jawline.

mütze: Germany. Old word for hood.

Mütze: United States of America. Amish man's frock coat with a split tail.

mu'u mu'u: United states of America. Hawaii. Woman's underslip or chemise; loose, yokeless, short-sleeved gown.

mu'umu'u moe po: United States of America. Hawaii. Literally "slip for sleeping at night," nightgown.

muwanna: Palestine. Shaded embroidery thread.

muzarkash: *See* zarqash.

mwa kwa: China. Mandarin-collared jacket.

mwa non: Thailand. Woman's lampshade shaped, wide brimmed, palm leaf hat.

mwaandaan: Zaire. Official belt.

myllion: Renaissance (1450–1550 C.E.) to Elizabethan (1840–1865 C.E.). Milanese fustian.

myojushil: Korea. Silk thread.

myongju: Korea. Lightweight silk fabric woven in plain weave of irregular threads of raw silk. Very soft and warm.

myonsa: Korea. Cotton yarn.

mysore: United Kingdom. Plain weave, dyed cotton fabric made for export.

N

na krilo: Bulgaria. Woman's hairstyle where hair is braided into many small braids which gradually become one large braid.

naajuban: Japan. Full-length under kimono worn over a cotton undershirt and half-slip.

naal: Denmark. Needle.

naald: Holland. Needle.

naaldhak: Holland. Stiletto heel.

nabchet: Renaissance (1450–1550 C.E.) to Elizabethan (1550–1625 C.E.). Slang term for a hat or cap.

nabob: Early Georgian (1700–1750 C.E.) to Late Georgian (1750–1790 C.E.). Thin East India fabric.

naboika: Russia. Printed fabric.

nácar: Portugal. Mother-of-pearl.

nacarat: 1. Directoire and First Empire (1790–1815 C.E.). Light red. 2. Fine linen or crepe dyed red orange.

naccarat: Directoire and First Empire (1790–1815 C.E.). United Kingdom. Orange.

Nachtgewand: *See* Nachthemd.

Nachthemd: Germany. Nightdress.

nachtjapon: Holland. Nightgown.

nachttabbaert: Elizabethan (1550–1625 C.E.) to Charles I and the Commonwealth (1625–1660 C.E.). Holland. From 1600 to 1660, term meaning night wear.

nacre: France. Mother-of-pearl.

nacre burgau: Bustle (1865–1890 C.E.). Dark mother-of-pearl used for accessories.

nacré velvet: Iridescent velvet with the back of one color and the pile of another color creating changeable appearance.

nada: India. A skirt drawstring.

Nadel: Germany. Needle.

nādela: Germany. Old word for needle.

nādele: Germany. Old word for needle.

Nadelspitze: Germany. Needlepoint lace.

nadoknada: Bosnia. Makeup.

nadoz: France. Breton for needle.

naemet: *See* namda.

naeui: *See* sokot.

naewang: Korea. Undergarment.

naga-juban: Japan. The long undergarment worn with the kimono.

nagarā: India. Plain leather shoes hooked at the ankle.

naga-tenuge: Japan. A rural woman's kerchief.

nagdeh: Charles I and the Commonwealth (1625–1660 C.E.). Persia. Compound weave fabric.

nages: Full mourning black frieze skirts.

nagrudnik: Bulgaria. Bodice front with strings of coins attached to it.

naguilla: *See* enagua.

náhrdelnú: Czechoslovakia. Necklace.

nail: United Arab Emirates. Sandal.

náilon: Portugal. Nylon.

nailoni: Samoa. Nylon.

nailron: Korea. Nylon.

nainsook: India. Soft, light, bleached, plain weave cotton with a lustrous finish on one side. Solid colored or striped.

nainsukh: *See* nainsook.

naizhào: China. Brassiere.

najon: Korea. Nacre.

naka: *See* nam-king.

nakara color: Directoire and First Empire (1790–1815 C.E.). Popular in 1812 and after, pearl color.

naksatramala: India. Necklace of 27 strings of pearls.

nakshi kantha: India. A kantha with elaborate pictorial embroidery.

nål: 1. Norway. Old word for needle. 2. Sweden. Needle; pin.

nama ha zome: Japan. Dyeing with fresh indigo.

namaakbusten: Holland. Falsies.

namaksin: *See* totnamaksin.

nambawi: Korea. Man's lined silk cap for winter. It has back flap, ear muffle, and circular opening in the top. It is trimmed with fur and held on with sashes under the chin.

namda: India. Felt.

nam-king: India. Nankeen.

ñañaca: Ecuador and Guatemala. Incan woman's headcloth.

ñañacas: Bolivia. Inca term for a headcloth.

ñañaka: *See* ñañaca.

nanako-kokechi: Japan. Very fine tie-dyeing.

nankeen: China. Imported from Nankin, China, a durable, light tan cotton fabric.

nankin: 1. Dense, plain weave, cotton fabric with a white warp and a colored weft. 2. Spain. Nankeen.

Nankin nishiki: Japan. Nishiki from Nankin.

nansú: Spain. Nainsook.

naočare: Bosnia. Spectacles.

nao-halu'a: United States of America. Hawaii. Tapa pattern with lines.

nao-ua-ha'ao: United States of America. Hawaii. Tapa pattern.

nao-ua-nanahuki: United States of America. Hawaii. Tapa pattern.

nap: Fuzzy surface projecting on some fabric. Forms direction when brushed.

napa leather: Originally from Napa, California, a tanned sheepskin or lambskin used for gloves.

napery: Linen for household use.

napkin: Elizabethan (1550–1625 C.E.). Handkerchief for the nose.

napkin hook: Elizabethan (1550–1625 C.E.) to Restoration (1660–1700 C.E.). Waistband hook for the handkerchief. Popular gift to young girls from young men.

napkin-cap: Early Georgian (1700–1750 C.E.) to Late Georgian (1750–1790 C.E.). Man's nightcap to cover the unwigged head.

Naples lace: Elizabethan (1550–1625 C.E.) to Restoration (1660–1700 C.E.). Made in Naples, Italy, a black silk lace.

náplitsi: Greece. Beaded trimming for braids.

napoleon: Directoire and First Empire (1790–1815 C.E.). Top boot designed by Napoleon.

Napoleon collar: Standing, turned-down collar popularly worn with wide revers.

Napoleon costume: (1900–1910 C.E.). In 1905, a dress with a straight stand collar with turndown, wide revers, and braid trim.

Napoleon necktie: Romantic (1815–1840 C.E.). United Kingdom. Man's narrow necktie that crosses in the front without tying and is attached to the suspenders. Violet colored. After 1830, called the Corsican tie.

napoleon

Napoleons: Crinoline (1840–1865 C.E.). United Kingdom. Man's long military boots that reached above the knee and were dipped in behind the knee to allow movement. Popular for horseback riding. Named for the Prince, later Napoleon III.

nappina: Italy. Tassel.

napron: Byzantine and Romanesque (400–1200 C.E.) to Renaissance (1450–1550 C.E.). United Kingdom. Middle English word for apron.

naqsha: Renaissance (1450–1550 C.E.) to Restoration (1660–1700 C.E.). Persia. Woman's trousers.

Nara sarashi: Japan. The best quality ramie made in Nara.

náramek: Czechoslovakia. Bracelet.

naramiennik: Poland. Bracelet. *See also* bransoletka.

narandžast: Bosnia. Orange colored.

narangi: India. The color orange.

narcorat: Crinoline (1840–1865 C.E.). Dark claret.

narmma-haripha: India. A soft stuff from Hira or Herat.

narukvica: Bosnia, Croatia, and Serbia. Bracelet.

näsduk: Sweden. Handkerchief.

nasgadh: Ireland. Gaelic word for collar.

nasheq rohoh: Palestine. White fabric with a border. Used for underdresses.

nasij: India. A silk stuff embroidered with gold.

nasitergium: Roman (753 B.C.E.–323 C.E.). Nose handkerchief.

nasta: *See* nath.

nastalik: India. Plain white muslin full court dress turban.

nastro: Italy. Ribbon.

nasture: Romania. Button.

naszyjnik: Poland. Necklace.

Natalie: Crinoline (1840–1865 C.E.). Introduced in 1862, black silk pardessus with pagoda sleeves and black lace inserted at the sides. Trimmed with narrow velvet strips.

nath: India. Woman's nose-ring.

nati: *See* natiyo.

natiyo: India. A hood worn as a sunscreen by a child.

natté: Bustle (1865–1890 C.E.). Introduced in 1874, firm silk that resembled cane plaiting.

Natalie

natural beaver: Crinoline (1840–1865 C.E.). In 1858, light brown or fawn.

Naugahyde: Trade name for vinyl coated fabric used mostly in upholstery.

Navailles: Crinoline (1840–1865 C.E.). In 1854, taffeta shawl-mantelet trimmed with lace and fringe.

Navarino smoke: Romantic (1815–1840 C.E.). Shade lighter than London smoke.

navershnik: Russia. Child's tunic which is worn as an outer garment.

navette: France. Tatting shuttle.

navoi: Bulgaria. Rectangular pieces of white woolen that are wound around the feet to below the knee. Held on with white hemp cords.

navy: Medium dark blue.

navy blue: Dark purple blue with a gray tint.

nawame-irokawa: Japan. Leather dyed in a zigzag pattern.

ncak: 1. Zaire. Women's dress. 2. Kuba. *See* nshak.

ncaka ishyeen: Zaire. Short overskirt.

ncok: Zaire. Conical hat.

ndeve: Kikuyu. Circular, wooden ear ornament.

ndik'a': Navaho. Cotton.

ndop: Cameroon. Blue-dyed strip fabric with white resist patterns.

nduli: Sierra Leone. White cotton cloth.

ndului: Sierra Leone. Pure white color.

nèapaicin anhaich: Ireland. Neckerchief.

nèapaicin pòca: Ireland. Pocket handkerchief.

Neapolitan bonnet: Directoire (1790–1815 C.E.). United Kingdom. Ladies' leghorn bonnet with straw flowers and ribbons.

Neapolitan hat: Hat of lacy fiber or horsehair braid.

Neapolitan headdress: Romantic (1815–1840 C.E.). United States of America. In 1817, full dress hat of striped gauze and silver trim.

neas-nam-fuar-thìrean: Ireland. Ermine.

neat's leather: Early Gothic (1200–1350 C.E.). Leather made from the hide of oxen and used for footwear.

nebula headdress: Late Gothic (1350–1450 C.E.). United Kingdom. 19th-century term for a woman's headdress. Also known as the goffered veil.

neck button: Charles I and the Commonwealth (1625–1660 C.E.). United Kingdom. Decorative button with loop at the neck of a doublet. Sometimes left undone to expose the shirt beneath it.

neck-chain: Early Gothic (1200–1350 C.E.). Decorative chain worn by men. In 17th century, called jack chain.

neck handkerchief: Early Georgian (1700–1750 C.E.) to Crinoline (1840–1865 C.E.). Cravat or tie.

neckatee: Late Georgian (1750–1790 C.E.). Handkerchief.

neckband: Fitted band around neck; especially band to which collar is attached.

neckcloth: Obsolete term for cravat or necktie.

necked bonnet: Renaissance (1450–1550 C.E.). United Kingdom. Man's cap with a deep back flap.

neckerchief: Square of fabric worn around neck.

neckstock: Early Georgian (1700–1750 C.E.) to Late Georgian (1750–1790 C.E.). Folded cravat with buckle in back.

nedle: Byzantine and Romanesque (400–1200 C.E.) to Renaissance (1450–1550 C.E.). United Kingdom. Middle English word for needle.

needle painting: A method of needlework that imitates oil painting.

needlecord: (1930–1940 C.E.). United Kingdom. In 1938, a velvet or fine rib corduroy used for men's shirts.

needlepoint lace: Lace made with a sewing needle.

neerstick: Elizabethan (1550–1625 C.E.) to Charles I and the Commonwealth (1625–1660 C.E.). Holland. From 1600 to 1660 C.E., a tucker.

negligee: 1. Early Georgian (1700–1750 C.E.). Informal attire for either gender. 2. Romantic (1815–1840 C.E.). Ladies' jet mourning girdle with a nine-inch pendant. Worn in public mourning of Princess Charlotte in 1818. 3. Term referring to ladies' nightwear or lingerie.

negligee de la volupte: *See* gown à la levantine.'

negligee garters: Garters worn on belt.

négrillon: Bustle (1865–1890 C.E.). In 1875, brown that is almost black.

negro: Portugal. Black.

negro carbón: Spain. Carbon black.

negro como azeviche: Portugal. Jet black.

negulrije: *See* silnaebok.

Nehru cap: Medium-crowned, brimless cap with a deep front-to-back crease, and cuff-like flaps around the crown.

Nehru jacket: (1960–1970 C.E.). United States of America. Introduced in 1968, jacket with standing collar that buttoned up the front to the neck and was fitted at the waist.

nei tao: China. Qing dynasty (1644–1911 C.E.). Long, blue silk gown with horse-hoof cuffs worn by graduates of the Manchu civil exam.

neiguse: Bustle (1865–1890 C.E.). Introduced in 1877, twill woolen fabric with a rough surface.

nèiyi: China. Underwear.

nekhau: Egyptian (4000–30 B.C.E.). Pendant amulet in the shape of a fish.

nekhaw: Egyptian (4000–30 B.C.E.). Metal fish pendant typically worn on child's side-lock.

nek'och ìpù: *See* mokdori.

nekt'ai: Korea. Necktie.

Nell Gwynne cap: Crinoline (1840–1865 C.E.). In July 1860, lace breakfast cap with violet ribbon at top.

nelpiloni: Mexico. Aztec sash.

Nelson hat: Gay Nineties (1890–1900 C.E.). United Kingdom. Introduced in 1895, straw hat with turned up brim. Trimmed with a front plume and side ribbon bows.

nemehef: Egyptian (4000–30 B.C.E.). Unidentified green stone used to make some scarabs.

Nemes headdress: Egyptian (4000–30 B.C.E.). Symbol of the pharaoh. Large rectangular scarf worn with two corners tied at nape of the neck.

neora: Shiny, synthetic straw.

nēÞla: Early Gothic (1200–1350 C.E.) to Late Gothic (1350–1450 C.E.). United Kingdom. Needle.

nerc: Bosnia. Mink. *See also* vison.

nerinuku: Japan. Plain weave fabric with raw silk warps and degummed silk wefts.

Nerz: Germany. Mink fur.

nesga: Spain. Gore; gusset.

nesgada: Renaissance (1450–1550 C.E.). Spain. Gored.

nestel: Holland. Aglet.

Nestel: Germany. Lace for fastening clothing.

nesti: *See* dalkr.

Nestila: Germany. Old High German word for a lace for fastening clothing.

netcha: United States of America. Eskimo sealskin coat.

neteldoek: Holland. Muslin.

nether integuments: *See* unmentionables.

nether stocks: Renaissance (1450–1550 C.E.) to Elizabethan (1550–1625 C.E.). United Kingdom. Lower portion of men's hose. In 16th century, referred to women's stockings.

netra: India. A kind of silk cloth.

nettlecloth: Elizabethan (1550–1625 C.E.) to Restoration (1660–1700 C.E.). Linen made from nettle fibers.

Netzstickerei: Germany. Embroidered netting.

neud: France. Breton for thread.

neura: India. Jeweled anklets.

Newgate fringe: Romantic (1815–1840 C.E.) to Crinoline (1840–1865 C.E.). United Kingdom. Common term for a fringe of beard under the jaw.

Newmarket coat: Romantic (1815–1840 C.E.). United Kingdom. Single-or double-breasted man's tailed riding coat with rounded fronts. Had cuffed sleeves and flap hip pockets. By 1850, referred to as cutaway and by 1870 it became the morning coat.

Newmarket jacket: Gay Nineties (1890–1900 C.E.). Introduced in 1891, single- or double-breasted women's hip-length day coat with a masculine turned collar and silk lapels. Had flap hip pockets and fitted sleeves.

Newmarket overcoat: Bustle (1865–1890 C.E.). United Kingdom. 1. In 1881, man's short-waisted single-breasted frock overcoat with long skirts. Commonly had a velvet collar and cuffs. 2. In 1889, woman's single- or double-breasted coat with long skirts. Had flap hip pockets, fitted sleeves, velvet collar, lapels, and cuffs.

Newmarket top frock: Gay Nineties (1890–1900 C.E.). United Kingdom. In 1895, man's overcoat similar to a frock coat with a velvet collar, waist pockets, and long skirts. Commonly made of cheviot.

Newmarket vest: Gay Nineties (1890–1900 C.E.). United Kingdom. In 1894, man's plaid or check waistcoat popular with sportsmen.

nezumi-iro: Japan. Gray.

ngac: Vietnam. Crocodile.

ng'andu: Swahili. Gold.

ngân-tinh công-vu: Vietnam. Silver necklace.

ngau hui suck: Crinoline (1840–1865 C.E.). United States of America. Chinese Hawaiian term for the color lotus root gray.

ngoc trao: Vietnam. Pearl.

ngoc-bích: Vietnam. Jasper.

ngoc-miên: Vietnam. Jade crown.

ngoc-thach: Vietnam. Jade.

ngore: Australia. Maori general term for cloaks covered in pompons.

ngore paheke: Australia. Maori cloak trimmed with decorative stitches and optional pompons.

ngozi ya kioo: Swahili. Patent leather.

nguyêt-bach: Vietnam. Bluish white.

nhac-ky: Vietnam. Tabard.

nhãn-kính: Vietnam. Eyeglasses.

nhung-trang: Vietnam. Military uniform.

ní: China. Wool fabric.

nibi: *See* kochi.

nic': Poland. Thread.

nicho-kinran: Japan. Kinran with one or two additional background colors.

Nicholas blue: Romantic (1815–1840 C.E.). New blue color in 1817.

niciane rekawiczki: Poland. Thread gloves.

nickel gray: Bustle (1865–1890 C.E.). In 1889, dark silver tint.

nicola: India. A long robe.

nicula: *See* nicola.

nificí forescá: Greece. Bridal costume.

nifles: Late Gothic (1350–1450 C.E.) to Renaissance (1450–1550 C.E.). Veil.

night coif: Elizabethan (1550–1625 C.E.) to Restoration (1660–1700 C.E.). United Kingdom. Woman's embroidered cap worn to bed. Sometimes worn with a forehead cloth.

night corset: Larger-waisted version of the day corset, a corset worn while sleeping in order keep the tight lacing consistent day and night.

night of France blue: Bustle (1865–1890 C.E.). France. In 1888, light watery green.

night rail: Renaissance (1450–1550 C.E.) to Early Georgian (1700–1750 C.E.). United Kingdom. Woman's lawn, holland, silk, or satin waist-length cape. Worn in or out of doors.

nightcap: Late Gothic (1350–1450 C.E.). 1. Man's skull cap with a small turned up brim. Worn indoors instead of a wig. 2. Man's plain cap for sleeping. 3. Women's mob cap that tied under the chin and was worn for sleeping.

night-cap wig: Early Georgian (1700–1750 C.E.). Man's wig with rolled curls circling the back of the head side to side.

nightgown: Late Georgian (1750–1790 C.E.). Informal gown with back pleats that were stitched down. It was worn for receiving guests at home.

Nightingale: Crinoline (1840–1865 C.E.). In 1856, woman's moiré shawl with velvet trim.

night-kercher: Elizabethan (1550–1625 C.E.) to Restoration (1660–1700 C.E.). United Kingdom. Night neckerchief.

nigitae: Japan. A smooth cloth.

niho-li'ili'i: United States of America. Hawaii. Literally "small teeth," a tapa design.

niho-mano: United States of America. Hawaii. Literally "shark tooth," a tapa design.

nihsvasaharya: India. Gown of very fine, white fabric.

nihyakusan-koti: Meizi (1867–1912 C.E.). Japan. A woman's hairstyle with a very high forelock.

niigashi: Japan. The finest quality banana fiber cloth.

nikautang: Micronesia. Woman's long, loose, puffed-sleeve dress.

nil: Bustle (1865–1890 C.E.). France. In 1888, a light watery green color.

nīlāmbarī: India. Blue sari.

nilaniradanicola: India. A dark blue tunic.

nilapatora: India. A blue silk.

nilavata: India. An indigo-dyed silk.

nile green: Yellowish green.

nileh: Palestine. Indigo, the most important dye.

nillae: India. Kind of blue cloth.

ni-lông: Vietnam. Nylon.

niluhura: India. A stuff dyed in indigo.

nimā: India. Mid-thigh length, short-sleeved tunic.

nima-pot: Guatemala. Ceremonial blouse or tunic.

nimbus: Greek (3000-100 B.C.E.). Gold embroidered linen headband.

nimtanah: India. Jacket.

nine-djere: Timbuktu. A filigree nose ring.

nine-tenths coat: (1960–1970 C.E.). Woman's A-line coat reaching below the knee.

nine-tenths coat
See also photospread
(Outerwear).
Dover Publications

ninikea: United States of America. Hawaii. White tapa worn by priests during ceremonies.

ninnoko: Ethiopia. Koma ritual scarring, usually consisting of five horizontal lines on many parts of the body.

ninon: 1. Lightweight soft silk. 2. Sheer, smooth, plain weave fabric.

nirangi: India. A wimple or veil.

nirmokinam: India. Fabric like snake's slough.

nirnejaka: India. A dyer.

níróng: China. Wool fabric.

nirya: India. Front pleats of the dhoti.

nisara: India. A warm cadar.

nishijin: Japan. A kind of rich brocade.

nishiki: Japan. Silk woven or brocaded in colors and gilt.

nishka: India. A necklace of coins.

nishra: Egypt. Large, black, finely woven rectangle with a fine plaid of red and white. Edges are fringed. Worn as a wrap.

niska: India. Necklace.

nit: Croatia and Serbia. Thread.

nit': 1. Czechoslovakia. Thread. 2. Russia. Thread.

nitambavastra: India. Woman's undergarment worn over the hips.

nithsdale: Early Georgian (1700–1750 C.E.). United Kingdom. Large bad-weather hood. Named for the Countess Nithsdale, famous for helping her husband escape from the Tower of London by dressing him in women's clothing and a large hood.

nitka: 1. Poland. Thread. *See also* nic'. 2. *See* nit'.

niukòu: China. Button.

niupàn: China. Button loop.

niúzaikù: China. Fitted pants; trousers.

niuzi: China. Button.

nivasana: India. Lower body garment; skirt.

Nivernois: Late Georgian (1750–1790 C.E.). United Kingdom. Small tricorne popular with the Macaronies who wore it with a cadogan wig. Named for the French writer Nivernois.

nivi: India. Lower body garment; an apron-like undergarment.

nivi bandha: India. The preliminary bow made to tie the anteriya to the waist.

nízi: China. Wool fabric.

njekloe: Sierra Leone. Black dye made from soot and vegetable matter.

njiru: Kikiuyu. Coil of brass wire worn in the ear.

nkrawou: Ashanti. Garment of appliquéd, embroidered colored felt.

nnup: Zaire. Type of mask.

nobleza: Spain. Duchesse.

nocna koszula: Poland. Nightgown.

nodder: Hat pin with ornament on a tiny spring which nods as head moves.

nodwydd: Wales. Needle.

nœdl: United Kingdom. Old English word for needle.

noeuds: France. Bow or knot of ribbon.

noeuds d'amour: Late Georgian (1750–1790 C.E.). France. Literally "love knots," referred to the bows or ties used as decoration on ladies' gowns.

noggui-hongsang: Korea. Bride's traditional set consisting of a green jacket and a red skirt.

noir: France. Black.

noisette: Bustle (1865–1890 C.E.). In 1867, new shade of brown.

nokmal: Korea. Starch.

noksaek: Korea. Green.

nometas: Lithuania. Married woman's headdress or veil.

nón: Vietnam. Conical hat.

nón lá: Vietnam. Hat made of latania leaves.

nón lông: Vietnam. Feather hat.

nón sat: Vietnam. Soldier's helmet.

none-so-pretty: Late Georgian (1750–1790 C.E.). United States of America. Narrow linen ribbons or tapes with a colored design woven in.

nonomea: United States of America. Hawaii. Reddish color.

nono-obi: Japan. A style of obi.

nora-gi: Japan. A field worker's clothes.

norat'a: Korea. Yellow.

*Norfolk jacket
See also photospread
(Outerwear).*

Norfolk jacket: Bustle (1865–1890 C.E.). Gentlemen's jacket with box pleats from shoulder to hem and commonly self-belted. Worn for sport occasions.

Norfolk shirt: Bustle (1865–1890 C.E.). United Kingdom. Jacket similar in cut to the Norfolk jacket but with collar and cuffs like a shirt. Had front flap pockets and a self-belt. Always worn buttoned up. Commonly made in tweeds for country wear.

norigae: Korea. Hair ornaments.

norki: Poland. Mink.

Norma corsage: Crinoline (1840–1865 C.E.). United Kingdom. Introduced in 1844, ladies' evening bodice with loose center front fold that was held in place with a gold pin.

Normande cap: Bustle (1865–1890 C.E.). In 1871, large white muslin bow worn on top of head.

Normandy bonnet: Bustle (1865–1890 C.E.). In 1866, lady's bonnet.

Northampton lace: Charles I and the Commonwealth (1625–1660 C.E.) to Late Georgian (1750–1790 C.E.). United Kingdom. Bobbin lace similar to Flemish lace.

Norwegian slippers: Nickname for loafers.

Norwich crepe: Elizabethan (1550–1625 C.E.). Silk and wool blend fabric similar to bombazine. Manufactured in Norwich.

Norwich paramatta: (1890–1900 C.E.). United Kingdom. A paramatta with a worsted weft and a silk warp.

nos: Ireland. Gaelic word for white.

noshime: Japan. Inner robe worn by male. No characters.

nosine: Lithuania. Handkerchief.

nosnja: *See* kostim.

nostle: Byzantine and Romanesque (400–1200 C.E.). United Kingdom. Band, secured around the leg and fastening the meo. Also a band used as a fillet.

Nottingham lace: United Kingdom. Flat lace made in Nottingham, United Kingdom.

nouet: France. Small linen bag for holding herbs, etc.

nouveautés: Crinoline (1840–1865 C.E.). In 1863, poplin with detached figures, usually of silk.

Novado: Crinoline (1840–1865 C.E.). In 1854, square cut pelisse trimmed with ribbon and deep falls of lace.

novato: Charles I and the Commonwealth (1625–1660 C.E.). Wool or silk fabric.

noyer: Bustle (1865–1890 C.E.). In 1871, walnut color.

nozelenn: France. Breton for button.

nsa: Ashanti. Camel's hair and wool cloth.

nsaduaso: Ghana. Very best kente cloth.

nshak: Kuba. Mid-calf length ornamental skirt.

nshiing: Zaire. Thread.

ntoa: Ashanti. Waist belt.

nuamhanair: Ireland. Gaelic word for embroidery.

nubia: Soft, light, scarf or head covering.

nudo: Spain. Bow.

nugi-sage: Japan. Karaori kosode worn with the right arm out of the sleeve.

nuihaku: Japan. Kosode decorated with embroidery and metallic foil. This style fell out of favor in the early 17th century.

nuikiri: Japan. Satin embroidery stitch used to outline broad areas.

nukkadar: India. A small pointed cap.

nula: India. A raw silk.

núm: Vietnam. Button.

numbda: *See* namda.

numda: *See* namda.

nummud: *See* namda.

numna: *See* namda.

numud: *See* namda.

nunda: *See* namda.

nuno: Japan. Fabric woven of vegetable fibers.

nun's cloth: Bustle (1865–1890 C.E.). Introduced in 1881, fine, thin wool. Previously called mousseline de laine. *See also* nun's veiling.

nun's thread: Elizabethan (1550–1625 C.E.). Made in convents in Italy and Flanders, thin white thread used for lace.

nun's veiling: 1. Bustle (1865–1890 C.E.). Introduced in 1879, thin wool barege. *See also* nun's cloth. 2. Sheer, soft, plain weave fabric, usually of worsted, silk, or cotton.

nun's work: Late Gothic (1350–1450 C.E.). United Kingdom. Similar to modern embroidery.

nuometas: Lithuania. Woman's headdress or veil.

nupura: India. An anklet.

nūr-ī-bādlā: India. Dress with decoration.

nurki: India. Gold or silver hoop earring.

nurse's cape: Three-quarter length navy cape, lined in red, buttoned with brass buttons.

nurse's cloth: Bleached, plain weave cotton fabric.

nurse's gingham: Heavy blue and white striped cotton fabric.

nursing dress: Romantic (1815–1840 C.E.) to Bustle (1865–1890 C.E.). Ladies' dress with a bodice front that was removable through the use of hooks and eyes at the shoulders. Underbodice had pleats or folds that concealed a small slit to allow the woman to nurse her infant. Used from c1820 to 1850.

nur-trang: Vietnam. Jewelry.

nussbraun: Germany. Nut brown.

nut: *See* nath.

nutria: 1. *See* grege. 2. Dark brown South American fur similar to beaver.

nwumu: False kente cloth made from imported silk or linen.

nyakas szür: Hungary. Literally "necked szür," szür with front and back cut in separate pieces.

nycette: Renaissance (1450–1550 C.E.). Ladies' light wrap for the neck.

nyeeng: Zaire. Type of mask.

nylon: Man-made polyamide yarns that are very strong and resilient, with a high wet strength.

nyoro: Rhodesia. Shona word for cicatrization.

O

ô: Vietnam. Umbrella.

oashyr voynee: Isle of Man. Men's long, knitted, footless stockings.

oashyr-slobbagh: *See* oashyr voynee.

Oatland village hat: Directoire and First Empire (1790–1815 C.E.). United Kingdom. Introduced in 1800, ladies' day hat with curved brim and dome-shaped crown. Made of straw, twist, or leghorn. Named for the country house of the Duchess of York.

oatmeal cloth: Soft, durable fabric made with a fine warp and coarse weft yarns.

obair-ghréis: Ireland. Arras; embroidery.

obair-gréise: Ireland. Embroidery.

obair-shnàthaid: Ireland. Needlework; embroidery.

obalenka: Slovakia. Pad or frame around which a woman's hair is arranged.

obang-nangja: Korea. Small pouch worn suspended from the sash that served as a pocket. Used the five directional colors (East, blue; West, white; South, red; North, black; Center, yellow).

obi: Japan. Ladies' broad sash of very heavy silk or satin and embroidered or brocaded.

obi hat: Directoire and First Empire (1790–1815 C.E.). Introduced in 1804, straw chip hat with high flat crown and narrow brim. Tied under the chin.

obi makura: Japan. Pad under the obi.

obi-age: Japan. A bustle sash. *See also* obiage.

obiage: Japan. Silk scarf used to cover the bow pad on a woman's back.

obi-dome: Japan. An obi tie.

obijime: Japan. Five foot long cord used to fasten the obi.

oblaciti: *See* odjesti.

oblec: *See* ubrac.

oblek: *See* saty.

oblékati: *See* odíti.

oboro-zome: Japan. Shaded dyeing ranging from white to grayish blue.

obraczka slubna: Poland. Wedding ring.

obradový kroj: Slovakia. Ritual costume.

obucá: Bosnia, Croatia, and Serbia. Shoe.

obuv: *See* sapog; strevíc.

obuwie: *See* trzewik.

oc xà-cù: Vietnam. Nacre.

occularium: Renaissance (1450–1550 C.E.). Eye-slit in the helm.

ocelot: Italy and France. Fur of large spotted cat, *Felix pardalis*.

ocelote: Spain. Ocelot.

ochre: Yellow similar to mineral.

ochtendjas: Holland. Housecoat.

ocra: Italy. Ochre.

ocre: 1. France. Ochre. 2. Portugal. Ochre.

ocreae rostratae: Byzantine and Romanesque (400–1200 C.E.). United Kingdom. Pointed toed boots.

octagon tie: Crinoline (1840–1865 C.E.). United Kingdom. Popular from the 1860s on, man's scarf worn with four points above the tie pin and secured with a band around the neck.

óculas: Portugal. Spectacles.

odet': Russia. To clothe or to dress.

odev: *See* saty.

odezda: Russia. Clothing.

odhar: Ireland. Gaelic word for dun colored.

odijelo: *See* odjeca.

odíti: Czechoslovakia. To clothe or to dress.

odjeca: Bosnia, Croatia, and Serbia. Clothing.

odjesti: Croatia and Serbia. To clothe or to dress.

odonarium: Roman (753 B.C.E.–323 C.E.). Handkerchief.

odonium: Roman (753 B.C.E.–323 C.E.). Handkerchief.

odziac: *See* ubrac.

odzienie: *See* suknie.

odziez: 1. Poland. Clothing. 2. *See* suknie.

oes: Renaissance (1450–1550 C.E.). Small eyelets used in decorative designs on women's garments.

oet'u: Korea. Overcoat.

ofer-braedels: Byzantine and Romanesque (400–1200 C.E.). United Kingdom. Outer garment, often ecclesiastical.

ofer-feng: Byzantine and Romanesque (400–1200 C.E.). United Kingdom. Clasp on the shoe.

oferlaeg: Byzantine and Romanesque (400–1200 C.E.). United Kingdom. Outer garment or cloak.

oferlagu: *See* oferlaeg.

ofer-slop: Byzantine and Romanesque (400–1200 C.E.). United Kingdom. Cloak.

ofer-slype: *See* ofer-slop.

off-the-horse bun: China. Woman's hairstyle.

off-the-peg: Readymade clothing.

'ofu: Samoa. Robe.

'ofuta 'ele: Samoa. Bathing dress.

'ofutino: Samoa. Shirt.

'ofuvae: Samoa. Trousers.

'ofuvae pupu'u: Samoa. Shorts.

ogami: Japan. Literally "worship," embroidery with converging stitches that resemble praying hands.

oganadi: *See* 'okanaki.

oggaegori: *See* syool.

ogi: Japan. Folding fan.

ogrlica: 1. Bosnia. Necklace. 2. Croatia and Serbia. Collar.

ogrtač: Bosnia. Overcoat.

'ohelohelo: United States of America. Hawaii. Pink.

ohi: Japan. Priest's arm stole.

Ohrring: Germany. Earring.

'ohule: United States of America. Hawaii. To be bald.

oi dai booi dai: (1900–1910 C.E.). United States of America. Chinese Hawaiian term for a baby carrier made like a square blanket with four fabric straps used to tie the child to the mother's back.

oilcloth: Heavy muslin that is coated on one side with oil, clay, and pigment.

oiled leather: Early Georgian (1700–1750 C.E.). Leather oiled with fish oil in imitation of chamois. Popular for use in workmen's breeches.

oiled silk: Silk fabric that has been waterproofed with oil.

oilets: Early Georgian (1700–1750 C.E.). Eyelets of lacing holes.

oilskin: Fabric treated with oil to make it waterproof.

òir-chrios: Ireland. 1. Studded belt. 2. Gold necklace.

oir-ghreus: Ireland. Gaelic word for embroidery, tapestry, or needlework.

oiseau: Romantic (1815–1840 C.E.). Chartreuse yellow.

oisionair: Ireland. Gaelic word for tabard.

ojak norigae: Korea. Accessory with five pendants.

ojal: Spain. Buttonhole.

ojales: Renaissance (1450–1550 C.E.). Spain. Loops.

ojete: Spain. Eyelet.

okana: Ghana. Gold bracelet worn by a councilor when on a royal errand.

'okanaki: United States of America. Hawaii. Organdy.

okara: Ibo. Raffia and cotton cloth.

okers: *See* hoggers.

okhaben: Russia. Charles I and the Commonwealth (1625–1660 C.E.) to Restoration (1660–1700 C.E.). Woman's summer cloak.

'oki pahu: United States of America. Hawaii. To bob the hair.

oko: Ibo. Raffia cloth.

okolepu'u: United States of America. Hawaii. Literally "humped buttocks," a bustle-style dress.

okovratnik: Bosnia. *See* kragna.

okrel: Bulgaria. Back kilted skirt.

okulary: Poland. Spectacles.

okulary sloneczne: Poland. Sunglasses.

okumi: Japan. The front overlap of the kimono.

okura-nishiki: Japan. A type of nishiki named for the imperial treasure house.

okuru: Ibibio. Cloth woven by youths from raffia and cotton.

okyangmok: Korea. Calico. *See also* mosulrin.

olann: Ireland. Gaelic word for wool.

Old Navajo Dyes: (1940–1950 C.E.). United States of America. Packaged synthetic dyes.

old rose: Soft, dull rose color.

Oldenburgh bonnet: Directoire and First Empire (1790–1815 C.E.). Introduced in 1814, ladies' large bonnet with wide brim and flat crown. Decorated with ostrich feathers and a ribbon tie. Named for the Duchess Oldenburgh, a visitor to the Peace celebration of 1814.

oldham: Coarse cloth made in Norfolk.

olicula: Roman (753 B.C.E.–323 C.E.). Ladies' hooded cape.

olino: Nigeria. Pleated cloth bound with raffia before it is dyed.

oliva: Spain. Olive color.

olivâtre: France. Olive color.

olive: Dark grayed green.

olive button: Late Georgian (1750–1790 C.E.). Long oval silk covered button.

olive drab: Dull greenish yellow.

olivenfarbig: Germany. Olive color.

olivet: A large button covered in cloth or thread.

olivette: Late Georgian (1750–1790 C.E.). Olive button of Brandenburg.

oliwny: Poland and Portugal. Olive color.

ollaodach: Ireland. Gaelic word for woolen fabric.

ollyet: Charles I and the Commonwealth (1625–1660 C.E.) to Restoration (1660–1700 C.E.). Wool fabric made in Norwich.

ol-ogarenji: Ogiek. A skull cap made from a goat's stomach.

olojémiti: Greece. Shawl filled with rows of heavy silk and gold.

Olympic: (1950–1960 C.E.). Man's hairstyle.

òmar: Ireland. Amber.

ombari: Namibia. Woman's necklace.

ombre: France. To be graduated in tone.

ombrelle: France. Parasol.

Omer mantle: Crinoline (1840–1865 C.E.). In 1855, mantle of thin material. Ruffles were bordered with velvet ribbon or braid and a heavy fringe.

omeshi: Japan. A fine silk crepe.

omophorion: Worn by officials of the Greek Church, strip of white embroidered fabric worn around the neck, crossing the left shoulder with ends hanging to the knees.

omote kon'ya: Japan. Shop that specializes in dyeing fabric.

omslagdoekje: Holland. Fichu.

ondergoed: Holland. Underwear.

onderriem: Elizabethan (1550–1625 C.E.). Holland. Popular 1600–1660, a chain.

onderzieltje: Elizabethan (1550–1625 C.E.). Holland. Under-bodice.

ondina crinoline: Crinoline (1840–1865 C.E.). United Kingdom. Introduced in 1860s, a cage crinoline.

ondine: Bustle (1865–1890 C.E.). Introduced in 1871, soft and brilliant silk and wool blend fabric. Reintroduced in 1893, as a corded silk crepon.

ondule: Bustle (1865–1890 C.E.). Introduced in 1865, fabric with surface that appeared to be wavy.

onechte juwelen: Holland. Costume jewelry.

ông tay áo: Vietnam. Coat sleeve.

ongebleekte Chinese zijde: Holland. Pongee.

oni didi: Nigeria. Cloth tied in knots before dyeing.

oni lilo: Nigeria. Cloth that is folded, twisted, and then tied before dyeing.

onigegemerin: Yoruba four-sided crown.

oniko: Nigeria. Raffia-tied adire.

onion white brown: China. Yuan dynasty. Shade of brown.

onrijp: *See* groen.

onuga: Ibo. Cloth made from narrow indigo bands.

onyx: Semi-precious stone.

oogschaduw: Holland. Eye shadow.

oogscherm: Holland. Eyeshade.

ooze calf: Bustle (1865–1890 C.E.). In 1889, soft, dull black leather.

opal: Precious stone with no one characteristic color.

opala: Portugal. Fine muslin.

opanky: Balkans. Leather sandal with a wide sole that lashed to the foot and ankle with thongs.

opas: Bulgaria. Waistband.

opasa: India. Woman's hairstyle with a loose chignon on the top of the head.

opera cloak: Fancy loose cloak or wrap worn when attending the opera or other formal evening events.

opera glove: Long glove, sometimes thumbless.

opera hat: Romantic (1815–1840 C.E.). Gentlemen's tall silk top hat that collapsed. It had an internal spring that allowed it to collapse so that it could be carried under the arm or be placed under a seat.

opera pump

opera pump: Ladies' plain heeled pump.

opera slipper: Dress slipper.

Ophelia: Crinoline (1840–1865 C.E.). 1. In 1850, taffeta mantelet trimmed with ruches of quilled ribbon and a white blonde fall. 2. In 1857, woman's cloth cloak trimmed with velvet galloons and a three-inch fringe. 3. In 1858, woman's velvet or cloth cloak that was loosely fitted with flowing sleeves. The hood was lined with satin. 4. Introduced in 1864, red violet.

opinak: Bulgaria. Rough hide shoes.

opinci: Romania. Women's peasant sandals.

opinki: Bulgaria. Leather boatlike sandals that are tied on the foot.

opossum: Italy and France. Long-haired fur with grayish hair and gray white underfur.

Opossum: Germany. Opossum.

Oposum: Spain. Opossum.

opperkleed: Holland. Surcoat.

opreg: Romania. Woman's short back apron. Richly woven or embroidered panel with a fringe that reaches to the skirt hem.

opus anglicanum: Early Gothic (1200–1350 C.E.). United Kingdom. Early English needlework of a chain stitch and fine split stitch.

opus araneum: Handmade bobbin lace.

opus consutum: Late Gothic (1350–1450 C.E.). United Kingdom. Sections of needlework that were stitched together. Figures were outlined in brown silk or painted.

opus filatorium: Late Gothic (1350–1450 C.E.). United Kingdom. Thread embroidery on network.

opus pectineum: Late Gothic (1350–1450 C.E.). United Kingdom. Woven work imitating embroidery.

opus phrygium: Late Gothic (1350–1450 C.E.). United Kingdom. Gold-outlined embroidery.

opus plumarium: Late Gothic (1350–1450 C.E.). United Kingdom. Feather-stitch embroidery.

opus pulvinarium: Late Gothic (1350–1450 C.E.). United Kingdom. Cross-stitch embroidery.

'opu'u kaimana: United States of America. Hawaii. A cut diamond.

orange-butter: Charles I and the Commonwealth (1625–1660 C.E.) to Late Georgian (1750–1790 C.E.). Pomade.

or: France. Gold.

or nué: Renaissance (1450–1550 C.E.) to Elizabethan (1550–1625 C.E.). A method of couching that used colored silks to create a shaded pattern on gold thread.

or trect: Renaissance (1450–1550 C.E.). Spain. Drawn gold.

orange: Reddish yellow.

orange tawny: Elizabethan (1550–1625 C.E.). Orangey brown.

orangegelb: Germany. Orange color.

oranje: Holland. Orange color.

orarion: Ecclesiastical stole.

orarium: Roman (753 B.C.E.–323 C.E.). Large handkerchief used by men.

orbace: Italy. Sardinian dyed wool fabric used for fezes.

òr-bhann: Ireland. Gold lace.

òrbhuidhe: Ireland. Yellow.

orbiculi: Roman (753 B.C.E.–323 C.E.). Decorative motifs at base of clavi.

orbis: Roman (753 B.C.E.–323 C.E.). Wire frame that supported the front of women's elaborate hairstyles.

orchell: Ireland. Purple dye.

orchid: Blue red.

or-choilear: Ireland. Gaelic word for golden collar.

ordinaria: *See* puntada recta.

ordnasc: Ireland. Gaelic word for thumb ring.

orecchino: Italy. Earring.

oreille d'ours: Bustle (1865–1890 C.E.). Warm brown.

oreilles de chien: Directoire and First Empire (1790–1815 C.E.). France. Man's very long side-locks.

orel: Byzantine and Romanesque (400–1200 C.E.). United Kingdom. Secular term for a veil.

orenjibich'ui: Korea. Orange colored.

orgagis: Early Georgian (1700–1750 C.E.). Rough Indian cotton cloth.

organdi: France and Spain. Organdy.

Organdin: Germany. Organdy.

organdy: Very fine, transparent cotton with a crisp finish.

organpipe folds: Even, deep folds.

organza: 1. Silk or synthetic fabric similar to organdy. 2. Germany and Italy. Organdy.

orhna: India. Two yards long and one and a half yards wide scarf of voile, silk, or other light fabric. Elaborately embroidered.

ori: Japan. Weaving.

oriellettes: Elizabethan (1550–1625 C.E.). France. Moveable steel plates that covered the ears on a helmet. May have been hinged.

oriental crepe: Handwoven crepe from China or Japan.

oriental embroidery: Various embroidery done in Asian countries.

oriental lace: Lace with design woven through net.

oriental satin: Bustle (1865–1890 C.E.). Introduced in 1869, wool or wool and silk blend fabric.

orikogbofo: Yoruba crown.

orla: *See* aba.

orle: Early Gothic (1200–1350 C.E.). Wreath or chaplet worn around the helmet of a knight.

orleans: Plain weave fabric with a cotton warp and worsted weft.

Orleans brown: Romantic (1815–1840 C.E.). Shade of brown.

orlo: Italy. Hem.

ormesine: India. Armozeen.

ormuzine: Persia. Silk fabric.

ornamento de gioielli: *See* spillo da petto.

oro de orilla: Renaissance (1450–1550 C.E.). Spain. Edging gold.

oro hilado: Renaissance (1450–1550 C.E.). Spain. Spun gold.

orphelian: Crinoline (1840–1865 C.E.). Claret color.

orphreys: Elizabethan (1550–1625 C.E.). Bands of embroidery on the cope and chasuble.

orrice: (17th century). United States of America. Lace or gimp trim with a gold and silver thread.

orris: Early Georgian (1700–1750 C.E.) to Late Georgian (1750–1790 C.E.). Elaborate gold or silver lace. Originally made in Arras, France.

orso: Italy. Bear fur.

ortie: Bustle (1865–1890 C.E.). In 1889, bluish gray.

orzechowy: Poland. Nut brown.

ósain: 1. Byzantine and Romanesque (400–1200 C.E.). Ireland. Trews. 2. Scotland. Trews.

osanachd: Ireland. Gaelic word for hosiery.

osatiti: *See* odíti.

Osbaldiston tie: Romantic (1815–1840 C.E.). Popular from 1830s through 1840s, man's necktie tied with barrel-shaped knot.

osbro: Charles I and the Commonwealth (1625–1660 C.E.). Worsted fustian.

oseille cuite: Bustle (1865–1890 C.E.). In 1877, yellowish green.

osito lavador: Spain. Raccoon.

osnabrug: *See* osnaburg.

osnaburg: Plain, rough flax or cotton fabric. Named for its place of manufacture, Osnaburg, Germany.

osnaburgo: Spain. Osnaburg.

oso: Spain. Bear.

osode: *See* hirosode.

osprey: Certain feathers, not osprey, used for hats.

ossenbrigs: *See* osnaburg.

ostaigrette: Imitation aigret.

ot: Korea. Clothes; garment.

otcharak: Korea. Skirt; train.

otgam: *See* ch'on.

otkam: Korea. Cloth.

otomana: Spain. Ottoman.

otomana imperial: Spain. Imperial ottoman.

otter: Dark brown fur of otter (*Lutra lutra*).

ottoman: Plain heavy fabric with crosswise ribs.

ottoman cord: Plain, corded silk fabric.

ottoman plush: Bustle (1865–1890 C.E.). Introduced in 1882, silk fabric with plush figures on a corded ground.

ottoman rep: Bustle (1865–1890 C.E.). Introduced in 1882, repped satin.

ottoman rib: Ribbed fabric where warp forms rib.

ottoman silk: Bustle (1865–1890 C.E.). Introduced in 1882, any silk with a horizontal cord.

ottoman velvet: Bustle (1865–1890 C.E.). Introduced in 1869, velvet with a colored brocade. Reintroduced in 1879, as a rich uncut velvet.

otu: India. Wool; woof.

oubosyuuju: *See* totsin.

ouch: Early Gothic (1200–1350 C.E.) to Late Gothic (1350–1450 C.E.). Jeweled pin or buckle.

ouderwetse vrouwenmuts: Holland. Mob cap.

ouhe: China. Pale pinkish purple.

ourle: Early Gothic (1200–1350 C.E.) to Late Gothic (1350–1450 C.E.). Fur border.

ourlet-bord: France. Hem.

ousè: China. Pale pinkish gray.

out-coat: Restoration (1660–1700 C.E.). Man's overcoat.

outing flannel: *See* flannelette.

outnal thread: Renaissance (1450–1550 C.E.) to Elizabethan (1550–1625 C.E.). Flemish flax thread.

ouvrage a l'aiguille: France. Needlework.

oval beaver hat: Romantic (1815–1840 C.E.). United Kingdom. Man's oval hat made of beaver.

over-all: *See* balandrana.

Overall: Germany. Overalls.

overalls: Romantic (1815–1840 C.E.). United Kingdom. Men's loose white cord or leather trousers. Worn for riding.

overcoat: *See* greatcoat.

overgaiter: Spat.

overhemb: Holland. Shirt.

overschoen: Holland. Galosh.

overseas blue: Grayed light navy worn by Air Force in World War II.

overseas cap
See also photospread
(Headwear).

overseas cap: United States of America. Small military cap worn by soldiers in World War I.

overslop: Byzantine and Romanesque (400–1200 C.E.) to Late Gothic (1350–1450 C.E.). Gown, stole, cassock, or surplice. Term in use from 950 to 1400.

owa sibi: Ekine. A dance headpiece.

'owaynet al-sus: Palestine. Literally "chick's eye," zigzag stitch used for applique.

'owili: United States of America. Hawaii. Bolt of cloth.

Oxford and Cambridge mixture: Bustle (1865–1890 C.E.). Introduced in 1885, two shades of iron gray.

Oxford bags: (1920–1930 C.E.). United Kingdom. Extremely loose knickers worn by gentlemen for golf. Very popular with male college students. *See also* plus fours.

Oxford blue: Navy blue.

Oxford chambray: Oxford cloth with a colored warp and a white weft.

Oxford cloth: Plain or basket weave, cotton shirting fabric with two fine warps and heavy weft years.

Oxford gillies: Bustle (1865–1890 C.E.). United Kingdom. Man's sports shoe that laced and then the laces were tied around the ankle.

Oxford gloves: Elizabethan (1550–1625 C.E.) to Charles I and the Commonwealth (1625–1660 C.E.). United Kingdom. Gloves scented with the Earl of Oxford's perfume.

Oxford jacket
See also photospread
(Outerwear).

Oxford gray: Any fabric of black and white mixed yarns, woven or knitted.

Oxford jacket: Crinoline (1840–1865 C.E.). A woman's or young boy's lightly fitted jacket with an Eton or Peter Pan collar.

Oxford shirting: Variety of coarse weaves in mercerized cotton. In white, colors, or stripes.

Oxford tie: Gay Nineties (1890–1900 C.E.). United Kingdom. Man's narrow, straight tie.

oxide: Bustle (1865–1890 C.E.). France. In 1888, dark slate color.

Oxonian boots: Romantic (1815–1840 C.E.). United Kingdom. Popular in 1830s and 1840s, man's short boot with a wedge cut from the top to assist in putting them on.

Oxonian jacket: Crinoline (1840–1865 C.E.). United Kingdom. Popular in 1850s and 1860s, man's oxford coat in bright blue with two buttons and many pockets.

oya: Hebrew. Fringe.

oya isi: Turkey. Airy needlework lace.

oyah: Turkey. Crocheted lace.

oyam: *See* oyuan.

oyokoman: Ashanti. Cloth for those of the royal family.

oyster: Light grayish white color with a blue tint.

oyuan: Nigeria. Mushroom-shaped lumbar ornament.

Ozelot: Germany. Ocelot.

ozenbridge: *See* osnaburg.

ozerel'e: Russia. Necklace.

ozherelok: Russia. Necklace.

oznaburg: *See* osnaburg.

ozura: Japan. Large vine-like scroll pattern.

P

pà: China. Handkerchief.

pa'a kama'a: United States of America. Hawaii. Pair of shoes.

pa'a lole: United States of America. Hawaii. Suit of clothes.

pa'a mua: United States of America. Hawaii. Ready-made, as clothes.

paakee: Australia. Maori general term for rain capes.

paakee nui: Australia. Maori full length cape.

paakee tikumu: Australia. Maori cape decorated with skin of tikumu (*Celmisia spectabilis*).

paaneter: India. A red silk piece of fabric with silver leaf borders.

paaraerae: Australia. Maori sandal with sole of plaited flax.

paardestaart: Holland. Ponytail.

paarengarenga: Australia. Maori lace-up leggings.

paars: Holland. Purple.

pabagu: Nigeria. A Tiv man's ceremonial coat.

paboudj: Hebrew's slipper shoes.

pabuç: Turkey. Shoe.

pac: Moccasin.

pachedī: India. Man's scarf.

packcloth: Heavy, coarse cotton fabric.

packing white: Renaissance (1450–1550 C.E.). United Kingdom. Wool fabric.

pacotilla: Ecuador. Low quality shawl.

pactole: Bustle (1865–1890 C.E.). France. In 1884, golden brown.

pād: Byzantine and Romanesque (400–1200 C.E.). United Kingdom. Outer garment, probably shaped like a tunic. *See also* rocc.

pada: India. Sandals.

pada-bandhati: India. Anklets.

padamsuka: India. A fine-gauze silk.

padapatra: India. A garter-like ornament for the thigh.

paddles: *See* wheat ears.

paddock coat: Gay Nineties (1890–1900 C.E.). United Kingdom. Man's single-or double-breasted overcoat with a fly front. It had no waist seam, but was fitted by a side seam to the pocket. Reintroduced in 1893 as the New Paletot.

padigunthima: India. A type of boot.

padiniansanam: India. A night garment.

padisoy: *See* paduasoy.

padom: Medes. Hood that surrounded the face and concealed the chin.

pa-ðo-suv: Vietnam. Overcoat.

padou: Early Georgian (1700–1750 C.E.) to Late Georgian (1750–1790 C.E.). Silk ribbon made in Padua, Italy.

paduasoy: Early Georgian (1700–1750 C.E.) to Crinoline (1840–1865 C.E.). Corded, strong silk fabric, first made in Padua, Italy. *See also* peau de soie.

paduka: India. A wooden sandal.

padukakrt: India. A peddler.

padura: India. A white stuff.

padusoy: *See* paduasoy.

pa'eke: United States of America. Hawaii. Pocket.

paekkum: Korea. Platinum.

paenang: Korea. Knapsack.

paencha: India. Pants leg.

p'aench'u: *See* paji.

paenula: Roman (753 B.C.E.–323 C.E.). Hooded cape of a waterproofed leather or wool.

paepaeroa: New Zealand. Maori term for a large cloak.

pafte: Yugoslavia. Metal waist clasp and coin decoration.

páfti: Bulgaria and Greece. Large silver buckle.

pag: *See* pagri.

pāg: India. Loosely folded turban. *See also* pecā.

pagarakhā: India. Leather shoes embroidered with gold or silver or silver thread. They are hooked at the toe.

pagari: *See* pugaree.

pagdī: *See* pagri.

page boy bob: Chin-length hair worn straight with only the bottom curled under.

paghadi: India. A turban.

pagi-sore: Indonesia. Literally "morning-evening," used to refer to batik divided into two different patterns.

pagliaccetto: Italy. Rompers.

paglietta: Italy. Boater.

pagne: Loincloth or skirt worn in tropical countries.

pagoda parasol: Directoire and First Empire (1790–1815 C.E.) to Crinoline (1840–1865 C.E.). Parasol that, when opened, was shaped like a pagoda.

pagoda sleeve

pagoda sleeve: Crinoline (1840–1865 C.E.). Funnel-shaped sleeve, narrow at the armseye and full at the bottom. By 1857, some had a slit in front from cuff to armseye. By 1859, called the funnel sleeve.

pagoda toque: Small, brimless hat similar in shape to an Oriental tower.

pagonazzo: *See* pavonazzo.

pagote: *See* pagri.

pāgrā: *See* pāg.

pagri: India. Long silk or cotton turban, 10 to 50 yards long, worn by Hindu men.

pag-sankla: India. Loose-fitting layers of chain worn at the ankle.

paheran: *See* kudtā; kurta.

pah-jungobein: Cambodia and Thailand. A hip wrap.

pah-poosh: Persia. Ladies' high-heeled velvet slippers. Often embroidered in gold and studded with jewels.

pahu papale: United States of America. Hawaii. Hatbox.

pahuñchi: India. Barrel-shaped armlet.

paiafzar: India. Shoes.

paida: Early Gothic (1200–1350 C.E.) to Late Gothic (1350–1450 C.E.). United Kingdom. Generic term for coat.

paidirean: Ireland. Gaelic word for rosary or necklace; bracelet; or chaplet.

paiki pa'alima: United States of America. Hawaii. Handbag.

paillasson: France. Straw hat.

paille: France. Straw.

paille de riz: France. Rice straw.

paille d'italie: France. Italian straw.

paillette: France. Small, scalelike glittering disks; sequins.

paimak: A variety of gold or silver lace.

painetta: Spain. Traditional high hair comb.

painntin: Ireland. Gaelic word for patten.

painter's pants: (1970–1979 C.E.). Ecru or white overalls.

pa'ipa'inaha: United States of America. Hawaii. Tapa cloak worn like a cape.

pairan: *See* kurta.

pàirt-dhathach: Ireland. Particolored.

pais-a-gwn bach: Wales. Gown with a snugly fitted bodice and a skirt split in front to the waist. Skirt is worn drawn back at the sides to expose the striped underskirt.

paisin: Thailand. Sarong-like skirt.

paisley: Intricate pattern involving abstract, curving shapes.

paisley shawl: Shawl woven in one piece, five or six feet square.

paison: Greek (3000-100 B.C.E.). Persian trousers.

pa'iua: United States of America. Hawaii. Fine, white tapa.

pajama: (1930–1940 C.E. to present). From the Hindustani word *epai-jama*, shirt and trouser combination. Worn for day or evening, formally or informally, at home and in public. Trouser legs were cut very full, suggesting skirts in their fullness.

pajama check: Barred nainsook used for men's underwear.

pajani: India. A sari dyed in blue, yellow, black, green, and red.

paji: Korea. Trouser part of the national costume.

pakama: United Kingdom. Cotton fabric made for export.

pakan: Borneo. Woof in weaving or plaiting.

pakana: United States of America. Hawaii. Waist; shirtwaist; blouse.

pakiri mbola: Sumba. A skirt trimmed with shells and beads.

pakjwiu san: *See* usan.

paklari: India. A five stringed necklace.

paklinnen: Holland. Sacking.

pala 'ehu: United States of America. Hawaii. Reddish yellow.

pala'a: United States of America. Hawaii. Silky, brown tapa.

palaka aloha: United States of America. Hawaii. Aloha shirt.

palalei: United States of America. Hawaii. Uncut tapa fringe.

palampore: *See* palempore.

palandrano: Italy. Gabardine.

palang posh: *See* palempore.

pălărie: Romania. Hat.

palatine: Directoire and First Empire (1790–1815 C.E.). Small fur or swansdown stole reaching below the waist.

palatine royal: Crinoline (1840–1865 C.E.). United Kingdom. Introduced in 1851, fur tippet with quilted hood.

palazzo pajamas: (1960–1970 C.E.). United States of America. Woman's pants cut as full as evening skirts.

pale: 1. Late Gothic (1350–1450 C.E.) to Renaissance (1450–1550 C.E.). Vertical stripe or series of stripes. 2. United States of America. Hawaii. Garment lining.

pale hanai: United States of America. Hawaii. Infant's bib.

pale kila: United States of America. Hawaii. Literally "steel shield," armor.

pale lilac brown: China. Yuan dynasty. Shade of brown.

pale maka: United States of America. Hawaii. Veil that conceals the face, as worn by Arab women.

pale pakaukau 'aila: United States of America. Hawaii. Oilcloth.

pale papale: United States of America. Hawaii. Hat lining.

pale wawae: United States of America. Hawaii. House slipper.

palelei: United States of America. Hawaii. Tapa worn as a head covering.

palema'i: United States of America. Hawaii. Underdrawers.

palempore: India. Chintz bed cover.

palepai: Indonesia (Sumatra). Long ceremonial textiles.

palestine: Bustle (1865–1890 C.E.). Introduced in 1883, dark blue violet.

palet: Renaissance (1450–1550 C.E.). Small skull-cap of cuir-bouilli or steel.

paletó: Portugal and Spain. Jacket.

paletoque: Renaissance (1450–1550 C.E.). Spain. Paltock.

paletot: 1. Romantic (1815–1840 C.E.). France. Man's short greatcoat with no side pleats or back vent. 2. Romantic (1815–1840 C.E.). Ladies' stiffly pleated three-quarter-length cloak with a short overcape. 3. Crinoline (1840–1865 C.E.). Pleated knee-length, cape-like garment for women. 4. Crinoline (1840–1865 C.E.). Man's yachting jacket.

paletot-cloak: Crinoline (1840–1865 C.E.). Popular in 1850s, short hip-length cloak with armhole slits.

paletot-mantle: Bustle (1865–1890 C.E.). Introduced in 1867, ladies' three-quarter-length caped cloak with hanging sleeve.

paletot-redingote: Bustle (1865–1890 C.E.). United Kingdom. Introduced in 1867, ladies' fitted long coat cut without a waist seam. It had revers and buttoned down the front. They sometimes had capes.

paletot-sac: Crinoline (1840–1865 C.E.). France. Popular in early part of the period, a man's short, straight single- or double-breasted paletot with a hood instead of a collar.

palettes: Early Gothic (1200–1350 C.E.). Steel or cuir-bouilli protection for the armpits.

palhaço: *See* calção.

paliacate: Mexico. Head kerchief.

palisade: Restoration (1660–1700 C.E.). Muslin cap worn over the fontange frame in the mornings. The term also referred to the wire frame itself.

palisandre: Romantic (1815–1840 C.E.). Purple brown.

palito: Guatemala. Back-strap loom.

p'aljji: Korea. Bracelet.

pall: 1. Obsolete for rich fabric or garment. 2. *See* cloke.

palla: 1. Roman (753 B.C.E.–323 C.E.). Roman equivalent of the Greek himation, made of wool, worn draped around the body. Women's version of the pallium. 2. India. A panel of fabric.

pallatine: Restoration (1660–1700 C.E.) to Early Georgian (1700–1750 C.E.). United Kingdom. Woman's sable shoulder wrap.

pallav: 1. India. The decorated end of a sari. 2. Bolivia. Generic term for a woven pattern.

pallets: *See* palettes.

pallettes: *See* palettes.

palliolum: Roman (753 B.C.E.–323 C.E.). Woman's veil, sometimes held in place with a wreath.

pallium: 1. Roman (753 B.C.E.–323 C.E.). Outdoor garment cut as a long square or rectangle of wool, then draped and fastened at the shoulder or neck with a fibula. Considered signature garment of the scholar and philosopher. Female version was the palla. 2. Ecclesiastical dress. In sixth century, worn by the pope over the left shoulder. In eighth century, V-shaped band worn over the chest over the other garments. In 10th century, became round-necked scarf with ends that hung down front and back. Today, woven band of white lamb's wool worn by Catholic archbishops over the chasuble. Decorated with four crosses.

pallustache: Greek. Cretan thigh-length shenti.

Palm Beach: Trade name for lightweight suiting made with cotton warp and mohair filling.

palmas: Ecuador. Palm tree–shaped silver earrings.

Palmerston wrapper: Crinoline (1840–1865 C.E.). United Kingdom. Popular 1853–1855, man's single-breasted full overcoat with wrapped front. It had wide, cuffless sleeves, a wide collar and lapel, and side flap pockets. Named after a popular politician.

palmilha: Portugal. Sole of a shoe.

p'almok sigye: Korea. Wristwatch.

Palmyra broché: Bustle (1865–1890 C.E.). In 1878, fine wool fabric, closely ribbed.

palmyrene: Romantic (1815–1840 C.E.). Introduced in 1827, silk-embroidered textile similar to poplin.

palmyrienne: Romantic (1815–1840 C.E.). Introduced in 1831, wool and silk fabric similar to mousseline de soie.

palo de lione: Renaissance (1450–1550 C.E.). Italy. Literally, "skin of lion," yellow color similar to a lionskin.

palomita: Spain. Bow tie.

palpulana: India. Lye.

palto: Russia. Crinoline (1840–1865 C.E.). In 1855, an officer's greatcoat.

paltock: Early Gothic (1200–1350 C.E.). Short jacket. Precursor of the pourpoint.

paludamentum: 1. Roman (753 B.C.E.–323 C.E.). Military mantle worn by the general in command or the emperor on the field. Cut like a chlamys, in the shape of a semicircle. 2. Byzantine (400–1200 C.E.). The imperial mantle, a half circle of richly embroidered purple velvet.

palulu maka: United States of America. Hawaii. Eyeshade.

pamela: 1. Directoire and First Empire (1790–1815 C.E.). United Kingdom. Popular 1800–1815 C.E., woman's small bonnet that tied with large ribbons under the chin. 2. Spain. Boater.

Pamela bonnet (Crinoline period) See also photospread (Headwear).

Pamela bonnet: 1. Crinoline (1840–1865 C.E.). United Kingdom. Popular 1845–1855, woman's small straw bonnet with a small lace frill at the nape of the neck. Brim and the crown were made in one piece. Trimmed with ribbons and often with flowers. Named after the heroine of Richardson's novel. 2. Bustle (1865–1890 C.E.). Similar to the Pamela bonnet of the Crinoline period, but with a more pointed brim and longer lace frill. It was commonly decorated with wide ribbons and heavy floral sprays.

pamela hat: Crinoline (1840–1865 C.E.). United Kingdom. Introduced in 1845, small gypsy hat of straw.

Pamico: Trade name for cotton plain weave fabric in solid colors.

pampa: Bolivia. In a textile, the monochrome space between stripes or patterned bands.

pampanilla: Peru. Tribal woman's loincloth.

pampilion: Renaissance (1450–1550 C.E.). Italy. Type of felt or a black fur from Navarre.

pamsukula: Thailand. Buddhist monk's robes made from discarded fabric.

Pamela bonnet (Bustle period) Dover Publications

pamuk: Croatia and Serbia. Cotton.

pamutos vászon: Hungary. Cotton and linen blend fabric.

pana: Ecuador, Guatemala, and Spain. Corduroy; velvet.

pana con cervaduras muy finas: Spain. Pin corduroy.

panache: France. 1. Plume or bunch of feathers worn erect in a headdress. 2. Bunch of tassels or ribbons.

panache blanc: France. White plume.

panache de coque: France. Plume of rooster feathers.

panaena: Australia. Maori sandal with toe protection.

panaeva: Russia. Worn under the sarafan; long wool skirt.

panama canvas: Heavy, colored basket weave, cotton fabric used for embroidery.

panama cloth: Millinery fabric whose texture suggests Panama hats.

Panama hat: (20th century). Originally made of exotic leaves, they were later made in poplar wood (latanier) and today are made of a fine straw from Ecuador or Colombia. In shape, they have a rounded crown.

panaúla: Greece. Apron.

panba: Iran. Cotton.

pancake bag: Flat circular handbag.

pancake beret: Broad flat beret.

pancake sleeves: *See* beret sleeve.

pancauna: India. A five-colored silk.

pancavarnapadi: India. A five-colored silk stuff.

pance: *See* dhoti.

pañchaphalaka: India. Necklace of five flat gems.

pandin: Borneo. Buckle.

pandjesjas: Holland. Tailcoat.

pandva: India. An unbleached or dyed cotton or silken stuff.

pane: India. Worn by young girls, a length of fabric worn wrapped around the body.

panel skirt: Gay Nineties (1890–1900 C.E.). United Kingdom. Woman's double day skirt with an overskirt that was two inches shorter than the underskirt and open on the left side showing a decorative panel of velvet.

paneter: India. Special red and white tie-dyed wedding sari.

pang' adari norigae: Korea. Pendant in the shape of a treadmill (symbol of strong legs).

panghyang: *See* hyangsu.

panier a coudes: *See* panniers.

paniers a bourelets: *See* panniers.

paniers anglais: *See* panniers.

panjam: Cotton fabric.

panjóva: *See* plakhta.

panne: 1. Directoire and First Empire (1790–1815 C.E.). Deep piled velvet used mostly for upholstery. Silk panne from Lyons was much sought after. 2. Gay Nineties (1890–1900 C.E.). Introduced in 1899, silk fabric between velvet and satin. 3. Finish for velvet or satin created by flattening the fabric.

panne satin: Satin treated by heat and pressure.

panne velvet: Velvet similar to mirror velvet.

panni diasperati: *See* diasper.

panni imperiales: Roman (753 B.C.E.–323 C.E.). Literally "imperial fabrics."

pannicelli: Renaissance (1450–1550 C.E.). Italy. Linen cloths worn by women over the head and/or shoulders.

pannier crinoline: Bustle (1865–1890 C.E.). United Kingdom. Popular in 1870s, combination cage crinoline and bustle.

pannier dress: Bustle (1865–1890 C.E.). United Kingdom. Introduced in 1868, woman's double skirted day dress with the upper skirt gathered up in the back and sides and a trained underskirt.

panniers
See also photospread
(Undergarments).

panniers: Early Georgian (1700–1750 C.E.). First appearing around 1718 and in fashion until 1800, skirts stretched over metal hoops. Initially round and called encouple or en gueridon. Later were oval, and called paniers a coudes. Top hoop was referred to as the traquenard. Panniers with a thick roll at the bottom edge were called paniers a bourelets. Panniers made with eight hoops were called paniers anglais. By 1750, the one-piece pannier was replaced by a two piece, with one section over each hip, called jansenistes.

panno: Italy. Felt cloth.

panno e pannino: Italy. Woolen cloth.

pannus: *See* textum.

pannus sine grano: Renaissance (1450–1550 C.E.). Ireland. Undressed English wool fabric that was dressed in Ireland.

Pannuscorium: Trade name for leather cloth.

pano: 1. Egyptian (4000–30 B.C.E.). Ankle-length transparent overskirt worn by both genders. 2. Portugal. Fabric.

paño: 1. Ecuador and Guatemala. Plain-weave wool fabric. 2. Spain. Cloth.

paño berbi: Peru. Uncombed wool fabric.

paño de brunete: Renaissance (1450–1550 C.E.). Spain. Cheap black cloth.

paño de la tierra: Renaissance (1450–1550 C.E.). Spain. Local cloth.

paño tuntido: Renaissance (1450–1550 C.E.). Spain. Sheared cloth.

pañolones: Peru. Blankets worn as shawls.

Panovraki: Greece. Man's long under-trousers.

panseron: Elizabethan (1550–1625 C.E.). France. Peascod belly.

panses: Elizabethan (1550–1625 C.E.). France. Peascod-belly.

pansid slops: *See* slops.

pansiere: Early Gothic (1200–1350 C.E.). Armor worn to protect the lower front of the body.

pansomae: Korea. Half-length sleeve.

pansomae syossu: Korea. Short-sleeved shirt.

pansy: *See* pensée.

p'anta: Bolivia. Headcloth.

pantadoe: *See* pintado.

pantalettes: Directoire and First Empire (1790–1815 C. E.) to Crinoline (1840–1865 C.E.). Worn from ca. 1812 to 1840s, woman's undergarment with long straight legged white drawers reaching almost to the ankle. Trimmed with lace or decorative tucks. Could be seen reaching below the skirt until c.1850.

pantalon: France. Trousers; slacks.

pantalon de travial: France. Overalls.

pantalone: Bosnia. Trousers.

pantalones: Spain. Trousers.

pantalones bermuda: Spain. Bermuda shorts.

pantalones cerrados por debajo de la rodilla: Spain. Knickers.

pantalones cortos: 1. Ecuador. A man's short, knee-length pants. 2. Spain. Shorts.

pantalones de baño: Spain. Bathing trunks.

pantalones de equitación: Spain. Jodhpurs.

pantalones de gimnasia: Spain. Gym shorts.

pantalones de golf: Spain. Knickerbockers.

pantalones largos hasta media pantorrillas: Spain. Pedal pushers.

pantalones rajados: Guatemala. Man's heavy woolen trousers of black, blue, or brown. They are worn over cotton under-trousers.

pantalones sueltos: Spain. Slacks.

pantalones tejanos: Spain. Jeans.

pantalones vaqueros: *See* pantalones tejanos.

pantaloni: 1. *See* abito da pantalone. 2. Romania and Russia. Trousers.

pantaloni alla zuava: Italy. Knickerbockers.

pantaloni corti: Italy. Shorts.

pantalons à pont: France. Directoire and First Empire (1790–1815 C.E.). Trousers that opened in front with panel buttoned to vest with three buttons.

pantaloon trousers: Romantic (1815–1840 C.E.). United Kingdom. Variation of the pantaloon that was loose from the calf down. Did not have side slits.

pantaloons: 1. Restoration (1660–1700 C.E.). Petticoat breeches. 2. Directoire and First Empire (1790–1815 C.E.). Popular from 1790 to 1850, initially snug fitting tights that ended just below the calf. After 1817, reached to the ankles and had short side slits, and were strapped under the foot. 3. Romantic (1815–1840 C.E.). Another name for the pantalette.

pantaplis: *See* šliuré.

panteen collar: Bustle (1865–1890 C.E.). United Kingdom. Popular in 1880s, high collar worn with women's jackets.

pantera: Italy and Spain. Panther.

panther: Fur from the *Felix pardus*, a leopard with a rare form of melanism.

Panther: Germany. Panther.

panthère: France. Panther.

panti: Bolivia. A wine or deep red color.

panties: Woman's short undergarment with practically no leg portion.

pantile: Charles I and the Commonwealth (1625–1660 C.E.). United Kingdom. Popular from 1640s to 1665, another name for the sugarloaf hat.

pántlikaskökö: Hungary. Apron trimmed with flowered ribbon.

pantofel: 1. Czechoslovakia. Slipper. 2. Poland. Slipper.

pantoffel: Holland. Slipper.

Pantoffel: Germany. Slipper.

pantofle: Renaissance (1450–1550 C.E.) to Charles I and the Commonwealth (1625–1660 C.E.). Mule or slipper overshoe with a wood or cork sole, worn to protect the shoe.

pantofola: Italy. Slipper.

pantoufle: France. Slipper.

pantouflenn: *See* arc'henad-kambr.

pantserhandschoen: Holland. Gauntlet.

pantuflas: Spain. Slippers.

pantuflo: Elizabethan (1550–1625 C.E.). Spain. Slipper.

panty corselette: (1960–1969 C.E.). Full body corselette with under crotch snaps.

pañu sumbriru: Ecuador. Small fedora.

pañuelo: 1. Philippine Islands. Square scarf folded in a triangle and worn as a collar or neck ruffle. 2. Spain. Handkerchief. 3. Ecuador. Shawl.

pañuelo para el cuello: Spain. Cravat.

panujil: Korea. Needlework.

panul: Korea. Needle.

panung: Thailand. Long wide strip of fabric worn shaped into a loincloth or skirt by both genders.

panungh: *See* panung.

pănură: *See* stofă.

panutzutzu ukufachallina: Ecuador. Woman's embroidered shawl worn for fiestas.

Panzer: *See* Brustharnisch.

panzo de burro: *See* zhutu.

páo: China. Gown.

paon velvet: Velvet with a thick pile. Pile is pressed in one direction.

paonazzo: *See* pavonazzo.

pàopàosha: China. Seersucker.

paoxié: China. Running shoes.

páozi: China. Gown.

papa: Samoa. Brassiere.

papa 'aiana: United States of America. Hawaii. Ironing board.

papaha: Russia. Fur cap.

papakha: Russia. Tall Caucasian hat.

papaki: *See* rapaki.

papale: United States of America. Hawaii. Generic term for hat.

papale ali'i: United States of America. Hawaii. Crown.

papale hainika: United States of America. Hawaii. Miter.

papale 'ie: United States of America. Hawaii. Hat made by sewing a long plaited strip into a hat.

papale kahuna: United States of America. Hawaii. Miter; priestly hat.

papale kapu: United States of America. Hawaii. Cap.

papale la'a: United States of America. Hawaii. Holy crown or head covering.

papale mu'ou'ou: United States of America. Hawaii. Literally "blunt hat," poke bonnet.

papale 'o'oma: United States of America. Hawaii. Literally "flared hat," bonnet; sunbonnet.

papale waiokila: United States of America. Hawaii. Panama hat.

papalu: United States of America. Hawaii. Apron.

papanaky: 1. Greek (3000-100 B.C.E.). Woman's head-pad. 2. Roman (753 B.C.E.–323 C.E.). Head pad embroidered with gold and worn high on head.

papari: Australia. Maori sandal and legging combination of green flax, stuffed with moss.

pápçes: Greece. Side opening of a dress.

papeline: Late Georgian (1750–1790 C.E.). France. Poplin.

paper cambric: Thin, narrow cambric, glazed and stiffened.

paper muslin: Tin, narrow muslin.

paper taffeta: Crisp, lightweight taffeta.

papillote comb: Romantic (1815–1840 C.E.). Introduced in 1828, decorative tortoiseshell three- to four-inch hair comb.

papillotes: Early Georgian (1700–1750). Paper hair curlers.

papoon: United Kingdom. Cotton fabric made for export.

papuc: Romania. Slipper.

papuca: Croatia and Serbia. Slipper.

papuča: Bosnia. Slipper.

papute: Romania. Shoes.

paquebot capote: Romantic (1815–1840 C.E.). Introduced in 1830s, bibi with brim trimmed with ribbons and lace.

parachute bag: Pouch style handbag.

parachute hat: *See* balloon hat.

parachute fabric: Lightweight, plain weave fabric of silk, cotton, nylon, or rayon.

paradise feather: Plume from bird of paradise.

paragaudion: Byzantine and Romanesque (400–1200 C.E.). Gold embroidered band presented by the Byzantine emperor to vassal sovereigns.

paragod: Biblical (Unknown–30 C.E.). Hebrew's bordered garment.

paragon: 1. Restoration (1660–1700 C.E.). Fabric similar to camlet. 2. Tightly woven fabric of wool or silk.

paraguas: Spain. Umbrella.

Paraguay lace: Spider-web style lace in wheel designs.

paragunda: Roman (753 B.C.E.–323 C.E.). Bordered garment.

parakiri: New Zealand. Maori term for a large cloak.

paramani: Italy. Cuffs.

paramatta: Lightweight fabric similar to bombazine or twill.

parament: Early Georgian (1700–1750 C.E.). Ornamental cuffs.

paramentos sacerdotais: Portugal. Clerical vestments.

paran: India. The color leaf green.

paranchah: Uzbekistan. Close-meshed horsehair veil worn by women over the age of ten.

p'arang: Korea. Blue; green.

paraplu: Holland. Umbrella.

parapluie: 1. Late Georgian (1750–1790 C.E.). Folding rain umbrella. 2. France. Umbrella.

parasisol: Linen-weave straw.

parasol: Small umbrella, usually not waterproof, carried by women for effect.

párasol: Portugal. Parasol.

parasol à canne: Late Georgian (1750–1790 C.E.). France. Parasol that doubled as a cane.

parasol skirt: Multi-gore skirt.

parasole: Italy. Parasol.

parasolka: Poland. Umbrella.

parasol-whip: Crinoline (1840–1865 C.E.). Popular in 1840s, parasol mounted halfway up the driving whip. Lost favor in 1870s.

paravalia: India. A coral colored stuff.

parawai: New Zealand. Maori term for a large cloak.

parchment: Pale tan.

parchment calves: Late Georgian (1750–1790 C.E.). Parchment shapes worn inside the breeches to improve the look of the leg.

parchment lace: Raised design lace made with parchment strips (cartisane).

parchmentier: (19th century). United Kingdom. Thin wool fabric made in Norwich.

pardessus: Crinoline (1840–1865 C.E.). Generic term for any outer garment of knee or three-quarter length.

pardessus redingote: Crinoline (1840–1865 C.E.). Introduced in 1850s, French term for the frock coat.

pardillo: 1. Peru. Coarse, dun-colored wool fabric. 2. Renaissance (1450–1550 C.E.). Spain. Grayish brown.

pardo: 1. India. Curtain. 2. Portugal and Spain. Brown.

pardo amarillento: Spain. Russet.

pardo opaco: Spain. Drab color.

pardo rojizo: Spain. Rust color.

parduzco: Spain. Drab color.

pare: Australia. Maori headband or chaplet.

parel: Holland. Pearl.

parements: *See* facings.

parements d'aube: *See* facings.

parements interrompus: *See* facings.

parengarenga: New Zealand. Maori. Leggings made of flax, woven in a wide piece and then laced on the body.

pareo: *See* pareu.

pareu: Rectangular cotton cloth worn as a skirt or loincloth.

parevau pata: India. A pigeon gray silk fabric.

parfait-contentement: Late Georgian (1750–1790 C.E.). France. Bow that covered the pin at the neck.

pari muka: Maori. Bodice of flax fiber.

paridhana: *See* dhoti.

parihasta: India. Bracelet.

parikara: India. A tight waistband.

Paris embroidery: White cord embroidery on pique.

Paris hat: Silk hat.

Parisian satin: (1900–1910 C.E.). Extremely soft satin fabric.

Paris-Pekin: Bustle (1865–1890 C.E.). In 1874, striped fancy fabric.

parivesa: India. Decorative waistband.

parka: Hooded jacket, usually with zipper in front.

parkala: India. Kind of spangled robe set with pieces of glass.

parkesine: Crinoline (1840–1865 C.E.). Invented in 1856, but only in general use after 1862, a plastic made from pyroxyline.

Parma violet: 1. Romantic (1815–1840 C.E.). In 1827, a new color. 2. Gay Nineties (1890–1900 C.E.). In 1896, a pale shade of heliotrope.

parmnaram: India. Shawl.

parniyan: India. A type of silk.

parnoe: Russia. Lace designs worked onto net or tulle.

parochka: Bustle (1865–1890 C.E.). Russia. Woman's suit consisting of a skirt and blouse made of the same fabric.

parricides: *See* Vatermörder.

parrock: Late Gothic (1350–1450 C.E.) to Renaissance (1450–1550 C.E.). Man's loose cloak with armseyes.

parrot green: Medium yellowish green.

parrucca: Italy. Periwig.

parson's hat: Clerical felt hat with low crown and wide brim.

part: Poland. Coarse hempen cloth.

part lace: Any bobbin lace in which the sections are made separately and then joined.

párta: 1. Romantic (1815–1840 C.E.). Austro-Hungarian Empire. Woman's cap of tinsel adorned with metal plates and disks that hung from it by ribbons or leather strips. Young women decorated it with pearls and enameled agrafes. Married women wore it covered in flat metal plates that were decorated with pearls. 2. Hungary. Girl's wreath of pearls or artificial flowers.

particolored: Early Gothic (1200–1350 C.E.). Garment made of two or more different fabrics.

partidor de crencha: Renaissance (1450–1550 C.E.). Spain. Hair parter.

partlet: Renaissance (1450–1550 C.E.). United Kingdom. Collared and ruffled covering for the neck and shoulders. Women's were made in linen; men's of richer fabric and ornamented.

parure: Directoire and First Empire (1790–1815 C.E.). France. Matched set of jewelry, including a necklace, bracelet, earrings, pin etc. Grand parure includes a headpiece. Demi-parure includes everything except the headpiece.

parure cornouailles: Bustle (1865–1890 C.E.). In 1870, velvet collar with bow, velvet band for hair, and velvet bodice bow. Embroidered with beads.

paryanka: India. *See* paryastika.

paryastaka: *See* rasana.

paryastika: India. A kamarband.

pas: Poland. Belt.

pás: Czechoslovakia. Belt.

pasa montañas: Spain. Stocking cap.

pāsābandhi kediyū: India. A short coat-like angarakha with strings for closures.

pāsābandi kediyoo: *See* pāsābandhi kediyū.

pasamanos: Ecuador and Guatemala. Trim; edging.

pashm: *See* cashmere.

pashmina: *See* cashmere.

pasoúmia: Greece. Sandal.

pass: Elizabethan (1550–1625 C.E.) to Restoration (1660–1700 C.E.). Front of a hat.

passacaille: *See* passecaille.

passagers: Charles I and the Commonwealth (1625–1660 C.E.). Curled lock worn near the temple.

passamontagna: Italy. Balaclava.

passanastro: Italy. Trim insertion.

passe: Crinoline (1840–1865 C.E.). Introduced in 1864, group of flowers or trim under the brim of a bonnet.

passecaille: Early Georgian (1700–1750 C.E.). Ribbon on which the muff was hung. Name came from a fashionable dance, the passacaglia.

passe-filon: Renaissance (1450–1550 C.E.). France. Fringe of hair worn across the forehead or a braid kept in place at the temples by a circlet.

passemayne lace: France. A term referring to both braid and early bobbin lace.

passemente: Early Gothic (1200–1350 C.E.). Braid of gold, silver, or other colors.

passementerie: Trim, especially heavy embroidery, guimp, braid, beads, tinsel, etc.

passementier: France. Maker of passementerie.

passementier-boutonnier: France. Maker of passementerie and buttons.

passements: France. Generic term for trims.

passionee: Patch worn at the corner of the eye.

passium: Egyptian (4000–30 B.C.E.). Very wide collar-like necklace.

passives: Many of the threads involved in bobbin lace; similar to the warp threads of a loom.

paste: Glass cut and polished into imitation of gems.

pastrano: Italy. Frock coat.

pastura: Romania. Apron worn over petticoats.

pasuāj: India. Full skirt.

pasvāj: *See* pasuāj.

pat gat: India. A man's bathing apron.

pata: *See* amsuka; badhani.

pataccara: India. Old, worn out clothing or any old fabric.

patagium: Roman (753 B.C.E.–323 C.E.). Similar to clavi, a band of purple or gold decoration worn down the fronts of women's tunics.

patalani: India. Rose color.

pataniya sacopa: India. An embroidered silk or velvet of Patan origin.

pata-pallavah: India. A bordered silk fabric.

patatúka: Greece. Wide, black overcoat with long, narrow sleeves.

patch dye: Dye process where one or more dyes are added to the fabric in an uneven or patchy manner.

patch pocket: (20th century). Pocket sewn on the outside of a garment.

patch veil: Gay Nineties (1890–1900 C.E.). Veil with large velvet wafers.

patelet: Renaissance (1450–1550 C.E.). Padded vest worn under armor.

patent kid: Kid leather finished with a transparent lacquer.

patent lace: Directoire and First Empire (1790–1815 C.E.). United Kingdom. Machine made lace.

patent leather: Any leather with a varnished finish.

patent leather boots: Bustle (1865–1890 C.E.). United Kingdom. Worn from 1870s, men's ankle high button boots of patent leather uppers.

patent net: Directoire and First Empire (1790–1815 C.E.). Knitted net made on the point net machine.

patentni zatvarač: *See* rajferšlus.

paternostri: Italy. Thick beads.

pateshehon: Biblical (Unknown–30 C.E.). Hebrew man's breeches.

patka: India. 1. A girdle made from a band of cloth worn wrapped around the body many times. It may be embroidered or brocaded. 2. A woman's decorative panel of cloth worn at the waist over the anteriya.

patna: Charles I and the Commonwealth (1625–1660 C.E.). One of first imported fabrics, this printed cloth came from Patna, Egypt.

pato'i: Samoa. Jet black.

patola: India. Silk double-ikat textile or silk cloth.

patolaka: India. A variegated silk fabric.

patolla: *See* patola.

patolo: *See* patola.

patondon: Indonesia. Sa'dan-Toraja man's hairstyle where the hair is made into a knot on the front of the head.

patorī: India. Sari with silk border.

patori: India. Sari with a silk border.

patrakarnika: India. Leaflike ear pendant.

Patrician: Crinoline (1840–1865 C.E.). Mantle cut somewhat on the bias. Center back seam was covered with embroidery.

patrol jacket: Bustle (1865–1890 C.E.). United Kingdom. 1. Man's hip-length, single-breasted jacket with five buttons, Prussian collar, and a military cut. 2. Introduced in 1889, woman's hip-length, fitted jacket cut without center back seam. It had front military trim, snug sleeves, and small cuffs.

patrona: India. Bleached silk.

patrontache: Russia. Cossack cartridge pouch.

patrorna: India. A variety of wild silk.

pat-sari: India. Silk sari.

patta: India. Cloth worn by women as a waist belt.

pattabandha: India. An ornamented gold strip used to hold the turban in position.

pattadukula: India. A silk and linen blend.

pattahari: India. A silk fabric from Herat.

pattala: *See* patola.

pattamsuka: India. A plain white silk.

pattamsuya: India. A fine silk fabric.

patte: *See* guleron.

pattens: Early Gothic (1200–1350 C.E.) to Elizabethan (1550–1625 C.E.). Chopines.

patti: India. Handwoven fabric that is 9–18 inches wide.

patti jets: Bustle (1865–1890 C.E.). United Kingdom. Introduced in 1869, balls of polished jet worn hanging from a ribbon necklace with matching earrings.

pattika: India. 1. A cotton dhoti. 2. An elaborate band of embroidery used as a cummerbund.

pattu: India. Homespun wool or tweed.

patu hitau: Maori. Stone club used to beat the flax fiber.

patúnes: Greece. White cotton ankle socks.

patynek: *See* pantofel.

patzeb: India. Loincloth.

pa'u: United States of America. Hawaii. Woman's skirt; sarong; skirt worn by female horseback riders.

pa'u heihei: United States of America. Hawaii. Sarong made of leaves.

pa'u meme'i: Samoa. Elastic.

pauku: New Zealand. Maori. A thick mat-like cloak.

pauldron: Early Gothic (1200–1350 C.E.). In armor, shoulder piece.

pauma: United States of America. Hawaii. Large curved needle.

pautener: Early Gothic (1200–1350 C.E.). Bag worn hung from the girdle.

pavediens: Lithuania. Thread.

pavo real: Mexico. Peacock embroidery pattern done by the Zoque Indians.

pavonazzo: Renaissance (1450–1550 C.E.). Italy. Peacock colored.

pavot: Bustle (1865–1890 C.E.). In 1886, ruby color.

paysanne bonnet: Directoire and First Empire (1790–1815 C.E.). Worn after 1800, the cottage bonnet.

pea: Samoa. Woman's costume.

pe'a: Samoa. Tattoo.

pea jacket: Romantic (1815–1840 C.E.) to Crinoline (1840–1865 C.E.). United Kingdom. Man's short double-breasted coat with wide lapels and a velvet collar. In 1850s, had huge buttons and a short back vent. After 1860, called the reefer.

peach: 1. Elizabethan (1550–1625 C.E.). Deep pinkish orange. 2. Bright tint of red orange.

peacock: Bright, dark blue green or green blue color.

pea-green: Directoire and First Empire (1790–1815 C.E.). Fashionable after 1809.

peak lace: Elizabethan (1550–1625 C.E.) to Restoration (1660–1700 C.E.). Lace with an irregular outer edge.

peallaid: Ireland. Gaelic word for sheepskin without the wool.

pealltag: Ireland. Gaelic word for patched cloak.

pearl gray: Neutral gray color.

pearl of beauty: Elizabethan (1550–1625 C.E.). United Kingdom. Striped worsted fabric.

pèarluinn: Ireland. Fine linen.

peasant fichu: Crinoline (1840–1865 C.E.). In 1856, woman's white fichu.

peasant lace: 1. Bobbin lace. 2. Torchon style lace.

peasant look: (1960–1970 C.E.). Late 1960s style generally consisting of a flounced skirt, head kerchief, and peasant blouse.

peasant skirt: Bustle (1865–1890 C.E.). United Kingdom. Introduced in 1885, full circle tennis skirt made with two or three tucks.

peasant's lace: *See* bavarian lace.

peascod belly: Elizabethan (1550–1625 C.E.). Doublet with padded front shaped like a peascod.

peau d'agneau: France. Lambskin.

peau d'ange: *See* angel skin.

peau de béte: Bustle (1865–1890 C.E.). In 1886, stiff plush used to imitate fur.

peasant look
See also photospread
(Women's Wear).
Dover Publications

peau de chevrette: Gay Nineties (1890–1900 C.E.). In 1893, a heavy peau de soie.

peau de cygne: France. Soft lustrous fabric.

peau de daim: France. Doeskin.

peau de soie: 1. Directoire and First Empire (1790–1815 C.E.). France. Particularly fine taffeta. 2. Bustle (1865–1890 C.E.). Dull, twill weave silk. *See also* paduasoy.

peau de suede: Bustle (1865–1890 C.E.). In 1887, a French silk.

pebasa: Sumbawa. A cloth worn draped over the shoulder.

peç: Iran. Fringed length of fabric.

peca: Balkans. Embroidered scarf worn over the poculica.

pecā: India. A turban of a folded strip of nine-inch-wide cotton that is 18–25 yards long.

peccary: Fine grained leather.

peche: France. Peach.

pechschwartz: Germany. Jet black.

pectoll: Renaissance (1450–1550 C.E.) to Elizabethan (1550–1625 C.E.). United Kingdom. Breast of a man's shirt.

pectoral: Egyptian (4000–30 B.C.E.). Piece of jewelry worn on a string or chain around the neck. Worn by nobility.

pectorale: Roman (753 B.C.E.–323 C.E.). Breastplate.

pedal pushers: (1950–1959 C.E.). Snug fitting pants ending below the knee, with or without a cuff.

pedal straw: Straw woven from foot of stalk.

pedaline: Synthetic straw.

pedimental headdress: *See* gable headdress.

pedraria: Portugal. Jewelry.

pedule: 1. Byzantine and Romanesque (400–1200 C.E.). Short hose, often worn turned down at the knee. 2. Early Gothic (1200–1350 C.E.). Boot-shaped leg covering of flannel, leather, or other fabric.

pee: Renaissance (1450–1550 C.E.) to Charles I and the Commonwealth (1625–1660 C.E.). Man's coat or jacket.

peek-a-boo waist: (1900–1910 C.E.). United Kingdom. Eyelet or sheer fabric shirtwaist.

peel: Crinoline (1840–1865 C.E.). United Kingdom. Man's light jacket.

peeler cotton: United States of America. Cotton used for combed yarns.

pegged boot: Boot with sole and upper fastened together with pegs.

Peggy collar: Round, flat collar similar to Peter Pan.

peg-top skirt: (20th century). Skirt very full at the waist and tapering to the hem.

peg-top sleeves: Crinoline (1840–1865 C.E.). United Kingdom. In fashion from 1857 to 1864, men's sleeves cut full at the armseye and tapering to the wrist. Revival of the gigot.

peg-top trousers: (1910–1920 C.E.). In 1911 and 1912, worn by college boys, trousers that were pleated and very wide at the waist and very narrow at the ankles.

peigné: France. Worsted.

peigne Josephine: Crinoline (1840–1865 C.E.). France. Woman's high hair comb decorated with small gilt balls. Worn at the back of the head for evening.

peg-top skirt
See also photospread (Women's Wear).

peignoir: 1. Crinoline (1840–1865 C.E.). Dress with unboned bodice. 2. Bustle (1865–1890 C.E.). France. Woman's loose unboned wrapper of light material.

peinadore: Renaissance (1450–1550 C.E.). Spain. Combing jacket.

peinture à l'aiguille: France. Literally "painting with the needle," pictorial embroideries.

peiteag: Ireland. Gaelic word for waistcoat; doublet; and woolen shirt.

peiteag-mhuinicheallach: Ireland. Gaelic word for jacket.

pejar: India. Footwear.

pekerere: New Zealand. Maori. A shoulder cape.

pekin: Bustle (1865–1890 C.E.). Used ca. 1879, term for any striped textile of alternating matte and shiny stripes.

pekin Aneline: Crinoline (1840–1865 C.E.). In 1861, soft woolen shawl with border of Chinese pattern.

pekin bournous: Crinoline (1840–1865 C.E.). In 1861, Canton crepe zouave for evening.

pekin crepe: Pekin fabric with a crepe weft.

pekin point: Crinoline (1840–1865 C.E.). Introduced in 1840, very rich white silk painted with flowers or foliage.

pekin satin: Directoire and First Empire (1790–1815 C.E.). Introduced in 1807, heavy satin with a self-stripe.

pelanu vastu: India. Literally "the stuff of the past," to be out of fashion.

pele de cordeiro: *See* pelica.

pelego: *See* pelica.

pelele: 1. Chitonga. A lip ornament. 2. Spain. Rompers.

pelerine: Late Georgian (1750–1790 C.E.). France. Woman's short shoulder cape of fur, velvet, or muslin.

pelerine

peleryna: Poland. Cape.

peleue: Samoa. Jacket.

pelica: Portugal. Lambskin.

pelicon: Byzantine and Romanesque (400–1200 C.E.) to Renaissance (1450–1550 C.E.). France. Fur-lined garment worn between the chemise and the cote.

pelise: *See* pelisse.

pelisse: Directoire and First Empire (1790–1815 C.E.). Long loose cloak that opened in the center front. Sometimes had a hood and was lined with fur.

pelisse-mantle: Romantic (1815–1840 C.E.) to Crinoline (1840–1865 C.E.). United Kingdom. Popular from 1838 to 1845, three-quarter to full-length caped cloak that draped over the arms, forming pseudo-sleeves. In the 1840s, cinched in at the waist in the back.

pelisse-robe: Romantic (1815–1840 C.E.) to Crinoline (1840–1865 C.E.). United Kingdom. Popular from 1817 to 1850, woman's day dress shaped like a pelisse and tied down the center front with bows. Called the redingote after 1840.

pelisson: Early Gothic (1200–1350 C.E.) to Renaissance (1450–1550 C.E.). Furred overgarment. *See also* pilch.

pellanda: Renaissance (1450–1550 C.E.). Italy. Fur lined overgarment with full sleeves ending in decorative edges.

pelliccia: Italy. Fur.

pellicea: Byzantine and Romanesque (400–1200 C.E.). An 11th-century fur-lined cassock.

pellicia: *See* pellicea.

Pelliz: Germany. Old High German term for fur.

pelliza: Spain. Fur.

pelo de castor: Spain. Beaver hair.

pelo de liebre: Spain. Hare hair.

pelo di castora: Italy. Beaver hair.

pelo di lepre: Italy. Hare hair.

pels: Denmark and Sweden. Fur.

peluca: Spain. Wig.

peluche: France. Plush or plush velvet.

peluche a poils: France. Literally "hairy plush," long-haired plush.

peluche de soie: France. Literally "silk plush," hatter's plush felt.

Pelz: Germany. Fur.

Pembroke paletot: Crinoline (1840–1865 C.E.). United Kingdom. Man's long-waisted, double-breasted calf-length overcoat with wide lapels, vertical breast pocket, flapped side pockets, and self-cuffs.

penache: *See* panache.

penang: India. Heavyweight, plain weave, native cotton fabric.

penang lawyer: Romantic (1815–1840 C.E.) to Bustle (1865–1890 C.E.). United Kingdom. Man's walking stick made from the stem of a palm from Penang.

peñas veras: Renaissance (1450–1550 C.E.). Spain. Ermines.

pencilled: Late Georgian (1750–1790 C.E.). Colors that were hand painted on fabric.

pendants d'oreille: Long drop earrings.

pendeloque: Pendant pear-shaped diamond or other gem.

pendej: Romania. Petticoat of a rough fabric.

pendely: Hungary. Woman's linen skirt with a high waistband and two shoulder straps.

pendicle: Elizabethan (1550–1625 C.E.). Man's drop earring. Only one was worn at a time.

penduricalho: Portugal. Pendant.

penelope: Sleeveless, knitted jacket.

penelope canvas: Double-thread canvas used for tapestry work.

peniascoe: *See* pinasco.

peniche lace: Portugal. Pillow lace in black and white.

penina: Samoa. Pearl.

penistone: United Kingdom. Once made in Penistone, coarse woolen fabric. *See also* forest white.

penitentials: Colloquial term for clothes of black.

penna di fagiano: Italy. Pheasant's feather.

penna di gallo: Italy. Cock feather.

pennbazh: France. Walking stick with knobbed head, often used as a bludgeon.

pensée: Romantic (1815–1840 C.E.). Dark purple.

pentadoe: *See* pintado.

penteado: Portugal. Coiffure.

pentes: Bustle (1865–1890 C.E.). Introduced in 1886, pyramid shaped panels of silk or velvet forming an underskirt, with an overskirt or tunic worn draped to expose the underskirt.

pentlení: Slovakia. Very ornate bridal wedding headdresses.

peoth: Hebrew. Hair, specifically side locks.

pepa de zapallo: Ecuador. Squash seed–shaped silver earring.

pepeiao: United States of America. Hawaii. Scallops in lace.

pepetu: Transvaal. Ndebele pubescent girl's beaded rectangular apron. It is 15 x 11 inches.

peplo: Spain. Peplum.

peplos: Greek (3000-100 B.C.E.). Overfold of the Doric chiton.

peplos chiton: Greek (3000-100 B.C.E.). Woman's garment cut in a large rectangle. Worn with a fold on the left side and the right side open to fall in loose drapery. Folded down at the top edge and pinned at the shoulders.

peplum basque: Bustle (1865–1890 C.E.). United Kingdom. Introduced in 1866, woman's peplum-shaped basque on a belt.

peplum bodice: Bustle (1865–1890 C.E.). United Kingdom. Woman's evening bodice with panniers.

peplum dolman: Bustle (1865–1890 C.E.). United Kingdom. Introduced in 1872, woman's dolman with long side points.

peplum imperatrice: France. Basque bodice with draped tunic or panniers.

peplum jupon: Bustle (1865–1890 C.E.). United Kingdom. Introduced in 1866, woman's gored petticoat with three hoops at the bottom and a pleated flounce. Replaced the cage crinoline.

peplum overskirt: Gay Nineties (1890–1900 C.E.). United Kingdom. Introduced in 1894, overskirt of a drape that was pleated into the waistband, short in the back but gradually lengthening to hem length in the front.

peplum rotonde: Bustle (1865–1890 C.E.). United Kingdom. Introduced in 1871, woman's waist-length circular cloak. Had a back vent and fringe on the edges.

pepper and salt: Any fabric made of black and white yarns.

pepperbox: Walking stick with a hidden automatic firearm.

percale: Tightly woven, plain weave, cotton fabric available in prints and solids. One of the most popular fabrics.

percale taffeta: Crinoline (1840–1865 C.E.). Introduced in 1859, cambric sarcenet.

percaline: Crinoline (1840–1865 C.E.) to present. Introduced in 1848, fine, thin, plain weave, cotton fabric with a glassy surface.

percatka: Russia. Glove.

percaula: *See* parkala.

perches: France. Medium grade linen.

percollae: *See* parkala.

percolle: *See* parkala.

Perdita chemise: Late Georgian (1750–1790 C.E.). United Kingdom. Woman's day dress with a V-neck and a falling collar that closed in the center front with buttons or ribbon bows from neck to hem. Had a broad waist sash that tied in back.

perednik: Russia. Apron. *See also* fartuk.

peridot: Semiprecious light green stone.

perineal strap: Strap connected to the corset which attaches to menstruation napkins/towels.

periwinkle: Light blue purple.

perizoma: Greek (3000-100 B.C.E.). Short, close-fitting Etruscan man's trunks with contrasting trim around the legs.

perkal: Poland. Calico.

perla: 1. Ecuador, Guatemala, and Poland. Pearl. 2. *See* biser.

perle: Renaissance (1450–1550 C.E.). Spain. Pearl.

perlehatt: Norway. Beaded hat.

perlin: Renaissance (1450–1550 C.E.) to Restoration (1660–1700 C.E.). Scotland. Lace.

perna da calça: Portugal. Trouser leg.

pērō: Roman (753 B.C.E.–323 C.E.). Agricultural boot of hairy undressed hide.

pérola: Portugal. Pearl; bead.

peropus: Elizabethan (1550–1625 C.E.) to Restoration (1660–1700 C.E.). Watered double camlet.

perpets: *See* perpetuana.

perpetuana: Elizabethan (1550–1625 C.E.). Very durable fabric.

perraje: Ecuador and Guatemala. Woman's cotton or cotton and wool blend shawl with fringed ends. Usually striped.

perramus: Spain. Raincoat.

perreje o tapado: Guatemala. Shawl.

perriwigg: Periwig.

perruche: Bustle (1865–1890 C.E.). In 1873, parrot color.

perrukes à bourse: Bagwig.

perruque quarrée: France. Early Georgian (1700–1750 C.E.). Literally, "squared wig." Worn by magistrates and serious men, a section of hair was worn at the nape in a queue and the rest shorter with a squared bottom edge.

perse: 1. Early Gothic (1200–1350 C.E.). Bluish gray. 2. Early Georgian (1700–1750 C.E.). Painted cloth from Coromandel Coast. Very fashionable in 18th century and again in mid-19th century.

Persian: Early Georgian (1700–1750 C.E.) to Late Georgian (1750–1790 C.E.). Thin silk used in linings.

persian broadtail: Beautiful pelts of young or premature Persian lamb.

Persian cap: Directoire and First Empire (1790–1815 C.E.). Introduced in 1811, fashionable riding hat.

persian cord: Plain weave, ribbed fabric.

Persian drape tunic: (1910–1920 C.E. until 1940 C.E.). Tunic with a full cut and draped skirts.

Persian lamb: Lustrous, black, brown, or gray fur with very tight curls. *See also* astrakhan.

Persian lawn: Sheer, plain weave, cotton fabric that is usually white and lustrous. Similar to India linon.

Persian lilac: Gay Nineties (1890–1900 C.E.). In 1891, a new color.

Persian pickle: Paisley.

Persian scarf: Directoire and First Empire (1790–1815 C.E.). Popular in 1812, cashmere or silk scarf with a Persian border.

Persian vest: United Kingdom. Restoration (1660–1700 C.E.). Introduced by Charles II in 1666, a loose coat held by a sash or belt.

Persianer: Germany. Persian lamb.

persienne: Persia. Cotton or silk fabric in an elaborate print.

perspective glass: Elizabethan (1550–1625 C.E.) to Restoration (1660–1700 C.E.). United Kingdom. Small lens for seeing distant objects and worn on a chain or ribbon around the neck.

pertla: Bosnia. Shoelace.

peruça: Portugal. Periwig.

Peruvian cotton: Peru. Rough, hairy cotton.

Peruvian hat: Romantic (1815–1840 C.E.). Woman's hat made of the braided leaves of the Cuban palm.

pervenche: Bustle (1865–1890 C.E.). In 1876, new color.

perwyke: Periwig.

perzikbloesemkleurig: Holland. Peach colored.

pesa: India. An embroidered skirt.

pesas: India. A gold embroidered fabric.

peshgir: India. Skirt.

peshkir: Bulgaria. Kerchief.

peshwas: India. Long-sleeved coat that buttons down the center front. It is worn over other clothes as a robe.

peski: Lapland. Smock-shaped reindeer coat with the fur worn on the inside.

pespuntaderas: Renaissance (1450–1550 C.E.). Spain. Stitchers.

pespuntado: Spain. To be quilted; backstitched.

pespunte: Spain. Backstitch.

pestelci: Romania. Apron from the Southern part of the country. Ornamented with colorful florals and geometrics.

pestiman: Roman (753 B.C.E.–323 C.E.). Black or dark blue woolen skirt that opened in the front.

pestryad: Russia. Cotton fabric with varicolored woolen threads.

pet: *See* muts.

petaa: Borneo. A bead cap.

petal collar: Collar made of petal-shaped sections.

petals Marguerite: Bustle (1865–1890 C.E.). France. In 1875, very closely plaited trim.

petasos

petasos: Greek (3000-100 B.C.E.). Broad brimmed, low crowned hat that tied under the chin with strings. First recorded brimmed hat.

petassos: *See* petasos.

petasus: *See* petasos.

pet-en-l'air: Early Georgian (1700–1750 C.E.) to Late Georgian (1750–1790 C.E.). France. Popular from 1745 to 1770s, thigh- or knee-length, sac-back jacket with elbow-length sleeves and a stomacher. Worn with a plain skirt.

Peter Pan collar

Peter Pan collar: (20th century). Small, soft, round, turnover collar. Popularized by the stage production of *Peter Pan*.

petersham: Rough woolen fabric, usually navy blue.

Petersham cloth: Heavy wool cloth with a thick nap.

Petersham cossacks: Romantic (1815–1840 C.E.). United Kingdom. Popular from 1817 to 1818, man's loose cossack flared around the ankles. Named for the Regency Buck, Charles, Viscount Petersham.

Petersham frock coat: Romantic (1815–1840 C.E.). United Kingdom. Popular in 1830s, man's double-breasted coat with velvet collar, lapels, and cuffs. Had large flap hip pockets.

Petersham greatcoat: Romantic (1815–1840 C.E.). United Kingdom. Man's overcoat with a short shoulder-cape.

Petersham greatcoat

Petersham ribbon: Crinoline (1840–1865 C.E.). United Kingdom. Double ribbons which were watered, plain, figured, or striped.

petershams: *See* Petersham ribbon.

petit bord: Romantic (1815–1840 C.E.) to Crinoline (1840–1865 C.E.). France. Popular from 1835 to 1850, woman's small elaborate evening hat. Early version was small crowned hat with a halo brim and ribbon and aigrette trim. Smaller and made of velvet in 1840s. Always worn at the back of the head at a slight sideways tilt.

petit point: France. Small, close, thread-count embroidery.

petit velours: France. Lightweight cotton velvet.

petite pois: Bustle (1865–1890 C.E.). In 1886, pea dot velvet with spots embroidered in contrasting color.

petite robe unie: Late Georgian (1750–1790 C.E.). France. Robe that was worn over panniers. Underskirt was of the same fabric as the overdress.

petit-gris: France and Italy. Fur from the gray squirrel (*Sciurus carolinensis*).

Petit-gris: Germany. Petit-gris.

petit-maître: Late Georgian (1750–1790 C.E.). France. Dandy.

petit-maîtresse: Late Georgian (1750–1790 C.E.). France. Woman dandy.

petits bonhommes: Early Georgian (1700–1750 C.E.). France. Cuff trim of frills of fine linen used on the gown à la française.

peto: Renaissance (1450–1550 C.E.). Spain. Breastplate.

petroméni: Greece. Cap sewn so thickly with coins that it is stiff.

pettabotta: Italy. Breastplate.

pettibockers: (1900–1910 C.E.). Ankle-length, silk jersey pantaloons for women.

petticoat: 1. Woman's underskirt. 2. Short coat worn by men. 3. Wide garment of waterproofed fabric worn by fisherman.

petticoat bodice: Gay Nineties (1890–1899 C.E.). United States of America. Corset cover.

petticoat breeches: Charles I and the Commonwealth (1625–1660 C.E.). United Kingdom. Full-cut upper-stocks elaborately decorated. Fashionable from 1650 to around 1675.

petticoat suspenders: Crinoline (1840–1865 C.E.). In 1857, five-inch-wide strip that fastened to the corset and buttoned to the petticoat.

petticoat suspenders

pettinato: Italy. Worsted.

petto: Renaissance (1450–1550 C.E.). Italy. Breastplate.

petuna: Glossy, durable fabric.

petunia: Gay Nineties (1890–1900 C.E.). In 1892, a softer version of magenta.

peupliere: Bustle (1865–1890 C.E.). In 1888, light yellow green.

pha ap nam fon: Laos and Thailand. Monk's bathing cloth.

pha beang: Laos. Sash.

phaa: Laos and Thailand. Cloth.

phaa biang: *See* phaa pat chieng.

phaa chet: *See* phaa pat chieng.

phaa chet naa: Thailand. Small square of patterned cloth used as a ceremonial gift. In Sumatra, it is called lamak or tampan.

phaa chet paak: Laos and Thailand. Handkerchief.

phaa khaaw maa: Thailand. Man's multi-purpose cloth used as a shoulder cloth, belt, or carrying cloth.

phaa pat chieng: Thailand. Woman's narrow shoulder cloth worn under one arm with the loose ends over the opposite shoulder. It is worn by men as a shoulder scarf or belt.

phaa sarong: Thailand. Man's skirt.

phaa sin: Laos. Skirt.

phaa yao: Thailand. Man's long, elegantly woven piece of cloth worn as a skirt.

phada: India. A waistband.

phaecassium: Roman (753 B.C.E.–323 C.E.). Woman's soft white leather shoe laced with colored silks.

phāgniā: India. White scarf with a red tie-dyed border.

phainoles: Greek (3000–100 B.C.E.). Cloak or mantle.

phalaka: India. Slab-like gems.

phalaka hara: India. A necklace with slab-like gems at intervals.

phalaka valaya: India. A bracelet with slab-like gems set into it.

phali: Peru. Short skirt worn by children until the age of eight.

phalinges: Ireland. One-piece breeches and stockings.

phãn sáp: Vietnam. Makeup.

phãn son: *See* phãn sáp.

phanatopa: India. A hood.

pháp-y: Vietnam. Monk's robe.

pharos: Greek (3000–100 B.C.E.). 1. Linen version of the himation. Worn only by nobles. 2. Peplos chiton worn belted at the waist.

phatoi: *See* bandi.

phatui: *See* bandi.

phenta: India. A turban or strip of cloth.

phentā Mohammadī: India. Style of turban.

pheran: India. Kashmiri man's long, sleeved robe worn belted.

pheta: India. A middle-class Parsee miter-like turban. Originally a round turban.

phetia: India. Narrow piece of cloth worn over the skirt to indicate that the wearer's husband is alive. An upper class woman's ghāgrā.

pheto: India. A turban that is folded fresh each time it is worn.

phicchi: Bolivia. Pin used to fasten mantles.

philibeg: Scotland. Kilt.

Philip and Cheney: Restoration (1660–1700 C.E.) to Late Georgian (1750–1790 C.E.). United Kingdom. Wool fabric similar to camlet.

Philip and China: *See* Philip and Cheney.

Philippine embroidery: Embroidery with dainty floral patterns.

philiselie: *See* filozella.

phillamot: Color of a dead or faded leaf.

philoselle: Charles I and the Commonwealth (1625–1660 C.E.). Variety of camlet.

phiren: India. A woolen smock worn by the Kashmiris.

phoinos: Greek (3000–100 B.C.E.). Blood red color.

phoque: France. Seal fur.

phosphorescent: Gay Nineties (1890–1900 C.E.). In 1892, a changeable fabric.

phrygian bonnet: Greek (3000–100 B.C.E.). Cap or bonnet of felt or leather. Rome made it a symbol of liberty by giving one to freed slaves. In France during the Revolution, known as le bonnet rouge, a symbol of French freedom.

phrygian bonnet

phrygian cap: Byzantine and Romanesque (400–1200 C.E.). Worn from ninth century to the end of the 12th century, a pointed cap with the point slightly bent toward the front. Common cap.

Phrygian needlework: Needlework with silk and gold.

phrygium: Byzantine and Romanesque (400–1200 C.E.). White version of the phrygian cap worn by popes.

phubati: *See* kochi.

phuc-súrc: Vietnam. Clothing.

phul gulabi: India. The color pink.

phu-la: Vietnam. Scarf.

phulam: India. A silk and cotton blend fabric.

phulkari: 1. India. Embroidery done in India. 2. Fabric embroidered with Indian embroidery.

phullu: Bolivia. Woman's rectangular mantle worn pinned on one shoulder.

phulphagarno ghaghro: India. A spaciously sinuous skirt.

phutā lugā: India. Widow's sari without a colored border.

phutadu: India. A black or red cotton stuff.

phylactery: 1. Amulet worn on body as protection. 2. Fringe or other border.

physical wig: Late Georgian (1750–1790 C.E.). United Kingdom. Man's long bob wig. Popular with the learned professions.

pí' ao: China. Fur-lined jacket.

pi bian: China. Man's ridged hat made from white reindeer or woven rattan covered in gauze.

pi ling: China. Qing dynasty (1644–1911 C.E.). Man's court shoulder collar. Usually embroidered with dragon designs.

p'i ling: *See* piling.

pianelle: Renaissance (1450–1550 C.E.) to Elizabethan (1550–1625 C.E.). Italy. Shoe similar to the pantoufle.

pianeta di prete: Italy. Chasuble.

piazi: India. Flesh pink.

picadilly Johnny: *See* masher.

picado: Renaissance (1450–1550 C.E.). Spain. Pinked.

picaporte: Spain. Traditional door-knocker hairstyle of Andalusia.

picaranga pāgadi: *See* picaranga peco.

picaranga peco: India. A five-color tie-dyed version of the turban.

piccadil: Elizabethan (1550–1625 C.E.). Decorative tabs worn at the armseye on the doublet.

Piccadilly collar: Bustle (1865–1890 C.E.). United Kingdom. Popular from 1860s on, man's separate standing collar.

piccadilly fringe: Bustle (1865–1890 C.E.). Bangs cut straight or fringed.

piccadilly weepers: *See* dundrearys.

piccolo punto: Italy. Petit point.

picheh: Persia. Woman's black horsehair face mask.

pichodī: *See* pachedī.

pichu anaku: Ecuador. A full-length anaku.

pichu jerga: Ecuador. Woman's tunic worn pinned at the shoulders.

pici: Java. A black velvet cap.

pickadil: Standing collar, often with a scalloped edge.

pickelhaube: Germany. Spiked helmet.

picklock: Fine grade of merino and Siberian wool.

picot: Finished pointed edge on fabric.

picoté: To be edged in picot.

picture hat: Gay Nineties (1890–1900 C.E.). United Kingdom. Woman's large wide-brimmed straw hat trimmed in strongly contrasting colors.

pidan: Korea. Silk.

pidjak: Russia. Peasant man's jacket.

pidjama: Bosnia. Pajamas.

pidzak: Russia. Coat.

pie: *See* enredos.

pie frill: (1910–1920 C.E.). Small crisp ruffle around woman's round neckline.

pie plate: Very flat beret.

piecette: Gusset in a glove.

pied: *See* particolored.

Piedmont gown: Late Georgian (1750–1790 C.E.). United Kingdom. Introduced around 1775, variation of the sac-back gown.

piedra de añil: Guatemala. Indigo.

piegatura: Italy. Fold.

piegatura a punte: Italy. Multipointed fold.

piegatura triangolare: Italy. Triangle fold.

pieghettato: Italy. Plissé.

piel de angel: Spain. Peau d'ange.

piel de becerro: Spain. Calfskin.

piel de cisne: Spain. Peau de cygne.

piel de foca: Ecuador. A heavily felted wool cloth.

piel de seda: Spain. Peau de soie.

piel de tiburón: Spain. Sharkskin.

piele: Romania. Leather.

pieptar: Romania. Short, sheepskin vest trimmed with strips of leather.

pieptarita: *See* pieptar.

pierrot: Late Georgian (1750–1790 C.E.). France. Worn from 1784 until the Revolution, a caraco with fanciful trim.

pierrot cape: Gay Nineties (1890–1900 C.E.). United Kingdom. Three-quarter length cloak with a shoulder cape and a pierrot ruff.

pierrot ruff: (1890–1899 C.E.). United Kingdom. Fur-edged ruff worn on capes.

pierścień: Poland. Finger ring.

pietra dura: Colored stones inlaid with black marble and used in jewelry.

pifferaro bonnet: Bustle (1865–1890 C.E.). United Kingdom. Introduced in 1877, woman's flat-crowned, narrow brimmed felt bonnet with feather trim.

pifferaro hat: Bustle (1865–1890 C.E.). United Kingdom. Woman's chimney pot shaped hat with an aigrette in front.

pigache: Byzantine and Romanesque (400–1200 C.E.). Shoe with a long pointed turned up toe. Plural is pigaciae.

pigache

pigeon fan: Bustle (1865–1890 C.E.). In 1877, stuffed head and breast of bird with spread wings as a fan mounted on ivory handle.

pigeon's breast: Gay Nineties (1890–1900 C.E.). In 1896, a new color.

pigeon's throat: Gay Nineties (1890–1900 C.E.). In 1896, a new color.

pigeon-winged toupee: Late Georgian (1750–1790 C.E.). Man's toupee with one or two horizontal rolls above the ears. Worn with various queues.

pi-gia-ma: Vietnam. Pajamas.

pigskin: Tough, durable leather made from the skins of wild hogs.

pigtail wig: Early Georgian (1700–1750 C.E.) to Late Georgian (1750–1790 C.E.). Man's wig with a long curled queue or a braided queue that was tied at the top and bottom with a black ribbon.

pihapiha-'o-kohola: United States of America. Hawaii. Pleated ruffle.

pihi: United States of America. Hawaii. Button.

pihi pulima: United States of America. Hawaii. Cuff button.

pijama: Portugal. Pajama.

pijian: China. Cape; shawl.

pijjekker: Holland. Pea jacket.

pigtail wig

pijpekrullen: Netherland. Long curls.

pikaklė: Lithuania. Collar.

piked shoe: Late Gothic (1350–1450 C.E.) to Renaissance (1450–1550 C.E.). Popular from 1370 to 1410 and again from 1460 to 1480, shoes with long pointed toes.

Pikee: Germany. Piqué.

pilch: Elizabethan (1550–1625 C.E.). Fur or leather outer garment.

pilche: *See* pilch.

pile: Fabric surface of standing threads.

pilece: Byzantine and Romanesque (400–1200 C.E.). United Kingdom. Skin or fur garment worn by both genders.

pileolus: Non-liturgical skull cap worn under miter and tiara by Catholic prelates.

pileus: 1. Rome. Man's felt cap. 2. Elizabethan (1550–1625 C.E.). Skull cap or a round, pointed, brimless cap favored by academics.

pilgrim: Cape or ruffle on back of bonnet to cover neck.

pilgrim's hat: Directoire and First Empire (1790–1815 C.E.). Introduced in 1811, Carmelite brown hat with a cockleshell ornament on the front.

piling: China. Manchu man's triangular court collar.

pilion: Biblical (Unknown–30 C.E.). Hebrew's felt cap.

piliyā: India. Yellow scarf with red dot tie-dye color with black border.

pillbox

pillbox: Small round hat.

pilleus: Roman (753 B.C.E.–323 C.E.). Hat.

pilling: The formation of broken fibers into ball on the surface of fabric.

pillion: Early Gothic (1200–1350 C.E.). Ecclesiastical hat or cap.

pillow lace: *See* bobbin lace.

pillu: Bolivia. Man's headdress.

pīlo: 1. *See* manchester. 2. *See* pomaco.

pilos: Greek (3000-100 B.C.E.). 1. Cape, worn by commoners. 2. Hat with a round, high crown and little or no brim.

pilot cloth: Coarse, thick, twill weave, woolen cloth napped on one side. Usually navy blue.

pilsc: *See* pilsn.

pilsn: Poland. Felt.

pilu saluf: Timbuktu. Headhunters' garb.

pilus tinctus: Renaissance (1450–1550 C.E.). Ireland. Dyed fabric.

pima cotton: United States of America. Long staple fiber cotton grown in Arizona.

pimento: Evergreen wood used for parasol handles.

pimpalia: India. A green cotton stuff.

pin check: Fine check, usually woven.

pin dot: Smallest dot used in fabric design.

pin stripe: Narrowest stripe used in fabrics.

piña cloth: Philippine Islands. Delicate, soft, transparent fabric made from leaf fibers of the pineapple plant.

pinafore costume: Bustle (1865–1890 C.E.). United Kingdom. Introduced in 1879, tennis dress made with bibbed pinafore front worn over a princess line, kilted skirt. Made of a fancy fabric.

pinafore heel: Nearly flat heel on children's shoes.

pinasco: India. Cloth made from pineapple fiber.

pinatikan: Celebes. A fabric woven on a back-tension loon with a continuous warp.

pinayusa: Philippine hemp fabric dyed with local dye.

pinch back coat: (20th century). Coat with inverted pleats at the back.

pinchbeck button: Late Georgian (1750–1790 C.E.). Used after 1769, button made from a copper and zinc alloy that cheaply imitated gilt buttons.

pince: France. Dart.

pincheck: Very tiny check.

pindileu: Romania. Loose, much pleated skirt of hemp or hemp and cotton. Trimmed on the waistband and hem.

piñe: Peru. Silver pendant.

pine: Samoa. Safety pin.

pine cloth: Delicate, transparent fabric made from pineapple leaf.

pine kaiapa: United States of America. Hawaii. Literally "diaper pin," safety pin.

pine kaula'i: United States of America. Hawaii. Literally "hanging pin," clothespin.

pine marten: *See* baum marten.

pine umauma: United States of America. Hawaii. Brooch.

pineapple fabric: *See* mousseline de soie.

pinga: India. Lower body garment.

piniki: Samoa. Pink color.

pinion: Elizabethan (1550–1625 C.E.) to Restoration (1660–1700 C.E.). Dropped shoulder line.

pink: 1. Tint of red. 2. To cut the edge of fabric. 3. Scarlet coat. 4. Scarlet hunting coat. The name refers to the color of a well-worn hunting coat.

pinking: Elizabethan (1550–1625 C.E.). Decorative treatment of fabric involving punching holes in the material.

pinks and green: (1940–1950 C.E.). United States of America. Olive drab semi-dress uniform worn by Army officers and warrant officers.

pinlán: China. Reddish blue.

pinlù: China. Light green.

pinner: 1. Charles I and the Commonwealth (1625–1660 C.E.). Elaborate apron. 2. Early Georgian (1700–1750 C.E.). Woman's headdress of two long flaps, one on each side of the head, and pinned in place.

pinson: Early Gothic (1200–1350 C.E.) to Restoration (1660–1700 C.E.). Term in use from 14th century to end of the 16th century for a light indoor shoe. Term was later replaced by pump.

pintada: Ecuador. To be of a color.

pintado: 1. Charles I and the Commonwealth (1625–1660 C.E.) to Restoration (1660–1700 C.E.). East Indian fabric. 2. India. Spotted or painted cloth.

pintadoe: *See* pintado.

pinthadoe: *See* pintado.

pinyuè: China. Pale blue.

pînza: Spain. Dart.

pînză: Romania. Linen.

pio borong: Indonesia. Sa'dan-Toraja long rectangular cotton loincloth.

piorko: Poland. Feather.

pipi: United States of America. Hawaii. Kind of tapa.

pipkin: Elizabethan (1550–1625 C.E.). United Kingdom. Woman's small hat with a flat crown and usually trimmed with jeweled hat-band and feathers.

piqué: 1. Firm, corded fabric of cotton, silk, or rayon. 2. Glove seam where one piece overlaps the other. 3. Inlay of metal, tortoiseshell, etc.

pique devant: Elizabethan (1550–1625 C.E.). United Kingdom. Popular from 1570s to 1600, short pointed beard.

piquet: France, Italy. Piqué.

piquets: Bustle (1865–1890 C.E.). France. Ornamental sprays worn on lace evening caps by matrons.

pirahan: 1. Persia. Woman's thin muslin shirt that is richly embroidered and studded with pearls. 2. Iran. Man's white cotton shirt with long pointed cuffs.

pirahan-e zananeh: Iran. Woman's flowing gown.

pirkstaine: *See* cimds.

pirned: Scotland. Having colored stripes or brocade.

pirnie: Scotland. Term for a striped wool nightcap.

pirny: *See* pirnie.

pirpiri: Sleeveless garment with a full skirt.

pirštinė: Lithuania. Glove.

piryiellya: Greece. Gold bobbin lace.

pisany lapti: Slovakia. Fancy bast sandals.

pishka: Peru. Rectangular cloth or leather bag used to carry salt, coca, money, etc.

piskalaka: *See* sucisutra.

pîslă: Romania. Felt.

pistache: Romantic (1815–1840 C.E.). Fashionable in 1819, very soft shade of green.

pistachio color: *See* pistache.

pistai: India. Pea green.

pistak: India. A pistachio green color.

pistent: Iran. Sash.

pístres: Greece. Pleats.

pitambara cadara: India. A yellow silk cadar.

pith helmet

pith helmet: Light pith hat for tropical wear.

pitji: Tall cap.

piuma: Italy. Feather.

piuma di struzzo: Italy. Ostrich plume.

piupiu: Australia. Grass skirt.

piwa haka: United States of America. Hawaii. Beaver hat.

píyi: China. Fur clothing.

pizama: Poland. Pajamas.

pizane: Renaissance (1450–1550 C.E.). France. Breastplate.

pizzo: Italy. Lace.

pizzo ad ago: Italy. Needlepoint lace.

pizzo ad ago a fuselli: Italy. Bobbin lace.

pizzo punto in aria: Italy. Venetian lace.

pizzo rinasciemento: Italy. Tape lace made with woven tapes and needle lace fillings.

placard: Elizabethan (1550–1625 C.E.). Stomacher.

placardo: Renaissance (1450–1550 C.E.). United Kingdom. Garment worn beneath the coat or gown.

placcards: *See* placcates.

placcates: Renaissance (1450–1550 C.E.). Small steel plates used to strengthen the breastplate armor.

plackard: Renaissance (1450–1550 C.E.). United Kingdom. 1. Man's stomacher filling in the V- or U-shaped gap in the doublet. 2. Front panel or stomacher in a surcoat. Often embroidered or trimmed with fur.

placket: Elizabethan (1550–1625 C.E.). United Kingdom. 1. Slit in the side of a petticoat. 2. Petticoat. 3. Woman wearing a petticoat.

plaid: Scotland. Square or rectangular tartan garment worn as cloak.

plaid neuk: Sewn up corner of plaid.

plain bow stock: Romantic (1815–1840 C.E.). United Kingdom. Man's stock of black silk with a bow in the front.

plain weave: Simplest and most common weave.

plait: 1. Braid, as in straw. 2. Variation of pleat.

plaits: *See* wheat ears.

plakhta: Ukraine. Woman's paneled skirt that opens in the front. Woven in a square fancy pattern.

plangi: Indonesia. Tie-dye.

plantillas: Renaissance (1450–1550 C.E.). Spain. Insoles.

plasc: Russia. Cloak.

plast: Croatia and Serbia. Cloak.

plást: Czechoslovakia. Cloak.

plastron: Romantic (1815–1840 C.E.) to Bustle (1865–1890 C.E.). 1. Front panel in a woman's gown made from different color or fabric from the rest of the gown. 2. Separate front of a woman's dress. 3. Man's unpleated shirt front.

płaszcz: Poland. Cloak; overcoat.

płat: 1. Braid of hair or straw. 2. Cords braided.

plat'e: *See* odezda.

plateado: Renaissance (1450–1550 C.E.). Spain. Silvered.

plateau: 1. Disk like hat. 2. Flat piece of fabric.

platform sole: Usually of cork or wood, one-half-inch to three-inch-thick shoe sole.

platilla: Silesia. White linen fabric.

platinum: 1. Grayish white precious metal. 2. Neutral gray color.

Platner: Renaissance (1450–1550 C.E.). Germany. Armorer.

platno: Croatia and Serbia. Linen.

plátno: Czechoslovakia. Linen.

platform sole
See also photospread
(Foot and Legwear).

plato de lo gorro: Spain. Flat crown of a hat.

Platoff cap: Directoire and First Empire (1790–1815 C.E.). United Kingdom. Woman's pale pink satin evening cap with a scalloped front and a row of pearls and a pearl tassel from the crown.

Platoff costume: Directoire and First Empire (1790–1815 C.E.). Style of dress named for the daughter of General Platoff who supposedly offered his daughter's hand to any soldier who would bring him Napoleon's head.

platok: Russia. Light summer scarf worn tied at the neck.

Plauen lace: Machine lace on muslin with the non-embroidered part of the fabric removed.

pleasance: Renaissance (1450–1550 C.E.) to Elizabethan (1550–1625 C.E.). Fine quality lawn.

pleated shirt: Directoire and First Empire (1790–1815 C.E.) to Bustle (1865–1890 C.E.). United Kingdom. Popular from 1806 to 1870s, man's day shirt with narrow vertical pleats down the front. Also worn for evening dress after 1840. Closed with studs.

pleated trousers: *See* cossacks.

pleureuses: France. After 1900, ostrich feathers lengthened by gluing or gumming strands together.

pliage: France. Fold.

pliage en pointe: France. Multipointed fold.

pliage en triangle: France. Triangle fold.

pliakthi: Greece. Everyday chemises worn by older women. The chemises are embroidered with dark colored cotton.

plimsoll: Australia. Canvas shoe.

plisado: Spain. Pleat.

plisado en abanico: Spain. Sunray pleats.

plisado en acordeón: Spain. Accordion pleat.

plisado en sierra: Spain. Knife pleat.

plisado encontrado: Spain. Box pleat.

plisîrani: Romania. Woman's short skirted frock.

plissé: France. Cotton fabric finished with a puckered effect.

plissé crepe: Seersucker like fabric.

plissiert: Germany. Plissé.

plivers: Lithuania. Veil.

plodan: Renaissance (1450–1550 C.E.). Rough wool checked fabric used for women's cloaks.

plomb: Bustle (1865–1890 C.E.). In 1885, lead color.

plooi: Holland. Pleat.

ploščius: *See* apsiustas.

płotno: Poland. Linen.

ploughman's gauze: Directoire and First Empire (1790–1815 C.E.). Introduced in 1801, fine gauze fabric with satin spots. Used for ladies' evening gowns.

pluderhose: Elizabethan (1550–1625 C.E.). Germany. Term for baggy breeches with wide vertical panes and silk linings between the panes. Linings sometimes overhung the panes below.

pluette: Gay Nineties (1890–1900 C.E.). Heavy waterproof fabric.

plug oxford: Oxford shoe with circular vamp.

pluie d'argent: Bustle (1865–1890 C.E.). In 1867, poplin dotted with yellow.

pluie d'or: Bustle (1865–1890 C.E.). In 1867, poplin dotted with white.

pluinnseag: Ireland. Gaelic word for large coarse apron.

plum: Soft, dark blue purple.

pluma de avestruz: Spain. Ostrich plume.

pluma de gallo: Spain. Cock feather.

plumach: Obsolete term for plume.

plumage: Early Georgian (1700–1750 C.E.). Italy. Ostrich feather trim around the edge of the hat brim.

plumbet: Silk or wool fabric.

plume: *See* aigrette.

plume d'autruche: France. Ostrich plume.

plume de coq: France. Cock feather.

plume de faisan: France. Pheasant's feather.

plume velvet: Romantic (1815–1840 C.E.). Introduced in 1820, velvet with a narrow satin stripe of the same color.

plumes fantaisies: France. A milliner's term for feathers other than ostrich.

plumetis: 1. France. Feather-stitch. 2. Dress muslin.

plummet: Elizabethan (1550–1625 C.E.) to Restoration (1660–1700 C.E.). Drop earring.

plumpers: Restoration (1660–1700 C.E.). Round balls to fill out the cheeks.

plunket: 1. Early Gothic (1200–1350 C.E.). Colored cloth. 2. Elizabethan (1550–1625 C.E.). Light blue.

plus fours: (1920–1930 C.E.). Men's full-cut knickers that bloused on to a band that buttoned or buckled at the knee. When unbuttoned they fell four inches below the knee.

plush: Directoire and First Empire (1790–1815 C.E.). Pile fabric, usually of wool, with a longer pile than velvet.

plush velveteen: Cotton plush.

plushette: Inferior plush.

pluvial: Long ceremonial robe worn by priests and kings.

po: Korea. Embroidered dragon insignia.

pòca: Ireland. Pocket.

poche: France. Pocket.

poches: Late Georgian (1750–1790 C.E.). France. Small pads worn at the hips to replace panniers.

pochette: France. Handbag; pocket handkerchief.

pocket cascade: Pocket in a folded and draped section of the skirt. When they appear on both sides, it gives the illusion of a peg-top skirt.

pocket handkerchief: Regular handkerchief worn in man's jacket pocket.

pocket siphonia: *See* siphonia.

poculica: Balkans. Embroidered cap.

poddyovka: Russia. Woman's long-waisted coat.

pó-de-arroz: Portugal. Face powder.

podhiá: Greece. Long, one piece, sleeveless, ankle-length garment.

podkapnik: Bulgaria. Skullcap.

podkolanówki: Poland. Knee socks.

podkošulja: Bosnia. Vest.

podopleka: Russia. Shoulder lining in a man's shirt.

podszewka: Poland. Lining.

podvika: Slovakia. Woman's fine rectangular shawl.

pœll: *See* hacele.

poes: Bulgaria. Man's black woolen waistband.

poetsdoek: *See* glazendoek.

pofbroek: Holland. Trunkhose.

poffer: Holland. Woman's over-bonnet.

pofi: Norway. Old word for felt.

pogoni: Russia. Shoulder boards.

pohaku 'oma'oma'o: United States of America. Hawaii. Emerald.

pohoi: New Zealand. Maori. An ear ornament made from bird skins.

poignée: France. Cuffs.

poil: Thread of raw silk used to make core of tinsel.

poil de castor: France. Beaver hair.

poil de saxe: Crinoline (1840–1865 C.E.). In 1862, cotton and wool blend fabric.

poile de chevre: Crinoline (1840–1865 C.E.). France. Introduced in 1861, goat's hair textile with a satiny surface.

point: *See* aglet.

point à la vierge: France. Rose ground lace.

point à l'aiguille: France. Applique lace.

point à reseau: France. Point lace on a net ground.

point Colbert: France. A modern term for a mid-19th-century lace.

point coupé: France. Cutwork.

point d'Alençon: France. 1. Alencon point lace. 2. Herringbone stitch.

point d'Angleterre lace: France. Fine-ground pillow lace.

point de Bayeux: Romantic (1815–1840 C.E.). France. A bobbin lace made of flax or cotton.

point de chainette: Crinoline (1840–1865 C.E.). New braid trim.

point de cordonnet: France. Couching stitch.

point de croix: France. Cross-stitch.

Point de Fée: Bobbin lace made in the Province of Antwerp.

point de feston: France. Buttonhole stitch.

point de France: *See* Argentan lace.

point de gaze: Belgium. Fine needlepoint lace.

point de gaze lace: France. Belgian needlepoint applique lace.

point de Hongroie: France. Canvaswork stitch.

point de Hongrye: *See* Hungerland lace.

point de neige: Decorative mesh of cloudy spots used in Flemish bobbin lace.

point de Paris: 1. Narrow, light, dainty bobbin lace. 2. Machine lace similar to Val lace.

point de raccroc: Romantic (1815–1840 C.E.). France. Invisible stitch to sew strips of bobbin lace into large flounces or shawls.

point de rose: France. Needle lace similar to Venetian gros point.

point de sedan: Restoration (1660–1700 C.E.) to Early Georgian (1700–1750 C.E.). France. Form of point de France.

point de tige: France. Stem stitch.

point de toile: France. Whole stitch.

point de Venise à reseau: Fine, flat, mesh-grounded needle lace made in Brussels.

point de Venise a rose: Small gros point de Venise.

point d'Espagne: France. Variation of the chain stitch.

point d'espagne: Spain. Needlepoint lace with gold or silver threads.

point d'esprit: 1. Net or tulle with dots. 2. A cotton lace with small oval or square dots. 3. Small figures in guipure lace.

point en sabretache: France. Border trim in pattern of sabretache.

point lace: Needlepoint lace.

point noué: France. Knotted buttonhole stitch.

point passé: France. Satin stitch.

point plat: France. Flat point lace.

point Turc: France. Flat, decorative way to finish a seam used on handmade lingerie.

pointed fox: Fox fur with white guard hairs inserted to simulate silver fox.

poire: Directoire and First Empire (1790–1815 C.E.). France. Drop earrings.

Poiret twill: Named for the French dress designer, Paul Poiret, worsted fabric similar to gabardine.

poissarde: Directoire and First Empire (1790–1815 C.E.). France. Earring with a semicircular or S-shaped hinged back.

poitrel: France. 1. Armor breastplate. 2. Stomacher resembling a breastplate.

poitrine: France. Chest or bosom.

pojagi: Korea. Wrapping cloth.

pojas: 1. Croatia and Serbia. Girdle. 2. Russia. Belt.

pójas: Greece. Polychrome, striped woven belt.

poka'a lopi: United States of America. Hawaii. Spool of thread.

poka'a-pilali: United States of America. Hawaii. Sewing machine's bobbin winder.

poke: Elizabethan (1550–1625 C.E.). Pouch or bag.

poke bonnet: Directoire and First Empire (1790–1815 C.E.) to Bustle (1865–1890 C.E.). United Kingdom. Popular from 1799 to end of the 19th century, woman's bonnet with large brim.

poke collar: Standing collar.

poke sleeve: Long, loose sleeve.

pokeka: New Zealand. Maori. The generic term for a rough cloak.

poket: Byzantine and Romanesque (400–1200 C.E.) to Renaissance (1450–1550 C.E.). United Kingdom. Middle English word for pocket.

pokeys: Late Gothic (1350–1450 C.E.). Enormously long false sleeves.

poking stick: Elizabethan (1550–1625 C.E.). Rod used to adjust the pleats of a ruff.

pokinikini: *See* kiniki.

pokkuri: Japan. Dressy lacquered geta for girls.

polaina: Spain. Gaiter; spat.

polakem: Early Georgian (1700–1750 C.E.). Russia. Cloth or felt cap with flaps that turned down to cover ears and neck.

Poland mantle: Directoire and First Empire (1790–1815 C.E.). Introduced in 1806, woman's mantle of light silk and fastened with a clasp or brooch on the right shoulder.

polayn: Early Gothic (1200–1350 C.E.). Fur of the black squirrel.

polca: Peru. Woman's short jacket with a ruffle on the lower edge.

poldavis: Elizabethan (1550–1625 C.E.). Coarse linen fabric.

polecat: Thick, light yellow fur from the *Mustela putorius*.

polera: Spain. Polo shirt.

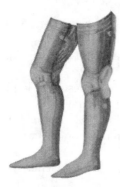

poleyns
Dover Publications

poleyns: Early Gothic (1200–1350 C.E.). Knee-caps of iron from a suit of armor.

policeman's cape: Gay Nineties (1890–1900 C.E.). United Kingdom. Introduced in 1895, one-piece circular cape.

Polish: High, laced shoe or boot.

Polish boots: Crinoline (1840–1865 C.E.). United Kingdom. Popular in 1860s, women's tall boots with a tassel and colored high heels.

Polish greatcoat: Directoire and First Empire (1790–1815 C.E.). United Kingdom. Introduced in 1810, man's long, fitted coat with Russian lambskin collar, cuffs, and lapels. It closed with frogs. Worn for evening.

Polish jacket: Crinoline (1840–1865 C.E.). United Kingdom. Introduced in 1846, woman's waist-length cashmere jacket with revers and collar cut in the masculine line. It had sleeves slit to the elbow on the inner side. Lined in quilted satin and worn for country.

Polish mantle: Romantic (1815–1840 C.E.). United Kingdom. Introduced in 1835, woman's knee-length satin mantle with a cape. Trimmed in fur.

polished cotton: Cotton fabric with a shiny face.

polka: 1. Crinoline (1840–1865 C.E.). United Kingdom. Introduced in 1844, woman's short cashmere or velvet mantle or jacket with loose sleeves. Lined with silk. 2. Short, button-down blouse.

Polka: Crinoline (1840–1865 C.E.). In 1853, surplice front mantle with pagoda sleeves. Black was the most popular color. Trimmed in many ways.

polka dot: Dot used in allover pattern.

pollera: 1. Peru and Spain. Skirt. 2. Bolivia. Woman's European-style full gathered or pleated skirt. 3. Ecuador. Waistband.

polmesenic: Romania. Woman's white cotton head veil. Worn over the caita.

polo belt: Wide leather belt.

polo cloth: Heavy coating fabric of wool and/or camel's hair.

polo collar: Gay Nineties (1890–1900 C.E.). United Kingdom. In 1899, a starched white stand-fall collar.

polo dot: Large dot printed on fabric.

polo shirt: Informal, short sleeved shirt, often collarless.

polonaise: *See* gown à la polonaise.

polonaise à deux fins: Late Georgian (1750–1790 C.E.). France. Literally "a two-purpose polonaise," gown with the skirt back intended to drape up or train.

polonaise pardessus: Crinoline (1840–1865 C.E.). Popular in 1840s, woman's half-length pardessus that buttoned to the waist and then sloped away to reveal the dress beneath it. Sometimes had a short cape.

polonese: Charles I and the Commonwealth (1625–1660 C.E.) to Early Georgian (1700–1750 C.E.). United States of America. Long-sleeved coat-like garment that opened down the front. Had large hood.

poloneze: *See* gown à la polonaise.

polonia: Charles I and the Commonwealth (1625–1660 C.E.). United Kingdom. Fashionable high heel shoe so high that it caused the wearer to stagger as they walked.

polos: Greek (3000–100 B.C.E.). Woman's high cylindrical hat.

polotno: Russia. Linen.

polrock: Directoire and First Empire (1790–1815 C.E.). United Kingdom. Polish coat with black hussar braid on the front.

polu-kaftan: Russia. Literally "half kaftan," a tunic.

polushubka: Russia. Short sheepskin coat.

polverino: Crinoline (1840–1865 C.E.). United Kingdom. Introduced in 1846, woman's large silk unlined cloak that wrapped around the body, sometimes with a hood.

pomaco: India. Woman's scarf.

pomade: Fragrant cosmetic, usually for the hair.

pomander: 1. Late Gothic (1350–1450 C.E.). Hollow ornament, often a filigreed ball, which held a sponge of perfume. Worn suspended from the girdle. 2. Elizabethan (1550–1625 C.E.). Metal case in which was an aromatic substance or perfume.

pomaranczowy: Poland. Orange color.

pomatum: Perfumed ointment used on hair.

pomchā: India. Woman's head veil.

pomegranate: Brilliant yellowish red.

pomme d'ambre: France. Ball- or apple-shaped pomander.

pomme de pin: Early Gothic (1200–1350 C.E.). France. Literally "pinecone," a name for the pomegranate pattern in fabric.

pomme de senteur: *See* pomme d'ambre.

Pomona green: Directoire and First Empire (1790–1815 C.E.). Introduced in 1812, shade of green similar to apple green.

pompadour: 1. *See* hip bags. 2. Late Georgian (1750–1790 C.E.). Red violet. 3. Dainty floral pattern.

pompadour bodice: Bustle (1865–1890 C.E.). United Kingdom. Woman's day bodice with a square neckline and snug-fitting sleeves ending in frills.

pompadour chiné: Crinoline (1840–1865 C.E.). Wool twill fabric with a chiné pattern and minute horizontal stripes.

pompadour duchesse: Crinoline (1840–1865 C.E.). France. Introduced in 1850, striped satin with alternating plain and flowered stripes.

pompadour heel: Late Georgian (1750–1790 C.E.). France. Popular in 1750s and 1760s, high slender heel that curved to a narrow base.

pompadour pardessus: Crinoline (1840–1865 C.E.). France. Popular in 1850s, colored silk pardessus with fringe, elbow-length sleeves. Often fastened only at the neck.

pompadour polonaise: Bustle (1865–1890 C.E.). Introduced in 1872, woman's black foulard polonaise with large, bright flowers. Paired with a plain skirt.

pompadour shantung: Bustle (1865–1890 C.E.). Introduced in 1880, thick, patterned washing silk.

pompeian red: Bustle (1865–1890 C.E.). In 1879, dull scarlet.

pompeian silk sash: Crinoline (1840–1865 C.E.). Popular in 1860s, woman's wide black sash with mythological subjects. Generally worn with a white summer jacket, bodice, and a colored skirt.

pompon: 1. Early Georgian (1700–1750 C.E.) to Late Georgian (1750–1790 C.E.). Popular from 1740s to 1760s, ornament for a woman's hat or cap. Named for Madame Pompadour. 2. Round, ball-shaped trim.

pomposa: Directoire and First Empire (1790–1815 C.E.). Worn after 1807 by children, high-cut slipper that laced up the front.

ponceau: Crinoline (1840–1865 C.E.). In 1862, very bright shade of scarlet.

ponchito: 1. Guatemala. Man's small woolen blanket worn as a hip wrap or apron. 2. Bolivia. Small poncho worn like a yoke or apron.

ponchiyā: India. Bracelet studded with precious stones and pearls.

poncho: 1. Crinoline (1840–1865 C.E.). United Kingdom. Popular in 1850s, man's double-breasted overcoat with pagoda sleeves. 2. Crinoline (1840–1865 C.E.). United Kingdom. Woman's loose three-quarter caped cloak that buttoned from the neck to the hem. It had a small stand collar and sleeves that tapered to the wrist. 3. South America. Large rectangle of unsewn cloth with an opening for the head. 4. Crinoline (1840–1865 C.E.). In 1856, plaid mantelet with a slightly gathered hood. Outside of hood and lower edge of a different solid fabric. Mantelet trimmed with vandyke velvet ribbon and large pearl buttons.

poncho amarrado: Ecuador. Warp-resist patterned ponchos.

poncho boliviano: Bolivia. Man's contemporary poncho in red, green, and orange (colors of the Bolivian flag).

poncho cuadrada: Ecuador. Plaid poncho.

poncho jijún: *See* poncho cuadrada.

poncho rosado: Ecuador. Pink warp-resist dyed poncho.

poncho tiñiska: *See* poncho tintoridao.

poncho tintoridao: Ecuador and Guatemala. Ikat poncho.

ponczocha: Poland. Stocking.

poneva: Russia. Woman's peasant skirt made from three lengths of checked woolen homespun.

Poney: France. Pony.

pongee: 1. Bustle (1865–1890 C.E.). Introduced in 1870s, shantung. 2. Thin, plain weave silk fabric with a natural tan color.

ponit: Korea. Bonnet.

ponto de cruz: Portugal. Cross-stitch.

pony: Short-haired fur from the *Equus caballus*.

ponyet: 1. Early Gothic (1200–1350 C.E.) to Charles I and the Commonwealth (1625–1660 C.E.). Foresleeve of a man's doublet when made in a contrasting fabric. 2. Elizabethan (1550–1625 C.E.) to Restoration (1660–1700 C.E.). Men's bodkins.

po'o hina: United States of America. Hawaii. Gray haired; ash colored.

po'o ke'oke'o: United States of America. Hawaii. White haired; platinum blonde.

po'o kuakea: United States of America. Hawaii. Literally "bleached head," gray haired.

poodle cloth: Fabric similar to the coat of a French poodle.

pootae taua: Australia. Maori mourning cap of rushes or feathers.

popatiya: India. A parrot green stuff.

popelina: Spain. Poplin.

popeline: 1. Rep fabric with a silk warp and wool weft. 2. Holland. Poplin.

popes ministers: Elizabethan (1550–1625 C.E.) to Restoration (1660–1700 C.E.). Possibly a linen manufactured in Munster.

popielaty: *See* szary.

popinjay: Elizabethan (1550–1625 C.E.). Bluish green.

pople: Late Gothic (1350–1450 C.E.) to Renaissance (1450–1550 C.E.). Fur from the back of a squirrel.

poplin: Named from papeline, 15th-century fabric woven at Avignon, France. Durable medium weight, plain weave fabric with fine cross ribs. Made from cotton, silk, wool, or a blend.

poplin lactee: Romantic (1815–1840 C.E.). Introduced in 1837, poplin shot with white.

poplin lama: Crinoline (1840–1865 C.E.). Introduced in 1864, softer and thicker version of mousselaine de laine.

poplinette: Crinoline (1840–1865 C.E.). Introduced in 1859, wool, linen, or other fiber woven with glazed threads in imitation of poplin.

popolohua: United States of America. Hawaii. Purplish blue.

poppy red: Bright yellow red.

pora: New Zealand. Maori. A rough cape.

porasz: Romania. Thick woolen laces used to tie the sandals or boots.

poratpit: Korea. Purple.

porcelain: Romantic (1815–1840 C.E.). United Kingdom. Wedgwood color.

porcelain button: Late Georgian (1750–1790 C.E.). Patented in 1785, fashionable decoration on men's garments.

porc-epic: *See* porcupine headdress.

porcupine headdress: Directoire and First Empire (1790–1815 C.E.). Popular in 1798, hairstyle with the hair cut very short and standing up like bristles.

porfira: Greece. A royal crimson color.

poriaan: South Africa. Ndebele man's front apron made from fur and beaded in geometric designs.

poritutu roto: Celebes. A ceremonial banner.

pork pie

pork-pie hat

pork pie: 1. A round, pillbox shaped hat worn by women. 2. *See* trilby.

porkhani: India. Lower ear earrings.

pork-pie hat: Crinoline (1840–1865 C.E.). United Kingdom. Popular in 1860s, woman's hat with a low flat crown and a narrow turned up brim.

poro-toroa: New Zealand. Maori. Two-inch pendants of albatross bones.

porphura: Greek (3000–100 B.C.E.). Purple.

porphyry: Bustle (1865–1890 C.E.). In 1884, a tint between brick red and garnet.

porpora: Italy. Purple.

porraye: Early Gothic (1200–1350 C.E.). Green cloth.

port manteau sunshade: Bustle (1865–1890 C.E.). United Kingdom. Introduced in 1879, en-tout-cas that fit in a medium size trunk.

portaligas: Spain. Garter belt.

porte-bonheur: Bustle (1865–1890 C.E.). In 1874, bracelet consisting of five armlets, each with a different stone.

portefraes: Elizabethan (1550–1625 C.E.) to Charles I and the Commonwealth (1625–1660 C.E.). Holland. Pleated collar.

porte-jupe pompadour: Bustle (1865–1890 C.E.). Popular in 1860s, belt worn by women with suspenders to hitch up the skirt when walking.

porte-jupe pompadour

portemonnaie: Bustle (1865–1890 C.E.). France. Woman's purse carried in the pocket or muff, not in the hand.

porte-train: Petticoat worn to support train.

portki: *See* spodnie.

portnoj: Russia. Tailor.

portrait collar: Wide collar that narrows in front, forming frame for the neck.

Portuguese farthingale: Restoration (1660–1700 C.E.). United Kingdom. Popular for a few years around 1662, woman's farthingale that was flat in front and in back. Brought to United Kingdom by Catherine of Braganza on her marriage to Charles II.

Portuguese knot: Outline stitch knotted at center of each stitch.

posahuanco: Mexico. Woman's wraparound skirt.

pósta: Greece. Belt of a dress.

postav: *See* stofă.

postavu: Bulgaria. Lining.

postboy hat: Bustle (1865–1890 C.E.). Introduced in 1885, woman's small straw hat with a high flat crown and a narrow sloping brim. Had a plume of feathers in the front and was worn on the top of the head.

posteen: East Indian leather garment with fleece left on.

posten: India. Leather garment with the hair or fleece still on it. *See also* posteen.

postiche: Egyptian (4000–30 B.C.E.). Fake beard of leather, felt, or metal. Worn only by royalty.

postilion coat: Greatcoat modeled after those worn by postilions.

postillion: High-crowned hat with a narrow brim that rolls on the sides.

postillon: Crinoline (1840–1865 C.E.). Fashionable around 1860, gathered or ruffled basque at the bottom of the bodice back.

postin: *See* posten.

postola: *See* obuca.

posy: Single flower or bouquet of flowers.

posztólájbi: Romania. Overcoat.

pot: Guatemala. Woman's covering, shawl, tzut, blouse, or tunic.

pot derby: Pot shaped hat.

pot hat: *See* pot derby.

pot lace: Rare bobbin lace.

potae taua: New Zealand. Maori. Mourning fillet worn by widows.

pothia: Greece. An apron.

poti: India. A short cotton waistcloth.

potkošulja: Bosnia. Undershirt.

pottala: India. A cotton fabric.

potur

potur: Turkey. Serge breeches.

poturi: Bulgaria. Men's breeches of white serge that are cut wide in the top with tapering legs.

pou dula bunga: Roti, Ndao, and Savu. Woman's skirt cloth.

pouch: Byzantine and Romanesque (400–1200 C.E.). to Elizabethan (1550–1625 C.E.). Worn from 12th century through early 16th century, bag or wallet hung from a man's belt or girdle. Commonly worn with a knife or dagger stuck through the straps supporting it.

pou-de-soie: *See* poult-de-soie.

pou-fou: China. Pectorals.

poufs au sentiment: Late Georgian (1750–1790 C.E.). France. Worn around 1780, women's huge hairstyles with elaborate and fanciful trimmings.

poukamiso: Greece. A woman's chemise.

poulaines
See also photospread (Foot and Legwear).

poulaines: Late Gothic (1350–1450 C.E.). France. Shoes in Polish style with long pointed toes. Number of edicts were passed to limit their length and eventually to outlaw them. All were ineffective.

poult de soir: Crinoline (1840–1865 C.E.). France. Introduced in 1863, fabric blend of silk and alpaca with a shiny surface.

poult-de-soie: France. Heavy, plain weave silk with a slight rib.

pound blanket: United States of America. Any piece of coarse, handspun, aniline dyed yarn Navajo blanket.

pounghí: Greece. Bag.

pourpoint: Late Gothic (1350–1450 C.E.). Short jacket with tight sleeves. Worn under the cotehardie.

pourpre: 1. Early Gothic (1200–1350 C.E.). Purple. 2. Directoire and First Empire (1790–1815 C.E.). Crimson red dye made from cochineal. 3. France. Purple.

pourpre gris: Early Gothic (1200–1350 C.E.). Gray crimson.

pourpre sanguine: Early Gothic (1200–1350 C.E.). Purple.

poussière: Bustle (1865–1890 C.E.). In 1869, dust color.

poussière de Paris: Romantic (1815–1840 C.E.). France. Introduced in 1819, shade of light brown.

poussière des ruines: Romantic (1815–1840 C.E.). In 1827, a new color.

poussin lace: Made in Dieppe, France. Fine, narrow lace similar to Valenciennes lace. *See also* Dieppe point lace.

poustomániko: Greece. Bolero jacket.

poutouri: Greece. Man's dark woolen trousers.

powder blue: Soft medium blue.

powdering dress: *See* powdering jacket.

powdering gown: *See* powdering jacket.

powdering jacket: Early Georgian (1700–1750 C.E.) to Late Georgian (1750–1790 C.E.). United Kingdom. Loose wrapper worn over the clothes to protect them while the wig was being powdered.

poyas: Bulgaria. Man's festive sash.

poynte: *See* aglet.

ppipu ppipu ahuaska: Peru. A closely woven fabric.

pracchadapata: *See* nicola.

prachchhada: India. Wrap.

prada: Indonesia. Application of gold dust, leaf, or paint to a textile.

praðr: Norway. Old word for thread.

praetexta: Roman (753 B.C.E.–323 C.E.). White robe with purple border.

praghata: India. A loose, long, unwoven fringe on a nivi.

prāiscīn: *See* aprūn.

prakhotaeo: Laos and Thailand. Waistband; belt.

pramana-krtsna: India. A shoe with two, three, or four soles.

pranken: Early Gothic (1200–1350 C.E.). Term meaning to arrange the folds of a gown.

prapadina: India. Woman's tunic that reaches to the feet.

pratidhi: India. Piece of fabric worn to cover a woman's breasts; a breast band worn tied in back.

pratigraha: India. Thimble.

pratinivasana: India. Undergarment.

pravara: India. Upper body garment.

pravatra: India. Earrings.

praveni: India. A plait of hair.

prawing-spinel: Byzantine and Romanesque (400–1200 C.E.). United Kingdom. Hairpin.

preen: Byzantine and Romanesque (400–1200 C.E.) to Renaissance (1450–1550 C.E.). United Kingdom. Middle English word for pin.

pregaca: Croatia and Serbia. Apron.

pregnant stay: Directoire and First Empire (1790–1815 C.E.). United Kingdom. Introduced in 1811, woman's corset that reached from the shoulders to below the hips and heavily boned to hide the woman's delicate condition.

prēon: Byzantine and Romanesque (400–1200 C.E.). United Kingdom. In 10th century, brooch or pin worn by women.

press cloth: Piece of fabric used between iron and fabric while pressing.

prestilka: Bulgaria. Front apron, 50 x 80 cm.

prêt-à-porter: France. Ready to wear clothing.

pretina: Renaissance (1450–1550 C.E.). Spain. Breeches waistband.

prétintailles: Early Georgian (1700–1750 C.E.). Elaborate cutout ornaments of lace or gold embroidery sewn to women's gowns.

preto: Portugal. Black.

prevez: Bulgaria. Bridal veil.

priccses nadrág: Hungary. Breeches.

priejuoste: Lithuania. Apron.

prieksauts: Lithuania. Apron.

prievite: Latvia. Belt less than two cm wide and 2-1/2 to four m long.

prijuostė: Lithuania. Apron.

primrose: Elizabethan (1550–1625 C.E.). Pale yellow.

Prince Albert: *See* frock coat.

Prince of Wales check: The Glen Urquart check.

Prince of Wales jacket: Bustle (1865–1890 C.E.). United Kingdom. Introduced in 1868, man's loose reefer with three pair of buttons.

Prince Oxford: Trade name for Dan River's oxford cloth.

Prince Rupert: Gay Nineties (1890–1900 C.E.). In 1896, a woman's figure-fitting, velvet jacket worn open at the front. Resembled a Louis XV coat.

prince's sleeve: Romantic (1815–1840 C.E.). United Kingdom. Man's sleeve with a pointed gore in the seam at the wrist.

prince's stuff: Early Georgian (1700–1750 C.E.) to Late Georgian (1750–1790 C.E.). Black wool, plain weave fabric. Used for clerical garb, legal gowns, and mourning.

princesa: Spain. Princess line dress.

princess: Close fitting style of garment with no horizontal seam from shoulder to floor.

Princess Augusta poke: Directoire and First Empire (1790–1815 C.E.). Introduced in 1813, woman's poke bonnet of white satin with a white feather that fell on the left side. Tied with a large bow under the right cheek.

princess dress: Bustle (1865–1890 C.E.). United Kingdom. Popular around 1865, a woman's dress cut in one piece (without a waistband). Possibly names for Princess Alexandra.

Princess Elizabeth lilac: Directoire and First Empire (1790–1815 C.E.). United Kingdom. Lavender.

princess lace: Very delicate variation of duchesse lace.

princess paletot

Princess of Wales bonnet: Directoire and First Empire (1790–1815 C.E.). Named for Princess Caroline in 1812. Round crowned woman's bonnet with the brim turned up on one side of the front.

princess paletot: Crinoline (1840–1865 C.E.). A girl's woolen paletot featuring a mock military style overcoat and trimmed with cording and military-cut pockets.

princess petticoat: Crinoline (1840–1865 C.E.). United Kingdom. Popular from 1840s on, woman's petticoat and bodice combination cut without a waist seam and buttoning in the back. By 1882, buttoned in front.

princess polonaise: Bustle (1865–1890 C.E.). United Kingdom. Popular in 1870s, woman's polonaise dress cut in princess line.

princess robe: Crinoline (1840–1865 C.E.). United Kingdom. Introduced in 1848, woman's day dress cut in the princess line. Buttoned down the entire front and had descending lines of ribbons on the sides. Three-quarter length sleeves worn with engageantes.

Princess Royal: Crinoline (1840–1865 C.E.). In 1858, woman's deep, flowing mantle trimmed with chenille-spotted braid or gimp and a light French lace.

princess slip: *See* princess petticoat.

Princess Wagram: Crinoline (1840–1865 C.E.). In 1854, guipure mantilla with a crocheted, scalloped border and fringe.

princesse: *See* principessa.

principessa: Italy. Princess line dress.

prine: Ireland. Gaelic word for pin used to fasten clothes.

prine feilidh: Scotland. Kilt pin. Traditionally worn fastened to lower right corner of front flap.

Prinzesskleid: Germany. Princess line dress.

Priora: Crinoline (1840–1865 C.E.). In 1854, double talma set on a pointed yoke and collar. Trimmed with a very rich fringe and eight rows of narrow velvet.

pristelca: Bulgaria. Richly embroidered apron.

pristídha: Greece. Heavily pleated skirt worn over the podhiá.

privy coat: Elizabethan (1550–1625 C.E.). Coat of defense worn under an outer garment.

procardium: Egyptian (4000–30 B.C.E.). Worn by both genders, wrapped garment made from a rectangular length of fabric wound around the body. In the woman's version, it sometimes had suspenders. Sometimes worn belted.

prœd: United Kingdom. Old English word for thread.

prokandaka: India. Pearl necklace.

prosaponcho: Peru. Fine cotton poncho worn folded around the neck and thrown back over the shoulders.

próstena: Greece. Everyday apron.

provincial bonnet: Directoire and First Empire (1790–1815 C.E.). Woman's fine straw bonnet trimmed simply.

provincial rose: Elizabethan (1550–1625 C.E.). Shoe rosette.

prsluk: *See* podkošulja.

prsten: Croatia, Czechoslovakia, and Serbia. Finger ring.

prudent: Late Georgian (1750–1790 C.E.). Man's winter wrap.

pruik: Holland. Periwig.

prune: Dull dark purple.

prune de Monsieur: Late Georgian (1750–1790 C.E.). France. Shade of purple.

prune Dumas: Bustle (1865–1890 C.E.). Introduced in 1883, dark blue violet.

prunell: Heavy, twill weave cashmere.

prunella: 1. Twill or satin weave, worsted dress fabric that is yarn-dyed. 2. Popular in 18th and 19th centuries, a wool or blend fabric with a smooth surface.

Prussian collar: Romantic (1815–1840 C.E.) to Bustle (1865–1890 C.E.). Man's stand-fall collar with the points nearly meeting in the front.

przedna: Poland. Darning thread.

pshente: Egyptian (4000–30 B.C.E.). Double crown, symbol of the pharaoh.

psila: Roman (753 B.C.E.–323 C.E.). Cloth with one side shorn.

psyche knot: Knot of hair worn at the nape of the neck styled after the hairstyle of Psyche from Greek mythology.

pteruges: Roman (753 B.C.E.–323 C.E.). Soldier's padded shirt with dags or tabs at the waist and sleeve.

pu fa'amau: Samoa. Buttonhole.

pu fu: China. Qing dynasty (1644–1911 C.E.). Woman's plain surcoat.

pu zi: China. Introduced in 1391, insignia badges used to denote rank.

pua: Borneo. Blankets.

puahi: New Zealand. Maori. A cloak of the skins of white haired dogs.

pualena: United States of America. Hawaii. Yellow.

puamoamoa: United States of America. Hawaii. A frock coat.

puava: Samoa. Ribbon.

puce: 1. Romantic (1815–1840 C.E.). Color of amethyst. 2. Purplish brown. 3. Croatia and Serbia. Button.

puch'ae: Korea. Folding fan.

puckery: *See* pugaree.

pudding cap: Late Georgian (1750–1790 C.E.). Padded roll or cap worn by children to prevent injury when falling.

pudding head: *See* bourrelet.

pudding sleeve: Early Georgian (1700–1750 C.E.) to Late Georgian (1750–1790 C.E.). Man's long, loose sleeve, often seen on a clergyman's gown.

pudding-basin cut: Late Gothic (1350–1450 C.E.). United Kingdom. Man's hairstyle where the hair was shaved on the neck and temples, leaving a skullcap of hair on top. Popular in Italy, United Kingdom, and France, but never in Germany.

puertas: Renaissance (1450–1550 C.E.). Spain. Buckles.

puff: Directoire and First Empire (1790–1815 C.E.). Thin gore of fabric in the back of the waistband of men's breeches or trousers. Sides of the gore had laces to draw the pants tight, creating a puff in the gore.

puff ring: Hollow finger ring.

Puffärmel: Germany. Puffed sleeves.

puffjacke: Elizabethan (1550–1625 C.E.). Germany. Literally "puffed jacket," short man's coat, either wide or narrow in cut, worn for riding.

pug: Elizabethan (1550–1625 C.E.) to Restoration (1660–1700 C.E.). Short, hooded cape, usually of silk or velvet.

pug hood: Early Georgian (1700–1750 C.E.). Woman's short hood made with pleats from a single point at the back of the head. Usually black with a colored lining that folded back to frame the face. Tied under the chin with a ribbon that matched the lining.

pugaree: Version of the turban originating in India that began as a form of protection from the sun. Evolved into a scarf-like hatband worn around the crown of a straw hat. *See also* pagri.

puggaree: *See* pugaree.

puggerie: *See* pugaree.

puggree: *See* pugaree.

pugovico: Russia. Button.

puhaszárú csizma: Hungary. Lightweight, soft, calf-high, black boots.

'pujok: Korea. Amulet.

puk: Korea. Bobbin.

puka: Ecuador. Red.

puka kui kele: United States of America. Hawaii. Needle slot of a sewing machine.

puka pihi: United States of America. Hawaii. Buttonhole.

pukaha: New Zealand. Maori. A very rough cape.

pukai: United States of America. Hawaii. Lime bleach for the hair.

puke: 1. Early Gothic (1200–1350 C.E.). Color puce or a common fabric used in making hose and gowns. 2. Elizabethan (1550–1625 C.E.). Dirty brown color.

puke pakeke: United States of America. Hawaii. Pocketbook.

puki: United States of America. Hawaii. Boot.

pukta: Korea. Red; crimson.

pukupuku: *See* pauku.

pulakabandha: *See* badhani.

puletasi: Samoa. Woman's long, loose, puff-sleeved dress.

puljka: *See* puce.

pullicat: Elizabethan (1550–1625 C.E.) to Late Georgian (1750–1790 C.E.). Cotton fabric for handkerchiefs from Pulicat.

pullings out: Elizabethan (1550–1625 C.E.). Inner lining of a garment when it was visible through slashes, cuts, or panes.

Pullman slipper: Soft bedroom slipper that folds flat for storage.

pullo: Peru. Thick, coarse baise blanket.

pull-over: Garment that pulls on over head.

pullover: Italy and Spain. Sweater.

Pullover: Germany. Sweater.

p'ullu: *See* phullu.

pulo: Tibet. Leather.

pulou: Samoa. Hat or headgear.

pulou fa'afao: Samoa. Helmet.

pulou pepe: Samoa. Baby's bonnet.

p'ulrannel: Korea. Flannel.

pulrausu: Korea. Blouse.

pulsera: *See* brazalete.

Pulswärmer: *See* Fausthandschuh.

Pultney cap: Late Georgian (1750–1790 C.E.). Popular in 1760s, a woman's indoor cap wired up with a dip in the center. Sometimes had two lappets in the rear.

Pumphose: Germany. Breeches.

pumpkin: Dull, deep orange.

pun alai: Borneo. A huge yellow bead.

punch: Bustle (1865–1890 C.E.). Introduced in 1884, color of blue gray smoke.

punchetto: Italy. A needle lace densely worked in a double knotted buttonhole stitch.

puncocha: Czechoslovakia. Coarse laced peasant's shoe.

punge: Early Gothic (1200–1350 C.E.). Purse.

punjam: *See* panjam.

punjang: *See* hwajang.

punk: (1970–1980 C.E.). Street fashion characterized by use of leather, chains, torn clothes, and brightly colored exotic hairstyles.

puño: Ecuador, Spain. Cuff.

puño ajustado: Spain. Sleeve wristband.

puño doble: Spain. French cuff.

punta: Renaissance (1450–1550 C.E.). Point that reinforced a ribbon or cord used for lacing. Later the word meant the entire lace.

punta roma: Renaissance (1450–1550 C.E.). Spain. Blunt toe of a shoe.

puntada limeña: Ecuador. Closed double chain stitch.

puntada recta: Spain. Literally, a straight stitch.

puntas: Renaissance (1450–1550 C.E.). Spain. Toes of shoes.

puntilla: Spain. Lacework.

puntilla de Venecia: Spain. Venetian lace.

punto: Italy. Point or stitch.

punto a feston: Italy. A looped mesh like point de gaze.

punto a giorno: Italy. Hem stitch.

punto a giorno cordonetto: Italy. Couching stitch.

punto a giorno croce: Italy. Cross-stitch.

punto a giorno festone: Italy. Buttonhole stitch.

punto a giorno indietro: Italy. Backstitch.

punto a gropo: Italy. Knotted buttonhole stitch.

punto a maglia quadra: Italy. Term for lacis.

punto a relievi: Italy. Needle lace with raised details.

punto de almorafán: Renaissance (1450–1550 C.E.). Spain. Chain stitch.

punto de cruz: Spain. Cross-stitch.

punto de España: *See* Spanish needlepoint.

punto de malla: Spain. Embroidered netting.

punto de oro llano: Renaissance (1450–1550 C.E.). Spain. Couched gold threads.

punto de tallo: Spain. Stem stitch.

punto erba: Italy. Stem stitch.

punto gothica: Reticella needle lace.

punto in aria: Renaissance (1450–1550 C.E.) to Restoration (1660–1700 C.E.). Early form of needle lace.

punto llano: Renaissance (1450–1550 C.E.). Spain. A stitch used in couching gold thread.

punto neve: Italy. Snowflake pattern in lace.

punto passato: Italy. Satin stitch.

punto real: Renaissance (1450–1550 C.E.). Spain. Literally "royal stitch," used to make raised, concentric curves.

punto tagliato: Italy. Cutwork.

punto tagliato a fogliani: *See* gros point de Venise.

punto tirato: Italy. Drawn work.

puoga: Lithuania. Button.

pupu hoaka: United States of America. Hawaii. Shell bracelet.

pupu lauoho: United States of America. Hawaii. Topknot.

purdah: India. Cotton cloth for curtains.

purée de pois: *See* oseille cuite.

pureke: *See* pukaha.

purfle: Early Gothic (1200–1350 C.E.). Border of trim.

puri: India. Bobbin.

Puritan: Crinoline (1840–1865 C.E.). In 1854, woman's full-circle wrap with a quilted lining. Trimmed with broad satin galloon and two rows of velvet ribbon. In France, called la Puritana.

Puritan bonnet: Gay Nineties (1890–1900 C.E.). United Kingdom. Woman's small, flat, crownless bonnet with a point in the front. Trimmed with lace or an aigrette.

puriya: India. A cloth stuffed with cotton.

purki: Bulgaria. Smock embroidered with a tightly worked stripe.

purl: Elizabethan (1550–1625 C.E.). 1. Pleat in a ruff. 2. Small edging lace.

purnellow: Early Georgian (1700–1750 C.E.) to Late Georgian (1750–1790 C.E.). Worsted fabric.

purpaidh: Ireland. Gaelic word for purple.

purper: *See* paars.

purple: Dye from the *Murex brandis*. When first collected, it is yellow and it alters to red then violet with exposure to light.

purple gown: China. Song dynasty. Gown worn by a scholar.

purpua: Spain. Purple.

púrpura: Portugal. Purple.

purpurea: Biblical (Unknown–30 C.E.). Hebrew word for purple.

purpuren: Holland. *See* paars

purpúreo: Portugal. Purple colored.

purpurfarben: *See* purpurrot.

purpurowy: *See* szkarlatny.

purpurrot: Germany. Purple.

purse: Small bag for carrying money, etc.

purse strings: Drawstrings used on purses.

p'uruda: Korea. Blue.

p'urun: Korea. Blue.

pusher lace: Directoire and First Empire (1790–1815 C.E.). Introduced in 1813, lace made on the patented Pusher machine. Imitation of Chantilly lace.

pushk kurta: Pakistan. Long tunic-like shirt with almost completely embroidered front and cuffs. It was worn with full trousers that tapered at the ankles.

püsküllü: Turkey. Tassels.

puspapatta: India. A floral fabric, with the pattern either woven in or printed on top.

Pussy Willow: Trade name for radium.

pussy-cat bonnet: Directoire and First Empire (1790–1815 C.E.). United Kingdom. Worn from 1814 to 1818, woman's bonnet of catskin.

pust: Croatia and Serbia. Felt.

pustin: India. A fur-lined coat.

putalya: India. A gold coin necklace of Maharashtra.

putan: Ireland. Gaelic word for button.

putois: France. Polecat.

puttee: (1910–1920 C.E.). Spiral bound legging.

putting stick: *See* poking stick.

puuahi: Australia. Maori dogskin cloak made of strips of hairless white dogskin.

pu'ukohukohu: United States of America. Hawaii. Gray tapa.

pu'ukukui: United States of America. Hawaii. Tapa colored with a dye made from the breadfruit blossom and kukui tree bark.

puzzola: Italy. Polecat.

pyajama: *See* pajama.

pyjamā: India. At home trousers.

pynn: *See* preen.

pyonbal: Korea. Queue.

pyramid style: Crinoline (1840–1865 C.E.). United Kingdom. Introduced in 1845, woman's day skirt trim in a series of horizontal bands that were wider at the bottom of the skirt than at the top.

Pyramid talma: Crinoline (1840–1865 C.E.). In 1854, gored silk talma. Seams were covered in a braid. Trimmed with nine tabs that reached one third down the garment. Embroidered and had a netted fringe.

pyramids: Crinoline (1840–1865 C.E.). United Kingdom. Introduced in 1858, woman's day skirt trim of triangular panels of fabric in a color different that the dress.

pyrope: Deep red garnet stone.

Q

qabā: Arabia. Rich, sleeved robe with a slit in the front.

qababand: *See* qatifah-i-purbi.

qabbeh: Palestine. Decorative chest panel.

qabbet anbar: Palestine. Elaborately embroidered chest panel of a woman's gown.

qadar: India. Long coat.

qadifeh: Afghanistan. Woman's long chiffon scarf edged with lace.

qaftan: 1. Morocco. Jewish woman's corselet. 2. Palestine. Full-length robe, with or without sleeves.

qalansuwa: Arabia. 1. High, miter-like hat. 2. Hood or cowl.

q'alaq'awa: Bolivia. Yellowish brown color.

qalasuva: Arabia. Persian hat.

qalush: Palestine. Man's cap.

qamha hamra: Palestine. Red and yellow striped silk fabric.

qamis: Palestine. Man's long white shirt cut in the European style.

qamīs: Arabia. Man's mid-thigh to ankle-length shirt with long or short sleeves.

qarawi: Palestine. Fine linen fabric used for veils.

qasab: Palestine. Silver cord used in fabric.

qasabiyeh: Palestine. Striped Syrian silk fabric.

qatifah-i-purbi: India. Plain silk cloth.

qaz: Palestine. Coarse silk fabric used for women's coats.

qaziyeh: Palestine. Unlined black or purple silk dura'ah.

q'epirina: *See* phullu.

qi: China. Figured silk damask.

qi pao: (1920–1930 C.E.) China. Literally "banner gown," one-piece gown introduced in 1925. Considered a very daring item of dress.

qian hua: China. White lead worn as makeup.

qiana: (1960–1970 C.E.). United States of America. Introduced in 1968 by DuPont, silklike synthetic fabric, soft and drapey.

qiapàn: China. Uygur or Tajik front-buttoning robe.

qibù: China. Varnished cloth.

qigé: China. Patent leather.

qiladeh dhahab: Palestine. Woman's gold necklace.

qilim: China. Under the Zhengde emperor (r. 1505–1521 C.E.), fourth and fifth rank of embroidery on a gown; unicorn.

qinglù: China. Dark green.

qirmizi: India. The color carmine.

qirmizi don: Turkmenistan. Man's long-sleeved coat.

qiú: China. Fur coat.

qladeh: Palestine. Lengthy necklace of chains of figure-eight silver links in between which are hollow silver balls which suspend coins.

qladet 'anbar: Palestine. Amber bead necklace.

qladet morjan: Palestine. Coral necklace.

qladet qrenfol: Palestine. Necklace of four sections of cloves, beads, corals, and tassels.

qompi: Peru. Incan finest quality textile.

quachtli: Aztec. Large, rectangular piece of fabric used as medium of exchange.

quadricorn hat: Hat with four points or corners.

quadrille head: Late Georgian (1750–1790 C.E.). Lappets embroidered with aces of spades, hearts, diamonds, and clubs.

quail-pipe boot: Elizabethan (1550–1625 C.E.). United Kingdom. Man's high, soft leather boot which fell softly in wrinkles on the leg.

Quaker chambray: Dan River's trade name for cotton fabric used for children's clothes.

Quaker collar: Broad, flat collar.

Quaker hat: Early Georgian (1700–1750 C.E.) to Late Georgian (1750–1790 C.E.). Man's tricorne with a tall crown.

Quaker skirt: Crinoline (1840–1865 C.E.). In 1863, small, lightweight hoop.

qualitie: Early Georgian (1700–1750 C.E.) to Directoire (1790–1815 C.E.). Coarse tape for binding or strings.

quan: Vietnam. Trousers.

quan cao-boi: Vietnam. Jeans.

quan cháo lòng: Vietnam. Dirty white trousers.

quan coc: Vietnam. Breeches; shorts.

quan con áo-cánh: Vietnam. Underwear.

quân đùi: Vietnam. Shorts.

quan soóc: Vietnam. Bermuda shorts.

quàn ta: Vietnam. Vietnamese trousers that are side pleated, low crotched, pocketless, and flyless.

quan xà-lón: Vietnam. Drawers; undershorts.

quande: Sierra Leone. Russet, cotton cloth.

quân-phuc: Vietnam. Military uniform.

quân-phuc đai-le: Vietnam. Full dress uniform.

quân-phuc làm viêc: Vietnam. Work uniform.

quartered cap: Late Georgian (1750–1790 C.E.). Boy's cap with flat circular crown on a headband and visor.

quat quì: Vietnam. Precious fan.

qubā: India. Short, fitted coat with sleeves.

qubpa: Turkmenistan. Jeweled finial worn on the bork.

quechquemitl

quechquemitl: Mexico. Woman's triangular folded outer garment. May be worn with or without a blouse.

querpo: Elizabethan (1550–1625 C.E.) to Restoration (1660–1700 C.E.). Spain. Man without a cloak or outer garment.

querpo hood: Elizabethan (1550–1625 C.E.) to Restoration (1660–1700 C.E.). Woman's plain soft hood.

queue: Restoration (1660–1700 C.E.). France. Braid of hair in the back of a wig.

quezote: Renaissance (1450–1550 C.E.). Spain. Linen jerkin.

quich: Morocco. Undergarment of light material.

quiff: United Kingdom. Slang term for man's hairstyle where hair is oiled and brushed back from the forehead.

quilitl: Mexico. Zoque Indian term for the color green.

quilted petticoat: 1. Early Georgian (1700–1750 C.E.). Elaborate petticoat exposed by a front slit in woman's gown. 2. Early Georgian (1700–1750 C.E.) and Crinoline (1840–1865 C.E.). Undergarment intended to expand the skirt and provide warmth. Made of silk or alpaca.

quimono: *See* saiote escocês.

quintin: France. Fine lawn fabric.

quintise: *See* cointise.

quiret: Cuirass.

quirk: Clock, as in hosiery.

quitasol: 1. Early Georgian (1700–1750 C.E.). United States. Large fan carried by matrons. 2. *See* kittysol.

quitta soll: *See* kittysol.

quittesol: *See* kittysol.

quizzing glass: Early Georgian (1700–1750 C.E.) to Bustle (1865–1890 C.E.). Monocle that hung from a neck chain. In 1820s, dandies had the monocle affixed to the head of their cane.

qulaqça: Iran. Fitted cap.

qumbaz: Palestine. Man's long-sleeved, calf- or ankle-length coat. Open in the center front and worn right over left.

qún: China. Skirt.

qungo: Ethiopia. Knee-length rain cloak made of long knotted strands of grass.

qúnzi: China. Skirt.

quôc-phuc: Vietnam. National dress.

qusak: Turkmenistan. Man's loosely tied silk girdle.

qutbah fallahi: Palestine. Literally "village stitch," cross-stitch.

qutn: United Arab Emirates. Cotton.

qutni: *See* qatifah-i-purbi.

qutun: *See* qutn.

quynh: Vietnam. Ruby.

R

ra: Japan. An early fancy gauze weave fabric.

rab: Poland. Seam.

rabagas bonnet: Bustle (1865–1890 C.E.). United Kingdom. Introduced in 1872. Woman's small, high-crowned, small brimmed bonnet that tied under the chin in a large bow. Brim turned up all around. Named for Sardou's satire of the same name (1871).

rabanna: Madagascar. Raffia fabric used for draperies.

rabat

rabat: 1. Renaissance (1450–1550 C.E.) to Charles I and Commonwealth (1625–1660 C.E.). Man's turned down collar that fell over the shoulders. 2. Restoration (1660–1700 C.E.). Linen or lace cravat with a vertically pleated or gathered fall. 3. (19th century). Lingerie ornament worn on women's bodices.

rabatine: Collar that falls over the shoulders like a cape or ruff.

rabbi: Short, bib-like collar or rabat worn by Roman Catholic ecclesiastics.

rabbit: Very soft, light fur that can be dyed to resemble many other furs.

rabot: Vertically pleated muslin stock that fastened in back.

raccoon: Thick fur with dense light gray under fur and long, silver guard hairs tipped in black.

raccoon coat: (20th century). Very bulky overcoat of raccoon fur. Popularly worn at football games.

rachdan: Ireland. Gaelic word for tartan plaid worn like a mantle or cloak.

Rachel cloak: Crinoline (1840–1865 C.E.). In 1853, woman's fitted, wadded cloak that was lined. Trimmed with silk or mohair lace.

racket: Broad wooden shoe.

radhanagri: India. Silken fabric made in Rhadha Nagar.

radielfo: (1920–1930 C.E.). Italy. A man's helmet that was fitted with radio receivers in hinged ear flaps.

radium: Fine, soft, plain weave fabric.

radnor: Mercerized cotton upholstery fabric.

radzimir: 1. Crinoline (1840–1865 C.E.). Introduced in 1949, black silk used for mourning. 2. Fine silk or rayon fabric with cross-wise ribs.

raffia: Straw made from strong palm fiber.

rafia: *See* rofia.

rafraf: Arabia. Back flap on a sabgha.

rafugar: India. Needleworker.

rafugari: India. Darning stitch embroidery.

raggiera: Italy. Long hairpins placed in a woman's hair to form a halo.

Raglan: Crinoline (1840–1865 C.E.). In 1855, velvet shawl lined with quilted satin. Trimmed with rich guipure lace and long fringe at false yoke and hem.

raglan boot: Crinoline (1840–1865 C.E.). United Kingdom. Worn in 1850s, man's soft black leather thigh-high boot worn when hunting. Named for the Crimean general.

raglan cape: Crinoline (1840–1865 C.E.). United Kingdom. Worn from 1857 on, man's sac, single-breasted overcoat with no vents. Had a type of sleeve, now known as the raglan sleeve. Commonly made of waterproof material.

raglan covert coat: Gay Nineties (1890–1900 C.E.). United Kingdom. Introduced in 1897, man's covert coat with raglan sleeves.

raglan overcoat: Gay Nineties (1890–1900 C.E.) to present. United Kingdom. Introduced in 1898, revival of 1850s version of the poncho but with raglan sleeves. Had side vents that buttoned with two buttons and was usually made of waterproof material. Replaced the mackintosh.

raglan sleeve: Crinoline (1840–1865 C.E.). Worn from 1857 on, sleeve that reached up into a point on the outer seam where it joined the body of the garment at the neckline.

raglan sleeve

Ragusa guipure: Type of cutwork.

raiglin: *See* rang.

railroad trousers: Romantic (1815–1840 C.E.). United Kingdom. Worn from 1837 to 1850. Men's vertically striped trousers.

railway pockets: Crinoline (1840–1865 C.E.). United Kingdom. Worn from 1857 on, flat bag worn under the dress in which a woman hid her valuables when traveling.

raing: *See* rang.

rainy daisy skirt: Gay Nineties (1890–1900 C.E.). Walking skirt, two to three inches off the ground. Worn by women belonging to the Rainy Day Club.

raised work: Any three dimensional detail in lace.

rajai: *See* razai.

rajaka: *See* nirnejaka.

rajapatta: India. Literally "a silk fit for kings."

rajata: India. Silver.

rajferšlus: Bosnia. Zipper.

rajstopy: Poland. Pantyhose.

raju: India. A striped cloth.

raktambara: India. A red silk.

raktani: India. The color red.

Raleigh bars: Venetian bars with loose loops at the bottom edge.

ráli: Greece. Good quality, white cotton cloth.

rallaka: India. A girdle.

ramall: Elizabethan (1550–1625 C.E.) to Late Georgian (1750–1790 C.E.). United States of America. Neckerchief or small shawl worn over the shoulders.

ramie: 1. Strong fiber of the Asian ramie plant. Sometimes called China grass. 2. Garment made of ramie.

Ramillies wig: Early Georgian (1700–1750 C.E.). Popular with military men, man's wig with one or two plaits tied at top and bottom with a black ribbon. Named in honor of the Battle of Ramillies. After 1780, plait was sometimes turned up and tied in a loop at the nape of the neck.

ramio: Spain. Ramie.

Ramillies wig

Ramona cloth: Linen-finished, plain weave cotton fabric.

ramoneur: Bustle (1865–1890 C.E.). In 1883, color of a Brazil nut.

rampoor-chuddar: Romantic (1815–1840 C.E.) to Bustle (1865–1890 C.E.). Fine twill weave wool shawl from India.

rān: Arabia. Leggings.

ranch pants: Full-length, straight pants.

randa: Guatemala. Hand sewn joining of two pieces of fabric with embroidered yarns.

randas: Renaissance (1450–1550 C.E.). Spain. Insertions.

randosel: *See* paenang.

Ranelagh mob: Late Georgian (1750–1790 C.E.). United Kingdom. Popular in 1760s, gauze handkerchief folded into triangle worn over the head, tied under the chin. Based on the fashion commonly worn by market women.

ranetz: Russia. Knapsack.

rang: India. Transparent muslin.

rangi: India. The process of dyeing.

rank: Iran. Men's voluminous trousers.

rankava: India. A woolen cloth.

rankavapata: India. A goat hair shawl.

rapaki: New Zealand. Maori term for a rainproof kilt.

Raphael dress: Crinoline (1840–1865 C.E.). In 1859, double-skirted dress with a deep square neckline filled in with lace and insertion. Sleeves had four puffs and a deep bell cuff.

raploch: Scotland. Coarse, rough homespun fabric.

raploch white: Renaissance (1450–1550 C.E.) to Elizabethan (1550–1625 C.E.). Coarse undyed wool homespun.

rapolin: Switzerland. Millinery braid.

raquettes: Directoire and First Empire (1790–1815 C.E.). Flat ornamental braid ends used on different helmet cords.

rara: Indonesia. Sa'dan-Toraja necklace of wooden cylinders covered in gold.

ras: France. Short napped fabric.

ras de Sicile: Early Georgian (1700–1750 C.E.) France. A brown and white tabby weave silk fabric.

ras du more: Early Georgian (1700–1750 C.E.) to Late Georgian (1750–1790 C.E.). Made in Ras de St. Maur and later called radzimir, heavy black silk similar to armozeen. Used for mourning.

rasana: India. A waist ornament.

rash: Smooth textile of silk called silk rash or worsted called cloth rash.

rasha: 1. Heavy rayon fabric. 2. Japan. Wool felt.

rasi: Swahili. Cape.

rasimal: India. A cheap silk fabric.

raso: 1. Renaissance (1450–1550 C.E.). Italy. Satin weave fabric forming the ground of a figured fabric. 2. Italy. Satin. 3. Spain. Satin.

raso cinese: Italy. China silk.

raso de la China: Spain. China silk.

raso de zapatillas: Spain. Slipper satin.

raso imperial: Spain. Imperial sateen.

raso liberty: Spain. Art Nouveau silk.

raso muy brillante: Spain. Pane satin.

raso piel de angel: Spain. Peau d'ange.

raso piel de cisne: Spain. Peau de cygne.

raso piel de seda: Spain. Peau de soie.

raso por trama: Spain. Sateen.

raso por urdimbre: Spain. Satin.

raspberry: Reddish color.

rat: 1. Gay Nineties (1890–1900 C.E.). A large coil of wire over which the hair was combed. 2. Pad worn inside the hair to make it extend.

rat musqué: France. Muskrat fur.

rat-tail: Small, firm, round braid.

rateen: Woolen fabric like frieze.

ratiné: 1. Loosely woven plain weave cotton or wool fabric. 2. *See* frise.

ratine lace: Machine made lace similar to Turkish toweling.

rational: Worn by bishops, a short ornamental vest.

rationals: Gay Nineties (1890–1900 C.E.). United Kingdom. Another name for the popular bicycle knickerbockers worn by women.

ratmusqué: Italy. Muskrat fur.

ratna: India. Precious stones.

ratnajali: India. A net of braid and pearls worn around a woman's chignon.

ratnakambala: India. A costly shawl from Goa.

ratnangulia: India. Finger rings studded with precious stones.

ratnapariksha: India. The art of the appreciation of precious gems.

ratnavali: India. A single string of pearls necklace with gold globules or a jeweled net worn around a woman's chignon.

ratnodgrathi tottariyam: India. Scarves with gems woven into them.

raton laveur: France. Raccoon fur.

rat's color: Elizabethan (1550–1625 C.E.). Dull gray.

rattan: Elizabethan (1550–1625 C.E.) to Late Georgian (1750–1790 C.E.). Cane from the East Indian palm.

ratteen: *See* ratiné.

rattinet: Woolen fabric, thinner than frieze.

râu cam: Vietnam. Beard.

râu dê: Vietnam. Goatee.

râu mép: Vietnam. Moustache.

râu som: Vietnam. Long beard.

rawā: India. Veil.

rawai: Borneo. Woman's corset of split rattan rings with brass rings threaded on them.

raxete: Ecuador and Guatemala. Coarse wool fabric.

ray: Late Gothic (1350–1450 C.E.) to Renaissance (1450–1550 C.E.). Striped cloth.

raye de comtesse: Bustle (1865–1890 C.E.). In 1883, corded cloth.

raymond: Romantic (1815–1840 C.E.). Powder blue.

raynes: Early Gothic (1200–1350 C.E.). Originally from Rennes, a fine linen.

rayon: *See* artificial silk.

rayon taffeta: Taffeta of rayon yarns.

rayonne: France. Name for synthetic fabrics. Replaced old name of soie artificielle.

rayonné: United States of America. Type of hood.

rayure travers: Gay Nineties (1890–1900 C.E.). In 1893, a silk and wool bengaline with horizontal stripes.

razai: India. Coverlet quilted with cotton.

razao: India. Bed cover.

razsouchal: Bulgaria. Kerchief worn by women as a hat.

reach-me-down: (1920–1930 C.E.). United Kingdom. Term for a ready-made clothier.

reaf: Byzantine and Romanesque (400–1200 C.E.). United Kingdom. Garment or clothes. A very common word.

real lace: Handmade tatted lace.

realce: Ecuador. A leaflike embroidery design.

rebato: Elizabethan (1550–1625 C.E.). 1. White lace collar wired to stand up around the low necked bodice. 2. Brass wired support of a collar or ruff.

rebozo: Bolivia, Ecuador, and Guatemala. Red woolen shawl sometimes draped and used to carry item behind the back like a pack cloth.

rebras: Early Gothic (1200–1350 C.E.) to Restoration (1660–1700 C.E.). Revers on a coat, glove, or undergarment.

recal: Romania. Brown woolen cloak.

Recamier sash: Bustle (1865–1890 C.E.). Sash with long purse-ends ending in tassels.

red: Color of blood or a ruby.

red cross gingham: Heavy cotton fabric with alternating blue and white dyed stripes.

red fox: Red to fawn colored fox fur.

red lilac: Romantic (1815–1840 C.E.). United Kingdom. Red lavender.

red rippers: *See* brogans.

red russels: *See* brogans.

redes: Spain. Lace.

redicella: Spain. Netting.

redil: Guatemala. Wool spinning wheel.

redingote: 1. Bustle (1865–1890 C.E.). France. A woman's long overcoat cut to fully cover the bustle. 2. *See* frock coat.

redingote à l'amazone: Late Georgian (1750–1790 C.E.). France. Coat cut in the style of a woman's riding habit.

redingote du matin: Late Georgian (1750–1790 C.E.). Morning gown cut in the style of a riding costume.

Recamier sash
Dover Publications

redingote
Dover Publications

redingote en Backmann: Late Georgian (1750–1790 C.E.). France. Redingote styled after Backmann, first man in Paris to wear a simple outer coat.

reed hat: Bustle (1865–1890 C.E.). United Kingdom. Introduced in 1879, woman's woven reed hat worn for tennis or bathing.

reefer: 1. Bustle (1865–1890 C.E.). Short, double-breasted, snug-fitting jacket with a low collar, short lapels, and no back seam. Sometimes worn as an overcoat. 2. (1930–1939 C.E.). Man's double-breasted, tweed coat with wide lapels and six or eight large buttons.

reefer jacket: Gay Nineties (1890–1900 C.E.). Woman's double-breasted blue serge jacket similar to the man's reefer.

refafo: Guatemala and Mexico. Underskirt.

refajo envuelto: Guatemala. Woman's wraparound skirt.

refajos: Guatemala. Women's skirts. The most common color of these skirts is indigo blue.

refajos plegados: Guatemala. Woman's full skirt with a drawstring waist.

refirha: Tuareg. A man's full-cut blouse.

regatta: Sturdy, twilled cotton fabric, usually blue and white striped.

regatta faille francais: Bustle (1865–1890 C.E.). In 1889, soft, flexible, rich fabric.

regatta shirt: Crinoline (1840–1865 C.E.). United Kingdom. Man's striped cambric shirt for summer outdoor wear. Front was cut plain.

regatta shirting: Crinoline (1840–1865 C.E.). Cotton fabric with narrow colored stripes.

regence: 1. Bustle (1865–1890 C.E.). Introduced in 1889, silk fabric with a ribbed satin face. 2. *See* charvet.

regency cap: Directoire and First Empire (1790–1815 C.E.). Introduced in 1813, white satin cap trimmed with satin rouleaux and ostrich feathers.

regency hat: Directoire and First Empire (1790–1815 C.E.). United Kingdom. Woman's fur hat with a belled crown, turned up brim, and trimmed with a gold hatband, cord, and tassel and a feather.

regency mantle: Directoire and First Empire (1790–1815 C.E.). Introduced in 1813, black mantle with a small cape and a high collar. Trimmed with black tassels and a side silk band edged in cording that trimmed the outer edges of the garment.

regency wrapper: Directoire and First Empire (1790–1815 C.E.). Introduced in 1813, trained, long sleeved wrap that laced up the front with a silk cord. It had a band of velvet or sealskin around the edges and had a pointed collar.

regenjas: Holland. Mackintosh.

regenmantil: *See* kabanica.

regina: Fine, lightweight, twill weave, cotton fabric.

Regina: 1. Crinoline (1840–1865 C.E.). In 1853, embroidered taffeta mantle with a deep knotted fringe. 2. Bustle (1865–1890 C.E.). In 1867, pink lilac color.

regine purple: Bustle (1865–1890 C.E.). Deep, intense purple.

reink'ot'u: Korea. Raincoat.

reion: *See* injogyonsa.

reister cloak: Elizabethan (1550–1625 C.E.) to Restoration (1660–1700 C.E.). United Kingdom. Man's full-length cloak.

reitrocke: *See* puffjacke.

rekaw: Poland. Sleeve.

rekawica: Poland. Mitten.

rekawiczka: Poland. Glove.

rékli: Hungary. Blouse worn outside the skirt. Cut to fit the body.

relevés à la Marie Stuart: Crinoline (1840–1865 C.E.). France. In 1851, woman's hairstyle with a center part. The mass of hair covered the ears and formed a rouleau in back.

religieuse sleeve: Crinoline (1840–1865 C.E.). In 1863, undersleeve with deep five-inch wristband.

religious petticoat: Charles I and the Commonwealth (1625–1660 C.E.). United Kingdom. Woman's petticoat embroidered with religious stories. Worn by Puritan women.

rempli: France. Needle lace with an area of buttonholing.

ren: 1. China. Small flap on the chao fu used to cover the fastening. 2. Vietnam. Lace.

Renaissance embroidery: Cutwork embroidery.

Renaissance lace: Modern lace with woven tape motifs. *See also* Battenburg lace.

renard: France. Fox fur.

rendalo: Portugal. Lacework; lace trimmed.

rendi: India. A tattered garment.

rendilhado: Portugal. Lacy.

renforcée: Restoration (1660–1700 C.E.). France. Introduced in 1685, strong silk fabric.

rennrocklein: Elizabethan (1500–1625 C.E.). Germany. Literally "racing doublet," a doublet with tails longer than 14 cm. Worn almost exclusively by nobility as part of the jousting outfit. Popular later in the middle class.

renque: Mexico. Netlike weave created by the Zoque Indians.

reowe: Byzantine and Romanesque (400–1200 C.E.). United Kingdom. Fabric piece used interchangeably as a rug or blanket, perhaps even as a cloak. Believed to have been of a shaggy texture.

rep: Fabric similar to poplin with heavier weft yarn.

rep bluet: Romantic (1815–1840 C.E.) to Bustle (1865–1890 C.E.). France. Dark blue silk rep patterned with cornflowers in black satin.

rerebrace: Early Gothic (1200–1350 C.E.). Plate armor for the upper arm.

reseau: France. Ground for lace.

réseau rosacé: France. Elaborate hexagon-shaped needle ground used for lace.

reseda: France. Grayish green.

resi: *See* kiski.

resille: France. Net or hood for the hair.

restagno d'oro: Italy. Patterned brocade with a gold weft.

reta: Renaissance (1450–1550 C.E.). Italy. Hairnet made of knotted silk of gold threads with pearls or other gems woven in.

rete: Italy. Net of all kinds.

reticella: Italy. Fine, snowflake-like lace. First form of needlepoint lace.

reticella lace: *See* reticella.

reticello: *See* drawn work.

reticulated headdress: Early Gothic (1200–1350 C.E.). Woman's style involving wearing crespine over hair padded at sides and veil falling to shoulders.

reticule
Dover Publications

reticule: Romantic (1815–1840 C.E.) to present. A woman's small purse, generally with short strings or cords, worn carried in the hand or draped over the wrist.

retículo: Spain. Reticule.

retrós: Portugal. Twisted sewing silk.

revers: Turned-back edge of a coat, waistcoat, or bodice.

revers en pelerine: Crinoline (1840–1865 C.E.). United Kingdom. The pleats, folds, or trim that extended from the shoulders to the waist on a woman's gown. In the 1850s, they were renamed bretelles.

rhabdoskidophoros: Cane with a hidden fan.

rhadames: Bustle (1865–1890 C.E.). Introduced in 1883, a soft satin with a diagonal grain.

rhason: Worn by Eastern Church clergy, long loose garment similar to the cassock.

Rhea: India. Chinese ramie or China grass.

rheno: Byzantine and Romanesque (400–1200 C.E.). Hoodless mantle.

rhinegraves: *See* petticoat breeches.

rhodophane: France. Glass fabric made by Colombet. Used for hats, bags, jackets, and accessories.

rholwani: South Africa. Ndebele married woman's very large collar made from twisted grass and encrusted with beads.

riabhach: Ireland. Gaelic word for yellow gray.

riband: Ribbon band.

ribbed crepón: Gay Nineties (1890–1900 C.E.). In 1892, a finely ribbed light woolen fabric.

ribbed satin: Ribbed fabric with satin face.

ribbon corset: (1900–1910 C.E.). Introduced in 1904, a lightweight corset for sport or relaxation.

ribean: Ireland. Gaelic word for ribbon.

ribete: Bolivia. Woven tubular edge on some llijllas and ak'sus.

ribfluweel: *See* manchester.

ribine: *See* lipine.

ribon: Korea. Ribbon.

ricamo: Italy. Embroidery.

ricamo in bianco: Italy. Household linen embroidery.

ricamo in bianco a reticello: Italy. Embroidered netting.

ricamo in bianco ad intaglio: Italy. Cutout embroidery.

ricamo in bianco inglese: Italy. Broderie anglaise.

rice net: Coarse cotton net.

rice powder: Face powder made of pulverized rice.

ricebraid: Braid made to resemble grains of rice strung lengthwise.

Richilieu embroidery: France. Type of cutwork.

ricinium: Roman (753 B.C.E.–323 C.E.). Square veil worn by women when offering sacrifices.

rick-rack: Colored zigzag braid.

ridā: Arabia. Man's mantle.

Ridgeway buckle: United States of America. Wide, gold-plated, commercial belt buckle adopted for Army use with a webbing belt.

ridicule: 1. Directoire and First Empire (1790–1815 C.E.) to Crinoline (1840–1865 C.E.). Popular name for reticule from 1800 to 1850. *See also* reticule. 2. Bustle (1865–1890 C.E.). A large exterior pocket.

riding dress frock coat: Romantic (1815–1840 C.E.). United Kingdom. Popular in 1820s, man's frock coat with a deep collar and large lapels.

riding habit: 1. Early Georgian (1700–1750 C.E.). Woman's riding costume consisting of a coat and waistcoat cut like men's garments. Worn with a skirt called a petticoat. 2. Late Georgian (1750–1790 C.E.). In 1780, the skirt developed a train. 3. Directoire and First Empire (1790–1815 C.E.). Gown resembling the earlier riding habit was worn. Trimmed with brandenburgs. 4. Crinoline (1840–1865 C.E.). In 1840, habit consisted of a jacket and a long trained skirt. In 1860, skirt was cut to fit over the saddle pommel. 5. Bustle (1865–1890 C.E.). Women began to wear trousers under the habit skirt. 6. (1890–1899). C.E. Skirts were made without trains.

riding hoop: Early Georgian (1700–1750 C.E.). United Kingdom. Small hoop petticoat worn by women when riding.

riese: *See* flieder.

rifeling: Byzantine and Romanesque (400–1200 C.E.). United Kingdom. Sandal or boot of rawhide. Probably worn by rural people.

rift: Byzantine and Romanesque (400–1200 C.E.). United Kingdom. Piece of material used as a cloak, a curtain, or a veil.

riga: Nigeria. Large loose robe with elaborate embroidery.

rigolette: Lightweight, scarf-like women's head covering.

Rigoletto mantle: Romantic (1815–1840 C.E.). United Kingdom. Woman's knee-length caped mantle of satin and edged with fur.

rigona: Nigeria. Robes.

riha: Bangladesh. Scarf with a fringe of tassels.

rijnsteen: *See* soort bergkristal.

Rikan cha: Japan. A shade of tea color named for the actor Arashi Rikan.

rilling: *See* riveling.

Rimini: Crinoline (1840–1865 C.E.). In 1850, taffeta cloak trimmed with a double taffeta ruche.

ring buckle: Buckle made of two rings.

ring cloth: Bustle (1865–1890 C.E.). In 1884, sheer black wool fabric similar to nun's veiling, so delicate that width of fabric can be drawn through wedding ring.

ring purse: *See* miser's purse.

ringetje: Holland. Ringlet.

rinrin wallka: Ecuador. A beaded, shoulder-length necklace.

rinzu: Japan. Silk damask.

rio verde: Crinoline (1840–1865 C.E.). Introduced in 1862, lightweight pardessus with pagoda sleeves. Edges trimmed with ruffles.

Rio Verde: Crinoline (1840–1865 C.E.). In 1855, mantilla trimmed with broad bands of velvet, falls of lace, and knotted fringe.

ripple cloth: Wool dress fabric with long silky hair on one side. *See also* zibeline.

Ripplesheen: Plain weave cotton fabric with faint corded effect.

Ripplette: Trade name for type of seersucker.

ripresa: Italy. Dart.

riso sopra riso: Elaborate gold cloth.

Ristori shawl: Crinoline (1840–1865 C.E.). In 1856, woman's shawl made from alternating stripes of moiré antique and velvet. Had a pointed yoke and was trimmed with a crochet-headed fringe.

ritssluiting: Holland. Zipper.

ritterhute: Renaissance (1450–1550 C.E.). Germany. Man's low crowned barrette frequently made of felt and covered in velvet or silk.

riveling: Byzantine and Romanesque (400–1200 C.E.). Shoe of raw hide with hair on the outside.

rivière: France. Necklace of precious stones, usually of several strands.

rivieres de jais: Bustle (1865–1890 C.E.). In 1874, bands of threaded jet beads.

riza: 1. Bulgaria. Shirt. 2. Czechoslovakia. Long garment. 3. Russia. Chasuble.

rizá: Greece. Scarf.

rizarato: Greece. Bride's sigouni.

rjsó: Peru. Tribal man's silver disc worn hanging from a pierced nose.

ro: Japan. A kind of silk gauze.

roach: Slang for hair brushed up from forehead.

roafia: *See* rofia.

roanes: Renaissance (1450–1550 C.E.). France. Made in Rouen, fine wool cloth.

roanne: France. Cotton and linen fabric used for sheeting.

robe à l'américaine: Late Georgian (1750–1790 C.E.). France. Simple style of dress epitomized by the immigrants to the United States of America.

robe à l'anglais: Late Georgian (1750–1790 C.E.). France. Gown that was shaped and fitted in the body. Curved down in the center front and center back. Skirt opened down the center front and revealed the underskirt.

robe à l'anglais
See also photospread (Women's Wear).

robe à la circassienne: Late Georgian (1750–1790 C.E.). France. Polonaise variation with short, funnel-shaped sleeves, and oriental trim.

robe à la française: Late Georgian (1750–1790 C.E.). France. Inspired by the grand habit, this consisted of three pieces: a sack back gown with a fitted bodice front, a long petticoat with side hoops, and a stomacher.

robe à la Joconde: Romantic (1815–1840 C.E.). France. Introduced in 1817, long gown open over a petticoat. Fastened on the left shoulder with a rose.

robe à la levantine: Late Georgian (1750–1790 C.E.). France. Loose, shaped, fur-trimmed, short-sleeved gown worn over undergown.

robe à la polonaise: *See* robe a la Reine.

robe à la prêtesse: *See* robe torque.

robe à la Reine: Late Georgian (1750–1790 C.E.). France. Popular from 1776 to 1787, bodice with an attached overskirt swagged back to show the underskirt. Bodice featured a pin in the center covered by a bow below which the bodice was open to show the vestee beneath. Gown was short sleeved and elaborately decorated.

robe à la Turque: Late Georgian (1750–1790 C.E.). France. Very tight bodice with trained over-robe with funnel sleeves and a collar. Worn with a draped sash.

robe à plis gironnés: *See* robe gironnée.

robe anglaise: Bustle (1865–1890 C.E.). Child's dress.

robe de cérémonie à la française: Late Georgian (1750–1790 C.E.). France. Sack dress worn with hoops and elaborately trimmed. Allowed at court for all but the most formal occasions.

robe de chambre: Charles I and Commonwealth (1625–1660 C.E.). France. Gown worn to the chambers of the royal apartments.

robe de chez: Crinoline (1840–1865 C.E.). House dress commonly worn with an ornamental apron.

robe de commune at ancienne guise: Renaissance (1450–1550 C.E.). France. Ordinary clothes.

robe de noce: France. Wedding dress.

robe de nuit: France. Nightdress.

robe de style: France. Bouffant frock with fitted bodice and full skirt.

robe déguisée: Renaissance (1450–1550 C.E.). France. Elegant garments on the cutting edge of fashion.

robe d'interieur: Romantic (1815–1840 C.E.). At-home negligee for men.

robe drapée: Bustle (1865–1890 C.E.). In 1873, single skirted dress, usually elaborately trimmed.

robe du soir: France. Evening dress.

robe en calecons: Directoire and First Empire (1790–1815 C.E.). Woman's dress with underdrawers built in and fullness in back of skirt.

robe gironnée: Renaissance (1450–1550 C.E.). France. Loose gown with pleats which were stitched in at the waist and then allowed to hang freely.

robe longue: Early Georgian (1700–1750 C.E.). France. Long robes worn by academics.

robe parée: Late Georgian (1750–1790 C.E.). France. Gown worn for evening events and elaborately trimmed and worn over hoops.

robe princesse: France. Princess line dress.

robe torque: Directoire and First Empire (1790–1815 C.E.). France. Introduced in 1803, overdress worn wrapped across the body like a Greek robe. By 1810, it had evolved into the redingote. *See also* sack gown.

robe volante: *See* robe de chambre.

robes à guille: Crinoline (1840–1865 C.E.). In 1857, plain-skirted gown with flounces on each side of the center. Had a border on the sleeves and skirt flounces.

robes de fantaisie: Late Georgian (1750–1790 C.E.). France. Gown worn without a hoop.

robes en calecon: First Empire (1790–1815 C.E.). France. Woman's very tight dress worn with only one petticoat underneath it.

Robespierre collar: Directoire (1790–1815 C.E.). High, turned over collar commonly worn with a frilly jabot and stock. Named for the French statesman.

robijn: Holland. The gemstone ruby.

robin: Early Georgian (1700–1750 C.E.) to Bustle (1865–1890 C.E.). Broad flat trim used on gowns around the neck and down the bodice front. It was sometimes also used down edges of open overskirt.

robin front: Romantic (1815–1840 C.E.). United Kingdom. Bodice trimmed with robins from shoulders to waist point.

robings: *See* robin.

Robinson hat: Directoire and First Empire (1790–1815 C.E.). United Kingdom. Silk hat with a narrow brim.

rôbo: *See* ankanjo.

robótka: Poland. Needlework.

Roc: Germany. Coat.

rocal: Ireland. Gaelic word for coarse clothing.

rocana: India. The color yellow.

rocc: Byzantine and Romanesque (400–1200 C.E.). Garment, probably a wrap. Sometimes made of fur.

rocher: Bustle (1865–1890 C.E.). In 1872, rock color.

rochet: Charles I and Commonwealth (1625–1660 C.E.). France. Small collarless coat with elbow-length sleeves slit to armseye. Originally worn by gentlemen, later worn by lackeys and buffoons in comedy.

rock: Sweden. Coat.

Rock: Germany. Coat; skirt.

rock and reel: Scotland. The distaff and spindle.

rocket: Early Gothic (1200–1350 C.E.) to Late Georgian (1750–1790 C.E.). Woman's white linen dress.

rococo: 1. To be extravagant. 2. Victorian hat.

rococo embroidery: Embroidery worked with narrow ribbons.

rodillera: Guatemala. Man's small woolen blanket, usually woven in black and white check, worn wrapped around hips from the waist to the knees.

rofia: Madagascar. Raffia.

roghan: India. A thick pigment applied to fabric, creating encrusted patterns.

roguelo dress: Directoire and First Empire (1790–1815 C.E.). Morning dress with a loose back and bias cut front.

Rohseide: Germany. Tussore silk.

ròibeag: Ireland. Moustache.

ròin: Ireland. Haircloth.

ròin-aodach: Ireland. Haircloth.

roinne-bhaidhe: Ireland. Gaelic word for haircloth.

ròinn-léine: Ireland. Hairshirt.

roisean: Ireland. Gaelic word for the train of a skirt.

rojario: Korea. Catholic rosary.

rojo: Spain. Red.

rojo Congo: Spain. Congo red.

rok: Holland. Kirtle. *See also* buis.

rokechi: Japan. Wax resist dyeing.

roketsu: Japan. Wax dyeing.

rokk: Hungary. Lined, black broadcloth, sleeved coat with pockets, and a fur collar. Reaches below the waist.

rokkr: Norway. Old Norse word for coat.

roklengte: Holland. Hemline.

Roko cha: Japan. A shade of tea color named for an actor.

rokoja: Romania. Skirt.

rokolya: Hungary. Homespun woolen skirt with vertical stripes in red and blue or red and black.

roll collar: Standing turnover collar; a shallower version of the shawl collar.

rolled hem: Narrow hem made by rolling edge of fabric and slipstitching in place.

rollers: *See* roll-up stockings.

rolling stockings: *See* roll-up stockings.

rollo: Renaissance (1450–1550 C.E.). Spain. Roundlet.

roll-up breeches: Restoration (1660–1700 C.E.) to Early Georgian (1700–1750 C.E.). United Kingdom. Men's breeches that buttoned at the knee and were worn with roll-up stockings.

roll-up stockings: Restoration (1660–1700 C.E.) to Early Georgian (1700–1750 C.E.). United Kingdom. Long men's stockings worn pulled up over the knee of the breeches and then rolled down.

rollups: *See* roll-up stockings.

rom: Laos and Thailand. Umbrella.

romagnuolo: Early Gothic (1200–1350 C.E.). Italy. Coarse cloth used by country folk.

romaine: Sheer, basket weave, silk fabric.

romaine crepe: Heavy sheer crepe.

romall: *See* ramall.

Roman cutwork: Openwork embroidery outlines in purl stitches.

Roman lace: Geometric needlepoint lace.

Roman pearl: Type of imitation pearl.

Roman sandal: Romantic (1815–1840 C.E.). Fashionable sandals introduced in 1817.

Roman stripe: Contrasting colored stripes.

Romeo: Man's house slipper.

rompers: 1. (1910–1920 C.E.). United States of America. Child's one-piece, short-sleeved, short-legged suit. Bottom of leg gathered with elastic. 2. (1980–1989 C.E.). Adult woman's version of child's romper, usually with long legs and a large collar.

roncadoras: Peru. Spurs.

rond: Charles I and the Commonwealth (1625–1660 C.E.). Sausage-shaped pad over which women built their hair.

rondastakken: Norway. Woman's striped long skirt.

rondel: 1. Round, flat bead. 2. *See* roundel.

rondz: Renaissance (1450–1550 C.E.). Spain. Decorative discs.

rong: India. A muslin.

róngbù: China. Flannelette.

róngkù: China. Sweatpants.

róngmiàngé: China. Suede.

róngyi: China. Sweatshirt.

rood: Holland. Red.

roodbruin: Holland. Russet.

roons hat: Directoire and First Empire (1790–1815 C.E.). Ubiquitous by 1812, woman's conical hat with rolled up brim.

rooskleurig: Holland. Rose colored.

ropa: 1. Elizabethan (1550–1625 C.E.). Spain. Woman's outer garment worn open all the way down the front. It had a standing band collar and sleeves cut full at the top, tapering to the wrist. *See also* simarra. 2. *See* vestidos.

ropa bastarda: Renaissance (1450–1550 C.E.). Spain. Man's short gown.

ropa bordado: Peru. Embroidered clothing.

ropa de estado: Renaissance (1450–1550 C.E.). Spain. State gown.

ropa larga: Renaissance (1450–1550 C.E.). Spain. Long gown.

ropa rozagnte: Renaissance (1450–1550 C.E.). Spain. Trailing gown.

ropilla: Elizabethan (1550–1625 C.E.). Spain. Doublet with snug-fitting basques and hanging sleeves.

roquelaure: Early Georgian (1700–1750 C.E.). 1. Large caped overcoat, named for the Duc de Roquelaure. 2. Heavy cloak with two small shoulder capes.

roquet: *See* rochet.

rosa: Palestine. Bleached silk fabric woven mainly in Majdal and Gaza.

ròsach: Ireland. Rose red.

rosadimoi: *See* ras du more.

rosado: Spain. Rose color.

rosalba: (1930–1940 C.E.). Luminous, soft artificial silk.

Rosaline: 1. Crinoline (1840–1865 C.E.). In 1855, mantilla with plain body and box-pleated skirt. Trimmed with ostrich plumes, gauze ribbon, and lace. 2. A Belgian bobbin lace.

Rosamond: Crinoline (1840–1865 C.E.). In 1854, shawl cut in one yard half circle. Made of velvet sewn to tulle with sections of the velvet cut away. Had heavy corded fringe.

rosaniline: Crinoline (1840–1865 C.E.). Color name for first aniline dye.

rosario: *See* lei kolona.

rosato: Renaissance (1450–1550 C.E.). Italy. Pinkish shade of red.

Rose: Crinoline (1840–1865 C.E.). In 1858, silk robe à lev. Had plain underskirt, tartan plaid upper skirt, sleeves, waist, and lappets. Trimmed with bows.

rose: Dull shade of soft red.

Rose de parnasse: Romantic (1815–1840 C.E.). France. Color name for cyclamen pink.

rose des Alpes: Crinoline (1840–1865 C.E.). In 1960, new color; very lightest shade of fuchsia.

rose point lace: Italy. Venetian needlepoint lace.

rose sublime: Crinoline (1840–1865 C.E.). In 1861, new color, ruby scarlet; color of currants.

rose tendre: Gay Nineties (1890–1900 C.E.). In 1895, a faded pink.

Rosebery collar: Gay Nineties (1890–1900 C.E.). United Kingdom. Introduced in 1894, white linen detachable collar that stood three inches high with rounded points in the front. Named for Prime Minister, Lord Rosebery.

rosehube: Switzerland. Black lace cap.

rosenadel: Switzerland. Long silver pin used to hold the rosehube in place.

rosette: France. Bow.

Roshanara: Trade name for silk fabric with heavy crepe texture. Copied in rayon and wool, rayon and cotton.

rosille de soie: Crinoline (1840–1865 C.E.). France. Silk with roses woven into it.

roskyn: Early Gothic (1200–1350 C.E.). Squirrel fur.

roso: Italy. Red.

Ross: Germany. Pony.

rossetto: Italy. Russet.

rossiccio: *See* rossetto.

rossignol: Bustle (1865–1890 C.E.). In 1872, nightingale color.

rot: Germany. Red.

ro-ten-kechi: *See* rokechi.

rotonde: 1. Directoire and First Empire (1790–1815 C.E.). France. Short circular cape that buttoned down the front. 2. Crinoline (1840–1865 C.E.). Woman's short circular mantle.

rotonelle: Directoire and First Empire (1790–1815 C.E.). Man's round elbow-length cape. Later, reached to the knees or below.

rotonne: Early Georgian (1700–1750 C.E.). Lower collar of a man's redingote.

Roubaix velvet: Bustle (1865–1890 C.E.). In 1874, cotton-backed velvet with silk face.

roucha: Bulgaria. Cloth.

rouge: France. Red.

Rough Rider shirt: Gay Nineties (1890–1900 C.E.). Khaki shirt popularized by Theodore Roosevelt and his Rough Riders in Cuba in 1898.

rouille: Bustle (1865–1890 C.E.). In 1874, rust color.

rouleaux: Romantic (1815–1840 C.E.). France. Puffed tubes of fabric used for trim on dresses and skirts in 1820s.

round dress: Late Georgian (1750–1790 C.E.) to Crinoline (1840–1865 C.E.). United Kingdom. Dress with the bodice and skirt made in one.

round gown: *See* round dress.

round seam: Glove seam.

roundabout: Short fitted jacket.

roundel: 1. Early Gothic (1200–1350 C.E.). Doughnut-shaped roll headdress with a scarf hanging down one side. 2. India. Obsolete term for umbrella.

roundlet: Elizabethan (1550–1625 C.E.) to Restoration (1660–1700 C.E.). United Kingdom. Roll of chaperon of 15th century.

ròusè: China. Yellowish pink.

roussâtre: France. Russet.

rowel: Early Gothic (1200–1350 C.E.). Round of yellow cloth worn by Jews in the 13th century, imposed by the Lateran Council and the Narbonne Council.

roxalene bodice: Romantic (1815–1840 C.E.). United Kingdom. Low-necked bodice with wide strips of pleated folds around the neck. Front waist ended in a point.

roxalene sleeve: Romantic (1815–1840 C.E.). United Kingdom. Bouffant evening sleeve caught in at the elbow with a fringed band.

roxano: *See* crepoline.

Roxburgh muff: Romantic (1815–1840 C.E.). United Kingdom. Introduced in 1816, swansdown muff bound with white satin.

roxo: Portugal. Violet.

Royal George stock: Romantic (1815–1840 C.E.). United Kingdom. Popular in 1820s and 1830s, man's stock of black Genoa velvet and satin.

Royal turquoise: (1930–1940 C.E.). A new color.

royale: 1. Closely woven, ribbed silk fabric. 2. Bustle (1865–1890 C.E.). In 1889, silk fabric of honeycomb mesh.

rozah: Palestine. Thick, white silk fabric used for veils, dresses, and men's coats.

rozenkrans: Holland. Rosary.

ro-zome: *See* roketsu.

rozye: *See* razai.

ru: China. Zhuong dynasty. Woman's waist-length, narrow-sleeved, fitted jacket. Often worn with checked skirt.

ruadh: Ireland. Gaelic word for reddish.

ruadh-bhuidhe: Ireland. Gaelic word for auburn.

ruaithne: Ireland. Gaelic word for reddish green.

ruana: 1. Colombia. Man's dark poncho. 2. Ecuador. *See* poncho cuadrada.

ruanduàn: China. Soft, satin weave, silk fabric.

rubaca: *See* kosulja.

rubái: China. Cream color.

rubakha: Russia. Embroidered long shirt or shift of homespun linen.

rubakha kosovorotka: Russia. Man's holiday shirt with side fastening.

ruban: France. Ribbon; hat band.

ruban d'amour: Directoire and First Empire (1790–1815 C.E.). France. Ribbon on which was written republican mottoes, insignia, or cockades. Worn conspicuously in the middle of the bodice.

rubas: Czechoslovakia. Short underskirt.

rubasca: Romania. Man's gay-colored loose shirt that opened on the side of the neck.

rubaska: Russia. Shirt.

Rubens bonnet: Bustle (1865–1890 C.E.). United Kingdom. Introduced in 1872, woman's small bonnet with a turned up brim on one side. Trimmed with a bow and a feather.

Rubens hat: Bustle (1865–1890 C.E.). United Kingdom. Woman's high-crowned hat with the brim turned up on one side.

rubi: Portugal. Ruby, a gemstone.

rubin: Poland. Ruby.

rubina: Balkans. Sleeved linen chemise vertically embroidered on the sleeves and bodice.

rubro: Portugal. Ruby red.

ruby: 1. Intense red. 2. Hard, deep red precious stone.

ruché: France. Ruffle or quilling of lace or ribbon.

ruche contraire: Crinoline (1840–1865 C.E.). Ruching where top edge of folds was turned one way and bottom edge the other way.

ruchika: India. Wristlet.

rudge wash: Kind of kersey made of unwashed fleece.

ruedas: Spain. A form of cut and drawn-thread work in which the residual threads are pulled into a spoke-like formation.

ruedo: Renaissance (1450–1550 C.E.). Spain. Skirt-foot (hem) of a woman's garment.

ruff

ruff: Elizabethan (1550–1625 C.E.). Starched collar in varied sizes and forms. In Spain, called the gran gola. Worn for most of 17th century.

ruffled shirt: Early Georgian (1700–1750 C.E.) to Crinoline (1840–1865 C.E.). Man's shirt with a goffered frill down the front. Frill was as deep as three inches. Originally worn for both day and evening, but after 1840, only worn for evening.

rug gown: Gown of coarse, shaggy fabric.

ruga: Ireland. Gaelic word for rough cloth.

ruhbani: Palestine. Dress linen.

ruho: *See* odjeca.

ruiterrock: Elizabethan (1550–1625 C.E.). Holland. Riding coat.

rukavica: Croatia and Serbia. Glove.

rukavica sa jednium prstom: Bosnia. Mitten.

rullion: Elizabethan (1550–1625 C.E.) to Restoration (1660–1700 C.E.). Shoe of undressed hide.

rūmāl: India. A square cloth rolled diagonally and wound into a turban.

rumala: India. A 12-inch square cloth, usually white, worn rolled along the diagonal and folded around the head.

Rumanian embroidery: Double sided, outline embroidery.

rumi: Palestine. Dress linen.

rum-swizzle: Crinoline (1840–1865 C.E.). Introduced in 1850, Irish frieze of undyed wool.

rumswizzle: Ireland. Imported, undyed wool fabric.

runa: Ecuador. General term for wool garments.

run-about dress: (1930–1940 C.E.). Shirt-style dress.

rundell: *See* roundel.

running shoe: Soft leather shoe with spiked sole.

ruosa secha: Color of old roses.

rupehri: India. Silver printing.

rupya: India. Silver.

Rüschen: Germany. Flounce.

russ hat: A man's short crowned straw hat with a drooping brim.

russ hat

russaline: Early Georgian (1700–1750 C.E.) to Late Georgian (1750–1790 C.E.). Wool fabric from Norwich.

russell: Renaissance (1450–1550 C.E.). United Kingdom. Black wool fabric first made in Norwich.

russell cord: Gay Nineties (1890–1900 C.E.). Fabric similar to coarse corded alpaca.

russell satin: *See* russells.

russells: Renaissance (1450–1550 C.E.) to Elizabethan (1550–1625 C.E.). United Kingdom. Worsted with a shiny surface made in Norwich.

russet: 1. Early Gothic (1200–1350 C.E.). Dark brown. 2. Renaissance (1450–1550 C.E.). Reddish brown or gray worn by countrymen. 3. Ireland. Coarse homespun woolen fabric in reddish brown, gray, or neutral.

Russia leather: Calfskin or other leather, bark, or chrome tanned.

Russian: Crinoline (1840–1865 C.E.). In November, 1859, black velvet mantle lined with deep violet or mauve quilted silk, trimmed with border of sable.

Russian blouse: Gay Nineties (1890–1900 C.E.). United Kingdom. Woman's loose knee-length tunic-blouse worn belted.

Russian bonnet: Bustle (1865–1890 C.E.). Specific style of bonnet.

Russian boot: Boot extending to calf of leg.

Russian braid: Narrow, flat decorative braid.

Russian cord: Madras type shirting with heavy corded stripes.

Russian crash: Strong, unbleached linen.

Russian crepe: Bustle (1865–1890 C.E.). Introduced in 1881, coarsely woven mat cloth.

Russian embroidery: Washable outline embroidery on holland or canvas.

Russian flame: Directoire and First Empire (1790–1815 C.E.). United Kingdom. Red.

Russian jacket: Bustle (1865–1890 C.E.). United Kingdom. Introduced in 1865, woman's short, sleeveless jacket worn over a sleeved vest.

Russian muskrat: Silvery gray fur of Russian muskrat.

Russian sergette: Gay Nineties (1890–1900 C.E.). In 1892, a fancy woolen fabric streaked with silk.

Russian suit: (1910–1920 C.E.). United States of America. Boy's suit consisting of a bloused tunic top and straight short pants.

Russian velvet: Gay Nineties (1890–1900 C.E.). In 1892, a light wool fabric with a raised, twisted stripe.

rust: Reddish yellow.

Rüstung: Germany. Armor.

rutí: Greece. White cotton chemise.

Rutland poke: Directoire and First Empire (1790–1815 C.E.). Introduced in 1813, woman's small bonnet of wadded satin. Trimmed with swansdown and an ostrich feather and tied under the chin.

ruwana: Ecuador and Guatemala. Poncho.

ruzhào: China. Brassiere.

ryasa: Russia. Housecoat.

ryssedamast: Charles I (1625–1660 C.E.). Sweden. Russian damask.

ryssekläde: Charles I (1625–1660 C.E.). Sweden. Russian cloth.

ryssewerk: Charles I (1625–1660 C.E.). Sweden. Russian work.

Ryūkū-gasuri: Japan. An Okinawan silk kasuri.

S

S curve
Dover Publications

S curve: (1900–1910 C.E.). The fashionable woman's silhouette created by a corset that pushed the upper body forward, the stomach and abdomen flat, and the buttocks back severely, creating an S silhouette.

sa: Korea. Lightweight, silk gauze.

sa din: Bustle (1865–1890 C.E.). United States of America. Chinese Hawaiian term for an inexpensive cotton sateen.

saba: Philippine Islands. Fabric made from the fiber of a banana-like plant.

sabaa: Egypt. V neckline.

sabada: Nigeria. Diagonally striped adire.

sabai: Thailand. Shoulder wrap.

sabaleh: Palestine. Literally "ears of corn," herringbone stitch used to join seams, applique, and decorate hems.

sábana: 1. Ecuador and Guatemala. Bed covering. 2. Ecuador. White cotton cloth, 12 feet 4 inches long, used to tie a baby to the mother's back.

sabanilla: *See* sábana.

sabeldier: Holland. Sable.

sable: Rarest and most desired kind of marten fur, next in value to ermine, from the *Martes zibelina*. Very deep, soft, medium brown fur with blue tint.

sablé: Early Georgian (1700–1750 C.E.). France. Cloth made of very fine beads.

sabong: Laos and Thailand. Lower garment worn by Buddhist monk.

sabot: A wooden shoe popular in a variety of European countries and distinguished by a strap across the instep.

sabot pantaloons: Gay Nineties (1890–1900 C.E.). Pantaloons that were wide at the bottom.

sabot sleeve: Sleeve on the gown à la polonaise that fit tightly over the elbow.

sabotine: (1910–1920 C.E.) Shoes worn by soldiers in World War I.

sabretache: 1. Early Georgian (1700–1750 C.E.). France. Worn by soldiers, leather dispatch bag. 2. Directoire and First Empire (1790–1815 C.E.). Leather bag worn by women.

sabrina: Neckline similar to the bateau neckline.

Sabrina work: Type of floral applique.

sabz moongia: India. Mung bean green.

sac: *See* Albert driving-cape.

sac de voyage: France. Traveling bag.

sac overcoat: 1. Crinoline (1840–1865 C.E.). Man's knee-length overcoat with welted front pockets. Had full-cut sleeves. 2. Crinoline (1840–1865 C.E.). Popular in 1860s, overcoat with a very narrow collar and lapels.

sacapallay: Bolivia. Embroidery sampler.

saccharine alum: Directoire and First Empire (1790–1815 C.E.). Popular cosmetic in 1808.

saccus: Greek (3000-100 B.C.E.). Hair binding.

sace: Nigeria. Middle-class man's very wide gown with a lined lower edge of white cotton.

sacha pullki: *See* yutu.

sack dress: (1950–1960 C.E.). Woman's loose, unbelted dress that hung straight from the shoulder to the hem.

sack dress
See also photospread (Women's Wear).
Dover Publications

sabot

sack gown: Early Georgian (1700–1750 C.E.). France. Popular from 1704 to 1835, loose dress that flared at the bottom.

sack suit: Crinoline (1840–1865 C.E.). Loose fitting man's three piece suit. Coat sleeves hung to the fingertips and had high, short lapels. Popular for sportswear.

sack-back: (1950–1960 C.E.). The back of a woman's blouse or dress that mimicked a Watteau pleat gown (robe à l'anglais).

sackcloth: Coarse, heavy, unbleached muslin.

saco: Peru. Long-sleeved jacket.

saco de abrigo: Peru. Western-style sweater.

sacred uraeus: Egyptian (4000–30 B.C.E.). Rearing viper, the symbol of royalty.

sacristan: Restoration (1600–1700 C.E.). Spain. Worn from 1675 to 1680, light brass farthingale of five or six hoops.

sacque: 1. Early Georgian (1700–1750 C.E.). Watteau-style gown. 2. Loose blouse.

sadarā: *See* kudtā.

sadaraa: *See* kurta.

saddle oxford: Oxford type of shoe with a saddle.

saddle shoe

saddle shoe: (1950–1960 C.E.). Two-colored oxford shoe.

sadeti: Ethiopia. Eight cubit garment given to the mother of the bride by the groom.

sadi: India. A kind of sari.

sadiaka: Madagascar. Skirt.

sadlo: India. A Gujarati woman's wrap, worn over a petticoat and blouse in the manner of a sari.

saekduresu: *See* charuot.

saenggosa: Korea. Raw silk fabric.

safa: India. A freshly wound turban.

safadiyeh: Palestine. Large, yellow and black striped, silk veil that is five meters long.

safari jacket: Belted, single-breasted, hip-length jacket with a notched collar, patch pockets, and elbow-length or full-length sleeves.

safed: India. The color white.

safeguard: 1. Elizabethan (1550–1625 C.E.) to Early Georgian (1700–1750 C.E.). Woman's overskirt worn when horseback riding to protect the clothes from dirt. Sometimes in the shape of an apron. 2. Man's colored apron, worn by bakers, etc. 3. Swathing band for a baby.

safety skirt: Bustle (1865–1890 C.E.). In 1875, a woman's riding skirt which could be opened up the back while in the saddle and fastened again when the rider dismounted.

saffeh: Palestine. Woman's headdress from Ramallah.

saffier: Holland. The gemstone sapphire.

saffron: Reddish yellow.

saffron shirt: *See* léine.

safira: Portugal. The gemstone sapphire; the color blue.

safsarī: Tunisia. Woman's enveloping loose cotton cloak.

saga: Lithuania. Button.

sagathie: *See* sagathy.

sagathy: Elizabethan (1550–1625 C.E.) to Late Georgian (1750–1790 C.E.). United States of America. Wool fabric.

sageo: Japan. A cord from which the sword is suspended.

sagetta: Renaissance (1450–1550 C.E.). Casque or helmet.

saggum: Roman (753 B.C.E.–323 C.E.). Military wrap of the Roman army.

sagiya guakari: India. A green stuff from Goa.

saglia: Italy. Twill.

sagmatogene: Roman (753 B.C.E.–323 C.E.). A coarse cotton used for stuffing and padding.

sagos: Greek (3000–100 B.C.E.). Coarse woolen mantle or blanket.

sagum: Byzantine and Romanesque (400–1200 C.E.). Goatskin with the hair still on worn draped over the shoulder and pinned on the right shoulder.

sahuli: India. A type of lower garment.

saia: 1. *See* aba. 2. Early Gothic (1200–1350 C.E.). Italy. Light fabric with combed wool weft or warp.

saiat: Morocco. Jewish woman's petticoats.

saider: India. Short coat.

saie: *See* sagum.

sail cloth: Heavy canvas.

sailor cap: Small, stiff, brimless cap.

sailor collar: Collar with square back and V-shaped front.

sailor suit: Crinoline (1840–1865 C.E.). United Kingdom. Suit for young boys based on the dress of the French and English sailors. It had a square collar trimmed with a narrow white braid. The version for girls developed with a pleated skirt instead of trousers.

sailor's reef knot tie: Bustle (1865–1890 C.E.). United Kingdom. Popular way to tie a man's tie showing vertical borders on the sides. Particularly fashionable in the 1890s.

sainre: Ireland. Gaelic word for reddish purple.

Saint Etienne velvet: Bustle (1865–1890 C.E.). In 1874, a lightweight cotton backed velvet with a silk nap.

Saint Gall lace: Imitation Venetian lace.

Saint Martin's lace: Renaissance (1450–1550 C.E.) to Restoration (1660–1700 C.E.). United Kingdom. Cheap copper braid lace.

Saint Omer: Elizabethan (1550–1625 C.E.) to Restoration (1660–1700 C.E.). United Kingdom. Worsted fabric.

saione: *See* giacchetto.

saiote: Portugal. Jupon.

saiote escocês: Portugal. Kilt.

sairpaich: India. A cluster of jewels set in gold or silver and worn on the turban.

sajás: *See* kaváði.

sakala: India. Terra-cotta red.

sakallat: *See* suclat.

sakayaki: Japan. The tonsured part of a man's head.

sakete: Samoa. Skirt.

saki: Nigeria. Pile cloth woven in Ijebu-Ode.

sakko: Crinoline (1840–1865 C.E.). Germany. Man's single-breasted, full-length coat that reached from shoulder to hip without a waist seam.

sakkos: Greek (3000-100 B.C.E.). Pointed cap with tassel trim. It had a small front brim.

sakma: *See* kabanica.

sako: Bosnia. Jacket.

saktapar: India. A sari with a checkerboard design.

šal: *See* marama.

şal kuşak: Turkey. Shawl.

salade: Late Gothic (1350–1450 C.E.) to Restoration (1660–1700 C.E.). Helmet with a low round crown.

salaka: Madagascar. Loincloth.

Salamanca: Crinoline (1840–1865 C.E.). In 1854, woman's yoked wrap. In back, the skirt was box-pleated; in front, plain. It had a deep lace fall at the skirt and yoke edges.

salampe: *See* pebasa.

salampy: *See* kisaly.

salapok: Borneo. Skull-cap made of rattan or pandanus.

salara: India. Native cotton, plain weave fabric.

salari: India. Handwoven, cotton fabric.

salem shahī: India. Embroidered slippers with gold or silver threads.

salembaree: India. Coarse, heavy cotton fabric.

salempoory: India. Kind of chintz. *See also* salempore.

salempora: 1. *See* salempoory.

salempore: 1. United Kingdom. Cotton fabric. 2. *See* palempore.

salempury: *See* salempoory.

salendang: Cotton fabric.

salim shahi: Pakistan. Worn by both genders, shoes with long curled toes. The right and left shoes are identical.

salisbury: United Kingdom. White woolen fabric.

salla: India. Cotton fabric.

sallet: *See* salade.

sallo: India. Plain weave, cotton fabric that is always dyed red.

salloo: Red twill weave cotton used in India but made in United Kingdom.

salmah: *See* simlah.

salmā-sitārā: India. Gold or fancy silver lace embroidered with sequins.

salmon: Reddish red yellow.

salopette: France. Overalls.

salovana: Madagascar. Woman's cotton body wrap.

salta: *See* damer.

salt-box pocket: Directoire and First Empire (1790–1815 C.E.). United Kingdom. Popular name for a man's rectangular flapped waistcoat.

salteh: 1. Egypt. Short coat often of velvet or broadcloth and lavishly embroidered. 2. Iran. Short jacket.

salto de cama: Spain. Dressing gown; negligee.

sālū: India. A kind of odhni. *See also* pomaco.

salūkā: India. Woman's shaped shirt.

salura: India. A fine quality red muslin, usually embroidered or brocaded.

salvar: Turkey. Woman's extremely full, ankle-length trousers worn under the gomlek.

Salvation Army Lassie bonnet: Black straw or felt bonnet lined with dark blue silk. It tied with silk ties.

salwar: India. Very full trousers cut extra long and banded at the ankle.

salwar-kameez: India. Woman's outfit of salwar and tunic.

sám ánh: Vietnam. Iron gray.

sám bac: Vietnam. Pearl gray.

Sam Browne belt: (1910–1920 C.E.). United States of America. Worn by World War I army officers, a wide, brown leather belt with a narrow strap that passed over the right shoulder. It was used to carry a pistol.

sám ðõm: Vietnam. Flea-bitten gray.

samaksika: India. The cloak of Buddhist monks.

samare: Lady's jacket like the English sacque.

samasama: Samoa. Yellow.

samasmiyeh: Palestine. Gaza man's turban patterned red and yellow. Worn with a skull cap.

sambatsi: Nigeria. Red and black weather sandals.

sambelatra: Madagascar. An unstitched body wrap that opens in the front.

sambhal: India. Plain weave, cotton fabric.

sambu' bongi: Indonesia. Sa'dan-Toraja man's sleeping sarong.

samghati: India. 1. Gown. 2. Buddhist monk's double cloak.

samit: *See* samite.

samite: Early Gothic (1200–1350 C.E.). Rich silk fabric with gold thread woven in. Silk warp and weft were supported by a wire that was finely woven into the fabric.

samittum: *See* samite.

samjak norigae: Korea. Accessory with three pendants.

samo: Korea. Fez-like, black silk gauze hat worn by high-ranking officials.

sampot: Cambodia. Length of silk worn wrapped around the waist, then drawn up in front between the legs, giving the effect of the wearer wearing trousers.

sampour: Java. Scarf.

samson: Gay Nineties (1890–1900 C.E.). In 1893, a grass green.

samt: Bosnia. Velvet.

Samt: Germany. Velvet.

Samt gerippt: Germany. Ribbing.

samurai-ebosi: Japan. A warrior's ebosi.

samyt: *See* samite.

sana: India. Hemp cloth.

šanāfilō: Ethiopia. Colored cotton shorts ornamented with linear patterns.

sanasati: India. General term referring to the dress of farmers and weavers.

sanbaf: India. A very thin muslin from Bengal.

sanbenito: 1. Robe of sackcloth worn by penitents. 2. Robe of yellow or black with painted designs worn by penitents during the Inquisition.

sancaq: Iran. Brooch.

sand crepe: Crepe with sandy or grainy surface.

sandaal: Holland. Sandal.

sandal: 1. Open shoe, often with slashed upper. 2. Sole of shoe strapped to foot. 3. Strap for holding shoe on foot.

Sandale: Germany. Sandal.

sandale: France. Sandal.

sandali: India. The color of sandalwood.

sandália: Portugal. Sandal.

sandalias: Guatemala. Sandals that cover the foot completely.

sandalium: Greek (3000-100 B.C.E.). Leather sole worn strapped onto foot by women. It had a leather upper to protect toes.

sandalo: Italy. Sandal. *See also* zoccolo.

sandalon: Greek (3000–100 B.C.E.). Sandal.

sandals à la greque: Directoire and First Empire (1790–1815 C.E.). France. Sandal with a leather sole and thongs of leather or ribbon. Worn laced to the top of the heel.

sang chau: Crinoline (1840–1865 C.E.). United States of America. Chinese Hawaiian term for a dark maroon or black double woven fabric.

sangati: India. Quality, handwoven muslin.

sangbok: Korea. Mourning clothes.

sanghati: India. The loincloth of Buddhist monks and nuns.

sanghhati: Laos. Doubled upper robe worn by Buddhist monks. This doubles as a blanket.

sangi: India. Silk cloth.

sangkhatti: Thailand. Doubled upper robe worn by Buddhist monk. This doubles as a blanket.

sanguine: Early Gothic (1200–1350 C.E.). Scarlet.

sangyn: Elizabethan (1550–1625 C.E.). Blood red.

sania: India. A hempen cloth.

sani-gani: India. A rough hempen fabric.

sanitary ball dress: Gay Nineties (1890–1900 C.E.). United Kingdom. Woman's ball dress with a cream or pink underbodice.

sanjaku-obi: Japan. A man's dress kimono sash. It is three feet long.

sanjharavau: India. A type of red cloth.

sankha: India. Mother-of-pearl.

sankhavalaya: India. Bracelet made of pearls.

sankla: India. A thick chained anklet.

sanmai-gusi: Meizi (1867–1912 C.E.). Japan. A set of three hair combs made of tortoiseshell, metal, or rubber. They were worn on three sides of a woman's hairknot.

sannaha: India. Mail coat or quilted cotton coat.

sans-culottes: Directoire and First Empire (1790–1815 C.E.). In France, this term referred to those who wore trousers. This term separated them from the aristocracy and later referred to all patriots.

sansflectum crinoline: Crinoline (1840–1865 C.E.). United Kingdom. Introduced in 1860, washable cage crinoline.

santipur cloth: India. Fine. Handwoven, cotton fabric embroidered with floral designs.

santon: Romantic (1815–1840 C.E.). France. Popular in 1820s, colored silk cravat worn with a small ruff.

sanubapha: India. A superior type of muslin.

sanyan: Nigeria. Native silk cloth woven by the Yoruba and used for special occasions.

sapaea: *See* kapa ea.

sapara: Nigeria. Yoruba man's lightweight gown worn over the buba. It is embroidered at the neck.

sapata: Portugal. Shoe.

sapato: Portugal. Shoe.

şapcă: Romania. Cap.

sapeiro: *See* kapa ea.

sapka: 1. *See* kapa. 2. Russia. Cap.

sapog: Russia. Shoe.

sapogi: Russia. Leather boots.

sapphire: 1. Rich, transparent blue precious stone. 2. Tone of blue.

saptaki: India. A seven stringed girdle.

saput: Indonesia. A brocade textile worn over the kamben.

sar: *See* qatifah-i-purbi.

sarafan: 1. Russia. Full skirt of rich brocade. Part of national dress of Russian peasant women. 2. Scandinavia. Pinafore with a high yoke or bodice.

saraga: *See* seragu.

Saragossa: Crinoline (1840–1865 C.E.). 1. In 1857, shawl with crocheted trim and a deep silk chenille fringe. 2. In 1859, pusher lace shawl with two deep flounces.

sarampura: *See* salempoory.

saranala: India. A cotton stuff from Sarnala.

sarandrana: Madagascar. Sash.

sarasa: 1. Japan. Chintz. 2. Japan. Resist-dyed cotton fabric from India.

sarashi: Japan. Bleached cotton or ramie.

sarashi nuno: Japan. A white, lightweight cotton fabric similar to cheesecloth.

sarassang: *See* sassang.

sarata shirting: Bustle (1865–1890 C.E.). Introduced in 1870, linen shirting fabric.

saratoga hat: Crinoline (1840–1865 C.E.). Introduced in 1862, girl's straw hat with a low crown and a turned down brim. It was trimmed with Solferino velvet band and short white plume.

sarawil: Early Gothic (1200–1350 C.E.). Turkey. Woman's white pajama-like trousers.

sarbal: Hebrew. Cloak without an opening on the right side. By 1200s, used for prayer.

sarbalehon: Biblical (Unknown–30 C.E.). Jewish man's cloak.

sarcenet: Byzantine and Romanesque (400–1200 C.E.). Originally from the Orient, a fine, thin gauze.

sarciatus: Early Gothic (1200–1350 C.E.). Coarse wool cloth worn by the lower classes.

sarcillus: Ecuador. Costume jewelry earrings.

sarde: Bustle (1865–1890 C.E.). In 1872, stone gray color.

Sardinian mantle: Directoire and First Empire (1790–1815 C.E.). Worn in 1808, knee-length scarf of thin fabrics like net, muslin, etc. with the ends in a knot or rosette.

Sardinian sac: Crinoline (1840–1865 C.E.). United Kingdom. Man's single-breasted sac overcoat with a square collar, full sleeves, and tied with a cord and tassel.

sardius: Roman (753 B.C.E.–323 C.E.). Cornelian.

sardonyx: Opaque semi-precious stone with alternating brown and white bands.

sare: Bosnia. Leggings.

saredonuka: *See* kalekonuka.

saree: *See* sari.

sárena: Greece. Festival apron.

sarga: Spain. Serge.

sargenes: Biblical (Unknown–30 C.E.). Ankle-length, white linen overgarment with big sleeves. Worn by bridegrooms and the head of the house during the Passover seder. *See also* kittel.

sari: India. Gauzy wrap worn by Hindu women. Wraps around the body with one end thrown over the shoulder.

sarja: Portugal. Serge; twilled woolen or silk cloth.

sarkan wuya: Nigeria. Necklace made of multiple chains.

sarkandai: *See* gul-i-sarrai.

sarong: 1. Java and Ceylon. Long, wide strip of fabric worn wrapped around the waist like a skirt. 2. Indonesia. Sa'dan-Toraja woman's large bamboo hat.

sarong billá: Indonesia. Sa'dan-Toraja hat made from bamboo bark.

sarong kadojo: Indonesia. Sa'dan-Toraja black sewn bamboo hat.

sarong kaledo: Indonesia. Sa'dan-Toraja pointed bamboo hat.

sarong lambing: Indonesia. Sa'dan-Toraja hat made from strips of bamboo skin woven together.

sarong lombok: Indonesia. Sa'dan-Toraja man's large coarsely plaited hat.

sarong pakolong: Indonesia. Sa'dan-Toraja hooded cape made of bamboo leaves.

sarpe: Late Gothic (1350–1450 C.E.) to Renaissance (1450–1550 C.E.). Man's decorative collar.

sarpech: India. Ornament of gold, silver, or jewels that is worn on the front of the turban.

sarsenet: Very fine, soft silk fabric.

sarseneta: Spain. Sarsenet.

sart: Sikkim. Vest.

sarta: Ecuador and Guatemala. String of pearls.

sarto: Italy. Tailor.

saru: 1. Palestine. Embroidery of cypress trees. One of the most popular motifs in this country. 2. Hungary. Boot-like shoe.

sarzil: *See* sarciatus.

sassang: Indonesia. Sa'dan-Toraja apron made from the leaves of the supar palm.

sastre: Spain. Tailor.

satalian: Coarse, plain weave cotton fabric.

sa-tanh: Vietnam. Satin.

satarra cloth: Gay Nineties (1890–1900 C.E.). In 1893, a lustrous, ribbed wool fabric.

satasutra: India. Necklace made of 100 metal wires twisted together.

satavalika: India. An athraiya worn with several folds.

sateen: 1. Bustle (1865–1890 C.E.). Introduced in 1878, cotton fabric with a satin face. 2. Satin weave fabric with floats in the direction of the weft.

sateen berber: Bustle (1865–1890 C.E.). In 1884, plain sateen.

sateen paré: Bustle (1865–1890 C.E.). In 1884, sateen with small, self-colored figure.

satén: Spain. Sateen.

satijn: Holland. Satin.

Satin: Germany. Satin.

satin: Silk or rayon fabric woven in a satin weave.

satin antoinette: Romantic (1815–1840 C.E.). Introduced in 1834, satin with a white ground and stripes and bouquets of flowers.

satin berber: Strong, worsted, satin weave fabric.

satin cashmere: Gay Nineties (1890–1900 C.E.). In 1893, a wool fabric with a silk surface.

satin checks: Lightweight satin fabric with a checked pattern.

satin chinois: France. China silk.

satin crepe: Rich, satin-faced fabric with a crepe back.

satin damask: Jacquard weave linen damask with satin figures.

satin de chine: Crinoline (1840–1865 C.E.). Introduced in 1850, silk and worsted satin.

satin de laine: Gay Nineties (1890–1900 C.E.). In 1892, a fabric with a surface smooth as silk.

satin de Lyon: Satin with a ribbed back.

satin de Mai: Crinoline (1840–1865 C.E.). In 1862, a new fabric.

satin duchesse: Bustle (1865–1890 C.E.). Introduced in 1870, thick, plain, strong satin.

satin faconne: Jacquard fabric with a satin weave ground.

satin fontange: Crinoline (1840–1865 C.E.). Introduced in 1841, broadly striped satin with alternating white and colored stripes.

satin foulard: Crinoline (1840–1865 C.E.). Introduced in 1848, silk satin with stripes or dots.

satin jean: Bustle (1865–1890 C.E.). Introduced in 1870, twilled cotton with a satin face.

satin liberty: France. Art Nouveau silk.

satin lisse: Satin weave cotton with tiny figures.

satin merino: Crinoline (1840–1865 C.E.). Introduced in 1846, fabric with one side like cashmere and the other like plush.

satin merv: Bustle (1865–1890 C.E.). Introduced in 1886, broad ribbed satin.

satin merveilleux: 1. Bustle (1865–1890 C.E.). Introduced in 1881, twill weave silk satin fabric. 2. Fine, soft silk fabric.

satin orientale: Gay Nineties (1890–1900 C.E.). In 1894, a satin brocaded in narrow stripes and faint tracery of leaves and flowers.

satin rouleaux: Directoire and First Empire (1790–1815 C.E.). Rolls or folds of ribbon used as piping.

satin stitch: Closely spaced stitch which forms a padded effect.

satin sultan: India. Worsted fabric with a satin face.

satin surah: Shiny surah.

satin turc: Bustle (1865–1890 C.E.). Introduced in 1868, very shiny wool fabric.

satin velouté: Romantic (1815–1840 C.E.). France. Introduced in 1837, satin fabric.

satin Victoria: Crinoline (1840–1865 C.E.). United Kingdom. Introduced in 1854, striped wool fabric similar to silk.

satin weave: Shiny weave with characteristic floats; warp yarns which pass over many weft yarns before going under one.

satiné playé: Bustle (1865–1890 C.E.). France. Introduced in 1873, striped cotton and wool blend fabric, the face satin and the stripes twilled.

satiné velouté: Bustle (1865–1890 C.E.). France. Introduced in 1873, striped cotton and wool blend fabric.

satinesco: Early Georgian (1700–1750 C.E.). United Kingdom. Poor satin.

satinet: Holland. Sateen.

satineta: Spain. Satinette.

satinette: Satin woven of silk or silk and cotton with closely twilled face.

satingle Holland: Bustle (1865–1890 C.E.). In 1868, fabric with silk on one side, satin on reverse.

satlara: India. A seven-stringed necklace.

satlari: India. A seven-stringed necklace.

satthaka: India. Scissors.

satula: India. Lower body wrap.

saty: Czechoslovakia. Clothing.

satyna: Poland. Satin.

saucer brim: Shallow turned up hat brim.

saucer-collar: Gay Nineties (1890–1900 C.E.). United Kingdom. In 1898, a woman's high, wide collar on a day dress.

saula: India. The border of a garment.

Saum: Germany. Hem.

sauma: Norway. Old Norse word meaning to sew.

sausani: India. Mauve.

saut-en-basque: Crinoline (1840–1865 C.E.). Sack.

sautoir: Directoire and First Empire (1790–1815 C.E.). France. 1. Chain necklace with a pendant. 2. Chain worn by women. 3. *See* santon.

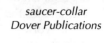

saucer-collar
Dover Publications

sauvarnapatta: India. A gold brocade.

savadi copacchudahu: India. An embroidered and dyed stuff from Savada.

savate: France. Worn out shoe.

savonnette watch: Pocket watch with spring lid.

savrikin: Biblical (Unknown–30 C.E.). Hebrew woman's tunic.

sawa 'id: Israel. Triangular inset in a woman's gown.

Saxon embroidery: Ancient outline embroidery.

saxony: Generic term referring to fine quality woolens of short staple botany wools.

Saxony lace: Imitation Brussels lace.

say: Byzantine and Romanesque (400–1200 C.E.) to Renaissance (1450–1550 C.E.). Wool cloth.

saya: 1. Philippine Islands. Ankle-length skirt. 2. Bulgaria. Woman's gown with a deeply curving bodice and sleeves. 3. Japan. Silk fabric with twill weave patterns on a plain weave ground. 4. Renaissance (1450–1550 C.E.). Spain. French dress.

sayal: Peru. Very coarse woolen fabric, mostly used for saddlebags.

saye: *See* sagum.

sayiaki: Greece. A thick white fabric.

šayō: Ethiopia. Belts.

saz: India. An Ottoman design of a round stemless blossom surrounded by a curling leaf.

sbernia: Renaissance (1450–1550 C.E.). Long scarf worn pinned on the left shoulder by women.

sbornik: Russia. Headdress.

scabilonians: Elizabethan (1550–1625 C.E.). Men's drawers.

scahwere: Early Gothic (1200–1350 C.E.). Veil.

scalings: Elizabethan (1550–1625 C.E.). United Kingdom. New fashion in men's breeches.

scallop: 1. Circular curve. 2. Restoration (1660–1700 C.E.). In 1662, a lace-edged band; forerunner of the tie.

scamato: Greece. A spun cotton.

scamiciato: Italy. Jumper.

scapulari: Elizabethan (1550–1625 C.E.). Chasuble worn by the Benedictines, Dominicans, and Carthusians.

scarab: Egyptian (4000– 30 B.C.E.). Beetle-like symbol of the sun god often used as a form of decoration.

scarabee: Bustle (1865–1890 C.E.). France. In 1888, dark yellowish green.

scaraboid: Egyptian (4000–30 B.C.E.) Animal shape carved into a scarab back.

Scarborough hat: Crinoline (1840–1865 C.E.). United Kingdom. Very popular woman's hat with a deep turned up brim.

Scarborough ulster: Gay Nineties (1890–1900 C.E.). United Kingdom. In 1892, a man's caped, hooded, sleeveless ulster.

scarf: Wide band of fabric worn loosely in various ways about body.

scarf drapery: Bustle (1865–1890 C.E.). United Kingdom. Popular in 1870s, form of trim on the front of a woman's skirt. Consisted of a fold or drape of fabric trimmed with flounces, frills, and ribbon.

scarf volant: Crinoline (1840–1865 C.E.). In 1854, silk shawl with a closed square front. It had a festooned flounce and was trimmed with bands of velvet and narrow lace. The lower edge was fringed.

scarlatto: Italy. The color scarlet.

scarlet: 1. Late Georgian (1750–1790 C.E.). Bright orange. 2. Brilliant red.

scarpa: Italy. Leather shoe.

scarpe: Italy. Shoe.

scarpetti: Shoe worn when rock climbing.

scavilones: *See* scabilonians.

sceanc-bend: Byzantine and Romanesque (400–1200 C.E.). United Kingdom. Band worn around the shin.

sceanc-gegirla: Byzantine and Romanesque (400–1200 C.E.). United Kingdom. Decorative band worn around the shin.

sceorp: Byzantine and Romanesque (400–1200 C.E.). United Kingdom. Men's clothes, particularly fancy clothes.

scépa: Greece. Everyday white kerchief.

schackelhaube: *See* shako.

Schafspelz: Germany. Mongolia fur.

schalavery: *See* esquavar.

Schaller: Germany. Sallet.

schapevel: Holland. Sheepskin.

schappe silk: Fabric made from carded spun silk.

schappel: Germany. Traditional Black Forest wedding hat in the general form of a crown in the style of those worn in statues of the Virgin Mary. Varies in size and shape. Honored sign of virginity.

Schäppeli: Switzerland. High, richly decorated crown or hat.

scharlaken: Holland. Scarlet.

schaubelein: Elizabethan (1550–1625 C.E.). Man's short, flaring jacket.

schauslooper: Directoire and First Empire (1790–1815 C.E.). South Africa. Greatcoat.

schecke: *See* scheckenrock.

scheckenrock: Late Gothic (1350–1450 C.E.). Germany. Wammes.

scheenplaten: Holland. Greaves.

scheibenbart: Austria. Bunch of feathers in hatband.

Scheitelstuck: Renaissance (1450–1550 C.E.). Germany. Skull of the helmet.

schenti: Egyptian (4000–30 B.C.E.). Loincloth. *See also* shenti.

Schiessstöcke: Germany. Literally "shooting stick," a seat cane.

Schiffchenspitze: Germany. Tatting lace.

schir: Germany. Fine cloth.

Schirm: Germany. Umbrella.

Schirmmütze: (1940–1949 C.E.). Germany. S.S. officer's peaked cap decorated with a black band with a death's head emblem.

Schlafanzug: Germany. Pajamas.

Schlafenzug: *See* Nachthemd.

Schlapp Hut: Germany. Squash hat.

schlappe: Switzerland. Woman's small white cap with wide black wings.

Schleier: Germany. Veil.

Schleife: Germany. Bow.

Schleswig lace: Denmark. Needlepoint lace.

Schlips: *See* Halsbinde.

Schneider: Germany. A tailor.

Schnupftuch: *See* Taschentuch.

Schnupftücher: Switzerland. Handkerchief.

Schnurrstich: Germany. Couching stitch.

schoen: Holland. Shoe.

schoenveter: Holland. Shoestring.

schöpen: Switzerland. Worn by women in the home, a loose gown.

Schornsteinkappe: *See* Mönchskappe.

schort: Holland. Apron.

schorteband: Holland. Apron string.

Schotse baret: Holland. Tam-o'-shanter.

Schotse Hooglanders: Holland. Kilt.

Schotse muts: Holland. Glengarry.

Schotse omslagdoek: Holland. Plaid.

Schottenröckchen: Germany. Kilt.

Schottenstoff: Germany. Tartan.

schoudermantel: Holland. Cloak.

schoudertas: Holland. Shoulder bag.

Schrōtœre: Germany. Tailor.

Schuh: Germany. Shoe.

schuifspeldje: *See* haarspeld.

Schuoch: Germany. Shoe.

Schürtze: Germany. Apron.

Schürze: Germany. Old word for apron.

Schurze: Germany. Pinafore.

Schutzhelm: Germany. Crash helmet.

schwartz: Germany. Black.

Schweizergelb: Switzerland. Literally "Swiss yellow."

schynbaldes: Early Gothic (1200–1350 C.E.). Armor shin guards.

sciameto: Early Gothic (1200–1350 C.E.). Italy. Rich heavy damask silk.

sciccels: 1. Byzantine and Romanesque (400–1200 C.E.). United Kingdom. Rectangular cloak, probably of fur. Worn by men. 2. *See* hacele.

sciccing: Byzantine and Romanesque (400–1200 C.E.). United Kingdom. Cloak.

scimmia: Italy. Monkey fur.

scipio eburneus: Byzantine and Romanesque (400–1200 C.E.). Scepter of ivory with an eagle at the top. Used by a consul or magistrate at the games.

sclaveyn: *See* sclavyn.

sclavine: *See* sclavyn.

sclavyn: Early Gothic (1200–1350 C.E.) to Renaissance (1450–1550 C.E.). Pilgrim's mantle.

scogger: United Kingdom. Footless worsted stockings.

scōh: Byzantine and Romanesque (400–1200 C.E.). United Kingdom. Shoe or shoes.

scollatura: Italy. Neckline.

scone cap: Scotland. Similar in shape to a scone; broad, flat, round cap with a visor. Popular in lowlands.

scoop bonnet: Crinoline (1840–1865 C.E.). Popular name for long narrow bonnet worn in 1840.

Scotch cambric: Fine cotton cambric.

Scotch cap: Brimless wool cap.

scotch gingham: Quality, closely woven, cotton gingham fabric.

Scotia: Crinoline (1840–1865 C.E.). In February, 1860, gray cloth cloak with plaid trim.

Scotia silk: Directoire and First Empire (1790–1815 C.E.). Introduced in 1809, cotton and silk fabric, similar to broché.

scozzese: Italy. Tartan.

scratch bob: Early Georgian (1700–1750 C.E.) to Late Georgian (1750–1790 C.E.). United Kingdom. Popular from 1740 to the end of the century, bob wig that covered only the back of the head with the wearer's own hair brushed back from the front to cover the edge. Name derived from the fact that when wearing it, wearer could reach and scratch his head.

scratch wig: *See* scratch bob.

scrip: Early Gothic (1200–1350 C.E.). Pouch or wallet.

scrōtari: Germany. Old word for tailor.

scrud: Byzantine and Romanesque (400–1200 C.E.). United Kingdom. Clothes. Used for either gender. Used frequently in papers dealing with arrange-ments to provide clothing for monks and nuns.

scrydan: United Kingdom. Old English word meaning to clothe or to dress.

scuird: Byzantine and Romanesque (400–1200 C.E.). Ireland. Shirt, tunic, or cloak.

Scuoh: Germany. Old High German term for shoe.

scye: Directoire and First Empire (1790–1815 C.E.). Tailoring term referring to the curved lower portion of armseye of coat.

scyfel: Byzantine and Romanesque (400–1200 C.E.). United Kingdom. Woman's hat or hood.

scyrte: Byzantine and Romanesque (400–1200 C.E.). United Kingdom. Originally term for tunic that appeared simultaneously with cyrtel. Worn by men.

sea coat: Renaissance (1450–1550 C.E.) to Elizabethan (1550–1625 C.E.). United Kingdom. Worn by seamen, man's lined and hooded coat.

sea green: Yellowish green.

Sea Island cotton: Fine, silky cotton grown on islands off southern coast of United States of America.

sea-gown: Renaissance (1450–1550 C.E.) to Elizabethan (1550–1625 C.E.). United Kingdom. Wrap worn at sea.

seal: Soft, thick, fine, mouse-colored fur. Often dyed black or brown.

sealskin cloth: Fabric imitating sealskin.

sealskin coat: Bustle (1865–1890 C.E.). United Kingdom. Fashionable in 1880s, coat cut full in the back. From 1882 to 1888, trimmed with a broad flat bow over the bustle.

sealskin sacque: (1900–1910 C.E.). A long, fitted cap of sealskin.

sēamere: United Kingdom. Old English word for tailor.

sebki: India. An apple green color.

sebnia: Morocco. White or green foulard silk scarf.

Second Empire costume: Crinoline (1840–1865 C.E.). United Kingdom. Popular from 1850 to 1867, gown with a snug-fitting bodice, pagoda sleeves, and a full skirt.

secque: Lightweight sabotine.

secrete: *See* jupe.

seda: Ecuador, Guatemala, Portugal, and Spain. Silk.

seda chape: Spain. Schappe silk.

seda cruda: Spain. Raw silk.

seda de corbatas: Spain. Tie silk.

seda floja: Guatemala. Silk floss from China.

seda silvestre: Spain. Tussah silk.

sedalina: Guatemala. Pearl cotton.

Sedan lace: Charles I and the Commonwealth (1625–1660 C.E.). Cutwork lace made in Sedan.

seed beads: Small beads used in allover effects.

seed embroidery: Germany. Embroidery done with seed beads.

seed pearl: Tiny pearl.

seeds: *See* wheat ears.

Seehund: Germany. Seal fur.

seerband: India. Turban.

seershaud: *See* sirshad.

seersucker: France. Lightweight, plain weave fabric with a crinkled effect made by making the warp very loose. It is derived from the Persian shiroshakkar, a puckered cotton fabric imported from India.

se'evae: Samoa. Sandals.

seghosen: Nigeria. Cloth used in festivals.

segmentae: Roman (753 B.C.E.–323 C.E.). Decorative stripes sewn on over the shoulders of garments.

segu: Senegal. Finely woven lightweight cloth woven from European yarns.

segúna: Greece. Everyday mantle.

sehan: India. Silk cloth.

Seide: Germany. Silk.

seigo: Japan. 1. A heavy, stiff silk fabric often used in stage costumes. 2. Taffeta-like silk.

seileadach: Ireland. Gaelic word for pocket handkerchief.

seïméniko: Greece. Three-quarter length overcoat.

seircean: Ireland. Gaelic word for jerkin.

seircin: Ireland. Gaelic word for jerkin.

seiric: Ireland. Gaelic word for silk.

seiz: France. Breton for silk.

sejodae: Korea. Silken cord worn by young men around the upper chest on ceremonial occasions.

sekernil: Denmark. Pants.

Sekhemty: Egyptian (4000–30 B.C.E.). Double crown of Egypt.

sela: India. A silk headscarf.

selari: India. A silk sari with breadthwise borders.

selba: Timbuktu. A woman's red slipper.

selendang: Indonesia. Long stole worn draped over the shoulder.

seleulu: Samoa. Scissors.

selimut: Timbuktu. Man's cloth.

selisie lawn: Early Georgian (1700–1750 C.E.). Cambric made in Silesia.

selk: 1. Russia. Silk. 2. Byzantine and Romanesque (400–1200 C.E.) to Renaissance (1450–1550 C.E.). United Kingdom. Middle English word for silk.

sella: Renaissance (1450–1550 C.E.). Italy. Saddle-shaped headdress from which hung a fine silk veil.

selvage: Finished edge on woven or knitted fabric.

semea: Samoa. Yellowish brown.

semfiti: Nigeria. A fringed scarf.

semnar: *See* samare.

sempringham: Early Gothic (1200–1350 C.E.). Lincolnshire fabric.

semptress bonnet: Directoire and First Empire (1790–1815 C.E.). United Kingdom. Introduced in 1812, woman's bonnet with very long wide ribbons that crossed under the chin and were then brought up to the top of the crown and tied in a bow.

šemsija: *See* kišobran.

sen: Japan. Felt.

Sendai Hira silk: Japan. A stiff, flat weave silk with a fine glossy warp and an untwisted raw silk woof. It is made on the Sendai Plains.

sendal: Early Gothic (1200–1350 C.E.). Lightweight gold cloth.

sendelbinde: *See* flieder.

sennit: Rough straw used for men's hats.

señor: Bolivia. Tied with a thick wide belt, a large burgundy cloth worn wrapped around the waist.

señora llijlla: Bolivia. Llijlla with bands of red, green, and wine color.

señore: Bolivia. Cummerbund.

señorita jacket: Bustle (1865–1890 C.E.). Woman's sleeveless jacket of colored silk with draped tabs in back over the bustle. Edges trimmed with a band of black velvet and aiguillettes of black silk cord on the shoulders.

sensuji: Japan. A heavy-duty cotton fabric like lightweight canvas.

seod: Ireland. Jewel.

seolac: *See* siolac.

sepia: Dark, dull brown.

sepu': Indonesia. Small cotton bag used by the Sa'dan-Toraja to carry betel.

Seraceta: Trade name for rayon made by acetate process.

seragu: India. Breadth-wise border on a sari.

serai topi: India. The Sindhi topi.

serape: Mexico. Blanketlike outer garment.

serapis: Persia. Long tunic of fine pleated fabric.

seraser: Turkey. Velvet in which the use of silver thread dominates.

seray: *See* ankanjo.

serc: Byzantine and Romanesque (400–1200 C.E.). United Kingdom. Man's simple shirt or tunic. Term applied to a tunic worn by monks during day and night. *See also* scyrte.

serekh: Egyptian (4000–30 B.C.E.). Rectangular plaque decorated with palace facade and topped with falcon. Used in jewelry.

serenk: Turkey. Colorful type of brocaded silk.

serge: 1. Cotton lining material. 2. Soft, strong, wool fabric. 3. Silk. 4. France. Twill.

serge de soy: Late Georgian (1750–1790 C.E.). Silk or silk and wool blend fabric used for men's vests.

serge royale: Bustle (1865–1890 C.E.). Introduced in 1871, flax and wool blend fabric with a silky surface.

sergedesoy: *See* desoy.

sergedusoy: Early Georgian (1700–1750 C.E.). Coarse silk fabric used for coats.

sergette: Thin serge.

sergia: France and Italy. Serge.

sēricum: Roman (753 B.C.E.–323 C.E.). Silk.

serih: *See* sīda.

serkr: Norway. Old Norse word for shirt.

serouel: *See* charoul.

seroval: Morocco. Loose, full trousers.

serpe: *See* sarpe.

serpent: Bustle (1865–1890 C.E.). In 1872, green.

serpentaux: Charles I and the Commonwealth (1625–1660 C.E.). France. Woman's hairstyle with lightly curled hair.

serpentine crepe: Plain weave fabric with lengthwise crinkled effect.

serpentine skirt: *See* morning glory skirt.

serpeych: *See* sarpech.

šerret: Ethiopia. Ankle-length apron.

serre-tête: Late Georgian (1750–1790 C.E.). France. Hat ribbon.

serribaf: *See* shirinbaf.

serst: Russia. Wool.

serud: *See* clāpes.

serul: Morocco. Bloused, long trousers that end below the knee.

service cap: *See* nehru cap.

service shoe: Military shoe, usually with plain toe.

servilla: Elizabethan (1550–1625 C.E.). Spain. Slipper.

sesir: Croatia and Serbia. Hat.

sēt: *See* delg.

sēt argait: Ireland. Old Gaelic word for silver brooch.

seta: Italy. Silk.

sethi: India. Banker's turban.

setim: Portugal. Satin.

setimeta: Portugal. Sateen.

setre: Turkey. Frock coat.

settee: Restoration (1660–1700 C.E.). Double lappets on woman's indoor cap.

seuchd: Ireland. Gaelic word for mantle or tunic.

seud-ghlasaidh: Ireland. Gaelic word for locket.

sevani: *See* suci.

Sevastopol: Crinoline (1840–1865 C.E.). In 1854, woman's cloak with a deep cape. Trimmed with deep plush, fur, or velvet.

seven-eighths coat: (1920–1930 C.E.). Woman's knee-length, double-breasted suit coats with large notched lapels, buttons, and braid trim. Worn with long slender skirts and high-necked blouses.

Seville: Crinoline (1840–1865 C.E.). Introduced in 1862, woman's violet silk bonnet trimmed with bunches of white roses and grapes on one side. Inside of brim was trimmed with blonde, roses, and grapes.

Sevillian: Crinoline (1840–1865 C.E.). In 1858, taffeta double shawl with a goffered ruche on the tower edge. Shawl had guipure hood and was edged with narrow fringe trimmed with jet beads.

Sèvres blue: Gay Nineties (1890–1900 C.E.). In 1891, a new color.

seyamitum: *See* samite.

sfifeh: Palestine. Cuffs.

sfilatura: Italy. Drawn-thread work.

sgaball: Ireland. Gaelic word for helmet.

sgaileagan: Ireland. Gaelic word for fan.

sgàilean-uisge: Ireland. Umbrella.

sgail-uisge: Ireland. Gaelic word for umbrella.

sgala: Ireland. Gaelic word for an ill-shaped hood or a tunic.

sgian-dubh: Scotland. Black-knife worn tucked into the top of a man's stocking on right leg. Held in place by garter band.

sgrog: Ireland. Gaelic word for skull cap.

sgrogaid: Ireland. Gaelic word for old hat or cap.

sgrogan: Ireland. Gaelic word for skull cap.

sguain: Ireland. Gaelic word for the train on a dress.

sgùird: Ireland. 1. Smock. 2. Apron. 3. Skirt.

sgulair: Ireland. Gaelic word for a large, old hat.

sgùman: Ireland. Skirt worn with the train tucked up.

sgyrt: Wales. Skirt.

sha: Japan. Soft, open weave, silk gauze.

sha 'iriyya: Libya. Choker necklace with many pendants.

sha 'riyeh: Palestine. Woman's silver necklace with many narrow pendants.

shaal: *See* ghoutra.

shabakat al-kharaz: Palestine. Literally "bead-net," crocheted cap decorated with small glass beads.

shabnam: India. Literally "morning dew," a transparent fabric.

shade: Late Georgian (1750–1790 C.E.) to Romantic (1815–1840 C.E.). Sheer piece of net, lace, or gauze worn by women to fill in or shade the décolletage. Sometimes had an attached neck ruff.

shade cloth: Heavy cotton fabric treated until opaque.

shadow: Elizabethan (1550–1625 C.E.) to Charles I and the Commonwealth (1625–1660 C.E.). United Kingdom. Bongrace without a hood and made of velvet, linen, or lace edged lawn.

shadow embroidery: Embroidery done with catch stitch on wrong side of fabric.

shadow lace: Very lightweight machine-made lace.

shadow organdy: Organdy printed with faint self-pattern.

shag: Charles I and the Commonwealth (1625–1660 C.E.). Used until end of 18th century, fabric with velvet nap on one side, of silk or worsted.

shag mittens: Directoire and First Empire (1790–1815 C.E.). United States of America. Mittens that were fringed all over.

shagreen: 1. Untanned leather of horse, shark, ass, or seal with a rough surface. Frequently dyed green. 2. Fabric with a grained ground.

shag-ruff: Elizabethan (1550–1625 C.E.) to Restoration (1660–1700 C.E.). Ruff with an irregular edge.

shagshu zamarro: Ecuador. Riding cape made of sheepskin.

shah ajidah: India. Coat with 60 ornamental stitches.

shahab: India. Red dye.

shahajidah: India. Double lined, royal coat with ornamental stitches. Sometimes it is quilted.

shahasi: Kiamu. A nose ornament.

shajak: Albania and Hungary. Heavy goat hair twill.

shakefold: Renaissance (1450–1550 C.E.) to Elizabethan (1550–1625 C.E.). United Kingdom. Early form of the farthingale made of a stiffened pad on a wire frame.

shaker: Heavy jersey.

shaker flannel: Lightweight, white, cotton flannel napped on both sides.

Shakespere collar: Crinoline (1840–1865 C.E.). United Kingdom. Man's turned down collar.

Shakespere vest: Bustle (1865–1890 C.E.). United Kingdom. Man's waistcoat with a turned down collar and a notched lapel. Popular 1876–1877.

shakkeh: Palestine. Woman's headdress ornament; row of gold coins on a band.

shako
See also photospread
(Headwear).

shako: Directoire and First Empire (1790–1815 C.E.). Hat wider at the top than at the edge on the head. It had a visor and was decorated with a plume on top. Reached popularity after the Italian Campaign.

shaksheer: Orient. Women's long, full trousers.

shal: 1. Russia. Winter long wool scarf worn tied under the chin. 2. Palestine. Flowered, fringed shawl in pink or maroon wool, cotton, or silk.

shale: *See* babushka.

shaleh: Palestine. 'Abayeh made of woolen fabric in black, blue, brown, or cream. May be embroidered at the neck.

shalloon: Lightweight, wool fabric made in Chalons, France.

shalwar: Orient. Trousers.

shambar: Palestine. Ceremonial veil.

shamew: *See* chammer.

shamiya: Bulgaria. Headcloth of white, red, or green. When tied over the crown it shows the wearer to be a maiden, when tied beneath the chin, to be married.

shamla: *See* shimla.

shamlah: Palestine. Woman's gold girdle worn with black dresses.

shams: *See* half shirt.

shan ku: China. Qing dynasty (1644–1911 C.E.). Han man's cotton, thigh-length gown worn by coolies. Worn with loose-fitting trousers.

shanf: Palestine. Gold earring comprised of a thick wire and semicircular disc. Worn through the upper ear or the nose.

shang: China. Ming dynasty (1368–1644 C.E.). Man's seven-paneled skirt.

Shanghai gown: *See* cheongsam.

shantung: 1. Bustle (1865–1890 C.E.). Popular in 1870s, thin, soft, undyed China silk. 2. Plain weave fabric with heavy weft yarns.

shao: China. Wei, Jin and Northern dynasties. Triangular lengths of silk hung from a woman's short upper skirt.

shapka: Russia. Cossack cap made of fur ranging in size to head size to as large as two feet high by two feet wide.

sharb: Egypt. Woman's square headscarf worn folded into a triangle. Sometimes trimmed with crochet, beading, or tassels.

sharbati: India. Very transparent cotton cloth; light buff color.

sharbūsh: *See* dubbahah.

sharf: Russia. Sash.

sharkskin: Twill or basket weave worsted suiting of a color crossed with white.

sharovary: Russia. Wide trousers.

sharps: Small, thin needles used for hand sewing.

shash: 1. Married Afar woman's black voile shawl. 2. Oman. White muslin veil. 3. Palestine. White muslin used for women's veils.

sha-sha: Egypt. Generic term for bead.

shatweh: 1. Muslim. Fez-like hat worn by married women under the white khirka. 2. Palestine. Woman's headdress similar to the tarbush. Made from red or red and green broadcloth, cotton, or linen and is padded and topped with a harbeh.

shaving hat: Early Georgian (1700–1750 C.E.). Man's hat of plaited wood-shavings.

shawal: Palestine. Woman's ankle-length, narrow-skirted dress.

shawl: Straight, square, oblong, or triangular piece of fabric worn across shoulders.

shawl collar

shawl collar: Romantic (1815–1840 C.E.). Wide turned down collar cut without a notch on a coat or waistcoat.

shawl Josephine: Crinoline (1840–1865 C.E.). In 1856, woman's lady's cloth talma with a slashed hood. Trimmed in black velvet.

shawl waistcoat: Romantic (1815–1840 C.E.) to Bustle (1865–1890 C.E.). Man's waistcoat with a shawl collar or a waistcoat made from a shawl.

shawl wool: *See* cashmere.

sheath dress: 1. Egyptian (4000–30 B.C.E.). Straight dress cut below the breasts with shoulder straps. 2. (1950–1960 C.E.). Woman's knee-length tightly fitted dress, strapped or strapless.

sheath dress
See also photospread
(Women's Wear).
Dover Publications

sheep's gray: Charles I and the Commonwealth (1625–1660 C.E.). Homespun undyed cloth of wool.

sheep's russet: Elizabethan (1550–1625 C.E.) to Restoration (1660–1700 C.E.). Fearnought.

sheitel: Wig worn by Jewish women after marriage.

shell: 1. Early Georgian (1700–1750 C.E.) to Late Georgian (1750–1790 C.E.). Curl of hair forming a bow in women's hairstyles. 2. Restoration (1660–1700 C.E.). Scotland. Cuirass. 3. (1960–1970 C.E.). Sleeveless, slip-on blouse.

shell pink: Pink with orange red tint.

shema: Tibet. Durable wool fabric.

shen dai: China. Zhuong dynasty. Scholar's girdle.

shen yi: China. Man's under-robe with a straight collar band, full sleeves with narrow cuffs, and paneled skirt. It fastened over to the right. Made of 12 pieces of fabric.

shenandoah: Thick-soled, high-heeled, mid-calf-high, leather boot.

shendot: Egyptian (4000– 30 B.C.E.). Symbol of the Pharaoh, a skirt similar to the gala skirt but cut with two curved and pleated edges in front.

shenti: Egyptian (4000–30 B.C.E.). Loincloth.

shenu: Egyptian (4000–30 B.C.E.). Flax.

shepherdess bonnet: Crinoline (1840–1865 C.E.). Woman's soft straw hat with a slightly turned up brim and usually adorned with flowers. It is worn toward the back of the head.

shepherd's check: Any fabric with small even black and white checks.

shepherd's cloth: *See* dreadnought.

shepherd's plaid: *See* shepherd's check.

shepherdess bonnet
Dover Publications

sherihah: Palestine. Leather belt.

sherry-vallies: Charles I (1625–1660 C.E.) to Late Georgian (1750–1790 C.E.). of America. Man's legging that buttoned up the outside of the trousers. Worn to protect the trousers from mud when riding.

sherte: Byzantine and Romanesque (400–1200 C.E.) to Renaissance (1450–1550 C.E.). United Kingdom. Middle English word for shirt.

sherwani: India. Angarakha that buttons down the center front. *See also* achkan.

shesh: Morocco. Man's long white or blue scarf worn around the head and neck as protection from the sun and sand.

shetland: Lightweight fabric made from Shetland sheep wool.

Shetland lace: Lightweight bobbin lace made of Shetland wool.

Shetland wool: Fine worsted yarn.

shibori: Japan. Tie-dyeing.

shibori-zome: Japan. Dapple dyeing.

shift: Early Georgian (1700–1750 C.E.) to Late Georgian (1750–1790 C.E.). Term replacing smock. Later replaced by chemise.

shige-meyui: Japan. Tiny knotted tie-dyeing.

shigoki-obi: Japan. A white crepe or cotton sash.

shigra: *See* linchi.

shihan: Japan. Literally "one-fourth," a type of kerchief.

shike-ito: Japan. Strong hemp thread used for tie-dyeing.

shima: Japan. Striped fabric.

shimabaori: India. An unlined jacket for mid-summer use.

shimba: Ecuador and Guatemala. Braid of hair.

shimla: India. A broad brimmed turban decorated with gold thread embroidery.

shimmy: Crinoline (1840–1865 C.E.). United States of America. Slang for chemise.

Shimokyo-zome: Japan. The dyeing done in lower Kyoto.

shin: Korea. Shoes; boots.

shinbar: *See* shambar.

shinel: Russia. Soldier's greatcoat.

shingle: Hair cut close to head.

shinobugusa: Japan. Grass used to produce a greenish stain for rubbed dyeing.

shintiyan: Egypt. Women's voluminous trousers similar to salvar. Very long with drawstrings to tie them at the knee where they blouse to the ankle.

shinyah: Palestine. Panel at lower back of woman's dress.

shinyar binaqleh talis: Palestine. Panel of solid embroidery.

shioze: Japan. Thick silk similar to taffeta.

ship-tire: Elizabethan (1550–1625 C.E.). United Kingdom. Woman's high coiffure.

shirastra: India. A helmet.

shirastra jala: A helmet for soldiers.

shireenbaf: *See* shirinbaf.

shirinbaf: India. Kind of fine cotton cloth.

shirinka: Russia. Scarf made from the entire width of the fabric. It is embroidered in satin stitch with silk and metallic threads.

shiromuku: Japan. A pure white bridal kimono.

shiroshakkar: Persia. A puckered cotton fabric imported from India.

shirt-drawers: Calf-length man's shirt with slits in center front and center back.

shirting flannel: Plain or twilled, lightweight woolen flannel.

shirtwaist: Crinoline (1840–1865 C.E.). Ladies' bodice cut in masculine style with a high collar.

shirvani: *See* qatifah-i-purbi.

shisha: India. Mirrored glass used in embroidery work.

shirtwaist
Dover Publications

shitagi: Japanese. Underkimono.

shiu tian yi: China. Literally "paddy field dress," woman's patchwork gown that fastened on the side.

shliapa: Russia. Hat.

shmar: Palestine. Cord used to tie back the sleeves of the thob.

shnat: Palestine. Gold nose-ring.

shnur: Russia. Hussar's shoulder cord.

sho: Byzantine and Romanesque (400–1200 C.E.) to Renaissance (1450–1550 C.E.). United Kingdom. Middle English word for shoe.

shoaizome: Japan. Method of indigo dyeing.

shoddy: Fabric made from rags of worsted and other wool scraps.

shoe horn: Renaissance (1450–1550 C.E.). Piece of metal or horn used to assist the foot to slip into a tight shoe or boot.

shoe satin: Strong, closely woven, semi-glossy satin.

shoe velvet: Heavy velvet used for making shoes.

shoen: Holland. Shoe.

shoepack: Late Georgian (1750–1790 C.E.). United States of America. Moccasin-like shoe of tanned leather.

shoe-tie necktie: Crinoline (1840–1865 C.E.). United Kingdom. Very narrow necktie that tied in a bow in front of passed through a ring allowing the ends to dangle freely.

shohakuzan: Japan. Literally "little white mountain," ancient nishiki pattern.

shokko-nishiki: Japan. Imported nishiki with hexagonal pattern.

shooting coat: Crinoline (1840–1865 C.E.) to Bustle (1865–1890 C.E.). United Kingdom. Popular name in 1860s through 1880s for a morning coat.

short shorts: *See* hot pants.

shortcuts: *See* hot pants.

shorties: (1950–1959 C.E.). Woman's gloves that just reached the wrists.

shorts: Romantic (1815–1840 C.E.). United Kingdom. Evening dress breeches.

shot silk: Changeable silk fabric.

shotten-bellied doublet: Elizabethan (1550–1625 C.E.). United Kingdom. Short-fronted doublet.

shoubiao: China. Wristwatch.

shoujuàn: China. Handkerchief.

shoulder belt: Elizabethan (1550–1625 C.E.) to Restoration (1660–1700 C.E.). United Kingdom. Baldrick.

shoulder heads: Elizabethan (1550–1625 C.E.). United Kingdom. Shoulder straps connecting front and back of a woman's gown.

shoulder knots: Restoration (1660–1700 C.E.). United Kingdom. Bunch of ribbon, cord, or lace loops worn as an ornament on the right shoulder.

shoulder straps: *See* shoulder heads.

shoulderette: Scarf or stole worn in place of jacket or sweater, often knitted or crocheted.

showing horn: *See* shoe horn.

shozoku: Japan. Theater costumes.

shribrik: Palestine. Couched stitch.

shrimbawi: Palestine. Plain linen fabric used for everyday dresses.

shrimp: Bright red orange.

shtany: Russia. Trousers.

shuba: Russia. Overcoat or cloak of fur.

shubnam: India. Thin pellucid muslin.

shuchin: Japan. Brocaded satin.

shudiya: Nigeria. Sace of dyed cotton.

shugga: Egypt. Wide, floor-length cloak that envelops the entire body.

shughl bet lahm: *See* shughl talhami.

shughl talhami: Palestine. Bethlehem work; embroidery couched in silver, gold, and silk cord.

shui tian yi: China. Ming dynasty. Paddy-field dress; gown made of scraps of satin patchworked together.

shuilù: China. Light green.

shuìyì: China. Night clothes; pajamas.

shuka: East African warrior's wrap worn wrapped around the body and tied on one shoulder.

shukina: Peru. Multicolored wool hat.

shukuy: Peru. Untanned leather slippers edged with colored wool fibers.

shu'lush: United States of America. Choctaw Indians' moccasins.

shumzil: India. Part of the Manipuri festival dress, a foot high horn-shaped cane headdress covered by a white turban.

shunbar: *See* shambar.

shunbar ahmar: Palestine. Bride's red veil.

shushpan: Russia. Peasant woman's holiday tunic.

shusu: Japan. Satin.

shuwayhiyyeh: Palestine. Woman's belt.

sialoa: Polynesia. A loincloth made of the bark of *Cypholophus macrocephalus*.

siamoise: France. Silk and cotton fabric from Thailand.

siang-malam: Sumatra. Changeable silks.

siapo: 1. Samoa. Bark cloth. 2. Polynesia. A wrapper made from the bark of the paper mulberry tree. *See also* tapa.

sic: India. An embroidered border or fringe.

sica-sicaya: *See* amsuka.

sich'ida: Korea. To baste.

sichóu: China. Silk fabric.

sicilian: Plain weave lining fabric.

Sicilian bodice: Bustle (1865–1890 C.E.). United Kingdom. Introduced in 1866, evening bodice with a low square décolletage. Worn with knee-length skirt panels, two in front, and two behind.

Sicilian embroidery: Lacelike work created using braid and buttonhole stitch

sicilienne: 1. Plain weave fabric with a silk warp and a cotton or wool weft. 2. Lightweight, plain weave silk fabric.

sickly green: Bustle (1865–1890 C.E.). United Kingdom. Green color made from natural vegetable dye, not commercial aniline dye.

sic-sik: *See* amsuka.

sīda: Germany. Old word for silk.

sidài: China. Silk ribbon.

sidan: Wales. Silk.

sidari: Egypt. Short vest.

side: Renaissance (1450–1550 C.E.) to Elizabethan (1550–1625 C.E.). United Kingdom. Term meaning long, i.e., sidegown.

Sīde: Germany. Silk.

side body: Crinoline (1840–1865 C.E.). United Kingdom. Separate panel in a coat below the armseye.

side edge: Romantic (1815–1840 C.E.) to Bustle (1865–1890 C.E.). Scalloped flap imitating a narrow vertical pocket. It was sewn into back vent of coat skirt. First appeared in greatcoats in 1810. Shortly after 1820, appeared in frock coats and made into day coats by 1829. Style was revived in the 1840s and again in 1873.

sideburns: Side whiskers.

sideless surcoat: Late Gothic (1350–1450 C.E.). Low-necked, sleeveless woman's overgarment worn to reveal the sleeves and front of the kirtle.

siden: *See* silke.

sidriyeh: Palestine. Man's satin waistcoat trimmed with braid and bobble fastenings.

sifsari: *See* safsari.

sigele: *See* mene.

siglat: Byzantine and Romanesque (400–1200 C.E.). Germany. Rich heavy damask silk.

siglatoen: Byzantine and Romanesque (400–1200 C.E.). Holland. Samite.

siglaton: Early Gothic (1200–1350 C.E.). Eastern gold brocade fabric used for dress garments.

sigle: 1. Byzantine and Romanesque (400–1200 C.E.). Clasp or brooch. 2. *See* mene.

signet ring: Ring with large intaglio initials.

signum: Roman (753 B.C.E.–323 C.E.). Finger ring with a key to a trunk mounted on it.

sigouni: Greece. Woman's long, sleeveless vest.

siguni: Hungary and Macedonia. Long coat with a large rectangular collar. It is worn over the shoulders.

sigúni: Greece. White woolen sleeveless coat worn open down the center front.

sihrang: *See* qatifah-i-purbi.

siiwaun: Laos. Upper robe worn by a Buddhist monk.

sikhamani: India. Man's crown ornamented with pearls.

sikhandaka: India. Lock of hair worn on the side of the head.

siki: 1. *See* salovana. 2. *See* wasa.

sikinchina: Ecuador. A shawl.

siklat: Byzantine and Romanesque (400–1200 C.E.). Norway. Samite.

sikma: *See* potur.

silahati: India. A silk or cotton stuff of Sylhet.

silai: *See* sari.

silecho: *See* sīda.

silesia: Early Georgian (1700–1750 C.E.). Germany. Originally made in Silesia, Germany, strong, lightweight, twill weave cotton fabric.

silika: Samoa. Silk.

silipa: Samoa. Slipper.

silistrienne: Bustle (1865–1890 C.E.). Introduced in 1868, wool and silk fabric.

siliva: Samoa. Silver.

silk: Protein fiber from the cocoon of the silk worm. Each fiber may be as long as 4,000 feet. Very strong, absorbent, resilient, and elastic.

silk Damascene: Bustle (1865–1890 C.E.). Introduced in 1876, silk and wool fabric with fine stripes of wool and satin alternately.

silk gauze: Thin silk curtain fabric.

silk linen: Rough spun, plain weave, silk fabric.

silk rash: *See* rash.

šilkai: Lithuania. Silk.

silkaline: Soft, thin cotton fabric with a glazed face.

silke: 1. Denmark. Silk. 2. Sweden. Silk.

silki: Norway. Old Norse word for silk.

silnaebok: Korea. Negligee.

silver fox: Fox fur with blue black fur and silver guard hairs.

silver lace: Lace or braid made with silk weft threads covered in foil or leaf.

silver taupe uniform: (1950–1960 C.E.). United States of America. Introduced in 1950, an Army woman's summer semi-dress uniform of light taupe wool gabardine.

silver tissue: Sheer metal fabric or silver threads.

silverets: Late Georgian (1750–1790 C.E.). United Kingdom. A silk and wool fabric. A cheaper version of Norwich crape.

silver-gray: (1900–1909 C.E.). In 1902, a new color.

simada: Edo (1600–1867 C.E.). Japan. A woman's hairstyle.

simarra: Late Gothic (1350–1450 C.E.). Man's outer robe with wide revers that turned back. Sometimes worn girdled. *See also* simarre; in Spain ropa; in France marlotte.

simarre: 1. *See* simarra. 2. Ecclesiastical gown shaped like a simarra.

simlah: Biblical (Unknown–30 C.E.). Long rectangle of fabric worn by Israelite Jews. Equivalent of himation.

simpa: Bolivia. Man's hair worn in a long single braid.

simtakvaldis: Lithuania. Woman's long jacket with a pleated basque.

sin: Laos. Woman's sarong.

sinamay: Stiff coarse fabric from abaca fiber.

sindon: 1. Egypt. Large draped piece of fabric worn as a cloak. 2. Early Gothic (1200–1350 C.E.). Fine linen fabric.

sindu: India. An Indian cotton.

singar patti: *See* dauni.

singe: France. Monkey fur.

singelos: Peru. Everyday skirt of woolen fabric.

singep: Indonesia. Cloth used to cover a child at his or her first haircut.

singlet: Unlined waistcoat.

siniki: Greece. Ink used to draw embroidery patterns on fabric.

sinus: Roman (753 B.C.E.–323 C.E.). Overfold on the toga.

sīoda: Ireland. Silk.

sioda bun-duirn: Scotland. Lace cuffs and jabot worn for evening.

siolac: United Kingdom. Old English word for silk.

siphonia: Crinoline (1840–1865 C.E.). Popular in 1850s and 1860s, man's long, weatherproofed overcoat. Pocket siphonia was a version that could be rolled up and carried.

sipu anaku: Ecuador. Quichua term for a pleated anaku.

sirastrana: India. Man's turban.

sirat: Borneo. Men's 18-inch by 15- or 16-feet-long cotton loincloth, made of red or blue cotton.

sire: *See* sari.

siree: *See* sari.

siren suit: (1940–1950 C.E.). Coveralls for women.

sirge debaragon: Elizabethan (1550–1625 C.E.) to Restoration (1660–1700 C.E.). Light variety of serge.

sirghe: Manchuria. Silk.

sīric: *See* sīta.

sirinbaf: India. A very fine muslin.

siring: *See* shirinbaf.

sirkek: Mongolia. Silk.

siróng: China. Velvet.

siropāu: India. Yellow or saffron colored tie-dyed turban.

sirottarapattika: India. A turban.

sirpeach: *See* sarpech.

sirsa kataha: India. A soldier's helmet.

sirsaka: 1. Romantic (1815–1840 C.E.). Introduced in 1835, silk fabric with lengthwise light colored stripes and horizontal dark colored stripes. 2. India. Pearl necklace.

sirshad: India. Kind of turban or veil.

sirsobha: India. Cap.

sirwaal: United Arab Emirates. Woman's trousers.

sirwal: Palestine. Baggy striped or solid colored pants. Vary widely in cut and length.

sirwall: Egypt. Black pants very baggy in the crotch and fitted at the calf and ankle.

sirwat: Sarawak. As long as 15 yards, a waistcloth of bark cloth, silk, or cotton.

sis sobha: India. Kulah.

sisal: Strong, durable fibers from agave plant.

sismusilis: *See* chisamus.

sissin kara: Indonesia. Sa'dan-Toraja woman's ring of white shell.

sister's thread: *See* nun's thread.

sīta: Ireland. Old Gaelic word for silk.

sitapuri: *See* qatifah-i-purbi.

sitara: India. A forehead ornament for women.

sits: Holland. Chintz.

siu fung sin: (1900–1910 C.E.). United States of America. Chinese Hawaiian term for a Shanghai collared blouse. The six-inch collar was worn folded down onto the shoulders.

siūlas: Lithuania. Thread.

siuvėjas: Lithuania. Tailor.

siwash sweater: *See* cowichan sweater.

siwy: *See* szary.

sizhipin: China. Silk fabrics.

sjaal: Holland. Shawl.

sjako: Holland. Shako.

skandakarani: India. Woman's square shawl.

skarabigion: Persia. Long fur-lined gown that buttoned shut at the sides.

skarpetka: Poland. Sock.

skaut: Norway. Older woman's starched white headdress.

skelat: Borneo. Red flannel.

skeleton suit: Directoire and First Empire (1790–1815 C.E.). United Kingdom. Boy's suit of a snug jacket with two rows of buttons, ankle-length trousers that buttoned to the jacket around the waist.

ski boot: Sturdy boot of special construction for skiing.

škidrauts: Lithuania. Thin cloth.

skilkja: *See* feldr.

skilts: Late Georgian (1750–1790 C.E.). United States of America. Full (a yard wide) trousers that reached just below the knee. Popular with country people.

skimskin: *See* snoskyn.

skin-coat: Renaissance (1450–1550 C.E.). Man's leather jerkin commonly worn by peasants and shepherds.

skinnsaum: Iceland. A form of open braid or gimp lace.

skiradion: Byzantine and Romanesque (400–1200 C.E.). Oval tiara worn by the Byzantine Empress. Fabric circlet trimmed with pearls and a plume. Color ranged from white to scarlet to green.

skirduk: Charles I and the Commonwealth (1625–1660 C.E.). Sweden. Gauzy veiling.

skirt ruff: Bustle (1865–1890 C.E.). United Kingdom. Thick ruching of fabric sewn to the inside of the hem of a skirt to make it stand out.

skitty boot: United Kingdom. Heavy half boot.

skiver: Cheap, soft sheep leather.

skjorta: Sweden. Shirt.

skjorte: Denmark. Shirt.

sklat: *See* skelat.

sko: Denmark and Sweden. Shoe.

skofium: Charles I and the Commonwealth (1625–1660 C.E.). Sweden. Gilt silver wire used in embroidery.

skōhs: Early Gothic (1200–1350 C.E.) to Late Gothic (1350–1450 C.E.). United Kingdom. Generic term for shoe.

skokie: (1920–1930 C.E.). United States of America. Variation of the Norfolk jacket with a set-in pleat in back and pleats or gathers for fullness.

skor: Norway. Old word for shoe.

skóra: Poland. Leather.

skort: (1960–1970 C.E. to present). Miniskirt combined with shorts.

skört: Sweden. Skirt.

skørt: Denmark. Skirt.

skräddare: Sweden. Tailor.

skraddari: Norway. Old Norse word meaning a tailor.

škrlet: Hungary. Broadcloth.

skrœdder: Denmark and Germany. Tailor.

skrybélé: Lithuania. Hat.

skuinsdoek: Romantic (1815–1840 C.E.). South Africa. Triangular scarf worn knotted as a neckcloth.

skull cap: Early Gothic (1200–1350 C.E.). Small snug-fitting cap.

skúña: Greece. Wool stockings.

skunk: Durable, long-haired, coarse, dark brown pelt with two white stripes which are dyed black or cut away.

skūra: Lithuania. Leather.

sky blue: Light blue.

skyrt: Byzantine and Romanesque (400–1200 C.E.) to Renaissance (1450–1550 C.E.). United Kingdom. Middle English word for skirt.

skyrta: *See* serkr.

skyteen: United Kingdom. Heavyweight cotton shirting fabric, usually with dark stripes on a sky blue ground.

slaapmuts: Holland. Nightcap.

slabbetje: Holland. Bib.

slammerkin: Early Georgian (1700–1750 C.E.) to Late Georgian (1750–1790 C.E.). Woman's loose unboned trained sac back morning gown worn with a petticoat. Named for character of Mrs. Slammerkin in *The Beggar's Opera. See also* trollopee.

slapaireachd: Ireland. Gaelic word for the train on a long robe.

slat bonnet

slash pocket: Directoire and First Empire (1790–1815 C.E.) to Bustle (1865–1890 C.E.). Horizontal pocket without flap.

slashed sleeve: *See* Spanish sleeve.

slashings: Renaissance (1450–1550 C.E.). Decorative cuts in clothing.

slat bonnet: Bonnet with brim held in place with thin wooden slats.

slat-rioghail: Ireland. Gaelic word for scepter.

slaucis: Lithuania. Handkerchief.

slave blanket: United States of America. Southwestern blanketry combining Navajo upright loom techniques and designs with minor motifs from the Spanish colonists.

slave bracelet: Bracelet of several narrow rings.

slavin: *See* sclavyn.

slavnostný kroj: Slovakia. Ceremonial costume.

sleasy holland: Early Georgian (1700–1750 C.E.) to Late Georgian (1750–1790 C.E.). Term referring to all Holland fabrics.

sleaved silk: Renaissance (1450–1550 C.E.) to Elizabethan (1550–1625 C.E.). Raw floss silk.

sleeve à la Louis Quinze: Bustle (1865–1890 C.E.). Introduced in 1872, elbow-length sleeve with scalloped flounces covered with flounce of Alencon lace.

sleeve à la Minerva: Directoire and First Empire (1790–1815 C.E.). Full short sleeve caught up in the front with a jeweled pin.

sleeve hand: Charles I and the Commonwealth (1625–1660 C.E.). Place in the sleeve through which the hand goes.

sleeve tongs: Gay Nineties (1890–1900 C.E.). United Kingdom. Decorative metal tongs used to pull the dress sleeves through the sleeves of the overcoat.

Sleier: *See* Sloier.

slendang: Indonesia. Shoulder cloth.

slesia lawn: Elizabethan (1550–1625 C.E.) to Restoration (1660–1700 C.E.). Fine linen similar to cambric.

slicker: (1920–1930 C.E. to present). United States of America. Yellow oilcloth raincoat worn by both sexes.

slicker fabric: Plain cotton fabric waterproofed for slickers.

sliehppa: Norway. Insert of broadcloth worn inside the V-neck of a gappte.

slife-scoh: Byzantine and Romanesque (400–1200 C.E.). United Kingdom. Bag-like foot covering.

slim jims: *See* ranch pants.

sling pump: Woman's backless shoe with strap across the back of the heel.

sling sleeve: Bustle (1865–1890 C.E.). United Kingdom. Introduced in 1885, woman's sleeve resembling a cape.

sling-duster: Bustle (1865–1890 C.E.). United Kingdom. Woman's dust cloak with sling sleeves. Commonly made of black and white checked silk.

sling pump

slipēir: Ireland. Slipper.

slipe-scoh: *See* slife-scoh.

slipper satin: Strong, durable, rayon or silk fabric used for evening footwear.

slippers: House shoes; so named because they slip on the foot with no form of closure (buckles or lacings).

slips: Renaissance (1450–1550 C.E.) to Charles I and the Commonwealth (1625–1660 C.E.). Individual floral motifs.

šliuré: Lithuania. Slipper.

slivers: *See* slyders.

sljapa: Russia. Hat.

sljem: Bosnia. Helmet.

slobkousen: Holland. Spatterdashes.

Sloier: Germany. Veil.

slöja: Sweden. Veil.

slop work: Romantic (1815–1840 C.E.). United Kingdom. Cheap basic clothing for sailors and for export to the colonies.

sloppy joe: (20th century). United States of America. Style for women consisting of oversized man's shirt worn over cuffed blue jeans.

slops: 1. Elizabethan (1550–1625 C.E.). Large unpadded knee-length men's breeches. 2. Late Georgian (1750–1790 C.E.). United States of America. Generic term for cheap ready-made clothing.

slør: Denmark. Veil.

slouch hat: Soft hat.

sluier: Holland. Veil.

slyders: Early Georgian (1700–1750 C.E.) to Late Georgian (1750–1790 C.E.). Overalls.

smadeh: Palestine. Married woman's embroidered cap with a padded rim shaped like a horseshoe. Row of coins was sewn to the rim.

small slops: Elizabethan (1550–1625 C.E.). Men's short breeches with open legs.

smàrag: Ireland. Emerald.

smaragd: Holland. Emerald.

smaragdfarben: Germany. Emerald green.

smaragdgrün: *See* smaragdfarben.

smaragdus: Roman (753 B.C.E.–323 C.E.). Emerald, a gemstone.

smezzati moro: Italy. Very small carved bead of coral used in jewelry.

smicket: Obsolete term for woman's smock.

smigeadach: Ireland. Gaelic word for chin cloth or bib.

smiotag: Ireland. Gaelic word for fingerless glove.

smoc: Byzantine and Romanesque (400–1200 C.E.). United Kingdom. Shirt or undergarment. Possibly decorated in some fashion.

smock: Woman's innermost garment worn next to the skin.

smock petticoat: Charles I and the Commonwealth (1625–1660 C.E.). Under petticoat.

smock-frock: Bustle (1865–1890 C.E.). 1. Man's loose homespun gown. Usually smocked or gauged in front. Commonly worn by agricultural workers. 2. Popular in 1880s, woman's informal garment influenced by the aesthetic movement.

smoking: Portugal. Tuxedo; dinner jacket.

smoking jacket: Crinoline (1840–1865 C.E.). United Kingdom. Popular from 1850s on, short, single- or double-breasted man's jacket of merino, velvet, cashmere, or plush and brightly lined. Ornamented with decorative closures.

smugadair: Ireland. Gaelic word for pocket handkerchief.

smuig-aodach: Ireland. Gaelic word for handkerchief.

smuigeadach: Ireland. Gaelic word for pocket handkerchief.

snail: Early Georgian (1700–1750 C.E.) to Late Georgian (1750–1790 C.E.). Short for chenille.

snail button: Early Georgian (1700–1750 C.E.) to Late Georgian (1750–1790 C.E.). Covered button decorated with French knots.

snaim na banaraich: Ireland. Gaelic word for the way a milkmaid fastens her skirt at the back after lifting it.

snajder: *See* krojac.

snake: Charles I and the Commonwealth (1625–1660 C.E.). Common term referring to men's love locks.

šnala: *See* kopča.

snāth: Ireland. Thread.

snàthad: Ireland. Needle.

snāthad: Ireland. Needle.

snāthat: Ireland. Old Gaelic word for needle.

snàth-clòimhe: Ireland. Woolen yarn.

snàth-cuir: Ireland. Weft.

snāthe: Ireland. Old Gaelic word for thread.

snàth-fuaidhle: Ireland. Sewing thread.

snàth-lìn: Ireland. Linen thread or yarn.

snàth-olla: Ireland. *See* snàth-clòimhe.

snàth-righailt: Ireland. Basting thread.

snàth-sioda: Ireland. Silk thread.

sneachd-gheal: Ireland. Gaelic word for snow white.

sneaker: Rubber soled, lace up sports shoe.

sniegowce: Poland. Galoshes.

sniezobialy: Poland. Snow white colored.

snod: Byzantine and Romanesque (400–1200 C.E.). Filet or band worn on head.

snood: Early Gothic (1200–1350 C.E.) to modern times. In 13th century, a net used to cover hair. In 15th and 16th centuries, the nets were decorated with pearls and gems. Disappeared from fashion at end of 16th century and reappeared around 1800 as covers for the fashionable low chignons.

snor: Holland. Moustache.

snoskyn: Elizabethan (1550–1625 C.E.). United Kingdom. Woman's small muff.

snow cloth: Knitted or woven fabric that is heavily pulled or felted. Often water repellent.

Snowdrop: Crinoline (1840–1865 C.E.). In 1854, mantilla with ruched hem. Had revers in front and a deep fringe on lower edge. Heavily embroidered.

snowflake: United Kingdom. Woolen fabric with white nubs on the surface.

snowskin: *See* snoskyn.

snufkin: *See* snoskyn.

snuftkin: *See* snoskyn.

šnura: *See* pertla.

sobaquera: Spain. Dress shield.

sobol: Poland. Sable.

sobre pantalón: Guatemala. Overpants.

sobrecapa: Portugal. Overcoat; raglan.

sobrecasaca: Portugal. Frock coat.

sobrepantalón rajado: Guatemala. Black woolen overtousers split to the thigh.

sobrepeliz: Portugal. Surplice.

sobretudo: Portugal. Overcoat.

sobretudo sôlto: Portugal. Balmacaan.

socas: Wales. Socks.

socc: Byzantine and Romanesque (400–1200 C.E.). United Kingdom. Bag-like foot covering. Similar to the meo.

soccae: Roman (753 B.C.E.–323 C.E.). Light shoes.

soccus: 1. Early Gothic (1200–1350 C.E.). Wide ceremonial cloak worn open and fastened on the right shoulder. Worn by the king for his coronation and other ceremonies. 2. Greek (3000–100 B.C.E.). Slipper or shoe without fastening. In Rome, worn only by women and comic actors.

socka: Sweden. Sock.

socke: Byzantine and Romanesque (400–1200 C.E.) to Renaissance (1450–1550 C.E.). United Kingdom. Middle English word for sock.

Socke: Germany. Sock.

soco: *See* socc.

socq: *See* socc.

sode: Japan. 1. Sleeves. 2. Sleeve guards in armor.

sode-guchi: Japan. The sleeve opening.

sode-nashi: Japan. Literally "no sleeves," a haori jacket with no sleeves.

sode-tsuke: Japan. The armseye seam.

soga: Indonesia. Brown dye used primarily for batik.

sogot: Korea. Underwear.

sohofa: Ethiopia. Man's copper collar which is open in front and ends in two rings.

soi: Vietnam. Shantung silk.

soie: France. Silk.

soie de Padoue: *See* paduasoy.

soie demantine: Crinoline (1840–1865 C.E.). In 1855, new fabric.

soieries à double face: Crinoline (1840–1865 C.E.). In 1862, silks with each face of different color.

soieries bizarres: Restoration (1660–1700 C.E.). France. Literally "bizarre silks," fabrics of rare sumptuousness made by mixing gold and silver with bright or muted colors.

Soiesette: Trade name for plain weave cotton fabric.

soilleir-dhonn: Ireland. Gaelic word for light brown.

sok: Denmark and Holland. Sock.

so-kanoko: Japan. Soli or allover kanoko.

sokch'ima: Korea. Woman's petticoat.

sokkr: Norway. Old Norse word for sock.

sokophouder: Holland. Sock suspenders.

sokot: Korea. Underclothes.

sokoto: Nigeria. Yoruba man's narrow trousers.

sokoto kafo: Nigeria. Yoruba man's trousers that taper to embroidered bands at the cuffs.

sokoto kembe: Nigeria. Yoruba man's wide legged trousers.

sokuhatu: Meizi (1867–1912 C.E.). Japan. Literally "knotted coiffure," a woman's hairstyle.

sokutai: Heian (794–1185 C.E.). Japan. A man's formal court costume.

sola topi: India. Pith helmet.

solapa: Spain. Lapel; revers.

solea: Roman (753 B.C.E.–323 C.E.). Simple sandal consisting of a wooden sole with a cord passing over the foot.

soled hose: Byzantine and Romanesque (400–1200 C.E.) to Renaissance (1450–1550 C.E.). Worn until end of 15th century, men's soled stockings of wool or leather that were worn without shoes. In 15th century, joined in the groin to form tights.

soleil: Wool fabric with warp twill weave.

solers: *See* slippers.

soletila: Elizabethan (1550–1625 C.E.). Spain. Thin sole.

solette: *See* soulette.

solferino: Crinoline (1840–1865 C.E.). Fuchsia, one of the first aniline dyes.

solitaire: 1. Early Georgian (1700–1750 C.E.). Black string which extended from the back hair bag on a bag wig and was brought around the neck to the front where it tied into a bow. Ancestor of the modern black bow tie. 2. Crinoline (1840–1865 C.E.). Lead colored silk mantilla.

solje: Norway. Symbol of matrons, a large brooch. Often handed down for generations.

søljer: Norway. Brooches.

solleret: 1. Early Gothic (1200–1350 C.E.). Overlapping plates of armor forming the mailed shoe of a knight. 2. Renaissance (1450–1550 C.E.). Round toed shoe.

söllstötter: Sweden. Silver ornaments, similar to bolo tips, which cover the end of a green silk ribbon worn tied in a bow around the shirt collar.

solo: Samoa. Duster.

solosolo: Samoa. Handkerchief.

som: Korea. Cotton.

somae: Korea. Sleeve.

somaega tchalbun: Korea. Short sleeved.

somaegakin: Korea. Long sleeved.

sombrerera: Spain. Hat box.

sombrero Cordobès

sombrero: Elizabethan (1550–1625 C.E.). Spain. Man's soft hat with a wide brim. Worn with brim turned up on one side.

sombrero Cordobès: Spain. Man's wide-brimmed hat.

sombrero de ala ancha: Spain. Broad-brimmed hat.

sombrero de caballero: Spain. Man's trilby.

sombrero de copa chistera: Spain. Top hat.

sombrero de dos picos: Spain. Cocked hat.

sombrero de paja: Spain. Straw hat.

sombrero de tela: Spain. Cloth hat.

sombrero flexible: Spain. Homburg.

sombreros de lana de lado de Ambato: Ecuador. Woman's white felt hat.

sombrinha: Portugal. Parasol; sunshade.

sombrinha chapeau de sol: Portugal. Parasol.

somi: Vietnam. Shirt.

so-mi carô: Vietnam. Checked shirt.

so-mi-dét: Vietnam. Short sleeved shirt.

somitum: *See* samite.

sommiere: France. Soft, wool serge napped on one side.

somot: Korea. Padded clothes.

somoyo: Japan. An allover design.

sonehri: India. Gold printing.

songabang: Korea. Handbag.

songkabang: Korea. Handbag.

songket: Indonesia. Brocade, particularly one using metallic threads.

sonko: Timbuktu. A silver bracelet.

sonkoli cap: India. Worn by the fishermen of Bombay, a tall red cap with a horseshoe-shaped opening over the forehead.

Sonnenschirm: Germany. Parasol.

sonsugon: Korea. Handkerchief.

sontag

sontag: Crinoline (1840–1865 C.E.). A woman's knitted jacket, sometimes sleeved and other times a simple knitted shawl.

sook chau: Bustle (1865–1890 C.E.). United States of America. Chinese Hawaiian term for a refined, black chau material with a light texture. It had floral designs woven into the fabric.

soort bergkristal: Holland. Rhinestone.

soort rijbroek: Holland. Jodhpurs.

soosey: 1. Early Georgian (1700–1750 C.E.) to Late Georgian (1750–1790 C.E.). India. Silk and cotton blend fabric with stripes. 2. *See* susi.

soosie: *See* susi.

sopagas: *See* batas.

sopanaka: India. String of pearls necklace on a gold wire.

soppravvesta: Italy. Tabard.

soprabito: Italy. Greatcoat.

sora-iro: Japan. Sky blue.

sorket: Late Gothic (1350–1450 C.E.). Germany. Term meaning surcote.

sorō: Ethiopia. Leather shirts.

soroki: Russia. Woman's horned headdress.

sorority pin: *See* fraternity pin.

sorquenie: Early Gothic (1200–1350 C.E.) to Crinoline (1840–1865 C.E.). Worn from 13th to 19th centuries, woman's tunic worn snugly fitted over the bust.

sorrel: Yellowish brown.

Sorrento edging: Lace edging similar to Brussels edging.

sorro: Timbuktu. A pear-shaped ornament worn in the middle of a woman's forehead.

șorț: Romania. Apron.

sorti: Restoration (1660–1700 C.E.). France. Small knot of ribbon worn between pinner and apron.

sortie: 1. *See* sorti. 2. Holland. Opera cloak.

sortie de bal: Crinoline (1840–1865 C.E.) to Bustle (1865–1890 C.E.). United Kingdom. Popular in 1850s through 1870s, hooded woman's evening cloak of silk, satin, or cashmere. Generally had quilted lining.

sortija: Spain. Finger ring.

sortixa: Ecuador and Guatemala. Finger ring.

sosni: India. The color purple.

sostén: Spain. Brassiere.

sotaina: *See* batina.

sottana: 1. Byzantine and Romanesque (400–1200 C.E.) to Early Georgian (1700–1750 C.E.). In 12th and 13th centuries, woman's tunic-shaped undergown. Sometimes plain, sometimes striped. Worn by young girls as outer gown. 2. Italy. Cassock. 3. *See* gonella.

sottogonna: Italy. Petticoat.

soucane: *See* sorquenie.

soudagir: India. Trade cloths (fabric made for export).

soudarion: Greek (3000–100 B.C.E.). Kerchief for neck or arm.

soufflet sleeve: Romantic (1815–1840 C.E.). United Kingdom. Popular in 1832, woman's evening sleeve that was very short with full vertical puffs.

soukno: Bulgaria. Homespun woolen petticoat striped in different colors.

soulette: Charles I and the Commonwealth (1625–1660 C.E.). France. Leather band passing over the instep and under the patten to hold it to the shoe or boot.

soulier: *See* chaussure.

soup and fish: United Kingdom. A slang term for the tuxedo.

souquenilles: *See* sorquenie.

sourés: Bustle (1865–1890 C.E.). In 1875, mouse color.

souris éffrayée: Restoration (1660–1700 C.E.). France. Dull gray.

soutache: Narrow decorative braid.

soutane: 1. Cassock worn by Roman Catholic priests. 2. *See* gonelle. 3. France. Cassock.

sou'wester: United States of America. Waterproof fisherman's hat with a brim wider in front than in back.

sovanel: Romania. Woman's muslin cap.

sowback: Scotland. Woman's cap with lengthwise fold.

sowlar: Iran. Wide trousers.

soyacal: Guatemala. Rain cape.

soyate: Mexico. Woman's sash.

soyeaux linsey: Bustle (1865–1890 C.E.). Introduced in 1869, lightweight wool poplin.

spa bonnet: Romantic (1815–1840 C.E.). Introduced in 1819, fancy straw hat, sometimes in two colors, worn without trim.

spad-choisbheart: Ireland. Gaelic word for gaiters.

spagnolet: Elizabethan (1550–1625 C.E.) to Late Georgian (1750–1790 C.E.). Gown with narrow sleeves a l'espagnole.

spaier: Early Gothic (1200–1350 C.E.). Vertical slit in a garment.

spair: Crinoline (1840–1865 C.E.). In use from 1850s on, fall in a man's breeches.

spandex: Synthetic fiber with super elastic qualities. *See also* Lycra.

spang: 1. Early Gothic (1200–1350 C.E.). Metal fastening. 2. Holland. Agraffe.

spangehelm

spangehelm: Cone-shaped helmet of boiled leather studded with small pieces or bands of iron and sometimes topped with a knob of wood or colored glass.

spangles: Late Gothic (1350–1450 C.E.) to present. United Kingdom. Small discs of metal used as trim. By 16th century, used on clothes of both genders and on hats and stockings. By 17th century, used on garters, pantofles, and shoe roses. By 18th century, used on men's coats and women's fans. By late 19th century, only used occasionally, and then on women's bonnets and evening dresses.

spaniel's ears: Crinoline (1840–1865 C.E.). Corkscrew curls worn on each side of the face.

Spanish blue: Directoire and First Empire (1790–1815 C.E.). Popular shade of dark blue used for men's morning coats in 1809.

Spanish boots: Charles I and the Commonwealth (1625–1660 C.E.). Short leather boots with falling tops.

Spanish breeches: Charles I and the Commonwealth (1625–1660 C.E.). Popular from 1630 to 1635 and revived from 1663 to 1670, men's high-waisted, full-length breeches that narrowed from the thighs to end below the knees where they closed with rosettes or bows or were left open over the stockings. Trimmed down outside edge of leg with braid or buttons.

Spanish cloak: 1. Elizabethan (1550–1625 C.E.). Man's short hooded cloak. 2. Romantic (1815–1840 C.E.). Worn from 1836 on, man's short round evening cloak fitted to the shoulders and lined with a bright silk. 3. *See* Italian cloak.

Spanish coat: Directoire and First Empire (1790–1815 C.E.). Fashionable in 1814, woman's pelisse with a standing collar and epaulettes on the shoulders.

Spanish comb: High comb worn in hair.

Spanish embroidery: 1. Herringbone stitching on muslin. 2. Designs of muslin, cambric, and braid buttonhole.

Spanish farthingale: Elizabethan (1550–1625 C.E.). United Kingdom. Worn from about 1545 to 1600, woman's underskirt held out by round hoops of rushes, wood, wire, or whalebone, creating a funnel-shaped, domed, or bell-shaped skirt. Made of muchado, fustian, buckram, or wool, although some were made of silk or velvet.

Spanish fly: Directoire and First Empire (1790–1815 C.E.). Introduced in 1809, dark green.

Spanish hat: Directoire and First Empire (1790–1815 C.E.). United Kingdom. Woman's large velvet, satin, or sarcenet hat trimmed with feathers. Worn for evening or promenade.

Spanish heel: Heel similar to French.

Spanish heel

Spanish hose: *See* Spanish breeches.

Spanish jacket: Crinoline (1840–1865 C.E.). United Kingdom. Woman's short jacket that met down the front and then cut away toward the back at waist level.

Spanish kettledrums: Elizabethan (1550–1625 C.E.). United Kingdom. Worn from 1555 to 1570s, the common term for trunk hose.

Spanish lace: Any lace made in Spain; most commonly silk with heavy flat floral design.

Spanish leather: *See* cordouan.

Spanish mantle: Crinoline (1840–1865 C.E.). In 1853, mantilla-shaped garment lined with quilted silk.

Spanish morion: *See* cabasset.

Spanish needlepoint: Elizabethan (1550–1625 C.E.). Mexico. Fine flax enriched with gold and silver thread.

Spanish paper: Late Georgian (1750–1790 C.E.). Little papers of red powder made into books which ladies would then tear out and rub on their faces as rouge.

Spanish sleeve: Directoire and First Empire (1790–1815 C.E.). United Kingdom. Popular from 1807 to 1820, woman's short evening sleeve puffed at the cap and slashed on sides to reveal a silk lining.

Spanish slops: Elizabethan (1550–1625 C.E.). Trunk hose without padding. Full slops were long enough to bag at the knees. Pansid slops were a shorter version.

Spanish stitch: *See* blackwork.

Spanish work: *See* blackwork.

spartiate: *See* sandal.

spats

spats: Bustle (1865–1890 C.E.). Coverings for the ankles and shoe tops. Made of felt or leather.

spatter dashes: Early Georgian (1700–1750 C.E.). First appearing around 1700, high leather leggings that covered the top of the shoe and the calf to protect them from spatters.

spavaćica: Bosnia. Nightgown.

Spazierstock: Germany. Walking stick.

spectator: Pump shoe with contrasting toe and heel, often perforated in a decorative pattern.

speilp: Ireland. Gaelic word for armor.

speld: Holland. Pin.

spencer: Directoire and First Empire (1790–1815 C.E.). 1. Very short-waisted jacket worn by women. Made of color that contrasted with the dress. Named for Lord Spencer. 2. Man's short, buttoned, long-sleeved, tailless jacket. Generally made of light-colored velvet or wool. Attributed to Lord Spencer.

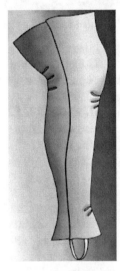

spatter dash

spencer cloak: Directoire and First Empire (1790–1815 C.E.). United Kingdom. Introduced in 1804, woman's cloak of worked net with short elbow-length sleeves.

spencer

spencer wig: Early Georgian (1700–1750 C.E.) to Late Georgian (1750–1790 C.E.). United Kingdom. Man's wig the exact shape unknown.

spencerette: Directoire and First Empire (1790–1815 C.E.). United Kingdom. Introduced in 1814, woman's fitted spencer with a low-cut neck edged with a lace frill.

spendlík: Czechoslovakia. Pin.

spenel: Germany. Old word for pin.

spennels: Byzantine and Romanesque (400–1200 C.E.). United Kingdom. Clasp or brooch.

spere: Elizabethan (1550–1625 C.E.) to Restoration (1660–1700 C.E.). Opening of a garment.

spets: Sweden. Generic name for lace.

speyer: *See* spere.

sphendome: Greek (3000-100 B.C.E.). Filet of felt, leather, or metal.

spice: Lithuania. Lace.

spider helmet: Elizabethan (1550–1625 C.E.). United Kingdom. A helmet with the skull covered by iron bars which hinged down to the shoulders and could be pushed up out of the way when desired.

spider work: Directoire (1790–1815 C.E.) to Bustle (1865–1890 C.E.). Cheap machine-made lace.

spiders: Czechoslovakia. Elaborate fillings in cutwork.

Spiderwork: United Kingdom. Opus araneum.

spiked shoes: Crinoline (1840–1865 C.E.). Men's shoes with spikes on soles for playing cricket. Patented in March, 1861.

spilenn: France. Breton for pin.

spillo: Italy. Pin.

spillo da petto: Italy. Brooch.

spinki: Poland. Cufflinks.

Spinula: Germany. Old High German word for a pin.

spiochag: Ireland. Gaelic word for purse or bag.

spiral witney: Crinoline (1840–1865 C.E.). Introduced in 1861, soft fabric with curls on the face, similar to a fur.

spit curl: *See* beau-catcher.

spit-boot: Early Georgian (1700–1750 C.E.) to Crinoline (1840–1865 C.E.). Man's shoe and gaiter combination forming boot that closed down the outside.

spitalfields: Silk fabric used to cover umbrellas.

Spitze: Germany. Lace.

spitzkappe: Austria. Woman's conical mushroom-shaped hat.

splay-footed shoes: *See* duck-billed shoes.

spleuchdan: Ireland. Gaelic word for a pair of spectacles.

splinter hat: *See* splyter-hat.

splints: Early Gothic (1200–1350 C.E.). Overlapping plates that protected the inside of the elbow in plate armor.

split stitch: A needlework in which the soft untwisted silk thread is split with the needle.

spliùchan: Ireland. Tobacco pouch.

splyter-hat: Renaissance (1450–1550 C.E.) to Elizabethan (1550–1625 C.E.). United Kingdom. Straw hat made of braided strips of split straw called splints.

spodic: Poland. Jewish man's high fur hat trimmed with plush.

spodky: Czechoslovakia. Trousers.

spódnica: Poland. Skirt.

spódniczka: Poland. Miniskirt.

spodniczka szkocka: Poland. Kilt.

spodnie: Poland. Trousers.

sponge cloth: Coarse, open leno weave, cotton fabric used for dishcloths.

spoon back: Bustle (1865–1890 C.E.). United Kingdom. Term used c.1885 for rounded folds of drapery on overskirt of a wool walking dress.

spoon bonnet: Crinoline (1840–1865 C.E.). United Kingdom. Popular from 1860 to 1864, woman's bonnet with a narrow brim reaching a tall spoon-shaped peak over the eyes.

spoon ring: Ring made from handle of sterling silver spoon.

sporan: Scotland. Purse of leather, fur, or long hair, plain or ornamented, worn hung from chain or strap around man's waist over kilt. Evening versions of hair or fur and hung from chain. Worn as part of the men's national dress suspended from a belt in the center front.

sportcolbert: Holland. Sport jacket.

sportjasje: Holland. Blazer.

sportpantalon: Holland. Jeans.

spring: Directoire and First Empire (1790–1815 C.E.). United Kingdom. Green.

spring boots: Late Georgian (1750–1790 C.E.). United Kingdom. Introduced in 1776, men's boots with a whalebone spring in the center back seam to control wrinkling.

sprzaczka: Poland. Buckle.

Spun-lo: Trade name for low luster rayon knitted fabric.

sraing: Ireland. Gaelic word for decorative lace.

sraja: India. Garland of flowers worn on the head.

srebro: Bosnia. Silver.

sribapha: India. A good quality muslin, sometimes dyed red or blue.

sringa: India. A crown made of horm.

srnkhalika: India. Necklace made of graduated beads.

sròin-eudach: Ireland. Pocket handkerchief.

stadium boot: Warm, insulated boot worn over shoes.

staeppe-scoh: Byzantine and Romanesque (400–1200 C.E.). United Kingdom. Term meaning a slipper.

stafford cloth: United Kingdom. Heavy curtain or drapery fabric.

stagbe: Nigeria. Handwoven cloth worn as a part of Ogboni Fraternity regalia.

stagen: Indonesia. Stiff cotton tie used to tie the kain in place.

staighinean: Ireland. Gaelic word for stays.

stalcadair: Ireland. Gaelic word for starch.

stalk button: Early Georgian (1700–1750 C.E.). Button with shank made of catgut.

stambouline: Turkey. Long coat worn by officials on formal occasions.

stamel: Early Gothic (1200–1350 C.E.). Coarse wool fabric, usually red in color.

stametto: *See* saia.

stamfortis: Early Gothic (1200–1350 C.E.). Strong, expensive fabric.

stamin: Coarse wool fabric, usually red.

stammel: Coarse wool fabric, usually red. Probably the same as stamin.

stamped velvet: Velvet with design stamped or crushed into the pile.

stamyn sengill: Renaissance (1450–1550 C.E.). United Kingdom. Worsted fabric made in Norfolk.

stanamsuka: India. 1. Woman's bodice-like garment. 2. A Persian-influenced knee or thigh-length tunic.

stand-fall collar: Directoire and First Empire (1790–1815 C.E.) to Bustle (1865–1890 C.E.). United Kingdom. Man's turned over collar. Inner layer referred to as the stand and the turned over part as the leaf or cape.

stand-fall collar

stanik: Poland. Bodice.

stany: Russia. Trousers.

star of the morning: Bustle (1865–1890 C.E.). Pale gray.

starch: Elizabethan (1550–1625 C.E.). United Kingdom. First used in 1560s for stiffening ruffs etc. Occasionally colored yellow or blue. Other countries used other colors.

starcher: Directoire and First Empire (1790–1815 C.E.) to Bustle (1865–1890 C.E.). United Kingdom. Man's starched cravat.

starrs: Ireland. Gaelic word for starch.

star-studded sky: China. Woman's hairstyle.

startop: *See* startups.

startups: Elizabethan (1550–1625 C.E.) to Restoration (1660–1700 C.E.). United States of America. Ordinary buckskin. Popular in 16th and 17th centuries with country folk.

statute cap: Elizabethan (1550–1625 C.E.). United Kingdom. Knitted cap. In 1570s, Queen Elizabeth ordered that all her countrymen should wear this cap on Sundays and holy days. This was an effort to promote the English hat making and wool industries.

staubfarbig: Germany. Khaki color.

stavaraka: India. A costly silk fabric made in Persia and imported to India.

stavrak: India. A heavy brocade.

stay hook: Early Georgian (1700–1750 C.E.) to Late Georgian (1750–1790 C.E.). Small decorative hook attached to the front of women's stays. From it hung the watch.

steatitis: Roman (753 B.C.E.–323 C.E.). Soapstone.

Stecknadel: Germany. Pin.

stecknōlde: *See* spenel.

steeple headdress: *See* hennin.

Steinkirk: Restoration (1660–1700 C.E.) to Early Georgian (1700–1750 C.E.). United Kingdom. Worn from c.1692 to 1730, long man's cravat, edged in lace, and worn loosely knotted under the chin with the ends pinned or left loose. Named for the Battle of Steinkirk, August 1692. Worn by women with the riding habit.

Steinmarder: Germany. Stone marten.

Stella: Crinoline (1840–1865 C.E.). In 1850, taffeta pardessus trimmed with ruches.

stem stitch: Diagonal, stepped stitches used for edges and lines.

stemma: Byzantine and Romanesque (400–1200 C.E.). Appearing around 430 C.E., variation on the diadem flared out at the top and had chains of gold that hung over the temples onto the cheeks. Later made with gemstones mounted on it.

stencil dye: A technique where stencils are used to retain undyed areas in the design.

stephane: Greek (3000-100 B.C.E.). Woman's tiara-like filet that was broad over the forehead and tapered on the sides. Originally it fitted the head; later versions stood out from the head and were decorated with repoussé.

stephanie: *See* stephane.

stephanos: Byzantine and Romanesque (400–1200 C.E.). Fabric diadem decorated with gems. Tied at the back of the head.

Steppnaht: Germany. Backstitch.

sternstichl: *See* stirnbindel.

stethodesme: *See* apodesme.

steutelreecx: Elizabethan (1550–1625 C.E.). Holland. Bunch of keys worn suspended from the waist.

stevige schoen: Holland. Brogue.

stibium: Egyptian (4000–30 B.C.E.). Compound used for staining eyelids and eyebrows.

sticharion: 1. White linen ecclesiastical robe worn in the Eastern Church. 2. Greek (3000–100 B.C.E.). Short-sleeved jacket.

stickerei: Even weave braid with an embroidered, scalloped, or notched edge.

Stickereiapplikation: Germany. Tuck embroidery.

sticking-plaster dress: Gay Nineties (1890–1900 C.E.). In 1893, a woman's tight black satin evening dress.

Stiefel: Germany. Boot.

Stiefelette: Germany. Bootee.

Stielstich: Germany. Stem stitch.

Stiful: Germany. Old High German term for boot.

stijf linnen: Holland. Buckram.

stikhar: Russia. Robe worn in religious ceremonies.

stiliaga: (1960–1970 C.E.). Russia. A male cool dresser.

stiog: Ireland. Gaelic word for a stripe on fabric.

stiom: Ireland. Gaelic word for hair lace; ribbon; or belt.

stiomag: Ireland. Gaelic word for small headband or hair fillet.

stìom-amhaich: Ireland. Scarf.

stìom-bhràghaid: Ireland. Neckband.

stippels: Holland. Polka dots.

stirnbindel: Poland. Jewish woman's forehead-band. Variously ornamented.

stirrup hose: Charles I and the Commonwealth (1625–1660 C.E.). United Kingdom. Men's long stockings with an instep strap instead of a sole. Worn over finer stockings when riding.

stirrup stockings: *See* stirrup hose.

stithópano: Greece. Breast kerchief.

Stival: Germany. Boot.

stivale: Italy. Boot.

stivaletto: Italy. Bootee.

stivali: 1. Early Gothic (1200–1350 C.E.). Lightweight, high, soft, summer boots usually black in color, although sometimes red. In France, were worn fitted to the leg; in United Kingdom, looser.

stivali grossi: Italy. Jackboot.

stoat: *See* stote.

stoca: Ireland. Stocking.

stocainn: Ireland. Gaelic word for stocking or hose.

stocainnis: Ireland. Gaelic word for stockings.

stock: Broad band worn as neck-cloth, usually fastened in back.

stock

stock buckle: Early Georgian (1700–1750 C.E.) to Crinoline (1840–1865 C.E.). Buckle fastening the stock at the back of the neck. Often decorated in gold, silver, or even set with jewels.

stock-drawers: Elizabethan (1550–1625 C.E.). United Kingdom. Stockings.

Stöcke mit Seele: Germany. Gadget cane.

stockinette: Knitted fabric made on circular machines.

stocking-purse: Directoire and First Empire (1790–1815 C.E.). Worn until 1820, small purse worn tucked through the belt or waistband. Usually made with a pair of metal rings and decorated with beaded tassels. *See also* miser's purse.

stof: *See* tkanina.

stofă: Romania. Cloth.

stoffelkappe: Switzerland. Woman's headdress.

Stoffhut: Germany. Cloth hat.

stoic: Ireland. Gaelic word for string of beads.

stola: 1. Roman (753 B.C.E.–323 C.E.). Typical garment of Roman woman, similar to men's tunica. Sleeved and worn over the tunica intima and belted twice, one on waist and other on hips. It had an insita, a panel, that hung from the belt in back where it trailed to the ground. 2. Holland. Stole. 3. Italy. Stole.

stole: Liturgical scarf worn by the priest over the amict and under the chasuble.

stölebelte: Norway. Silver belt made of discs of silver-gilt.

stomacher: 1. Renaissance (1450–1550 C.E.). United Kingdom. V- or U-shaped ornamental chest piece worn with the doublet. 2. Elizabethan (1550–1625 C.E.). Long elaborate panel in the center front of a bodice.

stomacher bodice: Romantic (1815–1840 C.E.). United Kingdom. Popular in 1820s, woman's bodice with revers (pelerine lapels) that ran from the shoulders to a V at the waist. Center of the V was filed with tucking.

stomper: Heavy shoe.

stone marten: Weasel fur that has a gray white underfur with dark brown guard hairs from the *Martes foina*.

storm serge: Hard, lightweight serge.

stote: Romantic (1815–1840 C.E.) to Bustle (1865–1890 C.E.). Method of sewing two pieces of fabric together so that there is no visible seam.

stövel: Sweden. Boot.

stovepipe hat: *See* chimney pot hat.

støvle: Denmark. Boot.

straight English skirt: Gay Nineties (1890–1900 C.E.). Woman's ankle-length day skirt with the fullness in the back made with gathers or pleats. Front and sides fitted with darts. It had a 12-inch pleated muslin balayeuse.

straight trousers: Romantic (1815–1840 C.E.) to Bustle (1865–1890 C.E.). United Kingdom. Men's trousers with legs an even width from top to bottom.

straight waistcoat: Romantic (1815–1840 C.E.) to Bustle (1865–1890 C.E.). United Kingdom. Tailoring term referring to single-breasted, lapel-less waistcoat.

strammel: Elizabethan (1550–1625 C.E.). Red.

Strampelhose: Germany. Rompers.

strandschoenen: Holland. Sand shoes.

stranlyng: Early Gothic (1200–1350 C.E.). Autumn fur of the squirrel.

strapontin: Bustle (1865–1890 C.E.). An 1885 bustle.

strapped pantaloons: Romantic (1815–1840 C.E.). United Kingdom. Men's pantaloons held down with straps under instep. Worn fashionably from 1820s to 1850; unfashionably to 1860.

strapul: Byzantine and Romanesque (400–1200 C.E.). United Kingdom. Laced legging worn by both genders.

strapula: Byzantine and Romanesque (400–1200 C.E.). United Kingdom. Laced legging.

Strasbourg cloth: Bustle (1865–1890 C.E.). Introduced in 1881, fabric resembling corduroy without the plush face.

Straussfeder: Germany. Ostrich plume.

stravestito a la todesco: Italy. Literally "dressed as a German."

straw: Elizabethan (1550–1625 C.E.). Light yellow.

streachlan: Ireland. Gaelic word for garter.

street sweeper: *See* balayeuse.

streimel: Poland. Jewish man's saucer hat with a flat fur brim worn on the sabbath.

strevíc: Czechoslovakia. Shoe.

strilinn: Ireland. Gaelic word for garter.

string glove: Glove crocheted or knitted in yarn.

string tie: Very narrow necktie.

stringbean: (1950–1960 C.E.). A long, narrow look in women's fashion.

stringhe: Renaissance (1450–1550 C.E.). Italy. Ribbons or laces which hung decoratively from garments.

striop: Ireland. Gaelic word for a red striped camlet used for the best clothes.

strips: Restoration (1660–1700 C.E.). United Kingdom. Bands of fabric, decorated or not, that crossed the shoulders where they met in a V to fill in a low-cut bodice.

Strohhut: Germany. Straw hat.

strój: Poland. Costume.

strokleurig: Holland. Strawberry colored.

strømpe: Denmark. Hosiery.

strophion: Greek (3000-100 B.C.E.). Early form of the corset made of linen, wool, or soft leather.

strophium: *See* strophion.

strossers: Elizabethan (1550–1625 C.E.). Men's knee- or ankle-length undergarments cut on the cross-grain to provide a snug fit over the legs.

strouding: United States of America. English scarlet red or dark navy blue fabric.

štrumfhozne: *See* triko.

strumpa: Sweden. Stocking.

Strumpf: Germany. Hosiery.

Strumpfhalter: Germany. Suspenders.

Strumpfhosen: Directoire and First Empire (1790–1815 C.E.). Germany. Literally "stocking breeches," men's breeches knitted so they might be as tight as possible.

stsepnoe: Russia. Chain-like lace.

stump work: Heavily padded or stuffed embroidery.

stupa: 1. Bulgaria. Young married woman's conical hat wrapped with a red kerchief. 2. India. A cone-like head ornament for men.

sturraic: Ireland. Gaelic word for a cap worn turned to one side.

sturraicean: Ireland. Gaelic word for undress for a woman's head.

stuth: Ireland. Gaelic word for camlet.

styfill: *See* boti.

su kom: India. Laos. Man's short coat.

sua hii: Laos. Woman's long-sleeved long coat.

sua saband thaut: Laos. Woman's ankle-length coat with inner and outer faces.

sua yan: Thailand. Talismanic handspun cotton jacket inscribed with a yantra.

suaicheantas: Scotland. Crest badge worn on band of boineid.

stringbean
See also photospread (Women's Wear). Dover Publications

sualef: Morocco. Jewish woman's wig.

sualef ez zoher: Morocco. Jewish bride's miter trimmed with pearls, jewels, and coins.

suarrow boots: Directoire and First Empire (1790–1815 C.E.). Popular boot name for the Polish general. Went out of fashion in 1802.

suba: *See* bunda.

subermalis: Roman (753 B.C.E.–323 C.E.). Coat or garment worn under the cuirass.

subha: Islamic rosary containing 39 or 99 beads.

sublagaculum: Roman (753 B.C.E.–323 C.E.). Loincloth, worn under the toga. Fashion taken from the Greeks, who got it from the Egyptians.

subligaculum: *See* sublagaculum.

sublime: *See* rose sublime.

sublom: *See* shubnam.

subnom: *See* shubnam.

subrichion: Greek (3000–100 B.C.E.). Woman's tunic.

subucula: *See* tunica interior.

suburban coat: (1960–1970 C.E.). United States of America. Woman's three-quarter-length car coat.

succinctorium: Band or scarf hanging from the girdle. Worn by the pope.

succinta: Roman (753 B.C.E.–323 C.E.). Wide belt worn by both genders to tuck up the garments at the waist for walking.

sucelaka: India. A generic term for costly garments.

suchi: India. A needle.

suci: India. Needles.

sucihastah: India. A needle.

sucisona: India. A silk embroidered with gold.

sucisutra: India. Sewing thread.

suckenie: Early Gothic (1200–1350 C.E.). Sideless gown.

suckeny: *See* surkney.

suclat: India. European broadcloth.

sucna: Romania. Pleated homespun woolen skirt with vertical stripes.

suculla ccahua: Bolivia. Worn by male children, a black tunic interwoven with three vertical red stripes.

sudan: Korea. Wide white cuffs on a bride's gown to cover her hands.

Sudanette: Trade name for pima cotton fabric in plain weave.

sudar: Biblical (Unknown–30 C.E.). Hebrew handkerchief. Worn on neck, shoulder, or forearm.

sudar sheal zero-othav: Biblical (Unknown–30 C.E.). Hebrew kerchief for the arm.

sudar shebetsavaro: Biblical (Unknown–30 C.E.). Hebrew kerchief for the head.

sūdārium: Roman (753 B.C.E.–323 C.E.). Literally "sweat cloth," a small piece of embroidered linen, similar to the modern handkerchief. Used by men to wipe perspiration from the face and hands.

suddha-ekavali: India. A pearl necklace with a gem at the center.

suddhaota: India. A bleached cotton.

suède: Leather with napped face.

suede cloth: Woven or knitted fabric finished to resemble suede leather.

suede kid: Kid leather that is napped on the flesh side.

suédoise: Bustle (1865–1890 C.E.). In 1875, deep blue gray.

suela: 1. Ecuador. A shoe sole. 2. Elizabethan (1550–1625 C.E.). Spain. Cowhide.

suéter: Portugal. Sweater.

suffibulum: Roman (753 B.C.E.–323 C.E.). Large white rectangle of fabric worn on the head, hanging down in the back and fastened under the chin with a brooch. Worn by the vestal virgins and priests during sacrifices.

súfres: Greece. Pleats.

sugar: Ireland. Gaelic word for a band for the neck.

sugar-loaf bonnet: Renaissance (1450–1550 C.E.). France. Man's high cap.

sugar-loaf bonnet

suggan: 1. United States. Common term for a long wool scarf. 2. Ireland and Scotland. Common term for a thick bed quilt or coverlet.

suit: 1. Ensemble of garments for men consisting of waistcoat, jacket, and trousers in the same material. 2. Late Georgian (1750–1790 C.E.). Set of matching cap, apron, handkerchief, and sleeve ruffles.

suit of ruffs: Elizabethan (1550–1625 C.E.) to Charles I and the Commonwealth (1625–1660 C.E.). United Kingdom. Neck ruff with matching hand ruffs.

suivez moi, jeune homme: *See* beau-catcher.

suji: Japan. Lines or stripes.

súkenice: Slovakia. Girl's fancy skirt.

sukhumasuttani: India. A fine thread.

sukienka: Poland. Frock.

sukkosa: Korea. Prepared or processed silk fabric.

śukla dhardīa: India. Sari with a simple border or white border.

suklang: Philippine Islands. Bachelor's basketry hat shaped like a shallow basket and tied in back with a looped cord.

suklatin: *See* suclat.

suklutun: *See* suclat.

sukmán: Bulgaria. Closed A-line tunic made of heavy fabric for winter and linen for summer.

sukmanki: *See* kaftany.

sukne: Czechoslovakia. Skirt.

sukni: *See* suckenie.

suknia: Poland. Gown or coat.

suknie: Poland. Clothing.

suknja: Bosnia, Croatia, and Serbia. Skirt.

sukno: *See* tkan'.

suk'oot'u: *See* sokch'ima.

sul: Korea. Tassel.

suliya: Nigeria. Yoruba man's lightweight agbada.

sulo bannang: Indonesia. Sa'dan-Toraja dark blue bead.

sulraeksu: *See* paji.

sultan sleeve: Romantic (1815–1840 C.E.). *See* sultana sleeve.

Sultana: Crinoline (1840–1865 C.E.). In 1853, mantle with revers in front. Had full sleeves bowed at elbow.

Sultana opera cloak: Crinoline (1840–1865 C.E.). In January, 1860, semicircular cloak with tasseled hood. Closed in front with loop and buttons.

sultana scarf: Crinoline (1840–1865 C.E.). United Kingdom. Woman's loose scarf of Oriental design worn over a canezou and tied below the waist.

sultana sleeve: Crinoline (1840–1865 C.E.). Woman's large hanging sleeve slit in the front. Popular with the casaque.

sultane: 1. Bustle (1865–1890 C.E.). Introduced in 1866, silk and mohair fabric, similar to alpaca, with alternating stripes in plain or satin. 2. Plumes of the purple gallinule, a sea bird.

sultane dress: Bustle (1865–1890 C.E.). United Kingdom. Introduced in 1877, woman's princess style day dress with a scarf fancifully draped to one side.

sultane jacket: Bustle (1865–1890 C.E.). United Kingdom. Introduced in 1889, woman's sleeveless zouave.

sulu: Fiji. Loincloth.

suman: Ashanti. Amulet.

sumane: Romania. Brown drugget coat embroidered with woolen cord.

šumbeqō: Ethiopia. Bronze.

šumboqō: *See* šumbeqō.

sumi: Japan. Black.

sumitsubo: Japan. Dressmaker's marking device.

sunburst: Brooch with jewels set in radiating pattern.

suncobran: *See* kišobran.

sundown: Broad-brimmed sun hat.

sungkit: Borneo. Bone needle used for embroidery.

sunglasses: Glasses with dark lenses.

sun-gum: Korea. Pure gold.

sunkit: *See* sungkit.

sun-ray skirt: Gay Nineties (1890–1900 C.E.). Accordion pleated skirt.

śunthiā: *See* phutā lugā.

suo: 1. Japan. A crested linen costume worn by the samurai. 2. Japan. Red dye.

suoyi: China. Palm-bark or straw rain cape.

super tunic: Byzantine and Romanesque (400–1200 C.E.). 1. Man's overgarment worn over the cote or tunic. Knee length, although ceremonial super tunics were ankle length. Sleeves were most commonly loose to elbow or wrist. 2. Woman's loose garment worn over the kirtle or tunic. Long loose sleeves.

superfine: Early Georgian (1700–1750 C.E.) to Late Georgian (1750–1790 C.E.). Broadcloth made of merino wool.

superhumeral: Byzantine and Romanesque (400–1200 C.E.). Wide jeweled collar worn by the ladies of the court.

superplie: Holland. Surplice.

supertasse: Elizabethan (1550–1625 C.E.). United Kingdom. Underproper used to support the large ruffs.

supertotus: *See* balandrana.

supha-kamkha: India. A brocaded woolen stuff.

supparium: Roman (753 B.C.E.–323 C.E.). Woman's short linen garment worn over the subucula.

suppléants: *See* appas postiches.

supportasse: *See* supertasse.

surabhi: India. Well-fitted clothing.

surah: Bustle (1865–1890 C.E.). India. Introduced in 1873, soft and brilliant silk fabric, twilled on both sides.

surangi: *See* al.

surat: Low-grade cotton fabric.

suravala: *See* coramo.

suravāla: *See* pyjamā.

suravara: *See* ijara.

suravarā: *See* pyjamā.

surc: *See* koteny.

surcingle: Ecclesiastical belt or girdle worn with the cassock.

surdut: Poland. Coat. *See also* suknia.

surf satin: (1910–1920 C.E.). United States of America. Heavy quality silk taffeta used for bathing costumes.

surfle: Obsolete term meaning to embroider.

suria: Tunisia. Woman's white or patterned slip worn under the mellia.

suriek: Borneo. Striped.

surihaku: Japan. Application of metallic foil on fabric.

surik: Borneo. Stripes.

surjan: Indonesia. Man's long sleeved jacket.

surkney: Early Gothic (1200–1350 C.E.). Man's loose cloak. Popular with shepherds and carters.

surmai: India. Navy blue.

surowa bawelna: Poland. Cotton wool.

surpaish: *See* sarpech.

surpied: *See* soulette.

surplice: Elizabethan (1550–1625 C.E.). Liturgical white linen robe with wide hanging sleeves. Knee or ankle length. Worn instead of the alb over the cassock.

surplice bodice: Bustle (1865–1890 C.E.). Introduced in 1881, woman's day bodice made with full gathers from the neck over the bust.

surplice collar: Collar with extended neckline that overlaps in front.

surplis: France. Surplice.

surt: *See* pastura.

surtout: Term referring to any man's long cloak or coat.

surtout àla Sultane: Directoire and First Empire (1790–1815 C.E.). Introduced in 1802, trained overdress worn over a white frock.

surtuk: Russia. From the French surtout, a frock coat.

surubuli: India. Red bordered sari.

suruwali ya Kolombo: Swahili. Bill-bottomed trousers.

suruwali ya uchinjo: Swahili. Literally "cut-off trousers," drainpipe trousers.

survāla: *See* corano.

surveyor's stick: Walking stick with a hidden pencil, pen, and inkstand.

susae: *See* susi.

susi: India. Cotton fabric with contrasting color stripes of cotton or silk.

suso: Japan. The hem or bottom edge of the skirt.

susomoyo: Japan. A design done diagonally across the bottom of the skirt; a woman's formal kimono.

susoyoke: Japan. Woman's wraparound slip.

suspender: One of pair of bands worn over shoulders to support trousers or skirt.

suspensor atletico: Spain. Jockstrap.

suspensores: Spain. Suspenders.

sussapine: Renaissance (1450–1550 C.E.) to Elizabethan (1550–1625 C.E.). Expensive silk fabric.

suthila: India. Any type of cotton stuff.

sutra: India. A neck chain.

sutradharah: India. Thread.

sutrahara: India. A chain necklace.

suvarna: India. Gold.

suvarnapadi: India. A gold brocade or tinsel printed stuff.

suvasana: India. A splendid garment.

suvasas: India. To be well dressed.

süveg: Hungary. Man's high, cylindrical cap.

suwak: Poland. Zipper.

suwet'o: Korea. Sweater.

suyacal: Guatemala. Rain cape.

suzushi: Japan. Raw silk.

svålltjá: Norway. Suede tunic.

švarkas: Lithuania. Coat.

svārki: *See* svarkas.

svasatura di abito-sbieco: Italy. Bell shaped.

svasthana: India. Loose trousers tied at the waist with silk tape.

svatební roucho: Slovakia. Wedding attire.

svechchhitika: India. Bracelet.

svetacinamsuka: India. A white Chinese cloth.

sviatocný kroj: Slovakia. Holiday costume.

svila: Bosnia, Croatia, and Serbia. Silk.

svityancali: India. A white fabric.

svyta: Ukraine. Man's brown woolen cloth coat trimmed in black.

swadeshi: India. Indian-made cloth.

swagger coat: (20th century). Coat with a very loose body or a flared body.

swagger stick: Short military stick carried in hand.

swallow's nests: Late Georgian (1750–1790 C.E.). Austria. Small cap sleeves set in the armseye over the normal sleeve. They could be of contrasting fabric.

swallow-tail bangs: China. Woman's bangs cut like the tail of a swallow.

swallow-tails: Crinoline (1840–1865 C.E.). United Kingdom. Man's evening coat.

Swami: Warp knit fabric of rayon and cotton.

swamy jewelry: India. Kind of gold and silver jewelry covered with grotesque mythological figures.

swanbill corset: Bustle (1865–1890 C.E.). United Kingdom. Introduced in 1876, woman's long, back-laced corset with a long metal busk in the center front to curve over the abdomen.

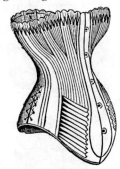

swanbill corset
Dover Publications

swan's down: Late Georgian (1750–1790 C.E.) to Crinoline (1840–1865 C.E.). Soft underplumage of a swan used to trim dresses, make powder puffs, pelerines, and muffs.

swansdown: *See* swan's down.

swanskin: Early Georgian (1700–1750 C.E.) to Crinoline (1840–1865 C.E.). Thick, twill weave flannel with a soft surface.

swar: Palestine. Simple copper bracelet.

swarry-doo: Gay Nineties (1890–1900 C.E.). In 1893, a brightly colored twill weave silk fabric.

Swatow grass cloth: China. Handwoven fabric of ramie fibers.

sweater: (1890–1900 C.E.). Bohemia. Made from Scottish Highland wool, a smooth white, black, or checkered tricot blouse with a roller collar.

sweater girl bra: (1950–1959 C.E.). Woman's bra with stiffened cones held together with whorls of stitching.

Swedish cuffs: Directoire and First Empire (1790–1815 C.E.). Deep cuffs with three buttons.

Swedish hat: Large felt hat style popularized by the musketeers. Inspired by the Swedish troops in the Thirty Years' War.

Swedish lace: Sweden. Simple torchon pillow lace.

sweter zapinany: *See* welniana kamizelka.

swiftlere: Byzantine and Romanesque (400–1200 C.E.). United Kingdom. Low slipper.

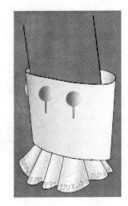

Swedish cuff

swing skirt: (1930–1940 C.E.). United States of America. Full circle or wide gored skirt popularized by teenagers to wear when dancing to swing music.

swire: Early Gothic (1200–1350 C.E.). Twist in embroidery.

Swiss belt: Romantic (1815–1840 C.E.). United Kingdom. Fashionable in 1815 and 1816, revisited in 1860s, 1880s, and 1890s, woman's waistband wider in the center front where it pointed on top and bottom. After 1860s, sometimes laced in the center front.

Swiss bodice: Bustle (1865–1890 C.E.). United Kingdom. Woman's velvet bodice with a Swiss belt and worn over a sleeved chemisette.

Swiss cambric: Muslin or lawn.

Swiss embroidery: Eyelet embroidery.

switch
Dover Publications

Swiss mountain hat: Romantic (1815–1840 C.E.). Introduced in 1819, hat with soft brim that drooped over the face. Trimmed with ostrich plumes.

swiss muslin: Thin, sheer muslin with raised dots or figures.

switch: A length of hair, human or artificial, used to pad out, enhance, or lengthen a woman's hairstyle.

sworl: *See* swire.

swyrell: *See* swire.

syassu: Korea. Pleats.

šydas: Lithuania. Veil.

synthesis: Roman (753 B.C.E.–323 C.E.). Tunic worn for meals. Only worn in public during the Saturnalia.

syool: Korea. Shawl.

šyras: Lithuania. Crepe; veil.

syrma: Greek (3000-100 B.C.E.). Long, trailing robe worn by actors.

szafir: Poland. Sapphire.

szal: Poland. Shawl.

szary: Poland. Gray.

szkarlat: Poland. Crimson. *See also* purpura.

szkarlatny: Poland. Crimson.

szlafrok: Poland. Dressing gown.

sznurowadlo: Poland. Shoelace.

szpilka: Poland. Hairpin.

sztruks: Poland. Corduroy.

szük gatya: Hungary. Fitted trousers.

szür: Hungary. Long white felt coat with full-cut sleeves, wide lapels, and a broad sailor collar. It is worn like a cape, being held in place across the chest with a decorative leather strap and large buttons. It is often elaborately decorated with cotton or silk embroidery or applique in patterns of carnations, roses, or tulips.

szür-kabát: Hungary. Shepherd's szür with sleeves which are used.

szürke: Hungary. Gray.

szurtuk: Romania. Fabric.

T

ta: New Zealand. Maori term meaning to net.

taahuka: Australia. Maori large inner garment.

taalapat: Thailand. Monk's ceremonial fan.

taapahu: Australia. Maori dogskin cloak made by sewing whole skins together.

taapeka: Australia. Maori bandolier made in tapestry.

taatara: Australia. Maori thick, warm cape decorated with short pieces of undressed flax.

taatua hume: Australia. Maori bleached flax or flax fiber belt with ends that taper to a point.

taawakawaka: Australia. Maori cloak with weft ends highlighted.

tab collar: Standing band collar with a front opening.

tabard: Late Gothic (1350–1450 C.E.). Ceremonial military coat with free hanging front and back and short wing sleeves. Worn primarily in tournaments.

tabardo: 1. *See* manto militar. 2. Spain. Tabard.

tabaret: Strong silk upholstery fabric with satin stripes.

tabarete: Spain. Tabaret.

tabbaard: *See* tabberd.

tabbaert: Elizabethan (1550–1625 C.E.). Holland. Tabard.

tabberd: Holland. Tabard.

tabbinet: *See* tabinet.

tabby: 1. Early Georgian (1700–1750 C.E.). Plain weave silk moiré taffeta. *See also* attaby. 2. *See* plain weave.

tabi

tabi: Japanese. Ankle-high, white cotton stockings with a stiffened sole and a separate stall for the large toe.

tabie-nishiki: Japan. Japanese imitations of European textiles.

tabijn: Holland. Tabby.

tabine: *See* tabby.

tabinet: Ireland. Poplin fabric, sometimes watered.

tablet: Elizabethan (1550–1625 C.E.). United Kingdom. Rare term used to refer to an apron. Derived from the French tablier.

tablier: France. Apron.

tablier skirt: Crinoline (1840–1865 C.E.). United Kingdom. Popular in 1850s and 1860s, skirt with descending trim in center front to suggest a decorative apron.

tablier tunic: Bustle (1865–1890 C.E.). United Kingdom. Popular in 1875, triangular overskirt with one corner reaching the hem of the skirt in front and the others fastened to the basque of the bodice.

tablion: Byzantine and Romanesque (400–1200 C.E.). Very elaborate decorative oblong or square patch on the front and back edge of the imperial mantle. Often embroidered and jeweled. Color indicated status of the wearer.

taboret: Embroidery frame.

tabouret: *See* taboret.

tabrizi: India. A silk or brocade fabric from Tabriz in Persia.

taces: Early Gothic (1200–1350 C.E.). Skirt of plate metal reaching from the waist to mid-thigh.

tache: Early Gothic (1200–1350 C.E.). Clasp.

tachi-kake: Japan. A trouser style.

tackies: South Africa. Tennis shoes.

tackover: Early Gothic (1200–1350 C.E.). United Kingdom. Overlap of the pleat at the top of the back vent of a man's skirted coat.

tacley: China. Beads of all kinds.

taenggi: Korea. Pigtail ribbon.

taenia: Greek (3000-100 B.C.E.). Headband or filet.

t'aesahye: Korea. Silk shoes worn by upper class men and boys.

tafailah: *See* qatifah-i-purbi.

tafetá: Portugal. Sarsenet.

tafetán: Spain. Taffeta.

taffeta: Smooth, glossy, plain weave fabric that is the same on both sides. Has considerable body.

taffeta coutil: Crinoline (1840–1865 C.E.). Introduced in 1847, silk and cotton blend fabric with blue or lilac stripes on a white ground.

taffeta crape: Crinoline (1840–1865 C.E.). New taffeta with creped face.

taffeta d'Annecy: Crinoline (1840–1865 C.E.). Introduced in 1862, cotton and wool blend fabric.

taffeta de Suez: Crinoline (1840–1865 C.E.). Introduced in 1862, thin cotton and wool blend fabric.

taffeta lustré: Late Georgian (1750–1790 C.E.). France. Lustring.

taffetaline: Bustle (1865–1890 C.E.). Introduced in 1876, form of mohair.

taffetán: Ecuador and Guatemala. Taffeta.

taffetane: Ecuador and Guatemala. Taffeta.

taffetas: France. Taffeta.

taffetine: Plain weave, lightweight lining fabric.

Taft: Germany. Taffeta.

tafta: 1. Turkey. Monochrome, lightweight, satin weave, silk fabric. 2. *See* qatifah-i-purbi.

tafuchóu: China. Taffeta.

tafzijde: Holland. Taffeta.

tagal straw: Straw from Manila hemp.

tagalsaek: Korea. Yellowish brown.

tagelmoust: Tuareg man's headcloth. Usually blue or white and is tied to cover the face.

tagikeri: Samoa. Dungarees.

tagilmus: Algeria. Ten-foot-long strip of indigo blue linen worn as a man's turban.

taglioni: Crinoline (1840–1865 C.E.). United Kingdom. Man's greatcoat, commonly double breasted, with very large flat collar and wide lapels. The coat had a fitted waist with full, short skirts without pleats. Each side of the skirt had a cross or slit pocket. The sleeves had turned-back cuffs. The collar, lapels, and cuffs were of quadrilled satin velvet. The entire coat was edged in twill binding. It was named for the ballet-master Filippo Taglioni.

Taglioni frock coat: Romantic (1815–1840 C.E.). United Kingdom. Popular from 1838 to 1842, a man's single-breasted frock coat with short, full skirts. It had a wide collar and cape. The hips had slash or flap pockets. The back vent was not pleated, but did have a tack-over.

tagora: Mexico. Loincloth.

tagulemust: Tuareg. A man's veil worn at all times.

tahrireh: Palestine. Cotton cord used in embroidery.

taifeid: Ireland. Gaelic word for taffeta.

taihakuzan: Japan. Literally "great white mountain," ancient nishiki pattern.

taiko obi: Japan. Drum-shaped obi worn by married women.

tai-k'ou: *See* daikou.

tail clout: Elizabethan (1550–1625 C.E.) to Restoration (1660–1700 C.E.). United Kingdom. Baby's napkin or diaper.

tail coat: Man's full-dress coat.

tailasân: Arabia. In ninth century C.E., yellow Persian mantle worn by Christians and non-Islamic believers.

tailleur: France. Tailor.

tãilliūr: Ireland. Tailor.

taillour: Byzantine and Romanesque (400–1200 C.E.) to Renaissance (1450–1550 C.E.). United Kingdom. Middle English term for tailor.

tailored coat: (1910–1920 C.E.). Introduced in 1910, a woman's coat cut in severe English cut. Always worn buttoned.

tailored suit: Bustle (1865–1890 C.E.). A woman's jacket and skirt combination suit, cut in a masculine line.

tailor's goose: Heavy, pointed iron heated by setting on a hot stove or radiator.

taisha: Japan. Brown.

tai-shih: *See* daishi.

taist: Ireland. Gaelic word for button.

tàiyángjìng: China. Sunglasses.

taj: 1. India. A small conical cap worn by Muslims. 2. Mohammedan. Tall, conical hat.

tāj: Arabia. Low crown or coronet.

tajehbaf: *See* qatifah-i-purbi.

tajvu: India. A tattoo.

takai buriet: Borneo. Seat mat.

takajo-tabi: Japan. Literally "falconer's tabi," tabi with hard soles so they may be worn without shoes.

takan: *See* qatifah-i-purbi.

takaschiya: India. Long coat with a round skirt that is tied on the right side.

takashimada: Japan. Formal bridal hairdo.

takauchiyah: India. Unlined coat that ties on one side.

takelmi: Nigeria. Poor man's sandals of undressed cowhide or car tires.

takenaga: Edo (1600–1867 C.E.). Japan. A broad band used to fasten a woman's hairstyle.

takhfīfa: Arabia. Simple winding cloth.

takitaki: Australia. Maori single layer sandal made of Cordyline.

takke: 1. Hebrew woman's cotton bonnet. 2. Turkey. Skull cap.

tala: China. Slippers.

talabanr: China. Wooden slippers; clogs.

talabo: Indonesia. Flat copper armband worn by upper class Sa'dan-Toraja boys.

talafa: Samoa. Side whiskers.

talama: Samoa. Black dye.

talapaga: India. Small piece of cloth worn as a headdress.

talar: Ankle-length robe.

talaria: Winged shoes or sandals.

talaris tunic: Long-sleeved, long-girded tunic worn by women and elderly men.

talavantika: India. Anantariya worn in a fan-shaped style.

talaria
See also photospread (Foot and Legwear).

talede: Indonesia. Sa'dan-Toraja man's penis support. *See also* tusuk.

talee: *See* tali.

talepā: India. Turban.

talepaga: *See* talapaga.

talhakimt: Nigeria. Glass or agate amulet formed like a ring.

talhatina: Nigeria. Neck ornament.

tali: India. Gold ornament worn on a slender cord about the neck. It is given to a bride by the groom in wedding ceremony, similar to the wedding ring of the Western World. *See also* talee.

tali bate': Indonesia. Sa'dan-Toraja headcloth.

tali 'ele 'ele: Samoa. Apron.

tali katarrung: *See* tali tarrung.

tali pakkaridi': Indonesia. Plaited hairband.

tali tarrung: Indonesia. Sa'dan-Toraja headdress in the shape of fruit. *See also* tali katarrung.

talika: India. A single soled shoe.

talisman: Charm or amulet worn on person for protection.

Talleyrand collar: A stand-up collar used on coats. *See also* Robespierre collar.

tallien redingote: Bustle (1865–1890 C.E.). United Kingdom. Introduced in 1867 by Worth, a redingote cut with heart-shaped neckline and a full back. It was trimmed with a sash that bowed on the sides with the ends hanging down and ending in bows. It was made in a fabric to match the dress, or in black silk.

tallith: Hebrew. Prayer shawl worn by men age 13 years and up. It is made of silk or wool; in white, with black or blue stripes across the ends. Silk talliths are 54–96 inches long and 36–72 inches wide; wool talliths are larger. A wool tallith is made of two lengths sewn together with a stitching covered by a narrow band of silk ribbon that is woven with silver or gold.

tallith katan: *See* arba kanphoth.

talma: *See* poncho.

Talma cloak: Crinoline (1840–1865 C.E.). United Kingdom. 1. Popular in 1850s, a man's evening knee-length cloak with a wide turned-down collar and a silk lining. It was named for a French actor of the Empire period. 2. In 1851, a woman's large circular silk cape with no lining.

Talma lounge: Gay Nineties (1890–1900 C.E.). United Kingdom. Introduced in 1898, a man's lounge jacket with raglan sleeves and a straight cut front.

Talma maltese: Crinoline (1840–1865 C.E.). A 29-inch-long talma, cut in a three-quarter circle and the hood cut bias. It buttoned up the front.

Talma mantle: Crinoline (1840–1865 C.E.). United Kingdom. Popular from 1850 to 1867, a circular velvet or satin cloak, resembling a shawl. It occasionally had a hood, cape or collar.

Talma overcoat: Gay Nineties (1890–1900 C.E.). United Kingdom. Introduced in 1898, a man's raglan overcoat with extra wide armseyes.

talma Zuleika: Crinoline (1840–1865 C.E.). In 1855, a taffeta talma with two lace flounces. It was trimmed with satin ribbon.

talonera: Ecuador. The heel strap of a sandal.

talpa: Italy. Mole.

taluqdari cap: India. A black velvet cap with a pointed front and back that are joined with a piece of fabric on the top of the head.

tamanco: Portugal. Clog, wooden shoe.

tamatis: Thong sandal with straw sole with rubber bottom. The thongs are made of velvet.

tamative: Crinoline (1840–1865 C.E.). Introduced in 1863, a light material similar to a heavy grenadine.

Tamba cloth: Japan. Striped cotton fabric. It was first made in Saji-machi, in the Temba district, but it is now made in many other places. It has an undyed waste silk woof and a cotton warp.

tambour: 1. *See* farthingale. 2. A circular frame made of one hoop that fits inside another. It is used to hold embroidery while it is worked. 3. Chain stitch embroidery on cloth or net.

tambour lace: Chain-stitch lace worked on a net ground.

tambour muslin: Plain weave cotton fabric.

tambour work: Used to decorate machine net, a technique in which surface chain stitches are form with a hooked needle.

tambourine bag: Round, flat handbag.

tambouring: Late Georgian (1750–1790 C.E.) to Crinoline (1840–1865 C.E.). Popular from 1780 to 1850, a form of white-work embroidery done on a frame resembling a drum. It was done with a hook which creates a continuous chain stitch.

tamein: Burma. Woman's draped garment similar to Indian sari.

tamentika: Tuareg. A man's blue cotton cummerbund.

tamise: Bustle (1865–1890 C.E.). Introduced in 1876, a soft wool fabric with a little silk woven in.

tammy: Early Georgian (1700–1750 C.E.). Fine worsted cloth, often with glazed finish. *See also* stamin.

tam-o'-shanter: Scotland. Cap with a tight headband and a full, flat top. Traditionally topped with a large pompon of heavy brushed wool.

tamoto: Japan. The bag-like pockets of kimono sleeves.

tampa: *See* touca.

tampan: Indonesia (Sumatra). Small rectangular ceremonial cloth. *See also* phaa chet naa.

tamra: India. Copper.

Tamsui hat: Straw hat similar to Panama.

tan: 1. Korea. Heavyweight, opaque silk fabric. 2. Yellowish brown color.

tanasukha: India. A fine muslin.

tanbal: Korea. Bobbed hair.

tanch'u: Korea. Button; shirt stud.

tanch'u kumong: Korea. Buttonhole.

tanga: Portugal. Loincloth.

tangalia: India. A woman's woolen loincloth worn by the Bharwad caste.

tangerine: Brilliant yellowish orange.

tanggi: Borneo. Sun hat.

tanggok: Borneo. Necklaces.

tango corset: (1910–1920 C.E.). Short, lightweight corset worn for dancing.

tang-phuc: Vietnam. Mourning clothes.

tanhwa: Korea. Shoes.

taniko: New Zealand. Maori term for ornamental colored borders on fabric or garments.

tanjeeb: *See* tanjib.

tanjib: India. Muslin. *See also* tanzeb.

tantoor: Syria. A headdress consisting of a 20-inch silver horn and two veils. The horn is worn atop a snug-fitting cap and tied to the forehead with two cords that hang to the ground, ending in tassels. A long fringed veil hangs from the end of the horn and a second, thinner veil covers the face.

tantra: India. The warp of fabric.

tantu: India. Yarn or thread.

tanutra: India. A bodice.

tanzeb: India. Fine white cotton fabric; jacket.

tanzen: Japan. A cotton padded kimono worn in the winter months.

tao 'ofu: Samoa. Waistcoat.

t'ao t'ieh: China. Monster mask, a common embroidery pattern.

taonga: Samoa. Flax cloth.

tàoshan: China. Pullover.

tàoxié: China. Overshoes.

tàoxiù: China. Oversleeve.

taozi: China. Silk ribbon; silk braid.

tap shoe: Shoe with special metal toe and heel.

tapa: Polynesia. A cloth made from the pounded bark of the paper mulberry. *See also* siapo.

tapa cloth: Fabric made from the beaten fibers of paper mulberry tree.

tapada: Peru. Woman's skirt, cloak, and shawl worn to completely cover the figure.

tapalo: Coarse fabric scarf worn in Spanish American countries.

taparrabos: Spain. Loincloth.

tap-de: Vietnam. Apron.

tape lace: Any lace made mainly of tape.

tapih: Java. A rectangular textile worn wrapped around a woman's hips.

tapis: 1. Indonesia (Philippine Islands). Wide sash or girdle. 2. Sumatra. Woman's heavy cotton sarong.

tapisserie: France. Literally "tapestry," a weaving in the tapestry technique.

tapisserie de broderie: France. Embroidered wall hanging.

tapisserie de petit point: France. Wall hanging worked in petit point.

tapiz: Ecuador and Guatemala. Tapestry.

tappert: Late Gothic (1350–1450 C.E.). Germany. A man's gown with the sleeves edged in fur.

taqiyeh: Palestine. A man's white cotton skull cap worn under the libbadeh.

taqsireh: Palestine. A woman's expensive short jacket, usually lined with a bold checked cotton. It is a square-cut, waist-length jacket with short sleeves. It is made of broadcloth, felt, velvet, or silk.

tara: *See* taatara.

tarabulsi: Palestine. Woman's colored sash.

tarahara: India. A single strand of big pearls.

taralapratibandha: India. Pearl necklace.

tarangaka: India. Ear ornament inset with rubies.

taratara: *See* taatara.

tarbi'ah: Palestine. Fine silk veil.

tarboosh: Arabia. Brimless felt skullcap of Greek origin.

tarbouch: Italy. Large, stiff, red or black fez decorated with suede.

tarbush istanbuli: Palestine. Man's tall, stiff hat shaped like an inverted flowerpot. It is worn by Ottoman officials, Turkish soldiers, and urbanites.

tarbush maghribi: Palestine. Man's red felt hat worn on top of the libbadeh.

tarbuzi: India. Bottle green.

tarf: *See* turf.

tarfe: Obsolete term for brim of hat.

targe: Scotland. The circular shield, ornamented with brass studs, carried by the Highlanders.

tarbush istanbuli

tarha: Egypt. Woman's head veil.

tarlatan: Thin, loosely woven, transparent, slightly stiffened muslin.

Tarleton helmet: Bustle (1865–1890 C.E.) to 1920s. Named for Sir Banastre Tarleton, a helmet with a leather skull, a peak, a puggaree-like sash on the bottom edge, and a fore-and-aft bearskin crest.

tarong-bugalong: Philippine Islands. Long skirt of pineapple cloth.

tarpus: Turkey. Woman's tall, pointed cap.

tarpya: India. A rough silk cloth.

tars: Obsolete silk fabric.

tarse: *See* tars.

tartan: Scotland. Twilled woolen or worsted plaid fabric woven in distinctive patterns and colors. It was originally worn only by members of the clan who bore the name of the chief or were his blood relatives.

tartan velvet: Short-napped velvet patterned in a tartan plaid.

tartanella: Tartan plaid fabric made from a combination of cotton or linen and wool.

tartarian: Romantic (1815–1840 C.E.). Introduced in 1823, a soft, light fabric that supposedly never creased.

tartarin: Early Gothic (1200–1350 C.E.). Cloth from Tarsus that was very fine and costly.

tartarine: Silk fabric made by the Tartars.

tartaryn: Early Gothic (1200–1350 C.E.). Expensive fabric, composition unknown.

tas van de Hooglanders: Holland. Sporran.

tasca: Italy. Pocket.

Tasche: Germany. Pocket.

Taschentuch: Germany. Handkerchief.

tash: East Indies. Silk and gold or silver thread fabric.

tashashit: Skullcap with tassel.

tashka: Russia. Sabretache.

tasiemka: *See* wstazka.

tāsile: *See* komānam.

tasna: Bosnia. Handbag.

tassar: 1. India. A good quality fabric. 2. *See* qatifah-i-purbi.

tasse: Early Gothic (1200–1350 C.E.). One of overlapping plates forming the skirt in armor.

tasseau: Renaissance (1450–1550 C.E.). Triangle of fabric, often black, that filled in the neckline.

tassel: *See* tasseau.

tasseled handkerchief: Elizabethan (1550–1625 C.E.). Pocket handkerchief trimmed with tassels at the corners. It often had fringed edge.

tasses: Late Gothic (1350–1450 C.E.). Small rectangular plates worn over the thigh in a suit of armor.

tasset: *See* tasse.

tassettes: Elizabethan (1550–1625 C.E.) to Restoration (1660–1700 C.E.). Steel pieces attached to the bottom of the corselet and worn to protect the thighs in armor.

tasso: Italy. Badger fur.

tasuki: Japan. The cord used to tie up the kimono sleeves and still allow the arms freedom of movement.

tàszli: Romania. Puckered collar.

tatamis: Thong sandal with a straw sole with a rubber bottom. The thongs are made of velvet.

tatara: New Zealand. Maori term for a cape with a white ground covered on the outside with black dried and curled flax.

tatas: *See* leading strings.

tatbandpuri: *See* qatifah-i-purbi.

tātē ukō: Ethiopia. Kafa king's crown.

tātēn dībabō: Ethiopia. King's parasol of bamboo and green cloth with a bamboo handle.

tate-nishiki: Japan. Nishiki with pattern woven in warp threads.

tater: Late Gothic (1350–1450 C.E.) to Renaissance (1450–1550 C.E.). Phonetic spelling for the tetour, a hood.

tatibin: Indonesia (Sumatra). Small, narrow ceremonial cloth.

tatquevluq: United States of America. Eskimo's sacred wooden mask.

tattersall: Gay Nineties (1890–1900 C.E.). Introduced in 1891, a vividly checked fabric similar to horse cloth.

tattersall vest: Gay Nineties (1890–1900 C.E.). United Kingdom. Popular from 1895 on, a man's single-breasted sport waistcoat in small checks. It had no collar, six buttons down the front, and four flap pockets.

tatting: Knotted lace worked with the fingers and a shuttle.

tatting lace: *See* tatting.

tattsuke: Japan. A style of trousers.

tatua: New Zealand. Maori generic term for belts.

tatua-pupara: New Zealand. Maori man's five- to six-inch-wide belt of woven flax.

tau: Indonesia (Timor). Indigo dye.

taulima: Samoa. Bracelet.

taupe: 1. Very dark, warm gray. 2. France. Mole.

tauri: New Zealand. Maori anklet or bracelet.

tauri koomore: New Zealand. Maori term for a wrist or ankle band.

tautaliga: Samoa. Earring.

tauvae: Samoa. Anklet.

tavancher: France. Breton for apron.

tavestock: Early Gothic (1200–1350 C.E.). Broadcloth.

tavlin: Biblical (Unknown–30 C.E.). Hebrew word for clavi.

tawar: *See* qatifah-i-purbi.

tawdry lace: Obsolete name for lace or braid worn at neck as tie.

tawney: Early Gothic (1200–1350 C.E.). Yellowish tan color.

Taxíria: Greece. Full, ankle-length, silk knickers.

tay áo: Vietnam. Sleeve.

tayu-kanoko: Japan. Painted imitation of tied kanoko.

tayyet sunnára: Palestine. Woman's round, cotton crochet cap. It is sometimes trimmed with glass beads or coins and is worn at home.

tchapka: *See* czapka.

tche djenji: Timbuktu. A C-shaped anklet with knobs on the ends of the C.

tchédik: Hebrew's soft boots.

tcherkeska: Russia. Lightweight, full-skirted wool coat.

tdinjok: Laos. Separately woven border attached to a woman's sarong.

tea jacket: Bustle (1865–1890 C.E.). United Kingdom. Introduced in 1887, this jacket slowly replaced the teagown in popularity. Fitted in the back and loose in the front, it had tight sleeves trimmed with lace.

tea rose: Dainty yellowish pink.

teagown: Bustle (1865–1890 C.E.). United Kingdom. Loose dress worn without corsets. It was commonly worn with a lace and muslin mob cap. Originally worn only by married women, in the 1880s it became an acceptable fashion for young ladies.

teakete: United States of America. Hawaiian term for jacket.

tear: Portugal. Weaver's loom.

tebenna: Greek (3000-100 B.C.E.). This Etruscan wrap was a semi-circular cloak worn under one arm, over the other shoulder or around the back. Commonly made of wool with colored borders.

techeleth: Biblical (Unknown–30 C.E.). Hebrew word for the color sky blue. Made from a mollusk.

tecidos: Portugal. Textiles.

teck: *See* four-in-hand.

teddies: United States of America. *See* camibockers.

teddybear coat: Winter coat of alpaca pile fabric.

teddy-bears: United States of America. *See* camibockers.

tegua: Buckskin sandal.

teia: Portugal. Cloth; textile.

teiliwr: Wales. Tailor.

tejadillo: *See* touca.

tejano: Spain. Denim.

tejedor: Ecuador and Guatemala. Weaver.

tejer: Ecuador and Guatemala. To weave.

tejido: Ecuador and Guatemala. Fabric.

tejido arrugado: Spain. Seersucker.

tejido calado: Spain. Eyelet fabric.

tejido con pelo largo: Spain. Fleece.

tejido de punto elástico: Spain. Rib knit.

tejido de punto liso: Spain. Jersey.

tejido esponjoso: Spain. Terry cloth.

tejido liso: Spain. Jersey.

tejón: Spain. Badger fur.

tekat menekat: Malaysia. Gold and silver embroidery on velvet and silk.

tekhelet: Hebrew. Blue purple.

tekko: Japan. A hand protector; essentially a mitten with the fingertips cut off.

tela: 1. Italy. Linen. 2. *See* paño.

tela caucho: Ecuador. Synthetic fabric.

tela cerata: Italy. Oilcloth.

tela de algodón mercerizado: Spain. Tussore.

tela de aspecto granulado: Spain. Granite.

tela de Jouy: Spain. Toile de Jouy.

tela de lino: Italy. Linen cloth.

tela grossolana: Italy. Lockram.

tela para carpa: Spain. Canvas.

tela Tagliata: Italy. Cut linen edged with buttonhole stitches and linked into a guipure lace.

tela tirata: Italy. Drawn-thread work.

telar de otale: Guatemala. Woman's hip loom.

telegraph blue: Bustle (1865–1890 C.E.). In 1882, a color similar to cadet blue. It was named for the blue telegraph paper used in France.

telescope parasol: Directoire and First Empire (1790–1815 C.E.). Introduced in 1811, this parasol had a stick that could be lengthened by pulling it out like a telescope.

telescope-crown hat: Hat with high draped crown resembling a section of a telescope.

telia rumal: India. A square double-ikat headcloth or loincloth.

tellex: Greek (3000-100 B.C.E.). Hair binding worn by athletes.

telpek: Turkmenistan. Man's flamboyant cap shaped like a pillbox. It has a wide, turned-up brim.

tembe: *See* kere.

tembleques: Peru. Ornamental comb of very fine metal threads which tinkle as they move.

temiak: Eskimo jacket or coat.

temple spectacles: Early Georgian (1700–1750 C.E.). Introduced in 1727 by Edward Scarlett, London optician, these spectacles were held in place with rigid sidepieces.

templers: Late Gothic (1350–1450 C.E.). Ornamental bosses worn over the hair in chignons over the temples. They were held up by a band circling the head across the forehead.

temples: *See* templers.

templettes: *See* templers.

tencel: (1990–1999 C.E.). A fabric that drapes like rayon and takes dye well.

tene: *See* teniske.

teneçir: Turkmenistan. Temple pendants that hang on each side of an unmarried woman's face.

Tenerife lace: Canary Islands. Lace of wheel and circle design.

ten-gallon hat: Large, broad-brimmed cowboy hat.

tenggak: Ecuador. Necklace.

tenida de gimnasia: Spain. Gym suit.

teñir: Ecuador and Guatemala. To dye.

teniske: Bosnia. Sneakers.

tenisówski: Poland. Canvas shoes.

tennis cloth: United Kingdom. Bleached cotton, basket weave fabric.

tennis flannel: United Kingdom. Lightweight, worsted, twill weave fabric.

tennis shoe: Elizabethan (1550–1625 C.E.) to present. United Kingdom. Men's soft-soled shoes invented for playing tennis. In 1878, tennis shoes with India rubber soles were introduced for playing lawn tennis.

tenugui: Japan. A headcloth.

tenzin-mage: Meizi (1867–1912 C.E.). Japan. A woman's hairstyle.

tephillin: Hebrew. Two small leather or wooden boxes containing passages from the Pentateuch worn strapped to forehead and left arm in obedience to directions in the Pentateuch.

terai hat: Bustle (1865–1890 C.E.). United Kingdom. Introduced in 1880s, a riding hat for wear in tropical lands. It was made of fur or wool felt with a short crown, a three- to five-inch brim and a metal vent through the crown for ventilation.

terbi' a: Palestine. Common veil of white, light silk or translucent cotton. It is worn over the shatweh.

terciopelo: 1. Guatemala and Mexico. Rayon velvet. 2. Ecuador and Spain. Velvet.

terciopelo acordonado: Spain. Gros velours.

terciopelo aplastado: Spain. Crushed velvet.

terciopelo chifón: Spain. Chiffon velvet.

terciopelo con dibujo multicolor: Spain. Genoa velvet.

terciopelo de Utrect: Spain. Utrecht velvet.

terciopelo en relieve: Spain. Raised velvet.

terciopelo labrado: Spain. Cisele velvet.

Teresa: Late Georgian (1750–1790 C.E.). Popular in 1770s and 1780s, a ladies' light gauze scarf worn over the head. *See also* Thérèse.

tergal: Madagascar. Imported French polyester.

terlik: Turkey. Woman's soft leather indoor boots.

terliz: Spain. Drill.

terra-cotta: Red orange.

terranine: Bustle (1865–1890 C.E.). In 1886, a shade of brown.

terre de Cuba: Romantic (1815–1840 C.E.). United Kingdom. Warm tan color.

terre de Pologne: Romantic (1815–1840 C.E.). France. Deep shade of yellow, almost brown.

terre d'Egypte: Romantic (1815–1840 C.E.). France. Brick red.

terrendam: Directoire and First Empire (1790–1815 C.E.). Introduced in 1806, an Indian muslin.

terrier overcoat: Crinoline (1840–1865 C.E.). United Kingdom. Introduced in 1853, a man's pilot coat.

terry cloth: Soft cotton fabric with uncut loops on both sides, often used for toweling.

Terylene: (1940–1950 C.E.). First discovered in 1941, a polyester fiber produced in the United Kingdom.

terzi: *See* darzi.

tesashi: United States of American. Hawaii. Denim elbow-length arm protector.

tesoura: Portugal. Scissors.

testière: Renaissance (1450–1550 C.E.). France. Metal skull-cap.

tête de mouton: Early Georgian (1700–1750 C.E.). France. Literally "sheep's head," a coiffure with the hair arranged close to the head in small, tight curls.

teud-bhràghad: Ireland. Collar.

tewke: *See* tuke.

textīle: *See* textum.

textum: Roman (753 B.C.E.–323 C.E.). Cloth.

teybaraten djendji: Timbuktu. A prophyry ring worn above the elbow.

thanapatta: India. Breast band.

thanh-lam: Vietnam. Turquoise.

thaub: Turkey. Early Gothic (1200–1350 C.E.). Woman's knee-length, long-sleeved robe worn belted at the waist.

thawb: Arabia. 1. Long or short sleeved robe. 2. General work for a garment.

the: Vietnam. Silk; gauze.

theke: Greece. Silk or gold bobbin lace.

theo tie: Open throated, tongueless shoe.

Thérèse: Late Georgian (1750–1790 C.E.). Loose head-dress shaped like a hood and worn over a tall bonnet. It continued in usage until 1840. *See also* Teresa.

Thibet cloth: Bustle (1865–1890 C.E.). Introduced in 1874, a soft, thick flannel with long goat's hair on the face.

Thibetine: Bustle (1865–1890 C.E.). In 1877, a fancy woolen fabric.

thicksets: Ireland. Coarse fustian with dense nap.

thiers red: Bustle (1865–1890 C.E.). In 1878, rich, dark garnet.

thiet-hài: Vietnam. Tap dance shoes.

thi-kính: Vietnam. Eyeglasses.

thirmā: India. White sheet worn by women as a wrap.

thistle: Reddish violet color.

thistle-green: Gay Nineties (1890–1900 C.E.). In 1891, a new color.

thistlewood: Bustle (1865–1890 C.E.). Lightweight wood with knots used for parasol handles.

thob: Palestine. Man's plain, ankle-length shirt or tunic. The sleeves are cut very full to the wrist and are tied up with a shmar to keep them out of the way when working. The robe is worn hitched up in a leather belt.

thob al-khidmah: Palestine. Woman's plain dress.

thob al-tal'ah: Palestine. Woman's elaborately decorated dress.

thob basitah: Palestine. Woman's simple dress.

thob mukhmal azraq: Palestine. Woman's blue velvet thob.

tholia: Greek (3000-100 B.C.E.). Woman's hat with pointed crown and flat brim.

thorakion: Byzantine and Romanesque (400–1200 C.E.). Empress's coat of arms.

thorex: Greek (3000-100 B.C.E.). Corselet of metal plates fastened on cloth worn tight over the tunic.

thorn: Common blackthorn (*Prunus spinosa*) often used for driving whips, walking sticks, and umbrella handles. Natural knots are left on the wood.

thread lace: Linen lace.

threde: Byzantine and Romanesque (400–1200 C.E.) to Renaissance (1450–1550 C.E.). United Kingdom. Middle English term for thread.

three-decker: Bustle (1865–1890 C.E.). United Kingdom. Popular from 1877 on, a three caped ulster.

three-fold linen button: Crinoline (1840–1865 C.E.). United Kingdom. Introduced in 1841 by John Aston, a button covered with three layers of linen.

three-seamer: Crinoline (1840–1865 C.E.). United Kingdom. Popular from 1860 on, a man's round jacket with a center back seam and side seams (as opposed to the traditional five seam coat).

three-stories-and-a-basement: Bustle (1865–1890 C.E.). United Kingdom. Popular name in 1886 for the very high crowned ladies' hats.

thrown silk: Needled silk made into thread.

thrum: Extremity of weaver's warp which cannot be woven.

thrum cap: Early Georgian (1700–1750 C.E.). United Kingdom. Cap knitted of thrum, popular with workmen.

thrummed hat: Renaissance (1450–1550 C.E.) to Elizabethan (1550–1625 C.E.). United Kingdom. A thrummed hat was made of felt or silk with a long nap. It was replaced by finer felt hats in the 1560s.

thunder and lightning: Early Georgian (1700–1750 C.E.) to Late Georgian (1750–1790 C.E.). Worsted warp and woolen weft serge made in glaring colors. *See also* German serge.

thung: Laos and Thailand. Shoulder bag.

thúy-ngoc: Vietnam. Emerald.

thymel: United Kingdom. Literally "thumb stall," thymel is the source word for thimble.

tí: China. Orange red color.

tì: China. Silk and cotton fabric.

tian 'éróng: China. Velvet.

tian ze: China. Qing dynasty (1644–1911 C.E.). Woman's festive headdress made of woven rattan or wire shaped like an inverted basket and covered with black gauze or silk net. It was trimmed with jeweled ornaments.

tianlán: China. Sky blue; azure.

tianqing: China. Reddish black.

tiao tuo: China. Jade bracelet.

tiáoróng: China. Corduroy.

tiara: Soft or metal crown in a narrow style. National headdress of southwest Asiatic nations.

Tibet cloth: Goat's hair fabric.

Tibetisches Lamm: Germany. Tibet lamb fur.

tibi: Crinoline (1840–1865 C.E.). Popular from 1840 on, the loop that fastened button to button at the top of a coat instead of the usual button to buttonhole closure.

tibilaes: Roman (753 B.C.E.–323 C.E.). High leggings worn by huntsmen or soldiers.

tibiteika: Uzbekistan. National symbol, a round, felt hat with a scalloped edge.

ticket pocket: Crinoline (1840–1865 C.E.). United Kingdom. Appearing after 1859, a small pocket for the rail ticket above the right flap pocket on the overcoat. In 1875, it was switched to the left side. In the 1890s, it appeared on the lounge jacket on the right side. In 1895, it appeared on morning coat.

ticklenburg: Charles I and the Commonwealth (1625–1660 C.E.) to Late Georgian (1750–1790 C.E.). Coarse linen from Tecklenburg.

tie-back skirt: Bustle (1865–1890 C.E.). United Kingdom. Trained day or evening skirt with tapes sewn into the side seams on the inside of the skirt. By tying these tapes together, the back was fluffed out and the front flattened, creating a hobble skirt.

Tierfibeln: (Fifth century B.C.E.). Austria. Brooches with quadrupeds modeled in the round.

tifa: Samoa. Mother-of-pearl.

tiffany: Early Georgian (1700–1750 C.E.). 1. Thin transparent silk fabric. 2. Transparent gauze, muslin, or cobweb lawn.

tifsireh: Palestine. Satin stitch.

tige d'aillet: Bustle (1865–1890 C.E.). In 1882, light bronze green.

tight: Italy. Man's morning coat.

tights: Romantic (1815–1840 C.E.) to Bustle (1865–1890 C.E.). Term used to refer to evening pantaloons.

tight-slacks: Bustle (1865–1890 C.E.). United Kingdom. Men's trousers that were very tight at the knees and loose at the hem.

tignon: Crinoline (1840–1865 C.E.). United States of America. A New Orleans word for a headwrap.

tiin: Thailand. Decorative border of a woven textile.

tiin sin: Laos. Supplemental lower skirt borders.

tijajin d'mahduh: Morocco. Jewish woman's coif of silver threads and cloisonné enamel.

tikamist: Tuareg. A man's long white cotton shirt.

tikamist kore: Tuareg. A man's embroidered indigo blue overgarment.

tiki: Australia. Maori woman's sacred neck pendant.

t'ikita: Bolivia. Octagon motif.

tikka: Arabia. Drawstring.

tikkeh: Palestine. The silk drawstring in sirwal. It is often elaborately trimmed.

tilari: India. A three-stringed necklace.

tilavasa: India. Brocade.

tilbi: Nigeria. A man's long shirt that is open at the sides.

Tilbury hat: Romantic (1815–1840 C.E.). United Kingdom. Popular in 1830s, a man's small hat with a high tapering crown, a flat top, and a narrow, round brim.

tile red: Bright red orange.

tilleul: Bustle (1865–1890 C.E.). Introduced in 1877, light green.

tilmatli: Mexico. 1. Cloak worn by the Tarahumara Indians. 2. Aztec man's mantle; basically a rectangle of fabric. There were 54 different styles.

tilter: Bustle (1865–1890 C.E.). Bustle where shirring that contained the springs was made of separate piece of fabric than the rest of the bustle. It was fitted to the figure with a belt.

tilting-helm: Early Gothic (1200–1350 C.E.). Large helmet worn over other armor helmets at tournaments.

timbre: Renaissance (1450–1550 C.E.). France. Skull of a helmet.

timu: New Zealand. Maori term for a rough, strong, serviceable cloak.

tin chiang chiang chau: Bustle (1865–1890 C.E.). United States of America. Chinese Hawaiian term for a slightly rough form of chau used for pants, bridal trousseaus, and birthday clothes. It was a very dark purplish red color.

tinaku azul: Ecuador and Guatemala. Indigo.

tinbiteh: Palestine. Zigzag applique.

tingmiak: Denmark. Blouse.

tini: *See* kochi.

tiñiska: Ecuador and Guatemala. Dyed.

tinsel printing: India. Patterns created with gold powder mixed into roghan.

tinte: Ecuador and Guatemala. General term for dye.

tintillano: Early Gothic (1200–1350 C.E.). Italy. Woolen cloth dyed before it is spun.

tintoriado: Ecuador and Guatemala. Dyed.

tinturar: Ecuador and Guatemala. To dye.

tinturero: Ecuador and Guatemala. Dyer.

tippet: 1. Early Gothic (1200–1350 C.E.). Streamer that hung from the sleeve of a garment. 2. Renaissance (1450–1550 C.E.). A short shoulder cape. 3. Romantic (1815–1840 C.E.). Flat collar with long ends that hung down to the waist in front. It was made of silk or velvet and fur.

tippling cane: Cane with a concealed flask.

tiputa: Polynesia. A woman's serape-like garment that is 5 feet by 30 inches.

tira: Ecuador. Commercial tape trim.

tira dorado: Ecuador. Gilt thread.

tiracolo: Portugal. Shoulder belt; baldric.

tirantes: Spain. Braces; straps.

tiraz band: India. An ornamented braid that is used to decorate the upper part of the sleeve.

tirchha: India. Striped fabric used for trousers.

tiretaine: 1. Early Gothic (1200–1350 C.E.) to Renaissance (1450–1550 C.E.). Fine wool fabric, often scarlet colored. 2. France. Linsey-woolsey.

tirita: India. Woman's diadem.

tirkô: Madagascar. T-shirt.

tirodhana: India. Woman's marriage dress; a long cloth wrapped around the body and worn girdled.

tissu: *See* étoffe.

tissu satiné: France. Sateen.

tissue: Any lightweight open fabric.

tissue d'Alma: Crinoline (1840–1865 C.E.). In 1855, a new fabric.

tissue gingham: Lightweight semitransparent gingham.

tissue taffeta: Fine lightweight taffeta.

tissutier-rubanier: France. Maker of weavings, trims, and ribbons.

titi: Polynesia. A girdle of plant leaves.

titian: Red or reddish brown.

titi-le-'au: Polynesia. A man's apron of leaves from the ti plant.

tittirapattika: India. A shoe shaped like a partridge wing.

Titus haircut: Short fuzzy haircut.

tiu camisa: Ecuador. A man's handmade shirt.

tjap: Indonesia. Fabric with block-work print made by men.

tjeld: Norway. Woman's shawl, usually striped.

tjindai: Indonesia. Sa'dan-Toraja term for batik cloth.

tkan': Russia. Cloth.

tkanina: 1. Poland. Fabric. 2. Bosnia. Fabric.

tkanina dziana: Poland. Jersey fabric.

tkanitsa: Bulgaria. Belt worn over the waistband. It is woven in multicolored wool with geometric ornaments.

tl'aakal: Navajo. Skirt.

tlahuiztli: Aztec. Fitted garment worn by warriors.

tlws: Wales. Jewel.

to hoá-hoc: Vietnam. Artificial silk.

tobacco cloth: Loosely woven cotton fabric similar to cheesecloth.

toban: Ireland. Gaelic word for cowl or hood.

tobe: 1. Africa. White cotton shirt that reaches the ankles. A man's tobe is blue cotton, while a woman's is blue, black, or red. 2. Ethiopia. A cotton sheet worn as a wrap.

tobi: Nigeria. Yoruba woman's strip of cloth worn pleated from waist to knees as an undergarment.

tobin: 1. Elizabethan (1550–1625 C.E.) to Restoration (1660–1700 C.E.). Striped wool or silk fabric made in Norwich. 2. Early Georgian (1700–1750 C.E.) to Late Georgian (1750–1790 C.E.). Twilled silk similar to florentine. 3. Romantic (1815–1840 C.E.) to Bustle (1865–1890 C.E.). Heavy twilled silk.

tobine: *See* tobin.

toboggan: Norway. Man's black wadmal coat trimmed with black velvet with a high collar and silver buttons down the center front and around the cuffs.

toboggan cap: Long knitted cap worn when tobogganning.

toby ruff: Gay Nineties (1890–1900 C.E.). United Kingdom. Woman's chiffon or lisse neck ruff gathered into two or three layers and tied at the throat with a ribbon for day wear.

toby ruff

toca: Spain. Wimple.

toca de camino: Renaissance (1450–1550 C.E.). Spain. Traveling headdress.

tocado: Spain. Headgear.

tocapu: Bolivia. Incan waist high row of ornamental squares on ccahua.

tocco: Late Gothic (1350–1450 C.E.). Italy. Bright red cap with turned up brim worn by Florentine citizens.

tochtlatten: Holland. Muttonchop whiskers.

tock: *See* toque.

tocoyales: Guatemala. Colored yarns woven into women's hair.

tocuyo: Peru. Coarse cotton cloth.

toda: India. Anklet.

Todenkopf: Germany. An armored headpiece with piercing over the eyes, nose, and mouth in the manner of a skull.

toer: Holland. *See* poffer.

toering: South Africa. Pagoda-shaped cane hat.

toffel: Sweden. Slipper.

tøffel: Denmark. Slipper.

toga: 1. Roman (753 B.C.E.–323 C.E.). Basic garment that was the signature garment of the Roman citizen. It was characteristically white and varied in size from its beginnings in 200 B.C.E. (16′ by 6′) to its largest size in 400 C.E. (21′ by 6′). It was cut in a semi-circle and worn draped around the body in a variety of styles. It finally went out of fashion because of its inconvenience due to size and elaborate drapery. 2. Poland. Judge's robe.

toga candida: Roman (753 B.C.E.–323 C.E.). Plain bleached white wool toga worn by candidates for political office. It was sometimes whitened with chalk.

toga contabulatum: *See* toga umbo.

toga gabiana: Roman (753 B.C.E.–323 C.E.). Tight-fitting toga worn with one fold over the head and the other end around the hips to form belt.

toga palmata: Roman (753 B.C.E.–323 C.E.). Toga embroidered with a palm branch pattern and worn only for special ceremonies.

toga picta: Roman (753 B.C.E.–323 C.E.). Official toga of the emperor; a purple toga embroidered in gold.

toga praetexta: Roman (753 B.C.E.–323 C.E.). Toga worn by senators, some officials, and priests. It had a purple band woven on the edge.

toga pulla: Roman (753 B.C.E.–323 C.E.). Toga worn for mourning or sacrifice. It was black, dark gray, or brown. It was worn by accused persons and the lower classes.

toga pura: Roman (753 B.C.E.–323 C.E.). Worn by Roman citizens, a toga made of natural-colored wool with no ornamentation.

toga sordida: *See* toga pulla.

toga trabea: Roman (753 B.C.E.–323 C.E.). Worn by equestrian knights, a small toga with a red or purple stripe.

toga umbo: Roman (753 B.C.E.–323 C.E.). Ordinary toga with a red or purple band that was popular toward the end of the second century C.E. It was worn draped so as to create a pocket or pouch in front. It became fashionable with the high dignitaries in the end of the second century C.E.

toga virilis: Roman (753 B.C.E.–323 C.E.). Worn by young males, aged 14 to 16, an all-white wool toga.

toghe: Late Gothic (1350–1450 C.E.). Italy. Man's shoulder cape reaching to the feet and worn gathered at the breast.

toi: *See* banat.

tøi: Denmark. *See* klœde.

toil colbert: France. Basket cloth.

toile: *See* étoffe.

toile à gros poil: France. Crash.

toile cirée: France. Oilcloth.

toile d'Alsace: Bustle (1865–1890 C.E.). In 1876, a soft, unglazed cotton fabric.

toile de jouy: Literally "cloth of joy," an elaborate design on cotton, linen, or silk.

toile de lin: France. Linen.

toile de religieuse: France. Nun's veiling.

toile de soie: Gay Nineties (1890–1900 C.E.). In 1898, a thick silk and cotton blend, thick ribbed fabric shot with two colors.

toile de Valeuce: Crinoline (1840–1865 C.E.). In 1863, a poplin-like fabric.

toile d'esprit: Bustle (1865–1890 C.E.). In 1879, a delicate spotted lace.

toile grossière: France. Lockram.

toile Nankin: Crinoline (1840–1865 C.E.). In 1863, a mixed unfigured fabric for travel, generally in brown or gray.

toile peinte: France. Painted cotton fabric.

toilet: 1. Elizabethan (1550–1625 C.E.). Loose linen wrapper worn by men when being shaved. 2. Early Georgian (1700–1750 C.E.). A loose wrapper worn by women when having their hair or wig styled.

toilet cap: Elizabethan (1550–1625 C.E.) to Restoration (1660–1700 C.E.). Man's plain nightcap worn when being barbered.

toilinet: Wool weft and cotton and silk warp fabric used for waistcoats.

toilinette: *See* toilinet.

toilonette: Directoire and First Empire (1790–1815 C.E.). Introduced in 1810, a fine wool fabric similar to merino.

toise mouvante: France. Telescopic measuring cane.

tok: France. Breton for hat.

t'okbaji: Korea. Bib.

tokeine: United States of America. Hawaiian term for stockings.

toley: Early Gothic (1200–1350 C.E.). Scarlet.

t'oljanggap: Korea. Fur gloves.

toll-cnaip: Ireland. Gaelic word for buttonhole.

toloboni: Romania. Boots.

tolomi: Timbuktu. A spiral shaped gold earring.

t'olshil: Korea. Woolen yarn.

tolsil: Korea. Worsted.

t'ol-sil: Korea. Woolen yarn.

toma: Ashanti. Waist beads.

tombeaux: Crinoline (1840–1865 C.E.). United States of America. The distinctive design on the chest of a Zouave's jacket.

tombodama: Japan. Complex multicolored glass beads.

tombolo: Italy. Lace-pillow.

tom-bons: Afghanistan. Cotton trousers cut very full in the waist and hips and tapering to a snug fit at the ankles.

tonaca: *See* tunica.

tonach: Ireland. Gaelic word for garment.

tonder lace: Denmark. Drawn work lace on muslin.

toneelkijker: Holland. Opera glasses.

tong xiu kai: China. Wei, Jin, Southern and Northern dynasties. Tubular mail coat made of scale- or shell-shaped pieces. It was joined at the sides with two tubular sleeves.

tongbok: Korea. Winter clothes.

tongs: Elizabethan (1550–1625 C.E.) to Late Georgian (1750–1790 C.E.). United States of America. Coarse cotton or linen overalls.

tongue pump: (1910–1920 C.E.). Introduced in 1914, a colonial pump with no throat ornament.

tonlet
(15th and 16th century)
See also photospread
(Armor).
Dover Publications

tonlet: 1. Early Gothic (1200–1350 C.E.). Horizontal band used to form a short armored skirt. 2. Late Gothic (1350–1450 C.E.) and Renaissance (1450–1550 C.E.). A short armored skirt.

tonnag: Scotland. Tartan square worn by women over the shoulders and fastened on the breast.

tontillo: Elizabethan (1550–1625 C.E.) to Restoration (1660–1700 C.E.). Spain. Heavy farthingale of steel hoops. It was replaced in the late 17th century with a lighter version.

toocke: *See* toque.

toog: Holland. Cassock.

top boot

toopuni: Australia. Maori dog-skin cloak with dark body and white hair on the side and neck borders.

toorua: Australia. Maori two-layer sandal of Cordyline.

toothpick: Bustle (1865–1890 C.E.). Extremely pointed toe of man's shoe.

top: *See* toupee.

top boot: 1. Late Georgian (1750–1790 C.E.). Boot made from a black leather with the flesh side down. It had a strap around the knee. 2. Romantic (1815–1840 C.E.) through Bustle (1865–1890 C.E.). Snugly fitted boot with buff or white leather tops.

top button: Button with only the face gilded.

top frock: Romantic (1815–1840 C.E.). Worn from 1830 on, man's overcoat cut like a frock coat. It was commonly double breasted.

topas: Ireland. Gaelic word for topaz.

topaz: 1. Semiprecious stone of varying shades of yellow. 2. A clear brown.

topaza: *See* kopako.

topazo: *See* kopako.

topazon: Roman (753 B.C.E.–323 C.E.). Chrysolite.

topee: 1. Pith hat. 2. *See* topi.

topi: 1. India. Generic term for a hat. 2. Nepal. Man's flat, woven wool hat with a round rolled brim.

topiwala: India. Literally "hat man," an Indian term used to describe a European (as opposed to pagriwala, a turban man).

topo: Spain. Mole.

topola: Nigeria. Yoruba woman's expensive crimson cloth with perforated edges that is used as a bridal cloth.

topper: Woman's mid-thigh length overcoat.

topuni: New Zealand. Maori term for a cloak of the skins of black haired dogs.

toque: 1. Renaissance (1450–1550 C.E.) and Elizabethan (1550–1625 C.E.). Woman's head scarf or coif. 2. Romantic (1815–1840 C.E.). Worn from 1815 to 1820, a triangular frame over which the woman's hair was arranged. 3. Romantic (1815–1840 C.E.). Snug turban shaped hat worn outdoors or for evening. It could be made of silk, satin, or straw. 4. Directoire and First Empire (1790–1815 C.E.). Soft, draped, snug woman's hat. It was sometimes trimmed with flowers or feathers. 5. *See* tuque.

toque à la Basile: Late Georgian (1750–1790 C.E.). France. Woman's hat style.

toque à la Grande Pretesse: Late Georgian (1750–1790 C.E.). France. Woman's hat style.

toque à la Susanne: Late Georgian (1750–1790 C.E.). France. Woman's hat style.

toque à l'Iphigénie: Late Georgian (1750–1790 C.E.). France. Woman's hat style.

toque de fourrure: France. Busby.

toquet: Crinoline (1840–1865 C.E.). Woman's small satin or velvet toque with a small brim turned up in front and trimmed with an ostrich feather. It was worn for evening on the back of the head.

toquette: France. High crowned bulky turban.

toque-turban: Crinoline (1840–1865 C.E.). Popular in 1840s, a woman's turban shaped like a toque and worn for evening.

toquilla: Fiber used in Panama hats.

toraco: (1920–1930 C.E.). A man's sleeveless shirt.

toran: India. A fabric door hanging; long embroidered flap on the lower edge of a helmet.

tora-tora: Indonesia. Necklace of crocodile's teeth worn by Sa'dan-Toraja hunter.

torchon lace: Coarse, durable bobbin lace of linen or cotton.

toreadoll pajamas: (1960–1970 C.E.). United States of America. Woman's sleep pajamas with mid-calf-length pants.

toreador hat: Gay Nineties (1890–1900 C.E.). Woman's circular, shallow crowned hat of felt or straw. It was worn with a net.

toreador pants: (20th century). Women's pants snug-fitting to the knee where they button.

torebka damska: Poland. Handbag.

t'orot: Korea. Fur (woolen) garment.

torque: Roman (753 B.C.E.–323 C.E.). Necklace in the form of an ornamented circle.

torquēs: *See* monīle.

torsade: Crinoline (1840–1865 C.E.). 1. Introduced in 1840, a twisted fringe trim. 2. Twisted or braided coronet of velvet or tulle with long lappets for evening wear. It was introduced in 1864.

tortoiseshell: Brownish yellow, semi-transparent turtle shell once used for accessories. Now banned in the United States of America where a faux tortoiseshell of plastic is used.

toruphulli: India. Lemon yellow.

torzal: Renaissance (1450–1550 C.E.). Spain. Cord.

tosaek: Korea. Pink.

tosca net: Firm, durable net.

toshikhana: India. Storehouse seal used to mark backs of chintzes used in India.

totnamaksin: Korea. Patten.

totoga: Samoa. Accessories.

totsin: Korea. Overshoe.

tot'urak taenggi: Korea. Woman's hair ribbon. This style was adopted from the Chinese.

tóu jim: China. Curved neck opening on a gown.

tou tu: *See* doudu.

touaille: Late Gothic (1350–1450 C.E.). France. Soft wimple.

touca: Portugal. Hood.

toujin: China. Scarf.

toupee: 1. Early Georgian (1700–1750 C.E.) to Late Georgian (1750–1790 C.E.). Roll facing the back on the forehead of a man's wig. 2. Bustle (1865–1890 C.E.). Fringe or forehead frizz of fake hair.

toupet: *See* toupee.

tour de cheveux: France. Fake hair worn on the front of the head.

touret: Early Gothic (1200–1350 C.E.) to Elizabethan (1550–1625 C.E.). Originally woman's veil covering the forehead. Later it was a mourning headdress consisting of a veil in two pieces; one piece covering the top of the face, the second covering the chin (later called the barbette). In the 16th century, the term referred only to the edge of the veil.

touret de nez: Early Gothic (1200–1350 C.E.). France. Band of fabric attached to the earflaps of the hood and covering the eyes. It had a pane of crystalline allowing the wearer to see. It was worn in winter.

tourie: A tuft or small pompon on the top of a cap or bonnet.

tourmaline: Semiprecious stone varying from red to green.

tournure: Bustle (1865–1890 C.E.). Bustle made with steel springs placed inside the shirring around the back of the petticoat. The term was commonly used as a polite term for the bustle.

tournure

tourterelle: 1. Romantic (1815–1840 C.E.). United Kingdom. Mushroom brown. 2. Crinoline (1840–1865 C.E.). Turtledove color.

tovaglia: 1. *See* bavolet. 2. Italy. Woman's folded headdress of white linen.

tow: Crinoline (1840–1865 C.E.). United States of America. Rough finished fabric.

tow cloth: First Empire (1790–1815 C.E.). United States of America. Rough linen fabric made from short fibers remaining from combed flax.

town blouse: (1920–1930 C.E.) Long, V-necked, short sleeved overtunic popularly worn with suits.

toyama: Japan. Literally "distant mountain," type of kesa decorated with cloudlike patterns in patchwork and stitches.

toyo: Shiny, rice-paper straw.

tozali: Nigeria. Powdered antimony used as an eye shadow.

traad: Denmark. Thread.

trabea: Byzantine and Romanesque (400–1200 C.E.). Brocaded scarf worn by consuls in Basilean period of the Byzantine.

tracht: Austria. General term referring to folk dress.

tråd: Sweden. Thread.

Trafalgar dress: Directoire and First Empire (1790–1815 C.E.). Named for the Battle of Trafalgar in 1806, a white satin evening gown trimmed with silver.

Trafalgar turban: Directoire and First Empire (1790–1815 C.E.). United Kingdom. Named for the Battle of Trafalgar in 1806, a woman's evening turban embroidered with the name of Nelson.

Träger: Germany. Braces.

traguardo: Renaissance (1450–1550 C.E.). Italy. Visor.

traheen: Ireland. Soleless stocking.

trahilia: Greece. Dickey.

trailer thread lace: Czechoslovakia. Bobbin lace made from very fine flaxen thread.

traje: Portugal. Dress; clothes.

traje de baño: Spain. Swimsuit.

traje de baño de dos piezas: Spain. Bikini.

traje de baño de una pieza: Spain. Maillot.

traje de novia: Spain. Bridal gown.

traka: *See* vrpca.

trancinha: Portugal. Narrow braid.

trang bong: Vietnam. Pure white.

trang nõn: Vietnam. Very white.

transformation: (1910–1920 to 1920–1930 C.E.). Worn 1914–1927, a natural-looking wig worn by women with thinning hair.

transparent velvet: Rayon fabric with rayon or silk back, usually crush-resistant finish. Transparent when held to light.

trapeze: (1950–1960 C.E.). United States of America. Introduced by Yves St. Laurent in 1958, a woman's short dress with free tent-shaped back and high belted front.

trappers: *See* tappert.

trapphant: *See* tappert.

trapuntato: Italy. Quilted.

trapunto: A dimensional design created by parallel stitches that are stuffed with yarn or batting.

traquenard: *See* paniers.

Traue: Germany. Mourning.

Trauring: Germany. Wedding ring.

trawerbandes: Elizabethan (1550–1625 C.E.) to Restoration (1660–1700 C.E.). Mourning bands.

treble ruff: Directoire and First Empire (1790–1815 C.E.). Worn in 1813 and later, a ruff made from three full layers of pointed lace or sheer muslin edged with lace. It fastened at the back of the neck.

treille: Belgian name for ground.

treillis: Early Georgian (1700–1750 C.E.). Buckram.

tremolanti: Renaissance (1450–1550 C.E.). Italy. Small pieces of decorative work often used on head-dresses.

Tremont hat: (1940–1950 C.E. to 1950–1960 C.E.). Worn 1947–1952, a man's hat with a tapered crown, center crease, and a narrow brim.

trench coat: Loose, rainproof overcoat with many pockets and flaps.

trencher hat: Directoire and First Empire (1790–1815 C.E.). Introduced in 1806, a woman's silk hat with a triangular brim that rose to a point in the center front.

trenerka: Bosnia. Sweatshirt.

trepats: Renaissance (1450–1550 C.E.). Spain. Perforated.

tresse: France. Plait.

Tresse: Germany. Galloon.

tressoir: Early Gothic (1200–1350 C.E.). Golden plait of silk worked with metal and gems.

tresson: Early Gothic (1200–1350 C.E.). Headdress or caul of net, often ornamented.

tressour: Early Gothic (1200–1350 C.E.) to Late Gothic (1350–1450 C.E.). Chaplet of gold or material.

treugolka: Russia. Tricorne.

trews: Scotland. Snug-fitting breeches with stockings attached.

triangle fold: Handkerchief folded so that only one corner shows out of a pocket.

tribon: Greek (3000–100 B.C.E.). Small oblong cloak worn by Spartan adult males (age 12 and over), often as the only garment.

tricô: Portugal. Stockinet; jersey.

tricolette: Knitted rayon, silk, or cotton. Fabric similar to jersey cloth.

tricolina: Portugal. Kind of poplin.

tricorn: Three cornered hat with upturned brim.

tricornio: Spain. Tricorne.

tricorno: Italy. Tricorne.

tricot: Soft, ribbed fabric.

tricot de Berlin: Directoire and First Empire (1790–1815 C.E.). Introduced in 1808, a very light knitted fabric similar to cotton gauze.

tricota: Portugal. Tricot.

tricotine: Soft, firm worsted fabric similar to gabardine.

trieu-phuc: Vietnam. Court dress.

trikarnas: India. Man's earring made of three interlocking rings.

triko: Bosnia. Tights.

Trikot: Germany. Tricot.

trilby: (1930–1939 C.E.). United States of America. Man's unlined felt hat.

Trilby hat: Gay Nineties (1890–1900 C.E.) to present. United Kingdom. Man's soft, black felt hat named for the hat worn by Beerbohm Tree when he played Svengali.

trilby

trim insertion: Embroidered lace or fabric in which a ribbon passes through vertical slits.

trimming à la greque: Crinoline (1840–1865 C.E.). France. Introduced in 1862, a form of key pattern in ruched ribbon.

trina: Italy. Originally a three pointed lace; today it refers to any lace. *See also* merletto.

trinzale: Renaissance (1450–1550 C.E.). Italy. Fine cloth worn over the hair.

tripe: Obsolete term for fabric woven like velvet.

triphalaka: India. Necklace of three gems or a gem set in three or five gold leaves.

triple ruff: *See* treble ruff.

triple voile: *See* ninon.

tripoline: Bustle (1865–1890 C.E.). Introduced in 1874, a twilled satin turc.

trip-sammet: Switzerland. Mock velvet.

triubhas: *See* trius.

triubhsair: Ireland. Gaelic word for trousers.

trius: Ireland. Close-fitting, ankle-length pants with strap under the instep. Some end above the knees.

triveni: India. Necklace made of three strings.

trocadero: Romantic (1815–1840 C.E.). United Kingdom. Orange color.

troche: Button set with three or more jewels.

tro-c'houzoug: France. Breton for necklace.

Troddelchen: Germany. Tassel.

troighthíní: *See* mairtíní.

Trolldals-trøya: Norway. Literally "Troll Valley coat," man's red, double-breasted short coat with long sleeves and wide revers.

trollekant: Simple bobbin lace made with a thick gimp thread.

trolley lace: English bobbin lace.

trollopee: Obsolete word for negligee.

trollopée: Early Georgian (1700–1750 C.E.). France. Long, flowing gown worn open in front and drawn up in back.

trolly cap: Late Georgian (1750–1790 C.E.). United Kingdom. Woman's indoor cap trimmed with trolly lace.

trolly lace: *See* trolley lace.

trompeurs: *See* liars.

Tropenhelm: Germany. Sun helmet.

tropenhelm: Holland. Pith helmet.

troqilla: Bolivia. Sombrero band.

trotcozy: Scotland. Cowl-like wrap used to cover the head and shoulders while riding.

trotteur: (1900–1909 C.E.). Introduced by Paul Poiret, a walking skirt above ankle length.

trouse: Trousers, trews, or knee-breeches.

trouser press: Gay Nineties (1890–1900 C.E.). United Kingdom. Set of two long flat boards between which a pair of trousers was laid. Boards were tightened together, thus creasing the trousers fashionably down the front of the trouser leg.

trouser stretcher: Bustle (1865–1890 C.E.). United Kingdom. Appliance used to stretch the leg of trousers when they were not being worn. One type consisted of an oblong steel loop placed in the end of the trouser leg. Another form was a wooden frame that tightly held each end of the garment and stretched it lengthwise.

trouserettes: Bloomers.

trousers: First worn by the early horse-riding steppe people, introduced to Western world by Italians in 16th century. They were accepted as informal dress in the Directoire (1790–1815 C.E.). They became a part of semi-formal dress around 1815 and became worn commonly after 1830.

trouses: Renaissance (1450–1550 C.E.) to Restoration (1660–1700 C.E.). Common name for men's undergarment (drawers).

trousseau: France. Household linens to accompany the bride.

troussoir: Late Gothic (1350–1450 C.E.). Hook used to lift the long gowns worn by women.

troussoire: *See* chatelaine.

trou-trou: France. Trim insertion.

trouwring: Holland. Wedding ring.

trovrec'h: France. Breton for bracelet.

trowses: *See* trouses.

trowsus: *See* llodrau.

trrsa: India. Necklace made of three strings.

tru: Vietnam. Military helmet.

trúc-bâu: Vietnam. Calico.

truffe: *See* truffeau.

truffeau: Late Gothic (1350–1450 C.E.). False hair or pads used to fill out the natural hairline. May also have referred to ornaments of gold to wear on a necklace.

truis-bhràghad: Ireland. Gaelic word for necklace.

trunk hose: Renaissance (1450–1550 C.E.). Upper hose that extend to the upper thigh.

trurng sáo: Vietnam. Light blue colored.

trus: Ireland. Gaelic word for belt or girdle.

trusgan: Ireland. Gaelic word for clothes or a suit of clothes.

trusses: Elizabethan (1550–1625 C.E.). United Kingdom. Tight venetian breeches.

trutag: Ireland. Gaelic word for wet weather cape.

trykotaze: Poland. Hosiery.

trykoty: Poland. Tights.

trzewik: Poland. Shoe.

tsala: Nigeria. Trousers with a wide drawstring waist and long narrow legs.

tsan: *See* zan.

tsangiá: Greece. Leather boots lined with wool.

tsarvouli: Bulgaria. Leather sandals.

tsavága: Norway. Red, yellow, and green vuoddaga that end in tassels.

tsaxínia: *See* Taxíria.

tselévo: Greece. Dirty stain.

tsemberi: Greece. A woman's triangular scarf with a rolled section in front.

tsepen: Bulgaria. Satin stitch.

tshapan: Hungary and Turkestan. Kandys-type garment.

tshoga: Punjab. Kandys-type garment of brown camel wool.

tsípes: Greece. Large pins for the headdress.

tsithsith: Hebrew. Tassels. Regarded as sign of orthodoxy.

tsitseróña: Greece. Long, red, silk kerchief.

tsubo-ori: Japan. Karaori kosode worn with the hem tucked into the hakama.

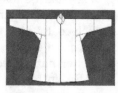

tshapan

tshoga

tsujigahana: Japan. Popular in the late 16th century, the kosode style.

tsumugi: Japan. Handspun silk fabric; pongee.

tsupári: Greece. Red fez.

tsupráci: Greece. Silver belt buckle.

tsurápe: Greece. White cotton bridal stockings.

tsuzure-nishiki: Japan. Early tapestry-weave brocade, sometimes with touches of gold.

tsuzure-ori: Japan. Literally "vine weaving," tapestry weave.

tti: *See* ribon.

ttisnu: Bolivia. Woven strap on ch'uspa.

ttoljam: Korea. Woman's hair ornament of gilt metal, semi-precious stones, pearls, and cloisonné. Worn in sets of three.

ttuggong: *See* moja.

tu kartu: New Zealand. Maori term for a woman's belt or waist-girdle of 10 or 12 plaited strands of sweet grass.

tuaka: New Zealand. Maori term for feather quills used as needles.

tuapora: *See* pora.

tūba: Lithuania. Felt.

tubao: Philippine Islands. Turban.

tubayt: Palestine. Cotton sateen.

tubbeck: Burma. Woman's sash, usually red.

tubsi: Palestine. White fabric with two red silk or cotton stripes on the border.

tubular necktie: Crinoline (1840–1865 C.E.). United Kingdom. Patented in 1852, a necktie woven in a tube.

Tuch: Germany. Woolen cloth.

tüchli: Switzerland. White church headdress.

tuck: *See* toque.

tuck embroidery: Embroidery made by applying one fabric to another with different stitches.

tucked skirt: Gay Nineties (1890–1900 C.E.). United Kingdom. In 1895, a woman's day skirt with a front wide box pleat, pleats in the back stiffened with horsehair, and side pleats.

tucker: 1. Elizabethan (1550–1625 C.E.) to Restoration (1660–1700 C.E.). Narrow piece of cloth used to fill in the décolletage of a woman's gown. 2. Early Georgian (1700–1750 C.E.). White trim on the neckline of a décolleté gown.

tudor cape: Gay Nineties (1890–1900 C.E.). United Kingdom. Woman's circular cape with a pointed yoke and a velvet Medici collar. It was commonly made of embroidered fabric.

tufel': *See* tuflja.

tuflja: Russia. Slipper.

tuft: 1. Late Gothic (1350–1450 C.E.). Tassel. 2. Tassel on a mortarboard.

tuftaffeta: Early Georgian (1700–1750 C.E.) to Late Georgian (1750–1790 C.E.). United States. Taffeta with chenille stripe worn in New United Kingdom.

tufted dimity: Early Georgian (1700–1750 C.E.) to Late Georgian (1750–1790 C.E.). Fustian with tufted surface commonly used for petticoats.

t'ugu: *See* ch'olmo.

tu-hou: New Zealand. Maori term for a rude apron of shrub leaves worn by priests.

tuichje: Elizabethan (1550–1625 C.E.). Holland. Items worn on the chatelaine.

tuikkoji: Korea. Floral motif hairpins.

tuil-aodach: Ireland. Gaelic word for apron.

tuille: Early Gothic (1200–1350 C.E.). Hinged steel plates attached by straps to the tasses in medieval armor. They helped to protect the thighs.

tuillinn: Ireland. Gaelic word for canvas.

tuithoed: Holland. Poke bonnet.

tujurka: Russia. Generally leather, a casual jacket.

Tukanitsa: Bulgaria. Man's patterned, checkered, or striped waistband worn over a long coat or under a short jacket.

tuke: Late Gothic (1350–1450 C.E.) to Renaissance (1450–1550 C.E.). Canvas or a similar fabric.

tukula: Zaire. Powdered camwood which is mixed with water or oil to use as a cosmetic.

tul: Spain. Tulle.

tulakoti: India. Heavy anklets with enlarged ends at their meeting point.

tulapansi: India. A lightweight cotton from central India.

tulapunnika: India. A shoe padded with cotton wool for warmth.

tulband: Holland. Turban.

tule: Holland. Tulle.

tulip collar: Roll collar, often with petal effect.

tulis: Indonesia. Hand-drawn form of batik done by women.

tulle: Late Georgian (1750–1790 C.E.) to present. France. Fine meshed net first made by machine in 1768 in Nottingham. It was named for the city Tulle, first place it was manufactured.

tullmas: Bolivia. Braid ties.

tulup: Russia. Long sheepskin coat.

tuly: Renaissance (1450–1550 C.E.) to Elizabethan (1550–1625 C.E.). Silk or thread fabric.

tuman: Iran. Woman's skirt worn over a petticoat (ic tuman) and under an outer skirt (ust tuman).

tumana: *See* ijara.

tumatukuru: New Zealand. Maori term for a snadla-legging combination garment.

tu-maurea: New Zealand. Maori term for a bright reddish yellow belt.

tumbaga: Colombia. Gold-copper alloy.

tumbe: Peru. Blanket worn as a shawl or mantle.

tumpal: Indonesia. A line of triangles that indicates the fringe end of the patola.

tu-muka: New Zealand. Maori term for a belt of 12 strands of dressed flax fiber. Four are white, four black, and four red.

tundikeri: India. A fine muslin.

tundra: Romania. White or black winter jacket with no trim.

tunece: Byzantine and Romanesque (400–1200 C.E.). United Kingdom. Man's tunic or woman's gown of a dark color. Also refers to a form of nightwear worn by monks. Valuable enough to be bequeathed by 10th century.

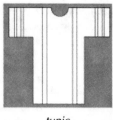
tunic

tunic: 1. Byzantine and Romanesque (400–1200 C.E.). Loose body garment similar to the kirtle. 2. Restoration (1660–1700 C.E.). Man's loose knee-length coat that buttoned down the front. It was worn with a waistcoat. It was introduced to United Kingdom by Charles II. 3. Crinoline (1840–1865 C.E.). Popular in 1840s and 1850s, a boy's jacket fitted to the waist, below which it flared into a gathered or pleated skirt. The sleeves were elbow or wrist length. It was worn with ankle- or knee-length trousers.

tunic à la juive: *See* tunic à la mameluck.

tunic à la mameluck: Directoire and First Empire (1790–1815 C.E.). France. Popular in 1801 and 1802, a woman's short tunic with short or long sleeves. *See also* juive.

tunic à la Romaine: Directoire and First Empire (1790–1815 C.E.). France. High-waisted, long, gauze or lawn tunic with long sleeves.

tunic dress: Romantic (1815–1840 C.E.) to Bustle (1865–1890 C.E.). Dress with a tunic-like overskirt. It was worn in various lengths and designs.

tunic shirt: Crinoline (1840–1865 C.E.). United Kingdom. Patented in 1855, a man's shirt that opened all the way down the front so that it did not have to go on over the head.

tunic skirt: Crinoline (1840–1865 C.E.) to 1890–1899 C.E. United Kingdom. Popular from 1856 on, a double skirt. In 1850s, the overskirt was trimmed with lace, the lower with a deep flounce. In 1897, the style reappeared minus the trim.

tunica: 1. Roman (753 B.C.E.–323 C.E.). Man's wool or linen knee-length garment with short or long sleeves. It was sometimes ornamented with clavi or segmentae. 2. Italy. Tunic. 3. Holland. Tunic.

túnica: Portugal. Tunic.

tunica alba: Roman (753 B.C.E.–323 C.E.). White tunic.

tunica augusticlavia: Roman (753 B.C.E.–323 C.E.). Worn by Equites; a tunic with narrow stripes.

tunica interior: Roman (753 B.C.E.–323 C.E.). 1. Another name for the colobium. 2. Innermost tunic, worn next to the body, and cut the same width from top to bottom. It was first made of wool and later made of cotton or silk.

tunica intima: *See* tunica interior.

tunica laticlavia: Roman (753 B.C.E.–323 C.E.). Worn by the senators, a tunic with broad stripes.

tunica manicata: Roman (753 B.C.E.–323 C.E.). Long sleeved tunic.

tunica palmata: Roman (753 B.C.E.–323 C.E.). Tunica richly embroidered with gold embroideries of palm branches and worn as part of official garb of the emperor. It was usually worn ungirdled.

tunica taleris: Roman (753 B.C.E.–323 C.E.). Ankle-length tunic with long, loose sleeves. It was popular during the fourth century C.E.

tunicle: Ecclesiastical garb. Narrow sleeved dalmatic worn by deacons at Mass.

tuniek: *See* tunica.

tunika: Germany and Poland. Tunic.

tunique: France. Tunic.

tunique à la Juive: *See* tunic à la mameluck.

tunnavaya: India. A tailor.

Tuoch: Germany. Cloth.

Tuoh: *See* Fane.

tuósè: China. Camel color; light tan.

tupele: Lithuania. Slipper.

tupu: 1. Ecuador. Shawl pin. 2. Peru. Large silver pin.

tupullina pichu jerguita: Ecuador. A small straight pin used to secure the pichu jerga.

tupy: *See* topi.

tuque: Canada. Long knitted tube of a hat worn for winter sports.

turamaggie: Korea. Long overcoat that ties on the right breast and reaches to eight inches from the ground.

turban: Scarf usually of fine linen worn wound around the head. The Mohammedan versions are from 20 to 30 inches wide and 6–9 yards long or as large as 6–8 inches wide and 10–50 yards long.

turban bonnet: Late Georgian (1750–1790 C.E.). France. In the 1780s, a woman's hat with no brim and a very high crown. It had three feathers and a sash that tied at the top back.

turban-diademe: Directoire and First Empire (1790–1815 C.E.). France. Thin headband of muslin, velvet, brocade, silver moiré, satin, or silver gauze.

turbante: Italy, Portugal, and Spain. Turban.

turchino: Renaissance (1450–1550 C.E.). Italy. Turquoise blue.

turco poplinnes: Bustle (1865–1890 C.E.). Introduced in 1867, a wool fabric with a soft, silky sheen.

turesu: *See* kin koot.

turf: 1. Late Gothic (1350–1450 C.E.). Turn-up or facing of a hood or sleeve. 2. Renaissance (1450–1550 C.E.). Turn-up of a cap.

turf hat: Romantic (1815–1840 C.E.). United Kingdom. Man's hat with tall crown, a flat top, and broad brim that turned up on the sides.

turin velvet: Crinoline (1840–1865 C.E.). Introduced in 1860, a silk and wool fabric similar to terry.

Türken-kappen: Switzerland. Head cloths made for export to Turkey.

turkey bonnet: Late Gothic (1350–1450 C.E.). Tall cylindrical brimless hat.

turkey gown: Renaissance (1450–1550 C.E.). United Kingdom. Long coat with long narrow sleeves that was worn loose or fastened down the front with loops or buckles. It was most commonly worn as a lay gown and was later worn by Puritan ministers.

turkey red: 1. Red dye made from vegetable madder or synthetic madder. 2. Plain red calico dyed with turkey red.

turkils: Early Gothic (1200–1350 C.E.). Turquoise.

Turkish brilliantine: Bustle (1865–1890 C.E.). In 1870, a wool fabric similar to beaver mohair.

Turkish point lace: *See* oyah.

Turkish polonaise: *See* Irish polonaise.

Turkish turban: Directoire and First Empire (1790–1815 C.E.). Popular in 1808, a turban made of folds of silk and gauze.

turkus: Poland. Turquoise.

turmkrone: Jewish bride's traditional bold headband set with little towers.

turno: Ecuador and Guatemala. Spinning wheel.

turnover: Elizabethan (1550–1625 C.E.) to Restoration (1660–1700 C.E.). Woman's head kerchief.

turquesa: Portugal. Turquoise, the gemstone.

turquoise: Greenish green blue.

turra: *See* turro.

turrah: India. Crested plume of gold or silver worn on top of the turban.

turrā-i-mārwadī: India. Flounced feathered tassels of gold, tied on the right side of the turban.

turret bodice: Bustle (1865–1890 C.E.). United Kingdom. Bodice with the basque cut into tabs.

turri: *See* turrah.

turro: India. The fanlike projection made by the end of the turban.

turudam: India. A muslin.

turumagi: Korea. Man's long overcoat.

tus: India. The color gray.

tusbahh: Somalia. Muslim prayer beads.

tusc: Poland. Mascara.

tuscan: Fine, yellow straw. When woven into lacelike braids, one of the finest braids. It was named for Tuscany, Italy, where it originated.

tüsjö: Romania. Wide leather belt.

tussah: Strong, lightweight fiber or the cloth woven or tussah fiber.

tusseh: *See* tussah.

tussoire: Early Gothic (1200–1350 C.E.) to Renaissance (1450–1550 C.E.). Chain and clasp combination which hung from the waist and were used to hold up one side of the long skirt.

tussore: *See* tussah.

tussore de Longchamps: Bustle (1865–1890 C.E.). In 1870, a reversible silk pongee; violet on one side, ecru on other.

tusuk: *See* talede.

tuszo: Hungary. Very wide leather belt made of tanned or smeared horse or cattle hide.

tuta: (1920–1930 C.E.). Italy. Designed by an Italian artist around 1926 as a protest against the vagaries of fashion, it was not very popular. It was an all-in-one, buttoned, belted jumpsuit.

tutki: India. A parrot green color.

tuttulik: Boot with caribou soles. Worn by Inuits for inland hunting.

tutu: Very full, short overskirt worn by ballerinas.

tutu mu'u: United States of America. Hawaii. A loose-fitting gown with a high neckline, yoke, and gathered bodice. It may be knee or ankle length.

tutulus: Roman (753 B.C.E.–323 C.E.). Woman's coiffure where the hair is piled in a conical shape on the top of the head.

tuu hangoroa: Australia. Maori girdle of shells.

tuu kaaretu: Australia. Maori woman's girdle of perfumed Hierochloe redolens.

tuu maro: Australia. Maori rough girdle of flax tow.

tuu muka: Australia. Maori decorative girdle of dressed flax fiber.

tuu ure: Australia. Maori penis string attached to waist belt.

tuumatakuru: Australia. Maori sandal and legging combination.

tuutum: Ghana. The color black.

tuxedo: Man's formal evening jacket. It is named for its first official presentation at the Tuxedo Park Club.

tuyn: Vietnam. Tulle.

túyt-xo: Vietnam. Tussah; tussore.

tweed: Romantic (1815–1840 C.E.). Soft, lightweight, wool fabric. It was so named in the 1830s when a Scottish clerk misread tweel (twill).

tweedside: Crinoline (1840–1865 C.E.). United Kingdom. Popular from 1858 on, a man's loose, single-breasted, high button lounge jacket. It varied in length from hip to thigh and had patch or slit pockets.

tweedside overcoat: Crinoline (1840–1865 C.E.). United Kingdom. Popular in 1850s, a knee-length tweedside jacket.

Twelve Apostles: Charles I and the Commonwealth (1625–1660 C.E.). Sweden. Collar bandolier belt carrying 12 charges for a musket.

Twenty Grands: *See* brogans.

twill weave: Strong weave characterized by a diagonal ridge running from lower left to upper right.

twillet: *See* toilet.

twine: Crinoline (1840–1865 C.E.). United Kingdom. Man's double-breasted paletot-sac, similar to a loose Chesterfield.

twinset: (1950–1960 C.E.). Sweater set consisting of cardigan and shell.

twist button: Crinoline (1840–1865 C.E.). Used in 1860s, a button covered in strong cotton twist.

twitkkoj: Korea. Married woman's hairpin worn with the cchok.

tyasen-gami: Japan. A man's tonsure with a string wound around the hair to hold it erect.

tye
See also photospread (Headwear).

tye: Early Georgian (1700–1750 C.E.) to Late Georgian (1750–1790 C.E.). Man's wig with a tied-back ponytail.

tyelambu: Timbuktu. Sandals.

tyes: Bustle (1865–1890 C.E.). United States. Girls' aprons.

tyg: *See* kläde.

tylesent: Renaissance (1450–1550 C.E.) to Elizabethan (1550–1625 C.E.). Tinsel or another fabric with metallic fibers.

typewriter cloth: Very fine, tightly woven, cotton fabric used for typewriter ribbons.

tyrasol: *See* kittysol.

tyrf: *See* turf.

Tyrian purple: Mesopotamia. Most expensive dye of its time, blue red or garnet color dye made from the murex, a sea animal. It was first manufactured in the Phoenician city Tyre.

Tyrolese cloak: Directoire and First Empire (1790–1815 C.E.). United Kingdom. Woman's knee-length shoulder cape made of sarcenet and trimmed with lace.

Tyrolese hat: Bustle (1865–1890 C.E.). United Kingdom. Woman's small flat top felt hat with a tapering crown and a narrow brim that turned up on the sides. It was trimmed on one side with a feather cockade.

tyubeterka: Uzbekistan. Brightly colored turban.

tyubetevka: Uzbekistan. Embroidered velvet skull cap worn by both genders.

tzakos: Greece. A woman's short, closely fitted bodice with elbow-length fitted sleeves.

tzanga: *See* zancha.

tzute: Guatemala. Square piece of fabric worn by men as a cloak or neckerchief.

tzutes: Guatemala. Head kerchief worn on the head by both men and women.

U

uaine: Ireland. Gaelic word for green.

uaine-donn: Ireland. Gaelic word for bronze green.

uaine-dorcha: Ireland. Gaelic word for olive.

uainicionn: Ireland. Gaelic word for lambskin.

uaki: *See* uwaki.

uati: *See* uwaki.

uauahi: United States of America. Hawaii. Smoky gray.

Überschuh: Germany. Galosh.

ubong: Borneo. Cotton thread.

ubong mata: *See* kain mata.

ubrac: Poland. To clothe or to dress.

ubrus: Slovakia. Type of shawl.

ubuhlalu: Rhodesia. Ndebele. Small beads used on a woman's waistband.

üçetek: Turkey. Woman's anteri with skirt deeply slit from each hip to hem.

uchdach: Ireland. Gaelic word for breastplate.

uchd-bheart: Ireland. Gaelic word for cuirass.

uchd-chrios: Ireland. Gaelic word for stomacher.

uchidashi-kanoko: Japan. Painted kanoko with printed dots with raised centers.

uchikake: Japan. Quilted robe worn over a kimono.

uchilla maki chumbi: Ecuador. A narrow belt.

uchiwa: Japan. Open fan.

uçkar: Turkey. 1. Waist drawstring of cream cotton or linen. Ends are embroidered. 2. Kerchief.

ugly

udbandha: India. A silken stuff from Khanaka.

udju: Egyptian (4000–30 B.C.E.). Ground green malachite used for eye shadow.

udo: Roman (753 B.C.E.–323 C.E.). Foot covering similar to the modern slipper.

udones: Roman (753 B.C.E.–323 C.E.). Stockings of sewn fabric.

ufanta: Bolivia. Long scarf or sash.

ugly: Crinoline (1840–1865 C.E.). 1. United Kingdom. Used from 1848 to 1864, popular name for extra brim on a hat or bonnet. Made from semi-circles of cane covered in silk that could be collapsed up against the brim when not in use. Used to protect the face from the sun. 2. Combination walking stick and sunscreen carried by ladies at the seaside to protect their faces.

ugurulik: Worn by Inuits, boots made of caribou or bearded sealskin.

'uha hipa: United States of America. Hawaii. Leg-of-mutton sleeve.

uhi maka: United States of America. Hawaii. Veil; mask.

uibok: *See* uiryu.

uilebril: Holland. Horn-rimmed glasses.

uiose: Romania. Man's woolen vest.

uiryu: Korea. Clothing.

ujjas: *See* kurti.

ujuta: Bolivia. Sandals.

ukara: Nigeria. Tie-dyed cloth with alternating blue and white triangles.

ukaw: *See* oko.

ukon: Japan. Canary yellow.

ukrasavanje: *See* vez.

uku churana: Ecuador. Pollera.

ukunchina: Ecuador. 1. Quichua word for an underskirt. 2. Woman's white woolen wrapper worn under the anaku.

ula: Ireland. Gaelic word for beard.

'ula: United States of America. Hawaii. Red; scarlet.

'ula hiwa: United States of America. Hawaii. Purplish red.

'ula maku'e: United States of America. Hawaii. Dark or purplish red.

'ula palani: United States of America. Hawaii. Bright red percale.

'ula waina: United States of America. Hawaii. Wine red.

'ula weo: United States of America. Hawaii. Dark red.

ulach: Ireland. Gaelic word for beard.

'ulahea: United States of America. Hawaii. Faded red.

'ula'okoko: United States of America. Hawaii. Blood red.

ulchadh: Ireland. Gaelic word for beard.

uld: Denmark. Wool.

ulimi: Zulu man's bandolier.

uliuli: Samoa. Bronze.

ulkhaulik: Afghanistan. Under-tunic.

ull: 1. Norway. Old Norse word for wool. 2. Sweden. Wool.

ulos godang: Indonesia. Skirt cloth worn as sarong.

ulos lobu-lobu: Indonesia. A circular cloth used to encircle the bridal couple while they eat a ritual meal.

ulos suri-suri: Indonesia. Cloth given on birth of a child. Worn as a shoulder drape.

ulster: Bustle (1865–1890 C.E.). United Kingdom. 1. Man's single- or double-breasted overcoat with waist belt. Initially had hood, but by 1870s was detachable. In 1875, the ticket pocket was added on the left sleeve above the cuff. 2. After 1877, a woman's long, sometimes trained, overcoat similar the men's version. Often made of waterproof material.

ulsterette: Lightweight ulster.

ultramarine: Intense dark blue color with purple tint.

ulub: Borneo. Shell beads.

uma tazina: Ecuador. Quichua word for a headwrap.

uma watana: Ecuador. Quichua word for a woman's headwrap.

uma watarina tazina: Ecuador. Quichua word for a kind of woman's headwrap.

uma-no-tsura: Japan. Literally "horse's face," a long bonnet worn to protect the face from falling snow.

umavadi: India. A linen cadar.

umber: Dark brown.

umbo: Roman (753 B.C.E.–323 C.E.). Pouch or fold made by draping the upper left portion of the toga to enclose the right hand.

umbrela: *See* sombrinha chapeau de sol.

umbrella: Initially a Chinese sunshade used to protect skin from the sun's harmful rays. By 17th century, used for decorative rather than utilitarian purposes.

umbrella cloth: Tightly woven fabric used to cover umbrellas.

umbrella gingham: Silk, cotton, or rayon gingham fabric used to cover umbrellas.

umbrella pleats: Flared seams resembling lines of an umbrella.

umbrella robe: Early Georgian (1700–1750 C.E.) to Late Georgian (1750–1790 C.E.). Long overgarment.

umbrella silk: Taffeta or twilled fabric of silk, synthetic, or cotton with finished selvage.

umbrella skirt: Gay Nineties (1890–1900 C.E.). United Kingdom. In 1891, a woman's skirt cut on cross grain. One seam down center back hidden by double box

pleats. Fitted with the use of darts. Most commonly lined and might be trained.

umgingqo: Zulu man's fabric roll covered in beads. It is worn on the arm, neck, chest, waist, or loin.

'umi'i kuapo: United States of America. Hawaii. Belt buckle.

'umi'i lauoho: United States of America. Hawaii. Hair clasp.

'umi'umi: United States of America. Hawaii. Whiskers; beard; mustache.

umpal: Indonesia. Silk scarf.

umritzur: Bustle (1865–1890 C.E.). Introduced in 1880, rough surfaced fabric of camel hair. Soft and very lightweight.

umsisi: *See* ishiwaba.

umtika: Rhodesia. Ndebele. A kilt of twisted skins of monkeys and wild cats.

umutsha: Zulu. Loincloth made with a thin cowhide belt that suspends a calf-skin flap in the back and twisted strips of civet, monkey, or genet fur in the back.

una: United States of America. Hawaii. Tortoiseshell.

uncut velvet: Deep pile velvet with loops uncut.

undaweya: Swahili. Underpants.

under cap: Renaissance (1450–1550 C.E.) to Elizabethan (1550–1625 C.E.). Indoor cap, worn by either gender similar to coif. Worn under hat, cap, or bonnet for additional warmth.

under proper: Elizabethan (1550–1625 C.E.). Frame that held up the large lace collars.

underhandkerchief: Crinoline (1840–1865 C.E.). Another name for a chemisette.

under-serc: Byzantine and Romanesque (400–1200 C.E.). United Kingdom. Literally "undershirt."

undersleeve: Crinoline (1840–1865 C.E.). Woman's sleeve, worn under the sleeve of a jacket or coat. The undersleeve was not attached permanently to a blouse but rather was basted into place with each wearing.

undersleeve

undervest: Crinoline (1840–1865 C.E.) to 1890–1899 C.E. In 1840s, woman's merino thigh-length, sleeved under-waist-coat. In 1875, women began to wear colored version of washable silk with gussets for the breasts. In 1890s, of natural wool with ventilating perforations in armpits. Men's version referred to as undershirts.

underwraedel: Byzantine and Romanesque (400–1200 C.E.). United Kingdom. Possibly loincloth.

Undine: Crinoline (1840–1865 C.E.). In November 1859, a plush or velvet mantle with mousquetaire sleeves and crocheted medallions.

undonghwa: Korea. Sneakers.

undress: Early Georgian (1700–1750 C.E.) to Romantic (1815–1840 C.E.). Term referring to everyday dress.

ungen-nishiki: Japan. Early weft patterned nishiki in a rainbow striped design.

ungkoi: Borneo. Red or black trimming on the collar of a jacket.

unhye: Korea. Upper-class woman's or girl's silk shoe.

union: Fabric woven with linen weft and cotton warp or cotton weft and wool warp.

union suit: Undergarment of shirt and drawers in one piece.

unitard: One-piece, fitted bodysuit. Reaches from neck or shoulders to ankles, sometimes ending in stirrup straps.

university athletic costume: Bustle (1865–1890 C.E.). United Kingdom. Uniform worn by university students in athletic classes consisting of short sleeved vest, knee-length knickerbockers, waist sash, ankle socks, and laced shoes.

university vest: Bustle (1865–1890 C.E.). United Kingdom. Introduced in 1872, man's double-breasted waistcoat worn with university coat.

unkelai: Biblical (Unknown–30 C.E.). Hebrew's under-tunic.

unkhuña: Bolivia and Peru. Small square of fabric used in pastoral rituals.

'unku: Ecuador. Aztec man's knee-length tunic.

unku: Bolivia and Peru. Tunic.

unkucha: Peru. Woolen petticoat.

unmentionables: Romantic (1815–1840 C.E.) to Bustle (1865–1890 C.E.). One of many euphemisms for men's trousers. *See also* inexpressibles.

unmunsa: Korea. Cloud patterned sa silk.

unnabi: India. The color mauve.

unnatasikharavestana: India. An elaborate, tall turban.

unpich'ui: Korea. Silver colored.

unpit: Korea. Silver, the color.

unterrock: Switzerland. Woman's house dress.

Unterrock: Germany. Petticoat.

unwhisperables: *See* unmentionables.

'upa 'oki nihoniho: United States of America. Hawaii. Literally "shears for cutting points," pinking shears.

upanah: India. Ritual sandals of antelope or bearskin.

upanat: India. Generic term for shoes.

uparanī: *See* pachedī.

uparanū: *See* pachedī.

uparivastra: India. Hem of a garment.

uparna: India. Silk or muslin scarf worn as a shawl or veil. May have gold or silver threads woven into it.

upasampanna: India. A well-dressed person.

upasamvyana: India. Man's loincloth-like garment, generally white.

upasirsaka: India. Pearl necklace.

upavasana: India. Woman's dupatta.

upavastra: *See* pachedī.

upavita: India. An upper body garment worn over the left shoulder and under the right arm.

up-legen: Byzantine and Romanesque (400–1200 C.E.). United Kingdom. Pin or ornament for the hair.

upper stocks: Elizabethan (1550–1625 C.E.). Breeches or hose reaching from waist to mid-thigh.

uraeus: Egyptian (4000–30 B.C.E.). Standing cobra. Symbol of royalty.

uraq-awa: Bolivia. Yellowish brown.

urasala: India. Camlet.

urbāi: India. Footwear.

urbasī: India. Dress worn as a top garment.

urdimbre: Guatemala. Warp on a loom.

urdir: Ecuador. To warp.

urku: Bolivia. A wrapped dress.

urna: India. Goat's or sheep's wool.

urna sutra: India. Woolen thread.

urumali: *See* rumala.

usala: Somalia. Beaded belt.

usan: Korea. Umbrella.

usgaraidh: Ireland. Gaelic word for jewelry.

usgar-bhràghad: Ireland. Necklace.

usgar-mheur: Ireland. Gaelic word for jeweled ring.

ushiro-migoro: Japan. The back panel of a kimono or haori.

ushnisa: India. A turban.

ushnisha: India. Turban.

ushuta: Ecuador. Sandals with leather or tire soles.

usnìsa: India. Man's headdress; turban.

üst tuman: Iran. Woman's outer skirt worn over middle skirt (tuman) and petticoat (ic tuman).

usuaka: Japan. Pink.

usugake: Japan. Medium blue.

'usut'a: Ecuador. Leather sandals.

usuta: Peru. Sandals made from the soft untanned leather from the neck of the camelids. The sandals are tied on with cords of colored wool or leather.

usuzumi: Japan. Gray.

utcu: Ecuador. Quichua word for cotton.

utrecht velvet: Cotton velvet.

utskurdsøm: Norway. Very fine cut-thread work.

uttarasanga: India. 1. Gown. 2. Woman's bodice-like garment.

uttariya: 1. India. Upper body garment. 2. *See* chaddar.

uwaki: United States of America. Hawaii. Watch.

uwaki pulima: United States of America. Hawaii. Wristwatch.

V

vachóris: Greece. Persian shawl worn as a belt.

vað: *See* klœði.

vadata: Lithuania. Needle.

Vadem: Germany. Thread.

vadhuya: India. Bride's dress. After the marriage ceremony, the robe is given to a Brahmin.

vadkyu: India. Embroidered corners of the phaphro.

vadmal: Norway. Coarse woolen fabric.

vadmala: Lithuania. Cloth.

vaga: India. A knee-length jacket.

vagabond hat: Brimmed sports hat.

vagem de ervilhas: Portugal. Peascod.

vagho: India. Coat in the jama style.

vahitha: India. An early variety of woolen cloth.

vahitika: India. Woolen fabric.

vài: Vietnam. Cloth.

vài bò: Vietnam. Denim.

vài bông: Vietnam. Cotton cloth; flannelette.

vài hoa: Vietnam. Printed fabric.

vai long-ðình: Vietnam. Shoulders of a coat.

vài màn: Vietnam. Mosquito netting.

vài to: Vietnam. Coarse fabric.

vài trorn: Vietnam. Plain fabric.

vài vóc: Vietnam. Generic term for cloth.

vaijayantika: India. Necklace made of groups of five gems each.

vaikaksaki: India. Woman's bodice worn tied on the right shoulder.

vaikaksha: India. Straps crossed on the chest.

vaio: Italy. Vair.

vair: Fur of northern gray squirrel that is blue gray on top and white on the underside. When sewn together in squares alternating color, called menu vair; with larger squares, grand vair or gros vair. Worn only by kings or some magistrates.

vajo: Italy. Squirrel belly fur.

vajramsuka: India. An asbestos fabric imported from China.

vakala: India. A pure gold or silver fabric.

văl: Romania. Veil.

Val: *See* Valenciennes lace.

valaya: India. Bangle bracelet.

valencia: Crinoline (1840–1865 C.E.). Fabric with a silk or cotton warp and a wool weft. Used for riding habits.

Valencia: Crinoline (1840–1865 C.E.). 1. In 1854, yoked cloak. Skirt was box-pleated in back, plain in front. The portion over the arms was scalloped. 2. In 1856, woman's semi-circular cloth cape trimmed with velvet, silk fringe tassels, and ribbon.

Valencian: Crinoline (1840–1865 C.E.). 1. Introduced in 1862, woman's ankle-length black velvet shawl that came to point in the center front and center back. It was wrist length on sides and embroidered along the hem in a floral pattern. 2. In 1857, woman's shawl with a deep gathered flounce. 3. In 1858, a woman's satin and cloth wrap with double sleeves. Trimmed with tassels.

Valenciennes lace: Fine bobbin lace made in one piece. Commonly referred to as Val.

valenki: Russia. High felt boots.

valentia: Fabric similar to toilinet.

Valentia: Crinoline (1840–1865 C.E.). In 1858, woman's cloth cloak with full-circle skirt trimmed with velvet bands. The waist-length bertha was trimmed with brandenbourgs.

vali: Samoa. Makeup.

valkala: India. Bark-strip garments worn by Hindu ascetics.

váll: Hungary. Woman's red cloth vest trimmed with black lace.

vallancy: Late Georgian (1750–1790 C.E.). Very large wig that shaded or partially hid the face.

vambraces: Early Gothic (1200–1350 C.E.). Armor plate for lower arm.

vampay: United States. Short sock of wool.

vân: Vietnam. Silk fabric with a woven cloud design.

vanadana: India. A loom.

vanakara: India. A weaver.

vandyke: Late Georgian (1750–1790 C.E.). 1. Dentate border or lace or material. 2. Lace-bordered handkerchief.

vandyke dress: Late Georgian (1750–1790 C.E.). United Kingdom. Fashion similar to that of the Van Dyke period.

vàng ánh: Vietnam. Shining yellow.

vàng đo: Vietnam. Gold jewels.

vàng huyên: Vietnam. Earring.

vàng khè: Vietnam. Very yellow.

vàng muròi: Vietnam. Pure gold.

vàng ròng: *See* vàng muròi.

vàng y: *See* vàng muròi.

vangala: India. A plain cotton stuff.

van-hài: Vietnam. Scholar's shoes.

vân-phuc: Vietnam. Evening dress.

varabana: India. A man's thick quilted coat.

varasi: India. A very coarse cadar.

varedira: Ecuador. Machine-made edging.

varens: Crinoline (1840–1865 C.E.). United Kingdom. Introduced in 1847, woman's short outdoor jacket with loose sleeves. It was made of cashmere or velvet and lined in silk. It was a combination in cut of the casaweck and the polka.

vareuse: France. Loose, rough jacket.

Varna: Crinoline (1840–1865 C.E.). In 1854, mantle with arm slits, plain front, and box-pleated back on a yoke. Trimmed with velvet and deep fringe.

varna-krtsna: India. Shoes of white or colored leather.

varsikasatika: India. A loincloth.

varti: *See* dasa.

varvana: India. Coat-like upper garment.

vasa: India. Lower body garment.

vasas: *See* amsuka.

vasconso: Portugal. Basque.

vashti: *See* dasa.

vasquine: *See* basquine.

vastagkabát: *See* rokk.

vastra: India. 1. Hem of garment. 2. *See* amsuka.

vastragrantha: India. A woman's waistcloth.

vastrañchala: India. Hem of garment.

vat: Vietnam. Skirt of a Vietnamese dress.

Vatermörder: Crinoline (1840–1865 C.E.). Germany. Man's tall collar with two points on the cheeks.

vati: India. A fabric, the specifics are unknown.

vaturinapada: India. The heavy foot guards worn by soldiers in battle.

vavr: India. Buckskin.

váy: Vietnam. Skirt; petticoat.

vaya: India. A weaver.

veau velours: Soft finished calfskin.

vedla: India. Upper ear earrings.

vegachiya: *See* vaikaksaki.

vegetable ivory buttons: Crinoline (1840–1865 C.E.). Introduced in 1862, ball buttons made from the South American palm tree seed.

veile: Byzantine and Romanesque (400–1200 C.E.) to Renaissance (1450–1550 C.E.). United Kingdom. Middle English word for veil.

veldschoen: South Africa. Shoe of untanned hide.

veldschoen

veletine: Directoire and First Empire (1790–1815 C.E.). Introduced in 1812, small figured silk fabric.

velette: Renaissance (1450–1550 C.E.). Italy. Horse soldier's coat.

veli: Samoa. Veil.

velleres fulvi: Roman (753 B.C.E.–323 C.E.). Tawny fleeces.

velleres nigri: Roman (753 B.C.E.–323 C.E.). Black fleeces.

velludillo: Spain. Velveteen.

velludo: Portugal. Velvet.

vellum: 1. Fine skin of lamb, kid, or calf. 2. Roman (753 B.C.E.–323 C.E.). Fleece. 3. Fine, plain weave, smooth cotton fabric made to imitate calfskin parchment.

vellum cloth: Fine transparent linen or cotton fabric.

velluto: Italy. Velvet.

velo: 1. Spain. Black lace scarf worn for shopping and attending mass. 2. Italy. Crepe.

velonísça: Greece. Lace made with a sewing needle.

velour: Soft, closely woven fabric with a short pile.

velour de coton: France. Velveteen.

velours: France. Velvet.

velours de coton croisé: France. Velveteen.

velours de laine: Gay Nineties (1890–1900 C.E.). In 1894, a wool fabric with velvet stripes or checks.

velours de Venise: Gay Nineties (1890–1900 C.E.). In 1891, a very expensive figured velvet.

velours frappé: Velvet with raised patterns.

velours Grégoire: Directoire (1790–1815 C.E.). France. The art of creating a picture woven in velvet. It was named for Gaspard Grégoire (1751–1846 C.E.), a velvet maker who perfected the technique.

velours Impératrice: Crinoline (1840–1865 C.E.). In 1858, white corded silk.

veloutine: Merino wool corded fabric with velvety finish.

velure: Velvet or similar fabric.

velveret: Crinoline (1840–1865 C.E.). Fustian with velvet face.

velvet: Satin, plain, or twill weave fabric with a short, soft, thick pile.

velvet imperatrice: Crinoline (1840–1865 C.E.). Introduced in 1860, dark terry velvet.

velveteen: All cotton fabric similar to velvet.

vema: *See* vanadanda.

veman: India. A loom.

Venediger Spitze: Germany. Venetian lace.

venera: *See* benerica.

venetian: Strong sateen.

Venetian bars: Embroidered lace made with bars of buttonhole stitches.

Venetian bonnet: Directoire and First Empire (1790–1815 C.E.). United Kingdom. Popular in 1800, woman's small straw bonnet trimmed with straw wreaths or flowers. Ribbons bowed in back and tied loosely in the front.

Venetian cloak: Romantic (1815–1840 C.E.). United Kingdom. Introduced in 1829, woman's black satin caped cloak with a collar and wide hanging sleeves.

Venetian cloth: 1. Mercerized cotton fabric with warp-face satin. Formerly called farmer's satin. 2. Soft wool fabric similar to prunella.

Venetian crape cloth: Gay Nineties (1890–1900 C.E.). A dull, heavy mixture of silk and wool.

Venetian edging: Crinoline (1840–1865 C.E.). In 1856, lace edging like Brussels edging.

Venetian embroidery: Openwork embroidery.

Venetian lace: Italy. Variety of laces including reticella, cutwork, drawn work, raised point, etc.

Venetian sleeve: Crinoline (1840–1865 C.E.). United Kingdom. Introduced in 1858, woman's day sleeve fitted at the top and flared to the forearm from where it was slit nearly to the shoulder. Worn with an engageante.

venetians: Elizabethan (1550–1625 C.E.). Bouffant breeches tied at the knee with ribbons.

veni: India. A small hair fillet of flowers.

Venice: Crinoline (1840–1865 C.E.). In 1857, woman's flounced cloak with deep Grecian folds that formed a collar.

Venice pearls: Crinoline (1840–1865 C.E.). Fake pearls.

venise: Fine damask table linen.

ventail: On an armored helmet, the part below the visor made with hinges to allow the passage of air.

ventilated pants: (1930–1940 C.E.). United Kingdom. Term used in the press for men's shorts.

ventoye: Elizabethan (1550–1625 C.E.) to Restoration (1660–1700 C.E.). Italy. Short stemmed fan with a rectangular vane.

ventus textilis: Roman (753 B.C.E.–323 C.E.). A fine muslin.

veo: Croatia and Serbia. Veil.

verd Nile: Bustle (1865–1890 C.E.). In 1869, gas light green.

verde: Portugal and Spain. Green.

verde celedón: Spain. Celadon green.

verde césped: Spain. Grass green.

verde limón: Spain. Lime green.

verde nilo: Spain. Nile green.

verde salvia: Spain. Sage green.

verde trébol: Spain. Irish green.

verdigris: Bluish or yellowish green.

verdingale: *See* farthingale.

verdugado: Spain. Farthingale.

vergette à la chinoise: Early Georgian (1700–1750 C.E.). France. Literally "Chinese dusting brush," it refers to the front roll of hair on forehead of a wig.

vermelhão: Portugal. Vermilion.

vermelho: 1. Portugal. Red. 2. *See* carmezim.

vermicelli: Late Georgian (1750–1790 C.E.). Italy. Fine motifs applied to a fabric in a swirling pattern.

vermilion: Intense red.

Vermummung: Germany. Fancy dress.

Veronese cuirasse: Bustle (1865–1890 C.E.). United Kingdom. Jersey bodice that laced up the back.

Veronese dress: Bustle (1865–1890 C.E.). United Kingdom. Popular in 1880s, knee-length, woolen, princess line tunic with deep points on the bottom that reached to the hem of the box-pleated silk under-skirt.

vert: France. Green.

vert malachite: Bustle (1865–1890 C.E.). In 1866, luminous green.

vertugadin: *See* farthingale.

vertugadin francais: *See* farthingale.

vertugale: Spain. Farthingale.

veš: *See* donje rublje.

vesa za cipele: *See* pertla.

vesh: India. Generic term for clothes.

veshovi meshok: Russia. Haversack.

vesses: Renaissance (1450–1550 C.E.) to Elizabethan (1550–1625 C.E.). Type of worsted fabric.

vest: 1. Short fitted upper body sleeveless garment. 2. Extra piece of trim on blouse front. 3. Short for undervest. 4. Obsolete term for robe, ecclesiastical vestment, or outer clothing.

vestana: India. Man's headdress; turban.

veste: *See* jaquette.

veste da camera: Italy. Nightgown.

veste di camera: Italy. Dressing gown.

veste Russe: Crinoline (1840–1865 C.E.). In 1862, ladies' braided blouse.

vest

vestee: Imitation vest or blouse front.

vestes: Roman (753 B.C.E.–323 C.E.). Piece of woven cloth draped by the wearer.

vesti: *See* dhoti.

vestido: Portugal. Dress; frock.

vestido de noche: Spain. Evening dress.

vestidos: Spain. Clothing.

vestimentum: *See* vestis.

vestir: 1. Portugal. Clothing. 2. Spain. To clothe or to dress.

vestire: Italy. To clothe or dress.

vestīre: Roman (753 B.C.E.–323 C.E.). To clothe or to dress.

vestis: Roman (753 B.C.E.–323 C.E.). Clothing.

vestiti: Italy. Generic term for clothing.

vestito da sera: Italy. Evening dress.

vestitus: *See* vestis.

veston: *See* gilet-veste.

vestuário: Portugal. Clothing.

vésure: Crinoline (1840–1865 C.E.). In 1862, orange color.

vêtement à la Créole: Late Georgian (1750–1790 C.E.). France. Style similar to that worn by women in the New World.

vétements: France. Clothing.

vethaka: India. A simple sash cummerbund.

vettam: India. A kind of very white fabric.

vét-tông: Vietnam. Suit coat; jacket.

Vevai cap: Romantic (1815–1840 C.E.). Worn in 1820, woman's snug black velvet cap with a heron's plume.

vexillum: Elizabethan (1550–1625 C.E.). Scarf worn tied about the crozier. *See also* infula.

vez: Bosnia. Embroidery.

vézane: Greece. Richly embroidered stockings.

vezzo: *See* collana.

vhulungu ha madi: Zimbabwe. Literally "beads of the water," translucent pale blue, blue green, or blue gray beads.

ví tay: Vietnam. Handbag.

viatu vyu Johanna: Swahili. Shoes with long straps that wrap up the shin.

viatu vyu kliipa: Swahili. Shoes with thick crepe soles.

viatu vyu malapa: Swahili. Backless shoes or slippers.

viatu vyu matende: Swahili. Shoes with crepe soles and thick heels.

vibushana: India. An elaborate necklace of looped strings of pearls and gems.

vichy: Stiff, yarn dyed cotton fabric similar to gingham.

vicitra: India. A variegated or figured silk.

victoria: 1. Romantic (1815–1840 C.E.). United Kingdom. Blue. 2. (1890–1899 C.E.). In 1895, a reddish violet.

Victoria: Crinoline (1840–1865 C.E.). 1. In 1853, promenade mantle of appliqued silk on silk net. It had a scalloped border. 2. In 1854, round mantelet with deep fringe at lower edge. It had a large bow of silk between the shoulder blades. 3. In 1855, velvet mantle trimmed with rich galloon, velvet, satin moiré, and deep fringe. 4. In 1856, woman's velvet mantle with very wide sleeves. It was trimmed with passementerie, buttons, and fringe. 5. In 1858, mauve, the Queen's purple. 6. In 1858, silk gown with plain underskirt. The overskirt was en tablier and was trimmed with plush. The bodice had a pointed corsage, two puff sleeves, and deep cuffs.

Victoria bodice: Gay Nineties (1890–1900 C.E.). United Kingdom. In 1899, a décolleté evening bodice with shoulder straps to support it. It was often trimmed with tulle ruchings and ruffles.

Victoria bonnet: Romantic (1815–1840 C.E.). United Kingdom. Introduced in 1838, small-crowned, small brimmed satin bonnet with ties under the chin. It had a long bavolet and was often trimmed with flowers.

Victoria cage: Bustle (1865–1890 C.E.). Trade name for steel skeleton skirt.

Victoria corset: Crinoline (1840–1865 C.E.). United Kingdom. Named for Queen Victoria, a heavily curved corset with deep bust gores that supported a woman's bust in an era before brassieres. It was particularly popular with full-figured women.

Victoria corset

Victoria crepe: Crinoline (1840–1865 C.E.) to Bustle (1865–1890 C.E.). United Kingdom. A cheap cotton version of crimped silk mourning crape.

Victoria lawn: *See* bishop's lawn.

Victoria mantle: Crinoline (1840–1865 C.E.). United Kingdom. Popular from 1850 to 1867, knee-length mantle with a collar and wide hanging sleeves. Often had wide, deep colored border.

Victoria pardessus: Crinoline (1840–1865 C.E.). In 1859, gray or speckled fabric pardessus framed with a wide border. The hood had pointed border around the face. The border was trimmed with rows of narrow black ribbon velvet.

Victoria pelisse-mantle: Crinoline (1840–1865 C.E.). United Kingdom. Introduced in 1855, double-breasted, knee-length mantle with flat collar, short wide sleeves, and side pockets.

Victoria silk: Gay Nineties (1890–1900 C.E.). In 1893, a silk and wool blend fabric used to make petticoats. Guaranteed to rustle.

Victoria sleeve: Romantic (1815–1840 C.E.) and 1890–1899 C.E. United Kingdom. Popular in 1838 and 1840s, fitted day sleeve with large flounce at elbows topped with two smaller ones. Revived in 1890s.

victorieuse: Bustle (1865–1890 C.E.). In 1882, repped silk.

victorine: United Kingdom. 1. Crinoline (1840–1865 C.E.). Popular in 1850s, narrow, flat neck tippet with short ends and fur edging. Tied at throat with ribbon. 2. (1890–1899 C.E.). In 1899, a waist- or ankle-length cloak with a high fluted collar ending in fur flounce.

vicuna: Wool from South American goat.

vidrilho: Portugal. Glass bead.

vieil argent: Bustle (1865–1890 C.E.). In 1875, subdued silver color.

Vielfraß: Germany. Wolverine fur.

vientre de ardilla gris: Spain. Vair.

viereckiger schleier: Jewish woman's square head covering worn only for synagogue and Sabbath. Cap with two starched wings of white linen. Covers the hair.

vierspitzige Faltung: Germany. Multipointed fold.

vigogna: Italy. Vicuna.

vigogne: France. Vicuna.

Vigogne: Germany. Vicuna.

vigone: Charles I and the Commonwealth (1625–1660 C.E.). Man's vicuna wool hat.

vihita kappasa: India. Calendered cloth.

vijayachchhanda: India. Necklace made from 504 strings of pearls.

vijayantika: India. A necklace made of pearls, rubies, emeralds, blue stones, and diamonds.

villi: Roman (753 B.C.E.–323 C.E.). Shaggy tufts on the surface of an unshorn fabric.

vilna: Lithuania. Wool.

vîlnic: Romania. Cotton or woolen skirt richly embroidered.

vilnos: Lithuania. Wool.

vilt: Holland. Felt.

Vilz: Germany. Felt.

vincha: Ecuador. Quichua term for barrettes.

vindi: Ecuador and Guatemala. Spinning wheel.

vinti: India. Gold finger ring.

Violet: Crinoline (1840–1865 C.E.). In 1855, very full mantilla trimmed with satin or taffeta ribbons in rows.

violet of the Alps: Crinoline (1840–1865 C.E.). In 1860, new color.

violeta: Portugal. Violet; violet colored.

violin bodice: Bustle (1865–1890 C.E.). United Kingdom. Introduced in 1874, day bodice with violin-shaped piece of dark material inserted in the center back.

virago sleeve: Long sleeve with periodic horizontal ties of elastic that create a series of puffs.

virágozás: Hungary. Literally "flowering," embroidery on szür.

viramo: India. Particularly coveted form of dupatta.

virgin wool: Any wool not previously manufactured into fabric.

virly: Early Gothic (1200–1350 C.E.). Green fabric made in Vire, Normandy.

visagière: France. Open part of hood around face.

visera: Spain. Peak of a cap.

visiera de berretto: Italy. Peak of a cap.

visité: Crinoline (1840–1865 C.E.). France. Introduced in 1845, large printed shawl that buttoned down center front. Came in various lengths and fabrics and stayed in usage until around 1885.

vison: France. Mink fur.

visón: Spain. Mink fur.

visone: Italy. Mink fur.

visor: Elizabethan (1550–1625 C.E.). Face guard of steel helmet.

visscherspij: Elizabethan (1550–1625 C.E.). Holland. Fisherman's smock.

vitha: India. A kamarband clasp.

vitis: Roman (753 B.C.E.–323 C.E.). Official baton of centurion.

vitses: Greece. Designs knitted on wool stockings.

vitta: Roman (753 B.C.E.–323 C.E.). Bandeau worn by freeborn women to hold back their hair.

Vittoria: Crinoline (1840–1865 C.E.). In 1857, Chantilly lace talma with a bertha.

vivos: Renaissance (1450–1550 C.E.). Spain. Pipings.

viyella: United Kingdom. Lightweight twill fabric in a wool and cotton blend.

Vlahs: Germany. Flax.

vlas: Holland. Flax.

vlieger: Elizabethan (1550–1625 C.E.). Holland. Woman's garment similar in cut to Spanish ropa. Literally "flyer."

vlno: Czechoslovakia. Wool.

voering: Holland. Lining.

voided shoe: Renaissance (1450–1550 C.E.) to Elizabethan (1550–1625 C.E.). Very fashionable in first half of 16th century, a shoe with a sole, toe-cap, and instep strap.

voile: 1. *See* nun's veiling. 2. France. Veil.

voile de laine: France. Wool voile.

voilette: Crinoline (1840–1865 C.E.). Very fashionable small veil.

vojlok: Russia. Felt.

volan: Romantic (1815–1840 C.E.) to Bustle (1865–1890 C.E.). Small flounce used to trim a sleeve.

volant: 1. Romantic (1815–1840 C.E.). Light unlined jerkin with no pockets, buttons, or buttonholes. Buttoned only at the neck. 2. Crinoline (1840–1865 C.E.). In 1854, promenade scarf with three rows of taffeta ruffles. Most made in green, tans, and drabs.

volante: 1. Renaissance (1450–1550 C.E.). Spain. Thin silk. 2. Spain. Flounce.

volanten: Switzerland. Loose gown.

volcan: Bustle (1865–1890 C.E.). France. In 1888, reddish terra-cotta.

volet: Early Gothic (1200–1350 C.E.). Short veil worn at back of head by women.

volpe: Italy. Fox fur.

volpe o renard: Italy. Fox fur.

volubilis: Gay Nineties (1890–1900 C.E.). In 1895, a shade of purple.

volupere: Early Gothic (1200–1350 C.E.) to Elizabethan (1550–1625 C.E.). Cap or headdress.

vòng huyèn: Vietnam. Jet bracelet.

vòng tai: Vietnam. Earrings.

vonica: Slovakia. Nosegay.

voorschoot: *See* schort.

vorotnicek: *See* vorotnik.

vorotnik: Russia. Collar.

vrai reseau: True net ground for lace.

vraka: Greece. Men's very full trousers with fullness between the legs. Plural is vraki.

vrpca: Bosnia. Ribbon.

vú già: Vietnam. Falsies.

vual': Russia. Veil.

Vulcanite buttons: Bustle (1865–1890 C.E.). Introduced in 1888, buttons made from ebonite, a hard form of vulcanized rubber.

vulcanized rubber bands: Crinoline (1840–1865 C.E.). Patented in 1845, manufactured for garters and belts.

vulnenik: Bulgaria. Kilted back skirt.

vulotó: Greece. Striped, colored silk.

vuna: Croatia and Serbia. Wool.

vuoddaga: Norway. Braided ribbons used to lace the gábmaga.

vyalapanktirmañjari: India. Necklace made of stone beads.

W

wà: China. Socks; stockings; hose.

wa leng mao: China. Mongolian man's hat of strips of rattan.

Waborne lace: Elizabethan (1550–1625 C.E.). Braid lace made in Waborne, Norfolk.

Wachstuch: Germany. Oilcloth.

wàdài: China. Suspenders; garters.

wadasan: Java. A textile pattern resembling rocks.

wadded hem: Romantic (1815–1840 C.E.). In use from 1820 to 1828, hem of skirt padded out with cotton wool.

wadmal: Lapland. Thick fabric.

wadmel: Early Gothic (1200–1350 C.E.). Coarse fabric.

waed-braec: Byzantine and Romanesque (400–1200 C.E.). United Kingdom. Loincloth.

waefels: Byzantine and Romanesque (400–1200 C.E.). United Kingdom. Covering which could be used as wrap.

waffenrock: Kind of doublet or tabard worn with armor.

wahi: United States of America. Hawaii. Wrapper.

wai 'ele: United States of America. Hawaii. Black tapa dye.

wai 'ele'ele: United States of America. Hawaii. Black dye.

wai gula: *See* wai kula.

wai kula: United States of America. Hawaii. Gold colored.

wài tào: China. Qing dynasty (1644–1911). Pu fu without a badge. Worn as mandatory dress by men after 1759 for formal occasions.

waikawa: Maori. Clothing made of grass mats.

waili 'ili'i: United States of America. Hawaii. Decorated tapa.

waist cincher: (1940–1950 to 1950–1960 C.E.). United States of America. Introduced in 1947, woman's tiny girdle necessary to the New Look.

waist seam: Romantic (1815–1840 C.E.). From 1823 on, horizontal seam at waist uniting torso of a coat with the skirts.

waisyooch'u: Korea. Shirt.

wàiyi: China. Coat.

wàizhào: China. Outer garment.

wajrapallay: Bolivia. In woven fabric, a scroll motif.

w'aka: *See* chumpi.

wak'a: Peru. Woven wool sash dyed in dark and light reds.

waki: *See* uwaki.

Walachian embroidery: Solid embroidery done with single purl buttonhole stitch.

walka: 1. Ecuador and Guatemala. Bead necklace. 2. Peru. Necklaces made from the seeds of jungle plants.

walking suit: (1900–1910 C.E.). In 1901, a woman's suit with a skirt that barely missed the ground. In 1902, the hem was three to four inches above the ground.

walking out dress: (1910–1920 C.E.). United Kingdom. In the British Army, the nickname in 1914 for a full dress uniform.

Wallachian cap: Directoire and First Empire (1790–1815 C.E.). Introduced in 1812, woman's round dark sable cap worn with matching tippet.

wallka: Ecuador. Bead necklace.

wallkarina: Ecuador. Rectangular shawl.

walnut brown: Soft, warm, taffy brown.

walutu: Ecuador. A twill-weave handspun wool fabric.

wambuis: *See* buis.

wammes: Late Gothic (1350–1450 C.E.). Indoor dress worn by knights. It opened down the front where it laced or buttoned. It was open at the sides from the hip down, although these openings could

wambuis

button. It always had long tight sleeves and rarely was trimmed or embroidered. In United Kingdom, it was called the gambeson; and in France, the gambesson.

wammiss: Switzerland. House jacket.

Wams: *See* Weste.

wamus: Cardigan or heavy outer jacket.

wandabo: *See* kamis.

wandelcostuum: Holland. Lounge suit.

wandelstok: Holland. Walking stick.

wanggwan: Korea. Crown.

wangu: Ecuador. Woman's ponytail wrapped in a thin white band.

wanjang: Korea. Crown.

wano: Philippine Islands. Man's loincloth.

want: Holland. Mitten.

wantus: Fine kid mitten lined with fur. Sometimes trimmed with jewels and fur on the outside.

wapenrusting: Holland. Armor.

wappenrock: Elizabethan (1550–1625 C.E.). Germany. Worn by heralds, wide cape worn open at the sides. Generally knee length and had armorial signatures.

wara: 1. Ecuador and Guatemala. Incan breechcloth. 2. Japan. Straw. 3. Peru. Incan loincloth worn by adults, beginning at age 14 or 15.

waraji: Japan. Flat, plaited sandals of rice straw.

warak: India. Thin gold leaf used for gold-printing on fabric.

waraka: Peru. Leaves used to hold the dress up around the pelvic region while a woman works.

Wardle hat: Directoire and First Empire (1790–1815 C.E.). United Kingdom. Woman's straw hat with conical crown.

warmi camisa: Ecuador. Quichua term for a blouse.

warp: The long threads that run lengthwise in fabric.

was and tam: Egyptian (4000–30 B.C.E.). Two scepters used by dignitaries to show the support of heaven. The was was straight and the tam was curved.

wasa: Bolivia. Poncho-like garment worn over the buttocks.

Waschbär: Germany. Raccoon fur.

wasdoek: Holland. Oilcloth.

wash silk: *See* habutai.

washa fachalina: *See* washajatana.

washajatana: Ecuador. A shawl.

washing leather gloves: Romantic (1815–1840 C.E.). Popular from 1817, gloves made of washing leather.

wasjun: Byzantine and Romanesque (400–1200 C.E.) to Renaissance (1450–1550 C.E.). To clothe or dress.

wasserfall: Directoire and First Empire (1790–1815 C.E.). Austria. Piece of fringe hanging from center back of waist.

wasti: Early Gothic (1200–1350 C.E.) to Late Gothic (1350–1450 C.E.). United Kingdom. Cloak.

wastjōs: Early Gothic (1200–1350 C.E.) to Late Gothic (1350–1450 C.E.). United Kingdom. General term for clothing.

wasy: Poland. Moustache.

wat: *See* kleit.

wāt: Germany. Old High German for clothing.

wata: Palestine. Common hide shoe.

watabōshi: Japan. Silk floss cap worn by brides.

wàtào: China. Socks; ankle socks.

watashinui: Japan. Embroidery with patterned couching over long, loose threads.

watch cap: United States. Knitted navy blue cap worn by Navy.

watchet: 1. Early Gothic (1200–1350 C.E.). Blue fabric. 2. Elizabethan (1550–1625 C.E.). Pale greenish blue.

wāten: *See* werien.

waterfall back: Bustle (1865–1890 C.E.). Popular from 1868 to 1889, dress with back of skirt hooked up at intervals with string beneath the gown.

waterproof cloak: Bustle (1865–1890 C.E.). United Kingdom. Introduced in 1867, woman's cloak of waterproofed fabric. Had small tasseled hood.

Watteau body: Crinoline (1840–1865 C.E.). United Kingdom. Popular from 1853 to 1866, day basquine bodice with low square neckline. Front edges did not meet but were filled in with a chemisette crisscrossed with ribbons. Elbow-length sleeves ending in ruffles.

Watteau costume: Bustle (1865–1890 C.E.). United Kingdom. Introduced in 1868, fichu front bodice worn with skirt ending in deep pleats. Watteau pleated overdress looped up on the sides of the skirt.

Watteau hat: Early Georgian (1700–1750 C.E.). Woman's small straw hat worn tilted forward.

Watteau pleat: Early Georgian (1700–1750 C.E.). Box pleat at center back top of the neckline of a gown causing the back to be full and loose. Fronts of these gowns were fitted.

Watteau pleat

Watteau polonaise: Bustle (1865–1890 C.E.). United Kingdom. Watteau back polonaise of white fabric with flowers.

Watteau robe: Crinoline (1840–1865 C.E.). United Kingdom. Popular in 1850s, Watteau pleated ball gown worn open in front over a lace inset.

watu: Ecuador. A narrow handwoven band.

wawa chumbi: Ecuador and Guatemala. Literally "baby belt," a long narrow belt worn over the mama chumbi.

waya: Ethiopia. Man's toga-like robe.

wāyăč attāmitō: Ethiopia. Gold earrings with chains of 22 silver bells which lie on the king's chest.

wayeta: Bolivia. Woman's head covering.

waz: Poland. Hose.

wàzi: China. Socks; stockings; hose.

wealca: Byzantine and Romanesque (400–1200 C.E.). United Kingdom. Full-cut garment, worn wrapped around the body by women. Used in reference to biblical dress.

wearing sleeves: Renaissance (1450–1550 C.E.). United Kingdom. Sleeves actually worn on the arm (not the false hanging sleeves).

wedding garter: Renaissance (1450–1550 C.E.) through present. United Kingdom. Blue garter worn about leg of bride. Following the ceremony, tossed into crowd. In Renaissance, fragments of garter were worn and proudly displayed on the crowns of young men's hats.

wedding gloves: Elizabethan (1550–1625 C.E.). White gloves distributed among the wedding guests as presents.

wedding knives: Late Gothic (1350–1450 C.E.) to Restoration (1660–1700 C.E.). Pair of knives in a shared sheath given as wedding present to bride and then worn as symbol of her married status.

wedding ring hat: (1970–1980 C.E.). Introduced in 1979 by Frank Olive, a rounded crown, rolled brim hat made of shiny straw.

wedding ring velvet: Fine, lightweight velvet. Supposedly so fine that a width could be pulled through a wedding ring.

wede: *See* weed.

wedge weave blanket: United States of America. Navajo blanketry with characteristic zigzag patterns.

wedgie: Shoe with high heel and sole created in one wedge-shaped piece.

wedgwood: Dark purple blue.

wedja: Egyptian (4000–30 B.C.E.). Eye-shaped oyster shell amulet thought to keep the wearer healthy.

weed: Early Gothic (1200–1350 C.E.). Medieval term referring to garments in general.

weepers: 1. Romantic (1815–1840 C.E.). Wide muslin hatbands worn around hat of a mourner. The end of the hatband hung down in back to the waist. Generally black, but might be white if the deceased was a maiden. 2. *See* pleureuses.

weeping willow bangs: China. Woman's hairstyle with bangs cut into sweeping half circle.

weft: The threads that run selvedge to selvedge in fabric.

Weicher Hut: Germany. Homburg.

wéijin: China. Muffler.

wéiqún: China. Apron.

Weissstickerei: Germany. Household linen embroidery.

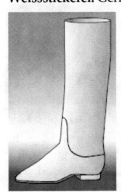

Wellington boot

Welch wig: Romantic (1815–1840 C.E.). Man's worsted cap, commonly worn by travelers.

weleweka: United States of America. Hawaii. Velvet.

Wellesley wrapper: Crinoline (1840–1865 C.E.). United Kingdom. Man's short saclike double-breasted wrapper edged in fur. Fastened in front with brandenburgs.

Wellington boot: Heavy black leather boot lined in chamois. Worn by Napoleon.

Wellington coat: Romantic (1815–1840 C.E.). United Kingdom. Fitted knee-length coat popular from 1820 to 1830.

Wellington frock: Romantic (1815–1840 C.E.). United Kingdom. Worn from 1816 through 1820s, early version of frock coat. Early version was single breasted, with roll collar, no lapels, full knee-length skirt, center back vent, side pleats, and hip-buttons. In 1818, a horizontal dart appeared at waist to give better fit. In 1823, the dart became a seam.

Wellington half-boot: Romantic (1815–1840 C.E.) and Crinoline (1840–1865 C.E.). United Kingdom. Short boot worn under the trousers which fastened under the sole with a strap.

Wellington hat: Romantic (1815–1840 C.E.). United Kingdom. Popular in 1820s and 1830s, a tall beaver hat that belled out slightly at the top.

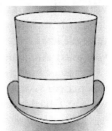

Wellington hat

Wellington pantaloons: Romantic (1815–1840 C.E.). United Kingdom. Men's pantaloons slit from calf down. Slit was held closed with buttons and loops.

wełna: Poland. Wool.

welniana kamizelka: Poland. Cardigan.

welniane skarpetki: Poland. Woolen socks.

welon: *See* kwef.

Welsh flannel: Fine flannel made from wool of Welsh sheep.

welt: Renaissance (1450–1550 C.E.). Strengthened border of garment.

Wendelring: 7–6 B.C.E. Germany. Neck ring worn by high-ranking women.

wentke: Holland. Woman's woolen gown associated with the town of Hindelopen in Friesland.

weo: United States of America. Hawaii. Red.

weret: Egyptian (4000–30 B.C.E.). White Crown of Egypt, a tall conical hat with a bulbous top. It was made of starched linen or white leather on a wicker frame.

werien: Germany. Old High German for to clothe or dress.

werkbroek of overall van stevig katoen: *See* sportpantalon.

werkpak: Holland. Dungarees.

wesekh: Egyptian (4000–30 B.C.E.). Broad collar with many strands of beads.

Weste: Germany. Waistcoat.

weyd: *See* weed.

whakatipu: *See* timu.

whalebone bodice: Renaissance (1450–1550 C.E.) to Restoration (1660–1700 C.E.). Bodice stiffened with whalebone strips.

whalebone bodies: *See* whalebone bodice.

whanake: Australia. Maori cape of cabbage tree leaves and fiber.

whang: Leather thong.

whangee: Pale yellow bamboo with large knots.

whatu: New Zealand. Maori term indicating to weave.

wheat ears: United Kingdom. Name for little oval and square motifs used in many bobbin laces.

wheel farthingale: Elizabethan (1550–1625 C.E.). United Kingdom. Wire or whalebone wheel-shaped apparatus covered in material, most commonly silk. It was worn snugly fitted around waist with front tilted down slightly. Variation on French farthingale. *See also* Catherine wheel farthingale.

wheel trimming: Romantic (1815–1840 C.E.). Silk soft puff trim formed into wheel shapes. Popular in 1824.

whey: Elizabethan (1550–1625 C.E.). Pale whitish blue.

whiitiki: Australia. Maori elongated rectangular belts made of bleached strips of flax or dress flax fiber.

whipcord: Worsted fabric with pronounced twill.

whisk: Charles I and the Commonwealth (1625–1660 C.E.). Woman's wide falling collar trimmed in wide lace.

white fox: Very delicate, long white, silky fox fur.

white scarlet: Late Gothic (1350–1450 C.E.). Fabric with undyed white background and scarlet cross-grain dyed-in design.

white turquoise: Chalky turquoise.

whitework: Any embroidery worked in white thread on a white background.

whittle: Charles I and the Commonwealth (1625–1660 C.E.). Countrywoman's large white Welsh flannel shawl.

whole backs: Romantic (1815–1840 C.E.) to present. Coats made without center back seam.

wickler: Romantic (1815–1840 C.E.). Austro-Hungarian Empire. In 1820s, redingote cut full, without cinched waist.

wide-awake

wide-awake: Romantic (1815–1840 C.E.) to Bustle (1865–1890 C.E.). Countryman's wide-brimmed, low-crowned felt hat.

widow's peak: 1. Hair growing in point in center of forehead. 2. Mourning bonnet with point in center of forehead.

wigan: Stiff, canvaslike fabric.

wijde kniebroek: Holland. Knickerbockers.

wikolia: United States of America. Hawaii. Fine lawn used for dresses; Victoria lawn.

wildbore: Early Georgian (1700–1750 C.E.) to Late Georgian (1750–1790 C.E.). Sturdy, closely woven tammy.

willow: Elizabethan (1550–1625 C.E.). Light green.

willow green: Directoire and First Empire (1790–1815 C.E.). Popular in 1811 and after, soft shade of green.

wimpel: Byzantine and Romanesque (400–1200 C.E.). United Kingdom. Headdress.

wimple: 1. Byzantine and Romanesque (400–1200 C.E.). Long piece of white linen or silk worn wrapped around neck and head. Commonly worn with veil or filet. 2. Directoire and First Empire (1790–1815 C.E.). In 1809, gauze covering for head worn for evening.

wimpled: Renaissance (1450–1550 C.E.). 1. Term meaning to be disguised. 2. To be arranged in folds.

wincey: Fabric woven with cotton or linen warp and woolen weft. Probably word derivative of linsey-woolsey.

winceyette: United Kingdom. Cotton flannel generally used for nightwear.

wincha: 1. Bolivia. Woman's headband beaded with flora and fauna. 2. Ecuador. Aztec term for a headband.

Windhaube: Germany. Balaclava.

Windsor tie: Black silk scarf cut on bias, hemmed all around, tied in loose bow at front neck.

wing: Elizabethan (1550–1625 C.E.) to Charles I and the Commonwealth (1625–1660 C.E.). Band of stiff material hiding the armseye. It might be decorated in a number of ways.

wing collar: Standing collar that opens in front with two front points folded and turned down. *See also* Gladstone collar.

wing collar

wings: 1. Renaissance (1450–1550 C.E.). Stiff, padded bands sewn into armseye as decoration. 2. Crinoline (1840–1865 C.E.). Side flaps of dormeuse.

wining: Byzantine and Romanesque (400–1200 C.E.). United Kingdom. Worn by monks, band worn around shins. Plural is winingas.

winingas: *See* wining.

winkers: Romantic (1815–1840 C.E.). United Kingdom. Term used from 1816 to 1820 to mean high points of man's shirt collar, reaching up to the eyes.

winkle-picker: (1950–1959 C.E.). Extremely pointed toe on woman's shoe.

Winslow lace: United Kingdom. Lace made in the Buckinghamshire village, Winslow.

wit: Holland. White.

witch hat: Tall pointed hat with a small brim. Based on the steeple hennin worn at the time of the first persecution of witches in England.

winkle-picker

witchoura: Romantic (1815–1840 C.E.). Hooded, fur-trimmed Polish overcoat. Often worn like cloak with sleeves left hanging.

witch's hat: Directoire and First Empire (1790–1815 C.E.). Woman's hat similar to gypsie hat with brim bent down by ribbon which reached down from crown.

witney: Heavy woolen fabric.

witschoura: *See* witchoura.

witte: Holland. Dimity.

woad: Natural blue dye similar to indigo.

wœfels: *See* hacele.

woeten: Germany. To clothe or to dress. *See also* kleiden.

woko: Nigeria. Man's tailored garment for the upper body. It is worn with a wrapper or trousers.

wol: Holland. Wool.

Wolla: Germany. Old High German term for wool.

Wolle: Germany. Wool.

wolle: Byzantine and Romanesque (400–1200 C.E.) to Renaissance (1450–1550 C.E.). United Kingdom. Middle English word for wool.

wollen goederen: Holland. Woolens.

wollen mousseline: Holland. Delaine.

wollen stof: *See* fijne.

Woodstock gloves: Early Georgian (1700–1750 C.E.) to Late Georgian (1750–1790 C.E.). United Kingdom. Riding gloves made of fawn skin.

wool: Fiber made from coat of sheep, 1-1/2 inches to 15 inches long and has natural crimp.

wool batiste: Fine, lightweight, smooth wool fabric.

wool bengaline: Gay Nineties (1890–1900 C.E.). In 1892, a wool and silk blend.

wool chiffon: Sheerest wool fabric.

wool crepe: Woolen fabric with texture like crepe.

wool plain: Crinoline (1840–1865 C.E.). In the 1860s, a white wool.

woolenet: Thin woolen fabric.

wooloes: Trinidad. Bells hung around the base of the Carnival Pierrot Grenade costume.

woolward: Renaissance (1450–1550 C.E.) to Elizabethan (1550–1625 C.E.). To be dressed entirely in wool.

worms: Early Georgian (1700–1750 C.E.). United Kingdom. Colored stripes on the lace in regimental dress.

worsted: Fabric made of long strand wool combed straight and smooth before it is spun.

worsted work: Any embroidery made with worsted wools.

wotenall thread: *See* outnal thread.

wraed: Byzantine and Romanesque (400–1200 C.E.). United Kingdom. Filet.

wrapping front dress: Directoire and First Empire (1790–1815 C.E.). United Kingdom. Bodice of dress cut to fasten one side crossed over other.

wrapping gown: Early Georgian (1700–1750 C.E.). Woman's dress with wrap-over bodice and skirt.

wrap-rascal: Early Georgian (1700–1750 C.E.) to Crinoline (1840–1865 C.E.). United Kingdom. Man's loose overcoat.

wraprascal: *See* wrap-rascal.

wrigels: Byzantine and Romanesque (400–1200 C.E.). United Kingdom. Veil worn by nuns.

wstazka: Poland. Ribbon.

wu bian: China. Man who had the queue removed, a form of punishment.

wu guan: China. Han dynasty (260 B.C.E.–7 C.E.). Headdress worn by military officials on formal occasions.

wùla: China. Leather boots.

wull: United Kingdom. Old English word for wool.

wulla: Early Gothic (1200–1350 C.E.) to Late Gothic (1350–1450 C.E.). United Kingdom. Wool.

wulle: *See* wull.

wundi: Nigeria. Middle-class man's wide gown with a round neckline and two pocket slits on the chest.

wuqa: *See* wuqayeh.

wuqayat al-darahem: Palestine. Bride's money hat.

wuqayat ed-derahim: *See* wuqayat al-darahem.

wuqayeh: Palestine. Woman's simple head cover. Large coin may be sewn on front edge. *See also* saffeh.

Wurtenburg frock: Directoire and First Empire (1790–1815 C.E.). Fashionable in 1813, dress or gown fastened in front under trim forming a jacket-like appearance. Featured long lace sleeves.

wyliecoat: Scotland. Petticoat, undervest, or nightdress.

X

xà-cap: Vietnam. Leggings.

xà-cùr: Vietnam. Nacre.

xale: Portugal. Shawl; plaid.

xám xì: Vietnam. Ash gray colored.

xamete: Late Gothic (1350–1450 C.E.) Spain. Heavy, rich silk, often embroidered with gold thread.

xám-xit: Vietnam. Dark gray.

xanh biec: Vietnam. Emerald green colored.

xanh biéc: Vietnam. Deep sky blue colored.

xanh da giò-i: Vietnam. Blue.

xanh da tròi: Vietnam. Sky blue colored.

xanh ðam: Vietnam. Dark green.

xanh dòrn: Vietnam. Green.

xanh durorng: Vietnam. Blue.

xanh lá cây: Vietnam. Green.

xanh lo: Vietnam. Blue.

xanh ngát: Vietnam. Very green; dark blue.

xanh tham: Vietnam. Dark blue; dark green.

xà-rông: Vietnam. Sarong.

xhurdine: Albania and Hungary. Short coat of heavy black goat-hair twill. It was trimmed with braids and a fringed collar.

xhyrdin: *See* xhurdine.

xi: China. Zhou dynasty. Most sophisticated shoes with wooden soles.

xia pei: China. 1. In Ming dynasty (1368–1644 C.E.), woman's embroidered neckband trimmed with gold and lace. 2. In Qing dynasty (1644–1911 C.E.) in China, Han woman's sleeveless tabard tied at sides. It reached below the knees where it ended in fringed pointed hem. First worn on wedding day and later for special occasions.

xian: China. Wei, Jin and Southern dynasties. Long ribbons hung from upper short skirt.

xian yi: China. Zhou dynasty. Ceremonial black clothes worn by emperors, kings, and officials.

xiang se: China. Greenish yellow, limited in Qing dynasty (1644–1911 C.E.) to daughters of the emperor and low ranking consorts.

xiàngliàn: China. Necklace.

xiàngquàn: China. Necklace.

xianhóng: China. Bright red; scarlet.

xiao yao jin: China. Jin dynasty. Older woman's hairnet trimmed with jade ornaments pinned on randomly.

xicolli: Mexico. Man's sleeveless garment.

xie: China. Zhou dynasty. Ordinary high-heeled shoes. Originally made from sheepskin and later from silk and hemp.

xie zhai: China. In Ming dynasty (1368–1644 C.E.), badge worn by some officials that had a mythical beast with a scaly body and a horn.

xiêm áo: Vietnam. Clothes.

xighu: Aztec. Huipil.

xi-líp: Vietnam. Man's briefs or bathing trunks.

xinghóng: China. Scarlet.

xinghuáng: China. Apricot.

xiu shang: China. Zhou dynasty. Embroidered trousers.

xiùbiáo: China. Armband.

xiùkou: China. Sleeve cuff.

xiùzhang: China. Armband.

xiùzi: China. Sleeve.

xong: Vietnam. Skirt.

x-ray dress: (1910–1920 C.E.). A transparent gown.

xu-chiêng: Vietnam. Brassiere.

xue: China. Zhou dynasty. Boots.

xueqing: China. Lilac.

xuyen: Vietnam. Glossy silk.

xylorite: *See* celluloid.

Y

ya hoo lam: Bustle (1865–1890 C.E.). United States of America. Chinese Hawaiian term for a robin's egg blue polished cotton.

yachting jacket: Crinoline (1840–1865 C.E.) to Bustle (1865–1890 C.E.). United Kingdom. Popular from the 1860s to the 1880s, a woman's short, square, single- or double-breasted, hip-length coat with large buttons and loose sleeves.

yacolla: Peru. Incan large, square robe worn over the shoulders. It was sometimes worn knotted on the left shoulder.

yagliq: Iran. Bandeau.

yak lace: Bustle (1865–1890 C.E.). 1. A coarse, heavy lace made from the hair of the yak. It was fashionable for shawls. 2. A coarse bobbin lace from Northampton, United Kingdom.

yaka: Turkey. Collar.

yakulla: Ecuador and Guatemala. Incan man's rectangular cloak.

yallow: Late Georgian (1750–1790 C.E.). Yellow.

yaluk: Turkmenistan. Woman's headscarf worn over the alan dangi. The ends are pulled over the face to serve as a veil.

yama-bakama: Japan. Literally "mountain trousers," tight fitting trousers.

Yamato nishiki: Japan. Domestic Japanese nishiki.

yan: China. Blackish red.

yana: Bolivia and Ecuador. Quichua term for the color black.

yana poncho: Ecuador. A black wool poncho with a thin band of colored machine embroidery on the shoulders.

yang zhi: China. Rouge made from wild safflowers.

yangbok paji: Korea. Trousers.

yangmal: Korea. Socks; stockings.

yangmal taenim: Korea. Garter.

yangsan: Korea. Parasol.

yangzhiyu: China. Literally "mutton fat," white jade.

yanhóng: China. Dark red.

yantraka: India. A dyer.

yapanji: India. Rainy weather coat.

yar chiki: Nigeria. Short-sleeved tunic with a standing collar on a slit neck, three patch pockets, and a smocked front.

yar pariahan: India. Trousers.

yareta: Bolivia. A shade of yellow.

yari yankunne: Nigeria. Earrings.

yashmak: *See* shash.

yashti: India. A necklace of gems and gold beads, with a large central bead.

yasti: India. Single string of pearls necklace with a gem in the center.

yata: Panel of beadwork worn by Yoruba dancers.

yatshmagh: Iraq. Checkered kuffuja.

yeddo crepe: Bustle (1865–1890 C.E.). Introduced in 1880, a soft cotton fabric printed in Chinese patterns.

yelek: *See* jellick.

yellow jacket: China. A golden yellow silk jacket worn on formal occasions as a symbol of imperial power or honor.

yelpaze: Turkey. A woman's fan.

yem dai: Vietnam. Bib.

yemeni: Turkey. A block-printed cotton scarf.

yeoman hat: Directoire and First Empire (1790–1815 C.E.). A woman's hat with a deep, soft crown that gathered onto a band and a small turned up brim.

yeri: *See* tobi.

yezmeh: Palestine. A horseman's red or yellow leather boots with iron soles.

yi'chit tal: United States of America. Hupa Indians' moccasins.

yín: China. Silver colored.

ying long: China. In the Ming dynasty (1368–1644 C.E.), a five clawed dragon with bat-like wings worn only by the emperor.

ying luo: China. Necklace of precious stones.

yinggelù: China. Parrot green.

yiordani: Greece. A net of gold plated beads that is worn as a chest ornament by women.

yoji-nori: Japan. Resist paste used for fine line dyeing.

yoke bodice: Bustle (1865–1890 C.E.) to 1890–1899 C.E. United Kingdom. Popular in the 1880s and 1890s, a woman's yoked bodice or blouse.

yoke shirt: Gay Nineties (1890–1900 C.E.). United Kingdom. In 1898, a woman's dual walking skirt with a pointed front yoke.

Yokohama crepe: Bustle (1865–1890 C.E.). Introduced in 1880, a cotton fabric with printed stripes in Japanese flower patterns.

yoko-nishiki: Japan. Nishiki with pattern woven in the weft threads.

yonboratpit: Korea. Lilac.

yonmibok: Korea. Tail coat.

York tan gloves: Directoire and First Empire (1790–1815 C.E.). Worn in 1807 and after, rough undressed kid leather gloves without a specific fit.

York wrapper: Directoire and First Empire (1790–1815 C.E.). United Kingdom. Introduced in 1813, a woman's high-necked jaconet muslin dress that buttoned in the back. It was trimmed with diamonds of lace or another form of needlework.

yoroi-hitatare: Japan. A large square-cut silk coat and trousers worn under the armor.

Yoshinaka-zome: Japan. Dyeing process named for the printmaker Yoshinaka Hambei.

youghal: Ireland. A flat needle lace with a distinctive pattern.

γoûva: Byzantine and Romanesque (400–1200 C.E.). Fur coat.

y-phuc: Vietnam. Clothes.

Ypres lace: Belgium. Lace made to imitate Valenciennes lace.

yslopan: Wales. Slipper.

ysnoden: Wales. Lace.

yuage: Japan. Baby towel.

yùdài: China. Jade belt.

yuèbaí: China. Literally "moon white," robin's egg blue.

yuhada-kawa: Japan. Tie-dyed leather.

yuishiba-komon: Japan. Dotted design resembling ends of a bundle of fagots.

yukata: Japan. A summer cotton garment; an unlined cotton kimono for bath or summer wear; the fabric used for these garments.

yukue-humei: Meizi (1867–1912 C.E.). Japan. Literally "missing," a woman's hairstyle.

yulin baizhequn: China. Woman's pair of aprons.

yumào: China. Rain cap.

yun jian: China. In the Qing dynasty (1644–1911 C.E.), a Han woman's four-pointed collar with the four lobes worn over the chest, back, and shoulders.

yunatárja: Greece. Pair of stockings.

yura poncho: Ecuador. A plain white poncho.

yurak: Ecuador. Quichua term for the color white.

yùsè: China. Jade green.

yusha: China. Camlet.

yusoku orimono: Japan. Fabrics of Chinese origin that were adapted by the Japanese.

yutu: Bolivia. Ornamental bird motif.

yuxié: China. Rubber boots.

yuyi: China. Raincoat.

yùzan: China. Jade hairpin.

Yuzen: Japan. Fine multicolored paste-resist dyeing process named for master dyer Yuzen.

Yuzen birodo: Japan. Velvet with chiseled cut-pile designs.

yuzen makinori: Japan. Traditional form of yuzen using sown paste method. It creates a pointillist effect.

yuzen-zome: Japan. Starch dyeing.

Z

zābaks: Lithuania. Boot.

zaboon: Iraq. Man's long wrapped coat. Also calle saya.

zache: Late Gothic (1350–1450 C.E.). Italy. Doublet.

zadblauwen: Late Gothic (1350–1450 C.E.). Ghent. Deep blue.

zafiro: Spain. Sapphire color.

zafroni: *See* chamelia.

zagalejo: Spain. Petticoat.

zaituni: India. An olive green color.

zak: Holland. Pocket.

zakdoek: Holland. Handkerchief.

zakiet: Poland. Woman's coat.

zakkengoed: Holland. Burlap.

zakkenlinnen: Holland. Sackcloth.

zalmkleurig: Holland. Salmon colored.

zamarra: Spain. Sheepskin coat favored by shepherds.

zamarro: *See* zamarra.

zambellotto: Italy. Black fabric imported from Near East.

zamitum: *See* samite.

zamliyeh: Palestine. Woman's green, yellow, and black striped headband worn to weddings.

zammarros: Ecuador. Sheepskin chaps.

zamora: Crinoline (1840–1865 C.E.). In 1856, a taffeta shawl with bertha.

zamsz: Poland. Suede.

zamurradi: India. An emerald green color.

zan: China. Hairpin.

zancha: Roman (753 B.C.E.–323 C.E.). Tall, snug fitting boot made of soft black leather. Worn by Eastern tribes under their trousers.

zane: Nigeria. Wrapper that is worn as a belt.

zanella: Crinoline (1840–1865 C.E.). Introduced in 1848 and re-released in 1870s, sateen-like fabric used to cover umbrellas.

zanella cloth: Twilled fabric used to made umbrella covers. *See also* gloria.

Zanfretti mantle: Crinoline (1840–1865 C.E.). In 1859, almost circular mantle, significantly longer in back.

zanga: *See* zancha.

zànglán: China. Purplish blue.

zàngqing: China. Dark blue.

zante lace: Reticella lace made in Greece.

Zanzibar: Bustle (1865–1890 C.E.). In 1872, a sandy brown.

zaohóng: China. Purplish red.

zapáska: Russia. Woman's back apron.

zapatillas: Spain. Slippers.

zapato: Spain. Shoe. *See also* calzado.

zapato de mujer sin correas: Spain. Pump.

zapato oxford: Spain. Oxford shoe.

zapon: Russia. Apron.

zaragüelles: Elizabethan (1550–1625 C.E.). Spain. Wide breeches.

zarcillos: Ecuador. Earrings.

zardozī: India. Very heavy embroidery with gold or silver done on velvet or satin.

zarī: India. Metal thread embroidery; silver lace.

zarost: Poland. Beard.

zarrin: India. A golden color.

zarzahan: Renaissance (1450–1550 C.E.). Spain. Thin striped silk.

zástera: Czechoslovakia. Apron.

zavelci: Romania. Apron with vertical designs.

zaveska: Bulgaria. Checked or striped piece of fabric wrapped around the body from under the arms to the ankle and tied with a knitted cord at the top edge.

zaybaqah: Palestine. Necklace.

záyres: Greece. Everyday shoes.

zazzara: Renaissance (1450–1550 C.E.). Italy. Coiffure involving fluffing out of the hair.

zbroja: Poland. Armor.

zé: China. Man's headdress worn in ancient China.

zebra feathers: Romantic (1815–1840 C.E.). Introduced in 1816, feathers artificially striped in two colors.

zéédééldoi: Navajo. Necktie.

zeemleer: Holland. Chamois.

zegelring: Holland. Seal ring.

zeghe: Romania. Man's long, thick drugget overcoat.

zeke: *See* condra.

zelfkant: Holland. Selvedge.

zelluuami: Hausa. Plaid cloth with a silk border.

zenaq: Palestine. Chin chain used to hold the shatweh in place.

zendado: Renaissance (1450–1550 C.E.). Italy. Very light silk fabric from the Orient.

zendale: *See* zendado.

zenith blue: Medium light blue.

zenne: Hausa. A plaid cloth.

zenne alffowa: Hausa. A light blue plaid cloth.

zephirina: Crinoline (1840–1865 C.E.). Introduced in 1841, blend fabric used for coats.

zephyr: Bustle (1865–1890 C.E.). Introduced in the 1880s, light, fine gingham. Often woven with colored warp and fine weft. *See also* French gingham.

zephyr armure: Bustle (1865–1890 C.E.). In 1879, lightly crinkled crepe.

zephyr cloak: Romantic (1815–1840 C.E.). Woman's long cloak of lace or net with ankle-length points in front. It was worn tied at the waist with a sash.

zephyr cloth: Thin, fine cassimere.

zephyr gingham: *See* zephyr.

zephyr shawl: Soft, lightweight shawl, often embroidered.

zerbaft: 1. India. Gold brocade. 2. Turkey. Velvet in which a lot of gold thread was used.

Zerlina dress: Crinoline (1840–1865 C.E.). In 1858, a gown with triple skirt. Bodice trimmed with quilted pattern of diamonds that was repeated on the sleeves.

zersej: Bosnia. Jersey.

zgarda: *See* ghiordan.

zgardan: *See* ghiordan.

zha jia: China. Han dynasty (206 B.C.E.–7 C.E.). Coat of mail that tied over the shoulders.

zhaijiepai: China. Qing abstinence plaque worn at the girdle to indicate the person was fasting as a part of a religious ceremony.

zhan: China. Felt.

zhàopáo: China. Overall.

zhàoshán: China. Overall.

zhàoyi: China. Overall.

zhe: China. Reddish brown.

zhe ji: China. Pleated coat with many variations in length and closures.

zhéshàn: China. Folding fan.

zhi huan: China. Finger ring.

zhi sun: China. Yuan dynasty. One-color clothes worn by the emperor and his courtiers.

zhòu: China. Crepe.

zhòubù: China. Cotton crepe.

zhuanglián: China. Trousseau.

zhuhóng: China. Bright red.

zhùmá: China. Ramie.

zhuó: China. Women's bangle bracelet.

zhutu: Ecuador. Women's handmade felt hat with a round top and a narrow brim.

zi: China. Purple; violet.

zibelina: *See* marta.

zibeline: 1. Thick wool fabric with long, silky hairs on one side. *See also* ripple cloth. 2. France. Sable fur.

zibellino: Italy. Sable.

zibun: United Arab Emirates. Man's sleeveless wrapover garment worn over the kaftan.

zīds: Lithuania. Silk.

žiedas: Lithuania. Finger ring.

zielony: Poland. Green.

Ziertaschentuch: Germany. Pocket handkerchief.

zihóng: China. Purplish red.

zijde: Holland. Silk.

zijden japon of toga: *See* zijde.

Zillon braid: Crinoline (1840–1865 C.E.). Straw resembling chip.

zimarra: Renaissance (1450–1550 C.E.). Italy. Man's overcoat, rarely worn girdled. Made of heavy patterned silk or velvet and lined with silk or fur.

zimbelline: Crinoline (1840–1865 C.E.). Introduced in 1856, mourning fabric between barege and paramatta.

ziurstai: Lithuania. Apron.

zivka: Turkey. Man's black or brown trousers fitted below the knee.

zlalzil: Berber wool shawl.

znak: Russia. Insignia; badge.

zobe: Nigeria. Finger ring.

zobel: Imitation sable.

Zobel: Germany. Sable.

zoccolo: 1. Italy. Generic term for sandal. 2. Renaissance (1450–1550 C.E.). Italy. Chopines with a leather shoe-like top.

zoeaaf: Holland. Zouave.

zogan: Japan. Applied gold decoration on cloth; damascene.

zolty: Poland. Yellow.

zona: Greek (3000–100 B.C.E.). Wide, flat belt worn by girls and removed by their husband in the wedding ceremony and never worn again.

zoccolo
*See also photospread
(Foot and Legwear).*

zonar: Belt worn by the Jews and Christians of the Levant.

zonder schouderbandjes: Holland. To be strapless.

zone: Late Georgian (1750–1790 C.E.). United Kingdom. Popular in 1770s and 1780s, fabric piece used to fill in open bodice of a gown.

zoni: Greece. A woman's belt.

zonnebril: Holland. Sunglasses.

zonnebruin: Holland. Suntan.

zonnenscherm: Holland. Parasol.

zoot suit: (1940–1950 C.E.). United States of America. Man's suit with coat extending almost to knees and trousers cut very full. Commonly worn with highly exaggerated accessories.

Zopfzeit: Late Georgian (1750–1790 C.E.). Germany. A man's pigtail wig.

zōri: Japan. Sandals consisting of flat soles held on with a thong that passes between the first and second toes.

zorro: Spain. Fox.

zoster: Greek (3000-100 B.C.E.). Belt or girdle worn by men.

zouave jacket: Crinoline (1840–1865 C.E.) to 1890–1899 C.E. United Kingdom. 1. Woman's silk, velvet, or cloth jacket with rounded front corners that fastened only at the neck. Based on jackets worn by the Algerian Zouave troops in Italian war of 1859. Popular 1859–1870 and in 1890s. 2. Little boy's jacket similar to women's style.

zouave paletot: Crinoline (1840–1865 C.E.). United Kingdom. Popular in 1840s, man's paletot of waterproofed llama wool.

zouave pantaloons: Gay Nineties (1890–1900 C.E.). United Kingdom. Wide pantaloon gathered in at knee, ending there in frilled band.

zsáknadrág: Hungary. Literally "sack trousers," full-cut trousers made of hemp or a rough fabric.

zuan: China. Qing dynasty. Bowl-shaped cap of palm fiber or hemp and covered in silk. Popular with middle-aged women.

zubun: Bosnia-Herzegovina. Woman's short, sleeveless vest which ends several inches above the waist.

zucchetto: Small, round, ecclesiastical skull-cap.

zueco: Elizabethan (1550–1625 C.E.). Spain. Sabot.

zukin: Edo (1600–1867 C.E.). Japan. Literally "head-cloth," a cloth cap or hood worn in inclement weather or at night.

Zuleka: Crinoline (1840–1865 C.E.). In 1858, woman's street basque fitted in the body. It had a vandyked bertha of net and ribbon. The basque was trimmed with guipure and gimp.

Zulima: Crinoline (1840–1865 C.E.). In 1856, woman's taffeta mantilla trimmed with moss velvet and crimped fringe.

Zulu cloth: Twilled fabric of a tight weave.

zunnar: Palestine. Sash. Square scarf striped or patterned. Rolled diagonally to form sash.

zunnar asmar: Palestine. Woman's black girdle.

zunnar maqruneh: Palestine. Sash of green, red, and yellow silk.

zunnar tarabulsi: Palestine. White, red, and green striped sash.

zuòcán: China. Tussah silk.

zuòsichóu: China. Pongee.

zurband: Palestine. Woman's silk veil that may have doubled as veil and sash.

zuyacal: Guatemala. Palm leaf raincoat.

zwanedons: Holland. Swansdown.

zwart: Holland. Black.

zwarte: *See* fijne.

zwempak: Holland. Bathing suit.

Zwickel: Germany. Gusset.

Zylinder: Germany. Top hat.

zywr: Renaissance (1450–1550 C.E.). Hungary. Gray fabric.

bell suit
Dover Publications

Big Look
Dover Publications

cheongsam

coat-dress
Dover Publications

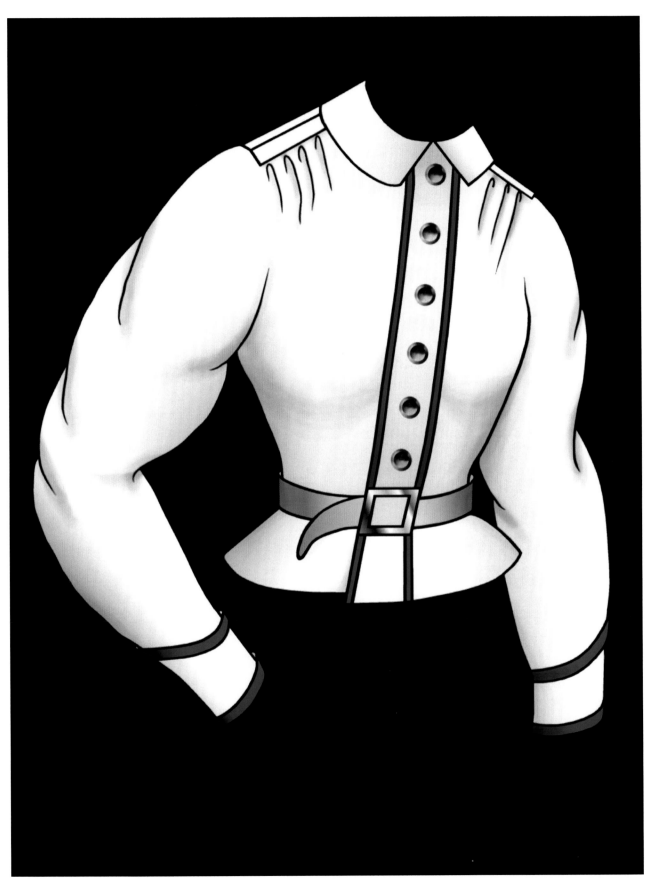

Garibaldi blouse

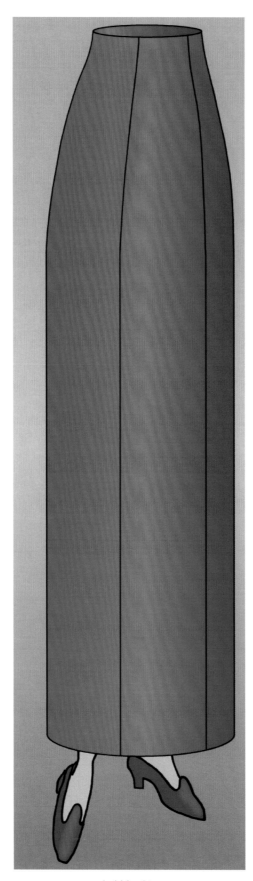

hobble skirt

peasant look
Dover Publications

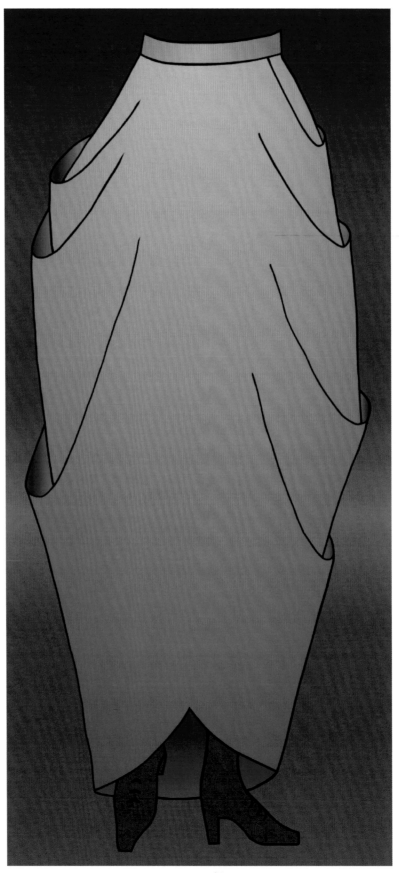

peg-top skirt

robe à l'anglais

sack dress
Dover Publications

sheath dress
Dover Publications

stringbean
Dover Publications

back-strap shoe

balmoral

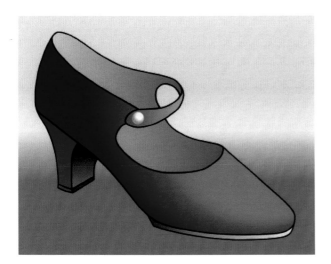

bar shoe

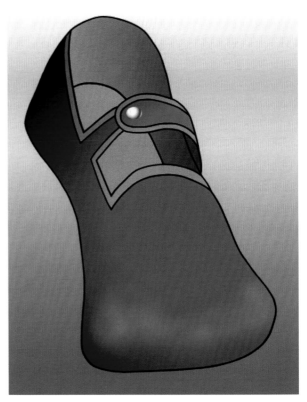

bear's paw

caite

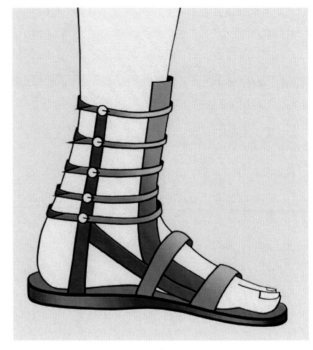

caliga

Chelsea boot

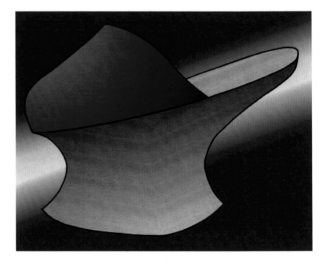

chopines

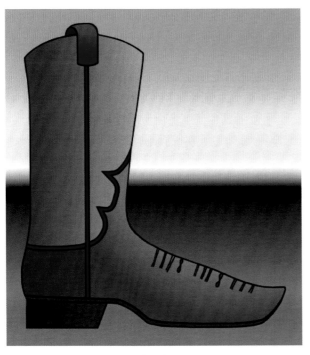

cowboy boots

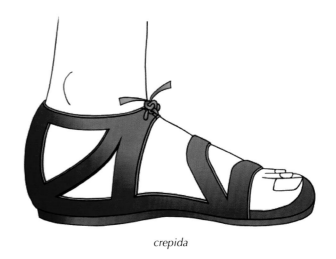

crepida

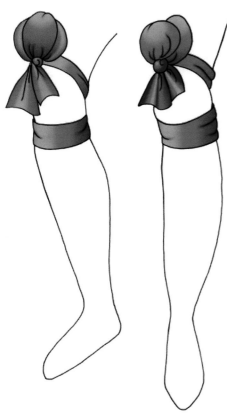

cross gartering

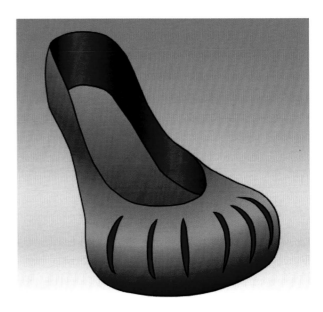

cut-fingered pumps

derby shoe

d'Orsay pump

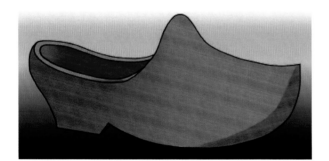

esclaud

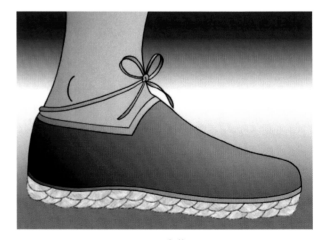

espadrille

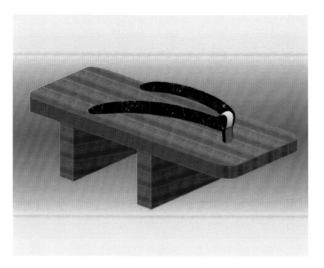

geta

Hessian boot

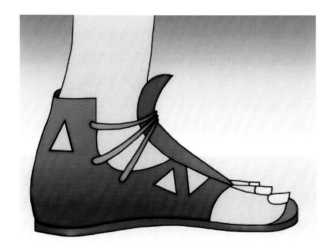

krepis

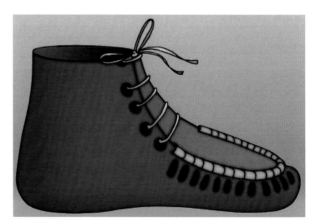

mukluk

platform sole

poulaines

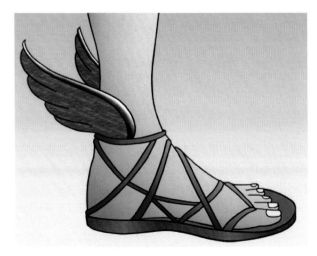

talaria

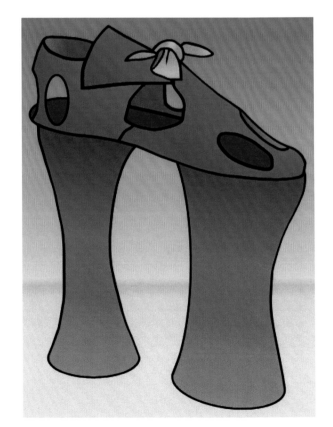

zoccolo

HEADWEAR

biretta

bob-wig

deerstalker hat

garcettes

gipsy bonnet

Muller-cut-down

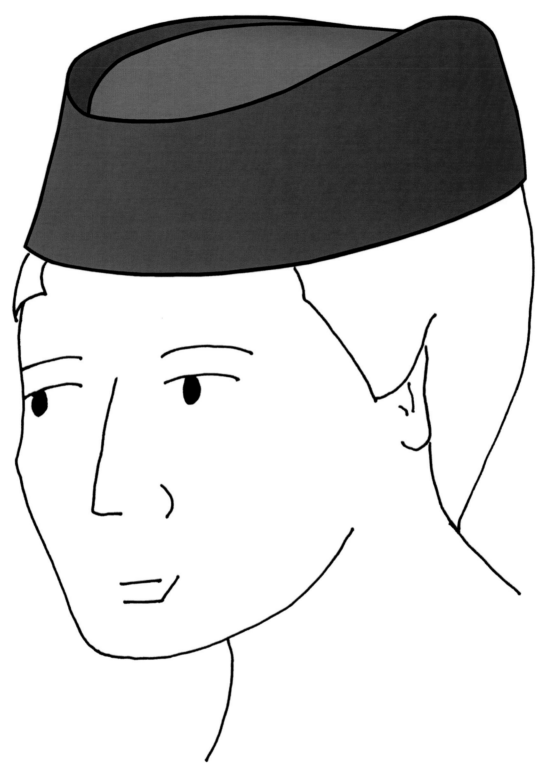

overseas cap

Pamela bonnet (Crinoline period)

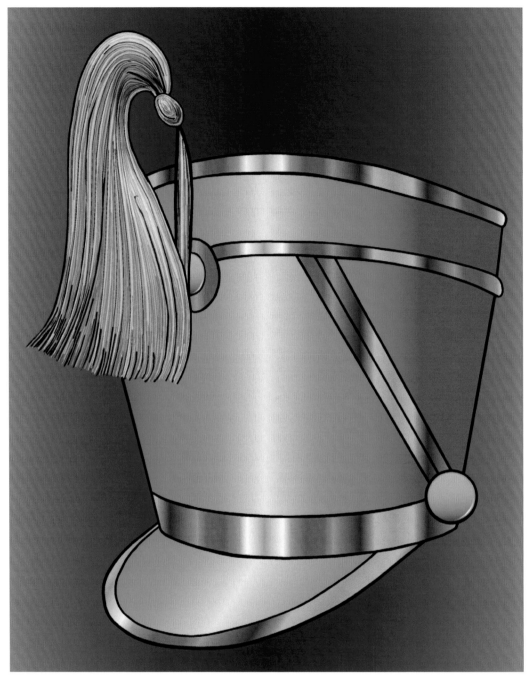

shako

tye

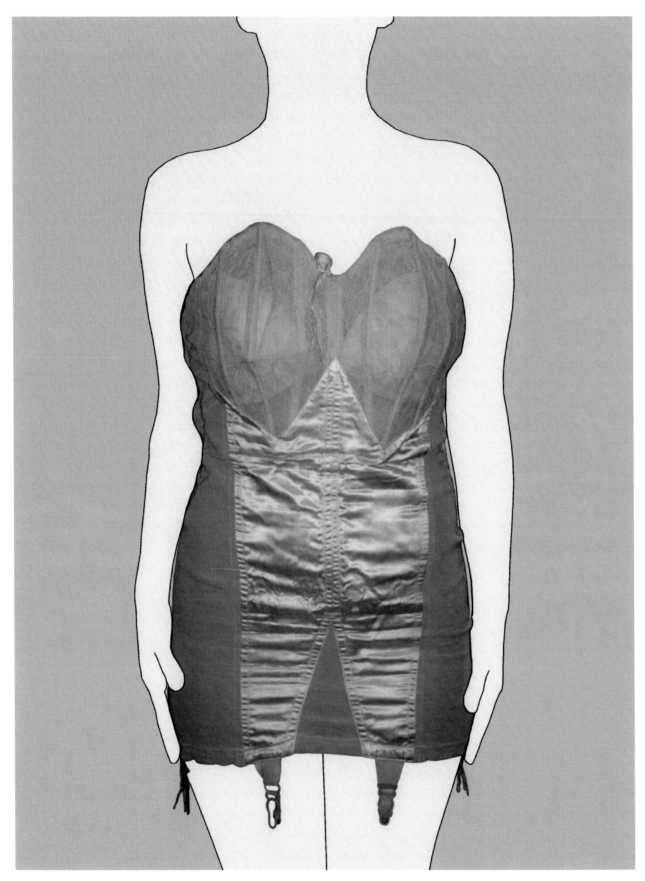

all-in-one

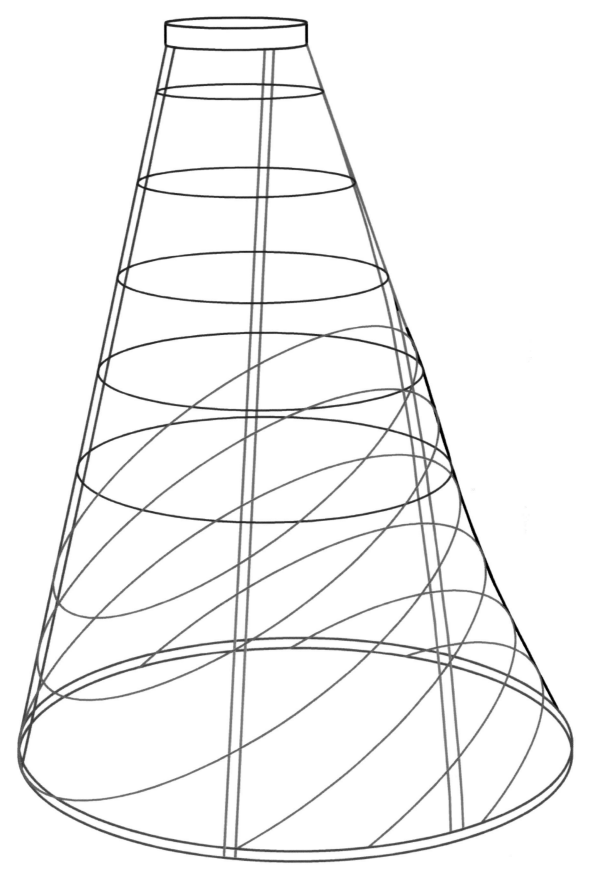

cage

panniers

nine-tenths coat
Dover Publications

Norfolk jacket

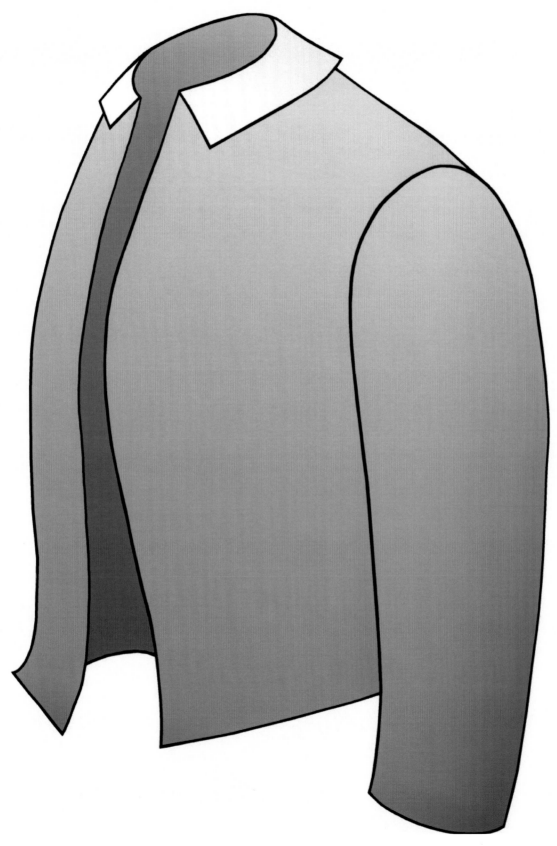

Oxford jacket

tonlet (15th and 16th century)
Dover Publications

Appendix A: Garment Types

ACCESSORIES

à l'espignole
'a'a puhaka
ačē gumbō
acessório
aglet
agrafe
agraffe
agulhade
aiglet
airmchrios
'ajami
alforja
anantu hwinie
anteojos
aparsaig
appas postiches
Austrian belt
avasakthika
bacchetta
badine
bahu
baju
balg
balgan
balg-bannaig
balg-thional
ball-serice
bälte
baltion
balusu
Balz
bandanna
basma
bastão
baston con anima
batistă

batom
beannag
beauty patches
beidai
bellotas
belti
benoiton chains
Berlin gloves
Berlins
bigotera
bikini chain belt
birbíla
bisha
bít-tāt tay
bœlte
boiseid
bokshandschoen
boquilha
bosom bottles
bosom flowers
bouffant mecanique
boulanger umbrella
bouquet de corsage
boutonniere
bracan
braces
bragueta
brandestoc
brandistocchi
breast hook
bretelle
brezekouki
brezikúci
bril
briosaid
bronnach

brumánika
builg
bulavka
bust forms
butung
bwoom
cabestrillo
cabriole
cachecol
cachelaid
cadach
cadenat
caefing
calico china button
can
cañari
canne
canne à système
cannes demi-solde
cannes-dard
cân-quac
capacho
caracule
ceinture
cenojil
ceruse
chai-chieh-p'ai
changgap
chao dai
charretera
chatelaine
chauri
chicken skin glove
chip'angi
chumbi banderilla
chumpi

ch'úspas
chustka
ciarsūr
cimds
cinch belt
cīnctus
cingătoare
cingillum
cingulum militaire
cinta
cintaliga
cintura
cinturão
circingle
cneaball
colan
colmar
concha
coquette
cordeliere
corking pins
coron Muire
correia articulada
coudières
countenances
court plaster
crambaid
crios
criosan
criosan biodag
crios-ceangail
crioslachan
crios-pheilear
crios-tarsainn
criss
cummerbund

curea	funda	haling hands	kajuk hyokdae
cut-fingered gloves	fusi	halsdoek	kakorízika
dabao	gadget cane	hances	kakshyabandha
dai kou	gadget stick	händschen	kaku obi
daishi	gairda	handschoen	kalabaku
d'Angri	galante	hand-scio	kaliki
dannocks	Galatea comb	handske	kalima hamo
danpiàn yanjìng	gallowses	haneeka	kamarband
datemaki	galluses	han-eri	kangha
degenkoppel	gant	Hantschuoch	kanzashis
degenstok	gants de Swède	Hantscuoh	kanzasi
digitalia	gants Régence	hanzki	kapesník
doramché	gartain	heiyanjìng	kardhani
dornag	garter	heko-obi	kashmir
dou dou	gaucho belt	hemavaikaksha	kaula uaki
downy calves	ge dai	hezaam	kayabandh
drapi	geideal	hezam	k'eša
dress clip	gemelos	hinaka	ketoh
dress holder	geolan	hinaka 'a'i	khan mùi-soa
ear string	ghungru	hinaka paeke	khan tay
eau de veau	ginglers	hiogi	kính trang
end of the day	giraffe comb	hiranya-sraj	knijpbril
endima	girdel	hohos	knobkerry
English chain	girdle à la victime	hoo tau dai	knoflik
enjouee	girdle glass	hoofddoek	knope haak
epauleti	Gladstone bag	horitti	kohl
equipage	glōf	hose-bend	kokade
esmouchoir	glofi	huaaca	koloa
etui	glùinean	huaka	kombologion
faixa	gordel	huallquepo	kooi
faja	gördel	huayaca	ko'oko'o 'amana
falt-dhealg	gouriz	humujìng	kshat
familla	guanto	hunting belt	kumshigye
faxiolion	guard chain	hwajang	kusak
fazolo	gul yaqa	hyanggap norigae	kushak
fazzoletto	guo luo dai	hyire	kusi
fengjìng	gurda	'ili kuapo	kusti
ferenn	Gürtel	irbora	kyaphi
fetel	Gurtil	istalla	kyara-abura
fetels	gwregys	itsembéri	laine foulard
fibula	gyrdel	jambee cane	lájish
ficheall	gyrdel-hring	japamala	lāmann
fivela	gyrdels	jarreteira	làmhain
flabells	gyrdels-hringe	jarretiere	làmhan
flower bottle	gyrðill	jatun chumbi	lamhas
fob ribbon	habit glove	jemmy cane	lāmind
fóci	haer-naedl	jessamine butter	laska
fogle	hagorah	jessamy gloves	lei
folly bells	hainaka	jiao dai	lei 'a'i
freiseau	hainaka 'a'i	josie	lei ali'i
frutilla	hainaka lei	juosta	lei hala
fucus	hainaka pa'eke	juostos	lei hulu
fue	hainaka pakeke	ka'ai	lei kamoe
fukás	hair strings	kadémi	lei kukui
fukube-dana	hakoseko	kadife	lei leho

lei pani'o
lei papa
lei papahi
lei pauku
lei pawehe
lei po'o
lei wiliwili
lenço
li kakini
li kaliki
liga
Limerick gloves
lindi
loo mask
loongee
lucky bells
má hong
maaporeth
maddavina
màineag
majestueuse
makarika
makhila
malabar
Malacca cane
maldā
manag
manchetknoop
maneg
manitergium
mantaqa
mănuşă
marama
maramica
marate
marguerite
mariposa
martō
maru-obi
mata tioata
mayad
meanaigean
megane
melbbang
melppang
mendil
mikini lima
minyiing
miotag
mirchal
mitons
mòjing
mokdori
monétra
monócula

mouche
mouchoir
mouchoir Alma
mouchoir de Venus
mouchoir Victoria
mouchouer
moufles
mousquetaire
muckender
muff bracelet
muffetees
mukyeeng
murchal
muscadine
mùtan
mwaandaan
namaakbusten
napkin
napkin hook
näsduk
nasitergium
nèapaicin amhaich
nèapaicin pòca
neckatee
nek'och ìpù
nelpiloni
nhãn-kính
niciane rekawiczki
nnup
nodder
nono-obi
norigae
nosine
ntoa
nyeeng
ô
obang-nangja
obi
obi-age
obi-dome
obijime
odonarium
odonium
ogi
òir-chrios
ojak norigae
oogschaduw
oogscherm
opera glove
orarium
Oxford gloves
padapatra
paenang
pafte
pafti

p'almok sigye
palulu maka
pang' adari norigae
pantserhandschoen
pañuelo
pañuelo para el cuello
papilotte comb
papillotes
paraguas
parchment calves
parfait-contentement
parure cornouailles
paryanka
paryastika
pás
passionee
patka
patrontache
patta
peigne Josephine
penang lawyer
pennbazh
pepperbox
percatka
perspective glass
petticoat suspenders
pha beang
phaa chet paak
phãn sáp
phãn son
pirkstaine
pirštinė
pishka
pistent
plumpers
pochette
pogoni
point
pojas
pójas
poking stick
pollera
pomander
pomme d'ambre
pomme de senteur
pompeian silk sash
porte-jupe pompadour
pósta
poyas
poynte
prakhotaeo
prawing-spinel
prievite
provincial rose
puch'ae

pugovico
punjang
puoga
putting stick
quat quì
qubpa
quitasol
quizzing glass
qusak
raggiera
ramall
randosel
ranetz
rasana
rat
Recamier sash
rekawica
rekawiczka
rhabdoskidophoros
Ridgeway buckle
romall
rond
rosenadel
Roxburgh muff
rukavica
saccharine alum
samjak norigae
sanjaku-obi
saptaki
sarandrana
šayō
scépa
Schiessstöcke
Schnupftücher
schoudertas
seileadach
seleulu
señore
sgaileagan
shag mittens
sharf
shash
shen dai
sherihah
shigoki-obi
shnur
shoe horn
shoujuàn
showing horn
shuwayhiyyeh
skimskin
slat-rioghail
slaucis
sleeve tongs
smiotag

smugadair
smuig-aodach
smuigeadach
snoskyn
snowskin
snuftkin
sokophouder
solosolo
sonsugon
soudarion
soyate
Spanish paper
Spazierstock
spendlík
spleuchdan
spliùchan
sròin-eudach
stagen
stay hook
steutelreecx
stibium
stithópano
Stöcke mit Seele
stölebelte
streachlan
strilinn
Strumpfhalter
subha
succinta
sudar
sudar sheal zero-othav
sūdārium
suppléants
surveyor's stick
Swiss belt
taalapat

taapeka
taatua hume
taiko obi
tai-k'ou
tai-shih
tàiyángjìng
talede
tali pakkaridi'
tamentika
tanch'u
t'ao t'ieh
tas van de Hooglanders
Taschentuch
tashka
tasseled handkerchief
tatquevluq
tatua
tatua-pupara
tauri koomore
tekko
temple spectacles
teneçir
tephillin
thi-kính
thung
tippling cane
tiracolo
tirantes
titi
tkanitsa
toise mouvante
t'okbaji
t'oljanggap
toneelkijker
totoga
tou tu

tozali
Träger
trahilia
troussoir
truffeau
trus
tsitseróña
tti
tu kartu
tubbeck
tuichje
tukula
tu-maurea
tu-muka
tussoire
tusuk
tuszo
tuu hangoroa
tuu kaaretu
tuu maro
tuu muka
tuu ure
Twelve Apostles
uchilla maki chumbi
uchiwa
ugly
uilebril
uku churana
up-legen
usala
vachóris
vali
vandyke
ventoye
veshovi meshok
vethaka

vonica
vú già
wàdài
w'aka
wak'a
wandelstock
wanjang
want
wantus
was and tam
washing leather gloves
wawa chumbi
wedding garter
wedding gloves
wedding knives
whiitiki
Woodstock gloves
yangmal taenim
yelpaze
yem dai
York tan gloves
zakdoek
zhaijiepai
Ziertaschentuch
znak
zona
zonar
zoni
zonnebril
zoster
zunnar asmar
zunnar maqruneh
zunnar tarabulsi

APRON

aparan
apch'ima
apron
aprūn
avental
barber's apron
barclod
barmcloth
barmecloth
barmfell
barmskin
barvell
bavette
bearm-clap
boscele
bracconiere

bréid-bronn
bruinneadach
byala houta
carpenter's apron
catrintoi
changalli
chef's apron
cialdini apron
cocktail apron
coverslut
cretinta
criosan
crios-ceangail
csipkeskötö
delantal
delantal de cintura

demi-tablier
diaraogenn
eip'uron
'epane
epani
fartuch
fartuk
fertuch
ffedog
fig leaf
förkläde
forklœde
fotaforkle
fúta
gavacha
grembiule

gremial
hoover apron
houta
jocolo
kaldoh
karinca
kecelja
korenka
koteny
koto
kruneforkle
kurligatka
lùireach leathair
luirg-bheairt
maaporeth
màilleach

mapoto
maro
maro huka
maro kaakaapoo
maro kaukau
maro kopua
maro kura
maro kuta
maro waero
maro waiapu
menagere
mrezhena prestilka
mukhu-wara
muna-medare
napron
opreg

panaúla
pántlikaskökö
papalu
pastura
pat gat
pepetu
perednik
pestelci
pinner
pluinnseag
poriann
pothia
prāiscīn
pregaca
prieksauts
prijuostė

pristelca
sarassang
sárena
sassang
schort
schorteband
Schürtze
Schürze
šerret
sorti
surc
tablet
tablier
tali 'ele 'ele
tap-de
tavancher

titi-le-'au
trus
tu-hou
tuil-aodach
Tukanitsa
tyes
'umi'i kuapo
voorschoot
wéiqún
yulin baizhequn
zapáska
zástera
zavelci
ziurstai

ARMOR

adaabo
ailette
almain rivet
almete
anima
anime
anlet
annelet
annulet
áo giáp
armadura
armadura del busto
armatura
armet
arming bolster
arming doublet
arming points
bacinet
baguette
bainbergs
balteum militare
bambergs
barbute
bascinet
basinet
bath-throid
baticol
beaver
bevor
bicoquet
biorraid
bishop's mantle
borstplaat
bouchette
bourguignotte
bracer

braconniere
braguette
brannamh
brassard
brayette
bridle-gauntlet
brigandine
brium
Brustharnisch
buckler
burganet
burgonet
byrnie
cabaset
cabasset
cailmhion
camail
capacete
cap-a-pie armor
cappelina
casco
casque
casque à la Tarleton
casquetel
ceann-bheart
celada de engole
cerveliere
chapel-de-fer
chapelle-de-fer
china cola
cimier
cingulum militiae
close-gauntlet
cnemis
coif-de-mailles
coiffette

combed helmet
corazza
corium
corr-léine
corselet
cotun
couraca
couters
crios-claidheimh
cruth-lachd
cubitiere
cūdō
cuerbully
cuir-bouilli
cuirie
cuish
cuissard
cuissart
cuisse
culet
curace
cuth-bhàrr
demijambe
demipauldron
demivambrace
elmo di giostra
enarme
epauliere
frog-mouthed helm
gadlings
gadlyngs
galea
galerum
galerus
gambeson
gamboised cuisses

gangkai
gardebras
garde-collet
garde-de-rein
gauntlet
genouillieres
giáp
giáp-bào
giáp-y
greaves
habergeon
haidate
hakoseko
hankotana
hao mao
haubergeon
hauberk
haubert à maille double
haubert clavey de double
    maille
haubert doublier
hausse col
hausse cul
heko-obi
helm
helmet
here-pād
heume
iron-pot
jamb
jambart
jambe
jambeau
jazerant
jumps
kabuto

kaijia
kaku obi
kancuyao
kapa kila
kask
kaska
koshiate
kote
kuras
Kurass
kyne
lamboys
lambrequin
leis-bheart
liang dang kai
lobster helmet
lorg-bheart
lorica
lorica hamata
lorica plumata
lorica segmentata
lorica squamata

lùireach mhàilleach
luirg-bheairt
màilleach
mammelieres
manica
mentonières
Milan coat
ming guang kai
montera
morion
mufflers
oriellettes
pale kila
palettes
pallets
pallettes
pansiere
Panzer
pauldron
pectorale
pickelhaube
placcards

placcates
poitrel
privy coat
quiret
rerebrace
Rüstung
salade
sallet
sannaha
Schaller
scheenplaten
schynbaldes
sgaball
shell
shihan
shirastra
shirastra jala
sirsa kataha
sode
solleret
spangehelm
speilp

spider helmet
splints
taces
tasse
tasset
tassettes
tilting-helm
Todenkopf
tong xiu kai
tonlet
tou tu
tuille
uchdach
uchd-bheart
vambraces
ventail
visor
wapenrusting
zbroja
zha jia
zhu

BODICES, BLOUSES, AND SMOCKS

à la du Barry corsage
à la Grecque corsage
à la Louis XV corsage
Agnes Sorel bodice
Agnes Sorel corsage
amazon corsage
Anglo-Greek bodice
antique bodice
áo bà-ba
áo cánh
áo côc
áo cut
aupakaksiki
baby bodice
bag bodice
baju bodo
baju kurung
Balkan blouse
balmoral bodice
bàn
bàn-gheal
baro
basque waistband
basque-habit
basquin body
batakari
bavlnka
beur
bewar

bib blouse
blusa
bluska
bluza
bò-lu
bow blouse
buba
burausu
burchanka
bust bodice
camisón
caroline corsage
casaque bodice
casaquin bodice
cased body
choli
circassian bodice
Clarissa Harlowe corsage
cliabhan-ceangail
coat-bodice
codiarte
cofta
corpetto
corpiño
corsage à la Maintenon
corsage en corset
cot
coton
cottage front

cuerpo baxo
cufaica
cuirasse bodice
culeco
cutaveica
dhumani
Directoire coat
Directoire jacket
Dutch waist
empire bodice
enagua
fanfreluche bodice
fuubu
Gallo-Greek bodice
Garibaldi blouse
Garibaldi bodice
genthulla
gilet
gonbaiz
Grecque corsage
guimpe
guj
gùn na h-eaglaise
gùn odhar
gypsy blouse
habit bodice
halter top
hatte
huepilli

huipil
huipil grande
huipil ranciado
iie
Isabeau corsage
jabot blouse
jhaggā
jhaggī
josephine bodice
kabátek
kācali
kācavo
kamis
kamkho
kanchali
kanchulika
kancuka
kebaya
keptar
kiel
kittel
koshoulya
kosnyo
kurpasaka
kurti
la vierge
Laibli
lakeke
leefekye

Leibchen
léine-bhàn
lemba
lembe
lijf
lijfje
Louis XIII corsage
luto huipil
Maintenon Corsage
Marie Stuart bodice
marquise bodice
middy blouse
Montespan corsage
nagrudnik
naguilla

Norma corsage
pakana
pari muka
peek-a-boo waist
peplum basque
peplum bodice
pirahan
plastron
pompadour bodice
pulrausu
refirha
rékli
robin front
róngyi
roxalene bodice

Russian blouse
sgùird
shell
shirtwaist
Sicilian bodice
siu fung sin
stanamsuka
stanik
stomacher bodice
surplice bodice
sweater
Swiss bodice
tanutra
tingmiak
town blouse

turret bodice
tzakos
Veronese cuirasse
veste Russe
Victoria bodice
violin bodice
Watteau body
Watteau costume
whalebone bodice
xighu
yoke bodice

COLLARS AND RUFFS

'a'i kala
ai ling
'a'iku
'a'ilepe
'akala
Albert collar
Alexandra collar
all-rounder
amazon collar
anglaise
apikaklé
apkakle
arched collar
argile
band
band strings
bann-muineal
berta
bertha
Betsie
bōna
bouleau
burrail collar
Buster Brown collar
Byron collar
cabbage-ruff
cáqui
carcaille
cardinal
cardinal pelerine
cartoose collar
ceabet
chal
chelsea
Chelsea collar
cô' con

cô' tay
coilēar
coileir
coler
collar à la Vandyke
collar of esses
collare
collerette
collet monte
colletto
collo
corsage à la vierge
cowl collar
Cromwell collar
cuello
cuello bebés
cuello bote
cuello burberry
cuello capuchon
cuello chal
cuello chino
cuello de pajarita
cuello eton
cuello mandarín
dux collar
elliptic collar
eri
esclavina
Eton collar
falling band
fanling
fichu-canezou
flip
fraise
fraise à la confusion
fraise à la Gabrielle

French ruff
gadroon
garde Française
gau liang
Geneva print ruff
Gladstone collar
gola
golilla
goller
Gollier
gouzougenn
gran gola
guler
guleras
halsboord
hault collet
Hungerland band
Italian collar
jaka
Judenkragen
kata-eri
kletje
klier
kola
kolnierz
kraag
krage
Kragen
krave
lá sen
lechugilla
lettice ruff
límec
ling tao
ling yue
lingzi

maniakes
masher collar
m-cut collar
Medici collar
military stock
moat collar
muinead
muinge
Napoleon collar
nasgadh
ogrlica
or-choilear
panteen collar
parricides
Peter Pan collar
Piccadilly collar
pierrot ruff
p'i ling
piling
plain bow stock
polo collar
portefraes
portrait collar
Prussian collar
rabat
rabatine
rabbi
rebato
Robespierre collar
Rosebery collar
rotonde
rotonne
ruff
sarpe
saucer-collar
shag-ruff

Shakespere collar	superhumeral	treble ruff	wing collar
shawl collar	Swedish cuffs	Vatermörder	winkers
stand-fall collar	tab collar	vorotnicek	yaka
stìom-bhràghaid	tàszli	vorotnik	yun jian
sugar	teud-bhràghad	Wendelring	
suit of ruffs	toby ruff	whisk	

COLOR

abiyad	argent	beni	broithdheanta
absinthe	arghwani	berettino	bronze
acajou	army green	bermejo	bruin
acier	arroxeado	bermellon	brun
acter	arruivado	bianco	brunatny
adelaide	asagi	bích-không	bruno
Adelaide blue	ashantee	biec	bruschino
adhranga	asli	bigio	buidhe
adriatic green	asmani	bìji	buidhe-bhan
aerdhaite	asmar	bìlán	buidhe-dhonn
aetherial	atshi	bìlù	buidhe-ruadh
ago duku	aubergine	bird of paradise	buidhe-shoilleir
'ahiehie	auburn	birinji	buidh-liath
alabaster	aurifère	birisi	burak
alesan	aurora	birodo	burdeos
alezan	autumn tea brown	bishop's blue	burgoyne
alfi	aventurine	bister	burgundy
alicante	avocado	bistre	cachou
Alice blue	awondwa	blanc	cadet blue
alizarina	azafran	blanco	cadet gray
all	azul	blanco cremoso	cafe
alma brown	azulado	blau	cafe au lait
amaranth	azulmarinho	blauw	cafe claro amrillento
amaranthus color	azur	blé de Turquie	cafe rojizo
amarelo	azure	blé mur	càin
amarillo	azuren	blé vert	caiqing
ambohai	azurline	bleu	cairtidh
amelie	azuur	bleu Anglais	caldron
amelle	azzurro	blondine	California
American	baby blue	bois de rose	camel
American green	baby pink	borak	camelite
amphibole	bacchante	boreal	camelolepard
amuva	baço	borgeon	canary yellow
anamite	badami	bosphore green	cane color
ananas	badshah pasand	bottle-green	cang
anaranjado	bàin-dearg	bouffon	cangcang
anguri	baise	bouffron	canghuang
anil	baizi	boulanger	cánh dán
ao-iro	balílà	bouton d'or	cánh-kien
Apollo	ballpark blue	bracach	canoque
apple green	bàn	branquidão	capri
apricot	banafsai	braun	capri blue
araignée méditant un	bàn-gheal	brazowy	capuchin
crime	banker's blue	breac-liath	capucine
ardoise	barbel	bròc	caqui
argaman	basc	broith	cáqui

cardinal red
carmelite
carmezim
carmin
carmine
carminio
carnation
caroubier
caspian
cassis
castagnino
castanho
castano
castillian red
castor
ceara
céire
celadon
celeste
celestial
cendre de rose
centre de Cedra
cereja
cereza
cerulea
cerulean blue
cetrino
chaetpit
chajutbit
chàm
chamelia
champai
chase
chasseur
châtain
chatiagne
chaudron
chaume
cheng
chermisi
chermisino
chihese
chìhóng
chilum
chinbunhongui
chinese green
chinhongsaek
chocolat au lait
chocolate
choksaek
ch'ongsaek
ch'oroksaekui
chu
ciel blue
cihrai

cineraire
cini
cinzento
citrine
clair de lune
clarence blue
clearc
cobalt blue
cobhrach
coccum
coeur de melon
colar de pérolas
color aceitung
colorado
colori corozoso
congbái
conglù
congo
congo red
convolvulus
coomassie
coquelicot
cor
cor de laranja
cor de rosa
coral
corbeau
corcuir
corcur
corcurachd
corinth blue
corinthe green
cornflower
corozoso
couleur-de-roi
couroncon
crà-gheal
crambaid
cramoisi
crane color
crapaud mort d'amour
crapaud saisi
crèach
cream
crema
cremisi
cremorne
crimson
crn
crnac
cròchach
crò-dhearg
cronnt
crottin
Crown pearl

crubhas
crubhasg
crushed strawberry
cui
cuìù
cuir
cuoroncou
cyan blue
cypress
czarny
czarny jak smola
czerwony
Dagmor blue
dàhóng
dàilù
dam-thanh
ðan
Danjuro cha
dànqing
dàoguàjinzhong
datilado
de Berri
de France
de Roi
dead Spaniard
dearg
deirge
ðen lánh
Devonshire brown
dian
dilbahar
dilhil
dima
dò choé
dò chói
dò chót
donkerblauw
donn
donn laugh-na-h-éilde
donn-ghlas
donn-uaine
douanier
drab style
dreach-bhuidhe
dubh-bhuidhe
dubh-ghlas
dubh-ghorm
dubh-ruadh
dudhai kanjai
dudhia khaki
dunkelblau
durazno
dust of Paris
dust of ruins
'ea malani

'ea 'ula
eabonach
eaglewood brown
ebomvu
eburneo
ecarlate
ecarlate blanches
ecorce
ecru
'efu 'efu
Egyptian brown
éhuáng
elderberry
eldergreen
'ele hiwa
'ele'ele
'ele'i
'eleuli
'emelala
emerala
emerald
emeraude
eminence
'ena
'ena'ena
'ena'ena mumu
encarnado
engkudu
English scarlet
epingles de nourrice
escarlata
escarlata subido
escarlate
esterhazy
Eugenie blue
eveque
fa 'ataelama
fakhtai
falwe
fei
feihóng
feisè
fenhóng
feòil-dhaith te
feòil-dhath
ferozai
feutre
firozi
flamme de punch
flann
flannach
flann-dhearg
flea
flesh
fleur de peche

fleur de soufre
flexine
florentine
floxine
fly's wing
fo-bhuidhe
fond de casserole
forester's green
fo-ruadh
framboise
fuchsia
Fuchsie
fufuo
fuigheag
fuiliche
fuilidh
fumee
fumee de Londres
gahra gulabi
gai pee jau sa
gàn
gandhaki
gànqing
garnet
gay
geal
geel
giall' antique
giallo
giallo antico
gitzwart
glas
glauco
gobelin blue
goirridh
golden tea brown
goose-turd
gooseturd greene
Gordon blue
gorge de pigeon
gorm
gorm-aotrom
gorrym
goud
goudbruin
gouden
grant
grape brown
grasshopper green
grau
grauw
gré
grege
grey lilac
gridelin

grigio
grijs
grijs blauw
grin
gris
gris Anglaise
gris de fer
gris humo
gris parduzco
gris ratón
grisalho
groen
gros bleu
gros vilain vert
groseille
grun
guinda
guirmean
gulbi
gul-e-anar
gulenar
gul-i-sarrai
gulpumbah
gurača
gusanillo
haiena
hair
halba
halchii'
hamo 'ula
ha'ula
ha'ula'ula
havane
havannah
hazel
hè
he'a
hei
hellviolet
hemelsblauw
heron
himmelblau
hi'ohi'o
hoa cà
hoesaek
hóng
hongsaek
hóngyànyàn
huángcàncn
Humboldt purple
hunhuáng
húsè
hwangsaek
iar
iar-dhonn

ijzergrauw
imperatrice
Imperial gold
incarnat
incarnate
indaco
Indian
Indian green
indigo
Indigoblau
ink gray
ipsiboe
Isabella
Isabella color
Isley green
ivory
jacqueminot
Japanese rose
Japonais
jaquemar
jastai
jaune
jiàng
jiàngsè
jiàngzì
jigari
jin huang
jonquille
josie
Judas color
júhóng
júhuáng
k'aak'isaekui
kafuri
kahi
kaironan
kaki
kalsaek
kama'ehu
kamalaharitacchaya
kamalena
kame-nozoki
kamsaek
kanjai
kapasi
karmesin
karmijn
karminrot
karmozijnrood
kasaya
kasni
kastanienbraun
kastanjebruin
kasumbi
kasztanowaty

keear
keorai
kersrood
kesariya
khaki
knight's blue
kobaltblauw
kodongsaek
kohlschwartz
kokoo
kolor granatowny
kolor khaki
kombukta
komp'uruda
komun
kon
korozen
kotai
kumbit
kumkuma
kuning
kunono
labang
lal
lanumoana
laranja
lavanda
lavende
lavender
Lavinia
laylock
lazur
lazurowy
leetsoii
lelieblank
leth-ruadh
lézard
lhani
liath
liath ghorm
liath-ghuirme
liath-phurpur
libá
lichen
lichíí
lichtbruin
lie de Bordeaux
lienzo de algodón
lightgroen
lila
lilac
lilac gray
lilack
lila-röz
lilás

lino
lino irlandes
lionceau
lìsè
lizhin
loden green
lona
London dust
London mud
London smoke
loutre
lovat
lucifer
lustie-gallant
ma canh gián
mã da cam
madas
madow
magenta
maiden hair
maide's blush
mais
majithi
maku'a
maku'e
mallow-color
malvenfarbig
mama'o
mandarin
manilla
manilla brown
máolán
ma'oma'o
marfil
Marie-Louise blue
marine blue
marineblauw
marmotte
maroon
marrom
marron
marshmellow
martinpècheur
maryland
mashi
massereen blue
mãu da giòi
mãu do
mauve
méihóngsè
melemele
melemele 'ili 'alani
mésange
Metternich
mexican

midori
Milan
milk and water
misè
mo gà
Modena red
moegi
moiré
mòlù
monachino
monster green
montebello
morado
morello
morone
motia
motiya
mulberry
mulot
mummy brown
mumu sesega
mumusali
murasaki
murray
murrey
murry
musqin
mustard
nacarat
naccarat
nakara color
narangi
natural beaver
Navarino smoke
navy
navy blue
ndului
négrillon
negro
negro carbón
negro como azeviche
nezumi-iro
nguyêt-bach
Nicholas blue
nickel gray
night of France blue
nil
nima-pot
noir
noisette
noksaek
nonomea
norat'a
nos
noyer

nsa
nussbraun
ocra
ocre
odhar
'ohelohelo
oiseau
oliva
olivâtra
olive
olive drab
olivenfarbig
oliwny
òmar
onion white brown
onrijp
Ophelia
orange
orange tawny
orangegelb
oranje
òrbhuidhe
orchid
oreille d'ours
orenjibich'ui
Orleans brown
orphelian
ortie
orzechowy
oseille cuite
ouhe
ousè
oxide
oyokoman
oyster
paars
pactole
pagonazzo
pala 'ehu
pale lilac brown
palestine
palisandre
palo di lione
pansy
panti
paonazzo
paran
p'arang
pardillo
pardo
pardo amarillento
pardo opaco
pardo rojizo
parduzco
Parma violet

patalani
pato'i
pavonazzo
pavot
peach
peacock
pea-green
pearl gray
pechschwartz
pensée
periwinkle
perruche
perse
Persian lilac
pervenche
perzikbloesemkleurig
petunia
phillamot
phoinos
phul gulabi
piazi
pigeon's breast
pigeon's throat
piniki
pink
pinlán
pinlù
pinyuè
pistache
pistachio color
pistai
pistak
plomb
plum
plunket
pomaranczowy
Pomona green
pompadour
pompeian red
ponceau
po'o hina
popielaty
popinjay
popolohua
poratpit
porcelain
porfira
porphura
porphyry
porpora
pourpre
pourpre gris
pourpre sanguine
poussière
poussière de Paris

poussiere des ruines
preto
primrose
Princess Elizabeth lilac
prune de Monsieur
prune Dumas
pualena
puce
puke
pukta
punch
purée de pois
purpaidh
purper
púrpura
purpurea
purpuren
púrpureo
purpurfarben
purpurowy
purpurrot
p'uruda
p'urun
q'alaq'awa
qinglù
qirmizi
quilitl
raktani
ramio
ramoneur
raso
rat's color
raymond
red
red lilac
regina
regine purple
riabhach
Rikan cha
rocana
rocher
rojo
rojo Congo
Roko cha
rood
roodbruin
rooskleurig
ròsach
rosado
rosaniline
rosato
Rose de parnasse
rose des Alpes
rose sublime
rose tendre

roso
rossetto
rossiccio
rossignol
rot
rouge
rouille
ròusè
roussâtre
roxo
Royal turquoise
ruadh
ruadh-bhuidhe
ruaithne
rubái
rubro
ruby
russet
Russian flame
sabz moongia
safed
safira
sainre
sakala
salmon
sám ánh
sám bac
sám ðõm
samasama
sandali
sanguine
sangyn
sarde
sausani
scarabee
scarlatto
scarlet
scharlaken
schwartz
Schweizergelb
sebki
semea
serpent
Sèvres blue
sharbati
shell pink
shrimp
shuilù
sickly green
siwy
smaragdfarben
smaragdgrun
sneachd-gheal
snieznobialy
soi

soilleir-dhonn
solferino
sora-iro
sorrel
sosni
sourés
souris éffrayée
Spanish blue
Spanish fly
spring
star of the morning
staubfarbig
strammel
straw
strokleurig
sublime
suédoise
sumi
surmai
suzushi
szary
szkarlatny
tagalsaek
taisha
tarbuzi
taupe
tawney
techeleth
tekhelet
telegraph blue
terra-cotta
terranine
terre de Cuba
terre de Pologne
terre d'Egypte
Thibetine
thiers red
thistle-green
tí
tianlán
tianqing
tige d-aillet
tilleul
toley
toruphulli
tosaek
tourterelle
trang bong
trang nõn
trocadero
trurng sáo
tuose
turchino
turkils
turquoise

tus
tutki
tuutum
uaine
uaine-donn
uaine-dorcha
uauahi
ukon
'ula
'ula hiwa
'ula maku'e
'ula waina
'ula weo
'ulahea
'ula'okoko
ultramarine
unnabi
unpich'ui
unpit
uraq-awa
usuaka
usugake
usuzumi
vàng ánh
vàng khè
verd Nile
verde
verde celedón
verde césped
verde limón
verde nilo
verde salvia
verde trébol
vermelhão
vermelho
vermilion
vert
vert malachite
vésure
victoria
vieil argent
violet of the Alps
violeta
volcan
volubilis
wai kula
watchet
wedgewood
weo
whey
willow
wit
xám xì
xám-xit
xanh biec

xanh da trời
xanh dòrn
xanh durorng
xanh lá cây
xanh lo
xanh ngát
xanh tham
xiang se
xianhóng
xinghóng

xinghuáng
xueqing
yallow
yan
yana
yanhóng
yareta
yin
yinggelù
yonboratpit

yuèbaí
yurak
yùsè
zadblauwen
zafroni
zaituni
zalmkleurig
zamurradi
zànglán
zàngqing

Zanzibar
zaohóng
zarrin
zhe
zhuhóng
zi
zielony
zihóng
zolty
zwart

DYE AND DYEING TOOLS

aal
acid dye
'ahina
akane
aka-ume-zome
ákna
al
alizarin
aniline
Arimatsu shibori
bandhani
batik
bingata
bokashi
brillantes
brok
cochineal
cochinilla
colorante acido
cremesino
deargan
Diamond dyes
dubhach
Egyptian indigo
esono

fuchina
garanza
geru
gobaishi
gorocana
guirmean
haldi
henna
hitta-zome
ho
ikat
indigo
kachi
kanoko
kariyasu
kasuri
katagami
katatsuke
kata-zome
katazome
kazuki
khombu
kna
kokechi
koketsu

kuro-ume-zome
Kyo-zome
lacca
laharia
leheria
Lincoln green
madder
magenta
mame-shibori
mat mii
mokume-shibori
moro
murasaki
nama ha zome
nanako-kokechi
nileh
njekloe
oboro-zome
Old Navajo Dyes
omote kon'ya
patch dye
piedra de añil
plangi
pourpre
praveni

purple
rokechi
roketsu
ro-ten-kechi
shahab
shibori
shike-ito
Shimokyo-zome
shoaizome
sickly green
stencil dye
suo
talama
tau
tinte
Tyrian purple
wai 'ele
wai 'ele'ele
woad
Yoshinaka-zome
Yuzen
yuzen makinori
yuzen-zome

FABRIC

'a'a lole
'a'a niu
'a'a'a
'a'amo'o
abba
ábbasi
abbot's cloth
abe
ab-i-hawa
ab-i-rawan
abougedid
abrasam
absinthe

abu hizz ahmar
abu miten
abu sab'in
acala cotton
acanalado
acca
Acele
aceta
acetaat
acetate
acetato
Acrilon
Ada canvas

adanudo cloth
adati
addhacina
Adelaide wool
adinkra cloth
adire cloth
adire eleko
Admiralty cloth
adrianople
aeolian
aerophane
agala
agihila

Agra gauze
ahata tantrika
'ahina
ahinvala
ahuasca
ahuaska
Aida canvas
ailanthus silk
'ainakini
airplane cloth
aizome momen
akathorasbhagarvako-
     mala

akoko
akongo
akpwem
aksamit
aksun
alaballee
alacha
aladzás
alajah
ālamgīrī
ālamjarī
alamode
'alapaka
alapine
alari
alaska
albangala
albatross
Albert cloth
Albert crepe
alchah
aleejah
alepin
alepine
alessandrino
alexander
alexander twill
Algerian stripe
algerienne
algerine
algodón
alkilla
allapeen
alleja
alliballi
allieballie
alloutienne
allucciolati
alma
alpaca
alpaga
alpagas
alpago
Alpaka
altibajo
alto e basso
amazon
ambara
ambaram
ambari
amen
American cloth
amphimalla
amphitapa
amsuka

amsu-patta
amsuyam
Amy Robsart satin
amyan ikondo
anabas
anart garbh
Anasazi stripe twill
Anatolian silk
Anatolian wool
andalusian
angel skin
anger
anglo-merino
angora
anserine
anterne
antique finish
antique satin
antique taffeta
appicciolato
applebloom
appleblue
aranzel
aratae
Argentine cloth
armazine
armoire
armoisin
armozeau
armozine
armure
armure satinee
armure-laine
armurette
arnel
arpillera
arras
artificial silk
asaweri
Asbestall
asbestos
ashira
ashish
ashrafī
asisa
asmodée
asi-ebi
aso-oke
asparasanumeya
assam cotton
assili cotton
astar
astrakhan
atataakoro
Atlas

atlas
atlas khasu
atlas silk
atsuita
attaby
au dekls
audeklas
Augusta
Augusta cloth
aurna
Australian wool
Austrian shade cloth
ava cotton
avaska
avignon
awasqa
awning
aya
Aylesham
Azetat
babadu
baby flannel
badara
badhani
badstof
baeta
bafota
bafota malandy
baft
bafta
bag Holland
bag sheeting
bagdad
bagdad wool
bagging
bagheera
bahia sheeting
baiberek
baibu
bainin
bairam
bairami
baise
baize
balandran
balayeuse
balbriggan
baldachin
baldekin
balernos
baline
balloon cloth
balmoral
balmoral cloth
balmoral crape

balzarine
balzerine
bamagia
bambak
bambulo
bandekin
bandhani
bandhej
bandle
bandle linen
bankuo
bannockburn
bao bó
bao táo
báosha zhiwù
barasi
baratea
barathea
Barchent
barège
barège Anglais
barège de laine
barège de Pyrenees
barège-grenadine
baréza
bari
bark cloth
bark crepe
barlingham
barmillian
baronette
barpour
barracan
barracano
barragan
barras
barratee
barratine
barre
bashōfu
basin de laine
basma
basta cloth
batavia cloth
Batist
batist
batista
batiste
batiste de laine
batiste de soie
batswing
Battist
batyst
baudekin
baudekyn

Baumwollsamt
bavalla
bavlna
bawełna
bayadère
bayadère poplin
bayeta
bayonnaise
bays
bayt al-sham
bazayl
beabhar
bearams
beatelle
beatilla
Beatrice twill
beaudoy
beaupers
beaver cloth
beaver fustian
beaverteen
beche-cashmere
bedford cloth
Bedford cord
bedrukt katoen
bedrukte katoenen stof
beetling
beige
beige damasse
beiramee
Belgian lace
Belgian linen
Bemberg
benares
bendera
bengal
bengal stripes
bengalina
bengaline
bengaline constellation
bengaline de soie
bengaline poplin
bengaline russe
beram
berber
Berlin canvas
Berlin wool
beronis
beteele
betteela
bez
bhaga
bhagela
bhurra

biancherie dammaschinate
bianchetto
bibizári
bietta
bihari
bili javali
birisi
birisii
bishop cotton
bishop's lawn
bivertina
black-a-lyre
blanc
blancard
blanket cloth
blauwe duffel
blazer cloth
bó
bobbinet
bocací
bocaran
boccaccino
bodkin cloth
bofeta
Boi
bokasyn
bolivar
bolivia
bombasette
bombasino
bombazet
bombazina
bombazine
bombei
bombycina
bomuld
bomull
boneette
bông
bongos
bont
book linen
boomwol
borada crape cloth
boratto
borgana
Boston net
botany
Botany wool
bouche
bouclé
boumwolle
bouracan
bourbon cotton

bourdon lace
bourette
bourette mousse
bovelna
box cloth
brabant
bracecloth
brakan
branched velvet
Brazilian corded sarcenet
breacán
breadeen
breakan
bréid
bréidín
brēit
bretenne lace
brethyn
Bretonne lace
bridgwater
Brighton nap
brillianette
brilliante
brilliantine
brilliants
brim
brissimi
Bristol red
Brittany
Brittany cloth
broadcloth
brocade
brocado
brocado raso de pelo
brocantine
brocart
brocatel
brocatelle
brocatine
brocato
broche
broché
broché silk serge
broella
brogetie
broglio-broglio
brokaat
Brokat
brown Holland
brown linen
brown sheeting
brunete
Brunswick cloth
brushed wool

Brussels camlet
bù
buac
bùbó
bucaran
Buddun khas
buffalo cloth
buffin
bugis
bukskin
bulbulchasm
bulgara cira
Bulgarian cloth
bumbac
bunting
burak
buratto
burberry cloth
bure
burel
buridan
buriel
burlap
burnet
burnley
burrah
bustian
butcher's linen
butternut
buttery cotton
buzu
byatilha
byramee
byrampaut
byrams
byramy
Byrd cloth
byssine
byssus
byzantine
byzantine granité
caballeros
caban
cabeca
cabesa
cable net
cabot
caceres
cachemira
cachemire
cachemire de soie
cachemire marguerite
cachemire royal
cachimira

cadadh
cadās
cadet cloth
caen
caffa
caffoy
caichóu
cailmleid
cainb
cainb-aodach
cainsil
cakresvari
calamanco
calamatta
calavia
Caledonian silk
calibri
calico
calicó
calimanco
calmuc
calton
camaca
camacaa
camall
camayeux silk
cambaia
cambali
cambaye
cambelloto
cambray
cambray liso
cambresine
cambric
câm-châu
caméléon
cameleon antique
camelin
cameline
camelot
camel's hair cloth
camlee
camlet
cammaka
cammello
cammocca
câ'm-nhung
camoca
camocas
camocato
camocho
canabhas
canach
canaichean
cañamazo doblado

canavaccio
candlewick
cangan
canganes
caniche
cannellato
cannequin
cantaloon
canton crepe
canton flannel
cantoon
canvas
capichola
caracule material
carda
cardinal cloth
cardinal white
carmeline
carmelite
carnagan
caroline
carpmeal
carpmeal white
carreau amazone
carrel
carrickmacross
carrickmacross lace
carrodary
carthagena
casbans
casement cloth
casemira
casha
cashmere
cashmere de baize
cashmere syrien
cashmere twill
cashmerette
cashmerienne
cashmire de bège
casimir
casimir de soie
casimira
casimiro
casket cloth
cassenet
cassimere
cassimerette
cassinette
castellan delaine
castor
castorina
catalowne
catalpha
catgut

çatma
caungeantries
caurimauri
Cavalry
cayenne
ceadach
cealtar
cebtí
celam
Celanese
cellular cloth
celtic weave
cendal
cendryn
cerata
cetim
ceylon
ceylonette
chaconada
chaddar
chadoe
chagrin
chainsil
chaisel
chalinet
challie
challis
chambery gauze
chambertine
chamblette
chambord
chambray
chamois cloth
chamoisette
champaigne cloth
champeyn
chana-chani
chandtara
changeable taffeta
channon cloth
charmè
charmeen
charmelaine
charmés
charmeuse
charmeuse felt
charvet
charvet et fils de Paris
chatoyante
chau
cheater's cloth
cheesecloth
cheklaton
chekmak
chènbù

cheney
chenille
cherryderry
Cheviot
cheviot
cheviot tweed
chevron de laine
cheyney
chhint
chiang chau
chicon
chicoree
chiffon
chiffon batiste
chiffon lace
chiffon net
chiffon taffeta
chiffon velvet
chifón
chifón terciopelo
chijimi
chillo
China calico
China cotton
China damask
China gauze
China grass
china patta
China silk
Chinaseide
chinchilla cloth
chiné
chino
chint
chintes
chintz
chirimen
chita
chitão
chite
chitra
chitta
chivaret
chlopok
cholst
ch'on
chóu
chóuduàn
chóuzi
chubut wool
chuca
chudan
chunari
chusi
chya mun bo

cicilian cloth
ciclaton
ciclatoun
cina
cinamsuka
ciolar
circas
circassian
ciré
ciselé velvet
citra-kapardaka
citravastra
cittalam
clāp
Clay worsted
clòimh
cloister cloth
cloth of gold
cloth rash
clouded lustrings
coācta
coburg
cobweb lawn
cogware
colbertine
collar canvas
collodion silk
comley
concertina cloth
constitution cord
constitutionals
convent cloth
corde du Roi
cordeliere
cordellate
corduroy
corinna
corset batiste
cossas
cotan
cote de Cheval
cote de Genève
côtelé
cotelé fino
cotelette
coteline
cotone
cô-tông
cotonia
cotoun
cotswold
cotton
cotton back satin
cotton cambric
cotton crepe

cotton flannel
cotton foulard
cotton pongee
cotton taffeta
cotton velvet
cottonade
cottonette
cotwm
Courtauld crape
Courtauld's new silk
  crepe
coutil
cover coat
Covercoat
covert
coyoichcatl
cranky checks
crape
craquelé net
crash
cravenette
cremyll
crepe
crepe aerophane
crepe anglaise
crepe back satin
crepe charmeuse
crepe de Chine
crepe de laine
crépe de Suisse
crepe georgette
crepe imperial
crepe lisse
crepe marocain
crepe maretz
crepe meteor
crepe myosotis
crepe plissé
crepe poplin
crepe royal
crepe-de-china
crepeline
crepelle
crepoline
crepon
crepon milleraye
crepon Persian
crep-satén
crespe
crespo
crespón
crespón arena
crespón de Cantón
Crespón de China
crespón de lana

crespón georgette
crespón marroqui
crespón musgo
crespón romano
cress cloth
crest cloth
cretona
cretonne
crinolina
crisp
croché
crocus
croise cloth
croizette blue
cubica
cubù
cudari
cuille
culgee
cumábù
cumáoyàng
cumbi
cumbly
cumly
cummul
cumpi
cuppalium
cùrainn
cùrainn-chneas
curled silk
currac
curracag
cursey cloth
cut velvet
cutar
cuttanee
cuyuscate
cynara
cyprus
dacca muslin
dagswain
dai fong chau
daisy belle
daisy cloth
dalahany
damas
damas lisere
damaschino
damasco
damascus
damasellours
damask
damaskin
damassé
damassin

Damast
damast
Damhirschfell
dandaprakara
da-n-katanga
deboan
degummed silk
delaine
delinere
demerara
demi-mousseline
dendeki
dengxinróng
denim
denkuro-zome
Denmark satin
deogir
deriband
derries
desoy
desvadusya
devadusa
devagiru
devanga
devanga-cira
devil skin
dhautakanseya
dhautapatta
dhota-patta
dhoti
dhumarai
dhurrie
diaper
diaper cloth
diaphane
diasper
diaspurum
dibahae cin
dima
dimie
dimity
dindilliam
djedda
dobby cloth
docrease
doeskin
Doitsu ahina
domette
donegal
donsu
dorea
doria
doriya
dorneck
dorretteen

dorsetteen	dunster	estameña	filet lace
dosooty	durance	estamene	filozella
do-suta	Durene	estamine	filozetta
do-suti	Duretta	estampado	filt
doti	duretty	estopa	Filz
dotted swiss	duroy	estopilla	fingroms
dowlas	durzi	estrella	Flahs
DPM	dutis	estrich	Flanders serge
drab	dutty	estridge	flannel
drabbet	duvetina	estrith	flannelette
drap	duvetine	etamine	flanyela
drap d'Alma	duvetyn	etamine broché	flat crepe
drap d'Argent	dzaan	étoffe	Flaxon
drap de Berry	e sa	etoile	fleax
drap de billard	ēadach	Etruscan cloth	fleece
drap de France	ebolo	etu	Flehtan
drap de Paris	eccelide	everlastings	Flemysshe cloth
drap de soldat	echizen	exhibition checks	fleur de thé
drap de velours	ecossais	express stripes	flex
drap de Venice	egasuri	eyelash	floki
drap d'ete	egenni bitte	eyelet embroidery	floramedas
drap d'or	Egyptian cloth	ezo nisbiki	florence
drap fourreau	Egyptian cotton	faglia	Florence satin
drap laitiere	eiderdown	faille	florentine
drap o drapé	'ekemau'u	faille crepe	florinelle
drap roulier	ekpe cloth	faillette	flurt-silke
Drapé	elastic	falánróng	flushings
drapo	elatch	falding	fluweel
drappus	elatcha	Falkland Island wool	fong chau
drawboys	electra cloth	falla contrama crespón	footing
dreadnought	elephant cloth	fanbù	forest cloth
Dresden silk	Eliottine silk	fandewai	forest white
Dresden work	ellementes	Fane	forestry cloth
dríli	elminetta	fangchóu	forfar
drill	elysian	farandine	Fortuny print
drillette	embroidered batiste	farmer's satin	foulard
drobé	empress cloth	fat quarter	foulard de laine
drògaid	empress gauze	fearnothing	foulard poile de chevre
droghette	encerado	fearnought	foulé
droguet	English mohair	feilt	foundation net
droguete	ensign cloth	félpa	franela
drugget	entretela	felt	franela de Canton
druid's cltoh	eolica	feltro	franela ligera
duàn	eolienne	ferret-silke	fregio
duànzi	eolienne diagonal	fessagida	French back serge
ducape	epangeline	feutre	French back twill
duchesse	epingle	fibre chamoise	French cambric
duchesse satin	epingline	fieltro	French crepe
duck	epingline chevron soie	figurero	French gingham
duffel	epingline flotté soie	figuretto	French merino
ðui	epingline raye	figury	French net
dukr	epinglorie brochée	fijne	French percale
dukula	eponge	fil de Chevre	friar's cloth
dulápi	escuaypiles	fil de vierge	Fries
dungaree	esparto	filé	fries

frieze
frisa
frise
frisé
frisé brocade
frizado
frizé
frou-frou
frou-frou gauze
fuchou
fuigheag
fuji
fustaine
fustan
fustao
fustein
fustian
fustian anapes
futro
fututam
fuya
gaas
ga-ba-ðin
gabardina
gabardine
gabardyna
gabbano
gach
gage de Inde
gajavadi
gajipali
galashiels
galatea
gãm
gãm vóc
gambroon
gamuza
gangasagara
gangetic
gao
garbbhasutra
garha
garlicks
garri cloth
garza
gates of Paris cloth
gatugatu
gau chau
gaunaka
gausapa
gauze
gaza
gazar
gaze
Gaze

gaze à bouquets
gaze de Chambery
gaze de fantaisie
gaze d'Orient
gaze gauffree
gazeline barege
gazzatum
gebauw
gelumbė
genappe cloth
Genoa plush
Genoa velvet
gentish
georgette
georgette crepe
Georgian cloth
German serge
German wool
gestreepte of geruite
    katoenen stof
ghabani
gimmoru
Gingang
gingerline
gingham
glacé Marguerite
glass cloth
glass toweling
glazendoek
glen checks
glissade
gloan
gloria
glove silk
goaly
gobanji
godo
godweb
golf cloth
Gore-Tex
gorgoran
gossamer
gossamer satin
gourgourans
Grain
grain
grain de poudre
grana encarnada
granilla
granit de laine
granite
granite cloth
grassets
grazzets
grebe cloth

Greek stripes
greige goods
grenadine
grenadine rayée
grinsing
grisaglia
grisaille
grisalla
grisette
grober Wollstoff
grobes Wollzeug
grof weefsel
grogram
groilleach
gros de Londres
gros de Naples
gros de Rome
gros de Suez
gros de Tours
gros d'Eccose silk
gros drap
grosgrain
gualescio
guayanilla
gudia
guinea cloth
guinga
guingan
gule-baqli
gulik holland
gulix
gunpowder silk
gurrah
guzzy
gwlan
gyolcs
habassie
habutai
habutaye
hachijo
hailìsi cuni
hair line stripe
hairbines
haircloth
haircord
haji
hakata
half silk
halshemd
Hamburg homespun
hammock cloth
handewarpes
handkerchief lawn
handkerchief linen
hangra

har
harden
hardhanger cloth
haren stof
harir asli
harir nabati
hariry
harlem stripes
harlequin plaid
harrateen
harrington
harris
harris tweed
harry tweed
Haru
harvard sheeting
harvards
haryani
hattan
hatter's plush
haustuch
hechtgrau
hedvábí
hei jiao chou
Helanca
hema-netrapata
Henrietta cloth
Henrietta glace
heremzi
hernani
herringbone
hessian
hickory
hilda
Himalaya carreau
himru
hirivastra
hodden
hol
holanda
holei
holland
Holland cloth
Holland shade cloth
hollmes
Hollywood gauze
homespun
honan
honeycomb
hopsack
hopsacking
hörr
houndstooth check
hounscot say
huabù

huádaní
huaduan
huanaco
huccatoon
huckaback
hule
hulu hipa
huluhulu
hum-hum
hummums
hungback
hwamunsa
hwap'o
Iceland wool
ichcatl
Ida canvas
'ie
'ie mafiafia
'ie valavala
ikat
ikhdari
ilhó
illusion
imperial
imperial ottoman
imperial sateen
imperial serge
imperial valley cotton
imperial velvet
in
inaka yuzen
inderlins
India chintz
India linen
India muslin
Indian
Indian dimity
Indian head
Indian lawn
Indian work
indiennes
injogyonsa
inkin
inkle
irengan
Irish lawn
Irish linen
Irish poplin
ispahanis
itagbe
Italian cloth
ixcaco
iyegbe
jaconas
jaconet

jaconette
jadara
jalaka
jamdani
jamete
jamiwar
janna wa-nar
Janus cloth
Janus cord
Japanese crepe
Japanese grass cloth
Japanese piqué
Japanese pongee
Japanese silk
jarajari
jardiniere
jaspè
jaspeado
jasper
Java canvas
Java stripes
jean
jedwab
jerga
jérsei
jersey
jhamaratali
jhanbartali
jhuna
jhuni
jiaki-kanoko
jian
jianchóu
jiljeleh
jinneh-u-nar
jirnavastra
jofu
jouy
juàn
Jugendstil satin
jukh
jungle khassa
jusi
kaasdoek
kabrí
kaci
kaciyau pitha
kadali-garbha
k'aenbosu
kageyapatte
kain bentenan
kain chelum
kain engkudu
kain mata
kain simbut

kains
kaishìmí
kakeda
kakimea
kakinia
kalakamsuka
kalakoa
kalamkari
kalandari
kalikone
kalmuks
kalómala
kaltsoskúti
kamakh
kamalaveli
kambala
Kambrick
Kamelhaar
kamkha
kamkhab
kamkhwab
kamrtušky
kanekopa
kanggan
kaniki
kano cloth
kanseya
kantha
kanto
kapa
kapa 'ino'ino
kapa lau'i
kappa
kapsa
kapuraveli
kapurnur
kara-aya
karagumi
karamini
kara-mushi
kara-nishiki
karaori
karayari
karitone
karnaysh
karpasa
karpata
karppura-tilaka
Kaschmir
kaseyyaka
kasha
kasha cloth
kasiam
kasimea
kasjmier

kassa
kasturiya
kasuri
katana jhuna
kata-ori
kataza-kanoko
katifés
katoen
katoenfluweel
kattan
Kattūn
kauseya
kauseyaka
kausheya
kausumbha
kažuoks
kelantan kain songket
kelt
kendal
kente cloth
kenting
ke'oke'o maoli
ke'oke'o pia
ke'oke'o wai
kermezot
kersey
kerseymere
kerseynette
khaddar
khaiki
khajalia
khaki
khanga
kharma
kharwa
khasata
khazz
kheenkaub
khemkaub
khinkhwab
khirodaka
khuri
kihachijo
kikoi
kilika
kilika lau
kilika nehe
kimkhab
kimkhwab
kimmoru
kimono flannel
kim-thuyen
kinamu
kincob
kingcob

kinham
kinihama
kinkhab
kinkhaib
kinran
kinsha
kinu
Kirmees
kirpas
kithaika
kläde
klœði
kluteen
knickerbockers
Kobe flannel
kobene
kobene cloth
koffo
kon-gasuri
kongdan
koprena
koprina
Korin-nami
kornaysh
kosa
kosi
kotoñs
ko-watari-tozan
koza
Krepp
krimija
Krinoline
krzno
Kshauna
kshouma
ksirodaka
kuakalikea
kulia
kumach
kummul
kumpi
kuntunkuni
kuokvilna
kuri-ume
Kurume-gasuri
kusabhia
kuttan
k'uyu
kuzufu
kuzununo
kwasida adinkera
kyoniingmul
lã
la Ciré
label cloth

Lachen
lacis
lady's cloth
laeloa
lafun
lagos
lah
lahalile
lai kee wat chau
lainakini
laine
laine foulard
lake
laken
lalatantuja
lamak
lamb mena
lamba
lamba maitso
lamba soratra
lambsdown
lambskin
lamé
lamouxa
lampas
lan
lana
lāna
landy
láng
lānh
lanilla estampada
lansdowne
Lapland beaver
lappa cloth
lärft
lasa
lasoa
lauhitaka
laundry duck
lawn
leather cloth
leatherette
leatherine
Leda cloth
lein
Leinen
Leinwand
lemister
lemster
len
leno brocade
leþer
levantine
levantine folicé

leviathan canvas
liàn
Liberty art silks
lièn
lienzo
lienzo de la India
lijnwaad
lilina
limbrick
limiste
limousine
līn
lînă
linai
lindiana
linen
līnen
Līnen
linen mesh
linene
linenette
líng
linge
Lingette
linho
lini
linne
linned
linnen
linnseach
linnseach thrusaidh
lino
lino irlandes
linon
linsey
linsey-woolsey
linteum
līnum
Līnwāt
līon
lipa garrusu
lisle
lisse
Lissue
lista
listadoes
llawban
lliain
llica llica ahuaska
llin
lockram
loden
lodix
lœrred
loft

lole lauoho
longcloth
longotte
looking glass silk
loretto
louisine
lovadi
lowell cloth
lowerings
lurik
lurot
lustre
lustrene
lustrina
lustring
lutestring
lutherine
Lycra
lyons velvet
ma sa
maa'
mábù
macabre
macana
mackinaw cloth
madapolam
madras
madras gingham
madras muslin
madvia
mahadhana
mahimudisahi
mahmudi
mahyu-salu
makabala
makalena
makalena pu'u
malak
malak abu wardeh
malamala sahi
malas
malausiu
malines
malir
malle-molle
malmal
mamoodie
manasasa
manchester
Manchester velvet
manchira
mandalia
mandiléño
manjira
manta

mantling
mantua
máobù
máogé
máoliào
máozhipin
marabou
marabout silk
marakatajadara
marcela
marceline
marcella
margine
Marguerite silk
mariposa
marocain
marocain crepe
marquisette
marramas
marseilles
marseillies quilting
marsella
marška
mashru
mashru sha'ri
Masulipatam chintz
mat mii
mătase
matelasé
matelassé
māteria
materija
matting oxford
mau'u-la'ili
mawa'
mayau
mbal
mbala
mbala badinga
mecca
mecklenburgh
medley
medvilnė
megha-udumbara
meghavarna
meisen
melton
merino
merinos
merinos ecossais
merveilleux
mescolato
messaline
metal cloth
metallic gauze

Mexican cloth
Mexicans
meyui
mezeline
mezer
miánbù
miánmáoshan
miánróng
middy twill
mikado
mila
Milanese
Milanese taffeta
milas
milk and water
millium
miroir silk
mirror velvet
misaru
misri
misru
mission cloth
mission net
mistake
mistral
mobondam
mockado
modacrylic
mogadore
mohair
moiré
moiré françiase
moiré velours
Moiréseide
moirette
moleskin
moletón
moletón reversible
molleton
mollitan
molochine
momie cloth
momie crepe
monache
mon-chirimen
monkey skin
monsha
montagnac
Montpensier cloth
mooree
moorie
moreen
morga
moruori
mosaic gauze

moscovite
moscow
mosi
mosolin
moss cloth
mossy crepe
mosulrin
mothadā
moticuri tamaru
moultan muslin
mountain moss
mousceline
mousselin aboukir
mousseline
mousseline de laine
mousseline de soie
mousseline grenadine
mousseline soie
Mozambique
muaré
mudhahhab
muduveya javali
muga
mukhmal
muletón de lana
mull
mulmul khās
mulmull
mumavadi
mungo
musaftaj
musayyar
Muscovite
Muscovite velvet
muselina
muselina de la india
mushajjar
mushru
muslin
muslin de laine
muslinet
mussolen
mussolina
mussolo
must deviles
mustard villars
mustardevelin
mustardevillers
mutarraz bil-dhahab
myllion
myongju
mysore
nabob
naboika
nacré velvet

naemet
nagdeh
náilon
nailoni
nailron
nainsook
nainsukh
naka
namda
nam-king
nankeen
nankin
Nankin nishiki
nansú
narmma-haripha
nasheq rohoh
nasij
natté
ndik'a'
ndop
nduli
neigeuse
neþla
nerinuku
neteldoek
netra
nettlecloth
ní
nicho-kinran
nigitae
niigashi
nilapatora
nilavata
nillae
ni-lông
niluhura
nirmokinam
niróng
nishijin
nishiki
nízi
nkrawou
nobleza
nometas
Norwich crepe
Norwich paramatta
nouveautés
novato
nsaduaso
nula
numbda
numda
nummud
numna
numud

nunda
nuno
nun's cloth
nun's veiling
nurse's cloth
nurse's gingham
nwumu
nylon
oatmeal cloth
oganadi
oilcloth
oiled silk
'okanaki
okara
oko
okura-nishiki
okuru
okyangmok
olann
oldham
olino
ollaodach
ollyet
omeshi
ondine
ondule
ongebleekte Chinese zijde
oni didi
oni lilo
oniko
onuga
opala
orbace
orgagis
organdi
Organdin
organdy
organza
oriental crepe
oriental satin
orleans
ormesine
ormuzine
osbro
osnabrug
osnaburg
osnaburgo
ossenbrigs
otgam
otkam
otomana
otomana imperial
ottoman
ottoman cord
ottoman plush

ottoman rep
ottoman rib
ottoman silk
ottoman velvet
otu
outing flannel
Oxford chambray
Oxford cloth
Oxford gray
Oxford shirting
ozenbridge
oznaburg
packing white
padamsuka
padisoy
paduasoy
padura
padusoy
paisley
pajama check
pakama
paklinnen
palandrano
pale pakaukau 'aila
Palmyra broché
palmyrene
palmyrienne
Pamico
pampilion
pamuk
pamutos vászon
pana
pana con cervaduras muy
    finas
panama canvas
panama cloth
panba
pancauna
pancavarnapadi
pandva
panjam
panne
panne satin
panne velvet
panni diasperati
panni imperiales
panno
panno e pannino
pannus
pannus sine grano
paño
paño berbi
paño de brunete
paño de la tierra
paño tuntido

pantadoe
pănură
paon velvet
pàopàosha
papeline
papoon
parachute fabric
paragon
paramatta
paravalia
parchmentier
pardillo
parevau pata
Parisian satin
Paris-Pekin
parniyan
pashm
pashmina
pataccara
pataniya sacopa
pata-pallavah
patna
patola
patolaka
patolla
patolo
patrona
patrorna
pattadukula
pattahari
pattala
pattamsuka
pattamsuya
patti
pattu
pearl of beauty
pèarluinn
peau d'ange
peau de béte
peau de chevrette
peau de cygne
peau de daim
peau de soie
peau se suede
peigné
pekin
pekin crepe
pekin point
pekin satin
peluche a poils
penelope canvas
peniascoe
pentadoe
pepper and salt
percale

percale taffeta
percaline
perches
perkal
peropus
perpetuana
perpets
perse
Persian
persian cord
Persian lawn
persienne
Peruvian cotton
pesas
pestryad
petersham
Petersham cloth
petit velours
petite pois
pettinato
phaa
Philip and Cheney
Philip and China
philiselie
phosphorescent
phulam
phulkari
phutadu
pidan
pieghettato
piel de angel
piel de cisne
piel de foca
piel de seda
piel de tiburón
Pikee
pīlo
pilot cloth
pilus tinctus
pima cotton
pimpalia
pin check
piña cloth
pinasco
pintado
pintadoe
pinthadoe
pînza
pînză
piqué
piquet
pîslă
pistai
płat
platilla

platno
plátno
plissé
plissiert
plodan
płotno
ploughman's gauze
pluette
pluie d'argent
pluie d'or
plumbet
plume velvet
plunket
plush
poetsdoek
pofi
poil de saxe
poile de chevre
point d'espagne
Poiret twill
poldavis
polished cotton
polo cloth
polotno
pompadour chiné
pompadour duchesse
pompadour shantung
pongee
poodle cloth
popatiya
popelina
popeline
popes ministers
poplin
poplin lactee
poplin lama
poplinette
porraye
postav
pottala
pou-de-soie
poult de soir
poult-de-soie
ppipu ppipu ahuaska
Prince of Wales check
prince's stuff
prunell
prunella
psila
pulakabandha
pullicat
p'ulrannel
punjam
purdah
puriya

purnellow
puspapatta
Pussy Willow
pust
qababand
qarawi
qasabiyeh
qatifah-i-purbi
qaz
qi
qiana
qibù
quande
quintin
qutn
qutni
qutun
ra
radhanagri
radium
radnor
radzimir
raiglin
raing
rajapatta
raju
raktambara
ráli
Ramona cloth
rang
rankava
raploch white
ras de Sicile
ras du more
rash
rasha
rasimal
raso
raso cinese
raso de la China
raso de zapatillos
raso imperial
raso liberty
raso muy brillante
raso piel de angel
raso piel de cisne
raso pile de seda
raso por trama
raso por urdimbre
ratine
ratteen
ray
raye de comtesse
raynes
rayon

rayon taffeta
rayonne
rayure travers
red cross gingham
regatta faille francais
regatta shirting
regence
regina
reion
renforcée
rep
rep bluet
restagno d'oro
rhadames
Rhea
rhodophane
ribbed crepón
ribfluweel
rigona
ring cloth
rinzu
ripple cloth
Ripplesheen
Ripplette
riso sopra riso
ro
roanes
roanne
Rohseide
ròin
ròin-aodach
roinne-bhaidhe
romagnuolo
romaine
romaine crepe
rong
róngbù
rosa
rosadimoi
rosalba
Roshanara
rosille de soie
Roubaix velvet
roucha
roxano
royale
rozah
ruanduàn
ruga
ruhbani
rum-swizzle
russaline
russell
russell cord
russell satin

russells
russet
Russian cord
Russian crash
Russian crepe
Russian sergette
Russian velvet
ryssedamast
rysseklade
Ryūkū-gasuri
sa
sa din
saba
sabada
sablé
saenggosa
sagathie
sagathy
sagiya guakari
sagmatogene
saia
Saint Etienne velvet
Saint Omer
saki
salara
salari
salembaree
salempoory
salempora
salempore
salempury
salendang
salisbury
salla
sallo
salloo
salura
sambhal
samit
samite
Samt
samyt
sana
sang chau
sangati
sangi
sania
sani-gani
sanjharavau
santipur cloth
sanyan
saput
sar
saranala
sarasa

sarashi
sarashi nuno
sarata shirting
sarcenet
sarciatus
sarga
sarja
sarsenet
sarzil
sa-tanh
satarra cloth
sateen
sateen berber
sateen paré
satén
satijn
Satin
satin
satin antoinette
satin berber
satin cashmere
satin checks
satin chinois
satin crepe
satin damask
satin de chine
satin de laine
satin de Lyon
satin de Mai
satin duchesse
satin faconne
satin fontange
satin foulard
satin jean
satin liberty
satin lisse
satin merino
satin merv
satin merveilleux
satin orientale
satin rouleaux
satin sultan
satin surah
satin turc
satin velouté
satin Victoria
satiné playé
satiné velouté
satinesco
satinet
satineta
satinette
satingle Holland
satyna
sauvarnapatta

savadi copacchudahu
saxony
say
saya
sayal
sayiaki
scamato
schappe silk
Schotse muts
sciameto
Scotch cambric
scotch gingham
Scotia silk
Sea Island cotton
sealskin cloth
seda
seda chape
seda cruda
seda de corbatas
seda silvestre
sedalina
seersucker
seghosen
segu
sehan
Seide
seigo
seiric
seiz
selisie lawn
selk
selvage
sempringham
sen
Sendai Hira silk
sendal
sensuji
seolac
Seraceta
seraser
serenk
serge
serge de soy
serge royale
sergedesoy
sergedusoy
sergette
sergia
sēricum
serih
serribaf
serst
seta
setim
setimeta

sha
shabnam
shag
shaker flannel
shalloon
shambar
shantung
sharbati
shash
shawl wool
sheep's gray
sheep's russet
shema
shenu
shepherd's check
shepherd's cloth
shepherd's plaid
shetland
shima
shioze
shireenbaf
shirinbaf
shirvani
shoddy
shoe velvet
shokko-nishiki
shrimbawi
shubnam
shuchin
shusu
siamoise
siang-malam
siapo
sichóu
sicilian
sicilienne
sīda
sidan
Sīde
siden
siglat
siglatoen
siglaton
sihrang
siklat
silahati
silecho
silesia
silika
silistrienne
siliva
silk
silk Damascene
silk gauze
silk linen

silk rash
šilkai
silkaline
silke
silki
silverets
sindu
sīoda
siolac
sirat
sirge debaragon
sirghe
sīric
sirinbaf
siring
sirkek
siróng
sirsaka
sisal
sīta
sitapuri
sits
sizhipin
skelat
škidrauts
skirduk
sklat
škrlet
skyteen
sleasy holland
sleaved silk
slesia lawn
slicker fabric
slipper satin
snail
snow cloth
snowflake
soie
soie de Padoue
soie demantine
soieries à double face
soieries bizarres
soiesette
som
sommiere
sook chau
soosey
soosie
soudagir
soyeaux linsey
spandex
spiral witney
spitalfields
sponge cloth
Spun-lo

sribapha
stafford cloth
stagbe
stamel
stametto
stamfortis
stamin
stammel
stamped velvet
stamyn sengill
stavaraka
stavrak
stijf linnen
stockinette
stof
stofă
Strasbourg cloth
striop
strouding
stuth
sublom
subnom
sucisona
suclat
Sudanette
suddhaota
suède
suede cloth
sukkosa
sukno
sultane
suoyi
superfine
supha-kamkha
surah
surf satin
surowa bawelna
susae
susi
sussapine
suthila
suvarnapadi
svetacinamsuka
svila
swadeshi
Swami
swanskin
swarry-doo
Swatow grass cloth
Swiss cambric
swiss muslin
šyras
sztruks
szurtuk
tabaret

tabarete
tabbinet
tabby
tabie-nishiki
tabijn
tabine
tabinet
tafailah
tafetá
tafetán
taffeta
taffeta coutil
taffeta crape
taffeta d'Annecy
taffeta de Suez
taffeta lustré
taffetán
taffetane
taffetas
taffetine
Taft
tafta
tafuchóu
tafzijde
taifeid
tajehbaf
takan
tamative
Tamba cloth
tamein
tamise
tammy
tan
tanasukha
tanjeeb
tanjib
tanzeb
tapa
tapa cloth
tarlatan
tarletan
tarpya
tartan
tartan velvet
tartanella
tartarian
tartarin
tartaryn
tassar
tatbandpuri
tate-nishiki
tattersall
tavestock
tawar
tayu-kanoko

tecidos
teia
tejano
tejido
tejido arrugado
tejido calado
tejido con pelo largo
tejido de punto elástico
tejido de punto liso
tejido esponjoso
tejido liso
tela
tela caucho
tela cerata
tela de algodón mercer-
  izado
tela de aspecto granulado
tela de Jouy
tela de lino
tela grossolana
tela para carpa
tela Tagliata
tennis cloth
tennis flannel
terciopelo
terciopelo acordonado
terciopelo aplastado
terciopelo chifón
terciopelo con dibujo
  multicolor
terciopelo de Utrect
terciopelo en relieve
terciopelo labrado
tergal
terliz
terrendam
terry cloth
tewke
textīle
textum
the
Thibet cloth
thicksets
thunder and lightning
tì
tian'eróng
tiáoróng
ticklenburg
tiffany
tilavasa
tin chiang chiang chau
tirchha
tiretaine
tissu
tissu satiné

tissue
tissue d'Alma
tissue gingham
tissue taffeta
tjap
tjindai
tkan'
tkanina
tkanina dziana
to hoá-hoc
tobin
tobine
tocuyo
toile
toile à gros poil
toile cirée
toile d'Alsace
toile de jouy
toile de lin
toile de soie
toile de Valeuce
toile d'esprit
toile grossiére
toile Nankin
toile peinte
toilinet
toilinette
toilonette
topola
tow
tow cloth
treillis
tricô
tricolette
tricolina
tricot
tricot de Berlin
tricota
tricotine
Trikot
triple voile
tripoline
trip-sammet
trúc-bâu
tsumugi
tsuzure-nishiki
tūba
tubayt
tubsi
Tuch
tuftataffeta
tufted dimity
tuillinn
tuke
tul

tulapansi
tule
tulis
tulle
tuly
Tuoch
Tuoh
turco poplinnes
turin velvet
turkey red
Turkish brilliantine
turudam
tussah
tusseh
tussore
tussore de Longchamps
tuyn
túyt-xo
tweed
tylesent
typewriter cloth
ubong mata
uchidashi-knaoko
udbandha
ukara
ukaw
'ula palani
uld
ull
umbrella cloth
umbrella gingham
umbrella silk
umritzur
uncut velvet
ungen-nishiki
union
unmunsa
urasala
utrecht velvet
vað
vadmal
vahitha
vahitika
vài
vài bò
vài bông
vai hoa
vài màn

vài to
vài trorn
vài vóc
vajramsuka
vakala
valencia
valentia
vân
vangala
veletine
velludillo
velludo
vellum
velluto
velo
velour
velour de coton
velours
velours de coton croisé
velours de laine
velours de Venise
velours frappé
velours Grégoire
velours Impératrice
veloutine
velure
velveret
velvet
velvet imperatrice
velveteen
venetian
Venetian cloth
Venetian crape cloth
venise
ventus textilis
vesses
vettam
vichy
vicitra
Victoria crepe
Victoria lawn
Victoria silk
victorieuse
vicuna
vigogna
vigogne
Vigogne
vihita kappasa

vilna
vilnos
vilt
Vilz
virgin wool
virly
viyella
Vlahs
vlas
vlno
voile de laine
vojlok
volante
vuna
Wachstuch
wadmal
wadmel
walutu
warp
wasdoek
wash silk
watchet
wedding ring velvet
weft
wełna
whipcord
white scarlet
wikolia
wildbore
wincey
winceyette
witte
wol
Wolla
Wolle
wolle
wollen goederen
wollen mousseline
wollen stof
wool
wool batiste
wool bengaline
wool chiffon
wool crepe
wool plain
woolenet
worsted
wull

wulla
wulle
Yamato nishiki
yeddo crepe
Yokohama crepe
yoko-nishiki
yukata
yusha
yusoku orimono
Yuzen birodo
zakkengoed
zakkenlinnen
zambellotto
zanella
zanella cloth
zarzahan
zelluuami
zendado
zendale
zenne
zenne alffowa
zephyr
zephyr armure
zephyr cloth
zephyr gingham
zerbaft
zhan
zhòu
zhòubù
zhùmá
zibeline
zīds
zijde
zijden japon of toga
zimbelline
Zulu cloth
zuòcán
zuòsichóu
zwarte

FEATHERS

aigrette
amazon plume
amazones
'at'a'

autruche
banditti
canache
coq

coque
coquearde
coquillicot feathers
cross aigrette

culgee
demiplume
eiderdown
ekawa

esprits
Feder
femina
flues
fulu
gossamer feathers
goura feather
gourah feather
grebe

hulu
jiqa
marabou
marabout feathers
ostaigrette
panache
panache blanc
panache de coque
penache

piorko
piuma
piuma di struzzo
pleureuses
pluma de avestruz
pluma de gallo
plumach
plumage
plume

plume d'autruche
plume de coq
plume de faisan
plumes fantaisies
weepers
zebra feathers

FUR AND LEATHER

Affenpeltz
agneau
agneau du Tibet
agneau karakul
agnelin
agnellino de Persia
agnello
aincis
ajina
ajina yajnopavita
Alaska sable
alligator
almizclera
alpaca
American badger
American broadtail
Angora goat
Angora rabbit
antelope
aquerne
arctic hare
ardilla
Armenian rat
arminho
armiño
astracán
astrakan
Astrakan
avika
badana
badger
baldrés
Bär
baronduki
basen
basil
baum marten
bauson skin
bazan
béabhar
beaver
Belliz
Bessarabian lamb

besshe
Biber
bice
Bisamratte
bise
bisshe
black bear
blaireau
blană
blaunchmer
blaundemer
blaundever
blauner
blue fox
boicionn
bolgar
borgal
breitschwantz
Breitschwantz
broadtail lamb
buckskin
budge
bulgar
bulger
bulghar
bullgarry
burunduki
cabra de China
cabretta leather
cabrito
caddice
caddis leather
calaber
calfskin
canepin
capeskin
capra china
caracul lamb
caracule
carolina beaver
castor
castorino
castoro

cazapo
chamois
charol
chele
cheveril
chèvre de Chine
chèvre de Mongolie
chevreau
chevrette
Chinaziege
chinchilla
chisamus
comadreja
conejo
coney
coracinus color
cordero
cordero de Rusia
cordero del Tibet
cordero mongoliano
cordobán
cordoban leather
cordouan
corium
cristygrey
croppes
cross fox
cuero
cuero de ante
cuero de cerdo
cuero de cocodrilo
cuero de marroqui
cuero napa
cuir
cuoio
curóugé
da boc-can
da láng
da linh
da lon
Dachs
Danakillisches Böcklein
dankalia capretto della

dankalie
diaopí
diphera
doeskin
dogskin
Eichhörnchen
ermellini
ermellino
ermine
esquilo
esquirole
Feh
Fettschwanzschaf
ffwr
fionnadh
flea-fur
Florentine leather
foca
fourrure
foynes
Fuchs
fuine
fycheux
galyac
galyak
gamsbart
gamuza
gaopí
gatos de lomos
genet
ghiottone
glacé kid
glazed kid
glotón
glouton
godalming
gold and silver kid
grand vair
gris
grise
gros vair
guanaco
Guanako

guanaquito
hermelijn
Hermelin
hermine
hertevel
hiladillo
hua yu
huarizo
'ili
'ili hinuhinu
'ili pipi
'ilio-hulu-papale
jack leather
Jap marten
Jap mink
Japanese mink
juchten
kailiniai
kailis
kalgan
kangaroo leather
Kanin
kaunakes
kawa
kid leather
kolinsky
koza
kozesina
krimmer
läder
lambskin
Lamm
lan yu
leder
leðr
leopard
Leopard
lerion
lethar
lether
lettice
lince
lledr
lobe
lœder

lontra
loup
loutre
Luchs
lupo
lynx
mapache
Marder
marmot
marmota
marmotta
marmotte
marta
marta cebellina
marta comú
marten
martora
martre
martre zibeline
mat kid
mech
mentýk
miniceag
minicionn
minicionn-laoigh
miniver
mink
mocha
mofeta
mongolia
mono
murmel
Murmeltier
muskrat
musquash
napa leather
nawame-irokawa
neas-nam-fuar-thìrean
neat's leather
Nerz
nutria
oiled leather
olann
ooze calf
opossum

Oposum
orbace
orso
osito lavador
oso
patent kid
patent leather
peallaid
peau d'agneau
pele de cordeiro
pelego
pelica
pelliccia
Pelliz
pelliza
pelo de castor
pelo de liebere
pelo di castora
pelo di lepre
pels
peñas veras
persian broadtail
Persian lamb
Persianer
petit-gris
phoque
piel de becerro
piele
pigskin
pointed fox
polayn
pople
pulo
qigé
rabbit
raccoon
ratmusqué
raton laveur
red fox
renard
róngmiàngé
roskyn
sable
sabeldier
schapevel

scheibenbart
scimmia
seal
Seehund
shagreen
silver fox
singe
skóra
skunk
skūra
sobol
Spanish leather
stone marten
stranlyng
suède
suede kid
suela
swan's down
tasso
tejón
Tibetisches Lamm
uainicionn
urna
vair
vajo
vavr
velleres fulvi
velleres nigri
vellum
villi
vison
visón
visone
volpe
volpe o renard
Waschbär
white fox
yuhada-kawa
zeemleer
zibelina
zibeline
zibellino
zobel
Zobel
zorro

GOWNS AND TUNICS

A line
aba
abba
achkan
agbada
agun-pat sari
akome

aksu
alb
almilla
anacu
andalusian casaque
angarkha
angarkhi

ankanjo
antaravasaka
áo bông
áo da
áo lanh lót vài bông
aoidai
apron tunic

attigra
attila
attush
aymilla
badan
bai na yi
ballerina dress

baluchar
bata corta
bata de casa
bata de mañana
Bavarian dress-style
Bavarian pelisse robe
Beatrice
bedla
bei zi
beramen
biedermeier
bil
binary chiton
bla lome
bliand
bliant
bliaunt
bliaus
blouse polonaise
brial
broderie anglaise
broigne
bròn
Brunswick
bui-bui
caftan
cai-ao
calasiris
calypso chemise
cancan dress
caraco
caraco à coqueluchon
caraco à la francaise
caraco à la polonaise
caraco gown
cazavacka
ccahua
ccahuas
cettelle
chang fu
chang shan
chángpáo
chángshan
chao pao
chapkan
charuot
chayazome
chemise à la greque
chemise à la Reine
chemise à l'anglaise
chemise dress
chemise gown
cheongsam
Cherbourg
chiton

chun sam
chungch'imak
cira
circassienne gown
coat-dress
cocktail dress
cola
colobium
Colson
Constance
convertible jumper
cool gown
corset dress
corset frock
costume à la Constitution
cote
cotehardie
cotelettes
cotellae
coton
cotta
cotte
cuirass tunic
curricle dress
cushma
cyrtel
dadiyā
dagba gulai
dàguà
dalephuc
dalmatic
dalmatica
dalmatikon
demi-gown
devantiere
diploidion
djubba
dogaline
Dolly Varden dress
Dolly Varden polonaise
doni
doric chiton
duster
earthquake dress
ebu
eillets panaches
English gown
exomia
exomide
false gown
Fatima robe
fliegende Nachtrok
flocket
fly-suit
Fortuny tea gown

fourreau dress
fourreau tunic
French polonaise
frou-frou dress
Gabrielle dress
galabijeh
galabiyeh bi wist
galerilla
gamurra
ganache
gandoora
gandoura
gandurah
gáppte
garchola
gare
garnache
gbariye
German gown
gharacholoo
gharcholu
gilaharā
gilbah
girki
gite
glandkin
gonelle
gonellone
gonne
goshodoki
gown
gown à la francaise
gown à la levantine
gown à la polonaise
gown à la sultane
gown à la turque
gown à l'anglaise
gown à l'insurgente
gown and coat
granatza
grande robe à corps
  ouvert
grande robe à la francaise
greatcoat dress
Grecian robe
gui yi
gùn na h-eaglaise
gùn odhar
gunachan
habit de demi-gala
habit degage
habit d'escalier
habit-redingote
haincelin
handkerchief dress

handkerchief tunic
haol
haori
hashimi
herigaute
Himmutsatha
H-line
hofkledij
holoku
holomu
homongi
houppelande
houppelande a mi-jambe
houppelande courte
house dress
hugue
hui yi
ichcahuipilli
indusium
interala
Ionic chiton
Irish polonaise
Isabeau style dress
Italian polonaise
japon
ji fu
jinashi
jinashi-nuihaku
jubba
jubbah
juive
juppo
kaeshi
kaftan
kaftani
kala-pat sari
kanakagi
kanca-pat sari
kancuka
kappa dachi
kasturia
kaun
kawakī
khalaga
khurkeh
kimono
ki-mô-nô
kimono dress
kin koot
kinumo
kirtle
kitel
kittel
koller
kolob

kolobus

kopin

koshimaki

koshipiri

kosode

koynek

kras

kubba

kudtā

kuftan

kyrtill

lampshade dress

Laveuse costume

Leine

léine-bhàn

lendener

levite

levite gown

liányiqún

little black dress

lobas compridas

long pao

Lonjumeau dress

losse japon

lucco

lugadoo

mameluke robe

mandā paradiyā

mang ao

Manon robe

manteau

mantelletta

mantua

matinée

mayūrakanthiā

Medici dress

meghadambara

melas

morning gown

mother hubbard

mshono wa Elizabethi

mshono wa Rosi

muslin deaths

mu'u mu'u

Napoleon costume

ncak

negligee de la volupte

nei tao

nightgown

nikautang

nīlāmbarī

nilaniradanicola

nimā

nugi-sage

nuihaku

nūr-ī-bādlā

nursing dress

'ofu

okolepu'u

pais-a-gwn bach

pajama

pajani

pallustache

pamsukula

pannier dress

páo

páozi

patori

pat-sari

peignoir

pelisse-robe

peplos chiton

Perdita chemise

Persian drape tunic

petite robe unie

pharos

phutā lugā

Piedmont gown

pinafore costume

pirahan-e zananeh

Platoff costume

plisîrani

polonaise

polonaise àdeux fins

poloneze

polu-kaftan

pompadour polonaise

prapadina

princesa

princess dress

princess polonaise

princess robe

princesse

principessa

Prinzesskleid

puletasi

purple gown

qiapàn

Raphael dress

raso

robe à la circassienne

robe à la française

robe à la Joconde

robe à la levantine

robe à la polonaise

robe à la prêtesse

robe à la Reine

robe à la Turque

robe à l'américaine

robe à l'anglais

robe à plis gironnés

robe anglaise

robe de chambre

robe de cérémonie à la

    française

robe de chez

robe de commune at an-

    cienne guise

robe de noce

robe de style

robe déguisée

robe d'interieur

robe drapeé

robe du soir

robe en calecons

robe gironnée

robe longue

robe parée

robe princesse

robe torque

robe volante

robes à quille

robes de fantaisie

robes en calecon

rôbo

rocket

roguelo dress

rok

ropa bastarda

ropa de estado

ropa larga

ropa rozagnte

Rose

round dress

round gown

sace

sack dress

sack gown

sack-back

saekduresu

samghati

sanitary ball dress

sapara

sari

savrikin

saya

schöpen

scyrte

Second Empire costume

selari

serapis

seray

sgùird

shan ku

shawal

sheath dress

shiromuku

shiu tian yi

shudiya

silai

sire

siree

slammerkin

sorquenie

soucane

souquenilles

soutane

spagnolet

stanamsuka

sticking-plaster dress

stola

subrichion

suckenie

suculla ccahua

śukla dhardīa

sukmán

sukni

suknia

suliya

sultane dress

sunthiā

surubuli

susomoyo

synthesis

tablier tunic

talaris tunic

tanzen

tappert

teagown

thaub

thawb

thob al-khidmah

thob al-tal'ah

thob basitah

thob mukhmal azraq

tonaca

Trafalgar dress

traje de novia

trapeze

trappers

trapphant

trollopee

tsubo-ori

tunece

tunic

tunic à la juive

tunic à la mameluck

tunic à la Romaine

tunic dress

tunica

túnica
tunica alba
tunica augusticlavia
tunica interior
tunica intima
tunica laticlavia
tunica manicata
tunica palmata
tunica taleris
tunicle
tuniek
tunika
tunique

tunique à la Juive
turesu
turkey gown
Turkish polonaise
tutu mu'u
uchikake
unku
unterrock
urbasī
urku
uttarasanga
vandyke dress
Veronese dress

vestido
vestido de noche
vestito da sera
Victoria
vlieger
volanten
wai tao
waterfall back
Watteau polonaise
Watteau robe
waya
wentke
woko

wrapping front dress
wrapping gown
wundi
Wurtenburg frock
x-ray dress
yar chiki
York wrapper
yukata
Zerlina dress

HAIRSTYLES AND WIGS

à la Maintenon
à la plaquette
à la Titus
à la Victime
Academician
accroche-coeur
Adonis wig
agemaki
aile de pigeon
'aki
alaka
amlag
Apollo knot
as
asbeh ruwaysiyeh
au globe fixe
Author
'ava
'avaaluga
badger whiskers
bag wig
bakkebaarden
barba
beau-catcher
beehive coiffure
berger
bhrameraka
bím
binette
bob-wig
bodkin
bodkin-beard
Borghesé
bras-ghruag
breug-chiabh
brodé
Brutus cut
Brutus head wig
buckled wig

búi tó
búi tóc
bull's head fringe
butterfly bun
cabeleira
cabeleira postiça
cache-folies
cadanette
cadenette
cadogan
cais-chiabh
caisean-feusaig
caisreag
camag
camalag
campaign wig
capillamentum
çargat
cas-urladh
catagan
catagan head-dress
cathedral beard
catogan
cauliflower wig
cavanhaque
caxon
chain buckle
chancellor
chignon
chignon flottant
chinó
choux
chucu
chuda
churna-kuntala
ciabhag
ciabh-chasta
clann
cleachd

cleachdag
clearc
clubwig
clytie knot
coiffure à la Ceres
coiffure à la Chinoise
coiffure à la conseillere
coiffure à la Dauphine
coiffure à la enfant
coiffure à la Eurydice
coiffure à la Flore
coiffure à la herisson
coiffure à la Junon
coiffure à la moutonne
coiffure à la Nino
coiffure à la Pomone
coiffure à la qu' es aco
coiffure à la Reine
coiffure à la zazzera
coiffure à l'Agnes Sorel
coiffure à l'anglomane
coiffure à l'indisposition
coiffure au chien couchant
coiffure Egyptienne
coiffure en bouffons
coiffure en cadenettes
coiffure en chien couchant
coiffure en moilin à vent
coiffure en parterre galant
coiffure en raquette
coiffure Maintenon
confidents
Continental
costeleta
coups de vent
courrone Ristori
crape
creve-coeur
croimeal

crop
cruches
cuach-chiabh
cuach-fhalt
culan
curls à la Greque
cutlets
dancing phoenix bun
dhanush
dildo
Director
djnne-djnne
djorro-marabu
dosan-banntraich
Droop Snoot
dual
dundreary whiskers
dundrearys
durol bedyeli
durol bedyeli puDaaDo
durol cakaol
durol chuddito
durol pila dorungol
durol tyeli
durol yesool
Duvillier wig
Editor
ekaveni
en beret
en colimaçon
en dos d'ane
faces
falbala
fantail wig
favoris
favorite
favourite
feather-top wig
Flying Saucer

foloara
fontanges
forked beard
fortop
fouriaux
frenello
frisette
frizette
frizz wig
frouze
fuafuati
full bottomed wig
furbelow
gaforinha
glib
goatee
gold ingot bun
gurnakuntala
hair à la Recamier
hair à la Romaine
hamaku'u
hammercut beard
heart-breaker
hectorean
hedgehog hairdo
Horus lock
hurluburlu
hurlupe
imperial
Irene Castle bob
ityogaesi
jasey
jata-bhara
jata-mukuta
jiu
kabal
kabari bandha
kaisika
kamozi
kampū
kaparda
kapitsáli
kapsel
kata-hazusi
katsura
kemba

kes
kesapasa
khopa
knevel
kogai
kolbe
korte pruik
k'ossuyom
krul
krulletje
kumbi
k'unmori
kurira
la coiffure Diane
lauoho
lauoho ku'i
Lily Langtry coiffure
llautu
long Duvallier
loth
mae-gami
mage
major wig
maku'a
marcel wave
marcelling
marquisetto beard
marteaux
marumage
mechones
mechuelas
mimi-kakusi
mitu-ori
mituwa
momo-ware
Montague curls
musk melon bun
muttonchops
na krilo
Newgate fringe
night-cap wig
nihyakusan-koti
obalenka
off-the-horse bun
'oki pahu
Olympic

opasa
orbis
oreilles de chien
paardestaart
page boy bob
parrucca
passagers
passe-filon
patondon
peluca
penteado
peoth
perriwigg
perrukes à bourse
perruque quarrée
peruça
perwyke
physical wig
picaporte
piccadilly fringe
piccadilly weepers
pigeon-winged toupee
pigtail wig
pijpekrullen
pique devant
po'o ke'oke'o
po'o kuakea
porcupine headdress
postiche
poufs au sentiment
pruik
psyche knot
pudding-basin cut
pupu lauoho
pyonbal
queue
Ramillies wig
râu cam
râu dê
râu mép
râu som
ringetje
ròibeag
sakayaki
sanbenito
scratch bob

scratch wig
serpentaux
sheitel
shell
ship-tire
sikhandaka
simada
simpa
snake
snor
sokuhatu
spencer wig
spit curl
star-studded sky
sualef
swallow-tail bangs
takashimada
talafa
tanbal
tenzin-mage
tête de mouton
tignon
tochtlatten
top
toupee
toupet
tour de cheveux
transformation
tyasen-gami
tye
ula
ulach
ulchadh
'umi'i lauoho
'umi'umi
vallancy
vergette à la chinoise
wasy
weeping willow bangs
Welch wig
weleweka
zarost
zazzara
Zopfzeit

HATS AND HEADDRESSES

à la Farare
à la Marie Stuart
'a'ahu a po'o
adagan
afia

agal
aision
Alampasand
alan dangi
Albanian hat

Albert pot
alceste
Alesjo
almuzi
alpine hat

ammana
ampyz
anadem
androsame
androsman

angelus cap
anglesea
Angouleme bonnet
Angouleme hat
angrakhâs
anhaho
Anne Boleyn mob
'aqal
'aqal mqassab
Aragonese bonnet
arak-chin
'araqiyeh
Armenian toque
ascanta
atef
attiffet
avagunthana
babet bonnet
babet cap
babushka
baby cap
baby Stuart cap
bag bonnet
bag cap
baigneuse
bairēad
bakhramā
bakwala
balaclava
balloon hat
balmoral cap
balzo
bambino hat
bandeau beehive crown
    hat
bandelet
bandelette
bandore
bandore peak
Bangalore cap
bao tou
baori
baranice
barbe
barbette
barbichet
barbúli
barbute
baret
Barett
barraighin
barret
barrete
barretino
barrette

bascinet
basco
bashlik
bashlyk
basinet
basque beret
bath-throid
batwat
bavolet
bayō
bēabhar
beanie
beatilla
beaver
bebedi
bee-gum hat
beefeater
beehive bonnet
beguin
bellboy hat
bend
benda
bendigo
beret
beret basque
bergere hat
berretino
berretto
berretto alla marinara
bersagliere
Bethlehem headdress
bewdley cap
béza
Bhayyā-cap
bian
bibi bonnet
bibi capote
bicorne
bigean
biggin
biggon
biggonet
biliment
billicock
binde
binnogue
biorraid
biretta
birritta
blangkon
bluebonnet
boater
boina
boina vasca
boineid

boineid bhall-ach
boineid biorach
boineid chath-dath
bolero toque
Bolivar hat
bollinger
bombetta
Bonaparte helmet
boné
bongrace
bonnet à barbes
bonnet à flamme
bonnet à la crete de coq
bonnet à la laitiere
bonnet à la moresque
bonnet à la Richard
bonnet à la victoire
bonnet assassin
bonnet aux trois ordres
    reunis
bonnet beehive
bonnet cabriolet
bonnet de police
bonnet demi-negligee
bonnet negligee
bonnet pamela
bonnet rond
bonnet sylphide
bonneto
boonie hat
börk
borla
borsalino
bosses
botchi
boudoir cap
bourbon hat
bourdalou
bourrelet
bréid
bréid geal
breton
brewer's cap
brides
brium
brud
Buchanan
bullycock
bumper
busby
bush hat
butterfly cap
bycocket
bycoket
cabriolet

cache-peigne
caciula
caeppe
cagoule
cahouk
caille
cailmhion
caipīn
cais-chiabh
caissia
caita
cake hat
calash
calata
cale
calêche
Caledonian cap
callaid
calotte
calpac
calyptra
camargo hat
camauro
cameleurion
campaign hat
canotier
cantab hat
cap à la Charlotte Corday
cap of maintenance
capacete de Indias
capadüsli
capeline
caperuza
capilla
capirote
capka
capot
capota
capote
capot-ribot
capouch
cappa
cappe
cappelina
cappello
cappello a cencio
cappello a cilindro
cappello a lobbia
cappello a tagliere
cappello a tesa larga
cappello da uomo
cappello di paglia
cappello floscio
cappucio
capriole

capuce
capuch
capucha
capuche
capuchinho
capuchon
capulet
caputium
carapuça
caravan
çârma
carmeillette
carmeñola
caroline hat
carpote
cartola
cartwheel
casco
caseac
casque
casque à la Tarleton
casque colonial
casquette
cassis
castle hat
castor
catagan net
cater-cap
catiole
cát-két
caubeen
caudebec hat
caul
causia
cawdebink
ceanna-bhrat
ceann-aodach
ceann-bhàrr
ceann-bhàrr eas-buig
ceann-éideadh
ceapsâ
ceimhleag
ceimh-mhileach
ceimh-phion
cepec
cepice
cepure
cerevis
cervelliera
ceryphalos
chaffers
chakvidar
chambergo
chang guan
chao guan

chapeau
chapeau à borne
chapeau à la Basile
chapeau à la Ceres
chapeau à la Charlotte
chapeau à la Cherubin
chapeau à la Colonne
chapeau à la Devonshire
chapeau à la Grenade
chapeau à la turque
chapeau à l'egyptienne
chapeau à l'italienne
chapeau à plumes
chapeau au bateau ren-
 versé
chapeau-bras
chapeau claque
chapeau de Cardinal
chapeau de paille
chapeau d'homme
chapeau jockei
chapeau melon
chapeau mou
chapeau souple
chaperone
chapéu cardinalício
chapiron
chaplet
chapska
charlotte
Charlotte Corday bonnet
chaugoshia
chechia
chechias
child's pudding
chimney pot hat
chin stays
chip hat
chobawi
choi-ngon
chokturi
chol
chola derby
ch'olmo
chongjagwan
chou hat
chouquette
chucu
chudamani
chullo
ch'ullu
chullu
chungjolmo
chungsanmo
cillāwālī

cimarosa
cinta
cipcic
circassian hat
circumfolding hat
clac
Clarissa Harlowe bonnet
cloche
cloche de feutre
cloche de fieltro
cloche di feltro
clock-mutch
close cap
coalman's hat
coalscuttle bonnet
Coburg bonnet
Coburg cap
cockle hat
coeffes
coffer headdress
cofia
cofia de tranzado
coif
coif cooil corran
coiffe
coiffure à la Ceres
coiffure à la Chinoise
coiffure à la corseillere
coiffure à la Dauphine
coiffure à la enfant
coiffure à la Eurydice
coiffure à la Flore
coiffure à la herisson
coiffure à la Junon
coiffure à la moutonne
coiffure à la Ninon
coiffure à la Pomone
coiffure à la Reine
coiffure à la zazzera
coiffure à l'Agnes Sorel
coiffure à l'anglomane
coiffure à l'indisposition
coiffure auchien couchant
coiffure Egyptienne
coiffure en bouffons
coiffure en cadanettes
coiffure en chien couchant
coiffure en moulin à vent
coiffure en parterre gab-
 ant
coiffure en raquette
coiffure Eugenie
coiffure Louis Treize
coiffure Mantenon
coiffure Zouave

coke
colbac
colbacco
colback
combed helmet
conch
conciu
confidents
conque
conversation bonnet
conversation hat
coolie hat
copitank
copotain
coquard
coqueluche
cordey cap
cordyback hat
corner cap
cornet
cornet hat
cornette
cornette à la Diane
corno
cornu
coroa
coron
coron òir
corona
corona etrusca
corona muralis
corona navalis
corona radiata
coronal
coronet
cossack cap
cossack hat
cottage bonnet
couvre-chef
cowl
coxcomb
cramignole
crants
cravate
crespine
crispine
crispinette
croisgileid
cross-cloth
cruinneacan
crùn
crùn-easbuig
csepesz
cucullus
cudamani

cūdō
cudon
cuffia
cuffie
cuircinn
Cumberland hat
cunua
curch
curchef
curling-cloud crown
currac
curracag
cushion headdress
cusma
cuth-bhàrr
cuth-bharran
czapka
czapska
czepek
czepesz
czólka
dan kura
dastar
dastar boongga
dastmal
dauni
Davy Crockett cap
dealg-fhuilt
demi-castor
demicaul
demi-turban
Denmark cock
deshret
dessous
Dettingen cock
Devonshire hat
diadem bonnet
diadem comb
diadem fanchon bonnet
Diana Vernon bonnet
Diana Vernon hat
dinner cap
Directoire bonnet
Directoire hat
disissik
doll hat
Dolly Varden bonnet
Dolly Varden cap
Dolly Varden hat
dopairi
dorelet
dormeuse
dormouse
d'Orsay roll
doulì

dragoonka
drawn bonnet
Dreispitz
dreumelthoelje
duchowny
dulándle
dulbén
dullemoese
Dutch bonnet
Dutch cap
Easter bonnet
ebo
eboshi
ebosi
écossaise hat
elastic hat
elmo di giostra
empire cap
Empress Eugenie hat
en ravanche
English cottage bonnet
English hood
eobhrat
escoffion
Eton cap
Eugenie hat
fa guan
fachalina
fachalina de cabeza
facóli
failtean
faldetta
fall
falt-dhealg
faluchos
fanchon
fanchon cap
fantail hat
farrukhshāhi
fascinator
fatas
fatumar saki
faufautu
feax-clap
feax-net
fedora
feluca
féngmào
festoul
feusag-bheòil
fez
field cap
field service cap
filead
Filzglocke

firmament
Fitzherbert hat
flammeum
flandan
flipe
floddermuts
Florentine hat
Florentinerhut
flügelmütze
flushing hat
flycap
foileid
foloara
fools hood
forage cap
fore-and-aft cap
foundling bonnet
fouraschka
French hood
friso
frontiere
fu tou
furashka
gable headdress
gahper
Gainsborough bonnet
Gainsborough hat
galatea
Galatea comb
Galatea hat
galero
galerum
galerus
Garibaldi hat
garrison cap
gartan
gebreide muts
geknauften kogeln
Geneva hat
ghatra
ghoutra
ghudfeh
ghughi
ghutra
gibus
gigolo
gig-top
gipsy bonnet
gipsy hat
Glengarry
gluga
gob cap
gondolier net
gorra
gorra deportiva

gorra escocesa
gorro
gorro de dormir
gorro de marinero
gorro de pieles
goshpech
gothic cap
Graham turban
granny bonnet
grenadier cap
grenadierka
grun
gu gu guan
gua pi mao
guanmiãn
gugel
gus-to-weh
gyöngyös bokréta
hachimaki
haet
haiduk
hair-lace
half handkerchief
half-beaver
halo
halssieraad
harbeh
harsa
hastrigánky
hat à la reine
hata
hatt
hatta
hattah
haube
haut de forme
havelock
headrail
heafod-clap
heafod-gewaede
Helen cap
helmet cap
helmet hat
hemispherical hat
hengjehuva
Henley boater
hennin
Herrenhut
het
hire
hitai-ebosi
hive
hod
hodnhue
hodnhuva

hoed
hœtt
hoge hoed
hoge zijden
homburg
hoofdband
hoofdtooi
hottr
houve
hovdatyet
howve
hūba
hue
hufá
hufa
hufe
huif
huke
hukkō
hul
hula saki
hulle
Huntley bonnet
Huot
hupé
hure
huve
huvet
hvivklaede
Hyde Park bonnet
hydrotobolic hat
igaal
ihram
ikar-hay
ikori
indlugula
infula
iricinium
'isāba
ishkay fachalina
Ivanhoe cap
jalika
Japanese hat
jarrawiyah
jelly bag
Jenny Lind riding hat
ji guan
Jim Crow hat
jin xian guan
jipajapa
jíros
Joan
jockey bonnet
jockey cap
John Bull

Judenhut
juk'ullu
Juliet cap
kaap
kabuto-sita
ka'ei papale
kaffiyeh
kafiyyeh
kaga-boshi
kahi 'omou
kaitsa
kakofnitch
kalabi
kalabousenn
kalansuwa
kalauna
kalaunu
kalaunu bihopa
kalimáfkia
kall
kalotje
kalpac
kalpak
kalpáki
kalpush
kalyptra
kamelaukion
kammuri
kamrukhi
kantopa
kap
kapa
kapelusz
Kapp
kappa
kappel
kapperoellike
kappie
kapsel
karabousenn
karaori
karauna
kartriz
kasa
kasaba
kaska
kasket
kat
katabira
katapu
kat-no
katsura-zutsumi
keffieh
keffiyeh
kelle

kepi
keppelche
kepresh
kepuré
kesapasa
kesg'han
keshghan
kettle hat
kettyl hat
kevenhuller
khamar
khamout
khan đôi đàu
khan ngang
khan tang
khimara
khirkidar
khirki-dar-pagri
khirqa
kidaris
kilmarnock bonnet
kim-khôi
kirita
kirita-mukuta
kiss-me-quick
kissing-strings
kite-high dandy
kiver
klaft
klapove hitl
Klapphut
klaw-i jnan
klaw-i pyawan
klobouk
klobuk
knipmuts
kogel
kokoshnik
kola
kolah
kolitsa
kolpak
konfederatka
Kopftuch
kopplak
kornek
korona
koruna
Kossuth
kova sheberosho
krachoom
ksoulia
kubba'ah
kugel
kulah

kulahā
kulah-e kordi
kulahī
kulah-i pahlavi
kule
kullah
kunba
kundala
kupasi
kupiah
kupkeh
kusulaka
kutusoff hat
kwef
kyrbasia
la
labarikada
labong
lad
Lady Diana hat
laffayef
laffeh
Lamballe bonnet
Langtry bonnet
Langtry hood
lapa
Lapland bonnet
lappenmutze
laseh
láurea
Lavinia hat
le crapaud
lei kolona
lettice bonnet
lettice cap
leung mo
lì
liang mao
libbadeh
lihaf
limào
lìon-cinn
liripium
little hennin
llautu
llawto
lokalio
lunardi
madras turban
maekko moja
mafors
magiostrine
maharmah
mahrameh
malafa

mameluke turban
Mandarin hat
mandel
Mandel
mandil
mandīl
mant
mantellina
màokuir
mappelana
marafiya
marama
marate
Marie Anglais bonnet
Marie Stuart bonnet
Marie Stuart hat
Marlborough hat
marmotte bonnet
marmotte cap
marquis
Mary Queen of Scots cap
Mary Stuart cap
masla
mauli
mauli bandha
Mazarin hood
Mazarine hood
Mecklenburg cap
melone
mendil
mendil hajj
mercury
merry widow hat
mezzaro
mian guan
mighfar
Milan bonnet
millma sumbriru
millma sumbru
mindīl
Minerva bonnet
mirliton
mistake hat
mitra
moab
Moabite turban
mob-cap
moja
Monmouth cap
Montana peak
montera
montero
monteroe
Montespan hat
morikkoji

mortier
mös sa
mountero
mu da
mu mán
mu miên
mubaf
mubarshi bakin fara
mudang morikkoji
muffin hat
mugiwara bō
muibaf
mukla
muktajala
mukut
mukuta
Muller-cut-down
mundash
mundāsi
mundil
mushroom
mushroom hat
mutch
muts
mutsje
mütze
Mütze
mwa non
nabchet
naga-tenuge
nambawi
ñañaca
ñañacas
napkin-cap
nastalik
nati
natiyo
ncok
Neapolitan bonnet
Neapolitan hat
Neapolitan headdress
nebula headdress
necked bonnet
Nehru cap
Nell Gwynne cap
Nelson hat
Nemes headdress
night coif
nightcap
nimbus
nirangi
nithsdale
Nivernois
nón
nón lá

nón lông
nón sat
Normande cap
Normandy bonnet
nukkadar
nuometas
Oatland village hat
obalenka
obi hat
Oldenburgh bonnet
ol-ogarenji
opera hat
orle
ouderwetse vrouwenmuts
oval beaver hat
pāg
pagdī
paghadi
paglietta
pagoda toque
pagote
pāgrā
pagri
painetta
pălărie
paliacate
palisade
palliolum
pamela
Pamela bonnet
pamela hat
Panama hat
pannicelli
p'anta
pantile
pañu sumbriru
pañuelo para el cuello
papaha
papakha
papale
papale ali'i
papale hainika
papale 'ie
papale kahuna
papale kapu
papale la'a
papale mu'ou'ou
papale 'o'oma
papale waiokila
papanaky
paquebot capote
parachute hat
pare
parta
pasa montañas

passamontagna
paysanne bonnet
pecā
penteado
pentlení
perlehatt
Persian cap
Peruvian hat
pet
petaa
petasos
petassos
petasus
petit bord
petroméni
phanatopa
phenta
phentā Mohammadī
pheta
pheto
phrygian bonnet
phrygian cap
phrygium
picaranga pāgadi
picaranga peco
pici
picture hat
pifferaro bonnet
pifferaro hat
pileus
pilgrim's hat
pilleus
pillion
pillu
pilos
pinner
pipkin
pirnie
pirny
pith helmet
piwa haka
Platoff cap
poculica
podkapnik
poffer
poke bonnet
polakem
polmesenic
polos
pomchā
ponit
pootae taua
pork-pie hat
postboy hat
potae taua

Princess Augusta poke
Princess of Wales bonnet
provincial bonnet
pshente
pudding cap
pug hood
pugaree
puggaree
puggerie
puggree
pulou
pulou fa'afao
pulou pepe
Pultney cap
Puritan bonnet
pussy-cat bonnet
qalansuwa
qalasuva
qalush
quadricorn hat
quadrille head
Quaker hat
quartered cap
querpo hood
qulaqça
rabagas bonnet
radielfo
Ranelagh mob
ratnajali
ratnavali
rayonné
razsouchal
reed hat
regency cap
regency hat
relevés à la Marie Stuart
resille
reta
ricinium
rigolette
ritterhute
Robinson hat
rollo
rosario
rosehube
roundel
Rubens bonnet
Rubens hat
rumal
rumala
Russian bonnet
Rutland poke
safa
saffeh
sakkos

salapok
Salvation Army Lassie
    bonnet
samasmiyeh
samo
samurai-ebosi
şapcă
sapka
sarong
sarong billá
sarong kadojo
sarong kaledo
sarong lambing
sarong lombok
saucer brim
sbornik
Scarborough hat
schackelhaube
schappel
Schäppeli
Schirmmütze
Schlapp Hut
schlappe
Schotse baret
Schutzhelm
scone cap
scoop bonnet
scyfel
seerband
seershaud
Sekhemty
sela
sella
semptress bonnet
service cap
sesir
sethi
settee
sgaball
sgrog
sgrogaid
sgrogan
sgulair
shaal
shako
shale
shambar
shamiya
shamla
shapka
sharb
sharbūsh
shatweh
shaving hat
shimla

shinbar
shirastra
shliapa
shukina
shumzil
shunbar
sikhamani
singar patti
sirastrana
siropāu
sirottarapattika
sirshad
sirsobha
sjako
skaut
skrybélé
skull cap
slaapmuts
slat bonnet
sljapa
sljem
smadeh
snod
snood
sombrerera
sombrero
sombrero Cordobès
sombrero de ala ancha
sombrero de caballero
sombrero de copa chistera
sombrero de dos picos
sombrero de paja
sombrero de tela
sombrero flexible
sombreros de lana de
    lado de Ambato
sonkoli cap
soroki
sou'wester
sovanel
sowback
spa bonnet
Spanish hat
sphendome
spitzkappe
splinter hat
splints
splyter-hat
spodic
spoon bonnet
sraja
sringa
statute cap
steeple headdress
stemma

stephane
stephanie
stephanos
stiom
stiomag
stoffelkappe
Stoffhut
stovepipe hat
streimel
Strohhut
stupa
sturraic
sturraicean
sualef
sudar shebetsavaro
suffibulum
sugar-loaf bonnet
suklang
süveg
Swedish hat
Swiss mountain hat
tagelmoust
tagilmus
taj
tāj
takenaga
takke
talapaga
talepā
talepaga
tali bate'
tali katarrung
tali tarrung
taluqdari cap
tanggi
taqiyeh
tarboosh
tarbouch
tarbush istanbuli
tarbush maghribi
tarha
Tarleton helmet
tarpus
tātē ukō
tater
tayyet sunnára
tchapka
tellex
telpek
templers
temples
templettes
tenugui
terai hat
Thérèse

tholia
three-stories-and-a-base-
    ment
thrum cap
thrummed hat
tian ze
tiara
tibiteika
tijajin d'mahduh
Tilbury hat
tirita
toban
toca
toca de camino
tocado
tocco
tock
tocoyales
toer
toering
toilet cap
tok
toocke
topee
topi
toque
toque à la Basile
toque à la Grande Pretesse
toque à la Susanne
toque à l'Iphigénie
toque de fourrure
toquet
toquette
toque-turban
toreador hat
torsade
tot'urak taenggi
touaille

touret
touret de nez
Trafalgar turban
Tremont hat
trencher hat
tresson
tressour
treugolka
tricornio
tricorno
trilby
Trilby hat
trinzale
trolly cap
Tropenhelm
tropenhelm
trotcozy
tru
tsan
tsupári
ttoljam
ttuggong
tubao
tüchli
tuck
tuikkoji
tuithoed
tulband
tupy
tuque
turban
turban bonnet
turban-diademe
turbante
turf hat
Türken-kappen
turkey bonnet
Turkish turban

turmkrone
turnover
turra
turro
tutulus
twitkkoj
Tyrolese hat
tyubeterka
tyubetevka
tzute
tzutes
uçkar
ugly
uma tazina
uma watana
uma-no-tsura
under cap
unnatasikharavestana
ushnisa
ushnisha
usnìsa
Venetian bonnet
veni
vestana
Vevai cap
Victoria bonnet
viereckiger schleier
vigone
vitta
voilette
volet
volupere
wa leng mao
Wallachian cap
wanggwan
Wardle hat
watabōshi
watch cap

Watteau hat
wayeta
wedding ring hat
Weicher Hut
Wellington hat
welon
weret
wide-awake
wimpel
wimple
wincha
Windhaube
witch hat
witch's hat
wraed
wrigels
wu guan
wuqa
wuqayat al-darahem
wuqayeh
xiao yao jin
yagliq
yaluk
yatshmagh
yeoman hat
yumào
zamliyeh
zan
zé
zhutu
zuan
zucchetto
zukin
zurband
Zylinder

JACKETS

acton
aketon
Albert jacket
Albert riding coat
Albert top frock
Alexandra jacket
almain coat
alpine jacket
americana
angia
Angouleme spencer
anorak
áo bành-tô

áo bò
áo da-le
áo đuôi-tôm
áo vét-tông
arqalix
avqueton
badan
badiyān
baishan
baju
balmoral jacket
barouche
base coat

basquine a l'espagnole
batín
Battenburg jacket
battle jacket
bed jacket
beer jacket
bekecs
beshmet
bietle
bigouden
bi-swing
blanchet
blazer

blezer
bolero
bò-lu-dông
brasserole
British warm
Brunswick
buff jerkin
buis
bujka
bum-freezer
bunte Sportjacke
bush jacket
caban

cadet jacket
camara
camargo
cambridge coat
campaign coat
canezou
caprice
casaco esportiva
casaque
casaquin en juste
cased body
cassock
cassock vest
caubagalā
chak'et
chalong phra ong long raja
chaman
chanchanko
chaqué
chaqueta
chaqueta corta de marino
chaqueta corta y gruesa
chaqueta deportiva
chaqueta para casa
cheats
chinese spenser
chogon
chogori
chuppaun
cicuilli
cinduse
ciupag
clawhammer tails
coatee
coatlet
coin de feu
condra
coraco Eugenie
corsage
corse
corsetka
costume au grand Figaro
còta biorach dubh
còta-goirid
coteron
cotla-gearr
coureur
cowbandi
cowes
crispin
cutaway
dalian
damer
dandine
daróc

deacaid
demi-tunique
demob
dinner jacket
divolgatore
dolman
dolmanette
doloman
doublet
dress lounge
duck-hunter
duffer
duffle coat
duibleid
dulumás
dushgreia
dushegreya
'éétsoh 'alts'íígíí
Eisenhower jacket
elek
espécie de jaqueta
Eton jacket
eyelet doublet
fearnothing jacket
félkabát
Figaro jacket
flying Josie
frock coat
gambeson
Garibaldi jacket
giacchetto
gipon
gippon
goon lhiabbee
habit noir
hacketon
haftel
hanten
hauketon
Henrietta jacket
Hibenian vest
hikeshi hanten
hongreline
hoqueton
houri-coat
huang ma qua
hug-me-tight
Hungarian vest
hussar jacket
inar
isticharion
jackanapes
jacket
jacket coat
Jan de Bry coat

japona
jaqueta
jaquette
jaquette coloriée
jaseran
jaserant
Jean de Bry coat
jekkertje
jemmy
jerkin
jerkinet
jhulwa
jiakè
joseph
jupe
jupel
jupon
justcoat
kabaya
kaftany
kalambi
kanjianr
kasacken
kawa
kazaka
kodmen
ködmön
kolder
kort wollen jasje
krauss
kuppasam
kurti
kurtka
kusak
Lancer jacket
leiber
Leicester jacket
leth-bhòt
M. B. waistcoat
ma gua
ma-coual
magoja
maiwai
mandeville
mandilion
mang ao
Mao jacket
Mark of the Beast
marlota
marsina
marynarka
mess jacket
military frock coat
min nap
mintiyan

morning coat
mundir
Mütze
mwa kwa
Nehru jacket
netcha
Newmarket coat
Newmarket jacket
nimtanah
Norfolk jacket
Oxonian jacket
paletó
paltock
patrol jacket
pea jacket
peinadore
peiteag-mhuinicheallach
peleue
pet-en-l'air
Petersham frock coat
pidjak
pierrot
pijjekker
pinch back coat
polca
Polish jacket
pourpoint
poustomániko
powdering dress
powdering gown
powdering jacket
Prince of Wales jacket
Prince Rupert
puffjacke
quezote
reefer
reefer jacket
reitrocke
rennrocklein
riding dress frock coat
rochet
rokk
ropilla
ru
ruiterrock
Russian jacket
saco
safari jacket
saione
sakko
sako
salta
salteh
samare
seircean

seircin
semnar
senorita jacket
seven-eighths coat
shimabaori
shooting coat
shotten-bellied doublet
simtakvaldis
skin-coat
skokie
smoking
smoking jacket
sobrecasaca
Spanish coat

Spanish jacket
spencer
spencerette
sportcolbert
sportjasje
stambouline
sticharion
sua yan
sukmanki
sultane jacket
surjan
tabard
tabbaert
Talma lounge

tanzeb
taqsireh
tea jacket
teakete
three-seamer
tight
tujurka
tundra
tuxedo
tweedside
ujjas
vaga
varens
vastagkabát

vét-tông
volant
waffenrock
wambuis
wammes
wammiss
whole backs
yachting jacket
yellow jacket
yonmibok
zache
zeke
zoeaaf
zouave jacket

JEWELS AND JEWELRY

ac cu gămălie
ačē attāmitō
ačē kéčō
ačē saččō
achates
adaftō
adamas
adjagba beads
agait
agrafes de centure
águamarinha
aigeallan
aigilean
ailbheag
ailbheag cluais
ailbheagan airgid
àilleag
āinne
aision
alankara
alfinete
aliança
allura mai-kai
âmbar
amethyst
amethystus
ametist
ametista
amulet
amuleto
anello
angada
angulia
anguliya
anguliyaka
angūthī
anthrax

ānulus
apavartaka
apo kula
apo lima
apruoce
'aqd anbar
'aqd wazari
ardhaguchchha
ardhamanavaka
argolas
armbaand
armband
Armband
armil
armilla
armillae
Armspange
arracadas
arsi
asawir 'iradh
asimojórdano
asinan
attāmitō
avaghataka
baby pins
bach-ngoc
bague
bahu
baiya
baju
bali
bane
bangle
bangle bracelet
banzhi
bar pin
barjura

basc
baugr
bāzūband
bēag
beah
bedelarmband
beg
beledzík
belette
beryl
beryllus
bezelikia
bezelitsa
bich-ngoc
biezhen
bignere
bijou
bijouterie
bijoutier
bina
bindi
biorān
bitug
bizou
bizuteria
black turquoise
blue john
bortspeld
Bouc
bouchons de carafe
boucle d'oreille
Boug
boukrania
bracaille
braccialetto
bracelete
brachiāle

bractiates
brāislēad
bràist
bràisteachan
braistich
brangenybé
brangus akmuo
bransoletka
braoig
braslet'
brăţara
breichled
brilhante
brinco
broche
brochetta
broszka
brummaggem
bughma
bughmeh
bul
bulla
bzima
cabestrillo
cadenat
caefing
caicmhe
camaieu
camee
candanhār
candongas
carbunculus
carcanet
carkanett
carkanette
carkenet
catula

cebolão
chachal
chai
chaine de forçat
chalchihuitl
chalong phra ong long raja
chao zhu
charanalankara
charm string
chaulari
chipana
chitika
choclos
choggā
choker
chrysolithus
chuỗi hat trai
chuo
chuoi
chupetes
ciondolino
clach-mhara
cluas-sheud
coire
cokar
colar
colar de pérolas
coler
colier
collana
collier
collier de chien
cordoni
coron
coron òir
corona
corona etrusca
corona muralis
corona navalis
corona radiata
coronal
coronet
creoles
cridhachan
crios-muineil
crochag
crotalia
cruinneacan
crùn
crystallus
cùirnean
curi
cyanus
dalc
dali dali

dalk
dārgums
dealg-gualainn
dehri
ðerdan
dhammilia
djore
ðôi bông
ðông-hò ðeo tay
ðông-ho quá quít
dormilonas
dorn-nasq
dragocennost'
dragulj
drahokam
drilbu
dwete 'ka
eha
ekavali
electrum
er
er dang
erdif
erhuán
esawra
esclavage
fail
faileach-an
fāinne
fàinne-pòsaidh
fantasia
fausse montre
feax-preon
fermaglio
fermail
ferroniere
fibula
fifele
figgragulþ
finic
firmale
foil
fraternity pin
friendship bracelet
furtuchsklemmer
gallang
gemma
ghiordan
ghungru
ghwayshat
giardinetti rings
gim
Gimma
gimme
gimstān

gimsteinn
giogan
gioielle
gioiello
girandole
girri
glasag-muineil
Glauvina pin
gleindorch
gólfi
gørsemi
graiveyaka
granaat
gredzens
gualcas
guard ring
gu'ut
gwddfdorch
halsbaand
halsband
Halsband
Halsbouc
Halsboug
halsgjorð
Halsgolt
halsketting
halssnoer
hamarti
hamsakah
handboei
handu djere
hanga-korbo
hāns
hār
hara
harasekhara
haravsti
harayasti
hastávali
hasti
hemasutra
hoa tai
hoakakala
hong-ngoc
horloger
hring
hringr
huáibiao
huttu
igbiri
ilbora
indrachchhanda
iner
ioring
irbora

iuele
iziketsho
jaatl'óól
jaseran
jeanette
jièzhi
jimiki
jiqa
joaillerie
joaillier
joalharia
jonc
jordáni
joshan
juste au cou
juvel
juweel
Juwel
juwelen
kadā
kakla ruota
kaklaryšis
kalasakha
kalathaki
kallača
kamba iri
kambánes
kamea
kanakakamaklaihkarma
kanakakirita
kanakaneyura
kancala
kanchanakundala
kandaure
kangan
kantha
kanthamala
kanthī
kantje
kapaladharina
kara
karakchi
karfitsa
karieliai
karnabharana
karnabhusana
karnapura
karnavalaya
karnika
karnotkilaka
karnphul
kataka
kaula ho'olewa
keččō
keyura

khalkhal
kharaz azraq
khatim
khawatim
khsur
kila
kinkini
kipini
kirdan
Kleinod
kleinood
kleinōt
klejnot
klenot
kniepe
knol
kobe gani
kol'co
kolczyk
komo lima
kostbaarheden
kotuly
krul
krulletje
kugunni
kullu
kundala
kundalas
kunna
kupe'e
kupe'e niho 'ilio
kuru
kwigoi
kyorhon panji
kyorhon yak'on panji
labret
lagidigba
lalatika
lambana
làmh-fhàil
langar
langgu lungping
languette
látsíní
lavaliere
lei hoaka
lei niho 'ilio
lei ole
lei 'opu'u
lei palaoa
lemmetørklœde
leug
lozi
ma'a taua
mabiim

màilleag
mālā
mālāband
malai
malda
malwa
manavaka
mangamelai
mani
mani nupura
manik ata
manik barata
manik bura bura
manik kalaa'
manik sekke'
manik tai anda'
manik tinggi
mani-karnika
manilha
manillas
maninupura
manivalaya
manjira
marfim
margarita
marik
maskotka
matab
mauktika alankara
mauli mani
mdama kofe
meanbh-ghàirdean
me-ðay
mekhala
men
menat
Menni
mentel-preon
menyet
minda
mkufu
modrwy
mokgori
monīle
morse
muddī
mudrika
muince
muintorc
muktavali
muktika-hara
mullu
murkī
nácar
náhrdelnú

naksatramala
náramek
naramiennik
narukvica
nasta
naszyjnik
nath
ndeve
neck-chain
nekhau
nekhaw
neura
ngoc trao
ngoc-bích
ngoc-miên
ngoc-thach
nine-djere
nishka
niska
njiru
nupura
nurki
nur-trang
nut
obraczka slubna
Ohrring
okana
òmar
ombari
onderriem
onechte juwelen
ordnasc
orecchino
ornamento de gioielli
ouch
owa sibi
oyam
oyuan
ozerel'e
ozherelok
pada-bandhati
pag-sanklā
pahuñchi
paidirean
paklari
p'aljji
palmas
pañchaphalaka
parel
parihasta
parure
passium
patrakarnika
pectoral
pedraria

pelele
pendicle
penduricalho
pepa de zapallo
pérola
phalaka
phalaka hara
phalaka valaya
phicchi
pierścień
piñe
pine umauma
platok
plummet
pohoi
poire
poissarde
ponchiyā
poro-toroa
porte-bonheur
pou-fou
pravatra
preen
prēon
prine feilidh
prokandaka
prsten
'pujok
pupu hoaka
putalya
pynn
qiladeh dhahab
qladeh
qladet 'anbar
qladet morjan
qladet qrenfol
quynh
rara
rasana
ratna
ratnangulia
ratnavali
rholwani
rijnsteen
ringetje
rinrin wallka
rivière
rivieres de jais
rjsó
robijn
rosenadel
rubi
ruchika
saffier
safira

sairpaich
sancaq
sankhavalaya
sankla
sarcillus
sardius
sarkan wuya
satasutra
satlara
satlari
savonnette watch
scaraboid
seod
serekh
sēt
sēt argait
seud-ghlasaidh
sha 'iriyya
sha 'riyeh
shabakat al-kharaz
shahasi
shanf
shnat
shoubiao
signet ring
signum
sirsaka
sissin kara
sitara
smàrag
smaragd
smaragdus
sohofa
solje
søljer
sonko

soort bergkristal
sopanaka
sorority pin
sorro
speld
spenel
spennels
spilenn
spillo da petto
spinki
Spitze
spoon ring
srnkhalika
steatitis
stecknõlde
stoic
sua yan
suddha-ekavali
suman
sutra
sutrahara
svechchhitika
swamy jewelry
swar
szpilka
talabo
talhakimt
talhatina
tali
tanggok
tarahara
taralapratibandha
tarangaka
taulima
tauri
tauri koomore

tautaliga
tauvae
tche djenji
tembleques
teybaraten djendji
thanh-lam
tiao tuo
Tierfibeln
tiki
tilari
tlws
tolomi
topas
topazon
tora-tora
torque
torquēs
Trauring
trikarnas
triphalaka
triveni
tro-c'houzoug
trouwring
trrsa
truis-bhràghad
tulakoti
tupu
tupullina pichu jerguita
turquesa
tusbahh
uaki
uati
upasirsaka
usgaraidh
usgar-bhràghad
usgar-mheur

uwaki
uwaki pulima
vaijayantika
valaya
vàng ðo
vành huyên
vezzo
vibushana
vijayantika
vòng huyèn
vòng tai
vyalapanktirmañjari
waki
walka
wallka
wāyāč attāmitō
wedja
white turquoise
xiàngliàn
xiàngquàn
yangzhiyu
yari yankunne
yashmak
yasti
ying luo
yiordani
zarcillos
zaybaqah
zegelring
zgarda
zgardan
zhi huan
zhuó
žiedas
zobe

LACE

à jour
ajour
Alençon lace
Alençon point
aloe lace
antique lace
Antwerp lace
Antwerp pot lace
Argentan lace
Ärmelaufschlag
Armenian lace
Arras lace
Ave Maria lace
baby lace
banat

barleycoms
basane
bâti
Battenburg lace
Bavarian lace
Bedfordshire Maltese lace
Bedfordshire plaited lace
beggar's lace
Belgian lace
Belgium Venise
bibíla
binche lace
black lace
blonda
blonde

blonde lace
blondes de Caen
bobbin lace
Bohemian lace
bonnes grâces
bordado suizo
bourbon lace
bourdon lace
Branscombe point
bretenne lace
Bretonne lace
Bruges lace
Brussels bobbin lace
Brussels edging
Brussels ground

Brussels lace
Brussels needle lace
Brussels net
Brussels point
Brussels wire-ground
Buckingham lace
Buckinghamshire lace
bullet-hole lace
bullion lace
burano lace
buratto lace
buta
buti
campaigne
campane

carrez de gaze
carrickmacross lace
catgut lace
chain lace
champ
chantilly
chemical lace
chenille blonde
chenille lace
cheyne lace
Chinese Venise
chutki
cipka
cipky
cluny lace
creme de cachemire lace
Crete lace
cutwork
cutworks
Damascene lace
ðang-ten
dantelă
dantelez
death lace
dentelle
dentelle Angleterre
dentelle Arabe
dentelle au fuseaux
dentelle aux fuseaux
dentelle cachmire
dentelle d'application
dentelle de Cambrai
dentelle de fil
dentelle de laine
dentelle la vierge
dentelle renaissance
dentelle torchon
Devonshire lace
dhanak
Dieppe ground
Dieppe point lace
dotted Venetian bars
drawn thread work
Dresden point lace
duchesse lace
Dutch lace
encaje
encaje chantilli
encaje de aguja
encaje de àngel
encaje de bolillos
encaje de Lila
encaje de Malinas
encaje de malla cuadrada
encaje de Milano

encaje estrecho de algodón
encaje frivolité
encaje hecho a maquina
encaje suizo
English bars
English edging
entre-deux
ficelle
fil de retour
filet lace
fili tirati
five hole lace
fleco morisco
fond à la marriage
fond clair
fond double
fond simple
frivolité
fuseau
fuselli
galão
galon d'argent
galon d'or
gassed lace
gaze neige
Genoa lace
Genoese lace
gota
grains
Greek lace
Greek Venise
grillé
groppo
gros point
gros point de Venise
ground
gueuse
guipure
guipure arabe
guipure de Bruges
hair-pin crochet
Hamilton lace
hamsa
head-side
hollie point lace
hollow lace
holly point
holy point
Honiton lace
Honiton point
Huguenot lace
Hungerland lace
insertion
Irish crochet
Irish lace

ivory stitch
kant
karbatkos
kasida
Katherine of Aragon lace
kināri
klosant
knipling
kniplinger
krajky
kruzeno
kruzhevo
lāsa
lasdadh
leadworks
leaves
lierre lace
Lille à fond clair
Lille lace
Limerick lace
Lisle lace
little Venetian edging
livery lace
madagascar lace
mailles carées
Maltese lace
mantle lace
Margot lace
maskel lace
matt stitch
mazzette
Mechlin lace
Medici lace
mennuet
merletto
merletto-trina chiaacchi-
    erino
metal lace
mezza mandolina
mezzo punto
mignonette
mignonette lace
Milan lace
Milanese lace
Minuit
modano
Moorish lace
Moravian work
mukhta
Naples lace
needlepoint lace
Northampton lace
Nottingham lace
nun's thread
opus araneum

òr-bhann
oyah
paddles
paimak
Paraguay lace
parchment lace
parnoe
part lace
passemayne lace
passives
patent lace
peak lace
peasant lace
peniche lace
perlin
piryiellya
pizzo
pizzo ad ago a fuselli
pizzo punto in aria
pizzo rinasciemento
plaits
Plauen lace
point à la vierge
point à l'aiguille
point à reseau
point Colbert
point coupé
point d'Alencon
point d'Angleterre lace
point de Bayeux
point de Fée
point de France
point de gaze
point de gaze lace
point de Hongrye
point de neige
point de Paris
point de sedan
point de toile
point de Venise à reseau
point d'espagne
point d'esprit
point lace
point plat
poussin lace
princess lace
punchetto
puntilla de Venecia
punto a feston
punto a maglia quadra
punto a relievi
punto gothica
punto in aria
punto neve
purl

pusher lace
raised work
Raleigh bars
ratine lace
real lace
redes
redicella
rempli
ren
Renaissance lace
rendalo
réseau rosacé
rete
reticella
reticella lace
retículo
Roman lace
Rosaline
rose point lace

ruedas
Saint Gall lace
Saint Martin's lace
salmā-sitārā
Saxony lace
Schiffchenspitze
Schleswig lace
Sedan lace
seeds
sfilatura
shadow lace
Shetland lace
silver lace
skinnsaum
Sorrento edging
Spanish lace
spets
spice
spider work

Spitze
sraing
stsepnoe
Swedish lace
tambour lace
tambour work
tape lace
tatting
tela Tagliata
tela tirata
Tenerife lace
theke
thread lace
toi
tonder lace
torchon lace
trailer thread lace
treille
Tresse

trina
trollekant
trolley lace
trolly lace
Turkish point lace
Valenciennes lace
Venediger Spitze
Venetian bars
Venetian edging
Venetian lace
Waborne lace
wheat ears
Winslow lace
yak lace
youghal
Ypres lace
ysnodan
zarī

LEGGINGS, LOINCLOTHS, AND TROUSERS

abito da pantalone
afrikin
almain hose
American trousers
ankle-breeches
ashigappa
avagraha
bags
balaq
bante
barn-door britches
barrel hose
bas
bas à cotes
bas à jour
bas de laine
bas de soie
bas de soy
bawelna
bearskin pants
bebed
beli potouri
bell bottoms
benevretsi
bermuda shorts
bhagawān
birnetsi
bít-tāt
bloomers
bobo
bogatya
boje

bombachas
boot hose
bordāra pyjamā
boti
boulevart
braccae
braccas
bracco
braecce
bragas
bragon braz
bragou
bragou-braz
braies
brayes
brec
brēc
brec-hraegel
breeches
brīste
briuki-dudochki
brōc
broek
brœkr
broekrok
brogs
brok
Bruch
bruki
Bruoch
bryczesy
bukser

bullion hose
burzighino
buskins
byxor
cabin boy breeches
caeles
caiquan
caksire
calanika
calçáo
calçâo de banho
calçâo de montaria
calças
calças de couro
calce
calcetería
calcetin
calcetines
calza
calzamaglia
calzas conpies
calzas enteras
calzas largas
calzaz de aguja
calzettoni
calzón
calzoncillo
calzoneras
calzoni
canions
capri pants
carapa

čarapa
chakchiri
chalana
chalwar
chambangi
chángkù
chàngtongwà
chaparajos
charahuilla
charicari
chariwari
charoul
chausettes
chausse
chaussembles
chausses
chausses en bourses
chausses larges à l'antique
chausses semellees
chaussette
chaussette montant
chaussures à cric
chaussures à point-levis
chirpa
cholana
churridah
ciorap
cloak-bag breeches
cockers
cocrez
cokers
cool pants

coranā
corano
cossack trousers
cossacks
cross-gartering
cuaran
cūdīdār
cuecas
culok
culot
culote
culotte
culotte courte
dai seong siu kwun
Danish trousers
darpe
dedo
detachi
dhile paenche
dhoti
dimii
dodot
ðôi bit-tāt
don't mentions
dungaree
dunniattham
dvipadi
eelskin trousers
een broek
elbas
esquavar
etam
ezor
falda-pantalón
famalniya
farthingale breeches
feminalia
femoralia
fleshings
French bottoms
French hose
fu ku
full slops
fungomi
gaiter bottoms
galligaskins
gamashes
gaskin
gatě
gatya
gaucho pants
gebreid of geweven on-
  dergoed
geldem

ghaghara
gharara
ghutanna
giosān
gomeda lugadu
gregesque
gregs
gregues
habaki
hakama
Hallingdal breeches
hansworst
harisnya
harlot
haut-de chausses
heerpauke
hetchi pansu
hip huggers
hipsters
hlace
hoi nong hu
hoo
hoo geok kwun
hosa
Hosa
hosan
hose
hosen
Hosen
hot pants
howling bags
'ie-tonga
ineffibles
inexpressibles
izār baftā
Jack Tar trousers
Jamaica shorts
janghia
jarretelle
jhangias
jjalbunyangbokbaji
jodhpurs
kach
kachcha
kadillam
kahan
kalhoty
kalidar pyjama
kaltsá
kamben
kameez
kandal
kaputula bombo
kaputula forpoketa

kaputula ya Kenya
katitra
keilhose
kelinės
kickies
kitamby
klapbroek
knee breeches
kniebroek
Kniehosen
Kniestrümpfe
kojinė
koksya
komānam
konam
korte
kous
krótkie spodnie
ku
kufia
kuitbroek
Kurze hose
kutsani gashti
kyahan
lambahoany
Lange hose
langooty
langoti
lava-lava
lavreg
lederhosen
ledersen
lehnga
leis-bheart
leis-bhrat
leotardo
liànjiaokù
libas
llodrau
loer
loincloth
lóipíní
lole wawae
lole wawae moe po
lole wawae puha'uha'u
lower stocks
lungee
lungi
macchavalaka
mairtíní
malo
malo kai
malo wai
Mantua hose

maolag
martingale breeches
martō
maxtlatl
maxtli
mechnesayim
media
medias y calcetines
meia
meia calça
meias de lã
melon hose
meo
mest
miánkù
miánmáokù
mi'zar
mocota
mogan
mogan briogais
moggan
momohiki
mompe
monpe
moschettos
môt chiec
môt ðôi
moulds
naqsha
nether integuments
nether stocks
niúzaikù
nivasana
nostle
oashyr voynee
oashyr-slobbagh
'ofuvae
'ofuvae pupu'u
ósain
osanachd
overalls
Oxford bags
paarengarenga
p'aench'u
pah-jungobein
painter's pants
paison
paji
palhaço
pampanilla
Panovraki
pansid slops
pantalon
pantalon de travial

pantalone
pantalones
pantalones bermuda
pantalones cerrados por
   debajo de la rodilla
pantalones cortos
pantalones de baño
pantalones de equitación
pantalones de gimnasia
pantalones de golf
pantalones largos hasta
   media pantorrillas
pantalones rajados
pantalones sueltos
pantalones tejanos
pantalones vaqueros
pantaloni
pantaloni all zuava
pantaloni corti
pantalons à pont
pantaloon trousers
pantaloons
panung
panungh
papari
parengarenga
paridhana
pateshehon
patzeb
pedal pushers
pedule
peg-top trousers
perizoma
perna da claça
Petersham cossacks
petticoat breeches
pio borong
pluderhose
podkolanówki
pofbroek
poignée
polaina
portki
potur
poturi
poutouri
priccses nadrág
Pumphose
puttee
quan
quan cao-boi
quan cháo lòng
quan coc
quân ðùi
quan soóc

quan ta
quat quì
railroad trousers
rajstopy
rān
ranch pants
rank
rationals
rhinegraves
rollers
rolling stockings
roll-up breeches
roll-up stockings
rollups
róngkù
sabot pantaloons
salaka
salvar
salwar
sambu' bongi
sampot
šanāfilō
sanghati
sans-culottes
sarawil
satavalika
scalings
schalavery
schenti
scogger
sekernil
serouel
seroval
serul
shaksheer
shalwar
sharovary
shenti
sherry-vallies
shintiyan
short shorts
shortcuts
shorts
shtany
sialoa
sikma
sirwaal
sirwal
sirwall
skarpetka
skilts
skúña
slim jims
slivers
slops

slyders
small slops
sobre pantalón
sobrepantalón rajado
socas
socc
socka
socke
sok
sokkr
sokoto
sokoto kafo
sokoto kembe
soled hose
soort rijbroek
sowlar
Spanish breeches
Spanish hose
Spanish kettledrums
Spanish slops
spatter dashes
spodky
spodnie
sportpantalon
stany
stirrup hose
stirrup stockings
stoca
stocainn
stocainnis
stock-drawers
straight trousers
strapped pantaloons
strapul
strapula
strømpe
strumpa
Strumpf
Strumpfhosen
styfill
sublagaculum
subligaculum
sulraeksu
sulu
suruwali ya Kolombo
suruwali ya uchinjo
survāla
svasthana
szük gatya
tabi
tachi-kake
tagikeri
tagora
tail clout
talavantika

tanga
tangalia
taparrabos
tapih
tasile
tattsuke
tibilaes
tights
tight-slacks
tokeine
tom-bons
tongs
toreador pants
traheen
trews
triubhas
triubhsair
trius
troighthíní
trouse
trousers
trouses
trowses
trowsus
trunk hose
trusses
trykotaze
trykoty
tsala
tsurápe
tumatukuru
tuumatakuru
udones
umutsha
underwraedel
unmentionables
unwhisperables
upasamvyana
upper stocks
vampay
varsikasatika
vastragrantha
venetians
ventilated pants
vraka
wà
wano
wara
wàtào
waz
wàzi
welniane skarpetki
werkbroek of overall van
   stevig katoen
werkpak

wijde kniebroek   xiu shang   yar pariahan   zōri
wining   yama-bakama   yunatárja   zsáknadrág
winingas   yangbok paji   zaragüelles
xà-cap   yangmal   zivka

LITURGICAL DRESS

alb   felon   mozzetta   sotaina
albe   Geneva gown   omophorion   soutane
amice   gremial   orarion   sticharion
analabos   humeral   paramentos sacerdotais   stikhar
batina   koorhemd   phrygium   stole
casul   léine-aifrionn   pianeta di prete   superplie
casulo   mandyas   pillion   surcingle
chimere   maniple   pluvial   surplice
Chorhemd   mantle and ring   rational   surplis
chorrock   Messgewand   rhason   toog
colletin   Messrock   riza   tunicle
cope   miter   scapulari   zucchetto
cotta d'ecclesiastico   monial   simarre
crùn-easbuig   mozetta   sobrepeliz

NECKLINES

à la chale   bote cuello   escote   murabba
à la Raphael   camisole neckline   escote en U   sabaa
'ahuua   crew neckline   Florentine neckline   sabrina
'a'i   décolletage   gorge à la Gabrielle   scollatura
bateau neckline   en coeur   d'Estrees   tou jim
beffschen   en Marquise   halslijn

NIGHTWEAR

baby doll pajama   lole moe po   negulrije   slaapmuts
bigotera   lole wawae moe po   padiniansanam   suravalā
camisola   long-drawers   pajama   suravarā
chamot   mogul breeches   pi-gia-ma   toreadoll pajamas
coramo   mu'umu'u moe po   pijama   tumana
dunne ochtendjas   nachtjapon   pyjama
ijara   nachttabbaert   pyjamā
Indian nightgown   negligee   silanebok

ORNAMENTAL TRIM (OTHER THAN LACE)

à la vielle   aiguillette   amanqonqo   Arabian embroidery
abla   akertjes   angleterre   araneous
acanthus   alas   Anglo-Saxon embroidery   arápis
acollé   álises   ankh   arokah
adai   aljófar   anuenue   Arrasene embroidery
adzalotí   almenadas   apparel   arricciatura
afshan   Alsatian bow   Appenzell embroidery   arrowhead
agrements   altita   applique   asanoha

ashasana
ásimozúnaro
asprocéndi
assisi embroidery
ata
atrocelado
aubusson stitch
Austrian knot
awakipa
Ayreshire
Ayrshire work
babag
babhaid
Babylonian work
bādlā
baende
baize
balza
balzana
band
banda arricciata
ba'o barit
ba'o bata'
ba'o burur
ba'o rawir
barbui
barros miudas
bâti
bavolet
bead lace
beading stitch
beauvais embroidery
bellotas
benerica
Berlin work
bersáña
bertita
beten
billiment
bishop's knot
blackerybond
blackwork
blistering
bluff edge
Blumenkränzchen
bonnaz
bordado
bordado a mano
bordado con caladaos
bordado con perlas
bordado cortado
bordado en blanco
bordado plano
bordado suizo
borduurwol

borla
borrillonnées
Borte
bottoni
botwm
bouffette
bouillion
bouillioné
boutis
bouton
boutons d'oreille
bozal
bragoenen
brahón
brandenbourgs
Brandenburg fringe
breast knot
bretelle
Brittany work
broderie
broderie anglaise
broderie en blanc
borderie en jais
broderie perse
bubúces
búles
Bulgarian embroidery
bullion embroidery
butti
button
buzáña
byzantine embroidery
cabachon
cable cord
cabos
cadena
cadeneta
cadenilla
cairel
Californian embroidery
campanoni d'ori
Canadian embroidery
candramā
cannelé
cannetille
cañutillos
capitonné embroidery
cardows
cartisane
cermuk
chain stitch
ch'aska
chasu
cherusque
cherusse

cheval de frise
chevaux de frise
chevron
chicken
chikan
chimpato
chite
chitterlings
chou
chugata
cicisbeo
clavi
clavos
clock
cloissoné
cnaipe
cnap
cnapan-trusgaidh
cneap
cneap-tholl
cocar
cocarde
cockade
codini
comh-dhualadh
contado
coque
coquillage
coquille
coral currant button
corchete
cordon
cordoncillo con alma
cordonnet
couronne
crepine
crewel work
crochê
culgah
culgee
cuprius
cushion work
cut linen work
czechoslovakian embroi-
   dery
Danish embroidery
danshichi-goshi
darázsolás
dasa
de lazo
de todo lazo
death's head button
Delhi work
dentalium
dentes de loup

deshilado
device
dhardi
diseño
diseño a cuadro
diseño a cuadros escocés
diseño a rayas
diseño con lunares
diseño raya de alfiler
diseño tradicional de pi-
   ñones
dival
dival isi
djéli
Dorset thread button
dou niu
drawn work
druin
dualadh
dubbahah
duchess
dugme
dZi bead
ecaille work
echelle
echelon
embozalada
en coulisse
en echelle de Jacob
en platitude
enbraude
English rosette
English work
espèce d'ouvrage à jour
estofado
estofée
fa'amau
facings
faja rizada
falbala
Falbel
falpalà
fancies
fandaráca
favors
featherstitch
fei yu
fers
festoons
fichu-robings
fijne punt
fil tiré
filete
fiocco
fitelho

flame embroidery
fleco
fleco bullion
fleur de lis
fleur de lys
fleur volant
fleuron
Flitter
flitter braid
floconné
flóra
Florentine embroidery
flossing
flots
flounce
flounce à disposition
flourish
flow-flow
fly-fringe
franja
franjas
French jet
French work
frilal
frill
frilling
frisure d'or
frog
froncés
frounce
frúta
fterotó
fúndes
fundítses
furbelow
fustan
gacchakā-kī-tūrrī
gadroon
galants
gallants
gallone
galloon
galon
gammadion
gaufrure
gauging
gedilim
Geneva bands
Geneva embroidery
Genoese embroidery
ghirlanda
gimp
glove string
glove-band
goat's hair fringe

gobanji
grand broché
grass embroidery
Greek embroidery
gréis
gréiseadaireachd
gréiseadh
gréis-obair
grelot
grunong
guards
guazzerone
guilloche
guirlande
guirnalda
güldenstick
guosaga
haakwerk
habkeh
haku-e
hamsa
hamsa mithuna
hardanger embroidery
hasp
havanese embroidry
hedbo embroidery
hembras
Hercules braid
herrete
hevilla
Hibernian embroidery
hip buttons
holán
holbi
horrō
houppe
huckaback embroidery
humu kaulahao
humu puka pihi
humuka
humulau
humupa'a
humuwili
Hungarian cord
Hungarian embroidery
iall
igne oyasi
incroyable bows
Indian embroidery
intarsia
Irish work
išānō
Italian ferret
Jacobean embroidery
Japanese embroidery

jari
jet buttons
jhalar
jigger button
jin be wun
jirones
Josephine knot
Jugoslavian embroidery
káçes
kalabattun
kalghi
kāmdānī
kara-nui
karfitsa
kasináci
kasuti
katab
kathipa
katikinari
kesdi
keshinui
khatwa
kināri
k'inkus
kirin
kiri-osa
kiski
klídja
klimatáca
klonári
knap
knapp
knee-fringe
knop
kogin
komon
Komparu
kopseró
kornish
kosárky
koshi
kosírek
kraspeda
Kräuseln
krósça
kselitsi
kuka weke
kulgie
kutchi bharat
labrada
lacet
lacis
laka
lampasi
langkit

languette
larga
laticlaves
lazouri
lazúrja
le Savage
Leek button
leki
lelingkok
lentejuela
let
liagh-dhealg
lilit
lint
lipine
lipine silika
listónes
Litze
llambu
llano
long
loraypu
lovertje
lustrini
madeira embroidery
magatama
maljor
malong andon
Maltese embroidery
mang
margarite
margaritte
Marseilles embroidery
mascaipacha
maspilli
Mathilde
matsu-nori
megamendung
mériza
middy braid
mlawlaw
moisson
morisco work
moti
mua
mullutuma
náplitsi
nasture
neck button
needle painting
noeuds d'amour
none-so-pretty
nuamhanair
nudo
nuikiri

núm
nun's work
obair-ghréis
obair-gréise
obair-shnàthaid
ogami
oir-ghreus
ojales
olive button
olivet
olivette
opus anglicanum
opus consutum
opus filatorium
opus pectineum
opus phrygium
opus plumarium
opus pulvinarium
or nué
ordinaria
oro de orilla
oro hilado
orphreys
orrice
orris
ourle
ouvrage à l'aiguille
'owaynet al-sus
oya
oya isi
ozura
páfti
paillette
pale
pallav
paragaudion
parament
passe
passementerie
passements
patagium
paternostri
patti jets
pattika
pavo real
peinture à l'aiguille
pencilled
pendants d'oreille
pepeiao
pespuntado
petals Marguerite
Petersham ribbon
petershams
petits bonhommes
phulkari

picado
piccadil
picot
picoté
pihapiha-'o-kohola
pihi
pihi pulima
pinchbeck button
pinking
piquets
pístres
plateado
plumage
po
podvika
point de chainette
point de cordonnet
point de croix
point de festoon
point de Hongroie
point de raccroc
point de rose
point de sedan
point de toile
point d'espagne
point d'Espagne
point nuré
point passé
point Turc
pomme de pin
pompon
ponto de cruz
porcelain button
praghata
pretintailles
pu fa'amau
pu zi
puava
puce
puertas
puka pihi
pullings out
pun alai
puntada limeña
puntilla
punto de almorafán
punto de España
punto de oro llano
punto llano
punto real
punto tagliato
punto tirato
purfle
püsküllü
putan

pyramid style
pyramids
qilim
qutbah fallahi
rabat
rafugari
randa
randas
raquettes
realce
rendalo
rendilhado
resi
reticello
revers en pelerine
ribean
ribete
ribine
ribon
ricamo
ricamo in bianco
rick-rack
robin
robings
roghan
rondz
rosette
rouleaux
ruban
ruban d'amour
ruché
ruche contraire
rupehri
Rüschen
ryssewerk
sabaleh
sacha pullki
saga
sarpech
saru
saula
saz
sceanc-gegirla
Schleife
segmentae
serpeych
shakkeh
shao
sharbush
sha-sha
shisha
shohakuzan
shoulder knots
shughl bet lahm
shughl talhami

sic
sirpeach
skofium
slips
smezzati moro
snail button
söllstötter
somoyo
sonehri
sorti
sortie
soutache
spangles
Spanish embroidery
Spanish needlepoint
spiders
split stitch
stalk button
stickerei
stringhe
strips
sul
surihaku
surpaish
swire
tablion
tacley
taenggi
taihakuzan
taist
tambouring
tanch'u
tanch'u kumong
taniko
tapisserie
targe
tavlin
tdinjok
tekat menekat
three-fold linen button
tifsireh
tiin
tiin sin
t'ikita
tinbiteh
tinsel printing
tira
tiraz band
tocapu
toll-cnaip
tombodama
top button
torsade
torzal
tourie

trancinha
trapunto
tremolanti
trepats
Tresse
trimming à la greque
tsavága
tsepen
tsithsith
tti
tuft
tumpal
turrā-i-mārwadī

twist button
ubuhlalu
ukrasavanje
ulub
ungkoi
utskurdsøm
vandyke
varedira
varti
vashti
vegetable ivory buttons
venera
vermicelli

vez
vhulungu ha madi
vidrilho
vivos
volante
Vulcanite buttons
vuoddaga
wadasan
wasserfall
watashinui
Weissstickerei
wheel trimming
whitework

wings
worms
worsted work
xian
xie zhai
ysnoden
yutu
zardozī
zarī
zogan

OUTERWEAR

abaaya
abayah
abbé cape
Abocchnai
abolla
abrigo
abrigo cruzado
abrigo en forma de capa
abrigo polo
abrigo raglan
abrigo trinchera
achchhadanaka
achkan
ackhan
Adèle
adhivasa
agbada
ahuayo
'ahuna
'ahu'ula
ajrak
alberoce
Albert cape
Albert driving-cape
Albert overcoat
Alboni
albornoz
Albuera
Alcamina
Alexandrine
Alice Maud
alicula
alkhalak
alkhaliq
Alma
Alma Escharpe
Almain coat
almerian
Alsatian

amautik
amictorium
amictus
amusse
anbijāniyya
Andaluse cape
Andalusia
Andalusian
andrienne
Aneline shawl
Angouleme spencer
Angouleme tippet
anterí
Antoinette
ao
áo baðò-suy
áo bành-tô
áo bò
áo choàng
áo ðan
áo ði mura
áo lanh lót vāi bông
áo lông
áo muta
áo toi
appilion
aprapadina
apsiustas
Aramis mantelet
Arctic
argūbō
arisard
arkhalukh
Armenian cloak
Armenian mantle
armilausa
aronui
Arragon
artois

Asturian
atigi
atka
autui
avondcape
awarua
awayu
azr
azur
bachelik
bachlik
backlik
bagalbandi
bagh
bagnolette
baju
bakku
balagnie cloak
Balaklava
balandrana
balmacaan
balmoral cloak
balmoral mantle
bandera
band-gale-kā-coat
bandi
bāndiā angarkhā
bandvai gujarati
bành-tô
bann-bhràighe
barani
Barbour jacket
Barcelona
bard
barracan
basing
bautta
bayeta de lishtas
Belle

Belvidera
Bernhardt mantle
bernia
Bijou
birda
birrus
Biscayan
bisht
bitusca
bivouac mantle
blusão
boemio
bohemio
boisson
boliviano
boorka
boubou
bournouse
Braganza
Brandenburg
brat
bratt
broché shawl
bubou
bucksain
bui-bui
bunda
burka
burnous
burnouse
buros
burqah
byrrus
çabut
caddow
cadows
caeppe
cagoule
calcheña llijlla

camail
cambolim
cambridge paletot
Camilla mantelet
Campan
campera
candakanta
canezou
capa
capa corta
capa larga
capa magna
capa morisca
cape à l'espanole
capellar
capixaij
capixay
capote
cappa clausa
cappa magna
cappa nigra
capuchin
caputrock
caradori
cardinal
careless
Cariola
carmeillette
caroline spencer
carrick
çarsof
casaca
casaco
casaco de peles
casaco para uso caseiro
casag
casag-mharcachd
casaque
casaweck
cashmere shawl
casōg
cassock mantle
Castiglione
Castilian
casul
chaddar
chadri
chakva chir
chal
chale
châle de brodie
chalet
chalina
challapata
chamarre

chambard mantle
chamford mantle
chamma
chammer
chang
chang-ot
ch'ao fu
chapan
chape
chape à aige
charwa
chasuble
cheo
cherkeska
Chesterfield overcoat
chi fu
chinacholaka
chlaine
chlamus
chlamydon
chlamys
chloene
choga
chonbok
chope
chuddah
chuddar
chugha
chulla cara
chunadi
chupa
chupkun
chymer
chyrpy
cifatten
cifraszür
cinnteagan
cioppa
cira
circular
cleòc
cleòca Gaidhealach
cleòcan
cloca
clog
cloke
coamery
cochall
cochl
codrington
čoha
Colleen Bawn cloak
collet
Columbine
copricappa

Cora mantle
Coraline
Cordovan
corso
cosar
cot
còta biorach dubh
còta de chadadh nam ball
còta-cathdath
còta-craicinn
còta-fada
còta-gearr
còta-glas
còta-uisge
cote
cote à armer
còt-iochdair
cottage cloak
còt'-uachdair
courtepy
courtepye
Crimea
crispin
crispin cloche
cubhrag
cuculla
curricle cloak
curricle coat
curricle pelisse
cyclas
czarina
dáábalii
dachang
dadhikali
daimon
damesmantel
dangdong
Darro
date-gera
dauphiness
dekmantel
del
demi-converti
demi-surtout
dengue
Desdemona
dimayeh
diphtera
diplax
Directoire coat
djebba
djellaba
dobuku
dochu-gi
dofuku

dogi
dolaktanka
dolama
domino
donariere
Doncaster riding coat
dorina
d'Orsay coat
doschella
doshala
doshāllā
dou bo
douillette
douillette à la Russienne
doupeng
drapi
duandàyi
Duchess
Duchesse
duffle coat
dukulottariya
dupattā
dura'ah
dusa
dushegreya
duster
Dutch cloak
eddimō
eglantine
elbow cloak
Emily
Empress
Empress pardessus
English wrap
epanechka
epitoga
Escurial
Esmerelda
Estramadura
étole
Eureka
fachalina
fachallina
faldetta
Faliero
fallaing
falluing
falnis
faraguja
fargal
fargī
farwah
feldr
Felix
ferace

feridge'
ferka
ferraiuolo
ferreruelo
fichu Ristori
fieltro
Flora
Florentine
for-bhrat
Fornarina
fota
frac
frakke
French cloak
frileuse
fūan
fugi
fugitive coat
gabán
gabano
gabardine
gabbano
gadar
gambeto
gansey
gansy
garannō
garbh-chulaidh
garde-corps
gardecors
garrick greatcoat
gestaltrock
ghava-ye zananeh
ghost coat
giacca
giboun
gig coat
giná
gipsy cloak
Gitana
giubea
giumedanii
gla Halstuch
Gladstone overcoat
glinne
glocken
glouhché
godweb-cynn
gole
govillam
gramalla
grand domino
grande pelisse d'hiver
grande redingote à
   l'allemande

grego
Grisi
guba
gueules
guleron
gun fu
gunia
gunoberonicia
guõc
hacele
Hachul
haik
haik royal
hainǎ
hakuls
halena
haleny
halstuch
hana
haori
harzkappe
hendira
henke
henri deux cape
Hermione
herreruelo
heuke
hidim
hidim al-khal
hi-goza
himation
hinggi
hiranyan atkan
Hispania
hitoe
hiyyak
hong-bào
hop-pada
Hortense mantle
housse
houtje-touwtje-jas
hrycg-hraedel
huallas
huik
huke
Hungarian wrap
huque
huru kurii
hwitel
ichella
ihupuni
Imogen
Imperial
inar
Incroyable

Inverness
ionar
isallo
iscayo
isigula
Isir
istela
Italian cloak
itstela
izar
jabul
jāmāh
jamawar
jas
jelab
jellab
jellaba
jellabia
jellib
jellick
Jenny Bell
Jenny Lind sortie de bal
jibbeh
jillayeh
jimbaori
jirga poncho
Jocelyn mantle
Josephine
jubba
jubbah
jube
jupen
júrda
justaucorps
kaabe
kaap
kabanica
kabát
kachabia
kadroun
kaftan
kahu huruhuru
kahu kaakaapoo
kahu kekeno
kahu kiwi
kahu kura
kahu kuri
kahu toi
kahu waero
kaidori
kain kudu
kain lemar
kaiser-rock
kaitaka
kalambi

kalambiara
kalasiris
kalavadi
kalmus
kambal
kambalaghana
kamzar
kanchuka
kandys
kapa
kapishay
kaplamás
kapoto
kappa
kappe
kaput
kaross
kashabia
katra
kaupapa
kaváði
kepa
kera-mino
kerry cloak
kesa
khalat
khalaty
khan tua
khirka
khirkah
khirqa
kho
kiber
kidara
ki-gomo
kihei
kihei 'a'ahu no'eno'e
kirk
kisaly
klashnik
kodot
koloka
kontush
kooletah
koreddō
korowai
koti oversaizi
kountouch
koyava
kozhoushé
kozhukh
kozsók
k'sa
kudtā
kuka

kuka'aila
kunka unku
kurochō
kurpasaka
kurteh
kurti
kutapa
kutusoff mantle
la Bretelle
la comptesse Walewski
la Esmeralda
la Grange
la Hermione
la Manuela
la Marguerite
la Ophelia
la Puritana
la Stella
lacerna
lamba
le Caprice
le Gitana
le printemps mantilla
lefhah
lembe
lenn
Leonese
letnik
Lexington cloak
liburnica
lijnne
Lily Benjamin
linaga
Lindbergh jacket
listao ponch
litewka
llacota
llakolla
lliclla
lliglla
llijlla
lliklla
loden
London Fog
Lou Lura cloak
Louisa mantilla
Louise mantelet
Lucie
lùireach
lukka
lulu ali'i
lumman
lung p'ao
lusekufte
luto poncho

macaña
Macfarlane
mackinaw
mackintosh
Madrid
mai
Maintenon cloak
malabary
mameluck
mameluke
manaeka
Mandel
manga
mangaeka
mangt'o
mang-tô
manta
mantal
Mantal
manteau
manteau à la cavaliere
manteau à l'italienne
manteau de cocher
mantee
manteel
mantel
mantelet
mantelet à la grand mere
mantelet au lever de
   l'aurore
mantelette
manteline
mantell
mantello
mantilla
mantita
mantle
manto
manto de oraciones
manton de mantilla
mantones de Manila
mantua marguerite
Marian
Marie Antonette fichu
Marion
marlota
marlotte
Marquise
marquise mantle
Mary Stuart
masher dust wrap
Mathilde mantilla
matinée
matschigote'
mattal

Maud
Medina
mekkō
melaya liff
melote
mentel
mentik
mentlíky
messaria
mētelis
miktorin
milakatra
mino
mintean
Mirandella
mirjāi
mishlah
mi'zar
Modena
Moldavian mantle
mong pao
Montana
Montebello
montenegrin
Montpensier mantle
monty-coat
Moresco
Morresca
Moscow wrapper
Mother Hubbard cloak
mousquetaire
mousquetaire mantle
mptull
mui dat
mulabbada
musa
Muscovite
mushal
Navailles
navershnik
Newmarket overcoat
Newmarket top frock
ngore
ngore paheke
nicola
nicula
night rail
Nightingale
nine-tenths coat
nisara
nishra
Novado
nurse's cape
oet'u
ofer-braedels

oferlaeg
oferlagu
ofer-slop
ofer-slype
oggaegori
okhaben
olicula
olojémiti
Omer mantle
opera cloak
Ophelia
opperkleed
out-coat
over-all
paakee
paakee nui
paakee tikumu
pabagu
pacotilla
pād
paddock coat
pa-ðo-suv
paenula
paepaeroa
paida
paisley shawl
pa'iua
palestine
paletó
paletot
paletot-cloak
paletot-mantle
paletot-redingote
paletot-sac
pall
palla
pallatine
pallium
Palmerston wrapper
palto
paludamentum
pandjesjas
pañolones
pañuelo
panutzutzu ukufachallina
parakiri
parawai
pardessus
pardessus redingote
parmnaram
parrock
partlet
pāsābandhi kediyū
pasabandi kediyoo
patatúka

Patrician	policeman's cape	rachdan	salampy
patte	Polish greatcoat	Rachel cloak	salim shahi
pauku	Polish mantle	Raglan	salmah
pealltag	polka	raglan cape	salteh
peasant fichu	Polka	raglan covert coat	sālū
pebasa	polonaise pardessus	raglan overcoat	samaksika
pekerere	polonese	rampoor-chuddar	samghati
pekin Aneline	polrock	rankavapata	Saragossa
pekin bournous	polushubka	rasi	sarbal
pelerine	polverino	ratnakambala	sarbalehon
peleryna	pompadour pardessus	rebozo	sarong pakolong
pelise	ponchito	recal	saut-en-basque
pelisse	poncho	redingote a l'amazone	saya
pelisse-mantle	poncho amarrado	redingote du matin	saye
pelisson	poncho boliviano	redingote en Backmann	Scarborough ulster
pellanda	poncho cuadrada	regency mantle	scarf volant
pellicea	poncho jijún	regency wrapper	schauslooper
pellicia	poncho rosado	regenjas	schoudermantel
Pembrocke paletot	poncho tiñiska	Regina	sciccels
peplum dolman	poncho tintoridao	reink'ot'u	sciccing
peplum rotonde	pora	reister cloak	sclaveyn
perraje	postin	rheno	sclavine
perramus	posztólájbi	ridā	sclavyn
perreje o tapado	pot	riga	Scotia
Persian vest	pracchadapata	Rigoletto mantle	sea coat
peshwas	prachchhada	Rimini	sea-gown
peski	princess paletot	rio verde	sealskin coat
Petersham greatcoat	Princess Royal	Rio Verde	sealskin sacque
phaa biang	Princess Wagram	Ristori shawl	seïméniko
phaa chet	Priora	Roc	señora llijlla
phaa khaaw maa	prosaponcho	rocc	serape
phaa pat chieng	prudent	rock	setre
phainoles	pu fu	Rock	seuchd
pharos	puahi	rodillera	Sevastopol
phatoi	puamoamoa	rokkr	Sevillian
phatui	pug	ropa	shadow
pheran	pukaha	roquelaure	shah ajidah
phullu	pukupuku	Rosaline	shahajidah
pi'ao	p'ullu	Rosamond	shal
pidzak	pureke	rotonde	shaleh
pierrot cape	Puritan	rotonelle	shamew
pijian	pustin	ruana	shash
pilch	puuahi	Russian	shawl Josephine
pilche	Pyramid talma	sabai	sherwani
pilos	qabā	sac overcoat	shinel
pink	qadar	sadlo	shuba
pitambara cadara	qaziyeh	safsarī	shugga
plasc	q'epirina	sagos	shuka
plást	qirmizi don	sagum	siapo
płaszcz	qiú	saider	sideless surcoat
ploščius	qubā	saie	sifsari
podvika	quechquemitl	sajás	sigúni
pœll	qumbaz	şal kuşak	siki
pokeka	qungo	Salamanca	sikinchina
Poland mantle	raccoon coat	salampe	simarra

simarre
simlah
sindon
siphonia
sjaal
skandakarani
skarabigion
skilkja
slavin
slicker
sling-duster
Snowdrop
sobrecapa
sobrecasaca
sobretudo
sobretudo sôlto
soccus
solo
soprabito
sorket
sortie
sortie de bal
soyacal
Spanish cloak
Spanish coat
Spanish mantle
spenser cloak
Stella
su kom
sua hii
sua saband thaut
suba
suburban coat
Sultana
Sultana opera cloak
sumane
supertotus
surdut
surtout
surtoutà la Sultane
surtuk
suyacal
švarkas
svārki
svyta
syool
szal

szür
taapahu
taatara
taawakawaka
taglioni
Taglioni frock coat
tailored coat
takaschiya
takauchiyah
talar
tallien redingote
tallith
Talma cloak
Talma maltese
Talma mantle
Talma overcoat
talma Zuleika
tamein
taonga
tapa
tara
taratara
tatua
tcherkeska
tebenna
terrier overcoat
three-decker
tikamist kore
tilmatli
timu
tippet
tiputa
tjeld
tobe
toboggan
toga
toga candida
toga contabulatum
toga gabiana
toga palmata
toga picta
toga praetexta
toga pulla
toga pura
toga sordida
toga trabea
toga umbo

toga virilis
toghe
toopuni
top frock
topper
topuni
tribon
Trolldals-trøya
trutag
tshapan
tshoga
tuapora
tudor cape
tulup
tumbe
turamaggie
turumagi
tweedside overcoat
twine
Tyrolese cloak
ubrus
uchikake
ulster
umavadi
umbrella robe
Undine
uttariya
vagho
Valencia
Valencian
Valentia
varabana
varasi
Varna
varvana
Venetian cloak
Venice
Victoria
Victoria mantle
Victoria pardessus
Victoria pelisse-mantle
victorine
Violet
viramo
visité
Vittoria
waefels

wahi
wàitào
wàiyi
wàizhao
wallkarina
wappenrock
wasa
washa fachalina
washajatana
wasti
waterproof cloak
Wellesley wrapper
Wellington coat
whakatipu
whanake
whittle
wickler
witchoura
witschoura
wœfels
wrap-rascal
xale
yacolla
yana poncho
yapanji
γoûva
yura poncho
yuyi
zaboon
zamora
zane
Zanfretti mantle
zeghe
zephyr cloak
zephyr shawl
zhàoshán
zhaoyi
zhe ji
zimarra
zlalzil
zouave paletot
Zuleka
Zulima
zuyacal

PERFUME

aegyptium
boltrachan

frangipani perfume
hyangsu

lukini
panghyang

PLEATS

accordion pleats
bulgare pleat
chikara-age
duchesse pleat
fluting

gadroon
godet pleat
kick pleat
knife pleats
Montespan pleats

plisado
plisado en abanico
plisado en acordeón
plisado en sierra
plisado encontrado

plooi
purl
Watteau pleat

PURSES

'a'a moni
abgar
alforja
Algerian purse
almoner
alner
amonieres sarrasinoises
aulmoniere
aumoniere
balantine
ballantine
barrel purse
beurs
bolso
borsa
bourse
bourserie en lisse

bursa
butung
buzunar
chatelaine bag
chigap
chuspa
ch'uspa
ch'ūspa
Coralie
dasko
escarelle
Eugenie purse
Eulalie
gibeciere
gipciere
gipser
gypciere

hakoseko
handubaek
indispensible
long Melford
mala
Milanie
miser's purse
morrales
musette bag
paiki pa'alima
pautener
pishka
pochette
poke
portemonnaie
pouch
puke pakeke

punge
reticule
ridicule
ring purse
sabretache
schoudertas
scrip
sepu'
songabang
songkabang
spiochag
sporan
stocking-purse
tasna
ví tay

SHIRTS

aba
akanjo
akanjobe
aloha shirt
anart garbh
aquatic shirt
barong tagalong
bluey
body shirt
boiled shirt
bosom shirt
bredzon
bubu
busserull
caimmse
cămaşă
cambja
camicia
camicia rossa
camisa
camisa chaki picada
camisa de homem
camisa de lā
camisa de la tela amarilla

camisa de rigor
camisa polo
camise
cemes
cheats
chemise d'homme
chènshan
chuga
cilice
coat shirt
comboy
corazza
cotón
crys
culeco
deiji'ée'
deraa
derekas ing
derrara
dish dasha
emperor shirt
etibo
frontje
fugu

Fusex shirt
fustar
Gekko shirt
gesteven overhemb
gimnasterka
guernsey
habit shirt
haihúnshan
hair shirt
half shirt
haluk
ham
hemd
Hemd
Hemde
hemeþe
henley shirt
historical shirt
hringofinn serkr
jumper
jupe
kabaa
kameez
kanzu

kasuri no shatsu
kazachock
kolobium
kosile
kosovorotka shirt
kósula
kosulja
koszula meska
krekls
krez
kudtā
kumya
kurta
labaada
leine
lêine
léineag
léine-chaol
léine-chròich
léine-sheacair
léine-thuilinn
léinteag
lēne
lobogós

maršliniai
messauria
nimā
'ofutino
overhemb
paheran
pairan
pala 'ehu
pansomae syossu
pisany lapti
pleated shirt
podopleka
polera
pteruges

pushk kurta
qamis
qamīs
regatta shirt
riza
ròinn-léine
Rough Rider shirt
rubaca
rubakha
rubakha kosovorotka
rubasca
rubaska
rubina
ruffled shirt

sadarā
sadaraa
saffron shirt
salūkā
scyrte
serc
serkr
sherte
shirt-drawers
skjorta
skjorte
skyrta
smoc
somi

so-mi ca-rô
so-mi-dét
sorō
thob
tikamist
tilbi
tirkô
tiu camisa
tobe
toraco
tunic shirt
waisyooch'u
warmi camisa

SHOES AND SHOE PARTS

a tsi'kin
acrobatic shoe
Adelaide boot
ahaddha
ah'ta qua o weh
al-aqrāq al-zarrariyya
alaska
Albert boots
alcorque
alpargata
aluta luxor
amageta
amanyatelo
antigropolis
apron front
aqraq
aratóbocskor
arc'henad-kambr
arctics
artois buckle
ashida
avampié
babouche
baboutcha
baby doll shoe
baby French heel
baby Louis heel
babysokje
bachelor shoes
back-strap shoe
bagging shoe
bal
balga
balmoral
balt
bandhana-krtsna
bar shoe

basmak
batas
batts
bear's paw
biànxié
bicycle bal
blucher
bocskor
bolzegin
bootikin
borceguí
bota
botas
bote
botez
botforti
botina
botinicos
botte
botte à genouillere
bottekin
bottine
bòtuinn
bow shoes
breaban-deiridh
breaban-toisich
brodekin
brodequin
brōg
brogan tionndaidh
brogans
bròg-bhréid
bròg-chalpach
bròg-fhiodha
brogues
buatais
bucket-top boot

buckskin
bulgha
bulldog toe
buskins
but
çabat
cabbage shoestring
cacci
cack
cactli
caisbheart
caite
calbhthas
calc
calçado
calcarapedes
calceolus
calceus
calceus patricius
caliga
caligula
callaid
calzado
calzatura
caméléon
campagus
canipo
caoxié
carabitina
carpet slippers
carranes
caucho pargate
čebatas
cebot
cepök
chanclas
changhwa

chappals
charan dharan
chāubwalī jootī
chaussure
Chelsea boot
chinela
chopines
chukka boot
cipela
çipsip
cizmă
clabaran
clarence
clog
clot
cockers
colonial pump
comforts
congress gaiter
congress shoe
corked shoes
corned shoe
cothurnes
coturno
crackow shoes
cracow
creedmore
crepida
crinc
Cromwell shoe
croquet boots
csizma
cuaran
Cuban heel
cut-fingered pumps
dameslarrje
dan garagai

Derby shoe
Dom pedro
d'Orsay pump
dress Wellington
duantongxue
duck-billed shoes
eared shoe
elastic-sided boots
eminii
empeines
escaffignons
escarpins
eschapins
esgid
espadrille
esqui
external high shoes
Faust slipper
ferradura
finnesko
flight boot
flokati
fotgewaed
fragrance on the surface
    of the soles
fragrant leaves
French fall
fudag
gábmaga
gaiter
gallicae
galliochios
galloshoes
galocha
galoche
galoscia
galosh
galosses
gambade
gambado
gamoshes
gaogenxié
gau dai hai
geta
gheată
gheta
ghillie
giay ta
giay tây
giay tuyet
gillie
giveh
go-go boot
golosh
gomushin

Grecian sandal
guêtre
gymschoentjes
hakimono
half boot
han'pa
hemming
hessian
heuz
heuze
highlows
hiscu
hock see hai
hoge laars
hoge toneelschoen
hoggers
hok see hai
hoseaux
huarache
hupodema
hussar boots
Hussar buskins
iallachrann
ihu kama'a
'ili pale o kama'a
impilayoth
impilia
încalţa minte
Italian heel
Italian slipper
jack boot
Jackson shoes
jarbā
Jemima
jemmy boots
jiaxié
jiaxue
jika-tabi
jockey boot
jojky
jootī
ju
jue
Juliet
kalíca
kalikia
kaltsi
kaltsouni
kama'a
kama'a hakahaka
kama'a hawele
kama'a 'ie
kama'a ili
kama'a laholio
kama'a la'i

kama'a lo'ihi
kama'a pale wawae
kama'a puki
kamiks
kampskatcha
kampskatcha slipper
kanjiki
kanonenstiefel
karanko geta
ké deigo danineezi
ké'achogii
kee ha hai
keményszárú csizma
khapusa
kheaya el kebira
khuff
kierpce
klompen
komag
komager
komusin
kopa
krepis
krpce
kubi najûn kudo
kubi nop'ûn kudu
kurpė
kwitsa pargates
laars
lacing studs
laggosszárú csizma
landrines
lapot
larrigan
lasting boots
latchet
leperhose
leth-bhòt
li kama'a
llanque
loafer
lotus flowers
lotus seeds
lu
lustriña
ma xue
madas
maolas
méstia
mezz
minalim
mizz
mocassin
moccasin
mock see hai

mojdī
mokasyny
mok'kus sin
Moorish boot
mule
muleus
musha''ara
naaldhak
nagarā
namaksin
Napoleons
ngozi ya kioo
Norwegian slippers
obucá
obuv
obuwie
ocreae rostratae
okers
opanky
opera pump
opera slippers
opinak
opinci
opinki
oubosyuuju
overschoen
Oxford gillies
Oxonian boots
pa'a kama'a
paaraerae
paboudj
pabuç
pada
padigunthima
paduka
pagarakhā
pah-poosh
paiafzar
painntin
pale wawae
panaena
pantaplis
pantofel
pantoffel
Pantoffel
pantofle
pantofola
pantoufle
pantuflas
pantuflo
paoxié
papari
papuc
papuca
papute

pasoúmia
patent leather boots
pattens
patynek
pejar
pērō
phaecassium
pianelle
pigache
piked shoe
pinson
pisany lapti
plantillas
plimsoll
pokkuri
Polish boots
polonia
pompadour heel
pomposa
postola
poulaines
pramana-krtsna
puhaszárú csizma
puki
puncocha
punta roma
puntas
pushk kurta
quail-pipe boot
raglan boot
red rippers
red russels
rifeling
rilling
riveling
Roman sandal
rullion
sabot
sabotine
saddle oxford
saddle shoe
salemshahī
salim shahi
sambatsi
sandaal
sandal
Sandale
sandale
sandália
sandalias

sandalium
sandalo
sandalon
sandals à la greque
sapata
sapato
sapog
sapogi
saru
savate
scarpa
scarpe
schoen
schoenveter
scōh
Scuoh
secque
se'evae
selba
servilla
shenandoah
shin
shoen
shoepack
shukuy
shu'lush
silipa
sko
skōhs
slife-scoh
slipēir
slipe-scoh
šliuré
slobkousen
sniegowce
soccae
soccus
solea
sopagas
soulier
spad-choisbheart
spats
spatter dashes
spectator
spiked shoes
spit-boot
splay-footed shoes
spring boots
staeppe-scoh
startop

startups
stevige schoen
Stiefel
Stiefelette
Stiful
Stival
stivale
stivaletto
stivali
stivali grossi
stövel
støvle
strandschoenen
strevíc
suarrow boots
swiftlere
tackies
takajo-tabi
takelmi
takitaki
talabanr
talaria
talika
tamanco
tanhwa
taoxié
tatamis
tchédik
tenisówski
tennis shoe
terlik
thiet-hài
tittirapattika
toffel
tøffel
toloboni
tongue pump
toorua
top boot
totnamaksin
totsin
trzewik
tsangiá
tsarvouli
tufel'
tuflja
tulapunnika
tupele
tuumatakuru
Twenty Grands

tyelambu
tzanga
Überschuh
udo
ugurulik
ujuta
undonghwa
unhye
upanah
upanat
urbāi
ushuta
'usut'a
usuta
valenki
van-hài
varna-krtsna
vaturinapada
veldschoen
viatu vya Johanna
viatu vya kliipa
viatu vya malapa
viatu vya matende
voided shoe
waraji
wata
wedgie
Wellington boot
Wellington half-boot
wùla
xi
xie
xue
yezmeh
yi'chit tal
yslopan
yuxié
zābaks
zancha
zapatillas
zapato
zapato de mujer sin cor-
  reas
zapato oxford
záyres
zoccolo
zōri
zueco

SKIRTS

à l'innocence reconnue
aba
adhivikartana
ajsu
amabejhu
anacu
anaku
angel overskirt
bagazia
ballet-skirt
balloon skirt
bases
basquina
bavlnka
bezulánky
bhairnavasani
bidang
bikla
bogazie
bolsicón
borda
bouwen
broz
buba
calanaka
calani
camargo puff
camboys
candataka
carana
centro
centro de lana
ceòis
cháng
charak
ch'ima
chimphullani
chiripá
cias
ciasan
cirb
comboy
cornet skirt
corte
cottereau
cueitl
de caracolillo
debajero
desplegada
Directoire skirt
dirndl
divided skirt
dodo

doso
dudda
eel skirt
el costal
eleven gore ripple skirt
empire skirt
enagua
enredo
enredos
envuelto
etapi
falda
falda con tabla añadida
falda envuelta
falda escocesa
falda-pantalón
faldellin
featherbrush skirt
filibeg
fimbria
fota
fourreau skirt
fralda
fustă
fústa
fustanéles
fustanella
gaghra
gergueta
ghaggharo
ghagra
ghagri
godet skirt
gonella
gonna
gonna pantalone
gored bell skirt
grannie'skirt
gun
gyolocsfersling
hanina
harem-hem skirt
hau'ina
hobble skirt
hondorgo
Hosenrock
housemaid skirt
huali
hula skirt
ihenga
ishiwaba
iupca
jeltesta

jelteta
joeb
jubka
jupe
jupe-pantalon
kain lepas
kain sampin
kamben
kampu anaku
kandys
kaunace
kebaya
kiki skirt
kikois
kilt
kilted skirt
kinkini
kuntunkuni
kusulaka
ku'uwelu
kwun
lahra patora
lau pahudu
lipa bannang
lipa garrusu
liùsb
longyi
lostenn
malong
malong andon
malong pandi
mang chu
mapel
maxi
mermaid's tail
midi
milkmaid skirt
minifalda
minigonna
minijupe
Minirock
minirok
mo
morga
morning glory skirt
mshono wa mwavuli
musui
muszuj
nages
ncak
ncaka ishyeen
nshak
okrel

orla
otcharak
pagne
paisin
pakiri mbola
panaeva
panel skirt
panjóva
pano
panung
papaki
parasol skirt
pareo
pareu
pasuāj
pasvāj
pa'u
pa'u heihei
peasant skirt
peg-top skirt
pendely
peplum overskirt
pesa
peshgir
pestiman
phaa sarong
phaa sin
phaa yao
phali
pichu anaku
pie
pindileu
piupiu
plakhta
pokinikini
pollera
poneva
posahuanco
pristídha
quimono
qún
qúnzi
rainy daisy skirt
rapaki
refajos
refajos plegados
Rock
rok
rokoja
rokolya
rondastakken
sadiaka
safeguard

safety skirt
saia
saiote escocês
sakete
sarafan
saya
Schotse Hooglanders
sgùman
sgyrt
shang
shendot

sin
singelos
sipu anaku
skört
skørt
sottana
spódnica
spódniczka
spodniczka szkocka
straight English skirt
sucna

súkenice
sukne
suknja
sun-ray skirt
swing skirt
tablier skirt
tapis
tembe
tie-back skirt
tl'aakal
tucked skirt

tuman
tunic skirt
umbrella skirt
umtika
üst tuman
vat
váy
vîlnic
vulnenik
xà-rông
xong

SLEEVES

à gomito
à gozzo
à la jardiniere
ailerons
amadis
amadis sleeve
angel sleeve
Ariadne sleeve
Ärmel
balloon sleeve
batwing
bellows sleeve
beret sleeve
bishop sleeve
bouffante sleeve
butterfly bow sleeve
cannon sleeves
cap sleeve
caroline sleeve
cased sleeve
cavalier sleeve
circassian sleeve
coat-sleeve
Donna Maria
double bouffant sleeves
du Barry sleeve
eelskin sleeve
elephant sleeve
false sleeves
farthingale sleeves

French gigot sleeves
French sleeves
furisode
Gabrielle sleeve
Garibaldi sleeve
gigot sleeve
grande-assiette sleeves
Grecian sleeve
half bishop sleeve
hanging sleeve
irdan
Isabeau sleeve
Italian sleeve
jockey sleeve
kato manikia
kum
Lady Alice sleeve
leg of mutton sleeves
lekmann detsmira
lima
lima puha'uha'u
Louis XIV sleeve
mamelouk sleeve
manche
manche à gigot
mancheron
manchette de cour
manchettes
manege averte
maneras

manga
manga ahuecada
manga caída
manga dolman
manga gitana
manga kimono
manga murciélago
manga raglán
mangas perdidas
manica
manica a buffo
maniche á comeo
Margaret of Valois
Marie sleeve
Marie-Antoinette sleeve
marino faliero sleeve
medias mangas
Medici sleeve
melon sleeve
mitten sleeve
Montespan
Montespan sleeve
mousquetaire sleeve
mouw
musequí
mushroom sleeve
pagoda sleeve
pancake sleeves
pansomae
peg-top sleeves

pokeys
ponyet
prince's sleeve
pudding sleeve
Puffärmel
raglan sleeve
rekaw
religieuse sleeve
roxalene sleeve
sleeve à la Louis Quinze
sleeve à la Minerva
sling sleeve
sode
sode-guchi
somae
soufflet sleeve
Spanish sleeve
sultan sleeve
sultana sleeve
swallow's nests
tamoto
tàoxiù
tay áo
'uha hipa
Venetian sleeve
Victoria sleeve
virago sleeve
wearing sleeves

STRAW

abaca
agave
aloe hemp
Baden hemp
bakou
baku

ballibuntal
ballibuntl
bangkok
Belgian split straw
bombanas
buntal

buriti
Cebu hemp
Davao hemp
estrain
French chip
Italiaans stro

Japanese mocha
jipijapa
koffo
liseré
Manila hemp
paillasson

parasisol	rattan	wara	
ramie	tuscan	Zillon braid	

SWEATERS

áo ðan	coltrui	lammie	suéter
áo len	cowichan sweater	lammy	suwet'o
Aran Isle sweater	cricket sweater	pullover	sweter zapinany
chandail	gebreid vest	Pullover	twinset
chompas	jersey sweater	saco de abrigo	welniana kamizelka

TIES AND SCARVES

à la Byron	das	lahariyo	riha
à la Napoleon	disa	lahasyo	Royal George stock
abnet	dopatta	lamballe	rūmāl
amhcha	ecrouellique	lingjié	sailor's reef knot tie
angavastra	Elbert Hubbard tie	lingjin	sālū
ascot tie	fichu	loros	sampour
ballroom neckcloth	fichu Antoinette	lorum	santon
bann-bhràghad	fichu Corday	macaroni cravat	sautoir
belcher	fichu la Valiere	maharatta	sbernia
berdash	fichu menteur	mail coach	scallop
bib-cravat	fichu raphael	mandili	Schlips
bilqusak	fichu Ristori	military stock	sebnia
boa	fichu-pelerine	mofeler	semfiti
bolia	fly plaid	moktor	shal
bufanda	focale	Napoleon necktie	shesh
buffonts	follette	neck handkerchief	shirinka
bukhani	foulard	neckcloth	shoe-tie necktie
carthage cymar	four-in-hand	neckstock	skuinsdoek
ca-vát	French boa	neerstick	starcher
chaconne	fu-la	nekt'ai	Steinkirk
chalina	giall-bhrat	obiage	stìom-amhaich
chemisette	gravata	octagon tie	succinctorium
ciotag	Halsbinde	orhna	suggan
cleòcan	halsneusdoek	Osbaldiston tie	sultana scarf
cloud	Halstuch	Oxford tie	tapalo
coilichin	hunting necktie	pachedī	Teresa
comforter	hunting stock	palomita	tóu jim
corbata	Huntley scarf	pañuelo	trabea
corbata ascot	Indian necktie	pañuelo para el cuello	tubular necktie
cravat	infula	Persian scarf	ufanta
cravat cocodes	jabot	phāgniā	umpal
cravat strings	joinville	phu-la	uparanī
cravate	kājaliyā	pichodī	uparanū
cravate à la Bergami	kasumbo	piliyā	uparna
cravate cocodes	khan vaông	pīlo	upavastra
cravate de bureaucrate	kidungas	plain bow stock	velo
cravate mathematique	king klipper	platok	vexillum
cravatta	Kravatte	pomaco	volant
Cremona cravat	krawat	qadifeh	wéijin
cūndad	Krawatte	rabat	zéédéeldoi
cunnī	kroplap	ratnodgrathi tottariyam	

UMBRELLAS AND PARASOLS

bamkyinie
barraca
Beatrice parasol
bee chaha'ohí
cái
chapeo
chatta
chattra
en tout cas
fa'amalu
fan parasol
fasgadan
gamp
grian-sgàil
grian-sgàilean
ketesal
kettysol

kippe-sole
kitsol
kittasol
kittasole
kittesaw
kittisal
kittsol
kittysol
kittysoll
kitysol
krambuno
ombrelle
pagoda parasol
pakjwiu san
paraplu
parapluie
parasol

párasol
parasol à canne
parasole
parasolka
parasol-whip
port manteau sunshade
quitasol
quitta soll
quittesol
rom
rondel
roundel
rundell
Schirm
sgàilean-uisge
sgail-uisge
sombrinha

sombrinha chapeau de sol
Sonnenschirm
tātēn dībabō
telescope parasol
tyrasol
umbrela
umbrella
usan
yangsan
zonnenscherm

UNDERGARMENTS

Alexandra petticoat
alforje
all-in-one
amazon corset
amplificateur
anacholus
anágua
áo lót
áo lót mình
áo nit
áo njt
apodesme
Apollo corset
avagraha
bajera
balmoral
balmoral petticoat
bandeau
bandleg brief
banyan
basque belt
basquine
bell hoop
berundjuk
bidang
bielizna
bishop
bodies, pair of
body stichet
body-stychet
bosom friends
brasserole

brassiere
brayette
breost-lin
breost-rocc
Brummel bodice
bum-barrel
bustehouder
bustier
cache corset
caderas postizas
cage
cage Americaine
cage empire
caleçons
calzon bombacho
calzoncillo
camibockers
camicia da donna
cami-knickers
camiseta
camiseta con mangas
    cortas
camisola
camisole
candataka
Catherine wheel farthin-
    gale
ceroulas
chalanika
chandataka
chemiloon
chemise

chènkù
chènqún
chènyí
cingulum
cintaliga
combinations
considerations
cork rump
corps piqué
corse
corset
corset waist
còta
cóta coirí
còta-ban
còta-bhioran
còta-cathdath
còtan
criardes
crinoletta
crinolette
crinolette petticoat
crinolina
crinoline
cue de Paris
cul de crin
cul de Paris
cul postiche
Cumberland corset
cupola coat
cushionet
Directoire knickers

divorce corset
dou dou
drawers
dress improver
drum farthingale
empire jupon
empress petticoat
enagua
enagua de lana
English farthingale
envelope combination
espartilho de senhora
faja-calzón
falda combinación
faldia
faldrilla
false hips
fan hoop
fardegalijn
farthingale
foot-mantle
friponne
fústa
fuste
gegendas
gipon
gomlek
gordel
gördel
gorset
gougandine
gourgandine

guard-infanta
guepiere
gueridons
guimpe
Gürtel
hadajuban
halka
hànbèixin
han-jubon
hànshan
hiyoku
hoepelrok
hoop petticoat
horsehair petticoat
iç tuman
Italian farthingale
Jaeger underclothes
jahanaroho
jansenistes
juban
jube
jubon
jupe
jupel
kaliki
kaliki waiu
kamis
kanchli
katasárci
kedelys
kinderbroekje
kolaristó
korsaza
korset
Korsett
koshimaki
kósula
koszula damska

ktef
kurta
lencería
Liberty bodice
lodier
luhinga
majtki
mamillare
Matinee skirt
may-ô
Merry Widow
mesofori
modeste
mu'u mu'u
naajuban
naeui
naewang
naga-juban
naizhào
nèiyi
night corset
nitambavastra
nivi
ondergoed
onderzieltje
ondina crinoline
palema'i
panier a coudes
paniers a bourelets
paniers anglais
pannier crinoline
panniers
pantalettes
panty corselette
papa
pendej
peplum jupon
pettibockers

petticoat bodice
placket
poches
Portuguese farthingale
praghata
pratidhi
pratinivasana
pregnant stay
princess petticoat
princess slip
Quaker skirt
quan con áo-cánh
quàn xà-lón
quilted petticoat
rawai
refafo
religious petticoat
ribbon corset
riding hoop
rubas
ruzhào
saiat
sansflectum crinoline
scabilonians
scavilones
secrete
shakefold
smock petticoat
sogot
sokch'ima
sokot
sostén
sottana
sottogonna
Spanish farthingale
staighinean
strapontin
strophion

strophium
strossers
suk'oot'u
susoyoke
suspensor atletico
swanbill corset
tambour
tango corset
Taxíria
teddies
teddy-bears
tilter
tontillo
tournure
traquenard
tsaxínia
üçetek
ukunchina
ulkhaulik
undaweya
underhandkerchief
under-serc
undervest
unkelai
unkucha
Unterrock
vasquine
verdingale
verdugado
vertugadin
vertugadin francais
Victoria cage
waist cincher
wandabo
wheel farthingale
wyliecoat
xi-líp
xu-chiêng

VESTS

albagcā
American vest
antery
áo gi-lê
bei xin
benjy
bondita
booie sum
borstrok
brustfleck
bústos
camiciuola
camisole
chaleco

chanbagala
chao gua
ch'aokua
chemisette
choggi
chokki
chupa
colera
colête
corpiño
cotorina
daku
drapi
dulamás

dzákos
firmla
French opening vest
French vest
gabā
geamantan
ghlila
gi-lê
gilet-veste
golf vest
griza
guzjók
hsia-pei
hussar point

ilic
jaleco
jaque
jelek
jockey waistcoat
kamiselka
kamizelka
kamizóla
kamzol
kanjian
kápa
keptar
kersetka
kiklikas

kisibao
klistó jiléci
lájbi
le gilet
lecric
liang dang
mejrevaló
Newmarket vest

peiteag
pieptar
pieptarita
rational
salt-box pocket
sart
Shakespere vest
shawl waistcoat

sidari
sidriyeh
sigouni
straight waistcoat
tao 'ofu
tattersall vest
uiose
university vest

váll
veston
Wams
Weste
zubun

Appendix B: Garments by Country

ABYSSINIA

abougedid
chamma
hamarti

kaldoh
matab

AFGHANISTAN

boorka
burqa
chadri
chapan
cheo
kubba

kupasi
loongee
qadifeh
tom-bons
ulkhaulik

ALGERIA

Bazna
çârma
djubba
gandoora
gandoura

gandurah
ghlîla
haik
jaseran
tagilmus

ANDAMAN ASLANDS

bôd-da

ANNAM

cai-ao

caiquan

ARABIA

al-aqrāq al-zarrariyya
anbijāniyya
aqrāq
ashrafī
badan

bulgha
burnous
burqu'
chechia
ghutra

hezaam   musaftaj
jubba   musayyar
keffieh   musha''ara
khirqa   qabā
kuffieh   qalansuwa
kufiyeh   qalasuva
mandīl   qamīs
mantaqa   rafraf
marlota   rān
mayāthir humr   ridā
mighfar   safsarī
mindīl   sharbūsh
mintaqa   tailasân
miqna'   tāj
miqna'a   takhfīfa
mi'zar   tarboosh
mizz   thawb
mudhahhab   tikka
mulabbada

ARGENTINA

chiripá   faja
chubut wool

ARMENIA

bambak

AUSTRALIA

Adelaide wool   paarengarenga
Australian wool   panaena
awarua   papari
bluey   pare
hana   piupiu
huru kurii   plimsoll
ihupuni   pootae taua
kahu huruhuru   puuahi
kahu kaakaapoo   taahuka
kahu kekeno   taapahu
kahu kiwi   taapeka
kahu kura   taatara
kahu kuri   taatua hume
kahu toi   taawakawaka
kahu waero   takitaki
kangaroo leather   tara
koopuu   taratara
kopa   tiki
mai muka   toopuni
ngore   toorua
ngore paheke   tuu hangaroa
paakee   tuu kaaretu
paakee nui   tuu maro
paakee tikumu   tuu muka
paaraerae   tuu ure

whanake whiitiki

AUSTRIA

blaukappe	haiduk
brustfleck	juppo
dentelle Angleterre	lederhosen
fazzelkappe	scheibenbart
festracht	spitzkappe
fürtuchsklemmer	Tierfibeln
gamsbart	tracht
goller	wasserfall
haftel	

AUSTRO-HUNGARIAN EMPIRE

à la jardiniere	dolman
corsage à la vierge	mente
csakora cut	parta
csizma	wickler
diszmagyar	

BALI

geringsing	kamben
kain prada	lamak

BALKANS

opanky	poculica
peca	rubina

BANGLADESH

riha

BELGIUM

Bruges lace	point de gaze
Brussels lace	Rosaline
kant	treille
klosant	Ypres lace
Point de Fée	

BOHEMIA

kaiser-rock sweater

BOLIVIA

ahuasca	awayu
ahuayo	aymilla
ajsu	bandera
aksu	bayeta
alforja	boliviano
almilla	brillantes
awakipa	calcheña llijlla

cañari
capacho
ccahua
ccahuas
challapata
ch'aska
chimi
chola derby
chucu
chullo
ch'ullu
chumpi
ch'uspa
cumbi
hiscu
huaka
huallas
huallquepo
huayaca
inti
isallo
iscayo
istalla
juk'ullu
khallus
killa
k'inkus
kunka unku
k'uyu
listado
listao ponch
llacota
llakolla
lliclla
llijlla
lliklla
lloq'e
loraypu
luto
luto poncho
manta
mantita

montera
mullutuma
p'anta
panti
phicchi
phullu
pillu
pollera
ponchito
poncho boliviano
p'ullu
q'alaq'awa
q'epirina
rebozo
ribete
sacapallay
sacha pullki
señor
señora llijlla
señore
siki
simpa
suculla ccahua
t'ikita
tocapu
troqilla
ttisnu
tullmas
ufanta
ujuta
unkhuña
unku
uraq-awa
urku
wajrapallay
w'aka
wasa
wincha
yana
yareta
yutu

BORNEO

a-a
anyam
baju
bane
ba'o barit
ba'o burur
ba'o rawir
bedong
bekatapu
bekengkang

bidang
borak
buchai
burak
chelum
chilum
dadong
dangdong
dilak bedong
engkudu

gari
gasieng
gasing
grunong
kain chelum
kain engkudu
kain mata
kalambi
kalambi ara
kanggan
karong
katapu
kebat
kelalin lambai
kengkang
klapong sirat
kuning
labang
labong
lelingkok
let
lilit
marau

marik
pakan
pandin
petaa
pua
pun alai
rawai
salapok
sirat
skelat
sklat
sungkit
sunkit
suriek
surik
takai buriet
tanggi
tanggok
ubong
ubong mata
ulub
ungkoi

BOSNIA

bakar
bluza
boje
crn
crnac
dorina
dugme
farba
kapa
kecelja
kopa
materija
narukvica
obuca
odjeca

okovratnik
platno
pregaca
puljka
Pumphose
sako
sljem
snala
stof
tasna
tkanina
ukrasavanje
vez
zersej
zubun

BRAZIL

bahia sheeting

Dom pedro

BULGARIA

abgar
beli potouri
belodreshnik
benevretsi
birnetsi
burchanka
byala houta
chernodreshnik

ciupag
dimii
diz
dolaktanka
dolama
doramché
dulboka pazva
elek

eminii
geamantan
glouhché
houta
ilic
jaka
jube
kaitsa
kalets
kaltsi
kaltsouni
klashnik
kolitsa
koprina
korenka
koshoulya
kozhoushé
kurligatka
kusak
kutsani gashti
leiber
mrezhera prestilka
na krilo
nagrudnik
okrel
opas

opinak
opinki
páfti
peshkir
podkapnik
poes
postavu
poturi
poyas
prevez
pristelca
purki
razsouchal
riza
roucha
shamiya
soukno
stupa
sukmán
tkanitsa
tsarvouli
tsepen
Tukanitsa
vulnenik
zaveska

BURMA

ainyi
khamout
longyi

tamein
tubbeck

CAMBODIA

hol

sampot

CAMEROON

leppi

ndop

CANADA

Chilkat blankets
cowichan sweater
siwash sweater

toque
tuque

CAUCASUS

arkhalukh
burka

cherkeska

CELEBES

baju bodo
fuya
kain bentenan
lelesepun

lipa bannang
lipa garrusu
maa'
mawa'

pinatikan

poritutu roto

CEYLON

bakou
baku

camboys
comboy

CHILE

chaman
charahuilla

ichella
k'isas

CHINA

ái
ao
autumn tea brown
bai na yi
bai shou yi
bai tong
báibù
báisè
baishan
baize
balílà
ban hi
banzhi
bao tou
báosha zhiwù
bei xin
bei ze
bei zi
beidài
bèifú
ben'àn
bi xi
biàn
biànxié
biézhen
bìji
bìlán
bìlù
bìsha
bó
bow shoes
bù
bùbó
butterfly bun
caichóu
càiqing
cang
cangan
canganes

cangcang
canghuáng
caoxié
chai
chai-chieh-p'ai
cháng
chang fu
chang guan
chang shan
chángkù
chángpáo
chángshan
chàngtongwà
ch'ao fu
chao guan
chao pao
chao gua
ch'aokua
charwa
chásè
chau fu
chènbù
chéng
chènkù
chènqún
chènshan
chènyí
chi
chi fu
chìhèsè
chìhóng
chong er
chóu
chóuduàn
chu
chuàn
chuandài
chuanzhuó
chu-chu

chunzhuang
chuo
congbái
conglù
cool gown
cubù
cuìlù
cumábù
cumáoyàng
curling-cloud crown
curóugé
cuzhi xianwéi
da dai
dabao
dàchang
dàguà
dàhóng
dai kou
dàilù
daishi
dalian
dancing phoenix bun
dang
danpiàn yanjìng
dànqing
danyi
dàoguàjinzhong
dengxinróng
dian
diaopí
dilun
dou
dou bo
dou dou
dou niu
doudu
doudoukur
doulì
doupeng
douzi
duàn
duandàyi
duantongxue
duànwén
duànzi
eaglewood brown
éhuáng
er
er dang
erhuán
external high shoes
fa guan
fàjia
falánróng
fanbù

fangchóu
fanling
fàqia
fayi
fei
fei yu
feihóng
feisè
feng huang
fengjìng
fengmào
fenhóng
fragrance on the surface of the soles
fragrant leaves
fú
fu ku
fu tou
fuchou
fuo
fúzhuang
gàn
gangkai
gànqing
gao
gaogenxié
gaopí
gaosù
ge dai
gen
gold ingot bun
golden tea brown
gongzhuangkù
grape brown
gu gu guan
guà
gua pi mao
guanmiãn
gui yi
gun
gun fu
gun mian
guo luo dai
haihúnshan
hailìsi cuni
hànbèixin
hànshan
haol
hè
héfú
hei
hei jiao chou
heiyanjìng
hóng
hóngyànyàn
hòugen

hòujin

hsia-pei

hua yu

huabù

huádání

huaduan

huáibiao

huang ma qua

huángcàncn

hù'er

hui yi

hùmùjìng

hunhuáng

húsè

ji fu

ji guan

jiakè

jian

jiàng

jiàngsè

jiàngzì

jianzhang

jiao dai

jiaxié

jiaxue

jièzhi

jin huang

jin xian guan

jin zi

jiu

ju

juàn

jue

júhóng

júhuáng

kaijia

kaishìmí

kanjian

k'o ssŭ

koo

ku

ku zhe

laliàn

lan yu

lasuor

leung mo

lì

liàn

liang dang

liang dang kai

liang mao

lianjiaokù

liányiqún

lifú

lily feet

limào

líng

ling tao

ling yue

lingjié

lingjin

lingkòu

lingzi

lìsè

long

long pao

lotus flowers

lotus seeds

lu

luan

lung p'ao

ma gua

ma xue

mábù

ma-coual

mang ao

mang chu

mang pao

máobù

máogé

màokuir

máolán

máoliào

máoyi

máozhipin

màozi

mèi

méihóngsè

mian fu

mian guan

miánbù

miánkù

miánmáokù

miánmáoshan

miánróng

miányi

ming guang kai

misè

mòjing

mòlù

musk melon bun

mwa kwa

naizhào

nankeen

nei tao

nèiyi

ní

níróng

niukòu

niupàn

niúzaikù

niuzi

nízi

off-the-horse bun

onion white brown

ouhe

ousè

pà

pale lilac brown

páo

pàopàosha

paoxié

páozi

pí ao

pi bian

pi ling

p'i ling

pijian

piling

pinlán

pinlù

pinyuè

píyi

pou-fou

pu fu

pu zi

purple gown

qi

qi pao

qian hua

qiapàn

qibù

qigé

qilim

qinglù

qiú

qún

qúnzi

ren

róngbù

róngkù

róngmiàngé

róngyi

ròusè

ru

ruanduàn

rubái

ruzhào

shan ku

shang

shao

shen dai

shen yi

shiu tian yi

shoubiao

shoujuàn

shui tian yi

shuilù

shuìyi

sichóu

sidài

sirghe

siróng

sizhipin

star-studded sky

suoyi

swallow-tail bangs

tacley

tafuchóu

tai-k'ou

tai-shih

tàiyángjìng

tala

talabanr

t'ao t'ieh

tàoshan

tàoxié

tàoxiù

taozi

tí

tì

tian'éróng

tian ze

tianlán

tianqing

tiao tuo

tiáoróng

tong xiu kai

tóu jim

tou tu

tsan

tuósè

wà

wa leng mao

wài tào

wàiyi

wàizhào

wàtào

wàzi

weeping willow bangs

wéijin

wéiqún

wu bian

wu guan

wùla

xi

xia pei

xian

xian yi

xiàngliàn

xiàngquàn
xianhong
xiao yao jin
xie zhai
xinghóng
xinghuáng
xiu shang
xiùbiáo
xiùkou
xiùzhang
xiùzi
xueqing
yan
yang zhi
yangzhiyu
yanhóng
yellow jacket
yín
ying long
ying luo
yinggelù
yùdài
yuèbai
yulin baizhequn
yumào
yun jian
yùsè
yusha
yuxié

yuyi
yùzan
zan
zànglán
zàngqing
zaohóng
zé
zha jia
zhaijiepai
zhan
zhàopáo
zhàoshán
zhàoyi
zhe
zhe ji
zhéshàn
zhi huan
zhi sun
zhòu
zhòubù
zhuanglián
zhuhóng
zhùmá
zhuó
zi
zihóng
zuan
zuòcán
zuòsichóu

COLOMBIA

ruana

tumbaga

CZECHOSLOVAKIA

bavlna
bota
camara
capka
cepice
cipky
death lace
drahokam
halena
hedvábí
jehla
kabát
kalhoty
kapesník
kapsa
klenot
klobouk
knoflik

kosile
kotuly
kozesina
krajky
krejci
len
límec
náhrdelnú
náramek
niť
oblékati
obuv
odíti
osatiti
pantofel
pás
plást
plátno

prsten
puncocha
riza
rubas
saty
spendlík
spiders

spodky
strevíc
sukne
trailer thread lace
vlno
zástera

DENMARK

armbaand
Barcelona scarf
bœlte
bomuld
bukser
dullemoese
filt
flip
forklœde
frakke
halsbaand
Hamburg homespun
handske
hedbo embroidery
hose
hue
hvivklaede
joeb
juvel
kaabe
kamiks
kappe
kapperoellike
kasket
klœde
klœder
knap

knipling
kniplinger
krave
lemmetør klœde
linned
lœder
lœrred
lomme
naal
pels
Schleswig lace
sekernil
silke
skjorte
sko
skørt
skrœdder
slør
sok
støvle
strømpe
tingmiak
tøffel
tøi
tonder lace
traad
uld

EAST INDIA

assam cotton
beteele
cabeca
chadoe

kalamkari
langooty
luhinga
nabob

ECUADOR

alli churana
anaku
ascanta
bajera
bayeta de lishtas
bolsicón
bozal

bufanda
cachimira
cadena
camisa chaki picada
camisa de la tela amarilla
candongas
caucho pargate

centro
chaleco
chalina
changalli
chompas
chulla cara
chumbi
chumbi banderilla
cinta
cruz churuku
cuerpo
debajero
embozalada
enagua
fachalina
fachalina de cabeza
fachallina
festones
filete
frutilla
gergueta
gualcas
hombrera
jatun chumbi
jerga
jirga poncho
kampu anaku
kwitsa pargates
larga
lienzo
linchi
lista
llano
lliglla
macana
maki
maki punta
maki watana
manilla
mantones de Manila
millma sumbriru
millma sumbru
mullu
ordinaria
pacotilla
pantalones cortos
pañu sumbriru
pañuelo
panutzutzu ukufachallina

panzo de burro
pepa de zapallo
pichu anaku
pichu jerga
piel de foca
pollera
poncho amarrado
poncho cuadrada
poncho jijún
poncho rosado
puño
puntada limeña
realce
rinrin wallka
ruana
runa
sábana
sabanilla
sarcillus
shagshu zamarro
shigra
sikinchina
sombreros de lana de lado de Ambato
suela
talonera
tela caucho
tira
tira dorado
tiu camisa
tupu
tupullina pichu jerguita
uchilla maki chumbi
uku churana
ukunchina
ushuta
'usut'a
varedira
wallka
wallkarina
walutu
wangu
washa fachalina
washajatana
yana poncho
yura poncho
zammarros
zarcillos
zhutu

EGYPT

abayah
afef
as

assili cotton
atef
bedla

birda

boukrania

bulgha

bur'a'

burqa

byssus

cahouk

calasiris

charoul

deshret

faraguja

ferka

futa

galabiyeh bi wist

ghatra

gilbah

giná

haik royal

henna

heqat and nekhekh

herset

Horus lock

jubba

jubbah

kalasiris

kepresh

khenmet

khepesh

khesbed

khimara

klaft

kohl

kornish

kuftan

kyaphi

libas

mandil

mefkat

melas

melaya liff

menat

menyet

mezz

mukla

murabba

nekhau

nekhaw

nemehef

Nemes headdress

nishra

pano

passium

patna

pectoral

postiche

procardium

pshente

sabaa

sacred uraeus

salteh

scarab

scaraboid

Sekhemty

serekh

serouel

sharb

sha-sha

sheath dress

shendot

shenti

shenu

shintiyan

shugga

sidari

sindon

sirwall

stibium

tarha

udju

was and tam

wedja

weret

wesekh

ETHIOPIA

ačē attāmitō

ačē gumbō

ačē kéčō

ačē saččō

ačō

adaftō

argūbō

attāmitō

bayō

birawō

bofeta

čadu

chamma

dima

dudda

eddimō

fota

garannō

geldem
girri
gošō
gurača
gurda
gu'ut
horrō
hukkō
ilbora
irbora
išānō
kallača
kamis
keččō
koreddo
kurni
maldā

martō
mekkō
ninnoko
qungo
sadeti
šanāfilō
šayō
serret
šohofa
sorō
šumbeqō
šumboqō
tātē ukō
tātēn dībabō
tobe
waya
wāyāč attāmitō

FRANCE

à jour
à la Byron
à la du Barry corsage
à la Farare
à la Figaro
à la Grecque corsage
à la Louis XV corsage
à la Maintenon
à la Marlborough
à la Napoleon
à la plaquette
à la Titus
à la Victime
à l'innocence reconnue
abaissé
acajou
accollé
accroche-coeur
adoucir
affiquet
agneau
agneau du Tibet
agneau karakul
agnelin
Agnes Sorel style
agrafe
agraffe
agrandir
agrements
agulhade
aigrette
aiguille
aiguille a reprises
aiguille a tricoter

aiguillette
aile
aile de pigeon
ailette
ajour
Albanian hat
Alençon lace
alezan
alliance
allongé
alloutienne
alpaga
alpargata
amazone
amigaut
amincir
amonieres sarrasinoises
amortir
androsmane
Angouleme bonnet
aplatir
appas postiches
araignée méditant un crime
arc'henad
arc'henad-kambr
ardoise
argent
Argentan lace
armes à l'épreuve
armoisin
armure cannelée
arras
Arras lace
arrêter

arrondir
astrakan
au globe fixé
aulmoniere
aumoniere
aune
aurifère
autruche
Ave Maria lace
aviver
azur
badine
bague
baiseuse
baisser
balagnie cloak
balandran
baleinage
barboteuse
barrette
bas
bas à cotes
bas à jour
bas de laine
bas de soie
bas de soy
basque
basque beret
bâti
batiste
bavarel
beauvais embroidery
benoiton chains
beret basque
beret de marin
Bernhardt mantle
bicoquet
bigouden
bijou
bijouterie
bijoutier
binette
bizou
black lace
blaireau
blanc
blanc haubert
bleu
blondes de Caen
blousant
bois de rose
boisson
bonnes grâces
bonnet à flamme
bonnet à la crete de coq

bonnet à la laitiere
bonnet à la moresque
bonnet à la Richard
bonnet à la victoire
bonnet aux trois ordres réunis
bonnet de police
bonnet demi-negligee
bonnet negligee
bord
borrillonnées
botez
botte
botte à genouillère
bottine
bouchons de carafe
bouclé
boucle d'oreille
boucle d'oreille à la guillotine
bouffant mecanique
bouffette
bouillion
bouillioné
boulanger
bourbon hat
bourguignotte
bourse
bourserie en lisse
boutis
bouton
bouton d'or
boutonnière
bragou
bragou-braz
braguette
braoig
brassière
Brittany
Brittany cloth
Brittany work
brocart
broche
brodequin
broderie
broderie en blanc
broderie en jais
broigne
broz
brun
bure
burnouse
caban
cache-folies
cachelaid
cachemire
cache-peigne

caen
cage Americaine
cagoule
California
calque
camaieu
cambresine
cambric
camelot
cancan dress
canepin
canezou
canne
canne à système
cannes demi-solde
cannes-dard
canotier
canvas
cap à la Charlotte Corday
cape a l'espanole
capulet
caraco à coqueluchon
caraco à la francaise
caraco à la polonaise
carda
carmagnole
carrez de gaze
casaquin en juste
casimir
casque
casque à la Tarleton
casque colonial
casquette
castor
catiole
cavalry
cayenne
cazavacka
ceinture
celeste
châle
chamarre
chameau
chandail
chape à aige
chapeau
chapeau à la Basile
chapeau à la Ceres
chapeau à la Charlotte
chapeau à la Cherubin
chapeau à la Colonne
chapeau à la Devonshire
chapeau à la Grenade
chapeau à la turque
chapeau à l'egyptienne

chapeau à l'italienne
chapeau au bateau renversé
chapeau claque
chapeau de Cardinal
chapeau de paille
chapeau d'homme
chapeau jockei
chapeau mou
chapeau souple
chapeau-bras
chapel d'acier
chapel de Montauban
chapel-de-fer
charvet
charvet et fils de Paris
chasuble
châtain
chausettes
chausse
chausses en bourses
chausses larges à l'antique
chausses semellees
chaussette
chaussette montant
chaussure
chaussures à cric
chaussures à pont-levis
chemise
chemise à la greque
chemise à la Reine
chemise de nuit
chemise d'homme
chenille lace
cheval de frise
cheveux de frise
chevesaille
cheviot
chèvre de Chine
chèvre de Mongolie
chevreau
chevrette
chicoree
chinchilla
chou
chou hat
chouquette
civette
cloche de feutre
cloqué
cocarde
coeffes
coiffe
coiffure à la conseillere
coiffure à la Dauphine
coiffure à la enfant

coiffure à la Eurydice
coiffure à la Flore
coiffure à la Junon
coiffure à la Ninon
coiffure à la qu' es aco
coiffure à la Reine
coiffure à l'Agnes Sorel
coiffure à l'anglomane
coiffure à l'indisposition
coiffure au chien couchant
coiffure en bouffons
coiffure en cadenettes
coiffure en chien couchant
coiffure en moulin à vent
coiffure en parterre galant
coiffure en raquette
coiffure Eugenie
coiffure Louis Trieze
coin de feu
cointise
col
colberteen
colbertine
collerette
collet
collet monte
collier
colmar
comperes
conch
conque
coq
coque
coquelicot
coqueluche
coquillage
coquille
corbeau
cordeliere
cordon de soulier
cordouan
cornette
cornette à la Diane
corp a baleine
corps piqué
corsage
corsage à la Maintenon
corsage en corset
costume à la Constitution
costume au grand Figaro
cote à armer
cote de Cheval
coton
cotte d'armes
cottereau

couleur-de-roi
countenances
coureur
couronne
courreges
courtepy
courtepye
couvre-chef
couvrechef
couvre-oreille
cramoisi
crapaud
crapaud mort d'amour
crapaud saisi
cravate
cravate à la Bergami
cravate cocodes
cravate de bureaucrate
cravate mathematique
crêpe
crepelle
crepon milleraye
crepon Persian
creve-coeur
creves
crinoline
cuir
cuir-bouilli
culot
culotte
culotte courte
cuoroncou
damas
damassé
dandine
dankalie
dantelez
de frivolité
décolletage
defrise
deguisement
demi-castor
demiceint
demi-converti
demijambe
demi-mousseline
demi-tablier
demi-tunique
dentelle aux fuseaux
dentelle de Cambrai
dentelle de fils
dentelle de la vierge
dentelle renaissance
dessous
deuil

devantiere
diamanté
diaraogenn
Dieppe point lace
dillad
donariere
dossière
doublure
doublure du chapeau
douillette
douillette à la Russienne
drap
drap d'Alma
drap d'Argent
drap de Berry
drap de billard
drap de France
drap de Paris
drap de velours
drap de Venice
drap d'ete
drap d'or
drap feutre
drap fourreau
ecaille work
écarlate
echancre
echarpe
echelle
echelon
ecossais
ecrouellique
ecureuil
effronter
elegant
eleganté
emeraude
en beret
en coeur
en colimaçon
en coulisse
en echelle de Jacob
en fourreau lace
en manche
en platitude
en pouf
en pouf à la Luxembourg
en ravanche
en tablier
engageantes
enjoueé
enseigne
entre-deux
epaules Americaines
epauliere

épingle
épingle à chevaux
epomine
escarelle
esclavage
espèce d'ouvrage à jour
esprits
estaches
etamine broché
étoffe
étoffe écossaise
étole
etui
faconné
faille
fausse montre
fautre
favoris
feltr
ferroniere
feur
feutre
fichu la Valiere
fichu menteur
fichu raphael
fichu-canezou
fichu-pelerine
fil
fil tiré
filé
fitchet
fleur de lis
fleur de lys
fleur volant
florence
flounce à disposition
follette
fond
fond à la marriage
fond clair
fontanges
Fortuny tea gown
fouine
foulard poile de chevre
foulé
foulinenn
fouriaux
fourisseur d'arme
fourrure
frac
fraise
frangipani perfume
freiseau
frileuse
frise

frisé

frivolité

frizé

froissé

froncés

frontiere

fuseau

fustaine

galante

galants

galoche

galon d'argent

galon d'or

gant

gants de chevreau

garçon d'honneur

gazar

gaze à bouquets

gaze de fantaisie

gilet

gilet-veste

gipciere

gipser

girdle à la victime

gland

gloan

glouton

god

godell

gorge à la Gabrielle d'Estrees

gorge de pigeon

gougandine

gouriz

gousset

gouzougenn

gown à la turque

gown à l'insurgente

grand habit de cour

grande pelisse d'hiver

grande robe à corps ouvert

grege

gregues

grillé

grisaille

gros drap

gros vilain vert

grosgrain

guêtre

guingan

guipure arabe

guirlande

guiterre

gwel

gwiska

gwiskamant

gypciere

habiller

habit de demi-gala

habit degage

habit d'escalier

habit noir

habits

haincelin

harris

hat à la reine

haubergeon

haubert à maille double

haubert clavey de double maille

haubert doublier

haut de forme

haute couture

havane

herigaute

hermine

heron

heume

heuz

Hombourg

hongreline

horloger

houppe

houppelande à mi-jambe

housse

huke

huque

indienne

Jan de Bry coat

jaquette

jaquette coloriée

jardiniere

jarretelle

jarretiere

jaune

joaillerie

joaillier

jonc

joyau

jupe

jupen

jupon

juste au cou

kalabousenn

karabousenn

kemener

kornek

kotoñs

krez

laine

lapin

lavende

lavreg
léopard
ler
lièn
ligne empire
Lille à fond clair
lin
linge
linon
lionceau
loer
longotte
lostenn
loup
loutre
loutre de Sibérie
luciole
maheutres
mahoîtres
mailles carées
makhila
manche
manche à gigot
manchette de cour
maneg
manege averte
manteau
mantelet au lever de l'aurore
mantell
mariage
marinière
marmotte
marseilles
Marseilles embroidery
martre
martre zibeline
matelassé
Mazarin hood
Medici lace
mezail
mezer
minijupe
mirliton
mitaine
moisson
monté la haute
mouche
mouched
mouchoir
mouchouer
mousquetaire
mousseline
mousseline de laine
mousseline de soie
nadoz

navette
neud
noeuds
noeuds d'amour
noir
nozelenn
nutria
ocelot
ocre
olivâtre
ombrelle
opossum
oreilles de chien
organdi
oriellettes
orris
ourlet-bord
pactole
paillasson
paille
paille de riz
paille d'italie
paillette
paletot
paletot-sac
panache
panache blanc
panache de coque
panseronpanses
pantalon
pantalon de travial
panthère
pantouflenn
parapluie
parasol à canne
pardessus redingote
parfait-contentement
parure
passe-filon
passementier
passementier-boutonnier
passements
peau d'agneau
peau d'ange
peau de cygne
peau de daim
peau de soie
peigné
peigne Josephine
peignoir
peinture à l'aiguille
pelerine
pelicon
peluche
peluche a poils

peluche de soie
pennbazh
perches
perruque quarrée
petals Marguerite
pet-en-l'air
petit bord
petit point
petit velours
petite robe unie
petit-gris
petits bonhommes
peupliere
phoque
pierrot
pince
piquet
piquets
pizane
pliage
pliage en pointe
pliage en triangle
plissé
plume
plume d'autruche
plume de coq
plume de faisan
plumes fantaisies
poche
poches
pochette
poignée
poil de castor
poile de chevre
point à la vierge
point à l'aiguille
point à reseau
point Colbert
point coupé
point d'Alençon
point d'Angleterre lace
point de Bayeaux
point de cordonnet
point de croix
point de feston
point de France
point de Hongroie
point de raccroc
point de rose
point de sedan
point de tige
point de toile
point d'Espagne
point noué
point passé

point plat
point Turc
poire
poitrel
poitrine
polonaise a deux fins
pomme d'ambre
pomme de pin
pomme de senteur
pompadour duchesse
pompadour heel
pompadour pardessus
Poney
portemonnaie
pou-de-soie
poufs au sentiment
poulaines
poult de soir
poult-de-soie
pourpre
poussière de Paris
poussin lace
prêt-à-porter
prune de Monsieur
putois
quintise
ras
ras de Sicile
rat musqué
ratine
raton laveur
redingote
redingote à l'amazone
redingote en Backmann
relevés à la Marie Stuart
rempli
renard
renforceé
rep bluet
reseau
réseau rosacé
resille
rhodophane
rivière
roanes
robe à la circassienne
robe à la française
robe à la Joconde
robe à la levantine
robe à la Reine
robe à la Turque
robe à l'américaine
robe à l'anglais
robe à plis gironnés
robe de cérémonie à la française

robe de chambre
robe de commune at ancienne guise
robe de noce
robe de nuit
robe de style
robe déguisée
robe du soir
robe gironnée
robe longue
robe parée
robe princesse
robe torque
robes de fantaisie
robes en calecon
rochet
roquet
Rose de parnasse
rosette
rosille de soie
rotonde
rouge
rouleaux
roussâtre
ruban
ruban d'amour
ruché
sablé
sabretache
sack gown
salopette
sandale
sandals à la greque
sans-culottes
santon
satin
satin chinois
satin liberty
satin velouté
sautoir
savate
scarabee
seersucker
seiz
serge
sergia
serpentaux
serre-tête
singe
soie
soieries bizarres
solette
sommiere
sorti
sortie
soulette

soulier
souris éffrayée
soutane
spilenn
sugar-loaf bonnet
suppléants
surpied
surplis
tablier
taffeta lustré
taffetas
tailleur
tapisserie
tapisserie de broderie
tapisserie de petit point
taupe
tavancher
terre de Pologne
terre d'Egypte
testière
tête de mouton
tiretaine
tissu
tissu satiné
tissutier-rubanier
toile
toile à gros poil
toile cirée
toile de lin
toile de religieuse
toile grossière
toile peinte
toise mouvante
tok
toque à la Basile
toque à la Grande Pretesse
toque à la Susanne
toque à l'Iphigénie
toque de fourrure
tour de cheveux
touret de nez
tresse
trimming à la greque
tro-c'houzoug
trollopée
trousseau
trou-trou
trovrec'h
tulle
tunic à la juive
tunic à la mameluck
tunic à la Romaine
tunique
tunique à la Juive
turban bonnet

turban-diademe
velour de coton
velours
velours de coton croisé
velours Grégoire
vergette à la chinoise
vert
veste
vêtement à la Créole

vétements
vigogne
visagière
visité
vison
voile
voile de laine
volcan
zibeline

GERMANY

Affe
Affenpeltz
Ajorstick
almain coat
Alpaka
Armband
Ärmel
Ärmelaufschlag
Armspange
Astrakan
Atlas
Aufschlag
Augsburg checks
Ausstattung
Azetat
Balz
Banddurchzug
Bär
Barchent
Barett
barthaube
Batist
Battist
Baumwolle
Baumwollsamt
Belliz
Beringt
Berlins
Biber
Biberhaar
biedermeier
Bisamratte
bishop's mantle
blau
Blumenkränzchen
Blusig
Boi
Borte
Bouc
Boug
boumwolle
braun

Breitschwantz
Brokat
Bruch
Brunswick
Brunswick cloth
Bruoch
Brustharnisch
bruststück
bunte Sportjacke
buntes Kopftuch
Cavalry
Cerevis
Cheviot
chevron de laine
Chinaseide
Chinaziege
Chinchilla
Chorhemd
chorrock
circas
Covercoat
Dachs
Damast
Damhirschfell
Danakillisches Böcklein
dilge
Drapé
dreieckige Faltung
Dreispitz
Dresden point lace
dunkelblau
Edelmarder
Eichhörnchen
Eisenkappe
Fadam
Faden
Falbel
Fane
Fasanerfeder
Fausthandschuh
Faustling
Feder

Feh
Fettschwanzschaf
Feuerwiesel
Filz
Filzglocke
Filztuch
Flachs
Flahs
Fleckenskunk
Flehtan
flieder
Flitter
Florentinerhut
Fries
Fuchs
Fuchsie
Futter
Fütterung
gansbauch
Gaze
geknauften kogeln
gelb
Geschützlafette
gestaltrock
Gimma
gimme
Gingang
giwāti
glocken
Gollier
Grain
grau
grober Wollstoff
grobes Wollzeug
Guanako
gugel
Gürtel
Gurtil
Haarnadel
Hachul
Hahnenfeder
Halsband
Halsbinde
Halsbouc
Halsboug
Halsgolt
halshemd
Halstuch
Handschuh
Hantschuoch
Hantscuoh
Har
harris tweed
Hasenhaar
haube

heerpauke
hellviolet
Hemd
Hemde
Hemidi
Hentzen
Hermelin
Heroldsrock
Herrenhut
heuke
himmelblau
Hosa
Hosen
Hosenrock
hūba
hulle
Huot
Hut
Hutband
Hutfutter
Hutkopf
inderlins
Indigoblau
Juchten
Jugendstil satin
Juwel
Kambrik
Kamelhaar
Kamfhandschuhe
Kanin
kanonenstiefel
Kapuze
Kardiert
karmesin
karminrot
Kaschmir
kastanienbraun
Kattūn
kittel
Klapphut
kleiden
kleider
Kleiderrock
kleidunge
kleinōt
kleit
klöppel
Knickebockers
Kniehosen
Kniestrümpfe
Knopf
Knopfloch
Knopflochblume
kohlschwartz
Kokarde

Kolinsky

Kopftuch

Korsett

Krage

Kragen

Kräuseln

Kravatte

Krawatte

Krempe

Krepp

Kreuzstich

Krinoline

Kürass

Kurze hose

Lachen

Laibli

Lamm

Lange hose

lapa

Lapin

Lätzchen

Leder

ledersen

Leibchen

leibi

Lein

Leinen

Leinwand

lendener

Leopard

Lintrock

Litze

Lochstickerei

Luchs

malvenfarbig

Mantal

Mantel

Marabu

Marder

Matrosenanzug

Maulwurf

Mauwiesel

melone

Menni

Messgewand

Messrock

Minirock

Moiréseide

Mönchskappe

Mongolia

Murmeltier

mütze

Nachtgewand

Nachthemd

Nadel

nãdela

nãdele

Nadelspitze

Nerz

Nestel

Nestila

Netzstickerei

nussbraun

Ohrring

olivenfarbig

Opossum

orangegelb

Organdin

organza

osnaburg

Overall

Ozelot

Panther

Pantoffel

Panzer

parricides

pechschwartz

Pelliz

Pelz

Persianer

Petit-gris

pickelhaube

Pikee

Platner

plissiert

pluderhose

Prinzesskleid

Puffärmel

puffjacke

Pullover

Pulswärmer

Pumphose

purpurfarben

purpurrot

reitrocke

rennrocklein

riese

ritterhute

Roc

Rock

Rohseide

Ross

rot

Rüschen

Rüstung

Samt

Samt gerippt

Sandale

Satin

Saum

Schafpelz
Schaller
schappel
schecke
scheckenrock
Scheitelstuck
Schiffchenspitze
schir
Schirm
Schlafanzug
Schlafenzug
Schlapp Hut
Schleier
Schleife
Schlips
Schneider
Schnupftuch
Schnurrstich
Schornsteinkappe
Schottenröckchen
Schottenstoff
Schrōœre
Schuh
Schuoch
Schürtze
Schürze
Schurze
Schutzhelm
schwartz
scrōtari
Scuoh
Seehund
Seide
sendelbinde
serih
sīda
Sīde
siglat
silecho
silesia
Sleier
Sloier
smaragdfarben
smaragdgrün
Socke
Sonnenschirm
sorket
Spazierstock
spenel
Spinula
Spitze
staubfarbig
Stecknadel
stecknōlde
Steinmarder

Steppnaht
Stickereiapplikation
Stiefel
Stiefelette
Stielstich
Stiful
Stival
stof
Stoffhut
Strampelhose
Straussfeder
Strohhut
Strumpf
Strumpfhalter
Strumpfhosen
Taft
tappert
Tasche
Taschentuch
Tibetisches Lamm
Träger
trappers
trapphant
Traue
Trauring
Tresse
Trikot
Troddelchen
Tropenhelm
Tuch
tunika
Tuoch
Tuoh
Überschuh
Unterrock
Vadem
Vatermörder
Venediger Spitze
Vermummung
Vielfraß
vierspitzige Faltung
Vigogne
Vilz
Vlahs
Wachstuch
wammes
Wams
wappenrock
Waschbär
wāt
wāten
Weicher Hut
Weisstickerei
Wendelring
werien

Weste
Windhaube
woeten
Wolla
Wolle

Ziertaschentuch
Zobel
Zopfzeit
Zwickel
Zylinder

GHANA

adaabo
adinkra cloth
adjagba beads
akambo
akwaba doll
asinan
atataakoro
awondwa
batakari
birisi
birisii
cifatten
fufuo

fugu
fututam
fuubu
hyire
kente cloth
kobene
kobene cloth
kokoo
kuntunkuni
kwasida adinkera
nsaduaso
okana
tuutum

GREECE

adzalotí
ajári
ákna
aladzás
alaménes
álises
amalia
anterí
arápis
arfanítica
asimojórdano
áspri
asprocéndi
bála
barbúli
baréza
béla
béledzik
bersáña
betúnici
béza
bezelitsa
bibíla
bibizári
bidémña
birbíla
bolia
brezekouki
brezikúci

brissimi
brumánika
bubúces
búles
bulla
búloma
bústos
buzáña
caissia
capash
carabitina
causia
ceryphalos
cestus
chiton
chlaine
chlamus
chlamydon
chlamys
chloene
coccum
cordoni
cothurnes
Crete lace
diphtera
diplax
diploidion
djéli
doric chiton

dríli
dulamás
dulápi
dulbén
dzákos
exomia
exomide
facóli
fandaráca
faxiolion
félpa
filati
fitili
flokati
flóra
fóci
foundi
frúta
fterotó
fukás
fúndes
fúndi
fúndítses
fústa
fustanéles
fustanella
fúta
gólfi
griza
gurgurlya
guzjók
himation
ibrisimidzís
Ionic chiton
itsembéri
jeléci
jíros
jordáni
jortiní fortescá
júrda
kabrí
káçes
kadémi
kakorízika
kalathaki
kalíca
kalikia
kalimáfkia
kalómala
kalpáki
kaltsá
kaltsoskúti
kaltsovelónes
kambánes

kamizóla
kápa
kapitsáli
kaplamás
karfitsa
kasináci
katasárci
kátça
katifés
kato manikia
kaváði
kazázis
klídja
klimatáca
klistó jiléci
klonári
kna
kólan
kolaristó
kolobium
kolobus
kolonáto
kolpos
kombologion
kondó
kopseró
kósula
kremezi
krósça
krupáca
kselitsi
ksoulia
kyne
lacerna
lamouxa
lazouri
lazúrja
linon
logia
lustríña
maístra
mandiléño
mandili
manicísco
manikéttia
mesofori
messaria
méstia
misofori
monétra
náplitsi
nificí forescá
nimbus
olojémiti

páfti
paison
panaúla
Panovraki
papanaky
pasoúmia
patatúka
patúnes
peplos
peplos chiton
perizoma
petasos
petassos
petasus
petroméni
pharos
phrygian bonnet
pilos
piryiellya
pistres
pliakthi
podhiá
pójas
porfira
pósta
pothia
poukamiso
pounghí
poustomániko
poutouri
pristídha
próstena
ráli
rizá
rizarato
rutí
saccus
sajás
sakkos
sandalium
sayiaki
scamato
scépa
seïméniko
sigouni

sigúni
siniki
skúña
soccus
soco
socq
sphendome
stephane
stephanie
stithópano
strophion
strophium
súfres
syrma
taenia
Taxíria
tebenna
tellex
theke
tholia
trahilia
tribon
tsangiá
tsaxínia
tselévo
tsemberi
tsípes
tsitseróña
tsupári
tsupráci
tsurápe
tzakos
vachóris
velonísça
vézane
vitses
vraka
vulotó
yiordani
yunatárja
záyres
zona
zoni
zoster

GREENLAND

amant

bearskin pants

GUATEMALA

algodón
alpargata

anaku
ascanta

aswashka
atole
awana
azul
balones
banco
baño reservado
batz
bayeta
blanco
blusa
caite
calum labrada
calzón
camisa
camiseta
capisayo
capixaij
capixay
capote
cardador
chachal
chaquira
chuku
chumbi
ch'úspa
codiarte
colorado
corte
cot
cuenta
cumbe
cumbe camentera
cuyuscate
desborrador
envuelto
espuelas
espuma
fachalina
faja
gabán
gavacha
guashmi
hilador
hilar
huipil
huso
ixcaco
jaspé
jaspeado
jiquilite
kálluwa
kapishay
killu
kushma

lana
lanzadera
lejfa
llautu
lustrina
luto huipil
mama chumbi
manilla
manta
maxtli
medias
merino
millma sumbru
morado
morga
ñañaca
ñañaka
nima-pot
palito
pana
paño
pantalones rajados
pasamanos
perla
perraje
perreje o tapado
piedra de añil
ponchito
poncho tiñiska
poncho tintoridao
pot
puka
randa
raxete
rebozo
redil
refajo envuelto
refajos
refajos plegados
rodillera
ruwana
sábana
sandalias
sarta
seda
seda floja
sedalina
shimba
sobre pantalón
sobrepantalón rajado
sortixa
soyacal
suyacal
taffetán
taffetane

tapiz
tejedor
tejer
tejido
telar de otale
teñir
terciopelo
tinaku azul
tiñiska
tinte
tintoriado
tinturar
tinturero

tocoyales
turno
tzut
tzute
tzutes
urdimbre
vindi
walka
wara
wawa chumbi
yakulla
zuyacal

HAUSA

alkilla
da-n-katanga
fessagida
godo

zelluuami
zenne
zenne alffowa

HEBREW

arba kanphoth
kittel
kraspeda
oya
peoth

sarbal
tallith
tallith katan
tephillin
tsithsith

HOLLAND

acetaat
agaat
akertjes
albe
amethist
armband
azuren
azuur
babysokje
badstof
bakkebaarden
balein
band
baret
barras
batist
bead lace
bedelarmband
bedrukt katoen
bedrukte katoenen stof
beenwindsel
beuk

beurs
blauw
blauwe duffel
boershabijt
bokshandschoen
bont
borduurwol
borst
borstplaat
borstrok
bortspeld
bouwen
bragoenen
bril
broche
broek
broekrok
brokaat
bruin
buis
bukskin
bustehouder

camee
clock-mutch
collier
coltrui
damast
dameslarrje
damesmantel
das
degenkoppel
degenstok
dekmantel
donkerblauw
dop
draad
dreumelthoelje
duikerpak
dunne ochtendjas
Dutch cap
een broek
fardegalijn
fijne
fijne punt
floddermuts
fluweel
foulard
fries
frontje
fustein
gaas
galon
gebauw
gebreid of geweven ondergoed
gebreid vest
gebreide muts
geel
geer
geklede jas
gesteven overhemb
gestreepte of geruite katoenen stof
gitzwart
glazendoek
gordel
goud
goudbruin
gouden
granaat
grijs
grijs blauw
groen
grof weefsel
gymschoentjes
haakwerk
haarspeld
halsboord
halsdoek

halsketting
halslijn
halsneusdoek
halssieraad
halssnoer
handboei
handschoen
hansworst
haren stof
hemd
hemelsblauw
hermelijn
hertevel
hoed
hoedeband
hoepelrok
hofkledij
hoge hoed
hoge laars
hoge toneelschoen
hoge zijden
Holland cloth
hoofdband
hoofddoek
hoofdtooi
houtje-touwtje-jas
huif
ijzergrauw
Italiaans stro
japon
jas
jaspand
jekkertje
juk
juweel
juwelen
kaap
kaasdoek
kaki
kalotje
kamerjas
kant
kap
kapsel
karmijn
karmozijnrood
kasacken
kasjmier
kastanjebruin
katoen
katoenfluweel
kersrood
kiel
kinderbroekje
kinderschort

kleeden
kleederen
kleedermaker
kleeding
kleinood
kletje
klier
klompen
klos
knevel
kniebroek
knijpbril
knipmuts
knol
knoop
knoopsgat
knop
knopehaak
kobaltblauw
kolder
koorhemd
kopplak
korset
kort wollen jasje
korte
korte pruik
kostbaarheden
kostuum
kous
kraag
kroplap
krul
krulletje
kuitbroek
kuras
laars
laken
leder
lelieblank
lichtbruin
lightgroen
lijf
lijfje
lijnwaad
lila
linnen
lint
losse japon
lovertje
manchester
manchetknoop
mantel
mantille
marineblauw
merinos

minirok
mocassin
moesje
molton
monnikskap
monty-coat
mouw
mutsje
naald
naaldhak
nachtjapon
nachttabbaert
namaakbusten
neerstick
nestel
neteldoek
ochtendjas
omslagdoekje
ondergoed
onderriem
onderzieltje
onechte juwelen
ongebleekte Chinese zijde
oogschaduw
oogscherm
opperkleed
oranje
ouderwetse vrouwemuts
overhemb
overschoen
paardestaart
paars
paklinnen
pandjesjas
pantoffel
pantserhandschoen
paraplu
parel
perzikbloesemkleurig
pet
pijjekker
plooi
pofbroek
poffer
popeline
portefraes
pruik
purper
purpuren
regenjas
ribfluweel
rijnsteen
ringetje
ritssluiting
robijn

rok
roklengte
rood
roodbruin
rooskleurig
rozenkrans
ruiterrock
sabeldier
saffier
sandaal
satijn
satinet
schapevel
scharlaken
scheenplaten
schoen
schoenveter
schort
schorteband
Schotse baret
Schotse Hooglanders
Schotse muts
Schotse omslagdoek
schoudermantel
schoudertas
schuifspeldje
shoen
siglatoen
sits
sjaal
sjako
slaapmuts
slabbetje
slobkousen
sluier
smaragd
snor
sok
sokophouder
soort bergkristal
soort rijbroek
sortie
spang
speld
sportcolbert
sportjasje
sportpantalon
steutelreecx
stevige schoen
stijf linnen
stippels
stola
strandschoenen
strokleurig
superplie

tabbaard
tabbaert
tabberd
tabijn
tafzijde
tas van de Hooglanders
tochtlatten
toer
toneelkijker
toog
tropenhelm
trouwring
tuichje
tuithoed
tulband
tule
tunica
tuniek
uilebril
vilt
visscherspij
vlas
vlieger
voering
voorschoot
wambuis
wandelcostuum
wandelstok
want
wapenrusting
wasdoek
wentke
werkbroek of overall van stevig katoen
werkpak
wijde kniebroek
wit
witte
wol
wollen goederen
wollen mousseline
wollen stof
zak
zakdoek
zakkengoed
zakkenlinnen
zalmkleurig
zeemleer
zegelring
zelfkant
zijde
zijden japon of toga
zoeaaf
zonder schouderbandjes
zonnebril
zonnebruin

zonnenscherm
zwanedons
zwart

zwarte
zwempak

HUNGARY

aba-posztó
aratóbocskor
attila
azur
bagazia
bekecs
bikla
bocskor
bögatya
bogazie
bujka
bunda
cepök
chepeneag
cifraszür
condra
csepesz
csispkèsköttö
cuha
daku
darázsolás
daróc
derekas ing
dulándle
epingeaua
félkabát
füdzö
gallér-szür
gatya
gatyamadzag
guba
guna
gunia
gunoberonicia
gyolcs
gyolocsfersling
gyöngyös bokréta
haiduk
haraszt
harisnya
hondorgo
Hungarian embroidery
imurluc
ipingea
ipingeaua
karazsia
keményszárú csizma
kepen'
kepenek

kodmen
ködmön
kopeniak
köpönyeg
koteny
kötö
kozsók
kurti
kusljak
laggosszaru csizma
lajbi
mejrevalo
mellrevaló
musui
muszuj
nyakas szür
pamutos vaszón
pántlikaskökö
párta
pendely
priccses nadrág
puhaszárú csizma
rékli
rokk
sakma
saru
shajak
siguni
skrlet
suba
sukno
surc
süveg
szük gatya
szür
szür-kabát
szürke
tshapan
tshoga
tuszo
váll
vastagkabát
virágozás
xhurdine
xhyrdin
zeke
zsáknadrág
zywr

IBIBIO

okuru

IBO

asisa

egeni bitte

okara

onuga

ICELAND

hringofinn serkr

hufá

hupé

Iceland wool

skinnsaum

INDIA

aaca

aal

aar

'abā

ábbasi

abe

ab-i-hawa

ab-i-rawan

Abocchnai

abrasam

achchhadanaka

achkan

ackhan

adai

adana

adati

addhacina

adhivasa

adhivikartana

adhotari

adhranga

afshan

agala

agihila

agun-pat sari

ahaddha

ahata tantrika

ahinvala

ajarakh

ajina

ajina yajnopavita

akalpa

akathorasbhagarvakomala

akhi laj

aksun

al

alaballee

alaka

ālamgīrī

ālamjarī

Alampasand

alankara

albagcā

albangala

alcah

alchah

alfi

alkhalak

alkhaliq

alleja

alliballi

allieballie

ambara

ambari

ambohai

ammana

amsuka

amsu-patta

amsuyam

amuva

anahata

anga

angada

angarkha

angarkhi

angavastra

angi

angia

angrakhâs

angulia

anguliya

anguliyaka

anguri
angūthī
anhaho
antaravasaka
antariya
apavartaka
aprapadina
arak-chin
araluck
ardhaguchchha
ardhamanavaka
ardhi laj
ardhoruka
arghwani
arhi
ari
arokah
arsi
ashasana
asli
asmani
asparsanumeya
astar
ata
atka
ati
atlas
atlas khasu
atlas silk
atshi
aupakaksiki
aupakasaki
aurna
ava cotton
avaghataka
avagraha
avagunthana
avasakthika
avika
badami
badan
badara
badhani
badiyān
badshah pasand
bafta
bagalbandi
bagh
bahirivasani
bahu
bairam
bairami
baizi
baju
baka

bakhrama
balaba
bālābandī
bali
baluchar
bana
banafsai
banat
band-gale-kā-coat
bandhana-krtsna
bandhani
bandhej
bandi
bāndiā angarkhā
bandvai gujarati
Bangalore cap
bangle
banyan
barani
barasi
bard
bari
barjura
barros miudas
bashlyk
bāzūband
bearams
beatelle
beattillia
bebedi
beiramee
bengal
bengal stripes
beram
beronis
betteela
beur
bhaga
bhagawān
bhagela
bhairnavasani
Bhayyā-cap
bhrameraka
bihari
bili javali
bina
bindi
birinji
bokani
bolgar
boloya
bordāra pyjamā
borgal
boteh
Buddun khas

bukhani
bulbulchasm
bulgar
bulgara cira
bulger
bulghar
bullgarry
bundi
buta
buti
butti
byatilha
byramee
byrampaut
byrams
byramy
cādar
cakresvari
calanaka
calani
calanika
calavia
camacaa
camall
cambaia
cambali
cambay
cambaye
cambja
cambolim
camlee
cammaka
cammakara
cammocca
camoca
camocato
candakanta
candanhār
candataka
candramā
carana
carmakt
catto
catula
caubagalā
cchipas
cela
chadidāra sādi
chaila
chakva chir
chakvidar
chalana
chalanika
chamelia
champai

chana-chani
chanbagala
chandarvo
chandataka
chandlo
chandtara
chaniyo
channavira
chapkan
chappals
charan dharan
charanalankara
charka
charkha
chatta
chattra
chāubwalī jootī
chaugoshia
chauri
chela
cherryderry
chhint
chicken
chickenwalla
chicon
chikan
chillo
chimphullani
china cola
china patta
chinacholaka
chite
chitika
chitragupita
choga
choggā
cholaka
cholana
choli
chope
chorni
chuda
chudamani
chuddah
chuddar
chudder
chuga
chugha
chunadi
chunari
chundadi
chunnat
chupkun
churna-kuntala
churridah

chutki
cihrai
cillāwālī
cina
cinamsuka
cini
cīra
citra-kapardaka
citravastra
cittalam
coda
cogā
cokar
cola
colaka
coli
comboy
comley
coramo
coranā
corano
corso
cossas
cowbandi
cudamani
cūdīdār
culgah
culgee
cumbly
cumly
cummul
cundad
cunnī
cuppalium
cutar
dacca muslin
dadhikali
dadiyā
daglā
danda
dandaprakara
daniyu
darpana
darzi
dasa
dastar
dastar boongga
dastar khana
dauni
dehri
deogir
deriband
derries
desero
desvadusya

devadusa
devagiru
devanga
devanga-cira
dhablo
dhammilia
dhanak
dhanush
dhardi
dharmasastra
dhautakanseya
dhautapatta
dhautavata
dhile paenche
dhota-patta
dhotar
dhotara
dhotee
dhoti
dhumani
dhumarai
dibahae cin
didjee
dilbahar
dimity
dindilliam
dirge
dirzee
divyasudha
docrease
dooputty
dopairi
dopatta
dorea
dori
doria
doriya
doshala
doshāllā
dosooty
do-suta
do-suti
doti
drapi
dudhai kanjai
dudhia khaki
dukula
dukulottariya
dunniattham
dupattā
dusa
dusya
dvipadi
ekavali
ekaveni

elatch
elatcha
fakhtai
farajiyyat
fargal
fargī
farrukhshāh
ferozai
firozi
gabā
gacchakā-kī-turrī
gach
gadar
gaghra
gahra gulabi
gajajin
gajavadi
gajipali
gamcha
gandhaki
gangasagara
gangetic
garbbhasutra
garchola
garha
gātrikāgranthi
gaunaka
genthulla
geru
ghaggharo
ghaghara
ghagra
ghagri
gharacholoo
gharara
ghararas
gharcholu
ghughi
ghunghut
ghungru
ghutanna
gilaharā
gindhuam
gomeda lugadu
gorocana
goshpech
gota
govillam
graiveyaka
guchccha
gudia
guinea cloth
guj
gulbadan
gulbi

gul-e-anar
gule-baqli
gulenar
gul-i-sarrai
gulpumbah
gunji
gurnakuntala
guzzy
habassie
haldi
hamsa
hamsa mithuna
hamsa-chihna-dukula-vana
hamsakah
hans
har
hara
harasekhara
haravsti
harayasti
haryani
hastāvali
hasti
hatakape
hathisondaka
heer
hema-netrapata
hemasutra
hemavaikaksha
himru
hiranya
hiranyan atkan
hiranya-sraj
hirivastra
honkar-ki-kalangi
ihenga
ijara
ijarbund
indhoni
India muslin
India shawl
India silk
indrachchhanda
izar
izār baftā
izaree
jadara
jahanaroho
jalaka
jalika
jāmā
jāmā chakmān
jāmāah
jamawar
jamdani

jamewar
jamiwar
janghia
jarajari
jarbā
jari
jastai
jata-bhara
jata-mukuta
jhaggā
jhalar
jhamaratali
jhanbartali
jhangias
jhulwa
jhuna
jhuni
jigari
jigha
jimi
jimiki
jirnavastra
jootī
jors
joshan
jullaha
jungle khassa
kaacha
kaachadi
kabā
kabaa
kabari bandha
kācali
kācavo
kach
kachcha
kaci
kaciyau pitha
kadā
kadali-garbha
kadigi
kadillam
kafuri
kageyapatte
kahi
kaisika
kaj kulah
kājaliyā
kaksha
kakshyabandha
kalabaku
kalabattu
kalabattun
kalakamsuka
kalam

kalandari
kala-pat sari
kalasakha
kalavadi
kalavuka
kalidar pyjama
kalpush
kamakha
kamalaharitacchaya
kamalaveli
kamandha
kamarband
kambal
kambala
kambalaghana
kāmdānī
kameez
kamiz
kamkha
kamkhab
kamkho
kamkhwab
kamrukhi
kamzar
kanakakamalaihkarna
kanakakirita
kanakaneyura
kancala
kanca-pat sari
kanchali
kanchanakumkumakambalanam
kanchi
kanchli
kanchuka
kanchulika
kancis
kancuka
kancuyao
kangan
kangha
kanjai
kankan
kanseya
kantha
kanthamala
kanthī
kantopa
kapaladharina
kaparda
kapasi
kapdu
kapuraveli
kapurnur
kara
karayari

kardhani
karigar
karnabharana
karnabhusana
karnapura
karnavalaya
karnika
karnotkilaka
karnphul
karpasa
karpata
karppura-tilaka
kasaya
kaseyyaka
kasiam
kasida
kasni
kasturia
kasturiya
kasumbi
kasumbo
kasuti
katab
kataka
katana jhuna
katikinari
katisutra
katitra
kattan
kaupin
kauseya
kauseyaka
kaushambha
kausheya
kausumbha
kawakī
kayabandh
kediyun
keorai
keriya
kes
kesapasa
kesariya
kesg'han
keshghan
ketesal
kettysol
keyura
khaddar
khadi
khadi lehnga
khajalia
khapusa
kharma
kharwa

khasata
khatwa
khazz
kheenkaub
khemkaub
khila
khilat
khinkhwab
khirkidar
khirki-dar-pagri
khirodaka
khopa
khuri
khusulka
kila
kimkhab
kimkhwab
kināri
kincob
kingcob
kinham
kinkhab
kinkini
kippe-sole
kirita
kirita-mukuta
Kirmees
kirpas
kitsol
kittasol
kittasole
kittesaw
kittisal
kittsol
kittysol
kittysoll
kitysol
kochi
koksya
komānam
konam
kopin
kosa
kotai
koyava
krimija
kripani
Kshauna
kshouma
ksirodaka
kudtā
kulah
kulahā
kulahī
kulgie

kumbi
kumkuma
kunba
kundala
kundalas
kuppasam
kurira
kurpasaka
kurpasika
kurta
kurta pyjama
kurti
kusabhia
kusti
kusulaka
kutapa
kutchi bharat
kuttan
kuvala
kuvinda
labaada
labādā
ladva
lah
lahariyo
lahasyo
lahra patora
laj kadvu
laj karvu
laka
lal
lalatantuja
lalatika
langar
langooty
langoti
languti
lauhitaka
leheria
lehnga
lhani
long-drawers
lovadi
lugadoo
lungi
macchavalaka
maddavina
madras
madvia
mahadhana
mahimudisahi
mahmudi
mahyu-salu
majithi
makabala

makarika
makhi
mālā
mālāband
malai
malamala sahi
malausiu
malir
malle-molle
malmal
malya
mamoodie
manasasa
manavaka
manchira
mandā paradiyā
mandalia
mandel
mandil
mangamelai
mangulsutra
mani
mani nupura
mani-karnika
mani-kundala
maninupura
manivalaya
manjira
marakatajadara
mashi
mashru sha'ri
masla
mauktika alankara
mauli
mauli bandha
mauli mani
mayau
mayūrakanthiā
meghadambara
megha-udumbara
mekhala
mirchal
mirjāi
mirya
misaru
misri
misru
mochi
mocota
mojdī
molochine
monache
mooree
moorie
morchal

mosolin
mothadā
moti
motia
moticuri tamaru
motiya
mousceline
mubaf
muddi
mudrika
muduveya javali
muga
muibaf
mukhta
muktajala
muktavali
muktika-hara
mukut
mukuta
mulmul
mulmul khas
mulmull
mumavadi
mundasa
mundash
mundāsi
muraja
murassa-jadau
murchal
murkī
mushajjar
mushru
musqin
mussolen
mussolo
nada
naemet
nagarā
nainsook
nainsukh
naka
naksatramala
nakshi kantha
namda
nam-king
narangi
narmma-haripha
nasta
nastalik
nath
nati
natiyo
netra
neura
nibi

nicola
nicula
nihsvasaharya
nīlāmbarī
nilaniradanicola
nilapatora
nilavata
nillae
niluhura
nimā
nimtanah
nirangi
nirmokinam
nirnejaka
nirya
nisara
nishka
niska
nitambavastra
nivasana
nivi
nivi bandha
nukkadar
nula
numbda
numda
nummud
numna
numud
nunda
nupura
nūr-ī-bādlā
nurki
nut
opasa
orhna
ormesine
otu
paaneter
pachedī
pada
pada-bandhati
padamsuka
padapatra
padigunthima
padiniansanam
paduka
padukakrt
padura
paencha
pāg
pagarakhā
pagari
pagdī
paghadi

pagote

pāgrā

pagri

pag-sankla

paheran

pahuñchi

paiafzar

paimak

pairan

pajani

paklari

palang posh

palempore

palla

pallav

palpulana

pancauna

pancavarnapadi

pance

pañchaphalaka

pandva

pane

paneter

pantadoe

paran

paravalia

pardo

parevau pata

parihasta

parikara

parivesa

parkala

parmnaram

parniyan

paryanka

paryastika

pāsābandhi kediyū

pasuāj

pasvāj

pat gat

pata

pataccara

patalani

pataniya sacopa

pata-pallavah

patka

patola

patolaka

patolla

patolo

patorī

patrakarnika

patrona

patrorna

pat-sari

patta

pattabandha

pattadukula

pattahari

pattala

pattamsuka

pattamsuya

patti

pattika

pattu

patzeb

pecā

pejar

pelanu vastu

penang

percaula

percollae

percolle

pesa

pesas

peshgir

peshwas

phada

phāgniā

phalaka

phalaka hara

phalaka valaya

phanatopa

phatoi

phatui

phenta

phentā Mohammadī

pheran

pheta

phetia

pheto

phiren

phubati

phul gulabi

phulam

phulkari

phulphagarno ghaghro

phutā lugā

phutadu

piazi

picaranga pāgadi

picaranga peco

pichodī

piliyā

pīlo

pimpalia

pinasco

pinga

pintado

pintadoe

pinthadoe
piskalaka
pistai
pistak
pitambara cadara
pomaco
pomchā
ponchiyā
popatiya
porkhani
posteen
posten
postin
poti
pottala
pracchadapata
prachchhada
praghata
pramana-krtsna
prapadina
pratidhi
pratigraha
pratinivasana
pravara
pravatra
praveni
prokandaka
puckery
pugaree
puggaree
puggerie
puggree
purdah
puri
puriya
puspapatta
pustin
putalya
qababand
qadar
qatifah-i-purbi
qirmizi
qubā
quitasol
quitta soll
quittesol
radhanagri
rafugar
rafugari
raiglin
raing
rajai
rajaka
rajapatta
rajata

raju
raktambara
raktani
rallaka
rampoor-chuddar
rang
rangi
rankava
rankavapata
rasana
rasimal
ratna
ratnajali
ratnakambala
ratnangulia
ratnapariksha
ratnavali
ratnodgrathi tottariyam
rawā
razai
rendi
rocana
roghan
rong
roundel
rozye
ruchika
rūmāl
rumala
rundell
rupehri
rupya
sabz moongia
sadarā
sadaraa
sadi
sadlo
safa
safed
sagiya guakari
sahuli
saider
sairpaich
sakala
sakallat
saktapar
salampe
salara
salari
salembaree
salempoory
salempora
salempore
salempury
salim shahī

sallo
salmā-sitārā
sālū
salūkā
salura
salwar
salwar-kameez
samaksika
sambhal
samghati
sana
sanasati
sanbaf
sandali
sangati
sanghati
sangi
sania
sani-gani
sanjharavau
sankha
sankhavalaya
sankla
sannaha
santipur cloth
sanubapha
saptaki
sar
saraga
saranala
saree
sari
sarkandai
sarpech
satasutra
satavalika
satin sultan
satlara
satlari
satthaka
satula
saula
sausani
sauvarnapatta
savadi copacchudahu
sebki
seerband
seershaud
sehan
sela
selari
seragu
serai topi
serpeych
serribaf

sethi
sevani
shabnam
shah ajidah
shahab
shahajidah
shamla
sharbati
sherwani
shimla
shirastra
shirastra jala
shireenbaf
shirinbaf
shirvani
shisha
shubnam
shumzil
sic
sica-sicaya
sic-sik
sihrang
sikhamani
sikhandaka
silahati
silai
sindu
sirastrana
sire
siree
sirinbaf
siring
siropāu
sirottarapattika
sirpeach
sirsa kataha
sirsaka
sirshad
sirsobha
sitapuri
sitara
skandakarani
sola topi
sonehri
sonkoli cap
soosey
soosie
sopanaka
sosni
soudagir
sraja
sribapha
sringa
srnkhalika
stanamsuka

stavaraka
stavrak
stupa
sublom
subnom
sucelaka
suchi
suci
sucihastah
sucisona
sucisutra
suclat
suddha-ekavali
suddhaota
sukhumasuttani
śukla dhardīa
suklatin
suklutun
śunthiā
supha-kamkha
surabhi
surah
suravarā
surmai
surpaish
surubuli
survāla
susae
susi
suthila
sutra
sutradharah
sutrahara
suvarna
suvarnapadi
suvasana
suvasas
svasthana
svechchhitika
svetacinamsuka
svityancali
swadeshi
swamy jewelry
tabrizi
tafailah
tafta
taj
tajehbaf
tajvu
takan
takaschiya
takauchiyah
talapaga
talavantika
talee

talepā
talepaga
tali
talika
taluqdari cap
tamra
tanasukha
tangalia
tanjeeb
tanjib
tantra
tantu
tanutra
tanzeb
tarahara
taralapratibandha
tarangaka
tarbuzi
tarpya
tāsile
tassar
tatbandpuri
tawar
telia rumal
terzi
thanapatta
thirmā
tilari
tilavasa
tini
tinsel printing
tiraz band
tirchha
tirita
tirodhana
tittirapattika
toda
topee
topi
topiwala
toran
toruphulli
trikarnas
triphalaka
triveni
trrsa
tulakoti
tulapansi
tulapunnika
tumana
tundikeri
tunnavaya
tupy
turra
turrah

turrā-i-mārwadī
turri
turro
turudam
tus
tutki
udbandha
umavadi
unnabi
unnatasikharavestana
upanah
upanat
uparanī
uparanū
uparivastra
uparna
upasampanna
upasamvyana
upasirsaka
upavasana
upavastra
upavita
urasala
urbāi
urna
urna sutra
urumali
ushnisa
ushnisha
usnìsa
uttarasanga
uttariya
vadhuya
vadkyu
vaga
vagho
vahitha
vahitika
vaijayantika
vaikaksaki
vaikaksha
vajramsuka
vakala
valaya
valkala
vanadana
vanakara

vangala
varabana
varasi
varna-krtsna
varsikasatika
varti
varvana
vasa
vasas
vashti
vastra
vastragrantha
vastrañchala
vati
vaturinapada
vavr
vaya
vedla
vegachiya
veman
veni
vesh
vestana
vesti
vethaka
vettam
vibushana
vicitra
vihita kappasa
vijayachchhanda
vijayantika
viramo
vitha
vyalapanktirmañjari
warak
yantraka
yapanji
yar pariahan
yashti
yasti
zaituni
zamurradi
zardozī
zarī
zarrin
zerbaft

INDONESIA

baju
baju kurung
baju panjang
balusu
basta cloth

batik
blangkon
bunga bau
cermuk
dali dali

disissik
dodo
dodot
double ikat
fuya
gallang
geringsing
grinsing
hijo marstiogutoguan
hingghi
hohos
ikat
irengan
kain
kain panjang
kamben cerik
kandaure
kebaya
kepala
khombu
koffo
kombu
krambuno
kupiah
lau
lemba
lembe
lurik
manik ata
manik barata
manik bura bura
manik kalaa'
manik sekke'
manik tai anda'
manik tinggi
pagi-sore
palepai
patondon
pio borong
plangi
rara

sambu' bongi
saput
sarassang
sarong
sarong billá
sarong kadojo
sarong kaledo
sarong lambing
sarong lombok
sarong pakolong
sassang
selendang
sepu'
singep
sissin kara
slendang
soga
songket
stagen
sulo bannang
surjan
talabo
talede
tali bate'
tali katarrung
tali pakkaridi'
tali tarrung
tampan
tapis
tatibin
tau
tjap
tjindai
tora-tora
tulis
tumpal
tusuk
ulos godang
ulos lobu-lobu
ulos suri-suri
umpal

IRAN

arqalix
bagdad wool
çabat
çargat
chaddar
chitta
çuga
darpe
dastmal
dhoti

ghava-ye zananeh
iç tuman
jiqa
kamarband
kawa
klaw-i jnan
klaw-i pyawan
koynek
kras
kulah

kulah-e kordi
musa
panba
paridhana
peç
pirahan
pirahan-e zananeh
pistent
qulaqça

rank
salteh
sancaq
sowlar
tuman
üst tuman
uttariya
yagliq

IRAQ

dish dasha
farous
hashimi

jarrawiyah
yatshmagh
zaboon

IRELAND

adagan
aerdhaite
agait
aigeallan
aigilean
ailbheag airgid
ailbheag cluais
ailbheagan
àilleag
aincis
āinne
airmchrios
aision
ametist
amhcha
amlag
anart garbh
angadh
aodach solus
aodach tiusail
aparan
aparsaig
aprūn
babag
baban
babhaid
bàin-dearg
bairēad
balbriggan
balg
balgan
balg-bannaig
balg-thional
ball
ball-serice
baltaich

bàn
bandle
bandle linen
bàn-gheal
bann-bhràghad
bann-bhràighe
bann-dùirn leine
bann-muineal
barraighin
basc
bath-throid
bēabhar
beannag
beul-a-theach
bigean
binnogue
biorān
biorraid
boban
boicionn
boideachan
boineid
boineid bhall-ach
boineid biorach
boineid chath-dath
boiseid
boltrachan
bōna
borsa
bòtuinn
bracach
bracaille
bracan
brāislēad
bràist
bràisteachan

braistich
brakan
brannamh
bras-fhalt
bras-ghruag
brat
brat-dhearg
brayes
breaban-deiridh
breaban-toisich
breacán
breac-liath
breadeen
breakan
breathnas
brēid
bréid
bréid geal
bréid-bronn
bréidín
bréid-uchd
brēit
breug-chiabh
briosaid
brīste
brium
brōc
brōg
bròg-bhréid
bròg-chalpach
bròg-fhiodha
brogs
broith
broithdheanta
broiudneireachd
brok
bròn
bronnach
brucag
bruinneadach
buac
buaicean
buatais
buidhe
buidhe-bhan
buidhe-dhonn
buidhe-ruadh
buidhe-shoilleir
buidh-liath
builg
cadadh
cadās
caddow
cadows
caicmhe

caille
cailmhion
cailmleid
caimmse
càin
cainb
cainb-aodach
caipīn
cairtidh
caisbheart
cais-chiabh
caisean-feusaig
caisreag
calbhthas
call
callaid
camag
camalag
canabhas
canach
canaichean
carkanett
carranes
carrickmacross lace
casag
casag-mharcachd
casair
casōg
cas-urladh
ceadach
cealt
cealtar
ceanna-bhrat
ceann-aodach
ceann-bhàrr
ceann-bhàrr eas-buig
ceann-bheart
ceann-éideadh
ceara
ceimhleag
ceimh-mhileach
ceimh-phion
céire
ceòis
ciabhag
ciabh-chasta
ciarsūr
cias
ciasan
cinnteagan
ciolar
ciotag
cirb
clabaran
clach-mhara

clann
cleachd
cleachdag
clearc
cleòc
cleòcan
cliabh
cliabhan-ceangail
clōca
clòimh
cluas-sheud
cnàimh-deud
cnaipe
cnap
cnapan-trusgaidh
cneaball
cneap-tholl
coamery
cobhrach
cochall
cochlach
cochull
coilēar
coileir
coilichin
coire
cōirighim
còmhdach
comh-dhualadh
corcuir
corcur
corcurachd
coron
coron Muire
coron òir
corr-léine
cosar
còta
còta biorach dubh
cóta coirí
còta de chadadh nam ball
còta-ban
còta-bhioran
còta-cathdath
còta-craicinn
còta-fada
còta-gearr
còta-glas
còta-goirid
còta-uisge
cotan
còtan
còt'-iochdair
còt'-uachdair
cotun

crà-gheal
crambaid
crèach
cridhachan
crios
criosan
crios-ceangail
crios-claidheimh
crioslachen
crios-muineil
crios-pheilear
crios-tarsainn
criss
crò snàthaid
cròchach
crochag
crò-dhearg
croiméal
croisgileid
cronnt
crubhas
crubhasg
cruinneacan
crùn
crùn-easbuig
cruth-lachd
cuach-chiabh
cuach-fhalt
cuaran
cubhrag
cuille
cuircinn
culaidh-aodaich
culaidh-bainnse
culan
culpait
cumhais
cùrainn
cùrainn-chneas
currac
curracag
cuth-bhàrr
cuth-bharran
deacaid
dealg
dealg-fhuilt
dealg-gualainn
dearg
deargan
deirge
deise
deise-mharcachd
delg
dīllat
dlùth

donn
donn laugh-na-h-éilde
donn-ghlas
donn-uaine
dornag
dorn-nasq
dosan-banntraich
dreach-bhuidhe
dreas
driubhlach
drògaid
droineach
druin
dual
dualadh
dubhach
dubh-bhuidhe
dubh-ghlas
dubh-ghorm
dugh-ruadh
duibleid
duire
eabonach
ēadach
ēaduighim
earradh
éideadh
eobhrat
ētach
ētim
ētiuth
fail
faileach-an
failtean
fāinne
fàinne-pòsaidh
faitheam
fallaing
falluing
falt-dhealg
fasgadan
feilt
feòil-dhaith te
feòil-dhath
ferenn
feusag-bheòil
fīal
ficheall
filead
finic
fionnadh
flann
flannach
flann-dhearg
fo-bhuidhe

foil
foileid
fola
for-bhrat
fo-ruadh
fuaigheal
fūan
fudag
fuigheag
fuiliche
fuilidh
gairgre
garbh-chulaidh
gartan
geal
geideal
geolan
giall-bhrat
giogan
giosān
glas
glasag-muineil
glib
glinne
glùinean
goirridh
goon lhiabbee
gorm
gorm-aotrom
gòrsaid
grant
gré
gréis
gréiseadaireachd
gréiseadh
gréis-obair
grian-sgàil
grian-sgàilean
grin
groilleach
guirmean
guiseid
gunachan
hata
iall
iallachrann
iar
iar-dhonn
inar
intuiger
ionar
ionaradh
Irish crochet
Irish lace
Irish lawn

Irish linen
Irish poplin
Irish work
kerry cloak
laipeid
lāmann
lāmhain
làmhainn
làmhan
lamhas
lāmind
lāsa
lasdadh
leacadan
lēine
léineag
leíne-aifrionn
léine-bhàn
léine-chaol
léine-chròich
léine-sheacair
léine-thuilinn
léinteag
leis-bheart
leis-bhrat
lēne
lenn
lethar
leth-bhòt
leth-ruadh
leug
liagh-dhealg
liath
liath ghorm
liath-ghuirme
liath-phurpur
līn
linnseach
linnseach thrusaidh
liocadan
līon
lion-cinn
lóipíní
lorg-bheart
loth
lùireach
lùireach leathair
lùireach mhàilleach
luirg-bheairt
lumman
màilleach
màilleag
mairtíní
manag
mantal

maolag
maolas
mattal
meanaigean
meanbh-ghàirdean
miniceag
minicionn
minicionn-laoigh
miotag
mogan
mogan briogais
muince
muinead
muinge
muintorc
mùtan
nasgadh
nèapaicin anhaich
nèapaicin pòca
neas-nam-fuar-thirean
nos
nuamhanair
obair-ghréis
obair-gréise
obair-shnàthaid
odhar
òir-chrios
oir-ghreus
oisionair
olann
ollaodach
òmar
òr-bhann
òrbhuidhe
orchell
or-choilear
ordnasc
ósain
osanachd
paidirean
painntin
pàirt-dhathach
pannus sine grano
peallaid
pealltag
pèarluinn
peiteag
peiteag-mhuinicheallach
phalinges
pilus tinctus
pluinnseag
pòca
prāiscīn
prine
purpaidh

putan
rachdan
riabhach
ribean
rocal
rocket
ròibeag
ròin
ròin-aodach
roinne-bhaidhe
ròinn-léine
roisean
ròsach
ruadh
ruadh-bhuidhe
ruaithne
ruga
russet
saffron shirt
sainre
scuird
seileadach
seircean
seircin
seiric
seod
sēt
sēt argait
seud-ghlasaidh
sgaball
sgaileagan
sgàilean-uisge
sgail-uisge
sgala
sgrog
sgrogaid
sgrogan
sguain
sgùird
sgulair
sgùman
sīoda
sīric
sīta
slapaireachd
slat-rioghail
slipēir
smàrag
smigeadach
smiotag
smugadair
smuig-aodach
smuigeadach
snaim na banaraich
snāth

snāthad
snàthad
snāthat
snàth-clòimhe
snàth-cuir
snāthe
snàth-fuaidhle
snàth-lìn
snàth-righailt
snàth-sioda
sneachd-gheal
soilleir-dhonn
spad-choisbheart
speilp
spiochag
spleuchdan
spliùchan
sraing
sròin-eudach
staighinean
stalcadair
starrs
stiog
stiom
stiomag
stìom-amhaich
stìom-bhràghaid
stoca
stocainn
stocainnis
stoic
streachlan
strilinn
striop
sturraic
sturraicean
stuth
sugar
suggan
tabbinet
tabinet
taifeid
tāilliūr
taist
teud-bhràghad
thicksets
toban
toll-cnaip
tonach
topas
traheen
triubhas
triubhsair
trius
troighthíní

truis-bhràghad
trus
trusgan
trutag
tuil-aodach
tuillinn
uaine
uaine-donn
uaine-dorcha
uainicionn

uchdach
uchd-bheart
uchd-chrios
ula
ulach
ulchadh
usgaraidh
usgar-bhràghad
usgar-mheur
youghal

ISLE OF MAN

carranes
coamery
coif cooil corran
criss
goon lhiabbee

gorrym
keear
Manx plaid
oashyr voynee
oashyr-slobbagh

ISRAEL

benayeq
harir nabati

sawa 'ìd

ITALY

a gomito
a gozzo
abiti
abito da pantalone
agnellino de Persia
agnello
ago
almuzi
alpagas
alpargata
alta moda
anello
anime
appicciolato
applicazione
armadura del busto
armatura
arricciatura
astrakan
azzurro
baccello di piselli
bacchetta
balza
balzana
balzo
banda arricciata
barrettino
baschina

basco
baston con anima
batista
bautta
bavaglio
bavalla
benda
berettino
berretto
berretto alla marinara
bersagliere
berta
biancherie dammaschinate
bianchetto
bianco
bigio
blusa
blusante
boccaccino
bombasino
bombetta
borsa
borsalino
bottoni
braccialetto
bragetto
brandistocchi
bredon

broccato
brochetta
bruno
bruschino
burano lace
cachemire marguerite
calamatta
calza
calzamaglia
calzatura
calzettoni
calzoni
cambraia
camicia
camicia da donna
camicia rossa
camiciuola
cammello
camocho
campanoni d'ori
canavaccio
cannellato
cappello
cappucio
cardato
carmagnole
carminio
casco
casco coloniale
casentino
casimiro
castagnino
castorino
castoro
cavallino
cavalry
chermisi
chermisino
chinchillà
ciarpa de' Scozzesi
cintura
ciondolino
cioppa
cloche di feltro
coazzone
coccarda
cocuzzolo o cupola
codini
colbacco
collana
collare
colletto
collo
colori corozoso
conchiglie ciprее

confezione
coppo
corazza
corno
corpetto
corredo
cors
coru
cosetto
cotone
cotta de maglia
cotta d'ecclesiastico
cravatta
cremesino
crespo
crinolina
cuffia
cuoio
Cyprian gold
damaschino
damasco
dankalia capretto della
divolgatore
dogaline
dorso
drap o drapé
drapo
droghette
elmo di giostra
ermellini
ermellino
faglia
faina
falda o tesa
faldia
falpalà
fasciatrella
fazolo
fazzoletto
feltro
feluca
fermaglio
ferraiuolo
fettuccia
filetto
fili tirati
filo
fimbria
finestrella
fiocco
flabells
Florentine hat
foca
fodera
forcella

fregio
frenello
frontone de berretto
fuine
fuselli
fustian anapes
gabano
gabbano
galero
gallone
gamurra
garanza
garza
gassa
gatto civetta
Genoa lace
Genoa velvet
Genoese embroidery
gherone
ghiottone
ghirlanda
giacca
giacchetto
giall' antique
giallo
giallo antico
gibus
gioielle
gioiello
gonna
gonna pantalone
grana
grano d'orzo
grembiule
grigio
grisaglia
groppo
gros gren
gros point
gros point de Venise
gualescio
guanto
guanto senza dita
guazzerone
harris
impiraperle
impiraressa
indaco
kalgan
kolinsky
lacca
lana
lapin
lavanda
leopard

lince
linea imperio
lino
lista
lontra
lupo
lustrini
lutto
magiostrine
maglia piatta
manica
manica a buffo
maniche á comeo
manople
mantello
Mantua hose
mappelana
marabù
margarite
marinara
marmotta
marsina
martora
mascherata
maspilli
mazzette
medaglio
merletto
merletto-trina chiaacchierino
mescolato
mezzaro
minigonna
mitile
monachino
mongolia
morello
murmel
mussolina
myllion
Naples lace
nappina
nastro
ocelot
ocra
opossum
orecchino
organza
orlo
ornamento de gioielli
orso
padisoy
padou
paduasoy
padusoy
pagliaccetto

paglietta
pagonazzo
palandrano
palo de lione
pampilion
pannicelli
panno
panno e pannino
pantaloni
pantaloni alla zuava
pantaloni corti
pantera
pantofola
paramani
parasole
parrucca
passamontagna
passanastro
pastrano
paternostri
pavonazzo
pellanda
pelliccia
pelo di castora
penna di fagiano
penna di gallo
petit-gris
pettabotta
pettinato
petto
pianelle
pianeta di prete
piccolo punto
piegatura
piegatura a punte
piegatura triangolare
pieghettato
piquet
piuma
piuma di struzzo
pizzo
pizzo ad ago
pizzo ad ago a fuselli
pizzo punto in aria
pizzo rinasciemento
porpora
princesse
principessa
punchetto
punto a feston
punto a giorno
punto a giorno cordonetto
punto a giorno croce
punto a giorno festone
punto a giorno indietro

punto a gropo
punto a maglia quadra
punto erba
punto neve
punto passato
punto tagliato
punto tirato
puzzola
radielfo
raggiera
raso
raso cinese
ratmusqué
restagno d'oro
reta
rete
reticella
reticella lace
ricamo
ricamo in bianco
ricamo in bianco a reticello
ricamo in bianco ad intaglio
ricamo in bianco inglese
ripresa
romagnuolo
rosato
rose point lace
roso
rossetto
rossiccio
saglia
saia
saione
sandalo
sarto
scamiciato
scarlatto
scarpa
scarpe
sciameto
scimmia
scollatura
scozzese
sella
sergia
seta
sfilatura
smezzati moro
soppravvesta
soprabito
sottana
sottogonna
spillo
spillo da petto
stametto

stivale
stivaletto
stivali grossi
stola
stravestito a la todesco
stringhe
svasatura di abito-sbieco
talpa
tasca
tasso
tela
tela cerata
tela de lino
tela grossolana
tela Tagliata
tela tirata
tight
tintillano
tocco
toghe
tombolo
tonaca
tovaglia
traguardo
trapuntato
tremolanti
tricorno
trina
trinzale
tunica
turbante

turchino
tuscan
tuta
vaio
vajo
velette
velluto
velo
Venetian lace
ventoye
vermicelli
veste da camera
veste di camera
vestire
vestiti
vestito da sera
vezzo
vigogna
visiera del berretto
visone
volpe
volpe o renard
zache
zambellotto
zazzara
zendado
zendale
zibellino
zimarra
zoccolo

JAPAN

abarenoshi
agemaki
aizome momen
akane
aka-ume-zome
akome
amageta
ao-iro
aozuri
aratae
Arimatsu shibori
asagi
asanoha
ashida
ashifuki
ashi-maki
ashinaka-zori
atsuita
attush
awase-bodokko

aya
baori
bashōfu
beni
bingata
birodo
bokashi
burausu
chanchanko
chayazome
chijimi
chikara-age
chirimen
chugata
daimon
Danjuro cha
danshichi-goshi
date-eri
date-gera
datemaki

denkuro-zome
detachi
dobuku
dochu-gi
dofuku
dogi
donsu
ebo
eboshi
ebosi
echizen
Edo kanoko
egasuri
ei
ekawa
eri
ezo nisbiki
fugi
fukube-dana
fungomi
furisode
fusa
fusube
fusuma
geta
gheta
gimmoru
ginran
gobaishi
goburan-ori
habaki
habutai
habutaye
hachijo
hadajuban
haidate
haji
hakama
hakata
hakimono
hakoseko
haku-e
han-eri
han-juban
hanao
hancha
hankotana
hanten
haori
happi
hata
hattan
heko-obi
hidarimae
hi-goza

hikeshi hanten
hiogi
hirauchi
hire
hirosode
hitai-ebosi
hitatare
hitoe
hitta-zome
hiyoku
ho
hoju
homongi
hoso-zome
ichi-dome
Ichimatsu
ikan
inaka yuzen
inkin
irege
ishi-zoko
ityogaesi
izaribata
Jap mink
Japanese crepe
jiaki-kanoko
jika-tabi
jimbaori
jinashi
jinashi-nuihaku
jofu
juban
junihitoe
kabuto
kabuto-sita
kachi
kaeshi
kaga-boshi
kaidori
kakeda
kake-eri
kaki-sarasa
kaku obi
kame-nozoki
kamishimo
kammuri
kamozi
kampū
kanden-medare
kanjiki
kanoko
kanoko-zome
kanto
kanzashis
kanzasi

kappa
kappa dachi
kappu
kara-aya
karagumi
kara-mushi
kara-nishiki
karanko geta
kara-nui
karaori
kara-ori
kariginu
kariyasu
kasa
kasuri
kata-eri
kata-hazusi
kata-ori
katabira
katagami
katami-gawari
katasuso
katatsuke
kataza-kanoko
kata-zome
katazome
katsura
katsura-zutsumi
kawa
kazuki
kera-mino
kesa
keshinui
kesho
khaiki
kidara
ki-gomo
ki-hachijo
kimmoru
kimono
kinran
kinsha
kinu
kinumo
kiri-osa
kogai
kogin
kokechi
koketsu
ko-kinran
komon
Komparu
kon
kondosa
kon-gasuri

kooi
Korin-nami
korozen
koshi
koshiate
koshihimo
koshimaki
koshipiri
kosode
kote
ko-watari-tozan
kuri-ume
kuro
kuro montsuki haori
kurochō
kuro-ume-zome
Kurume-gasuri
kusi
kuzufu
kuzununo
kyahan
kyara-abura
Kyo-zome
mae-dare
mae-gami
mae-migoro
magatama
mage
maiwai
mame-shibori
marumage
maru-obi
matsuinui
matsu-nori
megane
meisen
meyui
midori
mimi-kakusi
mino
mitu-ori
mituwa
mo
moegi
mofuku
mokume-shibori
momohiki
momo-ware
mompe
mon
mon-chirimen
monpe
monsha
montsuki
moruori

moto-yui
mugiwara bō
muna-medare
murasaki
mutsuki
naajuban
naga-juban
naga-tenuge
nama ha zome
nanako-kokechi
Nankin nishiki
nawame-irokawa
nerinuku
nezumi-iro
nicho-kinran
nigitae
nihyakusan-koti
niigashi
nishijin
nono-obi
nora-gi
noshime
nugi-sage
nuihaku
nuikiri
nuno
obi
obi makura
obi-age
obiage
obi-dome
obijime
oboro-zome
ogami
ohi
okumi
okura-nishiki
omeshi
omote kon'ya
osode
ozura
pokkuri
ra
rasha
Rikan cha
rinzu
ro
rokechi
roketsu
Roko cha
ro-ten-kechi
ro-zome
Ryūkū-gasuri
sageo
sakayaki

samurai-ebosi
sanjaku-obi
sanmai-gusi
sarasa
sarashi
sarashi nuno
saya
seigo
sen
Sendai Hira silk
sensuji
sha
shibori
shibori-zome
shige-meyui
shigoki-obi
shihan
shike-ito
shima
Shimokyo-zome
shinobugusa
shioze
shiromuku
shitagi
shoaizome
shohakuzan
shokko-nishiki
shozoku
shuchin
shusu
simada
sode
sode-guchi
sode-nashi
so-kanoko
sokuhatu
sokutai
somoyo
sora-iro
suji
sumi
sumitsubo
suo
surihaku
suso
susomoyo
susoyoke
suzushi
tabi
tabie-nishiki
tachi-kake
taihakuzan
taiko obi
taisha
takajo-tabi

takashimada
takenaga
Tamba cloth
tamoto
tanzen
tasuki
tate-nishiki
tattsuke
tayu-kanoko
tekko
tenugui
tenzin-mage
tombodama
toyama
tsubo-ori
tsujigahana
tsumugi
tsuzure-nishiki
tsuzure-ori
tyasen-gami
uchidashi-kanoko
uchikake
uchiwa
ukon
uma-no-tsura
ungen-nishiki

ushiro-migoro
usuaka
usugake
wara
waraji
watabōshi
watashinui
yama-bakama
Yamato nishiki
yoji-nori
yoko-nishiki
yoroi-hitatare
Yoshinaka-zome
yuage
yuhada-kawa
yuishiba-komon
yukata
yukue-humei
yusoku orimono
Yuzen
Yuzen birodo
yuzen makinori
yuzen-zome
zogan
zukin

JAVA

bangbangan
bebed
belongkon
biron
burung hook
cinde kenanga
cinde parang
cinde wilis
dodot
iket
kabaya

kain
kawung
kemben
lokcan
megamendung
mengekudu
pici
sampour
tapih
wadasan

KENYA

bafta
bendera
bombei

kaniki
kikoi

KOREA

anjonp'in
apch'ima
cchok
chach'im'
chaetpit

chagae
chajutbit
chak'et
chambangi
chamot

changgap
changhwa
chang-ot
charak
charuot
chasu
chasujong
chigap
ch'ilbo norigae
ch'ima
chinbunhongui
chingmul
chinhongsaek
chip'angi
chobawi
choggi
chogon
chogori
chokki
choksaek
chokturi
chol
ch'olmo
ch'on
chonbok
chongbok
chongjagwan
ch'ongsaek
ch'oroksaekui
chudan
chungch'imak
chungjolmo
chungsanmo
eip'uron
gomushin
habok
hanbok
handubaek
hangra
hansam
hoesaek
hongsaek
horitti
hukjinju
hwajang
hwajangbok
hwamunsa
hwangsaek
hwap'o
hyanggap norigae
hyangsu
injo chinju
injogyonsa
ioring
jjalbunyangbokbaji

k'aak'isaekui
kabal
k'aenbosu
kajuk hyokdae
kalsaek
kamsaek
kapsa
karakchi
kat
kat-no
kaun
kin koot
kirin
kkokkaot
kkwemaeda
kodongsaek
kodot
kodulch'i
kombukta
komp'uruda
komun
kongdan
koong-soo
korum
k'ossuyom
kubi najûn kudo
kubi nop'ûn kudu
kuduggun
kule
kumbit
kumshigye
k'unmori
kwigoi
kyonjiingmul
kyorhon panji
kyorhon yak'on panji
maekko moja
magoja
mangt'o
melbbang
melppang
min-soo
mobondam
moja
mokdori
mokgori
moktor
morikkoji
moritkirum
mosi
mosulrin
mudang morikkoji
myojushil
myongju
myonsa

naeui

naewang

nailron

najon

namaksin

nambawi

negulrije

nek'och ìpù

nekt'ai

noggui-hongsang

nokmal

noksaek

norat'a

norigae

obang-nangja

oet'u

oggaegori

ojak norigae

okyangmok

orenjibich'ui

ot

otcharak

otgam

otkam

oubosyuuju

paekkum

paenang

p'aench'u

paji

pakjwiu san

p'aljji

p'almok sigye

pang' adari norigae

panghyang

pansomae

pansomae syossu

panujil

panul

p'arang

pidan

po

pojagi

ponit

poratpit

puch'ae

'pujok

puk

pukta

p'ulrannel

pulrausu

punjang

p'uruda

p'urun

pyonbal

randosel

reink'ot'u

reion

ribon

rojario

sa

saekduresu

saenggosa

samjak norigae

samo

sangbok

sejodae

shin

sich'ida

silanebok

sogot

sokch'ima

sokot

som

somae

somaega tchalbun

somot

songabang

songkabang

sonsugon

sudan

sukkosa

suk'oot'u

sul

sulraeksu

sun-gum

suwet'o

syassu

syool

taenggi

t'aesahye

tagalsaek

tan

tanbal

tanch'u

tanch'u kumong

tanhwa

t'okbaji

t'oljanggap

t'olshil

tolsil

t'ol-sil

tongbok

t'orot

tosaek

totnamaksin

totsin

tot'urak taenggi

tti

ttoljam

ttuggong

t'ugu
tuikkoji
turamaggie
turesu
turumagi
twitkkoj
uibok
uiryu
undonghwa
unhye
unmunsa
unpich'ui

unpit
usan
waisyooch'u
wanggwan
wanjang
yangbok paji
yangmal
yangmal taenim
yangsan
yonboratpit
yonmibok

LAOS

chong kra ben
hua
kruang tok
pha ap nam fon
pha beang
phaa
phaa chet paak
phaa sin
prakhotaeo
rom

sabong
sanghhati
siiwaun
sin
su kom
sua hii
sua saband thaut
tdinjok
thung
tiin sin

LAPLAND

finnesko
Lapland bonnet
lukka

peski
prievīte
wadmal

LIBYA

sha 'iriyya

LITHUANIA

ada
adata
apg'erbt
apikaklé
apkakle
apruoce
apsiustas
ápvilkti
au dekls
audeklas
batas
bovelna
brangenybé
brangus akmuo
čebatas
cepure
cimds

dalmonas
dārgums
delmonas
drabužis
drebe
drebes
drebnieks
drobé
gelumbė
g'erbt
gredzens
güldenstick
juosta
juostos
kailiniai
kailis
kakla ruota

kaklaryšis
karbatkos
karieliai
kazuoks
kedelys
kelinės
kepuré
k'eša
kiklikas
kišené
kniepe
knypkis
kojiné
krekls
kuokvilna
kurpé
linai
lindraki
lini
margine
marška
maršliniai
medvilné
mētelis
mila
milas
nometas
nosine
nuometas
pavediens
pirkstaine
pirštiné

plivers
ploščius
priejuosté
prieksauts
prijuosté
puoga
saga
šilkai
simtakvaldis
siūlas
siuvéjas
škidrauts
skrybélé
skūra
slaucis
šliuré
sopagas
spice
švarkas
šydas
šyras
tūba
tupele
vadata
vadmala
vilna
vilnos
zābaks
zeke
zīds
žiedas
ziurstai

MACEDONIA

brok
kiski

resi

MADAGASCAR

akanjo
akanjobe
ankanjo
bafota
bafota malandy
bui-bui
dalahany
deboan
foloara
hariry
helaka
kazaka
kemba
kisaly

kitamby
korsaza
lamb mena
lamba
lamba maitso
lamba soratra
lambahoany
landy
lasoa
malabary
rafia
roafia
rôbo
rofia

sadiaka
salaka
salampy
salovana
sambelatra

sarandrana
seray
siki
tergal
tirkô

MALAYSIA

baju
bidang
kain lepas

kain sampin
kelantan kain songket
tekat menekat

MANCHURIA

sirghe

MEXICO

arracadas
cactli
cadeneta
calzón
calzoncillo
calzoneras
chalchihuitl
chanclas
charmèécolera
contado
cotón
cotorina
coyoichcatl
cueitl
de caracolillo
ehuatl
el costal
enagua
enredo
enredos
fantasia
fuchina
holán
huarache
huepilli
huicó
huipil
huipil grande
huipile con labor

huipilli
ichcahuipilli
ichcatl
ixtle
la bolsa
listonés
malacateras
manga
máquina de gasa
maxtlatl
morrales
nelpiloni
paliacate
pavo real
pie
posahuanco
punto de Espana
quechquemitl
quilitl
refafo
renque
serape
soyate
Spanish needlepoint
tagora
terciopelo
tilmatli
xicolli

MICRONESIA

nikautang

MONGOLIA

del

sirkek

MOROCCO

alberoce
baboutcha
deraa
djellaba
ebbelo
endima
farrajiyah
festoul
firmla
gonbaiz
grun
hendira
hezam
hiyyak
jelab
jellab
jellaba
jellabia
jellib

jeltesta
jelteta
khamar
kheaya el kebira
ktef
kumya
lekmann detsmira
lezim
Moorish lace
qaftan
quich
saiat
sebnia
seroval
serul
shesh
sualef
sualef ez zoher
tijajin d-mahduh

NAMIBIA

eha
etapi

ombari

NAVAJO

'at'a'
bee chaha'ohí
dáábalii
deiji'éé'
dilhil
dootl'izh
'éétsoh 'álts'íígíí
halba
halbá
halchii'
hodootl'izh
jaatl'óól

ke' achogii
kétl 'óól
lájish
lashdóón
látsíní
leetsoii
libá
lichíí
lizhin
ndik'a'
tl' aakal
zéédééldoi

NATAL

isi Diya

umutsha

NEPAL

topi

NETHERLANDS

hul

NEW ZEALAND

aho
aronui
hinarunaru
horu
huruhuru
io
kahu kuri
kahu waero
kaitaka
kaka hu kura
karure
kaupapa
kokowai
korowai
kuru
mai
manaeka
mangaeka
maro
maro huka
maro kaakaapoo
maro kaukau
maro kopua
maro kura
maro kuta
maro waero
maro waiapu
miro
paepaeroa
parakiri
parawai

parengarenga
patu hitau
pauku
pekerere
pohoi
pokeka
pokinikini
pora
poro-toroa
potae taua
puahi
pukaha
pureke
rapaki
ta
taniko
tatara
tatua
tatua-pupara
tauri
timu
topuni
tu kartu
tuaka
tu-hou
tumatukuru
tu-maurea
tu-muka
whakatipu
whatu

NIGERIA

abe
adire cloth
afia
agbada
akoko
alabere
alari
allura mai-kai
asi-ebi
aso-alake
aso-oke
attigra
bakwala
bante

boje
dan garagai
dan kura
dansiki
dedo
disa
doni
ebolo
ebu
ekpe cloth
etibo
etu
fatumar saki
fila ab'eti

gare
gbariye
George
girike
girki
hula saki
ibante
ibobirin
iborun
ikori
iyegbe
kaftani
kalabi
labarikada
lagidigba
lappa
malafa
marafiya
messauria
mubarshi bakin fara
olino
oni didi
oni lilo
oniko
oyam
oyuan
pabagu
riga
rigona
sabada

sace
saki
sambatsi
sanyan
sapara
sarkan wuya
seghosen
semfiti
shudiya
sokoto
sokoto kafo
sokoto kembe
stagbe
suliya
takelmi
talhakimt
talhatina
tilbi
tobi
topola
tozali
ukara
woko
wundi
yar chiki
yari yankunne
yeri
zane
zobe

NORWAY

avve
baugr
belling
belti
bloeja
blonder
boti
brœkr
brud
buningr
busserull
ceabet
dalkr
dasko
dukr
feldr
floki
fotaforkle
gåat adahke
gábmaga
gahper

gamanjunni
gáppte
gimsteinn
gjorð
glofi
gørsemi
guosaga
Hallingdal breeches
halsgjørð
hanzki
hengjehuva
hodnhue
hodnhuva
holbi
hörr
hosa
hottr
hovdatyet
hringr
klœða
klœði

komag
komager
kruneforkle
lad
leðr
lerept
lijnne
lin
lindi
lissto
luer
lusekufte
men
mpttull
muoddá
nål
nesti
perlehatt
pofi
praðr
rokkr
rondastakken
sauma
serkr

siklat
silki
skaut
skilkja
skor
skraddari
skyrta
sliehppa
sokkr
solje
søljer
stölebelte
styfill
sválltjá
tjeld
toboggan
Trolldals-trøya
tsavága
ull
utskurdsøm
vað
vadmal
vuoddaga

OGBONI

itagbe

OMAN

familla
lihaf

shash
yashmak

PAKISTAN

abla
ajrak
bagh
jinnah cap

kola
pushk kurta
salim shahi

PALESTINE

aba
abaaya
abba
abiyad
abu hizz ahmar
abu miten
abu sab'in
'ajami
'aqal
'aqal mqassab

'aqd anbar
'aqd wazari
'araqiyeh
'arayjeh
asaweri
asawir 'iradh
asbeh ruwaysiyeh
asmar
barracan
bayt al-sham

bazayl
benayiq
beramen
bisht
brim
bughmeh
burak
burqo
busht
damer
dendeki
dikkeh
dikky
dima
dimayeh
dubbahah
dura'ah
durra'a
durzi
elbas
esawra
gazzatum
ghabani
ghabaniyyeh
ghudfeh
ghwayshat
habkeh
harbeh
harir asli
harir nabati
hatta
hattah
heremzi
hidim
hidim al-khal
hijab
hizam
ikhdari
irdan
'isāba
ishdad
iznaq
jibbeh
jihaz
jiljeleh
jiljileh
jillayeh
jinnehu nar
jukh
kafiyyeh
kamakh
kamr
karamil
karnaysh
kashmir

keffiyeh
kermezot
khalaga
kharaz azraq
khatim
khawatim
khirqa
khsur
khurkeh
kiber
kirdan
kornaysh
kshat
kubba'ah
kum
lafa'if
laffayeh
laffeh
laseh
lefhah
libas
libbadeh
lozi
madas
mahrameh
malak
malak abu wardeh
malas
malwa
mawaris
menajel
mendil
mendil hajj
mintiyan
mlawlaw
msayyaha
mukhmal
muwanna
nasheq rohoh
nileh
'owaynet al-sus
qabbeh
qabbet anbar
qaftan
qalush
qamha hamra
qamis
qarawi
qasab
qasabiyeh
qaz
qaziyeh
qiladeh dhahab
qladeh
qladet 'anbar

qladet morjan
qladet qrenfol
qumbaz
qutbah fallahi
rosa
rozah
ruhbani
rumi
sabaleh
safadiyeh
saffeh
salta
samasmiyeh
saru
sfifeh
sha 'riyeh
shabakat al-kharaz
shakkeh
shal
shaleh
shambar
shamlah
shanf
sharbush
shash
shatweh
shawal
sherihah
shinbar
shinyah
shinyar binaqleh talis
shmar
shnat
shribrik
shrimbawi
shughl talhami
shunbar

shunbar ahmar
shuwayhiyyeh
sidriyeh
sirwal
smadeh
tahrireh
taqiyeh
taqsireh
tarabulsi
tarbi'ah
tarbush istanbuli
tarbush maghribi
tayyet sunnára
thob
thob al-khidmah
thob al-tal'ah
thob basitah
thob mukhmal azraq
tifsireh
tikkeh
tinbiteh
tubayt
tubsi
wata
wuqa
wuqayat al-darahem
wuqayat ed-derahim
wuqayeh
yezmeh
zamliyeh
zaybaqah
zunnar
zunnar asmar
zunnar maqruneh
zunnar tarabulsi
zurband

PERSIA

avonet
kalmuks
khalkhal
kola
kullah
nagdeh
naqsha

ormuzine
pah-poosh
persienne
picheh
pirahan
serapis
skarabigion

PERU

alforja
anacu
avaska

bellotas
buriel
camisón

canipo
centro de lana
chalina
chaman
chimpato
chimpita
chipana
choclos
chuca
chumpi
chupetes
chusi
chuspa
cordellate
corpiño
cotón
culeco
cumpi
curi
cushma
desplegada
detente
dormilonas
faldellin
fustan
fuste
gunpowder silk
huali
jerga
katra
llanque
llautu
llawto
llica llica ahuaska
lliclla
manquitos
marate
mascaipacha

mascaypacha
milakatra
mukhu-wara
pampanilla
paño berbi
pañolones
pardillo
phali
piñe
pishka
polca
pollera
ppipu ppipu ahuaska
prosaponcho
pullo
qompi
rjsó
roncadoras
ropa bordado
saco
saco de abrigo
sayal
shukina
shukuy
singelos
tapada
tembleques
tocuyo
tumbe
tupu
unku
unkucha
usuta
wak'a
walka
wara
waraka
yacolla

PHILIPPINE ISLANDS

abaca
agamid
balibuntal
ballibuntal
ballibuntl
baro
barong tagalong
batavia cloth
bitug
butung
jabul
jusi

langkit
malong
malong andon
malong pandi
mayad
pañuelo
piña cloth
saba
saya
suklang
tubao
wano

POLAND

agrafka
aksamit
batyst
bawełna
bielizna
binde
bizuteria
blezer
bluska
bransoletka
brazowy
brode
broszka
brunatny
brusttuch
bryczesy
but
cerata
chapska
chusta
chusteczka
contoushe
czapka
czarny
czarny jak smola
czepek
czerwony
czolka
duchowny
fartuch
fartuszek
fraka
futro
gabardyna
gaza
gorset
guzik
halka
igla
jedwab
kaftany
kall
kamea
kamiselka
kamizelka
kapelusz
kaptur
kasztanowaty
kelle
kierpce
kieszen'
klapa

klapove hitl
klejnot
klobuk
kolczyk
kolnierz
kolor granatowny
kolor khaki
kolpak
konfederatka
kontush
korona
koronki
kostium damski
koszula damska
koszula meska
kountouch
krawat
krawiec
kredka
krochmal
krótkie spodnie
kupkeh
kwef
lappenmutze
laska
lazur
len
lila-röz
macica perlowa
majtki
marynarka
maskotka
medalionik
mokasyny
mosalka
naramiennik
naszyjnik
nic'
niciane rekawiczki
nitka
nocna koszula
norki
oblec
obraczka slubna
obuwie
odziac
odzienie
odziez
okulary
okulary sloneczne
oliwny
pantofel

parasolka
part
pas
patynek
peleryna
perkal
perla
pierścień
pilsc
pilsn
piorko
pizama
płaszcz
płotno
podkolanówki
podszewka
pomaranczowy
ponczocha
popielaty
portki
przednapurpurowy
rab
rajstopy
rekaw
rekawica
rekawiczka
robótka
rubin
satyna
siwy
skarpetka
skóra
sniegowce
sniezobialy
sobol
spinki
spodic
spódnica
spódniczka
spodniczka szkocka
spodnie
sprzaczka
stanik
sternstichl
stirnbindel
streimel
strój

suba
sukienka
sukmanki
suknia
suknie
sukno
surdut
surowa bawelna
suwak
sweter zapinany
szafir
szal
szary
szkarlat
szkarlatny
szlafrok
sznurowadlo
szpilka
sztruks
tasiemka
tchapka
tenisówski
tkanina
tkanina dziana
toga
torebka damska
trykotaze
trykoty
trzewik
tunika
turkus
tusc
ubrac
wasy
waz
welna
welniana kamizelka
welniane skarpetki
welon
wstazka
zakiet
zamsz
zarost
zbroja
zielony
zolty

POLYNESIA

'ie-tonga
maro
sialoa
siapo

tapa
tiputa
titi
titi-le-'au

PORTUGAL

aba
acessório
acetato
acetinado
águamarinha
agulha de tricô
albói
alfaiate
alfinete
alforje
algibeira
algodão
aliança
alpargata
amarelo
âmbar
ametista
amido
amuleto
anágua
anil
aranzel
argênteo
argolas
armadura
arminho
arroxeado
arruivado
avental
azul
azulado
azulmarinho
babador
baço
baeta
barba
barbante
barraca
barrete
bastão
bata
batina
batom
bibe
blusa
blusa de operário
blusão
bobina
bobo
boina
boné
boquilha

borda
bordado
borla
bota
botão
botina
botoeira
bracelete
braguilha
branquidão
brilhante
brim caqui
brinco
cabeleira
cabeleira postiça
cabeleirerio
cachecol
calçado
calção
calçao de banho
calçao de montaria
calças
calças de couro
calicó
camada
camafeu
cambolim
cambraia
camisa de baixo
camisa de força
camisa de homem
camisa de lã
camisa de muiher
camisa de rigor
camisa de senhoras
camiseiro
camiseta
camisola
capa
capacete
capota
capote
capucha
capuchinho
capuz
capuz de frade
cáqui
carapuça
carmezim
carmim
cartola
casa de botão

casaca
casaco
casaco de peles
casaco esportiva
casaco para uso caseiro
casemira
casimira
castanho
casulo
cavanhaque
cebolão
cerata
cereja
ceroulas
cerulea
cerzideira
cetim
chapeleiro
chapéu cardinalício
chinó
chita
chitão
cimeira
cinta
cintaliga
cinto
cinturão
cinzento
cocar
colar
colar de pérolas
colcha de renda
colchete
colête
cor
cor de laranja
cor de rosa
cordões de sapatos
coroa
correia articulada
cós
costeleta
costureira
costureiro
cota
coturno
couraça
crepe-de-china
crepon
cresta
croché
cuecas
culote
damasco
debrum

droguete
elmo di giostra
encerado
entretela
escarlate
espartilho de senhora
espécie de jaqueta
esqui
esquilo
estampado
estopa
faixa
farda
fatiota
fato
ferradura
fiapo
fita
fitelho
fivela
fôrma
fralda
franja
frisa
friso
fundilho
fundo de agulha
fustão
gaforinha
galão
galocha
gaze
gibão
gola
gorro
gravata
grisalho
ilhó
jaleco
japona
jaqueta
jarreteira
jérsei
joalharia
lã
lapela
laranja
latão
láurea
lenço
lenço de sêda da india
lepela
lilás
lingüeta
linha

linho
luva
macacão
mala
mancebo
manequim
mangas perdidas
manga
manilha
manquitos
manta
manto de pescoço
manto militar
marfim
marrom
marta
meia
meia calça
meias de lã
monócula
nácar
náilon
negro
negro como azeviche
ocre
óculas
oliwny
opala
orla
paletó
palhaço
palmilha
pano
paramentos sacerdotais
párasol
pardo
pedraria
pele de cordeiro
pelego
pelica
penduricalho
peniche lace
penteado
perna da calça
pérola
peruça
pijama
pó-de-arroz
ponto de cruz
preto
púrpura
purpúreo
quimono
rendalo
rendilhado

retrós
roxo
rubi
rubro
safira
saia
saiote
saiote escocês
sandália
sapata
sapato
sarja
scarf
scarlet
seda
setim
setimeta
smoking
sobrecapa
sobrecasaca
sobrepeliz
sobretudo
sobretudo sôlto
sombrinha
sombrinha chapeau de sol
sotaina
suéter
tabardo
tafetá
tamanco
tampa
tanga
tear
tecidos
teia
tejadillo
tesoura
tiracolo
touca
traje
trancinha
tricô
tricolina
tricota
túnica
turbante
turquesa
umbrela
vagem de ervilhas
vasconso
velludo
verde
vermelhão
vermelho
vestido

vestir
vestuário
vidrilho

violeta
xale
zibelina

PRUSSIA

esquavar
flügelmütze

jelek

RHODESIA

amabejhu
amanqonqo
amanyatelo
ebomvu
incwado
indlugula

ishiwaba
isigula
iziketsho
nyoro
ubuhlalu
umtika

ROMANIA

ac
ac cu gămălie
altita
balt
barbui
barito
basma
batistă
bernec
bertita
bete
bitusca
blană
bondita
boscele
brățară
brezarau
brîu
bubou
bumbac
buzunar
caciula
caita
cămaşă
canura
caseac
catrinta
catrintoi
ceapsâ
chepeneag
chimir
chinius

chite
cînduse
cingătoare
ciorap
cipcic
cizmă
cofta
colan
colier
conciu
cretinta
croĭtor
cufaica
cunua
curea
cusma
cutaveica
czepesz
dantelă
dimie
duluma
fir
fîstîc
flanyela
fodra
fota
fustă
fustar
gheată
ghiordan
giubea
giumedanii

giuvaer
gluga
guler
guleras
haină
haĭne
iie
îmbrăca
îmbrăcăminte
in
încalţa minte
iner
ităr
iupca
karinca
keptar
kurti
lájbi
lecric
libade
lînă
lobogós
manta
mănuşă
marama
mătase
mînecare
mintean
nasture
opinci
opreg
pălărie
pantaloni
pănură
papuc
papute
pastura

pendej
pestelci
pestiman
piele
pieptar
pieptarita
pindileu
pînză
pîslă
plisîrani
polmesenic
porasz
postav
posztólájbi
recal
rokoja
rubasca
şapcă
şorţ
sovanel
stofă
sucna
sumane
surt
szurtuk
tàszli
toloboni
tundra
tüsjö
uiose
ujjas
văl
vîlnic
zavelci
zeghe
zgarda
zgardan

RUSSIA

arctic hare
baiberek
baronduki
bashlik
basmak
beshmet
botforti
braslet'
briuki-dudochki
bruki
bulavka
caracul
cebot
cepec

chakchiri
cherkeska
chirinka
chlopok
cholst
cossack cap
culok
doloman
dragocennost'
dragoonka
dushagreia
dushegreya
epanechka
epauleti

fartuk
fatas
felon
fouraschka
furashka
gaitan
gimnasterka
grenadierka
igla
jubka
kaftan
kakofnitch
kamzol
karman
kartriz
kaska
kazachock
khalaty
kitel
kithaika
kiver
kokade
kokoshnik
kol'co
koruna
kosovorotka shirt
koza
kruzeno
kruzhevo
kumach
kurtka
kushak
lampasi
lapot
len
letnik
materija
mech
mentik
mundir
naboika
navershnik
nit'
obuv
odet'
odezda
okhaben
ozerel'e
ozherelok
palto
panaeva
pantaloni
papaha
papakha
parnoe

parochka
patrontache
percatka
perednik
pestryad
pidjak
pidzak
plakhta
plasc
plat'e
platok
poddyovka
podopleka
pogoni
pojas
polakem
polotno
polu-kaftan
polushubka
poneva
portnoj
pugovico
ranetz
riza
rubakha
rubakha kosovorotka
rubaska
ryasa
sapka
sapog
sapogi
sarafan
sbornik
selk
serst
shal
shale
shapka
sharf
sharovary
shinel
shirinka
shliapa
shnur
shtany
shuba
shushpan
sljapa
soroki
stany
stikhar
stiliaga
stsepnoe
sukno
surtuk

tashka
tcherkeska
tkan'
treugolka
tufel'
tuflja
tujurka
tulup
valenki

veshovi meshok
vojlok
vorotnicek
vorotnik
vual'
zapáska
zapon
znak

SAMOA

afe
ai
'apa memea
'apamemea
ario
'auli
'auro
'ava
'avaaluga
'efu'efu
'ena
'ena'ena
'ena'ena mumu
fa'amalu
fa'amau
fa'ataelama
faufautu
fuafuati
fue
fulu
fusi
gatugatu
'ie
'ie mafiafia
'ie valavala
kalauna
kola
kosi
la'au su'isu'i
la'ei
lalaga
lanumoana
lava-lava
lei
lipine
lipine silika
ma'a taua
malo
mata tioata
mitiafu
moti
mua

mumu sesega
mumusali
nailoni
'ofu
'ofuta 'ele
'ofutino
'ofuvae
'ofuvae pupu'u
papa
pato'i
pau'meme'i
pea
pe 'a
peleue
penina
pine
piniki
pu fa'amau
puava
puletasi
pulou
pulou fa'afao
pulou pepe
sakete
samasama
se'evae
seleulu
semea
siapo
silika
silipa
siliva
solo
solosolo
tagikeri
talafa
talama
tali 'ele 'ele
tao 'ofu
taonga
taulima
tautaliga

tauvae   uliuli
tifa   vali
totoga   veli
uati

SARAWAK

dangdong   sirat

SARDINIA

orbace

SCANDINAVIA

sarafan

SCOTLAND

arisard   kelt
Ayrshire work   kilmarnock
balmacaan   kilmarnock bonnet
bandle   kilt
bannockburn   leine croich
benn   lovat
biodag   maud
bluebonnet   moggan
boineid   monteith
breacan-feile   moultan muslin
breacan-guaille   ósain
brogan tionndaidh   perlin
brogues   philibeg
claidheamh-mor   pirned
cleòca Gaidhealach   pirnie
cotla-gearr   pirny
criosan biodag   plaid
dornick   prine feilidh
DPM   raploch
écossaise hat   rock and reel
feileadh-beag   scone cap
filibeg   sgian-dubh
fly plaid   shell
forfar   sioda bun-duirn
galashiels   sowback
gartain   spangles
gash   sporan
ghillie   suaicheantas
gillie   suggan
hodden   tam-o'-shanter
how   targe
hungback   tartan
Inverness skirts   tonnag
jirkinet   trews

trotcozy
tweed

wyliecoat

SENEGAL

kassa

segu

SIERRA LEONE

bla lome
dagba gulai
fandewai
garrankee
garri cloth

lappa
nduli
ndului
njekloe
quande

SLOVAKIA

aksamitka
baranice
bavlnka
bezulánky
cepec
fertuch
gate
haleny
hastrigánky
jojky
kabátek
kamrtusky
kazdodenný kroj
kosárky
kosírek

krpce
mentlíky
mentýk
obalenka
obradový kroj
pentlení
pisany lapti
podvika
slavnostný kroj
súkenice
svatební roucho
sviatocný kroj
ubrus
vonica

SOMALIA

lunghi
madow

tusbahh
usala

SOUTH AFRICA

kapparings
kappie
kaross
klapbroek
knobkerry
poriaan

rholwani
schauslooper
skuinsdoek
tackies
toering
veldschoen

SPAIN

abrigo
abrigo cruzado
abrigo en forma de capa
abrigo polo

abrigo raglan
abrigo trinchera
acanalado
acetato

acetato de celulosa
acordonado Bedford
aguja
ailerons
ajuar
ala
alas
albornoz
albusado
alcorque
alepin
alfiler
algodón
alhaya
alizarina
aljófar
aljuba
almenadas
almete
almizclera
alpaca
alpargata
alta costura
altibajo
amarillo
ambo
americana
anaranjado
añil
anteojos
ardilla
ardilla gris
ardilla parda
argentería
armiño
arpillera
asargado
astracán
atrocelado
avampiés
azafran
azufar
babero
badana
baldrés
banador
baratea
barcelona
barret
basquina
bata corta
bata de casa
bata de mañana
baticol
batín

batista
bayeta
beatilla
benerica
bengalina
bermejo
bermellon
bernia
bigotera
bilbo
bivertina
blanco
blanco cremoso
blonda
blusa
bocací
bocaran
boemio
bohemio
boina
boina vasca
bolsillo
bolso
bombazina
borceguí
bordado
bordado a mano
bordado con calados
bordado con perlas
bordado cortado
bordado en blanco
bordado plano
bordado suizo
borde
borla
bota
bote cuello
botinicos
botón
botón suelto con espiga
bragas
bragon braz
bragueta
brahón
brazalete
breitschwantz
brial
brocado
brocado raso de pelo
brocatel
brocato
bucaran
bufanda
burdeos
cabelleras postizas

caballeros
cabesa
cabestrillo
cabos
cabra de China
cabrito
caceres
cachemira
cadenilla
caderas postizas
cafe
cafe claro amarillento
cafe rojizo
cahemir
cairel
calcetería
calcetin
calcetines
calçons
calva
calzado
calzas conpies
calzas enteras
calzas largas
calzaz de aguja
calzón bombacho
calzoncillo
cámara
camarera mayor
cambray
cambray liso
camisa
camisa polo
camiseta
camiseta con mangas cortas
camiseta de mujer
campera
campos
cañamazo doblado
cañutillos
capa
capa corta
capa larga
capa morisca
capacete de Indias
capellar
caperuza
capichola
capilla
capirote
caqui
caracul
cardado
carmeñola
carmin

carnaza
casco
casimir
castaño
castor
castorina
cavalry
cazapo
cebtí
celada de engole
cenojil
cereza
cerrada
cetrino
cettelle
chaconada
chal
chaldera
chaleco
chalino
chambergo
chandal
chapeo
chapiron
chaqué
chaqueta
chaqueta corta de marino
chaqueta corta y gruesa
chaqueta deportiva
chaqueta para casa
charmés
charol
charretera
cheviot
chiffon
chifón
chifón terciopelo
chinchilla
chinela
chopines
chupa
cinta
cinto
cinturón
ciruela
clac
clavos
cloche de fieltro
cofia
cofia de tranzado
cojin para hacer puntilla
colbac
collar
color aceitung
colorado

colorante acido
comadreja
comadreja de Siberia
conejo
copa
corbata
corbata ascot
corchete
cordellate
cordero
cordero del Tibet
cordero mongoliano
cordobán
cordon de zapatos
cordoncillo con alma
cordonero
coronet
corpiño
corse
cotelé
côtelé fino
cover
crea
crema
cremallera
cremallera separable
crep-satén
crespón
crespón arena
crespón de Cantón
Crespón de China
crespón de lana
crespón georgette
crespón marroqui
crespón musgo
crespón romano
cretona
crinolina
cubica
cuello
cuello bebés
cuello bote
cuello burberry
cuello capuchon
cuello chal
cuello chino
cuello de pajarita
cuello eton
cuello mandarín
cuero
cuero de ante
cuero de cerdo
cuero de cocodrilo
cuero de marroqui
cuero napa

cuerpo baxo
damasco
datilado
de lazo
de todo lazo
delantal
delantal de cintura
dengue
deshilado
diseño
diseño a cuadro
diseño a cuadros escocés
diseño a rayas
diseño con lunares
diseño raya de alfiler
diseño tradicional de piñones
disfraz
doblados todos
dobladura
dos
durazno
dutis
duvetina
ebúrneo
empeines
enagua
enagua de lana
encaje
encaje chantilli
encaje de aguja
encaje de angel
encaje de bolillos
encaje de Lila
encaje de Malinas
encaje de malla cuadrada
encaje de Milano
encaje estrecho de aldgodón
encaje frivolité
encaje hecho a maquina
encaje suizo
encarnado
entretela
entretela fusible
eolica
escarlata
escarlata subido
esclavina
escocés
escote
escote en U
escudete
esmoquin
espulgeata
esquirole
estameña

estofado

estofée

estopilla

faja rizada

faja-calzón

fajin

falda

falda combinación

falda con peto

falda con tabla añadida

falda envuelta

falda escocesa

falda-pantalón

faldita

faldrilla

falla contrama crespón

faluchos

faralafents

ferreruelo

fieltro

firmale

fleco

felco bullion

fleco morisco

foca

forro

forro de sombrero

franela

franela de Canton

franela ligera

franjas

fruncidas

fruncido

fustan

gabán

gabardina

galerilla

galocha

galón

gambeto

gamuza

garduña

garvín

gatos de lomos

gayado

gayas

gemelos

glauco

glotón

golilla

gorguera

gorra

gorra deportiva

gorra escocesa

gorro

gorro de dormir

gorro de marinero

gorro de pieles

grain de poudre

gran gola

grana encarnada

granilla

gris

gris humo

gris parduzco

gris ratón

grisalla

gros gren

guanaco

guante

Guard infanta

guardamalleta

guinda

guinga

guirnalda

gusanillo

harris

hault collet

hembras

herreruelo

herrete

hevilla

hiladillo

hilo

holanda

hombrera

horsehair petticoat

hueco de la manga

huke

hule

ispahanis

jamete

jipijapa

jirones

jornea

joya

jubeteros

jubon

labrada

lana

lana de alpaca

lanilla estampada

lavanda

lazo de entorchado

lechugilla

lencería

lentejuela

leopard

leotardo

lienzo

lienzo de algodón
lienzo de la India
liga
limiste
lince
linea imperio
lino
lino irlandes
llano
loba
lobas compridas
lobe
lona
luto
madrás
mañanita
maneras
manga
manga ahuecada
manga caída
manga dolman
manga gitana
manga kimono
manga murciélago
manga raglán
manopla
mantellina
mantilla
manto
manto de oraciones
mapache
marabù
marcela
marfil
margaritte
marinera
marlota
marmota
marrn
marta
marta cebellina
marta comú
matelasé
mechones
mechuelas
media
medias mangas
medias y calcetines
minifalda
mofeta
Moiréseide
moletón
moletón reversible
monjil
mono

monograma
morado
muaré
muletón de lana
muselina
muselina de la india
musequí
mutria
nankin
nansú
negro carbón
nesga
nesgada
nobleza
nudo
nutria
ocelote
ojal
ojales
ojete
oliva
Oposum
or trect
organdí
oro de orilla
oro hilado
osito lavador
osnaburgo
oso
otomana
otomana imperial
painetta
paletó
paletoque
palomita
pamela
pana
pana con cervaduras muy finas
paño
paño de brunete
paño de la tierra
paño tuntido
pañofieltro
panolones
pantalones bermuda
pantalones cerradoes por debajo de la rodilla
pantalones cortos
pantalones de baño
pantalones de equitacíon
pantalones de gimnasia
pantalones de golf
pantalones largos hasta media pantorrillas
pantalones sueltos
pantalones tejanos
pantalones vaqueros

pantera
pantuflas
pantuflo
pañuelo
pañuelo para el cuello
paraguas
pardillo
pardo
pardo amarillento
pardo opaco
pardo rojizo
parduzco
partidor de crencha
pasa montañas
peinadore
pelele
pelliza
pelo de castor
pelo de liebre
peluca
peñas veras
peplo
perle
perramus
pespuntaderas
pespuntado
pespunte
petit point
peto
picado
picaporte
piel de angel
piel de becerro
piel de cisne
piel de seda
piel de tiburón
pinza
piqué
plantillas
plateado
plato de lo gorro
plisado
plisado en abanico
plisado en acordeón
plisado en sierra
plisado encontrado
pluma de avestruz
pluma de gallo
plume de faisán
point d'espagne
polaina
polera
pollera
pony
popelina

portaligas
pretina
princesa
puertas
pullover
pulsera
puño
puño ajustado
puño double
punta roma
puntas
puntilla
puntilla de Venecia
punto a festón
punto de almorafán
punto de cruz
punto de malla
punto de oro llano
punto de tallo
punto llano
punto real
purpua
querpo
quezote
ramio
randas
raso
raso de la China
raso de zapatillas
raso imperial
raso liberty
raso muy brillante
raso piel de angel
raso piel de cisne
raso piel de seda
raso por trama
raso por urdimbre
redes
redicella
redingote
retículo
rojo
rojo Congo
rollo
rondz
ropa
ropa bastarda
ropa de estado
ropa larga
ropa rozagnte
ropilla
rosado
ruedas
ruedo
sacristan

salto de cama
sarga
sarseneta
sastre
satén
satineta
saya
seda
seda chape
seda cruda
seda de corbatas
seda silvestre
servilla
shantung
skunk
sobaquera
solapa
soletila
sombrerera
sombrero
sombrero Cordobès
sombrero de ala ancha
sombrero de caballero
sombrero de copa chistera
sombrero de dos picos
sombrero de paja
sombrero de tela
sombrero flexible
sortija
sostén
suela
suspensor atletico
suspensores
tabardo
tabarete
tafetán
taparrabos
tejano
tejido arrugado
tejido calado
tejido con pelo largo
tejido de punto elástico
tejido de punto liso
tejido esponjoso
tejido liso
tejón
tela
tela de algodón mercerizado
tela de aspecto granulado
tela de Jouy
tela para carpa
tenida de gimnasia
terciopelo
terciopelo acordonado

terciopelo aplastado
terciopelo chifón
terciopelo con dibujo multicolor
terciopelo de Utrect
terciopelo en relieve
terciopelo labrado
terliz
tirantes
toca
toca de camino
tocado
tontillo
topo
torzal
traje de baño
traje de baño de dos piezas
traje de baño de una pieza
traje de novia
trepats
tricornio
tul
turbante
tweed
velludillo
velo
verde
verde celedón
verde césped
verde limón
verde nilo
verde salvia
verde trébol
verdugado
vertugale
vestido de noche
vestidos
vestir
vientre de ardilla gris
visera
visón
vivos
volante
zafira
zagalejo
zamarra
zamarro
zapatillas
zapato
zapato de mujer sin correas
zapato oxford
zaragüelles
zarzahan
zorro
zueco

SRI LANKA

hatte

SUMATRA

siang-malam   tampan

SUMBA

hinggi   lau pahudu
hinggi kombu   pakiri mbola

SUMBAWA

kere   pebasa

SUMERIA

kaunakes

SWEDEN

armband   mös sa
bälte   nål
bomull   näsduk
byxor   pels
fält-teken   rock
ficka   ryssedamast
filt   ryssekläde
flor   ryssewerk
förkläde   siden
gördel   silke
halsband   skirduk
handske   skjorta
hatt   sko
hatta   skofium
juvel   skört
kappa   skräddare
kareeta   slöja
kask   socka
kithaika   söllstötter
kläda   spets
kläde   stövel
kläder   strumpa
knapp   Swedish lace
la   toffel
läder   tråd
lärft   Twelve Apostles
linne   tyg
maljor   ull
mantel

SWITZERLAND

androsame
Appenzell embroidery
beffschen
bredzon
capadüsli
chapeau à borne
händschen
haustuch
menagere
rapolin
rosehube
rosenadel

Schäppeli
schlappe
Schnupftücher
schöpen
Schweizergelb
stoffelkappe
trip-sammet
tüchli
Türken-kappen
unterrock
volanten
wammiss

SYRIA

agabanee
izar

tantoor

THAILAND

Chalong phra ong long raja
chiiwaun
chong kra ben
hua
krachoom
mat mii
mwa non
pah-jungobein
paisin
pamsukula
panung
pha ap nam fon
phaa
phaa biang
phaa chet

phaa chet naa
phaa chet paak
phaa khaaw maa
phaa pat chieng
phaa sarong
phaa yao
prakhotaeo
rom
sabai
sabong
sangkhatti
sua yan
taalapat
thung
tiin

TIBET

chupa
djore
drilbu

dZi bead
pulo
shema

TIMBUKTU

baiya
balga
djnne-djnne
djorro-marabu
handu djere
hanga-korbo
huttu
kamba iri

kantje
kobe gani
kugunni
kullu
kunna
mdama kofe
nine-djere
pilu saluf

selba
selimut
sonko
sorro

tche djenji
teybaraten djendji
tolomi
tyelambu

TIV

akongo
akpwem
amaua
amyan ikondo

anger
ashira
ashish
dzaan

TRANSVAAL

ghabi
jocolo
linaga

mapoto
pepetu

TRINIDAD

fol
glenglen

kandal
wooloes

TUNISIA

chechias
dentelle Arabe
djebba
kachabia
kadroun

kashabia
kufia
mellia
safsari
suria

TURKEY

Anatolian silk
Anatolian wool
angora
anteri
antery
atlas
basma
basmak
berundjuk
bibila
bughma
burqu
çarsof
çatma
cepken
chalwar
chekmak
chyrpy
çipsip
dival
dival isi
dizge

ferace
feridge'
fez
gömlek
houri-coat
igne oyasi
jellick
kadife
kalghi
kalpak
kemha
kesdi
khuff
kirk
kulah
kulah-i pahlavi
kusak
maharmah
mendil
oya isi
oyah
pabuç

potur   terlik
püsküllü   thaub
şal kuşak   Türken-kappen
salvar   Turkish point lace
sarawil   üçetek
seraser   uçkar
serenk   yaka
setre   yelpaze
stambouline   yemeni
tafta   zerbaft
takke   zivka
tarpus

TURKMENISTAN

alan dangi   kurteh
balaq   qirmizi don
bilqusak   qubpa
börk   qusak
çabut   telpek
chargat   teneçir
gul yaqa   yaluk
köynek

UKRAINE

corsetka   kozhukh
keptar   plakhta
kersetka   svyta

UNITED ARAB EMIRATES

aba   igaal
abaaya   keffiyeh
al hilel   khirqa
asayib   kibr
baalto   kussabi
bisht   milfa
burga   mishlah
burnous   qutn
burqu'   shaal
farwah   siklat
gaib   sirwaal
ghoutra   zibun

UNITED KINGDOM

À la George V   alamode
adelaide   albangala
Adelaide boot   Albert boots
Admiralty cloth   Albert collar
aetherial   Albert driving-cape
Agnes Sorel bodice   Albert jacket
Agnes Sorel corsage   Albert overcoat

Albert pot
Albert riding coat
Albert shoe
Albert top frock
Albert watch-chain
Alexandra jacket
Alexandra petticoat
alnage
amelle
American
American cloth
American trousers
American vest
Andaluse cape
andalusian casaque
angel overskirt
angel sleeve
angle-fronted coat
Anglo-Greek bodice
anglo-merino
ankle-jacks
antigropolis
antique bodice
Apollo corset
Apollo knot
aquatic shirt
Aragonese bonnet
Armenian cloak
artois buckle
aurifrisium
Aylesham
azure
babet bonnet
baby bodice
baby cap
baby French heel
backsters
baende
bag plastron
bag-waistcoat
balesses
ballet-skirt
ballroom neckcloth
balmoral
balmoral bodice
balmoral cloth
balmoral crape
balmoral petticoat
bandle
Barbour jacket
barclod
barlingham
barmillion
basing
bēag

beah
bearm-clap
Beatrice parasol
Beatrice twill
beg
belcher
bend
beret sleeve
besague
bhurra
bibi bonnet
billicock
binde
bivouac mantle
blue john
body-stychet
bollinger
bonnet assassin
borada crape cloth
botas
bote
botoun
botwm
braccae
braccas
bracer
braces
braecce
brandestoc
bratt
brec
brēc
brec-hraegel
brech
breichled
breost-lin
breost-rocc
brethyn
brides
British warm
broc
brodekin
brolly
brummaggem
Brummel
bugis
bul
bulgare pleat
Bulgarian cloth
bum-barrel
bum-freezer
burnley
bursa
buskins
butterfly bow sleeve

cabbage
cadach
caefing
caeles
caeppe
cage
calc
camibockers
campaign coat
cap of maintenance
cappa
cappe
careless
caroline corsage
carpet slippers
carpmeal
cascade waistband
cased body
cased sleeve
cassock
cassock mantle
cassock vest
castle
casul
Catherine wheel farthingale
cauliflower wig
cavalier sleeve
celestial
cemes
ceylon
ceylonette
chaffers
chambard mantle
chamford mantle
chammer
Charlotte Corday bonnet
Charlotte Corday cap
chemise a l'anglaise
chemise gown
chinese green
chinese spencer
chitterlings
circassian bodice
circumfolding hat
clap
clāp
clapes
clāpes
clarence
Clarissa Harlowe bonnet
Clarissa Harlowe corsage
Clay worsted
cloak-bag breeches
clœp
clog

cloke
clothe
clove
coat shirt
coatlet
coat-sleeve
Coburg
cochl
cockle hat
codrington
cœppe
coke
coler
colley-westonward
combed helmet
combinations
comforter
comforts
continental hat
conversation bonnet
coral currant button
corde du Roi
cordey cap
cork rump
corned shoe
cornet hat
cornet skirt
Corsican tie
cossacks
cot
cote
coton
cotoun
cottage front
cotwm
Courtauld crape
cowes
cranky checks
cravat strings
crepe anglaise
crepe imperial
crepelle
crinc
Cromwell collar
Cromwell shoe
cross-cloth
crusene
crys
cuerbully
cuffia
cuffie
cuirass tunic
cuirasse bodice
cuir-bouilli
Cumberland corset

Cumberland hat
curricle cloak
curricle dress
curricle pelisse
cushion work
cut-fingered pumps
cutlets
cyrtel
dalc
Danish trousers
de Berri
de France
de Roi
demi-surtout
demob
de-mob suit
demy-teste
Denmark cock
devil skin
Devonshire
diadem bonnet
diadem comb
diadem fanchon bonnet
Diana Vernon bonnet
Diana Vernon hat
dillad
dilladu
Directoire bonnet
Directoire coat
Directoire hat
Directoire jacket
Directoire skirt
Directoire swallow-tail coat
divided skirt
divorce corset
Dolly Varden bonnet
Dolly Varden cap
Dolly Varden dress
Dolly Varden hat
Dolly Varden polonaise
Doncaster riding coat
dorneck
d'Orsay coat
d'Orsay roll
double
double bouffant sleeves
downy calves
drabbet
drape cut
dress clip
dress holder
dress lounge
dress protector
dress Wellington
dresse

drillette
driving-cape
Drummond
du Barry corsage
du Barry sleeve
duchesse pleat
duck-billed shoes
dundreary whiskers
dunster
durance
duretty
Dutch cloak
Dutch skeleton dress
Dutch waist
earthquake dress
edau
eel skirt
Egyptian brown
elephant sleeve
eleven gore ripple skirt
ell
elliptic collar
eminence
emperor shirt
empire bodice
empire jupon
empire skirt
empress petticoat
en tout cas
English work
esgid
Eton cap
Eton collar
Eton jacket
everlastings
exhibition checks
eyelet doublet
faces
Fair Isle sweater
false gown
false hips
fan parasol
fana
fancies
fanfreluche bodice
featherbrush skirt
feathertop wig
feax-clap
feax-net
feax-preon
fel
fetel
fetels
ffedog
ffwr

fichu Antoinette
fichu Corday
fichu-robings
fifele
fig leaf
figgragulÞ
Flanders serge
fleax
flex
florinelle
flower hole
flower pot hat
flow-flow
flycap
fly-fringe
fly's wing
folly bells
forage cap
forel
fotgewaed
foundling bonnet
French gigot sleeves
French gores
French hose
frilling
furre
Fusex shirt
fustian
gable headdress
Gabrielle dress
Gabrielle sleeve
gadlings
Gainsborough bonnet
gairda
gaiter bottoms
Galatea comb
Galatea hat
Gallo-Greek bodice
Garibaldi bodice
Garibaldi jacket
Garibaldi sleeve
gemme
Geneva print ruff
gerele
gerife
ge-scripla
gewœde
gewœdian
ghost coat
gimstān
gipsy hat
giraffe comb
girdel
girdle glass
Gladstone collar

Gladstone overcoat
Glauvina pin
gleindorch
glissade
glōf
godet skirt
godweb
godweb-cynn
golf vest
gorchudd
gored bell skirt
gothic cap
gray lilac
greatcoat dress
Grecian sleeve
Grecque corsage
Greek stripes
grenadier cap
guard-chain
guinea cloth
gwddfdorch
gwisg
gwisgo
gwlan
gwregys
gyrdel
gyrdel-hring
gyrdels
gyrdels-hringe
habit bodice
habit glove
habit-redingote
hacele
haer-naedl
haet
haetera
hairbines
ham
hances
hand fall
handewarpes
handkerchief dress
hand-ruffs
hand-scio
hare pocket
harvard sheeting
heafod-clap
heafod-gewaede
healsed
heavy swell
hed-clap
heden
helmet cap
helmet hat
hemepe

hemispherical hat
hemming
Henley boater
here-pād
het
highlows
hip buttons
hod
hœtt
hoop petticoat
hop-pada
Hortense mantle
hosa
hosan
hose-bend
hounds ears
house dress
housemaid skirt
hraegel
hraelung
hring
hrycg-hraedel
huccatoon
hufe
hug-me-tight
hunting belt
hunting necktie
hunting stock
hussar boots
hussar jacket
hussar point
hwitel
Indian
Indian necktie
indispensible
Irish polonaise
iron-pot
Isabeau corsage
Italian heel
Italian nightgown
iuele
iwede
jack
Jacobean embroidery
jaganath
jam
Japanese hat
Java supers
Jemima
Jenny Lind costume
Jerry hat
Joan-of-Arc bodice
jockey cap
jockey sleeve
jockey waistcoat

joinville
justcoat
kains
kampskatcha slipper
kaniki
kano cloth
Kate Greenaway costume
Katharine of Aragon lace
kendal
kendal-green
kevenhuller
khanga
kidungas
kiss-me-quick
kite-high dandy
knee buckles
knee-fringe
knee-string
krauss
lake
Lamballe bonnet
Langtry hood
languette
lavender
leather cloth
Leicester jacket
lein
leþer
leperhose
lether
limbrick
Limpet trunks
Lincoln green
linen
linsey
linsey-woolsey
Lissue
listadoes
lobster helmet
lockram
long Melford
Louis XIII corsage
M. B. waistcoat
macana
macaroni cravat
mackintosh
madras gingham
madras turban
Maintenon cloak
major wig
Mandarin hat
maneg
Manon robe
Mantel
manteel

mantelet
mantle lace
mantua
Marie Anglais bonnet
mariner's cuff
Mark of the Beast
Marlborough hat
marmotte bonnet
marmotte cap
marquise bodice
marquise mantle
marquisetto beard
marshmellow
martingale breeches
Mary Queen of Scots cap
masher
masher collar
masher dust wrap
matinée
Maud
Mecklenburg cap
Medici dress
Medici sleeve
Medusa wig
Melton
mene
mentel
mentel-preon
meo
mermaid's tail
mexican
Mexicans
Milan bonnet
military frock coat
military stock
milkmaid skirt
mitten sleeve
modesty bit
modrwy
mofeler
Moldavian mantle
Monmouth cap
Montague curls
Montespan corsage
Montespan hat
Montespan pleats
Montespan sleeve
Montpensier mantle
morning gown
morone
moschettos
Mother Hubbard cloak
moulds
muffin hat
mufflers

Muller-cut-down
mush
mushroom hat
mushroom sleeve
muslin deaths
musquash
naccarat
Napoleon necktie
Napoleons
napron
Neapolitan bonnet
nebula headdress
neck button
necked bonnet
nedle
needlecord
Nelson hat
neÞla
nether stocks
Newgate fringe
Newmarket coat
Newmarket overcoat
Newmarket top frock
Newmarket vest
night coif
night rail
night-kercher
nithsdale
Nivernois
nodwydd
nœdl
Norfolk shirt
Norma corsage
Northampton lace
Norwich paramatta
nostle
Nottingham lace
nun's work
Oatland village hat
ocreae rostratae
octagon tie
ofer-braedels
ofer-feng
oferlaeg
oferlagu
ofer-slop
ofer-slype
ondina crinoline
opus anglicanum
opus consutum
opus filatorium
opus pectineum
opus phrygium
opus plumarium
opus pulvinarium

orel
oval beaver hat
overalls
Oxford bags
Oxford gillies
Oxford gloves
Oxford tie
Oxonian boots
Oxonian jacket
packing white
pād
paddock coat
paida
pakama
palatine royal
paletot-redingote
pall
pallatine
Palmerston wrapper
pamela
Pamela bonnet
pamela hat
panel skirt
pannier crinoline
pannier dress
pantaloon trousers
panteen collar
pantile
papoon
parchmentier
partlet
patent lace
patent leather boots
patrol jacket
patti jets
pea jacket
pearl of beauty
peasant skirt
pectoll
peek-a-boo waist
peel
peg-top sleeves
pelisse-mantle
pelisse-robe
Pembroke paletot
penang lawyer
penistone
peplum basque
peplum bodice
peplum dolman
peplum jupon
peplum overskirt
peplum rotonde
Perdita chemise
Persian vest

Perspective glass
Petersham cossacks
Petersham frock coat
Petersham greatcoat
Petersham ribbon
petticoat breeches
Philip and Cheney
Philip and China
physical wig
Piccadilly collar
piccadilly weepers
picture hat
Piedmont gown
pierrot cape
pierrot ruff
pifferaro bonnet
pifferaro hat
pilece
pinafore costume
pipkin
pique devant
placardo
plackard
placket
plain bow stock
Platoff cap
pleated shirt
plus fours
pœll
poke bonnet
poket
policeman's cape
Polish boots
Polish greatcoat
Polish jacket
Polish mantle
polka
polo collar
polonia
polrock
polverino
pompadour bodice
poncho
porcelain
pork-pie hat
port manteau sunshade
Portuguese farthingale
powdering jacket
prawing-spinel
preen
pregnant stay
prēon
Prince of Wales jacket
prince's sleeve
princess dress

Princess Elizabeth lilac
princess petticoat
princess polonaise
princess robe
princess slip
prœd
pudding-basin cut
Puritan bonnet
pussy-cat bonnet
pynn
pyramid style
pyramids
rabagas bonnet
raglan boot
raglan cape
raglan covert coat
raglan overcoat
railroad trousers
railway pockets
Ranelagh mob
rationals
reach-me-down
reaf
red lilac
reed hat
regatta shirt
regency hat
reister cloak
religious petticoat
reowe
revers en pelerine
riding dress frock coat
riding hoop
rifeling
rift
Rigoletto mantle
robin front
Robinson hat
rocc
rollers
rolling stockings
roll-up breeches
roll-up stockings
rollups
Rosebery collar
round dress
roundlet
roxalene bodice
roxalene sleeve
Roxburgh muff
Royal George stock
Rubens bonnet
Rubens hat
russell
russell satin

russells
Russian blouse
Russian flame
Russian jacket
sailor suit
sailor's reef knot tie
Saint Martin's lace
Saint Omer
Salempore
salendang
salisbury
salloo
salt-box pocket
sanitary ball dress
sansflectum crinoline
Sardinian sac
satin Victoria
satinesco
saucer-collar
scalings
Scarborough hat
Scarborough ulster
scarf drapery
sceanc-bend
sceanc-gegirla
sceorp
sciccels
sciccing
scogger
scōh
scratch bob
scratch wig
scrud
scrydan
scyfel
scyrte
sea coat
sea-gown
sealskin coat
seamere
Second Empire costume
selk
semptress bonnet
seolac
serc
sgyrt
shadow
shakefold
Shakespere collar
Shakespere vest
sherte
ship-tire
sho
shoe-tie necktie
shooting coat

shorts
shotten-bellied doublet
shoulder belt
shoulder heads
shoulder knots
Sicilian bodice
sickly green
sidan
side
side body
silverets
siolac
skeleton suit
skimskin
skirt ruff
skitty boot
skyrt
skyteen
sleeve tongs
slife-scoh
sling sleeve
sling-duster
slipe-scoh
slop work
smoc
smoking jacket
snoskyn
snowflake
snowskin
snufkin
snuftkin
socas
socc
socke
sortie de bal
soufflet sleeves
soup and fish
spangles
Spanish farthingale
Spanish hat
Spanish jacket
Spanish kettledrums
Spanish sleeve
spencer cloak
spencer wig
spencerette
spennels
spider helmet
Spiderwork
splay-footed shoes
splyter-hat
spoon back
spoon bonnet
spring
spring boots

staeppe-scoh
stafford cloth
stamyn sengill
stand-fall collar
starch
starcher
statute cap
Steinkirk
stirrup hose
stirrup stockings
stivali
stock-drawers
stomacher
stomacher bodice
straight trousers
straight waistcoat
strapped pantaloons
strapul
strapula
strips
suit of ruffs
sultana scarf
sultane dress
sultane jacket
supertasse
swallow-tails
swanbill corset
swiftlere
Swiss belt
Swiss bodice
tablet
tablier skirt
tablier tunic
tackover
taglioni
Taglioni frock coat
tail clout
taillour
tallien redingote
talma
Talma cloak
Talma lounge
Talma mantle
Talma overcoat
tassets
tattersall vest
tea jacket
teagown
teiliwr
tennis cloth
tennis flannel
tennis shoes
terai hat
terre de Cuba
terrier overcoat

Terylene
threde
three-decker
three-fold linen button
three-seamer
three-stories-and-a-basement
thrum cap
thrummed hat
thymel
ticket pocket
tie-back skirt
tight-slacks
Tilbury hat
tlws
toby ruff
tourterelle
Trafalgar turban
Trilby hat
trocadero
trolley lace
trolly cap
trolly lace
trouser press
trouser stretcher
trowsus
trusses
tubular necktie
tucked skirt
tudor cape
tunece
tunic
tunic shirt
tunic skirt
turf hat
turkey gown
turret bodice
tweedside
tweedside overcoat
twine
Tyrolese cloak
Tyrolese hat
ugly
ulster
umbrella skirt
under-serc
underwraedel
university athletic costume
university vest
up-legen
vandyke dress
varens
veile
Venetian bonnet
Venetian cloak
Venetian sleeve

ventilated pants
Veronese cuirasse
Veronese dress
victoria
Victoria bodice
Victoria bonnet
Victoria corset
Victoria crepe
Victoria mantle
Victoria pelisse-mantle
Victoria sleeve
victorine
violin bodice
viyella
waed-braec
waefels
walking out dress
Wardle hat
Wasti
Wastjōs
waterproof cloak
Watteau body
Watteau costume
Watteau polonaise
Watteau robe
wealca
wearing sleeves
wedding garter
Wellesley wrapper
Wellington coat
Wellington frock
Wellington half-boot
Wellington hat
Wellington pantaloons
wheat ears
wheel farthingale
wimpel
winceyette
wining
winingas
winkers
Winslow lace
wœfels
wolle
Woodstock gloves
worms
wraed
wrapping front dress
wrap-rascal
wraprascal
wrigels
wull
wulla
wulle
yachting jacket

yak lace
yeoman hat
yoke bodice
yoke shirt
York wrapper

zone
zouave jacket
zouave paletot
zouave pantaloons

UNITED STATES OF AMERICA

'a 'iku
à la Marie Stuart
a tsi'kin
a 'ula
'a'a lole
'a'a moni
'a'a niu
'a'a puhaka
'a'a'a
'a'ahu
'a'ahu a po'o
'a'ahu ali'i
'a'ahu makaloa
'a'ahu 'oihana piha
'a'ahu pawehe
'a'amo'o
abalone
acala cotton
acetate
'ahapi'i
'ahiehie
'ahina
ah'ta qua o weh
'ahu
'ahu hinano
'ahuna
'ahunali'i
'ahuua
'ahu'ula
'a'i
'a'i kala
ai ling
'a'ilepe
'ainakini
akaaka
akaka
'akala
'aki
ala-niho
'alapaka
alaulau
alepin
Alice blue
Alsatian
amaranthus color
'ameki
American blade

American green
ameti
Anasazi stripe twill
Angouleme hat
Angouleme spencer
Angouleme tippet
Anne Boleyn mob
Annette Kellerman
anuenue
apo kula
apo lima
apo papale
artificial silk
artificial wool
ashigappa
Augusta cloth
babushka
baby doll pajama
bachelor shoes
badger whiskers
barn-door britches
barratine
barvell
Beatrice
Bedford cord
bellboy hat
Bemberg
bicycle clip
blouse suit
body stocking
boiled shirt
booie sum
Borghesé
Buchanan
burial blanket
bush hat
Buster Brown collar
Buster Brown suit
cadet jacket
calico china button
campaign hat
capa
cardinal
cathedral beard
chanchanko
Chanel suit
chau

cheongsam
chiang chau
China calico
chint
chukka boot
chun sam
chya mun bo
collodion silk
Constance
cool pants
coquillicot feathers
corset waist
cossack hat
crocus
cue de Paris
curch
curchef
curled silk
cursey cloth
dai fong chau
dai seong siu kwun
daimana
dam boo lau
dauphiness
desoy
Diamond dyes
din
diyugi
Doitsu ahina
doll hat
e sa
'ea malani
'ea 'ula
eau de veau
eboni
egasuri
Eisenhower jacket
'ekemau'u
'ele hiwa
'ele'ele
'ele'ele kanikau
'ele'i
'eleuli
'emelala
'epane
epani
'eponi
Fatima robe
favorite
favourite
flannelette
flight boot
Flying Saucer
fong chau
forester's green

forestry cloth
gai pee jau sa
gamoshes
garrison cap
gau chau
gau dai hai
gau liang
gobanji
golosh
grass embroidery
grassets
grazzets
gus-to-weh
hachimaki
Häftler
haiena
ha'imanawa
hainaka
hainaka 'a'i
hainaka lei
hainaka pa'eke
hainaka pakeke
hair à la Recamier
hair strings
halakea
halstuch
hamaku'u
hamo 'ula
hand
haneeka
hanina
han'pa
hau'ina
ha'ula
ha'ula'ula
he'a
Hershey bars
hetchi pansu
Hibernian vest
hikoni
hili ha
hili pa ha
hili pa kolu
hinaka
hinaka 'a'i
hinaka paeke
hi'ohi'o
hiyoku
H-line
hoakakala
hock see hai
hoi nong hu
hok see hai
hokua
holei

holoku
holomu
hōmongi
hoo
hoo tau dai
hoover apron
hot pants
huila kaulike
huka pihi
hula skirt
hulu
hulu hipa
huluhulu
hum-hum
hummums
humu
humu kaulahao
humu puka pihi
humuhumu ulana
humuka
humulau
humupa'a
humuwili
hunakana'i
Hungarian wrap
iakepi
iasepi
ihu kama'a
'ili
'ili hinuhinu
'ili kuapo
'ili pale o kama'a
'ili pipi
'ilio-hulu-papale
Imperial valley cotton
Isabella color
Italian slipper
jacket coat
Jackson shoes
jambieres
jin be wun
jungle fatigues
ka'ai
ka'ako'o
ka'ei papale
ka'ei po'o
kahan
kahi 'omou
kahiko
kahiko kaua
kaiapa
kaimana
kakau uhi
kakimea
kakinia

kaku obi
kalakoa
kalaunu
kalaunu bihopa
kalekonuka
kalewai
kaliki
kaliki waiu
kalikone
kalima hamo
kama'a
kama'a hakahaka
kama'a hawele
kama'a 'ie
kama'a ili
kama'a laholio
kama'a la'i
kama'a lo'ihi
kama'a pale wawae
kama'a puki
kama'ehu
kamaki
kamalena
kampū
kanakagi
kanekopa
kaomi lole
kapa
kapa ea
kapa 'ino'ino
kapa kila
kapa komo
kapa lau'i
kapeila
kapeilo
Kapp
kappa dachi
karanko geta
karauna
karitone
kasimea
kasuri
kasuri no shatsu
kaula ho'olewa
kaula li
kaula li kama'a
kaula uaki
kawiliwili humuhumu
kee ha hai
kela lole
ke'oke'o maoli
ke'oke'o pia
ke'oke'o wai
keshinui
kihei

kihei 'a'ahu no'eno'e
kilika
kilika lau
kilika nehe
kinamu
kinihama
Knöpflers
koloa
koloka
komo humuhumu
komo lima
ko'oko'o 'amana
kopako
kuakalikea
kueka
kui humahuma
kui kaiapa
kui kele
kui lihilihi
kui ulana
kuiki
kuka
kuka ua
kuka weke
kuka'a
kuka'aila
kukaenalo
kulia
kunono
kupe'e
kupe'e niho 'ilio
ku'uwelu
kwun
la'a
laeloa
lahalile
lai kee wat chau
lainakini
lakeke
lauoho
lauoho ku'i
lei
lei 'a'i
lei ali'i
lei hala
lei hoaka
lei hulu
lei kamoe
lei kolona
lei korona
lei kukui
lei leho
lei niho 'ilio
lei ole
lei 'opu'u

lei palaoa
lei pani'o
lei papa
lei papahi
lei pauku
lei pawehe
lei po'o
lei wiliwili
leki
li kakini
li kaliki
li kama'a
lihilihi 'ula
lilina
lima
lima puha'uha'u
Lindbergh jacket
lipine
lokalio
lole
lole komo
lole lauoho
lole moe po
lole paikau
lole wawae
lole wawae moe po
lole wawae puha'uha'u
lopi
lopi ho'oholoholo
lopi huluhulu
lopi kaholo
lowell cloth
lowerings
lukini
lulu ali'i
lu'u 'ili
ma gua
ma sa
mackinaw
makalena
makalena pu'u
makila
maku'a
maku'e
malo
malo kai
malo wai
mama'o
mameluke
mameluke robe
Mandel
Mao jacket
maolua
ma'oma'o
marseilles quilting

mau'u-la 'ili
mekala
melemele
melemele 'ili 'alani
mercury
Merry Widow
mikini humuhumu
mikini lima
millium
milo lopi
min nap
moelola
mok'kus sin
mong pao
Monmouth cap
Montana peak
Mütze
mu'u mu'u
mu'umu'u moe po
nao-halu'a
nao-ua-ha'ao
nao-ua-nanahuki
napa leather
Neapolitan headdress
Nehru jacket
netcha
ngau hui suck
niho-li'ili'i
niho-mano
ninikea
none-so-pretty
nonomea
oganadi
'ohelohelo
'ohule
oi dai booi dai
'okanaki
'oki pahu
okolepu'u
Old Navajo Dyes
'opu'u kaimana
orrice
overseas cap
'owili
pa'a kama'a
pa'a lole
pa'a mua
pa'eke
pahu papale
paiki pa'alima
pa'ipa'inaha
pa'iua
pakana
pala 'ehu
pala'a

palaka aloha
palalei
palazzo pajamas
pale
pale hanai
pale kila
pale maka
pale pakaukau 'aila
pale papale
pale wawae
palelei
palema'i
palulu maka
papa 'aiana
papale
papale ali'i
papale hainika
papale 'ie
papale kahuna
papale kapu
papale la'a
papale mu'ou'ou
papale 'o'oma
papale waiokila
papalu
pa'u
pa'u heihei
pauma
peeler cotton
pepeiao
petticoat bodice
pihapiha-'o-kohola
pihi
pihi pulima
pima cotton
pine kaiapa
pine kaula'i
pine umauma
pinks and green
pipi
piwa haka
pohaku 'oma'oma'o
poka'a lopi
poka'a-pilali
polonese
po'o hina
po'o ke'oke'o
po'o kuakea
popolohua
pound blanket
pualena
puamoamoa
puka kui kele
puka pihi
pukai

puke pakeke
puki
pupu hoaka
pupu lauoho
pu'ukohukohu
pu'ukukui
qiana
ramall
rayon
rayonné
red rippers
red russels
ribine
Ridgeway buckle
rompers
rosario
Russian suit
sa din
sagathy
Sam Browne belt
sang chau
sapaea
sapeiro
saredonuka
Scotia
Sendai Hira silk
sensuji
shag mittens
sherry-vallies
shimmy
short shorts
shortcuts
shu'lush
silver taupe uniform
siu fung sin
skilts
skokie
slave blanket
slicker
sloppy joe
slops
sook chau
sou'wester
startups
strouding
suburban coat
suggan
surf satin
swing skirt
tatquevluq
teakete
teddies
teddy-bears

tesashi
tignon
tin chiang chiang chau
tokeine
tombeaux
tongs
topaza
topazo
toreadoll pajamas
tow
tow cloth
trapeze
trilby
tuftaffeta
tutu mu'u
Twenty Grands
tyes
uaki
uati
uauahi
'uha hipa
uhi maka
'ula
'ula hiwa
'ula maku'e
'ula palani
'ula waina
'ula weo
'ulahea
'ula'okoko
'umi'i kuapo
'umi'i lauoho
'umi'umi
una
'upa 'oki nihoniho
uwaki
uwaki pulima
wahi
wai 'ele
wai 'ele'ele
wai gula
wai kula
waili'ili'i
waist cincher
waki
watch cap
wedge weave blanket
weleweka
weo
wikolia
ya hoo lam
yi'chit tal
zoot suit

URUGUAY

bombachas

UZBEKISTAN

chuppaun
khalat

paranchah
tyubetevka

VIETNAM

áo
áo bà-ba
áo ba-đò-suy
áo bành-tô
áo bò
áo bông
áo cam-bào
áo cánh
áo cà-sa
áo choàng
áo côc
áo cut
áo da
áo dài
áo đai-trào
áo da-le
áo đan
áo dãu
áo đi mura
áo đuôi-tôm
áo giáp
áo gi-lê
áo kép
áo lan
áo lanh lót vài bông
áo len
áo lông
áo lót
áo lót mình
áo mão
áo muta
áo ngù
áo nit
áo njt
áo tam
áo thày-tu
áo thung
áo toi
áo vét-tông
áo xiêm
áo xõng
aoidai
áp long-bào

Âu-phuc
âu-trang
bach-ngoc
bái ngà
bàn chài quan áo
bành-tô
bao bó
bao táo
bích-không
bich-ngoc
biec
bím
binh-phuc
bít-tãt
bít-tãt tay
bô cánn
bò-lu
bò-lu-dông
bông
bõ-y
búi tó
búi tóc
cái
câm-bào
câm-châu
câ'm-nhung
câ'm-y
can
cân-đai
cánh dán
cánh-kien
cành-phuc
cân-quac
cap tóc
cà-rá
cát-két
ca-vát
chàm
châm
châu báu
chí hong
choi-ngon
chuỗi hat trai

chuoi
cố' còn
cố' tay
com-le
cổ'n-bào
cô-tông
da
da boc-can
da láng
da linh
da lon
dalephuc
dam-thanh
ðan
ðang-ten
dây bang
dây giãy
ðen lánh
dinh cúc
do
dò choé
dò chói
ðò orí
ðõ sô gai
ðôi bit-tât
ðôi bông
ðông-hò ðeo tay
ðông-ho qua quít
ðung
fu-la
ga-ba-ðin
gãm
gãm vóc
gau
gay
ghim bang
giáp
giáp-bào
giáp-y
giá-trang
giay ta
giay tây
giay tuyet
gi-lê
gót
guõc
hieu-phuc
hoa cà
hoa tai
hoàng-bò
hoàng-ngoc
hòng-bào
hong-ngoc
hung-phuc
huyèn-ðai

kep quàn áo
kep tóc
khan ðôi ðàu
khan mùi-soa
khan ngang
khan tang
khan tay
khan trum
khan tua
khan vaông
khan voông
khiên-churong
kim cài ðãu
kim-bang
kim-curong
kim-khôi
kim-ngoc
ki-mô-nô
kim-thoa
kim-thuyen
kính trang
lá sen
láng
lãnh
le-phuc
lon
long-bào
long-con
lót
luroi gà
luroi-trai
lurort
ma canh gián
mã da cam
má hong
mã-não
mang-tô
mãu da giòi
mãu do
may san
may-ô
me-ðay
mo gà
môt chiec
môt ðôi
mu da
mu mán
mu miên
mui dát
ngac
ngân-tinh công-vu
ngoc trao
ngoc-bích
ngoc-miên
ngoc-thach

nguyêt-bach
nhac-ky
nhãn-kính
nhung-trang
ni-lông
nón
nón lá
nón lông
nón sat
núm
nur-trang
ô
oc xà-cù
ông tay áo
pa-đo-suv
phãn sáp
phãn son
pháp-y
phuc-súrc
phu-la
pi-gia-ma
quan
quan cao-boi
quan cháo lòng
quan coc
quan con áo-cánh
quân đùi
quan soóc
quàn ta
quan xà-lon
quân-phuc
quân-phuc đai-le
quân-phuc làm viêc
quat quì
quõc-phuc
quynh
râu cam
râu dê
râu mép
râu som
ren
sám ánh
sám bac
sám đõm
sa-tanh
soi
somi
so-mi ca-rô
so-mi-dét
tang-phuc
tap-de
tay áo
thanh-lam
the
thiet-hài

thi-kính
thuy-ngoc
to hoá-hoc
trang bong
trang nõn
trieu-phuc
tru
trúc-bâu
trurng sáo
tuyn
túyt-xo
vài
vài bò
vài bông
vài hoa
vài long-đình
vài màn
vài to
vài trorn
vài vóc
vân
vàng ánh
vàng đo
vàng huyên
vàng khè
vàng muròri
vàng ròng
van-hài
vãn-phuc
vat
váy
vét-tông
ví tay
vòng huyèn
vòng tai
vú già
xà-cap
xà-cur
xám xì
xám-xit
xanh biec
xanh biéc
xanh da giò-i
xanh da tròi
xanh đam
xanh dòrn
xanh durorng
xanh lá cây
xanh lo
xanh ngát
xanh tham
xà-rông
xiêm áo
xi-líp
xong

xu-chiêng   yem dai
xuyen   y-phuc

YORUBE

alari   etu

YUGOSLAVIA

pafte

ZAIRE

bwoom   mukyeeng
ilaam   mwaandaan
kiing   ncak
mabiim   ncaka ishyeen
mapel   ncok
mbal   nnup
mbala   nshiing
mbala badinga   nyeeng
minyiing   tukula
moro

ZAMBIA

bongos

ZIMBABWE

vhulungu ha madi

ZULU

ulimi   umgingqo

Appendix C: Garment Types by Era

EGYPTIAN (4000–30 B.C.E.)

aegyptium
afef
ankh
as
atef
boukrania
calasiris
crook and flail
deshret
haik royal
heqat and nekhekh
herset
Horus lock
kalasiris
kepresh
khenmet
khepesh
khesbed
klaft
kohl
kyaphi
mefkat
menat
menyet
nekhau

nekhaw
nemehef
Nemes headdress
pano
passium
postiche
procardium
pshente
sacred uraeus
scarab
scaraboid
schenti
Sekhemty
serekh
sheath dress
shendot
shenti
shenu
stibium
udju
was and tam
wedja
weret
wesekh

BIBLICAL (UNKNOWN–30 C.E.)

afrikin
appilion
ata
balneri
begadim levanim
bigdai tsivonim
buros

dalmatikon
ezor
falnis
famalniya
funda
hagorah
haluk

Himmutsatha
impilayoth
istela
isticharion
itstela
kalansuwa
kalmus
karbelathehon
kethoneth
kolob
kova sheberosho
liburnica
maaporeth
mechnesayim
miktorin
minalim
paragod

pateshehon
pilion
polos
purpurea
sarbalehon
sargenes
savrikin
serapis
simlah
sudar
sudar sheal zero-othav
sudar shebetsavaro
tavlin
techeleth
toga
unkelai

GREEK (3000–100 B.C.E.)

aegis
ampyz
anacholus
apodesme
apotygma
Armenian rat
armilla
baltion
binary chiton
birrus
byrrus
caissia
ceryphalos
cestus
chalmyeonchiton
chlaine
chlamus
chlamydon
chlamys
chloene
coccum
coracinus color
cothurnes
cricket
diphtera
diplax
diploidion
doric chiton
faxiolion
hectorean
Ionic chiton
kalyptra
kolobium
kolobus
kolpos

kredemnon
kyne
lacerna
linon
nimbus
peplos
peplos chiton
perizoma
petasos
phainoles
pharos
phoinos
phrygian bonnet
pilos
polos
porphura
saccus
sagos
sakkos
sandalium
sandalon
soccus
soudarion
sphendome
stephane
sticharion
strophion
strophium
subrichion
syrma
taenia
tebenna
tellex
tholia
thorex

tribon
zona

zoster

ROMAN (753 B.C.E.–323 C.E.)

abolla
achates
acus
adamas
alicula
aluta luxor
amethystus
amictorium
amictus
amphimalla
angusti clavi
anthrax
ānulus
armillae
babylonica stromata
balneari
balteum
balteum militare
balteus
beauty patches
beryllus
brachiale
braies
bursa
cacci
calamistrum
calceolus
calceus
calceus patricius
caliga
caligula
cameleurion
capillamentum
caracalla
carbunculus
chausse
chrysolithus
cinctus
cinctus gabinus
cineflone
cingillum
cingulum
cingulum militiae
clavi
cnemis
coācta
colobium
corium
corona

corona etrusca
corona muralis
corona navalis
corona radiata
crepida
crotalia
crystallus
cuculla
cucullus
cūdō
cuprius
cyanus
dalmatic
dalmatica
digitalia
drappus
electrum
epitoga
epomine
facitergium
fascia
feminalia
femoralia
fibula
filum
flammeum
focale
fucus
galerum
galerus
gangetic
gausapa
gemma
gonelle
greaves
impilia
induere
indumentum
indusium
infectore
infula
instita
interala
krepis
lana
laticlaves
linteum
lodix
lorica

lorica hamata
lorica plumata
lorica segmentata
lorica squamata
manica
manitergium
mappa
margarita
māteria
molochine
monache
monīle
muleus
nasitergium
odonarium
odonium
olicula
orarium
orbiculi
orbis
paenula
palla
palliolum
pallium
paludamentum
panni imperiales
pannus
papanaky
paragunda
patagium
pectorale
pērō
pestiman
phaecassium
pileus
pilleus
praetexta
psila
pteruges
ricinium
rose
saggum
sagmatogene
sardius
segmentae
sēricum
signum
sinus
smaragdus
soccae
solea
steatitis
stola
subermalis
sublagaculum

subligaculum
succinta
sūdārium
suffibulum
supparium
synthesis
textīle
textum
tibilaes
Tierfibeln
toga
toga candida
toga cantabulatum
toga gabiana
toga gibina
toga palmata
toga picta
toga praetexta
toga pulla
toga pura
toga sordida
toga trabea
toga umbo
toga virilis
topazon
torque
torques
tunica
tunica alba
tunica augusticlavia
tunica interior
tunica intima
tunica laticlavia
tunica manicata
tunica palmata
tunica taleris
tutulus
tzanga
udo
udones
umbo
velleres fulvi
velleres nigri
vellum
ventus textilis
vestes
vestimentum
vestire
vestis
vestitus
villi
vitis
vitta
zancha
zanga

BYZANTINE AND ROMANESQUE (400–1200 C.E.)

amusse
aurum filatum cyprense
aurum tractitium
baende
barbe
barbette
basing
beah
bearm-clap
beg
beguin
bend
binde
bliand
bliant
bliaunt
bliaus
bombycina
bote
botoun
braccae
braccas
bracco
bractiates
braecce
braies
bratt
brec
brech
brec-hraegel
breost-lin
breost-rocc
broc
broigne
brok
bul
caefing
caeles
caeppe
cagoule
cainsil
calc
calce
caleçons
calyptra
camise
camlet
campagus
cappa
cappe
capuce
capuchon

caracalla
carmeillette
casul
caul
cemes
chainsil
chainse
chape
chausses
chemise
ciclat
clap
clapes
cnaep
cnaipe
cochall
cope
corsage
corse
cote
cotoun
cotta
cotte
crinc
crispine
crispinette
crusene
cuffia
cuffie
culpait
cyrtel
dalc
dalk
diaper
English work
escaffignons
eschapins
facings
fallaing
feax-clap
feax-net
feax-preon
fel
fetel
fetels
fifele
flex
fotgewaed
fouriaux
freiseau
friponne
fustian

fycheux
galerum
gallicae
gerele
gerife
ge-scripla
girdel
girdelstede
glōf
godweb
godweb-cynnn
gonelle
gonellone
gonne
gown
gyrdel-hring
gyrdels
gyrdels-hringe
hacele
haer-naedl
haet
haetera
ham
handewarpes
hand-scio
headrail
heafod-gewaede
healsed
hed-clap
heden
hemepe
hemming
heuze
hod hop-pada
hosa
hoseaux
hose-bend
houppe
hraegel
hraelung
hring
hrycg-hraedel
hufe
hugue
hwitel
inar
inde
iricinium
ispahanis
iuele
jupe
jupel
lake
leine
leperhose

lerion
lether
lettice
loros
lorum
lumman
mafors
maniakes
mentel
mentel-preon
meo
mitons
modeste
mufflers
nedle
nostle
ocreae rostratae
ofer-braedels
ofer-feng
oferlaeg
oferlagu
ofer-slop
ofer-slype
orel
ósain
overslop
pād
paragaudion
pedule
pelicon
pellicea
pellicia
phrygian cap
phrygium
pigache
pilece
poket
pouch
prawing-spinel
preen
preon
reaf
reowe
rheno
rifeling
rift
rilling
riveling
rocc
sagum
saie
sarcenet
say
saye
sceanc-bend

sceanc-gegirla
sceorp
sciccels
sciccing
scipio eburneus
scōh
scrud
scuird
scyfel
scyrte
secrete
serc
sherte
sho
siglat
siglatoen
sigle
siklat
skiradion
slife-scoh
slipe-scoh
smoc
snod
socc
socke
soled hose
sottana
spennels
staeppe-scoh

stemma
stephanos
strapul
strapula
super tunic
superhumeral
swiftlere
tablion
thorakion
threde
trabea
tunece
tunic
under-serc
underwraedel
up-legen
waed-braec
waefels
wasjun
wealca
wimpel
wimple
wining
winingas
wolle
wraed
wrigels
γοûva

EARLY GOTHIC (1200–1350 C.E.)

acca
acton
aglet
agrafe
agraffe
aiglet
aketon
alexander
almoner
amigaut
anelace
anlace
applebloom
appleblue
aquerne
araneous
armure
attaby
aulmoniere
aumoniere
aumuce
Aylesham

baguette
bainbergs
balandrana
baleen
bambergs
barbette
barlingham
barmcloth
barmecloth
barmfell
barmskin
baselard
basen
basinet
batiste
bazan
belette
besague
besshe
beten
bice
bise

bisshe
black-a-lyre
blanchet
blaunchmer
blaundemer
blaundever
blauner
bosses
bouchette
bourdon
bracer
braguette
branched velvet
brassard
brasserole
brayes
brayette
breech-girdle
broella
brunete
burel
burnet
button
bycocket
bycoket
byrnie
byssine
calaber
camaca
camail
cambric
camelin
cameline
camericke
cammaka
camoca
camocas
capeline
cappa clausa
cappa nigra
carda
caul
caurimauri
cendal
cendryn
cervelière
chaisel
chape à aige
chapel-de-fer
chapelle-de-fer
chasuble
chausse
cheklaton
chele
chemise

chevesaille
chisamus
cicimus
ciclaton
ciclatoun
cilice
cimier
cingulum
cogware
coif-de-mailles
coiffette
cointise
cordwain
cornalia
cornu
coronet
corselet
corset
cotehardie
cotelettes
cottereau
couters
crants
cremyll
crespine
crisp
cristygrey
cubitière
cuir-bouilli
cuirie
cuish
cuissard
cuissart
cuisse
culan
culet
cyclas
Cyprian gold
demijambe
demivambrace
dentelle
device
diasper
diaspurum
dogaline
dorelet
doublet
dunster
ecarlate blanches
enarme
enbraude
engreynen
épaulière
epitoga
épomine

ermine
escarelle
esclavine
estrain
falding
falwe
fana
ferret-silke
figgragulÞ
fitchet
Flemysshe cloth
flieder
flurt-silke
foot mantle
foynes
frontière
frounce
fycheux
gadlyngs
gairda
galea
gambeson
gamboised cuisses
ganache
gardebras
garde-collet
garde-corps
gardecors
garde-de-rein
garnache
garnement
genouillieres
genuillieres
gibeciere
gige
gipciere
gipon
gippon
gipser
girdelstede
gite
godalming
gole
gorget
gowce
gris
grise
guarnache
gueules
guige
guimp
guleron
gypciere
habergeon
habit

hatere
haubergeon
hauberk
hausse col
heaume
henke
herigaute
herlot
heuke
heuze
Holland cloth
hollie point lace
hringofinn serkr
huke
hure
imperial
jack
jamb
jambart
jambe
jambeau
jaque
jaquette
jazerant
Judenhut
juppe
kendal
kendal-green
knop
la
lachet
lambrequin
lein
lettice
liripipe
liripium
mahoîtres
mamelieres
mammelieres
mantle and ring
marramas
melote
mescolato
misericorde
moufles
murrey
neat's leather
neck-chain
opus anglicanum
orle
ouch
ourle
paida
palettes
pallets

pallettes
paltock
panni diasperati
pansiere
particolored
passemente
patte
pattens
pauldron
pautener
pedule
pelisson
perse
pied
pillion
pinson
plunket
point
polayn
poleyns
pomme de pin
ponyet
porraye
pourpre
pourpre gris
pourpre sanguine
poynte
pranken
puke
punge
purfle
quintise
ray
raynes
rebras
rerebrace
reticulated headdress
riese
robe longue
rocket
romagnuolo
roskyn
roundel
rowel
russet
saia
samit
samite
samyt
sanguine
sarawil
sarciatus
sarsenet
sarzil
scahwere

schynbaldes
sciameto
sclaveyn
sclavine
sclavyn
scrip
sempringham
sendal
sendelbinde
siglaton
sindon
sismusilis
skōhs
skull cap
slavin
snood
soccus
solers
solleret
sorquenie
soucane
souquenilles
spaier
spang
splints
stamel
stametto
stamfortis
stivali
stranlyng
suckenie
suckeny
surkney
swire
sworl
swyrell
tabby
taces
tache
tackover
tartarin
tartaryn
tasse
tasset
tavestock
tawney
thaub
tilting-helm
tintillano
tippet
tiretaine
toley
tonlet
touret
touret de nez

tressoir
tresson
tressour
tuille
turkils
tussoire
vambraces
virly
volet
volupere
wadmel
wasti

wastjōs
watchet
wede
weed
weyd
worsted
wraed
wulla

LATE GOTHIC (1350–1450 C.E.)

almuce
almuzi
amônières sarrasinoises
armet
armilausa
aurifrisium
bacinet
bag cap
baldekin
bandekin
barbute
barlingham
bascinet
batwat
bellows sleeve
bicoquet
bourguignotte
bourrelet
bracconiere
bracer
braconniere
braguette
brigandine
butterfly headdress
caban
calata
candlewick
cappelina
carcaille
cassis
caurimauri
ceint
cervelliera
champaigne cloth
champeyn
channon cloth
chaperone
chaussembles
chausses semellées

cingulum militare
cloth of gold
collet
colletin
corozoso
corset
coudieres
courtepy
courtepye
cremisi
cress cloth
crest cloth
criss
cristygrey
cukar
cushion headdress
cushion work
dagswain
demysent
escoffion
estaches
false sleeves
fenetres d'enfer
fermail
figury
finger gauntlet
folly bells
forked beard
fret
frette
frog-mouthed helm
frontlet
frounce
fu tou
gaberdine
gadlings
galero
galoche
gimnel-ring

goffered veil
grande-assiette sleeves
haincelin
hanging sleeve
harlot
harlots
haube
haubert à maille double
haubert clavey de double maille
haubert doublier
heafod-clap
hennin
houppelande
houppelande à mi-jambe
housse
huke
huque
huve
journade
jupon
kall
kareeta
kettle hat
kettyl hat
kruseler headdress
lamboys
langet
langettes
lendener
maljor
mang
marbrinus
maskel lace
miniver
napron
nebula headdress
nifles
nightcap
nun's work
opus consutum
opus filatorium
opus pectineum
opus phrygium
opus plumarium
opus pulvinarium
pale
paltock

parrock
piked shoe
pokeys
pomander
pople
poulaines
pourpoint
pudding-basin cut
salade
sarpe
sarrasinoises
scheckenrock
serpe
shiu tian yi
sideless surcoat
simarra
simarre
sorket
spangles
steeple headdress
tabard
tappert
tarf
tater
templers
temples
templettes
tewke
tocco
toghe
tonlet
touaille
troussoir
truffe
truffeau
tuft
tuke
turf
turkey bonnet
tyrf
wammes
wedding knives
white scarlet
xie zhai
ying long
zache
zadblauwen

RENAISSANCE (1450–1550 C.E.)

à gomito
à gozzo
adarque
affiquet

aghetto
agugello
aiglet
ailerons

alas
albornoz
alessandrino
aljófar
aljuba
allucciolati
almain coat
almayne rivet
almenadas
almizclera
altibajo
anadem
anime
anteojos
appicciolato
argentería
armes à l'épreuve
arming-bonett
arming-hose
armure cannelée
atrocelado
attiffet
avampiés
azufar
badana
baft
bagging shoe
baize
baldrés
balesses
balza
balzana
balzo
bamagia
barbe
barbette
barret
barthaube
base coat
bases
basquine
baticol
Battenburg lace
baudekyn
bauson skin
bavolet
bear's paw
beatilla
beaupers
beck
beguin
benda
benerica
bents
berettino

Beringt
bernia
besague
bianchetto
bigio
blackerybond
blackwork
blanc haubert
bocaran
boccaccino
bodkin-beard
body stichet
body-stychet
bohemio
bokasyn
bombasino
bombast
bongrace
botinicos
bottoni
boulevart
bragetto
brahón
branc
brassière
bredon
breeches
brial
brichette
bridgwater
Bristol red
brocado raso de pelo
brochetta
brodekin
brogues
Brunswick cloth
bruschino
bruststück
Buckinghamshire lace
buckram
buffin
bufle
buratto lace
busc
busk
buske
busq
busque
caddice garter
caddis leather
cadenilla
caderas postizas
caffa
cairel
cale

calpac
calva
calzas conpies
calzas enteras
calzas largas
cámara
camarera mayor
cambelloto
camocho
cannequin
cañutillos
capelina
capellar
caperuza
capilla
capirote
carpmeal
carpmeal white
carrel
castle
cater-cap
caungeantries
cebtí
celada de engole
cenojil
ceruse
cettelle
chaffers
chamarre
chammer
chapel d'acier
chapel de Montauban
chapiron
chatelaine
chaussons
chianetta
chinela
chupa
chymer
cioppa
clavos
cloke
close-gauntlet
clot
cly
coazzone
cod-placket
coffer headdress
cofia de tranzado
colley-westonward
colorado
colori corozoso
conch
cophia
coppo

cordeliere
cordellate
cordonero
corked shoes
corned shoe
corner cap
cornet
cornette
corps a baleine
corps piqué
cotehardie
cotswold
cotta de maglia
couleur-de-roi
cramignole
cremesino
croppes
cuaran
cuerpo baxo
cut-fingered pumps
cyprus
dagged
dalk
damaschino
de lazo
demiceint
demi-gown
demipauldron
demy-teste
deshilado
dilge
doblados todos
dorneck
dorso
dos
dossière
dou niu
double
doublet
drawers
drum farthingale
duck-billed shoes
durance
duretty
eared shoe
Eisenkappe
elbow cloak
elbow gauntlet
elbow-cops
elmo di giostra
empeines
encarnado
English hood
English work
entretela

ermellini
escaffignons
espulgeata
esquirole
estameña
estofado
estofée
estrich
estridge
estrith
everlastings
falda
faldia
faldrilla
fall
farthingale
fautre
fazzoletto
fei yu
felted knitting
fents
fermaglio
filetto
finestrella
firmale
flea-fur
flipe
flocket
flourish
forest cloth
forest white
fraise
franjas
French cloak
French hood
frenello
frieze
frill
frisure d'or
frizado
frontlet
frose paste
fruncidas
gabano
gabardine
gabbano
gable headdress
galloshoes
galosses
gamurra
garanza
garvín
Gates of Hell
gatos de lomos
gayado

gayas
gefrens
gemmews
genouillieres
giardinetti rings
gimstān
glandkin
glib
goller
gömlek
gooseturd greene
gorgias
gorguera
grana
grana encarnada
grano d'orzo
graundice
gregues
grigio
gualescio
guards
guazzerone
halecret
half shirt
halshemd
handewarpes
harden
hault collet
hausse col
hembras
Hentzen
herrenhutte
herrete
heuke
hevilla
hiladillo
hive
hodtrene
holanda
hollow lace
hoqueton
horsehair petticoat
huke
inkle
Italian cloak
jirones
jornea
jubeteros
jubon
Kamfhandschuhe
kirtle
kyrtill
labrada
lacca
ledersen

leefekye
lemister
lemster
lienzo de la India
limiste
lista
little hennin
llano
loba
lobas compridas
lucco
maglia piatta
magliette
maheutres
mahoîtres
mainfaire
mairtíní
mancheron
maneras
maniche á comeo
manopla
manople
manteline
mantellina
manto
margaritte
marlota
marlotte
marquisetto beard
martingale breeches
Mary Stuart cap
maspilli
mechones
mechuelas
medaglio
medias mangas
mene
mezail
Milan bonnet
milk and water
mockado
mofeler
monachino
morello
morion
morisco work
musequí
must deviles
mustard villars
mustardevelin
mustardevillers
myllion
nabchet
naqsha
necked bonnet

nesgada
nether stocks
night rail
nycette
occularium
oes
ojales
or nué
or trect
oro de orilla
oro hilado
packing white
pagonazzo
palet
paletoque
palo di lione
pampilion
pannicelli
pannus sine grano
paño de brunete
paño de la tierra
paño tuntido
pantofle
pantuflo
paonazzo
pardillo
partidor de crencha
partlet
passe-filon
patelet
pavonazzo
pectoll
pee
peinadore
pellanda
peñas veras
perle
perlin
pespuntaderas
petto
pianelle
picado
pilus tinctus
pizane
placardo
placcards
placcates
plackard
plantillas
plateado
Platner
Pleasance
plodan
pretina
puertas

punta
punto de almorafán
punto de oro llano
punto in aria
punto llano
punto real
qilim
quezote
rabat
randas
raploch white
raso
reta
ritterhute
roanes
robe à plis gironnés
robe de commune at ancienne guise
robe déguisée
robe gironnée
rollo
rondz
ropa bastarda
ropa de estado
ropa larga
ropa rozagnte
rosato
ruedo
russell
russells
sagetta
Saint Martin's lace
saya
sbernia
Scheitelstuck
sea coat
sea-gown
sella
servilla
shakefold
shamew
shoe horn
showing horn
side
skin-coat
slashings
sleaved silk
slips
solleret
splay-footed shoes
splyter-hat
stamyn sengill
stomacher
stringhe
sugar-loaf bonnet

sussapine
tambour
tasseau
tassel
testière
thrummed hat
timbre
tippet
toca de camino
tock
toocke
toque
torzal
traguardo
tremolanti
trepats
trinzale
trouses
troussoire
trowses
trunk hose
tuck
tuly
turchino
turf
turkey gown
tylesent
under cap
velette
venera
verdingale
verdugado
vertugadin
vertugadin francais
vesses
vivos
voided shoe
volante
wearing sleeves
wedding garter
welt
whalebone bodice
whalebone bodies
wimpled
wings
woolward
zarzahan
zazzara
zendado
zendale
zimarra
zoccolo
zywr

ELIZABETHAN (1550–1625 C.E.)

aglet
alb
albangala
Albanian hat
Alcorque
almain hose
almain rivet
anima
ankle-breeches
anlet
annelet
annulet
apparel
armet
arming bolster
arming doublet
arming points
asooch
atlas
Ave Maria lace
baby cap
bag Holland
bairam
bairami
baldric
baldrick
band
band strings
bandileer
bandoleer
bandolier
barrel hose
barrette
basquine
baudekin
baudekyn
baudricke
bavarette
bawdric
bearams
bearing cloth
beaver
beiramee
bents
beram
beronis
bevor
biggin
biggon
bilbo
biliment
bill
billiment

biretta
bishop's mantle
black lace
bodies, pair of
bodkin
bodkin cloth
boemio
boershabijt
Bologna crape
bone lace
boratto
borceguí
borst
bouwen
bragoenen
bragueta
bride lace
brigandine
brogetie
brogs
buckler
budge
buff jerkin
bullion hose
bum-barrel
buratto
busk point
buske
buskins
busq
busque
bustian
byramee
byrampaut
byrams
byramy
cabaset
cabasset
cabbage shoestring
cabbage-ruff
cabestrillo
caleçons
calico
calimanco
calton
calzaz de aguja
cambric
camericke
cañamazo doblado
cane color
canions
cannon sleeves
cantaloon

capa
cap-a-pie armour
cape à l'espanole
capouch
capuch
caputium
carcanet
cardinal white
cardows
carkanette
carkenet
carnation
carnaza
carriages
cartoose collar
cased body
castor
catalowne
catalpha
catgut lace
cathedral beard
Catherine wheel farthingale
chamblette
chausses en bourses
chaussures à cric
chaussures à pont-levis
cheney
cheveril
chicken skin glove
chimere
chin-clout
chiveret
chopines
cloak-bag breeches
clog
close cap
cobweb lawn
cockle hat
codpiece
coiffure à la Ninon
coiffure en cadenettes
coiffure en raquette
conch
conque
copatain
copitank
copotain
coquard
cordobán
cordouan
cornet
countenances
crane color
crespe
cross gartering

cross-cloth
cuff strings
culot
cushionet
cut linen work
cuttanee
dalmatica
damasellours
damasin
datilado
de todo lazo
dead Spaniard
demi-castor
Dieppe point lace
dogskin
dowlas
drawings out
drawn work
dreumelthoelje
dust gown
duster
Dutch cloak
Dutch waist
ear string
eelskin sleeve
ellementes
English farthingale
etui
eyelet doublet
falling band
farandine
fardegalijn
farthingale
farthingale breeches
farthingale sleeves
ferreruelo
ferret
fers
fieltro
Flanders serge
floramedas
flower pot hat
flycap
forepart
French hose
French ruff
French sleeves
friponne
frislet
frouting
galerilla
galligaskins
galocha
gamashes
gansbauch

garlicks
gaskin
gauntlet
gestaltrock
gingerline
ginglers
Golconda chintz
golilla
goose-turd
gran gola
gregesque
Guard infanta
habit
hair
halsneusdoek
hammercut beard
hand-ruffs
hangers
harzkappe
heerpauke
herreruelo
hollow lace
huik
incarnate
Indian gown
Indian nightgown
indiennes
jack boot
jack chain
jack leather
jaseran
jerkin
jessamy gloves
Judenkragen
kanzasi
kasacken
kennel headdress
kirtle
kittel
kletje
klier
knee breeches
knee-string
kolbe
kolder
kroplap
kusi
kyara-abura
lap-mantle
latchet
lawn
lechugilla
lettice bonnet
lettice cap
lettice ruff

liga
lijf
Lincoln green
linsey-woolsey
linstock
loo mask
loretto
lower stocks
lustie-gallant
mage
maiden hair
maide's blush
mandilion
mantilla
marumage
Masulipatam chintz
Medici collar
milk and water
modeste
monial
monjil
Monmouth cap
montero
monteroe
Moorish lace
moto-yui
moulds
mountero
murrey
nachttabbaert
napkin
napkin hook
Naples lace
neerstick
nettlecloth
night coif
night-kercher
Norwich crepe
nun's thread
onderriem
onderzieltie
orange tawny
oriellettes
orphreys
Oxford gloves
panseron
panses
pantuflo
pass
peach
peak lace
pearl of beauty
peascod belly
pendicle
peropus

perpets
perpetuana
perspective glass
piccadil
pilch
pilche
pileus
pinion
pinking
pipkin
pique devant
placard
placket
pluderhose
plummet
plunket
poke
poking stick
poldavis
pomander
ponyet
popes ministers
popinjay
portefraes
primrose
privy coat
provincial rose
puffjacke
pug
puke
pullicat
pullings out
purl
putting stick
quail-pipe boot
querpo
querpo hood
ramall
rat's color
rattan
rebato
reister cloak
reitrocke
rennrocklein
reticello
ropa
ropilla
roundlet
ruff
ruiterrock
rullion
sagathy
safeguard
Saint Omer
sangyn

scabilonians
scalings
scapulari
scavilones
schaubelein
secrete
servilla
shadow
shag-ruff
shakefold
sheep's russet
ship-tire
shotten-bellied doublet
shoulder belt
shoulder heads
shoulder straps
simada
sirge debarabon
sister's thread
skimskin
slesia lawn
slops
small slops
snoskyn
snowskin
snufkin
snuftkin
soletila
sombrero
spagnolet
Spanish cloak
Spanish farthingale
Spanish hose
Spanish kettledrums
Spanish leather
Spanish morion
Spanish needlepoint
Spanish slops
spere
speyer
spider helmet
starch
startop
startups
statute cap
steutelreecx
stock-drawers
stomacher
strammel
straw
strossers
suela
suit of ruffs
supertasse
supportasse

surplice
tabbaert
tablet
tail clout
takenaga
tassettes
tennis shoe
tobin
tobine
toilet
toilet cap
tongs
tontillo
trawerbandes
trusses
tucker
tuichje
turnover
twillet
under proper
upper stocks

vasquine
venetians
ventoye
verdugado
vertugadin
vest
vexillum
visor
visscherspij
vlieger
Waborne lace
wappenrock
watchet
wedding gloves
wheel farthingale
whey
willow
wing
zaragüelles
zueco
zukin

CHARLES I AND THE COMMONWEALTH (1625–1660 C.E.)

Augusta
baby Stuart cap
balagnie cloak
batts
bei yen
bend-leather
bisette
bourdalou
bucket-top boot
bull's head fringe
cachelaid
cadanette
cadenette
casaque
chadoe
chang fu
chao dai
chao gua
chao guan
chao pao
chao zhu
chau fu
chivaret
coiffure à la moutonne
colberteen
colbertine
collet monte
cravat
devantiere
falling band

fält-teken
fancies
favors
figurero
figuretto
filozella
filozetta
firmament
fob pocket
French fall
French pocket
fustian anapes
galants
gallants
garcettes
Geneva print ruff
girdle glass
glove-band
gourgandine
gulik holland
gun fu
half-beaver
hand fall
historical shirt
hollmes
Hungerland band
Hungerland lace
Indiennes
iron-pot
jabot

jerkin
jerkinet
ji guan
kithaika
ling yue
lobster helmet
lodier
long pao
mandeville
mang pao
manteau
mantua maker
mantua woman
meurtriers
mogul breeches
monté la haute
morella de Venus
mouchoir
nagdeh
neck button
Northampton lace
novato
okhaben
ollyet
orange-butter
osbro
pantile
passagers
patna
petticoat breeches
philiselie
philoselle
pinner
pintado

polonese
polonia
pu fu
religious petticoat
rhinegraves
robe de chambre
robe volante
rochet
rond
roquet
Sedan lace
serpentaux
shag
sheep's gray
sherry-vallies
skirduk
skofium
sleeve hand
smock petticoat
snake
solette
soulette
Spanish boots
Spanish breeches
Spanish hose
stirrup hose
stirrup stockings
surpied
tian ze
ticklenburg
vigone
whisk
whittle
xiang se

RESTORATION (1660–1700 C.E.)

alamode
amadis sleeve
Antwerp lace
araignée méditant un crime
baiberek
banyan
barratine
berger
bib-cravat
binette
boot hose
Brandenburg
breadeen
breidin
camisole
campaign coat
campaign wig

campaigne
caroline hat
casaque
cassock
caudebec hat
caul
cawdebink
chaconne
cheats
chite
chitterlings
choux
confidents
cordyback hat
crapaud mort d'amour
crapaud saisi
cravat strings

creve-coeur
cruches
cul de Paris
culotte
dildo
duchess
echelon
elatch
elatcha
falbala
fal-lal
flandan
fontanges
frangipani perfume
frouze
full bottomed wig
furbelow
gamoshes
gougandine
heart-breaker
hip buttons
hounds ears
hurluburlu
hurlupe
jackanapes
Jacobean embroidery
jockey boot
jockey cap
jockey sleeve
jumps
justaucorps
knee buckles
knee-band
knee-fringe
knee-piece
knee-string

lavaliere
mante
manteau
Mazarin hood
mousquetaire
muff bracelet
out-coat
palisade
pallatine
pantaloons
paragon
Persian vest
Philip and Cheney
Philip and China
plumpers
point de sedan
Portuguese farthingale
queue
rabat
renforcée
rollers
rolling stockings
roll-up breeches
roll-up stockings
rollups
sacristan
scallop
settee
shell
shoulder knots
soieries bizarres
sorti
sortie
souris éffrayée
Steinkirk
strips

EARLY GEORGIAN (1700–1750 C.E.)

à la Maintenon
adrienne
aiguillette
ailette
alajah
aleejah
alepine
anabas
andrienne
anserine
anterne
armazine
armozeen
armozine
bag wig
bagnolette

bahut
bandore
bandore peak
barkit
barleycorn
beaudoy
beguin
bergere hat
bicoquets
binder
blancard
bob-wig
bonnet cabriolet
boot cuff
braiel
breast hook

breast knot
brillianette
broglio-broglio
Brunswick
buckled wig
busby
caffoy
cambresine
capote
carrodary
casaquin
caul
caxon
chain buckle
chancellor
chapeau-bras
chapska
chemisette
cherryderry
cockers
cocrez
coggers
coiffure en cadenettes
cokers
colmar
common dress
considerations
cotellae
crapand
crapaud
Cremona cravat
criardes
cross pocket
cupola coat
cut-fingered gloves
denim
desoy
Dettingen cock
domino
Dorset thread button
dorsetteen
drab
dragon's blood cane
drawboys
duroy
Duvillier wig
elbow cuff
elminetta
engageantes
English nightgown
English ringlet
equipage
facings
falbala
fall

falls
false gown
false hips
fan hoop
fantail wig
fearnothing jacket
festoons
filleadh beag
fingroms
fly-fringe
fly-suit
fob ribbon
follette
fortop
furbelow
gallowses
galluses
gentish
German serge
glove string
gown à la francaise
grassets
grazzets
gridelin
grogram
gros vilain vert
gulik holland
gulix
habit glove
habit shirt
haiduk
hair-lace
half handkerchief
Hamilton lace
harlem stripes
harrateen
hasp
hongreline
inderlins
jambee cane
jansenistes
jemmy cane
joseph
justcoat
kall
kilmarnock
kincob
kinkhaib
kissing-strings
kountouch
lappet
le crapaud
leading strings
livery lace
long Duvallier

lustring
lutestring
lutherine
Malacca cane
Manchester velvet
mantee
manteel
mantle
mantling
mantua
Marseilles embroidery
Mazarine hood
medley
modestie
modesty piece
moreen
muckender
muff
muffetees
nabob
napkin-cap
neck handkerchief
neckstock
negligee
night-cap wig
nithsdale
oiled leather
oilets
orgagis
orris
padou
paduasoy
panier a coudes
paniers a bourelets
paniers anglais
panniers
papillotes
parament
passacaille
passecaille
perruque quarrée
perse
Persian
pet-en-l'air
petits bonhommes
pigtail wig
plumage
polakem
pompon
powdering dress
powdering gown
powdering jacket
pretintailles
prince's stuff
pudding sleeve

pug hood
purnellow
Quaker hat
qualitie
queue
quilted petticoat
quitasol
quizzing glass
Ramillies wig
ras de Sicile
ras du more
riding habit
riding hoop
robe longue
robin
robings
roquelaure
rosadimoi
rotonne
ruffled shirt
russaline
sablé
sabretache
sack gown
sacque
sagathie
sagathy
satinesco
scratch bob
scratch wig
selisie lawn
sergedesoy
sergedusoy
shaving hat
shell
shift
silesia
slammerkin
sleasy holland
slivers
slyders
snail
snail button
solitaire
soosey
spatter dashes
spencer wig
spit-boot
stalk button
stay hook
stock buckle
superfine
swanskin
tabby
tabine

tammy
tatas
temple spectacles
tête de mouton
thrum cap
thunder and lightning
tiffany
tobin
toilet
top
toupee
toupet
treillis
trollopée
tucker

tuftaffeta
tufted dimity
tye
umbrella robe
undress
vergette a la chinoise
Watteau hat
Watteau pleat
wildbore
Woodstock gloves
worms
wotenall thread
wrapping gown
wrap-rascal
wraprascal

LATE GEORGIAN (1750–1790 C.E.)

à la Farare
à la Figaro
à la Marlborough
à la plaquette
à l'innocence reconnue
Adonis wig
adrienne
aile de pigeon
amadis
an nouveau desire
artois
artois buckle
au globe fixe'
badine
baigneuse
balloon hat
bavette
bicorne
blucher
boisson
bonnet à la crête de coq
bonnet à la laitière
bonnet à la moresque
bonnet à la Richard
bonnet à la victoire
bonnet aux trois ordres réunis
bonnet demi-negligee
bonnet négligée
bootikin
bosom bottles
bosom flowers
boudoir cap
bourrelet
Brussels camlet
buffon

buffonts
butterfly cap
cabriole
cadogan
calash
capuchin
caputrock
caraco
caraco à coqueluchon
caraco à la française
caraco à la polonaise
caraco gown
caravan
casaquin en juste
catogan
cauliflower wig
chapeau à la Basile
chapeau à la Cérès
chapeau à la Charlotte
chapeau à la Chérubin
chapeau à la Colonne
chapeau à la Devonshire
chapeau à la Grenarde
chapeau à la turque
chapeau à l'égyptienne
chapeau à l'italienne
chapeau au bateau renversé
chapeau de Cardinal
chapeau jockei
chapeau-bras
charlotte
chemise à la Reine
chignon flottant
chip hat
circassienne gown

clouded lustrings
clubwig
coiffure à la conseillere
coiffure à la Dauphine
coiffure à la enfant
coiffure à la Eurydice
coiffure à la Flore
coiffure à la Junon
coiffure à la qu' es aco
coiffure à la Reine
coiffure à l'anglomane
coiffure au chien couchant
coiffure en chien couchant
coiffure en moulin à vent
coiffure en parterre galant
cork rump
costume au grand Figaro
court habit
court plaster
crape
creoles
crocus
crop
cul de crin
cul postiche
curch
dannocks
dauphiness
de frivolité
death's head button
demi-tablier
Denmark cock
Devonshire hat
dittos
dormeuse
dormouse
downy calves
Dresden work
earthquake dress
en dos d'ane
en échelle de Jacob
en fourreau lace
en platitude
en pouf
en pouf à la Luxembourg
English gown
esclavage
esquavar
fantail hat
fausse montre
favorite
favourite
fazolo
feather-top wig
fichu

fichu menteur
Fitzherbert hat
flea
florinelle
flounce
frac
French frock
frizz wig
fustan
Gainsborough hat
galante
garnet
gaze à bouquets
gaze de fantaisie
geknauften kogeln
Genoa velvet
German gown
gilet vest
glocken
gorge à la Gabrielle d'Estreés
gorge de pigeon
gown à la française
gown à la levantine
gown à la polonaise
gown à la sultane
gown à l'anglaise
gown à l'insurgente
gown and coat
grand domino
grand habit
grand habit de cour
grande pelisse d'hiver
grande redingote à l'allemande
grande robe à corps ouvert
grande robe à la française
gueridons
habit
habit à la française
habit de demi-gala
habit d'escalier
hairbines
half silk
half-dress
hat screw
hedgehog hairdo
highlows
hoop petticoat
hum-hum
hummums
Irish polonaise
Italian heel
Italian nightgown
jasey
jin huang
Joan

kampskatcha
kampskatcha slipper
kenting
klapbroek
konfederatka
kurtka
lamballe
laylock
le gilet
levite
levite gown
liars
lilac
lilack
Limerick gloves
love lock
lunardi
macaroni cravat
macaroni suit
major wig
manchettes
manteau à la cavaliere
manteau à l'italienne
mantelet au lever de l'aurore
mariner's cuff
marsina
Mary Queen of Scots cap
massereen blue
Mecklenburg cap
mecklenburgh
menteurs
mercury
mignonette lace
military stock
mirliton
miser's purse
mob-cap
morning gown
neckatee
negligee de la volupte
nightgown
Nivernois
noeuds d'amour
none-so-pretty
olive button
olivette
papeline
parapluie
parasol à canne
parchment calves
parfait-contentement
pelerine
pencilled
Perdita chemise
petite robe unie

petit-maître
petit-maîtresse
physical wig
Piedmont gown
pierrot
pigeon-winged toupee
pinchbeck button
poches
polonaise
polonaise à deux fins
pompadour
pompadour heel
porcelain button
poufs au sentiment
prudent
prune de Monsieur
pudding cap
Pultney cap
quadrille head
quartered cap
Ranelagh mob
redingote à l'amazone
redingote du matin
redingote en Backmann
riding habit
robe à la circassienne
robe à la française
robe à la levantine
robe à la polonaise
robe à la Reine
robe à la Turque
robe à l'américaine
robe à l'anglais
robe de cérémonie à la française
robe parée
robes de fantaisie
round dress
round gown
scarlet
serge de soy
serre-tête
shade
shoepack
skilts
slops
Spanish paper
spring boots
suit
swallow's nests
swan's down
swansdown
taffeta lustré
tambouring
Teresa
Thérèse

top boot
toque à la Basile
toque à la Grande Pretesse
toque à la Susanne
toque à l'Iphigenie
trolly cap
trompeurs
tulle
turban bonnet

vallancy
vandyke
vandyke dress
vermicelli
vêtement à la Créole
wai tao
yallow
zone
Zopfzeit

DIRECTOIRE AND FIRST EMPIRE (1790–1815 C.E.)

à la Titus
à la Victime
aerophane
Agatha robe
alliballi
amadis
amaranth
amaranthus color
amazones
andalusian casaque
anglo-merino
Angoulême hat
Angoulême tippet
Anne Boleyn mob
Apollo corset
appas postiches
arched collar
Ayreshire
Ayreshire work
bag bonnet
balantine
balucher
banditti
barouche
basane
beehive bonnet
beehive hat
benjamin
Betsie
bishop's blue
bivouac mantle
Bonaparte helmet
bosom friends
bottle-green
boucle d'oreille à la guillotine
Brandenburg fringe
Brighton nap
brocatelle
Brummel bodice
Brutus cut
Brutus head wig
buckskin

cabriolet
cache-folies
cadenat
Caledonian silk
calypso chemise
canezou
cannetille
cantab hat
cantoon
cap à la Charlotte Corday
capot-ribot
capriole
carmagnole
carmine
caroline spencer
carthage cymar
casbans
cased sleeve
casimir
casque à la Tarleton
chapeau-bras
charicari
chemise à la greque
chemise à l'anglaise
chemise gown
chenille
cherusque
cherusse
chinese spenser
circassian hat
circassian sleeve
circassian wrapper
clarence blue
clawhammer tails
coalscuttle bonnet
coatee
cockade
coiffure à la Chinoise
coiffure à l'indisposition
coiffure en bouffons
colback
collerette

comforts
conversation bonnet
conversation hat
coquillicot feathers
cordey cap
cornet hat
cornette
corset
corset frock
cossack hat
cossacks
costume á la Constitution
cottage bonnet
cottage front
coups de vent
coureur
court sleeve cuff
crepine
curled silk
curls à la Greque
curricle cloak
curricle dress
czapska
demi-converti
demi-tunique
demi-turban
Devonshire brown
dinner cap
dorretteen
douillette
douillette à la Russienne
drab style
droguet
drugget
Dutch bonnet
eau de veau
ecrouellique
Egyptian brown
en colimaçon
English chain
escarpins
esprits
faces
fall
fan parasol
Fatima robe
fichu menteur
filé
fleshings
florence
Florence satin
flushing hat
flying josie
fogle
forage cap

French gores
French net
frisé
frizé
fugitive coat
garrick greatcoat
Georgian cloth
gipsy hat
girdle à la victime
Glengarry
gorgoran
gossamer satin
gown à la turque
Graham turban
greatcoat dress
Grecian robe
Grecian sandal
gros de Naples
gros de Tours
habit degage
hair à la Recamier
hair à la Romaine
half boot
helmet cap
hessian
Hibernian vest
Hungarian vest
Hungarian wrap
hunting belt
Huntley bonnet
hussar boots
Hussar buskins
Hyde Park bonnet
indispensible
Italian slipper
jaconas
jaconet
jaconette
Jan de Bry coat
Jean de Bry coat
jockei
jockey bonnet
jockey waistcoat
jonquille
joseph
juive
kerseymere
kutusoff hat
kutusoff mantle
lamé
lampas
Lavinia hat
Liberty cap
liseré
litewka

mameluck
mameluke
mameluke robe
mameluke turban
manchette de cour
manilla brown
marabout feathers
marceline
Mathilde
Medusa wig
melon sleeve
mexican
Minerva bonnet
mirliton
mistake
mistake hat
Moravian work
morone
moschettos
muscadin
muscadine
muslin deaths
nacarat
naccarat
nakara color
napoleon
Neapolitan bonnet
Oatland village hat
obi hat
Oldenburg bonnet
oreilles de chien
pagoda parasol
palatine
pamela
panne
pantalettes
pantalons à pont
pantaloons
parure
patent lace
patent net
paysanne bonnet
pea-green
peau de soie
pekin satin
pelise
pelisse
Persian cap
Persian scarf
pilgrim's hat
Platoff cap
Platoff costume
pleated shirt
pleated trousers
ploughman's gauze

plush
poire
poissarde
poke bonnet
Poland mantle
Polish greatcoat
polrock
Pomona green
pomposa
porc-epic
porcupine headdress
pourpre
pregnant stay
Princess Augusta poke
Princess Elizabeth lilac
Princess of Wales bonnet
provincial bonnet
puff
pusher lace
pussycat bonnet
raquettes
regency cap
regency hat
regency mantle
regency wrapper
ridicule
riding habit
robe à la prêtesse
robe torque
robes en calecon
Robespierre collar
Robinson hat
roguelo dress
roons
rotonde
rotonelle
ruban d'amour
Russian flame
Rutland poke
sabretache
saccharine alum
salt-box pocket
sandals à la greque
sans-culottes
Sardinian mantle
satin rouleaux
sautoir
schauslooper
Scotia silk
scye
semptress bonnet
shag mittens
shako
skeleton suit
slash pocket

slashed sleeve
sleeve à la Minerva
Spanish blue
Spanish coat
Spanish fly
Spanish hat
Spanish sleeve
spencer
spencer cloak
spencerette
spider work
spring
stand-fall collar
starcher
stocking-purse
Strumpfhosen
suarrow boots
surtout à la Sultane
Swedish cuffs
telescope parasol
terrendam
toilonette
toque
Trafalgar dress
Trafalgar turban
treble ruff
trencher hat

tricot de Berlin
triple ruff
tunic à la juive
tunic à la mameluck
tunic à la Romaine
tunique à la Juive
turban-diademe
Turkish turban
Tyrolese cloak
veldschoen
veletine
velours Grégoire
Venetian bonnet
Wallachian cap
Wardle hat
wasserfall
weepers
willow green
witch's hat
wrapping front dress
Wurtenburg frock
yeoman hat
York tan gloves
York wrapper
zephyr cloak

ROMANTIC (1815–1840 C.E.)

à la Byron
à la jardiniere
à la Napoleon
adelaide
Adelaide blue
Adelaide boot
aetherial
Albert boots
alizarin
alpaca
amelie
amelle
amen
American
American green
Amy Robsart satin
andalusian
Anglo-Greek bodice
Angoulême bonnet
Angoulême spencer
antique bodice
Apollo
Apollo knot
aquatic shirt

Aragonese bonnet
arcari
Armenian toque
armozeau
aurora
aventurine
avignon
azure
babet bonnet
babet cap
ballroom neckcloth
balzarine
barbel
barège
basque belt
Bavarian dress-style
Bavarian pelisse robe
beaverteen
beret sleeve
Berlin gloves
bertha
bibi bonnet
bibi capote
bird of paradise

bishop's knot
body coat
Bolivar hat
bonnet à barbes
bonnet beehive
bonnet pamela
bonnet sylphide
bottine
bouffant mecanique
bouffante sleeve
bouillion
Bourbon hat
box coat
brandenbourgs
Brazilian corded sarcenet
brides
brodequin
buridan
burrail collar
Byron collar
byzantine embroidery
Caledonian cap
camargo hat
cameloleopard
canezou spencer
capa
capot
careless
carmeillette
carnagan
caroline corsage
caroline sleeve
casaweck
cased body
cashmere shawl
cassenet
cavalier sleeve
celestial
chaine de forçat
cheats
chemisette
cheyney
chicoree
chin stays
chinese green
cifatten
circassian bodice
circumfolding hat
clarence
clotidienne
Coburg bonnet
coiffure a l'Agnes Sorel
corinna
corinth blue
cornette à la Diane

corsage à la Maintenon
corsage à la vierge
corsage en corset
corsage en Fourreau
cottage cloak
couchouc
cran
cravate à la Bergami
cravate mathématique
crispin
csakora cut
csizma
Cumberland corset
Cumberland hat
curricle coat
curricle pelisse
cushion headdress
dandizette
de Berri
de France
de Roi
demicaul
demi-surtout
dentes de loup
diadem comb
diszmagyar
divorce corset
dolman
Donna Maria
d'Orsay coat
d'Orsay pump
d'Orsay roll
double bouffant sleeves
draft
dress Wellington
dust of ruins
Dutch skeleton dress
eccelide
elastic hat
elastic-sided boots
elephant sleeve
elysian
eminence
English chain
English cottage bonnet
esterhazy
fanchon
ferroniere
fichu Corday
fichu-canezou
fichu-pelerine
fichu-robings
flushings
fly's wing
forester's green

fraise
French bearer
French boa
French bottoms
French work
frock coat
frog
Gabrielle sleeve
Gallo-Greek bodice
gauging
gibus
gipsy cloak
Glauvina pin
gothic cap
gourgourans
gray lilac
guard chain
hare pocket
harrington
Huguenot lace
hunting necktie
Huntley scarf
Hussar point
imbecile
Indian
Indian green
Indian necktie
Indian rubber
ineffibles
inexpressibles
ipsiboe
Isabella
Isabella color
Ivanhoe cap
Japanese rose
jeanette
Jemima
jemmy
jemmy boots
jet buttons
jigger button
jockey
jokey
kluteen
languette
lavender
Lavinia
leg of mutton sleeves
levantine
levantine folicé
Lily Benjamin
London dust
London mud
London smoke
macabre

mackintosh
madras turban
mail coach
mameluke
mantelette
Marie sleeve
Marie Stuart bodice
Marie Stuart bonnet
marino faliero sleeve
marmotte bonnet
marmotte cap
marquise mantle
marseilles quilting
marshmellow
Medici sleeve
mente
mentonnierres
metallic gauze
military frock coat
Moabite turban
Modena red
monster green
Montespan
Montespan sleeve
Moorish boot
mosaic gauze
mummy brown
Napoleon necktie
Navarino smoke
Neapolitan headdress
negligee
Newgate fringe
Newmarket coat
Nicholas blue
nursing dress
oiseau
opera hat
Orleans brown
Osbaldiston tie
oval beaver hat
overalls
Oxonian boots
paletot
palisandre
palmyrene
palmyrienne
pansy
pantaloon trousers
pantaloons
papillote comb
paquebot capote
Parma violet
parta
pea jacket
pelisse-mantle

pelisse-robe

penang lawyer

pensée

Peruvian hat

Petersham cossacks

Petersham frock coat

Petersham greatcoat

petit bord

pistache

pistachio color

plain bow stock

plastron

plume velvet

point de Bayeux

point de raccroc

Polish mantle

poplin lactee

porcelain

poussière de Paris

poussière des ruines

prince's sleeve

Prussian collar

puce

railroad trousers

rampoor-chuddar

raymond

red lilac

rep bluet

reticule

riding dress frock coat

Rigoletto mantle

robe à la Joconde

robe d'interieur

robin front

Roman sandal

rosadimoi

rose de parnasse

rouleaux

roxalene bodice

roxalene sleeve

Roxburgh muff

Royal George stock

santon

satin antoinette

satin velouté

sautoir

shawl collar

shawl waistcoat

shorts

side edge

sirkasa

skuinsdoek

slop work

soufflet sleeves

spa bonnet

Spanish cloak

stoat

stomacher bodice

stote

straight trousers

straight waistcoat

strapped pantaloons

sultan sleeve

Swiss belt

Swiss mountain hat

Taglioni frock coat

tartarian

terre de Cuba

terre de Pologne

terre d'Egypte

tights

Tilbury hat

tippet

tobin

top boot

top frock

toque

tourterelle

trocadero

tunic dress

turf hat

tweed

Venetian cloak

Vevai cap

victoria

Victoria bonnet

Victoria sleeve

volan

volant

wadded hem

waist seam

washing leather gloves

weepers

Welch wig

Wellington coat

Wellington frock

Wellington half-boot

Wellington hat

Wellington pantaloons

wheel trimming

whole backs

wickler

wide-awake

winkers

witchoura

witschoura

zebra feathers

zephyr cloak

CRINOLINE (1840–1865 C.E.)

à la du Barry corsage
à la Grecque corsage
à la Louis XV corsage
à la Marie Stuart
à la vielle
à l'espignole
Adèle
Agnes Sorel bodice
Agnes Sorel corsage
Agnes Sorel style
Albanian robe
Albert cape
Albert collar
Albert crepe
Albert driving-cape
Albert jacket
Albert overcoat
Albert pot
Albert riding coat
Albert shoe
Albert top frock
Alboni
Albuera
Alcamina
alceste
Alexandra collar
Alexandra jacket
Alexandra petticoat
Alexandrine
algerine
Alice mantle
Alice Maud
all-rounder
Alma
alma brown
Alma Escharpe
almerian
alpago
alpine
Alsatian
amazon collar
amazon corsage
amazon corset
American trousers
American vest
Andaluse cape
Andalusia
Andalusian
Aneline shawl
anglaise
ankle-jacks
antigropolis
Antoinette

Aramis mantelet
Arctic
Ariadne sleeve
Armenian cloak
Armenian mantle
armure
Arragon
Arragonese
Astracan de laine
Asturian
attila
Augusta cloth
aurifère
Austurian
azurline
baby French heel
bachelor shoes
badger whiskers
Balaklava
balmoral
balmoral cloak
balmoral petticoat
Barcelona
barège Anglais
barège de laine
barège de Pyrenees
barpour
basin de laine
basque
basquin body
Basquine
basquine a l'espagnole
batiste de laine
bavolet
bayadère poplin
Beatrice
Beatrice parasol
beche-cashmere
Belle
Belvidera
Bijou
Biscayan
blé de Turquie
bloomers
blue john
bolero
bollinger
bonnet assassin
Borghesé
borrillonnées
bosphore green
bouquet de corsage
bournouse

braces
Braganza
Branscombe point
brilliante
brilliants
broderie anglaise
brogans
Brussels point
bucksain
burnous
burnouse
cache-peigne
cage
cage Americaine
cage empire
calcarapedes
calico china button
California
camail
camayeux silk
cambridge paletot
caméléon
Camilla mantelet
Campan
caprice
capuche
capuchin
caradori
cardigan
cardinal
cardinal pelerine
Cariola
caroline corsage
carpet slippers
carpote
carrickmacross
casaque
casaweck
cascade waistband
cashmere de baize
cashmere syrien
cashmire de bètge
casimir de soie
casquette
cassock vest
Castiglione
Castilian
cazenou
ceinture dragonne
châle de brodie
chambard mantle
chamford mantle
Charlotte Cordey cap
charm
chatelaine

chatoyante
chau
chemise
Cherbourg
chimney pot hat
China calico
chinchilla cloth
chocolat au lait
chya mun bo
cialdini apron
cimarosa
Clarissa Harlowe corsage
codrington
coeur de melon
coiffure à la Ceres
coiffure à la Pomone
coiffure Egyptienne
coiffure Eugenie
coiffure Louis Trieze
coiffure Maintenon
coiffure Zouave
coin de feu
coke
collar à la Vandyke
Colleen Bawn cloak
Colson
Columbine
combed helmet
comforter
Constance
Cora mantle
coraco Eugenie
coral currant button
Coralie
Coraline
corazza
cordeliere
Cordovan
corinthe green
couronne Ristori
coutil
cravate cocodes
cravate de bureaucrate
crepe aerophane
crépe de Suisse
crepe maretz
Crimea
crinoline
crispin cloche
cuir
cutlets
czarina
dai fong chau
d'Angri
Darro

dentelle de Cambrai
dentelle de laine
derby
Desdemona
diphera
domette
Doncaster riding coat
drap de Paris
drap de velours
dress clip
dress protector
du Barry corsage
du Barry sleeve
Duchess
Duchesse
duck-hunter
dundreary whiskers
dundrearys
dust of Paris
dux collar
écossaise hat
eglantine
elephant sleeve
elliptic collar
Emily
emperor shirt
empire cap
empire jupon
Empress
Empress Eugenie hat
Empress pardessus
en beret
en Cavalier
en coulisse
en manche
en Marquise
en ravanche
en tablier
English wrap
epingline raye
epinglorie brochée
Escurial
Esmerelda
Estramadura
Eugenie blue
Eugenie hat
Eugenie purse
Eulalie
Eureka
exhibition checks
faldetta
Faliero
fanchon cap
favoris
Felix

fichu Antoinette
fichu Ristori
fig leaf
Figaro jacket
fil de Chevre
flamme de punch
fleur de peche
Flora
florence
Florentine
Flossing
flounce à disposition
flower bottle
flower hole
Fornarina
foulard de laines
fourreau dress
fourreau skirt
fourreau tunic
fraise à la Gabrielle
Francis the First sleeve
French cuff
French opening vest
French vest
frileuse
frilling
frog pocket
gage de Inde
gai pee jau sa
gaiter bottoms
gamp
gants de Swède
garde Français
Garibaldi blouse
Garibaldi bodice
Garibaldi hat
Garibaldi jacket
Garibaldi sleeve
gaze d'Orient
genappe cloth
giboun
Gitana
glacé Marguerite
goat's hair fringe
granit de laine
Grecian sleeve
Grecque corsage
grelot
Grisi
gros d'Eccose silk
groseille
guipure arabe
gypsy cloak
hair strings
half bishop sleeve

hand
Harrie sack
harris tweed
hat à la reine
havane
havannah
heavy swell
hechtgrau
Helen cap
hemispherical hat
Henriette hat
Hercules braid
Hermione
Hippolita
Hispania
hock see hai
horsehair petticoat
Hortense mantle
howling bags
hoxter
hug-me-tight
Humboldt purple
hydrotobolic hat
Imogen
imperatrice
imperial
Imperial
Incroyable
Inverness
Ionian
Isabeau corsage
Isabeau sleeve
Isabeau style dress
Isir
Isley green
Italien
Jackson shoes
jambieres
jardiniere
Jenny Bell
Jenny Lind costume
Jenny Lind riding hat
Jenny Lind sortie de bal
Jim Crow hat
Jocelyn mantle
John Bull
joinville
Josephine
kappie
kask
kite-high dandy
kittel
Kossuth
Krinoline
la Bretelle

la coiffure Diane
la comptesse Walewski
la Equestrienné
la Esmerelda
la Grange
la Hermione
la Manuela
la Marguerite
la Mignene
la Ophelia
la Princesse
la Puritana
la Stella
la vierge
Lady Alice sleeve
Lady Diana hat
lai kee wat chau
laine foulard
Lancer jacket
Lapland beaver
le Bijou
le Caprice
le Gitana
le jupon Imperatrice
le printemps mantilla
le Savage
Leek button
Leicester jacket
Leonese
levantine
Lexington cloak
Lille à fond clair
ling tao
Lonjumeau dress
Lou Lura cloak
Louis XIII corsage
Louis XIV sleeve
Louisa mantilla
Louise mantelet
Lowell cloth
lowerings
Lucia
Lucie
M. B. Waistcoat
ma gua
ma sa
Madrid
magenta
Maintenon cloak
Maintenon corsage
mallow-color
mamelouk sleeve
Mandarin hat
Manon robe
mantelet à la grand mère

mantelet Isabella
mantua marguerite
Margaret of Valois
Marguerite silk
Marian
Marie Antoinette fichu
Marie Stuart hat
Marie-Louise blue
Marion
Mark of the Beast
marquise
Marquise
Mary Stuart
Mathilde mantilla
matinée
Matinee skirt
Maud
Medina
merinos ecossais
Metropolitan jacket
mezzaro
mignonette
Milan
Milanie
min nap
Mirandella
mock see hai
Modena
Moldavian mantle
monkey skin
Montana
Montebello
Montespan corsage
Montespan hat
Montespan pleats
Montpensier mantle
Moresco
morning coat
Morresca
Moscow wrapper
mouchoir Alma
mouchoir Victoria
moultan muslin
mountain moss
mousquetaire
mousquetaire mantle
mousquetaire sleeve
mousselin aboukir
Mozambique
muffin hat
Muscovite
mutton leg sleeve
muttonchops
Napoleons
narcorat

Natalie
natural beaver
Navailles
Nell Gwynne cap
ngau hui suck
Nightingale
Norma corsage
nouveautés
Novado
octagon tie
Omer mantle
ondina crinoline
Ophelia
orphelian
Oxford jacket
Oxonian jacket
pagoda sleeve
palatine royal
paletot
paletot-cloak
paletot-sac
Palmerston wrapper
palto
Pamela bonnet
pamela hat
parasol-whip
pardessus
pardessus redingote
parkesine
parricides
passe
Patrician
peasant fichu
peel
peg-top sleeves
peigne Josephine
peignoir
pekin Aneline
pekin bournous
pekin point
Pembroke paletot
percale taffeta
percaline
Petersham ribbon
petershams
petticoat suspenders
piccadilly weepers
poil de saxe
poile de chevre
point de chainette
Polish boots
Polish jacket
polka
Polka
polonaise pardessus

polverino
pompadour chiné
pompadour duchesse
pompadour pardessus
pompeian silk sash
ponceau
poncho
poplin lama
poplinette
pork-pie hat
postillon
poult de soir
princess paletot
princess petticoat
princess robe
Princess Royal
princess slip
Princess Wagram
Priora
Puritan
pyramid style
Pyramid talma
pyramids
Quaker skirt
Rachel cloak
radzimir
Raglan
raglan boot
raglan cape
raglan sleeve
railway pockets
Raphael dress
red rippers
red russels
regatta shirt
regatta shirting
Regina
releves à la Marie Stuart
religieuse sleeve
revers en pelerine
riding habit
Rimini
rio verde
Rio Verde
Ristori shawl
robe de chez
robes à guille
Rosaline
Rosamond
rosaniline
Rose
rose des Alpes
rose sublime
rosille de soie
rotonde

ruche contraire
rum-swizzle
Russian
sac overcoat
sack suit
sailor suit
sakko
Salamanca
sang chau
sansflectum crinoline
Saragossa
saratoga hat
Sardinian sac
satin de chine
satin de Mai
satin fontange
satin foulard
satin merino
satin Victoria
saut-en-basque
Scarborough hat
scarf volant
scoop bonnet
Scotia
Second Empire costume
Sevastopol
Seville
Sevillian
Shakespere collar
shawl Josephine
shimmy
shirtwaist
shoe-tie necktie
shooting coat
side body
siphonia
smoking jacket
Snowdrop
soie demantine
soieries à double face
solferino
solitaire
sontag
sortie de bal
spair
Spanish jacket
Spanish mantle
spiked shoes
spiral witney
spoon bonnet
Stella
stovepipe hat
sublime
Sultana
Sultana opera cloak

sultana scarf
sultana sleeve
swallow-tails
tablier skirt
taffeta coutil
taffeta crape
taffeta d'Annecy
taffeta de Suez
taglioni
Talma cloak
Talma maltese
Talma mantle
talma Zuleika
tamative
terrier overcoat
three-fold linen button
three-seamer
tibi
ticket pocket
tignon
tissue d'Alma
toile de Valeuce
toile Nankin
tombeaux
toque-turban
toquet
torsade
tourterelle
tow
trimming à la greque
tubular necktie
tunic
tunic shirt
tunic skirt
turin velvet
tweedside
tweedside overcoat
Twenty Grands
twine
twist button
ugly
underhandkerchief
undersleeve
undervest
Undine
valencia
Valencia

Valencian
Valentia
varens
Varna
Vatermörder
vegetable ivory buttons
velours Impératrice
velveret
velvet imperatrice
Venetian edging
Venetian sleeve
Venice
Venice pearls
veste Russe
vésure
Victoria
Victoria corset
Victoria crepe
Victoria mantle
Victoria pardessus
Victoria pelisse-mantle
victorine
Violet
violet of the Alps
visité
Vittoria
voilette
volant
vulcanized rubber bands
Watteau body
Watteau robe
Wellesley wrapper
wings
wool plain
yachting jacket
zamora
zanella
Zanfretti mantle
zephirina
Zerlina dress
Zillon braid
zimbelline
zouave jacket
zouave paletot
Zuleka
Zulima

BUSTLE (1865–1890 C.E.)

à la chale
à la Raphael
absinthe
acier
acter

adrianople
adriatic green
agemaki
agrafes de centure
Albert watch-chain

alezan
algerienne
alicante
alpine jacket
amphibole
ananas
angel sleeve
angle-fronted coat
argile
armoire
armurette
ascot tie
ashantee
baby bodice
bacchante
bachelik
bachlik
backlik
bag bodice
bag plastron
bag-waistcoat
bagdad
balayeuse
balernos
Balkan blouse
ballet-skirt
balmoral bodice
balmoral jacket
balmoral mantle
balzerine
bambulo
barège-grenadine
basque waistband
basque-habit
bateau neckline
Battenburg jacket
bayadère
bayonnaise
beau-catcher
beige
beige damasse
Belgian linen
bengaline
bengaline poplin
benoiton chains
Bernhardt mantle
bicycle bal
bishop
blanc
blazer
blé mur
blé vert
bleu Anglais
blouse polonaise
boater

bois de rose
bolero toque
boneette
booie sum
borada crape cloth
boreal
borgeon
bouchons de carafe
boulanger
boulanger umbrella
bouleau
bouracan
bourette
bourette mousse
bouton d'or
broché silk serge
bulgare pleat
Bulgarian cloth
bullycock
bunting
bure
burgoyne
byzantine
byzantine granité
cachemire
cachemire marguerite
cachemire royal
cachou
calibri
camargo
camargo puff
cambridge coat
camelite
canoque
capuchin
carmeline
carmelite
caroubier
carrick
casaque bodice
casaquin bodice
cascade waistband
cashmerienne
cassis
cassock mantle
castellan delaine
castor
catagan
catagan head-dress
catagan net
celadon
celeste
celluloid
cendre de rose
centre de Cedra

chain-hole
chambertine
chambery gauze
chambray
Charlotte Corday bonnet
charm string
chasseur
chaudron
chaume
chemise
Chesterfield overcoat
Chevalier bonnet
cheviot
chevron de laine
chiang chau
China damask
China gauze
China grass
chrysoprase
chun sam
cicilian cloth
ciel blue
cineraire
ciselé velvet
Clarissa Harlowe bonnet
cloud
coat-bodice
coat-sleeve
congo
congress gaiter
congress shoe
coomassie
coquelicot
cote de Genève
côtelé
cotelette
coteline
couroncon
creme de cachemire lace
cremorne
crepe de Chine
crepe imperial
crepe poplin
crepe royal
crepeline
crepon
cretonne
crinoletta
crinolette
crinolette petticoat
croise cloth
croizette blue
Cromwell collar
Cromwell shoe
croquet boots

crottin
cue de Paris
cuirass tunic
cuirasse bodice
cuirasse tunic
cuoroncou
curtain drapery
cypress
Dagmor blue
dai seong siu kwun
dam boo lau
Danish trousers
dentelle cachmire
dentelle torchon
diadem bonnet
diadem fanchon bonnet
Diamond dyes
Diana Vernon bonnet
Diana Vernon hat
din
Directoire bonnet
Directoire coat
Directoire hat
Directoire jacket
Directoire swallow-tail coat
divided skirt
djedda
Dolly Varden bonnet
Dolly Varden cap
Dolly Varden dress
Dolly Varden hat
Dolly Varden polonaise
donariere
douanier
drap de France
drap de soldat
drap de Venice
drap fourreau
drap laitiere
drap roulier
dress holder
dress improver
dress lounge
duchesse pleat
dust ruffle
e sa
ecorce
eelskin trousers
Egyptian cloth
eillets panaches
elderberry
eldergreen
elephant cloth
emeraude
empire bodice

empire skirt
empress petticoat
English mohair
English velveteen
epangeline
estamine
Eton jacket
Etruscan cloth
faldellin
Fanfreluche bodice
fedora
feutre
ficelle
fichu la Valiere
fichu raphael
fishtail
flannelette
fleur de soufre
fleur de thé
florentine
flower bottle
flow-flow
fore-and-aft cap
foulard poile de chevre
foulé
foundling bonnet
four-in-hand
framboise
frisé brocade
frou-frou
frou-frou dress
frou-frou gauze
fumee
fumee de Londres
gabardine
gabnel
Gabrielle dress
Gainsborough bonnet
gants Régence
gau chau
gaze de Chambery
gaze neige
gazeline barege
Genoa plush
gig-top
gipsy bonnet
giraffe comb
Gladstone collar
Gladstone overcoat
goaly
gobelin blue
godet pleat
gondolier net
Gordon blue
grain de poudre

granite
Grecian bend
grenadine rayée
gris Anglaise
gris de fer
gros bleu
gros de Londres
gros de Rome
gros de Suez
habit backed skirt
habit bodice
habit-redingote
handkerchief dress
helmet hat
Henrietta glace
heron
hip bags
hok see hai
Hombourg
homburg
Honiton point
hoo
hoo geok kwun
hoo tau dai
house dress
housemaid skirt
Hungarian cord
hussar jacket
imperial velvet
impiraperle
incarnat
incroyable bows
incroyable coat
ink gray
ityogaesi
Jack Tar suit
Jack Tar trousers
jacket coat
Jaeger underclothes
Janus cord
Japanese hat
Japanese piqué
Japanese pongee
Japanese silk
Japonais
jaquette
jersey
jersey sweater
jin be wun
Joan-of-Arc bodice
josephine bodice
josie
kaironan
karamini
Kate Greenaway costume

kilted skirt
kiss-me-quick
knickerbockers
koller
kwun
laddie, come follow me
lai kee wat chau
Lamballe bonnet
Langtry bonnet
Langtry hood
lasting boots
Laveuse costume
lézard
Liberty art silks
lichen
lie de Bordeaux
Lily Langtry coiffure
limousine
lionceau
Little Lord Fauntleroy dress
louisine
lucifer
luciole
lyons loops
madapolam
mais
malines
mandarin
manteau de coceher
marabout
Marie Anglais bonnet
Marie-Antoinette sleeve
mariposa
Marlborough hat
marmotte
marquise bodice
marteaux
martinpècheur
maryland
masher
masher collar
masher dust wrap
matelassé
mecca
Medici dress
mermaid's tail
mésange
Metternich
Mexican cloth
mikado
Milanese
Milanese taffeta
milkmaid skirt
mimi-kakusi
mituwa

moab
moiré
molleton
momie cloth
momo-ware
Montague curls
montebello
Montpensier cloth
moscovite
Moscow wrapper
moss cloth
Mother Hubbard cloak
mousquetaire cuff
mousseline grenadine
mousseline soie
Muller-cut-down
mulot
murray
Muscovite
Muscovite velvet
mushroom hat
nacre burgau
natté
négrillon
neigeuse
Newmarket overcoat
nickel gray
night of France blue
nihyakusan-koti
nil
noisette
Norfolk jacket
Norfolk shirt
Normande cap
Normandy bonnet
noyer
nun's cloth
nun's veiling
ondine
ondule
ooze calf
oreille d'ours
oriental satin
ortie
oseille cuite
ottoman plush
ottoman rep
ottoman silk
ottoman velvet
Oxford and Cambridge mixture
Oxford gillies
oxide
pactole
palestine
paletot-mantle

paletot-redingote
Palmyra broché
pannier crinoline
pannier dress
panteen collar
Paris-Pekin
parochka
parure cornouailles
patent leather boots
patrol jacket
patti jets
pavot
peasant skirt
peau de béte
peau de soie
peau de suede
peignoir
pekin
pentes
peplum basque
peplum bodice
peplum dolman
peplum jupon
peplum rotonde
perruche
pervenche
petals Marguerite
petite pois
peupliere
picadilly Johnny
Piccadilly collar
piccadilly fringe
piccadilly weepers
pifferaro bonnet
pifferaro hat
pigeon fan
pinafore costume
piquets
plomb
pluie d'argent
pluie d'or
pompadour bodice
pompadour polonaise
pompadour shantung
pompeian red
pongee
porphyry
port manteau sunshade
porte-bonheur
portemonnaie
postboy hat
poussière
Prince of Wales jacket
princess dress
princess polonaise

prune Dumas
punch
puree de pois
rabagas bonnet
ramoneur
rationals
raye de comtesse
Recamier sash
redingote
reed hat
reefer
regatta faille francais
regence
Regina
regine purple
rhadames
ridicule
riding habit
ring cloth
rivieres de jais
robe anglaise
robe drapee
rocher
rossignol
Roubaix velvet
rouille
royale
Rubens bonnet
Rubens hat
Russian bonnet
Russian crepe
Russian jacket
sa din
safety skirt
sailor's reef knot tie
Saint Etienne velvet
sanmai-gusi
sarata shirting
sarde
sateen
sateen berber
sateen paré
satin duchesse
satin jean
satin merv
satin merveilleux
satin turc
satiné playé
satiné velouté
satingle Holland
scarabee
scarf drapery
sealskin coat
señorita jacket
serge royale

serpent
Shakespere vest
shantung
Sicilian bodice
sickly green
silistrienne
silk Damascene
skirt ruff
sleeve à la Louis Quinze
sling sleeve
sling-duster
smock-frock
sokuhatu
sook chau
sourés
soyeaux linsey
spats
spoon back
star of the morning
strapontin
Strasbourg cloth
street sweeper
suedoise
suivez moi, jeune homme
sultane
sultane dress
sultane jacket
surah
surplice bodice
swanbill corset
Swiss bodice
tablier tunic
taffetaline
tailored suit
tallien redingote
tamise
Tarleton helmet
tea jacket
teagown
telegraph blue
tenzin-mage
terai hat
terranine
Thibet cloth
Thibetine
thiers red
thistlewood
three-decker
three-stories-and-a-basement

tie-back skirt
tige d'aillet
tight-slacks
tilleul
tilter
tin chiang chiang chau
toile d'Alsace
toile d'esprit
toothpick
toupee
tournure
tripoline
trouser stretcher
turco poplinnes
Turkish brilliantine
turret bodice
tussore de Longchamps
tyes
Tyrolese hat
ulster
umritzur
university athletic costume
university vest
verd Nile
Veronese cuirasse
Veronese dress
vert malachite
Victoria cage
victorieuse
vieil argent
violin bodice
voile
volcan
Vulcanite buttons
waterfall back
waterproof cloak
Watteau costume
Watteau polonaise
ya hoo lam
yak lace
yeddo crepe
yoke bodice
Yokohama crepe
yukue-humei
Zanzibar
zephyr
zephyr armure
zephyr gingham

GAY NINETIES (1890–1900 C.E.)

angel overskirt
asmodée
aubergine

balloon sleeve
Balmoral crape
beauty spot veil

bengaline constellation
bengaline russe
blondine
bouffon
bouffron
brocantine
bust bodice
butterfly bow sleeve
cake hat
cameleon antique
cancan dress
caracule
caracule material
cardinal
carmelite
carreau amazone
cashmere twill
caspian
chiffon
circular
cleopatra
coat shirt
coatlet
combinations
concertina cloth
convolvulus
cornet skirt
Courtauld crape
Courtauld's new silk crepe
cowes
cravenette
crepon
crepon milleraye
crepon Persian
crushed strawberry
dead white
Directoire skirt
dolmanette
eel skirt
eleven gore ripple skirt
eminence
eolienne diagonal
epaules Americaines
epingles de nourrice
epingline chevron soie
epingline flotté soie
erinoid
etamine broché
eveque
faillette
featherbrush skirt
fil de vierge
flabells
flexine
floxine

fond de casserole
French gigot sleeves
French jet
gadroon
Galatea comb
Galatea hat
gaze gauffree
gegendas
godet skirt
golf vest
gored bell skirt
grannie skirt
granny bonnet
grasshopper green
Harvards
Henley boater
henri deux cape
Henrietta cloth
Henrietta jacket
Himalaya carreau
hopsack
hounscot say
Italian sleeve
jacqueminot
la pliant
lacing studs
lierre lace
lisse
looking glass silk
loutre
lucky bells
lustre
manilla
mignonette green
miroir silk
mirror velvet
mitten sleeve
moiré française
moiré velours
moirette
mushroom sleeve
Nelson hat
Newmarket jacket
Newmarket top frock
Newmarket vest
Oxford tie
paddock coat
panel skirt
panne
Parma violet
patch veil
peau de chevrette
peplum overskirt
Persian lilac
petunia

phosphorescent
picture hat
pierrot cape
pierrot ruff
pigeon's breast
pigeon's throat
pluette
policeman's cape
polo collar
Prince Rupert
Puritan bonnet
raglan covert coat
raglan overcoat
rainy daisy skirt
rat
rationals
rayure travers
reefer jacket
ribbed crepon
rose tendre
Rosebery collar
Rough Rider shirt
russell cord
Russian blouse
Russian sergette
Russian velvet
sabot pantaloons
samson
sanitary ball dress
satarra cloth
satin cashmere
satin de laine

satin orientale
saucer-collar
Scarborough ulster
Sèvres blue
sleeve tongs
sticking-plaster dress
straight English skirt
street sweeper
sun-ray skirt
swarry-doo
Talma lounge
Talma overcoat
tattersall
tattersall vest
thistle-green
toby ruff
toile de soie
toreador hat
Trilby hat
trouser press
tucked skirt
tudor cape
umbrella skirt
velours de laine
velours de Venise
Venetian crape cloth
Victoria bodice
Victoria silk
volubilis
wool bengaline
yoke shirt
zouave pantaloons

1900–1910 C.E.

ai ling
amplificateur
Audobon plumage law
baby Louis heel
Bakelite
bishop sleeve
bloomers
booie sum
Buster Brown collar
Buster Brown suit
colonial pump
crepelle
fibre chamoise
gau dai hai

gau liang
hoi nong hu
kee ha hai
mong pao
Napoleon costume
oi dai booi dai
Parisian satin
peau d'ange
peek-a-boo waist
pettibockers
ribbon corset
sealskin sacque
siu fung sin
walking suit

1910–1920 C.E.

aeroplane umbrella
artificial silk

balaclava
bandeau beehive crown hat

battle jacket
bellboy hat
blouse suit
campaign hat
castle hat
debutante slouch
Directoire knickers
envelope combination
Fortuny tea gown
hobble skirt
hoover apron
Irene Castle bob
kiki skirt
lampshade dress
Montana peak
mule

peg-top trousers
persian drape tunic
puttee
rompers
Russian suit
sabotine
Sam Browne belt
surf satin
tailored coat
tango corset
teddies
teddy-bears
tongue pump
transformation
walking out dress
x-ray dress

1920–1930 C.E.

acetate
all-in-one
Annette Kellerman
beer jacket
Bethlehem headdress
broderie anglaise
Brummel
Buchanan
bum-freezer
Cami-knickers
Chanel suit
cloche
dandine
fong chau

gigolo
krauss
monastic silhouette
Oxford bags
plus fours
qi pao
radielfo
reach-me-down
seven-eighths coat
skokie
slicker
toraco
town blouse
tuta

1930–1940 C.E.

aloha shirt
babushka
bambino hat
bust forms
chukka boot
cowl collar
crepe myosotis
Crown pearl
doll hat
drape cut
English scarlet
Fusex shirt
ghost coat
halo hat

Imperial gold
keilhose
knight's blue
Limpet trunks
little black dress
mess jacket
needlecord
pajama
rosalba
Royal turquoise
run-about dress
swing skirt
ventilated pants

1940–1950 C.E.

battle jacket
beanie
bikini
British warm
de-mob suit
Eisenhower jacket
flight boot
garrison cap
guepiere
jinnah cap

loafer
martingale belt
Old Navajo Dyes
pinks and green
siren suit
Terylene
Tremont hat
waist cincher
zoot suit

1950–1960 C.E.

Academician
army green
Author
baby doll pajama
banker's blue
beehive coiffure
bicycle clip
Continental
cosh-boy
courreges
Davy Crockett cap
Director

Droop Snoot
Editor
Flying Saucer
Hershey bars
H-line
Merry Widow
millium
Olympic
saddle shoe
silver taupe uniform
trapeze
twinset

1960–1969 C.E.

bell bottoms
body shirt
body stocking
briuki-dudochki
bush hat
cadet jacket
Chelsea boot
Chelsea collar
cool pants
go-go boot
gypsy blouse
hipsters
hot pants
jungle fatigues
khalaty

king klipper
les shorts
Mao jacket
maxi
midi
Nehru jacket
palazzo pajamas
qiana
shell
short shorts
shortcuts
skort
stiliaga
suburban coat
toreadoll pajamas

1970–1979 C.E.

DPM
Gore-Tex

punk
wedding ring hat

1980–1989 C.E.

Gekko shirt

Selected Bibliography

Abler, Thomas S. *Hinterland Warriors and Military Dress: European Empires and Exotic Uniforms*. Oxford: Berg, 1999.

Abu-Lughod, Lila. *Veiled Sentiments*. Berkeley: University of California Press, 1986.

Adams, J. Donaldson. *Naked We Came*. New York: Holt, Rinehart, and Winston, 1967.

Adams, Monni. Kuba embroidered cloth. *African Arts* 12 (1978): 24–39, 106–7.

Adelson, Laurie, and Arthur Tracht. *Aymara Weavings Ceremonial Textiles of Colonial and 19th Century Bolivia*. Washington, D.C.: Smithsonian Institution Traveling Exhibition Service, 1983.

Aldred, Cyril. *Jewels of the Pharaohs: Egyptian Jewelry of the Dynastic Period*. New York: Praeger, 1971.

Alexander, Helene. *Fans*. London: B. T. Batsford, 1984.

Alkazi, Roshen. *Ancient Indian Costume*. New Delhi: Art Heritage, 1983.

Allenby, Jeni. *Portraits without Names: Palestinian Costume*. Canberra: Palestine Costume Archive, 1996.

Anawalt, Patricia Rieff. Costume and control: Aztec sumptuary laws. *Archaeology* 33 (1980): 33–43.

Andersen, Ellen. *Folk Costumes in Denmark*. Copenhagen: Hassing, 1952.

Anderson, Lois E. *John F. Kennedy*. New York: Gallery Books, 1986.

Anderson, Ruth Matilda. *Hispanic Costume 1480–1530*. New York: Hispanic Society of America, 1979.

Antubam, Kofi. *Ghana's Heritage of Culture*. Leipzig: Koehler and Amelang, 1963.

Argenti, Philip P. *The Costumes of Chios*. London: B. T. Batsford, 1953.

Arnold, Janet. *Patterns of Fashion c1560–1620*. New York: Drama Book, 1985.

———. *Patterns of Fashion 1 c1660–1860*. Rev. ed. New York: Drama Book, 1977.

———. *Patterns of Fashion 2 c1860–1940*. New York: Drama Book, 1972.

———. *Perukes and Periwigs*. London: Her Majesty's Stationery Office, 1970.

Bailey, Margaret J. *Those Glorious Glamour Years: The Great Hollywood Costume Designers of the 1930's*. Secaucus, N.J.: Citadel Press, 1982.

Baker, Patricia. *Fashions of a Decade: The 1940's*. New York: Facts on File, 1992.

Barnes, R. Money. *Military Uniforms of Britain and the Empire, 1742 to the Present Time*. London: Seeley Service, 1968.

———. *The Uniforms and History of the Scottish Regiments*. London: Seeley Service, 1956.

Barwick, Sandra. *A Century of Style*. London: George Allen and Unwin, 1984.

Bastide, J. A. Jockin la, and G. van Kooten. *Cassell's English-Dutch Dutch-English Dictionary*. New York: Macmillan, 1978.

Batterberry, Michael, and Ariane Batterberry. *Fashion: The Mirror of History*. 2nd ed. New York: Crown, 1982.

———. *The Belle Epoque of French Jewellery*. London: Thomas Heneage, 1991.

Battersby, Martin. *Art Deco Fashion: French Designers 1908–1925*. New York: St. Martin's Press, 1974.

———. *The Decorative Thirties*. New York: Walker, 1971.

———. *The Decorative Twenties*. New York: Walker, 1971.

Battersley, C. W. *The Baganda at Home*. London: Frank Cass, 1968.

Beier, Uli. *Yoruba Beaded Crowns*. London: Ethnographica, 1982.

Bennett, Daphne. *Queen Victoria's Children*. New York: St. Martin's Press, 1977.

Bennett, Edna Mae. *Turquoise and the Indian*. Chicago: Sage Books, 1970.

Bennett-England, Rodney. *Dress Optional: The Revolution in Menswear*. Chester Springs, Pa.: Dufour Editions, 1968.

Ben-Yusef, Anna. *Edwardian Hats: The Art of Millinery (1909)*. Mendocino, Calif.: R. L. Shep, 1992.

Bergquist, Laura, and Stanley Tretick. *A Very Special President*. New York: McGraw-Hill Book, 1965.

Bernard, Barbara. *Fashion in the 60's*. New York: St. Martin's Press, 1978.

Bhushan, Jamila Brij. *The Costumes and Textiles of India*. England: F. Lewis, 1958.

Binder, Pearl. *Muffs and Morals*. New York: William Morrow, 1955.

————. *The Peacock's Tail*. London: George G. Harrap, 1958.

Bingham, Caroline. *The Crowned Lions: The Early Plantagenet Kings*. Totowa, N. J.: Rowman and Littlefield, 1978.

————. *The Stewart Kingdom of Scotland 1371–1603*. New York: St. Martin's Press, 1974.

Binks, H. K. *African Rainbow*. London: Sidgwick and Jackson, 1959.

Birbari, E. *Dress in Italian Painting: 1460–1500*. London: John Murray, 1975.

Black, J. Anderson, and Madge Garland. *A History of Fashion*. New York: William Morrow, 1975.

Blair, Claude. *European Armor*. London: B. T. Batsford, 1958.

Blomberg, Nancy J. *Navajo Textiles*. Tucson: University of Arizona Press, 1988.

Blum, André. *The Last Valois 1515–90*. London: George G. Harrap, 1951.

Blundell, Sir Michael. *So Rough a Wind*. London: Weidenfeld and Nicolson, 1964.

Bogatyreo, Petr. *The Functions of Folk Costume in Moravian Slovakia*. Paris: Mouton, 1971.

Bolitho, Hector. *Albert Prince Consort*. New York: Bobbs-Merrill, 1964.

Boller, Paul F., Jr. *Presidential Wives*. New York: Oxford University Press, 1988.

Bond, David. *The Guinness Guide to Twentieth Century Fashion*. Middlesex: Guinness Superlatives, 1981.

Branca, Patricia. *Silent Sisterhood: Middle-Class Women in the Victorian Home*. London: Croom Helm, 1977.

Breasted, James Henry. *A History of Egypt*. 2nd ed., rev. New York: Scribner's, 1924.

Brelsford, W. V. *The Tribes of Northern Rhodesia*. Lusaka: Government Printer.

Brion, Marcel. *The Medici: A Great Florentine Family*. New York: Crown, 1969.

Brooke, Iris. *Costume in Greek Classic Drama*. Westport, Conn.: Greenwood Press, 1973.

————. *English Children's Costume since 1775*. London: Adam and Charles Black, 1930.

————. *English Costume of the Later Middle Ages*. London: Adam and Charles Black, 1963.

————. *Footwear: A Short History of European and American Shoes*. New York: Theatre Arts Books, 1971.

————. *Medieval Theatre Costume: A Practical Guide to the Construction of Garments*. New York: Theatre Arts, 1967.

Brown, Dorothy Foster. *Button Parade*. Chicago: Lightner, 1942.

Buck, Anne. *Dress in Eighteenth-Century England*. London: B. T. Batsford, 1979.

Buck, Carl Darling. *A Dictionary of Selected Synonyms in the Principal Indo-European Languages*. Chicago: University of Chicago Press, 1949.

Burnham, D. K. *Cut My Cote*. Toronto: Royal Ontario Museum, 1973.

Buxton, David. *Travels in Ethiopia*. New York: Frederick A. Praeger, 1967.

Byrde, Penelope. *Nineteenth Century Fashion*. London: B. T. Batsford, 1992.

Calthrop, Dion Clayton. *English Dress from Victoria to George V*. London: Chapman and Hall, 1934.

Calvert, Albert F. *Spanish Arms and Armour*. New York: John Lane, 1907.

Carey, Margret. *Beads and Beadwork of East and South Africa*. Aylesbury: Shire Ethnography, 1986.

————. *Beads and Beadwork of West and Central Africa*. Aylesbury: Shire Ethnography, 1991.

Carlano, Marianne, and Larry Salmon, eds. *French Textiles from the Middle Ages through the Second Empire*. Hartford, Conn.: Wadsworth Atheneum, 1985.

Carlin, John. *Gulla the Tramp: An Ethnological Indiscretion*. London: Jonathan Cape, 1937.

Carnagy, Vicky. *Fashions of a Decade: The 1980's*. New York: Facts on File, 1990.

Cassin-Scott, Jack, and John Fabb. *Ceremonial Uniforms of the World*. New York City: Hippocrene Books, 1973.

Cawthorne, Nigel. *Sixties Source Book*. Secaucus, N.J.: Chartwell Books Inc., 1989.

Cecil, Lamar. *Wilhelm II Prince and Emperor 1859–1900*. Chapel Hill: University of North Carolina Press, 1989.

Cerulli, Ernesta. *Peoples of South-west Ethiopia and Its Borderland*. London: International African Institute, 1956.

Chandra, Moti. *Costumes, Textiles, Cosmetics, and Coiffure in Ancient and Medieval India*. Delhi: Oriental, 1973.

Charles, Anne, and Roger DeAnfransio. *The History of Hair: An Illustrated Review of Hair Fashions for Men throughout the Ages*. New York: Bonanza Books, 1970.

Chaturvedi, B. K. *Dresses and Costumes of India*. New Delhi: Diamond Pocket Books, 1980.

Churchill, Winston S. *The Second World War*. New York: Time, 1959.

Clancy, Deirdre. *Costume since 1945: Couture, Street Style and Anti-Fashion*. New York: Drama, 1996.

Clarke, A. A. *Police Uniforms and Equipment*. Buckinghamshire: Shire, 1991.

Cloulas, Ivan. *The Borgias*. New York: Franklin Watts, 1989.

Colle, Doriece. *Collars . . . Stocks . . . Cravats: A History and Costume Dating Guide to Civilian Men's Neckpieces 1655–1900*. Emmaus, Pa.: Rodale Press, 1972.

Connikie, Yvonne. *Fashions of a Decade: The 1960's*. New York: Facts on File, 1990.

Contini, Mila. *Fashion from Ancient Egypt to the Present Day*. London: Hamlyn, 1965.

Cooper, Wendy. *Hair, Sex, Society, Symbolism*. New York: Stein and Day, 1971.

Cordry, Donald Bush, and Dorothy M. Cordry. *Costumes and Weaving of the Zoque Indians of Chiapas, Mexico*. Los Angeles, Calif.: Southwest Museum, 1941.

Corson, Richard. *Fashions in Eyeglasses*. London: Peter Owen, 1967.

————. *Fashions in Hair*. London: Peter Owen, 1971.

————. *Fashions in Makeup from Ancient to Modern Times*. London: Owen, 1972.

Costantino, Maria. *Men's Fashion in the Twentieth Century*. New York: Costume and Fashion Press, 1997.

Crawford, M. D. C. *One World of Fashion.* New York: Fairchild, 1967.

Crill, Rosemary. *Hats from India.* London: Victoria and Albert Museum, 1985.

Cronin, Vincent. *Louis and Antoinette.* New York: William Morrow, 1975.

Cumming, Valerie. *Gloves.* New York: Drama Book, 1982.

———. *Royal Dress: The Image and the Reality: 1580 to the Present Day.* New York: Holmes and Meier, 1989.

———. *A Visual History of Costume: The Seventeenth Century.* London: B. T. Batsford, 1984.

Cummins, Genevieve E., and Nerylla D. Taunton. *Chatelaines: Utility to Glorious Extravagance.* Suffolk: Antique Collectors' Club, 1994.

Cunnington, C. Willett. *English Clothing in the Present Century.* London: Faber and Faber, 1952.

Cunnington, C. Willett, and Phyllis Cunnington. *Handbook of English Costume in the 16th Century.* London: Faber and Faber, 1970.

———. *Handbook of English Costume in the 17th Century.* 3rd ed. London: Faber and Faber, 1972.

———. *Handbook of English Costume in the 18th Century.* London: Faber and Faber, 1970.

———. *Handbook of English Costume in the 19th Century.* 3rd ed. London: Faber and Faber, 1970.

———. *Handbook of English Medieval Costume.* Rev. ed. London: Faber and Faber, 1973.

———. *The History of Underclothes.* London: Michael Joseph, 1951.

Cunnington, Phillis Emily. *Charity Costumes of Children, Scholars, Almsfolk, Pensioners.* London: Adam and Charles Black, 1978.

———. *Costume of Household Servants from the Middle Ages to 1900.* New York: Barnes and Noble, 1974.

Cunnington, Phillis Emily, and Catherine Lucas. *Costume for Births, Marriages and Deaths.* New York: Barnes and Noble, 1972.

Cunnington, Phillis Emily, and Alan Mansfield. *Handbook of English Costume in the Twentieth Century, 1900–1950.* Boston: Plays, 1973.

Dahmus, Joseph. *Seven Medieval Queens.* New York: Doubleday, 1972.

Davidoff, Leonore. *The Best Circles.* London: Croom Helm, 1973.

Davies, Stephanie Curtis. *Costume Language.* Malvern: Cressrelles, 1994.

Davis, Wade, Ian Mackenzie, and Shane Kennedy. *Nomads of the Dawn: The Penan of the Borneo Rain Forest.* San Francisco: Pomegranate Artbooks, 1995.

de Alcega, Juan. *Tailor's Pattern Book 1589.* New York: Costume and Fashion Press, 1999.

de Buzzaccarini, Vittoria. *Men's Coats.* Modena, Italy: Zanfi Editori, 1994.

de Castries, Duc. *The Lives of the Kings and Queens of France.* New York: Alfred A. Knopf, 1979.

de Courtais, Georgine. *Women's Headdress and Hairstyles in England from 600 AD to the Present Day.* London: B. T. Batsford, 1973.

de la Haye, Amy, and Cathie Dingwall. *Surfers, Soulies, Skinheads, and Skaters.* New York City: Overlook Press, 1996.

de la Sizeranne, Robert. *Celebrities of the Italian Renaissance.* Freeport, N.Y.: Library Press, 1969.

De Marly, Diana. *Christian Dior.* New York: Holmes and Meier, 1990.

de Negri, Eve. Yoruba men's costume. *Nigeria Magazine* 73 (1962): 4–12.

Dike, Catherine. *Cane Curiosa from Gun to Gadget.* Geneva: Catherine Dike, 1983.

Dorner, Jane. *Fashion in the Forties and Fifties.* London: Ian Allen, 1973.

———. *Fashion in the Twenties and Thirties.* London: Ian Allen, 1973.

Doughty, Robin W. *Feather Fashions and Bird Preservation: A Study in Nature Protection.* Berkeley: University of California Press, 1975.

Dreher, Denise. *From the Neck Up: An Illustrated Guide to Hatmaking.* Minneapolis, Minn.: Madhatter Press, 1981.

Dubin, Lois Shearr. *The History of Beads.* New York City: Harry N. Abrams, 1987.

Duff, David. *Mother of the Queen: The Life Story of Her Majesty the Queen Mother Elizabeth.* New York: Hawthorn Books, 1965.

Dunlevy, Mairead. *Dress in Ireland.* New York: Holmes and Meier, 1989.

Earle, Alice Morse. *Two Centuries of Costume in America: 1620–1820.* Rutland, Vt.: Charles E. Tuttle, 1971.

Edgar, Donald. *Britain's Royal Family in the Twentieth Century.* New York: Crown, 1979.

———. *An Elegant Art: Fashion and Fantasy in the Eighteenth Century.* New York: Harry N. Abrams, 1983.

Edwards, Elizabeth, and Lynne Williamson. *World on a Glass Plate.* Oxford: Pitt Rivers Museum, 1981.

Eicher, Joanne Bubolz. *Nigerian Handcrafted Textiles.* Ife, Nigeria: University of Ife Press, 1976.

Epton, Nina. *Josephine: The Empress and Her Children.* New York: W. W. Norton, 1975.

Espinosa, Carmen. *Shawls, Crinolines, Filigree.* El Paso: University of Texas at El Paso, 1970.

Evans, Joan. *Dress in Medieval France.* Oxford: Clarendon Press, 1952.

Ewing, Elizabeth. *Dress and Undress: A History of Women's Underwear.* New York: Drama Book Specialists, 1978.

———. *Fur in Dress.* London: B. T. Batsford, 1981.

———. *History of Twentieth Century Fashion.* England: Barnes and Noble, 1986.

———. *Women in Uniform through the Centuries.* London: B. T. Batsford, 1975.

Fax, Elton C. *West Africa Vignettes.* New York: American Society of African Culture, 1960.

Fél, Edit, and Tomás Hofer. *Proper Peasants: Traditional Life in a Hungarian Village.* Chicago: Aldine, 1969.

Feldman, Elane. *Fashions of a Decade: The 1990's.* New York: Facts on File, 1992.

Felford, A. A. *Yesterday's Dress: A History of Costume in South Africa.* Cape Town, South Africa: Purnell, 1972.

Femenias, Blenda. *Andean Aesthetics: Textiles of Peru and Bolivia.* Madison, Wis.: Elvehjim Museum of Art, 1987.

Ffoulkes, Charles. *The Armourer and His Craft.* New York: Dover, 1988.

Folk Russian Costume. Moscow: Historical Museum in Moscow, 1989.

Folledore, Giuliano. *Men's Hats.* Modena, Italy: Zanfi Editori, 1989.

Forde, Daryll. *Efik Traders of Old Calabar*. London: Oxford University Press, 1956.

———, ed. *The Shona and Ndebele of Southern Rhodesia*. London: International African Institute, 1954.

Forde, Daryll, and G. I. Jones. *The Ibo and Ibibio-Speaking Peoples of South-Eastern Nigeria*. Plymouth: Oxford University Press, 1950.

Fossnes, Heidi. *Folk Costumes of Norway*. Norway: J. W. Cappelen Forlag, 1995.

Fosten, D. S. V., and B. K. Fosten. *The Thin Red Line*. London: Windrow and Greene, 1989.

Foster, Vanda. *Bags and Purses*. London: B. T. Batsford, 1982.

Fox-Davies, Arthur Charles. *A Complete Guide to Heraldry*. New York: Bonanza Books, 1978.

Fraser, Beatrice. *Sunshine and Lamplight*. Cape Town: Howard Timmins, n.d.

Fry, Plantagenet, and Fiona Somerset. *The History of Scotland*. London: Routledge and Kegan Paul, 1982.

Fuchs, Peter. *The Land of Veiled Men*. New York: Citadel Press, 1956.

Fusero, Clemente. *The Borgias*. New York: Praeger, 1972.

Gaborjan, Alice. *Hungarian Peasant Costumes*. Budapest: Kossuth Printing, 1969.

Gailey, Henry A. *A History of the Gambia*. New York: Frederick A. Praeger, 1965.

Garland, Madge. *The Indecisive Decade: The World of Fashion and Entertainment in the Thirties*. London: Macdonald, 1968.

Garrett, Valery M. *Chinese Clothing: An Illustrated Guide*. Oxford: Oxford University Press, 1994.

Gattey, Charles Neilson. *The Bloomer Girls*. New York: Coward-McCann, 1967.

Geijer, Agnes. *Oriental Textiles in Sweden*. Copenhagen: Rosenkilde and Bagger, 1951.

Gere, Charlotte. *Victorian Jewelry Design*. Chicago: Henry Regnery, 1972.

Gernsheim, Alison. *Fashion and Reality*. London: Faber and Faber, 1963.

———. *Victorian and Edwardian Fashion*. New York: Dover, 1981.

Gervers-Molnar, Veronika. *The Hungarian Szur*. Toronto: Royal Ontario Museum, 1973.

Gervis, Pearce. *Of Emirs and Pagans*. London: Cassell, 1963.

Ghurye, G. S. *Indian Costume*. Bombay: Popular Prakashan, 1966.

Gibbs-Smith, Charles H. *The Fashionable Lady in the Nineteenth Century*. London: Her Majesty's Stationery Office, 1958.

Gilgun, Beth. *Tidings from the 18th Century*. Texarkana, Tex.: Rebel, 1993.

Gillow, John, and Nicholas Barnard. *Traditional Indian Textiles*. London: Thames and Hudson, 1991.

Gimbel's Illustrated 1915 Fashion Catalog. New York: Dover, 1994.

Gingerich, Melvin. *The Mennonites in Iowa*. Iowa City: State Historical Society of Iowa, 1939.

Gittinger, Mattiebelle, and H. Leedom Lefferts Jr. *Textiles and the Tai Experience in Southeast Asia*. Washington, D.C.: Textile Museum, 1992.

Gottlieb, Robert, and Frank Maresca, eds. *A Certain Style: The Art of the Plastic Handbag 1949–1959*. New York: Alfred A. Knopf, 1988.

Grange, H. M. D. *A Short History of the Scottish Dress*. New York: Macmillan, 1967.

Grant, Michael. *History of Rome*. New York: Charles Scribner's Sons, 1977.

Groves, Sylvia. *The History of Needlework Tools and Accessories*. New York: Arco, 1973.

Gunn, Harold D. *Pagan Peoples of the Central Area of Northern Nigeria*. London: International African Institute, 1956.

Haddon, Alfred C., and Laura E. Star. *Iban or Sea Dayak Fabrics and Their Patterns*. Cambridge: University Press, 1936.

Haertig, Evelyn. *Antique Combs and Purses*. Singapore: Gallery Graphics Press, 1983.

Hall, Carrie A. *From Hoopskirts to Nudity*. Caldwell, Ida.: Caxton Printers, 1938.

Hall, Rosalind. *Egyptian Textiles*. Aylesbury: Shire Egyptology, 1986.

Hamilton-Paterson, James, and Carol Andrews. *Mummies: Death and Life in Ancient Egypt*. New York: Viking Press, 1979.

Hanley, Clifford. *The Scots*. New York: Times Books, 1980.

Hargrave, Harriet. *From Fiber to Fabric*. Lafayette, Calif.: C and T, 1997.

Harrold, Robert. *Folk Costumes of the World*. London: Blandford, 1988.

Hart, Avril. *Ties*. New York: Costume and Fashion Press, 1998.

Hart, Avril, and Emma Taylor. *Fans*. New York: Costume and Fashion Press, 1998.

Harte, N. B., and K. G. Ponting, eds. *Cloth and Clothing in Medieval Europe*. London: Heinemann Educational Books, 1983.

Harvey, Nancy Lenz. *Elizabeth of York: The Mother of Henry VIII*. New York: Macmillan, 1973.

Hauglid, Roar, Randi Asker, Helen Englestad, and Gunvor Trattleberg. *Native Art of Norway*. New York: Frederick A. Praeger, 1967.

The Hausa of Northern Nigeria. Edinburgh: Royal Scottish Museum, 1981.

Hayashi, Tadaichi. *Japanese Women's Folk Costumes*. Tokyo: Ie-No-Hikari Assoc., 1960.

Higgins, Reynold. *Greek and Roman Jewellery*. 2nd ed. London: Methuen, 1961.

Hijlkema, Riet. *National Costumes in Holland*. Amsterdam: J. J. Meulenhoff, 1951.

Hill, Errol. *The Trinidad Carnival*. Austin: University of Texas Press, 1972.

Hilton, Alison. *Russian Folk Art*. Bloomington: Indiana University Press, 1995.

History of Russian Costume from the Eleventh to the Twentieth Century. New York: Metropolitan Museum of Art, 1982.

Hope, Thomas. *Costumes of the Greeks and Romans*. New York: Dover, 1962.

———. *Greek Gold: Jewelry from the Age of Alexander*. New York: Dover, 1962.

Horan, James D. *The Desperate Years: A Pictorial History of the Thirties*. New York: Bonanza Books, 1972.

Horse Capture, George P., et al. *Robes of Splendor*. New York: New York Press, 1993.

Hostetler, John H. *Amish Society*. 3rd ed. Baltimore: Johns Hopkins University Press, 1980.

Hough, Richard. *Born Royal: The Lives and Loves of the Young Windsors.* New York: Bantam Books, 1988.

Houston, Mary G. *Ancient Egyptian, Mesopotamian, and Persian Costume and Decoration.* London: Adam and Charles Black, 1947.

———. *Ancient Greek, Roman, and Byzantine Costume and Decoration.* London: A. and C. Black, 1931.

———. *Medieval Costume in England and France: The 13th, 14th and 15th Centuries.* London: Adam and Charles Black, 1979.

Houston, Mary G., and Florence Hornblower. *Ancient Egyptian, Assyrian and Persian Costumes and Decorations.* London: A. and C. Black, 1920.

Howe, Russell Warren. *Black Star Rising: A Journey through West Africa in Transition.* London: Herbert Jenkins, 1958.

Hunnisett, Jean. *Period Costume for State and Screen: Patterns for Woman's Dresses 1800–1909.* London: Unwin Hyman, 1988.

Ioannou-Giannara, Tatiana. *Greek Folk Art: The Greek Folk Costume.* Athens, Greece: Melissa, 1977.

Irwin, John, and Katharine B. Brett. *Origins of Chintz.* London: Her Majesty's Stationery Office, 1970.

Irwin, John, and Margaret Hall. *Indian Painted and Printed Fabrics.* Vol. 1. Ahmedabad, India: Calico Museum of Textiles, 1971.

Jarvis, Anthea, and Patricia Raine. *Fancy Dress.* London: Shire, 1984.

Jaslan, Janina, and Jan Stansilawski. *Wiedza Powszechna: Compact Polish and English Dictionary.* Chicago: National Textbook Company, 1994.

Jayakar, Pupul. *The Indian Printed Textiles.* All India Handicrafts Board, n.d.

Jenkins, Alan. *The Forties.* New York: Universe Books, 1977.

———. *The Twenties.* New York: Universe Books, 1974.

Jernigan, E. Wesley. *Jewellery through 7000 Years.* London: Trustees of the British Museum, 1976.

———. *Jewelry of the Prehistoric Southwest.* Albuquerque: University of New Mexico Press, 1978.

Johnson, Eleanor. *Fashion Accessories.* Aylesbury: Shire, 1980.

Johnson, Marion. *The Borgias.* New York: Holt, Rinehart and Winston, 1981.

Kahlenberg, Mary Hunt. *Textile Traditions of Indonesia.* Los Angeles: Los Angeles County Museum of Art, 1977.

Kaplan, Joel H., and Sheila Stowell. *Theatre and Fashion: Oscar Wilde to the Suffragettes.* Cambridge: Cambridge University Press, 1994.

Kawakami, Barbara F. *Japanese Immigrant Clothing in Hawaii 1885–1941.* Honolulu: University of Hawaii Press, 1993.

Kawakatsu, Ken-ichi. *Kimono.* 5th ed. Tokyo: Japan Travel Bureau, 1960.

Kaye, Barrington. *Bringing Up Children in Ghana.* London: George Allen and Unwin, 1962.

Kelly, F. M. *Shakespearean Costume for Stage and Screen.* 2nd rev. ed. London: Adam and Charles Black, 1970.

Kendrick, A. F. *Catalogue of Early Medieval Woven Fabrics.* London: Victoria and Albert Museum, 1925.

Kennedy, Alan. *Japanese Costume.* Paris: Editions Adam Biro, 1990.

Kennett, Frances. *Ethnic Dress.* New York: Facts on File, 1994.

Kent, Kate Peck. *Navajo Weaving: Three Centuries of Change.* Santa Fe, N.M.: School of American Research Press, 1985.

———. *Prehistoric Textiles of the Southwest.* Albuquerque: University of New Mexico Press, 1983.

Kidwell, Claudia B. *Women's Bathing and Swimming Costume in the United States.* Washington, D.C.: Smithsonian Institution Press, 1968.

Kidwell, Claudia B., and Margaret C. Christman. *Suiting Everyone: The Democratization of Clothing in America.* Washington, D.C.: Smithsonian Institution Press, 1974.

Kilgour, Ruth Edwards. *A Pageant of Hats Ancient and Modern.* New York: Robert M. McBride, 1958.

Koch, Ronald P. *Dress Clothing of the Plains Indians.* Norman: University of Oklahoma, 1977.

Korn, Afons L. Some notes on the origin of certain Hawaiian shirts: Frock, smock-frock, block and palaka. *Oceanic Linguistics* 15, no. 1–2.

Kozloski, Lillian D. *U. S. Space Gear: Outfitting the Astronaut.* Washington, D.C.: Smithsonian Institution Press, 1994.

Landor, A. Henry Savage. *Across Wildest Africa.* Vols. 1–2. London: Hurst and Blackett, 1907.

Laurence, Margaret. *New Wind in a Dry Land.* New York: Alfred A. Knopf, 1964.

Laver, James, ed. *The Dominance of Spain 1550–1660.* London: George G. Harrap, 1951.

———. *The Great Age of Holland 1600–1660.* London: George G. Harrap, 1951.

le Bourhis, Katell, ed. *The Age of Napoleon Costume from Revolution to Empire, 1789–1815.* New York: Metropolitan Museum of Art, 1989.

Lefferts, Charles M. *Uniforms of the American, British, French and German Armies in the War of the American Revolution 1775–1783.* Old Greenwich, Conn.: WE, 1926.

Leon, Luisa Castañeda. *Traditional Dress of Peru.* Lima: Museo Nacional de la Cutura Peruana, 1981.

Lepage-Medvey. *National Costumes.* London: Hyperion Press, 1939.

Lester, Katherine Morris, and Bess Viola Oerke. *Accessories of Dress.* Peoria, Ill.: Manual Arts Press, 1940.

Levey, Santina M. *Lace: A History.* London: W. S. Maney and Son, 1983.

Lindsay, Irina. *Dressing and Undressing for the Seaside.* Essex: Ian Henry, 1983.

Linthicum, Marie Channing. *Costume in the Drama of Shakespeare and His Contemporaries.* New York: Russell and Russell, 1963.

Lithuanian Folk Art. Los Angeles: UCLA Ethnic Art Galleries, 1967.

Little, Kenneth. *The Mende of Sierra Leone.* London: Routledge and Kegan Paul, 1967.

Lopez, Claude-Anne. *Mon Cher Papa Franklin and the Ladies of Paris.* New Haven, Conn.: Yale University Press, 1966.

Lystad, Robert A. *The Ashanti: A Proud People.* New Brunswick, N.J.: Rutgers University Press, 1958.

Mack, John. *Malagasy Textiles.* Aylesbury: Shire Ethnography, 1989.

Mackay-Smith, Alexander, Jean R. Ruesedow, and Thomas Ryder. *Man and the Horse*. New York: Simon and Schuster, 1984.

Mackenzie, Jean Kenyon. *African Clearings*. Boston: Houghton Mifflin, 1924.

Mackrell, Alice. *Paul Poiret*. New York: Holmes and Meier, 1990.

Mails, Thomas E. *Plains Indians*. New York: Bonanza Books, 1985.

Mann, Kathleen. *Peasant Costume in Europe*. London: Adam and Charles Black, 1935.

Martienssen, Anthony. *Queen Katherine Parr*. New York: McGraw-Hill, 1973.

Martin, Richard, and Harold Koda. *Haute Couture*. New York: Metropolitan Museum of Art, 1995.

———. *Jocks and Nerds: Men's Style in the Twentieth Century*. New York: Rizzoli International, 1989.

Marwick, Arthur. *Women at War 1914–1918*. London: Croon Helm, 1977.

Mascetti, Daniela, and Amanda Triossi. *Earrings from Antiquity to the Present*. London: Thames and Hudson, 1990.

Mathur, Pushpa Rani. *Costumes of the Rulers of Mewar*. New Delhi: Abhinav, 1994.

Mazzaoui, Maureen Fennell. *The Italian Cotton Industry in the Later Middle Ages, 1100–1600*. Cambridge: Cambridge University Press, 1981.

McCauley, Daniel, and Kathryn McCauley. *Decorative Arts of the Amish of Lancaster County*. Intercourse, Pa.: Good Books, 1988.

McClelland, Elisabeth. *History of American Costume: 1607–1870*. New York: Tudor, 1969.

McClintock, H. F. *Handbook on the Traditional Old Irish Dress*. Dundalk: Dundalgan Press, 1958.

———. *Old Irish and Highland Dress*. Dundalk: W. Tempest, Dundalgan Press, 1943.

McDowell, Colin. *The Man of Fashion: Peacock Males and Perfect Gentlemen*. London: Thames and Hudson, 1997.

McKendrick, Melveena. *The Horizon Concise History of Spain*. New York: American Heritage, 1972.

Mead, S. M. *Traditional Maori Clothing*. Sydney, Australia: A. H. and A. W. Reed, 1969.

Meen, V. B., and A. D. Tushingham. *Crown Jewels of Iran*. Toronto: University of Toronto Press, 1968.

Meis, Reinhard. *Pocket Watches*. Lancaster, Pa.: Schiffer, 1987.

Meisch, Lynn. *Otovalo: Weaving, Costume and the Market*. Quito, Ecuador: Ediciones Libri Mundi, 1987.

Mera, Harry Percival. *Navajo Textile Arts*. Santa Barbara, Calif.: Peregrine Smith, 1975.

———. *Pueblo Indian Embroidery*. Santa Fe, N.M.: William Gannon, 1975.

Miller, Peggy. *A Wife for the Pretender*. New York: Harcourt, Brace, and World, 1965.

Minnich, Helen Benton. *Japanese Costume and the Makers of Its Elegant Tradition*. Tokyo: Charles E. Tuttle, 1963.

Moeller, Walter O. *The Wool Trade of Ancient Pompeii*. Amsterdam: E. J. Brill, 1976.

Moers, Ellen. *The Dandy Brummell to Beerbohm*. New York: Viking Press, 1960.

Mollo, John. *Military Fashion*. New York: G. P. Putnam's Sons, 1972.

Moore, Doris Langley-Levy. *The Child in Fashion*. London: B. T. Batsford, 1953.

———. *Fashion through Fashion Plates 1771–1970*. London: Ward Lock, 1971.

———. *The Woman in Fashion*. London: B. T. Batsford, 1949.

Morse, Harriet Klamroth. *Elizabethan Pageantry: A Pictorial Survey of Costume and Its Commentaries from c1560–1620*. New York: B. Blom, 1969.

Municchi, Anna. *Furs for Men*. Modeno, Italy: Zanfi Editori, 1988.

———. *Ladies in Furs 1900–1940*. Modena, Italy: Zanfi Editori, 1992.

———. *Ladies in Furs 1940–1990*. Modena, Italy: Zanfi Editori, 1993.

Munsterberg, Hugo. *The Folk Arts of Japan*. Rutland, Vt.: Charles E. Tuttle, 1958.

Murray, Jane. *The Kings and Queens of England*. New York: Charles Scribner's Sons, 1974.

Newark, Tim. *Brassey's Book of Uniforms*. London: Brassey's, 1998.

Norris, Herbert. *Costume and Fashion: The Evolution of European Dress through the Earlier Ages*. London: J. M. Dent and Sons, 1927.

———. *Costume and Fashion*. Vol. 2, *1066–1485*. London: J. M. Dent and Sons, 1927.

———. *Costume and Fashion*. Vol. 3, *1485–1547*. London: E. P. Dutton , 1938.

Noss, Aagot. *Lad og Krone*. Oslo: Insituttet for Sammenlignende Kulturforskning, 1991.

NTC's Compact Portuguese and English Dictionary. Chicago: National Textbook, 1995.

Oaks, Alma, and Margot Hamilton Hill. *Rural Costume: Its Origin and Development in Western Europe and the British Isles*. New York: Van Nostrand Reinhold, 1970.

Ogawa, Masataka. *The Enduring Crafts of Japan*. New York: Walker/Weatherhill, 1968.

Paine, Sheila. *Embroidered Textiles: Traditional Patterns from Five Continents*. New York: Rizzoli, 1990.

Parker, Rozsika. *The Subversive Stitch Embroidery and the Making of the Feminine*. London: Women's Press, 1984.

Parry, Linda. *Textiles of the Arts and Crafts Movement*. London: Thames and Hudson, 1988.

Paulme, Denise, ed. *Women of Tropical Africa*. Berkeley: University of California Press, 1963.

Peacock, John. *Fashion Sketchbook: 1920–1960*. New York: Avon Books, 1977.

Peri, Paolo. *The Handkerchief*. Modena, Italy: Zanfi Editori, 1992.

Perry, George, and Nicholas Mason, eds. *The Victorians: A World Built to Last*. New York: Viking Press, 1974.

Peterson, Harold L. *Arms and Armor in Colonial America*. New York: Bramball House, 1956.

Petsopoulos, Yanni, ed. *Tulips, Arabesques and Turbans: Decorative Arts from the Ottoman Empire*. New York: Abbeville Press, 1982.

Pettersen, Carmen L. *The Maya of Guatemala: Their Life and Dress*. Guatemala City: Ixchel Museum, 1976.

Pick, Robert. *Empress Marie Theresa: The Earlier Years 1717–57*. New York: Harper and Row, 1966.

Picken, Mary Brooks. *The Fashion Dictionary*. New York: Funk and Wagnalls, 1957.

Pile, John. *Dictionary of 20th Century Design*. New York: Facts on File, 1990.

Plath, Iona. *The Decorative Arts of Sweden*. New York: Charles Scribner's Sons, 1948.

Polakoff, Claire. *African Textiles and Dyeing Techniques*. London: Routledge and Kegan Paul, 1982.

Poli, Doretta Davanzo. *Maternity Fashion*. Modena, Italy: Zanfi Editori, 1988.

Popova, L. P., ed. *NTC's Compact Russian and English Dictionary*. Chicago: National Textbook, 1994.

Powers, Stephen. *Tribes of California*. Berkeley: University of California Press, 1976.

Powys, Marian. *Lace and Lace-Making*. Boston: Charles T. Branford, 1953.

Prescott, Orville. *Princes of the Renaissance*. New York: Random House, 1969.

Pukui, Mary Kawena, and Samuel H. Elbert. *Hawaiian Dictionary*. Honolulu: University of Hawaii Press, 1971.

Rattray, R. S. *Religion and Art in Ashanti*. London: Oxford University Press, 1927.

Ray, Dorothy Jean. *Eskimo Masks: Art and Ceremony*. Seattle: University of Washington Press, 1967.

Reynolds, Reginald. *Beards*. London: George Allen and Unwin, 1950.

Ribiero, Aileen. *The Art of Dress Fashion in England and France 1750 to 1820*. New Haven, Conn.: Yale University Press, 1995.

———. *Fashion in the French Revolution*. New York: Holmes and Meier, 1988.

Roberts, Keith, and Angus McBride. *Soldiers of the English Civil War Infantry*. London: Osprey, 1989.

Robinson, Julian. *Fashion in the Forties*. New York: St. Martin's Press, 1976.

———. *Fashion in the Thirties*. New York: Two Continents, 1978.

Rothstein, Natalie. *Silk Designs of the Eighteenth Century*. London: Bulfinch Press, 1990.

Rowe, Ann Pollard. *Costume and Identity in Highland Ecuador*. Washington, D.C.: Textile Museum, 1998.

———, ed. *Costumes and Featherwork of the Lords of Chimor Textiles from Peru's North Coast*. Washington, D.C.: Textile Museum, 1984.

Rubens, Alfred. *A History of Jewish Costume*. London: Vallentine, Mitchel, 1967.

Rudofsky, Bernard. *The Unfashionable Human Body*. New York: Anchor Press, 1974.

Russell, Andrew J. *Russell's Civil War Photographs*. New York: Dover, 1982.

Saito, R. *Japanese Coiffure*. Tokyo: Board of Tourist Industry, 1939.

Salisburg, Charlotte Y. *Mountaintop Kingdom: Sikkim*. New York: W. W. Norton, 1971.

Salomon, Julian Harris. *The Book of Indian Crafts and Indian Lore*. New York: Harper and Row, 1928.

Sandberg, Gösta. *The Red Dyes: Cochineal, Madder, and Murex Purple*. Hong Kong: Lark Books, 1997.

Sann, Paul. *The Angry Decade: The Sixties*. New York: Crown, 1979.

———. *The 20s: The Lawless Decade*. New York: Crown, 1957.

Saunders, Catherine. *Costume in Roman Comedy*. New York: Columbia University Press, 1909.

Sayer, Chloe. *Arts and Crafts of Mexico*. San Francisco: Chronicle Books, 1990.

Schevill, Margot Blum. *Maya Textiles of Guatemala*. Austin: University of Texas Press, 1993.

Schevill, Margot Blum, Janet Catherine Berlo, and Edward B. Dwyer, eds. *Textile Traditions of Mesoamerica and the Andes*. New York: Garland, 1991.

Schneider, Jane. *The Anthropology of Cloth*. Palo Alto, Calif.: Annual Reviews, 1987.

Schroeder, Joseph J. Jr., ed. *The Wonderful World of Ladies' Fashions, 1850–1900*. Northfield, Ill.: Digest Books, 1971.

Sciama, Lidia D., and Joanne B. Eicher, eds. *Bead and Bead Makers*. Oxford: Berg, 1998.

Seaton, Henry. *Lion in the Morning*. Edinburgh: R. and R. Clark, 1963.

Seligman, C. G. *Races of Africa*. London: Oxford University Press, 1957.

Seward, Desmond. *Napoleon's Family: The Notorious Bonapartes and Their Ascent to the Thrones of Europe*. New York: Viking Penguin, 1986.

Sichel, Marion. *The Edwardians*. Boston: Plays, 1978.

Sieber, Roy. *African Textiles and Decorative Arts*. New York: Museum of Modern Art, 1972.

Simmons, Pauline. *Chinese Patterned Silks*. New York City: Metropolitan Museum of Art, 1948.

Simon, Kate. *A Renaissance Tapestry: The Gonzaga of Mantua*. New York: Harper and Row, 1981.

Skira, Albert, ed. *The Great Centuries of Painting: Byzantine Painting*. Geneva: Editions Albert Skira, 1953.

———. *The Great Centuries of Painting: Gothic Painting*. Geneva: Editions Albert Skira, 1954.

———. *The Great Centuries of Painting: Romanesque Painting*. Geneva: Editions Albert Skira, 1957.

Smith, Gene. *Maximilian and Carlota*. New York: William Morrow, 1973.

Smith, Robin. *American Civil War Zouaves*. London: Reed International Book, 1996.

Sronkova, Olga. *Gothic Woman's Fashion*. Prague: Artia, 1954.

Stanton, Shelby. *U.S. Army Uniforms of the Cold War*. Mechanicsburg, Pa.: Stackpole Books, 1994.

Stein, Kurt. *Canes and Walking Sticks*. Atgen, Pa.: Liberty Cap Books, 1974.

Stevenson, Pauline. *Bridal Fashions*. London: Ian Allen, 1978.

Stewart, Janice S. *The Folk Arts of Norway*. New York: Dover, 1972.

Stigand, Chauncy Hugh. *The Land of Zinj*. New York: Barnes and Noble, 1966.

Stillman, Norman A., ed. *Arab Dress from Dawn of Islam to Modern Times*. Leiden, Netherlands: Koninklijke Brill, 2000.

Stillman, Yedida Kalfon. *Palestinian Costume and Jewelry*. Albuquerque: University of New Mexico Press, 1979.

Strizhenova, Tatiana. *Soviet Costume and Textiles 1917–1945*. Moscow: Flammarion, 1991.

Strouhal, Eugen. *Life of the Ancient Egyptians*. Norman: University of Oklahoma Press, 1992.

Swann, June. *Shoes*. New York: Drama Book, 1982.

Tanaka, Toshio, and Reiko Tanaka. *A Study of Okinawan Textile Fabrics*. Tokyo: Meiji-Shobo, 1952.

Tannahill, Reay. *Food in History*. New York: Stein and Day, 1973.

Tanner, Clara Lee. *Southwest Indian Craft Arts*. Tucson: University of Arizona Press, 1968.

Taylor, Lou. *Mourning Dress: A Costume and Social History*. London: George Allen and Unwin, 1983.

Telford, A. A. *Yesterday's Dress: A History of Costume in South Africa*. Cape Town: Purnell, 1972.

Thornton, Peter. *Baroque and Rococo Silks*. New York City: Taplinger, 1965.

Tickner, Lisa. *The Spectacle of Women: Imagery of the Suffrage Campaign 1907–14*. London: Chatto and Windus, 1987.

Tily, John C. *The Uniforms of the United States Navy*. New York: Thomas Yoseloff, 1964.

Tincey, John. *Soldiers of the English Civil War: Cavalry*. London: Osprey, 1990.

Torrens, Deborah. *Fashion Illustrated: A Review of Women's Dress, 1920–1950*. New York: Hawthorn Books, 1975.

Tosa, Marco. *Evening Dresses 1900–1940*. Modena, Italy: Zanfi Editori, 1988.

Tozer, Jane, and Sarah Levitt. *Fabric of Society: A Century of People and Their Clothes 1770–1870*. Carno, Powys, Wales: Laura Ashley, 1983.

Trasko, Mary. *Daring Do's: A History of Extraordinary Hair*. Paris: Flammarion, 1994.

Travis, William. *The Voice of the Turtle*. London: George Allen and Unwin, 1967.

Tyrrell, Anne V. *Changing Trends in Fashion: Patterns of the Twentieth Century 1900–1970*. London: B. T. Batsford, 1986.

Tyrrell, Barbara. *Tribal Peoples of Southern Africa*. Cape Town: Books of Africa, 1968.

Uzicanin, Nikolina S. *Bosnian-English English-Bosnian Dictionary*. New York: Hippocrene Books, 1996.

Vansina, Jan. *The Children of Woot*. Dawson: University of Wisconsin Press, 1978.

Vaughan, Herman Millingschamp. *From Anne to Victoria*. London: Methuen Press, 1931.

Vaughan-Williams, H. *A Visit to Lobengula in 1889*. Pietermaritzburg: Shuter and Shooter, 1947.

Veyne, Paul, ed. *A History of Private Life from Pagan Rome to Byzantium*. Cambridge, Mass.: Belknap Press, 1987.

Villa, Nora. *Children in Their Party Dress*. Modena, Italy: Zanfi Editori, 1989.

Vincent, John Martin. *Costume and Conduct*. New York: Greenwood Press, 1935.

Vollmer, John E. *Decoding Dragons Status: Garments in Ch'ing Dynasty China*. Eugene: Museum of Art, University of Oregon, 1983.

von Falke, Otto. *Decorative Silks*. New York City: William Helburn, 1922.

Walkley, Christina. *The Ghost in the Looking Glass*. London: Peter Owen, 1981.

Waller, Jane. *A Man's Book: Fashion in the Men's World in the 20's and 30's*. London: Duckworth, 1977.

Waugh, Nora. *Corsets and Crinoline*. New York: Theatre Arts Books, 1954.

Weibel, A. Coulin. *2000 Years of Silk-Weaving*. New York: E. Weyhe, 1944.

Weiner, Annette B., and Jane Schneider, eds. *Cloth and Human Experience*. Washington, D.C.: Smithsonian Institution Press, 1989.

Weir, Shelagh. *Palestinian Costume*. Austin: University of Texas Press, 1989.

Wells, Evelyn. *Hatshepsut*. Garden City, N.Y.: Doubleday, 1969.

———. *Nefertiti*. Garden City, N.Y.: Doubleday, 1964.

Welters, Linda. *Women's Traditional Costume in Attica Greece*. Athens, Greece: Peloponnesian Folklore Foundation, 1988.

Wherry, Joseph H. *Indian Masks and Myths of the West*. New York: Funk and Wagnalls, 1969.

Wilcox, Ruth Turner. *The Mode in Footwear*. New York: Charles Scribner's Sons, 1948.

———. *The Mode in Furs*. New York: Scribner's, 1951.

Williams, Neville. *All the Queen's Men: Elizabeth I and Her Courtiers*. New York: Macmillan, 1972.

Wilson, Carrie. *Fashions since Their Debut*. Scranton, Pa.: International Textbook, 1939.

Wilson, Lillian M. *Clothing of the Ancient Romans*. Baltimore: Johns Hopkins University Press, 1938.

———. *The Roman Toga*. Baltimore: Johns Hopkins University Press, 1924.

Windraw, Martin, and Gerry Embleton. *Military Dress of North America 1665–1970*. New York: Charles Scribner's Sons, 1973.

Wood, Josephine, and Lilly de Jongh Osborne. *Indian Costumes of Guatemala*. Austria: Akademische Druck, 1966.

Worell, Estelle Arsley. *Children's Costume in America 1607–1910*. New York: Scribner, 1980.

Wright, Merideth. *Everyday Dress of Rural America 1783–1800*. New York: Dover, 1992.

Yefimova, L., and Belogorskaya, R. *Russian Embroidery and Lace*. New York: Thames and Hudson, 1987.

Yule, Henry, and A. C. Burnell. *Hobson-Jobson: A Glossary of Colloquial Anglo-Indian Words and Phrases, and of Kindred Terms, Etymological, Historical, Geographical and Discursive*. London: Routledge and Kegan Paul, 1968.

Zarina, Xenia. *Classis Dances of the Orient*. New York: Crown, 1967.

Zdatny, Steven, ed. *Hairstyles and Fashion: A Hairdresser's History of Paris 1910–20*. Oxford: Berg, 1999.

About the Author and Illustrator

Elizabeth J. Lewandowski is a professor of theatre at Midwestern State University, where she teaches costuming and stage makeup. She has designed costumes for more than 100 productions, ranging from drama to opera to dance. Her work has been exhibited regionally and nationally. She has served on the boards of a number of local, regional, and national organizations related to the theatrical industry.

She received her undergraduate degrees in theatre and music from Bradley University and her MFA from Texas Tech University, where her mentor was Dr. Forrest Newlin. She is passionate about all things costume related and has a special place in her heart for costume history–related subjects, from the history of undergarments to the use of drag in theatre. She is currently beginning work on an article on the history of fancy dress and a book on the history of drag.

In her spare time, she enjoys learning new gourmet recipes, sewing for local charities, reading voraciously, spending time with her three cats, and adoring her amazing husband, Dan.

Dan Lewandowski earned a BS in theatre, a BS in mass communications from Bradley University (where he met the author), and an AAS in electronics engineering technology from Amarillo College. He has worked in all of the above disciplines for a wide variety of educational and commercial organizations from Chicago to Houston and a few cities in between. Since he and Elizabeth formed a partnership business called Mostly Harmless in 1995, some of his clients have included KERA-Dallas, Sezmi.com, and Midwestern State University. He describes himself as a mostly harmless, mysterious, flirtatious, occasionally helpful, nocturnal, bipedal, carbon-based life form who is a proud and spectacularly successful house husband, persistently fond of the author (he had to sleep with her for 25 years to get this gig.). He dabbles in writing, reading, ice hockey, philosophy, civil activism, throwing legendary solstice parties, contemplating his cosmic insignificance, and taste testing anything that the world famous author cooks up in her amazing, magic kitchen. He describes the illustration process as starting with the highly talented author quickly and seemingly effortlessly creating a gorgeous line drawing, followed by him utilizing his merely mortal skills to take way too long to tweak the perspective and proportion, smooth the lines, and add shading, color, and texture using Jasc Paint Shop Pro 8.1. He is very grateful for the chance to collaborate on this project and for the author's and editor Stephen Ryan's enduring patience. He and Elizabeth reside in Wichita Falls, Texas.